HANDBOOK OF CLASSROOM MANAGEMENT

The *Handbook of Classroom Management, Third Edition*, is an authoritative treatment of the latest science and development in the study of classroom management in schools. Evidence-based classroom management practices and programs are essential to enhancing students' academic, behavioral, social-emotional, and motivational outcomes across grade levels. This comprehensive volume collects scholarship and cutting-edge research for graduate students and faculty of psychology, teacher education, curriculum and instruction, special education, and beyond. The book has been thoroughly revised and expanded with updated coverage of foundational topics such as effective instruction, preventative strategies, positive behavior intervention and supports, family-school relationships, legal issues, and other related topics, while also giving new attention to social justice, students on the autism spectrum, and adaptations across urban, rural, and virtual contexts.

Edward J. Sabornie is Professor in the College of Education in the Department of Teacher Education and Learning Sciences at North Carolina State University, USA.

Dorothy L. Espelage is William C. Friday Distinguished Professor of Education in the School of Education at University of North Carolina, USA.

HANDBOOK OF CLASSROOM MANAGEMENT

Third Edition

Edited by Edward J. Sabornie
and Dorothy L. Espelage

Routledge
Taylor & Francis Group

NEW YORK AND LONDON

Cover image: Getty Images

Third edition published 2023
by Routledge
605 Third Avenue, New York, NY 10158

and by Routledge
4 Park Square, Milton Park, Abingdon, Oxon, OX14 4RN

Routledge is an imprint of the Taylor & Francis Group, an informa business

First edition published by Routledge 2006

Second edition published by Routledge 2014

Library of Congress Cataloging-in-Publication Data
Names: Sabornie, Edward James, editor. |
Espelage, Dorothy L. (Dorothy Lynn), editor.
Title: Handbook of classroom management /
Edited by Edward J. Sabornie and Dorothy L. Espelage.
Description: Third edition. | New York, NY : Routledge, 2023. |
Includes bibliographical references and index.
Identifiers: LCCN 2022009359 (print) | LCCN 2022009360 (ebook) |
ISBN 9781032230344 (hardback) | ISBN 9781032224367 (paperback) |
ISBN 9781003275312 (ebook)
Subjects: LCSH: Classroom management–Handbooks, manuals, etc.
Classification: LCC LB3013.H336 2023 (print) |
LCC LB3013 (ebook) | DDC 371.102/4–dc23
LC record available at https://lccn.loc.gov/2022009359
LC ebook record available at https://lccn.loc.gov/2022009360

ISBN: 9781032230344 (hbk)
ISBN: 9781032224367 (pbk)
ISBN: 9781003275312 (ebk)

DOI: 10.4324/9781003275312

Typeset in Bembo
by Newgen Publishing UK

CONTENTS

List of Contributors   *viii*
Preface   *xvii*

PART I
Introduction   **1**

1   Introduction to the Third Edition   3
    Edward J. Sabornie and Dorothy L. Espelage

PART II
Methods of Classroom Management   **13**

2   Effective Instruction as the Basis for Classroom Management   15
    Terrance M. Scott and Jennifer Nakamura

3   Prevention Strategies for Classroom Management   31
    Sierra M. Trudel, Emily L. Winter, and Melissa A. Bray

4   Restorative Practices in Schools   54
    Sean Darling-Hammond and Trevor Fronius

5   First Step to Success: A Preventive, Early Intervention for Young
    Students with Disruptive Behavior Problems   74
    *Hill M. Walker, Andy J. Frey, Jason W. Small, Ed Feil, John R. Seeley,
    Jon Lee, Annemieke Golly, Shantel Crosby, and Steve Forness*

6   Current Trends in Positive Behavioral Interventions and Supports:
    Implications for Classroom Management   87
    Sara Estrapala and Timothy J. Lewis

Contents

7 Supporting Students' Social, Emotional, and Behavior (SEB) Growth
   Through Tier 2 and 3 Intervention within a Multi-Tiered System of
   Supports (MTSS) Framework   102
   Brandi Simonsen, Karen Robbie, Katherine Meyer, Jennifer Freeman,
   Susannah Everett, and Adam B. Feinberg

8 Adapting Classroom Management for Delivery Across Contexts:
   A Focus on Urban, Rural, and Online Settings   128
   Shanna E. Hirsch, Kristine E. Larson, Lydia A. Beahm,
   and Catherine P. Bradshaw

9 Classroom Management in "No-Excuses" Charter Schools   152
   Chris Torres

10 Emerging Issues in School Bullying Research and Prevention   167
   Chad A. Rose, Dorothy L. Espelage, and Luz E. Robinson

PART III
Context of Classroom Management   **187**

11 Teacher Stress and Classroom Management   189
   Christopher J. McCarthy, Kristen C. Mosley, and Jendayi B. Dillard

12 The New Jim Crow in School: Exclusionary Discipline
   and Structural Racism   211
   Russell J. Skiba, Edward Fergus, and Anne Gregory

13 Why Effective Classroom Management Depends on Teachers'
   Abilities to Engage Families   231
   Joan Walker and Jennifer Pankowski

14 Teacher Training and Classroom Management   249
   Marcia L. Montague and Andrew Kwok

15 School Administration and Classroom Management   271
   Lance D. Fusarelli, Lacey Seaton, and Claudia Saavedra Smith

16 The Contribution of School and Classroom Disciplinary Practices to
   the School-to-Prison Pipeline   288
   David Osher, Stephen Plank, Candace Hester, and Scott Houghton

17 Rethinking K–12 Disciplinary Policies and Practices in Virtual School
   Settings: Initial School Responses to the COVID-19 Pandemic   319
   Kevin P. Brady

18 Using Multimedia to Support Teacher Candidates' Knowledge and Use of
    Evidence-Based Classroom Management Practices   335
    Michael J. Kennedy, Rachel L. Kunemund, and Lindsay M. Carlisle

19 International Research on the Foci and Effectiveness of Classroom
    Management Programs and Strategies   350
    Hanke Korpershoek, Jolien M. Mouw, and Hester De Boer

PART IV
Social Perspectives of Classroom Management   **373**

20 Transformative Social-Emotional Learning and Classroom Management   375
    Dorothy L. Espelage, Luz E. Robinson, and Alberto Valido

21 Classroom Management at Different Timescales: An Interpersonal Perspective   388
    Theo Wubbels, Tim Mainhard, Perry den Brok, Luce Claessens, and Jan van Tartwijk

22 Teacher Aggression and Classroom Management   415
    Kent Divoll

23 An Equity-Driven Behavior Management Approach to Close the
    Discipline Gap   436
    Anna Long and Kelly Clark

PART V
The Classroom Management and Student Type Interaction   **455**

24 Critical Race Theory Insights on Issues of Classroom Management   457
    Patricia L. Marshall and Brittani N. Clark

25 Classroom Management Instruction in Teacher Education: A Culturally
    Responsive Approach   477
    Bettie Ray Butler, Deondra Gladney, Ya-yu Lo, and Altheria Caldera

26 Classroom Management to Support Students with Disabilities: Empowering
    General and Special Educators   499
    Kathleen Lynn Lane, Holly M. Menzies, Lucia Smith-Menzies, and Katie Scarlett Lane

27 Students with Autism and Classroom Management   517
    Edward J. Sabornie, Glennda K. McKeithan, and Jamie N. Pearson

28 Classroom Management in Early Childhood Education   534
    Marissa A. Bivona and Amanda P. Williford

Index   *558*

CONTRIBUTORS

Lydia A. Beahm (lar3h@virginia.edu) is a doctoral student at the University of Virginia in the School of Education and Human Development where she conducts research on bridging the research-to-practice gap and behavioral interventions. She is also interested in scaling up professional development to an online format to support teachers with improving student behavior in the classroom.

Marissa A. Bivona (mab2dx@virginia.edu) worked as an early childhood educator and consultant for eight years before beginning her doctoral studies in Clinical and School Psychology within the School of Education and Human Development at the University of Virginia. Her research and clinical interests attempt to create supports for teachers, families, and children in early childhood settings and are informed by her experience working in childcare.

Catherine P. Bradshaw (cpb8g@virginia.edu) is a University Professor and Senior Associate Dean for Research and Faculty Development in the School of Education and Human Development at the University of Virginia. Her interests include research on school-based violence prevention, mental health promotion, student engagement, and increasing the use of evidence-based programs and models in schools.

Kevin P. Brady (kpbrady@uark.edu) is a professor of educational leadership in the department of Curriculum and Instruction at the University of Arkansas, and Program Chair of the UCEA Center for the Study of Leadership and the Law. His primary areas of scholarship include educational law and policy, legal issues involving student discipline, students with disabilities, school finance litigation, and school leadership in isolated, rural school communities.

Melissa A. Bray (melissa.bray@uconn.edu) is a Professor and Director of the School of Psychology program at the University of Connecticut. She is a licensed psychologist and speech-language pathologist and a Fellow of both the American Psychological Association and the American Psychological Society.

Bettie Ray Butler (Bettie.Butler@uncc.edu) is an Associate Professor of Urban Education and the Director of the MEd in Urban Education program in the Department of Middle, Secondary, and K-12 Education at the University of North Carolina at Charlotte. Her research focuses on culturally responsive educational approaches, racial and gender disproportionality in school discipline, and restorative practices.

Altheria Caldera (altheriacaldera@icloud.com) is an Assistant Professor of Reading and Language Arts in the Curriculum and Instruction Department at Howard University, and director of the D.C.-Area Writing Project, a chapter of the National Writing Project. Her research and scholarship examines ways educators can advance racial equity in schools with specific attention to linguistic justice, Black girlhood, and equitable educational policies.

Lindsay M. Carlisle (lmc8ff@virginia.edu) is a PhD student in the School of Education and Human Development at the University of Virginia. Her research interests and scholarship are centered around the importance of effective communication across all facets of special education, including teacher practice, student well-being and achievement, and policy rhetoric, with an emphasis on implications for culturally and linguistically diverse students with disabilities.

Luce Claessens (L.C.A.Claessens@uu.nl) is an Associate Professor in the Department of Education at Utrecht University in the Netherlands, where she coordinates the Teacher Education Program for Primary Education. In both teaching and research, she is interested in teacher-student interactions and relationships, teacher education, and the position in schools of primary education teachers who graduated from research universities.

Brittani N. Clark (bnclark2@ncsu.edu) is a doctoral student in the Department of Teacher Education and Learning Sciences at NC State University. Her areas of interest and research include the representation of Black teachers in education, explorations of the broader social and political contexts that shaped Black teachers' pedagogies from a historical perspective, and racial inequities in US public school systems.

Kelly Clark (kellyclark@lsu.edu) is an Assistant Professor in the School Psychology Program at Louisiana State University. Her research is centered on promoting student mental health through a dual-factor consideration of risk (e.g., internalizing difficulties, suicidal ideation) and protective factors (e.g., social support, school belongingness).

Shantel Crosby (shantel.crosby@louisville.edu) is an Associate Professor in the Kent School of Social Work at the University of Louisville. Her scholarship focuses on childhood trauma and trauma-informed interventions in an effort to inform practice and policies in schools and other youth-serving organizations.

Sean Darling-Hammond (seandh@berkeley.edu) is a licensed attorney and a PhD candidate at UC Berkeley, as well as a researcher at WestEd. His research focuses on identifying school practices that can enhance school climates.

Hester De Boer (hester.de.boer@rug.nl) is a researcher at the GION Education/Research institute of the University of Groningen, the Netherlands. Her research interests include expectations and aspirations of teachers and parents and their influence on student academic performance, the effects of the attributes related to the implementation and evaluation of educational intervention studies, and learning strategy instruction.

Perry den Brok (perry.denbrok@wur.nl) is a professor of education and learning sciences at Wageningen University and Research in the Netherlands, and chair of the 4TU Centre of Engineering

Education, an innovation centre of the four universities of technology in the Netherlands. His research interests are innovation in higher education, learning environments, teaching, teacher learning, and professional development.

Jendayi B. Dillard (jbdillard@utexas.edu) is a doctoral candidate in the Department of Educational Psychology at the University of Texas at Austin. Her current scholarly focus is on educational disparities for minoritized students and teachers in the United States.

Kent Divoll (divoll@uhcl.edu) is an associate professor of teacher education in the department of Curriculum and Instruction at the University of Houston-Clear Lake. His areas of interest and scholarship include classroom management, relational pedagogy, teacher preparation, and the scholarship of teaching and learning.

Dorothy L. Espelage (espelage@unc.edu; Co-Editor) is a William C. Friday Professor of Education in the School of Education at the University of North Carolina at Chapel Hill. Her areas of interest and scholarship include prevention of youth violence, bullying, sexual violence, relationship aggression, social-emotional learning, and mental health interventions in K–12 settings.

Sara Estrapala (sle9bb@missouri.edu) is a Postdoctoral Fellow in the Department of Special Education at the University of Missouri. Her research interests include developing Tier 1 and Tier 2 teacher-delivered behavior interventions for students with challenging behaviors in high schools emphasizing student self-regulation development, teacher self-efficacy, and intervention social validity.

Susannah Everett (susannah.everett@uconn.edu) is an Assistant Professor in Residence at the University of Connecticut. Her research and clinical interests include the development of systems to support implementation of tier 2 interventions in schools, and to support school-based teams to use behavioral data for decision-making.

Ed Feil (edf@ori.org) is a school psychologist and Senior Research Scientist at Oregon Research Institute. He has authored papers and led federally funded research projects on screening and intervention with young children at risk for the development of behavioral disorders, and incorporating internet technology into the delivery of evidence-based interventions to hard-to-reach populations. He is a co-author of *First Step Next*.

Adam B. Feinberg (adam.feinberg@uconn.edu) is an Assistant Research Professor at the University of Connecticut and the Director of the Northeast PBIS Network. His research and clinical interests include the development and implementation of Multi-Tier Systems of Supports in schools and districts, with a focus on developing and supporting coaching knowledge, skills, and networks.

Edward Fergus (edward.fergus@temple.edu) is an Associate Professor of Urban Education and Policy at Temple University. His research focuses on racial disparity patterns in special education, discipline, and gifted/Honors/Ap programming.

Steve Forness is a distinguished professor emeritus at the UCLA Neuropsychiatric Hospital where he was also chief educational psychologist and hospital school principal from 1968–2003. He has published widely in learning disorders, school detection of children with psychiatric disorders, and classroom impact of psychopharmacologic treatments.

Jennifer Freeman (jennifer.freeman@uconn.edu) is an Associate Professor in the Department of Educational Psychology and is a research scientist for the Center for Behavioral Education Research at the University of Connecticut. She studies the effects of multi-tiered systems of support, such as Positive Behavior Interventions and Supports, and on outcomes at the high school level for high-risk student groups including students with disabilities.

Andy J. Frey (afrey@louisville.edu) is a professor at the Kent School of Social Work at the University of Louisville. His areas of interest include school mental health services, applications of motivational interviewing in school settings, and early intervention.

Trevor Fronius (tfroniu@wested.org) is a Senior Researcher within WestEd's Justice and Prevention Research Center (JPRC). His scholarship concerns the intersection of prevention and wellbeing where he researches and evaluates policies, practices, and programs aimed to improve school climate and safety, social capital and community violence, and outcomes for systems impacted youth and families.

Lance D. Fusarelli (lance_fusarelli@ncsu.edu) is Distinguished Professor of Educational Leadership and Policy at North Carolina State University. His research interests include the politics of education, federal education policy, and educational leadership.

Deondra Gladney (dgladney@uncc.edu) is a doctoral candidate in the Department of Special Education and Child Development at the University of North Carolina at Charlotte and an Instructional Coach at the University of North Carolina A&T. Her research interests include culturally responsive instruction for African American students and teacher support through effective professional development and coaching.

Annemieke Golly (agolly@uoregon.edu) is a co-author of *First Step Next* (FSN) and is the lead, master trainer of professionals who implement FSN. She also administers the program during implementation and works closely to coordinate issues between FSN developers and end user-consumers of the program.

Anne Gregory (annegreg@gsapp.rutgers.edu) is a Professor in the School Psychology Department at Rutgers Graduate School of Applied and Professional Psychology. Her research is in the area of racial and gender disparities in discipline, and she is currently examining school-wide restorative practices and equity-oriented social and emotional learning.

Candace Hester (chester@air.org) is a Principal Researcher at the American Institutes for Research. She has worked on several rigorous evaluations to examine the implementation and impact of policies and programs that have been designed to engender inclusive pathways to thriving, particularly for youth and young adults with prior justice system contact.

Shanna E. Hirsch (ShannaH@clemson.edu) is an Associate Professor of Special Education in the Department of Education and Human Development at Clemson University. She conducts research in the areas related to preparing and supporting teachers, implementing classroom management and intensive supports for students with challenging behavior, and evaluating instructional methods including technology adaptations.

Scott Houghton (shoughton@air.org) is a Researcher at the American Institutes for Research. His work includes projects aimed at supporting marginalized youth and young adults across K-12 and post-secondary settings, with particular attention to those impacted by the criminal and juvenile justice systems.

Michael J. Kennedy (mjk3p@virginia.edu) is an Associate Professor of Special Education at the University of Virginia's School of Education and Human Development. His research focuses on the intersection of teacher quality, professional development models, and effective implementation of multimedia to support teacher and student learning.

Hanke Korpershoek (h.korpershoek@rug.nl) is Professor (adjunct) of Educational Sciences, in particular educational innovation and school improvement, at the GION Education/Research institute of the University of Groningen, the Netherlands. Her research interests include school innovation and school improvement, evidence-informed decision making, school systems, research on choice behavior and motivation.

Rachel L. Kunemund (rk8vm@virginia.edu) is a Research Assistant Professor in the School of Education and Human Development at the University of Virginia. Her research interests include efforts to improve outcomes for young students with ongoing problem behavior in school settings including student–teacher relationships and interactions, teacher coaching models, and student behavioral and academic outcomes.

Andrew Kwok (akwok@tamu.edu) is an assistant professor in the Department of Teaching, Learning, & Culture at Texas A&M University. His research focuses on supporting beginning teachers with a particular emphasis on classroom management, teacher preparation, and teacher induction.

Kathleen Lynn Lane (kathleen.lane@ku.edu) is a Roy A. Roberts Distinguished Professor in the Department of Special Education and Associate Vice Chancellor for Research at the University of Kansas. Her current research interests focus on designing, implementing, and evaluating Comprehensive, Integrated, Three-tiered (Ci3T) models of prevention in schools related to learning and behavior challenges in students.

Katie Scarlett Lane (katie.lane@uconn.edu) is a doctoral student at the University of Connecticut studying research methods, measurement, and evaluation. Her research interests include behavior screening, primary prevention practices, and connecting educators to evidence-based practices.

Kristine E. Larson (klarson2@ndm.edu) is an Assistant Professor of Special Education at Notre Dame of Maryland University where she teaches special education courses and conducts research in classroom management, school climate, coaching, and comprehensive wellbeing/flourishing. She serves as a professional development school (PDS) liaison and is the founder and chair of the *Teacher Education for Flourishing Collaborative*.

Jon Lee (jon.lee@nau.edu) is an Associate Professor of early childhood education in the department of Teaching and Learning at Northern Arizona University. His research and teaching focuses on issues relating to family impact on very young children's emergent literacy development, factors pertaining to children's social, emotional, and behavioral adjustment to schooling, and applications of Motivational Interviewing in educational contexts.

Timothy J. Lewis (LewisTJ@missouri.edu) is a Curators' Distinguished Professor of Special Education at the University of Missouri and Co-Director of the OSEP Center for Positive Behavioral Interventions and Supports. His research interests include individual to school and district-wide systems of positive behavior support through a multi-tiered framework.

Ya-yu Lo (ylo1@uncc.edu) is a professor of special education in the Department of Special Education and Child Development at the University of North Carolina at Charlotte. Her areas of interest and scholarship include multi-tiered academic and behavioral interventions, applied behavior analysis, culturally responsive social skill instruction, and teacher training and coaching.

Anna Long (along@lsu.edu) is an Associate Professor in the School Psychology Program at Louisiana State University. Her research focuses on culturally relevant and responsive mental health practices and promotes implementing multi-tiered systems to prevent and remediate student social, emotional, and behavioral difficulties.

Tim Mainhard (m.t.mainhard@fsw.leidenuniv.nl) is a professor of educational science in the Department of Education and Child Studies at Leiden University in the Netherlands. He is interested in the social dynamics in school settings and classroom management, and uses micro-observations as well as questionnaire-based methods to study teacher-student relationships and how they affect teacher and student well-being and academic functioning.

Patricia L. Marshall (plmarsha@ncsu.edu) is a professor in the Department of Teacher Education and Learning Sciences at NC State University. Her scholarship includes multicultural-and anti-racist education, teachers' concerns about working with culturally diverse students, critical equity pedagogies in social studies and mathematics, cross-cultural competence among teacher educators, environmental justice education, and adult second language acquisition.

Christopher J. McCarthy (cjmccarthy@austin.utexas.edu) is a professor in the Department of Educational Psychology at the University of Texas at Austin. His current scholarly focus is on researching factors that cause stress for K-12 teachers and developing interventions to help teachers thrive.

Glennda K. McKeithan (gmckeithan@ku.edu) is an Associate Teaching Professor and autism program lead in the Department of Special Education at the University of Kansas. Her areas of interest and scholarship include autism spectrum disorder, classroom management, online student engagement, and the application of evidence-based practices across the continuum of services.

Holly M. Menzies (hmenzie@calstatela.edu) is Professor Emeritus in the Division of Special Education & Counseling at California State University, Los Angeles. Her research is in the areas of tiered systems of support and teachers' perceptions of managing student behavior.

Katherine Meyer (katherine.meyer@uconn.edu) is a Research Assistant with the Center for Behavioral Education and Research at the University of Connecticut. Her research and clinical interests include the development and implementation of multi-tiered systems of support such as Positive Behavior Interventions and Supports and Response to Intervention.

Marcia L. Montague (mmontague@tamu.edu) is a Clinical Assistant Professor in the Special Education Division of the Department of Educational Psychology at Texas A&M University. Her scholarship interests include inclusive special education teacher preparation and professional development, classroom management, and equity in access.

Kristen C. Mosley (k.mosley@utexas.edu) is a doctoral candidate in the Department of Educational Psychology at the University of Texas at Austin. Her current scholarly focus is on researching teacher working conditions, factors that cause stress for K-12 teachers, and resources that may help them thrive.

Jolien M. Mouw (j.m.mouw@rug.nl) is an assistant professor at the GION Education/Research institute of the University of Groningen, the Netherlands. Her research interests are educational innovations, purposeful implementation of educational technologies, simulation-based learning environments, pre-service teacher education, and professionalizing teachers' classroom management skills and educational technology use.

Jennifer Nakamura (jennifer.nakamura@sri.com) is an Education Researcher at SRI International. She contributes to mixed methods research and evaluation of educational programs and policies in PreK–12 schools, and her areas of interest include social-emotional learning, supporting students with disabilities, and tiered systems of support.

David Osher (Dosher@air.org) is Vice President and Institute Fellow at the American Institutes for Research. His areas of interest and scholarship include the science of learning development, robust equity, the social and emotional conditions for teaching and learning, student support, safety, cultural competence and responsiveness, collaboration, and implementation science.

Jennifer Pankowski (jpankowski@pace.edu) is a Clinical Assistant Professor and Program Coordinator for Alternative Certification Programs and Special Education in the School of Education at Pace University. Her background includes working as a childhood special education teacher which informs her research on classroom and behavior management for students with disabilities.

Jamie N. Pearson (jnpearso@ncsu.edu) is an Assistant Professor of Special Education in the Department of Teacher Education and Learning Sciences at North Carolina State University. Her research focuses on disparities in autism identification, the impact of parent-advocacy and empowerment training on child and family outcomes, and strategies to promote positive parent-professional partnerships between educators and historically marginalized communities.

Stephen Plank (splank@aecf.org) is vice president of Research, Evaluation, Evidence, and Data at the Annie E. Casey Foundation. In this role, he and his team are responsible for advancing evidence-based practices, commissioning social policy research, overseeing evaluations of Casey programs and initiatives, supporting innovative research methodologies and data resources, and building local capacity to produce and use data to inform programs, planning, and policy reform.

Karen Robbie (karen.robbie@uconn.edu) is a Research Assistant with the Center for Behavioral Education and Research at the University of Connecticut. She provides professional development and technical assistance to schools and districts throughout the Northeast and serves on several national, state, and local committees focused on promoting positive student outcomes and effective school environments.

Luz E. Robinson is a doctoral student in School Psychology at the University of North Carolina at Chapel Hill and her research interests include school-based protective and promotive factors for improving the mental health and well-being of Latinx youth and families. Specifically, her focus is on transformative social-emotional learning, culturally responsive practices, and school-based violence prevention strategies that center social and emotional skill development for marginalized students.

Chad A. Rose (rosech@missouri.edu) is an associate professor in the Department of Special Education at the University of Missouri, and Director of the Mizzou Ed Bully Prevention Lab. His areas of interest and scholarship include prevention of youth violence, including protective factors associated with bullying involvement, bullying among youth with disabilities, and bully prevention interventions within a multi-tiered system of support.

Claudia Saavedra Smith (cpsaaved@ncsu.edu) is a doctoral student and graduate assistant at North Carolina State University. Her research interests include bilingual education, equitable educational opportunities in schools, and educational leadership.

Edward J. Sabornie (ejsaborn@ncsu.edu; Co-Editor) is a Professor of Special Education in the Department of Teacher Education and Learning Sciences at NC State University. His areas of interest and scholarship include applied behavior analysis and classroom management, school violence, social status of students with disabilities in inclusive settings, and secondary-level instruction and behavioral interventions for students with disabilities.

Terrance M. Scott (t.scott@louisville.edu) is a professor and Distinguished University Scholar, and Director of the Center for Instructional and Behavioral Research in Schools at the University of Louisville. His areas of interest include the role of effective instruction in managing student behavior, classroom management, strategies for students with challenging behavior, and school-wide systems of support.

Lacey Seaton (seatonle@vcu.edu) is an Assistant Professor of Educational Leadership at Virginia Commonwealth University. Her research interests include educational leadership, creating inclusive school environments, and equity in education.

John R. Seeley (jseeley@uoregon.edu) is a professor in the Department of Special Education and Clinical Sciences within the College of Education at the University of Oregon. His areas of interest and scholarship include emotional and behavioral disorders, suicide prevention, substance abuse, behavioral health intervention, and implementation science.

Brandi Simonsen (brandi.simonsen@uconn.edu) is a Professor of Special Education in the Neag School of Education, and the Co-Director of the Center for Behavioral Education and Research at the University of Connecticut. She is also the Co-Director of the National Technical Assistance Center on Positive Behavioral Interventions and Supports, and Co-Principal Investigator of the National Multi-Tiered System of Supports Research Network.

Russell J. Skiba (skiba@indiana.edu) is Professor Emeritus, Department of Counseling and Educational Psychology at Indiana University. His research attempts to illuminate racialized practices of exclusionary discipline and school policing that create disparities and inequity, and to contribute to the process of transforming school discipline to promote supportive and nurturing school climates.

Jason W. Small (jasons@ori.org) is an Associate Scientist at the Oregon Research Institute. His current work focuses on the development of interventions for children experiencing social-emotional difficulties, the use of Motivational Interviewing in school-based settings, and the evaluation of training and assessment systems.

Lucia Smith-Menzies (007437073@coyote.csusb.edu) is a special education teacher and a doctoral student in the Educational Leadership program at California State University, San Bernardino. Her scholarly interests include classroom management, behavioral interventions for students with disabilities, and school discipline practices.

Chris Torres (ctorres@msu.edu) is an Associate Professor of Educational Administration in the College of Education at Michigan State University. His areas of interest and expertise focus on educator careers and turnover, policy implementation, district governance, student disciplinary methods, and no-excuses charter schools.

Sierra M. Trudel (sierra.trudel@uconn.edu) is a PhD Candidate of School Psychology at the University of Connecticut. She is a nationally certified school psychologist, licensed professional counselor, and certified yoga teacher with research interests in mind–body health, positive education, and strengths–based assessment.

Alberto Valido is a doctoral student in Applied Developmental Science and Special Education at the Peabody School of Education, University of North Carolina at Chapel Hill. His research interests include intersectionality and mental health among adolescents who experience discrimination or are victimized at school due to their sexual, racial, or gender identities.

Jan van Tartwijk (j.vantartwijk@uu.nl) is a Professor of education in the Department of Education at Utrecht University in the Netherlands, where he chairs the graduate school for teacher education. In his research and teaching he focuses on teacher-student communication processes in the classroom, learning and assessment of learning in the workplace, and on the development of teacher expertise.

Hill M. Walker (hwalker@uoregon.edu) is a Professor Emeritus in the College of Education at the University of Oregon. His research interests include universal screening of students having behavioral challenges, early identification and intervention, social skills training and curricular development, inclusion and social integration, and longitudinal studies of antisocial behavior in school.

Joan Walker (jwalker@pace.edu) is Associate Professor in the School of Education at Pace University. As a developmental psychologist, her research interests include children's development of self–regulation, family engagement in children's education, and teacher professional education for class–room management and family-school partnership.

Amanda P. Williford (williford@virginia.edu) is the Batten Bicentennial Professor of Early Childhood Education and the Associate Director for Early Childhood Education at the Center for Advanced Study of Teaching and Learning within the School of Education and Human Development at the University of Virginia. Her applied research focuses on young children's mental well-being, social-emotional, and school readiness development.

Emily L. Winter (emily.l.winter@uconn.ecu) is a PhD Candidate of School Psychology at the Neag School of Education at the University of Connecticut. She is a nationally certified school psychologist with research interests in eating disorders, athletics, and mind–body health.

Theo Wubbels (t.wubbels@uu.nl) is an Emeritus Professor of Educational Sciences on the faculty of Social and Behavioural Sciences at Utrecht University in the Netherlands. His main research interests developed from the pedagogy of physics education, via problems and supervision of beginning teachers, to studies of learning environments, and interpersonal relationships in education.

PREFACE

The third edition of the *Handbook of Classroom Management* follows the second edition by eight years, and the original version of the same text by 17 years. This edition of the *Handbook* is a clear indicator of how the field of classroom management has evolved and how we attempted to select topics that are timely; there are ten new chapters in this edition that were not found in the second edition. An indication of the relevance of this text can be found in the new chapter topics such as (a) classroom management and discipline practices in virtual school settings as a result of COVID-19, (b) classroom management in "no excuses" charter schools, (c) adapting classroom management across urban, rural, and virtual learning settings, (d) school administration and classroom management, and (e) Critical Race Theory and classroom management. At the same time, informed and original scholarship continues to grow in other traditional and established facets of classroom management (e.g., see Chapter 12 related to exclusionary discipline, Chapter 14 on teacher training and classroom management, and Chapter 6 on trends in Positive Behavior Intervention and Support). Opinions, scientific research, and related scholarship have expanded exponentially in all aspects of the field of classroom management as seen in the number of "hits" generated when one enters the term "classroom management" in a research library search. Last time we checked, we found 11,000+ related journal articles, dissertations, books, chapters, research reports, and other related publications available when the search term "classroom management" was used to generate other related literature available since 2015 in a research library exploration. The totality of implications related to classroom management from such a large amount of recently generated knowledge are too numerous to review in this Preface, but rest assured many chapters found herein address a multitude of such inferences.

The goal of this third edition is to review a large portion of the newly available classroom management information so that interested researchers, behavior analysts, teachers and teacher educators, school administrators, and students have a source of information that can guide their own work related to effective management of classrooms from many different perspectives. A *Handbook* such as this reduces the arduous task of locating a single, comprehensive source of information and allows the reader to gain a scholarly picture of the science and art of classroom management.

The creation of this text would not have been possible without the expertise provided by each of the invited peer reviewers who assisted in the review and revision process of each chapter found herein. Their opinions and proficiency in providing feedback and suggestions to the Co-Editors and chapter authors are truly invaluable and made the *Handbook* stronger and more scholarly. The peer reviewers include: Brittany Anderson, Sheri Bauman, Allison Bruhn, Chris Curran, Lisa De La Rue, Kent Divoll, Steve Evans, Lance Fusarelli, Robert Jagers, Tim Knoster, Dore LaForett, Tamika LaSalle,

Andrew Kwok, Sara McDaniel, Bruno Oldeboom, Drew Polly, Rami Benbenishty, Nancy Jo Schafer, Daniel Shepherd, Louise Southern, Melissa Stormant, Lisa Stulberg, Janet VanLone, and Stacy Weiss. Thank you everyone!

The field of classroom management would not be as important and respected without the earlier scholarship and tireless work of Carolyn M. Evertson and Carol S. Weinstein, the co-editors of the first *Handbook of Classroom Management*. Likewise, many thanks are due to Edmund T. Emmer, co-editor of the second *Handbook*. Without their pioneering work in the field this third edition of the *Handbook* would not be possible.

We would also like to thank the publisher, Routledge/Taylor & Francis, for their continuous support and assistance in creating this third edition of the *Handbook*. Very special appreciation is offered to Daniel Schwartz and Olivia Powers at Routledge/Taylor & Francis for having confidence in us to create and deliver this *Handbook*. We could not have completed all the steps in the process of organizing and producing the final version of the *Handbook* without their expert assistance.

Edward J. Sabornie
Dorothy L. Espelage

PART I

Introduction

1

INTRODUCTION TO THE THIRD EDITION

Edward J. Sabornie

NC STATE UNIVERSITY

Dorothy L. Espelage

UNIVERSITY OF NORTH CAROLINA AT CHAPEL HILL

Few experts in education are likely to argue that effective classroom management (CM) in schools is irrelevant for student success at all grade levels. The science, development, and scholarship of CM over time, however, does not appear to be as substantial as the study of reading or mathematics instruction in schools. Perhaps that is the way it should be considering the academic instructional priorities in schools. Nevertheless, much has changed in terms of CM knowledge and research since the first two editions (i.e., Emmer & Sabornie, 2015; Evertson & Weinstein, 2006) of the *Handbook of Classroom Management* were published. For example, Pomerance and Walsh (2020) concluded that five specific contingencies comprise effective CM:

> (a) establishing classroom rules and routines, (b) maximizing available student learning time in the classroom, (c) delivering frequent positive reinforcement to deserving students, (d) teacher redirection of minor disruptive and inappropriate behavior, and (e) addressing serious student misbehavior with consistent and fair consequences.
>
> *p. 11*

It should be noted, however, particularly related to CM, that the Pomerance and Walsh conclusions related to their "Big Five" contingencies above are not universally perceived as valid for effective CM. Stillman and Schultz (2021), for example, questioned the validity of the conclusions of Pomerance and Walsh in assuming that effective CM is a specific compendium that can be "observed and measured by a predetermined checklist" (i.e., the above Big Five list; p. 6). In essence, Stillman and Schultz determined that the CM suppositions of Pomerance and Walsh are "of little use" (p. 9). So, just as the "science of reading" instructional viewpoint has been questioned over time by the "balanced reading" teaching approach (and vice versa), so too does CM have sparring sides related to its composition, effectiveness, teacher preparation, and implementation.

Additionally, when considering ongoing findings from meta-analysis research (i.e., Kopershoek et al., 2016), it is now known which CM strategies and programs enhance students' academic, behavioral, social-emotional, and motivational outcomes in *primary* grades education. Kopershoek et al. stated that:

DOI: 10.4324/9781003275312-2

3

Implementation of effective classroom management interventions could be further stimulated…by providing schools with adequate information on those interventions with strong evidence on their effectiveness and those without. Moreover, teacher training programs should…integrate the existing knowledge about effective classroom management more strongly into their programs. By doing so, they can train their student teachers to manage classrooms effectively.

p. 670

Many (see Emmer & Sabornie, 2015; Evertson & Weinstein, 2006) have recommended that teachers in training need greater exposure to evidenced-based CM techniques to be effective in classroom environments, and Kopershoek et al. demonstrated support for such a concept with youth in the early grades. The Kopershoek et al. results are also similar to those of Flower et al. (2017) who found that most teacher training higher education institutions emphasize the foundations of CM in terms of "basic" classroom rules and physical arrangements. When students consistently misbehave and demonstrate serious and aggressive behavioral problems in classrooms, however, the basics of CM are insufficient for treating such inappropriate behavior by students (Flower et al., 2017). Another threat in a classroom where efficacious management is dangerously lacking is that students exposed to trauma in an environment achieve at less than optimum levels (Harper, 2020). No conscientious school personnel would want to be employed in or foster such an environment. School administrators also report that teacher candidates in higher education (i.e., student teachers) lacked the necessary skills when faced with CM issues in urban schools (Albright et al., 2017).

The Transformation of the Teaching Force

In an effort to provide a picture of who are the present "classroom managers," Ingersoll et al. (2018) contributed extensive information regarding the most recent characteristics of the teaching force in the USA, as collected by the National Center on Educational Statistics (NCES). In total, the NCES surveyed over 40,000 teachers, more than 9,000 school administrators, and roughly 5,000 school district level managers to determine who is teaching the children and youth in the USA. What is particularly interesting about this survey is that it confirmed the rather profound changes occurring in the teaching force in the country, yet the teacher population trends found in the Ingersoll et al. (2018) report have not been widely broadcast or known to the public.

The seven "trends" Ingersoll et al. (2018) found regarding the current teaching force in US schools include:

- The number of teachers has grown markedly while the number of students served in schools has not grown in parallel fashion
- The average age of US teachers has increased as well as the number of retirements
- As the average age of US teachers has increased, so too has the proportion of younger teachers with less teaching experience; most newly employed teachers are recent college graduates, but a sizeable number of new teachers are older and less experienced
- Historically, US school teachers are overwhelmingly female, and recently the teaching population is even more proportionally female
- US teachers are becoming more diverse in terms of race and ethnicity
- College students seeking to become teachers tend to have lower SAT and ACT scores, and this trend has not changed over the last few decades
- Teacher attrition is higher than that for nurses, lawyers, engineers, architects, and academics

To extrapolate, many population characteristic changes are occurring in the US teaching profession, and there is a need to determine how such variables interact with CM and its application. Additional teacher demographic questions to be answered deal with the predominantly female teaching force, and whether women are better classroom managers than their male peers. The same applies when comparing (a) the CM expertise of teachers of color versus those who are white, (b) what teacher characteristics (i.e., gender, age, years of experience) are closely related to CM success, and (c) what type of teacher is likely to experience higher levels of psychological stress (see below) on the job. All these issues are socially valid for experimentation and important to understand fully among educational researchers, teachers, school administrators, and teacher trainers.

The Importance of Effective Classroom Management

In a comprehensive research literature review regarding the effects of "professional learning programs" on CM, Paramita et al. (2020) repeatedly showed that CM is an important skill for teachers to master, but educators at all levels often express inadequacy in treating and responding to students' challenging classroom behavior. Not surprisingly, this same issue was raised in the original *Handbook of Classroom Management* by Brophy (2006). While time has marched onward since the first edition of the *Handbook*, it appears that some of the same problems related to CM and its interaction with teacher training are difficult to remedy. The more serious student misbehavior is in classrooms, the more comprehensive preparation and coaching in effective CM is required for educators before and during actual teaching experiences.

Included in the CM "much more needs to be done" realm is the requirement for teachers to learn exactly how to become successful classroom managers. Effective CM instruction is extremely important—perhaps more so today than ever before (Stevenson et al., 2020). A confounding variable is that it is probably beyond the capability of higher education, alone, to provide all pre-service teachers with the knowledge to become expert classroom managers in every aspect immediately following completion of a teacher education degree program. This is known as the "train and hope" (Stokes & Baer, 1977) paradigm related to generalization of behavior: preservice teachers are trained by being exposed to lectures, readings, classroom practice activities, and actual classroom teaching experiences, and school district employers and administrators hope that new teachers have retained and can apply all the important information and skills learned in higher education. In other words, school district employers have faith in the notion that their newly hired teacher employees are all expert classroom managers among other desirable characteristics.

The above train and hope concern can be corrected by following the implementation science model of teacher change recommended by Mitchell et al. (2017). The Mitchell et al. model specifically states that "if we want teachers to acquire and use new or different instructional or management approaches, we need to attend to maximally effective learning opportunities" (p. 143). Mitchell et al. do not recommend conventional teacher training via higher education as the only preferred way in which to prepare expert classroom managers. Instead, Mitchell et al. recommend the use of professional classroom *coaching* which provides direct, live, and wide-ranging assistance and feedback provided to teachers in classrooms by CM and content area experts. The direct CM coaching model ensures fidelity of instructional delivery and allows the educator to receive immediate feedback on student outcomes. The Mitchell et al. coaching model also includes (a) intensive teacher supervision in actual classrooms—not lecture halls, (b) "teaching the teacher" and extensive practice in ways to engage in effective CM, (c) direct behavioral assessment of teacher instruction implementation, and (d) encouragement and reinforcement directed toward the teacher for correct execution of newly learned and effective CM (or any other) teaching skills. Without a change in the teacher preparation status quo, and implementation of effective CM teaching skills acquired through coaching, new and experienced teachers are likely to struggle (as shown above in research) and lead to early exit from the profession.

Classroom Management Versus Behavior Management

It should be noted that the terms CM and behavior management (BM) have frequently been used synonymously in the literature because of their many similarities in application (see Chapters 24 and 27 in this volume). While the terms CM and BM do share many components, there is a key difference between the two descriptors that should be highlighted. Our view is similar to that of Stevenson et al. (2020) who stated that CM emphasizes interventions aimed at "instructional groups," while BM has a narrower focus on individual pupils in classrooms. It should be noted, however, that there is much overlap in the two terms simply because individual students do populate groups in classrooms, and it is difficult to determine which term should be emphasized primarily. Do we concentrate mainly on individual students, or the entire classroom with many students?

Effective classroom managers aim their behavioral interventions at both individual students who need special assistance (e.g., when using an intervention such as "Check-in, Check-out" [CICO] with one student), and directing additional interventions at an entire classroom group (e.g., when using a Tier 1 Positive Behavior Intervention and Support [PBIS] treatment such as catching students "being good" and reinforcing them for appropriate behavior with exchangeable tokens). A student receiving the CICO treatment (the BM factor) would still be eligible to receive the reinforcement associated with the classwide PBIS structure in place (the CM factor). Stevenson et al. (2020) stated that CM components included, among other factors, establishing behavioral expectations, reinforcement for following classroom routines, and instruction to reduce future behavioral problems. These CM treatments could also be applied on an individual student basis quite easily. We are not certain of this, but perhaps attempting to separate effective BM from evidence-based CM is unnecessary in light of their shared goals: to enhance organization and management in classrooms so that students and teachers have a chance to succeed.

Beyond contrasting CM with BM, Stevenson et al. (2020) also suggested three ways in which to strengthen the factors associated with CM so that it can be improved. We agree with the Stevenson et al. suggestions for they seem reasonable and worthy of implementation to strengthen CM for all concerned. Their first recommendation concerns the need to improve preparation of all teachers in training that includes a required course in CM. Such a course would emphasize "explicit, evidence-based, and culturally and contextually relevant classroom management skills" (p. 401). In this course teachers in training would learn in detail the importance of (a) reinforcing appropriate behavior in the classroom (e.g., student active engagement), and (b) responding appropriately to student off-task and inappropriate behavior in classrooms. The course would also provide opportunities for teachers in training to practice effective CM skills and receive performance feedback from university instructors. Additionally, the course would also provide case studies, instructional videos, and class-room simulations pinpointing actual CM skills.

The second recommendation provided by Stevenson et al. (2020) concerns revising student teaching requirements in actual schools and classrooms. The improved student teaching experience suggested in the Stevenson et al. model would provide "extensive support and coaching of classroom management skills" (p. 401). The coaching personnel would include university personnel as well as classroom instructors involved in supervising the teachers in training. Coaching behaviors would include active modeling of requisite behaviors by both types of mentors as well as performance feedback directed at the student teacher while practice teaching. This coaching recommendation is very similar to what Mitchell et al. (2017) suggested (see above).

The third recommendation offered by Stevenson et al. (2020) is the simplest in concept but perhaps the most difficult for implementation. It involves individual state Departments of Education, and the role that such governing bodies play in improving education (and CM) in schools. Stevenson et al. recommended that state Departments of Education should simply adopt both of their above proposals for training teachers in CM and require them through codification for all teachers in preparation in higher education. In other words, the Stevenson et al. guidelines would create statewide CM preparation regulations for all teachers in training. We agree with the need for such stringent directives related to CM teacher training. Without such protocols elementary and secondary level students in classrooms are likely to be negatively affected (see Stevenson et al., 2020).

Proactive Classroom Management

While a plethora of additional research on CM is now available since the last edition of the *Handbook of Classroom Management* was published 2015, new CM ideas and direct recommendations for practitioners are also available and need to be highlighted. Terada (2019), for example, provided the following suggestions—backed by research—that can assist teachers seeking better behavioral CM and eliminating disruptive student behavior.

- *Greeting students at the door at the beginning of a school day or instructional period.* By doing so, teachers can show interest in every student who enters the classroom and demonstrate to students that s/he cares about their welfare.
- *Establish and maintain personal relationships.* It has been shown that "checking-in" with students at various times throughout the school day (e.g., asking "How's it going?" "How are you doing now, after …" "Is there any way I can help you so that _____ doesn't happen again…") can direct teachers to focus on assistive solutions rather than punitive consequences to problem behaviors.
- *Use reminders and cues.* To help students focus on what is important in terms of their behavior in the classroom, it is wise to remind them of what is expected. This could be done with a tap on a wind chime (for younger students) or a verbal reminder of the classroom rules at the beginning of class for any students.
- *Optimize classroom seating.* To prevent disruptive behavior in the classroom, the informed classroom manager may want to control seat assignment for students. When students are allowed to select their own seats (usually with friends) misbehavior has a higher probability of occurring.
- *Give behavior-specific praise.* When attempting to reinforce students for appropriate behavior in the classroom, deliver any social praise with specificity rather than generality. Say, "I like the way that you started your work immediately after my directions," rather than saying the generic, "good job" to a student.
- *Set clear expectations.* Display the classroom rules where clearly visible to all, but also discuss with the students *why* the rules are necessary. Involve the students in creating classroom rules so that they understand the expectations at a personal level.
- *Be active in student supervision.* Watch what students are doing in the classroom at all times, and be active in staying in close physical contact with students. Diligently supervise students' individual seat work so that reinforcement or corrective feedback can be provided immediately.
- *Be consistent in applying rules.* Do not "play favorites" when applying behavioral expectations and classroom rules, and remind students that their behavior may be aberrant at times, but not their humanity. The student's behavior needs redirection, not his or her personality; teachers should also not allow minor student misbehavior to add to personal stress on the job (see Sparks, 2017).

The above suggestions by Terada (2019) are similar to the CM recommendations provided by Mitchell et al. (2017). Additional recommended, evidence-based CM strategies found in Mitchell et al. include: (a) arranging the classroom physical layout so that it is orderly and safe, (b) provide students with numerous opportunities to respond to task-related questions, and (c) the teacher follows the same rules, routines, and expectations as those prescribed for the students.

Current Classroom Management and Its Social Context

Classroom teaching is a rewarding yet difficult profession at times, and many teachers experience daily stress on the job (Steiner & Woo, 2021). Disruptive student behavior is a frequent reason for teacher stress (Freiberg et al., 2020). An overwhelming majority (i.e., 60%) of teachers admit that they experience job-related stress "frequently or always," and many teachers (i.e., 41%) acknowledge that their instructional effectiveness decreases when they feel stressed (Will, 2020; also see Chapter 11 in this volume). Moreover, teachers disclose that when they feel stress on the job, CM, along with relationships with students and quality of instruction, decrease in effectiveness (Will, 2020). Students feel the stress that teachers demonstrate in classrooms, and it can lead to less that desired student behavioral functioning and instructional involvement (Will, 2020). Add the stress of possibly being exposed to COVID-19 into classrooms, in addition to the typical stress levels that teachers experience on the job, and one can understand the troublesome issues that teachers face while trying to be effective educators.

The teacher stress in the classroom that can affect CM is gaining much recent attention, and even teacher trade publications are highlighting its serious nature. EdWeek Research Center (2021), for example, highlighted the classrooms challenges that COVID-19 placed on teachers and the stress they felt on the job. It was reported that "91% of educators experience job-related stress sometimes, frequently, or always" (p. 1). In the same EdWeek Research Center report, teachers also requested support for assisting their students' challenges in mental health and home life during the COVID-19 pandemic. Steiner and Woo (2021) stated that during the 2020–2021 school year, at the height of the pandemic, teachers reported "higher job-related stress and depression than the general population" (p. 2). Cardoza (2021) found that many teachers have reached the breaking point regarding teaching while COVID-19 is present in society, and they feel the need to be nurtured beyond typical levels. Lastly, Zamarro et al. (2021) claimed that the COVID-19 pandemic changed teachers' plans for continuing as a classroom teacher.

The above examples of teachers experiencing job-related stress related to COVID-19 are in addition to the level of pressure and anxiety that is typically found by teachers in schools every day. It is easy to understand how COVID-19 has had an extraordinary amount of influence on teachers and their stress levels, and it has—with reason—affected how CM operates in classrooms amid a pandemic. The COVID-19 pandemic has also uncovered the need for a different kind of CM application related to online instruction (see Chapter 8 in this volume). It will be necessary to pinpoint the specific kinds of CM needed in an online instructional environment that do not exist in face-to-face classroom instruction in traditional schools. We realize that parts of the following idiom are often overused in scholarly literature; however, additional research is indeed necessary to partial-out how, exactly, the COVID-19 pandemic has influenced CM, and what changes need to be implemented for effective teacher training under such troublesome health circumstances.

Organization and Content of the Third Edition

The third edition of the *Handbook of Classroom Management* will assist researchers, school and educational psychologists, teacher educators in training, school administrators, and a countless number of new and existing teachers on the latest information related to effectively managing classrooms at all school levels. With proven CM procedures appearing along with a discussion of related instructional issues, a current, updated vision of the entire field of CM is provided herein. More work is necessary related to research and ways to prepare teachers in effective CM, and this text is our attempt at doing so. Found below is a description of each handbook part, chapters, and other narrative. This brief introductory chapter forms Part I.

Part II: *Methods of Classroom Management*

Part II of this Handbook, *Methods of Classroom Management*, begins with Chapter 2 by Terrance Scott and Jennifer Nakamura covering effective instruction as the foundation of successful CM. They discuss the characteristics of explicit instruction in classrooms and how clear teacher communication, student engagement, and direct teacher feedback to students aids effective CM. In Chapter 3, Sierra Trudel, Emily Winter, and Melissa Bray provide prevention strategies that assist in efficacious CM. Included in Chapter 3 are recommendations and unique mind-body health strategies and exercises that can assist educators in working with students who need to keep emotions and behavior in check in educational environments. In Chapter 4, Sean Darling-Hammond and Trevor Fronius provide a thoughtful review of the history of implementation of restorative practices, or restorative justice, in US classrooms and schools. They highlight the quantitative studies on the impact of restorative practices and provide readers with specific strategies to maximize sustainability of these non-punitive approaches to building classroom climate and sense of community. Hill Walker, Andy Frey, Jason Small, Ed Feil, John Seeley, Jon Lee, Annemieke Golly, Shantel Crosby, and Steve Forness, in Chapter 5, discuss the particulars (e.g., history, features, research) of the *First Step* program, an intervention designed to prevent inappropriate student behavior in early elementary grades. The *First Step* (and its 2015 revision, *First Step Next*) program is a Tier 2 treatment regimen that attempts to serve students whose challenging overt behavior does not fit with the expectations found in school settings. In Chapter 6, Sara Estrapala and Timothy Lewis provide a discussion related to current trends in Class-wide Positive Behavioral Intervention and Supports (CWPBIS). Recent CWPBIS research is reviewed while focusing on classroom configurations, data-based decision making, critical implementation issues, and ways in which to improve teacher practice related to student behavior. Classroom management at intervention Tiers 2 and 3, and related issues, are discussed in detail in Chapter 7 by Brandi Simonsen, Karen Robbie, Katherine Meyer, Jen Freeman, Susannah Everett, and Adam Feinberg. Readers of this chapter will find a plethora of CM recommendations related to implementation of social, emotional, and behavioral support of students found within a multi-tiered system of support framework. Chapter 8, written by Shanna Hirsch, Kristine Larson, Lydia Beahm, and Catherine Bradshaw, focuses on the environment adaptations necessary for effective CM in schools. The authors focus on rural and urban schools, as well as online learning settings, to emphasize the need for a range of necessary instructional services to be implemented to ensure CM success. In Chapter 9, Chris Torres examines the controversial approaches to CM found in "no-excuses" charter schools. Torres reviews the important issues in no excuses charter schools from the perspective of teachers, administrators, parents, and students related to school policies and practices, and shortcomings of disciplinary strategies. Recognizing that bullying and violence in the classroom can be challenging behaviors for teachers to manage, Chad Rose, Dorothy Espelage, and Luz Robinson in Chapter 10 review the plethora of research on bullying prevention that has been published since the last edition of this *Handbook*. They focus on equipping teachers with strategies and approaches to minimize bullying and promote inclusivity and belongingness in their classrooms.

Part III: *Context of Classroom Management*

Part III of this Handbook, Context of Classroom Management, includes chapters that address the importance of building strong connections between those stakeholders that play a critical role in effective CM. These chapters speak to promoting strong connections among students, teachers, administrators, and families as well as the role of teacher institutions on the training and supervision of pre-service and in-service teachers. The issues in these chapters are situated within the larger social justice concerns of inequities in discipline approaches and CM. In Chapter 11 by Christopher McCarthy, Kristen Mosley, and Jendayi Dillard, the authors review the research on the intersection between CM and teacher stress, an issue that has been exacerbated during the COVID-19 pandemic. These authors provide concrete recommendations of best practices for reducing stress and increasing well-being in the classroom. Using research published since the last edition of the *Handbook*, in Chapter 12 Russell Skiba, Edward Fergus, and Anne Gregory analyze racialized disparities in exclusionary discipline through the lens of structural racism. Among other issues, Skiba et al. conclude that further analyses of color-blind racism, and the failure of recommended disciplinary strategies to reduce disciplinary disproportionality, comports with other recent reviews in calling for interventions that abandon race neutrality in favor of treatments that are conscious of and seek to overcome historical injustice.

Effective CM hinges on teacher communication with parents and engaging families in meaningful ways. This is the focus of Chapter 13 by Joan Walker and Jennifer Pankowski. They summarize the research on the connection between CM and family communication, argue that families provide teachers with the critical information about their children, and provide concrete strategies to engage families. In a revised Chapter 14 on teacher training and CM, Marcia Montague and Andrew Kwok focus on the importance of training in CM at both the pre-service and in-service levels. Updates in this revised chapter include greater attention to culturally responsive CM, inclusive classroom management, and universal design for learning.

In a new chapter found in this third edition of the *Handbook*, Lance Fusarelli, Lacey Seaton, and Claudia Smith in Chapter 15 explore the interaction between school principal supervision of teachers related to CM. Effective CM support of teachers provided by school principals is examined along with the challenges and limitations of such didactic assistance. Next, David Osher, Stephen Plank, Candace Hester, and Scott Houghton in Chapter 16 examine the recent research on the school-to-prison pipeline and document how institutionalized racism and privilege manifest in dynamic interactions and co-actions between and among adults and youth in classrooms. Critical to this conversation is the examination of promising strategies to mitigate racialized interactions in the classroom to prevent and promote student learning and wellbeing.

Kevin Brady, in Chapter 17, provides a review of the recent legal issues related to CM. What is particularly important in Brady's chapter is the review of current legal issues concerning CM as a result of the creation of virtual school environments due to the COVID-19 pandemic. Michael Kennedy, Rachel Kunemund, and Lindsay Carlisle discuss the role that technology plays in effective CM in Chapter 18. The authors review research related to Content Acquisition Podcasts, simulations, and video-aided reflections in an attempt to showcase how technology can support teachers seeking effective CM procedures. Chapter 19, written by Hanke Korpershoek, Jolien Mouw, and Hester De Boer, presents an overview of 18 recent CM studies that examined various multimodal and social-emotional learning programs. The authors' research review results show increased international interest in developing positive student-teacher relationships in classrooms.

Part IV: Social Perspectives of Classroom Management

Part IV of this Handbook, Social Perspectives of Classroom Management, includes chapters that address the importance of building strong connections between those stakeholders that play a critical role in effective CM. In Chapter 20, Dorothy Espelage, Luz Robinson, and Alberto Valido present an overview of Transformative Social Emotional Learning (TSEL), which focuses on equity by understanding and embracing student culture, identity, agency, belonging, and engagement to support the development of social and emotional skills. Through the implementation of TSEL, the authors provide teachers with strategies to promote a positive classroom environment by equipping youth with skills to manage emotions and peer relations. In Chapter 21, Theo Wubbels, Tim Mainhard, Perry den Brok, Luce Claessens, and Jan van Tartwijk examine the interpersonal perspectives of CM from recent published research. Social dynamic systems theory is reviewed so that the reader can understand the interpersonal interactions between students and teachers, and how such theory can guide effective CM. Kent Divoll, in Chapter 22, reviews recent teacher aggression research and how such a variable affects CM and student-teacher relationships. Studies included in the review of research found that teacher aggression and teacher-delivered corporal punishment simply result in additional behavior problems in students. Next, Anna Long and Kelly Clark, in Chapter 23, examine factors contributing to discipline disparities across race and ethnicity. They propose a model to reduce these disparities by examining school discipline policies and philosophies and improving teacher preparation and implicit racial bias training. The authors provide specific strategies for teachers to incorporate into their CM approaches to minimize bias.

Part V: The Classroom Management and Student Type Interaction

In Chapter 24, concerning Critical Race Theory (CRT) and CM, Patricia Marshall and Brittani Clark address the very timely and important issue of CM and race. For decades, the CM and race interaction issue has had a robust focus in the educational research literature, and the authors show that today it continues to be just as strong—if not more so—than the past. Continuing with a focus on multi-cultural issues, Bettie Ray Butler, Ya-yu Lo, Deondra Gladney, and Altheria Caldera, in Chapter 25, discuss culturally responsive CM. The authors' intent in this chapter is to assist experienced teachers as well as teachers in training so that discriminatory CM procedures have no place in effective class-room environments. In Chapter 26, Kathleen Lane, Holly Menzies, Lucia Smith-Menzies, and Katie Lane attempt to empower all teachers of students with disabilities—in any classroom environment—with effective CM techniques. The authors provide a discussion regarding proactive (rather than reactive) CM strategies which include the integrated system of Comprehensive, Integrated, Three-tiered model (Ci3T) of inappropriate behavior prevention. Edward Sabornie, Glennda McKeithan, and Jamie Pearson, in Chapter 27, provide a review of recent classroom and behavioral management research concerning students with autism. The authors highlight how problem behaviors of many students with autism interfere with smooth processes in classrooms and suggest methods from research to eliminate CM problems with such students. Lastly, in Chapter 28, Marissa Bivona and Amanda Williford examine recent research related to CM in early childhood education. The authors stress the numerous challenges faced by early childhood educators as well as support systems that can be used to enhance CM in early childhood educational settings.

Concluding Remarks

Significant advances in CM theory, research, and practice have been noted since the publication of the second Edition of the *Handbook of Classroom Management* in 2015. During the writing of this third Edition, K-12 schools across the globe have struggled to understand how to best manage classrooms both in-person and in online learning communities. Concurrently, a racial pandemic in our communities and schools has further uncovered racial disparities in how student behavior is managed and how well-intended CM approaches can lead to racist and discriminatory outcomes.

Considering these two pandemics, the authors of this third edition consider how the field of CM can contribute to greater equity in classrooms and ultimately contribute to greater learning and wellbeing outcomes for students, teachers, and families. We are therefore extremely grateful for the researchers who were willing to prepare updated and new chapters during a global pandemic, and we believe that this volume will offer readers evidence and scientifically-based strategies to improve their CM strategies and frameworks.

References

Albright, J. L., Safer, L. A., Sims, P. A., Tagaris, A., Glasgow, D., Sekulich, K. M. & Zaharis, M. C. (2017). What factors impact why novice middle school teachers in a large midwestern urban school district leave after their initial year of teaching. *NCPEA International Journal of Educational Leadership Preparation*, *12*(1). https://files. eric.ed.gov/fulltext/EJ1145460.pdf

Brophy, J. (2006). History of research on classroom management. In C. M. Evertson & C. S. Weinstein (Eds.), *Handbook of classroom management* (pp. 17–43). Erlbaum.

Cardoza, K. (2021, April 21). *'We need to be nurtured, too': Many teachers say they're reaching a breaking point.* NPR WUNC. www.npr.org/2021/04/19/988211478/we-need-to-be-nurtured-too-many-teachers-say-theyre-reaching-a-breaking-point

EdWeek Research Center (2021, September 14). What the data say. *Education Week, 41*(5), 7. www.edweek.org/leadership/educator-stress-anti-racism-and-pandemic-response-how-youre-feeling/2021/09

Emmer, E. T., & Sabornie, E. J. (2015). Introduction to the second edition. In E. T. Emmer & E. J. Sabornie, *Handbook of classroom management* (2nd ed., pp. 3–12). Routledge.

Evertson, C. M., & Weinstein, C. S. (Eds.). (2006). *Handbook of classroom management.* Erlbaum.

Flower, A., McKenna, J. W., & Haring, C. D. (2017). Behavior and classroom management: Are teacher preparation programs really preparing our teachers? *Preventing School Failure, 61*(2), 163–169. http://dx.doi.org/10.1080/1045988X.2016.1231109

Freiberg, H. J., Oviatt, D., & Naveira, E. (2020). Classroom management meta-review continuation of research-based programs for preventing and solving discipline problems. *Journal of Education for Students Placed at Risk, 25*(4), 319–337. https://doi.org/10.1080 /10824669.2020.1757454

Harper, S. R. (2020, May). Presidential statement on police killings of Black people. American Educational Research Association. www.aera.net/Newsroom/Presidential-Statement-on-Police-Killings-of-Black-People

Ingersoll, R. M., Merrill, E., Stuckey, D., & Collins, G. (2018). Seven trends: The transformation of the teaching force—updated October 2018. *Consortium for Policy Research in Education Research Reports.* https://repository.upenn.edu/cpre_researchreports/108

Korpershoek, H., Harms, T., de Boer, H., van Kuijk, M., & Doolaard, S. (2016). A meta-analysis of the effects of classroom management strategies and classroom management programs on students' academic, behavioral, emotional, and motivational outcomes. *Review of Educational Research, 86*(3), 643–680. https://doi.org/10.3102% 2F0034654315626799

Mitchell, B. S., Hirn, R. G., & Lewis, T. J. (2017). Enhancing effective classroom management in schools: Structures for changing teacher behavior. *Teacher Education and Special Education, 40*(2), 140–153. https://doi.org/10.1177/0888406417700961

Paramita, P. P., Anderson, A., & Sharma, U. (2020). Effective teacher professional learning on classroom behaviour management: A review of literature. *Australian Journal of Teacher Education, 45*(1), 61–81. https://ro.ecu.edu.au/ajte/vol45/iss1/5

Pomerance, L. & Walsh, K. (2020). 2020 *Teacher Prep Review: Clinical Practice and Classroom Management.* National Council on Teacher Quality. www.nctq.org/publications/2020-Teacher-Prep-Review:-Clinical-Practice-and-Classroom-Management

Sparks, S. D. (2017, June 7). *How teachers' stress affects students: A research roundup.* Education Week. www.edweek.org/education/how-teachers-stress-affects-students-a-research-roundup/2017/06

Steiner, E. D., & Woo, A. (2021). *Job-related stress threatens the teacher supply: Key findings from the 2021 state of the U.S. teacher survey.* Rand Corporation. https://doi.org /10.7249/RRA1108-1

Stevenson, N. A., VanLone, J., & Barber, B. R. (2020). A commentary on the misalignment of teacher education and the need for classroom behavior management skills. *Education and Treatment of Children, 43*, 393–404. https://doi.org/10.1007/s43494-020-00031-1

Stillman, J., & Schultz, K. (2021). 2020 *Teacher prep review: Clinical practice and classroom management.* National Education Policy Center. http://nepc.colorado.edu /thinktank/teacher-prep

Stokes, T. F., & Baer, D. M. (1977). An implicit technology of generalization. *Journal of Applied Behavior Analysis, 10*, 349–367. https://psycnet.apa.org/doi/ 10.1901/jaba.1977.10-349

Terada, Y. (2019, August 7). *8 proactive classroom management tips.* Edutopia. www.Edutopia.org/article/8-proactive-classroom-management-tips

Will, M. (2020, September 14). *Teachers are not ok, even though we need them to be.* Education Week. www.edweek.org/teaching-learning/teachers-are-not-ok-even-though-we-need-them-to-be/2021/09

Zamarro, G., Camp, A., Fuchsman, D., & McGee, J. B. (2021, September 8). *How the pandemic has changed teachers' commitment to remaining in the classroom.* Brookings Brown Center Chalkboard. www.brookings.edu/blog/brown-center-chalkboard/2021/09/08/how-the-pandemic-has-changed-teachers-commitment-to-remaining-in-the-classroom/

PART II

Methods of Classroom Management

2

EFFECTIVE INSTRUCTION AS THE BASIS FOR CLASSROOM MANAGEMENT

Terrance M. Scott

CENTER FOR INSTRUCTIONAL AND BEHAVIORAL RESEARCH
IN SCHOOLS, UNIVERSITY OF LOUISVILLE

Jennifer Nakamura

SRI INTERNATIONAL

Introduction

When queried, teachers report managing student behavior to be both the most challenging part of their job and the part for which they feel least prepared (Westling, 2010). While this is especially true of novice teachers (APA, 2006), classroom management has been widely cited as the greatest challenge for all teachers (Melnick & Meister, 2008). In fact, challenges related to student behavior have been cited as the leading cause of teacher burn-out and leaving the profession early (Aloe et al., 2014; Wang et al., 2015). In reality, student behavior can be considered and taught in the same manner as any academic content. To be clear, instruction is not merely a strategy for classroom management; it is the essential foundational component. This chapter describes how the key features of effective instruction can be applied to teaching behavior to lay the foundation for effective classroom management.

Effective instruction can be defined as the collective use of teacher instructional practices that maximize the probability of student success (Scott, 2017). Clearly, there are no sure strategies that are guaranteed to be successful; nothing works for every student or in every instance. But practitioners can consider practices in terms of their probability of producing a success and rank them according to their relative effectiveness. When considered in this light, good teachers are those who most consistently engage in teaching practices that have a high probability of achieving the intended result. Good teaching begets student success, and success begets additional successes. That is, a student experiencing a small success increases the probability of subsequent larger successes, which snowball into self-confidence and an ability to successfully transition skills to the world outside of the classroom and school setting. This all begins with a teacher designing instruction to make the student successful. In this manner of thinking, the definition of a teacher could be said to be one who thoughtfully creates presentations, wording, environments, and even tricks that push students into success—and then give the students all the credit for that success.

DOI: 10.4324/9781003275312-4

Effective instruction plays a critical role in fostering what is typically considered classroom management (Sindelar et al., 2010). First, classroom management refers to managing student behaviors so that they are behaving in ways that create a positive learning environment. The fact that we want students to engage in specific behaviors at specific times is a justification for teaching those behaviors; and if we're teaching behaviors, it makes sense to use effective instructional practices. Second, by definition, effective instruction means that students are more likely to be successful. Providing students with opportunities to succeed, even during purely academic instruction, greatly improves their behavior (McIntosh et al., 2006; Scott & Gage, 2020).

Within the broader field of education, some take issue with the concept of "managing" students, arguing that attempting to control others is unethical and counterproductive to authentic learning (e.g., Freiberg, 1999; Brantlinger & Danforth, 2006). For purposes of classroom management, the term "control" simply means predictability. We say a behavior is under control when we can predict that the student will engage with appropriate behaviors as the context requires. Under the context that a student has a conflict with a peer, we would like to predict that the student solve the conflict peacefully using conflict resolution methods that have been taught. That this happens predictably is referred to as control. But there is no force involved in control; it is the student's chosen behavior. Note that this is no different teaching academics. Given the context, "what's 2 + 2," we would like to predict that the student will say "4." Again, the behavior occurs without overt control of adults.

Of course, some have argued, any time that the adult controls consequences to affect a change in student behavior, it involves forcing the student to bend to their will. As such, the teaching of rules for behavior is potentially hegemonic as the teacher dictates right and wrong from their own ethnocentric point of view (Agostinone-Wilson, 2006). Because teachers are largely White, middle-class individuals, school becomes a party to the stripping of cultural mores from groups whose behaviors do not fit the White standard (Pitsoe & Letseka, 2013).

These are important and well-considered criticisms that warrant serious thought as we consider the nature of being a teacher. Clearly, curricular decisions need to be made by representative stakeholder groups that understand the sanctity of culture. As we believe behavior management is a form of instruction, the same processes need to be in place as teachers consider their classroom rules. To this end, we recommend first that classroom rules be tied to larger school expectations so as not to be too tied to individual decisions. Second, we discuss how teachers involve students in discussions of the rules rather than simply have them dictated. The overall concerns with any instruction is the degree to which it will result in dignity and success for students.

This chapter is guided by the simple question: What strategies provide students with the best chances for success? In this light, effective instruction can be considered within the concepts of (a) communication, (b) engagement, and (c) feedback (Hattie, 2009; McLeskey et al., 2019). This chapter is focused on definitions and examples of key practices within each of these three concepts. While the focus will be on the teaching of behavior, these same concepts apply equally to academic content and academic analogies are used to help make this point.

Communicating Classroom Expectations

Effective communication of information from a teacher to a student is perhaps the very essence of teaching. Students that don't know or don't understand the rules are more prone to errors (Engelmann, 1966). But continuing with our consideration of probability, not all communication styles, strategies, or practices are equal; some provide higher probabilities for success than others (see Ceylan, 2009: Sorakin-Balli et al., 2020). The key components of communicating as part of instruction are: (1) to help students understand what it being communicated and why it is important, (2) to teach them to discriminate between right and wrong across a range of examples, and (3) to build their capacity to generalize knowledge and skills to more natural circumstances in their lives (Engelmann & Colvin, 2006). To that end, we start with a discussion of what is known as explicit instruction. In its most basic form, the term "explicit" simply means to say something clearly and directly. While this is surely an important part of communication, in the context of effective instruction, the term explicit can be expanded to include a series of teacher behaviors that systematically help students to learn a skill or concept and to understand its importance and key features (Archer & Hughes, 2011).

Clarity Through Contextualized Information

The concept of explicit instruction is founded on communication. One manner of describing explicit instruction is to consider the concept of teacher clarity, or the degree to which the teacher relates information in a precise and unambiguous manner (McLeskey et al., 2019). To maximize clarity, effective teachers describe new ideas, rules, concepts, or relationships by couching new information within a familiar context. Context can be created through connections to larger concepts, prior learning, or students' real-life experiences.

The most logical application of explicit instruction to classroom management is in teaching class rules and expectations. To clarify, expectations are broad goals for student behavior (e.g., respect others), while rules are the specific behaviors in which the students should engage to meet the expectation (e.g., keep hands and feet to self). Sometimes expectations are described as "anchors" in that they provide a key concept by which to introduce the many smaller rules. Effective classroom managers develop and teach classroom expectations beginning on the first day of school. Many schools have defined these on a school-wide basis, so that students hear the same expectations in every location and every classroom. However, the individual behaviors that are necessary to demonstrate the expectation will likely vary by location. For example, a school may define "respect yourself" as keeping oneself safe and learning. But in a Math classroom the rules for behavior under this anchor are likely very different from the Art classroom. When entering the Math class students are asked to respect themselves by turning in homework before being seated. In Art class, respecting oneself is demonstrated by putting on aprons before beginning project work. In both cases the concept is staying safe and learning, but the behaviors are very different. Still, anchoring rules to larger conceptual expectations provide an important context connection and increases the probability of student success (Kirschner et al., 2006).

New information can also be clarified by presenting it in the context of prior learning. When content is part of a clear scope and sequence, this is an easy task; teachers simply describe what the class has covered previously and how the next step is a logical progression. In fact, a clearly communicated learning target can create an obvious connection across lessons that, while different, share a common goal. But when instruction is not so clearly sequenced, teachers must consider ways to make logical connections. Sometimes, the context is simply prevention, in which students are given a familiar context and provided with a rule to avoid the problem. For example, well into the school year, teachers often notice a predictable class behavior problem that results in frequent reprimands. In response, if the teacher develops a new rule aimed at preventing the problem, he or she can remind students of the reprimands they received previously when introducing the new rule, which will help students understand following the rule solves an existing problem. Student familiarity can be a powerful context for making connections; therefore, teachers do well to create authentic connections to students' lives, both inside and outside of school. For example, a rule about no sharing of food could be introduced by asking students if anyone in their family has a food allergy. The resulting discussion provides a perfect context for introducing the rule. The more that new information can be presented in ways that students can connect to their own lived experiences, the more likely they are to understand the associated skills and concepts. Figure 2.1 presents an example of how classroom rules can be anchored to larger expectations.

Mr. Carlson is a new teacher who will have different students during different periods of the day. Because he is working in a PBIS school, all students have previously been taught the

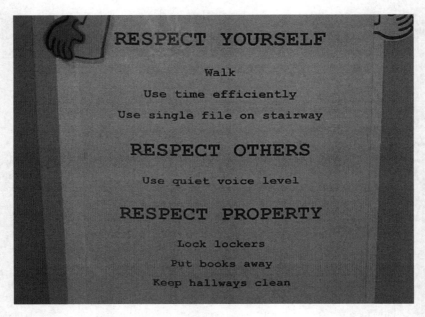

Figure 2.1   Behavior rules anchored to larger expectations

- expectations of respect yourself (keep safe and keep learning), respect others (treat others as you'd have them treat you), and respect property (treat others' property as you'd have them treat yours). On the first day of school, he takes time to talk to the class, engaging in a discussion that allows him to know more about the students. He has thought out what rules he wants to teach and has organized them by area (doorway, desks, sink, bookshelf). He continues his discussion with the students by asking about what problems could potentially happen in each area, and as they respond, he helps them to consider what rules might help to avoid these problems. As students offer suggestions, he provides examples of similar rules in their lives inside and outside the classroom to help them understand that such rules are helpful to all.

Clarity Through Example Selection and Sequencing

Providing relevant examples is an important component of effective instruction, but the selection and sequencing of examples is critically important—not all examples are equally effective. Research on effective instruction has established some key guidelines for the selection and sequencing of examples (Engelmann & Carnine, 1982; Horner et al., 1982). These guidelines, which are summarized in Table 2.1, have been demonstrated to be effective in teaching those classroom expectations necessary to maintain control of the lesson content and promote student engagement (Walters & Frei, 2007) and social behaviors related to effective communication (Chadsey-Rusch, 1993; Drasgow & Halle, 1995; Hicks et al., 2011, 2015; Knapczyk, 1989; O'Neill, 1990; O'Neill et al., 2000). The connections we make to students' lives inside and outside the school provide a fertile ground for identifying authentic examples that will ring true for students. Connecting to students' lives provides not only a range of authentic examples, but also an opportunity to consider the degree to which rules are culturally relevant for the classroom population and how they may need to be described to ensure clarity. Generally, each successive example should present equal amounts of new information by systematically varying relevant circumstances. For example, if a teacher is selecting examples of the appropriate use of hand raising in the classroom, it's better to use examples of hand raising

Table 2.1 Guidelines for selecting examples for teaching classroom rules (adapted from Horner, Sprague, & Wilcox, 1982)

1	Select examples that sample the range of variation in the classroom.
2	Select examples with equal amounts of new information.
3	Select examples that vary unimportant information.
4	Select examples that teach the learner what not to do as well as what to do.
5	Select examples that include significant exceptions.

during group discussion, independent study, and lecture. In each example, the students and physical conditions remain the same but the critical contextual features change, allowing students to key into what is important.

In teaching any rule for classroom behavior, the teacher should consider the range of circumstances under which the behavior is necessary. Many classrooms teach students to interact respectfully with one another and teachers provide examples of what it means to be respectful, what constitutes appropriate and inappropriate wording, and how to use respectful voice tone and volume. While this may cover all the relevant behaviors, the teacher must consider a range of examples. For instance, if all the examples involved someone saying thank you for a gift, this would be insufficient to help students understand what it means to be respectful in other encounters throughout their daily lives. More relevant examples might include circumstances in which someone is standing too close, when you believe someone has taken your belongings, and even when someone has been disrespectful to you. These are the circumstances in which students are most likely to be challenged to demonstrate respect and, thus, are necessary teaching examples. Watching students and considering conditions that might be more challenging for them is a key to identifying a range of effective teaching examples.

To summarize, it's important that the examples presented demonstrate how the expected behavior should be used across a range of classroom circumstances and a strong rationale for why the expected behavior is important and helps create a safe and effective classroom community. In addition to positive examples of rules for behavior, non-examples help students to discriminate between right and wrong. Negative examples demonstrate a behavior that is not correct in each situation and should be presented immediately after a positive example of the correct behavior, highlighting the difference between right and wrong. Ideally, the teacher would introduce and describe the rule, demonstrate multiple positive examples while pointing out the key behaviors, and then show a negative example, pointing out that it is not correct because one of the key features is missing. As instruction progresses, teachers present additional positive examples to students, asking them to determine whether it is appropriate (yes) and how they know (all the features are present). The negative example should be as similar as possible to the immediately preceding example, but with one of the features missing. The teacher again asks the student whether it is appropriate (no) and how they know (one feature is missing). By repeating this process with each of the key features of the rule, teachers provide students with clarity regarding the exact nature of the expected behavior.

With most rules for behavior there are exceptions. For example, students do not need to raise their hand to receive permission before speaking out in a class discussion if they have a warning of imminent danger. These exceptions should be taught as such, after other examples. The idea is to separate these unique exceptions from the general rule.

After using the first class meeting to get to know the students and engage in a discussion of the expectations and then logical rules for behavior across classroom settings, Mr. Carlson takes student suggestions and does some think aloud modeling. Noting that students might splash one another at the sink, the students suggested that the rule might be "keep water in the sink," which is tied to both respecting others and respecting property. He thinks through the different ways students use the sink and models several different scenarios that he believes are relevant. He first models washing hands, then getting a drink, then washing off materials, and finally he models wetting a towel to use for cleaning elsewhere. With each positive example he demonstrates the correct behavior while describing the rule: "Notice how I'm keeping the water in the sink, even as I move this wet paper towel to my desk." After this last example he says, "But I'm not doing it right this time, because even though I turned off the water, I'm still letting water drip outside the sink." After a few repetitions, he begins asking students to judge his modeling efforts, describing whether they believe his actions are correct or incorrect and how they know.

Engaging Students in Content

Even the best instruction is ineffective if the students are not attending or are disengaged. We broadly define engagement as the degree to which students are aware of and participating in the learning process. Engagement is built-in when students are involved in practice activities such as working on projects or discussing with peers. While the degree of interest may vary, there is an interaction with the curriculum that is key to learning (Greenwood et al., 2002). In fact, time engaged with instruction is perhaps the largest correlate of academic achievement. David Berliner (1990) summarized the literature on this point and has stated very clearly that the relationship between student engagement and achievement "has the same scientific status as the concept of homeostasis in biology, reinforcement in psychology, or gravity in physics" (p. 3).

For teachers, the question is not whether to engage students, it is how to engage them, and the method depends upon who and what is being taught. While young students may be easily engaged by connecting content to cartoons and animation, older students will likely require more creative teacher actions. Similarly, while teaching rules for abstract situations requires compelling stories, rules for how to use the classroom materials can be modeled directly in front of the students. Of course, when we undertake culturally relevant practices such as making lessons fit the context of students' real lives, making use of natural examples, interacting with students during modeling, striving to share personal stories, and sharing data with a student, the immediate goal is engagement. But engagement is a means to an end; we use it to maximize the probability of success with the lesson content. In any case, responsibility for creating and maintaining student engagement falls on the teacher. While there is a range of specific strategies to facilitate student engagement during instruction, it is also clear that the nature of the teacher and student relationship is critical.

Relationships

The importance of strong student–teacher relationships is well established; numerous studies indicate students who have strong relationships and connections with their teachers demonstrate higher levels of academic motivation, engagement, and achievement (Martin & Collie, 2016; Pianta et al., 2012; Wentzel, 2010). The interactive nature of instruction provides opportunities for teachers to initiate and maintain relationships with their students. This can be enhanced through clear and authentic instruction around the rules and by actively working toward creating an inclusive classroom environment. These strategies help students feel a sense of belonging and a comfort in taking chances to engage during instruction (Urszul et al., 2020).

Being a critically conscious practitioner, or in other words, engaging in ongoing self-reflection, is at the core of being an authentic teacher (Urszul et al., 2020). It is important for teachers to spend time reflecting on their personal biases and attitudes that may be impacting their interactions with students, specifically in the context of instruction. Biases are automatically developed as part of the human cognitive system; therefore, it is important for teachers to think through any biases they might have to determine whether they may be producing unintended results for their students during instruction. For example, a teacher's attitude, tone, and body language can all influence a student's sense of belonging in the classroom and the degree to which they absorb lesson content. Teachers may unintentionally interact with certain students differently than others during instruction, particularly students with challenging behaviors, which can lead to students feeling isolated and excluded from the classroom environment. As part of self-reflection, it is important that teachers are willing to take responsibility for their actions and adjust their self-knowledge and behaviors toward students.

Teachers can also engage in self-reflection around their own identity and role as an educator (Urszul et al., 2020). Teachers who find meaning in their role and feel empowered in their abilities as a teacher can engage with students more authentically. Further, students are able to perceive the extent to which teachers care about the subject material and the degree to which they are intentional in delivering lesson content. By demonstrating their passion for teaching and commitment to delivering lesson content in a way that is meaningful to students, teachers are also conveying that they care about their students both in and outside of the learning environment.

However, as mentioned previously, in order to learn what is important to students and make connections with lesson content, teachers must spend time getting to know their students both inside and outside of instruction. It is important that teachers make an effort to get to know *all* their students, even those with challenging behaviors. The degree to which students feel their teacher is interested in them as an individual has been shown to predict their academic motivation and engagement (Martin, 2012). One strategy teachers can use to get to know their students, particularly those with challenging behavior, is the 2x10 strategy, which involves talking with the student for at least 2 minutes each day for 10 days in a row about topics other than academics (Wlodkowski, 1983). Teachers feeling a sense of relatedness with their students not only allows them to engage in more effective instruction but can promote their own self-efficacy and even their long-term well-being (Spilt et al., 2011).

Engaging in meaningful dialogue during instruction is another way teachers can authentically engage with students. Teachers can provide students with opportunities to engage with classroom rules by: (1) including activities that promote the use of higher-order thinking skills (e.g., synthesizing, generalizing, explaining); (2) building deep knowledge of concepts covered during lessons (e.g., by addressing topics with appropriate thoroughness and clarity); (3) engaging in substantive conversations with students and allowing them opportunities to engage with peers; and (4) making connections between lesson content and public problems or personal experiences (Newman et al., 1995). Teachers establishing expectations for higher-level thinking and engagement from all students helps to promote a climate of mutual respect in the classroom. While the nurturing of positive relationships may provide several social and ethical advantages, its practical advantage is as a means to increase student success with lesson content.

There are a few students in Mr. Carlson's classroom during the day that have a history of misbehavior. He was warned about these students and some colleagues suggested that he "crack down hard" on these students early in the year. But Mr. Carlson knows that building relationships with students is a much better predictor of success. First, he considers each student and reflects on whether he has any biases that might cause him to act differently with each student. As a result, he realizes that one of these students, Hank, has at times in the past said some offensive things about an ethnic group to which Mr. Carlson is a member. He realizes that he will need to be especially self-aware when working with Hank and determines that he will make a special effort to call on him, use a calm tone, and engage him in personal conversations. Every day as students come into the classroom, Mr. Carlson meets them at the door, asking questions about what they've been watching on TV, what video games they play, and other trivial but personal conversation starters. On a couple of occasions Mr. Carlson singled out Hank to help him with a special task just as he entered the room, and; using the opportunity to have a personal chat and showing interest in Hank's interests. Over time, Mr. Carlson found that these efforts paid off in terms of Hank's behavior, but also he found that he had changed his own attitude toward Hank. Hank still at times engages in misbehavior, but because of their relationship, Mr. Carlson can work successfully to get Hank back to success.

Using Relationships to Facilitate Active Engagement

While effective example selection and descriptions from a culturally relevant mindset are helpful in creating engagement, teachers can make use of relationships with students to encourage engaging interactions. In considering strategies for engaging students, there is a critical distinction between active and passive engagement. Passive engagement approximates what is often referred to as "on task," which has traditionally been defined as the student simply doing as instructed. Under this definition, during instruction, we expect the student to be seated and to be looking at the teacher. However, students can be looking at the teacher, and even nodding in agreement, without really listening. In contrast, active engagement is defined as the degree to which the student is actively involved with the lesson content, demonstrated by observable actions (Whitney et al., 2021). There is strong evidence to associate active engagement with both increased achievement and decreased misbehavior (Scott & Gage, 2020). Teachers can facilitate active engagement by providing students with opportunities to respond (OTR) during instruction. An OTR can be defined as anything the teacher does to facilitate the student to think and act physically within the lesson content. The response must have a physical component to ensure that the student is actually involved. Simply asking a student to think or read is not considered an OTR because no active engagement is observed. There are several general strategies from which the teacher can create unique OTRs to fit the students and lesson content (see Whitney et al., 2021). These include verbalizations, gestures, and actions that can be delivered to individual students or to the group. Research has demonstrated that OTRs are most effective when delivered at rates of at least three times per minute during instruction (Partin et al., 2010; Sutherland et al., 2003). Importantly, instruction here refers to the part of the lesson where the teacher is delivering new information or reviewing. These are times in which there is no natural active engagement. Despite the demonstrated positive effects of OTRs in terms of creating active engagement and decreased disruptions (Gage et al., 2018), they are typically used at very low rates during instruction (Scott et al., 2017). Table 2.2 provides examples of a range of OTRs in the context of teaching behavior, followed by a non-example.

Although OTRs can be used to assess student understanding, the purpose of OTR is to engage students (Whitney et al., 2021). Teachers can create engagement as a means of teaching new rules, reviewing existing rules, providing prompts, or simply keeping students' attention. As with any instructional strategy, teachers do well to consider in advance what OTRs will fit best within a lesson plan. At the same time, OTRs can be used in a more impromptu manner to engage students when it becomes obvious that their engagement is waning.

As was previously mentioned, OTRs should be used in consideration of a student's age and ability, with the intention of creating high rates of success (i.e., engagement rather than assessment). An effective OTR is delivered in a genuine manner, with the intent of providing the student with an opportunity to be successful. Students should view these opportunities to respond as both natural and simple. When planning for older students and those with challenging behaviors, it's helpful to consider both the relationship with the student and the manner with which OTRs are delivered. First, teachers need to know their students and consider how their own verbal (e.g., volume, tone) and non-verbal (e.g., facial expressions, movement) behaviors might be interpreted by the student. When planning for older students and those with challenging behaviors, delivering OTRs to the group may be more effective than individual OTRs. In addition, delivering OTRs as a direction (please take your best guess at this answer) rather than a question (do you know the answer?) is recommended. Consider the student that is reluctant to respond during class. When asked a direct question it is too easy to simply say "I don't know," effectively cutting off the engagement. Rather than asking the

Table 2.2 Examples of typical OTR strategies for teaching behavior

OTR	Example
Verbal	Teacher says, "Someone from the blue table tell me what I'm doing at the sink right now that is not correct."
Response Card	Before beginning a class activity, students are given a red card and a green card. Teacher reads a statement about the rules for the activity and students hold up a green card if they agree with the statement or a red card if they disagree.
Gesture	Teacher says, "If you think I'm currently trying to get teacher attention correctly right now, please stand up."
Discussion	Teacher says, "Turn and talk to your partner about the best way to respect others when we're in the hallway – then I'll ask you what you learned."
Action	Teacher asks, "Who can demonstrate the best way to let someone know they are being too loud?"
Choral	Teacher points at each of the rules for using the pencil sharpener and the students are expected to read them out loud.
Not OTR	Teacher says, "Everyone read the list of rules for the pencil sharpener to yourselves and think about them."
	–There is no observable physical action so it's not clear whether there is engagement.

question, teachers can make this a demand by saying "thumbs up if you agree, thumbs down if you disagree—if you don't know make a guess." Some students will simply look around the room to see how others have responded— but this is fine. The student is still thinking about the question and the answer, which is a form of engagement.

Mr. Carlson's 4th period class is especially challenging in terms of getting their heads into the daily lesson content. They seem to either sit and stare into space while he begins, or they are talking with one another and not listening to or thinking about the lesson content. As a result, Mr. Carlson decides to start each class with an activity called the "whip around." He starts by saying something about yesterday's lesson and then tells the students he wants each of them to say one thing they know about the subject. He tells them he'll go down each row and each person should say one thing quickly. He also reminds them that it's OK to say the same thing someone else has already said. As he points at the first person in row 1, that student calls out a single word related to the lesson. "Good" says Mr. Carlson, moving immediately the next person. In all, this takes about 90 seconds, and when completed, all students are now looking at him as they've had their minds on the content during that time. Throughout the period he thinks about where students may be challenged to stay engaged and he uses additional opportunities to respond, "Raise your hand if you remember the first rule of using the sink." He then calls on individual students to provide specific answers. In addition, he often asks students to give him a finger count of how comfortable they are with the current lesson content; one means not very and five means total understanding. He uses these opportunities both to engage the students and to consider where additional instruction may be necessary.

Providing Effective Instructional Feedback

Providing feedback on student behavior is an essential component of effective instruction. Students must be informed as to whether they are behaving appropriately in order to know right from wrong. To many, classroom management, and in fact all behavior management, is simply the delivery of positive and negative consequences. This overreliance on consequences ignores all the other essential components of effective instruction. To provide an academic example, using only consequences to teach math would entail writing a problem (e.g., 2 + 2) and simply saying "yes" or "no" as students guessed at answers in a trial-and-error manner. Similarly, when considering classroom behavior relying only on consequences will not effectively teach students to sustain and generalize appropriate behaviors. While feedback is a necessary component, its use is dependent upon the effectiveness of instruction. That is, if instruction is effective, feedback will be positive; on the contrary, if it is ineffective, feedback will be largely corrective. Effective instruction creates circumstances under which students are more likely to be successful and receive positive feedback. The purpose of feedback, then, is to help students maintain success and extinguish errors. Still, if students continue with errors, it is an indication that instruction is not working—and it is the teacher that must consider change.

While success is the best predictor of success, just how much success is necessary to reasonably predict future success depends upon the individual, the content difficulty, and confidence from prior trials (Rozin & Royzman, 2001). But as a general rule, a ratio of success to failure somewhere between 3:1 and 6:1 predicts more sustained success once instruction is completed (Fredrickson, 2000; Fredrickson & Losada, 2005). An issue that is often tied to positive feedback is the notion that adult feedback inhibits students' ability to internalize their success, or to have self-confidence to perform without external feedback. Clearly, this is an important idea; but simply letting students know they were right through clear verbal affirmations (e.g., "yes") has not been demonstrated to harm students' longer-term self-concept (Cameron et al., 2001; Scott & Landrum, 2020). In fact, the evidence has long shown that students with high rates of adult affirmation for their successes have more confidence and higher self-esteem (e.g., Engelmann et al., 1988; Rosenshine, 1978).

As with clarity and engagement, the question is not whether feedback should be a part of instruction, but how it is best implemented within a given classroom. The simplest manner of providing feedback is to do so verbally. As humans, we have the ability to communicate feedback in a quick and concise manner (e.g., yes, no, thanks, try again, great, oops). When teaching new skills, research supports that feedback must occur immediately and consistently in order to help students discriminate between right and wrong (Engelmann & Carnine, 1982). As was noted, many educators conceive of classroom management purely as a system of contingent consequences, often structured in the form of a token economy or other point system. While these are examples of feedback systems, they are (1) typically far removed from the immediacy of verbal feedback during instructional interactions and (2) rarely delivered consistently enough to account for every instance of behavior. So, while such systems may have a role in providing longer-term feedback in the classroom, effective instruction requires the use of more effective and efficient feedback systems that likely are delivered directly to the student from the teacher.

Responding to Expected Behavior

Teachers' consistent use of reinforcement for desired student behavior is associated with increases in positive and on-task student behavior (Apter et al., 2010). The term "reinforcement" simply refers to circumstances in which an action or event occurring just after a behavior has the effect of making that behavior more likely to occur in the future (Alberto & Troutman, 2013). Positive reinforcement means that the action provides something desirable for the student. For example, a student holds a door for a peer and the teacher provides positive feedback by thanking her for respecting others. The success of this behavior makes the student more likely to do it again in the future. In contrast, negative reinforcement involves an action that removes something undesirable. For example, the student holds a door for a peer and the teacher lets her know that she can remove 5 minutes from her recess restriction for respecting others. In both cases, reinforcement made behavior more likely in the future. But because negative reinforcement requires that something undesirable be in place, it is not an effective planned strategy for instruction.

The ideal for providing reinforcement is to provide the least amount necessary to predict student success (Alberto & Troutman, 2013). While there is a range of possible positive reinforcers, including privileges or tangible items, the most effective reinforcer during instruction is verbal affirmation—simply letting the student know that he or she is correct. A larger and more obvious version of this might include more verbal praise (e.g., "Wow, I really like how you kept trying to solve that problem until you got it right!") or even public acknowledgement (e.g., "Everyone, I'm so impressed with Sally's hard work on this!"). On the other hand, a smaller and less obvious version might include only a simple smile or thumbs-up gesture without any verbal interaction.

Expectations generally refer to larger conceptual descriptions of comportment (e.g., respect others), while rules refer to the specific behaviors that demonstrate the expectation (e.g., use kind words). When teaching new rules, teachers should facilitate student engagement to initiate opportunities for early feedback. Providing ongoing reminders is an effective strategy for prompting appropriate behaviors and it provides additional opportunities for positive feedback to strengthen behavior. Again, effective instruction prescribes consistent and immediate feedback during instruction of new content. But as students become more fluent, feedback should become intermittent and less immediate. At some point, confidence and a history of success will ensure a student sustains appropriate learned behaviors in the absence of external sources of reinforcement, including genuine behavior-specific teacher praise.

> As part of his earlier reflection on what biases he might have, Mr. Carlson made a commitment to himself to increase his use of positive feedback to all students. He filled his left pocket with paper clips and every time he said something positive, he moved one paper clip over to his right pocket. He did this to help him keep track of his own behavior so that he could continually set goals for improvement. Often, he'd find that a particular student was not accessing as much positive feedback as others. In such cases, he provided a reminder to the student as a manner of prompting a positive behavior, which he could then praise. He also found that it was not always easy to provide verbal feedback across a quiet room, and he made efforts to use more eye contact, smiles, and other gestures to provide positive feedback on a regular basis. Finally, on a regular basis Mr. Carlson stopped the class and told them he was proud of them, thanking them for being good examples of the school expectations.

Responding to Misbehavior

Feedback for misbehavior or errors (i.e., negative feedback) is as important as positive feedback. Misbehavior due to a lack of fluency with the rule, forgetfulness, or simply to test the teacher's response are a normal part of learning the classroom rules. Feedback on these misbehaviors help the learner to discriminate right and wrong, lessening the likelihood of future errors. But the need for negative feedback is also a signal to the teacher that instruction has not been entirely effective and warrant remediation and additional prompting. To create effective positive to negative feedback ratios, the idea is not simply to reduce the use of negative feedback, but to reduce the need for it by using instruction to reduce errors. For certain, teachers could improve their ratio of positive to negative feedback by simply ignoring errors. But, using an academic analogy, if the student responded to the question of 2 + 2 with the answer, 5, ignoring would only serve to teach the student that this is an accurate response. Under such circumstances, additional instruction is warranted.

The teacher's ability to successfully provide feedback on misbehavior is at least in-part a function of his or her relationship with the student. When students believe that the teacher is caring and has their best interest at heart, they are more likely to accept feedback and correction. But a critical distinction can be made between informing a student that he or she has made an error and providing a correction. Considering again the academic analogy, when the student answers the 2 + 2 question with 5 the teacher can simply yell "no" at the student. While this may make it less likely the student answers with 5 in the future, it does not increase the likelihood of the correct answer and it very well may increase the probability of the student not answering at all—or even becoming aggressive. In fact, teacher reprimands are predictive of continued reprimands (Caldarella et al., 2021), indicating a lack of effect. In contrast, correction involves leading the student through a set of prompts to arrive at the correct answer. Correction is a less aversive response to misbehavior as it both sets the student up to end with a successful response and creates an opportunity for a positive interaction in the face of misbehavior.

At some point, continued misbehavior must be met with consequences that are undesirable to the student (e.g., lose privilege, receive reprimand). While such consequences are to be used as a last resort, there likely will be students whose behaviors warrant this step. As we continue to consider the teacher-student relationship, teaching a hierarchy of standard consequences is a helpful manner of helping the student to take responsibility for his or her behavior. When taught ahead of time, teachers can clarify that given misbehaviors result in specific consequences. Teachers can then suggest that it is their job to help make sure students do not make the errors necessitating such consequences. At the point where students misbehave, the relationship is not harmed because the consequence is framed as a result of the student's choice, not the teacher's. Of course, the key is that the teacher takes steps to avoid anger, disgust, or frustration when addressing misbehavior. The statement simply becomes, "I'm sorry you made that choice, let's talk about how I can help remind you so that you don't end up with this consequence again." In this manner, students take responsibility for their own misbehavior rather than blaming the teacher for "giving" them a consequence.

One of Mr. Carlson's students in 2nd period, Emily, has been exhibiting misbehavior on an increasing trend over the past couple of weeks. Mainly, she seems to just give up and toss a book or other materials on the floor when things aren't going her way. As a result, he has begun prompting her more often and has tried to find time to have some conversation time with her. But Emily has not been responsive to this and has even been surly in response. While Mr. Carlson wants to continue trying to find ways to help Emily, he also has to follow-through with the standard consequences for such disruptive behavior. One day as Mr. Carlson asks students to pair off and share ideas, Emily yells "I'm not doing this." Mr. Carlson calmly approaches Emily and speaks quietly to her, "This is the task for the day, Emily. If you get this done you get your grade – and you could use easy points like this." But Emily huffs and refuses to move. Mr. Carlson again uses a very calm and matter-of-fact voice, "Remember, Emily, if you don't do your work during class, you'll end up doing make-up work during your normal free period. I don't want you to miss your free period, but it's up to you. Look, you already have part of it done, you just need to share and write the response – but it has to be your choice." Emily continues to refuse and Mr. Carlson follows through with the consequence, "I'm sorry you've made this choice to miss your free time, Emily. Maybe we can talk then about how I can help make this work for you." For Emily, the consequence stands. But Mr. Carlson presented this so that she made her own choice for the consequence, and he presented himself as caring and wanting to help.

Historically, teachers have been found to use positive feedback at very low rates (Beaman & Wheldall, 2000). In fact, Scott, Hirn, and Cooper (2017) looked at over 7000 classrooms and found that the typical student receives positive feedback during instruction at a rate far less than even one per minute (.137 per minute) at the elementary level, dropping steadily as they progressed through middle and high school. These same students received negative feedback during instruction at similar rates averaging .0335 instances of negative feedback at elementary and middle school, but raising to .046 at high school, where the average student receives more negative than positive feedback. These observation data are summarized in Table 2.3. In terms of classroom management, none of these ratios

Table 2.3 Typical rates per minute of positive and negative feedback that the average student receives during classroom instruction and the ratio of positive to negative

	Positive Feedback	*Negative Feedback*	*Ratio*
Elementary School	.137	.038	3.60:1
Middle School	.061	.031	1.97:1
High School	.033	.046	.78:1

of positive to negative represent a high probability for student success. Moreover, research has consistently shown that students with a history of behavior problems and skill deficits receive less teacher affirmation, even when their behaviors are similar to other students (Hirn & Scott, 2014; Mayer & Patriarca, 2007).

Summary

Throughout this chapter the case has been made that effective instruction cannot be considered separately from classroom management. Attempting to teach without classroom management is a fruitless effort but working on classroom management without teaching is just as fruitless. Logically, effective instruction (for academics and classroom rules) makes students more successful, and as students are more successful, they are less inclined to exhibit challenging behaviors (Cameron et al., 2008). There is nothing complex about this relationship or the strategies that facilitate its success. Unfortunately, research has repeatedly shown that teacher preparation programs provide too little attention to the basics of classroom management to be effective (Hammerness et al., 2005; Freeman et al., 2014; Westling, 2010). Further, this fact is evinced in the number of teachers who cite burnout over behavior as their reason for leaving the profession (Dinkes et al., 2009; Ingersol et al., 2018). But, without training and support, there should be no surprise that effective instructional practices are not a part of the typical teacher's repertoire of skills. While it does not mean that classroom management is non-existent in schools, it does mean that a significant number of teachers do not have the knowledge or skills to do this with sufficient fluency to be effective (Butler & Monda-Amaya, 2016; Flower et al., 2017). In fact, there is compelling evidence that effective training in classroom management leads to higher job satisfaction and less burnout (Canrinus et al., 2012; Caprara et al., 2006). Given that the basic tenet of this chapter has been that classroom management and effective instruction are inextricably related, the first step toward a solution is to use these same tenets of effective instruction to train teachers in the use of effective instruction. At both pre-service and in-service, training must be explicit, engaging, and provide opportunities for practice with feedback.

References

Agostinone-Wilson, F. (2006). Downsized discourse: Classroom management, neoliberalism, and the shaping of correct workplace attitude. *Journal for Critical Education Policy Studies, 4*(2), 129–158. www.jceps.com/archives/523.

Alberto, P., Troutman, A. C., & Axe, J. B. (2013). *Applied behavior analysis for teachers.* Pearson.

Aloe, A. M., Shisler, S. M., Norris, B. D., Nickerson, A. B., & Rinker, T. W. (2014). A multivariate meta-analysis of student misbehavior and teacher burnout. *Educational Research Review, 12,* 30–44. https://doi.org/10.1016/j.edurev.2014.05.003

American Psychological Association (2006). Coalition for Psychology in Schools and Education. *Report on the teacher needs survey.* American Psychological Association. Center for Psychology in Schools and Education. www.apa.org/ed/schools/coalition/2006-teacher-needs-report.pdf

Apter, B., Arnold, C., & Swinson, J. (2010). A mass observation study of student and teacher behaviour in British primary classrooms. *Educational Psychology in Practice, 26*(2), 151–171. https://doi.org/10.1080/02667361003768518

Archer, A. L., & Hughes, C. A. (2011). *Explicit Instruction*. Guilford.

Beaman, R., & Wheldall, K. (2000). Teachers' use of approval and disapproval in the classroom. *Educational Psychology, 20*(4), 431–446. https://doi.org/10.1080/713663753

Berliner, D. C. (1990). What's all the fuss about instructional time. In M. Ben-Peretz & R. Bromme (Eds.), *The nature of time in schools: Theoretical concepts, practitioner perceptions* (pp. 3–35). Teachers College Press.

Brantlinger, E., & Danforth, S. (2006). Critical theory perspective on social class, race, gender, and classroom management. *Handbook of classroom management: Research, practice, and contemporary issues* (pp. 157–159). Erlbaum.

Butler, A., & Monda-Amaya, L. (2016). Preservice teachers' perceptions of challenging behavior. *Teacher Education and Special Education, 39*(4), 276–292. http://dx.doi.org/10.1177/0888406416654212

Caldarella, P. Larsen, R. A. A., Williams, L., Wills, H. P., & Wehby, J. H. (2021). "Stop doing that!": Effects of teacher reprimands on student disruptive behavior and engagement. *Journal of Positive Behavior Interventions, 23*(3), 163–173. https://doi.org/10.1177/1098300720935101

Cameron, J., Banko, K. M., & Pierce, W. D. (2001). Pervasive negative effects of rewards on intrinsic motivation: The myth continues. *The Behavior Analyst, 24*, 1–44. DOI: 10.1007/BF03392017

Cameron, C. E., Connor, C. M., Morrison, F. J., & Jewkes, A. M. (2008). Effects of classroom organization on letter-word reading in first grade. *Journal of School Psychology, 46*, 173–192. DOI: DOI: 10.1016/j.jsp.2007.03.002

Canrinus, E. T., Helms-Lorenz, M., Beijaard, D., Buitink, J., & Hofman, A. (2012). Self efficacy, job satisfaction, motivation and commitment: Exploring the relationships between indicators of teachers' professional identity. *European Journal of Psychology of Education, 27*(1), 115–132. https://doi.org/10.1007/s10212-011-0069-2

Caprara, G. V., Barbaranelli, C., Steca, P., & Malone, P. S. (2006). Teachers' self-efficacy beliefs as determinants of job satisfaction and students' academic achievement: A study at the school level. *Journal of School Psychology, 44*(6), 473–490. https://doi.org/10.1016/j.jsp.2006.09.001

Ceylan, R. (2009). An examination of the relationship between teachers' professional self-esteem and empathic skills. *Social Behavior and Personality: an international journal, 37*(5), 679–682. DOI: https://doi.org/10.2224/sbp.2009.37.5.679

Chadsey-Rusch, J., Drasgow, E., Reinoehl, B., Halle, J., & Collet-Klingenberg, L. (1993). Using general-case instruction to teach spontaneous and generalized requests for assistance to learners with severe disabilities. *Journal of the Association for Persons with Severe Handicaps, 18*(3), 177–187. https://doi.org/10.1177/154079699301800304

Dinkes, R., Kemp, J., & Baum, K. (2009). *Indicators of School Crime and Safety: 2009*. NCES 2010-012/NCJ 228478. National Center for Education Statistics. https://nces.ed.gov/pubs2010/2010012.pdf

Drasgow, E. & Halle, J. W. (1995). Teaching social communication to young children with severe disabilities. *Topics in Early Childhood Special Education, 15*(2), 164–186. https://doi.org/10.1177/027112149501500203

Engelmann, S. (1966). The structuring of language processes as a tool for thought. In D. Kestel (Ed.), National Catholic Educational Association Bulletin: *Curriculum for Renewal, 63*(1), 459–468.

Engelmann, S., Becker, W. C., Carnine, D., & Gersten, R. (1988). The direct instruction follow through model: Design and outcomes. *Education and Treatment of Children*, 303–317. www.jstor.org/stable/42899079

Engelmann, S., & Carnine, D. (1982). *Theory of Instruction*. Irvington.

Engelmann, S., & Colvin, G. (2006). Rubric for identifying authentic Direct Instruction programs. Engelmann Foundation.

Flower, A., McKenna, J. W., & Haring, C. D. (2017). Behavior and classroom management: Are teacher preparation programs really preparing our teachers? *Preventing School Failure: Alternative Education for Children and Youth, 61*(2), 163–169. https://doi.org/10.1080/1045988X.2016.1231109.

Fredrickson, B. L. (2000). Extracting meaning from past affective experiences: The importance of peaks, ends, and specific emotions. *Cognition and Emotion, 14*(4), 577–606. https://doi.org/10.1080/026999300402808

Fredrickson, B. L., & Losada, M. F. (2005). Positive affect and the complex dynamics of human flourishing. *American psychologist, 60*(7), 678. DOI: 10.1037/3333-066X.60.7.678

Freeman, J., Simonsen, B., Briere, D., & MacSuga-Gage, A. M. (2014). Pre-service teacher training in classroom management: A review of state accreditation policy and teacher preparation programs. *Teacher Education and Special Education, 37*(2), 106–120. https://doi.org/10.1177/0888406413507002

Freiberg, H. J. (1999). *Beyond behaviorism: Changing the classroom management paradigm.* Allyn & Bacon.

Gage, N., Scott, T. M., Hirn, R. G., & MacSuga-Gage, A. (2018). The relationship between teachers' implementation of classroom management practices and student behavior in elementary school. *Behavioral Disorders, 43*(2), 302–315. https://doi.org/10.1177/0198742917714809

Greenwood, C. R., Horton, B. T., & Utley, C. A. (2002). Academic engagement: Current perspectives on research and practice. *School Psychology Review, 31*(3), 328. https://psycnet.apa.org/record/2002-18945-004

Hammerness, K., Darling-Hammond, L., Grossman, P., Rust, F., & Shulman, L. S. (2005). The design of teacher education programs. In L. Darling-Hammond & J. Bransford (Eds.), *Preparing teachers for a changing world* (pp. 390–441). Jossey-Bass.

Hattie, J. A. C. (2009). *Visible Learning: A synthesis of over 800 meta-analyses relating to achievement.* Routledge Press.

Hicks, C. S., Bethune, K. S., Wood, C. L., Cooke, N. L., & Mims, P. J. (2011). Effects of Direct Instruction on the acquisition of prepositions by students with intellectual disabilities. *Journal of Applied Behavior Analysis, 44*(3), 675–679. DOI: 10.1901/jaba.2011.44-675

Hicks, C. S., Rivera, C. J., & Wood, C. L. (2015). Using Direct Instruction: Teaching preposition use to students with intellectual disability. *Language, Speech, and Hearing Services in Schools, 46*(3), 194-206. DOI: 10.1044/2015_LSHSS-14-0088

Hirn, R. G., & Scott, T. M. (2014). Descriptive analysis of teacher instructional practices and student engagement among adolescents with and without challenging behavior. *Education and Treatment of Children, 36*(4), 585–607. DOI:10.1353/etc.2014.0037

Horner, R. H., Sprague, J., & Wilcox, B. (1982). General case programming for community activities. In B. Wilcox & G. T. Bellamy, *Design of high school programs for severely handicapped students* (pp. 61–98). Paul H. Brookes Publishing Co.

Ingersoll, R., Merrill, L., Stuckey, D., & Collins, G. (2018). *Seven Trends: The Transformation of the Teaching Force.* Updated October 2018. Consortium for Policy Research in Education. https://repository.upenn.edu/cpre_researchreports/108/

Kirschner, P. A., Sweller, J., & Clark, R. E. (2006). Why minimal guidance during instruction does not work: An analysis of the failure of constructivist, discovery, problem-based, experiential, and inquiry-based teaching. *Educational Psychologist, 41*(2), 75–86. https://doi.org/10.1207/s15326985ep4102_1

Knapczyk, D. R. (1989). Generalization of student question asking from special class to regular class settings. *Journal of Applied Behavior Analysis, 22*, 77–83. DOI: 10.1901/jaba.1989.22-77

Martin, A. J. (2012). *Interpersonal relationships and student development (motivation, engagement, buoyancy, and achievement): What outcomes teachers, peers, and parents do and do not impact.* Keynote presented at International Conference on Interpersonal Relationships in Education (ICIRE), Vancouver, Canada.

Martin, A. J., & Collie, R. J. (2016). The role of teacher-student relationships in unlocking students' academic potential: Exploring motivation, engagement, resilience, adaptability, goals, and instruction. In K. R. Wentzel & G. Ramani (Eds.), *Handbook of social influences on social-emotional, motivation, and cognitive outcomes in school contexts* (pp. 158–177). Routledge.

Mayer, M. J., & Patriarca, L. A. (2007). Behavioral scripts and instructional procedures for students with learning and behavioral problems. *Preventing School Failure, 52*(1), 3–12. https://doi.org/10.3200/PSFL.52.1.3-12

McIntosh, K., Chard, D., Boland, J., & Horner, R. H. (2006). A Demonstration of Combined Efforts in School-Wide Academic and Behavioral Systems and Incidence of Reading and Behavior Challenges in Early Elementary Grades. *Journal of Positive Behavior Interventions, 8*, 146–154. https://doi.org/10.1177/10983007060080030301

McLeskey, J., Maheady, L., Billingsley, B., Brownell, M. T., & Lewis, T. J. (Eds.) (2019). *High leverage practices for inclusive classrooms.* Routledge.

Melnick, S. A., & Meister, D. G. (2008). A comparison of beginning and experienced teachers' concerns. *Educational Research Quarterly, 31*(3), 39–56. www.proquest.com/docview/215934753

Newman, F. M., Secada, W. G., & Wehlage, G. G. (1995). *A guide to authentic instruction and assessment: Vision, standards and scoring.* Wisconsin Center for Education Research.

O'Neill, R. E. (1990). Establishing verbal repertoires: Toward the application of general case analysis and programming. *The Analysis of Verbal Behavior, 8*, 113–126. DOI: 10.1007/BF03392852

O'Neill, R. E., Faulkner, C., & Horner, R. H. (2000). The effects of general case training of manding responses on children with severe disabilities. *Journal of Developmental and Physical Disabilities, 12*(1), 43–60. https://doi.org/10.1023/A:1009456210739

Partin, T. C., Robertson, R. E., Maggin, D. M., Oliver, R. M., & Wehby, J. (2010). Using teacher praise and opportunities to respond to promote appropriate student behavior. *Preventing School Failure 54*(3), 172–178. https://doi.org/10.1080/10459880903493179

Pianta, R. C., Hamre, B. K., & Allen, J. P. (2012). Teacher-student relationships and engagement: Conceptualizing, measuring, and improving the capacity of classroom interactions. In S. L. Christenson, A. L. Reschly, & C. Wylie (Eds), *Handbook of research on student engagement* (pp. 365–386). Springer.

Pitsoe, V., & Letseka, M. (2013). Foucault's discourse and power: Implications for instructionist classroom management. *Open Journal of Philosophy, 3*(01), 23. DOI: 10.4236/ojpp.2013.31005

Rosenshine, B. V. (1978). Academic engaged time, content covered, and direct instruction. *Journal of Education, 160*(3), 38–66. https://doi.org/10.1177/002205747816000304

Rozin, P., & Royzman, E. B. (2001). Negativity bias, negativity dominance, and contagion. *Personality and Social Psychology Review, 5*(4), 296–320. https://doi.org/10.1207/S15327957PSPR0504_2

Scott, T. M. (2017). *Teaching behavior: Managing classrooms through effective instruction.* Corwin Press.

Scott, T. M., Hirn, R. G., & Cooper, J. (2017). *Classroom Success: Keys to Success in Classroom Instruction*. Rowman and Littlefield Publishing.

Scott, T. M., & Landrum, T. J. (2020). An evidence-based logic for the use of positive reinforcement: Responses to typical criticisms. *Beyond Behavior, 29*(2), 69–77. https://doi.org/10.1177/1074295620917153

Sindelar, P. T., Brownell, M. T., & Billingsley, B. (2010). Special education teacher education research: Current status and future directions. *Teacher Education and Special Education, 33*, 8–24. https://doi.org/10.1177/08884 06409358593

Sorakin-Balli, Y., Basari, S., & Guldal-Kan, S. (2020). The relation between classroom management skills and empathic tendencies of high school teachers high school teachers' classroom management skills and empathic tendencies. *Cypriot Journal of Educational Sciences, 15*(1), 144–152. https://doi.org/10.18844/cjes.v15i1.4595

Spilt, J. L., Koomen, H. M. Y., & Thijs, J. T. (2011). Teacher wellbeing: The importance of teacher–student relationships. *Educational Psychology Review*, 23, 457–477. DOI:10.1007/s10648-011-9170-y

Sutherland, K. S., Adler, N., & Gunter, P. L. (2003). The effects of varying rates of opportunities to respond to academic requests on the classroom behavior of students with EBD. *Journal of Emotional and Behavioral Disorders, 11*, 239–248. https://doi.org/10.1177/10634266030110040501

Urszul, P., Murphy, D., & Joseph, S. (2020). A systematic review and metasynthesis of qualitative research into teachers' authenticity. *Cambridge Journal of Education*. https://doi.org/10.1080/0305764X.2020.1829546

Walters, J., & Frei, S. (2007). *Managing classroom behavior and discipline*. Shell Education.

Wang, H., Hall, N. C., & Rahimi, S. (2015). Self-efficacy and causal attributions in teachers: Effects on burnout, job satisfaction, illness, and quitting intentions. *Teaching and Teacher Education, 47*, 120–130. https://doi.org/ 10.1016/j.tate.2014.12.005

Wentzel, K. R. (2010). Students' relationships with teachers. In J. L. Meece & J. S. Eccles (Eds.), *Handbook of research on schools, schooling, and human development*. Routledge.

Westling, D. L. (2010) Teachers and challenging behaviors: Knowledge, views, and practices. *Remedial and Special Education, 31*, 48–63. https://doi.org/10.1177/0741932508327466

Whitney, T., Cooper, J., & Scott T. M. (2021). *Creating an actively engaged classroom: 14 strategies for student success*. Corwin Press.

Wlodkowski, R. J. (1983). *Motivational opportunities for successful teaching* [Leader's Guide]. Universal Dimensions.

3

PREVENTION STRATEGIES FOR CLASSROOM MANAGEMENT

Sierra M. Trudel, Emily L. Winter, and Melissa A. Bray

DEPARTMENT OF SCHOOL PSYCHOLOGY,
UNIVERSITY OF CONNECTICUT

Antecedent Strategies

Classroom Space Structuring

Perhaps not surprisingly, the physical environment of the classroom is a crucial foundation for classroom management. Rooting this notion of classroom interior design in theory, consideration of Maslow's (1943) Hierarchy of Needs (Maslow's Theory of Motivation), posits that people's basic needs have to be met before people can engage in any semblance of higher-level processing or functioning. Indeed, research (Makela et al., 2014) has echoed this statement, noting that a student's basic needs oftentimes must be addressed (e.g., food, clothes, safety, comfort) before any higher-order processes, such as learning, self-regulation, problem solving, and executive functioning, can be considered or expected to be appropriately utilized (Ford, 2016). Attention to the classroom's physical makeup and layout, therefore, are not just factors to leave to interior designers for mere aesthetic pleasure, but such considerations are imperative for educators and school-based personnel to consider in order for future student learning to occur. Additionally, these design characteristics are especially important to consider when supporting students who are facing prior trauma, which will be addressed below (Frey et al., 2020).

The modern-day classroom often was not designed in a "modern" way per se, that is, the physical structure of the classroom is often a product of design that is decades, if not centuries, old (Ford, 2016; Park & Choi, 2014). Thus, attention to present-day needs of students and the consequential diversification of layouts are best teaching practice and may require careful consideration and ingenuity in order to address physical layouts that may comprise the physical foundation and structure of the school building and classroom. Classrooms that are inherently organized to be flexible and adapt with changing hybrid curriculum (i.e., group work lecture, independent learning, online), are critical (Park & Choi, 2014). The classroom setting should be consciously designed, allowing for smooth movement and access throughout the classroom, for both teacher and students. Consideration of traffic flow should be planned so that students may move freely throughout the room and have clear entrance and exit points, with attention paid to minimize back-up in areas of high concentration (Sterling, 2009). Finally, emphasis should also be placed on decluttering the space and removing unnecessary furniture and materials for students to feel welcome and not overwhelmed by additional unneeded stimuli (Ford, 2016).

DOI: 10.4324/9781003275312-5

The interior layout of the classroom should also be considered to facilitate instruction and accompanying activities, with materials organized and easy to access for all in the class. Consideration of who needs to access materials (i.e., teacher versus student) should be identified in order to plan for allocation, storing of materials, as well as safety considerations (Sterling, 2009). Emphasis should be placed on efficiency in both navigating the classroom and keeping materials easy to access (Sterling, 2009).

Conscious attention of the layout from the perspective of students is also an important antecedent consideration. One rule of thumb states that students should never have their backs facing the instructor (Sterling, 2009). To combat this seating debacle, consider facing tables and desks so that students do not have to physically move their bodies to see the teacher, but rather just turn their heads (Sterling, 2009). Additional thought should be placed on making the arrangements relatively easy to move in case of group work or team projects (Sterling, 2009). Other attention to design may include tables or centers for group work and facilitation, a larger circle area for whole group lessons, as well as unique and individualized workspaces for students (Simonsen et al., 2015). Additionally, dedicated locations should be identified and clearly provided to students to deposit work that is completed as well as pick up any new work.

Resources related to learning should be posted on the walls for students to reference and use as a guide (Simonsen et al., 2015). Emphasis should be placed on curating an environment that is warm, inviting, and inclusive (Ford, 2016). For example, research suggests painting walls colors other than white (Grube, 2014; Tanner, 2015) as well as decorating with materials that show inclusivity and intentionality regarding gender, nationality, and race (Cheran et al., 2014). Such arrangements have been shown to produce positive effects on student learning (Ford, 2016). Regarding colors, lighter shades of blue, tones of purple, and hues of green provide an aura of spaciousness and serenity. Sharp reds and yellows, on the other hand, may communicate anxiety and increase feelings of tension, while white, greys, and beige may suggest an institutionalized atmosphere (Frey et al., 2020).

Trauma Sensitive Spaces

When considering the design and make up of a space, educators should also keep in mind trauma-sensitive practice. Trauma-sensitive practice extends to the classroom space, again, tying back the idea of Maslow's Hierarchy of Needs (1943). In this, considerations may address improvement of movement and accessibility through adding wheels to tables for easy and swift transitions, reduction of noise by using tennis balls on the bottom of chairs, addressing harsh lighting by adding dimmer switches and small table lamps to invite warmth into the space (Frey et al., 2020). With consideration of sensory overload, these suggestions help minimize student exposure to loud noises and harsh changes in lights.

Regarding decor, teachers may consider decorating classroom walls with positive messages, again, paying attention to intentionality and reduction of wall clutter (Frey et al., 2020). Special considerations should be considered for objects hanging from the ceiling as students may experience hypervigilance to these stimuli and perceive such dangling items from the ceiling as threats to safety. Overall, streamlining aesthetically pleasing, calming, and intentional stimuli may be most considerate for those who have experienced trauma (Frey et al., 2020).

Providing students with access to nature may also be appropriate, through live plants, small tabletop waterfalls, and soothing images of nature (Frey et al., 2020). Incorporation of nature has been demonstrated to have a positive impact on the physical and mental health of patients in hospital settings (Berman et al., 2008), with these findings extended to other settings beyond clinical medical facilities (Ryan et al., 2014). Classrooms may also benefit from the inclusion of a sheltered space, such as soft chairs, fidgets, and soft tactile items (e.g., pillow, stuffed animals; Frey et al., 2020). Such spaces may be helpful for students who have experienced trauma to have an established sense of safety and a physical location that communicates protection in the classroom.

Classroom Expectations

Establishing classroom rules is one simple solution to prevent challenging behaviors prior to occurrence. Classroom rules "are defined as the statements that teachers present to describe acceptable and unacceptable behaviors" (Alter & Haydon, 2017, p. 115). Within school systems, oftentimes there are behavioral frameworks such as Multi-Tiered Systems of Support that oversee behavior. One such system is Positive Behavior Interventions and Supports (PBIS). A core foundation of PBIS is universal expectations for behaviors, that is, a working agreement for appropriate behavior to be displayed by students. PBIS identifies that setting core expectations should combine "more globally stated expectations (e.g., 'be respectful') as well as routines that constitute effective functioning" (Alter & Haydon, 2017, p. 15; Gable et al., 2009). Schoolwide expectations vary from school to school and are often set and overseen by key stakeholders in the school, administration, and local community (Kilgus & Von Der Embse, 2019). Within the PBIS framework, behavioral expectations should be set schoolwide in order to ensure consistency across classrooms and environments in the school setting. Within each setting, the behavioral expectations should be further clarified and defined to clearly identify what the schoolwide expectations look like in specialized settings (e.g., gym, lunchroom, playground). The classroom is one such environment that requires further clarification beyond the general schoolwide expectations established earlier. Researchers have described the classroom to be a microsystem of society as a grander whole (Alter & Hyden, 2017). Thus, knowing that, rules and expectations in the class setting offer a similar function to that in society: to provide structure for the world and the role of the student (Alter & Haydon, 2017; Boostrom, 1991; Maag, 2004).

A 2017 review of effective practices related to classroom rules suggests seven features of effective rules: (a) number of rules, (b) created collaboratively with students, (c) positively stated, (d) specific in nature, (e) posted and shared in a public space, (f) taught to students, and (g) tied to positive and negative consequences (Alter & Hyden, 2017).

Regarding the number of rules, the overarching theme of setting classroom expectations seeks to provide clear guidelines so that students should be able to understand and identify what is expected of them for their behaviors in the classroom and the school setting. It is suggested that the number of expectations are low so that students are more likely to recall what behaviors are expected of them. Too many expectations may be overwhelming or hard for students to remember (Kilgus & Von Der Embse, 2019). Although the ideal number of expectations may vary depending on the cited literature, the maximum number of expectations proposed is seven (Maag, 2004), with "a small number" being the standout recommendation (Simonsen et al., 2008, p. 358).

For student collaboration, overwhelmingly, students should be involved and invested in the expectations that govern their classroom. Researchers Kerr and Nelson (2010) suggest that rules are more likely to be followed if they are created in collaboration with teachers and students as opposed to overseen and created only by the adult leaders in the classroom. Classroom teachers may consider creating a skeleton of expectations that they would like to see implemented in the classroom, and then ask for feedback from students to add or modify from that original foundation, thus scaffolding the conversation to incorporate the interests of all key stakeholders utilizing the classroom space (Bicard, 2000).

Rules should be positively stated. In this, instead of describing behaviors classroom teachers do not want in their classrooms, teachers should reword the statement to reflect replacement behaviors, or an alternative behavior that would be ideal to see in the classroom (Kerr & Nelson, 2010; Scott et al., 2011). Expectations, additionally, should be specific and clear. Oftentimes, the overarching schoolwide expectations may be worded more broadly (Alter & Hyden, 2017). These overarching expectations may be referred to as "principles," whereas classroom-based expectations should be clear and specific to the environment and tailored to typical activities and routines common to that teacher and classroom culture (Smith, 2004).

Research consensus suggests that expectations and classroom rules should be posted in a public place for students to read and revisit as needed. These postings may serve as prompts for students to consciously remind themselves of what is expected and appropriate behaviors. Along this line, scholars Scott and colleagues (2011) suggest making this "posting" more appropriate for students based on their age. For example, when working with younger students, teachers may consider incorporating pictures on the classroom expectation visual posted document, whereas for teachers in high school, students may be provided with a personal copy to keep for reference, or a digital copy could be posted to their online classroom.

The sixth recommendation is that expectations should be explicitly taught to students so that they are aware of what behaviors look like and how to follow the expectation guide. Different scholars provide differing amounts of time for when to review expectations and for how long. General consensus suggests that expectations should be reviewed in depth at the start of the year, during times of transition (i.e., after breaks), with mini lessons and reminders provided weekly throughout the school year (Center on Positive Behavioral Interventions and Supports, 2015). Research also suggests that for a student to learn a new skill, on average, they need to practice and repeat that skill eight times (Wong et al., 2005). This number increases for when a student is expected to unlearn a behavior and instead implement an appropriate replacement behavior, with researchers suggesting that the behavior should ideally be repeated for practice 28 times (Wong et al., 2005). Practice and instruction may involve explicit teaching of skills, and also may fold in other strategies to engage students in the learning process, such as role playing, providing examples and nonexamples of behaviors, as well as providing rationale for why the expectations were created and what function they serve the student and their community (Alter & Hyden, 2017; Scott et al., 2011).

The final component of classroom rules is that expectations should be linked to reinforcements and consequences (Alter & Hyden, 2017). Such reinforcements and consequences should seek to increase positive and prosocial behaviors, while decreasing negative and inappropriate behaviors. Scholars have suggested that when reviewing and teaching the expectations, reminders about potential consequences should be shared with students (Shores et al., 1993) so that the pupils are aware of what is expected of them and what consequences are connected with inappropriate behaviors. Additionally, and perhaps most importantly within the PBIS framework, is the call for consistent positive reinforcement for appropriate behaviors (i.e., "catch 'em doing good"). Reviews of the literature on classroom rules highlights the need for reinforcement using positive, specific praise as well as tangible rewards (Alter & Hyden, 2017).

Building Relationships

> Every child deserves a champion, an adult who will never give up on them, who understands the power of connection, and insists that they become the best that they can possibly be.
>
> *Pierson, 2013*

Classroom management is an interpersonal relationship that involves the synthesis of understanding student motivation, learning theory, and human development. As a social species, we learn through our observations and interactions with others (Bandura, 1971), and the school environment is a primarily social and interactive environment placing great importance on these relationships. Our first opinions of school form early and are greatly impacted by teacher–student relationships. Take a moment and think about one of your most memorable teachers. What is it about them that has made that relationship memorable? It is likely the way they enriched your education, spoke to you, inquired about your life, gave you feedback, or made you feel. In short, relationships matter.

Rita Pierson, renowned educator, shared in her 2013 TED Talk: "Kids don't learn from people they don't like" (2013). In a longitudinal study examining the quality of teacher-student relationships on academic achievement, Hajovsky et al. (2017) found that as the level of closeness decreased and conflict increased, academic achievement did as well, and as the level of closeness increased and conflict decreased, academic achievement improved. What is also interesting, in this study students from low socioeconomic status (SES) backgrounds and Black students experienced greater conflict and lower levels of closeness, whereas students from high SES backgrounds had higher levels of academic achievement and closeness and lower conflict. Additionally, Anderson et al. (2004) found that a quality teacher-student relationship was associated with improved engagement, attendance, persistence, preparation for class, and work completion. This evidence indicates a strong correlation between what happens when relationships are fostered versus when they are damaged. Therefore, cultivating positive relationships with students is imperative.

The evidence above suggests that students from diverse backgrounds and identities, including race, culture, linguistic, disability, socioeconomic status, gender identity, sexual orientation, and religion, who embody differences from our own identity or belief system, may require additional efforts to strengthen a relationship. Emdin (2020) notes that relationships and rigor in the classroom can co-occur if educators recognize and follow the seven rights of our students: (a) right to be here; (b) right to feel; (c) right to act; (d) right to love and be loved; (e) right to speak; (f) right to see; and (g) right to know. These rules are ultimately upheld through relationships with students and can also be a powerful message printed and posted on the classroom wall.

Howard et al. (2020) provides strategies and exercises to build relationships with diverse students to make them feel seen, heard, and valued in the classroom community. One strategy Howard et al. recommend is to use language that builds and protects self-esteem. This is done using micro-affirmations; a practice recognizing that the language we use matters. The use of frequent, subtle, and explicit acknowledgment of a student's character, values, efforts, accomplishments, and mere presence in the classroom support students to feel safe, welcome, included, and cared for (Rowe, 2008). This way of communicating with students puts into action Dr. Emdin's seven rights of our students. Micro-affirmations are especially important for students of color who may have experienced implicit bias and microaggressions in their educational experience and in life (Howard et al., 2020). Simple statements such as, "I missed you yesterday and am so happy to see you in class today," "Your curiosity and excitement is contagious!" or "Thank you for your thoughtful response," can cultivate a positive classroom climate, foster an authentic relationship, and make students feel seen.

The way in which micro-affirmations are delivered is also important. Students notice when positive tone and sincerity are missing and can have the opposite effect that educators intend; the student may shut down (Howard et al., 2020). To become more mindful of communication with students, Howard et al. suggest paying attention to student reactions to your communication. Does the student shut down or act out after your communication? What could you change in your communication to affirm and build self-esteem? What does your body language look like and say? Are you providing recognition to some students and not others? What is it about the students you do not provide recognition to that may bother you or that you find difficult? Begin to take notice of the way you communicate both verbally and nonverbally and how students in your classroom respond. Another strategy is to create and rehearse micro-affirmations about each of your students. Create a list of characteristics about each student that you admire and practice saying each out loud. Additionally, practice how you respond to challenging behavior. What wording can you use to avoid judgment? What face is most conducive to de-escalating challenging behavior? Teachers should practice these strategies in the mirror so when the opportunities arise in the classroom their responses come naturally.

Positive relationships are also a fundamental component of well-being (e.g., Positive Emotions, Engagement, Relationships, Meaning, Accomplishment [PERMA]; Seligman, 2011). Positive psychology research has indicated that as humans, the social creatures that we are, have the innate need for relationships to allow us to feel valued, supported, and loved by others (Seligman, 2011). One way to demonstrate this is by acknowledging something about the other person. In the classroom, a typical acknowledgement is to state something along the lines of, "Nice job reading that paragraph," "You did really well on that math problem," or "Great job cleaning up after our class project." These statements are positive in that they report a behavior expected at school that we like to see yet lack acknowledgement of an innate or personal quality about a student. Noting more personalized information or personality traits about a student supports the relationship-building process and supports the student in feeling understood, valued, and visible (Howard et al., 2020).

A student's character strengths are also associated with positive relationships and well-being (Wagner et al., 2020). Character strengths are visible positive personality traits. They are innate mechanisms that support individuals in their everyday lives. Character strengths encompass areas such as zest, love of learning, leadership, and curiosity—just to name a few (Peterson & Seligman, 2004). A wonderful and free resource to learn more about character strengths is www.viacharacter.org. To reword the examples above, acknowledgment that emphasizes positive personality traits and character strengths could be stated as: "Nice job reading that paragraph. I know you do not like reading in front of others, yet you demonstrated your strength of bravery and overcame something that was hard." "You did really well on that math problem, you tapped into your strength of perseverance and did not give up." and "Great job cleaning up after our class project, you demonstrated your strength of leadership and inspired the rest of the class to help out." Calling out and spotting strengths in students acknowledges traits that are innate and focus on more than just compliance. Again, this language supports students in feeling noticed, valued, and cared for.

Many of the classroom management strategies in this chapter double as meaningful ways to build relationships with students. Building relationships can take time, but the rewards far exceed the hurdles.

Mind-Body Health Strategies

Circles

One avenue to address problem behaviors in classrooms are restorative practices, a solution to challenge the negative outcomes associated with zero tolerance procedures (González, 2012). Restorative practices are frequently used frameworks aimed to create and foster positive school climates and connected communities by responding to behaviors as well as repairing relationships within the school environment and community context (Evanovich et al., 2020). Restorative practices are rooted in the Native American, First Nation, and other indigenous people of North America, as well as Aboriginal people (Mirksy, 2004) tradition and the community-based perspectives of the Mennonite practices (Evanovich et al., 2020; High, 2017; Payne & Welch, 2018), and originally were used under the title of "Restorative Justice" in the juvenile justice system. Practices have since extended to the school-based sector of practice starting in the 1990s (Payne & Welch, 2018). Restorative practices prioritize healing harm over punishment (Lustick et al., 2020). It is important to note that the evidence around restorative practices is still emerging, with exploratory studies suggesting promising findings related to the impact of such acts on school climate, behaviors of students, and fostering relationships between students and staff.

Restorative practices are a preventative approach at the core, focusing on community building, positive relationships, and positive responses to difficult situations and behaviors (Evanovich et al., 2020; González, 2012). Restorative practices have been linked to school climate efforts and are linked with a variety of data-based outcomes, especially when paired with an existing multi-tiered system of support, such as PBIS (Bradshaw et al., 2008). Research examining restorative practices suggests that positive outcomes associated with use of the framework are student ownership, targeting the school-to-prison pipeline, improving school relationships, prevention of inappropriate conflict resolution strategies, engagement in fruitful conversation, as well as improved outcomes for students on academic achievement and social outcomes (Ortega et al., 2016).

The most prominent preventative tools are Proactive Circles, which are used to foster connectivity among classmates via connection and sharing of personal experiences as well as concerns faced by a student (High, 2017). Use of Proactive Circles provides students with a model and a framework to engage in meaningful dialogue with peers, as well as fostering the opportunity for explicit instruction around behavioral skills. Researchers have suggested that the use of Proactive Circles may help students with social skills instruction through learning how to relate to others, add to a conversation, as well as share their own ideas and experiences (Evanovich et al., 2020).

What does a circle look like? Topographically, students and their teacher should be seated in a circular format, where all members of the circle can see each other. The overarching theme of the circle is that students sit shoulder to shoulder with their peers and the facilitator, both physically and metaphorically. That is, students and facilitators have equal opportunities to participate in the process and share their own personal experiences (Pranis, 2005; Pranis et al., 2003). Similar to PBIS, Circles encompass universal expectations for behavior, which may align with schoolwide behavior expectations.

A Proactive Circle should contain four key components: (a) greeting and a focusing moment, (b) connections and feelings check-in, (c) activity, and (d) closing. During the greeting and focusing moment students check-in with an introduction and the class may respond back with a "Good morning!" response. More elaborative check-in questions and prompts may be used when working on rapport building and connectedness. The focusing moment may include a brief mindfulness meditation or deep breathing exercise. This portion of the meeting should be relatively brief (Evanovich et al., 2020). The second component to the meeting is the connections and feelings check-in where students are asked to share how they are feeling emotionally. This provides the facilitator with information on the emotional pulse of the group, as well as allows the facilitator to make a mental list of any students who may need to be followed after the circle for an additional moment to touch-in (Evanovich et al., 2020). This is an opportunity to strengthen empathy skills and group cohesion as well and encourage students to listen more and speak less (Costello et al., 2010). The third component is the activity for the session, which is the main purpose for the meeting. This purpose may include problem solving and mediation, working on rapport and strengthening the community, or perhaps teaching explicit skills around academics, behaviors, or social skills instruction. As such, the function of the circle may be focused around repairing relationships, continued community building, or explicit instruction. The final component of a Proactive Circle is the closing. This portion of the circle focuses on ending the process and offering conscious time for reflection. Students may share something they learned, a thought or feeling connected to the circle, or stating a follow-up they plan to engage in as a result of the circle. The circle generally ends in a community circle-wide song, call and response activity, or a brief check-out activity (Evanovich et al., 2020). It is important for educators to consider implementation fidelity in order to ensure that the process is implemented as designed. Fidelity measures are easy to create or adapt for use, free of charge (see Evanovich et al., 2020).

Relaxation and Guided Imagery

One mindfulness practice that has been frequently used in the school-based setting is Relaxation and Guided Imagery (RGI). The RGI practice promotes images and feelings of relaxation both in the mind and the physical body (Costa & Barnhofer, 2016; deLeyer-Tiarks et al., 2020). One of the many benefits of incorporating RGI into the classroom is the inherent flexibility associated with the intervention (deLeyer-Tiarks et al., 2020). The RGI procedure relies on two distinctive and important principles to promote relaxation. One is through decreasing unwanted thoughts and emotions, and the second is through using distraction as a tool in order to think about certain imagery, locations, or events (Adeola et al., 2015; deLeyer-Tiarks et al., 2020).

Within Multi-Tiered Systems of Support, as a prevention agent, RGI may be relied on as a universal support practice for students (deLeyer-Tiarks et al., 2020). Scholars in the fields of mind-body health interventions suggest a multitude of benefits connected with use of RGI, such as decreased levels of reported depression and anxiety (Costa & Barnholder, 2016), as well as increased executive functioning skills needed for attending to classroom lessons (Hashim & Zainol, 2015).The practice of RGI has also been shown to be effective in higher levels of care, such as assisting children with a variety of medical health conditions, such as asthma (Dobson et al., 2015), abdominal pain (van Tilburg et al., 2009), and anxiety (van Tilburg et al., 2009), among other robust findings. deLeyer–Tiarks et al. (2020) suggest that RGI in schools may decrease negative emotions and increase coping behaviors in the school setting. deLeyer–Tiarks (2020) notes that an RGI script read before an exam in the classroom may decrease student worries and anxieties surrounding the exam.The RGI intervention may be efficacious when working with students during a public health crisis, such as COVID-19, as preliminary research suggests using RGI as an intervention to alleviate health-related trauma and anxieties for those who are caretakers (e.g., nurses; Sanadgol et al., 2020). Additionally, engagement in mindfulness activities during the COVID pandemic has been shown to be helpful for increasing positive mental health outcomes for educators (Matiz et al., 2020).

Regarding the length of the Relaxation and Guided Imagery script, for a universal classroom-based support procedure, teachers may consider using a short script (deLeyer–Tiarks et al., 2020). Lengths of scripts may include a few minutes at the start of the day during morning meetings (or during the school-wide announcements) in order to increase positive thought patterns and decrease school-related stress (deLeyer–Tiarks et al., 2020). Scripts for RGI are widely available online as well as videos and audio recordings to easily play in the classroom.With universal implementation and use of RGI at a school- or classroom-wide level, scripts should remain more general in nature, instead of targeting a specific audience or set of symptoms (e.g., trauma, depression, grief; deLeyer–Tiarks et al., 2020).

Gratitude Writing and Written Emotional Expression

Gratitude writing

In school-aged youth, gratitude has been linked to a variety of prosocial behaviors, relationships, and social interactions (Layous & Lyubomirsky, 2014).The mere experience of gratitude is connected with increased social wellbeing as well as strengthened social connectivity (Layous & Lyubomirsky, 2014). Across the literature, both increased prosocial and positive behaviors and outcomes are associated with practicing gratitude, as well as noted decreases in unhealthy mental health outcomes such as depression (Valois et al., 2004), substance use and abuse (Zullig et al., 2001), and psychopathology (Layous et al., 2014).

Gratitude practices may incorporate a variety of different practices and can be adjusted for use depending on teacher preference and the age of students. One gratitude practice is known as "Counting Blessings" where students are asked to reflect on five things in their life for which they experience gratitude (Froh et al., 2008).This is a free classroom-based support that can be quick and easy to implement.Additionally, it may be incorporated as part of an existing writing prompt in order to align with the academic goals or curriculum of the classroom, while sparking a mind–body and health-oriented classroom management strategy. Findings surrounding gratitude practices such as the "Counting Blessings" exercise have been linked to a variety of positive health outcomes immediately after engaging in the exercise as well as in follow-up assessment three weeks post-intervention (see Froh et al., 2008).

Another gratitude intervention to consider for use in the classroom setting are gratitude letters, which is a combination of both a journaling exercise as well as a gratitude practice (Winter et al., in press). The mere act of writing a letter to someone for whom you are grateful increases metrics related to positive wellbeing, including increases in measures of happiness as well as satisfaction with life (Froh et al., 2009; Toepfer et al., 2012).

Written Emotional Expression

Written Emotional Expression is a response allowing individuals to engage in, and reflect upon, their emotional experiences in order to improve mind-body health (Symth, 1998). This form of expressive writing asks students to write about difficult or traumatic emotional experiences and has been linked with decreased levels of depression (Symth, 1998). Similar to other mind-body health classroom management supports, the Written Emotional Expression management strategy has been linked with a variety of positive mental and behavioral outcomes for students (Symth, 1998; Pennebaker & Francis, 1996). A script for Written Emotional Expression may read as follows, as proposed by Symth (1998):

> Please write about your most stressful life experience(s) that you have ever undergone. Write continuously for 20 minutes without regard for spelling or stylistic concerns. You can use the same topic for 3 sessions OR you could write about a different stressful event each session. If necessary, repeat a previous topic rather than stop early. All essays will remain anonymous
>
> *Bray et al., 2003, p. 198*

In the classroom setting, engaging in Written Emotional Expression has been linked with decreasing classroom worry around exams, and increased exam scores overall (Ramirez & Beilock, 2011). Research has suggested that engagement in such reflective writing exercises may decrease worry placed on working memory, which may cause test-related anxieties. Engaging in Written Emotional Expression exercises as a whole class prior to high- and low-stakes exams may help students reassess the circumstances and eliminate the need to worry about the assessment (Klein & Boals, 2001; Ramirez & Beilock, 2011). The Written Emotional Expression intervention may be useful to incorporate classroom-wide in order to decrease internalizing concerns related to anxieties around performance or general stress.

Culturally Sensitive Meditation and Yoga

Culturally Sensitive Meditation

Public education is plagued by rising achievement demands and the common daily stressors associated with child and adolescent development (e.g., social and family demands, materialism; Pope, 2009). These experiences often lead to damaging health effects. Stress can lead to headaches, depleted immune systems, sleep deprivation, impaired brain functioning, relationship problems, anxiety, depression, digestive problems, and chronic illness; a symptom list most would want to avoid. Sadly, these effects are projected to continue to rise (de Bruin et al., 2017). Now imagine an activity that is easy to learn and that could alleviate the symptoms of stress and academic demands in as little as ten minutes a day. That activity is called meditation (Smith, 2014).

Meditation intervention studies have demonstrated significant health benefits (e.g., treatment of anxiety, depression, chronic pain, and immune functioning), positive impacts on affect (e.g., increased self-compassion, overall well-being, and adaptive emotional regulation; de Bruin et al., 2017; Menezes & Bizarro, 2015; Sears & Kraus, 2009), changes in brain development (e.g., strengthens connections within the brain that enhance perspective and understanding; Smith, 2014), benefits to academic resources (e.g., improved test performance, increased concentration, and overall better cognitive performance; Waters et al., 2014), and improved school climate (Wisner, 2013). These are benefits we clearly want students to experience.

It is important to note the use of meditation is not bound to neither spiritual or religious affiliation (Kabat-Zinn, 2013), nor cultural or ethnic backgrounds (DeLuca et al., 2018). Meditation is an inclusive practice and can be shared by all to experience the aforementioned benefits (DeLuca et al.,

2018). Still, to ensure meditation benefits students, Duane et al. (2021) provide insight to make meditation and mindfulness equitable, culturally responsive, and trauma informed. We cannot expect to drop meditation into a school where the climate and culture are hostile and expect positive outcomes. With this, it is important to examine a school's system and recognize how that impacts a student's feelings of safety, connectedness, and trust, while simultaneously understanding that though these strategies support student well-being, they do not eradicate systemic injustices. In the practice of mindfulness and meditation, classroom managers should encourage students to integrate their cultural values into the practice. This can include, but is not limited to, their personal religious beliefs, cultural terminology, and community traditions. Allow students to make this practice their own (Duane et al., 2021).

Educators also need to be cognizant of how they use meditation. Meditation should never be used as a strategy to silence students. For example, if your class is getting loud and not following directions, it would be inappropriate to enforce a "meditation break" to force students into silence. Additionally, when considering safety and making students feel safe in this practice, never force students to close their eyes. We do not always know a student's trauma history or comfort level and closing one's eyes can lead to feelings of vulnerability. You can make it an invitation, "I invite you to close your eyes if you feel comfortable," but it is encouraged to invite students to choose what feels best for them for their practice (Duane et al., 2021).

In a systematic review of the meditation interventions in schools, Waters et al. (2014) reported compelling evidence to support the inclusion of meditation in the classroom. In this examination of peer-reviewed research, meditation was found to support student well-being, social competence, and academic achievement. In the 15 studies included in the review, there were ten styles of meditation examined, with each technique being supported by an overarching theme; intentional attention and full concentration to internal or external stimuli (Waters et al., 2014). In general, there are three simple steps that guide meditation (Zylowska et al., 2008):

1. Direct attention and focus to a focal point (e.g., a person or being, the breath, an external object, a mantra)
2. Noticing internal and external distractions without judgment
3. Returning attention and focus to the focal point when distractions arise

General conclusions indicate that meditation implementation is most effective when delivered by the classroom teacher and is more efficacious when delivered for longer durations and offered twice daily. Still, the authors note that any little bit helps and any amount that can be implemented in the classroom is beneficial (Waters et al., 2014).

There are three meditation techniques that provide greater effects and are more feasible to deliver in the classroom setting: mindfulness, loving kindness, and transcendental (TM; Waters et al., 2014). Kabat-Zinn (2013) describes mindfulness meditation as being present to where you are and allowing you to authentically experience each moment, all the while free from judgment. Often personal thoughts become so overpowering that people may lose track of the present moment, or the mind tends to wander to tasks that need to be completed. There are an infinite number of reasons why the mind rapidly jumps from one thought to another, but through practicing mediation people can learn to be aware of the mind and body and elicit necessary change. "In order to release this tension, you first have to know it is there. You have to feel it. Then you have to know how to shut off the automatic pilot and how to take over the controls of your own body and mind" (Kabat-Zinn, 2013, p. 13). Mindfulness meditation often places emphasis on awareness of breathing, surrounding sounds, and bodily sensations. When thoughts or distractions arise, awareness is brought back to the breath. Often, in guided mindfulness meditations, themes may be assigned for the session, such as compassion, peace, or forgiveness of self and others (Sears & Kraus, 2009). de Bruin et al. (2017) stated:

We do not have much control over our life events and inner turmoil, but we do have control over how we relate to it. Mindfulness will not eliminate life's pressures, but it can help us to respond to them in a more deliberate and calm manner that benefits our mind and body, as well as our relationships with others.

p. 205

Mindfulness meditation is closely related to loving kindness meditation, where deliberate attention is placed on expressing positive thoughts and feelings toward self and others. Similarly, TM has the student focus on and silently repeat a single word or mantra and when distractions occur attention is brought back to the word(s) (Waters et al., 2014).

Examples of these meditation techniques can be found in print and online in both scripts and pre-recorded media to seamlessly integrate into the daily classroom routine. Examples of meditation print resources for classroom use include Snel (2013), Chopra (2018), and Allen and Klein (1997). Computer or other electronic device applications available online include *Calm, Headspace, Smiling Mind, Insight Timer, My.Life*, and *Liberate Meditation*. Other meditation online websites resources include Mindful.org, MindfulnessForTeens.com, and Happy Minds—Meditations and Sleep Stories (YouTube).

Yoga

Modern yoga, as most commonly practiced in western society, is described as the union of body, mind, and breath that is practiced as a means to improve bodily strength, flexibility, and cognitive functioning (Singleton, 2010). In the school-based setting, yoga has been shown to support students' physiology in response to stress (e.g., heart rate variability; Frank et al., 2020), enhanced coping skills, increased self-esteem, and self-regulation (Santangelo White, 2012), improved mood (Noggle et al., 2012), decreased hyperactivity and inattention (Chimiklis et al., 2018), and improved cognition and academic performance (Chung, 2018). In these studies, students were provided with lessons on several of the components of yoga, including, physical postures, breathing techniques, meditation training, and relaxation techniques. Khalsa and Butzer (2016), in their research review of yoga in schools, further emphasized that yoga in schools is efficacious in supporting student health and well-being.

To be clear, classroom teachers are not expected to lead elaborate 60-minute yoga classes for students, rather educators may consider strategies to integrate key practices of yoga (e.g., individual postures and breathing techniques) into the daily classroom routine. Suggestions on how to integrate yoga as a brain break is described in more detail below. Suggestions and strategies for integrating techniques of yoga are also discussed below.

Poses. Stretching and movement associated with yoga improves the circulation of cerebrospinal fluid and oxygenation of the brain. Taking the time to practice yoga also allows time for the eyes to relax and provides the body an opportunity to break from musculoskeletal tensions from sitting (Jensen, 2000). The following brief sequences, as shown in Figures 3.1, 3.2, and 3.3, can be integrated into the daily flow of the class and performed from the student's seat. Brief instructions that can be used for delivery with students are also provided. See Figures 3.1, 3.2, and 3.3 for a visual representation of the following scripts.

Seated Yoga Sequence 1. "Students, we are going to take a brief yoga movement break at your desks. If you feel comfortable, I invite you to close your eyes to provide your eyes some rest. Sit in your seat with your backs nice and tall. Bring your hands to your heart. Take a deep breath in, and a deep breath out. As you inhale, reach your arms up to the sky, leaning back over your chair a bit. As you exhale, fold over your legs and let your arms dangle to the floor. Inhale, sit up and bring your right knee to your chest, giving it a squeeze as you bring your forehead to your knee. Exhale, put your foot back on the floor. Inhale and reach your arms to the sky and gently bending over the back of your chair. Exhale and fold over your legs, letting your arms dangle to the floor. Inhale, sit up and bring your left knee to your chest, giving it a squeeze as you bring your forehead to your knee. Exhale, put your foot back on the floor. Inhale, raising your arms to the sky again. Exhale, folding your body over your legs and dangle your arms. Inhale again, raising your arms to the sky and gently bending over the back of your chair." Repeat sequence as desired (Tummee, n.d.a; see Figure 3.1).

Seated Yoga Sequence 2. "Students, we are going to take a brief yoga movement break at your desks. If you feel comfortable, I invite you to close your eyes to provide your eyes some rest. Sit up nice and tall and rest your hand on your knees. Take a deep breath in, and a deep breath out. Inhale and stretch your right hand to the ceiling, bending gently to your left. Hold on to your seat with your left hand for support if you need. Exhale and bend a little further. Inhale and switch sides, and stretch your left hand to the ceiling, bending gently to your right. Exhale and bend a little further. Inhale coming back to a regular seated position with your hand on your lap. Exhale. Shift your body so your legs are facing the left side of the classroom. As you inhale, hold on to the back of your chair and twist to the left. Exhale and twist a tiny bit more. Now, shift your body so your legs are facing the right side of the classroom. As you inhale, hold the back of your chair and twist to the right. Exhale and twist a tiny bit more. Come back to your regular seated position facing the front of the classroom. Inhale. As you exhale, reach your hand to your knees and round your back like a cat and bring your chin closer to your chest. On your next inhale, sit up tall, but this time push your heart to the front of the classroom arching your lower back. Exhale and relax in a comfortable position with your hands on your knees." Repeat sequence as desired (Tummee, n.d.b; see Figure 3.2).

Standing Yoga Chair Sequence. "Students, we are going to take a brief yoga movement break at your desks. Go ahead and stand behind your chair. Hold your hands at your heart. Feel your feet firmly on the ground. Take a deep inhale and deep exhale. Inhale and reach your arms to the sky and as you exhale place your hands on the back of your chair and fold towards the back of your chair, like

Figure 3.1   Seated Yoga Sequence 1

Note: All images are Tummee.com copyright. Tummee.com is a yoga sequencing platform for yoga teachers. Reprinted with permission (Tummee, n.d.a).

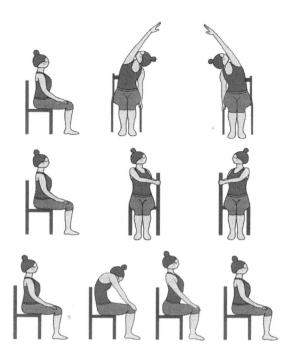

Figure 3.2 Seated Yoga Sequence 2

Note: All images are Tummee.com copyright. Tummee.com is a yoga sequencing platform for yoga teachers. Reprinted with permission (Tummee, n.d.b).

a little push-up. Inhale and step your left foot back. Exhale, straighten your arms and stand in a lunge. Feel free to move your left foot back if that feels comfortable to to get a little more stretch. Inhale, move your right foot back to meet your left foot and lower your torso while keeping your arms straight. Feel a nice stretch in your arms, legs, and shoulders. Inhale and put your weight into your hands on the back of your chair and lift your torso up and come up to your tippy toes if you are able. Exhale, rest your feet back down on the ground and again lower your torso while keeping your arms straight to give your shoulders, legs, and arms a nice stretch. Inhale, move your right foot forward so you are in a lunge position again. Adjust your left foot back or forward to give yourself the stretch you want. Exhale, place your hands on the back of your chair and fold towards the back of your chair, like a little push-up. Inhale, stand up straight with your arms reaching to the sky. Exhale and bring your hands back to your heart." Repeat sequence as desired (Tummee, n.d.c; see Figure 3.3).

Breathing. "Breathing is intimately linked with mental functions" (Zaccaro et al., 2018, p. 1). It is common for people to take short and shallow breaths, taking in less oxygen than needed, which leads to increased symptoms of anxiety (Conrad et al., 2007). Therefore, the ability to control one's breath is imperative to relaxation and regulating the stress response (Benson et al.,1974). Breathing techniques associated with yoga aim to regulate the frequency, deepness of breath, and the inspiration and expiration ratio of respiration (Jerath et al., 2006). Slowed and controlled breathing has been shown to improve parasympathetic regulation, increased heart rate variability, and increased central nervous system alpha power, which are indicators of emotional control and psychological well-being (Zaccaro et al., 2018). The literature is rich with benefits for deep breathing, and since breathing is something we all must do, it makes it a skill we must teach children.

Practicing deep, slow, and controlled breathing is a wonderful skill to teach and practice with students during circles or morning meeting time, and during brain breaks throughout the day (more information on brain breaks below). It is best used and practiced proactively so that when students

Figure 3.3 Standing Yoga Chair Sequence

Note: All images are Tummee.com copyright. Tummee.com is a yoga sequencing platform for yoga teachers. Reprinted with permission (Tummee, n.d.c).

do become aroused, breathing in this way to calm the nervous system becomes automatic. Still, when students become aroused, they may need adult support to regulate through modeling or using a visual prompt.

When first learning deep breathing, it can be helpful to first bring attention to how your students breathe naturally. One way to do this is by having students place one hand on their chest and the other on their stomach. As students breathe, have them bring their attention to which hand is moving. During natural breathing, the hand on their chest is likely to rise with each breath. To have students shift to deep breathing, have them imagine they are filling a balloon in their belly. The deeper they breathe, the larger their balloon gets. For younger students, this activity can also be done laying on the ground with a stuffed animal on their belly.

Next, to teach students about controlling their breath some props may be beneficial such as using bubbles, a feather, straws, or for older students a deep breathing GIF (e.g., https://youtu.be/u9Q8 D6n-3qw). These props teach students how to slowly and carefully control their breathing. With bubbles, specifically, students cannot blow too hard and fast or weak and slow or the bubbles don't form. Guide students to take deep breaths through their nose to fill their stomachs with air and at the same rate as they breathe in take a controlled breath out with pursed lips. It can be helpful to have students count while breathing in and out (e.g., counting to 4). This strategy can help the breath remain consistent. Using a straw on the outbreath can also help with controlling how much air is exhaled at one time.

Visual reminders of deep breathing can be beneficial. Students could benefit from traceable breathing guides, as shown in Figures 3.4, 3.5, and 3.6. These guides provide a discrete way for students to practice deep breathing during class. Students use their finger to trace each of the shapes and breathing as directed. To encourage students to use these guides, they can be used during brain breaks throughout the day and students can track how breathing in this way makes them feel. The

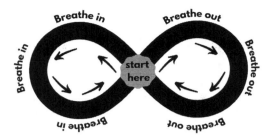

Figure 3.4   Lazy 8 Breathing

Note: Image created by first author, Sierra M. Trudel, for use in "Prevention Strategies for Classroom Management," by E. Sabornie and D. Espelage (Eds.), *Handbook of Classroom Management* (Third edition), 2023, Routledge (Trudel, 2022a).

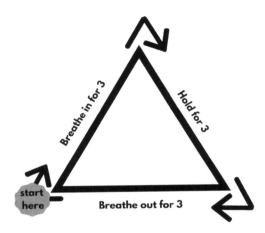

Figure 3.5   Triangle Breathing

Note: Image created by first author, Sierra M. Trudel, for use in "Prevention Strategies for Classroom Management," by E. Sabornie and D. Espelage (Eds.), *Handbook of Classroom Management* (Third edition), 2023, Routledge (Trudel, 2022b).

examples provided below start with practicing deep breathing alone (see Figure 3.4), then include an additional element of controlled breathing, briefly holding the breath at the top of the inhale (see Figure 3.5) and briefly holding the breath at the top of the inhale and exhale (see Figure 3.6). Allow students to choose which they prefer to use independently.

Some additional resources for teachers include YogaEd.com, KidsYogaStories.com, and Tummee. com.

Brain Breaks and Movement Breaks

"All work and no play makes Jack a dull boy."—Proverb. In the context of education, these words about Jack should still be cautionary. In other words, continuous engagement and production of work is not sustainable for those who do not receive breaks. The typical student is in school approximately 30 hours per week, nearly the length of a full-time job. With rising demands and increased rigor in curriculum this can leave students sitting at their desks for extended periods of time. The research is clear that such sedentary behavior has grave consequences on students' physical health (e.g., cardio-metabolic disease and obesity; Tremblay et al., 2011), but what is not often discussed is the impact

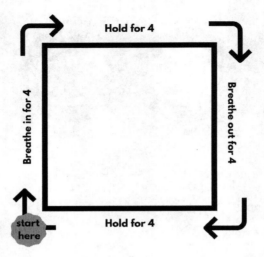

Figure 3.6   Square Breathing

Note: Image created by first author, Sierra M. Trudel, for use in "Prevention Strategies for Classroom Management," by E. Sabornie and D. Espelage (Eds.), *Handbook of Classroom Management* (3rd edition), 2023, Routledge (Trudel, 2022c).

of sedentary behavior on learning and psychological well-being. Tremblay and colleagues (2011) noted that sedentary children are more likely to have lower self-esteem, diminished social skills, and decreased academic achievement. In addition to being sedentary, the length and duration of lessons can impact a student's ability to absorb and retain knowledge. Student off-task behavior is a phenomenon no teacher wants to experience, yet in traditional learning settings (e.g., whole-group learning) student attention can dwindle after just ten minutes of continuous instruction (Godwin et al., 2016).

To combat these adverse effects, there is evidence to suggest that the increase of physical activity within the classroom and structured breaks (i.e., brain breaks) can support academic performance. Giving the brain time away from academic tasks can increase a child's capacity for productivity, emotional well-being, social skill development (Jensen, 2000), cognitive performance (Committee on Physical Activity and Physical Education in the School Environment et al., 2013), and engagement with learning (Ma et al., 2014). Additionally, executive functioning is impacted by an individual's level of physical activity and stress, and both play a pivotal role in learning, especially regarding reading and mathematics. Beyond academics, executive functioning encompasses emotional and behavioral regulation, working memory, the ability to plan and organize information, and flexible thinking. Improved executive functioning performance has been shown to be correlated with physical activity, making the inclusion of frequent movement breaks imperative to foster cognitive health (Committee on Physical Activity and Physical Education in the School Environment et al., 2013).

Brain breaks also support brain health by allowing the student to take a brief respite from the academic task by participating in physical activity or a fun mental task, fun being the key word (Institute of Positive Education, n.d.). These activities support cognition, memory, and mood (Jensen, 2011) by increasing circulation, which oxygenates the brain and increases attention to task, allows time for learning to consolidate in memory (the hippocampus can only store so much information and overloading students with information results in no new learning), and stimulates the release of key neurotransmitters, noradrenaline and dopamine, which support a sense of urgency and mood, respectively. In short, brain breaks can lead to improved storage and retrieval of information and ultimately support students to feel good (Jensen, 2000).

In the classroom brain breaks and movement breaks can be used to:

1. Increase energy or positively prime the class. There are inevitably times throughout the school day where students appear lethargic, unmotivated, or tired. To positively increase the energy of the classroom, brain breaks can be used to elicit positive emotions and engagement through the use of movement (Frederickson, 2013) and humor (Jensen, 2008).
2. Decrease energy or de-escalate the class. Similar to above, there will be times during the school day where students need support in shifting from a heightened state of arousal to a state of calm. Strategies noted above, such as meditation and mindful breathing, in addition to quiet coordination activities (Institute of Positive Education, n.d.), can be used to calm and refocus students. Teachers should be mindful of how they introduce the activity and can model the tone they wish to see in their students.
3. Cultivate co-regulation with the class. Sometimes the collective student arousal levels can be mismatched or a student may be experiencing a stressful moment. To co-regulate the whole class, emotional and behavioral regulation can be fostered or repaired through the use of rhythm and repetition (Brunzell et al., 2016). By providing students with a brain break that provides rhythmic repetitions, the body's stress response can begin to regulate. The heart rate for a healthy child is approximately 60–80 beats per minute, and students who have experienced trauma or are in a state of arousal can vastly exceed this number. One strategy to support students to co-regulate is to use a metronome that is set within the healthy range of 60–80 beats per minute (Brunzell et al., 2016). If the entire class or student is aroused, 80 beats per minute may be a good pulse with which to start. While the metronome is pulsing, providing students with opportunities for mindfulness (e.g., breathing and stretching), or quiet coordination activities to the pulse of the metronome, may be beneficial.

These breaks can be planned or implemented in the moment. It is still important to track how students respond to each type of break. For example, scheduling a relaxation break after lunch when students already appear lethargic may increase their sleepiness. It will be important to remain flexible in choosing a brain break based on the needs of your students at any particular time.

The following are tips and strategies for brain break implementation inspired by suggestions from the Institute of Positive Education (n.d.): (a) Create a routine for when students can expect brain breaks to occur. Flexibility in the type of brain break can be employed, however, teachers should still consider trialing a particular concept over a period of time to allow students to adapt. Time your brain breaks. (b) Choose activities that are developmentally appropriate, so students do not perceive the activity as childish. (c) Be transparent on how brain breaks support learning as students are more likely to engage in these activities when they know and understand *why* they are doing it. (d) Ask students for feedback! Asking for feedback cultivates teacher-student relationships and provides insight as to how brain breaks can be altered to meet student needs. Teachers might also consider having students rate their mood, feelings of engagement, and energy level throughout the day (Stokes et al., 2019). (e) Remember, the addition of brain breaks to your classroom routine is to promote student learning. Consider this time away from instruction an investment (Institute of Positive Education, n.d.). An excellent teacher resource for brain breaks is *Brain Breaks, Brain Breaks 2,* and *Brain Breaks 3* by Institute of Positive Education (n.d.), Geelong Grammar School.

Conclusion

Effective classroom management is rooted in structure, routine, and relationships (Marzano & Marzano, 2003) to cultivate positive and equitable classroom climate and moderate student behavior (Marzano & Marzano, 2003; Sieberer-Nagler, 2015). The classroom layout is the first, most basic step, for educators to consider in their classroom management. Controlling the physical environment allows for instruction to access the greatest number of students with low effort from the educator via attending to basic principles of student learning and trauma sensitivity. Similarly, established classroom expectations set the tone for how students are expected to behave, which decreases confusion and allows for consistency and stability in the classroom and school when implemented on a Tier 1 schoolwide level. At the heart of classroom management are relationships. Classrooms are social environments that can foster a positive culture and climate to influence both student behavior and learning. Teachers who take the time to get to know each student and communicate student strengths are more likely to gain student respect, see desired behaviors, and increase achievement in their classrooms.

Mind-body health strategies are efficacious in supporting classroom management by mitigating student emotional regulation, psychological stress, attentional difficulties, coping skills, and physical health challenges (Bray & Maykel, 2016), so students can best access learning opportunities. Circles, a common practice in the restorative practice movement, are one brief tool to increase classroom connectivity and tackle classroom conflicts when they emerge, thereby targeting the core of classroom management. Again, this practice is rooted in a proactive foundation, in that restorative practices use connectivity to stop conflict and issues from emerging in the first place, while simultaneously providing students and educators with the language to handle classroom conflict should it arise.

Relaxation and Guided Imagery (RGI), mediation, and yoga, are evidence-based mind-body health strategies that aim to decrease troubling emotions and offering a calming distraction for students during their school day. RGI and meditation can help students grapple with their emotions and access a strategy when they notice they are feeling distressed or upset, and support students to intentionally shift their attention to an internal or external stimuli. Similarly, Written Emotional Expression provides another mind-body health strategy to aid students in identifying their emotions and providing a subtle strategy to cope with tough circumstances and emotions. In the school-based setting, yoga has been shown to support students' physiology in response to stress, enhanced coping skills, increased self-esteem, and self-regulation, decreased hyperactivity and inattention, and improved cognition and academic performance.

Additionally, the length and duration of lessons can impact a student's ability to absorb and retain knowledge, with student attention dwindling after just ten minutes. Brain breaks, then, are a quick and efficient means of giving a student's brain time away from academic tasks, which can increase productivity, well-being, and engagement with learning.

Together, these strategies support teachers in cultivating positive learning environments where students learn important skills to regulate emotions and behavior. These actions are conducive to the successful delivery of instruction, fostering both student achievement and well-being.

References

Adeola, M.T., Baird, C.L., Sands, L., Longoria, N., Henry, U., Nielsen, J., & Shiels, C.G. (2015). Active despite pain: Patient experiences with guided imagery with relaxation compared to rest. *Clinical Journal of Oncology Nursing, 19*(6), 649–652. https://doi.org/10.1188/15.CJON.649-652

Allen, J. S., & Klein, R. J. (1997). Ready…set…R.E.L.A.X: A research-based program of relaxation, learning and self-esteem for children. Inner Coaching.

Alter, P., & Haydon, T. (2017). Characteristics of effective classroom rules: A review of the literature. *Teacher Education and Special Education, 40*(2), 114–127. https://doi.org/10.1177/0888406417700962

Anderson, A. R., Christenson, S. L., Sinclair, M. F., & Lehr, C. A. (2004). Check & Connect: The importance of relationships and promoting engagement with school. *Journal of School Psychology, 42*(2), 95–113. https://doi.org/10.1016/j.jsp.2004.01.002

Bandura, A. (1971). Social learning theory. *General Learning Press*, 1–46.

Benson, H., Beary, J. F., & Carol, M. P. (1974). The relaxation response. *Psychiatry, 37*(1), 37–46. https://doi.org/10.1080/00332747.1974.11023785

Berman, M. G., Jonides, J., & Kaplan, S. (2008). The cognitive benefits of interacting with nature. *Psychological Science, 19*(12), 1207–1212. https://doi.org/10.1111/j.1467-9280.2008.02225.x

Bicard, D. F. (2000). Using classroom rules to construct behavior. *Middle School Journal, 31*(5), 37–45. https://doi.org/10.1080/00940771.2000.11494651

Boostrom, R. (1991). The nature and functions of classroom rules. *Curriculum Inquiry, 21*(2),193–216. https://doi.org/10.2307/1179942

Bradshaw, C. P., Koth, C. W., Bevans, K. B., Ialongo, N., & Leaf, P. J. (2008). The impact of school-wide positive behavioral interventions and supports (PBIS) on the organizational health of elementary schools. *School Psychology Quarterly, 23*(4), 462–473. https://doi.org/10.1037/a0012883

Bray, M., & Maykel, C. (2016). Mind-body health in the school environment. *International Journal of School & Educaitonal Psychology, 4*(1), 3–4. https://doi.org/10.1080/21683603.2016.1130528

Bray, M. A., Theodore, L. A., Patwa, S. S., Margiano, S. G., Alric, J. M., & Peck, H. L.(2003). Written emotional expression as an intervention for asthma. *Psychology in the Schools, 40*(2), 193–207. https://doi.org/10.1002/pits.10078

Brunzell, T., Stokes, H. & Waters, L. (2016). Trauma-informed positive education: Using positive psychology to strengthen vulnerable students. *Contemporary School Psychology, 20*, 63–83. https://doi.org/10.1007/s40688-015-0070-x

Center on Positive Behavioral Interventions and Supports (2015) Positive behavioral interventions and supports (PBIS) implementation blueprint. University of Oregon. www.pbis.org.

Cheryan, S., Ziegler, S. A., Plaut, V. C., & Meltzoff, A. N. (2014). Designing classrooms to maximize student achievement. *Policy Insights from the Behavioral and Brain Sciences, 1*(1), 4–12. https://doi.org/10.1177/2372732214548677

Chimiklis, A. L., Dahl, V., Spears, A. P., Goss, K., Fogarty, K., & Chacko, A. (2018). Yoga, mindfulness, and meditation interventions for youth with ADHD: Systematic review and meta-analysis. *Journal of Child and Family Studies*, 27, 3155–3168. https://doi.org/10.1007/s10826-018-1148-7

Chopra, M. (2018). Just breathe: Meditation, mindfulness, movement, and more. Running Press Kids.

Chung, S. C. (2018). Yoga and meditation in youth education: A systematic review. *The Lancet, 392*(2). https://doi.org/10.1016/S0140-6736(18)32052-X

Committee on Physical Activity and Physical Education in the School Environment, Food and Nutrition Board, & Institute of Medicine (2013). Physical activity, fitness, and physical education: Effects on academic performance. In H. W. Kohl III & H. D. Cook (Eds.), *Educating the student body: Taking physical activity and physical education to school* (pp. 97–160). The National Academy Press.

Conrad, A., Müller, A., Doberenz, S., Kim, S., Meuret, A. E., Wollburg, E., & Roth, W. T. (2007). Psychophysiological effects of breathing instructions for stress management. *Applied Psychophysiology Biofeedback*, 32, 89–9. https://doi.org/10.1007/s10484-007-9034-x

Costa, A., & Barnhofer, T. (2016). Turning towards or turning away: A comparison of mindfulness meditation and guided imagery relaxation in patients with acute depression. *Behavioural and Cognitive Psychotherapy, 44*(4), 410–419. https://doi.org/10.1017/S1352465815000387

Costello, B., Wachtel, J., & Wachtel, T. (2010). *Restorative circles in schools: Building community and enhancing learning.* International Institute for Restorative Practices.

de Bruin, E. I., Formsma, A. R., Frijstein, G., & Bogels, S. M. (2017). Mindful2Work: Effects of combined physical exercise, yoga, and mindfulness medications for stress relieve in employees. A proof of concept study. *Mindfulness*, 8, 204–217. https://doi.org/10.1007/s12671-016-0593-x

deLeyer-Tiarks, J. M., Gammie, L. E., Bray, M., & Moriarty, S. (2020). Relaxation and guided imagery for mind-body health. In C. Maykel & M. A. Bray (Eds.), *Promoting mind-body health in schools: Interventions for mental health professionals* (pp. 173–186). American Psychological Association. https://doi.org/10.1037/0000157-012

DeLuca, S. M., Kelman, A. R., & Waelde, L. C. (2018). A systematic review of ethnoracial representation and cultural adaptation of mindfulness- and meditation-based interventions. *Psychological Studies, 63*, 117–129, https://doi.org/10.1007/s12646-018-0452-z

Dobson, R. L., Bray, M. A., Kehle, T. J., Theodore, L. A., & Peck, H. L. (2005). Relaxation and guided imagery as an intervention for children with asthma: A replication. *Psychology in the Schools, 42*(7), 707–720. https://doi.org/10.1002/pits.20119

Duane, A., Casimir, A. E., Mims, L. C., Kaler-Jones, C., & Simmons, D. (2021). Beyond deep breathing: A new vision for equitable, culturally responsive, and trauma-informed mindfulness practice. *Middle School Journal, 52*(3), 4–14. https://doi.org/10.1080/00940771.2021.1893593

Emdin, C. (2020). *Keynote* [Conference session]. 2020 Educator Summit, Philadelphia, PA, United States. https://educatorsummit.org

Evanovich, L. L., Martinez, S., Kern, L., & Haynes Jr, R. D. (2020). Proactive circles: A practical guide to the implementation of a restorative practice. Preventing School Failure: Alternative Education for Children and Youth, *64*(1), 28–36. https://doi.org/10.1080/1045988X.2019.1639128

Ford, A. (2016). Planning classroom design and layout to increase pedagogical options for secondary teachers. *Educational Planning*, *23*(1), 25–33.

Frank, J., Seifert, G., Schroeder, R., Gruhn, B., Stritter, W., Jeitler, M., Steckhan, N, Kessler, C. S., Michalsen, A., & Voss, A. (2020). Yoga in school sports improves functioning of autonomic nervous system in young adults: A non-randomized controlled pilot study. *PLOS ONE*, *15*(4). https://doi.org/10.1371/journal.pone.0231299

Frederickson, B. L. (2013). Positive emotions broaden and build. *Advances in Experimental and Social Psychology*, *47*, 1–52. http://dx.doi.org/10.1016/B978-0-12-407236-7.00001-2

Frey, N., Fisher, D., & Smith, D. (2020). Trauma-informed design in schools. *Trauma-Sensitive Schools*, *78*(2).

Froh, J. J., Kashdan, T. B., Ozimkowski, K. M., & Miller, N. (2009). Who benefits the most from a gratitude intervention in children and adolescents? Examining positive affect as a moderator. *Journal of Positive Psychology*, *4*, 408–422. https://doi.org/10.1080/17439760902992464

Froh, J. J., Sefick, W. J., & Emmons, R. A. (2008). Counting blessings in early adolescents: An experimental study of gratitude and subjective well-being. *Journal of School Psychology*, *46*(5), 213–233. https://doi.org/10.1016/j.jsp.2007.03.005

Gable, R. A., Hester, P. H., Rock, M. L., & Hughes, K. G. (2009). Back to basics: Rules, praise, ignoring, and reprimands revisited. *Intervention in School and Clinic*, *44*(4), 195–205. https://doi.org/10.1177/1053451208328831

Godwin, K. E., Almeda, M.V., Seltman, H., Kai, S., Skerbetz, M. D., Baker, R. S., & Fisher, A.V. (2016). Off-task behavior in elementary school children. *Learning and Instruction*, *44*, 128–143. https://doi.org/10.1016/j.learninstruc.2016.04.003

González, T. (2012). Keeping kids in schools: Restorative justice, punitive discipline, and the school to prison pipeline. *Journal of Law* and *Education*, *41*(2), 281–335.

Grube, K. J. (2013). Detrimental effects of white valued walls in classrooms. *Educational Planning*, *21*(2), 69–82.

Hajovsky, D. B., Mason, B. A., & McCune, L. A. (2017). Teacher-student relationship quality and academic achievement in elementary school: A longitudinal examination of gender differences. *Journal of School Psychology*, *63*, 119–133. https://doi.org/10.1016/j.jsp.2017.04.001

Hashim, H. A., & Zainol, N. A. (2015). Changes in emotional distress, short term memory, and sustained attention following 6 and 12 sessions of progressive muscle relaxation training in 10–11 years old primary school children. Psychology, Health & Medicine, *20*(5), 623–628. https://doi.org/10.1080/13548506.2014.1002851

High, A. J. (2017). Using restorative practices to teach and uphold dignity in an American school district. M*cGill Journal of Education*, *52*(2), 525–534. https://doi.org/10.7202/1044479ar

Howard, J. R., Milner-McCall, T., & Howard, T. C. (2020). *No more teaching without positive relationships* (N. K. Duke & M. C. Cruz, Series Eds.). Heinemann Publishers.

Institute of Positive Education (n.d.a). *Brain breaks: Activities for stimulating student engagement and enhancing teacher-student relationships*. Institute of Positive Education.

Institute of Positive Education (n.d.b). *Brain breaks 2: More activities for stimulating student engagement and enhancing teacher-student relationships*. Institute of Positive Education.

Jensen, E. (2000). Moving with the brain in mind. *Educational Leadership*, *58*(3), 34–38.

Jensen, E. (2008). *Brain-based learning: The new paradigm of teaching*. Corwin Press.

Jensen, E. (2011). Brain-based education in action. *Educational Horizons*, *90*(2), 5–6. https://doi.org/10.1177/0013175X1109000202

Jerath, R., Edry, J. W., Barnes, V. A., & Jerath, V. (2006). Physiology of long pranayamic breathing: Neural respiratory elements may provide a mechanism that explains how slow deep breathing shifts the autonomic nervous system. *Medical Hypotheses*, *67*(3), 566–571. https://doi.org/10.1016/j.mehy.2006.02.042

Kabat-Zinn, J. (2013). *Full catastrophe living: Using the wisdom of your body and mind to face stress, pain and illness*. Bantam Books.

Kerr, M. M., & Nelson, C. M. (2010). *Strategies for addressing behavior problems in the classroom* (6th ed.). Pearson.

Khalsa, S. B. S., & Butzer, B. (2016). Yoga in school settings: A research review. *Annals of the New York Academy of Sciences*, *1373*, 45–55. https://doi.org/10.1111/nyas.13025

Kilgus, K.P., & Von der Mebse, N.P. (2019). General model of service delivery for school-based interventions. In K. Radley & E. Dart (Eds.) *Handbook of behavioral interventions in schools: Multi-tiered systems of support*. Oxford University Press.

Klein, K., & Boals, A. (2001). Expressive writing can increase working memory capacity. *Journal of Experimental Psychology: General*, *130*(3), 520–533. https://doi.org/10.1037/0096-3445.130.3.520

Layous, K., Chancellor, J., & Lyubomirsky, S. (2014). Positive activities as protective factors against mental health conditions. *Journal of Abnormal Psychology*, *123*(1), 3–12. https://doi.org/10.1037/a0034709

Lustick, H., Norton, C., Lopez, S. R., & Greene-Rooks, J. H. (2020). Restorative practices for empowerment: A social work lens. *Children & Schools*, *42*(2), 89–97. https://doi.org/10.1093/cs/cdaa006

Ma, J. K., Mare, L. L., & Gerd, B. J. (2014). Classroom-based high-intensity interval activity improved off task behavior in primary school students. *Applied Physiology, Nutrition, and Metabolism, 39*(12), 1332–1337. https://doi.org/10.1139/apnm-2014-0125

Maag, J. W. (2004). *Behavior management: From theoretical implications to practical applications (2nd ed.).* Wadsworth/Thomson Learning.

Makela, T., Kankaanrant, M. & Helfenstein, S. (2014). Considering learners' perceptions in designing effective 21st century learning environments for basic education in Finland. *The International Journal of Educational Organization and Leadership, 20*(3), 1–13. https://doi.org/10.18848/2329-1656/CGP/v20i03/48481

Marzano, R. J., & Marzano, J. S. (2003). The key to classroom management. *Educational leadership, 61*(1), 6–13.

Maslow, A. H. (1943). A theory of human motivation. *Psychological Review, 50*(4), 370–396.

Matiz, A., Fabbro, F., Paschetto, A., Cantone, D., Paolone, A. R., & Crescentini, C. (2020). Positive impact of mindfulness meditation on mental health of female teachers during the COVID-19 outbreak in Italy. *International Journal of Environmental Research and Public Health, 17*(18), 6450. https://doi.org/10.3390/ijerph17186450

Menezes, C. B. & Bizarro, L. (2015). Effects of a brief meditation training on negative affect, trait anxiety and concentrated attention. *Paidéia, 25*(62), 393–401. https://doi.org/10.1590/1982-43272562201513

Mirksy, L (2004). Restorative justice practices of Native American, First Nation and other indigenous people of North America: Part two. www.iirp.edu/news/restorative-justice-practices-of-native-american-first-nation-and-other-indigenous-people-of-north-america-part-two

Noggle, J. J., Steiner, N. J., Minami, T., Khalsa, S. B. (2012). Benefits of yoga for psychosocial well-being in US high school curriculum: A preliminary randomized controlled trial. *Journal of Developmental and Behavioral Pediatrics, 33*(3), 193–201. http://dx.doi.org/10.1097/DBP.0b013e31824afdc4

Ortega, L., Lyubansky, M., Nettles, S., & Espelage, D. L. (2016). Outcomes of a restorative circles program in a high school setting. *Psychology of Violence, 6*(3), 459–468. http://dx.doi.org/10.1037/vio0000048

Park, E. L., & Choi, B. K. (2014). Transformation of classroom spaces: Traditional versus active learning classroom in colleges. *Higher Education, 68*(5), 749–771. https://doi.org/10.1007/s10734-014-9742-0

Payne, A. A., & Welch, K. (2018). The effect of school conditions on the use of restorative justice in schools. Youth Violence and Juvenile Justice, 16(2), 224–240. https://doi.org/10.1177/1541204016681414

Pennebaker, J., & Francis, M. (1996). Cognitive, emotional, and processes in disclosure. *Cognition and Emotion, 10*(6), 601–626. https://doi.org/10.1080/026999396380079

Peterson, C., & Seligman, M. E. (2004). *Character strengths and virtues: A handbook and classification.* Oxford University Press.

Pierson, R. (2013, May). *Every kid needs a champion* [Video]. TED Conferences. www.ted.com/talks/rita_pierson_every_kid_needs_a_champion

Pope, D. (2009). Beyond "doing school:" From 'stressed-out' to 'engaged in learning.' *Education Canada, 50*(1), 4–8.

Pranis, K. (2005). *The little book of circle processes.* Good Books.

Pranis, K., Stuart, B., & Wedge, M. (2003). *Peacemaking circles: From crime to community.* Living Justice Press.

Ramirez, G., & Beilock, S. L. (2011). Writing about testing worries boosts exam performance in the classroom. *Science, 331*(6014), 211–213. https://doi.org/ 10.1126/science.1199427

Rowe, M. (2008). Micro-affirmations and micro-inequities. *Journal of the International Ombudsman Association, 1*(1), 45–48.

Ryan, C. O., Browning, W. D., Clancy, J. O., Andrews, S. L., & Kallianpurkar, N. B. (2014). Biophilic design parameters: Emerging nature-based parameters for health and well-being in the built environment. *International Journal of Architectural Research: ArchNet-IJAR, 8*(2), 62–76. https://doi.org/10.1007/s10734-014-9742-0

Sanadgol, S., Firouzkouhi, M., Badakhsh, M., Abdollahimohammad, A., & Shahraki-vahed, A. (2020). Effect of guided imagery training on death anxiety of nurses at COVID-19 intensive care units: a quasi-experimental study. *Neuropsychiatria i Neuropsychologia/Neuropsychiatry and Neuropsychology, 15*(3), 83–88. https://doi.org/10.5114/nan.2020.101290

Santangelo White, L. (2012). Reducing stress in school-age girls through mindful yoga. *Journal of Pediatric Health Care, 26*(1), 45–56. https://doi.org/10.1016/j.pedhc.2011.01.002

Scott, T. M., Anderson, C. M., & Alter, P. J. (2011). *Managing classroom behavior using positive behavior supports.* Pearson.

Sears. S. & Kraus, S. (2009). I think therefore I om: Cognitive distortions and coping style as mediators for the effects of mindfulness meditation and anxiety, positive and negative affect, and hope. *Journal of Clinical Psychology, 65*(6), 561–573. https://doi.org/10.1002/jclp.20543

Seligman, M. (2011). *Flourish.* Free Press.

Shores, R. E., Gunter, P. L., & Jack, S. L. (1993). Classroom management strategies: Are they setting events for coercion? Behavioral Disorders, 18(2), 92–102. https://doi.org/10.1177/019874299301800207

Sieberer-Nagler, K. (2016). Effective classroom-management & positive teaching. *English Language Teaching, 9*(1), 163–172.

Simonsen, B., Fairbanks, S., Briesch, A., Myers, D., & Sugai, G. (2008). Evidence based practices in classroom management: Considerations for research to practice. *Education and Treatment of Children, 31*(3), 351–380. https://doi.org/10.1353/etc.0.0007

Simsonsen, B., Freeman, J., Goodman, S., Mitchell, B., Swain-Bradway, J. Flannery, B., Sugai, G., George, H., Putnam, B. (2015). Supporting and responding to behavior: Evidence-based classroom strategies for teachers. U.S. Office of Special Education Programs.

Singleton, M. (2010). *Yoga body: The origins of modern posture practice*. Oxford University Press.

Smith, O. (2014, Spring). 10 minutes of bliss. *Montessori Life, 26*(1), 48–50.

Smith, R. (2004). Conscious classroom management: Unlocking the secrets to great teaching. Conscious Teaching Publications.

Smyth, J. M. (1998). Written emotional expression: effect sizes, outcome types, and moderating variables. *Journal of Consulting and Clinical Psychology, 66*(1), 174–184. https://doi.org/10.1037/0022-006X.66.1.174

Snel, E. (2013). Sitting still like a frog: Mindfulness exercises for kids (and their parents). Shambhala Publications.

Sterling, D. R. (2009). Classroom management: Setting up the classroom for learning. *Science Scope, 32*(9), 29.

Stokes, H., Turnbull, M., Forster, R. & Farrelly, A. (2019). Young people's voices, young people's lives: A Berry Street Education Model (BSEM) project. Melbourne: Youth Research Center.

Tanner, C. K. (2015). Effects of school architectural designs on students' Accomplishments: A meta-analysis. Retrieved from the Education Facilities Clearinghouse (EFC) www.efc.gwu.edu/library/effects-of-schoolar chitectural-designs-on-students-accomplishments-a-meta-analysis/

Toepfer, S. M., Cichy, K., & Peters, P. (2012). Letters of gratitude: Further evidence for author benefits. *Journal of Happiness Studies, 13*, 187–201. https://doi.org/10.1007/s10902-011-9257-7

Tremblay, M. S., LeBlanc, A. G., Kho, M. E., Saunders, T. J., Larouche, R., Colley, R. C., Goldfield, G., & Connor Gorber, S. (2011). Systematic review of sedentary behaviour and health indicators in school-aged children and youth. *International Journal of Behavioral Nutrition and Physical Activity, 8*(98). https://doi.org/10.1186/1479-5868-8-98

Trudel. S. M. (2022a). *Lazy 8 breathing* [Image]. Prevention Strategies for Classroom Management. In E. Sabornie and D. Espelage (Eds.), *Handbook of Classroom Management* (3rd edition). Routledge.

Trudel. S. M. (2022b). *Triangle breathing* [Image]. Prevention Strategies for Classroom Management. In E. Sabornie and D. Espelage (Eds.), *Handbook of Classroom Management* (3rd edition). Routledge.

Trudel. S. M. (2022c). *Square breathing* [Image]. Prevention Strategies for Classroom Management. In E. Sabornie and D. Espelage (Eds.), *Handbook of Classroom Management* (3rd edition). Routledge.

Tummee (n.d.a). [Seated yoga sequence 1][Image]. Tummee. www.tummee.com/

Tummee (n.d.b). [Seated yoga sequence 2][Image]. Tummee. www.tummee.com/

Tummee (n.d.c). [Standing yoga chair sequence][Image]. Tummee. www.tummee.com/

Vagnoli, L., Bettini, A., Amore, E., De Masi, S., & Messeri, A. (2019). Relaxation-guided imagery reduces perioperative anxiety and pain in children: a randomized study. *European Journal of Pediatrics, 178*(6), 913–921. https://doi.org/10.1007/s00431-019-03376-x

Valois, R. F., Zullig, K. J., Huebner, E. S., & Drane, J. W. (2004). Life satisfaction and suicide among high school adolescents. *Social Indicators Research, 66*(23), 81–105. https://doi.org/10.1007/978-1-4020-2312-5_5

van Tilburg, M. A., Chitkara, D. K., Palsson, O. S., Turner, M., Blois-Martin, N., Ulshen, M., & Whitehead, W. E. (2009). Audio-recorded guided imagery treatment reduces functional abdominal pain in children: a pilot study. *Pediatrics, 124*(5), 890–897. https://doi.org/10.1542/peds.2009-0028

Wagner, L., Gander, F., Proyer, R. T., & Ruch, W. (2020). Character strengths and PERMA: Investigating the relationships of character strengths with a multidimensional framework of well-being. *Applied Research in Quality of Life, 15*(2), 307–328. https://doi.org/10.1007/s11482-018-9695-z

Waters, L., Barsky, A., Ridd, A., & Allen, K. (2014). Contemplative education: A systematic, evidenced-based review of the effect of meditation interventions in schools. *Educational Psychology Review, 27*, 103–134. https://doi.org/0.1007/s10648-014-9258-2

Winter, E., Maykel, C., Bray, M., Levine, M., & Graves, M. (In Press). Physical health as a foundation for well being: Exploring the RICH theory of happiness. In Deb, S. & Gerrard, B. (Eds.), *Health and Well-Being: A Concern for All*. Springer.

Wisner, B. L. (2013). An exploratory study of mindfulness meditation for alternative school students: Perceived benefits for improving school climate and student functioning. *Mindfulness, 5*, 626–638. https://doi.org/10.1007/s12671-013-0215-9

Wong, H. K., Wong, R. T., & Seroyer, C. (2005). *The first days of school: How to be an effective teacher*. Harry K. Wong Publications.

Zaccaro, A., Piarulli, A., Laurino, M., Garbella, E., Menicucci, D., Neri, B., & Gemignani, A. (2018). How breath-control can change your life: A systematic review on psycho-physiological correlates of slow breathing. *Frontiers in Human Neuroscience, 12*, 1–16. https://doi.org/10.3389/fnhum.2018.00353

Zullig, K. J., Valois, R. F., Huebner, E. S., Oeltmann, J. E., & Drane, J. W. (2001). Relationship between perceived life satisfaction and adolescents' substance abuse. *Journal of Adolescent Health, 29*(4), 279–288. https://doi.org/10.1016/S1054-139X(01)00269-5

Zylowska, L., Ackerman, D. L., Yang, M. H., Futrell, J. L., Horton, N. L., Hale, T. S., Pataki, C., & Smalley, S. L. (2008). Mindfulness meditation training in adults and adolescents with ADHD: A feasibility study. *Journal of Attention Disorders, 11*(6), 737–746. https://doi.org/10.1177/1087054707308502

4
RESTORATIVE PRACTICES IN SCHOOLS

Sean Darling-Hammond

UNIVERSITY OF CALIFORNIA, BERKELEY

Trevor Fronius

WESTED JUSTICE & PREVENTION RESEARCH CENTER

Introduction

This chapter provides an overview of research regarding restorative practices (RP) in U.S. K–12 schools. In the first section, we define "restorative practices." In the second, we summarize quantitative studies regarding the effectiveness of RP across outcomes related to classroom management. Finally, we provide policy guidance for how to ensure RP are leveraged in a manner that fosters student and community growth.

What Are School-Based Restorative Practices?

Restorative practices (RP) encompass an array of non-punitive, relationship-centered approaches for proactively avoiding harm, and repairing harm when it occurs. While many practices fall under the RP umbrella, the best-known category of practices is Restorative Justice (RJ). RJ was developed long before RP was a term, and much of the theory underpinning RJ extends to RP. We thus begin our exploration of school-based RP by explaining the genesis of, and theory underlying, RJ.

Before the Umbrella: Restorative Justice (RJ) as a Root of Restorative Practices (RP)

Restorative Justice is a relationship-centered system for responding to grievances, misdemeanors, and crimes. It can be leveraged in lieu of (or in addition to) traditional and often punitive justice system responses. Experts generally agree that the first recorded uses of RJ occurred in the pre-modern era in the South Pacific and Americas (e.g., Zehr, 2002). These cultures had an approach to conflict and social ills that emphasized the offender's accountability for the social harm they caused, along with a plan for repairing the hurt and restoring the offender to acceptance. The emphasis on the harm done rather than the act is a widely recognized principle across RJ literature.

Perhaps the most well-known framework for understanding RJ is called "reintegrative shaming theory" (Braithwaite, 2004). Critically, reintegrative shaming is distinct from typical "negative shaming" in that the ultimate goal is not simply deterrence, but reconciliation between all parties

DOI: 10.4324/9781003275312-6

involved and reintegration of the offender back into the community. Reintegrative shaming acknowledges the impact of wrongdoing on both the offender and those who were harmed. Zehr (2002) suggests that RJ requires society to move away from a system that emphasizes traditional retributive justice ("an eye for an eye"). Morrison and Vaandering (2012) argue that a system influenced by RJ would define "laws and rules as serving people to protect and encourage relationships and relational cultures" (p. 145) rather than protecting the status quo.

For at least five decades, many U.S. institutions—such as juvenile courts, domestic violence courts, universities, and K-12 schools—have used RJ as a means to divert people from punitive justice systems, reduce rates of recidivism, and repair and improve social connections. In 1972, the Minnesota Restitution Center guided its first cohort of property offenders and victims through mediated proceedings to collaboratively determine how offenders can repair harm they have caused while also securing parole (Hudson, 2012). Today, a majority of U.S. states have codified the use of RJ in statutes and / or codes (Pavelka, 2016).

Restorative Justice in K-12 Schools

In part due to promising research indicating that RJ can reduce recidivism (and, relatedly, offending) (e.g., Sherman & Strang, 2007), K-12 educators began developing and implementing school-based RJ programs to reduce the number of students suspended or expelled, and who ultimately fall victim to the "school-to-prison pipeline" (Losen, 2015, p. 241). According to Zehr (2002) and others (e.g., González, 2012; Karp & Breslin, 2001), in the K-12 setting, RJ is meant to bring together all stakeholders to resolve issues and build relationships rather than control student misbehavior through punitive exclusionary approaches. RJ programs in schools range from training for teachers in conflict-responsive dialogue techniques for the classroom to professionally guided restorative conferences with students, staff, and other stakeholders (Darling-Hammond et al., 2020). RJ is often used as an add-on to existing school discipline approaches. A common "add-on" approach is to divert some students who would typically be suspended for their offenses to engage in a formal restorative proceeding where they are guided to understand the harm their actions caused, take steps to repair the harm, and make a plan to avoid making the same mistakes in the future.

In more formal RJ proceedings, participants can include the victim(s), misbehaving student(s) (i.e., "respondents"), and facilitator(s), but may also include other community members (e.g., witnesses, friends, family) (Darling-Hammond et al., 2020). The victims could also include members of the school community who represent the school that was harmed by the respondents' actions (e.g., in the case of vandalism). Together, the conference participants aim to determine a reasonable and restorative response to the harm done. These can include community service, restitution, apologies, or agreements to change specific behaviors, such as the respondent agreeing to comply with certain conditions, sometimes in exchange for incentives (Stinchcomb et al., 2006). As evidenced above, RJ can take many forms, and while some models appear nearly identical to what one might find in the juvenile justice system (such as the Balance and Restorative Justice, or BARJ, model), others were developed specifically for school communities (Mirsky, 2007; Mirsky & Wachtel, 2007).

Opening the Umbrella: The Pivot to Restorative Practices (RP)

Restorative Justice (RJ) programs focus on how to respond once students have made mistakes. In that sense, they are reactive in nature. More recently, however, many schools and school districts have embraced a broader set of, often proactive, Restorative Practices (RP). While RP encompasses RJ, RP is broader, and includes practices that are designed to foster an interconnected school community and healthy school climate in which punishable transgressions are less common (Brown,

2017). Thus, as documented by Bazemore and Schiff (2009), there are a variety of practices that fall under the RP umbrella that schools may implement. These practices include RJ-style mediation conferences; training in affective communication techniques to bolster social connections; and various "circles" in and out of the classroom. Community-building circles are preemptive and designed to help students and staff deepen relationships and trust so that misbehavior becomes less common. Peace-making circles bring together parties who were involved in or impacted by harmful actions, often in a less formal manner than conference and mediation. And re-entry circles help students who have been removed from the school community (for example, due to out-of-school suspensions) re-integrate into the community to ensure they have the social support needed to thrive (and to avoid misbehaving). Practitioners often group RP into three "tiers" of practices (e.g., Kervick et al., 2019; Kidde, 2017)). Tier 1 practices are designed to enhance community connectedness, and include community building circles, activities to define and elevate community values, affective statements, and celebrations. Tier 2 practices are meant to repair relationships, and include affective questions, restorative conferences, and peer mediation. Finally, Tier 3 practices are designed to reintegrate members of the community after absences, and include circles of support and reentry circles.

The two basic models of RP implementation are "add-on" programs and "whole school" models. In the former, schools add limited RP functions to their existing disciplinary arrangements. This can take the form of diverting some students who would otherwise be suspended to restorative proceedings, or to hiring a single RP coordinator to oversee selective RP functions within the school. The latter, whole school, model involves providing RP training to all school personnel so restorative concepts and approaches are infused in as many school interactions as possible. The "whole school" model can be augmented with continuous professional development in the form of coaching and/or professional learning communities dedicated to expanding and improving the use of restorative practices.

Potential Benefits of RP

Proponents often turn to RP to reduce exclusionary discipline, which, research suggests, can cause declines in academic achievement and increases in adult criminal activity (Bacher-Hicks et al., 2019). Proponents (e.g., Tyler, 2006; Zehr, 2002) argue that RP mitigates reliance on exclusionary discipline by addressing root causes of misbehavior, all while improving school climate and academic engagement. They argue that while traditional discipline approaches manage student behavior, RP approaches develop students' social and emotional capacities and nurture school relationships so students are less likely to misbehave.

Restorative Practices have also gained popularity as a means of addressing disproportionalities in school discipline—a phenomena whereby some groups of students receive exclusionary punishment at higher rates than others. A recent report by the U.S. Government Accountability Office found that while Black students represent 15.5% of all students in the country, they represent 39% of students suspended from schools, and that while students with disabilities represent 13.7% of all students, they represent 25.9% of those suspended (Government Accountability Office, 2018). Psychologists have identified that one cause of racial disparities in discipline is that teachers are more likely to perceive a misbehavior by a Black student as indicating that the student is a "troublemaker"; but that enhancing student-teacher relationships can stem this tendency and reduce disparities (e.g., Okonofua et al., 2016; Okonofua et al., 2020; Okonofua & Eberhardt, 2015). Accordingly, RP advocates argue that RP can address disproportionalities by facilitating positive student-teacher relations regardless of student demographics (e.g., Gregory et al., 2016).

While research and writing regarding the *theory* underlying RP in schools is rich and well developed, the research on the *effects* of restorative practices in schools is still budding, but has grown considerably in recent years.

Quantitative Research Regarding the Effectiveness of Restorative Practices

Here, we summarize all available quantitative research regarding the effectiveness of Restorative Practices (RP) in U.S. K-12 schools published between January 1999 and August 2021. This summary expands on, and uses the same methods as a prior summary (Darling-Hammond et al., 2020). The review focuses on the outcomes that appeared most often in extant literature, which were student misbehavior, bullying, exclusionary discipline, disparities in discipline, student attendance, school climate, and academic outcomes.

Exclusionary Discipline and Student Misbehavior

RP theory suggests that a well-implemented program would reduce problem behavior over time which, in turn, would reduce discipline (Tyler, 2006). Critically, misbehavior and discipline are distinct phenomena. Misbehavior is a student action; discipline is a scholastic response. Many RP programs are "suspension diversion" programs which take students who would have been suspended under prior discipline regimes and instead "divert" them to engage in restorative proceedings. Almost by default, such programs reduce rates of exclusionary discipline, but they may or may not reduce student misbehavior. However, because exclusionary discipline can, itself, be harmful to students educational and carceral outcomes (Bacher-Hicks et al., 2019), we first review research regarding the relationship between RP programs and exclusionary discipline and then review research specifically related to misbehavior.

EXCLUSIONARY DISCIPLINE

To determine if RP causes a reduction in exclusionary discipline (among other outcomes, discussed later), Augustine et al. (2018) conducted a randomized controlled trial (RCT). RCTs are a common mechanism for ascertaining if a given program (here, RP) *causes* desired outcomes.[1] Relevant here, RCTs in educational contexts, and particular those evaluating RP, may suffer from compliance issues whereby schools assigned to receive RP training may struggle to implement the program as intended, and/or schools assigned *not* to receive training may nonetheless implement RP and become poor comparators. RCTs evaluating RP may also struggle to detect effects as successful implementation can take as many as five years (Evans & Lester, 2013), and researchers may not be able to evaluate programs for such a lengthy duration.

Braving these challenges, Augustine et al. (2018) conducted their RCT with 44 mid-sized Pittsburgh schools serving kindergartners through 12-graders. Half of the schools were randomly selected to received RP training by the International Institute of Restorative Practices (IIRP) in the 2014–2015 school year while the other half were put on a wait list for the duration of the study. The study team then reviewed outcomes in the following two school years. The authors note that their study may suffer from RCT-related concerns noted above as they did not verify that "treated" schools used RP; did not measure if "control" schools did not use RP; and only measured outcomes two years after implementation.

These caveats notwithstanding, Augustine et al. (2018) estimated that RP implementation caused a 16% reduction in days lost to suspensions, which was statistically significant ($p < .05$). The reported reduction in suspension days was statistically significant among Black, low-income, and special needs students.

In pre-post analyses leveraging administrative data from Minnesota, Texas, Denver (CO), and Oakland (CA), researchers found that suspension rates dropped after RP implementation by between 47% and 87% (Armour, 2014; Baker, 2009; González, 2015; Gregory et al., 2018; Riestenberg, 2003; Sumner et al., 2010). Research from individual schools shows similarly strong reductions in suspension rates (Fowler et al., 2016; Goldys, 2016; Katic, 2017), as does a pre-post analysis using data from the Los Angeles Unified School District (Hashim et al., 2018).

Researchers have also reviewed whether discipline rates tend to fall when students report higher rates of exposure to restorative practices. A recent study by Darling-Hammond et al. (2021) examined the relation between exposure to restorative practices and discipline. Reviewing records from over 800,000 California middle and high school students, the authors found that, across racial groups, students who indicated higher levels of exposure to restorative practices were less likely to have been suspended in the prior 30 days. This was true even after controlling for a suite of student, parent, and district level factors that may have influenced the outcome. Gregory et al. (2016) reviewed thousands of school records from two diverse east coast high schools, and surveys from 412 students and 29 teachers. They found that students who indicated being in classrooms that utilized an above average ("high") degree of restorative practices received fewer defiance and misconduct referrals than those who indicated they were in classrooms that utilized a below average ("low") degree of restorative practices. Specifically, among Black and Latino students (collectively), those in low restorative practice classrooms received three times more defiance and misconduct referrals than those in high restorative practice classrooms and this difference was statistically significant. Among White and Asian students (collectively), those in low restorative practice classrooms received 2.2 times more such referrals, but the difference was not statistically significant.

Some research has examined the kinds of RP programs that can reduce discipline rates. Jain, Bassey, Brown, and Kalra (2014) examined students in Oakland (CA) who participated in two RP programs: Whole School Restorative Justice (WSRJ) and Peer Restorative Justice (Peer RJ). They note that students were selected for WSRJ in part because they had higher suspension rates than average. After three years, these WSRJ students received statistically significantly fewer suspensions than students in the district overall, and fewer than students in Peer RJ.

MISBEHAVIOR

Cook et al. (2018) and Duong et al. (2019) report on randomized controlled trials in which elementary (for Cook et al.) and middle (for Duong et al.) school teachers were randomly assigned to receive training in the "Establish, Maintain, Restore" program, and to receive ongoing coaching. Both teams found that the program resulted in statistically significant reductions in disruptive behavior that were observed directly by the researchers rather than reported on by teachers or students. Notably, both studies collected post-intervention data only three months after initial RP trainings. Thus, while the trainings bore immediate effects, it is unclear whether those effects would diminish, sustain, or grow over time.

Many studies simultaneously note reductions in school discipline and reductions in student misbehavior. For example, Davis (2014) reports that after Oakland Unified implemented RP, they saw a 77% decrease in referrals for violence. Lewis (2009) reports that a West Philadelphia High School saw "violent acts and serious incidents" drop 52% in the first year of RP implementation, followed by an additional 40% drop in year two. McCold (2002) reports that RP preceded a 58% reduction in offending for youth participants in an alternative education program in Pennsylvania during a three-month follow-up. Based on a follow-up study of the same program, McCold (2008) reports that effects were sustained through two years of implementation, with reductions in offending of around 50%.

McMorris et al. (2013) report similarly positive results from their study of the "Family Group Conferencing" model adopted in Minnesota. In this model, the misbehaving student (i.e., "respondent") and victim do not meet face-to-face in the conference (distinguishing it from most types of restorative conferencing). Instead, family members, school staff, and the respondent work together to develop a plan to ensure that the youth takes responsibility for the youth's actions, improves any harmed relationships, and takes steps to ensure that the youth does not make the same mistakes in the future. The researchers reported a decrease in self-reported incidents of physical fighting and skipping school among conference participants in a six-week follow-up (which were validated by related drops in suspension rates and gains in attendance).

Some recent theses and dissertations have also reported positive results for RP on exclusionary discipline and misbehavior at the school, state, and district level. Ptacek (2021) reported statistically significant decline in juvenile arrests among Michigan secondary students after state implemented mandatory restorative practices in secondary schools. McCain (2015) found that 33 administrators in one large district reported RP as largely effective at addressing student behaviors relative to exclusionary discipline approaches. Nabors (2017) noted sizeable reductions in assaults on students, assaults on teachers, disorderly conduct, incidents of disrespect to teachers, and incidents of classroom disruption at two high schools implementing RP. Carroll (2017) reports that, in three high schools in Merced, California, all categories of suspensions dropped markedly after the implementation of facilitated restorative professional learning group (PLG) training. Henson-Nash (2015) found that overall disciplinary infraction rates, and those for physical aggression and weapon possession declined substantially in a public K–8 school in Illinois after the introduction of RP.

EXCEPTIONS TO GENERAL TRENDS

Armour (2014), Barkley (2018), DeAntonio (2015), and Sadler (2021) reported exceptions to the otherwise consistent finding that behavioral problems drop after RP implementation. Armour (2014) found that offense frequencies grew steadily over the course of RP implementation in a San Antonio middle school. Barkley (2018) reports that office discipline referrals per student increased over a five-year span following RP implementation in one middle school in Michigan. Importantly, Barkley notes that although staff at the school in the first two years received RP training, staff received "little to no training" (p. 77) in subsequent years, and only 33% of the staff who were at the school in year one remained in year five, suggesting fidelity of implementation issues. The school also experienced substantial changes in administrative leadership over the five-year period.

DeAntonio (2015) used a covariate matching based design to attempt to ascertain whether 19 Pennsylvania schools that received training in restorative practices (from the International Institute of Restorative Practices) saw larger reductions in student misbehavior than 19 matched schools. This approach is sensitive to the fullness of the list of variables used to match schools and the matching formula utilized. If the formula fails to identify proper matches, matched "control" schools might actually use RP (or have other systematic differences), and thus be poor comparators. That said, DeAntonio (2015) did not find a statistically significant difference in the frequency of misbehavior in schools utilizing RP compared to matched schools.

Sadler (2021) leveraged data from over 60,000 students attending a network of no-excuses charter schools, and finds that the number of student infractions increased significantly in the first year after RP implementation. Notably, however, the shift to RP coincided with marked shifts to student population, with significant increases in the proportion of students that were low-income, Black, special needs, and English language learning. Moreover, infractions began to decline over time in the second year of implementation. Sadler argued that the charter network's challenges with adopting RP may have been a function of the network's decision to adopt RP while continuing to implement a punitive discipline regime.

Bullying

Bullying remains prevalent in U.S. schools (Basile et al., 2020). Research suggests that bullying negatively impacts individual students' psyches and the overall school climate (Polanin et al., 2021). Because RP focuses on repairing relationships and reducing transgressions against the community, some have suggested that it is a viable strategy for ameliorating bullying (e.g., Christensen, 2009; Duncan, 2011; Molnar-Main, 2014; Morrison, 2006). In some cases, however, victims may not be comfortable facing the bully due to fear regarding potential consequences (Amstutz & Mullet, 2005). Theorists have also suggested that mediation led by students can be ineffective or even damaging (Haft & Weiss, 1998). To address these and other concerns, Molnar-Main (2014) provides a number of recommendations for how to integrate RP into bullying prevention, such as focusing on the emotional safety of the victim and ensuring that RP conferences are led by trained adult facilitators (rather than students).

While little research has directly addressed whether RP implementation reduces bullying, available evidence is mixed. Acosta et al. (2019) conducted an RCT in which seven Maine middle schools were randomly selected to receive RP training and six were randomly selected not to. As with the research conducted by Augustine et al. (2018), Acosta et al. reported evidence of compliance issues—based on student surveys, treatment schools used RP less, and control schools used RP more, than would be expected given the assignment scheme.

That said, assignment to treatment did not predict less bullying, suggesting that RP *training* did not have a statistically significant negative impact on bullying victimization. However, students who reported that their teachers used *more restorative practices* experienced statistically significantly less physical bullying ($p < .01$) and statistically significantly less cyber bullying ($p < .001$). More restorative practices predicted statistically significantly higher levels of peer attachment, positive peer relationships, school connectedness, and empathy ($p < .001$ in all cases), suggesting various mechanisms that might be responsible for lower levels of bullying.

In Augustine and colleagues' (2018) RCT of RP in 44 Pittsburgh K-12 schools, assignment to treatment produced an appreciable (albeit not statistically significant) reduction in bullying ($p < .1$). Henson-Nash (2015), meanwhile, reviewed surveys from students in an Illinois school district and found that many types of bullying behavior diminished after RP implementation. Notably, female students saw a statistically significant drop in bullying victimization. However, while declines were statistically significant for the subpopulation of female students, they were not statistically significant for the overall student population. One reading of these findings is that RP are particularly effective at reducing bullying between girls.

In contrast, Armour (2014) finds that a San Antonio middle school that implemented RP saw an increase in bullying after implementation. However, bullying was fairly rare at the school prior to implementation and remained so thereafter. The increase was small, in raw terms—an increase from 43 incidents in the "pre-RP" year to 53 incidents in the "post-RP" year. Notably, students in "RD pilot" classrooms saw a decrease in reported bullying (from 30 incidents to 9 incidents), suggesting that where RP exposure was higher, bullying abated.

Impacts on Disparities in Discipline

Research has indicated that exclusionary discipline rates are particularly high among racial minorities and students with disabilities in comparison with other students (Petrosino et al., 2017). One explanation for racial disparities in discipline (often called "disproportionality") is that students of certain backgrounds misbehave more often, or engage in more serious misbehaviors. However, Welsh and Little (2018) recently found in a comprehensive review of literature on discipline disparities that racial disparities in misbehavior do not, alone, explain racial disparities in discipline, and that adult conduct and school policy play a role in driving discipline disparities. Relatedly, psychologists have found that, at least under certain conditions, teachers treat Black students more harshly than White peers for identical misconduct (Okonofua & Eberhardt, 2015). Moreover, interventions designed to increase teacher empathy have been demonstrated to reduce racial disparities in discipline (Okonofua et al., 2016; Okonofua et al., 2020). Available research thus suggests that school practices could play a role in ameliorating racial disparities in school discipline.

Accordingly, RP has been introduced as one method for addressing disproportionalities (Gregory et al., 2016). Proponents have argued that RP can facilitate positive student-teacher relations for students of all backgrounds by guiding both teachers and students through a process of better understanding and respecting one another.

Quantitative research regarding the effect of RP at reducing discipline gaps is mixed, but largely supports the effectiveness of RP in this domain. A randomized controlled trial (RCT) that compared outcome measures in 22 RP schools to those in 22 control schools indicated that RP implementation led to a reduction in the racial discipline gap between Black and White students (Augustine et al., 2018).

Research reviewing correlates of either student exposure to RP or teacher utilization of RP suggest RP can bridge racial disparities. Reviewing surveys from over 800,000 California middle and high school students, Darling-Hammond et al. (2021) found that students with higher levels of exposure to RP evidence markedly smaller Black-White and Hispanic-White discipline disparities. Specifically, as authors detailed, "students with the highest levels of exposure to restorative practices experienced Black–White discipline disparities that were *five times* smaller than those experienced by students with the lowest levels of exposure to restorative practices" (3). Gregory et al. (2016)'s review of data from two large, diverse high schools surfaces similar findings. Comparing teachers who implemented RP frequently to those who implemented RP less, they find that frequent implementers exhibited less of a racial discipline gap.

Pre-post analyses of administrative data in Los Angeles (CA) and Denver (CO) find that racial and disability related disparities abridged after RP implementation. Reviewing data from Los Angeles (CA), Hashim et al. (2018) report discipline rate declines for all measured categories of students (Black, Latino, Asian, and White students; students with disabilities; English learner students; and students eligible for free or reduced-price lunch), and narrowing of discipline gaps related to race and disability. Meanwhile, reviewing Denver data, González (2015) reported that RP preceded suspension rate drops for Black, Latino, and White students; and a narrowing of the discipline gap between Black and White students and between Latino and White students. Also in Denver, Gregory et al. (2018) reported that suspension rates dropped for all racial categories and that the Black-White discipline gap narrowed nearly in half, from 9% to 5%, following the introduction of RP throughout the district. Armour (2014) found that both the Black-White and Latino-White discipline gaps narrowed after RP implementation in a San Antonio middle school. And in their dissertation, Clark (2019) reported evidence that after a middle school implemented RP, not only did the overall discipline rate fall, but the special education discipline disparity diminished by about 40%.

One study has compared types of RP implementation to ascertain which might better reduce disparities. Jain et al. (2014) examined 30 schools in Oakland (CA) and categorized each as "control" (no RP), "emerging" (just starting to use RP in a limited scope), or "developing" (using RP throughout the school). They found that "developing" schools closed the Black-White discipline gap by a few percentage points (from 12.6% to 9.2%) while the discipline gap actually grew in both "emerging" and "control" schools. They also surveyed adults connected to schools implementing RP and found that 11 out of 12 of the surveyed principals and assistant principals believed that RP had helped reduce disciplinary referrals for Black and Latino boys.

In contrast to the studies depicted above, in a review of administrative data from a large urban district Anyon et al. (2016) found that, following an RP intervention, discipline rates abated overall, but racial discipline gaps persisted.

Impacts on Attendance and Absenteeism

Chronic school absence and truancy have been linked to a wide range of negative childhood and adult outcomes, including low academic achievement, high dropout rates, difficulties in obtaining employment, poor health, increased chances of living in poverty, increased risk of juvenile deviance, and violent behavior (Baker et al., 2001; McCluskey et al., 2004). Proponents argue that, by improving school climate, RP may be able to encourage some chronically absent students to attend school more often.

The RP literature relevant to attendance vary widely in how outcomes are reported. Nonetheless, across the studies, school attendance tended to improve after RP implementation. Baker (2009), for example, reports that students who participated in at least three RP interventions over the course of a schoolyear experienced a 50% reduction in absenteeism during the first year of implementation and a school year in tardiness of about 64%. McMorris et al. (2013), reported that expelled students who participated in an RP program improved their attendance after participation. Reviewing data from a San Antonio middle school implementing RP in 6th and 7th, but not 8th, grades, Armour (2014) found that students in the implementing grades had markedly fewer tardies than the 8th grade students, and that the cohort of students who experienced two years of RP (7th graders) received less than half as many tardies as the cohort of students who experienced zero years of RP (8th graders). A study (Jain et al., 2014) in Oakland (CA) reports that middle schools implementing RP experienced a 24% drop in chronic absenteeism while schools not implementing the program experienced a 62% increase during the same period. But not all schools experienced such declines. Riestenberg (2003) reports that one school that implemented RP reported a 2% increase in absenteeism in the follow-up year. Sadler (2021) found that a charter network saw a decrease in attendance in the year after implementation, but that attendance returned to pre-intervention levels in subsequent years. Sadler attributed the network's implementation challenges to its dual adherence to punitive and restorative regimes. Augustine et al. (2018) did not find a statistically significant link between RP implementation and absenteeism in their two-year RCT of 44 K–12 schools in Pittsburgh, Pennsylvania.

Impacts on School Climate and Safety

Some researchers argue that educators and administrators who create a safe, supportive, and nurturing school climate help promote the social-emotional growth and positive development of students (Voight et al., 2013). One objective of addressing school climate is to foster healthy, resilient students who are ready for college and careers out of school. RP is one tool among many that educators may use to create and support a positive school climate (e.g., Health and Human Development Program, 2012).

Although the evidence is limited, there are findings to suggest that RP improves school climate. Based on their 44-school RCT, Augustine et al. (2018) reported that RP caused a statistically significant ($p < .05$) increase in teachers' perceptions of school climate. The authors noted that this impact was driven by large and statistically significant ($p < .05$) positive impacts on teachers' views about school safety and whether they understood school policies regarding student conduct. They also note statistically significant improvements in teachers' perceptions about working conditions being conducive to teaching and learning, opportunities for leadership, and school leadership. In Cook et al. (2018) and Duong et al. (2019)'s teacher-level randomized controlled trials of the "Establish, Maintain, Restore" program, results indicated that RP training caused a statistically significant improvement in student-teacher relationships. Acosta et al.'s (2019) school-level RCT painted a more mixed picture. RP implementation did not cause statistically significant improvements in school climate, but students who experienced more restorative practices by teachers experienced statistically significantly higher levels of school connectedness, positive peer relations, and peer attachment ($p < .001$ in all cases).

In her dissertation, Featherston (2014) reviewed results from an RCT of 48 Black adolescent girls attending a Mid-Atlantic high school that participated in Real Talk 4 Girls, a three-week social problem-solving program. The 24 girls assigned to the "treatment" condition took part in six, one-hour "restorative circle" sessions in which they learned and practiced cognitive and behavioral strategies for reducing and addressing conflict and aggression. Post-intervention student surveys indicated that, relative to those in the "control" condition, girls in the treatment condition exhibited statistically significant declines in social aggression ($p < .001$); and statistically significant increases in social problem solving ($p < .001$) and prosocial behavior ($p < .05$).

Similarly, in the aforementioned study of Family Group Conferencing in Minnesota, McMorris et al. (2013) reported increased school connectedness and improved problem solving among students in a six-week follow-up. The Lansing School District (2008) reported similar findings from a one-month-post survey of 289 RP participants, finding that 91% of students said they "learned new [conflict resolution] skills in the RP process" (p. 3) and 89% of their parents indicated that their children "learned new ways to resolve [disputes]" (p. 3). Students also generally indicated that they resolved their initial disputes through the RP process (92%) and had used these skills to resolve future disputes (90%), and their parents generally agreed that RP helped their children resolve the initial dispute (85%). Based on a survey in schools implementing RP in Oakland (CA), Jain et al. (2014) reported that 69% of staff believed that RP had improved school climate and 64% believed that it helped build caring relationships between teachers and students. Staff were about four times more likely to hold each of these positive opinions than to believe RP had had a negative impact on climate or relationships. However, parents' opinions were not as strongly positive. Whereas 100% of principals believed that RP improved school climate, only 40% of parents agreed; and whereas 92% of principals believed that RP improved teacher-student relationships, only 28% of parents did.

In more recent research, an elementary school saw a 55% decrease in physical aggression after implementing RP, and 97.7% of students reported feeling safe in school after implementation (Goldys, 2016). Gregory et al.'s (2016) research in two large, diverse, East Coast high schools similarly found that students' perceptions of their teachers' levels of RP implementation were predictive of students' depictions of their relationships with their teachers (whether the teachers respected them), even after controlling for student race and teachers' depictions of students' levels of cooperativeness. Focusing on three diverse, rural, West Coast schools, Terrill (2018) reported that teachers felt that implementing the Discipline that Restores program resulted in greater respect by students for other students. And Jain et al.'s (2014) survey found that 67% of staff in schools implementing RP indicated that RP helped students improve their social and emotional skills.

Impacts on Academic Outcomes

There is limited and mixed evidence that RP can improve academic achievement and progress. Darling-Hammond et al. (2021) review of over 800,000 student surveys from California middle and high school students found that, even after adjusting for student, parent, and district level controls, students with higher levels of exposure to restorative practices also had higher GPAs. This was true for students of each racial group assessed (including Black, White, and Hispanic).

In a review of data from a San Antonio middle school, Armour (2014) found that 6th grade students exposed to RP for a year saw 11% improvements on their statewide reading passage rates and a 13% improvement in math. These improvements were driven in part by growth by Black students (8% increase), Hispanic students (13%) and economically disadvantaged students (13%). Most notably, passage rates among special education students increased markedly in both reading (42%) and math (50%). Jain et al. (2014) reported that schools in Oakland (CA) that were implementing RP saw reading levels increase by 128% over three years while non-RP schools saw an increase of only 11%; four-year graduation rates increased by 60% in RP schools, compared to 7% for schools not implementing RP; and high school dropout rates decreased by 56% in RP high schools compared to 17% for non-RP high schools. Kerstetter (2016) compared outcomes at a restorative justice charter elementary school to a "comparable" no-excuses charter and found that the RP charter school outperformed the comparison charter in the percent of third grade students scoring proficient on the state standards. Specifically, in the study year (2012–13), 60% of the RP charter's students were proficient relative to the 36% students in the comparison charter, and 44% of students across the district overall.

McMorris et al. (2013) noted that for students in their sample who participated in Family Group Conferencing and remained enrolled in school the following academic year, participation was associated with a slight increase in the students' grade point averages. Although there was a sizeable drop in the number of students on track to graduate in the year of their participation in RP, this drop may have been due to the poor attendance prior to the program, and a majority of these students did get back on track in the following year.

Elsewhere, the results for academic outcomes are more mixed. For example, based on an RCT of RP in 44 schools in Pittsburgh, Pennsylvania, Augustine et al. (2018) reported that RP did not have a positive impact on math and reading scores, but rather led to significant ($p < .05$) reductions in elementary and middle school math performance and significant ($p < .01$) reductions in elementary and middle school academic performance among Black students. Similarly, Sadler (2021) found that academic performance for Black students in a large charter network diminished in the first year after RP adoption, but rose again in subsequent years. Norris (2009) reported no significant change in grade point average for RP participants (compared to non-participants). Lewis (2009) suggested that there was improvement in student test scores in one Pennsylvania school, but provides no data to support this finding. Based on reviewing the student records of 80 students in a diverse, rural California high school, Terrill (2018) reported that while grade point averages of students overall fell after RP implementation, grade point averages increased among students who had received office referrals and therefore encountered the Discipline that Restores program.

Limitations of the Literature Review

The evidence presented in this literature review is limited by how, when, and what we searched. We focused on research databases that compile peer-reviewed research; concluded our searches in August 2021; and limited our review to quantitative studies in U.S. K–12 contexts.

In addition, like any research review, our review of RP evidence is influenced by the quality of the studies that comprise the "sample." For each of the outcomes we reviewed, there is at least some evidence that suggests RP can benefit students. However, setting aside that results are often mixed, some of the more sanguine studies have small sample sizes, and most are correlational in nature. Studies most typically recruited a pre–post design which, as Weisburd, Petrosino, and Fronius (2014) explain, renders these studies low in internal validity. Even where researchers utilized more rigorous methods (such as RCTs), they often reported internal validity concerns such as challenges with compliance among treated and control cases, and intervention duration issues.

Final Thoughts on Restorative Practice Research

In general, the research evidence to support RP in schools is still in a nascent state. However, the preliminary evidence does suggest that RP could drive improvements in discipline, discipline disparities, misbehavior, and school climate. While mixed, available evidence favors the effectiveness of RP at reducing bullying and student absenteeism. Finally, evidence on the impact of RP on academic performance is mixed, with a number of correlational studies suggesting RP can yield impressive academic performance gains while a large-scale school-level RCT, and some correlational studies, suggest RP may harm academic performance.

Given the state of the research field, future research might accelerate the growth of knowledge about the effectiveness of RP in schools by addressing these research challenges:

- developing a clear and broadly usable mechanism (e.g., a survey instrument) for discerning where, and to what extent, RP is being utilized;
- examining the factors associated with a school's readiness to implement RP and how those factors interact with the effectiveness of a school's RP programming;
- identifying factors that determine high levels of implementation fidelity, including determining what kinds of training and professional development for school leaders enhance their ability to value and implement RP, and in turn ensure students get exposure to actual practices.
- determining rigorous research approaches that can identify the impacts of *student* exposure to restorative *practices* (rather than simply the impacts of *teachers* receiving restorative practice *training*);

- conducting deep, mixed-methods analysis in districts that have a track record of successful and sustainable RP implementation to uncover the conditions that have led to their success and might provide clues for replication; and
- examining the integration of RP with other alternatives to exclusionary discipline, such as Positive Behavioral Interventions and Support (PBIS) and Social and Emotional Learning (SEL) programs.

Policies to Help Restorative Practices Nurture Students and Communities

As detailed above, research indicates that RP may be a useful tool for, at minimum, improving school climates; reducing overall misbehavior and discipline; and bridging discipline disparities related to race and special education status. However, schools and school districts may experience a range of implementation challenges, and also may want to avail themselves of opportunities to accelerate and accentuate the positive benefits of RP. Below, we therefore discuss a few policy recommendations that we believe could enhance the potential of RP to realize positive outcomes. These recommendations are designed for educational decision makers at all institutional levels, including the Department of Education, state education agencies, local education agencies, and schools. Throughout this section, we also use the word "staff" to describe all adults employed by schools who interface with children (including, for example, teachers, guidance counselors, and school resource officers).

Commit to Culture Change

Recently, when we interviewed a restorative practice trainer, we were told that "restorative practices are a lifestyle, not just a program or something you can learn from reading a binder." From this and similar sentiments expressed by myriad researchers and practitioners, we intuit that to ensure RP realize intended impacts, schools must commit to a *cultural transformation* (Ashley & Burke, 2009; Beckman et al., 2012; Brown, 2017; Cavanagh et al., 2014; Evans & Lester, 2013; González, 2012; Gregory et al., 2021; Hantzopoulos, 2013; Lustick, 2020; Mirsky & Wachtel, 2007; Vah Seliskar, 2020) The first facet of this transformation is to shift the attitudes about discipline, relationships, and misbehavior. Educators, parents, and other stakeholders may find it difficult to believe that relational approaches can improve behavior, and to shift away from relying on punitive means. They may worry that restorative approaches are "too soft." Thus, schools may want to proactively help teachers and parents understand the evidence base in favor of the proposition that when students have positive relationships, they are less likely to misbehave; and that exclusionary discipline can be harmful and counterproductive. The second facet is to make a true shift to the disciplinary regime. Simultaneously implementing harsh exclusionary practices and restorative practices may cause culture incongruence (Sadler, 2021). Thus, we recommend that educational institutions seeking to implement RP encourage schools to make real shifts in their discipline frameworks (for example, abating the use of punitive discipline) and provide a context that enables staff to shift their teaching philosophies (relaxing reliance on punitive mechanisms to manage classrooms, and encouraging the use of relational approaches) to empower the cultural transformation necessary for RP to work. This could be achieved by modeling relational alternatives to managing common tricky classroom situations, and providing ample support and time for staff to practice relational approaches *before* they face classroom conflict.

Empower Perseverance, and Preempt Caregiver Concerns

In another recent interview with a practitioner, we were told that the "work [of shifting to RP] is not for the timid. It takes time, and patience, for these practices to work." In our review of RP implementation research, we see that changes over time to outcomes (like academic performance) are often "u-shaped," meaning there are short term declines followed by long-term gains (e.g., Sadler, 2021). This trajectory may indicate growing pains that must be weathered before positive impacts can be realized. Schools may be tempted to abandon RP during this early period of implementation if they fear that district funds will subside if immediate results (e.g., on discipline rates or discipline disparities) are not positive, or if they show potentially short-lived declines in academic performance. Thus, institutions hoping to realize the positive impacts of RP should seek (or provide) funding that is structured to support multiple years of implementation. They should also consider providing clear guidance that funding is not tied to near-term results, and communicating to stakeholders that it is important to persevere through growing pains.

One major threat to RP program perseverance is caregiver concerns that when schools adopt RP, their children will experience negative outcomes (such as more bullying and classroom disruptions; or declines in academic performance). In an article for the International Institute of Restorative Practices, Phillips (2017) provides five tips for ensuring parent and family buy-in for restorative practices, which are: (1) host sessions to introduce families to RP; (2) provide ongoing information online; (3) invite parents to serve on RP leadership groups; (4) have students bring RP information packets home; and (5) recruit an RP consultant to facilitate communication with caregivers. In another guide on this topic, Community Organizing and Family Issues (2016) suggests that schools recruit parents to join "Parent Peace Centers," providing RP training and employing parents to conduct RP circles and to provide intensive tutoring and mentoring to students exhibiting disruptive behavior as an alternative to suspension.

Close the Program/Practice Gap

In Acosta et al. (2019)'s RCT, they notably did not find that students randomly assigned to *teachers* who received RP *training* saw certain improvements (such as less bullying). However, they *did* find that *students* who got more *exposure* to RP did see these improvements. Their research thus demonstrated a program/practice gap. While exposure to RPs can have huge benefits, RP *programs* that provide trainings to *staff (e.g., teachers)* may not always accrue to staff actually using (and *students* getting exposed to) restorative practices. So, what can be done to close the program/practice gap and ensure students get exposure to these practices?

One potential solution is to ensure staff actually *want* RP training when they receive it. Via sophisticated, randomized controlled trials, Cook et al. (2018) and Duong et al. (2019) find that RP training for a cohort of willing teachers not only improved student-teacher relationships, but also reduced student misbehavior and improved student attention in class. Unlike Acosta et al. (2019) and Augustine et al. (2018)'s RCTs (which randomized at the level of schools, and *required* that *all* educators in the treatment schools participate in multiple RP trainings), Cook et al. (2018) and Duong et al. (2019)'s research processes began with the recruitment of a group of teachers who had *opted in* to RP training. The teams then randomized from a subset of *entirely willing staff* to determine which would actually receive the training. One explanation for their relatively superior results is that their research design ensured staff buy-in, and that staff buy-in is a precondition to program success. Indeed, Evans and Lester's (2013) review of implementation guidance surfaced the importance of securing staff buy-in *before* implementing RP, and specifically "recommended spending the necessary time for discussion and dialogue about school practices, as opposed to unilaterally deciding to implement" (62). And research regarding other forms of trainings indicated the importance of voluntary participation (Gegenfurtner et al., 2016).

In this light, we recommend that schools take one of two approaches. The first is to provide RP training to staff who would like to volunteer to receive them. This can avoid the drawbacks of requiring unwilling staff to use RP. However, RP practitioners (Kidde, 2017) and researchers (González et al., 2018) have argued that a whole-school RP model (where all staff receive RP training) is more effective. Relatedly, the second option then is to prepare staff for a whole school model by proactively facilitating discussions about school practices *before* choosing RP (let alone implementing it) to ensure *all* staff feel *they* have chosen RP for their schools (and for themselves).

Another challenge schools face when trying to close the program/practice gap is that even when staff receive RP training and are willing to use it, they may not be able to sustain their use of restorative practices. When faced with challenging relational dynamics or classroom conflicts, they may abandon RP and revert to prior punitive practices. Research (e.g., Evans & Lester, 2013) shows that staff sometimes worry RP is "too soft" and can encourage students to misbehave. This preconception (while out of step with extant research) could lead staff to abandon RP when the going gets tough. To address these issues, educational institutions can take a two-pronged approach. First, they can help staff shift their preconceptions by presenting relatable case studies and examples showing *declines* in misbehavior following sustained RP implementation. Second, they can provide continuous professional development, coaching, and partner learning so teachers can weather temptation to abandon RP, and can—slowly but surely—make RP their new modus operandi.

Educational institutions may also try leveraging insights from behavior science and "nudging" the use of restorative practices (such as "community building circles" or "restorative dialogue"). In one of the more famous nudge experiments, Ashraf et al. (2014) found that "social signaling" was a powerful driver of prosocial behavior. Specifically, business owners engaged in more prosocial behavior when they could "signal" their virtuous conduct through a thermometer display than when they were given financial incentives to engage in prosocial behavior. As an example of one of the many potential "nudge" approaches school leaders could adopt, schools could provide thermometer displays to be placed outside of teachers' doors where they could indicate the number of community building circles they have held.

Expand Access

Some research (Payne & Welch, 2015) suggests that RP exposure is lower for Black students and low-income students (two groups that are particularly at risk of exposure to exclusionary discipline). To ensure RP realizes its intended impacts, schools should take steps to ensure students of *all* backgrounds (and particularly those most often subjected to harsh discipline) are not only exposed to RP, but experience RP in a manner that deepens their connection to the school. Kervick et al. (2019) argued that a critical step in achieving widespread and productive exposure to RP is to ensure teachers receive training in equity literacy, critical consciousness, bias awareness classrooms, and culturally responsive teaching. These practices can help teachers identify and overcome structural barriers that discourage certain groups from participating in RP activities, and communicate with students of varied backgrounds in ways that make them want to engage in RP activities.

A critical driver of the extent to which teachers use RP, and the quality of implementation, is the strength of their relationships with students (Brown, 2017). Evidence from psychology (e.g., Okonofua et al., 2020) shows that, absent training, teachers may be more likely to label Black students as "troublemakers," and may be less likely to form positive relationships with Black students. To ensure teachers are able to leverage RP in their interactions with Black students, schools may want to help stem this "troublemaker labeling" process and empower teachers to improve relationships with Black students. On this topic, Okonofua et al. (2020) report on a randomized controlled trial finding that teachers encouraged to view student-teacher relationships as capable of improving over time, encouraged to view students as being capable of growing in their social and emotional skills, and provided with opportunities to hear students' perspectives showed smaller Black-White disparities in their disciplinary responses to misbehavior. Interventions akin to that implemented by Okonofua et al. (2020) may thus be a powerful tool in ensuring teachers can form positive relationships with, and subsequently leverage RP when interacting with, students of all backgrounds.

Discipline disparities also impact students with learning differences, and educational institutions may therefore seek to ensure teachers leverage RP when interacting with special education students.

Kervick et al. (2019) provided the following guidance for schools hoping to overcome accessibility issues, and ensure RP reach students with learning differences:

> [M]any common RP essential practices, such as sitting quietly in a circle, taking turns, and using perspective taking and affective statements, must be presented in optioned ways for all students to be able to participate in a restorative classroom. For example, circle facilitators could represent the circle prompts in multiple formats (projecting the circle prompts on a screen so all students have a visual prompt rather than delivering the question only in an auditory format). Circle facilitators could consider the size of the circle itself and consider flexible grouping to maximize student engagement and limit the amount of time needed to wait one's turn. Circle facilitators might also provide response options so that students with communication challenges can still respond to the prompts. For example, framing a question so that students can respond gesturally (e.g., thumb up, thumb down) ensures that all students can participate regardless of language ability.

Leverage RP in Unprecedented Times

While this chapter is largely written without reference to the COVID-19 pandemic, here we want to acknowledge the elephant in the room. The past two school years have been anything but normal. Millions of students (and caregivers) faced sweeping and intermittent school closures. Schools temporarily embraced universal remote instruction. Even after schools resumed in-person instruction, tens of thousands of students were absent for lengthy durations while fighting COVID infections. Some now face the lingering effects of long-COVID. And new variants continue to emerge. So while we all hope the pandemic will appear in schools only in history textbooks, we must acknowledge the possibility that the pandemic will drive school policy in the 2022-23 school year, and perhaps beyond. With due care, RP can be recruited in these unprecedented times.

A defining characteristic of school in the age of COVID-19 is the use of online learning platforms and the shift to remote instruction. How can schools continue to leverage RP in a remote framework? Das et al. (2019) discusses the potential of "virtualized" RP as a tool for reducing cyberbullying, and ensuring more inclusive and engaging online learning for K-12 students. They conceptualize restorative coordinators creating "virtual peace rooms" when a conflict arises. Facilitators could virtually invite relevant students to the room to help them address any conflicts and repair relationships. They note that because conflict often surrounds students' use of social media, students should be able to add content from popular social media platforms to the peace rooms. And they argue that virtual RP would provide students with new and exciting ways to become active participants in enhancing their school climate, such as participating in collective moderation and curation.

Another uncertainty in these times is how to reopen schools. Students may feel more anxiety than usual during school reopenings due to fears of contracting and spreading the COVID-19 virus, anxiety about interacting after a long hiatus, or fear related to growing social tensions. Community building circles are tailor-made to provide students with opportunities to share feelings about these big issues while learning (through teacher guidance) how to empathize with, and reassure, one another. Educational institutions that have already trained staff in RP may therefore want to strongly encourage teachers to use RP during the early phases of reopening; and institutions that have not provided RP training to staff may, time permitting, want to provide training for staff *before* reopenings occur.

Guide School Resource Officers Through Training, Trust, and Transformation

According to the most recent data available (Diliberti et al., 2019), 58% of schools employ an on-site police officer, and 45% specifically employ a school resource officer (SRO). While schools ostensibly employ SROs to enhance student safety, research regarding the impacts of SROs has been discouraging. Of particular importance to this report, Fisher and Hennessy (2016) find that SRO presence is associated with more exclusionary discipline; and Finn and Servoss (2014) find that schools that employ more security measures (such as employing SROs) also have larger Black–White discipline disparities. Relatedly, research indicates that Black students have more negative views of school police than their peers (Nakamoto et al., 2019). And qualitative research by Fisher et al. (2020) suggests that SROs may sometimes perceive Black, but not White, students as threats.

Given these challenges, can schools employ SROs while successfully implementing RP? Rosiak (2021) provided useful guidance on this front, arguing that SROs can indeed leverage RP, and should. The author indicated that for SROs to utilize RP successfully, educational institutions should ensure SRO buy-in by involving them in pre-implementation discussions and by helping SROs understand that a restorative regime actually requires *more* accountability for misbehavior than an exclusionary regime as only in the former, misbehaving students must take steps to "make things right" (p. 16). They also recommended providing universal RP training for SROs and taking steps to build student trust in SROs' abilities to facilitate relational repair. Finally, they note that SRO hiring and retention practices should reflect the goal of creating a restorative climate and culture.

To this list, we suggest the addition of one more critical point to ensure SROs can implement RP. Trainings should help SROs transform their view of their job. While, traditionally, SROs address student safety in large part by identifying and responding to "dangerous" students, in a restorative regime, SROs must shift their philosophical orientation and expand their work to include nurturing and repairing relationships to *proactively* enhance student safety. If SROs are unable to make this cognitive shift, RP implementation may prove at least challenging and potentially damaging.

Conclusion

Restorative practices (RP) are a powerful tool for improving school climates by proactively nurturing and reactively repairing school relationships. Research evidence indicates that RP can be a potent mechanism for reducing misbehavior, reducing discipline, reducing discipline disparities, and improving school climate. Research is more mixed on the impacts of RP on bullying and on academic performance. Certain policy approaches may help ensure RP realizes intended outcomes. These approaches include shifting from a "punitive" to a "relational" culture; closing the program/ practice gap such that professional development results in students getting exposure to RP; expanding RP access to Black and special education students via equity and accessibility minded approaches; leveraging RP virtually during school closures to maintain positive school climates; using in-person community building circles once schools reopen to help students overcome anxiety; and guiding school resource officers through training, trust, and transformation that allows them to successfully implement RP.

Note

1 By randomly assigning some schools to receive the "treatment" (here, RP training), researchers can theoretically ensure that the only systematic difference between treated and control units is treatment status, allowing
   researchers to attribute differences in mean outcomes to treatment, rather than other potential confounders.

References

Acosta, J., Chinman, M., Ebener, P., Malone, P.S., Phillips, A., & Wilks, A. (2019). Evaluation of a whole-school change intervention: Findings from a two-year cluster-randomized trial of the restorative practices intervention. *Journal of Youth and Adolescence, 48*, 876–890. https://doi.org/10.1007/s10964-019-01013-2

Amstutz, L. S., & Mullet, J. H. (2005). *The little book of restorative discipline for schools: Teaching responsibility, creating caring climates*. Good Books.

Anyon, Y., Gregory, A., Stone, S., Farrar, J., Jenson, J. M., McQueen, J., Downing, B., Greer, E., & Simmons, J. (2016). Restorative interventions and school discipline sanctions in a large urban school district. *American Educational Research Journal, 53*(6), 1663–1697. https://doi.org/10.3102/0002831216675719

Armour, M. (2014). *Ed White Middle School restorative discipline evaluation: Implementation and impact, 2012/2013 sixth & seventh grade* [PDF file]. The Institute for Restorative Justice and Restorative Dialogue. Retrieved from http://sites.utexas.edu/irjrd/files/2016/01/Year-2-Final-EW-Report.pdf

Ashley, J., & Burke, K. (2009). *Implementing restorative justice: A guide for schools* [PDF file]. Illinois Criminal Justice Information Authority. Retrieved from www.icjia.state.il.us/assets/pdf/BARJ/SCHOOL%20BARJ%20GUIDEBOOOK.pdf

Ashraf, N., Bandiera, O., & Jack, K. (2014). No margin, no mission? A field experiment on incentives for public service delivery. *Journal of Public Economics 120*, 1–17. https://doi.org/10.1016/j.jpubeco.2014.06.014

Augustine, C. H., Engberg, J., Grimm, G. E., Lee, E., Wang, E. L., Christianson, K., & Joseph, A. A. (2018). *Can restorative practices improve school climate and curb suspensions? An evaluation of the impact of restorative practices in a mid-sized urban school district* [PDF file]. RAND Corporation. Retrieved from www.rand.org/pubs/research_reports/RR2840.html

Bacher-Hicks, A., Billings, S., & Deming, D. (2019). The school to prison pipeline: Long-run impacts of school suspensions on adult crime. *NBER Working Paper Series*. www.nber.org/system/files/working_papers/w26257/w26257.pdf

Baker, M. (2009). *DPS Restorative Justice Project: Year three*. Denver Public Schools.

Baker, M. L., Sigmon, J. N., & Nugent, M. E. (2001). Truancy reduction: Keeping students in school. *Juvenile Justice Bulletin*. Retrieved from www.childtrends.org/?indicators=student-absenteeism#_edn4

Barkley, S. (2018). *A 5-year examination of data for non-minority and minority students from 2011–2016* (Publication No. 10746541) [Doctoral dissertation, Northcentral University, San Diego, CA]. ProQuest Dissertations Publishing.

Basile, K. C., Clayton, H. B., DeGue, S., Gilford, J. W., Vagi, K. J., Suarez, N. A., Zwald, M. L., & Lowry, R. (2020). Interpersonal violence victimization among high school students—Youth risk behavior survey, United States, 2019. *MMWR, 69*(1), 28–37.

Bazemore, G., & Schiff, M. (2009). *Addressing the school-to-jail pipeline: Restorative justice and theory for practice in real alternatives to zero tolerance*. Paper presented at the American Society of Criminology Annual Conference, Philadelphia, PA.

Beckman, K., McMorris, B., & Gower, A. (2012). *Restorative interventions implementation toolkit* [PDF file]. Minnesota Department of Education. Retrieved from https://education.mn.gov/mdeprod/idcplg?IdcService=GET_FILE&dDocName=048363&RevisionSelectionMethod=latestReleased&Rendition=primary

Braithwaite, J. (2004). *Restorative justice: Theories and worries*. United Nations Asia and Far East Institute for the Prevention of Crime and the Treatment of Offenders.

Brown, M. (2017). Being heard: How a listening culture supports the implementation of schoolwide restorative practices. *Restorative Justice: An International Journal, 5*(1), 53–69. https://doi.org/10.1080/20504721.2017.1294792

Carroll, P. G. (2017). *Evaluating attempts at the implementation of restorative justice in three alternative education high schools* (Doctoral dissertation). Retrieved from https://escholarship.org/uc/item/2t95r24f

Cavanagh, T., Vigil, P., & Garcia, E. (2014). A story legitimating the voices of Latino/Hispanic students and their parents: Creating a restorative justice response to wrongdoing and conflict in schools. *Equity & Excellence in Education, 47*(4), 565–579. https://doi.org/10.1080/10665684.2014.958966

Christensen, L. (2009). Sticks, stones, and schoolyard bullies: Restorative justice, mediation and a new approach to conflict resolution in our schools. *Nevada Law Journal, 9*(3), 545–579.

Clark, A. (2019). Fostering equitable learning opportunities for middle school students in special education by reducing their discipline disproportionality rates. Dissertation. City University of Seattle.

Communities Organizing for Family Issues (2016). Strategies for parent engagement. www.restorativeschoolstoolkit.org/sites/default/files/TSDC%20Administrator%20Guide-Implementing%20Parent%20Engagement_0.pdf

Cook, C.R., Coco, S., Zhang, Y., Fiat. A.E., Duong, M., Renshaw, T., Long, A.C., & Frank, S. (2018). Cultivating Positive Teacher–Student Relationships: Preliminary Evaluation of the Establish–Maintain–Restore (EMR) Method. *School Psychology Review, 47*(3), 226–243. https://doi.org/10.17105/SPR-2017-0025.V47-3

Darling-Hammond, S., Fronius, T. A., Sutherland, H., Guckenberg, S., Petrosino, A., & Hurley, N. (2020). Effectiveness of restorative justice in US K–12 schools: A review of quantitative research. *Contemporary School Psychology, 24*, 295–308. https://doi.org/10.1007/s40688-020-00290-0

Darling-Hammond, S., Trout, L., Fronius, T., & Cerna, R. (2021). Can restorative practices bridge racial disparities in schools? Evidence from the California Healthy Kids Survey. *WestEd*. www.wested.org/wp-content/uploads/2021/08/Restorative-Practices-Bridging-Racial-Disparity-Research-Brief-3.pdf

Davis, F. (2014). Discipline with dignity: Oakland classrooms try healing instead of punishment. *Reclaiming Children and Youth, 23*(1), 38–41.

DeAntonio, M. G. (2015). *A comparative study of restorative practices in public schools* (Publication No. 3734773) [Doctoral dissertation, Alvernia University, Reading, Pennsylvania]. ProQuest Dissertations Publishing.

Diliberti, M., Jackson, M., Correa, S., & Padgett, Z. (2019). Crime, violence, discipline, and safety in U.S. public school: Findings from the school survey on crime and safety: 2017-2018 (NCES 2019-061). *National Center for Education Statistics*. https://nces.ed.gov/pubs2019/2019061.pdf

Duncan, S. (2011). Restorative justice and bullying: A missing solution in the anti-bullying laws. *New England Journal on Criminal and Civil Confinement, 37,* 701.

Duong, M.T., Pullmann, M.D., Buntain-Ricklefs, J., Lee, K., Benjamin, K.S., Nguyen, L., & Cook, C.R. (2019). Brief teacher training improves student behavior and student–teacher relationships in middle school. *School Psychology, 34*(2), 212–221. https://doi.org/10.1037/spq0000296

Evans, K., & Lester, J. (2013). Restorative justice in education: What we know so far. *Middle School Journal, 44*(5), 57–63. https://doi.org/10.1080/00940771.2013.11461873

Featherston, T. (2014). *An experimental study on the effectiveness of a restorative justice intervention on the social aggression, social problem solving skills, and prosocial behaviors of African American adolescent girls* (Publication No. 3619936) [Doctoral dissertation, Capella University]. ProQuest Dissertations Publishing.

Finn, J.D., & Servoss, T.J. (2014). Misbehavior, suspensions, and security measures in high school: Racial/ethnic and gender differences. *Journal of Applied Research on Children, 5*(2).

Fisher, B., & Hennessy, E. (2016). School resource officers and exclusionary discipline in U.S. high schools: A systematic review and meta-analysis. *Adolescent Research Review, 1*(3), 217–233. https://doi.org/10.1007/s40 894-015-0006-8

Fisher, B., Higgins, E.M., Kupchik, A., Viano, S., Curran. F.C., Overstreet, S., et al. (2020). Protecting the flock or policing the sheep? Differences in school resource officers' perceptions of threats by school racial composition. *Social Problems,* 1–19. https://doi.org/10.1093/socpro/spaa062

Fowler, B., Rainbolt, S., & Mansfield, K. (2016). *Re-envisioning discipline in complex contexts: An appreciative inquiry of one district's implementation of restorative practices.* Paper presented at University Council for Educational Administration Annual Conference, Detroit, MI.

Gegenfurtner, A., Könings, A.D., Kosmajac, N., & Gebhardt, M. (2016). Voluntary or mandatory training participation as a moderator in the relationship between goal orientations and transfer of training. *International Journal of Training and Development, 20*(4), 290–301. https://doi.org/10.1111/ijtd.12089

Goldys, P. (2016). Restorative practices: From candy and punishment to celebration and problem-solving circles. *Journal of Character Education, 12*(1), 75–80.

González, T. (2012). Keeping kids in schools: Restorative justice, punitive discipline, and the school to prison pipeline. *Journal of Law and Education, 41*(2), 281–335.

González, T. (2015). Socializing schools: Addressing racial disparities in discipline through restorative justice. In D. Losen (Ed.), *Closing the school discipline gap: Equitable remedies for excessive exclusion* (pp. 151–165). Teachers College Press.

González, T., Sattler, H., & Buth, A.J. (2018). New directions in whole-school restorative justice implementation. *Conflict Resolution Quarterly, 36*(3), 207–220. https://doi.org/10.1002/crq.21236

Government Accountability Office (2018). *K-12 education: Discipline disparities for Black students, boys, and students with disabilities* (GAO-18-258). Retrieved from www.gao.gov/products/GAO-18-258

Gregory, A., Clawson, K., Davis, A., & Gerewitz, J. (2016). The promise of restorative practices to transform teacher-student relationships and achieve equity in school discipline. *Journal of Educational and Psychological Consultation, 26*(4), 325–353. https://doi.org/10.1080/10474412.2014.929950

Gregory, A., Huang, F. L., Anyon, Y., Greer, E., & Downing, B. (2018). An examination of restorative interventions and racial equity in out-of-school suspensions. *School Psychology Review, 47*(2), 167–182. https://doi.org/10.17105/SPR-2017-0073.V47-2

Haft, W.S., & Weiss, E.R. (1998). Peer mediation in schools: Expectations and evaluations. *Harvard Negotiation Law Review 3,* 213–270.

Hantzopoulos, M. (2013). The fairness committee: Restorative justice in a small urban public high school. *Prevention Researcher, 20*(1), 7–10. Retrieved from www.fsusd.org/cms/lib/CA01001943/Centricity/Dom ain/1271/TPR20-1-Hantzopoulos%20.pdf

Hashim, A., Strunk, K., & Dhaliwal, T. (2018). Justice for all? Suspension bans and restorative justice programs in the Los Angeles Unified School District. *Peabody Journal of Education, 93*(2), 174–89. https://doi.org/10.1080/0161956X.2018.1435040

Health and Human Development Program (2012). *Workbook for improving school climate & closing the achievement gap, 2nd edition* [PDF file]. California Department of Education. Retrieved from www.wested.org/online_p ubs/WB_1221_allv5.pdf

Henson-Nash, S. (2015). *A study of bullying: A school perspective with a restorative discipline model approach* (Publication No. 3728995) [Doctoral dissertation, St. Francis College of Education, New York]. ProQuest Dissertations Publishing.

Hudson, J. (2012). Contemporary origins of restorative justice programming: The Minnesota Restitution Center. *Federal Probation, 76*(2), 49–55. www.uscourts.gov/sites/default/files/76_2_9_0.pdf

Jain, S., Bassey, H., Brown, M., & Kalra, P. (2014). *Restorative justice in Oakland schools: Implementation and impacts* [PDF file]. Oakland Unified School District. Retrieved from www.ousd.org/cms/lib/CA01001176/Centricity/Domain/134/OUSD-RJ%20Report%20revised%20Final.pdf

Karp, D., & Breslin, B. (2001). Restorative justice in school communities. *Youth and Society, 33*(2), 249–272. https://doi.org/10.1177%2F0044118X01033002006

Katic, B. (2017). *Restorative justice practices in education: A quantitative analysis of suspension rates at the middle school level* (Master's thesis). Retrieved from https://scholarworks.lib.csusb.edu/cgi/viewcontent.cgi?article=1567&context=etd

Kerstetter, K. (2016). A different kind of discipline: Social reproduction and the transmission of non-cognitive skills at an urban charter school. *Sociological Inquiry, 86*(4), 512–539. https://doi.org/10.1111/soin.12128

Kidde, J. (2017). Whole-school restorative approach resource guide: An orientation to a whole-school restorative approach and guide toward more in-depth resources and current research. Vermont Agency of Education. https://education.vermont.gov/sites/aoe/files/documents/edu-integrated-educational-frameworks-whole-school-restorative-approach-resource-guide_0_0.pdf

Kervick, C. T., Moore, M., Ballysingh, T. A., Garnett, B. R., & Smith, L. C. (2019). The Emerging Promise of Restorative Practices to Reduce Discipline Disparities Affecting Youth with Disabilities and Youth of Color: Addressing Access and Equity. *Harvard Educational Review, 89*(4), 588–610.

Lansing School District (2008). *Lansing School District Restorative Justice Annual Report* [PDF file]. Retrieved from www.lansingschools.net/downloads/restorative_justice_files/lansing_school_district_restorative_justice_annual_report_07-08.pdf

Lewis, S. (2009). *Improving school climate: Findings from schools implementing restorative practices* [PDF file]. International Institute for Restorative Practices. Retrieved from www.iirp.edu/pdf/IIRP-Improving-School-Climate-2009.pdf

Losen, D. (Ed.). (2015). *Closing the school discipline gap: Equitable remedies for excessive exclusion.* Teachers College Press.

Lustick, H. (2020). Culturally responsive restorative discipline. *Educational Studies, 56*(5), 555–583. https://doi.org/10.1080/00131946.2020.1837830

McCain, M. (2015). *The impact of discipline policies on students of color and the inequities of suspensions and expulsions* (Publication No. 3738532) [Doctoral dissertation, California State University, East Bay, Hayward, CA. ProQuest Dissertations Publishing.

McCluskey, C. P., Bynum, T. S., & Patchin, J. W. (2004). Reducing chronic absenteeism: An assessment of an early truancy initiative. *Crime and Delinquency, 50*(2), 214–234. https://doi.org/10.1177%2F0011128703258942

McCold, P. (2002). *Evaluation of a restorative milieu: CSF Buxmont School/day treatment programs 1999–2001, evaluation outcome technical report* [PDF file]. International Institute of Restorative Practices. Retrieved from www.iirp.edu/pdf/erm.pdf

McCold, P. (2008). Evaluation of a restorative milieu: Restorative practices in context. *Sociology of Crime, Law and Deviance, 11*, 99–137.

McMorris, B. J., Beckman, K. J., Shea, G., Baumgartner, J., & Eggert, R. C. (2013). *Applying restorative justice practices to Minneapolis Public Schools students recommended for possible expulsion* [PDF file]. University of Minnesota. Retrieved from www.legalrightscenter.org/uploads/2/5/7/3/25735760/lrc_exec_summ-final.pdf

Mirsky, L. (2007). SaferSanerSchools: Transforming school cultures with restorative practices. *Reclaiming Children and Youth: The Journal of Strength-based Interventions, 16*(2), 5–12.

Mirsky, L., & Wachtel, T. (2007). "The Worst School I've Ever Been To": Empirical evaluations of a restorative school and treatment milieu. *Reclaiming Children and Youth: The Journal of Strength-based Interventions, 16*(2), 13–16.

Molnar-Main, S. (2014). *Integrating bullying prevention and restorative practice in schools: Considerations for practitioners and policymakers* [PDF file]. Highmark Foundation. Retrieved from www.safeschools.info/content/BPRPWhitePaper2014.pdf

Morrison, B. (2006). Schools and restorative justice. In G. Johnstone & D. Van Ness (Eds.), *Restorative justice handbook* (pp. 325–350). Willan Publishing.

Morrison, B., & Vaandering, D. (2012). Restorative justice: Pedagogy, praxis, and discipline. *Journal of School Violence, 11*(2), 138–155. https://doi.org/10.1080/15388220.2011.653322

Okonofua, J. A., & Eberhardt, J. L. (2015). Two strikes: Race and the disciplining of young students. *Psychological Science, 26*(5), 617–624. https://doi.org/10.1177/0956797615570365

Okonofua, J., Paunesku, D., & Walton, G. M. (2016). Brief intervention to encourage empathic discipline cuts suspension rates in half among adolescents. *Proceedings of the National Academy of Sciences, 113*(19), 5221–5226. https://doi.org/10.1073/pnas.1523698113

Okonofua, J., Perez, A., & Darling-Hammond, S. (2020). When policy and psychology meet: Mitigating the consequences of bias in schools. *Science Advances, 6*(42). https://doi.org/10.1126/sciadv.aba9479

Polanin, J. R., Espelage, D. L., Grotpeter, J. K., Spinney, E., Ingram, K. M., Valido, A., El Sheikh, A., Torgal, C., & Robinson, L. (2021). A meta-analysis of longitudinal partial correlations between school violence and mental health, school performance, and criminal or delinquent acts. *Psychological Bulletin, 147*(2), 115–133. https://doi.org/10.1037/bul0000314.

Nabors, L. (2017). *The level of fidelity in restorative practices and its impact on school-level discipline data in middle Tennessee* (Doctoral dissertation). Retrieved from www.cn.edu/libraries/tiny_mce/tiny_mce/plugins/file manager/files/Dissertations/Dissertations2017/LaQuilla_Nabors.pdf

Nakamoto, J., Cerna, R., & Stern, A. (2019). High school students' perceptions of police vary by student race and ethnicity: Findings from an analysis of the California Healthy Kids Survey, 2017/18. *WestEd.* www.wested.org/wp-content/uploads/2019/05/resource-high-school-students-perceptions-of-police.pdf

Norris, A. (2009). *Gender and race effects of a restorative justice intervention on school success.* Paper presented at American Society of Criminology Annual Conference, Philadelphia, PA.

Pavelka, S. (2016). Restorative Justice in the states: An analysis of statutory legislation and policy. *Justice Policy Journal, 2*(13), 1–23.

Payne, A., & Welch, K. (2015). Restorative justice in schools: The influence of race on restorative justice. *Youth and Society, 47*(4), 539–564. https://doi.org/10.1177%2F0044118X12473125

Petrosino, A., Fronius, T., Goold, C. C., Losen, D. J., & Turner, H. B. (2017). *Analyzing student-level disciplinary data: A guide for districts (Issues & Answers Report, REL 2017–No. 263)* [PDF File]. U.S. Department of Education, Regional Educational Laboratory Northeast and Islands. Retrieved from https://ies.ed.gov/ncee/edlabs/regions/northeast/pdf/REL_2017263.pdf

Phillips, R. (2017). Five keys for gaining parent and family buy-in for restorative practices. *International Institute of Restorative Practices.* www.iirp.edu/news/five-keys-for-gaining-parent-and-family-buy-in-for-restorative-practices

Riestenberg, N. (2003). *Restorative schools grants final report, January 2002–June 2003: A summary of the grantees' evaluation* [PDF File]. Minnesota Department of Education. Retrieved from http://crisisresponse.promoteprevent.org/webfm_send/1200

Rosiak, J. (2021). How school-based law enforcement can engage in restorative practices. *Journal of School Safety.* www.mydigitalpublication.com/publication/?m=9648&i=709622&p=14&ver=html5

Sadler, K. (2021). No-excuses in restorative justice clothing: The effects of adopting restorative justice in a no-excuse setting. Dissertation. University of North Carolina at Chapel Hill.

Sherman, L. W., & Strang, H. (2007). *Restorative justice: The evidence* [PDF file]. Smith Institute. Retrieved from www.iirp.edu/pdf/RJ_full_report.pdf

Stinchcomb, J. B., Bazemore, G., & Riestenberg, N. (2006). Beyond zero tolerance. *Youth Violence & Juvenile Justice, 4*(2), 123–147. https://doi.org/10.1177%2F1541204006286287

Sumner, D., Silverman, C., & Frampton, M. (2010). *School-based restorative justice as an alternative to zero-tolerance policies: Lessons from West Oakland* [PDF file]. University of California, Berkeley, School of Law. Retrieved from www.law.berkeley.edu/files/thcsj/10-2010_School-based_Restorative_Justice_As_an_Alternative_to_Zero-Tolerance_Policies.pdf

Terrill, S. (2018). *Discipline that restores: An examination of restorative justice in the school setting.* Paper presented at MidAmerica Nazarene University Colloquium, Olathe, KS.

Tyler, T. (2006). Restorative justice and procedural justice: Dealing with rule breaking. *Journal of Social Issues, 62*(2), 307–326. https://psycnet.apa.org/doi/10.1111/j.1540-4560.2006.00452.x

Van Seliskar, H. (2020). *Transforming a school community through restorative practices.* IGI Global.

Voight, A., Austin, G., & Hanson, T. (2013). *A climate for academic success: How school climate distinguishes schools that are beating the achievement odds* [PDF file]. WestEd. Retrieved from www.wested.org/online_pubs/hd-13-10.pdf

Weisburd, D., Petrosino, A., & Fronius, T. (2014). Randomized experiments. In G. Bruinsma & D. Weisburd (Eds.), *Encyclopedia of criminology and criminal justice* (pp. 4283–4291). Springer Press.

Welsh, R., & Little, S. (2018). The school discipline dilemma: A comprehensive review of disparities and alternative approaches. *Review of Education Research, 88*(5), 752–794. https://doi.org/10.3102%2F0034654318791582

Zehr, H. (2002). *The little book of restorative justice.* Good Books.

5

FIRST STEP TO SUCCESS

A Preventive, Early Intervention for Young Students with Disruptive Behavior Problems

Hill M. Walker

OREGON RESEARCH INSTITUTE
UNIVERSITY OF OREGON

Andy J. Frey

UNIVERSITY OF LOUISVILLE

Jason W. Small

OREGON RESEARCH INSTITUTE

Ed Feil

OREGON RESEARCH INSTITUTE

John R. Seeley

OREGON RESEARCH INSTITUTE
UNIVERSITY OF OREGON

Jon Lee

NORTHERN ARIZONA
UNIVERSITY

Annemieke Golly

OREGON RESEARCH INSTITUTE

Shantel Crosby

UNIVERSITY OF LOUISVILLE

Steve Forness

UNIVERSITY OF CALIFORNIA AT
LOS ANGELES

Original First Step Program Reviews

The original First Step program was positively reviewed by the Institute for Education Sciences (IES) regarding its intervention efficacy for achieving prevention outcomes.[1] The What Works Clearinghouse (WWC) uses a standardized format to evaluate programs as to their efficacy or effectiveness within a number of domains; the review process can take up to two years. In April 2012, the First Step program was certified by IES reviewers as a promising, evidence-based intervention that produces positive outcomes at a moderate level of magnitude. The First Step program has been recommended as an evidence-based intervention and included in more than a dozen reviews of effective early intervention programs for addressing challenging and problem behavior patterns among at-risk, K-3 students. This includes being listed in the Model Program Guide of the US Department of Justice's Office of Juvenile Justice and Delinquency Prevention.

First Step Program Foundations

First Step is a social ecological, tier 2 intervention designed to address the poor fit that often exists between a student's behavioral characteristics and the routines, demands, and social contingencies of school environments (Romer & Heller, 1983). The theoretical foundation and underpinnings of the First Step program are based on a social learning formulation of behavior. Negative, social

DOI: 10.4324/9781003275312-7

learning contingencies often characterize family ecologies in which coercive, child behavior patterns are inadvertently strengthened via parenting practices (Patterson, 1982). At-risk children and youth growing up in such environs learn coercive strategies and bring them to the schooling process where they eventually produce rejection, social isolation, and punishment from both teachers and peers (Patterson et al., 1992; Reid et al., 2002).

The primary focus of First Step is (1) to reverse these contingency arrangements with parents and teachers and (2) to teach at-risk students an equally efficient but adaptive set of school success skills. Parents, teachers, and peers are involved in the First Step intervention as participants and supportive collaborators. Their intervention roles are coordinated and supervised by a behavioral coach such as a school psychologist or school counselor, school social worker, PBIS implementer, or behavioral specialist.

First Step Goals

First Step seeks to (1) facilitate efforts by at-risk students in achieving the best start possible to their school careers, (2) effectively engage parents in collaborating with schools in developing their child's current and long-term school success, and (3) enhance the bonding and engagement of students with the schooling process (Walker et al., 1997). First Step Next is focused on a series of skills that enhance academic engagement and contribute to satisfactory teacher and peer-related adjustments, which are two of the most critically important relationships that all students must negotiate in their school careers (Walker et al., 2004).

First Step Structure and Implementation Procedures

First Step Next relies upon group dependent contingencies at school and individual contingencies at home to motivate the target student's participation. If the student meets a daily reward criterion at school, a brief free time activity is earned which is shared with classmates thus potentially encouraging their involvement in his or her success. The student also earns a prearranged reward at home for achieving the school reward. A "good day card" is used to communicate this information to parents who are urged to praise the child's school performance.

First Step operates for 30 continuous program days with a daily reward criterion which must be met in order to advance to the next program day. If the reward criterion for a particular day is not met, then the student is recycled to a prior successful program day. Thus, as a rule, approximately 2 to 3 months are required to complete the First Step program which begins with a 20-minute period where the student can earn points on a coach or teacher-administered card for following classroom rules and meeting the teacher's expectations. By the end of the intervention, it has been gradually extended to the full school day or to those periods of the day where the student struggles with teacher expectations.

A visual cueing system, in the form of a green-red point card, is used to record teacher praises and earned points. When the student is following classroom rules, the green side of the card is shown to him or her by either the coach or teacher and then turned to red when s/he is not. A return to appropriate behavior prompts the card to be turned back from red to green. The First Step program and how it operates is explained privately to the student, the cooperating teacher, and the child's parents. Consent to participate is secured from all these parties before the First Step program can begin.

The green-red point card can be used to easily extend the program to recess periods and to class periods other than homeroom. There are three phases to First Step Next: the coach phase; the teacher phase; and a post-intervention, maintenance phase. The coach phase lasts for the first ten program days and is coordinated and actively managed by the behavioral coach. During the remainder of implementation, the teacher has primary responsibility for the program and is supervised by the coach. At program day ten, the homeBase program component is introduced to the parents who are taught and supervised in how to support and encourage school success skills at home. The last ten days of implementation are focused on maintaining achieved program gains and includes four options ranging from increased teacher praise and support to a brief, temporary reinstatement of the FS program depending on a student's needs. Longer term, occasional booster shots, based on the work of Paine et al. (1982), have been successfully implemented as a means of helping preserve First Step Next behavioral gains.

The remainder of this chapter provides information on the following topics: (a) Development of the First Step program, (b) Revision of the original First Step program and Creation of First Step Next, (c) Evaluation research on the First Step program, (d) Synthesis of First Step Evidence from Randomized Controlled Trials, (e) Research on the Sustainability of First Step Program Adoption and Usage, (f) Cost analysis of First Step implementation, (g) Implications of First Step findings for managing the classroom context, and (h) Concluding remarks.

Development of the Original First Step Program

The original First Step program was developed through a four-year, model development grant from the US Office of Special Education Programs to the first author that ran from 1992 to 1996. This development grant involved four sets of collaborative partners representing the University of Oregon (U of O), the Oregon Social Learning Center (OSLC), Eugene School District 4J, and the Oregon Research Institute (ORI). Original First Step was designed as a tier 2, early intervention for achieving secondary prevention goals and outcomes and was jointly based upon a foundation of prior research on families and antisocial children conducted by the Oregon Social Learning Center (OSLC), under the direction of Gerald Patterson and his associates (Patterson, 1982; Patterson et al., 1992), and two decades of school-based screening and intervention research by Walker and his colleagues focused on students with challenging behavior (Walker et al., 1995).

Revision of Original First Step and Creation of First Step Next

Beginning in 2014, a year-long process was begun to update original First Step based on our implementation experience and feedback from end user consumers during the first decade of the program's existence. This process is described in Walker et al. (2018) and resulted in the development of First Step Next (Walker et al., 2015). First Step Next combines the original (K–3) First Step program with the First Step preschool version for 3–5 year-olds (see Feil et al., 2016) and now provides a seamless intervention for use from PreK and Kindergarten through grade two.

The 2014–15 First Step Next revision was guided by three goals: (a) to standardize the First Step Next program procedures and components and forge them into a single unified module, (b) to make the program more user friendly for implementers, especially cooperating parents, and (c) to increase the intervention's efficacy by adding new components and updating existing ones based on consumer feedback (see Walker et al., 2018).

The following developments spurred the revision. Over several decades of existence, end users had created a number of differing First Step innovations and adaptations that resulted in competing First Step Next versions which were circulating. Further, coaches indicated they needed more information about how to individualize the program more effectively. The coach phase also needed to be expanded to allow younger students and those with more intractable problems additional time to acquire new skills. First Step coaches found that for some parents, requiring them to directly teach school success skills at home proved to be a burden and resulted in a low-quality implementation effort leading to elimination of this requirement in the revised intervention. This and other valuable consumer and coach feedback was integrated into the revision process. The resulting First Step Next program is considered more streamlined, less complex, easier to implement with integrity, and more acceptable to consumers than the original.

The revised First Step Next program also has a more balanced academic and social–emotional focus and includes the addition of seven new Super Student Skills lessons, more robust maintenance and trouble-shooting options, and additional supplemental materials including parent and teacher workbooks, coloring books, behavioral skills charts, new and revised implementation forms, and new program task demonstration videos. The FSN super student skills are: *follows directions, be cool, be a team player, fix-ups are OK, ask for help in the right way, do your best work, and play well with others.* In addition, the homeBase component of First Step Next, as noted above, relieves parents of the responsibility for directly teaching school success skills at home as in original First Step. First Step Next is now considered a parent-supported rather than a parent-school intervention due to the changed implementation role of parents.

Trial Testing of First Step Intervention Components

A series of informal, quasi-experimental studies was used to trial test components of the First Step intervention during its initial developmental phase. The First Step screening procedures were derived from research conducted by Walker and colleagues on the use of teacher rankings, ratings, and behavioral observations in the universal screening and identification of students having challenging forms of behavior (Walker et al., 1988, 1990). The school intervention procedures were based upon an adaptation of the *Contingencies for Learning Academic and Social Skills (CLASS) Program* for acting out children previously developed and researched by Hops, Walker, and colleagues (Hops & Walker, 1988). Two investigators (Reid and Kavanagh) from the Oregon Social Learning Center designed an adaptation of their parent training-intervention model for antisocial children and youth that enabled parents to directly teach their child school success skills at home. These three modules (screening, school intervention, parent support and involvement) were then implemented, in combination, for a selected number of cases representing the K–3 grade range and examined as to feasibility, the occurrence of logistical problems, and identification of critical implementation-delivery issues. Finally, literature searches and reviews of published programs in these three domains were conducted to identify any needed enhancements that might improve the program's efficacy, consumer acceptability to end user professionals, and ease of delivery prior to publishing a manual and user's guide to enable implementation, replication, and adoption of First Step.

Evaluation Research on Original First Step and First Step Next

The empirical knowledge base on First Step and its revision has been largely developed over the past two decades by the Oregon School Study Group consisting of researchers from the Oregon Research Institute, the University of Louisville, the University of Oregon, Northern Arizona University, and UCLA. Our evaluation research was informed by the hierarchy evidence standard as opposed to the threshold standard of scientific evidence (see Drake et al., 2004) which allows for differing designs connected to investigations of a variety of research questions. A mix of single case and group designs was used to successfully investigate important questions in constructing and validating the First Step intervention (Walker et al., 2014b). Single case designs provided a robust information yield in relation to their required implementation effort—particularly as deployed in the early stages of our research and development process. We found their sensitivity to both behavioral process variables (during the intervention) and outcome variables (after the intervention) were instrumental to our First Step development efforts (Carter & Horner, 2007, 2009; Horner et al., 2005). Group experimental designs were used to address questions pertaining to First Step internal and external validity.

First Step Efficacy and Effectiveness Studies

There have been five studies of FS efficacy and three studies on the effectiveness of the original FS program version. Overall, our efficacy studies were carefully controlled by the FSN developers and produced robust effects. Our effectiveness studies produced less robust effects as expected (see Flay et al., 2005 for a further discussion of this distinction). Two of the efficacy studies and one of the effectiveness studies are briefly reviewed following.

Nelson et al. (2009) included original First Step as a selected intervention in a complex study investigating the impact of a 3-tiered behavioral intervention conducted over a 4-year period that focused on 407 students in grades K–3 drawn from 7 elementary schools. Students from one of four longitudinal cohorts participated in this study. There were 153 universal intervention students, 173 selected First Step students who received the tier 2 intervention, and 81 students who received the indicated MultiSystemic Therapy intervention. The demographic breakdown of the study sample was as follows: 130 girls and 277 boys; 35% students of color; and 61% who qualified for free and reduced lunch.

Thus, the three intervention levels of universal, selected, and indicated were represented respectively by the Behavior and Academic Support and Enhancement (BASE) intervention, First Step, and MultiSystemic Therapy (MST); dependent measures included a range of social skills, problem behavior, and academic performance measures. Employing a series of 2-level linear growth analyses, the authors concluded that the 3-tiered behavior model used in the study achieved hypothesized outcomes in social and behavioral domains but not in academic performance areas. The authors reported that First Step students showed significant gains on the study measures in these two domains and that gains were maintained at one- and two-year follow-up assessments.

Walker and his colleagues reported a large-scale, randomized controlled trial of FS that was funded by a 4-year grant from the Institute of Education Sciences (IES). The study was conducted in the Albuquerque Public Schools (APS) with a diverse sample of students in grades 1–3 (over 70% of the participants were students of color). Results of this study were reported in Walker et al. (2009) which describes an efficacy trial of the FS program. Year 1 of this study involved planning, student participant screening and identification, and recruitment of schools, teachers, and coaches, along with staff training. Years 2 and 3 were intervention years and involved two cohorts of 99 and 101 participants respectively who were randomly assigned to intervention and control conditions. Year 4 of this study was focused on follow-up and maintenance activities, training additional APS staff, data analysis, report writing and dissemination efforts. The APS sample of 200 cases was 73% male with 57% Hispanic and 24% Caucasian students. The remainder of the sample was distributed across four other underrepresented groups that included 7% African-American students. Eighty eight percent of the sample came from English-speaking households and more than 70% were eligible for free or reduced lunch.

School outcome measures examined social skills, classroom behavior (adaptive and maladaptive), academic performance, and oral reading fluency. These measures were in the form of teacher ratings and also direct performance assessments as well as behavioral observations of participating students. Teachers completed the SSRS rating scale measure of social skills (i.e. Social Skills Rating System, Gresham & Elliott (1990). Academic engaged time (AET) was recorded with a stopwatch in all experimental and control classrooms using the *Systematic Screening for Behavior Disorders* observation system (Walker et al., 2014a).

Pre and post assessments showed relatively strong effects for social, adaptive, and maladaptive behavior and AET domains but no effects on direct academic performance measures as measured by standardized achievement tests. However, the academic performance subscale of the Social Skills Rating System (Gresham & Elliott, 1990) was sensitive to the FS intervention with an effect size of .66. For maladaptive behavior, effect sizes ranged from .62 to .73; for adaptive behavior and social skills, effect sizes ranged from .54 to .87; and for academic performance, they ranged from .13 to .66.

This study was the first large-scale, randomized test of the FS program within a diverse, large urban school district. The relatively robust intervention effects achieved on our behavioral measures demonstrate the short-term benefits of the program. However, follow-up and maintenance effects were disappointing. One year after the end of intervention, most of the gains for FS students in the two cohorts had decayed with no differences detectable between experimental and control participants. This result prompted the design and implementation of a classroom-wide (i.e. universal) FS maintenance plan designed to reestablish and stabilize the initial program gains. However, its outcomes were judged to have been only modestly effective in meeting this goal.

First Step Effectiveness Study

The FS program has been the focus of one large-scale, national effectiveness study funded by the Institute of Education Sciences and reported by Sumi et al. (2013). This study involved a total of 48 schools, randomly assigned to intervention or control conditions with 142 intervention students and 144 control or comparison students. The implementation sites were in Illinois, West Virginia, Florida, California, and Oregon. In this study, the FS developers and associated investigators were much less involved in the FS implementation protocol than in previously reported First Step Next efficacy studies (see Walker et al., 1998, 2009). Their role was primarily limited to providing initial staff training in FS implementation procedures and in coordinating and the collection of study measures. Also, this study involved five FS implementation sites as opposed to one participating site as in the prior FS efficacy studies—thus substantially increasing its complexity and logistics. The dependent measures used in the study were identical to those reported in Walker et al. (2009).

Findings of the Sumi et al. (2013) effectiveness study generally replicated outcomes of the large-scale efficacy study reported by Walker et al. (2009) but effect sizes were of lower magnitude than in the Walker et al. study. Outcomes favored FS intervention students on 8 of 10 dependent measures. As in prior FS research, direct academic performance of oral reading fluency on the Woodcock Johnson Diagnostic Reading III Inventory (Schrank et al., 2004) were not positively impacted by exposure to the intervention but student behavior on all other teacher, parent and observational measures were. Effect sizes for the Sumi et al. study ranged from .11 to .67. In the efficacy study reported by Walker et al. (2009), they ranged from .57 to .87. Such reduced effects are expected when comparing effectiveness and efficacy studies (see Flay et al., 2005; Weisz & Jensen, 2001) where much tighter control is maintained over implementation procedures, dosage levels, and the trouble shooting of problems that arise during the intervention.

On the issue of implementation, large amounts of definitional, conceptual, and empirical work remains to be conducted on the relationship between the quality of implementation and intervention outcomes beginning with the quality of fidelity measures used to predict such outcomes. Sheridan et al. (2009), in a study of fidelity measurement in consultation, noted that the relationship between implementation fidelity and intervention outcomes may be more a function of adherence to meaningful intervention protocols over time (i.e., dosage). We have evidence from our First Step research that although good fidelity is associated with good outcomes, a less than perfect implementation of First Step Next does not insure poor outcomes. For example, in the Walker et al. (2009) efficacy study, the canonical correlation between our measure of fidelity and intervention outcomes was .50. In the Sumi et al. (2013) effectiveness study, there was a similar finding regarding this relationship with First Step.

In our view, these outcomes speak to the structure and power of applied interventions as key factors in accounting for intervention outcomes that produce meaningful behavior change. In addition to fidelity, a huge panoply of variables likely account for intervention outcomes such as the design and characteristics of the intervention, the severity of target student behavior problems, staff training and motivation, classroom ecology, supervision and consultation with implementers, parent and administrative support, and so on. We look forward to research that clarifies and isolates the role of these variables in future studies of intervention outcomes.

Although not expected, we argue that the implementation fidelity and intervention outcomes noted above can be considered a potential strength of the First Step Next program. That is, given the not infrequent, semi-chaotic ecologies and behavioral challenges that exist in many of today's classrooms and schools, if a targeted intervention such as First Step Next can be implemented, albeit with a lower level of fidelity and still produce acceptable student outcomes, it can be viewed as a positive result. Less than adequate implementation fidelity may actually be a more likely event than satisfactory fidelity in many "real world" applications of behavioral interventions. Because there is likely to be a less than ideal implementation of First Step Next in many instances, this outcome becomes a potentially noteworthy finding. However, regardless of the magnitude of achieved intervention effects, our research consistently shows that decay of FS behavioral outcomes begins occurring soon after termination of the intervention unless systematic maintenance procedures are in place.

Overall, the studies conducted on the original FS program from its development until the 2014–15 revision show it producing relatively robust outcome effects. However, as noted, the durability of achieved behavioral gains in these studies has been disappointing and is a challenge to be addressed going forward (Walker et al., 2014b).

First Step Next Research Following the 2014–15 Program Revision. Substantive changes were made to the original FS program in the 2014–15 revision that resulted in First Step Next. Following this revision, a question arose as to whether these changes would negatively influence the FSN program's outcomes and efficacy as compared to original First Step Next. Two recent IES-funded studies, conducted respectively with preschool and elementary student samples, provide evidence that they do not. These studies are briefly described below.

Feil et al. (2021) recently reported a validation study of FSN conducted in four preschool settings. One hundred and sixty students at risk for school failure, and their teachers, were randomized to the First Step Next intervention and control conditions. Results for the three prosocial outcome measures had Hedges' g effect sizes that ranged from 0.34 to 0.91 and favored the First Step Next intervention condition. For the problem behavior domain, Hedges' g effect sizes ranged from 0.33 to 0.63 again favoring the intervention condition.

Frey et al. (in press) conducted a comparative efficacy study of First Step Next where they identified a sample of 379 student-teacher-parent triads in which identified students were at elevated risk for disruptive behavior and school failure. Triads were randomly assigned to a school only condition, a home only condition, and combined condition along with a business as usual condition. Across prosocial, problem behavior and academic domains, results showed substantial support for the school only and combined conditions compared to business as usual. Modest support was obtained for the home only condition. Effect sizes in the school only and combined conditions averaged moderate to large magnitudes across domains and were small for the home only condition ranging from 0.09 to 0.26. Using the WWC Improvement Index, the mean percentile gains for the school only, combined, and home only conditions were respectively 18.9, 18.5, and 7.5.

First Step Next Applications to Attention Deficit Hyperactive Disorder and Other Psychiatric Disorders. An important condition affecting school performance and adjustment is Attention Deficit Hyperactive Disorder (ADHD). Attention Deficit Hyperactive Disorder has long been established as a co-occurring condition with conduct disorder (August et al., 1996). To date, there have been no formal, large-scale trials of First Step focused exclusively on students with disruptive behavior and ADHD. However, using data from the larger randomized efficacy trial (N=200) reported by Walker et al. (2009), Seeley et al. (2009) conducted a series of analyses for 42 participants (23 intervention and 19 control) who met eligibility criteria for co-occurring ADHD in order to determine FS outcomes for this subpopulation.

Students were identified for this ADHD subsample using Conner's DSM symptom cutoff for teacher-reported ADHD symptomatology. As part of the baseline assessment measures for the larger Albuquerque Public Schools (APS) study of 200 cases, intervention and control teachers completed an 18-item version of Conner's ADHD/DSM-IV scale (CADS-T; Conners, 1997). Thus, 21% (n=42) of our larger APS sample met ADHD diagnostic criteria. As compared with the larger sample, the ADHD subsample had significantly fewer females and significantly more Hispanic students. When this study was conducted, 1% of the students with ADHD in the control condition and 3% of students with ADHD in the intervention condition were receiving medication. Dependent measures were grouped into five areas or domains as follows: (a) school-based measures, (b) ADHD and disruptive behaviors and symptoms, (c) social functioning, (d) academic functioning, and (e) home-based outcome measures.

When the ADHD subsample was compared to the larger, remaining sample of students with disruptive behavior but without ADHD (n=158), the ADHD subsample had significantly more problematic profiles on measures of hyperactivity, attention, oppositional defiant disorder and maladaptive behavior. They also had less favorable profiles on measures of adaptive behavior and social skills. There were no differences between them in the areas of academic functioning and home-based measures completed by parents (i.e. SSRS problem behavior and social skills).

An overall multivariate model was tested for the four post-test behavioral symptom measures. Intervention students with ADHD had large overall gains compared to control students with ADHD on each of these measures with effect sizes ranging from d=.74 to 1.32. In the social functioning domain, effect sizes for these same students were (d=.80) for adaptive behavior and (d=1.01) for social skills. In the academic domain, there was a medium level difference between the groups on two academically related measures. These were the AET observational measure (d=.76) and teacher ratings on the SSRS academic competence subscale (d=.58). Parent ratings on the SSRS problem behavior subscale were in the predicted direction (d=.60) but there were no significant differences on the SSRS social skills scale (d=.31).

These outcomes were comparable in magnitude to school-home interventions that are directly focused on ADHD students without disruptive behavior (see Pfiffner et al., 2007). They also compare favorably to interventions that are focused on externalizing problem behavior among at-risk students (Conduct Problems Prevention Research Group, 2011). The ADHD sample showed a robust response to the original First Step intervention suggesting that it may have a positive impact on students with other externalizing problems and disorders.

A replication of the Seeley (2009) ADHD study was subsequently conducted by Feil et al. (2016) with preschoolers having co-occurring ADHD. This study involved a subsample from a relatively large RCT study of First Step for 126 preschoolers (Feil et al., 2014). Using a similar diagnostic measure for co-occurring ADHD, as in the study just described for elementary students, we retrospectively identified 45 preschoolers with ADHD symptoms, 26 from the intervention condition and 19 from the control or usual care condition. Preschoolers with ADHD who received the First Step Next intervention had statistically significant improvement compared to control preschoolers with ADHD on all teacher and parent-reported outcomes. For teacher-reported improvements in symptoms, Hedges' g effect sizes ranged from 0.80 to 1.4. As in the elementary-aged study above, parent-reported outcomes were smaller with effect sizes of 0.77 for symptoms and 0.65 for social functioning.

As there is some evidence that very young children with Autism Spectrum Disorder (ASD) may also be at risk for conduct or oppositional disorders (Kim et al., 2012) and that anxiety disorders have a high co-occurrence with disruptive behavior disorders (Franz et al., 2014), we used the same preschool sample from Feil et al. (2014) to also study subsamples having risk for ASD and anxiety disorders. In the ASD study, we used cutoffs on the autism diagnostic measure from the Early Childhood Inventory (ECI) (Gadow & Sprafkin, 2000) to retrospectively identify a subsample of 17 preschoolers with ASD who received the FS intervention and 17 with co-occurring ASD and who were in the usual care condition (Frey et al., 2015). Hedges' g effect sizes ranged from 0.65 to 1.12 in favor of the FS subsample in teacher-reported reductions in symptoms and from 0.29 to 1.18 in teacher-reported improvements in social functioning. Effect sizes in parent-reported improvements in social functioning ranged from 0.48 to 0.57 in favor of the FS subsample. All but one of the 11 outcome measures was statistically significant.

We then used the anxiety disorders diagnostic measure from the ECI to retrospectively identify a subsample of 38 preschoolers with anxiety disorders who were respectively assigned to the First Step intervention or to a usual care condition (19 per condition). Seven of 9 outcome measures were statistically significant in favor of the subsample assigned to First Step (Seeley et al., 2018). Hedges' *g* effect sizes ranged from 0.59 to 0.79 for disruptive behavior and 0.60 to 0.85 for social functioning improvements as reported by teachers; parent reported effect sizes on the same measures were 0.66 and 0.6 respectively. For both teacher and parent-reported outcomes for internalizing behavior, however, effect sizes were smaller at 0.42 and 0.23 suggesting that anxiety symptoms continued to be problematic. This was an expected finding as original FS was not designed to address internalizing anxiety problems; the achieved effects in this domain are likely a result due to disruptive students who also had co-occurring anxiety disorders.

Since the above studies were quite limited due to their small sample sizes, we are in the process of retrospectively identifying larger subsamples of children with co-occurring psychiatric disorders to also include depression. A recently completed RCT of nearly 400 elementary teacher-student-parent triads by Frey et al. (in press) will allow us to partially address this goal.

Synthesis of Original First Step and First Step Next Evidence from Randomized Controlled Trials

School professionals are well aware of the positive impact of early intervention and prevention efforts for successfully reducing disruptive behaviors and the likelihood of poor developmental outcomes (Hawkins et al., 1999). Following its development and initial testing in a small-scale RCT (Walker et al., 1998), the First Step intervention, as we have noted herein, was validated in a large-scale study conducted in the diverse Albuquerque School District (Walker et al., 2009) and via a national effectiveness study conducted by Sumi et al. (2013).

The Oregon School Research Group recently reviewed and synthesized five randomized controlled trials conducted between 2009–21 that included efficacy and effectiveness studies involving both FS and its revised FSN version along with several subsample analyses demonstrating impact across a range of co-occurring disorders and diverse target populations. Collectively, these studies show that the First Step intervention has resulted in small to large effect sizes and statistically significant improvements, compared to students randomized to control conditions, on multiple indicators of prosocial and problem behavior. A manuscript describing this best evidence synthesis is presently in press to Remedial and Special Education. This article provides professional consumers with accessible synthesized, First Step information that may facilitate program evaluation and adoption decisions.

Research on the Sustainability of First Step Next Program Usage

Flay et al. (2005) defined a set of evaluation standards for applied interventions which specify that (1) intervention programs should demonstrate replicable efficacy and effectiveness, (2) in addition to being judged as effective, they should meet criteria ensuring that agencies will adopt them, and (3) adopting agencies and organizations have the capacity and resources to make effective use of them. Loman et al. (2010) reported a comprehensive, long-term study of the sustainability of First Step that investigated these questions. These investigators systematically examined variables associated with the First Step program's usage and implementation over a ten-year period following First Step training and adoption by 29 Oregon schools located in 13 Oregon school districts. A survey, called the First Step Evaluation Tool was developed by the study's authors to investigate these questions. Each participating school was represented by one school-level respondent (i.e. personnel formally trained in First Step) and was included in the sample based on the following criteria: (a) being an elementary school with K-3 grades, (b) having personnel who received formal training in First Step, (c) having personnel who at one time implemented First Step in their school, and (d) having school personnel with past and present knowledge of First Step implementation in their school.

Results showed that 28% of adopting school districts continued to implement the First Step program up to 10 years after initial implementation. Six critical features were reported by school personnel as associated with First Step sustainability: (a) dedicated resources, (b) training and orientation activities, (c) district-level coordination, (d) selection of students who are a good fit for the program, (e) highly qualified coaches, and (f) administrative support. This was a well-designed and conducted study that produced valuable information on the differences between First Step sustaining and non- sustaining schools.

Cost Analysis of First Step Next Implementation

The long-term societal costs of disruptive behavior disorders are well known. However, there is a dearth of available information on the costs of interventions that are used to impact them. Frey et al. (2019) conducted a comprehensive cost analysis of First Step Next with 40 preschool and kindergarten students. The per child cost to implement the program with 29 triads in two cohorts was $4,330. The incremental cost per additional student was $2,970—a difference of $1,360. In a recent efficacy study involving 379 teacher-parent-student triads, we examined whether either First Step Next (FSN) alone or First Step Next plus a brief, home visitation intervention (i.e., homeBase) to support parents is more cost-effective in treating disruptive behavior problems among elementary aged students (Frey et al., in press). Intervention costs were estimated using an activities-based Ingredients Method (Levin & McEwan, 2001) and comparative cost effectiveness analyses involved calculating incremental cost-effectiveness ratios (ICERs). The average cost per student of $3,387 and the additional cost of serving one more student once the intervention was in place ($2,538) were similar to the costs identified in Frey et al. (2019) for preschoolers. Intervention effectiveness was defined as a student moving from the borderline range into the normative range or from the clinical range into the borderline or normative range at post-intervention. The combined intervention was always more cost-effective among co-occurring conditions (i.e., ADHD, CD, and co-occurring ADHD and CD).

Implications of First Step and First Step Next Findings for Classroom Management

There have been just over two decades of research and development conducted on First Step and its 2015 revision since it was published in 1997. This research has produced a number of important findings, empirical as well as experiential, that have implications for managing the classroom context. They are listed and briefly described below.

- First Step reduces conflict between teachers and students.
- Target students during First Step Next implementation experience a surge in their popularity with peers as the target student is instrumental in earning a preferred activity in which classmates all share.
- Sprague and Perkins (2009) found positive spillover effects from First Step to (a) other students with problem behavior in the same classroom, (b) with the teacher and (c) on the classroom's climate.
- Horner and colleagues found that First Step works well for students whose problem behavior is motivated primarily by attention seeking and less well for students motivated by escape from or avoidance of situations they perceive as aversive.
- First Step works best when there is a positive universal intervention, such as PBIS, already in place. Students who fail to respond to the universal intervention are likely good candidates for a Tier 2 intervention such as First Step.
- Target students with strong parental support tend to do better in the program.
- Target students who are younger (i.e., preschoolers) or whose problems are more severe tend to need a longer exposure to the program in order to see positive results.

- Behavioral gains achieved via First Step do not automatically maintain over the long term unless accompanied by regular monitoring and the provision of ongoing supports.
- It appears that First Step can be implemented with substantially less than perfect fidelity and still produce acceptable intervention outcomes.
- First Step produces positive changes in academically related behavior (i.e., AET and Teacher Ratings of Academic Performance) but not on standardized achievement tests.

Concluding Remarks

First Step is a well-researched early intervention and its accumulated evidence suggests that, on average, it produces moderate to strong effects, even when not implemented as well as desired or expected. There is solid evidence that the First Step program works effectively for a diverse array of Pre-K, and K-2 students and that it does not require specialized accommodations for such students to experience success. A recent What Works Clearinghouse review of a preschool, efficacy validation study of First Step Next by Feil et al. (2021) found that the study met WWC group design standards without reservations. Results of this review are available on the WWC website. However, it is also clear that while assigning the program moderate to high satisfaction ratings, some teachers see it as too much work in exchange for the benefits they perceive FS as delivering. Teacher comments suggest they believe the program pulls them away from teaching academics and other essential tasks as opposed to making these tasks easier. However, parents of target students tend to give the program high marks and slightly more positive satisfaction ratings than do teachers. A consistent finding from our research is that the First Step program does not impact direct academic performance measures but does impact important academically related measures such as academic engagement and academic competence-enablers (i.e., forms of student behavior that support direct academic performance such as being organized for instruction, working on assigned tasks, cooperating, responding to teacher directives, and so forth). It is gratifying to see the positive effects of First Step with ADHD students and those having autism and anxiety disorders.

The challenge for programs like First Step is to find ways to sustain their positive effects over the long term but without incurring unreasonable costs (time, effort, materials) in doing so. It has been argued that behavior change is a two-part process. That is, there is one set of procedures for producing it and determining efficacy-effectiveness and another set of procedures governing its durability and generalization. Part two of this change process continues to be laden with challenges that remain to be solved. It appears that First Step is robust in addressing part one of the behavior change process—at least in the relative short term (i.e., within a school year). We will address the issue of inducing longer-term intervention outcomes as an important component of a continuing program of First Step Next research.

Note

1 The authors are indebted to Ed Sabornie for his editorial assistance during the production of this manuscript. Portions of the material contained herein in the Evaluation Research section were previously included in Walker et al. (2014b). Thanks to Kristina Hulegaard for her assistance in finding URLs.

References

August, G., Realmuto, G., MacDonald, A., Nugent, S., & Crosby, R. (1996). Prevalence of ADHD and comorbid disorders among elementary school children screened for disruptive behavior. *Journal of Abnormal Child Psychology*, *24*, 571–595. https://doi.org/10.1007/BF01670101

Carter, D. & Horner, R. (2007). Adding functional behavioral assessment to First Step Next to Success: A case study. *Journal of Positive Behavior Intervention*, *9*(4), Fall, 229–238. https://doi.org/10.1177/1098300707009 0040501

Carter, D., & Horner, R. (2009). Adding function-based behavioral support to First Step Next to Success: Integrating individualized and manualized practices. *Journal of Positive Behavior Intervention*, *11*(1), 22–34. https://doi.org/10.1177/1098300708319125

Conduct Problems Prevention Research Group (2011). The effects of the Fast Track preventive intervention on the development of conduct disorder across childhood. *Child Development*, January–February, *82*(1), 331–345. https://doi.org/10.1111/j.1467-8624.2010.01558.x

Connors, C. (1997). *Connors' rating scales—revised technical manual*. Multi-Health Systems, Inc.

Drake, R., Latimer, E., Leff, S., McHugo, G., & Burns, B. (2004). What is evidence? *Child and Adolescent Psychiatric Clinics of North America*, *13*, 717–728. https://doi.org/10.1016/j.chc.2004.05.005

Feil, E., Frey, A., Walker, H., Seeley, J., Golly, A., & Forness, S. A. (2014). The efficacy of a home/school intervention for preschoolers with challenging behaviors: A randomized controlled trial of Preschool First Step Next to Success. *Journal of Early Intervention*, *36*(3), 151–170. https://doi.org/10.1177/1053815114566090

Feil, E., Small, J., Seeley, J., Walker, H., Golly, A., Frey, A., & Forness, S. (2016). Early intervention for preschoolers at risk for Attention-Deficit/Hyperactivity Disorder: Preschool First Step Next. *Behavioral Disorders*, *41*, 95–106. https://doi.org/10.17988/0198-7429-41.2.95

Feil, E., Walker, H., Frey, A., Seeley, J., Small, J., Golly, A., Lee, J., & Forness, S. (2021). Efficacy validation of the revised First Step Next program: A randomized controlled trial. *Exceptional Children*, *87*(2), 183–198. https://doi.org/10.1177/0014402920924848

Flay, B., Biglan, A., Boruch, R., Castro, F., Gottfredson, D., Kellam, S., Moscicki, E., Schinke, S., Valentine, J., & Ji, P. (2005). Standards of evidence: Criteria for efficacy, effectiveness, & dissemination. *Prevention Science*, *6*(3), September, 151–175. https://doi.org/10.1007/s11121-005-5553-y

Franz, L., Angold, A., Copeland, W., Costello, E., Towe-Goodman, N., & Egger, H. (2013). Preschool anxiety disorders in pediatric primary care: Prevalence and comorbidity. *Journal of the American Academy of Child and Adolescent Psychiatry*, *52*, 1294–1303. https://doi.org/10.1016/j.jaac.2013.09.008

Frey, A., Kuklinski, M., Bills, K., Small, J., Forness, S. R., Walker, H., Feil, E., & Seeley, J. (2019). Comprehensive cost analysis of First Step Next for preschoolers with disruptive behavior disorder: Using real-world intervention data to estimate costs to scale. *Prevention Science*, *20*, 1219–1232 https://doi.org/10.1007/s11121-019-01035-z

Frey, A., Small, J., Feil, E., Seeley, J., Walker, H., & Forness, S. R. (2015). First Step Next: Application to preschoolers at risk of developing autism spectrum disorders, *Education and Training in Autism and Developmental Disabilities*, *50*(4), 397–407.

Frey, A., Small, J., Seeley, J., Walker, H., Feil, E., Forness, S. R., Lee, J., Lissman, D., Crosby, S., & Golly, A. (in press). First Step Next and homeBase: A comparative efficacy study of children with disruptive behavior. *Exceptional Children*. https://urldefense.com/v3/__https://doi.org/10.1177/0014402920924848.

Frey, A., Small, J., Walker, H., Mitchell, B., Feil, E., Lee, J., & Forness, S. (in press). First Step Next: A synthesis of replication studies from 2009-2021. *Remedial & Special Education*.

Gadow, K., & Sprafkin, J. (2000). *Early childhood inventory-4 screening manual*. Checkmate Plus.

Gresham, F. & Elliott, S. (1990). *Social Skills Rating System. SSRS.* (test and manual), American Guidance Service.

Hawkins, D., Catalano, R., Kosterman, R., Abbott, R., & Hill, K. (1999). Preventing adolescent health risk behaviors by strengthening protection during childhood. *Archives of Pediatric and Adolescent Medicine*, *153*, 226–234. https://doi.org/10.1001/archpedi.153.3.226

Hops, H. & Walker, H. (1988). *CLASS: Contingencies for Learning Academic and Social Skills*. Educational Achievement Systems.

Horner, R., Carr, E., Halle, J., McGee, G., Odom, S., & Wolery, M. (2005). The use of single-subject research to identify evidence-based practice in special education. *Exceptional Children*, *71*(2) 165–179. https://doi.org/10.1177/001440290507100203

Kim, J., Freeman, S., Paparella, T, & Forness, S. (2012). Five year followup of preschoolers with autism and comorbid psychiatric disorders. *Behavioral Disorders*, *38*(1), Nov., 57–70. https://doi.org/10.1177/019874291203800105

Levin, M., & McEwan, J. (2001). *Cost effectiveness analysis: Methods and applications*. Sage.

Loman, S., Rodriguez, B., & Horner, R. (2010). Sustainability of a focused intervention package: First Step to Success in Oregon. *Journal of Emotional Disorders*, *18*(3), 178–191. https://doi.org/10.1177/1063426610362899

Nelson, R., Hurley, K., Synhorst, L., Epstein, M., Stage, S., & Buckley, J. (2009). The child outcomes of a behavior model. *Exceptional Children*, *76*(1), 7–30. https://doi.org/10.1177/001440290907600101

Paine, S., Hops, H., Walker, H., Greenwood, C., Fleischman, D., & Guild, J. (1982). Repeated treatment effects: A study of maintaining behavior change in socially withdrawn children. *Behavior Modification* https://doi.org/10.1177/01454455820062002

Patterson, G. R. (1982). *Coercive family process (Vol. 3): A social learning approach*. Castalia.

Patterson, G. R., Reid, J. B., & Dishion, T. J. (1992). *Antisocial boys*. Castalia.

Pfiffner, L., Mikami, A., Huang-Pollack, C., Easterlin, B., Zalecki, C., & McBurnett, K. (2007). A randomized, controlled trial of integrated home-school behavioral treatment for ADHD, predominantly intensive type.

Journal of the American Academy of Child and Adolescent Psychiatry, *46*(8), 1041–1050. https://doi.org/10.1097/chi.0b013e318064675f

Reid, J. B., Patterson, G. R., & Snyder, J. J. (Eds.). (2002). *Antisocial behavior in children and adolescents: A developmental analysis and the Oregon Model for Intervention*. American Psychological Association.

Romer, D., & Heller, T. (1983). Social adaptation of mentally retarded adults in community settings: A social–ecological approach. *Applied Research in Mental Retardation*, *4*, 303–314. https://doi.org//10.1016/0270-3092(83)90031-0

Schrank, F., Mather, N., & Woodcock, R. (2004). *Woodcock-Johnson IIIr Diagnostic Reading Battery*. (test and manual), (2004). Riverside Insights.

Seeley, J., Small, J., Feil, E., Frey, A., Walker, H., Golly, A., & Forness, S. (2018). Effects of the First Step Next intervention on preschoolers with disruptive behavior and comorbid anxiety problems. *School Mental Health*, *10*, 243–253. https://doi.org/10.1007/s12310-017-9226-3

Seeley, J. R., Small, J. W., Walker, H. M., Feil, E. G., Severson, H. H., Golly, A. M., & Forness, S. R. (2009). Efficacy of the First Step to Success intervention for students with ADHD. *School Mental Health*, *1*, 37–48. https://doi.org/10.1007/s12310-008-9003-4

Sheridan, S., Swanger-Gange', M., Welch, G., Kwon, K., & Garbacz, A. (2009). Fidelity measurement in consultation: Psychometric issues and preliminary examination. *School Psychology Review*, *38*(4), 476–495.

Sprague, J., & Perkins, K. (2009). Direct and collateral effects of the First Step to Success program. *Journal of Positive Behavior Interventions*, *11*(4), 208–221. https://doi.org/10.1177/1098300708330935

Sumi, C., Woodbridge, M., Javitz, H., Thornton, P., Wagner, M., Rouspil, K., Yu, J., Seeley, J., Walker, H., Golly, A., Small, J., Feil, E., & Severson, H. (2013). Assessing the effectiveness of First Step to Success: Are short-term results the First Step Next to long-term behavioral improvements? *Journal of Emotional and Behavioral Disorders*, *21*(1). https://doi.org/10.1177/1063426611429571

Walker, H. M. (2004). Commentary: Use of evidence-based interventions in schools: Where we've been, where we are, and where we need to go. *School Psychology Review*, *33*(3), 398–407. https://doi.org/10.1080/02796015.2004.12086256

Walker, H. M., Colvin, G., & Ramsey, E. (1995). *Antisocial behavior in school: Strategies and best practices*. Brooks/Cole, Inc.

Walker, H., Feil, E., Frey, A., Small, J., Seeley, J., Golly, A., Crosby, S., Lee, J., Forness, S. R., Sprick, M., Coughlin, C., & Stiller, B. (2018). First Step Next: An updated version of the First Step to Success early intervention program. *Perspectives on Early Childhood Psychology and Education*, *3*(1), 89–109.

Walker, H. M., Kavanagh, K., Stiller, B., Golly, A., Feil, E., & Severson, H. H. (1997). *First Step to Success: Helping young children overcome antisocial behavior (an early intervention program for grades K-3)*. Sopris West.

Walker, H. M., Kavanagh, K., Stiller, B., Golly, A., Severson, H. H., & Feil, E. G. (1998). First Step to Success: An early intervention approach for preventing school antisocial behavior. *Journal of Emotional and Behavioral Disorders*, *6*(2), 66–80. https://doi.org/10.1177/106342669800600201

Walker, H. M., Seeley, J. R., Small, J., Severson, H. H., Graham, B., Feil, E. G., Serna, L., Golly, A. M., & Forness, S. R. (2009). A randomized controlled trial of the First Step to Success early intervention: Demonstration of program efficacy outcomes in a diverse, urban school district. *Journal of Emotional and Behavioral Disorders*, *17*(4), 197–212. https://doi.org/10.1177/1063426609341645

Walker, H. M., Severson, H., & Feil, E. (2014a) (2nd Ed.). *Systematic Screening for Behavior Disorders*. SSBD. (test and manual). Ancora Publishing, Inc.

Walker, H. M., Severson, H., Seeley, J., Feil, E., Small, J., Golly, A., Frey, A., Lee, J., Sumi, W.C., Woodbridge, M., Wagner, M., & Forness, S. (2014b). The evidence base of the First Step to Success early intervention for preventing emerging antisocial behavior patterns. In H.M. Walker & F.M. Gresham (Eds.), *Handbook of evidence-based practices for emotional and behavioral disorders: Applications in schools* (pp. 518–537). Guilford.

Walker, H. M., Severson, H., Stiller, B., Williams, G., Haring, N., Shinn, M., & Todis, B. (1988). Systematic screening of pupils in the elementary age range at risk for behavior disorders: Development and trial testing of a multiple gating model. *Remedial and Special Education*, *9*(3), 8–14. https://doi.org/10.1177/074193258809000304

Walker, H. M., Severson, H. H., Todis, B. J., Block-Pedego, A. E., Williams, G. J., Haring, N. G., & Barckley, M. (1990). Systematic screening for behavior disorders (SSBD): Further validation, replication and normative data. *Remedial and Special Education*, *11*(2), 32–46. https://doi.org/10.1177/074193259001100206

Walker, H., Stiller, B., Coughlin, C., Golly, A., Sprick, M. & Feil, E (2015) *First Step Next* (2nd Ed.). Ancora Publishing.

Weisz, J., & Jensen, A. (2001). Efficacy and effectiveness of psychotherapy with children and adolescents. *European Child and Adolescent Psychiatry*, *10*, 112–118. https://doi.org/10.1007/s007870170003

6

CURRENT TRENDS IN POSITIVE BEHAVIORAL INTERVENTIONS AND SUPPORTS

Implications for Classroom Management

Sara Estrapala and Timothy J. Lewis

Introduction

Positive Behavioral Interventions and Supports (PBIS) is an evidence-based framework grounded in data-based decision making and involves a three-tiered continuum of social, emotional, and behavioral supports (Sugai & Horner, 2009). Within Tier 1, leadership teams establish systems and practices for ensuring all students are taught and practice socially appropriate behaviors across all school settings. Tier 2 includes targeted interventions (e.g., self-management, check-in/check-out [CICO], social skills groups) for small groups of students who need additional supports beyond Tier 1. Finally, Tier 3 may include intense, function-based behavior interventions, one-on-one counseling, and wraparound services for students who need individualized supports (Horner et al., 2010). Effective, sustainable PBIS implementation relies on the interconnected relationship between (a) implementing evidence-based practices; (b) collecting and monitoring data; and (c) establishing systems to ensure fidelity of implementation that leads to achieving socially relevant school, district, and statewide educational goals (Coffee & Horner, 2012).

For more than 25 years, empirical evidence supporting PBIS to improve school climate, safety, and student outcomes (e.g., academic performance, social-emotional wellbeing, graduation rates; Bradshaw, Waasdorp, et al., 2014; Freeman et al., 2016; Gage et al., 2015) while reducing exclusionary discipline (e.g., office discipline referrals [ODRs], suspensions, restraint and seclusion; Estrapala et al., 2020; Gage, Whitford, et al., 2018; Noltemeyer et al., 2018), has demonstrated the enduring utility of this systematic approach to school behavior. Whereas district and schoolwide PBIS (SWPBIS) are intended to establish consistency between buildings, classrooms, and shared spaces; in class-wide PBIS (CWPBIS) data, systems, and practices are adapted to suit individual classroom needs through evidence-based classroom management strategies.

At Tier 1, CWPBIS is a classroom management approach which utilizes the same foundational elements of SWPBIS: (a) explicitly taught universal expectations (e.g., respectful, responsible, safe); (b) establishment of procedures and routines; (c) acknowledgement systems (e.g., contingent

DOI: 10.4324/9781003275312-8

reinforcement, behavior specific praise); (d) behavior response systems focusing on error correction; and (e) data collection and management systems (e.g., School-Wide Information System [SWIS], PBISApps., 2021a; PBIS Assessment PBISApps., 2021b). Ideally, classroom teachers adapt the schoolwide expectations to suit the individual contexts of their classroom (e.g., grade level, content area) and teach, reinforce, and monitor these expectations using the same systems established at the schoolwide level. Continuity between SWPBIS and CWPBIS can improve overall school climate, culture, connectedness, and organizational health (Bradshaw et al., 2009; Bradshaw et al., 2021; Koth et al., 2008; Reinke et al., 2013) while reducing additional planning and organizational burdens for teachers (e.g., developing their own data management system; Freeman et al., 2020). At Tiers 2 and 3, school- and district-wide PBIS plans help classroom teachers determine (a) which students might require more intensive supports; (b) appropriate, resource-effective interventions; and (c) needed systems for monitoring and responding to intervention outcome data. In turn, implementing CWPBIS with fidelity provides essential data utilized across school- and district-wide implementation and planning efforts.

In this chapter, we will review recent literature on CWPBIS, and highlight current research and innovation related to data, systems, and practice. We will then discuss critical issues necessitating ongoing research related to classroom management and CWPBIS. Additional information on the schoolwide framework, including evidence to date, can be found at pbis.org as well as chapters in previous editions of this textbook.

CWPBIS Current Research and Innovations

As mentioned above, successful implementation of PBIS in any context (e.g., classroom, school, district, state) hinges on following the problem-solving framework of using *data* to identify and progress monitor evidence-based *practices*, and creating *systems* of support to increase implementation fidelity, consistency, and sustainability. The evidence base for foundational classroom management practices (e.g., physical arrangement of classroom structures, active supervision, increased opportunities to respond [OTR], behavior-specific feedback) has been well established and documented (c.f., Simonsen et al., 2008; Zaheer et al., 2019). As such, the following section highlights the data-based decision making and creation of systems of teacher support that are hallmarks of the PBIS framework.

Data

Systematically collecting, interpreting, reporting, and using data to identify areas for improvement and to determine effectiveness of interventions is often referred to as data-based decision making (DBDM). In CWPBIS, implementation fidelity and outcome data are the primary drivers of DBDM (Swain-Bradway et al., 2017). Implementation fidelity refers to the extent to which an intervention is implemented as designed, and can include data on procedures, quality, and content (e.g., Simonsen et al., 2019). CWPBIS fidelity data can be recorded with validated tools (e.g., Tiered Fidelity Inventory [TFI], Algozzine et al., 2014), and fidelity data should be collected and analyzed at regular intervals throughout the school year (e.g., each semester). Researchers have repeatedly demonstrated a positive correlation between implementation fidelity and improved outcomes, and that high SWPBIS fidelity may result in higher CWPBIS fidelity (Childs et al., 2016). Childs and colleagues further posit that since most ODRs originate from classrooms as opposed to common areas, high implementation fidelity of CWPBIS should significantly improve schoolwide outcome data. CWPBIS outcome data can include student behavior (e.g., ODRs; direct observation of academic engagement, disruptive behaviors, turn taking, etc.), academic achievement, and teacher instructional-related behaviors (e.g., OTRs, ratio of positive to negative feedback, active supervision). When interventions are implemented with fidelity, systematically reviewing outcome data can reveal the extent to which an intervention is impacting the variable of interest (e.g., teacher or student behavior). As such, school and district leadership teams can identify relevant, efficient, and cost-effective practices to codify within their systems.

Although systematic use of DBDM is directly linked to PBIS sustainability and improved student outcomes (Coffee & Horner, 2012), widespread use of behavioral DBDM by practitioners is sparse (Bruhn et al., 2020). For example, classroom teachers consistently report difficulty collecting and interpreting behavioral data (Fallon et al., 2014), are underprepared to use DBDM (Reeves et al., 2016), or are unaware of behavioral data collected and used within the district (Stormont et al., 2011). As a result, reliable reporting of student outcomes is limited, and the ability for leadership teams to adapt and improve existing systems and practices dissipates. Interestingly, results from a survey of perceptions of PBIS coaching supports indicated that assistance with DBDM was one of the most beneficial coaching activities (Bastable et al., 2020). Specifically, respondents (i.e., SWPBIS leadership team members with 3–9 or more years of implementation) ranked collecting, analyzing, reporting, and action planning as the most important coaching supports.

To illustrate, a study by Bruhn et al. (2020) reported statistically significant improvements in students' positive behaviors when teachers learned to implement systematic DBDM within the context of a technology-based self-monitoring intervention. In addition, participating teachers reported statistically significant gains in conceptual understanding, self-efficacy, and overall usability of DBDM after a year-long series of professional development activities (Bruhn et al., 2019). Perhaps one component contributing to the success of the Bruhn et al. studies was the data collection system which closely resembled direct behavior ratings (DBRs). DBRs are a reliable and valid assessment tool combining features of systematic direct observation (e.g., repeatedly observing behavior after a pre-specified amount of time) and behavior ratings scales (e.g., rating the degree to which a target behavior occurred; Riley-Tillman et al., 2008). The primary advantage of DBRs over other behavioral data collection methods is (a) it requires little training to conduct reliably, (b) the data are sensitive enough to detect responsiveness to intervention and make informed decisions, and (c) teachers can easily collect DBRs while teaching (Chafouleas et al., 2012; Maggin & Bruhn, 2018; Riley-Tillman et al., 2008). Since many teachers view data collection and analysis as a daunting task within the context of teaching and classroom management (Bruhn et al., 2019), researchers continue to develop simple and feasible data collection methods to track Tier 1 and Tier 2 CWPBIS outcomes.

Systems

PBIS systems are created to insure that (a) practices are consistently implemented with fidelity, (b) data are regularly collected, reviewed, and disseminated, (c) leadership teams adapt and adopt practices based on outcome data, and (d) all staff are fully trained to carry out their PBIS responsibilities (Horner et al., 2010). As a result, these organizational systems create large-scale interconnected state, district, school, and classroom channels for implementing equitable, socially relevant, and evidence-based practices (Fixsen et al., 2013; Horner et al., 2017). In recent years, systems research to promote uptake of evidence-based CWPBIS practices has included increasing district support and teacher professional development (PD).

Increasing District Capacity to Support CWPBIS. If teachers are to receive the support they need to improve classroom management practices within sustained systems, districts must plan accordingly through DBDM (e.g., time to attend trainings, coaching, access to materials, assessments and feedback, alignment across initiatives, etc.; Kittelman et al., 2019). Consistent with research in organizational systems (e.g., Fixsen et al., 2013), a district leadership team ensures executive drivers are in place to enable systematic change including: (a) funding for initiatives; (b) regular communication of initiative purpose and related data; (c) political support; and (d) initiatives incorporate district, region, or state policies regarding social, emotional, and behavioral wellbeing in schools (Fixsen et al., 2013; Horner et al., 2014). Limited research to date has shown a district-wide focus leads to sustained school level implementation at fidelity (Kittelman et al., 2019). As these executive drivers are put into place, leadership teams implement training, coaching, and evaluation functions. See Figure 6.1 for an illustration of this process.

The National Technical Assistance Center for PBIS (www.pbis.org) has recently developed a suite of tools to help districts increase capacity to implement PBIS, including CWPBIS. The District Systems Fidelity Inventory (DSFI; Center on PBIS, 2019) is an implementation fidelity assessment and action planning tool which helps districts target areas of strengths and weaknesses related to district-level implementation and to help differentiate professional development and technical assistance to individual schools, including classroom systems (see Figure 6.1 for core functions). Two essential district-level system components which directly effect CWPBIS include funding and alignment and increasing workforce capacity (e.g., streamlining job descriptions, hiring policies, and evaluation criteria to reflect a district-wide commitment to PBIS). Research in organizational systems suggests that explicitly defining jobs to include roles, responsibilities, and performance evaluation criteria related to new initiatives will increase the probability of successful implementation (Fixsen et al., 2013; Horner et al., 2017). That is, alignment of job descriptions and evaluation criteria across members of the district leadership team, district and school administrators, teachers and other school staff will increase accountability, commitment, and dissemination of initiatives. Given that classroom management is an area of high need yet often receives little attention, building CWPBIS into the essential functions of employees should highlight the importance of classroom management as a district priority. Finally, in order to ensure staff have the time to learn and execute their PBIS functions, districts must allocate funding to highlight and support these initiatives. Research on the impact of these district systems on classroom management and student outcomes is currently ongoing (Kittelman et al., 2019).

Systems to Support Professional Development. Researchers have continually documented teachers' struggles with behavior and classroom management (Beam & Mueller, 2017; Reinke et al., 2011) and these struggles are frequently top-cited reasons for leaving the field (Aloe et al., 2014;

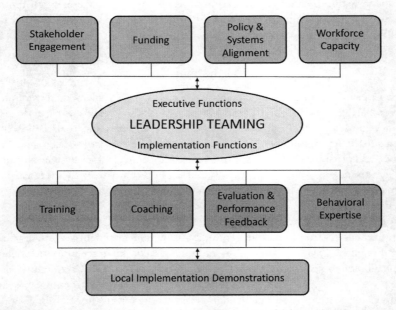

Figure 6.1   PBIS Leadership team functions to ensure implementation fidelity and student impact
Source: used with permission from the OSEP Center on PBIS

Gilmour & Wehby, 2020). Further, vast differences among state teacher licensing requirements for classroom management instruction results in an overall lack of teacher pre-service instruction on classroom management, minimal standards for states requiring classroom management for teacher certification, (Freeman et al., 2014), and infrequent use of evidence-based strategies for in-service teachers (Reinke et al., 2013; Scott et al., 2011). This unevenness of teacher preparation and certification is especially acute among general education teachers. For example, researchers examined the extent to which classroom management items were included on state-developed, required teacher evaluation rubrics for in-service teachers (Gilmour et al., 2019). The authors reported that while most evaluation rubrics included classroom management-related language, very few explicitly addressed evidence-based classroom management practices. As a result, the authors concluded that teachers who were evaluated with these required state-developed observation rubrics would not be provided actionable feedback to help them improve their classroom management practices. Finally, traditional and widely used methods of PD on classroom management where teachers attend a one-time informational session without follow-up have been repeatedly deemed ineffective (Simonsen, Freeman, Myers, et al., 2020). Taken together, there is ample evidence supporting the need for quality, in-service professional development with on-going performance feedback in classroom management (Simonsen et al., 2020).

A recent literature review by Wilkinson and colleagues (2021) synthesized peer-reviewed research reporting the effects of classroom management for in-service teachers PD included 74 studies published between 1984 and 2018. The authors found that the most common components of PD included explicit instruction (i.e., model, lead, test, Archer & Hughes, 2011; n = 39), coaching (i.e., instruction in teacher classrooms; n = 46), and performance feedback (i.e., observation data provided to teachers; n = 38), and that the studies demonstrating the greatest changes in teacher and student behaviors included multiple PD components. Further, a study of state-wide PBIS PD components found significant predictive relationships between overall PD effectiveness and the following components: (a) active learning opportunities (i.e., explicit instruction); (b) alignment of PD content with current school supports and initiatives; and (c) PD offered at the beginning of academic school years (Palmer & Noltemeyer, 2019). This research demonstrates complex relationships between delivery method (e.g., individualized, group, instructional method), intensity (e.g., time spent engaged in PD sessions, number of PD sessions required, resource allocation, personnel involved) and PD components (e.g., coaching, feedback, targeted classroom management strategy).

Given the effectiveness of multi-component PD, research in building classroom management fluency have called for a multi-tiered approach to support PD delivery (e.g., Gage, MacSuga-Gage, et al., 2017; Sanetti & Collier-Meek, 2015; Simonsen et al., 2014). The multi-tiered approach examined by Simonsen and colleagues (2014) included three tiers of supports which increased in intensity as teachers' needs increased and were designed to improve teacher use of evidence-based classroom management strategies. Tier 1 included instruction in universal, evidence-based classroom-management practices (e.g., active supervision, establishing rules and expectations, increasing OTRs) to all teachers using explicit instruction techniques, and provided a framework for teachers to self-monitor their use of these practices in their classrooms. To self-monitor, teachers recorded the number of times they delivered the classroom management practice using a small hand-held golf stroke counter or by recording tally marks on paper for 10–15 mins of instruction per day. They were also instructed to enter their data into a spreadsheet and review their data at least weekly, alongside an instructional coach, to determine the extent to which teachers were implementing the practice taught during the PD session. Further, Simonsen and colleagues recommend that school leaders should periodically observe and assess teacher classroom management using an empirically validated assessment tool (e.g., Classroom Management Observation Tool [CMOT], Simonsen, Freeman, Dooley, et al., 2020). Teachers who struggled with classroom management after Tier 1 PD move to Tier 2, which involved more intense self-management strategies as well as weekly check-ins with behavior coaches. Specifically, at Tier 2, teachers (a) identified a specific classroom management strategy to improve; (b) set a goal for improvement; (c) established a prompting system to promote use of the strategy; (d) self-monitored use of the strategy; (e) graphed and evaluated their data; and (f) self-reinforced when they meet their goals. To assess Tier 2 progress, behavior coaches reviewed teacher self-management data, conducted classroom observations, and reviewed student-level data. At Tier 3, teachers implemented the same self-management intervention developed at Tier 2, however the behavior coach identified key areas of improvement and provided more frequent consultation and formative feedback. Through a pilot case study, Simonsen and colleagues found that across four teachers, each required a differentiated level of support (i.e., tiered) to increase their delivery rates of behavior specific praise, however no functional relations were found due to design limitations.

Similarly, Gage and colleagues (2017) utilized a two-tiered framework to determine if a multi-tiered approach would increase teachers' use of behavior-specific praise. In their study, at Tier 1, four teachers were provided a 30-min explicit instruction session on behavior specific praise and were taught how to self-monitor their use of behavior specific praise using a golf stroke counter. Results showed little to no improvements in praise rates, teachers did not self-monitor with fidelity, and no teachers accurately self-monitored their praise rate delivery (compared to direct observation data). At Tier 2, researchers increased the intensity of PD for three of the four teachers by (a) providing individualized booster sessions on delivering behavior specific feedback, (b) graphing baseline specific praise rate data and setting goals, and (c) providing teachers with weekly visual performance feedback via email. Following the inclusion of intensified supports, all teachers improved their rates of delivering behavior specific praise, however the authors did not note whether teachers' self-monitoring fidelity improved or more accurately self-monitored their praise rates.

Sanetti and Collier-Meek (2015) focused specifically on improving fidelity of implementation of classroom management strategies across a continuum of supports approach. At Tier 1, teachers met individually with consultants who provided teachers a classroom management plan and to teach them a variety of evidence-based classroom management strategies. These plans were based on teacher interviews and classroom observations. After the consultation, teachers who failed to implement the plan with at least 80% fidelity moved to Tier 2, where they received additional consultation to identify implementation barriers, problem-solve solutions, and revise the plan as needed. Teachers who continued to struggle received Tier 3 supports, which included another consultation session to practice implementation with the consultant. Further, the consultant modeled implementation in vivo during the teachers' class where they struggled with classroom management, followed by independent teacher practice and another consultation session. Across six elementary teachers, mean implementation fidelity for Tier 1 ranged from 45.96% to 92.13%, thus four teachers moved to Tier 2 supports. Tier 2 mean fidelity ranged from 62.97% to 95.6%, and two teachers qualified for Tier 3 supports. At Tier 3, one teacher met fidelity (i.e., 84%) while the other continued to fall below the criterion (i.e., 75.76%).

Although the above reviewed studies by Simonsen et al. (2014), Gage et al. (2017), and Sanetti and Collier-Meek (2015) did not provide strong causal evidence linking the PD provided to improved classroom management behaviors, the collective preliminary data suggest that a multi-tiered systems approach to PD delivery holds promise. Research on these multi-tiered approaches indicated (a) teachers apply skills and knowledge related to classroom management PD at different rates, and (b) some teachers require more intensive supports to implement classroom management strategies with fidelity. These points are important because a multi-tiered system for PD could not only improve the uptake of evidence-based classroom management practices and implementation fidelity, but also could save valuable time and resources since some teachers responded well to Tier 1 supports (i.e., quality explicit instruction of evidence-based practices and self-monitoring). Further, all teachers should still receive assessments and/or observations by administrators or other building leaders which include classroom management competencies to provide feedback and determine which teachers require more extensive supports. Future research is needed to (a) refine decision rules for moving teachers through Tiers; (b) develop a variety of Tier 2 and 3 supports which can suit a variety of contexts (e.g., grade levels, content areas, resource availability); and (c) examine the long-term and distal effects on teacher and student behaviors.

Coaching. Coaching is a method of delivering PD via a content area expert (e.g., behavior specialist, school psychologist, experienced teacher) who typically meets with district teams, school teams, or individual teachers to teach new skills and develop implementation plans (Freeman et al., 2017). From a systems perspective, coaching is intended to build capacity and sustainability of evidence-based practice implementation with fidelity and utilize DBDM with action planning (Horner et al., 2017). Coaching typically involves regularly scheduled observations or assessment of skill implementation, data-based feedback, and action planning (Barrett & Pas, 2020). Numerous studies have demonstrated that coaching can improve teacher use of classroom management procedures with correlated improved student behavior (Bethune, 2017; Bradshaw et al., 2018; Kraft et al., 2018; Kretlow & Bartholomew, 2010; Simonsen, Freeman, Myers, et al., 2020; Simonsen et al., 2019).

Experts suggest that for coaching to be effective, schools should have a solid SWPBIS foundation upon which PD and coaching builds (Bradshaw et al., 2018). For example, to address overrepresentation of minority students receiving behavioral infractions, Bradshaw and colleagues (2018) developed and tested a comprehensive approach to SWPBIS, PD, and coaching utilizing the "Double Check" model (see Hershfeldt et al., 2009). The approach developed by Bradshaw and colleagues included (a) focused DBDM related to disaggregated ODR data; (b) five, one-hour PD sessions on Double Check strategies (e.g., linking students' cultural identities to lesson planning and classroom management, reflective thinking, and developing authentic relationships); and (c) coaching to support Double Check strategies with embedded DBDM. Results from a randomized controlled trial indicated that the teachers who received coaching supports versus PD alone significantly reduced ODRs for Black students, employed more proactive classroom management strategies, and provided fewer negative comments to students (Bradshaw et al., 2018). Further, students of teachers who were coached demonstrated significantly lower disruptive behaviors and increased cooperation. However, the addition of coaching to the PD series did not significantly change teacher perceptions of stress or self-efficacy related to disproportionality and equity. Interestingly, both groups received the same PD series on the Double Check model, and both groups demonstrated an overall reduction in ODRs yet there was no significant difference between groups on reported stress reduction.

Another related study by Bradshaw and colleagues (2021) compared the effects of typical state-provided training in Tier 1 PBIS compared to training and coaching provided by the Maryland Safe and Supportive Schools (MDS3) training model (see Bradshaw, Debnam, et al., 2014). The MDS3 coaches provided support to building-level leadership teams, held schoolwide PD sessions, and established connections with district-level administration. The researchers found that teachers who received schoolwide PD in Tier 1 classroom management practices from MDS3 coaches demonstrated significant reductions of reactive behavior management strategies, even though teachers did not work directly with coaches. This finding is significant, as it provides evidence that universal Tier 1 trainings on classroom management strategies can impact teacher practices without intensive, individualized coaching. Bradshaw and colleagues further demonstrated that effectively coaching school teams can scale up implementation efforts to reduce reliance on external supports. Unfortunately to date, little research is available on PD and coaching for Tier 2 or Tier 3 interventions (Bruhn & McDaniel, 2021).

Self-Management. Through a targeted self-management plan, teachers can develop their own strategies to increase use of evidence-based classroom management practices, and several studies cited throughout this chapter have implemented such self-management strategies (e.g., Gage, Scott, et al., 2017; Simonsen, Freeman, Myers, et al., 2020; Simonsen et al., 2019; Simonsen et al., 2014). Self-management comprises a series of interrelated skills and strategies which enables individuals to recognize and control their own behavior to achieve a goal (Arslan, 2014). The most often used self-management strategies include self-monitoring, whereby the teacher sets a cuing device (e.g., kitchen timer, MotivAider) to prompt implementation of a targeted classroom management practice (e.g., praise, OTRs, prompts, feedback; Wills et al., 2018) and to self-record the number of times they used a classroom management practice (e.g., OTRs, prompts; Simonsen et al., 2020) for comparison to benchmarks. Another frequently utilized self-management strategy is goal setting the number of times a practice should be implemented within a designated class period and often includes self-evaluation of self-monitoring data (Bradshaw et al., 2018; Gage et al., 2017; Simonsen et al., 2014, 2020). Initial goal criteria could be set through reviewing several data sources (e.g., observer-collected baseline data of both student and teacher behavior, structured interviewing; Bradshaw et al., 2018; Sanetti & Collier-Meek, 2015), self-estimates of current behavior (Simonsen et al., 2017), or recommendations from relevant literature (Gage et al., 2017; Grassley-Boy et al., 2021). In studies of multi-tiered coaching supports, goals could be used as either a Tier 1 (Sanetti & Collier-Meek, 2015) or Tier 2 support (Gage et al., 2017; Simonsen et al., 2014).

To date, most research has targeted a single classroom management practice for improvement with self-management; however, it is possible that once teachers learn how to develop their own self-management plan, they could generalize these strategies to target other practices. In addition, once teachers become fluent with self-management, reliance on coaching may be reduced to periodic observation and feedback. Important considerations for researchers as they continue to develop self-management interventions include (a) evaluating the effect of self-managing a range of classroom practices (e.g., active supervision, reinforcing expectations, etc.); (b) studying maintenance and generalization effects; and (c) component analyses to determine which self-management strategies are most efficient and effective for various teacher and classroom characteristics (e.g., grade level, content area).

Performance Feedback. As indicated in prior sections, feedback is a critical component for adopting new practices and shaping behavior, and recent research has provided empirical evidence supporting performance feedback as a mechanism for improving teacher use of evidence-based practices. Feedback is most effective when it specifies a behavior of interest, is sincere, and immediately follows the behavior, and can be either corrective or affirmative. Feedback can be delivered in a variety of methods, including verbal, written, visual, and combinations, and recently, to increase efficiency and reduce costs, researchers have begun studying the use of technology to deliver feedback (Grassley-Boy et al., 2021). For example, emailed visual and written performance feedback has effectively improved teacher delivered praise (Hemmeter et al., 2010; Gage et al., 2017, 2018; Barton et al., 2014). In addition, recent research has demonstrated increases in praise statements when teachers received written and visual feedback via text messages (Barton et al., 2019; Grassley-Boy et al., 2021). The studies by Gage et al. (2017, 2018) and Grassley-Boy et al. (2021) utilized visual performance feedback as a Tier 2 strategy within a multi-tiered PD model, and all demonstrated increased teacher use of targeted skills. Interestingly, Gage et al. (2018) and Grassley-Boy et al. (2021) demonstrated improvements in teacher-delivered praise with performance feedback alone without the addition of self-management.

Packaged Interventions with Teacher Support Built in. Class-Wide Function-Related Intervention Team (CW-FIT; Wills et al., 2018), a group contingency management strategy, has repeatedly demonstrated improved teacher and student behaviors across a variety of contexts (Caldarella et al., 2016; Kamps, Wills, et al., 2015; Kamps, Conklin, et al., 2015; Speight et al., 2020; Wills et al., 2016). Teacher training of CW-FIT combines several PD and coaching components described previously (e.g., feedback on fidelity, self-management, in-vivo modeling by experts). As part of the implementation package, teachers then implemented several classroom management practices such as explicit instruction of classroom expectations, pre-corrects, and contingent reinforcement. In addition to overwhelmingly positive findings, CW-FIT consistently yields high levels of social validity from teachers and students, while requiring minimal time and resources to implement (Speight et al., 2020).

Further, several studies added a Tier 2 intervention (e.g., self-monitoring, response cards) for students who failed to respond to Tier 1 CW-FIT supports, and all reported improvements in academic engagement and reduced disruptive behaviors (Kamps, Conklin et al., 2015; Wills et al.,

2018; Van Camp et al., 2020). The study by Van Camp et al. (2020) initially tested the effects of a Tier 2 self-monitoring intervention with a student with low academic engagement, and after several days of self-monitoring, the student yielded little to no improvements. Interestingly, the researchers decided to implement CW-FIT, a Tier 1 intervention, rather than moving the student to Tier 3 supports, because few class-wide Tier 1 supports were in place and class-wide engagement was low. Results indicated that the addition of CW-FIT bolstered the effects of the self-monitoring intervention, yielding high, stable levels of engagement for the target student, and class-wide engagement also increased. This research highlights the need to further study the relationship between Tier 1 CWPBIS supports and referral to Tier 2 interventions, as the effects of Tier 2 interventions may be significantly impacted by classroom context and teacher behaviors (Van Camp et al., 2020).

Critical Issues and Future Research

SWPBIS, CWPBIS, and Academic Achievement. While there is a clear relationship between behavior and academic achievement (Algozzine et al., 2011), limited research on the direct relationship between CWPBIS and academic achievement is available. A 2015 literature review and longitudinal analysis by Gage and colleagues examined the extent to which academic outcomes were studied within PBIS literature and the associated impact on academic outcomes (Gage et al., 2015). Results indicated minimal evidence supporting SWPBIS implementation with fidelity and improved academic achievement at the schoolwide level. Gage and colleagues (2015) further studied statewide longitudinal data to determine the relative impact of SWPBIS on academic achievement, and again, found no statistically significant relationship between academics and schools implementing SWPBIS. In fact, the researchers found greater improvements in academic achievement in schools not implementing with fidelity, and that there was no overall difference between schools implementing SWPBIS (with and without fidelity) and schools not implementing SWPBIS. The primary limitation to this study, with respect to connecting CWPBIS and academic achievement, is that all results were analyzed using fidelity scores with the Schoolwide Evaluation Tool (SET; (Horner et al., 2004). The SET does not include measures of classroom fidelity; thus, inferences of classroom practices and academic achievement cannot be made. Researchers should consider utilizing fidelity measures which include classroom management items (e.g., DSFI, Center on PBIS, 2019; TFI, Algozzine et al., 2014). Further, given the emerging evidence linking SWPBIS with CWPBIS (e.g., Bradshaw et al., 2021; Childs et al., 2016), utilizing tools which include schoolwide, and class-wide items can help researchers better understand relationships between implementation fidelity, contextual influences (e.g., grade level, mobility rates, socioeconomic status, etc.), and outcomes.

A related study by Pas and colleagues (2019) examined the relationship between fidelity and academic and behavioral outcomes using overall and subscale scores on the SET. In a sample of 180 schools, including elementary, middle, and high school, the researchers found that the only subscale item significantly related to improved academic achievement was "Responding to Behavioral Violations" (Pas et al., 2019). Again, the SET does not measure fidelity of classroom-level implementation, so direct relationships between behavior response systems, academic achievement, and classroom management cannot be inferred. However, when considering these results alongside the findings by Childs et al. (2016), it is plausible that consistent implementation of behavior response plans in classrooms can improve academic achievement, though further research is needed to understand the relationship.

High School Implementation. Although there are a growing number of research studies targeting high school classroom management (Bradshaw et al., 2021; Freeman et al., 2018; Hawkins & Heflin, 2011; Kennedy et al., 2017), there remains a dearth of knowledge regarding adoption, implementation, and sustainability of CWPBIS at the high school level (Bradshaw et al., 2021; Wilkinson et al., 2021). For instance, research has demonstrated that it takes high schools longer to achieve

SWPBIS Tier 1 fidelity than elementary and middle schools, yet detailed examination into why this delay occurs and how to improve uptake remains unstudied. Further, high school teachers consistently struggle to implement evidence-based classroom management practices even when provided high quality PD (Bradshaw et al., 2021; Freeman et al., 2018). For example, Freeman et al. (2018) replicated the multi-tiered PD system studied by Simonsen et al. (2014) within a high school and found no marked increases in teacher use of skills taught (e.g., specific praise). The authors posited variables related to the high school context (e.g., complex organizational structures, less preservice classroom management training, increased academic focus), may impact the generalized effects of research conducted in elementary and middle school settings. Future research should focus on (a) learning what effective and ineffective classroom management practices are currently being used by high school teachers; (b) how to deliver PD to high school teachers which will improve classroom management practices; and (c) how individual classroom variables (e.g., instructional format, class size, content area, teacher experience, special education inclusion) mediate or moderate impact.

Social Validity. Social validity is the perceived importance of intervention goals, usability and feasibility of intervention procedures, and perceived significance of intervention outcomes (Marchant et al., 2012; Miramontes et al., 2011), and researchers have long demonstrated the interconnected relationship between implementation social validity, fidelity, outcomes, and sustainability. That is, higher social validity ratings predict higher implementation fidelity (Lane et al., 2009), and higher implementation fidelity predicts better outcomes and sustainability (Childs et al., 2016; Freeman et al., 2016; Mathews et al., 2014). Further, for educational initiatives to be sustainable and implemented on a large scale, they must demonstrate strong social validity (Fixsen et al., 2013; Horner et al., 2017; Snodgrass et al., 2018). In other words, teachers, leadership teams, and administrators are more likely to adopt initiatives if they perceive the initiative as feasible, cost effective, and leading to improved student outcomes (State et al., 2017). Unfortunately, the systematic measuring of social validity from a variety of stakeholders (e.g., teachers, students, school and district leadership teams, parents, community members) is vastly understudied and underreported (Estrapala et al., 2020; Snodgrass et al., 2018; Spear et al., 2013; State et al., 2017). A closer examination of the social validity of CWPBIS systems and evidence-based practices could shed light on why they are consistently underutilized in classrooms (Freeman et al., 2018; Reinke et al., 2013; Scott et al., 2011; Simonsen, Freeman, Myers, et al., 2020). Future research should include (a) developing reliable and valid social validity measures for a variety of stakeholders and contexts, and (b) systematically studying and reporting stakeholder perceptions of educational initiatives and interventions.

Conclusion

Empirical evidence continues to document the impact of CWPBIS on improved student social, emotional, and behavioral skills. Specifically, effective classroom management decreases teacher use of reactive behavior management strategies and reduce exclusionary discipline, while increasing instructional time, academic engagement, and improving classroom climate, teacher-student relationships, and student-student relationships (Bradshaw et al., 2021; Larson et al., 2021). Key to successful implementation is following the problem-solving framework of examining data to identify needed practices, and building the systems to increase implementation fidelity, consistency, and sustained implementation. Recent research has documented the necessary inclusion of classroom-specific systems that target increased teacher implementation of key instructional and management practices. While the current literature base, as discussed in this chapter, points to the need for effective professional development and follow-up technical assistance through self-monitoring and/or performance feedback to improve classroom management practices, additional research on creating the most parsimonious classroom support systems is warranted. In particular, the logic of differentiating classroom supports along a similar three-tiered continuum, while showing promise, needs further study before codifying the process within school and district PBIS implementation.

References

Algozzine, B., Barrett, S., Eber, L., George, H., Horner, R., Lewis, T., Putnam, B., Swain-Bradway, J., McIntosh, K., & Sugai, G. (2014). School-wide PBIS Tiered Fidelity Inventory. OSEP Technical Assistance Center on Positive Behavioral Interventions and Supports. www.pbis.org

Algozzine, B., Wang, C., & Violette, A. S. (2011). Reexamining the relationship between academic achievement and social behavior. *Journal of Positive Behavior Interventions*, 13(1), 3–16. https://doi.org/10.1177/109830070 9359084

Aloe, A. M., Shisler, S. M., Norris, B. D., Nickerson, A. B., & Rinker, T. W. (2014). A multivariate meta-analysis of student misbehavior and teacher burnout. *Educational Research Review*, 12, 30–44. https://doi.org/10.1016/j.edurev.2014.05.003

Archer, A. L., & Hughes, C. (2011). *Explicit Instruction: Effective and Efficient Teaching*. Guilford Publications.

Arslan, S. (2014). An investigation of the relationships between metacognition and self-regulation with structural equation. *International Journal of Educational Sciences*, 6(3), 603–611. https://doi.org/10.15345/iojes.2014.03.009

Barrett, C. A., & Pas, E. T. (2020). A cost analysis of traditional professional development and coaching structures in schools. *Prevention Science*, 21, 604–614. https://doi.org/10.1007/s11121-020-01115-5

Bastable, E., Massar, M. M., & McIntosh, K. (2020). A survey of team members' perceptions of coaching activities related to Tier 1 SWPBIS implementation. *Journal of Positive Behavior Interventions*, 22, 51–61. https://doi.org/10.1177/1098300719861566

Beam, H. D., & Mueller, T. G. (2017). What do educators know, do, and think about behavior? An analysis of special and general educators' knowledge of evidence-based behavioral interventions. *Preventing School Failure*, 61, 1–13. https://doi.org/10.1080/1045988X.2016.1164118

Bethune, K. S. (2017). Effects of coaching on teachers' implementation of tier 1 school-wide positive behavioral interventions and support strategies. *Journal of Positive Behavior Interventions*, 19, 131–142. https://doi.org/10.1177/1098300716680095

Bradshaw, C. P., Debnam, K. J., Lindstrom Johnson, S., Pas, E. T., Hershfeldt, P., Alexander, A., Barrett, S. B., & Leaf, P. J. (2014). Maryland's evolving system of social, emotional, and behavioral interventions in public schools: The Maryland Safe and Supportive Schools Project. *Adolescent Psychiatry*, 4, 194–206. https://doi.org/10.2174/221067660403140912163120

Bradshaw, C. P., Koth, C. W., Thornton, L. A., & Leaf, P. J. (2009). Altering school climate through school-wide positive behavioral interventions and supports: Findings from a group-randomized effectiveness trial. *Prevention Science*, 10, 100–115. https://doi.org/ 10.1007/s11121-008-0114-9

Bradshaw, C. P., Pas, E. T., Bottiani, J. H., Debnam, K. J., Reinke, W. M., Herman, K. C., & Rosenberg, M. S. (2018). Promoting cultural responsitvity and student engagement through double check coaching of classroom teachers: An efficacy study. *School Psychology Review*, 47, 118–134. https://doi.org/10.17105/SPR-2017-0119.V47-2

Bradshaw, C. P., Pas, E. T., Debnam, K. J., & Johnson, S. L. (2021). A randomized controlled trial of MTSS-B in high schools: Improving classroom management to prevent EBDs. *Remedial and Special Education*, 42, 44–59. https://doi.org/10.1177/0741932520966727

Bradshaw, C. P., Waasdorp, T. E., Debnam, K. J., & Lindstrom Johnson, S. (2014). Measuring school climate: A focus on safety, engagement, and the environment. *Journal of School Health*, 84, 593–604. https://doi.org/10.1111/josh.12186

Briesch, A. M., Chafouleas, S. M., & Chaffee, R. K. (2018). Analysis of state-level guidance regarding school-based, universal screening for social, emotional, and behavioral risk. *School Mental Health*, 10, 147–162. https://doi.org/10.1007/s12310-017-9232-5

Bruhn, A. L., Estrapala, S., Mahatmya, D., Rila, A., & Vogelgesang, K. (2019). Professional development on data-based individualization: A mixed research study. *Behavioral Disorders*. https://doi.org/10.1177/019874291 9876656

Bruhn, A. L., Lane, K. L., & Hirsch, S. E. (2014). A review of Tier 2 interventions conducted within multitiered models of behavioral prevention. *Journal of Emotional and Behavioral Disorders*, 22, 171–179. https://doi.org/10.1177/1063426613476092

Bruhn, A. L., & McDaniel, S. (2021). Tier 2: Critical issues in systems, practices, and data. *Journal of Emotional and Behavioral Disorders*, 29, 34–43. https://doi.org/10.1177/1063426620949859

Bruhn, A. L., Wehby, J. H., & Hasselbring, T. S. (2020). Data-based decision making for social behavior: Setting a research agenda. *Journal of Positive Behavior Interventions*, 22, 116–126. https://doi.org/10.1177/109830071 9876098

Bruhn, A. L., Woods-Groves, S., & Huddle, S. (2014). A preliminary investigation of emotional and behavioral screening practices in K-12 schools. *Education and Treatment of Children*, 37, 611–634. https://doi.org/10.1353/etc.2014.0039

Caldarella, P., Williams, L., Jolstead, K. A., & Wills, H. P. (2016). Managing student behavior in an elementary school music classroom: A study of class-wide function-related intervention teams. *Update: Applications of Research in Music Education, 35*, 23–30. https://doi.org/10.1177/8755123315626229

Center on Positive Behavioral Interventions and Supports (2019). Positive Behavioral Interventions and Supports District Systems Fidelity Inventory (DSFI) – Pilot version 0.1 University of Oregon. Retrieved from www.pbis.org

Chafouleas, S. M., Sanetti, L., Kilgus, S. P., & Maggin, D. M. (2012). Evaluating sensitivity to behavioral change using direct behavior rating single-item scales. *Exceptional Children, 78*, 491–505. https://doi.org/10.1177/001440291207800406

Childs, K. E., Kincaid, D., & George, H. P. (2016). The relationship between school-wide implementation of positive behavior intervention and supports and student discipline outcomes. *Journal of Positive Behavior Interventions, 18*, 89–99. https://doi.org/10.1177/1098300715590398

Childs, K. E., Kincaid, D., George, H. P., & Gage, N. (2016). The relationship between school-wide implementation of positive behavior intervention and supports and student discipline outcomes. *Journal of Positive Behavior Interventions, 18*, 89–99.

Coffee, J. H., & Horner, R. H. (2012). The sustainability of schoolwide positive behavior interventions and supports. *Exceptional Children, 78*, 407–422. https://doi.org/10.1177/001440291207800402

Cohen, R., Kincaid, D., & Childs, K. E. (2007). Measuring school-wide positive behavior support implementation: Development and validation of the benchmarks of quality. *Journal of Positive Behavior Interventions, 9*, 203–213.

Educational & Community Supports, PBISApps. (2021a). PBIS Assessment [Online App]. University of Oregon. www.pbisapps.org

Educational & Community Supports, PBISApps. (2021b). School-wide Information System Suite [Online App]. University of Oregon. www.pbisapps.org

Estrapala, S., Rila, A., & Bruhn, A. L. (2020). A systematic review of Tier 1 PBIS implementation in high schools. *Journal of Positive Behavior Interventions*, 1–15. https://doi.org/10.1177/1098300720929684

Fallon, L. M., McCarthy, S. R., & Sanetti, L. (2014). School-wide Positive Behavior Support (SWPBS) in the classroom: Assessing percieved challenges to consistent implementation in Connecticut schools. *Education and Treatment of Children, 37*, 1–24. https://doi.org/10.1353/etc.2014.0001

Fixsen, D. L., Blase, K., Metz, A., & Van Dyke, M. (2013). Statewide implementation of evidence-based programs. *Exceptional Children, 79*, 213–230. https://doi.org/10.1177/001440291307900206

Forness, S. R., Kim, J., & Walker, H. M. (2012). Prevalence of students with EBD: Impact on general education. *Beyond Behavior, 21*(2), 3–10.

Freeman, J., Kowitt, J., Simonsen, B., Wei, Y., Dooley, K., Gordon, L., & Maddock, E. (2018). A high school replication of targeted professional development for classroom management. *Remedial and Special Education, 39*, 144–157. https://doi.org/10.1177/0741932517719547

Freeman, J., La Salle, T., Ferrick, M., Derian-Toth, M., Bouckaert, J., & Feinberg, A. (October, 2020). *Building Momentum for PBIS Implementation in High Need* Districts. OSEP TA Center on PBIS, University of Oregon. Retrieved from www.pbis.org.

Freeman, J., Simonsen, B., Briere, D. E., & MacSuga-Gage, A. S. (2014). Pre-service teacher training in classroom management: a review of state accreditation policy and teacher preparation programs. *Teacher Education and Special Education, 37*(2), 106–120. https://doi.org/10.1177/0888406413507002

Freeman, J., Simonsen, B., McCoach, D. B., Sugai, G., Lombardi, A., & Horner, R. H. (2016). Relationship between school-wide positive behavior interactions and supports and academic, attendancd, and behavior outcomes in high schools. *Journal of Positive Behavior Interventions, 18*, 41–51. https://doi.org/10.1177/1098300715580992

Freeman, J., Sugai, G., Simonsen, B., & Everett, S. (2017). MTSS coaching: Bridging knowing into doing. *Theory Into Practice, 56*, 29–37. https://doi.org/10.1080/00405841.2016.1241946

Freeman, J., Yell, M. L., Shriner, J. G., & Katsiyannis, A. (2019). Federal policy on improving outcomes for students with emotional or behavioral disorders: Past, present, and future. *Behavioral Disorders, 44*, 97–106. https://doi.org/10.1177/0198742918814423

Gage, N., Grassley-Boy, N. M., & MacSuga-Gage, A. S. (2018). Professional development to increase teacher behavior-specific praise: A single-case design replication. *Psychology in the Schools, 55*. https://doi.org/10.1002/pits.22106

Gage, N., MacSuga-Gage, A. S., & Crews, E. (2017). Increasing teachers' use of behavior-specific praise using a multitiered system for professional development. *Journal of Positive Behavior Interventions, 19*, 239–251. https://doi.org/10.1177/1098300717693568

Gage, N., Scott, T., Hirn, R., & MacSuga-Gage, A. S. (2017). The relationship between teachers' implementation of classroom management practices and student behavior in elementary school. *Behavioral Disorders*. https://doi.org/10.1177/0198742917714809

Gage, N., Sugai, G., Lewis, T. J., & Brzozowy, S. (2015). Academic achievement and school-wide positive behavior supports. *Journal of Disability Policy Studies*, 15, 99–209. https://doi.org/10.1177/104420731 3505647

Gage, N., Whitford, D. K., & Katsiyannis, A. (2018). A review of schoolwide positive behavior interventions and supports as a framework for reducing disciplinary exclusions. *The Journal of Special Education*, 52, 142–151. https://doi.org/10127274/0606292146867961788744678

Gilmour, A., Majeika, C. E., Sheaffer, A., & Wehby, J. H. (2019). The coverage of classroom management in teacher evaluation rubrics. *Teacher Education and Special Education*, 42, 161–174. https://doi.org/10.1177/088840641 8781918

Gilmour, A., & Wehby, J. H. (2020). The association between teaching students with disabilities and teacher turnover. *Journal of Educational Psychology*, 112(1042–1060). https://doi.org/10.1037/edu0000394

Grassley-Boy, N. M., Gage, N., Reichow, B., MacSuga-Gage, A. S., & Lane, H. (2021). A conceptual replication of targeted professional development to increas teachers' behavior-specific praise. *School Psychology Review*. https://doi.org/10.1080/2372966X.2020.1853486

Hawkins, S. M., & Heflin, L. J. (2011). Increasing secondary teachers' behavior-specific praise using a video self-modeling and visual performance feedback intervention. *Journal of Positive Behavior Interventions*, 13, 97–108. https://doi.org/10.1177/1098300709358110

Hershfeldt, P., Sechrest, R., Pell, K. L., Rosenberg, M. S., Bradshaw, C. P., & Leaf, P. J. (2009). Double-Check: A framework of cultural respon- siveness applied to classroom behavior. *Teaching Exceptional Children Plus*, 6, 2–18.

Horner, R., Kincaid, D., Sugai, G., Lewis, T., Eber, L., Barrett, S. B., Dickey, C. R., Richter, M., Sullivan, E., Boezio, C., Algozzine, B., Reynolds, H., & Johnson, N. (2014). Scaling up school-wide positive behavioral interventions and supports: Experiences of seven states with documented success. *Journal of Positive Behavior Interventions*, 16, 197–208. https://doi.org/10.1177/1098300713503685

Horner, R., Sugai, G., & Fixsen, D. L. (2017). Implementing effective educational practices at scales of social importance. *Clinical Child and Family Psychology Review*, 20, 25–35. https://doi.org/10.1007/s10 567-017-0224-7

Horner, R. H., Sugai, G., & Anderson, C. M. (2010). Examining the evidence base for school-wide positive behavior support. *Focus on Exceptional Children*, 42(8), 1–14.

Horner, R. H., Todd, A. W., Lewis-Palmer, T., Irvin, L., Sugai, G., & Boland, J. B. (2004). The school-wide evaluation tool (SET): A research instrument for assessing school-wide positive behavior support. *Journal of Positive Behavior Interventions*, 6, 3–12.

Kamps, D., Conklin, C., & Wills, H. (2015). Use of self-management with the CW-FIT group contingency program. *Education and Treatment of Children*, 38, 1–32. https://doi.org/10.1353/ etc.2015.0003

Kamps, D., Wills, H., Bannister, H., Heitzman- Powell, L., Kottwitz, E., Hansen, B., & Fleming, K. (2015). Class-wide function-related interven- tion teams "CW-FIT" efficacy trial outcomes. *Journal of Positive Behavior Interventions*, 17, 134–145. https://doi.org/10.1177/1098300714565244

Kittelman, A., McIntosh, K., & Hoselton, R. (2019). Adoption of PBIS within school districts. *Journal of School Psychology*, 76, 159–167.

Kennedy, M. J., Hirsch, S. E., Rodgers, W. J., Bruce, A., & Lloyd, J. W. (2017). Supporting high school teachers' implementation of evidence-based classroom management practices. *Teaching and Teacher Education*, 63, 47–57. https://doi.org/10.1016/j.tate.2016.12.009

Koth, C. W., Bradshaw, C. P., & Leaf, P. J. (2008). A multilevel study of predictors of student perceptions of school climate: The effect of classroom-level factors. *Journal of Educational Psychology*, 100, 96–104. https://doi.org/ 10.1037/0022-0663.100.1.96

Kraft, M. A., Blazar, D., & Hogan, D. (2018). The effect of teacher coaching on instruction and achievement: A meta-analysis of the causal evidence. *Review of Educational Research*, 88, 547–588. https://doi.org/10.3102/ 0034654318759268

Kretlow, A. G., & Bartholomew, C. C. (2010). Using coaching to improve the fidelity of evidence-based practices: A review of studies. *Teacher Education and Special Education*, 33, 279–299.

Larson, K. E., Pas, E. T., Bottiani, J. H., Kush, J. M., & Bradshaw, C. P. (2021). A multidimensional and multilevel examination of student engagement and secondary school teachers' use of classroom management practices. *Journal of Positive Behavior Interventions*, 23, 149–162. https://doi.org/10.1177/1098300720929352

Lane, K. L., Kalberg, J. R., Bruhn, A. L., Driscoll, S. A., Wehby, J. H., & Elliott, S. N. (2009). Assessing social validity of school-wide positive behavior support plans: Evidence for the reliability and structure of the Primary Intervention Rating Scale. *School Psychology Review*, 38, 135–144.

Little, S. G., Akin-Little, A., & O'neill, K. (2015). Group contingency interventions with children – 1980–2010: A meta-analysis. *Behavior Modification*, 39, 322–341. https://doi.org/10.1177/0145445514554393

Lloyd, B. P., Bruhn, A. L., Sutherland, K. S., & Bradshaw, C. P. (2019). Progress and priorities in research to improve outcomes for students with or at risk for emotional and behavioral disorders. *Behavioral Disorders, 44*, 85–96. https://doi.org/p1s0:/./1d1o7i.o7r/g0/190.81714772/9019887048249818580

Maggin, D. M., & Bruhn, A. L. (2018). Evidence-based assessment and single-case research: A commentary for the special issue on direct behavior ratings. *Assessment for Effective Intervention, 2018*, 71–78. https://doi.org/10.1177/1534508417738722

Marchant, M., Heath, M. A., & Miramontes, N.Y. (2012). Merging empiricism and humanism: Role of social validity in the school-wide positive behavior support model. *Journal of Positive Behavior Interventions, 14*, 221–230. https://doi.org/10.1177/1098300712459356

Mathews, S., McIntosh, K., Frank, J. L., & May, S. L. (2014). Critical features predicting sustained implementation of school-wide positive behavioral interventions and supports. *Journal of Positive Behavior Interventions, 16*, 168–178. https://doi.org/10.1177/1098300713484065

Miramontes, N.Y., Marchant, M., Heath, M. A., & Fisher, T. L. (2011). Social validity of a positive behavior intervention and support model. *Education and Treatment of Children, 34*, 445–468. https://doi.org/10.1353/etc.2011.0032

Mitchell, B. S., Kern, L., & Conroy, M.A. (2019). Supporting students with emotional or behavioral disorders: State of the field. *Behavioral Disorders, 44*, 70–84. https://doi.org/10.1177/0198742918816518

Noltemeyer, A., Palmer, K., James, A. G., & Wiechman, S. (2018). School-wide positive behavioral interventions and supports (SWPBIS): A synthesis of existing research. *International Journal of School & Educational Psychology*. https://doi.org/10.1080/21683603.2018.1425169

Palmer, K., & Noltemeyer, A. (2019). Professional development in schools: predictors of effectiveness and implications for statewide PBIS trainings. *Teacher Development, 23*, 511–528. https://doi.org/10.1080/13664530.2019.1660211

Pas, E.T., Johnson, S. R., Debnam, K. J., Hulleman, C. S., & Bradshaw, C. P. (2019). Examining the relative utility of PBIS implementation fidelity scores in relation to student outcomes. *Remedial and Special Education, 40*, 6–15. https://doi.org/10.1177/0741932518805192

Reeves, T. D., Summers, K. H., & Grove, E. (2016). Examining the landscape of teacher learning for data use: The case of Illinois. *Cogent Education, 3*, 1–21. https://doi.org/10.1080/2331186X.2016.1211476

Reinke, W. M., Herman, K. C., & Stormont, M. (2013). Classroom-level Positive Behavior Supports in schools implementing SW-PBIS: Identifying areas for enhancement. *Journal of Positive Behavior Interventions, 15*, 39–50. https://doi.org/10.1177/1098300712459079

Reinke, W. M., Stormont, M., Herman, K. C., Puri, R., & Goel, N. (2011). Supporting children's mental health in schools: Teacher perceptions of needs, roles, and barriers. *School Psychology Quarterly, 26*, 1–13. https://doi.org/10.1037/a0022714

Riley-Tillman, T. C., Chafouleas, S. M., Sassu, K. A., Chanese, J. A. M., & Glazer, A. D. (2008). Examining the agreement of direct behavior ratings and systematic direct observation data for on-task and disruptive behavior. *Journal of Positive Behavior Interventions, 10*, 136–143. https://doi.org/10.1177/1098300707312542

Sanetti, L., & Collier-Meek, M. A. (2015). Data-driven delivery of implementation supports in a multi-tiered framework: A pilot study. *Psychology in the Schools, 52*, 815–828. https://doi.org/10.1002/pits.21861

Scott, T. M., Alter, P. J., & Hirn, R. G. (2011). An examination of typical classroom context in instruction for students with and without behavioral disorders. *Education and Treatment of Children, 2011*, 619–641. https://doi.org/10.1353/etc.2011.0039

Simonsen, B., Freeman, J., Dooley, K., VanLone, J., Byun, S., Xu, X., Lupo, K., Kooken, J., Gambino, A. J., Wilkinson, S., Walters, S., & Kern, L. (2020). Initial validation of the classroom management observation tool (CMOT). *School Psychology, 35*, 179–192. https://doi.org/10.1037/spq0000357

Simonsen, B., Freeman, J., Myers, D., Dooley, K., Maddock, E., Kern, L., & Byun, S. (2020). The effects of targeted professional development on teachers' use of empirically supported classroom management practices. *Journal of Positive Behavior Interventions, 22*, 3–14. https://doi.org/10.1177/1098300719859615

Simonsen, B., Freeman, J., Swain-Bradway, J., George, H. P., Putnam, B., Lane, K. L., Sprague, J., & Hershfeldt, P. (2019). Using data to support educators' implementation of positive classroom behavior support (PCBS) practices. *Education and Treatment of Children, 42*, 265–290. https://doi.org/doi.org/10.1353/etc.2019.0013

Simonsen, B., MacSuga-Gage, A. S., Briere, D. E., Freeman, J., Myers, D., Scott, T. M., & Sugai, G. (2014). Multitiered support framework for teachers' classroom-management practices: Overview and case study of building the triangle for teachers. *Journal of Positive Behavior Interventions, 16*, 179–190. https://doi.org/10.1177/1098300713484062

Snodgrass, M. R., Chung, M.Y., Meadan, H., & Halle, J. (2018). Social validity in single-case research: A systematic literature review of prevalence and application. *Research in Developmental Disabilities, 74*, 160–173. https://doi.org/10.1016/j.ridd.2018.01.007

Spear, C. F., Strickland-Cohen, K., Romer, N., & Albin, R. W. (2013). An examination of social validity within single-case research with students with emotional and behavioral disorders. *Remedial and Special Education, 34*, 357–370. https://doi.org/10.1177/0741932513490809

Speight, R., Whitby, P., & Kucharczyk, S. (2020). Impact of CW-FIT on student and teacher behavior in a middle school. *Journal of Positive Behavior Interventions, 22*, 195–206. https://doi.org/10.1177/1098300720910133

State, T. M., Harrison, J. R., Kern, L., & Lewis, T. (2017). Feasibility and acceptability of classroom-based interventions for students with emotional/ behavioral challenges at the high school level. *Journal of Positive Behavior Interventions, 19*, 26–36. https://doi.org/10.1177/1098300716648459

Stormont, M., Reinke, W. M., & Herman, K. C. (2011). Teachers' knowledge of evidence-based interventions and available school resources for children with emotional and behavioral problems. *Journal of Behavioral Education, 20*. https://doi.org/10.1007/s10864-011-9122-0

Sugai, G., & Horner, R. H. (2009). Responsiveness-to-intervention and school-wide positive behavior supports: integration of multi-tiered system approaches. *Exceptionality 17*(4), 223–227. https://doi.org/10.1080/09362830903235375

Swain-Bradway, J., Putnam, R., Freeman, J., Simonsen, B., George, H. P., Goodman, S., Yanek, K., Lane, K. L. & Sprague, J. (December 2017). *PBIS Technical Guide on Classroom Data: Using Data to Support Implementation of Positive Classroom Behavior Support Practices and Systems.* National Technical Assistance Center on Positive Behavior Interventions and Support

Van Camp, A., Wehby, J. H., Copeland, B. A., & Bruhn, A. L. (2020). Building from the bottom up: The importance of Tier 1 supports in the context of Tier 2 interventions. *Journal of Positive Behavior Interventions.* https://doi.org/10.1177/1098300720916716

Wilkinson, S., Freeman, J., Simonsen, B., Sears, S., Byun, S., Xu, X., & Luh, H. (2021). Professional development for classroom management: A review of the literature. *Educational Research and Evaluation*, 1–31. https://doi.org/10.1080/13803611.2021.1934034

Wills, H., Kamps, D., Fleming, K., & Hansen, B. (2016). Student and teacher outcomes of the class-wide function-related interven- tion team (CW-FIT) program. *Exceptional Children, 83*, 58–76. https://doi.org/10.1177/0014402 916658658

Wills, H., Wehby, J. H., Caldarella, P., Kamps, D., & Romine, R. S. (2018). Classroom management that works: A replication trial of the CW-FIT program. *Exceptional Children, 84*, 437–456. https://doi.org/10.1177/00144 02918771321

Zaheer, I., Maggin, D. M., McDaniel, S., McIntosh, K., Rodriguez, B. J., & Fogt, J. B. (2019). Implementation of promising practices that support students with emotional and behavioral disorders. *Behavioral Disorders, 44*, 117–128. https://doi.org/10.1177/0198742918821331

7

SUPPORTING STUDENTS' SOCIAL, EMOTIONAL, AND BEHAVIOR (SEB) GROWTH THROUGH TIER 2 AND 3 INTERVENTION WITHIN A MULTI-TIERED SYSTEM OF SUPPORTS (MTSS) FRAMEWORK

Brandi Simonsen, Karen Robbie, Katherine Meyer, Jennifer Freeman, Susannah Everett, and Adam B. Feinberg

UNIVERSITY OF CONNECTICUT

Introduction

Today's classrooms are (a) racially and ethnically diverse, with minoritized groups making up the majority of the school-aged population (Vespa et al., 2020); (b) inclusive, with the majority of students with disabilities spending the majority of time in general education classrooms (Hussar et al., 2020); and (c) contextually varied, with instruction occurring in whole-group, small-group, individual, and/or remote learning contexts (Center on PBIS et al., 2021).[1] Consequently, "classroom management" needs to be reconceptualized as positive and proactive social, emotional, and behavioral (SEB) supports that meet the needs of increasingly diverse learners and learning contexts.

To enable educators to support the SEB needs of each and every learner, many states, districts, and schools invest in multi-tiered system of support (MTSS) frameworks (Center on PBIS et al., 2021). For example, more than 25,000 schools have adopted positive behavioral interventions and supports (PBIS)—an evidence-based MTSS framework for SEB (www.pbis.org). Using a MTSS approach, educators organize positive and proactive practices within a continuum of support, beginning with universal (Tier 1) support for all, layering on targeted (Tier 2) support for students whose SEB needs persist after effective universal support, and prioritizing intensive (Tier 3) support for individual students with significant or complex SEB needs (Center on PBIS, 2021).

Effective educators implement, differentiate, and intensify critical evidence-based and culturally relevant SEB practices to meet the needs of all learners in all learning contexts. To support all students (Tier 1), educators design a welcoming and inclusive physical environment; intentionally connect with each student and family; collaboratively develop a small number of positively stated, culturally

DOI: 10.4324/9781003275312-9

relevant expectations (e.g., take care of others, self, environment); explicitly teach expectations and other critical SEB skills; actively engage students in learning; and provide positive and supportive specific feedback to encourage growth (Calderella et al., 2020; Chaparro et al., 2015; Leverson et al., 2021; Simonsen et al., 2008; Simonsen & Myers, 2015). For students requiring additional support, educators use data to enhance implementation. For example, they may increase the dosage (e.g., frequency, duration), specificity (e.g., identified SEB skills, scripted lessons, system to prompt and reinforce), and/or other key implementation dimensions to further target (Tier 2) or individualize (Tier 3) SEB practices. Importantly, educators coordinate and align implementation throughout the continuum.

In this chapter, we describe how educators implement effective SEB support within a MTSS framework to meet the needs of all learners. We begin with a clear focus on how to implement and differentiate universal SEB practices to support each and every learner within a classroom. As other chapters in this text provide a foundation for universal classroom management (Chapter 2) and MTSS (Chapter 3), we move beyond the universal foundation to discuss how to (a) differentiate support within Tier 1 to increase the power of universal prevention and identify students who need additional support, (b) target SEB support within Tier 2 and identify students who require more intensive intervention, and (c) use team-based comprehensive assessment, including functional behavioral assessment (FBA), to develop and implement individualized intensive SEB supports documented on a positive behavior support plan (BSP). Within each section, we highlight empirical support and practical recommendations to support implementation. We conclude with a discission of issues, trends, and future directions for research and practice.

SEB Support within MTSS Framework

Throughout tiers and consistent with other comprehensive approaches (e.g., Dunlap et al., 2010), we emphasize four critical components of effective SEB support: prevent, teach, respond, and decide (see Figure 7.1).

- **Prevent** refers to antecedent strategies that set students up for success and minimize the likelihood of SEB challenges.
- **Teach** refers to strategies to explicitly teach critical SEB skills, including skills that replace contextually inappropriate behaviors.
- **Respond** refers to consequence strategies that (a) increase the likelihood that students engage in critical SEB skills and contextually appropriate behavior and (b) decrease the likelihood that students engage in contextually inappropriate behaviors.
- **Decide** refers to using data to guide implementation, including (a) identifying students who require additional support, (b) matching need to support, and (c) monitoring implementation and outcomes to adjust (e.g., intensify, adapt, or fade) support as needed.

Tier 1: Universal SEB Support

Educators establish effective learning environments by implementing tier 1 practices to provide a strong foundation of differentiated universal support for all students. Specifically, educators (a) prevent SEB challenges and set students up for success; (b) explicitly teach SEB expectations and skills; (c) respond to students in ways that promote positive, contextually appropriate outcomes; and (d) use data to decide whether they are implementing Tier 1 supports with fidelity, differentiating to provide a strong foundation of support for all students, and identifying students who require additional layers of support (Tier 2 and/or 3) to experience success. Table 7.1 summarizes each practice, describes considerations for implementation, and presents considerations to differentiate each practice to provide

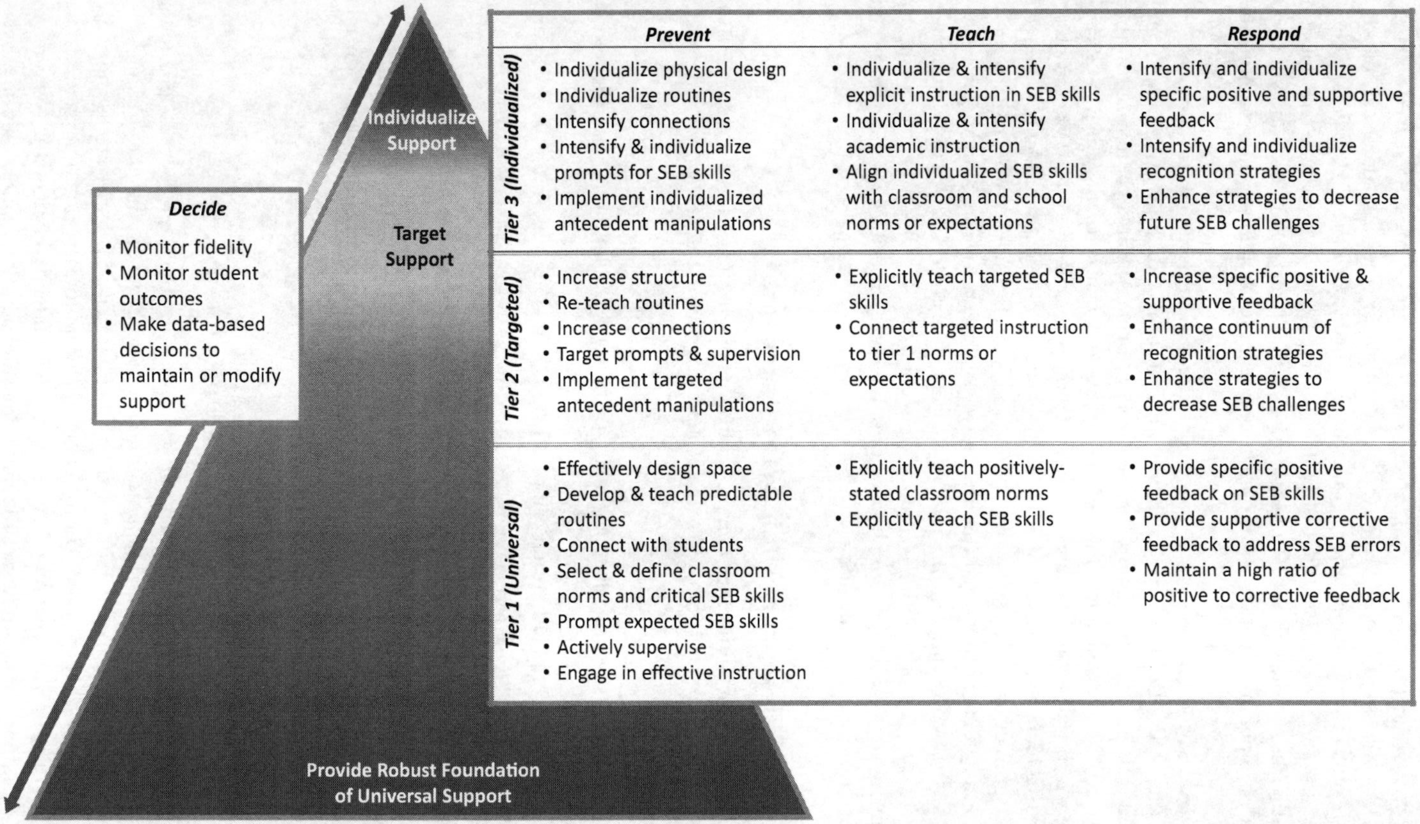

	Prevent	*Teach*	*Respond*
Tier 3 (Individualized)	• Individualize physical design • Individualize routines • Intensify connections • Intensify & individualize prompts for SEB skills • Implement individualized antecedent manipulations	• Individualize & intensify explicit instruction in SEB skills • Individualize & intensify academic instruction • Align individualized SEB skills with classroom and school norms or expectations	• Intensify and individualize specific positive and supportive feedback • Intensify and individualize recognition strategies • Enhance strategies to decrease future SEB challenges
Tier 2 (Targeted)	• Increase structure • Re-teach routines • Increase connections • Target prompts & supervision • Implement targeted antecedent manipulations	• Explicitly teach targeted SEB skills • Connect targeted instruction to tier 1 norms or expectations	• Increase specific positive & supportive feedback • Enhance continuum of recognition strategies • Enhance strategies to decrease SEB challenges
Tier 1 (Universal)	• Effectively design space • Develop & teach predictable routines • Connect with students • Select & define classroom norms and critical SEB skills • Prompt expected SEB skills • Actively supervise • Engage in effective instruction	• Explicitly teach positively-stated classroom norms • Explicitly teach SEB skills	• Provide specific positive feedback on SEB skills • Provide supportive corrective feedback to address SEB errors • Maintain a high ratio of positive to corrective feedback

Provide Robust Foundation of Universal Support

Individualize Support

Target Support

Decide
• Monitor fidelity
• Monitor student outcomes
• Make data-based decisions to maintain or modify support

Figure 7.1 Illustrates how to prevent, teach, respond, and decide within each tier of a MTSS framework

Adapted and reprinted with permission from MTSS in the Classroom (Center on PBIS Practice Brief; Simonsen et al., 2021)

Table 7.1 Tier 1 Prevent, Teach, Respond, and Decide Practices with Considerations for Implementation and Differentiation

Tier 1 Practice	Considerations for Implementation of Tier 1	Considerations for Differentiation of Tier 1
PREVENT Effectively design space	• Design the classroom environment to facilitate typical instructional activities (e.g., small group, whole group, individual, and/or remote learning), facilitate transitions (e.g., plan movement among parts of room, organize instructional materials), and minimize distractions. • Create purposeful visual prompts and displays to support learning (e.g., reminders of strategies), access to materials (e.g., labeled bins), and independent engagement with academic activities.	• Consider diverse mobility and other physical or mental health when designing the classroom environment (e.g., pathways that ensure wheelchair access, quiet or calming spaces). • Consider diverse language, reading, and related abilities when developing visual prompts (e.g., pair pictures with text).
Develop & teach routines	• Post and review schedule for the day or class period. • Define, explicitly teach, prompt, and regularly review procedures for common activities (e.g., arrival, dismissal, turning in homework, working in groups).	• Consider breaking common routines or procedures into discrete steps (i.e., develop a task analysis), and teach, prompt, and review simple steps for students who need additional support with the routine. • Adjust and reteach routines as needed. Some students will need more frequent review, structure, and opportunities to rehearse routines and/or visual supports (e.g., picture sequence of routine).
Connect with students	• At the start of each year, plan activities to get to know each student, connect with each family to establish a positive relationship, and deliberately create a welcoming environment. • Use simple strategies, like positive greetings at the door, to connect with students at the start of each day. • Throughout the day, provide opportunities for authentic connection (e.g., lunch bunch, peer-to-peer connections in academic routines, cooperative group work). • Engage families and students in bi-directional communication; for example, move beyond a newsletter where educators share information and invite feedback and participation to create an engaged and vibrant classroom community.	• Provide families and students with a variety of opportunities to connect that (a) honor family and student identity, (b) consider a range of needs (e.g., language, ability, transportation, scheduling), and (c) engage families and students across time (e.g., beyond back-to-school night or open house). • When implementing simple connection strategies (e.g., greetings), offer a range of ways for students to engage, ensure communication supports are in place to enable each student to participate, and differentiate content of greeting to meet the needs of each and every student.

(continued)

Table 7.1 Cont.

Tier 1 Practice	Considerations for Implementation of Tier 1	Considerations for Differentiation of Tier 1
Select & define classroom norms and critical SEB skills	• Adopt school norms, or expectations, for the classroom (if school has a few positively stated norms). If school norms do not exist, engage students in selecting a few (3–5) positively stated classroom norms (e.g., take care of others, environment, and self). • Define norms, or expectations, in the context of classroom routines. Consider using a matrix that specifies norms (row headers), routines (column headers), and examples of SEB skills that are consistent with norms within each routine (in each box of the matrix).	• Ensure all students are able to actively engage in selecting and defining classroom norms, or expectations. For example, consider diverse communication and language needs when planning activities to select and define norms. • With students, identify a range of critical SEB skills that are contextually, culturally, and developmentally appropriate for all students to ensure each student is able to "see" themself in the norms (representation) and engage in and skills represented in the matrix (skill differentiation).
Prompt Expected SEB Skills	• Remind students of critical SEB skills before presenting them with the opportunity to perform that skill (e.g., at the start of class, before transitions, prior to starting an activity). • Ensure prompts are specific and describe the expected SEB skill.	• Use non-verbal prompts, such as visuals, gestures, and modeling, in addition to verbal prompts, to support the understanding of all students. • Provide visual reminders (e.g., checklist, picture sequence of expected behaviors within routine) to promote independence
Actively supervise	• Regularly scan and circulate through entire classroom space (physical or virtual) during all classroom routines • While supervising, educators check in with individual students and use proximity, precorrections, and specific verbal praise to promote on-task behavior.	• Increase supervision and interactions for students who require additional prompts, praise, and redirection to stay engaged. • Adjust mode of supervision to meet the needs of students in diverse learning contexts (e.g., electronically monitor engagement in virtual environments) and/or with diverse needs (e.g., consider praise notes for students who do not benefit from adult attention)
Engage in effective instruction	• Engage students in instruction through frequent and various opportunities to respond (OTRs) that include a mixture of individual and choral or unison responding. • Vary OTRs to match the activity and provide a range of ways for students to participate across OTRs. Consider response modalities (e.g., verbal, gestural, written, or electronic responses); scope (individual, small-group, or whole class unison responses, or embedded in polls or chat during virtual instruction. • Select instructional materials that are evidence-based and culturally relevant, so students see their identities reflected in pictures, text, and other aspects of instructional materials.	• Pre-teach OTRs to students who require additional support to respond so that each and every student is able to successfully engage in OTRs. • Ensure alternative augmentative communication devices are available and programmed to enable participation.

TEACH	Explicitly Teach Positively Stated Classroom Norms	• Explicitly teach classroom norms, as defined in the classroom matrix described in prevent section, using a range of examples (and non-examples) to teach the "general case" of SEB skills that are consistent (and inconsistent) with norms during each routine. • Use a model (I do), lead (we do), and test (you do) format to ensure that each student has an opportunity to demonstrate and receive feedback on engaging in behaviors that are consistent with classroom norms within each routine.	• Enhance instruction with visuals and social narratives to ensure norms are clear to all students. Some students may benefit from visuals of norms that they can keep with them for reference. • Provide extra opportunities to practice and receive praise for modeling norms to students who may need it, especially prior to tasks or times that have presented challenges to students in the past.
	Explicitly Teach SEB Skills	• In addition to teaching SEB skills in the context of classroom norms and routines, educators may (a) use data to identify additional SEB skills (e.g., asking for help, problem solving) and develop lesson plans to teach these skills, (b) adopt an evidence-based curriculum, or (c) use a combination of these approaches to promote students' SEB growth. • Regardless of approach (e.g., curriculum or teacher developed lessons), engage students in explicit instruction (model, lead, test), make connections between skills and classroom norms, and provide practice opportunities and specific feedback throughout classroom routines.	• Consider diverse abilities and needs when prioritizing SEB skills to teach. • If adopting an evidence-based curriculum, consider contextual and cultural relevance of lessons. • Consider visual (e.g., picture sequence to prompt problem solving) and alternative or augmentative communication strategies that enable all students to engage in social/communication skill. • Provide additional opportunities to review, practice, and receive feedback on SEB skills that are challenging for some students.
RESPOND	Provide specific positive feedback for SEB skills	• Provide specific verbal praise that labels the specific SEB skill to acknowledge individuals and groups for engaging in SEB skills that are consistent with classroom norms. • Ask students to complete a survey for preferred praise or acknowledgement strategies to maximize the contextual and cultural relevance for all learners. • Match acknowledgement approaches to students' interest, developmental level, etc. and to ensure acknowledgement is reinforcing (i.e., enhances SEB skills).	• Provide even more specific verbal praise for students who experience error corrections. • Praise effort, improvement, and progress toward key SEB skills. • Consider additional acknowledgement approaches (e.g., group contingency, token economy) to increase opportunities for reinforcement during challenging routines or times of year

(continued)

Table 7.1 Cont.

Tier 1 Practice	Considerations for Implementation of Tier 1	Considerations for Differentiation of Tier 1
Provide supportive corrective feedback to address SEB errors	• Correct SEB errors in a supportive manner, similar to academic corrections: Calmly inform the student of the error and appropriate SEB skill for the context (e.g., "Instead of running, we agreed to walk in the classroom to be safe."). • Ensure corrections are brief, provide an opportunity for the student to perform the desired behavior and receive praise, and redirect the student to the desired skill. • Teach and use strategies to reduce implicit bias when responding to student SEB errors (e.g., identify vulnerable decision points, implement neutralizing routines)[2]	• Provide visual supports and additional opportunities to practice the appropriate behavior in addition to verbal error correction. • Re-teach SEB skills as necessary to reduce likelihood of future behavior errors. • Consider additional low-intensity response approaches (e.g., private conference, reflection sheet, planned ignoring, differential reinforcement).
Maintain a high ratio of positive to corrective feedback	• For every correction, provide at least 5 praise statements or positive interactions. This sets the tone for a reinforcing classroom environment.	• Maintain an even higher praise to correction ratio (i.e., 9:1 for students with disabilities and those requiring additional support) in order to increase engagement, decrease disruption, and maintain a positive environment.
Monitor fidelity	• Collect simple fidelity data to self-assess the use of the above practices (e.g., tally positive to corrective statements, count opportunities to respond).	• If data indicate fidelity of implementation is lower than desired, set a goal to improve (e.g., increase specific praise rate), continue to monitor, seek additional training and coaching support if appropriate, and celebrate implementation efforts and improvements in fidelity.
Monitor student outcomes	• Collect simple outcome data on students SEB skills to (a) guide implementation and differentiation of Tier 1 support for all students and (b) determine who is benefitting and who may need additional support. • Monitor outcomes for all student subgroups (i.e., race/ethnicity, gender, language status, disability status) to ensure equitable access and benefit.	• If data indicate that Tier 1 support is not meeting the needs of students, collect additional data on (a) students' skills (e.g., SEB, academic, engagement/attendance data) and (b) context associated with challenges (e.g., specific routines, content, activities, time of day) to more clearly define the concern and identify an action plan to enhance support.

DECIDE

| Make data-based decisions to maintain or modify support | • Implement universal screening process to identify students who may require additional SEB support to meet targeted (Tier 2) or intensive (Tier 3) support needs.
• Use a variety of data sources (fidelity, outcome, screening) to make decisions about (a) increasing or decreasing support to meet the needs of all students (Tier 1) or (b) considering additional support for some (Tier 2) or a few (Tier 3) students with more targeted or intensive needs, respectively. | • Monitor implementation and outcomes of enhanced Tier 1 support, and consider whether individual students also require targeted (Tier 2) or intensive (Tier 3) support in one or more areas (e.g., SEB skills, academic skills). |

Note: Adapted and reprinted with permission from *MTSS in the Classroom* (Center on PBIS Practice Brief; Simonsen et al., 2021) a robust foundation of Tier 1 support for all learners in the classroom. (See Chapter 2 for additional detail about the key features of Tier 1 classroom practice.)

At the school level, representative leadership teams use the MTSS framework to build positive and proactive systems to support educators that invest in effective and on-going professional development (explicit training and job-embedded coaching), prioritize wellness, actively engage stakeholders (representative educators, families, students, and community partners), and celebrate implementation successes (Center on PBIS et al., 2021). Beyond organizing practices and systems, the school leadership team members collect, summarize, and use data within the MTSS framework to match students' needs to practices within tiers, monitor implementation and outcomes, and enhance implementation of key practices or systems to improve supports for students and educators, respectively (Center on PBIS, 2020). By investing in systems and using data, school leadership teams can increase the likelihood of effective implementation and positive student outcomes.

Tier 2: Targeted SEB Support

Even when tier 1 classroom SEB support practices are robust and implemented with fidelity, some students experience SEB challenges that interrupt learning for themselves or others. As indicated in Table 7.1, the Tier 1 school leadership team may identify these students through universal screening and regular data review procedures. Educators target their approach and implement Tier 2 support to prevent, teach, respond, and decide to (a) address common needs among students (e.g., identified need for SEB skill instruction, enhanced prompting and feedback) and (b) increase the likelihood that students benefit from SEB support by layering targeted (Tier 2) support on a strong foundation of universal (Tier 1) support.

Targeted support practices. One common Tier 2 approach is Check-In, Check-Out (CICO; e.g., Hawken et al., 2021). In CICO, a student checks in with a preferred adult (e.g., teacher, instructional assistant) in the morning, carries a "daily progress report" (DPR: i.e., point card) based on Tier 1 expectations throughout the day to recruit feedback related to after each instructional activity or period, checks out with the same adult in the afternoon, and brings their DPR home to share with a family member. Another common approach is targeted small-group social skills instruction (e.g., Cho Blair et al., 2020; Kern et al., 2020; Lane et al., 2009). These approaches are not mutually exclusive. Educators may combine CICO and social skills instruction, though additional research is needed to guide the careful integration of these approaches (e.g., Eklund, et al. 2020). Table 7.2 provides considerations for educators to implement targeted practices to prevent, teach, respond, and decide in classrooms in general and within two common Tier 2 approaches (CICO and social skills instruction). There are other empirically supported Tier 2 approaches, including self-management (e.g., Briesch & Chafouleas, 2009; Van Camps, 2021), Check and Connect (e.g., Anderson et al., 2004), Check, Connect, & Expect (e.g., Cheney et al., 2009), and First Step to Success (e.g., Walker et al., 2009).

School systems to support Tier 2. To maximize success of Tier 2 support, a universal (Tier 1) school leadership team supports educators to ensure a strong foundation of Tier 1 (Van Camp et al., 2021). Then, a complementary school Tier 2 school team coordinates Tier 2 implementation. This team may also be known as a student/child study team, teacher assistance team, or similar team that uses data to meet students' targeted support needs. Smaller schools may combine school-level Tier 2 and Tier 3 teams to coordinate implementation of targeted and intensive support. School-based coaches facilitate this team, which includes a school administrator, a representative group of educators, and relevant community providers (e.g., mental health). Together, members of this team

- adopt a range of evidence-based and culturally-relevant Tier 2 approaches (e.g., CICO, social skills training, cognitive behavioral interventions) that (a) match targeted needs of their student population and (b) are efficient and standardized to ensure implementation is feasible;

Table 7.2 Tier 2 Prevent, Teach, Respond, and Decide Practices in Classrooms

Tier 2 Practice	Considerations for Implementing Tier 2 Practices in Classroom	Considerations for Implementing Check-In/Check-Out (CICO)	Considerations for Implementing Social Skills Instruction
Increase structure	• Consider strategies to increase structure within the classroom environment to further support students' SEB success (e.g., seating arrangement, designated space for calming routine, visual prompts for key SEB skills).	• Implement CICO to provide additional structure to student routines at the start (check-in) and end (check-out) of each activity and each day. • Design the physical space to accommodate CICO (e.g., basket or clipboard to collect paperwork, location for quick checks in/out).	• Select a space for targeted social skills instruction that maximizes structure and minimizes distractions (e.g., quite space in a conference room or office, table in classroom when all students are engaged in small group activities).
Re-teach routines	• Increase specificity and predictability in students' routines, including increased opportunities to practice SEB skills, take breaks, and other targeted adjustments to meet the needs of small groups of students.	• When introducing CICO, teach new CICO routines to students and communicate new routines to families. During this instruction, review or re-teach classroom routines and norms, as appropriate.	• Establish and teach predictable routines for targeted social skills instruction, which may occur in small groups in a pull-out context, including a re-entry routine for students to rejoin their classroom community after instruction.
Increase connections	• Provide targeted opportunities for peer-to-peer connections (e.g., provide opportunity to work with peers on tasks, peer-to-peer praise or acknowledgement). • Provide targeted opportunities for student-to-educator connections (e.g., lunch bunch, private conference, 1:1 walk during PE). • Provide targeted opportunities for family connections (e.g., virtual coffee hour, drop-in family time), and increase outreach to families of students with targeted SEB needs.	• Use CICO to enhance opportunities to connect with students (during check-ins at the start of day, end of each activity, and end of day), and provides another opportunity for students to connect with a family member (during home check in). • Share brief positive comments or other information with family members on the daily progress report (DPR), and invite a similar exchange from the family members by including space for family comments on the DPR.	• Intentionally create opportunities for students to practice SEB skills and connect with each other during and outside of targeted social skills instruction. • Because a range of trained educators (e.g., a school psychologist, counselor, special educator, and/or social worker) may facilitate targeted social skills instruction, this activity provides an opportunity to further enhance students' connections with the broader school community.

(continued)

PREVENT

Table 7.1 Cont.

Tier 2 Practice	Considerations for Implementing Tier 2 Practices in Classroom	Considerations for Implementing Check-In/Check-Out (CICO)	Considerations for Implementing Social Skills Instruction
Target prompts and supervision	• Increase visual and verbal prompts for targeted SEB skills • Use active supervision to increase proximity, provide additional opportunities for specific praise (as students are engaged in SEB or academic skills), and/or provide timely redirections to use SEB skills in context	• During morning check-in, provide prompts and precorrections for the day ahead, check to ensure the student has necessary materials, and give the student a blank DPR, if you are the CICO facilitator. • The DPR includes a written reminder of norms, as items to be rated. • At the start of each class period or activity, briefly check-in with each student participating in CICO (and collect their DPR). During this brief check-in, connect positively, prompt key SEB skills (connected to classroom norms), and transition to the first classroom activity.	• Provide an opportunity for students to communicate skills learned during social skills instruction with the educators and peers in their classrooms. • Consider a visual prompt (e.g., handout, poster, card) to prompt SEB skills learned during small group in the classroom. • Provide targeted prompt (e.g., verbal reminders, gesture to visual of targeted skills) to encourage SEB skills before and during each classroom activity.
Implement targeted antecedent manipulations	• Consider additional targeted adjustments to the classroom context to support students (e.g., increase opportunities for choice, adjust task difficulty, adjust response options)	• In addition to the enhanced routines provided by CICO, consider other opportunities to increase choice, prompt other classroom SEB skills during CICO, and remind of available reinforcers.	• In addition to prompting SEB skills taught during targeted social skills instruction, consider providing additional opportunities to practice, choice, and other relevant antecedent supports.
Explicitly teach targeted SEB skills	• Reteach and provide additional opportunities for practice for SEB skills taught in Tier 1 • When re-teaching, design lessons to be more explicit, more specific, and/or delivered in small-groups to support targeted SEB skills • Build in frequent opportunities for review	• When teaching CICO routines, re-teach critical SEB skills in the context of classroom and schoolwide norms • During brief check-ins at the beginning of each day, at the end of each activity, and at the end of each day, provide mini-lesson (or review) of critical SEB skills connected to norms where data indicate re-teaching would be beneficial	• With targeted social skills instruction, educators often adopt and implement an evidence-based curriculum that explicitly teaches SEB skills in targeted areas of need. Some curricula may be design to target a specific need (e.g., managing anxiety), and others may provide options for educators to select specific lessons based on targeted needs.

TEACH

RESPOND	Connect instruction to Tier 1 norms or expectations	• Connect targeted SEB skill instruction to overall classroom norms; teach, prompt, and reinforce SEB skills for all students. • Provide extra doses of instruction using varied examples and multiple opportunities to role-play, problem-solve, or demonstrate how to use the skills appropriately within the classroom	• Ensure the daily progress report is based on school and classroom norms (e.g., take care of others, environment, and self), so that written prompts on daily report card and verbal reminders, reteaching, and feedback are all directly connected to Tier 1 norms.	• Educators teach norms for the group activity that are consistent with school and classroom norms. • Explicitly connect SEB skills learned as part of social skills instruction with classroom norms. During social skills instruction, ensure educator is familiar with each student's classroom norms (if students are grouped across classrooms), and explicitly teach how each skill is connected to norms.
	Increase specific positive and supportive feedback	• Increase frequency of specific praise, and provide praise in a manner consistent with student preference. • Increase specificity of supportive feedback, and increase opportunities to practice targeted SEB skill following a SEB error (i.e., contextually inappropriate behavior).	• At the end of each class activity or period, (a) provide specific positive or supportive feedback on the students' behavior and (b) rate the students' behavior on the daily progress report (typically on a 3-point scale reflecting whether the student's behavior did not meet, met, or exceeded expectations). • At the end of the day, the CICO facilitator checks out with the student, reviewing the day, summarizing ratings and feedback, determining if the student met the goal for the day, giving the student a copy of the DPR to bring home, and entering data from the DPR into a CICO database.	• During targeted social skills instruction, provide specific positive and supportive feedback on engagement and use of specific SEB skills. • During typical classroom activities (i.e., outside of targeted social skills instruction), provide specific positive and supportive feedback to encourage and improve SEB skills, enhance fluency, and promote generalization and adaptation of skills across contexts.
	Enhance continuum of recognition strategies	• Implement a continuum of acknowledgement strategies that vary in form and function (e.g., attention, tangible items, activities, breaks from work, sensory), availability (e.g., continuously available vs. special occasion), and schedule (e.g., frequent vs. infrequent, predictable vs. unpredictable).	• In addition to providing feedback and ratings, consider developing a menu of acknowledgement activities (e.g., lunch with educator and peer, homework pass) students can chose from on days they meet their goal. (This could be a token economy, with activities priced at different values and "purchased" with points, or simply available on days students meet goals.)	• In addition to feedback, consider adopting an acknowledgement system (for entire class or small group of students participating in targeted social skills instruction) to recognize and reinforce key SEB skills.

(continued)

Table 7.1 Cont.

Tier 2 Practice	Considerations for Implementing Tier 2 Practices in Classroom	Considerations for Implementing Check-In/Check-Out (CICO)	Considerations for Implementing Social Skills Instruction
Enhance strategies to decrease SEB challenges	• Implement a least-to-most continuum to address SEB errors. For example, consider enhanced implementation of proximity, redirection, reteaching, and other targeted response strategies (e.g., differential reinforcement, problem-solving conference) based on targeted student need. • Continue to implement neutralizing routines to reduce implicit bias when implementing strategies to decrease SEB challenges	• In addition to providing supportive corrective feedback, consider re-teaching CICO routines during which students continue to experience challenges (e.g., accepting feedback, transitioning between activities). • Also consider strategies from least-to-most continuum (see box on left) to address SEB errors.	• In addition to providing supportive corrective feedback, consider re-teaching targeted SEB skills that replace contextually inappropriate behaviors (e.g., teach student to request help instead of ripping up classwork). • Provide additional targeted social skills instruction in natural contexts to facilitate generalization. • Consider additional strategies from least-to-most continuum (see box on left).
Monitor fidelity	• For each targeted strategy, monitor implementation fidelity to ensure strategies are implemented as intended.	• Monitor fidelity of each CICO component (check in and out activities, completion of daily progress report, home check-in).	• Monitor fidelity of targeted social skills instruction and re-entry routine.
Monitor student outcomes	• Monitor students' SEB skills in an efficient way to examine progress and benefit from targeted supports. • Monitor targeted outcomes for all student subgroups (i.e., race/ethnicity, gender, language status, disability status) to ensure equitable access and benefit.	• Count and summarize each student's daily progress report ratings (i.e., points) to monitor individual student outcomes, and aggregate data at the school, grade, and/or classroom levels to monitor overall program outcomes.	• Monitor students' use of SEB skills during targeted social skills instruction and in the natural context (during typical classroom and school routines). Summarize at individual student and group level.

DECIDE

114

Make data-based decisions to maintain or modify support	• Based on fidelity and outcome data, adjust implementation and/or type of targeted support to maximize benefit to students.
	• To support targeted practice implementation, consider self-management strategies including (a) increased prompting; (b) self-monitoring implementation of key practices (e.g., increased prompts or praise) with a paper and pencil tally, counter, or app on a smart device (e.g., Be+; Center on PBIS, 2019); and (c) celebrating implementation successes.
		• Based on fidelity and outcome data, adjust implementation support.
		• For individual students, decide to maintain or modify support.
		  o If a student has made consistent progress, consider fading to self-managed CICO and/or Tier 1 support.
		  o If a student is not benefiting from standard CICO, consider adaptations based on function of behavior (e.g., Breaks are Better; Boyd & Anderson, 2013), specific skill needs (e.g., academic/SEB skill support), or other adaptations (Majeika et al., 2020).
		  o If a student continues to display chronic or significant SEB challenges, consider intensive and individualized SEB support (Tier 3).
			• Based on fidelity and outcome data, adjust targeted social skills instruction groups to better meet the needs of all students in the group.
			• For individual students, decide to maintain or modify support.
			  o If students are making consistent progress, consider fading to SEB instruction in Tier 1.
			  o If a student is not benefiting from targeted social skills instruction, consider adjusting elements instruction (e.g., schedule, instructor, focus, peers) and/or introducing a different Tier 2 support (e.g., CICO).
			  o If a student continues to display chronic or significant SEB challenges, consider intensive and individualized SEB support (Tier 3).

Note: Adapted and reprinted with permission from *MTSS in the Classroom* (Center on PBIS Practice Brief; Simonsen et al., 2021)

- use data to identify students who need additional support (e.g., universal screening, reviewing existing data with clear decision rules, considering requests for assistance);
- select appropriate and efficient Tier 2 practices for groups of students with similar needs to further prevent, teach, and respond to SEB needs of students;
- support authentic educator, student, and family engagement in the Tier 2 support; and
- monitor fidelity and outcomes of Tier 2 implementation schoolwide to decide whether
  - access to schoolwide Tier 2 support is equitable,
  - the team is implementing Tier 2 systems (e.g., teaming, data review) with fidelity,
  - educators are implementing Tier 2 practices (e.g., CICO) with fidelity,
  - students receiving Tier 2 support are benefiting overall (schoolwide Tier 2 outcomes), and
  - individual students are making progress with Tier 2 support, require adaptations (e.g., fade to Tier 1, adjust practices), or may require individualized support in Tier 3 to experience benefit.

Tier 3: Intensive and Individualized SEB Support

Educators provide Tier 3 supports for students who require intensive and individualized supports matched to their specific needs. Educators implement Tier 3 supports in addition to and aligned with the other tiers, so that students engaged in Tier 3 continue to receive supports in Tiers 1 and 2. Students in need of Tier 3 supports may or may not qualify for special education or have an IEP—in other words, Tier 3 is not a synonym for special education, and students with disabilities may participate in supports throughout the tiers (Meyer et al., 2021). Tier 3 supports may be appropriate to address a variety of externalizing or internalizing student behaviors including severe disruption, aggression, suicidal ideation, depression, or anxiety. These behaviors may be affected by academic needs, mental health needs, trauma, or crisis situations and signify high risk of failure or dropout. Within an effective MTSS framework, about 1–5% of students are likely to require intensive, individualized supports at any given time (e.g., Walker et al., 1996). Therefore, in a classroom of 25 students, 0–2 students may require Tier 3 supports.

Team–driven individual student support. At Tier 3, individualized student support teams design, implement, monitor, and adjust intensive student support. Team membership is comprised of those who know and support the student, and members come from a variety of different backgrounds and knowledge bases. Members often include the student (when appropriate), family members, community members, administrators, teachers, social workers, school psychologists, and an individual with applied behavior expertise, among others. Tier 3 student support teams are responsible for (a) conducting comprehensive assessments, (b) developing and implementing comprehensive student support plans, and (c) meeting regularly to evaluate and monitor student progress and make adjustments to the plan as needed. By actively engaging the student, family member(s), and educator(s) in developing the comprehensive assessment and support plan, the team is more likely to develop a plan that is valued, feasible, and culturally/contextually relevant; and by actively engaging team members with relevant expertise (e.g., applied behavioral expertise), the team is more likely to develop a plan that emphasizes evidence-based features that promote student benefit (i.e., technical adequacy; Benazzi et al., 2006).

Comprehensive assessment. Student support teams conduct a comprehensive assessment to guide decisions about Tier 3 support. First, the team members collect comprehensive data, including SEB, academic, mental health, physical health, and other relevant areas of strength and need. They prioritize multiple sources of data (e.g., records review, interview, direct observation), collected from multiple individuals (e.g., educator, student, family member), that document strengths and needs over time. As part of this comprehensive assessment, the team examines the context (antecedents that predict and consequences that maintain) of SEB challenges (i.e., contextually inappropriate behavior), and develop a data-based summary statement that describes behavioral function (i.e., functional behavioral assessment).

Table 7.3 Tier 3 Prevent, Teach, Respond, and Decide Practices in Classrooms

Tier 3 Practice	Considerations for Implementing Tier 3 Practices in Classroom	Considerations for Individualized Comprehensive Support Plan Development
PREVENT Individualize effective design	• Adapt classroom design, layout, and materials to (a) encourage SEB skills and contextually appropriate behavior and (b) minimize opportunities for contextually inappropriate behavior. For example, design a designated space for students to engage in calming strategies, ensure students have easy access to the space, include accessible visual prompts for calming strategies that have been previously taught, practiced, and reviewed. • Consider other adjustments to physical space to meet the individual needs of students in the classroom.	• Consider student-specific needs for space (e.g., grouping, seating, visual barriers, access to materials) during classroom routines identified during comprehensive assessment. For example, consider whether the student need additional space, fewer distractions, or other individualized accommodations. • Consider additional individualized adaptations to the sensory environment based on comprehensive assessment (e.g., access to noise canceling headphones, opportunity to increase/decrease sensory stimulation). • Consider modifications to physical environment based on safety (e.g., reduce unsupervised access to sharp objects for student with history of self-harm).
Individualize predictable routines	• Consider an individualized schedule to enhance predictability throughout a student's day. This can be particularly helpful for students who are anxious, have difficulty with transitions, or whose schedules vary from the class schedule (e.g., due to services such as Speech and Language, counseling, visits to the nurse for medication, etc.). • When unanticipated changes to the schedule come up, such as a switch to indoor recess, alert students to the change in advance and provide additional support as needed. • Explicitly teach and rehears specific classroom routines. Create a task analysis of challenging routines (e.g., break routine into smaller steps), and teach the step-by-step sequence. For example, the routine for completing a task can be defined as: 1) Turn your classwork into the "IN" basket at the front of the room. 2) Return to your desk. 3) Choose to read your book or draw quietly. 4) If you need materials or assistance, raise a silent hand. 5) Wait for the teacher to call on you or check in.	• Depending on the needs of the student determined through the comprehensive assessment, incorporate planned breaks, non-contingent attention, or other individualized routines into the student's individual schedule to support engagement and minimize challenging behavior. • Consider designing individualized schedule to alternate between easier to more difficult activities (i.e., activities with higher and lower probabilities of success, respectively). • Enhance routines included in Tier 2 supports. For example, if access to attention is identified as a reinforcer that is preferred and/or maintains challenging behavior, enhance CICO routines to (a) provide more opportunities for check-ins and non-contingent attention or (b) build in check-ins with additional preferred adults and/or peers. • If a student engages in escalated or crisis-level behaviors, define, teach, and practice explicit routines for de-escalation.

(continued)

117

Table 7.1 Cont.

Tier 3 Practice	Considerations for Implementing Tier 3 Practices in Classroom	Considerations for Individualized Comprehensive Support Plan Development
Intensify connections	• Engage students and families in the Tier 3 assessment and support planning (as members of the individualized team), and establish frequent multidirectional communication to strengthen individualized supports, improve coordinated implementation, and share other important information (e.g., compliance with and changes to medications, success of components of the plan across settings, mood or behavior ratings). • Intensify connections to develop a strong student-teacher relationship and increase student SEB benefit (e.g., increased student confidence, satisfaction with school, peer relationships, and academic performance; LoCasale-Crouch et al., 2018; Solomon et al., 2000; Wentzel et al., 2010). For example, increase opportunities to discuss high-interest topics and engage with students during preferred activities.	• Consider more intensive or structured approaches to engage families during planning: • Person-Centered Planning (PCP) elevates student and family voice to (a) communicate goals and concerns for the student's future, (b) prioritize quality of life and connection with community, and (c) develop supports specific to identified goals and needs.[3] • Wraparound process incorporates PCP to provide holistic and layered supports that are child and family centered within a system of care. Wraparound results in a strengths-based, flexible service plan that (a) prioritizes student and family voice and (b) integrates and coordinates comprehensive and individualized supports across multiple agencies (e.g., child welfare, schools, individual agencies) and life domains.[4]
Intensify and individualize prompts and active supervision for SEB skills	• Individualize prompts for SEB skills and classroom norms based on individual student need. • Consider individualizing prompts embedded in Tier 2 supports. For example, if a student participates in CICO, the school norm of responsible may be personalized on the student's DPR to include an individualized SEB skill of asking for a break when frustrated (a Tier 3 modification). • Intensify active supervision during challenging routines. For example, provide increased prompts, proximity, and specific feedback for individual students with intensive needs while actively supervising all students.	• Provide visual (e.g., writing and/or pictures) and verbal reminders of (a) steps of individualized routines and/or (b) key SEB skills (e.g., those skills taught to replace challenging behaviors and/or other contextually appropriate SEB skills). As the student become fluent with routines and SEB skills, fade prompts to promote independence. • Consider individualized adaptations to active supervision (e.g., minimize attention for challenging behaviors that are reinforced by access to attention, ensuring safety during escalation).
Implement other individualized antecedent interventions	• Consider other factors that may be associated with SEB challenges for one or more students (e.g., hunger, activity level, transitions from preferred to less preferred activities), and develop individualized strategies to address these factors (e.g., snack, activity breaks, careful sequencing of activities).	• Implement additional antecedent interventions to address other factors that predict SEB challenges during comprehensive assessment (e.g., provide non-contingent attention on a fixed schedule to prevent periods of time without attention that predict challenges; intersperse sensory breaks for students who engage in behaviors to obtain sensory stimulation; schedule breaks for students who engage to escape instruction).

(continued)

TEACH

Individualize and intensify explicit instruction for SEB skills

- Further individualize and intensify SEB instruction through explicit instruction (i.e., modeling, practice opportunities, and specific feedback), and continue to review and practice until SEB skills to a predetermined criterion or level of fluency.
- For complex SEB skills, perform a task analysis to break a skill, such as "initiate a conversation," into smaller steps (e.g., say peers name, introduce a topic, ask a question, wait for peer to respond, take turns responding).

- Intensify and individualize explicit instruction on specific SEB skills identified in a student's individualized behavior plan that (a) replace challenging behaviors (e.g., hitting teacher when presented with difficult task) with functionally equivalent behaviors (e.g., asking for a break from difficult task) and (b) other contextually relevant SEB skills (e.g., communication).

Individualize and intensify academic instruction

- Match academic instruction to the student's instructional level, based on comprehensive assessment.
- Increase active engagement (e.g., high rates of response opportunities), and consider varying types of opportunities (e.g., closed vs. open choice, simple vs. complex concepts), numbers of respondents (e.g., choral vs individual), and response modes (e.g., written, oral, gestural, response cards, technology).
- Modify other task dimensions during instruction and practice activities (e.g., duration) and intersperse brief, easy tasks with longer, more difficult tasks.
- Incorporate choice (e.g., among assignments, materials to work with, where they will work, with whom they work, the order of tasks, and what they can do when finished).

- Use diagnostic academic data to target specific skills and/or starting place within an evidence-based program to build upon students' academic strengths and address areas of academic need.
- Prioritize evidence-based practices indicated for specific skill/need areas and use data to guide further adjustments to academic support.
- Further differentiate and individualize instructional support to help the student meet individualized academic goals (e.g., IEP objectives) and/or address unique needs.

Align individualized SEB skills with classroom and school norms or expectations

- Provide more intensive instruction and practice in SEB skills in the context of norms or expectations. For example, if a student has difficulty raising her hand and waiting to be called, initially teach this SEB skill (connected to a classroom norm of "respect" during whole-group instruction) to the entire class (Tier 1). Then, intensify instruction by providing additional practice opportunities that result in positive and supportive feedback.

- When selecting SEB skills to target in an individualized plan, select skills that are (a) valued by student, family member(s), and educators and (b) functionally-relevant (i.e., result in the same maintaining reinforcers as the challenging behavior.
- Define and teach the individualized SEB skills (e.g., ask for a break) in the context of classroom norms (e.g., taking care of self).
- During class instruction in SEB skills (Tier 1), make explicit connections to the skills included in individual plans. Consider teaching these skills to all students to enhance supports for all and minimize stigma of students using individualized skills.

Table 7.1 Cont.

Tier 3 Practice	Considerations for Implementing Tier 3 Practices in Classroom	Considerations for Individualized Comprehensive Support Plan Development
Intensify and individualize specific positive and supportive feedback	• Provide specific praise for individualized SEB skills that are consistent with classroom norms. • Provide specific, calm, respectful, private, and supportive error corrections that include opportunities for re-teaching (e.g., modeling) and practice of contextually appropriate SEB skills. Follow any performance or approximation of the appropriate behavior with specific praise or another form of reinforcement to strengthen the behavior. • Increase ratio of positive to corrective feedback to at least nine praise statements for every correction (Caldarella et al., 2019).	• Provide specific feedback for SEB skills that replace challenging behavior. For example, if a student's individualized behavior plan involves teaching self-calming strategies such as coloring or deep breathing to replace yelling and property destruction, provide explicit feedback and praise for approximating or effectively using any of the self-calming strategies. • Include a plan to shape replacement skills (e.g., ask for a break to escape task) into more contextually appropriate skills (e.g., begin task and ask peer or adult for help when needed) by reinforcing effort and approximations of contextually appropriate skill (e.g., once student fluently asks for a break, request that the student complete 30 seconds of work before taking a break).
Intensify and individualize recognition strategies	• Intensify and individualize the classroom continuum of recognition strategies (e.g., token economy, group contingency) to introduce variety, maintain engagement, and match the value of the reinforcer to the task. • Consider a range of preferences and behavioral functions in selecting recognition strategies to ensure that each student, including a student with intensive needs, is recognized in ways they value, prefer, and experience benefit. • Consider adopting an individualized recognition system, such as a token board or individualized DPR for student engaged in CICO, to provide more frequent and clear feedback across settings (e.g., classroom, music, cafeteria, Speech) and to facilitate generalization.	• Provide function-based reinforcement for SEB skills that replace challenging behaviors. For example, if a student asks for a break (instead of hitting) to escape, provide immediate access to the break; if a student appropriately initiates a conversation with a peer (instead of swearing at peer) to obtain peer attention, work with peers to appropriately engage in the conversation). • Assess preferences for additional reinforcers (e.g., reinforcer survey, stimulus preference assessment; DeLeon et al., 2001). Then, organize reinforcers into a hierarchy from most to least potent, and reinforce new or difficult skills with stronger reinforcers (e.g., playing a game with a friend or time with a preferred adult). • Further individualize recognition strategies in the moment by asking the student what they want to earn and/or offering a choice of known preferred items/activities.

RESPOND

(continued)

Enhance strategies to decrease SEB challenges

- To prevent escalation, provide a brief redirection to contextually relevant SEB skill (e.g., remember to raise your hand, ask for a break if needed).
- Differentially reinforce contextually relevant SEB skills (e.g., raise hand) and withhold/prevent reinforcement for contextually inappropriate behavior (e.g., talk out).

- Prevent reinforcement of contextually inappropriate behaviors that interfere with learning or safety of the student and others (e.g., withhold attention from contextually inappropriate behaviors that function to obtain attention; redirect student to task to prevent escape).
- Consider additional functionally-relevant approaches, based on differential reinforcement, to prevent reinforcement of contextually inappropriate behaviors while increasing reinforcement for contextually appropriate SEB skills.

Monitor fidelity

- Monitor implementation of classroom Tier 3 strategies using simple approaches to count or rate implementation of intensive and individualized strategies. For example, consider tracking data on the number of prompts, practice opportunities, and praise statements provided to support students SEB skills during challenging classroom routines.

- Collect data to monitor fidelity of plan implementation, including (a) consistent use of critical features across staff or settings, (b) the quality of delivery of critical features, and/or (c) the frequency of delivery of critical features.
- Select a feasible approach for monitoring fidelity across time and settings, including direct observation, self-assessment checklist, and/or permanent products resulting from plan implementation).

Monitor student outcomes

- Monitor student progress on a regular basis (e.g., daily, weekly) to enable timely consideration of student benefit. Organize progress monitoring data and identify overall patterns of strength and concerns and concerns are easily identified. Consider working with your school team to adopt a system that generates effective graphs to facilitate progress monitoring, such as Direct Behavior Ratings (https://dbr.education.uconn.edu) or Individual School-Wide Information System (www.pbisapps.org/products/i-swis).
- Monitor Tier 3 outcomes for all student subgroups (i.e., race/ethnicity, gender, language status, disability status) to ensure equitable access and benefit.

- Collaboratively with members of the student support team, develop individualized goals to measure progress related to the students' individualized comprehensive support plan.
- Select goals for each individualized SEB or academic skill (e.g., performing academic skills, increasing adaptive and prosocial skills, decreasing contextually inappropriate, and/or use of acceptable alternative behaviors).
- Ensure goals (a) clearly identify the SEB or academic skill (e.g., ask for help or independently begin work) and relevant features of the context (e.g., during difficult task that involves writing), (b) specify a criterion for meeting goal (e.g., on 90% of observed opportunities), and consider referencing the contextually inappropriate behavior being replaced by the skill (e.g., in lieu of ripping or throwing materials).
- Write goals in specific, objective, and measurable language.

DECIDE

121

Table 7.1 Cont.

Tier 3 Practice	Considerations for Implementing Tier 3 Practices in Classroom	Considerations for Individualized Comprehensive Support Plan Development
Make data-based decisions to maintain or modify support	• Based on fidelity and outcome data, adjust implementation and/or type of individualization of support to maximize benefit. • To support implementation of intensive and individualized practices, again consider self-management strategies including (a) increased prompting; (b) self-monitoring implementation of key practices (e.g., increased prompts or praise) with a paper and pencil tally, counter, or app on a smart device; and (c) celebrating implementation successes (as recommended for Tier 2).	• Summarize and regularly review data with Tier 3 student support team to inform decisions about maintaining or modifying implementation supports for educators and/or elements of the plan. • For individual students, decide to maintain or modify support. o If students are making consistent progress, consider fading to SEB supports in Tiers 1 and/or 2. o If a student is not benefiting from Tier 3 support, consider (a) revisiting the comprehensive assessment, (b) considering adaptations to prevent, teach, and respond practices, and/or (c) further intensifying supports to meet student need. o If a student continues to display chronic or significant SEB challenges, request support from school, district, or external experts with relevant areas of expertise (e.g., applied behavior analysis, mental health, trauma) to support plan revision and consider/ implement additional supports.

Note: Adapted and reprinted with permission from *MTSS in the Classroom* (Center on PBIS Practice Brief; Simonsen et al., 2021).

Educators play a critical role in comprehensive assessment process; they are directly involved in collecting and providing data to define and clarify student strengths and needs. Although someone with applied behavior (or other relevant areas of) expertise may facilitate the assessment process, educators likely participate in interviews, complete rating scales, and record data student SEB needs (e.g., the frequency, duration, or intensity of contextually inappropriate behavior), and share other relevant information (e.g., grades, progress monitoring data, effectiveness of previous interventions). Once team members have collected data, they summarize the comprehensive assessment in a report that guides development of a comprehensive student support plan.

Comprehensive student support plan. The comprehensive student support plan that includes strategies to (a) prevent SEB challenges through individualized antecedent strategies; (b) teach critical SEB skills that replace SEB challenges and meet the same function, and shape toward other contextually appropriate SEB skills (e.g., start work and request help when needed); and (c) respond in ways that strengthen key SEB skills (reinforcement) and decrease SEB challenges (additional response strategies). Thus, as an extension of previous tiers, Tier 3 supports build on and intensify the same prevent, teach, respond, and decide strategies. In this way, student support teams intensify and differentiate universal supports to meet the specific needs of individual students requiring Tier 3 supports. Table 7.3 provides considerations for individualizing and intensifying these strategies at Tier 3 to support students in the classroom and across settings in a comprehensive support plan.

Input from educators is critical during the development and implementation of individualized comprehensive plans to maximize feasibility, social validity, and ultimately effectiveness of the plan. Educators are often the primary implementors of individualized comprehensive support plans, and they may also be responsible for collecting progress monitoring data on the fidelity and outcomes of the plan to guide decisions about maintaining or modifying support. In addition to educator input, it is critical that student support teams actively engage family members, students, and other support providers from relevant disciplines (e.g., school or community mental health, social work, speech language, occupational therapy, physical therapy). To facilitate these efforts, teams often use person-centered (Kincaid & Fox, 2002) and/or wraparound (Eber, 2014; Eber & Nelson, 1997) approaches that center the student and family goals and needs in designing supports and flexibly coordinate services across multiple providers.

School systems to support Tier 3. To maximize the effectiveness and efficiency of Tier 3 support, a Tier 3 school systems team, which may be combined with the Tier 2 team in some schools, coordinates school-level development and implementation of assessment and support protocols, assembles student support teams for students identified as candidates for Tier 3, supports educators in implementing Tier 3 supports with fidelity, and monitors fidelity and outcomes to inform adjustments and enhancements to school-level Tier 3 supports. Tier 3 coordinators facilitate this team, which has a similar composition to the Tier 2 team (i.e., administrator; representative group of educators; and individuals with applied behavioral expertise, academic expertise, mental health and trauma experience, and other relevant areas of expertise). This team meets regularly to consider students who require Tier 3 supports and monitor implementation and outcomes of all students receiving Tier 3 supports to enhance school systems to support Tier 3.

Importantly, effective Tier 3 systems include providing professional development on the Tier 3 process and common strategies (e.g., basic behavioral theory, function-based intervention) to all staff as well as in situ coaching to educators implementing individualized plans to support high-fidelity implementation and accurate data collection. Educators are partners in the coaching process, raising questions, providing feedback on implementation of the plan, and problem-solving barriers.

Issues, Trends, and Future Directions for Research and Practice

To enhance benefit for each and every learner, researchers and educators strive to (a) better understand contextual variation in implementation to maximize benefit for all students, (b) enhance equitable implementation and outcomes for all student subgroups, and (c) invest in systems to support, sustain, and scale educators' implementation of classroom practices.

Understand Contextual Variation in Implementation

Though evidence supports each practice described in this chapter, additional research may illuminate contextual variations in implementation to maximize student benefit. Contextual variation considers what practices work for whom under what conditions. For example, beyond continuing to document the effectiveness of specific praise, researchers may ask:

1. What is an optimal specific praise rate (praise per minute)?
2. Are different optimal specific praise rates associated with different classroom routines (e.g., instruction, transitions)?
3. Do optimal rates and/or preferred praise dimensions (e.g., public vs. private) vary based on age, school level, or other demographic characteristic (e.g., gender, ability level)?
4. Does implementation of other classroom practices (e.g., high vs. low rates of response opportunities or prompts) affect optimal praise rates?

By understanding contextual variation, educators would be able to maximize the effectiveness and efficiency of classroom practice implementation.

Enhance Equitable Implementation and Outcomes for all Subgroups of Students

Whereas understanding contextual variation and optimizing implementation may maximize benefit, research has demonstrated historical and harmful variations in practice implementation. Specifically, research demonstrates that students from historically marginalized groups, especially Black students and students with or at risk for disabilities, are at greater risk of exclusionary/reactive discipline (e.g., suspensions, expulsions, restraint, seclusion; Lossen & Martinez, 2020; Morris & Perry, 2016; US Department of Education's Office of Civil Rights, 2018; Wagner & Newman, 2012). Contributing to disproportionate discipline, emerging research indicates that students from historically marginalized populations have less access to evidence-based practices to support SEB skills (e.g., specific praise and opportunities to respond; Gion, 2019; Green et al. 2020; Scott et al., 2011), and implicit bias may impact disciplinary decisions (Scott et al., 2019; Smolkowski et al., 2016). Therefore, additional research is needed to understand and enhance equitable practice implementation across student subgroups, including research on (a) professional development strategies to monitor and enhance equitable implementation of positive and proactive practices to support students SEB needs, (b) enhancing research on culturally and contextually relevant classroom practices (e.g., effectively engaging family, student, and community voice in practice selection and adaptation), and (c) on-going work to interrupt and reduce reactive practices that lead to disproportionate discipline (e.g., understanding vulnerable decision points and implementing neutralizing routines). For further guidance and resources, see Leversen et al. (2021).

Invest in Systems to Support, Sustain, and Scale Educators' Implementation of Classroom Practices

Finally, despite decades of research that have documented the importance of evidence-based practices, educators typically implement Tier 1 practices at lower levels than required for student benefit (e.g., Reinke et al., 2013). Although educators can independently develop habits of effective practice (Simonsen et al., 2021), many schools and districts invest in an implementation framework, like MTSS or PBIS, that prioritizes systems to support educators. Research demonstrates the importance of three critical systems features: explicit training, on-going coaching/mentoring support, and performance feedback to support educators' implementation of SEB supports (Wilkinson et al., 2021). At the school level, these systems features can be implemented, monitored, and enhanced to support all educators; and at the district-level, these systems features can be coordinated to promote sustained and scaled implementation (Freeman et al., 2017). However, additional research is needed to understand the contextual variation in staff support, and approaches that maximize efficiency and effectiveness in a manner that is sustainable and scalable across a range of school and district characteristics.

Summary

This chapter describes how educators implement a MTSS approach within classrooms to meet the needs of all learners through (a) robust universal support (Tier 1) implemented with fidelity and differentiated to meet the needs of each student, (b) targeted support (Tier 2) to further intensify support for groups of students with common needs, and (c) intensive individualized support (Tier 3) for individual students with chronic or complex needs. Within and across each tier of support, educators prevent, teach, respond, and decide.

Notes

1 Grant H326S180001 from the Office of Special Education Programs, US Department of Education for OSEP Center on Positive Behavioral Interventions and Supports (www.pbis.org) supported in part authors' time to develop this chapter. Opinions expressed herein are the authors' and do not necessarily reflect the position of the US Department of Education, and such endorsements should not be inferred.
2 See A 5 Point Intervention for Enhancing Equity in School Discipline (McIntosh et al., 2018) to learn more about vulnerable decision points, neutralizing routines, and other approaches to improve equity in discipline.
3 See Kincaid & Fox (2002) to learn more about person-centered planning.
4 See Eber et al. (1997) and Eber et al. (2014) to learn more about wraparound process.

References

Allen, G. E., Common, E. A., Germer, K. A., Lane, K. L., Buckman, M. M., Oakes, W. P., & Menzies, H. M. (2020). A Systematic Review of the Evidence Base for Active Supervision in Pre-K–12 Settings. *Behavioral Disorders*, *45*(3), 167–182. https://doi.org/10.1177/0198742919837646

Anderson, A. R., Christenson, S. L., Sinclair, M. F., & Lehr, C. A. (2004). Check & Connect: The importance of relationships for promoting engagement with school. *Journal of School Psychology*, *42*, 95–113. https://doi.org/10.1016/j.jsp.2004.01.002

Benazzi, L., Horner, R. H., & Good, R. H. (2006). Effects of Behavior Support Team Composition on the Technical Adequacy and Contextual Fit of Behavior Support Plans. *The Journal of Special Education*, *40*(3), 160–170. https://doi.org/10.1177/00224669060400003040

Boyd, R. J., & Anderson, C. M. (2013). Breaks are Better: A Tier II social behavior intervention. *Journal of Behavioral Education*, *22*, 348–365. https://doi.org/10.1007/s10864-013-9184-2

Briesch, A. M., & Chafouleas, S. M. (2009). Review and analysis of literature on self-management interventions to promote appropriate classroom behaviors (1988–2008). *School Psychology Quarterly*, *24*, 106–118.

Caldarella, P., Larsen, R. A., Williams, L., Downs, K. R., Wills, H. P., & Wehby, J. H. (2020). Effects of teachers' praise-to-reprimand ratios on elementary students' on-task behaviour. *Educational Psychology*, *40*(10), 1306–1322.

Center on Positive Behavioral Interventions and Supports (2019). Track Positive Reinforcement with Our Be+ App. [Webpage]. www.pbis.org/announcements/track-positive-reinforcement-with-our-be-app

Center on Positive Behavioral Interventions and Supports (December 2020). *Positive Behavioral Interventions and Supports (PBIS) Evaluation Blueprint.* University of Oregon. www.pbis.org

Center on Positive Behavioral Interventions and Supports (2021). *Tiered framework.* Positive Behavioral Interventions & Supports. www.pbis.org.

Center on Positive Behavioral Interventions and Supports, State Implementation and Scaling up of Evidence-Based Practices Center, National Integrated Multi-Tiered Systems of Support Research Network, National Center on Improving Literacy, & Lead for Literacy Center (March, 2021b). *Returning to school during and after crisis: A guide to supporting states, districts, schools, educators, and students through a multi-tiered systems of support framework during the 2020–2021 school year.* University of Oregon. www.pbis.org

Chaparro, E. A., Nese, R. N. T., & McIntosh, K. (2015). *Examples of engaging instruction to increase equity in education.* Center on Positive Behavioral Interventions and Supports. www.pbis.org

Cheney, D. A., Stage, S. A., Hawken, L. S., Lynass, L., Mielenz, C., & Waugh, M. (2009). A 2-year outcome study of the Check, Connect, and Expect intervention for students at risk for severe behavior problems. *Journal of Emotional and Behavioral Disorders*, *17*, 226–243. https://doi.org/10.1177/1063426609339186

Cho Blair, K., Park, E., & Kim, W. (2020). A meta-analysis of tier 2 interventions implemented within school-wide positive behavioral interventions and supports. *Psychology in the Schools, 58*, 141–161. https://doi.org/10.1002/pits.22443

Conroy, M. A., Sutherland, K. S., Snyder, A., Al-Hendawi, M., Vo, A. (2009). Creating a positive classroom atmosphere: Teachers' use of effective praise and feedback. *Beyond Behavior, 18*, 18–26.

Cook, C. R., Fiat, A., Larson, M., Daikos, C., Slemrod, T., Holland, E. A., ... Renshaw, T. (2018). Positive greetings at the door: Evaluation of a low-cost, high-yield proactive classroom management strategy. *Journal of Positive Behavior Interventions, 20*(3), 149–159. https://doi.org/10.1177/1098300717753831

Cooper, J. T., Gage, N. A., Alter, P. J., LaPolla, S., MacSuga-Gage, A. S., & Scott, T. M. (2018). Educators' self-reported training, use, and perceived effectiveness of evidence-based classroom management practices. *Preventing School Failure: Alternative Education for Children and Youth, 62*(1), 13–24. https://doi.org/10.1080/1045988X.2017.1298562

Cooper, J. O., Heron, T. E., & Heward, W. L. (2019). *Applied behavior analysis* (3rd Edition). Pearson Education.

Dunlap, G., Iovannone, R., Wilson, K. J., Kincaid, D. K., & Strain, P. (2010). Prevent-Teach-Reinforce: A Standardized Model of School-Based Behavioral Intervention. *Journal of Positive Behavior Interventions, 12*(1), 9–22. https://doi.org/10.1177/1098300708330880

Eber, L., Malloy, J. M., Rose, J., & Flamini, A. (2014). School-based wraparound for adolescents: The RENEW model for transition-age youth with or at risk of emotional and behavioral disorders. In H. M. Walker & F. M. Gresham (Eds.), *Handbook of evidence-based practices for emotional and behavioral disorders: Applications in schools.* (pp. 378–393). The Guilford Press.

Eber, L., Nelson, C. M., & Miles, P. (1997). School-based wraparound for students with emotional and behavioral challenges. *Exceptional Children, 63*(4), 539–555. https://doi.org/10.1177/001440299706300414

Eklund, K., Kilgus, S. P., Taylor, C., Allen, A., Meyer, L., Izumi, J., Beardmore, M., Frye, S., McLean, D., Calderon, F., & Kilpatrick, K. (2019). Efficacy of a combined approach to Tier 2 social-emotional and behavioral intervention and the moderating effects of function. *School Mental Health: A Multidisciplinary Research and Practice Journal, 11*, 678–691. https://doi.org/10.1007/s12310-019-09321-5

Ennis, R. P., Royer, D. J., Lane, K. L., & Griffith, C. E. (2017). A Systematic Review of Precorrection in PK–12 Settings. *Education and Treatment of Children 40*(4), 465–495. https://doi.org/10.1353/etc.2017.0021.

Freeman, J., Simonsen, B., Briere, D. E., & MacSuga-Gage, A. S. (2014). Pre-service teacher training in classroom management: A review of state accreditation policy and teacher preparation programs. *Teacher Education and Special Education, 37*(2), 106–120. https://doi.org/10.1177/0888406413507002

Freeman, J., Simonsen, B., Goodman, S., Mitchell, B., George, H. P., Swain-Bradway, J., Lane, K., Sprague, J., & Putnam, B. (2017). *PBIS technical brief on systems to support teachers' implementation of positive classroom behavior support.* Center on PBIS, University of Oregon. www.pbis.org.

Gion, C. (2019). Effects of a multifaceted classroom intervention on racial disproportionality [ProQuest Information & Learning]. In *Dissertation Abstracts International Section A: Humanities and Social Sciences* (Vol. 80, Issue 3–A(E)).

Hawken et al., (2021). *Responding to problem behavior in schools: The check-In, check-out intervention.* (3rd ed) Guilford Press.

Haydon, T., Conroy, M. A., Scott, T. M., Sindelar, P. T., Barber, B. R., & Orlando, A. M. (2010). A comparison of three types of opportunities to respond on student academic and social behaviors. *Journal of Emotional and Behavioral Disorders, 18*(1), 27–40. https://doi.org/10.1177/1063426609333448

Hussar, B., Zhang, J., Hein, S., Wang, K., Roberts, A., Cui, J., Smith, M., Bullock Mann, F., Barmer, A., & Dilig, R. (2020). *The Condition of Education 2020* (NCES 2020-144). U.S. Department of Education. National Center for Education Statistics. Retrieved [May 2021] from https://nces.ed.gov/pubsearch/pubsinfo. asp?pubid=2020144

Green, A. L., Lewis, T. J., & Olsen, A. A. (2020). General education teachers' use of evidence-based practices: Examining the role of student race and risk status. *Behavioral Disorders, 45*(3), 183–192. https://doi.org/10.1177/0198742919883570

Kern, L., Gaier, K., Kelly, S., Nielsen, C. M., Commisso, C. E., & Wehby, J. H. (2020). An evaluation of adaptations made to tier 2 social skill training programs. *Journal of Applied School Psychology, 36*, 155–172. https://doi.org/10.1080/15377903.2020.1714858

Kincaid, D., & Fox, L. (2002). Person-centered planning and positive behavior support. In S. Holburn & P. M. Vietze (Eds.), *Person-centered planning: Research, practice, and future directions.* (pp. 29–49). Paul H. Brookes Publishing Co.

Lane, K. L., Wehby, J., Menzies, H. M., Doukas, G. L., Munton, S. M., & Gregg, R. M. (2003). Social skills instruction for students at risk for antisocial behavior: The effects of small-group instruction. *Behavioral Disorders, 28*(3), 229–248. https://doi.org/10.1177/019874290302800308

Leverson, M., Smith, K., McIntosh, K., Rose, J., & Pinkelman, S. (March, 2021). PBIS Cultural Responsiveness Field Guide: Resources for Trainers and Coaches. Center on PBIS, University of Oregon. www.pbis.org

Losen, D. J., & Martinez, P. (2020). Is California doing enough to close the school discipline gap? The Center for Civil Rights Remedies at The Civil Rights Project, University of California Los Angeles. https://civilrightsproject.ucla.edu/research/k-12-education/school-discipline/is-california-doing- enough-to-close-the-school-discipline-gap/Final_CA_Report_06_29_2020-revised-for-post.pdf

MacSuga-Gage, A.S., & Simonsen, B. (2015). Examining the Effects of Teacher-Directed Opportunities to Respond on Student Outcomes: A Systematic Review of the Literature. *Education and Treatment of Children*, *38*(2), 211–239. https://doi.org/10.1353/etc.2015.0009

Majeika, C. E., Bruhn, A. L., Sterrett, B. I., & McDaniel, S. (2020). Reengineering tier 2 interventions for responsive decision making: An adaptive intervention process. *Journal of Applied School Psychology*, *36*, 111–132. https://doi.org10.1080/15377903.2020.1714855

McIntosh, K., Girvan, E. J., Horner, R. H., Smolkowski, K., & Sugai, G. (2018). A 5-point intervention approach for enhancing equity in school discipline. Center on Positive Behavioral Interventions and Supports. www.pbis.org

Meyer, K., Sears, S., Putnam, R., Phelan, C., Burnett, A., Warden, S., & Simonsen, B. (2021). Supporting students with disabilities with universal positive behavioral interventions and supports (PBIS): Lessons learned from research and practice. *Beyond Behavior*. Manuscript published on line first. https://doi.org/10.1177/10742956211021801

Morgan, P. L., Farkas, G., Hillemeier, M. M., Wang, Y., Mandel, Z., DeJarnett, C., & Maczuga, S. (2019). Are students with disabilities suspended more frequently than otherwise similar students without disabilities? *Journal of School Psychology*, *72*, 1–13. https://doi.org/10.1016/j.jsp.2018.11.001

Morris, E. W., & Perry, B. L. (2016). The punishment gap: School suspension and racial disparities in achievement. *Social Problems*, *63*, 68–86. https://doi.org/10.1093/socpro/spv026

Niwayama, K., Maeda, Y., Kaneyama, Y., & Sato, H. (2020). Increasing teachers' behavior-specific praise using self-monitoring and a peer teacher's feedback: The effect on children's academic engagement. *Preventing School Failure: Alternative Education for Children and Youth*, *64*(4), 271–280.

Reinke, W. M., Herman, K. C., & Stormont, M. (2013). Classroom-level positive behavior supports in schools implementing SW-PBIS: Identifying areas for enhancement. *Journal of Positive Behavior Interventions*, *15*, 39–50. https://doi.org/10.1177/1098300712459079

Scott, T. M., Gage, N., Hirn, R., & Han, H. S. (2019). Teacher and student race as a predictor for negative feedback during instruction. *School Psychology Quarterly*, *34*(1), 22–31. https://doi.org/10.1037/spq0000251

Simonsen, B., Fairbanks, S., Briesch, A., Myers, D., & Sugai, G. (2008). Evidence-based practices in classroom management: Considerations for research to practice. *Education and Treatment of Children*, *31*, 351–380. https://doi.org/10.1353/etc.0.0007

Simonsen, B., & Myers, D. (2015). *Classwide positive behavior interventions and supports: A guide to proactive classroom management*. The Guilford Press.

Simonsen, B., Robbie, K., Meyer, K., Freeman, J., Everett, S., & Feinberg, A. (2021). *MTSS in the Classroom*. Center on PBIS, University of Oregon. www.pbis.org.

Simonsen, B., Yanek, K., Sugai, G., & Borgmeier, C. (December, 2020). *Habits of Effective Classroom Practice*. Center on PBIS, University of Oregon. www.pbis.org

US Department of Education Office for Civil Rights (2018). School Climate and Safety: Data Highlights on School Climate and Safety in Our Nation's Public Schools. U.S. Department of Education. www2.ed.gov/about/offices/list/ocr/docs/school-climate-and-safety.pdf

Van Camp, A. M., Wehby, J. H., Copeland, B. A., & Bruhn, A. L. (2021). Building from the bottom up: The importance of tier 1 supports in the context of tier 2 interventions. *Journal of Positive Behavior Interventions*, *23*, 53–64. https://doi.org/10.1177/1098300720916716

Vespa, J., Medina, L., & Armstrong, D. M. (February 2020). Demographic Turning Points for the United States: Population Projections for 2020 to 2060. US Census Bureau: www.census.gov/content/dam/Census/library/publications/2020/demo/p25-1144.pdf

Wagner, M., & Newman, L. (2012). Longitudinal transition outcomes of youth with emotional disturbances. *Psychiatric Rehabilitation Journal*, *35*, 199–208. https://doi.org/10.2975/35.3.2012.199.208

Walker, H. M., Horner, R. H., Sugai, G., Bullis, M., Sprague, J. R., Bricker, D., & Kaufman, M. J. (1996). Integrated approaches to preventing antisocial behavior patterns among school-age children and youth. *Journal of Emotional and Behavioral Disorders*, *4*(4), 193–256. https://doi.org/10.1177/106342669600400401

Walker, H. M., Seeley, J. R., Small, J., Severson, H. H., Graham, B. A., Feil, E. G., Serna, L., Golly, A. M., & Forness, S. R. (2009). A randomized controlled trial of the First Step to Success early intervention: Demonstration of program efficacy outcomes in a diverse, urban school district. *Journal of Emotional and Behavioral Disorders*, *17*, 197–212. https://doi.org/10.1177/1063426609341645

Whitney, T., & Ackerman, K. B. (2020). Acknowledging Student Behavior: A Review of Methods Promoting Positive and Constructive Feedback. *Beyond Behavior*, *29*(2), 86–94. https://doi.org/10.1177/10742956210902474

Wilkinson, S., Freeman, J., Simonsen, B., Sears, S., Byun, S. G., Xu, X., & Luh, H. J. (2021). Professional development for classroom management: A review of the literature. *Educational Research and Evaluation*. Manuscript published on line first. https://doi.org/10.1080/13803611.2021.1934034

8

ADAPTING CLASSROOM MANAGEMENT FOR DELIVERY ACROSS CONTEXTS

A Focus on Urban, Rural, and Online Settings

Shanna E. Hirsch

CLEMSON UNIVERSITY

Kristine E. Larson

NOTRE DAME OF MARYLAND UNIVERSITY

Lydia A. Beahm

UNIVERSITY OF VIRGINIA

Catherine P. Bradshaw

UNIVERSITY OF VIRGINIA

There is growing awareness that evidence-based classroom management strategies can have a positive impact on a range of outcomes for students, yet there is limited uptake of these strategies in schools (Stormont et al., 2011).[1] One commonly cited barrier to their adoption is the perceived need for adaptation to optimize fit with the classroom context and student culture. Even more recently, the COVID-19 pandemic has underscored the importance of and need for effective classroom management in the online (i.e., remote) environment; moreover, the pandemic exposed several gaps in teacher preparation related to adapting their use of evidence-based practices across different platforms and settings to address a number of urgent student behavioral, emotional, and academic needs. The current chapter aimed to address this research to practice gap by providing an overview of research-based classroom management practices and strategies that can be adapted for use across a variety of contexts including urban, rural, and online settings. In addition, strategies for adapting and guiding teacher professional development are provided.

Important Role of Classroom Management

Classroom management is a common and core function of teacher practice, but is often more complex to execute on than one might anticipate. As Evertson and Weinstein (2006) noted in the first edition of

DOI: 10.4324/9781003275312-10

this *Handbook*, classroom management refers to "the actions teachers take to create an environment that supports and facilitates both academic and social-emotional learning" (p. 4). More recently, Myers and colleagues (2017) highlighted that "teachers who successfully support student behavior use a variety of practices and strategies that are efficient, effective, and appropriate for the student population" (p. 132). Myers et al. also noted classroom management focuses on what the teachers do to support and promote student behavior while considering individual student factors. As such, it also includes "teachers' ability to manage student learning… so that students can engage and participate meaningfully in the teaching and learning exchange—regardless of the subject matter being taught" (Milner, 2015, p. 170).

A host of classroom management practices have been developed and shown to be effective, including active supervision, opportunities for students to respond, praise, and provide specific feedback (for a review see Simonsen et al., 2008). In fact, in classrooms where teachers use a high rate of evidence-based classroom management strategies, the students experience several benefits including active student engagement and academic performance (Gage et al., 2018; Hirsch, Randall et al., 2021; Larson et al., 2021; Simonsen et al., 2008). As such, classroom management is a recommended practice for teachers across all grade levels. Despite this push for the use of evidence-based classroom management practices, there is variability in the extent to which teachers use these practices (Hollo & Hirn, 2015; Scott et al., 2011). Regrettably, many teachers do not receive sufficient training, either preservice or in-service, on how to proactively support students through classroom management (Flower et al., 2017; Freeman et al., 2014; Podolsky et al., 2016). Moreover, managing classroom disruptions is stressful for teachers (Herman et al., 2020; Westling, 2010), and if not adequately addressed, can lead to burnout and attrition (Aloe et al., 2014; Metlife Inc., 2013; Sutton et al., 2009). In the following section, we consider a number of different factors at the teacher, student, and school level which may account for the limited uptake of such practices, and serve as potential challenges for teachers aiming to implement these strategies.

Contextual Influences on Teachers' Use of Classroom Management Strategies

It is important to consider the range of possible factors, at the student, classroom, or school levels, that may influence, either consciously or unconsciously, teachers' use of evidence-based classroom management practices. For example, student factors, such as the increasing number of students with disabilities in general education settings (US Department of Education, 2021), may increase demand on teachers and challenge their ability to use classroom management strategies effectively. In fact, students with disabilities who spent 80% or more of their school day in a general education setting increased from 59% in the fall of 2009 to 65% in the fall of 2019. In the classroom, teachers report that both students with and without disabilities exhibit a range of challenging behaviors that exceed their skillset (Westling, 2010). These data, including the increasing trend toward increasing the amount of time students with disabilities spend in general education settings, highlight the importance of all teachers, including general teachers, to receive adequate training to support all of their students using research-based proactive behavior and classroom management strategies.

Classrooms across the United States are becoming increasingly more linguistically, culturally, and racially diverse (US Department of Education, 2018). English learners in the US represent 4.5 million students or an average of 9.2% of all students (with 18.7% in Texas and 19.4% in California). The US public school enrollment data revealed the percentages of students who were Hispanic increased (from 22% to 27%, between 2009 and 2018, respectively). As a nation, our public schools are now "majority-minority" yet there continue to be areas in the country where White students attend majority-White schools and Black students attend majority non-white schools (Orfield et al., 2012). This trend continues in states with high rates of English Language Learners such as Texas. When looking at the teacher workforce, however, teachers are overwhelmingly White (US Department of Education, 2016). As La Salle et al. (2020) described, this racial mismatch is having significant negative impacts on minoritized students' perceptions of school climate. They cite, for example, data on White students who were educated by a majority of White teachers who reported feeling an increased sense of cultural acceptance and connectedness, but there was no such effect for minoritized students. In addition, students of color generally report feeling less favorable school climate and less equitable discipline in school than their White peers (Bottiani et al., 2016).

Disproportionate discipline is viewed as a major reason for students not to feel a sense of belonging (La Salle et al., 2020). Black students with and without disabilities are suspended at a rate significantly higher than their proportion within the school population (Gage et al., 2019). In regards to corporal punishment, Black students without disabilities are statistically more likely to receive corporal punishment than White students (MacSuga-Gage et al., 2020). In addition, Black students with disabilities are more likely to receive corporal punishment compared to White students with disabilities (MacSuga-Gage et al., 2020). These findings highlight the harm of corporal punishment especially for Black students and those with disabilities.

In light of these and other such troubling findings, schools are strongly encouraged to implement frameworks to create more equitable outcomes for minoritized students (Bottiani et al., 2018; Larson et al., 2018; La Salle et al., 2020). Teachers need opportunities to increase their knowledge and skills for developing strategies to reflect culturally appropriate and relevant applications (Bradshaw et al., 2018). One way to do this is for teachers to use "specific culturally responsive classroom management practices to ensure that all students have a common understanding of what is expected of them and that all students feel valued and encouraged to contribute to their own learning and that of their peers" (Cartledge et al., 2015, p. 412). Ideally, teachers will include student, community, and local stakeholder values when developing culturally responsive classrooms (Bal, 2018). A guiding principle of culturally responsiveness is to consider the students' backgrounds as well as the learning context.

Relatedly, the broader context or environmental characteristics (e.g., history, social values, norms, resources) may influence teachers' use of classroom management strategies. As noted by Sugai et al. (2000), "the contextual fit between intervention strategies and the values of families, teachers, schools, support personnel, and community agency personnel may affect the quality and durability of support efforts" (p. 136). As such, there is a strong and urgent need for behavior and classroom management to shift to consider various aspects of the students' culture, as well as geographic context (e.g., rural, urban) of the school. Aspects of the schools' location (e.g., dense, large, metropolitan areas), student diversity (e.g., racial, ethnic, linguistic, and socioeconomic), and resources (e.g., technology, funding through federal programming, property taxes) are also important to consider when aiming to promote the implementation of any program, including effective classroom management (Domitrovich et al., 2008; Milner, 2015). Taken together, the extant research highlights the potential utility of classroom management practices on a range of student behavioral and academic outcomes. Yet, teachers' routine use of these practices is limited; a number of teacher, student, and contextual factors have been cited as possible reasons why uptake and adoption of these practices is limited. Perhaps even more important is the intersection and interactions among these various factors, including teacher characteristics, student factors, and the school setting (Sugai et al., 2000). Taking into consideration factors at these various levels may provide insight into how best to adapt evidence-based classroom management practices to increase their uptake and routine use.

Adapting Classroom Management Practices

Given the focus of understanding how to support all learners, there is an increased interest in adapting classroom management practices to meet students' needs (Sugai et al., 2012). Adaptation is the extent to which practices are adopted to consider student or contextual factors that enhance the overall effectiveness of a practice (Chen et al., 2021; Sterrett et al., 2021). Both differentiated instruction and adaptations are important, yet they are separate and distinct concepts. For example, differentiated instruction provides students with multiple options for content, process, and product (Tomlinson & McTighe, 2006), whereas adaptations change the support based on individual factors including school environment or context.

Sterrett et al. (2021) recently provided some helpful guidance on adapting Tier 2 interventions. Although the focus of that particular paper was related to Tier 2 interventions, many of their suggestions are relevant to classroom management. For example, when done correctly, adaptations should "not alter the core components of the intervention, but tailor interventions to match student need" (Sterrett et al., 2021, p. 134). As suggested above, planned adaptations should be based on data as well as contextual factors such as setting characteristics (e.g., underserved schools, culturally diverse schools). For example, when considering adaptations, it is critical to consider the resources, culture within and outside of the school contexts, and existing schoolwide frameworks (Sterrett et al., 2021). When considering preventative, adaptive, and responsive schoolwide frameworks to support students, it is critical to leverage the research on the adaptation process. One potentially helpful model is Multi-Tiered System of Supports (MTSS), which is designed to enhance student learning and social–emotional–behavioral well-being through (a) high-quality evidence-based instruction and behavioral supports; (b) on-going data monitoring of student progress; (c) opportunities for students to respond to strategies and interventions; and (d) monitoring of implementation to ensure research-based strategies are implemented with fidelity. The MTSS framework provides schools and districts with structure to organize practices, data, and systems to effectively identify students in need and provide appropriate support (Brownell et al., 2018).

One example of MTSS focused on behavior is Positive Behavioral Interventions and Supports (PBIS; Horner et al., 2010). PBIS is a three-tiered system designed to support the behavioral needs all of the students in the school (Tier 1), and provide targeted interventions (Tiers 2 and 3) in combination with the preventative (Tier 1) supports for those students with greater needs (Horner et al., 2010). A key component of the Tier 1 PBIS framework is classroom management or classwide positive behavior support (Office of Special Education Programs, 2015). Key classroom management practices include: designing the physical layout of the classroom, creating predictable classroom routines and procedures, establishing 3–5 positively stated expectations, delivering prompts and actively supervising students, providing a high rate and varied opportunities to respond, and acknowledging expected behaviors. The Office of Special Education Programs (2015) document provides an interactive map of classroom strategies along with a self-assessment and examples of the practices across elementary and secondary settings. They highlight several practices that are supported by research and in turn connected to positive student outcomes (i.e., increased student academic and behavior outcomes) as well as increased time teaching (e.g., Scott et al., 2011).

The aforementioned classroom management practices can be adapted across a variety of contexts such as geographic settings (e.g., McDaniel, Chaparro, et al., 2020) as well as to support diverse students (e.g., Bal, 2018; Rose et al., 2020), and students with disabilities (e.g., Loman et al., 2018). Importantly, both the universal and multi-tiered PBIS model are supported by decades of research (e.g., Bradshaw et al., 2008, 2009, 2010, 2012; Gage et al., 2018). As a result, the model has been widely disseminated, with over 26,000 schools implementing Tier 1 PBIS in the USA (Office of Special Education Programs, Technical Assistance Center on Positive Behavior Interventions and Supports, 2021). While the research on PBIS holds great promise as a possible framework for helping schools adapt and consistently implement classroom management and school-wide supports to reduce behavioral challenges, there remain a number of contextual issues that may require additional consideration; particular attention should be paid to cultural and contextual adaptations of these evidence-based models.

A Focus on Three School Contexts: Rural, Urban, and Remote Learning Environments

In the remaining sections of this chapter, we consider three broad types of cultural and contextual factors that may warrant additional attention during the adaptation process. Specifically, we focus on rural settings, urban settings, and the remote learning environment. After introducing each of these

Table 8.1 Classroom Management Adaptations

Context	Potential Considerations *	Adaptations			
		Expectations	Reinforcement	Engagement	Supporting Teachers
Rural	Limited resources, increased poverty, food insecurities, substance abuse, and mental health problems.	Develop behavioral expectations in various settings (e.g., bus, library, classroom)	Consider using the Remote Instruction Strategy Matrix to reach students at home with limited access to technology.	Include examples that are relevant to their environment, include activities that will be useful in their daily lives	Provide mental health support services for students, telecoaching and online professional development, train experienced school personnel to be PBIS coaches
Urban	Urban classroom management requires teachers to have an understanding about a wide range of student diversity that is beyond race.	Work with students, parents, and community members to identify and define acceptable expectations respectful of the community's norms.	Focus on student-teacher relationships and high expectations for students. Seek input from parents, students, and community members to identify reinforcement practices.	Meet the needs of learners and create supportive classrooms by using evidence-based instructional practices known to decrease the opportunity gap (Chaparro et al., 2015).	The Double Check CARES framework provides teachers with group-based professional development by a trained coach/trainer, along with coaching using an adapted version of the Classroom Check-up coaching model.
Online	Classroom management typically occurred in brick-and-mortar classrooms therefore few teachers prior to 2020 taught online.	Identify behavioral expectations across different virtual environments. Explicitly teach the expectations and provide frequent checks for understanding.	Students can earn points during instruction which can be exchanged in an online school store.	Frequent communication with learning managers is critical. It is also important to include a high rate of opportunities to respond within asynchronous and synchronous online instruction.	Leverage technology to provide online teacher professional development in classroom management.

settings and providing background on possible reasons for adaptation, we narrow more specifically into strategies for adaptation to optimize the fit of classroom management practices in each of those settings. The three settings discussed herein are examples. This is not an exclusive or required list of contexts or adaptations, rather they are considerations. Table 8.1 provides an overview of specific adaptations across the three settings. These examples are based on our work across rural, urban, and remote settings. Adaptations of classroom management are specifically relevant to PBIS through community expectations, reinforcement, reinforcement, and teacher support.

Challenges Faced in Rural Settings

Approximately 20 percent of students in the USA attend schools in the rural setting (USDA, 2017). The National Center for Educational Statistics (NCES) classifies rural areas based on their proximity to urban centers and is delineated into three classifications: fringe, distant, and remote (2013). This distinction is important to understanding differences in access to resources, economic drivers (e.g., tax base), and population density. For example, in more resource–rich rural communities, such as those near urban centers, resources to meet community needs are typically plentiful (Greenough & Nelson, 2015; Wilger, n.d.). In contrast, remote environments supported by a single industry that has declined and is no longer bountiful (e.g., agriculture or mining) are often characterized by a lack of access to services, jobs, and high–quality educational opportunities (Twaddell & Emerine, 2007). These remote communities tend to have a steady decline in population and job loss, leading to a lack of young, diverse, and educated residents, and therefore, fewer opportunities for growth (Twaddell & Emerine, 2007).

Moreover, remote rural communities are frequently plagued with challenges such as increased poverty, food insecurities, substance abuse, and mental health problems (Bares et al., 2019; Coleman-Jensen et al., 2013; Moon et al., 2017). It may come as no surprise that rural communities also have higher rates of opioid addiction, overdose, opioid–related deaths, as well as higher suicide and child abuse and neglect rates (Borders, 2018; Keyes et al., 2014; National Advisory Committee on Rural Health and Human Services, 2015). These factors contribute to higher rates of mental health concerns and severe mental health illnesses in rural settings compared to those living in urban and suburban areas (Meit et al., 2014).

Despite these increased public health burdens, rural communities experience formidable barriers to mental health and behavioral services. Barriers include geographic isolation, travel expenses, and a lack of public transportation that make it difficult for families to access behavioral and mental health resources (Berry et al., 2011). Not only do rural communities struggle to get access to services, but limited tax income means that nearby government-funded resources (e.g., schools or mental health services) struggle financially and, therefore, are typically underfunded and low quality (Reeves, 2003). Furthermore, the lack of mental health services prevents many rural individuals from seeking help. Additionally, rural communities tend to stigmatize mental health issues; as a result, those who do seek help frequently face prejudice and social rejection (Murimi & Harpel, 2010; Pullmann et al., 2010). Thus, rural residents are less likely to indicate a need for mental health services (Gamm et al., 2010), which may lead to increased drug usage, suicide, and harmful family situations (Centers for Disease Control and Prevention, 2017). With a lack of accessibility and acceptability of mental health services, teachers are frequently responsible for providing behavioral and mental health support services in the classroom (Wade et al., 2008). Despite this additional demand, rural teachers tend to be unprepared to provide behavioral and mental health services and lack access to adequate training (Arnold et al., 2005). Unfortunately, many rural teachers are often new to the profession, struggle with access to quality professional development opportunities, and are less likely to hold an advanced degree (i.e., master's degree, Johnson & Howley, 2015). Consequently, many rural teachers are inadequately prepared to efficiently implement research-based strategies (Schonert-Reichl et al., 2017). Additionally, rural schools have a high attrition rate that impacts the success of teachers and students

(Nguyen et al., 2019; Sutcher et al., 2016). High staff turnover rate makes it difficult to effectively implement schoolwide classroom management practices due to the inconsistency of trained teachers (Sutcher et al., 2016).

Adapting Strategies for Rural Schools

Despite a need for support in rural schools, there is a scarcity of research regarding rural classroom management. Therefore, it remains unclear what the best behavioral practices are for rural schools. However, we offer strategies for teachers to consider as they work with rural schools. Specifically we share strategies for adapting PBIS practices and supporting rural teachers using tele-coaching.

Rural Tier 1 Support. In order to support students in rural environments, teachers can use Tier 1 strategies in and outside of the classroom. Tier 1 strategies are to be implemented by the entire school staff (e.g., custodians, cooks, and secretaries) and as rural schools tend to rely heavily on bus transportation, schools may want to consider extending Tier 1 strategies to the bus. For example, bus drivers could model, practice, and reinforce appropriate bus behavior. Teachers could use video modeling right before the students get on the bus to remind them of the expectations. Additionally, the PBIS reinforcement system (e.g., tickets) could extend to the bus to help reinforce appropriate bus behavior.

Given the limited availability of technology and broadband at home, teachers must consider how to reach students both in and outside of the classroom. The Remote Instruction Strategy Matrix is useful for supporting rural students outside of the classroom (McDaniel, Chaparro, et al., 2020). The matrix provides a number of examples for adapting PBIS while connecting students and teachers (see McDaniel, Chaparro, et al., 2020 for the full matrix). Included in the matrix is a brief overview of various types of technology (i.e., computer with video, computer without video, phone, and tech-free) along with learning strategies such as providing positive recognition of students, increasing engagement, delivering instruction, and checking in for well-being/mental health (McDaniel, Chaparro, et al., 2020).

PBIS Teams may want to consider using the Working Smart Matrix to develop a plan for identifying potential problems and solutions (see Robbie et al., 2021 for more information). Robbie and colleagues (2021) describe a problem–solving approach to the PBIS framework using a Working Smarter Matrix. They suggest schools (a) identify problems with implementing PBIS within the school; (b) analyze the problem by determining what resources are necessary for implementation; (c) intervene by developing an action plan to re-allocate resources and involving community members; and (d) evaluate if it worked by collecting and analyzing data. In order for successful PBIS implementation, schools need to attempt to prevent any problems by determining how much funding and support is needed to ensure effective implementation. Another proactive method is for students to set short-term and long-term goals to motivate students to be successful in school (Hardré et al., 2008). These goals may not always be directly related to getting good grades, but may include learning a new skill. As such, students should not be celebrated based on their grades, but based on the effort they put into meeting that goal. Additionally, teachers may use these goals to help structure the materials they use in class. For example, if several students are interested in becoming mechanics, the teacher may want to include car-related books and find activities that teach students more about mechanical engineering. Incorporating students' interests into the class may increase their motivation and effort and decrease challenging behavior (Hardré et al., 2008).

Mental Health Supports. School-based mental health programs have been shown to improve students' mental health, academic performance, and have positive long-term implications for students' lives after school (Michael et al., 2016). Although several studies have shown the positive effects of PBIS (e.g., Bradshaw et al., 2008; Horner et al., 2009), relatively few studies were conducted in a rural setting. Historically, one of the greatest hurdles rural schools face is accessing PBIS training and support (Cavanaugh & Swan, 2015; Steed et al., 2013). While it may be challenging for rural schools to fully implement a PBIS framework, adopting one or two PBIS strategies may support students behaviorally, academically, and emotionally. Each PBIS tier consists of several different behavior strategies, such as token economies, self-management, social-emotional learning strategies, positive teacher–student relationships, and teaching expected behaviors. These strategies can be easily adapted to fit within the context of the rural environment.

Professional Development Considerations. Access to resources is a significant hurdle for rural schools, thus schools may consider utilizing online professional development platforms. For example, rural teachers responded positively to receiving PBIS training online and were motivated to implement what they had learned (McDaniel, Bloomfield, et al., 2020). The rural teachers also found PBIS tele-coaching to be a feasible and efficient way to communicate monthly with their PBIS coach who helped them implement PBIS in their school. This adaptation may be beneficial because neither PBIS coaches nor teachers are required to travel long distances.

Another method to support rural teachers with implementing PBIS is to train experienced teachers, school counselors, and school psychologists to be PBIS coaches. Given the urgency of supporting all students, school counselors and psychologists with training on mental health screeners and supporting teachers with administering is needed (Nichols et al., 2017). The counselors and psychologists could then support the teachers with analyzing the data from the screeners and finding appropriate social-emotional learning strategies for students in need. Using school personnel as coaches may reduce the demands of outside training and may increase "buy-in" from the teachers.

Challenges Faced in Urban Settings

According to Milner (2015), there are three types of "urban" environments: (1) urban intensive (i.e., large cities and dense communities of over 1 million people like Los Angeles, Chicago, New York); (2) urban emergent (populations close to but less than 1 million like Nashville, TN, Austin, TX, Columbus, OH); and (3) urban characteristic (areas that are located in suburban and rural areas, but that are experiencing shifts in the diversity of populations like increases in immigrant families and also families from lower socioeconomic backgrounds). Because of the increasing diversity of urban intensive, urban emergent, and urban characteristic spaces, urban classroom management requires teachers to have an understanding about a wide range of student diversity that is beyond race (Milner, 2015).

Underlying challenges, stemming largely from structural inequities in high-poverty urban areas, include higher rates of abuse (physical, psychological, and/or emotional), addiction (e.g., drug, alcohol, gambling), health and nutrition (asthma, ear infections, stomach and speech problems), and homelessness (Milner, 2015). Students experiencing these challenges are absent or tardy more often, move from place to place, and have difficulties concentrating and/or and socializing. Although students in suburban and rural environments may face similar challenges, these challenges are unique to urban environments because of the number and concentration of students who may experience these challenges in any given urban area or school. Moreover, social context, lack of school funding, and variance in the *type* of parent involvement may exacerbate the issues students in urban schools may face (Milner, 2015).

The challenges that students from urban environments face have been associated with teacher attrition (Smith & Smith, 2006). Specifically, one study found that teachers who left urban schools perceived these schools as "violent and chaotic places where anything can happen" (Smith & Smith, 2006, p. 34). Unfortunately, high turnover is a major barrier to adapting evidence-based practices (Forman et al., 2009). With a rotating staff, it is challenging for teams to continually onboard new staff, who often lack experience, appropriate certification, and in some cases any preparation at all (Smith & Smith, 2006). This issue is bi-directional in that lack of knowledge and implementation of classroom management practices is a contributor to teacher attrition, while high turnover is a barrier to adaptation of evidence-based practices. Without stabilizing the workforce, the adaptation challenges will likely continue and schools will ultimately fail to meet the needs of students. As such, it is important to provide appropriate pre-service and in-service training so that teachers can create supportive environments where students flourish.

Teacher Knowledge, Beliefs, and Emotions

In 2013, Jones et al. urged teachers to move away from discipline, conformity, and obedience and towards one that is richer in relationship and context. Specifically, they defined classroom management in urban environments as, "creating a place where students are not only free from physical, emotional, and psychological harm, but are also empowered to learn and grow as people" (p. 30). The emphasis on the eight components of managing a highly productive, safe, and respectful urban environment was founded upon student-teacher relationships, high expectations for students, non-verbal cues and redirection, teacher consistency, teacher perseverance and assertiveness, capitalizing on human resources, restorative justice, and schoolwide consistency for student behavior (Jones et al., 2013). These components begin to merge the components of traditional classroom management strategies (i.e., non-verbal cues and redirection) with *how* the teacher should approach these strategies (e.g., with authentic relationships, high expectations, consistency, perseverance, assertiveness). This approach is consistent with the concept of "warm demanders," in which teachers "embrace values and enact practices that are central to their students' success" (Bondy et al., 2013, p. 421). Moreover, a third theme emerged in the literature beginning at this time: restorative justice. Restorative justice is an approach that focuses on restoring relationships (Hurley et al., 2015). At the center of restorative justice is the relationship. Restorative justice, and restorative practices more generally, leverage a combination of strategies (e.g., restorative conferences and circles; Hurley et al., 2015) that can be used proactively and reactively. Specifically, circles can be used for relationship-building as well as to restore relationships when harm has been committed.

Program and Model Evaluation and Assessment

In a review on classroom management training for teachers in urban environments, teacher trainings up to that point focused on traditional classroom management strategies (e.g., clear expectations, praise), while only a few alluded to culturally responsive classroom management strategies (e.g., relationship building, creating caring environments that focus on learning, encouraging socialization and discussion, and teaching with assertiveness; Larson, 2016). Yet none of the articles addressed recognizing one's own ethnocentrism and having knowledge of students' cultural backgrounds (Larson, 2016), thereby exposing a research-to-practice gap that needed attention in urban classroom management training for teachers working with predominately African American students.

Graham (2018) highlighted the distinct perspectives on equitable classroom management in urban schools (one emphasizing democratic classrooms, the other emphasizing teacher authority) and reconciled the contradictory perspectives by noting that a balanced approach is necessary, as democracy and authority are "two sides of the same coin" (p. 511). Similar to Milner (2014), Graham noted that it is necessary to include student voice in conversations around classroom management, citing the movement in Restorative Justice Education. This balanced approach notes the rejection of zero tolerance discipline policies for more supportive approaches like Restorative Justice Education and social-emotional learning. He writes that we "must address issues of authority without resorting to mechanistic and punitive forms of control," thereby moving further away from the "preoccupation with behavioral regulation in urban schools" (p. 495).

This is not to say that traditional classroom management approaches should be abandoned in urban environments. Pre-correction (reading rules prior to class), explicit timing (letting students know when a transition was about to occur), and active supervision (scanning, providing non-verbal prompts, and offing a minimum of one positive feedback statement) have also been linked with as much as a 50% decrease in middle school student disruptions (Hunter & Haydon, 2019). However, a recent study suggests that first year urban teachers tend to prioritize behavioral strategies (e.g., rules, procedures, expectations, verbal, and non-verbal strategies) over academic and relational aspects of classroom management (Kwok, 2019). Moreover, there was little evidence to suggest that teachers used culturally responsive classroom management strategies, suggesting that pre-service and district training and mentoring programs for early career teachers may want to further support teachers in this critical area of training.

Teacher Learning and Teacher Education

Research by Caldera and colleagues (2020) offers an outline for a classroom management course in urban teaching. This research group identified five thematic units within their framework: (1) trauma-informed and trauma-sensitive classrooms; (2) facing cultural conflicts; (3) culturally informed care; (4) culturally relevant/responsive classroom management; and (5) restorative discipline philosophy and practices. These researchers noted the challenges of students of color living in urban areas (especially those in low-income areas) and insisted that teachers in urban schools consider contextual and cultural influences on student behavior. With regards to context, Caldera and colleagues noted that high-poverty areas can have higher levels of crime, which has been associated with higher levels of stress and trauma. They noted that, "it is… necessary for teachers to cultivate a warm, supportive, and inclusive environment to mitigate the negative effects of low income urban living" (p. 348). Creating trauma-informed and trauma-sensitive classrooms means that teachers not only understand how violence has impacted individuals, but they can create environments and use strategies to meet the needs of trauma survivors. They further highlighted that generic classroom management strategies are Eurocentrically-normed and fail to link classroom management with cultural diversity.

At the time of Milner's writing, it was unclear what teacher education programs taught in terms of "urban classroom management." Milner (2014) suggested that more studies focus on teachers' cultural knowledge in addition to practical knowledge on classroom management in urban settings, thereby aligning what teachers believe with what they actually do. Whether teacher education programs have moved past this is still to be determined, however, the research by Caldera and colleagues (2020) provides a start. Moreover, the literature highlighted by Milner (2015) suggested a more person-centered approach that incorporates support around student emotions and creating positive classroom climates. The research by Graham (2018) supports the notion that we need a balanced approach to classroom management in urban environments—one where we use behaviorist principles and approaches to classroom management, but whereby we also move towards more responsive classroom management techniques where teachers are focused on meeting the needs of their learners and creating psychologically supportive classrooms.

Double Check Student Engagement and Culturally-Responsive Practices Framework

Building on the PBIS literature, and its focus on data, systems, and practices within a multi-tiered infrastructure, the Double Check Student Engagement and Culturally-responsive Practices framework was developed to more directly address issues of student culture in the classroom (Bradshaw et al., 2018). Developed in direct response to concerns regarding the discipline gaps for students of color, the Double Check CARES framework was created, which outlines the following five core elements culturally-responsive practices: Connection to Curriculum, Authentic Relationships, Reflective Thinking, Effective Communication, and Sensitivity to Students' Culture (Bradshaw et al., 2018). The model incorporates three core elements: (1) Tier 1 School-wide Positive Behavioral Interventions and Supports, (2) the Double Check Professional Development series (DCPD), and (3) the Classroom Check-Up (CCU) coaching model. More specifically, teachers receive group-based professional development by a trained coach and trainer, along with coaching using the CCU model originally created by Reinke et al. (2008) to promote their use of the five CARES research-based core features. The CCU coaching incorporates elements of motivational interviewing, data-based decision-making, and on-going tailored supports and technical assistance to help teachers effectively and routinely use a variety of strategies aligned with the CARES framework. In addition to the DCPD and CCU coaching, schoolwide and team-based coaching occurs to further leverage the Tier 1 PBIS infrastructure to promote review of discipline data with an eye toward disproportionality and supports for the PBIS Team to address issues of diversity, equity, and inclusion. A series of studies has documented positive impacts of the Double Check version of the CCU coaching model on teacher and student outcomes, over and above the effects of DCPD and Tier 1 PBIS (Bradshaw et al., 2018; Pas et al., in press); efforts are currently underway to further scale the model through an online platform and promote its use in a variety of school contexts, including rural schools.

Challenges Faced in Online Settings

Historically, behavior and classroom management occurred in traditional brick-and-mortar classrooms. However, the COVID-19 pandemic changed what schools and classrooms looked like during and after the pandemic (Darling-Hammond et al., 2020). In March 2020, millions of students no longer entered schools in person, instead they began meeting their teachers online via Zoom or other web conferencing tools as part of emergency remote learning (UNESCO, 2020). In many instances, online learning continued into 2020–2021, however it varied based on the context, grade, and technology resources. By April 2021, most schools are offering face-to-face (brick-and-mortar) instruction (US Department of Education, 2021). Yet online or remote learning will likely remain an option for districts. For example, many districts are now opting to provide online instruction instead of closing schools for inclement weather or other reasons (Lieberman, 2020). Parents have also found online options to be feasible and are now able to enroll their children in public options.

Although different terms are often used to describe online learning (e.g., remote, virtual), we opted to use the term online learning as we find it encompasses a variety of different options, including synchronous (students meet online with their teachers or classmates), asynchronous (students learn on their time, discussion boards), and blended (a combination of synchronous, asynchronous or face-to-face). For the purpose of this paper, we will focus on online instruction; however many of the asynchronous strategies are relevant to the other modalities. Singh and Thurman (2019) provide a definition of online learning:

> Education being delivered in an online environment through the use of the internet for teaching and learning. This includes online learning on the part of the students that is not dependent on their physical or virtual co-location. The teaching content is delivered online and the instructors develop teaching modules that enhance learning and interactivity in the synchronous or asynchronous environment
>
> *p. 302*

As online instruction became a common modality during the COVID-19 pandemic, the transition to online learning for teachers and students was challenging as many teachers do not receive training in online instruction (Gunter & Reeves, 2017; Hirsch, Bruhn, et al., 2021). Prior to the pandemic, computers and technology were largely used to augment instruction, rather than the primary instructional platform (Hinostroza et al., 2015). In a survey of 75 elementary teachers, the majority of respondents (70%) indicated they received less than 3 hours of technology-related professional development during the previous 12-month period (Pittman & Gains, 2015). For this reason it is likely that only 18.7% of survey respondents were considered to be high-level technology integrators (Pittman & Gains, 2015).

Further compounding the challenges related to online learning is the digital divide or homework gap (lack of digital devices and reliable broadband; National Education Association, 2020). According to the American Community Survey data (2018) 25% of US students do not have an Internet-capable device or high-speed broadband at home. The homework gap is especially prominent in rural and urban areas of the USA (National Education Association, 2020). To respond to the homework gap, students urgently need technology resources to participate in online learning and their teachers need sufficient training on how to instruct and engage students online. The remainder of this section provides an overview of essential classroom management strategies to support students in online learning environments.

Online Tier 1 Support

In an effort to support students in online learning environments, teachers can adapt Tier 1 schoolwide and classroom systems for online learning (McDaniel, Chaparro, et al., 2020). Universal or Tier 1 support focused on proactively supporting student behavior by providing predictable and reinforcing environments. Three key elements include: establishing relationships, teaching expectations and routines, and utilizing strategies for increasing student engagement.

Establishing Relationships. Building relationships with students is considered a key component to classroom management (Marzano, 2003; Simonsen & Myers, 2015). Relationships are essential because they not only connect students with teachers and peers, but also can help connect "learning managers" with teachers, where a *learning manager* is an adult who helps support the student during online learning (i.e., parents, family members, tutors; Hirsch, McDaniel et al., 2021). Partnerships between learning managers and teachers have resulted in coordinated and consistent messages (Christenson & Sheridan, 2001), as well as articulating shared goals, implementation of consistent plans, and adoption of mutual and coordinated responsibility for problem solving (Clarke et al., 2009). Students with supportive relationships have higher levels of achievement and high school graduation (Rathvon, 2008).

One way to build an authentic relationship is through consistent and frequent communication. For example, greeting students, using their names frequently, and engaging in non-academic conversations can help teachers establish a relationship (Simonsen & Myers, 2015). In brick-and-mortar classrooms, the "greeting at the door" strategy is linked to increased engagement and increased speed-to-task engagement (Allday et al., 2011; Allday & Pakurar, 2007). This simple classroom management strategy can be adapted to an online environment (e.g., "Hi Avi, I am glad you are online with your headphones on today! I appreciate you being prepared to learn!"). Another option is for teachers to have students complete a brief polling question as they are joining the online meeting.

Online instruction requires teachers to communicate with students, but also with learning managers. Communication should include synchronous and asynchronous options. Synchronous options could include online open houses, office hours, and conferences. Asynchronous options could include pre-recorded videos, emails, or discussion boards.

Another strategy for building relationships is surveying students and learning managers. Brief surveys can include questions related to student interests, their needs, and identify potential barriers (Hirsch, McDaniel, et al., 2021). For example, one teacher created an online "morning check-in" on Google Forms. The form asked questions related to how the student is feeling that day with a smiley-face rating scale. It also included questions asking their goal for the day and how they wanted to meet with the teacher (e.g., telephone, online). Teachers can use survey data to adjust their daily schedules and communicate with the learning managers.

Teaching Expectations and Routines. Effective classroom management starts with integrating expectations (Office of Special Education Programs, 2015). Teaching and reinforcing behavioral expectations have been widely studied and connected to higher academic achievement and improved school climate (Horner et al., 2010, 2017). Paralleling brick-and-mortar classwide positive behavior supports (Simonsen et al., 2015), online contexts also incorporate teaching expectations and routines. If students are part of a brick-and-mortar school, this is a great opportunity to infuse the schoolwide expectations into the online classroom. Rather than reinvent the wheel, the online classroom can use the same three to five positively phrased expectations (e.g., Be Ready, Be Respectful, Be Safe). Using the same familiar language helps increase generalization across the settings.

Teachers can adapt the expectations matrix to include "online learning" as one setting similar to brick-and-mortar settings (e.g., bathroom, hallway, classroom). Another option is to create expectations for each online context or setting. The National Technical Assistance Center on PBIS (2020) developed guidance for creating remote instruction teaching matrices. They recommend using online activities and applications as the settings (e.g., teacher-led whole group instruction, small-group activities in breakout rooms, SeeSaw Application, EPIC Reading Application). Within the online learning matrix, expectations for technology specific behaviors are outlined such as when video is required and accessing school-approved sites.

Similar to brick-and-mortar, proactively teaching routines helps students and learning managers. Online learning routines may include topics such as how to get the teacher's attention, submit work, or cite sources of information and pictures. A daily schedule is also another important classroom management tool. The schedule will likely include synchronous meeting times along with asynchronous activities. Schedules also need to include breaks and lunch times. A predictable and developmentally appropriate schedule will help both students and learning managers navigate online learning (Hirsch, McDaniel, et al., 2021). This schedule should be posted, reviewed, and referenced on a daily basis. It is important to communicate schedule changes with both the students and learning managers. Many students (especially younger students and students with disabilities) may benefit from using paper copies of schedules and other materials. Teachers can provide printed packets containing information such as daily tasks and manipulatives. For example, a seventh grade student with a learning disability may need a daily schedule in the form of a checklist, detailing information about their daily tasks and meetings (Hirsch, McDaniel, et al., 2021).

Strategies for Increasing Student Engagement. As noted earlier, effective classroom management integrates strategies to increase student engagement (Office of Special Education Programs, 2015). In brick-and-mortar classrooms, these generally include opportunities to respond (OTR). OTRs provide students an opportunity to respond and then allow teachers to provide feedback (e.g., individual or group questions). Examples of individual OTRs include calling on students individually and round-robin responses. Examples of group or choral OTRs include responding aloud in union, think-pair-shares, holding up a cue card or response card, white boards. Across all grade levels, students perform better when there are frequent checks for their understanding (i.e., Hollo & Hirn, 2015; MacSuga-Gage & Gage, 2015). This holds true for students with disabilities such as those with emotional and behavioral disorders (e.g., Alter et al., 2011; Sutherland et al., 2003).

To promote student engagement, teachers can adapt and embed OTRs in their online instruction. Low-tech strategies such as physical actions (e.g., thumbs up, standing up) as well as materials (e.g., response cards, wipe-off boards) are easy to integrate into online instruction. There are high-tech programs available for teachers. These include programs such as Poll Everywhere and PearDeck. PearDeck is suitable for K–12 students and allows teachers to include a variety of different types of OTR strategies in their instruction. Regardless of the technology (low-high tech) used to deliver OTRs, it is helpful for the teacher to generate the questions ahead of time and embed them into their lesson. Another key is to make sure the students know how to respond prior to delivering the OTR. Teachers will need to model, practice, and provide feedback on the desired response prior to asking a question. Depending on the age-level of the students this information will need to be communicated with the learning manager prior to the lesson.

In summary, when creating online lessons, expectations, and routines, it is important to consider the student's access to technology, support at home, and age. The three aforementioned classroom management practices (i.e., establishing relationships, teaching expectations, and actively engaging students) are simply examples of practices that are traditionally used in brick-and-mortar classrooms as well as online spaces. Teachers can also look at adapting other practices such as reinforcement and choice.

Professional Development to Implement and Adapt Classroom Management Across Contexts

In response to the challenges associated with the lack of pre-service training in classroom management, the remainder of this chapter presents content on professional development. Many of the strategies can also be adapted for teacher preparation settings. In addition, they can be implemented across a variety of contexts such as rural, urban, and online settings.

Studies suggest that training in classroom management can have an impact on both teacher and student behaviors, as well as reduce teachers' risk for attrition for the field (Aloe et al., 2014; Metlife Inc., 2013; Sutton et al., 2009). In fact, there is a large and robust body of research documenting the positive impacts of training in classroom management on a variety of effective teacher practices, such as teachers' use of praise (Simonsen et al., 2020), positive behavioral expectations, the frequency of approvals, and ratings of teacher monitoring and anticipation (Pas, Johnson, et al., 2016). Similarly, providing training in classroom management can also improve teachers' use of individualization, transitions, and reinforcement (Akalin & Sucuoglu, 2015), and a reduction in the use of teacher reprimands (Reinke et al., 2014), as well as improvements in their own self-efficacy in classroom management (Dicke et al., 2015) and teacher wellbeing (Kennedy et al., 2021). Moreover, researchers have examined the association between classroom management training and student behavior as measured by office disciplinary referrals and suspensions (Reglin et al., 2012). Similarly, classroom management has also been linked with fewer disruptions and more prosocial behavior (Pas, Johnson, et al., 2016; Reinke et al., 2014), as well as greater on-task behavior and academic engagement (Reinke et al., 2014; Akalin & Sucuoglu, 2015), along with less overall negative behavior (Akalin & Sucuoglu, 2015).

Professional Development Content

It is important that classroom management training across contexts includes information and strategies on supporting both teacher *and* student behaviors. Specifically, comprehensive training packages may include evidence-based, culturally responsive, trauma-informed, and restorative practices and strategies (Caldera et al., 2020) to build psychologically supportive and inclusive classrooms that support pro-social student behaviors. In trauma-informed classrooms and schools, for instance, teachers (a) understand trauma, the impact of trauma, and paths for recovery; (b) know the signs of trauma; (c) create classrooms that support students who have been exposed to trauma; and (d) work to not re-traumatize students (Cavanaugh, 2016). Teachers also need information on classroom management (e.g., routines and procedures, responding to disruptions), as well as resources on relationship-building, effective instruction for students with special needs, and culturally responsive pedagogy (Caldera, et al., 2020). In addition, information about resolving conflict (Baker et al., 2016; Webster-Stratton et al., 2011), parent–teacher collaboration, and ways to promote students' emotional regulation, social skills, and problem-solving skills should also be considered (Webster-Stratton et al., 2011). Moreover, comprehensive classroom management training might also include content related to stress management and wellness since challenges with classroom management and student disruptions may increase stress that can eventually lead to burnout (Dicke et al., 2015; Kennedy et al., 2021). Scholars also recommend that the process of professional development in classroom management be systematic and collaborative, and that these processes are built into the intervention to allow for adaptation with high fidelity across contexts (Webster-Stratton et al., 2011).

Multi-tiered Support for Professional Development in Classroom Management

Using a Multitiered Support for Professional Development (MTS-PD; Grasley-Boy et al., 2019; Simonsen et al., 2014) framework to support teachers' classroom management practices aligns with the multicomponent professional development and may provide the flexibility and adaptability needed to facilitate training across contexts. This is particularly helpful given that teachers vary in their knowledge and skills to implement effective classroom management. As such, a MTS-PD framework may account for diverse teacher needs and ability in classroom management (Grasley-Boy et al., 2019; Simonsen et al., 2014). In general, MTS-PD includes: (1) a continuum of support (i.e., universal, targeted, and intensive PD) and assessment (i.e., universal screening and progress monitoring), and (2) a structured manner for differentiating, supporting, and supervising classroom teachers' needs (Simonsen, et al., 2014). An MTS-PD framework not only allows for adaptability and flexibility in training and support, but will also serve to organize the literature on classroom management training. Moreover, content across all tiers should include evidence-based classroom management strategies, culturally responsive practices, trauma-informed practices, and restorative practices (Caldera et al., 2020). Below we consider specific models for training teachers in classroom management across all three tiers.

Tier I Training Supports

A common method for supporting teachers is whole-group, in-service professional development training (Simonsen et al., 2014). In this tier, support and training is generally delivered to all teachers. Effective professional development likely requires follow-up sessions to support learning (Yoon et al., 2007). As such, some scholars have found success providing a one-day workshop and then supplementing that workshop with online support (Baker et al., 2016). This type of online support can be encouraging teachers to view online video clips of strategies they learned from the workshop, applying strategies in their classroom, and then engaging in online discussions about using the strategies (Baker et al., 2016). It is suggested that each professional development session include explicit modeling and opportunities to practice (Simonsen et al., 2014). Content support has also been offered to participants in the form of books and video supports that are representative of multiple cultural contexts (Webster-Stratton et al., 2011). One particular training model uses role-plays and small group break-out sessions, along with encouraging practice between monthly workshops (Webster-Stratton et al., 2011).

Tier II Training Supports

Tier II supports generally include more intensive supports outside of the whole group professional development. This may include self-monitoring (Simonsen et al., 2014) or small group coaching (Webster-Stratton et al., 2011). The Incredible Years Classroom Management Training Program (IY TCM), for example, trains two or three teachers per building who then provide small group coaching support to other teachers in their building. These trained coaches model skills and support teachers' efforts to generalize the principles of the training into their classroom (Webster-Stratton et al., 2011). Small group coaching is beneficial in that it may reduce isolation and stigma often experienced by those who struggle with classroom management (Webster-Stratton et al., 2011). In this way, teachers learn as much from each other as from the group leader in IY TCM (Webster-Stratton et al., 2011). Schools may even want to consider setting up professional learning communities focused on classroom management whereby members meet regularly for the purpose of professional growth to support both teacher and student behavior. In this form of training and support, teachers learn by working collaboratively, systematically, and interdependently to change their classroom practice in a way that benefits students and the school community (Riggins & Knowles, 2020).

Tier III Training Supports

The most intensive support involves individualized coaching (Simonsen, 2014). This type of support is more time consuming and resource-intensive than the supports offered to teachers at tiers I and

II. For instance, some classroom management training programs provide weekly coaching visits to teachers throughout the year (Webster-Stratton et al., 2011), while other classroom management coaching interventions might take three hours of active participation over a course of several weeks (Pas, Larson, et al., 2016). Some researchers have noted that the Classroom Check-Up (CCU) can be time consuming, and attempted to make the CCU approach more feasible by using explicit didactic training as well as booster training with verbal modeling (see for example Fallon et al., 2019); however, others have argued that the CCU is an economical and efficient method for coaching teachers (Pas et al., in press). Others have attempted to find time and cost-effective coaching that involves a targeted professional development (TPD) approach. This approach included brief (~20 minute) didactic training on a targeted skill, weekly scripted email prompts reminding teachers to focus on their skill, daily self-monitoring, and self-reinforcement (Simonsen et al., 2020). Although TPD increased targeted behaviors in specific praise, it was not as effective when the training shifted to a different skill (Simonsen et al., 2020).

Other examples of Tier III supports may involve technology like a mixed-reality simulation (Pas, Johnson, et al., 2016; Pas et al., 2019) or web-based communication software (Rock et al., 2013). This type of coaching support can be implemented in pairs or individually, depending on the needs of the teachers and the time allotted to the activity. In two coaching projects, Pas and colleagues (2016, 2019) used a modified version of the Classroom Check-Up (Reinke et al., 2008) to support teachers in classroom management for students with autism (Pas, Johnson, et al., 2016) and bullying (Pas et al., 2019). Findings from both studies suggest that a coaching intervention that combines mixed-reality simulation with the Classroom Check-Up coaching model is not only acceptable and feasible, but is also associated with teacher and student behavior change (Pas, Johnson, et al., 2016; Pas et al., 2019). Relatedly, researchers have found success using web-based, real time communication using Skype software to offer online coaching in evidence-based classroom management strategies (Rock et al., 2013). In general, research suggests that performance feedback has a positive effect on teachers' use of targeted classroom management skills (Akalin & Sucuoglu, 2015) and is therefore an important support to provide to teachers who need the most assistance with classroom management.

Methods for Providing Classroom Management Professional Development

Several classroom management professional development formats have been implemented and researched. These include: (1) whole-group professional development (Dicke et al., 2015); (2) coaching with performance feedback (Akalin & Sucuoglu, 2015; Fallon et al., 2019; Pas, Johnson, et al., 2016; Pas, Larson, et al., 2016; Reinke et al., 2012); (3) whole group professional development with embedded coaching (Reinke, et al., 2012, 2014; Webster-Stratton, et al., 2011); (4) virtual coaching (Rock et al., 2013),; (5) whole group professional development with online support (Baker et al., 2016),; and (6) targeted professional development (Freeman et al., 2018; Simonsen et al., 2020). Based on the various supports identified in the literature, it is evident that more attention should be placed on a multicomponent professional development model (Simonsen et al., 2014; Webster-Stratton et al., 2011).

Multicomponent professional development models generally include explicit training, coaching, performance feedback, and similar strategies that align with one another (Simonsen et al., 2020). These activities can be done online or in person. For example, research with pre-service teachers suggests that using short multi-media vignettes, referred to as Content Acquisition Podcasts (CAP) are an effective strategy to learn about PBIS as well as classroom management (Kennedy et al., 2017; Kennedy & Thomas, 2012). CAPs have been researched with both in-service teachers (Kennedy et al., 2017) as well as preservice teachers (Hirsch et al., 2015; Kennedy et al., 2015).

Infusing this type of universal, technology-based support can be implemented in conjunction with self-monitoring progress (Simonsen et al., 2014) using the strategies discussed between professional development sessions. Internal or external coaches are encouraged to remind teachers to use targeted strategies (via email, text messages, or bulletins), and coaching support (small group or individual)

Table 8.2 Classroom Management Professional Development Adaptations

Context	Considerations (Adaptations)	Included Content	Example
Rural	Professional development should include presenters familiar with the rural environment and understand the complexities that come along with being in a rural school	Include social–emotional learning curriculum and mental health training for teachers	Teachers can work with other local level educators or connect online with other rural educators.
Urban	Professional development should include diverse presenters and diverse examples	Include evidence-based, culturally responsive, trauma informed, and restorative practices and strategies	Discuss practices from Double Check
Online	Include videos of real-world examples, breakout rooms so teachers can meet with others in a small group, allow teachers to access materials after the session	If possible, include self-check quizzes or interactive lessons to keep teachers engaged	For example, include a Kahoot! Quiz on the topic and play with the teachers.

intensifies according to teacher need along each tier. When considering classroom management training, school leadership teams can determine how the classroom management practices can be adapted to align with their school's culture and context. See Table 8.2 for an example of adaptations across the three contexts (i.e., rural, urban, online).

Conclusion

The increased interest in and push for broad dissemination of evidence-based classroom management strategies has brought about a more concerted focus on program adaptation. While not a new concept, adaptation does require careful consideration and collaboration between practitioners and researchers. The empirical work on adaptation is still emerging and there are many aspects of this field yet to be fully explored. A complicating factor is that few teachers enter the field well-prepared to leverage the research base of effective classroom management strategies. And even fewer teachers are adequately trained on how to make planned adaptations of these models to meet their students' cultural and contextual needs, without compromising the integrity of the program or practice.

In this chapter, we have focused largely on three contexts—rural schools, urban schools, and online learning—which are important settings where evidence-based classroom management programs are sorely needed; however, they each pose some unique challenges that may require additional attention to the adaptation process. With these goals in mind, we emphasize the importance of professional development and coaching support, which are necessary to guide teachers in the adaptation process. We hope that this review and set of recommendations provide some insight for teachers and other school-based practitioners who seek guidance on strategies for adapting evidence-based classroom management strategies for these three contexts, and potentially other educational settings.

Note

1 Our work was supported by a grant awarded by the National Center for Special Education Research within the Institute for Education Sciences (Cooperative Agreement # R324A200061) to the University of Virginia (principal investigator: Michael Kennedy). No specific endorsement of the products reported herein on the part of the U.S. Department of Education should be inferred.

References

Akalin, S., & Sucuoglu, B. (2015). Effects of classroom management intervention based on teacher training and performance feedback on outcomes of teacher-student dyads in inclusive classrooms. *Educational Sciences: Theory & Practice, 15*(3). doi.org/10.12738/estp.2015.3.2543

Allday, R. A., Bush, M., Ticknor, N., & Walker, L. (2011). Using teacher greetings to increase speed to task engagement. *Journal of Applied Behavior Analysis, 44*(2), 393–396. https://doi.org/10.1901/jaba.2011.44-393

Allday, R. A., & Pakurar, K. (2007). Effects of teacher greetings on student on-task behavior. *Journal of Applied Behavior Analysis, 40*, 317–320. doi.org/10.1901/jaba.2007.86-06

Aloe, A. M., Amo, L. C., & Shanahan, M. E. (2014). Classroom management self-efficacy and burnout: A multivariate meta-analysis. *Educational Psychology Review, 26*, 101–126. https://doi.org/10.1007/s10648-013-9244-0

Alter, P. J., Brown, E. T., & Pyle, J. (2011). A strategy-based intervention to improve math problem solving skills of students with emotional and behavioral disorders. *Education and Treatment of Children, 34*, 535–550. www.jstor.org/stable/42900133

Arnold, M. L., Newman, J. H., Gaddy, B. B., & Dean, C. B. (2005). A look at the condition of rural education research: Setting a direction for future research. *Journal of Research in Rural Education, 20*(6), 1–25.

Baker, C., Gentry, J., & Larmer, W. (2016). A model for online support in classroom management: Perceptions of beginning teachers. *Administrative Issues Journal: Connecting Education, Practice, and Research, 6*, 22–37. DOI: 10.5929/2016.6.1.3

Bal, A. (2018). Culturally responsive positive behavioral interventions and supports: A process-oriented framework for systemic transformation. *Review of Education, Pedagogy, and Cultural Studies, 40*(2), 144–174. https://doi.org/10.1080/10714413.2017.1417579

Bares, C. B., Weaver, A., & Kelso, M. F. (2019). Adolescent opioid use: Examining the intersection of multiple inequalities. *Journal of Prevention and Intervention in the Community, 47*(4), 295–309. DOI: 10.1080/10852352.2019.1617382

Berry, A. B., Petrin, R. A., Gravelle, M. L., & Farmer, T. W. (2011). Issues in special education teacher recruitment, retention, and professional development: Considerations in supporting rural teachers. *Rural Special Education Quarterly, 30*(4), 3–11. https://doi.org/10.1177/875687051103000402

Bondy, E., Ross, D. D., Hambacher, E., & Acosta, M. (2013). Becoming warm demanders: Perspectives and practices of first year teachers. *Urban Education, 48*(3), 420–450. http://dx.doi.org/10.1177/0042085912456846

Borders, T. F. (2018). Portraying a more complete picture of illicit drug use epidemiology and policy for rural America: A competing viewpoint to the CDC's MMWR report. *The Journal of Rural Health, 34*(1), 3–5. DOI: 10.1111/jrh.12289

Bottiani, J. H., Bradshaw, C. P., & Gregory, A. (2018). *Nudging the gap: Introduction to the special issue Closing in on Discipline Disproportionality*. School Psychology Review, 47, 109–117. doi.org/10.17105/SPR-2018-0023.V47-2

Bottiani, J., Bradshaw, C. P., & Mendelson, T. (2016). A multilevel examination of racial disparities in high school discipline: Black and White adolescents' perceived equity, school belonging, and adjustment problems. *Journal of Educational Psychology, 109*(4), 532–545. http://dx.doi.org/10.1037/edu0000155

Bradshaw, C. P., Koth, C. W., Bevans, K. B., Ialongo, N., & Leaf, P. J. (2008). The impact of school-wide Positive Behavioral Interventions and Supports (PBIS) on the organizational health of elementary schools. *School Psychology Quarterly, 23*, 462–473. DOI: 10.1037/a0012883

Bradshaw, C. P., Koth, C. W., Thornton, L. A., & Leaf, P. J. (2009). Altering school climate through school-wide Positive Behavioral Interventions and Supports: Findings from a group-randomized effectiveness trial. *Prevention Science, 10*, 100–115. DOI:10.1007/s11121-008-0114-9

Bradshaw, C. P., Mitchell, M. M., & Leaf, P. J. (2010). Examining the effects of school-wide positive behavioral interventions and supports on student outcomes: Results from a randomized controlled effectiveness trial in elementary schools. *Journal of Positive Behavior Interventions, 12*, 133–148. DOI:10.1177.1098300709334798

Bradshaw, C. P., Pas, E. T., Bottiani, J., Debnam, K. J., Reinke, W., Herman, K., & Rosenberg, M. S. (2018). Promoting cultural responsivity and student engagement through Double Check coaching of classroom teachers: An efficacy study. *School Psychology Review, 47*, 118–134. DOI: 10.17105/SPR2017-0119.V47-2

Bradshaw, C. P., Waasdorp, T. E., & Leaf, P. J. (2012). Effects of school-wide positive behavioral interventions and supports on child behavior problems. *Pediatrics, 130*, 1136–1145. DOI:10.1542/peds.2012-0243

Brownell, M. T., Chard, D., Benedict, A., & Lignugaris/Kraft, B. (2018). Preparing general and special education preservice teachers for response to intervention: A practice-based approach. In P. C. Pullen & M. J. Kennedy (Eds.), *Handbook of response to intervention and multi-tiered systems of support* (pp. 121–145). Routledge.

Caldera, A., Whitaker, M. C., & Conrad Popova, D. A. (2020). Classroom management in urban schools: proposing a course framework. *Teaching Education, 31*(3), 343–361. ttps://doi.org/10.1080/10476210.2018.1561663

Cartledge, G., Lo,Y.-Y.,Vincent, C. G., Robinson-Ervin, P. (2015). Culturally responsive classroom management. In Emmer, E., & Sabornie, E. J. (Eds.), *Handbook of Classroom Management* 2nd ed., pp. 411–430. Routledge.

Cavanaugh, B. (2016). Trauma-informed classrooms and schools. *Beyond Behavior, 25*(2), 41–46. doi/10.1177/107429561602500206

Cavanaugh, B., & Swan, M. (2015). Building SWPBIS capacity in rural schools through building-based coaching: Early findings from a district-based model. *Rural Special Education Quarterly, 34*(4), 29–39. https://doi.org/10.1177/875687051503400404

Centers for Disease Control and Prevention. (2017). *CDC reports rising rates of drug overdose deaths in rural areas.* U.S. Department of Health and Human Services. www.cdc.gov/media/releases/2017/p1019-rural-overdose-deaths.html

Center on Positive Behavioral Interventions and Supports (March 2020). *Creating a PBIS behavior teaching matrix for remote instruction.* University of Oregon. www.pbis.org.

Chaparro, E. A., Nese, R. N.T., & McIntosh, K. (2015). Examples of engaging instruction to increase equity in education. Center on Positive Behavioral Interventions and Supports. University of Oregon.

Chen, C.-C., Sutherland, K. S., Kunemund, R., Sterrett, B.,Wilkinson, S., Brown, C., & Maggin, D. M. (2021). Intensifying interventions for students with Emotional and Behavioral Difficulties: A conceptual synthesis of practice elements and adaptive expertise. *Journal of Emotional and Behavioral Disorders, 29*(1), 56–66. https://doi.org/10.1177/1063426620953086

Christenson, S. L., & Sheridan, S. M. (2001). *Schools and families: Creating essential connections for learning.* Guilford Press.

Clarke, B. L., Sheridan, S. M., & Woods, K. E. (2009). Elements of healthy school–family relationships. In S. Christenson & A. Reschly. (Eds.), *Handbook of family-school partnerships* (pp. 61–79). Routledge.

Coleman-Jensen, A., McFall, W., & Nord, M. (2013). Food insecurity in households with children: Prevalence, severity, and household characteristics, 2010–11. *Economic Information Bulletin,* EIB-113. www.ers.usda.gov/publications/pub-details/?pubid=43765

Darling-Hammond, L., Schachner, A., & Edgerton, A. K., Badrinarayan, A., Cardichon, J., Cookson, P. W., Jr., Griffith, M., Klevan, S., Maier, A., Martinez, M., Melnick, H.,Truong, N., & Wojcikiewicz, S. (2020). *Restarting and reinventing school: Learning in the time of COVID and beyond.* Learning Policy Institute. http://learningpolicyinstitute.org/product/restarting-reinventing-school-covid.

Dicke,T., Elling, J., Schmeck, A., & Leutner, D. (2015). Reducing reality shock: The effects of classroom management skills training on beginning teachers. *Teaching and Teacher education, 48,* 1–12. https://doi.org/10.1016/j.tate.2015.01.013

Domitrovich, C. E., Bradshaw, C. P., Poduska, J., Hoagwood, K., Buckley, J., Olin, S., Romanelli, L. H., Leaf, P. J., Greenberg, M. T., & Ialongo, N. S. (2008). Maximizing the implementation quality of evidence-based preventive interventions in schools: A conceptual framework. *Advances in School Mental Health Promotion: Training and Practice, Research and Policy, 1*(3), 6–28. DOI:10.1080/1754730X.2008.9715730

Evertson, C. M., & Weinstein, C. S. (Eds.). (2006). *Handbook of classroom management: Research, practice, and contemporary issues.* Erlbaum.

Fallon, L. M., Collier-Meek, M. A., & Kurtz, K. D. (2019). Feasible coaching supports to promote teachers' classroom management in high-need settings: An experimental single case design study. *School Psychology Review, 48*(1), 3–17. https://doi.org/10.17105/SPR-2017-0135.V48-1

Flower, A., McKenna, J.W., & Haring, C. D. (2017). Behavior and classroom management: Are teacher preparation programs really preparing our teachers? *Preventing School Failure: Alternative Education for Children and Youth, 61*(2), 163–169. https://doi.org/10.1080/1045988X.2016.1231109

Forman, S. G., Olin, S. S., Hoagwood, K. E., Crowe, M., & Saka, N. (2009). Evidence-based interventions in schools: Developers' views of implementation barriers and facilitators. *School Mental Health, 1*(1), 26. https://doi.org/10.1007/s12310-008-9002-5

Freeman, J., Kowitt, J., Simonsen, B.,Wei,Y., Dooley, K., Gordon, L., & Maddock, E. (2018). A high school replication of targeted professional development for classroom management. *Remedial and Special Education, 39*(3), 144–157. https://doi.org/10.1177/0741932517719547

Freeman, J., Simonsen, B., Briere, D., & MacSuga-Gage, A. S. (2014). Pre-service teacher training in classroom management: A review of state accreditation policy and teacher preparation programs. *Teacher Education and Special Education, 37*(2), 106–120. https://doi.org/10.1177/0888406413507002

Gage, N. A., Scott, T., Hirn, R., & MacSuga-Gage, A. S. (2018). The relationship between teachers' implementation of classroom management practices and student behavior in elementary school. *Behavioral Disorders, 43*(2), 302–315. https://doi.org/10.1177/0198742917714809

Gage, N. A.,Whitford, D. K., Katsiyannis, A., Adam, S., & Jasper, A. (2019). National analysis of the disciplinary exclusion of Black students with and without disabilities. *Journal of Child and Family Studies, 28,* 1754–1764. https://doi.org/10.1007/s10826-019-01407-7

Gamm, L., Stone, S., & Pittman, S. (2010). Mental health and mental disorders – A rural challenge: A literature review. *Rural Healthy People, 1*(1), 97–114.

Graham, E. J. (2018). Authority or democracy? Integrating two perspectives on equitable classroom management in urban schools. *The Urban Review, 50*(3), 493–515. https://doi.org/10.1007/s11256-017-0443-8

Grasley-Boy, N., Gage, N. A., & MacSuga-Gage, A. S. (2019). Multitiered support for classroom management professional development. *Beyond Behavior, 28*(1), 5–12. doi:10.1177/1074295618798028

Greenough, R., & Nelson, S. R. (2015). Recognizing the variety of rural schools. *Peabody Journal of Education, 90*(2), 322–332. https://doi.org/10.1080/0161956X.2015.1022393

Gunter, G. A., & Reeves, J. L. (2017). Online professional development embedded with mobile learning: An examination of teachers' attitudes, engagement and dispositions. *British Journal of Educational Technology, 48*(6), 1305–1317. https://doi.org/10.1111/bjet.12490

Hardré, P. L., Sullivan, D. W., & Roberts, N. (2008). *Rural Teachers' Best Motivating Strategies: A Blending of Teachers' and Students' Perspectives. The Rural Educator, 30*(1), 19–31. https://doi.org/10.35608/ruraled.v30i1.458

Herman, K. C., Prewett, S., Eddy, C., Savale, A., & Reinke, W. M. (2020). Patterns of middle school teacher stress and coping: Concurrent and prospective correlates. *Journal of School Psychology, 78*, 54–68. DOI: 10.1016/j.jsp.2019.11.003

Hinostroza, J. E., Ibieta, A. I., Claro, M., & Labbe, C. (2015). Characterization of teachers' use of computers and Internet inside and outside the classroom: The need to focus on the quality. *Education and Information Technologies, 21*, 1595–1610. https://doi.org/10.1007/s10639-015-9404-6

Hirsch, S. E., Bruhn, A. L., McDaniel, S. M., & Mathews, H. (2021). A survey of educators serving students with emotional and behavioral disorders during the COVID-19 pandemic. *Behavioral Disorders, 47* (2), 95–107. https://doi.org/10.1177/01987429211016780

Hirsch, S. E., Kennedy, M. J., Haines, S. J., Thomas, C. N., & Alves, K. D. (2015). Improving preservice teachers' knowledge and application of functional behavioral assessments using multimedia. *Behavioral Disorders, 41*, 38–50. DOI:10.17988/0198-7429-41.1.38

Hirsch, S. E., McDaniel, S., La Salle, T., & Walker, A. C. (2021). Instructional management for students with emotional and behavioral disorders in remote learning environments. *Intervention in School and Clinic, 57*(2), 78–86. https://doi.10.1177/10534512211001825

Hirsch, S. E., Randall, K., Bradshaw, C. P., & Lloyd, J. W. (2021). Professional learning and development in classroom management for novice teachers: A systematic review. *Education and Treatment of Children.* https://doi.org/10.1007/s43494-021-00042-6

Hollo, A., & Hirn, R. G. (2015). Teacher and student behaviors in the contexts of grade-level and instructional grouping. *Preventing School Failure: Alternative Education for Children and Youth, 59*, 1, 30–39, DOI: 10.1080/1045988X.2014.919140

Horner, R. H., Sugai, G., & Anderson, C. M. (2010). Examining the evidence base for school-wide positive behavior support. *Focus on Exceptional Children, 42*(8), 1–14.

Horner, R. H., Sugai, G., Smolkowski, K., Eber, L., Nakasato, J., Todd, A. W., & Esperanza, J. (2009). A randomized, wait-list controlled effectiveness trial assessing school-wide Positive Behavior Support in elementary schools. *Journal of Positive Behavior Interventions, 11*(3), 133–144. https://doi.org/10.1177/1098300709332067

Horner, R. H., Sugai, G., & Fixsen, D. L. (2017). Implementing effective educational practices at scales of social importance. *Clinical Child and Family Psychology Review, 20*(1), 25–30. DOI:10.1007/s1056701702247

Hunter, W. C., & Haydon, T. (2019). Implementing a classroom management package in an urban middle school: A case study. *Preventing School Failure: Alternative Education for Children and Youth, 63*(1), 68–76. https://doi.org/10.1080/1045988X.2018.1504740

Hurley, N., Guckenburg, S., Persson, H., Fronius, T., & Petrosino, A. (2015). What further research is needed on restorative justice in schools? WestEd. Retrieved from: https://eric.ed.gov/?id=ED559727

Johnson, J., & Howley, C. B. (2015). Contemporary federal education policy and rural schools: A critical policy analysis. *Peabody Journal of Education, 90*(2), 224–241. https://doi.org/10.1080/0161956X.2015.1022112

Jones, K. A., Jones, J. L., & Vermette, P. J. (2013). Exploring the complexity of classroom management: 8 components of managing a highly productive, safe, and respectful urban environment. *American Secondary Education, 41*(3), 21–33.

Kennedy, Y., Flynn, N., O'Brien, E., & Greene, G. (2021). Exploring the impact of Incredible Years Teacher Classroom Management training on teacher psychological outcomes. *Educational Psychology in Practice*, 1–19. DOI: 10.1080/02667363.2021.1882944

Kennedy, M. J., Hirsch, S. E., Rogers, W. J., Bruce, A., & Lloyd, J. W. (2017). Supporting high school teachers' implementation of evidence-based classroom management practices. *Teaching and Teacher Education, 63*, 47–57. DOI: 10.1016.j.tate.2016.12.009

Kennedy, M. J., & Thomas, C. N. (2012). Effects of content acquisition podcasts to develop preservice teachers' knowledge of positive behavioral interventions and supports. *Exceptionality*, *20*(1), 1–19. https://doi.org/10.1080/09362835.2011.611088

Kennedy, M. J., Wagner, D., Stegall, J., Lembke, E., Miciak, J., Alves, K. D., Brown, T., Driver, M. K., & Hirsch, S. E. (2015). Using content acquisition podcasts to improve teacher candidate knowledge and application of curriculum-based measurement. *Exceptional Children*, *82*, 303–320. https://doi.org/10.1177/0014402915615885

Keyes, K. M., Cerdá, M., Brady, J. E., Havens, J. R., & Galea, S. (2014). Understanding the rural-urban differences in nonmedical prescription opioid use and abuse in the United States. *American Journal of Public Health*, *104*(2), e52–9. 10.2105/AJPH.2013.301709

Kwok, A. (2019). Classroom management actions of beginning urban teachers. *Urban Education*, *54*(3), 339–367. http://dx.doi.org/10.1177/0042085918795017

La Salle, T. P., Wang, C., Wu, C., & Neves, J. R. (2020). Racial mismatch among minoritized students and white teachers: Implications and recommendations for moving forward, *Journal of Educational and Psychological Consultation*, *30*(3), 314–343, DOI: 10.1080/10474412.2019.1673759

Larson, K. E. (2016). Classroom management training for teachers in urban environments serving predominately African American students: A review of the literature. *The Urban Review*, *48*(1), 51–72. https://doi.org/10.1007/s11256-015-0345-6

Larson, K. E., Pas, E. T., Bottiani, J. H., Kush, J. M., & Bradshaw, C. P. (2021). A multidimensional and multilevel examination of student engagement and secondary school teachers' use of classroom management practices. *Journal of Positive Behavior Interventions*, *23*(3), 149–162. https://doi.org/10.1177/1098300720929352

Lieberman, M. (2020, November 23). *No more snow days, thanks to remote learning? Not everyone agrees. Education Week*. www.edweek.org/leadership/no-more-snow-days-thanks-to-remote-learning-not-everyone-agrees/2020/11

Loman, S. L., Strickland-Cohen, M. K., & Walker, V. L. (2018). Promoting the accessibility of SWPBIS for students with severe disabilities. *Journal of Positive Behavior Interventions*, *20*, 113–123. DOI:10.1177/1098300717733976

MacSuga-Gage, A. S., & Gage, N. A. (2015). Student-level effects of increased teacher-directed opportunities to respond. *Journal of Behavior Education*, *24*, 273–288. https://doi.org/10.1007/s10864-015-9223-2

MacSuga-Gage, A. S., Gage, N. A., Katsiyannis, A., Hirsch, S. E., & Kinser, H. (2020). Disproportionate corporal punishment for students receiving special education services and Black and Hispanic Students. *Journal of Disability Policy Studies*. https://doi.org/10.1177/1044207320949960

Marzano, R. J. (2003). *What works in schools: Translating research into action*. ASCD.

McDaniel, S. C., Bloomfield, B. S., Guyotte, K. W., & Shannon, T. M. (2020). Telecoaching to support schoolwide positive behavior interventions and supports in rural schools. *Journal for Education of Students Placed At-Risk*. 10.1080/10824669.2020.1834395

McDaniel, S. C., Chaparro, E., Santiago-Rosario, M. R., Kern, L., & George, H. P. (November, 2020). *Adapting PBIS practices for rural settings: The remote instruction strategy matrix*. OSEP TA Center on PBIS, University of Oregon. Retrieved from www.pbis.org.

Meit, M., Knudson, A., Gilbert, T., Yu, A. T. C., Tanenbaum, E., Ormson, E., & Popat, S. (2014). The 2014 update of the rural-urban chartbook. *Bethesda, MD: Rural Health Reform Policy Research Center*.

MetLife Inc. (2013, February). *The MetLife survey of the American teacher: Challenges for school leadership*. www.metlife.com/content/dam/microsites/about/corporate-profile/MetLife-Teacher-Survey-2012.PLDf

Michael, K. D., George, M. W., Splett, J. W., Jameson, J. P., Sale, R., Bode, A. A., Iachini, A. L., Taylor, L. K., & Weist, M. D. (2016). Preliminary outcomes of a multi-site, school-based modular intervention for adolescents experiencing mood difficulties. *Journal of Child and Family Studies*, *25*(6), 1903–1915. https://doi.org/10.1007/s10826-016-0373-1

Milner IV, H. R. (2015). Research on classroom management in urban schools. In Emmer, E., & Sabornie, E. J. (Eds.), *Handbook of Classroom Management* 2nd ed., (pp. 167–185). Routledge.

Milner IV, H. R., Murray, I. E., Farinde, A. A., & Delale-O'Connor, L. (2015). Outside of school matters: What we need to know in urban environments. *Equity & Excellence in Education*, *48*(4), 529–548. https://doi.org/10.1080/10665684.2015.1085798

Moon, J., Williford, A., & Mendenhall, A. (2017). Teachers' perceptions of youth mental health: Implications for training and the promotion of mental health services in schools. *Children and Youth Services Review*, *73*, 384–391. https://doi.org/10.1016/j.childyouth.2017.01.006

Murimi, M. W., & Harpel, T. (2010). Practicing preventive health: The underlying culture among low-income rural populations. *Journal of Rural Health*, *26*(3), 273–282. https://doi.org/10.1111/j.1748-0361.2010.00289.x

Myers, D., Sugai, G., Simonsen, B., & Freeman, J. (2017). Assessing teachers' behavior support skills. *Teacher Education and Special Education*, *40*, 128–139. DOI: 10.1177/0888406417700964

National Advisory Committee on Rural Health and Human Services (2015). *Intimate partner violence in rural America*. www.hrsa.gov/advisory-committees/rural-health/publications/index.html

National Education Association (2020) *Digital equity for students and teachers*. www.nea.org/resource-library/digital-divide-and-homework-gap-your-state

NCES (2013). *The Status of Rural Education*. https://nces.ed.gov/programs/coe/indicator_tla.asp

Nguyen, T. D., Pham, L., Springer, M. G., & Crouch, M. (2019). The factors of teacher attrition and retention: An updated and expanded meta-analysis of the literature. *Annenberg Institute at Brown University*, 19–149. https://doi.org/10.26300/cdf3-4555

Nichols, L. M., Goforth, A. N., Sacra, M., & Ahlers, K. (2017). Collaboration to support rural student social-emotional needs. *The Rural Educator*, *38*(1). https://doi.org/10.35608/ruraled.v38i1.234

Office of Special Education Programs (2015). Supporting and responding to student behavior: Evidence-based classroom strategies for teachers. Office of Special Education Programs. Retrieved from www.pbis.org/resources/supporting-and-responding-to-behavior-evidence-based-classroom-strategies-for-teachers

Orfield, G., Kucsera, J., & Siegel-Hawley, G. (2012). E pluribus … Separation: Deepening double segregation for more students. The Civil Rights Project/Proyecto Derechos Civiles. https://civilrightsproject.ucla.edu/research/k-12-education/integration-and-diversity/mlk-national

Pas, E. T., Johnson, S. R., Larson, K. E., Brandenburg, L., Church, R., & Bradshaw, C. P. (2016). Reducing behavior problems among students with autism spectrum disorder: Coaching teachers in a mixed-reality setting. *Journal of Autism and Developmental Disorders*, *46*(12), 3640–3652. https://doi.org/10.1007/s10803-016-2898-y

Pas, E. T., Larson, K. E., Reinke, W. M., Herman, K. C., & Bradshaw, C. P. (2016). Implementation and acceptability of an adapted classroom check-up coaching model to promote culturally responsive classroom management. *Education and Treatment of Children*, *39*(4), 467–491. https://doi.org/10.1353/ETC.2016.0021

Pas, E. T., Waasdorp, T. E., & Bradshaw, C. P. (2019). Coaching teachers to detect, prevent, and respond to bullying using mixed reality simulation: An efficacy study in middle schools. *International Journal of Bullying Prevention*, *1*, 58–69. https://doi.org/ 10.1007/s42380-018-0003-0

Pittman, T., & Gains, T. (2015). Technology integration in third, fourth, and fifth grade classroom in a Florida school district. *Educational Technology Research and Development*, *63*(4), 539–554. https://doi.org/10.1007/s11423-015-9391-8

Podolsky, A., Kini, T., Bishop, J., & Darling-Hammond, L. (2016). *Solving the teacher shortage: How to attract and retain excellent teachers*. Learning Policy Institute. https://learningpolicyinstitute.org/product/solving-teacher-shortage

Pullmann, M. D., Vanhooser, S., Hoffman, C., & Heflinger, C. A. (2010). Barriers to and supports of family participation in a rural system of care for children with serious emotional problems. *Community Mental Health Journal*, *46*(3), 211–220. DOI: 10.1007/s10597-009-9208-5

Rathvon, N. (2008). *Effective school interventions: Evidence-based strategies for improving student outcomes* (2nd ed.). The Guilford Press.

Reeves, C. (2003). *Implementing the No Child Left Behind Act: Implications for rural schools and districts*. Educational Policy Publications.

Reglin, G., Akpo-Sanni, J., & Losike-Sedimo, N. (2012). The effect of a professional development classroom management model on at-risk elementary students' misbehaviors. *Education*, *133*(1), 3–18. https://link.gale.com/apps/doc/A302463826/AONE?u=anon~9ffc1d5b&sid=googleScholar&xid=60d8ccbf

Reinke, W. M., Lewis-Palmer, T., & Merrell, K. (2008). The classroom check-up: A classwide teacher consultation model for increasing praise and decreasing disruptive behavior. *School Psychology Review*, *37*(3), 315–332.

Reinke, W. M., Stormont, M., Herman, K. C., Wang, Z., Newcomer, L., & King, K. (2014). Use of coaching and behavior support planning for students with disruptive behavior within a universal classroom management program. *Journal of Emotional and Behavioral Disorders*, *22*(2), 74–82. https://doi.org/10.1177/1063426613519820

Reinke, W. M., Stormont, M., Webster-Stratton, C., Newcomer, L. L., & Herman, K. C. (2012). The Incredible Years Teacher Classroom Management program: using coaching to support generalization to real-world classroom settings. *Psychology in the Schools*, *49*(5), 416–428. https://doi.org/10.1177/1063426613519820

Riggins, C., & Knowles, D. (2020). Caught in the trap of PLC Lite: Essential steps needed for implementation of a true professional learning community. *Education*, *141*(1), 46–54.

Robbie, K., Van Lone, J., Kern, L., & George, H. P. (August, 2021). *Using a PBIS framework: Working smarter, not harder in rural schools*. Center on PBIS, University of Oregon. Retrieved from www.pbis.org.

Rock, M. L., Schoenfeld, N., Zigmond, N., Gable, R. A., Gregg, M., Ploessl, D. M., & Salter, A. (2013). Can you Skype me now? Developing teachers' classroom management practices through virtual coaching. *Beyond Behavior*, *22*(3), 15–23. https://doi.org/10.1177/107429561302200303

Rose, J., Leverson, M., & Smith, K. (April 2020). Embedding culturally responsive practices in Tier I. Center on PBIS, University of Oregon. Retrieved from www.pbis.org.

Schonert-Reichl, K. A., Kitil, M. J., & Hanson-Peterson, J. (2017). *To reach the students, teach the teachers: A national scan of teacher preparation and social & emotional learning.* A report prepared for the Collaborative for academic, social, and emotional learning (CASEL). University of British Columbia. https://files.eric.ed.gov/fulltext/ED582029.pdf

Scott, T. M., Alter, P. J., & Hirn, R. (2011). An examination of typical classroom context and instruction for students with and without behavioral disorders. *Education and Treatment of Children, 34*, 619–642. https://doi.org/10.1353/etc.2011.0039

Simonsen, B., Fairbanks, S., Briesch, A., Myers, D., & Sugai, G. (2008). Evidence-based practices in classroom management: Considerations for research to practice. *Education and Treatment of Children*, 351–380. www.jstor.org/stable/42899983

Simonsen, B., Freeman, J., Myers, D., Dooley, K., Maddock, E., Kern, L., & Byun, S. (2020). The effects of targeted professional development on teachers' use of empirically supported classroom management practices. *Journal of Positive Behavior Interventions, 22*(1), 3–14. https://doi.org/10.1177/1098300719859615

Simonsen, B., MacSuga-Gage, A. S., Briere III, D. E., Freeman, J., Myers, D., Scott, T. M., & Sugai, G. (2014). Multitiered support framework for teachers' classroom-management practices: Overview and case study of building the triangle for teachers. *Journal of Positive Behavior Interventions, 16*(3), 179–190. https://doi.org/10.1177/1098300713484062

Simonsen, B., & Myers, D. (2015). *Classwide positive behavior interventions and supports: A guide to proactive classroom management.* The Guilford Press.

Singh, V., & Thurman, A. (2019). How many ways can we define online learning? A systematic literature review of definitions of online learning (1988–2018). *American Journal of Distance Education, 33*(4), 289–306. https://doi.org/10.1080/08923647.2019.1663082

Steed, E. A., Pomerleau, T., Muscott, H., & Rohde, L. (2013). Program-wide positive behavioral interventions and supports in rural preschools. *Rural Special Education Quarterly, 32*(1), 38–46. https://doi.org/10.1177/875687705130320106

Sterrett, B. I., McDaniel, S. C., Majeika, C. E., & Bruhn, A. L. (2021) Using evidence informed strategies to adapt Tier 2 interventions. *Journal of Applied School Psychology, 36*(2), 133–154. DOI: 10.1080/15377903.2020.1714856

Stormont, M., Reinke, W., & Herman, K. (2011). Teachers' knowledge of evidence-based interventions and available school resources for children with emotional and behavioral problems. *Journal of Behavioral Education, 20*, 138–147. DOI 10.1007/s10864-011-9122-0

Sugai, G., Horner, R. H., Dunlap, G., Hieneman, M., Lewis, T. J., Nelson, C. M., Scott, T., Liaupsin, C., Sailor, W., Turnbull, A. P., Turnbull, H. R., Wickham, D., Wilcox, B., & Ruef, M. (2000). Applying positive behavior support and functional behavioral assessment in schools. *Journal of Positive Behavior Interventions, 2*(3), 131–143. https://doi.org/10.1177/109830070000200302

Sugai, G., O'Keeffe, B. V., & Fallon, L. M. (2012). A contextual consideration of culture and school-wide positive behavior support. *Journal of Positive Behavior Interventions, 14*(4), 197–208. https://doi.org/10.1177/1098300711426334

Sutcher, L., Darling-Hammond, L., & Carver-Thomas, D. (2016). *A coming crisis in teaching? Teacher supply, demand, and shortages in the US.* Learning Policy Institute. https://learningpolicyinstitute.org/product/coming-crisis-teaching

Sutherland, K. S., Adler, N., & Gunter, P. L. (2003). The effect of varying rates of opportunities to respond to academic requests on the classroom behavior of students with EBD. *Journal of Emotional and Behavioral Disorders, 11*, 239–248.

Sutton, R., Mudrey-Camino, R., & Knight, C. C. (2009). Teachers' emotion regulation and classroom management. *Theory into Practice, 38*, 130–137. https://doi.org/10.1080/00405840902776418

Tomlinson, C. A., & McTighe, J. (2006). *Integrating differentiated instruction & understanding by design: Connecting content and kids.* ASCD.

Twaddell, H., & Emerine, D. (2007). *Best Practices to Enhance the Transportation-Land Use Connection in the Rural United States.* Transportation Research Board.

UNESCO (2020). Global education coalition. UNESCO. https://en.unesco.org/covid19/educationresponse/globalcoalition

US Department of Education (2021, June 10). *Statement from U. S. Secretary of Education Miguel Cardona on results of April 2021 NAEP Survey on school reopening.* www.ed.gov/news/press-releases/statement-us-secretary-education-miguel-cardona-results-april-2021-naep-survey-school-reopening

US Department of Education, National Center for Education Statistics, Common Core of Data (CCD), "Local Education Agency Universe Survey (2018–19). See *Digest of Education Statistics 2020*, table 204.20.

US Department of Education, National Center for Education Statistics, Common Core of Data (CCD), "State Nonfiscal Survey of Public Elementary and Secondary Education (2009–10 and 2018–19). See *Digest of Education Statistics 2020*, table 203.50.

US Department of Education, Office of Special Education Programs, Individuals with Disabilities Education Act (IDEA) database (February 7, 2021). Retrieved from www2.ed.gov/programs/osepidea/618–data/state-level–data–files/index.html#bcc. See Digest of Education Statistics 2020, table 204.60.

USDA (2017). Rural America at a glance, 2017 Edition. Economic Research Service, United States Department of Agriculture. www.ers.usda.gov/publications/pub-details/?pubid=85739

Wade, T. J., Mansour, M. E., Guo, J. J., Huentelman, T., Line, K., & Keller, K. N. (2008). Access and utilization patterns of school-based health centers at urban and rural elementary and middle schools. *Public Health Reports*, *123*(6), 739–750. DOI: 10.1177/003335490812300610

Webster-Stratton, C., Reinke, W. M., Herman, K. C., & Newcomer, L. L. (2011). The Incredible Years Teacher Classroom Management Training: the methods and principles that support fidelity of training delivery. *School Psychology Review*, *40*(4), 509–529.

Westling, D. L. (2010). Teachers and challenging behavior: Knowledge, views, and practices. *Remedial and Special Education*, *31*(1), 48–63. https://doi.org/10.1177/0741932508327466

Wilger, S. (n.d.). *Special considerations for mental health services in rural schools*. SAMHSA: Now Is the Time Technical Assistance Center. https://rems.ed.gov/docs/resources/SAMHSA_Mental_Health_Services_Rural_Schools.pdf

Yoon, K. S., Duncan, T., Lee, S. W., Scarloss, B., & Shapley, K. L. (2007). *Reviewing the evidence on how teacher professional development affects student achievement* (Issues & Answers Report, REL 2007-No. 033). U.S. Department of Education, Center for Education Sciences, National Center for Education Evaluation and Regional Assistance, Regional Educational Laboratory Southwest. Retrieved from http://ies.ed.gov/ncee/edlabs/regions/southwest/pdf/REL_2007033.pdf

9
CLASSROOM MANAGEMENT IN "NO-EXCUSES" CHARTER SCHOOLS

Chris Torres

MICHIGAN STATE UNIVERSITY

Introduction

Classroom management and issues of exclusionary discipline have been a hot button issue in charter schools for the last two decades. Reports comparing suspension and expulsion rates between the charter and traditional public schools have generated intense criticism and debate (Barnum, 2018; Carr, 2014). But what is it exactly that "charter schools" do when it comes to classroom management, and what does this look like when charter schools are varied and heterogenous by nature?

This chapter first describes the sort of heterogeneity that exists in the charter sector, summarizing evidence regarding the kinds of charter schools and their purposes. Because of this variation, there is no single approach that "charter schools" take to classroom management, and even charter schools grouped in similar categories will vary based on the contexts, conditions, and sensemaking of individuals working within them. However, many charters employ younger, newer teachers compared to traditional public schools (Rich, 2013; Torres, 2016a), and new teachers classically struggle with classroom management, particularly those employed in high poverty urban schools. This is especially true in some of the highest-performing urban charter school networks in the country—national networks run by "no-excuses" Charter Management Organizations (CMOs) like the Knowledge is Power Program (KIPP), Uncommon Schools, YES Prep, and Achievement First (Abrams, 2016). For example, no-excuses CMOs often prefer to hire early career or novice teachers because they are amenable to learning the organization's way of doing things in ways that more experienced teachers might not be (Hashim et al., 2021; Torres, 2014). Leaders especially prefer hiring new teachers who are willing and able to follow the prescriptive disciplinary philosophy and practices of the organization (Torres, 2019).

The charter sector is ripe for mimetic isomorphism because these prominent CMO networks are rewarded with resources and attention for replicating practices that lead to increased academic outcomes (Ferrare & Settari, 2018; Renzulli et al., 2015). Mimetic isomorphism refers to the tendency of an organization to imitate another organization's structure because of the belief that the structure of the latter organization is beneficial (DiMaggio & Powell, 1983). Since no-excuses charter schools are widely touted as the most successful in terms of academic outcomes, significant incentive exists to expand their practices (Cohodes, 2018), including prioritizing authorization of CMO schools and practices over community-based charter school applications in urban areas (Henry Jr., 2019). The disciplinary practices I describe here and elsewhere (see Golann & Torres, 2020) are

152

DOI: 10.4324/9781003275312-11

viewed as a critical component of the no-excuses model. In a recent book, Golann (2021) eloquently described the philosophy behind no-excuses discipline and why it is perceived as necessary to the success of schools. In her ethnography, school leaders described not just the need to maintain order to focus on instruction, but they also focused heavily on behavioral "scripts" (defined as detailed and standardized behavioral codes or procedures) to explicitly teach middle-class values and skills to low-income students of color (Golann, 2021). These scripts for success are essential to the mission and vision of no-excuses schools, and their methods are explicitly taught across the country not just by charter networks, but in educator training programs founded by no-excuses charter leaders such as the Relay Graduate School of Education (Mungal, 2016). These reasons, along with others I detail in later sections, explain why we see mimetic isomorphism around discipline.

No-excuses schools have taken an especially prominent role within the charter school movement, receiving significant political and philanthropic support for their efforts at closing the achievement gap (Farrell et al., 2012; Fryer, 2014; Goodman, 2013). The appeal of scaling up the most successful charter networks to improve public education for the nation's neediest students has resulted in several high-profile reform attempts such as those documented in Dale Russakoff's (2015) *The Prize* or efforts by the Broad Foundation to increase the proportion of charter schools in Los Angeles. Researchers find that foundations are playing an outsize role in the expansion of market-based reforms like charter schools (Reckhow & Snyder, 2014; Scott, 2009; Scott & Jabbar, 2014). In particular, foundations are disproportionately spending philanthropic dollars on "academically successful" CMO networks that explicitly seek to serve minoritized, low-income students, helping to fuel and incentivize their expansion (Ferrare & Settari, 2018; Quinn et al., 2016).

While no-excuses schools and networks have received significant support, they have also been subject to much criticism. Researchers have compiled a significant body of evidence detailing the drawbacks of exclusionary discipline, defined as school disciplinary actions like expulsion or suspension that remove or exclude students from their usual educational settings (Skiba & Losen, 2016). One of the concerns raised about no-excuses schools is that their practices lead to greater rates of exclusionary discipline even as compared to traditional public schools serving similar students. As Golann and Torres (2020, p. 8) note:

> Students may also perceive no-excuses discipline as unfair because minor infractions can lead to major consequences, including suspensions and expulsions. According to a recent report released by Advocates for Children of New York (2015), 65% of the 164 charter school discipline policies reviewed violated state law because they permitted suspension or expulsion as a penalty for any infraction in their discipline policy, no matter how minor. Concern is growing that no-excuses charter schools are more likely than comparable traditional schools to use exclusionary discipline (Denise, Gross, & Rausch, 2015; Stern, Clonan, Jaffee, & Lee, 2015), which has been shown to have negative psychosocial and academic consequences, for both suspended individuals and their peers at school (Gregory et al., 2010; Perry & Morris, 2014). According to an analysis of publicly available data from 2011–2012, New York City charters suspended students at almost three times the rate of traditional public schools, with several of the largest no-excuses charter networks suspending more than 20% of their students at least once (Decker, Snyder, & Darville, 2015).

In sum, while no-excuses schools have received money and positive attention for their results as compared to traditional public schools serving similar students (Cohodes, 2018), they have been equally critiqued about their discipline being stricter and resulting in greater racial disparities.

In this chapter, I describe no-excuses disciplinary practices, including why they can lead to higher rates of exclusionary discipline compared to traditional public schools. I also detail the rationale and controversy over no-excuses disciplinary methods, how debates and practices have evolved over time, and future directions for practice and research.

Charter School Heterogeneity and Classroom Management

At least in theory, charters were meant to be unique spaces for educational innovation (Renzulli et al., 2015). One of the original theories of action behind the idea of charter schools was to develop a unique, specialized mission tailored to the particular needs of the communities they serve (Henry Jr., 2019). One report tackled this question of whether and how charters are different by looking at the diversity of charter school offerings in 17 cities. McShane & Hatfield (2015) coded all charter schools in these cities and found that about half could be categorized as "general" offerings with no particular pedagogical or curricular emphasis while the rest were "specialized" schools categorized as focusing on topics such as "progressive," "STEM," "arts," and "vocational" education. The largest proportion of specialized schools in this report were categorized as "no-excuses" charter schools.

There has been much debate about the term, "no-excuses" charter schools, but they generally emphasize high academic expectations, longer school days, intensive data use to drive instruction, frequent teacher observation and coaching, and their most controversial and debated characteristic is the use of strict and paternalistic approaches to student discipline to maintain order and maximize instructional time (Cohodes, 2018; Golann, 2021; Torres & Golann, 2018). These schools are often operated by academically successful Charter Management Organizations (CMOs) that help manage large networks of schools that have a common vision and pedagogical and behavioral models that are viewed as best practice (Lake et al., 2012). Of course, not all "no-excuses" models are part of CMOs and not all CMOs are "no-excuses" models. Available evidence, which is limited in scope and specificity, suggests that the highest-performing CMOs tend to subscribe to "no-excuses" disciplinary approaches (e.g., Lake et al., 2012). Further complicating this picture is the fact that no-excuses leaders often reject this label (Cuban, 2019). I contend that self-identification with this label is irrelevant if the practices themselves remain consistent with what the label intends to capture. In other words, organizations should be judged by what they *do* rather than what they *say*. Thus, for my purposes I describe what no-excuses schools and networks tend to do, and why. I also attempt to describe (where evidence is available) changes in the no-excuses sector as well as variations in approaches.

No-excuses organizations have historically emphasized control and zero tolerance of a range of student behaviors as foundational to their success (Torres & Golann, 2018). For example, a report on five of the most academically high-performing CMOs by the pro-charter Center on Reinventing Public Education (CRPE) found that these CMOs had zero tolerance policies and emphasized consistency in enforcement. The authors explained: "Although the CMOs [in the study] approach the creation of an orderly and respectful student culture in somewhat different ways, they all believe that success would be impossible without these policies" (Lake et al., 2012, p. 20). In an article published in the *American Educational Research Journal* (AERJ), Kevin Henry Lawrence (2019) analyzed charter applications in post-Katrina New Orleans and found that "no-excuses" discourses were prioritized over applications that were more community-based. This is another example of how accountability systems that prioritize reputation around raising test scores (while de-emphasizing other potentially desirable outcomes) have contributed to the isomorphism in the charter sector. I will argue that this isomorphism also applies to behavioral practices because they have historically been seen as foundational to the academic success of CMOs.

Background on "No-Excuses"

In the field of education, the term *"No-Excuses"* was coined by Samuel Casey Carter in his book *No Excuses: Lessons from 21 High-Performing, High-Poverty Schools*. The phrase was initially philosophical. For instance, Carter (2000) emphasized the idea that if these schools can help low-income children of color achieve at high levels, then all schools should be able to meet this standard. Carter (2000) wrote: "All children can learn. The principals and [No Excuses] schools profiled in this book have overcome the bureaucratic and cultural obstacles that keep low-income children behind in most public schools. No Excuses schools have created a culture of achievement among children whom most public schools would condemn to a life of failure" (p. 1). This term has been used to describe a particular kind of charter school and some associated practices or values. Some of these include: a longer school day and school year, highly defined standards for teacher hiring and "fit" with the school's culture, strict norms for student behavior, mandatory small group afterschool tutoring, and high expectations for students and staff, and these broadly defined practices or values are thought to help students achieve academically (Torres, 2019; Wilson, 2009). Therefore, the term "*No Excuses*" is a philosophy and a particular set of loosely defined practices. Some structures and practices, like the longer school day or small group tutoring, are easily defined. Others, such as the form that student behavior systems or "high expectations" take, are not.

Many CMOs, particularly the highest-performing CMOs, have subscribed to a *No Excuses* approach (Peyser, 2011; Lake et al., 2012). For instance, according to Peyser (2011, p. 37), "The highest-performing CMOs in the New Schools portfolio tend to be those that have embraced a "no excuses" approach to teaching and learning. These CMOs have created organizational and school cultures based on explicit expectations for both academic achievement and behavior, with meaningful consequences when those expectations are not met." It is precisely this association between a *No Excuses* school culture and their practices, and higher than average levels of student achievement (Fryer, 2014), that has fueled the initial popularity and growth of *No Excuses* charters and CMOs.

The Backlash: No-Excuses Falling Out of Favor?

Despite much attention and philanthropic support for scaling up no-excuses schools, growth has slowed in recent years. According to data from the National Association of Charter School Authorizers (NACSA) applications and approvals from no-excuses schools dropped by as much as 50% over the last five to seven years (Prothero, 2019). In a 2019 blog post, Larry Cuban, a professor emeritus at Stanford University, theorizes why the term fell out of favor:

> Criticism of classroom disciplinary codes, whole-class direct instruction, and less than stellar results in college completion have eroded the image of No Excuses schools… Epithets— "militaristic," "rigid," "rote learning"—spilled over mainstream and social media. The phrase lost its initial luster. Moreover, some charter networks (e.g., KIPP, Achievement First) questioned whether their students were acquiring the necessary skills to succeed at the next level of education. They began expanding student autonomy encouraging teachers to alter lessons to get students to think independently…

It is difficult to determine to what degree changes in beliefs or practices in no-excuses schools are due to public critiques such as those outlined by Dr. Cuban or organizational recognition that disciplinary practices are counter-productive. Likely it is a combination of both, as documented in public comments and media.

As one example, Taylor (2019) wrote an article in the *New York Times* examining how Achievement First and KIPP were responding to college completion rates that were above national averages but below their own expectations. She wrote:

> Was the schools' highly structured, disciplined approach to behavior and learning giving students the tools they needed to succeed at the next level?

Achievement First is not the only charter wrestling with that issue. "That is one of the questions everybody's been asking as they design high schools," Dave Levin, one of the co-founders of the KIPP network, said in an interview.

In the same article, Taylor (2018) describes how difficult it is to let go of disciplinary practices while promoting independence. And even though schools like Achievement First Amistad High School attempted to promote greater independence, students still held a walkout to demand more racial diversity on the staff and fairer discipline (Taylor, 2018). This illustrates the difficulty educators have in letting go of strict discipline and the challenges in promoting deeper learning and independence in the context of high teacher turnover and a largely novice teaching staff (see Debs et al., 2019 for more examples), an issue I take up in a later section.

Pushing Back: The Politics of Race and Disciplinary Change

At the same time, concerns about racialized discipline shaped how leaders responded to the term "no-excuses." In particular, the pandemic and George Floyd's murder resurfaced broader, ongoing problems with racism and racial equity ultimately leading to statements about change and apologies from networks like KIPP, Uncommon Schools, and Noble in Chicago for their disciplinary practices (Kunichoff, 2020; Morrison, 2020). Undoubtedly, pressure from students, families, educators, scholars, and the public influenced how the term "no-excuses" went from a point of pride to one that was rejected by many leaders and reformers. For example, Cuban (2019) wrote:

> In two decades, the phrase has gone from a proud label charter school advocates used to fierce rejection by many of the same boosters. Listen to Eva Moskowitz, founder of Success Academies in New York City in a 2017 interview: "We're not a no-excuses school. We're just not. I don't really know how to respond to that nomenclature….That doesn't mean you don't believe that high levels of learning can occur in chaos, and we do believe that students do need to say please and thank you to the lunch ladies. We do assign school uniforms to simplify things for parents … and really allow us to focus on learning [instead of clothes.]"

Yet simply rejecting this term does not equate to actual change in practice, which is the standard that schools should be held to regardless of the label. And on that measure, it is doubtful that changes are in fact occurring at networks like Success Academies. In a *Washington Post* op-ed, my co-authors and I note that public denunciations such as these are, at least in some cases, not producing actual change (Debs et al., 2019):

> In the past year, protests from students, parents and teachers revealed the persistence of these disciplinary practices and high levels of dissatisfaction. Earlier this year, for example, a scandal erupted at an Achievement First (AF) high school over video footage of a principal shoving a student into a locker and allegations of a coverup by the network. An AF spokesperson's statement on current disciplinary practices across the network speaks volumes in its omissions: "Not all our transitions are silent across all our schools." In 2018, high school students at Success Academy's new flagship high school led a protest against the school discipline as chief executive Eva Moskowitz installed her desk in the high school hallway and implemented tougher sanctions on students. Teachers at Chicago's Noble network protested school uniform and hair policies they found "dehumanizing" to students.

So what is actually happening inside of schools and why are these practices so hard to change? The next sections examine these key questions.

What Does Classroom Management in "No-Excuses" Charter Schools (NECSs) Look Like?

What are no-excuses disciplinary practices and why are they so enduring despite being so polarizing and controversial? To understand this, I first broadly define them according to existing literature and then summarize some of the most common views of proponents and critics.

There is a dearth of empirical research on CMOs, in part because they have only allowed the Center on Reinventing Publication (CRPE) and evaluation centers such as *Mathematica* to conduct research (that are *not* single case studies of a CMO or with teachers/principals volunteering as cases) rather than independent researchers. Based on the limited empirical work that exists and which looks at a varied number of CMOs, we know that many CMOs regard the creation of a calm, orderly school environment with high, consistent expectations for student behavior as a matter of high priority (Lake et al., 2010, p. 27). This belief can result in highly prescriptive student behavior systems. According to Lake et al. (2010), 54% of the 37 surveyed CMOs required their schools to implement a prescribed student behavior plan of highly structured, incentive-driven behavior systems. Lake et al (2010, p. 27) describe an example of an "ideally run" system:

> In an ideally run "Excellence School," students have so internalized routines and procedures that they can execute them without teacher guidance or input. Staff describes the culture as "warm-strict" and "very structured." One Excellence School uses a paycheck behavioral system, where students receive "dollars" or deductions based on behavior. Students can, and often do, get demerits for low-level behaviors, such as talking out of turn and not following directions immediately. Students who have high paychecks get rewards and students whose paychecks reach zero are put on a different status for two to three days. These students must wear a differently colored uniform, have restricted privileges, and meet with the behavior dean to reflect on their behavior. Anywhere from 20 to 50 students (out of 200) may be on this status at a given time. Students with good behavior receive rewards (limousine rides, trips, ice cream parties). Adult relationships with students are professional and demanding. Teachers may be encouraged to use strong, judgmental tones to correct minor child behavior throughout a lesson. Teachers constantly monitor child behavior and give quick, sometimes severe, feedback and consequences to behavior.

While descriptions such as these exist in reports, there is obviously variation in whether or how schools implement particular practices. For instance, some prominent no-excuses schools like those run by KIPP in San Francisco and elsewhere have adopted relational approaches to discipline, using practices consistent with the Responsive Classroom or restorative justice (see, for examples, Golann & Torres, 2020; Kerstetter, 2016). However, the vast majority of work on no-excuses charters and CMOs document and describe approaches consistent with the prior excerpt or the framework that follows. Below, I describe what no-excuses discipline generally looks like and why reformers and leaders tend to adopt these broad tenets.

The Four "C's:" Comprehensiveness, Clarity, Consequences, and Consistency

Golann and Torres (2020) reviewed the literature on no-excuses schools and their disciplinary practices and described a "four C's" model: comprehensiveness, clarity, consequences, and consistency. At least initially, the philosophy behind no-excuses discipline was characterized by a "broken windows" philosophy (Whitman, 2008). "Broken windows" is a theory historically used in crime and policing. The theory is to closely monitor and address minor violations to prevent larger disorder: for example, cracking down on vandalism and repairing a broken window helps maintain the appearance of law and order. This theory more or less represents the *comprehensiveness* behind the no-excuses disciplinary model. In one of the first books on these schools, Whitman (2008) described the broken windows theory and contended that these schools needed to be "paternalistic" in their approach in order to be effective. *Clarity* refers to the hyper-specificity of expectations—rather than saying "we need to be quiet," a teacher might be encouraged to point out highly specific behaviors (e.g., put your feet on the ground, mouths closed, hands folded) and dole out consequences for non-compliance. Golann and Torres (2020) report other examples of "clarity" from various studies describing discipline in these schools: "students are often forbidden to talk quietly in the hallway, enter and exit classrooms on their own, keep backpacks at their desk, wear jewelry, stare into space, slouch, put their head down, get out of a seat without permission, or refuse to track a teacher's eyes" (p. 620).

Consistent with broken windows theory, schools target minor behaviors and, rather than ignoring them, act decisively to address them. For instance, no-excuses organizations encourage schoolwide *consistency* in rewarding desired behaviors and enforcing *consequences* for undesirable ones. According to a report by the Center on Reinventing Public Education, no-excuses CMOs "constantly monitor child behavior and give quick, sometimes severe, feedback and consequences to behavior" (Lake et al., 2010, p. 27) such as talking out of turn or not following directions immediately (Golann, 2015). Reinforcing the idea that high-performing CMOs believe this kind of order is foundational to their success: in one study, principals in the highest-performing networks were much more likely to strongly agree compared to principals in other CMOs that their schools should have standard behavior codes with rewards and sanctions and that they should be enforced consistently schoolwide (Lake, et al., 2012).

In practice schools often use merit-demerit or scholar dollar systems for rewards and consequences, but because undesirable behaviors are often "minor," it can lead to an overwhelmingly punitive climate in some schools, particularly for students who are regularly non-compliant and who view such expectations as racist or deeply unfair (Golann & Torres, 2020; Golann, 2015; Goodman, 2013; Marsh & Noguera, 2018; Torres, 2016b). For example, if rolling your eyes or not regularly tracking the speaker is seen as undesirable or defiant behavior (behaviors that might be overlooked or go unpunished in most schools), a student might receive a demerit. Over time, these demerits can accumulate and turn into suspensions. As one example of the climate of constant consequences, Golann (2021) spent a year inside a no-excuses charter school and during her time there observed the school giving 15,243 such infractions to 250 students enrolled in the school. The frequency and nature of these kinds of punishments can lead to understandable defiance by some students and families and create a climate of control that normalizes shaming (Golann, 2015; Goodman, 2017).

Proponents of No-Excuses Discipline: The Allure of Order

Some feel that the means (e.g., control and paternalism) are justified for the ends (achievement, graduation, and college acceptance gains), or they do not acknowledge or agree that the disciplinary measures are as problematic or prominent as critics suggest (Boyd et al., 2014; Pondiscio, 2019). Cohodes (2018) reviewed the most rigorous quantitative studies on no-excuses charter schools and found they contributed to significant academic gains, arguing that as a result, policymakers should consider expanding them as a means to address racial achievement gaps. Torres & Golann (2018) agreed methodologically with Cohodes' review but questioned the inferences and recommendations made based on the review of evidence—in particular, they questioned whether the harsh disciplinary approaches found by many other scholars was (a) ethical and (b) necessary for these schools to realize their academic gains.

As previously noted, research suggests that school and CMO leaders believe these approaches are critical for achieving success. A four-year, multi-method study of 43 CMOs found that nearly all of the school leaders interviewed believed that they needed to create an orderly school environment to make their academic gains. The vast majority of CMOs placed a high priority on establishing consistent expectations for student behavior, and over half of the 37 surveyed CMOs required their schools to implement a prescribed student behavior plan of highly structured, incentive-driven behavior systems (Lake et al., 2010).

One reason that the practices outlined in the four C's persist is that they offer easy and replicable support for the novice teachers these schools attract. No-excuses organizations are characterized by young, energetic, mission-aligned teachers (Merseth, 2009; Wilson, 2008) and have higher than average turnover rates (Torres, 2016a). Kardos and colleagues (2001) argued that "novice-oriented" school cultures comprised of large proportions of new young teachers are unable to draw upon the knowledge and practice of established veterans and often must figure things out for themselves without support. Standardized disciplinary systems can help induct new teachers into organizational practices and support them in their efforts to manage students, a particular challenge in urban schools (Anyon, 1995; Noguera, 2003). Schoolwide behavioral expectations can also help schools maintain cultural continuity, minimizing the adverse consequences of higher-than-average teacher and principal turnover in charter schools (Ni et al., 2014; Torres, 2016b).

No-excuses behavioral systems aim to create common, schoolwide expectations, and this is crucial for many school leaders (Lake et al., 2010; Torres, 2019). So long as expectations are reasonable and fairly enforced, this preference is supported by research: schoolwide behavioral expectations for students and consistent teacher enforcement help promote student safety and a positive school climate (Ingersoll, 2004; Marzano et al., 2003). Consistent behavioral expectations and coherent codes of conduct are also associated with higher student achievement and teacher retention (Johnson et al., 2012).

Focusing on consistency and order is especially important for schools staffed by novice teachers. Rosenholtz and Simpson (1990) categorized organizational conditions affecting teachers' commitment into two categories: boundary and core (instructional) tasks. Boundary tasks involved arrangements outside of the core task of instruction, including behavior management and other foundational tasks that must be solved before teachers can progress to addressing the instructional core. Studying elementary teachers in Tennessee, Rosenholtz and Simpson (1990) found that novice teachers needed far more support for boundary tasks like behavior management while experienced teachers preferred supports targeted towards improving instruction. Thus, there is good reason to see such a strong focus on behavior management in no-excuses schools, as these schools are unlikely to improve instruction without first resolving boundary tasks. In turn, teachers are more likely to stay in schools that are perceived as orderly, safe, and where they are supported in their efforts to manage student behavior (Bosworth et al., 2011; Marinell & Coca, 2013).

Even scholars such as Dr. Joan F. Goodman at the University of Pennsylvania, who criticize no-excuses behavioral practices, acknowledge that these schools can provide children a sense of safety absent in many other urban schools and can, in theory, provide a strict but supportive environment (Goodman, 2013). In spite of the theoretical and practical advantages of no-excuses disciplinary systems, a growing chorus of scholars are highlighting theoretical, racial, ethical, and practical problems with the disciplinary methods, and even CMO leaders are increasingly acknowledging these problems and turning towards different solutions.

Critiques of No-Excuses Discipline: Ignoring Race, Structural Inequality, and Racism

Critics contend that the means do not justify the ends. They argue that the disciplinary means used to justify the ends are explicitly or implicitly racist and ignore how such practices detract from many other desirable outcomes such as socialization for independence in college, social and emotional outcomes, and culturally responsive and anti-racist approaches to schooling (Golann, 2015, Golann, 2021; Golann & Torres, 2020; Graham, 2019; Marsh, 2020; Sondel et al., 2019; White, 2015).

For example, White (2015) points out that disciplinary expectations found in no-excuses schools are a form of cultural racism: elevating White, middle-class norms over the cultural strengths of students of color. Through comparative case studies of four no-excuses charter schools in New York City, White (2015) argued that the overwhelming focus on test production and school expansion by White senior leaders was in tension with the cultural differences, strengths, and preferences of Black and Latino/a students and families.

Similarly, Hernandez (2016) used critical discourse analysis to examine the marketing materials of two prominent CMOs and found that there were negative racial depictions of the communities and racial groups they served. She emphasized how the discourse reified colorblindness (an ideology that ignores the role of race and racism in the production of inequality) and argued: "the discursive obfuscation of race affects the manner in which educational leaders imagine educational solutions and neglects the continued and unique impact that race has in everyday lives" (Hernandez, 2016, p. 47).

Sondel and colleagues (2019) conducted teacher interviews and observations in/from two no-excuses charter schools in New Orleans and used critical race theory as a primary analytic framework. The researchers analyzed policies and practitioner narratives through the lens of critical race theory and culturally responsive practice and found patterns across the qualitative data that strongly reflected theories of anti-blackness, white saviorism, and colorblind racism. For example, they note that beliefs such as this quote from a teacher interview exemplify deficit narratives and colorblindness: "Teaching them the skills their parents often don't have which is how to at least publicly check yourself and talk in a professional manner and interact with people correctly" (Sondel et al., 2019, p. 16). In essence, they argued that patterns of narratives and beliefs such as these across their interview data reflected deficit views of students and families.

Findings such as these represent an important critique leveled by various scholars—that no-excuses disciplinary practices and discourses ignore and are in tension with the cultural strengths of students and families of color, and can reproduce the same structural, racial inequities they aim to address (Golann, 2015; Graham, 2019).

Others provide critiques through more race-neutral avenues, focusing on questions of child development and whether methods achieve their intended behavioral aims. For example, in an article in *Phi Delta Kappan*, Goodman (2017) defined the practice of shaming and discussed why it was detrimental for child development and for ultimately addressing and correcting student behavior. She analyzed handbooks from nine large Charter Management Organization parent-student handbooks spanning roughly 500 schools for evidence of probable shaming. She found that two thirds of the handbooks included markers of probable shaming, such as mandatory public apologies and physical or simulated isolation from peers via silent lunches or clothing changes to mark a transgression (Goodman, 2017). These examples represent a common critique that, in effect and despite any "good intentions," no-excuses disciplinary practices control, coerce, and shame students of color in ways that white parents would find unacceptable for their own children (Lewis and Diamond, 2015; Marsh & Noguera, 2018; White, 2015).

Evidence on Teacher and Student Perceptions of No-Excuses Discipline

As noted earlier, proponents argue that disciplinary practices and systems should, in theory, support teachers to feel successful in no-excuses schools. If this were the case, and for the moment setting aside the question of whether the methods are actually good for children, research should document widespread teacher support for no-excuses disciplinary systems. What does research suggest about teacher perceptions and sensemaking of these practices?

Numerous recent studies highlight significant variation in teacher perceptions, including disagreement and doubts about whether no-excuses disciplinary practices are good for students. Sondel (2015) looked in no-excuses charters in New Orleans and found that some teachers struggled to enact their own vision of civic education given the constraints of the disciplinary structure. Analyzing interviews with novice teachers in no-excuses schools in the Northeast, Kershen & colleagues (2019) argued that many became socialized by disciplinary methods to understand "control as care." In an ethnography of one no-excuses charter in New York City, Marsh (2020) found that the pre-dominantly White teaching staff most often conceptualized student "success" as an ideal in which students took individual responsibility—working hard and demonstrating intrinsic motivation. Yet the researcher also observed and documented instances where, despite a few teachers expressing the need to teach students self-advocacy skills, students were instead punished for demonstrating such traits (Marsh, 2020), reinforcing findings from Golann's (2015) ethnographic study of a different no-excuses charter. As Lewis & Diamond (2015) point out when it comes to research on organiza-tional routines, there are *ostensive* (the ideal of the routine) and *performative* (the routine as practiced) aspects to routines and these tend to be misaligned especially when it comes to applying disciplinary rules and expectations to students of color. This same idea can be applied to the ideal of the systems that no-excuses proponents discuss and what teachers actually *do* and how they *feel* performing the routines.

For instance, despite the ostensive theory that disciplinary practices help novice teachers feel successful, researchers find a variety of teacher responses in practice, including substantial resistance to enforcing disciplinary expectations. For example, Golann (2018) categorized teachers' responses to dis-ciplinary expectations and found that teachers were conformers, imitators, adaptors, and rejecters, with the latter two making significant changes to or outright rejecting no-excuses disciplinary expectations.

Torres (2014) interviewed no-excuses charter teachers in New York City and found that those adaptors and rejecters who strongly disagreed with disciplinary methods and how students were being socialized in no-excuses schools are more likely to leave and they cited this as an important reason to leave the no-excuses environment or to leave teaching altogether. In a case study of one large no-excuses CMO, Torres (2019) surveyed and interviewed newly hired teachers before and after starting their jobs. These teachers provided very strong survey ratings of their fit with the organiza-tion *before* starting the job, but once they completed their first year, their ratings of fit dropped most sharply in the area of views of student discipline (moving from an average between "strongly agree" and "agree" on a 7-point Likert scale prior to starting to an average of "neutral" by the middle of the year). In the same study, interviews with principals and teachers highlighted strong pressure for teachers to follow schoolwide disciplinary methods and some teachers connected their discomfort doing so to feelings of failure and subsequent decisions to leave (Torres, 2019).

These feelings are echoed in other contexts. In an evaluation of the Knowledge is Power Programs (KIPP) Bay Area schools (Woodworth et al., 2008), found that nearly a third of surveyed teachers were uncomfortable with their school's disciplinary policies. Though the study is older, it again reinforces the variation and teacher discomfort documented by qualitative and mixed method researchers across a variety of settings and cities.

The same evaluation found that roughly half of surveyed KIPP students did not feel that the school rules were fair (Woodworth et al., 2008). Student perceptions are crucial to consider when thinking about the efficacy of disciplinary practices. Research on school climate illustrates how important perceptions of fairness are for the *relationship* dimension of climate, as these perceptions influence feelings of connectedness, engagement, and social support (Thapa et al., 2013). These are all critical to school effectiveness and broader notions of student success (Golann & Torres, 2020; Thapa, et al., 2013).

Though few in number, peer-reviewed studies of how students experience no-excuses discip-linary practices have common findings. For example, in a recent ethnography published in the *American Educational Research Journal* (AERJ), Graham (2019) spent nearly a year with 24 sixth-grade students in a no-excuses school in the mid-Atlantic region. He argued that the disciplinary structures ran counter to ideals of civic education and found that nearly all of the students viewed some rules as unreasonable and their enforcement as unfair, most often saying that they "got in trouble for no reason" (Graham, 2019, p. 672).

Extending findings from Goodman's (2017) study on probable shaming found in CMO handbooks, Marsh & Noguera (2019) analyzed interviews with Black students labeled "at-risk" and ethnographic observations and found that labeling practices perpetuated racialized stigmas, deficit narratives, and biases in ways that were detrimental to these students' well-being. Finally, Golann's (2015) ethnography found that students expressed numerous concerns about the rules. Students felt that they were generally not trusted to make decisions, had to defer to authority rather than question it, and the researcher observed that they generally had few opportunities to express their opinions (Golann, 2015).

Although there is little known about student perspectives on no-excuses schools, there is even less empirical or peer-reviewed work conducted on the perspectives of parents choosing these schools. This is critical to understand, as some advocates claim that low-income Black and Latinx parents must really want no-excuses charters and their practices because these schools are over-subscribed (Pondiscio, 2019). Analyzing interview data with 25 parents who chose a no-excuses charter, Golann and colleagues (2019) found that while they valued self-discipline and academic discipline, many found the school's disciplinary practices restrictive and problematic yet chose not to voice their concerns because they had been made to sign contracts agreeing to the school's practices. This reinforces the idea that although some parents may choose these schools, they are not necessarily making the choice because they agree with the way their children are treated.

Taken together, evidence across numerous studies in the last decade overwhelmingly suggests that the disciplinary climate in these schools is pervasive and often problematic, especially when viewed through lenses of anti-racism and cultural responsiveness. Although school leaders often feel that these disciplinary systems and expectations are necessary (Golann, 2021; Lake et al., 2010), studies show that teachers, students, and parents alike express significant concerns across time and a variety of no-excuses contexts which is partly why some of these networks have recently denounced and attempted to move away from such practices.

Future Directions for Policy, Practice, and Research

In recent years, a number of schools and networks have turned away from the no-excuses disciplinary practices described in this chapter. Even as early as 2009, a small number of schools such as those in KIPP San Francisco were adopting restorative justice and later, others in Indiana, Denver, New Orleans, and Philadelphia were publicly recognizing the problems with existing disciplinary practices and experimenting with research-based alternatives such as Positive Behavior Intervention and Supports (Golann & Torres, 2020; Kellogg, 2019). While these alternatives were not without their own challenges and faults, they represented some variation in the sector and foreshadowed dramatic changes in 2020 amidst calls for racial justice in the wake of George Floyd's murder (Kunichoff, 2020; Morrison, 2020) and backlash from years of accumulated criticism over discipline (Kellogg, 2019; Shapiro, 2019). The year 2020 saw some of the largest and most recognizable CMOs disavow and apologize for their approaches, with networks like Uncommon Schools and the Noble Network issuing apologies and detailed letters about how they would discontinue certain disciplinary practices and begin changing policies and practices to increase parent and student voice (Kunichoff, 2020; Morrison, 2020; Murphy, 2021).

Given these shifts, more research is needed documenting whether and how disciplinary practices are changing, and what effect they are having on a variety of important outcomes. Given the evolution in the thinking and practice of no-excuses schools and teachers/leaders, researchers should examine why these decisions were made, document what is happening in schools/classrooms, and measure the effect of these changes. Researchers should also dramatically expand their definition of desirable outcomes to focus on to determine the impact of no-excuses schools. In addition to test scores and attainment measures, researchers should prioritize other outcomes related to racial equity and school climate such as social-emotional outcomes, cultural responsiveness, and teacher, student, and parent perception measures. Policymakers can encourage such changes by building incentives and regulations that encourage schools to be successful on these other metrics that do not simply measure student attainment. For example, charter authorizers could require more reporting on disciplinary systems, focusing on data such as suspensions, expulsions, and even lower-level infractions such as removals, detentions, and other referrals.

It has also been difficult to access no-excuses schools and CMOs to conduct research on this topic, which leads to a dearth of research across a variety of no-excuses schools. The research I reviewed illustrates some of the strengths in the current research, which include rich case study data that take the form of single-site ethnographies (e.g., Golann, 2021; Marsh, 2020; Graham, 2019), as well as interviews and survey data from teachers, leaders, and parents. However, existing studies also illustrate some notable challenges that underscore issues of site access, as some scholars have had to turn to assessing website data and parent-student handbooks. While studies such as these can say something meaningful about the *ostensive* organizational routines, we know that what is on paper can differ from *performative* ones (Lewis & Diamond, 2015). Thus, comparative studies could document what is occurring, and how and why this varies based on the organizational context. This would move the literature towards a better understanding of how and why no-excuses schools vary in practice.

Surveys from independent researchers could answer questions such as: What are the largest CMOs *actually* doing when it comes to changes in discipline, how are these changes perceived, and how does this compare across various organizations that typically get identified as no-excuses schools? Because access is difficult, researchers also tend to lack nuance when discussing the beliefs, practices, and routines of no-excuses organizations, and this results in lumping many charter schools into a "no-excuses" category without an understanding of how or why they vary. Comparative data could help researchers and policymakers understand whether, why, and how organizations are implementing practices consistent with the way no-excuses discipline is typically portrayed. Qualitative analyses could compare multiple organizations and include classroom observations that get at variations in practice and allow us to understand how ostensive routines compare with the performative. Having access to a broader swath of organizations would help us understand variations and common patterns in perception and practice, and the conditions that foster or detract from outcomes of interest. Additionally, while some reformers and charter leaders may chafe at the "no-excuses" label, it is impossible to discern whether and how the disciplinary practices in individual schools or networks are or are not consistent with those detailed in this chapter unless researchers are allowed to system-atically analyze what is happening and provide feedback to these organizations and the public.

While *scripts* and scripted routines may be effective for assisting novice educators in pedagogy and classroom management (Golann, 2021), approaches like restorative justice, culturally responsive practice, and other pedagogical strategies that promote deeper learning may require increasingly complex levels of expertise for effective implementation (Mehta & Fine, 2019). Therefore, no-excuses practitioners interested in moving away from punitive disciplinary practices should consider ways to develop and then retain more experienced educators (Debs et al., 2019; Murphy, 2021).

In sum, there is much that is not yet known about changes in classroom management in no-excuses charter schools. What we do know is that if we are interested in racial equity, it is critical for us all to reflect on the critiques made and lessons learned along the way.

References

Abrams, S. E. (2016). *Education and the commercial mindset*. Harvard University Press.

Anyon, J. (1995). Race, social class, and educational reform in an inner-city school. Teachers College Record, 97(1), 69–94.

Barnum, M. (2018). Do charter schools suspend students more? It depends on how you look at the data. *Chalkbeat.* www.chalkbeat.org/2018/4/20/21104867/do-charter-schools-suspend-students-more-it-depends-on-how-you-look-at-the-data

Bosworth, K., Ford, L., & Hernandaz, D. (2011). School climate factors contributing to student and faculty perceptions of safety in select Arizona schools. *Journal of School Health, 81*(4), 194–201. https://pubmed.ncbi.nlm.nih.gov/21392011/

Boyd, A., Maranto, R., & Rose, C. (2014). The softer side of "no excuses." *Education Next*, *14*(1), 48–53. www.educationnext.org/the-softer-side-of-no-excuses/

Carr, S. (2014, December). How strict is too strict? The backlash against no-excuses discipline in high school. *The Atlantic*. www.theatlantic.com/magazine/archive/2014/12/how-strict-is-too-strict/382228/

Carter, S. C. (2000). *No excuses: Lessons from 21 high-performing, high-poverty schools*. Heritage Foundation.

Cohodes, S. (2018). Charter schools and the achievement gap. *The Future of Children*, 1–16. https://futureofchildren.princeton.edu/news/charter-schools-and-achievement-gap

Cuban, L. (2019, December 9). Whatever Happened to No-Excuses Schools? *Larry Cuban on School Reform and Practice*. https://larrycuban.wordpress.com/2019/12/09/whatever-happened-to-no-excuses-schools/

Debs, M., Golann, J., & Torres, A.C. (2019, August 29). "Some 'no-excuses' charter schools say they are changing. Are they? Can they?" *The Washington Post*. www.washingtonpost.com/education/2019/08/29/some-no-excuses-charter-schools-say-they-are-changing-are-they-can-they/

DiMaggio, P. J., & Powell, W. W. (1983). The iron cage revisited: Institutional isomorphism and collective rationality in organizational fields. *American sociological review*, 147–160. www.jstor.org/stable/2095101

Farrell, C., Wohlstetter, P., & Smith, J. (2012). Charter management organizations: An emerging approach to scaling up what works. *Educational Policy*, *26*(4), 499–532. https://journals.sagepub.com/doi/10.1177/0895904811417587

Ferrare, J. J., & Setari, R. R. (2018). Converging on choice: The interstate flow of foundation dollars to charter school organizations. *Educational Researcher*, *47*(1), 34–45. https://journals.sagepub.com/doi/abs/10.3102/0013189X17736524?journalCode=edra

Fryer, R. G. (2014). Injecting charter school best practices into traditional public schools: Evidence from field experiments. *The Quarterly Journal of Economics*, *129*(3), 1355–1407. https://academic.oup.com/qje/article-abstract/129/3/1355/1817328

Golann, J. W. (2015). The paradox of success at a no-excuses school. *Sociology of Education*, *88*(2), 103–119. https://journals.sagepub.com/doi/10.1177/0038040714567866

Golann, J. W. (2018). Conformers, adaptors, imitators, and rejecters: How no-excuses teachers' cultural toolkits shape their responses to control. *Sociology of Education*, *91*(1), 28–45. https://journals.sagepub.com/doi/10.1177/0038040717743721

Golann, J. W. (2021). *Scripting the moves: Culture and control in a "No-Excuses" Charter School*. Princeton University Press.

Golann, J. W., Debs, M., & Weiss, A. L. (2019). "To Be Strict on Your Own": Black and Latinx Parents Evaluate Discipline in Urban Choice Schools. *American Educational Research Journal*, *56*(5), 1896–1929. https://journals.sagepub.com/doi/abs/10.3102/0002831219831972

Golann, J. W., & Torres, A. C. (2020). Do no-excuses disciplinary practices promote success? *Journal of Urban Affairs*, *42*(4), 617–633. www.tandfonline.com/doi/abs/10.1080/07352166.2018.1427506

Goodman, J.F. (2013). Charter management organizations and the regulated environment: Is it worth the price? *Educational Researcher*, *42*(2), 89–96. https://journals.sagepub.com/doi/10.3102/0013189X12470856

Goodman, J. F. (2017). The shame of shaming. *Phi Delta Kappan*, *99*(2), 26–31. https://journals.sagepub.com/doi/10.3102/0013189X12470856

Graham, E. J. (2019). "In Real Life, You Have to Speak Up": Civic Implications of No-Excuses Classroom Management Practices. *American Educational Research Journal*, *57*(2), 653–693. https://journals.sagepub.com/doi/abs/10.3102/0002831219861549?journalCode=aera

Hashim, A., Torres, A.C., & Nader, J. (2021). Is more autonomy better? How school actors perceive school autonomy and effectiveness and the role of internal and external contingencies. *Journal of Educational Change*. https://doi.org/10.1007/s10833-021-09439-x

Hernández, L. E. (2016). Race and racelessness in CMO marketing: Exploring charter management organizations' racial construction and its implications. *Peabody Journal of Education*, *91*(1), 47–63. www.tandfonline.com/doi/full/10.1080/0161956X.2016.1119566

Henry Jr, K. L. (2019). Heretical discourses in post-Katrina charter school applications. *American Educational Research Journal*, *56*(6), 2609–2643. https://journals.sagepub.com/doi/abs/10.3102/0002831219853811

Ingersoll, R. M. (2003). *Who controls teachers' work: Power and accountability in America's schools*. Harvard University Press.

Johnson, S. M., Kraft, M. A., & Papay, J. P. (2012). How context matters in high-need schools: The effects of teachers' working conditions on their professional satisfaction and their students' achievement. Teachers College Record, *114*(10), 1–39. https://doi.org/10.1177/016146811211401004

Kardos, S. M., Johnson, S. M., Peske, H. G., Kauffman, D., & Liu, E. (2001). Counting on colleagues: New teachers encounter the professional cultures of their schools. *Educational Administration Quarterly*, *37*(2), 250–290. https://journals.sagepub.com/doi/10.1177/00131610121969316

Kellogg, A. (2019). Charter schools swap "no excuses" for a gentler approach to discipline. *Christian Science Monitor*. www.csmonitor.com/EqualEd/2019/0227/Charter-schools-swap-no-excuses-for-a-gentler-approach-to-discipline

Kershen, J., Weiner, J., & Torres, A.C. (2019). Control as Care: How Teachers in "No Excuses" Charter Schools Position Their Students and Themselves. *Equity and Excellence in Education*, 1–19. https://doi.org/10.1080/10665684.2018.1539359

Kerstetter, K. (2016). A different kind of discipline: social reproduction and the transmission of non-cognitive skills at an Urban Charter School. *Sociological Inquiry*, 86(4), 512–539. https://doi.org/10.1111/soin.12128

Kunichoff, Y. (2020). Amid a pandemic, a reckoning for a Chicago charter turning away from 'no excuses.' *Chalkbeat Chicago*. https://chicago.chalkbeat.org/2020/12/1/21755014/amid-a-pandemic-a-reckoning-for-a-chicago-charter-turning-away-from-no-excuses

Lake, R., Bowen, M., Demeritt, A., McCullough, M., Haimson, J., & Gill, B. (2012). *Learning from charter school management organizations: Strategies for student behavior and teacher coaching.* Center on Reinventing Public Education (CRPE) and Mathematica Policy Research. www.mathematica.org/publications/learning-from-charter-school-management-organizations-strategies-for-student-behavior-and-teacher-coaching

Lake, R., Dusseault, B., Bowen, M., Demeritt, A., & Hill, P. (2010). *The national study of charter management organization (CMO) effectiveness: Report on interim findings*: Center on Reinventing Public Education (CRPE) and Mathematica Policy Research. www.mathematica.org/publications/the-national-study-of-charter-management-organization-cmo-effectiveness-report-on-interim-findings

Lewis, A. E., & Diamond, J. B. (2015). *Despite the best intentions: How racial inequality thrives in good schools.* Oxford University Press.

Maranto, R., & Ritter, G. (2014). Why KIPP Is Not Corporate: KIPP and Social Justice. *Journal of School Choice*, 8(2), 237–257. http://doi.org/10.1080/15582159.2014.910052

Marinell, W. H., Coca, V. M. (2013). *Who stays and who leaves? Findings from a three part study of teacher turnover in NYC middle schools.* The Research Alliance for New York City Schools. https://steinhardt.nyu.edu/research-alliance/research/publications/who-stays-and-who-leaves

Marsh, L. T. S. (2020). "Raw Intelligence Does Not Help You": Exploring Teachers' Conceptualizations of Success at One "No-Excuses" Charter School. *Urban Education*, https://journals.sagepub.com/doi/abs/10.1177/0042085920979677

Marsh, L. T. S., & Noguera, P. A. (2018). Beyond stigma and stereotypes: An ethnographic study on the effects of school-imposed labeling on Black males in an urban charter school. *The Urban Review*, 50(3), 447–477. https://link.springer.com/article/10.1007/s11256-017-0441-x

Marzano, R. J., Marzano, J. S., & Pickering, D. J. (2003). *Classroom management that works: Research-based strategies for every teacher.* ASCD.

McShane, M. Q., & Hatfield, J. (2015). Measuring diversity in charter school offerings. *American Enterprise Institute (AEI)*. www.aei.org/research-products/report/measuring-diversity-in-charter-school-offerings/

Mehta, J., & Fine, S. (2019). *In search of deeper learning: The quest to remake the American high school.* Harvard University Press.

Merseth, K. K. (2009). *Inside urban charter schools: Promising practices and strategies in five high-performing schools.* Harvard Education Press.

Morrison, N. (2020). Uncommon U-Turn Should Help Consign No Excuses Schools To History. *Forbes*. www.forbes.com/sites/nickmorrison/2020/08/24/uncommon-u-turn-should-consign-no-excuses-culture-to-history/?sh=1ab5697f5591

Mungal, A. S. (2016). Teach For America, Relay Graduate School, and the charter school networks: The making of a parallel education structure. *Education Policy Analysis Archives/Archivos Analíticos de Políticas Educativas*, 24, 1–30. https://doi.org/10.14507/epaa.24.2037

Murphy, J. (2021, June 15). Rochester Prep rethinks 'no excuses' discipline policy after reckoning on racial injustice. *Democrat & Chronicle*. www.democratandchronicle.com/restricted/?return=https%3A%2F%2Fwww.democratandchronicle.com%2Fstory%2Fnews%2Feducation%2F2021%2F06%2F15%2Frochester-prep-rethinks-no-excuses-discipline-policy%2F5125739001%2F

Ni, Y., Sun, M., & Rorrer, A. (2015). Principal turnover: Upheaval and uncertainty in charter schools? Educational Administration Quarterly, 51(3), 409–437. https://doi.org/10.1177/0013161X14539808

Noguera, P. (2003). *City schools and the American dream: Reclaiming the promise of public education* (Vol. 17). New York: Teachers College Press.

Peyser, J.A. (2011). Unlocking the secrets of high-performing charters. *Education Next*. http://educationnext.org/unlocking-the-secrets-of-high-performing-charters/

Pondiscio, R. (2019). *How the Other Half Learns: Equality, Excellence, and the Battle Over School Choice.* Avery.

Prothero, A. (2019, March 19). 'No-Excuses' Charter Schools May Be Falling Out of Favor, Report Suggests. *Education Week*. www.edweek.org/policy-politics/no-excuses-charter-schools-may-be-falling-out-of-favor-report-suggests/2019/03

Quinn, R., Oelberger, C.R., & Meyerson, D. (2016). Getting to Scale: Ideas, Opportunities, and Resources in the Early Diffusion of the Charter Management Organization, 1999–2006. *Teachers College Record*, 118, 44. https://journals.sagepub.com/doi/abs/10.1177/016146811611800902

Reckhow, S., & Snyder, J. W. (2014). The Expanding Role of Philanthropy in Education Politics. *Educational Researcher*, *43*(4), 186–195. https://doi.org/10.3102/0013189X14536607

Renzulli, L. A., Barr, A. B., & Paino, M. (2015). Innovative education? A test of specialist mimicry or generalist assimilation in trends in charter school specialization over time. *Sociology of Education*, *88*(1), 83–102. https://journals.sagepub.com/doi/abs/10.1177/0038040714561866

Rich, M. (2013). At Charter Schools, Short Careers By Choice. *New York Times*. www.nytimes.com/2013/08/27/education/at-charter-schools-short-careers-by-choice.html?pagewanted=all

Rosenholtz, S. J., & Simpson, C. (1990). Workplace conditions and the rise and fall of teachers' commitment. *Sociology of Education*, *63*(4), 241–257. https://doi.org/10.2307/2112873

Russakoff, D. (2015). *The Prize: Who's in Charge of America's Schools?* Houghton Mifflin Harcourt.

Scott, J. (2009). The politics of venture philanthropy in charter school policy and advocacy. *Educational Policy*, *23*(1), 106–136. https://journals.sagepub.com/doi/abs/10.1177/0895904808328531

Scott, J., & Jabbar, H. (2014). The hub and the spokes: Foundations, intermediary organizations, incentivist reforms, and the politics of research evidence. *Educational Policy*, *28*(2), 233–257. https://doi.org/10.1177/0895904813515327

Shapiro, E. (2019). Why some of the country's best urban schools are facing a reckoning. *New York Times*. www.nytimes.com/2019/07/05/nyregion/charter-schools-nyc-criticism.html

Skiba, R. J., & Losen, D. J. (2016). From reaction to prevention: Turning the page on school discipline. *American Educator*, *39*(4), 4. https://eric.ed.gov/?id=EJ1086522

Snyder, J. W., & Reckhow, S. (2017). Political determinants of philanthropic funding for urban schools. *Journal of Urban Affairs*, *39*(1), 91–107. https://onlinelibrary.wiley.com/doi/abs/10.1111/juaf.12295?af=R

Sondel, B. (2015). Raising citizens or raising test scores? Teach for America, "no excuses" charters, and the development of the neoliberal citizen. *Theory & Research in Social Education*, *43*(3), 289–313. www.tandfonline.com/doi/abs/10.1080/00933104.2015.1064505

Sondel, B., Kretchmar, K., & Hadley Dunn, A. (2019). "Who Do These People Want Teaching Their Children?" White Saviorism, Colorblind Racism, and Anti-Blackness in "No Excuses" Charter Schools. *Urban Education*. https://doi.org/10.1177/0042085919842618

Taylor, K. (2018, January 11). Can a No-Excuses Charter Teach Students to Think for Themselves? *New York Times*. www.nytimes.com/2018/01/11/nyregion/can-a-no-excuses-charter-teach-students-to-think-for-themselves.html

Thapa, A., Cohen, J., Guffey, S., & Higgins-D'Alessandro, A. (2013). A review of school climate research. *Review of Educational Research*, *83*(3), 357–385. https://journals.sagepub.com/doi/10.3102/0034654313483907

Torres, A. C. (2014). "Are we architects or construction workers?" Re-examining teacher autonomy and turnover in charter schools. *Education Policy Analysis Archives*, *22*(124). https://doi.org/10.14507/epaa.v22.1614

Torres, A. C. (2016a). Is This Work Sustainable? Teacher Turnover and Perceptions of Workload in Charter Management Organizations. *Urban Education*, 1–24. https://journals.sagepub.com/doi/abs/10.1177/0042085914549367?journalCode=uexa

Torres, A. C. (2016b). Teacher Efficacy and Disciplinary Expectations in Charter Schools: Understanding the Link to Teachers' Career Decisions. *Journal of School Choice*, *10*(2), 171–199. www.tandfonline.com/doi/abs/10.1080/15582159.2016.1152528

Torres, A. C. (2019). If They Come Here, Will They Fit? A Case Study of an Urban No-Excuses Charter Management Organization's Teacher Hiring Process. *Urban Education*, https://journals.sagepub.com/doi/abs/10.1177/0042085919860564

Torres, A. C., & Golann, J. W. (2018). NEPC Review: "Charter Schools and the Achievement Gap." *National Education Policy Center*. http://nepc.colorado.edu/thinktank/review-no-excuses

White, T. (2015). Charter schools: Demystifying Whiteness in a market of "no excuses" corporate-styled charter schools. In B. Picower & E. Mayorga (Eds.), *What's Race Got To Do With It?* (pp. 121–145). Peter Lang.

Whitman, D. (2008). *Sweating the small stuff: inner-city schools and the new paternalism*. Thomas B. Fordham Institute.

Wilson, S. (2009). *Success at scale in charter schooling*. American Enterprise Institute. www.aei.org/research-products/report/success-at-scale-in-charter-schooling/

Woodworth, K.R, David, J.L, Guha, R., Wang, H., & Lopez-Torkos, A. (2008). *San Francisco Bay Area KIPP schools: A study of early implementation and achievement, final report*. SRI International. www.sri.com/publication/san-francisco-bay-area-kipp-schools-a-study-of-early-implementation-and-achievement-final-report/

10

EMERGING ISSUES IN SCHOOL BULLYING RESEARCH AND PREVENTION

Chad A. Rose

UNIVERSITY OF MISSOURI

Dorothy L. Espelage

UNIVERSITY OF NORTH CAROLINA AT CHAPEL HILL

Luz E. Robinson

UNIVERSITY OF NORTH CAROLINA AT CHAPEL HILL

Introduction

Bullying and peer victimization remain public health concerns for school-aged youth. Bullying research and prevention efforts can inform classroom management practices by assisting teachers with identifying incidents of bullying and responding effectively. Involvement in bullying is associated with detrimental short- and long-term outcomes that span across the educational, social, behavioral, psychosocial, and psychosomatic domains (McCree et al., 2022). For example, bullying involvement is associated with serious academic and psychosocial problems that can harm students' school performance in the form of school avoidance, lower levels of academic achievement, more conflictual relations with teachers and students, and poorer school adjustment (Cook et al., 2010; Espelage, Low, et al., 2013; Glew et al., 2008; Juvoven et al., 2000; Nansel et al., 2003). In addition to negative school consequences, youth who are victimized, engage in bullying, or both, often report adverse psychological effects, which have the potential to lead to subsequent victimization or perpetration (Espelage, Low, et al., 2012; Juvoven et al., 2000) and long-term effects into later adolescence and adulthood (Copeland et al., 2013; Espelage, Low, et al., 2013).

Definition of Bullying and Peer Victimization

Almost five decades of research has been conducted on bullying and peer victimization ranging from prevalence studies, etiological investigations, intervention implementation, and systematic reviews and evaluations of prevention and intervention programs (Espelage & Holt, 2012; Gaffney et al., 2019a, 2019b); National Academies of Sciences, Engineering, and Medicine [NASEM], 2016). However, over the past decade, a rigorous debate has emerged about how best to define bullying and how

DOI: 10.4324/9781003275312-12

to distinguish it from other forms of aggression and/or peer victimization (American Educational Research Association [AERA], 2013; Casper et al., 2015; NASEM, 2016; Rodkin et al., 2015). For example, NASEM (2016) concluded that "definitional and measurement inconsistencies lead to a variation in estimates of bullying prevalence, especially across disparate samples of youth" (p. 4). One of the first predominant definitions of bullying that continues to be used in the literature and in the legal arena is "A student is being bullied or victimized when he or she is exposed, repeatedly and over time, to negative actions on the part of one or more students" (Olweus, 2010, p. 11). Most contemporary definitions continue to emphasize observable or non-observable aggressive behaviors, the repetitive nature and intentionality of these behaviors, and the imbalance of power between the perpetrator(s) and victim (Espelage & Swearer, 2011; NASEM, 2016; Ybarra et al., 2014).

An imbalance of power exists when the perpetrator or group of perpetrators have more physical, social, or intellectual power than the victim. For example, in a nationally representative study, adolescents that perceived that their perpetrator had more power than them reported greater adverse outcomes (e.g., depression, suicidal ideation) than victims who did not perceive a power differential (Ybarra et al., 2014). Intent refers to purposeful behaviors engaged in by the perpetrator to willfully harm the victim. Therefore, intention requires the cognition necessary to recognize the social, emotional, or physical impact one's behaviors have on others (Green et al., 2017), while also possessing the behavioral and social skillset to communicate at an age-appropriate rate (Rose & Espelage, 2012). Finally, repetition should be evaluated carefully given that a perpetrator, or group of perpetrators, could engage in bullying repeatedly across a single victim, or fewer times across multiple victims. Youth who experience victimization often engage in avoidance behaviors in order to minimize the probability of reoccurrence (Batanova et al., 2014; Kingsbury & Espelage, 2007). Unfortunately, this may lead students to stop riding the bus, attending lunch, and/or avoiding school and other places where the victimization is likely.

Beginning in 2010, leading violence and victimization scholars convened several meetings hosted by the US Department of Education and the Centers for Disease Control and Prevention (CDC) to develop a uniform *research* definition. In 2014, The CDC issued the following definition of bullying: "any unwanted aggressive behavior(s) by another youth or group of youths who are not siblings or current dating partners that involves an observed or perceived power imbalance and is repeated multiple times or is highly likely to be repeated. Bullying may inflict harm or distress on the targeted youth including physical, psychological, social, or educational harm," (Gladden et al., 2014, p. 7). While this definition further operationalizes bullying, it maintains the three aforementioned domains: (1) power imbalance, (2) intentionality, and (3) repetition. It should be noted, however, that the unwanted behaviors referenced in the definition include physical, verbal, and relational aggression that range in severity from spreading rumors and social exclusion, to making verbal threats, and to physical attacks that cause injury—all of which can occur in physical or online environments (Rose, Simpson, et al., 2015; Rose & Tynes, 2015). Bullying which maintains its domains and occurs in online environments is referred to as cyberbullying. Cyberbullying is the act of receiving or sending/posting messages, videos or images that include negative, damaging, or abusive language or harassment through information and communications technology (Pearce et al., 2011). Finally, some bullying behaviors may overlap with aggression and may meet the legal definition of harassment but not all incidents of harassment constitute bullying (NASEM, 2016; Yell et al., 2016). Bullying is considered a chronic manifestation of aggression or harassment behaviors. Given the prevalence of these behaviors, successful classroom management hinges on a teacher's ability to identify, intervene and prevent aggression, harassment, and bullying behaviors within their classroom.

Prevalence of Bullying and Peer Victimization

According to the United Nations Educational, Scientific, and Cultural Organization (UNESCO, 2018), approximately one in three youth worldwide experience victimization at school. Recent national data in the United States suggests that approximately 22% of youth, aged 12–18, report experiencing victimization at school, representing more than 5.6 million students nationwide (Irwin et al., 2021). Over the past two decades, bullying behaviors have begun to manifest in online spaces as more youth gain access to the Internet and join social media platforms. It is important for teachers to know the prevalence of cyberbullying as it may influence classroom behaviors and peer dynamics. A recent meta-analysis on cyberbullying found that the prevalence rates for cyberbullying involvement among youth between the ages of 10 and 17 years (as a victim, perpetrator, or bully/victim) have been reported between 14% and 21% (Polanin, Espelage, Grotpeter, Ingram, et al., 2021). In 2017, The National Center for Education Statistics' (NCES) report from the School Crime Supplement to the National Crime Victimization Survey estimated that 15% of students ages 12 through 18 were victims of cyberbullying during the 2016–2017 school year (Zhang et al., 2019).

Whether in school or online, bullying behaviors peak and are most prevalent during early adolescence and middle school (Pepler et al., 2006). The rise in bullying during adolescence functions as a result of various developmental factors including the transition from child to adolescent, personal identity construction, peer influence and a strong desire to belong or "fit in" among peers. It is important to note that bullying behaviors can emerge sooner, and as early as preschool (Vlachou et al., 2011). Research in early childhood suggests that relative weaknesses in social and language skill development serve as predictors of bullying roles among younger children (Jenkins et al., 2017). These findings indicate the importance of learning and practicing social and emotional skills, such as communication in the home and providing early intervention at school. As students grow and develop their cognitive, social, and emotional skills at different rates as a function of their biological and environmental interactions, different types of bullying behaviors may emerge (e.g., physical, verbal, and relational/social). When discussing the prevalence of bullying behaviors, it is critical to emphasize that bullying does not target all children equally, with research indicating that students with one or more marginalized identities are at a greater risk of involvement. The emerging literature on bias-based or identity-based victimization is a call to action for all adults who work with children. As educators who support children in their developmental trajectories, including the formation of their identities, it is our responsibility to be explicit in promoting diversity, inclusion and equity in classrooms and schools such that bullying behaviors that target specific identities are directly addressed and significantly reduced.

Bias-Based/Identity-Based Victimization

Bias-based or identity-based victimization (also referred to as stigma-based bullying) represents the overlap between discrimination and bullying, such that the bullying behaviors are motivated by stigma towards individuals living with or perceived to live with certain identities, characteristics, or attributes (Earnshaw et al., 2018). Research findings consistently demonstrate that specific populations of school-aged youth are at increased risk of being victimized by their peers as a result of one or more marginalized identities, including youth with disabilities (Rose & Gage, 2017), racial/ethnic groups (Earnshaw et al., 2018), and lesbian, gay, bisexual, transgender or gender non-conforming youth (Espelage et al., 2008; Kahle, 2020). Some evidence suggests that bias-based bullying is associated with worse outcomes than non-bias-based bullying. Russell and colleagues (2012) found that youth who reported identity-based bullying, including bullying based on their sexual orientation, race, religion, sex/gender, or disability, were at greater risk of poor mental health outcomes (e.g., depression, suicide ideation and attempts), substance use, and low academic achievement than youth who reported bullying unrelated to their identities. While providing an exhaustive review of all marginalized youth identities (e.g., low SES, religious identity) that are particularly at risk for bias-based victimization or those who are overrepresented as bully perpetrators is beyond the scope of this chapter, three subsets of youth identities will be briefly discussed.

Bullying among students with disabilities. Early research on bullying and peer victimization emerged from the field of special education (Hoover & Hazler, 1994; Hoover et al., 1993), but a dearth of research evaluating the experiences and bullying involvement among youth with disabilities existed until recently. For example, when disability status is dichotomized (i.e., students with disabilities compared to students without disabilities), students with disabilities are twice as likely to experience victimization (Blake et al., 2012; Rose, Espelage, et al., 2011; Rose, Espelage, et al., 2015; Rose & Gage, 2017), and are significantly more likely to be identified as perpetrators (Rose et al., 2009; Rose & Espelage, 2012). Unfortunately, this disproportionate representation begins in preschool (Son et al., 2012), and persists through school exit (Rose & Gage, 2017). Specifically, Rose and Gage (2017) conducted a longitudinal evaluation of bullying involvement among youth with disabilities in grades 3 through 12 and determined that this subset of youth experienced higher rates of victimization and engaged in higher levels of bullying behaviors than their peers without disabilities over time.

While these discrepancies are alarming, bullying among youth with disabilities is more complex than dichotomization. Specifically, two of the most notable predictors of bullying involvement among youth with disabilities are social and communication skill deficits (McLaughlin et al., 2010; Rose, Monda-Amaya, & Espelage, 2011). The complexity is associated with the spectrum of disabilities and characteristics associated with a disability, as well as the services provided to support identified deficits associated with a specific disability (Rose, 2017). From a disability identification perspective, severity of the disability is predictive of involvement. Youth with learning disabilities (LD) tend to have comparative rates of involvement (Rose, Espelage, et al., 2015; White & Loeber, 2008), where youth with autism spectrum disorder (ASD) (Bear et al., 2015; Zablotsky et al., 2012) and intellectual disabilities (ID) (Rose, Stormont, et al., 2015) report higher rate of victimization, and youth with a behavioral disorder (BD) and other health impairment, including attention-deficit/hyperactivity disorder, report higher rates of perpetration (Rose & Espelage, 2012; Rose & Gage, 2017; Ryoo et al., 2015) when compared to youth without disabilities. When special education services are considered, Rose and colleagues (2009) argued that youth in more restrictive environments are more disproportionately involved in bullying than their peers with disabilities in more inclusive settings. However, it is important to note that variability exists within this subpopulation of students as it relates to classroom setting. For example, youth with ASD (Zablotsky et al., 2013) and LD (Rose, Stormont, et al., 2015) report higher rates of victimization in inclusive environments, whereas youth with ID and BD report higher rates of victimization in more restrictive environments (Rose, Stormont, et al., 2015) when compared to their peers with the same disability identification in the opposite setting. Therefore, Rose and Espelage (2012) argued that risk factors among this subset of youth hinges on a variety of complex factors.

Bullying among racial and ethnic identities. Many students with marginalized racial-ethnic identities demonstrate extraordinary resilience by drawing on cultural assets and familial strengths. However, repeated bullying encounters that include racial and ethnic discrimination can lead to significant emotional and psychological harm, also known as racial trauma (Helms et al., 2012). Identity-based bullying tied to race or ethnicity threatens a student's self-esteem and sense of safety, resulting in a variety of socio-emotional responses that may disrupt classroom management, including heightened depressive and other internalizing symptoms or increased violence and aggression (Price et al., 2019).

The literature on bullying experiences for youth with marginalized racial and ethnic identities in the US is limited and mixed, with majority of bullying research centering the experiences of White students and those with diverse samples using different measures. For example, Sawyer and colleagues (2008) found that Black students were less likely than White students to indicate that they were bullied when researchers used definition-based measures of bullying, but when they used behavior-based measures they found they were just as likely as White students to indicate that they were bullied. These findings suggest that students from different racial and ethnic groups may interpret bullying definitions and behaviors differently to White students. Thus, as US classrooms become more diverse, there is a need for additional research on historically marginalized identities and intersectionality to inform bullying prevention efforts. In addition, research suggests that students from marginalized racial and ethnic identities who do not fulfill stereotypes about their groups are more likely to be bullied than youth who fulfill stereotypes. For example, Black students who do not participate in sports and those who score high on standardized tests were more likely to be bullied among their Black peers (Peguero & Williams, 2013).

Earnshaw and colleagues (2018) conducted a review of stigma-based bullying interventions. They found that racially/ethnically marginalized youth and immigrants are disproportionately affected by contextual-level risk factors associated with bullying (e.g., adverse environments, community, home, and school), which may moderate or influence the effects of individual-level characteristics associated with bullying victimization or perpetration (e.g., depressive symptoms, acculturation stress, attitudes toward aggression) on bullying involvement and outcomes. Marginalized youth may be more likely to perpetrate bullying or be involved in the bully-victim dynamic, and are at a much higher risk for poor mental health and behavioral outcomes because of stigma-based bullying. Simultaneously, racial and ethnic groups who have experienced historical marginalization may be protected against bullying involvement and its negative outcomes as a result of resilience factors such as a strong ethnic identity, positive cultural and family values, and teacher support (Earnshaw et al., 2018). Classroom management practices for teachers with students from marginalized identities would benefit from learning about their students' culture and building relationships with them and their families. Cultural competency is imperative to ensuring classrooms are safe space for students of color and classrooms that are managed with inclusive and equitable activities that allow students, who are largely underrepresented, to develop positive cultural values for themselves and others.

Bullying and the Lesbian, Gay, Bisexual, Transgender, Queer or Questioning (LGBTQ+) community. A large percentage of bullying among youth involves the use of homophobic epithets and slurs, called homophobic teasing or victimization (Espelage, Basile, & Hamburger, 2012; Espelage et al., 2018; Poteat & Espelage, 2005; Poteat & Rivers, 2010). Bullying and homophobic victimization occur more frequently among LGBTQ+ youth in US schools than among students who identify as heterosexual or cisgender (Espelage et al., 2008; Kosciw et al., 2009; Robinson & Espelage, 2011, 2012). Some LGBTQ+ youth report greater symptoms of depression, anxiety, suicidal thoughts and behaviors, and truancy than their straight-identified peers (Espelage et al., 2008; Robinson & Espelage, 2011). However, peer victimization does not appear to explain all mental health disparities between LGBTQ+ and heterosexual or cisgender youth (Robinson & Espelage, 2012).

Russell, Kosciw, Horn, and Saewyc (2010) highlight four practices that have shown to promote safety and well-being for LGBTQ+ youth in schools. First, administrators and staff need to ensure that school nondiscrimination and anti-bullying policies specifically include protection for actual or perceived sexual orientation or gender identity or expression. Second, it is imperative that teachers receive training and ongoing professional development on how to intervene when homophobic teasing and/or name-calling occur. Third, school-based support groups or clubs (e.g., gay-straight alliances) should be created and supported, given their presence is associated with less victimization related to gender nonconformity and/or sexual orientation. Finally, it is important to include LGBTQ+ role models or issues in school curricula, including bullying-prevention programming, and access to information and resources through the library, school-based health centers, and other avenues.

Bullying, Peer Victimization, Academic Achievement, and Engagement

Several national and international research studies relying on cross-sectional data have documented those experiences of being victimized or engaging in bullying are associated with decreased academic achievement and school engagement (Espelage, Hong, et al., 2013; Rose, Espelage, et al., 2015). For example, in a large-scale, cross-sectional study of 16,302 adolescents from 52 high schools, youth who identified as experiencing victimization, engaging in bullying, and engaging in and experiencing bullying were 1.25, 1.54, and 1.67 times more likely, respectively, to report lower academic marks (Bradshaw et al., 2013). Similarly, Rose, Espelage, and colleagues (2015) found higher academic grades predicted lower self-reported bullying, victimization, and anger among a large sample of middle school youth. Negative associations between bullying involvement and grade point average and standardized test scores are also found when students are followed over time in longitudinal studies (Baly et al., 2014; Juvonen et al., 2011; Schwartz et al., 2005). For example, Riffle and colleagues (2021) reported a significant, negative association between bully perpetration and victimization on grade point average over the course of one academic year. Similarly, Juvonen and colleagues (2011) documented that peer victimization can account for an average of a 1.5 letter grade decrease in one academic subject, and an overall decrease in grade point average, across three years of middle school. Additionally, greater self-reported victimization was associated with lower grades and lower teacher-rated academic engagement.

However, in the first meta-analytic review of 33 studies assessing the relationship between victimization and academic performance, Nakamoto and Schwartz (2010) reported that empirical research on this association has produced an incongruent pattern of findings and modest correlations. In fact, these authors reported a small but significant negative correlation between peer victimization and academic achievement under both a random effects model ($r = -.12$, $p < .001$) and the fixed-effects model ($r = -.10$, $p < .001$). To complicate the picture, a small number of researchers have also concluded that peer victimization and academic performance are unrelated phenomena (Woods & Wolke, 2004). For example, Polanin, Espelage, Grotpeter, Spinney, et al., (2021) conducted a comprehensive meta-analysis on the association between school violence and mental health, school performance, and criminal or delinquent acts, and concluded that bully perpetration and victimization did not predict overall school performance outcomes, but bully perpetration predicted a trend towards lower grade point average ($r_p = .02$, $p < .01$) and victimization predicted an inverse relationship to later grade point average ($r_p = -.03$, $p < .01$), suggesting increased rates of victimization were associated with increased grade point average. This research suggests that peer victimization or engaging in bullying results in academic challenges for some students, but not all, and not all in the same way. Thus, there are likely risk and protective factors that explain this association. For example, poor academic performance might be a result of victimization at school through mediating influences of internalizing behaviors (DeRosier & Mercer, 2009; Graham et al., 2006; Nishina et al., 2005), or mental health factors such as depression, social anxiety, and low self-esteem, which then could contribute to academic challenges (Cook et al., 2010; Polanin, Espelage, Grotpeter, Spinney, et al., 2021).

In addition, some youth who are victimized blame themselves for their victimization, which leads to negative self-perceptions (Batanova et al., 2014; Graham & Juvonen, 1998) and difficulty concentrating on their schoolwork. Consequently, they are likely to receive lower grades (Graham et al., 2006; Lopez & DuBois, 2005; Nakamoto & Schwartz, 2010). Friendship quality and peer social support also have a complex moderating role in the association between peer victimization and academic performance (Rose, Espelage, et al., 2015; Schwartz et al., 2008).

Etiology of Bullying and Peer Victimization: Social-Ecology Perspective

The onset of bullying, aggression, and peer victimization is best understood from a social–ecological perspective, where individual biological characteristics of children interact with complex environmental and social factors to facilitate cognitive, emotional, and behavioral development (Basile et al., 2009; Espelage, 2004, 2012; Hong & Espelage, 2012; Preast et al., 2020). The social ecological framework, adapted from Bronfenbrenner's (1979) *Ecological Systems Theory*, has been applied to bullying involvement as a mechanism to understand the interaction of risk and protective factors, whereby child and adolescent behaviors are shaped by a range of nested contextual systems, including family, peers, school, community, and societal environments (Bronfenbrenner, 1979; Espelage & Swearer, 2011; Hong & Espelage, 2012; Preast et al., 2020). The social ecological perspective provides a conceptual framework for investigating the independent and combined impact of complex social contexts, environmental systems, and transactional influences on behavioral development (Preast et al., 2020). The *microsystem* includes structures in which an individual has direct contact, such as families, peers, and schools. The *mesosystem*, another component of the social ecological framework, comprises the interrelations among microsystems. This framework has been applied to the conceptualization of bullying perpetration and victimization, highlighting reciprocal influences on behavioral development and social interactions that vary within contexts and between individuals, families, schools, peer groups, communities, and societies (Espelage et al., 2003; Espelage, 2012; Hong & Espelage, 2012; Preast et al., 2020).

Individual Characteristics

Certain individual characteristics have been implicated in increasing the risk of bullying involvement. For example, dichotomized biological gender (i.e., male, female) remains a common factor associated with bullying involvement due to inconsistent outcomes. International data suggest that males and females experience similar rates of bullying (UNESCO, 2018), whereas estimates in the US suggest that approximately 26% of females and 19% of males report experiencing victimization at school (Irwin et al., 2021). While victimization rates are relatively similar, males tend to engage in higher rates of bully perpetration, or respond to victimization through increased perpetration (i.e., bully-victim) (Cook et al., 2010). The topography of behavior is also important, such that males tend to experience and engage in higher rates of physical and verbal bullying compared to females (Card et al., 2008). Another important individual characteristic is cognitive, social, and emotional skill weaknesses and strengths. For example, youth with relative weaknesses in social and communication skills tend to engage in and experience higher rates of bullying involvement, including students with disabilities (Rose, Espelage, et al., 2011).

Race and ethnicity are also an important consideration, yet limited research in this area make it difficult to discern differences across racial and ethnic groups (NASEM, 2016). Early studies suggest that Black youth report less victimization than White and Latinx youth, and Latinx youth engage in higher rates of perpetration than Black and White youth (Nansel, 2001). However, in a recent meta-analysis, Vitoroulis and Vaillancourt (2018) reported no significant differences between ethnic majority and minority youth in bully perpetration but acknowledged a limited literature base. Current national data in the US found that 37.1% of youth who identified as multi-racial, 24.6% of White youth, 22.2% of Black youth, 18.0% of Latinx youth, and 13.5% of Asian youth reported experiencing victimization at school (Irwin et al., 2021). These findings suggest how individual differences may impact bullying involvement and the different ways they may present and interfere with classroom management. However, it is critical for teachers to know that it is not the identity itself that places these students at an inherently higher risk, but rather it is the social norms and structures (e.g., racism, ableism, heteronormativity) upheld by all of us that creates this risk.

Family Characteristics

Parental monitoring and supervision play an important role in youth's experiences with bullying and victimization. Youth who engage in bullying tend to have parents who provide less than adequate supervision or are not actively involved in the lives of their children (Espelage et al., 2000; Georgiou & Fanti, 2010; Low & Espelage, 2013). Adolescents are more likely to engage in bullying behaviors when their daily activities are not monitored by adults, they are not held accountable for their actions, the family is not able to intervene, socially appropriate behaviors are not taught and reinforced, and socially appropriate communicative practices are not modeled within the household (NASEM, 2016). Additionally, parents who model aggression at home or encourage aggression as a means of retaliation have children with a higher likelihood of engaging in bullying behaviors at school (Espelage, Low, et al., 2013; Georgiou & Fanti, 2010). Conversely, youth who have a stronger sense of family belonging, report lower levels of bully perpetration (Slaten et al., 2019).

Children who are victims of bullying more often come from families with histories of abuse or inconsistent parenting (Espelage, Low, & De La Rue, 2012; Georgiou & Fanti, 2010), conceivably because they have not been modeled the skills necessary to respond to bullying in a safe and socially appropriate way. However, supportive familial relations can also buffer the negative physical and mental health impact associated with bullying involvement. When victims of bullying have warm, caring, and supportive relationships with their families, it is considered a protective factor, such that they have more positive outcomes, both emotionally and behaviorally than other victimized peers with lower levels of family support (Bowes et al., 2010; Holt & Espelage, 2007). These positive parent–child interactions provide children with the opportunity to talk about their bullying experiences in a safe environment, where parents can provide guidance on how to respond and cope with these events. Additionally, connections with other family members including supportive sibling relationships may serve to aid in bully-victims' resilience (Bowes et al., 2010).

School Characteristics

Teachers, Administrators, and Paraprofessionals. It has been noted that there are discrepancies between how teachers and staff perceive bullying in comparison to their students. Many teachers are unaware of how serious and extensive the bullying is within their schools, and are often ineffective in being able to identify bullying incidents (Bradshaw et al., 2007; Kochenderfer-Ladd & Pelletier, 2008). Divergence between staff and student estimates of the rates of bullying are seen in elementary, middle, and high school, with staff consistently underestimating the frequency of these events (Bradshaw et al., 2007). Bradshaw and colleagues (2007) reported these differences were most pronounced in elementary school, where less than 1% of elementary school staff reported bullying rates similar to that reported by students.

Very few teachers reported that they would ignore or do nothing if a student reported an incident of bullying, instead many teachers reported that they would intervene with the perpetrator and victim (Bradshaw et al., 2007). Despite the good intentions of school officials, many students feel that teachers and staff are not doing enough to prevent bullying (Bradshaw et al., 2007). For example, students may fear that teachers will not be able to assist, if they "tattle" the situation may become worse, teachers may not believe them, teachers may not be able to protect them, or believe they can resolve the situation independently (see Rose et al., 2018 for review), which may also explain why teachers perceive a lower prevalence of bullying (Craig et al., 2000).

Classroom-level predictors

Studies that employ social network analysis to examine classroom structure and its impact on aggression find that when classrooms have rigid hierarchical social structures, victimization occurs and becomes more stable because there are few opportunities to maneuver into different roles or social positions (Schäfer et al., 2005). When there are clear power differences, children who are victimized may not have the resources, support, or social and communication skills necessary to respond, thus the bully behavior remains unaddressed (Preast et al., 2020). On the other hand, when classrooms are more democratic and the social power is more evenly distributed, a less hostile environment for students is created (Ahn et al., 2010), which discourages bullying behaviors. Research suggest that schools and classrooms with a "culture of bullying" can serve as a catalyst that allows youth who engage in bullying to continue to behave aggressively without fear of sanction, encourage passivity of bystanders, and reduce the likelihood of help-seeking behavior (Bandyopadhyay et al., 2009). However, youth with a strong sense of school belonging report less bullying involvement (Slaten et al., 2019). These studies taken together suggest that prevention should intervene at all levels of the school's ecology.

Peers Characteristics

Peers can be a source of enormous support for students, and as such, when students lack a connection to their peers it can make incidents of bullying more severe. For example, peer social support has been found to predict lower levels of bully perpetration, physical aggression, victimization, and anger (Rose, Espelage, et al., 2015), especially when coupled with increased school belonging (Slaten et al., 2019). Peers serve various roles in bullying, such that they may choose to perpetuate bullying by actively joining in or passively accepting the bullying behaviors, while other peers may choose to engage in prosocial behaviors to intervene and stop bullying or defend the victim (Espelage, Green, & Polanin, 2012; Flaspohler et al., 2009; Salmivalli, 2010). Unfortunately, inaction on behalf of peers seem to be more prevalent, and many students reinforce bullying by passively observing (Flaspohler et al., 2009).

Decades of research point to the role of empathy in promoting prosocial behavior and inhibiting antisocial behavior, where studies specifically extended empathy to willingness to intervene in bullying scenarios or defender behavior (Caravita et al., 2009; Gini et al., 2007, 2008, 2011; Nickerson et al., 2008; Pöyhönen et al., 2010; Stavrinides et al., 2010). Taken together, these studies find that among early adolescent samples, defending behavior is associated with greater empathy (Gini et al., 2007, 2008; Nickerson et al., 2008; Stavrinides et al., 2010) and youth who engage in high rates of bullying behavior appear to be morally competent, but lack in morally compassionate behavior (Gini et al., 2011). For example, Pozzoli and Gini (2010) found that perceived positive peer pressure to defend a victim interacted with personal responsibility to predict defending. That is, students who held moderate or high levels of personal responsibility were more likely to defend a victim if they perceived their peers to hold a positive view toward defender behavior. These findings suggest the importance of teaching empathy and compassion to students to help them with managing their attitudes and behaviors towards themselves and others.

Increasingly, school-based bullying prevention programs are focusing their attention on encouraging bystanders to intervene. Polanin and colleagues' (2012) meta-analysis, which synthesized bullying prevention programs' effectiveness in altering bystander behavior to intervene in bullying situations, revealed that overall, the programs were successful (Hedges' $g = 0.20$, C.I.: 0.11, 0.29, $p <$ .001), with larger effects for high school samples compared to K-8 student samples (HS ES = 0.43, K-8 ES = 0.14; $p < .05$). Therefore, this meta-analysis indicated that programs were effective at changing bystander intervening behavior. Thus, teachers can shape bystander behaviors and facilitate a classroom culture that encourages empathy and compassion by incorporating activities that involve perspective-taking to help students better understand their own feelings, the feelings of others and the value of holding prosocial attitudes and behaviors.

Bystander approaches need to consider the developmental trends in role status. Traditional views of bullying contend that bullying is a linear process between a "pure bully" and "pure victim." However, contemporary views have determined that roles associated with bullying may be more fluid across time and context (Demaray et al., 2021; Gumpel et al., 2014; Rose, Simpson, & Moss, 2015; Ryoo et al., 2015). Additionally, the association between peers and bullying can also look different depending on the age of students. For elementary-aged youth, there tends to be a lack of stability for the victim role, while students who engage in high rates of bullying tend to remain relatively stable for a period of time (Schäfer et al., 2005). At this age, bullying perpetration seems to be directed at multiple targets, which results in multiple victims and lower stability. The environment of primary schools is such that social hierarchies are not as pronounced; therefore, students will more often respond directly when victimized. Therefore, it is critically important to teach, model, and reinforce social and communication skills necessary for effectively and appropriately responding to bullying (Preast et al., 2020)

What Works in Bullying Prevention?

Despite the personal and societal costs of youth aggression and bullying involvement and associated correlates, the efficacy of school violence and bullying prevention programs have varied across countries and contexts (NASEM, 2016; Gaffney et al., 2019a, 2019b; Ttofi & Farrington, 2011). While there has been an increase in bullying prevention and intervention programs, their efficacy varies tremendously across contexts, and program effects are often modest (Ttofi & Farrington, 2011) or have produced mixed results (NASEM, 2016; Pearce et al., 2011). In two recent meta-analyses, which included a review of 100 bully prevention program evaluations and randomized controlled trials; 65 bully prevention interventions were evaluated, with four programs representing 38% of the total sample (Gaffney et al., 2019a, 2019b). The US represented 28% of the studies evaluated, where prevention programs were 1.38 times more likely to reduce bully perpetration and 1.17 times more likely to reduce victimization when compared to control schools, which represented the fourth and seventh largest, out of 12 countries, respectively (Gaffney et al., 2019a). Overall, Gaffney et al. (2019a) found reductions in perpetration by approximately 20% and victimization by approximately 16%. In a separate meta-analysis, Gaffney and colleagues (2021) noted that whole-school prevention programs, anti-bullying policies, classroom rules, information for parents, informal peer involvement, and working with youth who are victimized were associated with larger reductions in bullying involvement. NASEM (2016) also reported that bully prevention programs that include multiple components, implemented across a variety of settings, and grounded in skill development are associated with reductions in bullying involvement. However, the disparities between outcomes associated with bully prevention programs in the US, in comparison to other countries, may be partially attributed to the competing demands on students' and teachers' learning and instructional time (NASEM, 2016).

The Olweus Bullying Prevention Program (OBPP) is considered by some to be the "gold standard" of bully prevention (Gaffney et al., 2019a, 2019b), is used in thousands of US school districts (OBPP, 2022), and supported by a number of State Departments of Education. For example, out of the 65 programs evaluated in the two meta-analyses, OBPP represented 18% of the total sample (Gaffney et al., 2019a, 2019b). However, the outcomes associated with OBPP in the US are inconsistent with Norwegian schools, where larger effect sizes were found in Norway, when compared to evaluations among US samples (Gaffney et al., 2019a). Gaffney et al. (2019a) argued, "These differences could be attributed to different evaluation methodologies, but they could also reflect cultural and societal differences between youth in Norway and youth in the USA." (p. 25). Therefore, research on the efficacy of the OBPP in US schools is ongoing, and it is important for program developers, implementers, and evaluators to demonstrate under what conditions this program yields reductions in bullying and for whom.

Social and Emotional learning (SEL) approaches. In contrast, school-based violence prevention programs that facilitate social and emotional learning (SEL) skills, address interpersonal conflict, and teach emotion management have been very successful in reducing youth violence and disruptive behaviors in classrooms (van de Sande et al., 2019; Wilson & Lipsey, 2007). Many of these social-emotional and social-cognitive intervention programs target risk and promotive factors that have consistently been associated with aggression, bullying, and violence in cross-sectional and longitudinal studies (Basile et al., 2009; Espelage et al., 2003, 2012; Espelage, Low et al., 2013, 2015; Espelage, Rose, & Polanin, 2015; 2016), including anger, empathy, perspective-taking, respect for diversity, attitudes supportive of aggression, coping, intentions to intervene to help others, and communication and problem-solving skills. Overall, SEL involves "the systematic development of a core set of social and emotional skills that help children more effectively handle life challenges and thrive in both their learning and their social environments" (Ragozzino & Utne O'Brien, 2009). SEL programs can provide schools, after-school programs, and youth community centers with a research-based approach to building skills and promoting positive individual and peer attitudes that can contribute to the prevention of bullying.

SEL as a framework emerged from influences across different movements that focused on resiliency and teaching social and emotional competencies to children and adolescents (Elias et al., 1997). SEL programs encompass five domains (i.e., self-awareness, self-management, social awareness, relationship skills, responsible decision making; CASEL, 2012) that employ social skill instruction to address behavior, discipline, safety, and academics to help youth become self-aware, manage their emotions, build social skills (e.g., empathy, perspective-taking, respect for diversity), friendship skill building, and make positive decisions (Zins et al., 2004). A study of more than 213 SEL-based programs found that if a school implements a quality SEL curriculum, they can expect better student behavior and an 11 percentile increase in academic test scores (Durlak et al., 2011). A growing number of schools are electing to implement these programs because of the gains that schools see in achievement and pro-social behavior. Students exposed to SEL activities report feeling safer and more connected to school and academics; SEL programs also help students build work habits in addition to social skills, such that teachers and students are able to build strong relationships (Zins et al., 2004).

SEL approaches to prevention are showing promise in reducing aggression, bullying involvement, and promoting prosocial behavior (Brown et al., 2011; Espelage, Low, Polanin, & Brown, 2013; Espelage, Low, et al., 2013, 2015; Espelage, Rose, & Polanin, 2015; 2016; Frey et al., 2005), while improving social and communication skills, which are two of the most notable predictors of bullying involvement (Mc Cree et al., 2022; Preast et al., 2020). This success is in large part due to SEL school-based programs paralleling the hallmarks of the prevention science framework. First, these programs draw from the scientific literature on the etiological underpinnings of aggression, bullying, school violence, and other problematic behaviors among children and adolescents (Merrell, 2010). Second, risk (e.g., anger, impulse control) and promotive (e.g., empathy, communication skills) factors are identified from the etiological literature and targeted through direct instruction of skills and opportunities to use skills in different contexts. Third, in relation to bystander intervention, these programs include discussions and content about the challenges (e.g., fear of being targeted, losing friends) that youth face when they attempt to intervene on behalf of a victim of aggression. Several randomized controlled trials (RCTs) have attended to the rigorous evaluation of the intervention effects (Brown et al., 2011; Espelage, Low, Polanin, & Brown, 2013; Espelage, Low et al., 2013, 2015; Espelage, Rose, & Polanin, 2015; 2016), which is an additional hallmark of prevention science. For example, Espelage, Rose, and Polanin (2015; 2016) demonstrated that SEL is an effective intervention for reducing bullying involvement, increasing willingness to intervene in bullying situations, and increasing academic outcomes for youth with disabilities. The Collaborative for Academic, Social, and Emotional Learning (CASEL, 2003) has reviewed many of SEL approaches and is a great resource for teachers who want to improve the social and emotional devlopment of their classrooms and schools.

Positive Behavioral Interventions and Supports (PBIS) framework. PBIS is a dominant paradigm in schools internationally and is a problem-solving framework designed to guide schools in the systematic implementation of social and behavioral interventions within a tiered system framework (Lewis et al., 2010). RCTs of school-wide PBIS in elementary schools have shown that high quality implementation of the framework is associated with significant reductions in office discipline referrals and suspensions (Bradshaw et al., 2010; Horner et al., 2009) and teacher-ratings of classroom behavior problems and aggression, emotion regulation problems, bullying perpetration and peer rejection (Bradshaw et al., 2012; Waasdorp et al., 2012). It should be noted, however, that PBIS is an intervention delivery framework, not an intervention. In a large-scale assessment of PBIS and bullying involvement, Gage and colleagues (2019) reported that the prevalence of bullying involvement was not significantly different between schools that implemented PBIS with fidelity, and match comparison schools without PBIS. However, Rose and colleagues (2019) argued that PBIS is a promising framework for bully prevention, as long as bully prevention is identified as a school-based need, and tiered interventions are purposefully implemented to address bullying and support social and communication skill acquisition at each tier. Rose and colleagues (2019) further their argument by presenting a comprehensive PBIS framework for bully prevention, grounded in social and emotional learning, that includes recommendations for assessment, school-wide SEL, targeted social and communication skill instruction, and individualized supports and prevention.

School climate interventions. Research suggests that both effective risk prevention (e.g., bullying and other forms of school violence) and health promotion (e.g., safe, supportive, engaging schools) efforts are, in essence, school climate reform efforts (Battistich, 2008; Berkowitz, 2000; Cohen,

2006, 2013). "School climate" or culture refers to the quality and character of the school community. School climate is based on patterns of people's experience of school life, and reflects norms, goals, values, interpersonal relationships, teaching, learning, leadership practices, and organizational structures (National School Climate Council, 2007). The school climate improvement process reflects a series of overlapping systemic or schoolwide processes that promote safe, supportive, engaging and flourishing schools (for review see Bradshaw et al., 2021): (i) *transparent, democratically informed leadership* (Berkowitz, 2011); (ii) *engaging multiple stakeholders* (students, parents, school staff and community members) to be co-learners and co-leaders in the improvement efforts (school-home-community partnerships) (Morton & Montgomery, 2011); (iii) *measurement practices* that recognize the social, emotional, and civic dimensions of learning and school life (Cohen et al., 2009); (iv) *tailored improvement goals* to meet the unique needs of all students and the school community (Espelage & Poteat, 2012); (v) *adult learning* and professional learning communities that supports capacity building (Davis et al., 2005); and (vi) *prosocial education* (Durlak et al., 2011; Espelage, Low, et al., 2013).

Bullying Prevention and Intervention: Moving the Field Forward

Much is understood about the correlates of bullying and the short-term and long-term outcomes for all youth involved. However, the reality is that school-based anti-bullying programs and efforts are yielding modest effects in reducing bullying and peer victimization (Gaffney et al., 2019a, 2019b). We have argued for many years that the efforts in place are flawed in several ways. First, many bully prevention programs included in previous meta-analyses did not stem from educational and developmental theory. Thus, the movement back to character education, problem-solving, social and emotional learning, and school climate reform as ways to promote positive relationships within schools offers some promise given its roots in psychology and education. Second, many bully prevention efforts in our schools are often short-term and do not routinely bring about sustainable change, because they often do not engage all members of the school community, including other school staff, parents and adults in the greater community (Mc Cree et al., 2022; Rose et al., 2019). Third, many prevention programs do not routinely direct interventions at the proximal peer social ecology that promotes and sustains bullying perpetration (Espelage, 2012; Espelage & Holt, 2012). For example, the overemphasis on unscientific bystander intervention approaches does not consider the complexity associated with youth defending a victim or intervening to help a victim (Espelage et al., 2011; Polanin et al., 2012), the necessity of teaching and reinforcing skills and behaviors associated with socially appropriate responses (Preast et al., 2020), or the fluidity of role affiliation (Rose, Simpson & Moss, 2015). Fourth, many evaluations of these programs do not address the changing demographics of communities, and do not incorporate components addressing key potential moderators of effects such as race, fidelity, and SES (Espelage & Poteat, 2012). Fifth, many do not target shared underlying risk factors (e.g., anger, impulsivity, lack of empathy) associated with persistent aggression. Sixth, many of the current programs are not designed to support students who are most at-risk for bullying involvement (e.g., students with disabilities; Rose et al., 2019), or do not assess, include, or report outcomes for youth with the most intensive needs (Espelage, Rose, & Polanin, 2015, 2016). Seventh, these programs often require resources (e.g., funding, teacher time, instructional time) that schools simply do not have, given the demands of meeting academic standards via core content instruction and standardized testing (Cohen, 2006). Finally, schools have unique ecologies with varying issues, administrative support, professional development opportunities, resources, and parental involvement that may need to be considered as programs are adapted and implemented (Espelage & Poteat, 2012).

Despite the challenges that schools face in effectively implementing bully prevention programs, teachers who understand the complexities of bullying, recognize the need for skill development, and recognize that successful interventions are multi-dimensional, have the potential to intervene and prevent bullying efficiently in their classrooms. Given that bullying involvement is associated with a variety of negative academic outcomes and internalizing and externalizing mental health problems that can disrupt classroom management, teachers are some of the first adults to notice, or have the opportunity to notice, bullying and subsequent behaviors. When teachers notice bullying behaviors or are summoned to respond to bullying either by a victim or a bystander, their response sets the tone for future incidents. Teachers are responsible for the physical and psychological safety of their students and when bullying behaviors are ignored, it teaches students that these behaviors are acceptable, and establishes the perception that not all students are deserving of a safe learning environment. This indirect and even unintentional consequence can exacerbate educational inequities and feelings of discrimination among students holding one or more marginalized identities. Thus, teachers who are aware of how bullying impacts certain subgroups of students and recognize the potential of positive prosocial attitude and behavioral development in decreasing bullying and shaping bystander behaviors, have the responsibility of infusing opportunities to learn and practice SEL, including social and communication skills, through examples of diversity, inclusion and equity that are relevant and representative of their classroom and school community.

References

Ahn, H., Garandeau, C. F., & Rodkin, P. C. (2010). Effects of classroom embeddedness and density on the social status of aggressive and victimized children. *Journal of Early Adolescence, 30*, 76–101. DOI:10.1177/0272431609350922

American Educational Research Association (2013). *Prevention of bullying in schools, colleges, and universities: Research report and recommendations*. American Educational Research Association.

Baly, M. W., Cornell, D. G., & Lovegrove, P. (2014). A longitudinal investigation of self- and peer reports of bullying victimization across middle school. *Psychology in the Schools, 51*, 217–240. DOI:10.1002/pits.21747

Bandyopadhyay, S., Cornell, D. G., & Konold, T. R. (2009). Validity of three school climate scales to assess bullying, aggressive attitudes, and help seeking. *School Psychology Review, 38*(3), 338–355. DOI:10.1080/02796015.2009.12087819

Basile, K. C., Espelage, D. L., Rivers, I., McMahon, P. M., & Simon, T. R. (2009). The theoretical and empirical links between bullying behavior and male sexual violence perpetration. *Aggression and Violent Behavior, 14*(5), 336–347. DOI:10.1016/j.avb.2009.06.001

Batanova, M., Espelage, D.L., & Rao, M. (2014). Early adolescents' willingness to intervene: what roles do attributions, affect, coping, and self-reported victimization play? *Journal of School Psychology, 52*, 279–293. DOI:10.1016/j.jsp.2014.02.001

Battistich, V. A. (2008). Character education, prevention, and positive youth development. *Journal of Research in Character Education, 6*, 81–90.

Bear, G. C., Mantz, L. S., Glutting, J. J., Yang, C., & Boyer, D. E. (2015). Differences in bullying victimization between students with and without disabilities. *School Psychology Review, 44*, 98–116. DOI:10.17105/SPR44-1.98-116

Berkowitz, M. W. (2000). Character education as prevention. In W. B. Hansen, S. M. Giles, & M. D. Fearnow-Kenney (Eds.), *Improving prevention effectiveness* (pp. 37–45). Thousand Oaks, CA: Tanglewood Research.

Berkowitz, M.W. (2011). Leading schools of character. In A. M. Blankstein & P. D. Houston (Eds.), *The soul of educational leadership series. Volume 9: Leadership for Social Justice and Democracy in Our Schools* (pp. 93–121). Corwin.

Blake, J. J., Lund, E. M., Zhou, Q., Kwok, O., & Benz, M. R. (2012). National prevalence rates of bullying victimization among students with disabilities in the United States. *School Psychology Quarterly, 27*, 210–222. DOI:10.1037/spq0000008

Bowes, L., Maughan, B., Caspi, A., Moffitt, T. E., & Arseneault, L. (2010). Families promote emotional and behavioural resilience to bullying: Evidence of an environmental effect *Journal of Child Psychology and Psychiatry, 51*(7), 809–817. DOI:10.1111/j.1469-7610.2010.02216.x.

Bradshaw, C. P., Cohen, J., Espelage, D. L., & Nation, M. (2021). Addressing school safety through comprehensive school climate approaches. *School Psychology Review, 50*(2–3), 221–236. DOI:10.1080/2372966X.2021.1926321

Bradshaw, C. P., Mitchell, M. M., & Leaf, P. J. (2010). Examining the effects of School-Wide Positive Behavioral Interventions and Supports on student outcomes: Results from a randomized controlled effectiveness trial in elementary schools. *Journal of Positive Behavior Interventions, 12*, 133–148. DOI:10.1177/1098300709334798

Bradshaw, C. P., Sawyer, A. L., & O'Brennan, L. M. (2007). Bullying and peer victimization at school: Perceptual differences between students and school staff. *School Psychology Review, 36*, 361–382.

Bradshaw, C. P., Waasdorp, T. E., Goldweber, A., & Johnson, S. L. (2013). Bullies, gangs, drugs, and school: Understanding the overlap and the role of ethnicity and urbanicity. *Journal of Youth and Adolescence, 42,* 220–234. DOI:10.1007/s10964-012-9863-7

Bradshaw, C. P., Waasdorp, T. E., & Leaf, P. J. (2012). Effects of school-wide positive behavioral interventions and supports on child behavior problems. *Pediatrics, 130*(5), 1–10. DOI:10.1542/peds.2012-0243

Bronfenbrenner, U. (1979). *The ecology of human development: Experiments by nature and design.* Boston, MA: Harvard University Press.

Brown, E. C., Low, S., Smith, B. H., & Haggerty, K. P. (2011). Outcomes from a school-randomized controlled trial of STEPS to RESPECT: A Bullying Prevention Program. *School Psychology Review, 40,* 423– 443.

Caravita, S., DiBlasio, P., & Salmivalli, C. (2009). Unique and interactive effects of empathy and social status on involvement in bullying. *Social Development, 18,* 140–163. DOI:10.1111/j.1467-9507.2008.00465.x

Card, N. A., Stucky, B. D., Sawalani, G. M., and Little, T. D. (2008). Direct and indirect aggression during childhood and adolescence: A meta-analytic review of gender differences, intercorrelations, and relations to maladjustment. *Child Development, 79*(5), 1185–1229. DOI:10.1111/j.1467-8624.2008.01184.x.

Casper, D. M., Meter, D. J., & Card, N. A. (2015). Addressing measurement issues related to bullying involvement. *School Psychology Review, 44*(4), 353–371. DOI:10.17105/spr-15-0036.1

Cohen, J. (2006). Social, emotional, ethical and academic education: Creating a climate for learning, participation in democracy and well-being. *Harvard Educational Review, 76*(2; Summer), 201–237. (www.hepg.org/her/abstract/8)

Cohen, J. (2013). Effective bully prevention efforts and school climate reform. In M. Masiello & D. Schroeder (Eds.), *A Public Health Approach to Bullying Prevention* (pp. 1–23). American Public Health Association.

Cohen, J., McCabe, E. M, Michelli, N. M & Pickeral, T. (2009). School Climate: Research, Policy, Teacher Education and Practice. *Teachers College Record, 111*(1), 180–213. (Available on: www.tcrecord.org/Content.asp?ContentId=15220)

Collaborative for Academic, Social, and Emotional Learning (CASEL) (2003). *Safe and sound: An educational leader's guide to evidence based social and emotional learning (SEL) programs.* CASEL.

Collaborative for Academic, Social, and Emotional Learning (2012). *Effective social and emotional learning programs: Preschool and elementary school edition.* CASEL.

Cook, C. R., Williams, K. R., Guerra, N. G., Kim, T. E., & Sadek, S. (2010). Predictors of bullying and victimization in childhood and adolescence: A meta-analytic investigation. *School Psychology Quarterly, 25,* 65–83. DOI:10.1037/a0020149

Copeland, W. E., Wolke, D., Angold, A., & Costello, E. J. (2013). Adult psychiatric outcomes of bullying and being bullies by peers in childhood and adolescence. *JAMA Psychiatry, 70*(4), 419–426. DOI:10.1001/jamapsychiatry.2013.504

Craig, W. M., Henderson, K., & Murphy, J. G. (2000). Perspective teachers' attitudes toward bullying and victimization. *School Psychology International, 21,* 5–21. DOI:0.1177/0143034300211001.

Davis, S., Darling-Hammond, L., LaPointe, M., & Meyerson, D. (2005). *School leadership study: Developing successful principals.* Stanford University, Stanford Educational Leadership Institute.

Demaray, M. K., Malecki, C. K., Ryoo, J. H., & Summers, K. H. (2021). Deconstructing bullying roles: A longitudinal latent profile analysis of bullying participant behavior for students in grades 4 through 12. *Journal of School Psychology, 86,* 32–48. DOI:10.1016/j.jsp.2021.02.006

DeRosier, M. E., & Mercer, S. H. (2009). Perceived behavioral atypicality as a predictor of social rejection and peer victimization: Implications for emotional adjustment and academic achievement. *Psychology in the Schools, 46,* 375–387. DOI:10.1002/pits.20382

Durlak, J. A., Weissberg, R. P., Dymnicki, A. B., Taylor, R. D., & Schellinger, K. B. (2011). The Impact of enhancing students' social and emotional learning: A meta-analysis of school-based universal interventions. *Child Development, 82,* 405–432. DOI:10.1111/j.1467-8624.2010.01564.x

Earnshaw, V. A., Reisner, S. L., Menino, D. D., Poteat, V. P., Bogart, L. M., Barnes, T. N., & Schuster, M. A. (2018). Stigma-based bullying interventions: A systematic review. *Developmental Review, 48,* 178–200. DOI:10.1016/j.dr.2018.02.001

Elias, M. J., Zins, J. E., Weissberg, K. S., Greenberg, M. T., Haynes, M., Kessler, R., et al. (1997). *Promoting social and emotional learning: Guidelines for educators.* Association for Supervision and Curriculum Development.

Espelage, D. L. (2004). An ecological perspective to school-based bullying prevention. *The Prevention Researcher, 11,* 3–6.

Espelage, D. L. (2012). Bullying prevention: A research dialogue with Dorothy Espelage. *Prevention Researcher, 19*(3), 17–19.

Espelage, D. L., Aragon, S. R., Birkett, M., & Koenig, B. W. (2008). Homophobic teasing, psychological outcomes, and sexual orientation among high school students: What influences do parents and schools have? *School Psychology Review, 37,* 202–216.

Espelage, D. L., Basile, K. C., & Hamburger, M. E. (2012). Bullying experiences and co-occurring sexual violence perpetration among middle school students: Shared and unique risk factors. *Journal of Adolescent Health*, *50*, 60–65.

Espelage, D. L., Bosworth, K., & Simon, T. R. (2000). Examining the social context of bullying behaviors in early adolescence. *Journal of Counseling and Development*, *78*, 326–333. DOI:10.1002/j.1556-6676.2000.tb01914.x

Espelage, D. L., Green, H., & Polanin, J. (2012). Willingness to intervene in bullying episodes among middle school students: Individual and peer-group influences. *The Journal of Early Adolescence*, *32*(6), 776–801. DOI:10.1177/0272431611423017

Espelage, D. L., & Holt, M. K. (2012). Understanding and preventing bullying and sexual harassment in school. In K. R. Harris, S. Graham, T. Urdan, S. Graham, J. M. Royer, & M. Zeidner, *APA educational psychology handbook, Vol 2: Individual differences and cultural and contextual factors* (pp. 391–416). American Psychological Association.

Espelage, D. L., Holt, M. K., & Henkel, R. R. (2003). Examination of peer-group contextual effects on aggression during early adolescence. *Child Development*, *74*(1), 205–220. DOI:10.1111/1467-8624.00531

Espelage, D. L., Hong, J. S., Merrin, G. J., Davis, J. P., Rose, C. A., & Little, T. D. (2018). A longitudinal examination of homophobic name-calling in middle school: Bullying, traditional masculinity, and sexual harassment as predictors. *Psychology of Violence*, *8*, 57–66. DOI:10.1037/vio0000083

Espelage, D. L., Hong, J. S., Rao, M. A., & Low, S. (2013). Associations between peer victimization and academic performance. *Theory into Practice*, *52*(4), 233–240. DOI:10.1080/00405841.2013.829724

Espelage, D. L., Low, S., & De La Rue, L. (2012). Relations between peer victimization subtypes, family violence, and psychological outcomes during adolescence. *Psychology of Violence*, *2*, 313–324. DOI:10.1037/a0027386

Espelage, D. L., Low, S., Polanin, J., & Brown, E. (2013). The impact of a middle-school program to reduce aggression, victimization, and sexual violence. *Journal of Adolescent Health*, *53*(2), 180–186. DOI:10.1016/j.jadohealth.2013.02.021

Espelage, D. L., Low, S., Polanin, J., & Brown, E. (2015). Clinical trial of Second Step© middle-school program: Impact on aggression & victimization. *Journal of Applied Developmental Psychology*, *37*, 52–63. DOI:10.1016/j.appdev.2014.11.007

Espelage, D. L., Low, S., Rao, M. A., Hong, J. S., & Little, T. (2013). Family violence, bullying, fighting, and substance use among adolescents: A longitudinal transactional model. *Journal of Research on Adolescence*, *24*(2), 337–349. DOI:10.1111/jora.12060

Espelage, D. L., & Poteat, V. P. (2012). School-based prevention of peer relationship problems. In B. Altmaier & J.-I. Hansen (Eds.), *The Oxford Handbook of Counseling Psychology* (pp. 703–722). Oxford, UK: Oxford University Press. DOI:10.1093/oxfordhb/9780195342314.013.0027

Espelage, D. L., Rose, C. A., & Polanin, J. R. (2015). Social-emotional learning program to reduce bullying, fighting, and victimization among middle school students with disabilities. *Remedial and Special Education*, *36*, 299–311. DOI:10.1177/0741932514564564

Espelage, D. L., Rose, C. A., & Polanin, J. R. (2016). Social-emotional learning program to promote prosocial and academic skills among middle school students with disabilities. *Remedial and Special Education*, *37*, 323–332. DOI:0741932515627475.

Espelage, D. L., & Swearer, S. M. (Eds.) (2011). *Bullying in North American schools (2nd Edition)*. Routledge.

Flaspohler, P. D., Elfstrom, J. L., Vanderzee, K. L., Sink, H. E., & Birchmeier, Z. (2009). Stand by me: The effects of peer and teacher support in mitigating the impact of bullying on quality of life. *Psychology in the Schools*, *46*(7), 636–649. DOI:10.1002/pits.20404

Frey, K. S., Hirschstein, M. K., Snell, J. L., Edstrom, L. V., MacKenzie, E. P., & Broderick, C. J. (2005). Reducing playground bullying and supporting beliefs: An experimental trial of the *Steps to Respect* program. *Developmental Psychology*, *41*, 479–491. DOI:10.1037/0012-1649.41.3.479

Gaffney, H., Farrington, D. P., & Ttofi, M. M. (2019a). Examining the effectiveness of school-bullying intervention programs globally: A meta-analysis. *International Journal of Bullying Prevention*, *1*, 14–31. DOI:10.1007/s42380-019-0007-4

Gaffney, H., Ttofi, M. M., & Farrington, D. P. (2019b). Evaluating the effectiveness of school-bullying prevention programs: An updated meta-analytical review. *Aggression and Violent Behavior*, *45*, 111–133. DOI:10.1016/j.avb.2018.07.001

Gaffney, H., Ttofi, M. M., & Farrington, D. P. (2021). What works in anti-bullying programs? Analysis of effective intervention components. *Journal of School Psychology*, *85*, 37–56. DOI:10.1016/j.jsp.2020.12.002

Gage, N. A., Rose, C. A., & Kramer, D. A. (2019). When prevention is not enough: Students' perceptions of bullying and school-wide positive behavior interventions and supports. *Behavioral Disorders*, *45*, 29–40. DOI:10.1177/0198742918810761

Georgiou, S. N., & Fanti, K. A. (2010). A transactional model of bullying and victimization. *Social Psychology of Education*, *13*(3), 295–311. DOI:10.1007/s11218-010-9116-0

Gini, G., Albiero, P., Benelli, B., & Altoè, G. (2007). Does empathy predict adolescents' bullying and defending behavior? *Aggressive Behavior*, *33*, 467–476. DOI:10.1002/ab.20204

Gini, G., Pozzoli, T., Borghi, F., & Franzoni, L. (2008). The role of bystanders in students' perception of bullying and sense of safety. *Journal of School Psychology*, *46*, 617–638. DOI:10.1016/j.jsp.2008.02.001

Gini, G., Pozzoli, T., & Hauser, M. (2011). Bullies have enhanced moral competence to judgerelative to victims, but lack moral compassion. *Personality & Individual Differences*, *50*, 603–608. DOI:10.1016/j.paid.2010.12.002

Gladden, R.M., Vivolo-Kantor, A.M., Hamburger, M.E., & Lumpkin, C.D. (2014). *Bullying Surveillance Among Youths: Uniform Definitions for Public Health and Recommended Data Elements, Verson 1.0*. National Center for Injury Prevention and Control, Centers for Disease Control and Prevention and U.S. Department of Education.

Glew, G. M., Fan, M., Katon, W., & Rivara, F. P. (2008). Bullying and school safety. *The Journal of Pediatrics*, *152*, 123–128. DOI:10.1016/j.jpeds.2007.05.045

Graham, S., Bellmore, A. D., & Mize, J. (2006). Peer victimization, aggression, and their co–occurrence in middle schools: Pathways to adjustment problems. *Journal of Abnormal Child Psychology*, *34*(3), 363–378. DOI:10.1007/s10802-006-9030-2

Graham, S., & Juvonen, J. (1998). Self-blame and peer victimization in middle school: An attributional analysis. *Developmental Psychology*, *34*(3), 587–599. DOI:10.1037/0012-1649.34.3.587

Green, J. G., Furlong, M. J., & Felix, E. D. (2017). Defining and measuring bullying across the life course. In C. Bradshaw (Ed.), *The Handbook on bullying prevention: A lifecourse perspective* (7–20). National Association of Social Workers (NASW) Press.

Gumpel, T. P., Zioni-Koren, V., & Bekerman, Z. (2014). An ethnographic study of participant roles in school bullying. *Aggressive Behavior*, *40*(3), 214–228. DOI:10.1002/ab.21515

Helms, J. E., Nicolas, G., & Green, C. E. (2012). Racism and ethnoviolence as trauma: Enhancing professional and research training. *Traumatology*, *18*(1), 65–74. DOI:10.1177/1534765610396728

Holt, M. K., & Espelage, D. L. (2007). Perceived social support among bullies, victims, and bully-victims. *Journal of Youth and Adolescence*, *36*(6), 984–994. DOI:10.1007/s10964-006-9153-3

Hong, J. S., & Espelage, D. L. (2012). A review of research on bullying and peer victimization in school: An ecological systems analysis. *Aggression and Violent Behavior*, *17*, 311–312.

Hoover, J. H., & Hazler, R. J. (1994). Bullies and victims. *Elementary School Guidance and Counseling*, *25*, 212–220.

Hoover, J. H., Oliver, R., & Thomson, K. (1993). Perceived victimization by school bullies: New research and future direction. *Journal of Humanistic Education and Development*, *32*, 76–84.

Horner, R. H., Sugai, G., Smolkowski, K., Eber, L., Nakasato, J., Todd, A. W., Esperanza, J. (2009). A randomized, wait-list controlled effectiveness trial assessing school-wide positive behavior support in elementary schools. *Journal of Positive Behavior Interventions*, *11*, 133–144. DOI:10.1177/1098300709332067

Irwin, V., Wang, K., Cui, J., Zhang, J., and Thompson, A. (2021). *Report on Indicators of School Crime and Safety: 2020* (NCES 2021-092/NCJ 300772). National Center for Education Statistics, U.S. Department of Education, and Bureau of Justice Statistics, Office of Justice Programs, U.S. Department of Justice. Washington, DC.

Jenkins, L. N., Mulvey, M., & Flores, M. T. (2017). Social and language skills as predictors of bullying roles in early childhood: A narrative summary of the literature. *Education and Treatment of Children*, *40*(3), 401–417. DOI:10.1353/etc.2017.0017

Juvonen, J., Nishina, A., & Graham, S. (2000). Peer harassment, psychological adjustment, and school functioning in early adolescence. *Journal of Educational Psychology*, *92*(2), 349–359. DOI:10.1037/0022-0663.92.2.349

Juvonen, J., Wang, Y., & Espinoza, G. (2011). Bullying experiences and compromised academic performance across middle school grades. *Journal of Early Adolescence*, *31*(1), 152–173. DOI:10.1177/0272431610379415

Kahle, L. (2020). Are sexual minorities more at risk? Bullying victimization among lesbian, gay, bisexual, and questioning youth. *Journal of Interpersonal Violence*, *35*(21–22), 4960–4978. DOI:10.1177/0886260517718830

Kingsbury, W. L. & Espelage, D. (2007). Attribution style and coping along the bully-victim continuum. *Scientia Paedagogica Experimentalis*, *64*, 71–102.

Kochenderfer-Ladd, B., & Pelletier, M. E. (2008). Teachers' views and beliefs about bullying: Influences on classroom management strategies and students' coping with peer victimization. *Journal of School Psychology*, *46*, 431–453. DOI:10.1016/j.jsp.2007.07.005

Kosciw, J. G., Greytak, E. A., & Diaz, E. M. (2009). Who, what, where, when, and why: Demographic and ecological factors contributing to hostile school climate for lesbian, gay, bisexual, and transgender youth. *Journal of Youth Adolescence*, *38*, 976–988. DOI:10.1007/s10964-009-9412-1

Lewis, T. J., Jones, S. E. L., Horner, R. H., & Sugai, G. (2010). School-wide positive behavior support and students with emotional/behavioral disorders: Implications for prevention, identification, and intervention. *Exceptionality*, *18*(2), 82–93. DOI:10.1177/2332858417711428

Lopez, C., & DuBois, D. D. (2005). Peer victimization and rejection: investigation of an integrative model of effects on emotional, behavioral, and academic adjustment in early adolescence. *Journal of Clinical Child and Adolescent Psychology*, *34*, 25–36. DOI:10.1207/s15374424jccp3401_3

Low, S., & Espelage, D.L. (2013). Differentiating cyber bullying perpetration from other forms of peer aggression: Commonalities across race, individual, and family predictors. *Psychology of Violence*, *3*, 39–52. DOI:10.1037/a0030308

McCree, N., Romero, M. E., Hopkins, S., Mirielli, L. G., & Rose, C. A. (2022). Bully prevention and social and emotional learning: impact on youth with disabilities. In Lemons, Lane & Powell (Eds.), *Handbook of Special Education Research, Vol. II* (272–290). Routledge.

McLaughlin, C., Byers, R., & Vaughn, R. P. (2010). *Responding to bullying among children with special educational needs and/or disabilities.* Anti-Bullying Alliance.

Merrell, K. W. (2010). Linking prevention science and social and emotional learning: The Oregon Resiliency project. *Psychology in the Schools*, *47*(1), 55–70. DOI:10.1002/pits.20451

Morton, M., & Montgomery, P. (2011). *Youth empowerment programs for improving self-efficacy and self-esteem of adolescents.* Campbell Systematic Reviews, 6. DOI:10.4073/csr.2011.5

Nakamoto, J., & Schwartz, D. (2010). Is peer victimization associated with academic achievement? A meta-analytic review. *Social Development*, *19*, 221–242. DOI:10.1111/j.1467-9507.2009.00539.x

Nansel, T. R., Haynie, D. L., & Simons-Morton, B. G. (2003). The association of bullying and victimization with middle school adjustment. *Journal of Applied School Psychology*, *19*, 45–61. DOI:10.1300/J008v19n02_04

Nansel, T. R., Overpeck, M., Pilla, R. S., Ruan, W., Simons-Morton, B., & Scheidt, P. (2001). Bullying behaviors among US youth: Prevalence and association with psychosocial adjustment. *Journal of the American Medical Association*, *285*(16), 2094–2100. DOI:10.1001/jama.285.16.2094

National Academies of Sciences, Engineering, and Medicine (NASEM) (2016). *Preventing bullying through science, policy, and practice.* The National Academies Press.

National School Climate Council (2007). *The school climate challenge: Narrowing the gap between school climate research and school climate policy, practice guidelines and teacher education policy.* Author. Retrieved January 29, 2012, from www.schoolclimate.org/climate/documents/policy/school-climate-challenge-web.pdf

Nickerson, A.B., Mele, D., & Princiotta, D. (2008). Attachment and empathy as predictors of roles as defenders or outsiders in bullying interactions. *Journal of School Psychology*, *46*, 687–703. DOI:10.1016/j.jsp.2008.06.002

Nishina, A., Juvonen, J., & Witkow, M. R. (2005). Sticks and stones may break my bones, but names will make me feel sick: The psychosocial, somatic, and scholastic consequences of peer harassment. *Journal of Clinical Child and Adolescent Psychology*, *34*(1), 37–48. DOI:10.1207/s15374424jccp3401_4

Olweus, D. (2010). Understanding and researching bullying: Some critical issues. In S. R. Jimerson, S. M. Swearer, & D. L. Espelage (Eds.), *Handbook of bullying in schools: An international perspective* (pp. 9–34). Routledge.

Olweus Bully Prevention Program (2022). *About the Olweus Bullying Prevention Program.* Olweus bullying prevention program, Clemson University. Retrieved January 10, 2022, from https://olweus.sites.clemson.edu/about.php

Pearce, N., Cross, D., Monks, H., Waters, S., & Falconer, S. (2011). Current evidence of best practice in whole-school bullying intervention and its potential to inform cyberbullying interventions. *Australian Journal of Guidance Counselling*, *21*, 1–21. DOI:10.1375/ajgc.21.1.1

Peguero, A. A., & Williams, L. M. (2013). Racial and ethnic stereotypes and bullying victimization. *Youth & Society*, *45*(4), 545–564. DOI:10.1177/0044118X11424757

Pepler, D. J., Craig, W. M., Connolly, J. A., Yuile, A., McMaster, L., & Jiang, D. (2006). A developmental perspective on bullying. *Aggressive Behavior: Official Journal of the International Society for Research on Aggression*, *32*(4), 376–384.

Polanin, J. R., Espelage, D. L., Grotpeter, J. K., Ingram, K., Michaelson, L., Spinney, E., Valido, A., El Sheikh, A., Torgal, C., & Robinson, L. (2021). A Systematic Review and Meta-Analysis of Interventions to Decrease Cyberbullying Perpetration and Victimization. *Prevention Science*, 1–16.

Polanin, J. R., Espelage, D. L., Grotpeter, J. K., Spinney, E., Ingram, K. M., Valido, A., El Sheikh, A., Torgal, C., & Robinson. L. (2021). A meta-analysis of longitudinal partial correlations between school violence and mental health, school performance, and criminal or delinquent acts. *Psychological Bulletin*, *147*(2), 115–133. DOI:10.1037/bul0000314

Polanin, J., Espelage, D. L., & Pigott, T. D. (2012). A meta-analysis of school-based bullying prevention programs' effects on bystander intervention behavior and empathy attitude. *School Psychology Review*, *41* (1), 47–65. DOI:10.1080/02796015.2012.12087375

Poteat, V. P., & Espelage, D. L. (2005). Exploring the relation between bullying and homophobic verbal content: The Homophobic Content Agent Target (HCAT) Scale. *Violence and Victims*, *20*(5), 513–528. DOI:10.1891/vivi.2005.20.5.513

Poteat, V. P., & Rivers, I. (2010). The use of homophobic language across bullying roles during adolescence. *Journal of Applied Developmental Psychology*, *31*(2), 166–172. DOI:10.1016/j.appdev.2009.11.005

Pöyhönen, V., Juvonen, J., & Salmivalli, C. (2010). What does it take to stand up for the victim of bullying? The interplay between personal and social factors. *Merrill-Palmer Quarterly*, *56*(2), 143–163. DOI:10.1353/mpq.0.0046

Pozzoli, T., & Gini, G. (2010). Active defending and passive bystanding behavior in bullying: The role of personal characteristics and perceived pressure. *Journal of Abnormal Child Psychology, 38*(6), 815–827. DOI:10.1007/s10802-010-9399-9

Preast, J. L., Bowman, N., & Rose, C. A. (2020). Creating inclusive classroom communities through social and emotional learning to reduce social marginalization among students. In Management Association, Inc. (Ed.), *Accessibility and Diversity in Education: Breakthroughs in Research and Practice* (pp. 102–120). PA: IGI Global.

Price, M., Polk, W., Hill, N. E., Liang, B., & Perella, J. (2019). The intersectionality of identity-based victimization in Adolescence: A person-centered examination of mental health and academic achievement in a US high school. *Journal of Adolescence, 76*, 185–196. DOI: 10.1016/j.adolescence.2019.09.002

Ragozzino, K., & Utne O'Brien, M. (2009). *Social and emotional learning and bullying prevention* [Issue Brief]. Retrieved from http://casel.org/downloads/2009_bullyingbrief.pdf.

Riffle, L. N., Kelly, K. M., Demaray, M. L., Malecki, C. E., Santuzzi, A. M., Rodriguez-Harris, D. J., & Emmons, J. D. (2021). Associations among bullying role behaviors and academic performance over the course of an academic year for boys and girls. *Journal of School Psychology, 86*, 49–63. DOI:10.1016/j.jsp.2021.03.002

Robinson, J. P., & Espelage, D. L. (2011). Inequities in educational and psychological outcomes between LGBTQ and straight students in middle and high school. *Educational Researcher, 40*(7), 315–330. DOI:10.3102/0013189X11422112

Robinson, J. P., & Espelage, D. L. (2012). Bullying Explains Only Part of LGBTQ-Heterosexual Risk Disparities: Implications for Policy and Practice. *Educational Researcher, 41*(8), 309–319. DOI:10.3102/0013189X12457023

Rodkin, P. C., Espelage, D. L., & Hanish, L. D. (2015). A relational framework for understanding bullying: Developmental antecedents and outcomes. *American Psychologist, 70*(4), 311–321. DOI:10.1037/a0038658

Rose, C. A. (2017). Bullying among youth with disabilities: Predictive and protective factors. In C. Bradshaw (Ed.), *The Handbook on bullying prevention: A lifecourse perspective* (113–123). National Association of Social Workers (NASW) Press.

Rose, C. A., & Espelage, D. L. (2012). Risk and protective factors associated with the bullying involvement of students with emotional and behavioral disorders. *Behavioral Disorders, 37*(3), 133–148. DOI:10.1177/019874291203700302

Rose, C. A., Espelage, D. L., Aragon, S. R., & Elliott, J. (2011). Bullying and victimization among students in special education and general education curricula. *Exceptionality Education International, 21*(3), 2–14. DOI:10.5206/eei.v21i3.7679

Rose, C. A., Espelage, D. L., & Monda-Amaya, L. E. (2009). Bullying and victimisation rates among students in general and special education: A comparative analysis. *Educational Psychology, 29*(7), 761–776. DOI:10.1080/01443410903254864

Rose, C. A., Espelage, D. L., Monda-Amaya, L. E., Shogren, K. A., & Aragon, S. R. (2015). Bullying and middle school students with and without specific learning disabilities: An examination of social-ecological predictors. *Journal for Learning Disabilities, 48*(3), 239–254. DOI:10.1177/0022219413496279

Rose, C. A., & Gage N. A. (2017). Exploring the involvement of bullying among students with disabilities over time. *Exceptional Children, 83*(3), 298–314. DOI:10.1177/0014402916667587

Rose, C. A., Hopkins, S., McGillen, G., & Simpson, J. (2019). Current trends in bully prevention: An examination of tiered interventions. In D. Bateman, J. Cline, & M. Yell (Eds.), *Current Trends and Legal Issues in Special Education* (157–175). Corwin Publishing.

Rose, C. A., Monda-Amaya, L. E., & Espelage, D. L. (2011). Bullying perpetration and victimization in special education: A review of the literature. *Remedial and Special Education, 32*(2), 114–130. DOI:10.1177/0741932510361247

Rose, C. A., Monda-Amaya, L. E., & Preast, J. L. (2018). Preservice special and general educators' perceptions of bullying. *Exceptionality Education International, 28*(2), 33–54.

Rose, C. A., Simpson, C. G., & Moss, A. (2015). The bullying dynamic: Prevalence of involvement among a large-scale sample of middle and high school youth with and without disabilities. *Psychology in the Schools, 52*(5), 515–531. DOI:10.1002/pits.21840

Rose, C. A., Stormont, M., Wang, Z., Simpson, C. G., Preast, J. L., & Green, A. L. (2015). Bullying and students with disabilities: Examination of disability status and educational placement. *School Psychology Review, 44*(4), 425–444. DOI:10.17105/spr-15-0080.1

Rose, C. A., & Tynes, B. M. (2015). Longitudinal associations between cybervictimization and mental health among U.S. adolescents. *Journal of Adolescent Health, 57*(3), 305–312. DOI:10.1016/j.jadohealth.2015.05.002

Ryoo, J. H., Wang, C., & Swearer, S. M. (2015). Examination of the change in latent statuses in bullying behaviors across time. *School Psychology Quarterly, 30*(1), 105–122. DOI:10.1037/spq0000082

Russell, S. T., Kosciw, J. G., Horn, S. S., & Saewyc, E. (2010). Safe Schools Policy for LGBTQ Students. *Social Policy Report, 24*(4), 1–24. Society for Research in Child Development.

Russell, S. T., Sinclair, K. O., Poteat, V. P., & Koenig, B. W. (2012). Adolescent health and harassment based on discriminatory bias. *American Journal of Public Health, 102*(3), 493–495. DOI:10.2105/AJPH.2011.300430

Salmivalli, C. (2010). Bullying and the peer group: A review. *Aggression & Violent Behavior, 15*(2), 112–120. DOI:10.1016/j.avb.2009.08.007

Sawyer, A. L., Bradshaw, C. P., & O'Brennan, L. M. (2008). Examining ethnic, gender, and developmental differences in the way children report being a victim of "bullying" on self-report measures. *Journal of Adolescent Health, 43*(2), 106–114. DOI:10.1016/j.jadohealth.2007.12.011

Schäfer, M., Korn, S., Brodbeck, F. C., Wolke, D., & Schulz, H. (2005). Bullying roles in changing contexts: The stability of victim and bully roles from primary to secondary school. *International Journal of Behavioral Development, 29*, 323–335. DOI:10.1177/01650250544000107

Schwartz, D., Gorman, A. H., Dodge, K. A., Pettit, G. S., & Bates, J. E. (2008). Friendships with peers who are low or high in aggression as moderators of the link between peer victimization and declines in academic functioning. *Journal of Abnormal Child Psychology, 36*(5), 719–730. DOI:10.1007/s10802-007-9200-x

Schwartz, D., Gorman, A. H., Nakamoto, J., & Toblin, R. (2005). Victimization in the peer group and children's academic functioning. *Journal of Educational Psychology, 97*(3), 425–435. DOI:10.1037/0022-0663.97.3.425

Slaten, C. D., Rose, C. A., & Ferguson, J. (2019). Understanding the relationship between youth sense of belonging and bullying behavior: An SEM model. *Educational and Child Psychology, 36*(2), 50–63.

Son, E., Parish, S. L., & Peterson, N. A. (2012). National prevalence of peer victimization among young children with disabilities in the United States. *Children and Youth Services Review, 34*(8), 1540–1545. DOI:10.1016/j.childyouth.2012.04.014

Stavrinides, P., Georgiou, St., & Theofanous, V. (2010). Bullying and empathy: A short-term longitudinal investigation. *Educational Psychology, 30*(7), 793–802. DOI:10.1080/01443410.2010.506004

Ttofi, M. M., & Farrington, D. P. (2011). Effectiveness of school based programs to reduce bullying: A systematic and meta-analytic review. *Journal of Experimental Criminology, 7*, 27–56. DOI:10.1007/s11292-010-9109-1

United Nations Educational, Scientific, and Cultural Organization (2018). *School violence and bullying: Global status and trends, drivers and consequences.* UNESCO.

van de Sande, M. C. E., Fekkes, M., Kocken, P. L., Diekstra, R. F. W., Reis, R., & Gravesteijn, C. (2019). Do universal social and emotional learning programs for secondary students enhance the competences they address? A systematic review. *Psychology in the Schools, 56*(10), 1545–1567. DOI:10.1002/pits.22307

Vitoroulis, I., & Vaillancourt, T. (2018). Ethnic group differences in bully perpetration: A meta-analysis. *Journal of Research on Adolescence, 28*(4), 752–771. DOI:10.1111/jora.12393

Vlachou, M., Andreou, E., Botsoglou, K., & Didaskalou, E. (2011). Bully/victim problems among preschool children: A review of current research evidence. *Educational Psychology Review, 23*(3), 329–358. DOI:10.1007/s10648-011-9153-z

Waasdorp, T. E., Bradshaw, C. P., & Leaf, P. J. (2012). The impact of schoolwide positive behavioral interventions and supports on bullying and peer rejection: A randomized controlled effectiveness trial. *Archives of Pediatrics & Adolescent Medicine, 166*(2), 149–156. DOI:10.1001/archpediatrics.2011.755

White, N. A., & Loeber, R. (2008). Bullying and special education as predictors of serious delinquency. *Journal of Research in Crime and Delinquency, 45*(4), 380–397. DOI:10.1177/0022427808322612

Wilson, S. J., & Lipsey, M. W. (2007). School-based interventions for aggressive and disruptive behavior: Update of a meta-analysis. *American Journal of Preventive Medicine, 33*(2), S130–S143. DOI:0.1016/j.amepre.2007.04.011

Woods, S., & Wolke, D. (2004). Direct and relational bullying among primary school children and academic achievement. *Journal of School Psychology, 42*(2), 135–155. DOI:10.1016/j.jsp.2003.12.002

Yell, M., Katsiyannis, A., Rose, C. A., & Houchins, D. (2016). Bullying and harassment of students with disabilities in schools: Legal considerations and policy formation. *Remedial and Special Education, 37*(5), 274–284. DOI:10.1177/0741932515614967

Ybarra, M., Espelage, D. L., & Mitchell, K. J. (2014). Differentiating youth who are bullied from other victims of peer-aggression: the importance of differential power and repetition. *Journal of Adolescent Health, 55*(2), 293–300. DOI:10.1016/j.jadohealth.2014.02.009

Zablotsky, B., Bradshaw, C. P., Anderson, C., & Law, P. (2012). Involvement in bullying among children with autism spectrum disorders: Parents' perspectives on the influence of school factors. *Behavioral Disorders, 37*(3), 179–191. DOI:10.1177/019874291203700305

Zablotsky, B., Bradshaw, C.P., Anderson, C. M., Law, P. (2013). Risk factors for bullying among children with autism spectrum disorders. *Autism, 18*(4), 419–427. DOI:10.1177/1362361313477920

Zhang, A., Wang, K., Zhang, J., & Oudekerk, B. A. (2019). Indicators of school crime and safety: 2018. NCES 2019–047/NCJ 252571. *National Center for Education Statistics.*

Zins, J. E., Weissberg, R. P., Wang, M. C., & Walberg, H. J. (Eds.). (2004). *Building School Success Through Social and Emotional Learning.* Teachers College Press.

PART III

Context of Classroom Management

11

TEACHER STRESS AND CLASSROOM MANAGEMENT

Christopher J. McCarthy, Kristen C. Mosley, and Jendayi B. Dillard

UNIVERSITY OF TEXAS AT AUSTIN

Introduction

> A courage which looks easy and yet is rare; the courage of a teacher repeating day after day the same lessons—the least rewarded of all forms of courage.
>
> *Honore de Balzac (1799–1850)*

Teaching is a rewarding and challenging profession. Being in front of a classroom of students day in and day out is not for the faint of heart. One of the most frequently cited factors contributing to teacher stress is classroom management (Friedman-Krauss et al., 2014; Lecavalier et al., 2006; Lopez et al., 2008; Sutton et al., 2009). When student behavior disrupts the learning process (McGrath & van Bergen, 2015), it can add to teacher stress, and conversely, teachers who are already experiencing stress will likely find classroom management more difficult (Friedman, 1995; Lewis et al., 2011; Sutton et al., 2009). Tsouloupas and colleagues (2010), for example, found that the act of disciplining students was associated with emotional exhaustion for teachers. Ingersoll and Smith (2003) noted that student discipline problems are the second leading cause of beginning teachers leaving the profession due to dissatisfaction.

Considered alongside other realities of teachers' daily lives, such as time pressure, low pay, and bureaucratic requirements (Boyle et al., 1995; Carver-Thomas & Darling-Hammond, 2017; Ingersoll, 2001; Schonfeld, 2001; Zhai et al., 2011), classroom management can represent a tipping point for teachers, turning an already challenging job into a stressful one (Friedman, 2006; Kuzsman & Schnall, 1987). The ongoing COVID-19 pandemic has only added to the stress of being a teacher, particularly in the realm of classroom management (Brackett & Cipriano, 2020), as teachers were required to teach in person and online, in some cases simultaneously.

Given that expertise on specific classroom management practices are included in other chapters of this book, we will examine when and how classroom management is associated with teacher stress, and to discuss best practices for reducing stress and increasing teacher well-being in the classroom. While teacher well-being has been defined in several ways, we take from Aldrup and colleagues' (2018) definition to understand this phenomenon as the presence of positive psychological and work functioning (e.g., job satisfaction) amidst the absence of negative functioning (e.g., stress). In order to provide a foundation for the topics reviewed in this chapter, we will first present an integrative

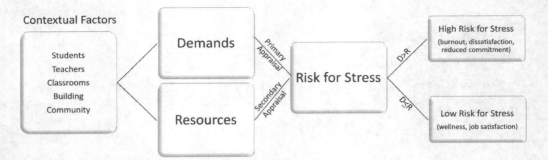

Figure 11.1 Teachers' appraisal of classroom demands as exceeding their resources for coping are at risk for stress

theoretical framework drawn from recent research on teacher stress. We then examine the teaching conditions and aspects of classroom management that are most likely to put teachers at risk for stress, followed by resources and practices that have the potential of lowering stress and increasing teacher well-being.

Theoretical Perspectives on Teacher Stress, Coping, and Well-Being

Imprecision in defining stress has plagued the stress literature for decades, so we will first describe current thinking on what is meant by teacher stress. Collie et al. (2017) described three overlapping definitions of teacher stress. The first definition is borrowed from the field of engineering, in which stress refers to the amount of pressure placed on an object, which can cause it to "break." In the context of teaching, this "pressure" comes from classroom demands on the teachers, including classroom management (Klassen & Chiu, 2011). A second definition of stress focuses on the emotional and behavioral consequences of stress. Emotions such as distress and anxiety result from the complex cognitive, behavioral, and physiological systems that are activated as part of the stress response (Kyriacou, 2001). Third, the predominant models of stress and coping harken to Lazarus and Folkman's (1984) transactional theory, which suggests that stress results when teachers appraise classroom management demands as exceeding their appraised resources for coping.

While Lazarus and Folkman (1984) pioneered the notion that stress results from appraised imbalances in demands and resources, it is important to note that other such "balance" models have also been proposed, including the job demand–control model (Theorell et al., 1990), job demands-resources model (Bakker & Demerouti, 2007), and the effort–reward imbalance model (Siegrist, 1996; Siegrist et al., 1986). Each of these models defines demands as the physical, psychological, social, or organizational facets of a job that necessitate continued physical and psychological effort (Schaufeli & Bakker, 2004). In order to avoid stress, demands must be appraised as consistent or "balanced" with resources, defined as the physical, psychological, social, or organizational features of a job that either reduce job demands, promote individual growth, or support the achievement of goals (Lazarus & Folkman, 1984).

Teachers' Appraisals and the Stress Process

Understanding stress as a transaction between person and environment helps address an important question asked by Chang (2009): "If classroom disruptive behavior is identified as the prominent source of teacher burnout, how does one teacher manage to survive while another is depleted by it?" (p. 202). Teachers make appraisals about their classroom demands and the sufficiency of resources to meet those demands (Steinhardt et al., 2011), and when there is an imbalance, teachers are vulnerable to stress.

Using the language of transactional theory, a further important distinction is made between primary and secondary appraisals. Primary appraisals refer to appraisals about demands, which occur automatically whenever potential threats emerge. Secondary appraisals then follow as the individual evaluates whether they have sufficient resources to address an appraised demand. This process is translated into the context of teaching in Figure 11.1.

At the left of Figure 11.1, several of the contextual factors identified in the literature as making up a teachers' daily reality are depicted. For example, students are integral to the context of classroom management, because every teacher has a certain group of students, each of whom has a unique background and set of experiences and abilities. Teachers have their own backgrounds and identities, including their unique professional skills, training, personality, and identity (e.g., gender, race, ethnicity, age, sexual identity). Classrooms are of course made up of teachers and students, along with physical aspects such as instructional resources and materials. Classrooms are also nested in buildings and communities which have their own unique characteristics. While not exhaustive, all of these factors constitute the daily fabric of a teacher's life, presenting both demands and resources which contribute to a teacher's ability to successfully manage their classroom.

Once demands are identified, a reflexive, cognitive balancing act is triggered in which the teacher weighs the nature of the event using primary appraisals (i.e., How serious is it? What implications does it have for my students and me?) along with the teacher's secondary appraisal about perceived capabilities (i.e., Is this something I can handle? What resources are available to address this demand?). Classroom management skills are particularly important to the demand/resource equation, as they are critical to effective teaching (Betoret, 2009) and are used every day (Dicke et al., 2018).

Lazarus (2001) suggested that appraisals, as a psychological process, include an objective component ("That student is clearly not working on their assignment") leavened with individual interpretation ("That student is being defiant"). Thus, even when presented with seemingly similar types of classroom management issues, one teacher could appraise the demand as "no big deal" while another teacher could be overwhelmed. Secondary appraisals are hypothesized to converge with primary appraisals, resulting in an overall evaluation of whether or not the demand constitutes a stressor or simply a challenge that can be met (Lazarus, 2000). This convergence of appraisals is depicted as risk for stress in Figure 11.1. We label this construct risk for stress, since it refers to a state in which a teacher's appraised demands exceed their appraised resources, which can, but does not always, result in the physiological, cognitive, and emotional symptoms of stress (McCarthy et al., 2014).

As an example of this process, consider one scenario with two possible appraisal outcomes. If a student is off-task after the teacher asks them to follow directions, the teacher might evaluate the situation by thinking, "I need them to follow directions because their behavior is incongruent with my goals for the class (primary appraisal), so I need to think about what resources I have to address this off-task behavior (secondary appraisal). Since I have a variety of effective techniques that have worked in the past with this student, I am going to choose one of them to address this behavior." This example might result in the evaluation that the teacher has resources to handle the situation ($R \geq D$), and the teacher would view the event as a challenge, not a stressor. On the other hand, when faced with the same off-task student, a different teacher could appraise the behavior in this way: "I need them to follow directions because their behavior is incongruent with my class goals (primary appraisal). I am pretty sure, however, that I have previously tried everything with this student and nothing will work (secondary appraisal)." This appraisal, that the teacher does not have the resources to handle the situation ($R < D$), puts the teacher at higher risk for classroom management stress.

Negative Consequences of Stress for Teachers

As is shown along the right side of Figure 11.1, once the stress response occurs, a number of negative consequences are likely to result. Teachers who are stressed because of student misbehavior can experience emotions such as anger, and teachers who are angry are less likely to be successful in managing their classroom (Sutton et al., 2009). Anger can also cause teachers who experience a high level of stress to blame students for their misbehavior and to be less likely to attribute student misbehavior to anything within the teacher's control (Brouwers & Tomic, 2000).

A number of pernicious consequences can ensue for teachers when demands are chronically appraised as outstripping resources. For example, long-term stress can result in burnout for teachers. Freudenberger (1974) first identified burnout as a construct consisting of reduced idealism and enthusiasm, and more recently, Maslach and colleagues (2001) refined the meaning and measurement of burnout and identified three essential components: (1) emotional exhaustion, the central construct of burnout, referring to feeling overwhelmed by emotional contact with others at work; (2) depersonalization, which describes the development of a cynical attitude and emotional distancing; and (3) reduced personal accomplishment, which involves reduced feelings of competence and personal achievement. Schaufeli and Enzmann (1998) described teachers as one of the most frequently studied occupational groups in burnout research. In addition to a range of psychological and emotional consequences, teacher burnout has also been associated with physiological symptoms such as high blood pressure (Moya-Albiol et al., 2010) and systemic inflammation known to contribute to atherosclerosis (von Känel et al., 2008). In addition to burnout, chronic stress for teachers has many destructive consequences, such as job dissatisfaction and reduced occupational commitment (López et al., 2010). We will next examine factors most likely to be associated with stress.

Student Factors Associated with Classroom Management Stress

Research makes it clear that, despite a teacher's classroom management facility, some types of classroom events are routinely associated with teacher stress (e.g., Abdullah & Ismail, 2019; Klassen, 2010). In this section, we focus on student behaviors that are shown in research to be associated with classroom management stress. Beyond specific behaviors, literature is emerging on how students with trauma histories can present challenges for teachers that can be addressed through trauma-informed practices.

Student Behaviors Associated with Teacher Stress

Clunies-Ross and colleagues (2008) tested 12 behaviors and identified three that contributed most to teacher stress: students talking out of turn, students hindering other students, and students being idle or slow. A student talking out of turn means that a student is talking at an inappropriate time; for example, not raising her/his hand when a teacher has asked the class to do so before answering or interrupting a lesson by talking. Hindering other students involves distracting other students from the lesson, while idleness/slowness involves students doing work deliberately slowly on an assignment. The authors found it noteworthy that the three behaviors causing most concern for teachers were relatively minor misbehaviors, rather than major misbehaviors, such as physical aggression (Clunies-Ross et al., 2008), suggesting that small misbehaviors occurring frequently may be primary contributors to teacher stress. Friedman (1994, 1995) found that disrespectful behaviors were most often cited as stressful for teachers. Lopez et al. (2008) found support for Friedman's claim that student disruptive attitude/behavior (included in the category of "disrespectful behaviors") was the largest factor predicting negative emotions and a stress response in teachers.

Much of what we know about stress and classroom management predates the COVID-19 pandemic of course. Most teachers, in the U.S. and around the world, switched to online learning in Spring of 2020 after the pandemic was declared, during which roughly 55 million students experienced in-person learning loss and school closures (EdWeek.org, 2020). Online instruction continued throughout the 2020–21 school year in many countries, as the pandemic turned into a chronic, society-altering public health crisis. Classroom management was obviously much different under these circumstances, as varying formats (e.g., online, face-to-face, and hybrid) pose unique challenges for classroom management and teacher stress.

As one example, we were part of a longitudinal study in a central Texas school district during the 2020–21 school year that assessed teachers' appraisals of demands and resources on a monthly basis (Blaydes et al., 2021). A random sample of the district's 10,000 teachers (*n* = 335) completed brief monthly surveys of stress from December 2020 through April 2021. Throughout the study, we also asked how teaching formats shifted from month-to-month in response to the pandemic, and teachers reported using three different formats throughout the year: in-person, online-only, or hybrid (a mixture of students in-person and online) classrooms. Not surprisingly, when teaching face-to-face, teachers reported greater demands associated with student misbehavior, on average, than their online-only counterparts. However, the inverse occurred in reports of demands associated with student assignment submission and attendance: teachers in online-only environments experienced greater demands with these responsibilities than teachers whose students were in-person.

During the 2021–22 school year, school districts across the country struggled to balance pressure to return to typical, in-person instruction, and the need to maintain a safe and healthy environment for students and teachers. Many speculate the trauma from the many life challenges and changes due to COVID-19 will persist for students and teachers, alike, for years to come (Crosby et al., 2020). Existing literature on the topic of trauma does provide some guidance, which we review next.

Students with Trauma Histories and Teacher Stress

Even before the pandemic, the likelihood of U.S. teachers working with students who have experienced trauma was quite high. A recent report from the Centers for Disease Control and Prevention (CDC, 2015) assessed the prevalence of child abuse and/or neglect has impacted at least one in seven US children. Similarly, analysis of The National Survey of Children's Exposure to Violence conducted by Finklehor and colleagues (2013) found that roughly half of U.S. children had experienced an assault-related injury in the prior year. Trauma permeates today's classrooms, yet the effect of students with trauma histories on teachers' work is curiously missing from much of the research on teacher stress.

Trauma is understood as resulting from a short or single event or as an ongoing experience that may involve multiple incidences of threats, violations, or violence. Regardless of the nature of the trauma, though, students who have trauma histories experience the world in ways that feel less safe (Brunzell et al., 2015). When teachers are not trained in how trauma can impact a student's life, the student's behaviors may be categorized as "problematic" and appraised as a demand for which the teacher has inadequate resources (see Figure 11.1). For example, a teacher who works with trauma-affected students likely takes on roles similar to that of mental health professionals, even if their background excludes such training (Brunzell et al., 2015), introducing a demand for which a teacher has no resource.

It has been documented that adults who work with trauma-affected children experience unique demands in meeting their needs (Newell & MacNeil, 2010): trauma-affected students trying to focus on learning has been noted as akin to "trying to play chess in a hurricane" (Wolpow et al., 2009, p. 24). It follows that teachers working with this vulnerable group experience additional demands, which likely also take place in schools where resources are lacking.

The resultant demands alongside inadequate resources can feed the cycle of trauma, as the teacher's increased likelihood for stress may also increase the student's difficulties in the classroom (Woods-Jaeger et al., 2018). Van der Kolk (2014), identified multiple ways in which children's development is thwarted by trauma, such as causing delays in their overall maturation, executive functioning skills, and stress responses. Such sequelae are necessary to classroom functioning and therefore pose demands for the students and teachers of students who struggle in these areas (Brunzell et al., 2015). Indeed, relationship building, concentration, and self-regulation set students up for successful learning, and the absence of these skills can exact additional classroom demands for teachers working with trauma-affected students.

Teacher- and School-Related Contextual Factors

As can be seen in Figure 11.1, teacher- and school-related contextual factors can play an important role in whether classroom management situations are likely to result in stress. It has become clear that feeling like an ineffective classroom manager, no matter what management strategy a teacher uses, can increase teacher stress. For example, Evers and colleagues (2004) found that teachers' perceived inability in managing student misbehavior led to higher levels of stress, and Tsouloupas and colleagues (2010) found that teachers reported student misbehavior and classroom management as significant demands in their work. Teachers bring with them their own perspectives, ideals, and tendencies, which can influence both their primary appraisals of demands and secondary appraisals of resources. We review these factors next.

Teacher Personality

Though psychologists have often disagreed on how best to measure and describe an individuals' personality, the Five Factor model has been widely accepted and utilized among researchers of personality and individual differences (Costa & McCrae, 2009). This model assesses individuals in terms of five domains of personality: conscientiousness (e.g., self-discipline, self-regulating, and responsible), neuroticism (e.g., likelihood of experiencing anxiety, anger, or depression), extraversion (e.g., extent to which one enjoys and gains energy from interactions with others), agreeableness (e.g., extent to which one values social cohesion and "getting along"?), and openness or openness to experience (e.g., extent to which one values variety of experience?; McCrae & Costa, 2008).

Using this model, Kokkinos and colleagues (2005) found that certain aspects of teachers' personality were significantly correlated with their appraisals of student behaviors. Specifically, they found that teachers high in conscientiousness were more likely to rate antisocial behavior, oppositional or defiant behavior, and negative affect in students as being more severe while teachers high in neuroticism were more likely to rate interpersonal sensitivity or conflict in students as being more severe. This work was extended by Kokkinos (2011), who found that along with student misbehavior, neuroticism was also significantly positively associated with teacher reports of burnout. Other aspects of personality are associated with less stressful conditions and outcomes for teachers. For example, extraversion and openness positively predict classroom management self-efficacy for early childhood teachers (Bullock et al., 2015), while extraversion and conscientiousness were associated with healthy coping behaviors among first-year teaching students (Reichl et al., 2014).

Though researchers have demonstrated associations between aspects of teacher personality and various stress-related outcomes, little has been done to advise educational stakeholders on what the implications of these findings might be. Research suggests that personality is relatively stable over time and unlikely to change (Cobb-Clark & Schurer, 2012; Ortet et al., 2020), leaving teachers and administrators with few tools to manage stress related to teacher personality. More research is needed which evaluates the extent to which targeted interventions may affect this relationship between teacher personality, classroom management, and stress and that explores potential protective factors that may be leveraged to support stressed-out teachers.

Teacher (and Student) Race, Ethnicity, and Gender

Given that schools are mainly staffed by women, it is interesting to note that female teachers report more stress related to student behavior (Klassen, 2010), less classroom management self-efficacy (Klassen & Chiu, 2010), and more emotional exhaustion (Antoniou et al., 2006). Bottiani and colleagues suggested that the social pressure experienced by women to play multiple social roles likely increases job demands and feelings of job-related stress. Others point out that women are often expected to take on the greater share of responsibilities in non-work domains as well, which could influence stress appraisals at school (Greenglass & Burke, 2003).

U.S. public schools, along with the country as a whole, are undergoing a demographic shift as students of color make up the majority of U.S. public school students (NCES, 2019a). However, while U.S. public school students are increasingly diverse, the teacher workforce is 80% White and female (NCES 2019b). While student demography is increasingly diverse, it is also very concentrated, with more than half of students attending schools where the demography is either 75% White or 75% students of color. Disturbingly, majority White school districts receive $23 billion more in funding than majority non-White schools (EdBuild, 2019).

Some research also finds that teachers who identify as White also experience more stress than teachers of color in schools composed primarily of students of color (McCarthy et al., 2021). Bottiani and colleagues (2019) surveyed 255 urban middle school teachers and found that even when accounting for both job demands and resources, White teachers and female teachers were more likely to report feelings of stress and burnout. Fitchett and colleagues (2020) examined a large, nationally representative dataset and found that teachers working in schools where the majority of students were Black or Latinx were more likely to report being at risk for experiencing occupational stress compared to teachers working in schools where there was no clear majority or where the majority of students were White.

There are a number of reasons why these associations may exist. For White teachers, cultural conflicts and difficulties engaging with issues around race may pose additional demands (Bottiani et al., 2019; Lowenstein, 2009). Research also suggests that teachers often appraise the behavior of racial minority students more harshly than that of White children (e.g., Losen et al., 2015), which can increase tensions between teachers and their students. Since majority White schools tend to be more resourced in the U.S. than majority non-White schools (EdBuild, 2019), the association of teacher stress with demography is likely conflated with the lack of resources in majority-minority schools.

Recent research finds that culturally responsive pedagogy is important for teachers working in diverse classrooms, yet research reviewed here suggests that White teachers still appraise working in diverse schools as more demanding regardless of resources available (Dillard et al., 2021; Mosley et al., 2021). Educational stakeholders should continue to acknowledge the immense effect resource inequities continue to have on teacher well-being and teachers' ability to be effective classroom managers. For example, the association between teachers' reported susceptibility to stress and student race changes dramatically when accounting for student SES (McCarthy et al., 2019), implying that what could be understood as an issue of cultural insensitivity or bias may in fact be a reflection of systemic inequalities. Researchers and educational stakeholders need to focus on the factors that can empower teachers to disrupt these patterns. This may include tools like multicultural competency for pre-service teachers (Sleeter, 2008) or protective factors like teacher autonomy or teacher self-efficacy (described below). However, the extant literature mainly focuses on patterns of teacher stress associated with these identity factors. Clearly more research is needed to uncover how such factors play out in the work of teachers and, where stress is identified, how to remedy its causes.

Teacher Autonomy

Teacher autonomy, or teachers' feelings of control or influence over their classroom and school (Parker, 2015), is negatively related to teacher stress (Pearson & Moomaw, 2005) and positively related to teachers' job satisfaction and engagement (Skaalvik & Skaalvik, 2014). In fact, in a survey of long-term high school teachers, participants highlighted the role that autonomy plays in their valuing of the teaching profession (Brunetti, 2001). Researchers have also found that teacher autonomy has a broader impact on school climate and functioning. Ingersoll (1996) found that among high school teachers, feelings of autonomy in the classroom and faculty influence over school policy were both significantly negatively associated with conflicts between staff and students. Additionally, Blömeke And Klein (2013) found that among beginning mathematics teachers, teacher autonomy was positively associated with both mathematics instruction and general teacher quality, including classroom management.

Conceptually, the supportive benefits of autonomy play into the development of intrinsic motivation. Along with feelings of competence and relatedness, individuals need to feel a sense of autonomy or control in order to build intrinsic motivation to re-engage in a task (Deci & Ryan, 2000). Individuals who feel control over their choice to complete a task or not are more likely to engage for internally driven reasons, as opposed to externally driven ones. More practically, strict policies around curriculum, classroom and behavior management, professional development, and so on, restrict teachers' opportunities to express their creativity, limit responsiveness to individual student and family needs, and represents yet another additional demand on teachers' workloads. Teachers who may already feel overwhelmed attending to disruptive student behavior within their classroom, for example, must not only attend to the behavior itself, but also navigate guidelines and policies restricting their options, which can reduce their autonomy and intrinsic motivation (Shepard, 2018). In contrast, a teacher with more autonomy may be free to focus their resources on addressing the problem at hand, and not the restrictive policies that go with them (Pearson & Moomaw, 2005).

Despite the many benefits associated with teacher autonomy, teachers of differing experience levels may respond to autonomy differently. For new and early-career teachers, too much autonomy can be perceived as a lack of support or direction (Kauffman et al., 2002; Pitt, 2010). Taking this into account, Grant and colleagues (2020) advocate for a graduated model of teacher autonomy, in which school leadership takes into account individual teachers' level of proficiency in the various domains of their job and respond with the appropriate level of autonomy and control for the teachers. For beginning teachers who are still building necessary skills, schools provide more structure and guidelines. For more advanced teachers who have gained proficiency, schools allow more decision-making power. Researchers argue that this model allows not only for both early career and veteran teachers to have what they need, but also allows for the flexibility to support teachers of any experience level who might need additional support in one domain, but not another.

Teacher Efficacy

Teacher self-efficacy is composed of instructional, engagement, and classroom management efficacy (Tschannen-Moran & Woolfolk-Hoy, 2001), all of which determine the extent to which a teacher believes in their own ability to attain educational goals (Skaalvik & Skaalvik, 2007). These three dimensions of teacher self-efficacy, particularly that of classroom management efficacy, are critical to effective teaching (Betoret, 2009; Brouwers & Tomic, 2000; Friedman & Farber, 1992; Good & Lavigne, 2017), as well as representative of some of the resources most frequently linked to the stress process (McCarthy et al., 2021).

Research has shown that teachers with lower levels of general self-efficacy are more vulnerable to stress. Schwerdtfeger et al. (2008) found that teachers with low self-efficacy had greater health complaints along with higher levels of burnout. In addition, Hong (2012) found that low self-efficacy teachers tend to experience higher levels of stress when faced with managing a classroom and handling disruptive behaviors. Lastly, Schwarzer and Hallum (2008) found that low general self-efficacy (measuring general coping resources not specific to teaching) and teacher self-efficacy preceded burnout symptoms in a longitudinal study completed over the course of one school year.

Research on teacher self-efficacy emphasizes the importance of classroom management self-efficacy for a teacher's overall confidence in their job. In a review of research on teacher burnout, Betoret (2009) found that a positive perception of both classroom management self-efficacy and instructional self-efficacy provided a buffer against classroom stressors; having high self-efficacy "mitigated the impact that the potential stressors have on the teaching work" (p. 61), causing teachers to operate at an optimal level of functioning, while low self-efficacy predicted higher teacher burnout (Betoret, 2009). Additionally, Aloe et al. (2014) conducted a meta-analysis to examine the relationship of classroom management self-efficacy and burnout, of which stress is a common precursor. Aloe and colleagues reviewed 16 studies and suggested that there is a significant relationship between classroom management self-efficacy and burnout, such that teachers with greater classroom management self-efficacy are less likely to experience burnout. It therefore follows that classroom management self-efficacy can serve as a viable resource for reduced teacher stress.

Researchers have elaborated on why teachers with low self-efficacy might face greater levels of stress (e.g., Skaalvik & Skaalvik, 2016), with recent research supporting the relationship between teachers' low self-efficacy and school-related stressors (Barouch Gilbert et al., 2014; Collie et al., 2012). Teachers with low classroom management self-efficacy are also more likely to give up easily when faced with continuous disruptive behavior, believing that their actions have little influence (Brouwers & Tomic, 2000; Emmer & Hickman, 1991). This in turn can cause more disruptive behavior that teachers find stressful (Lewis et al., 2011; Sutton et al., 2009), thus illustrating the relationship between perceived self-efficacy and awareness of environmental stressors: as self-efficacy declines, feelings of ineffectiveness and stress increase (Brouwers & Tomic, 2000). Consistently poor classroom management by a teacher has been described as "tantamount to failure" (McCormick & Barnett, 2011, p. 290), and linked to less on-task student behavior and negative classroom climate (Marzano et al., 2003). Cast in the light of transactional models of stress, teacher self-efficacy and classroom management self-efficacy can be thought of as important coping resources, and as such, must be taken into account when attempting to prevent teacher stress. Recent research suggests that self-efficacy may be important to teachers not only in "withstanding" stress, but in helping them avoid stress altogether (Schwerdtfeger et al., 2008). We next turn to the topic of teacher well-being as a resource for effective classroom management.

Teacher Well-being as a Resource for Effective Classroom Management

The preceding section identified likely sources of stress for teachers that could impact their classroom management capacities, as well as resources such as self-efficacy and teacher autonomy that could counteract such demands. Whether ineffective classroom management is a contributing factor to teacher stress or the result of it, efforts must be made to enhance the wellbeing of teachers in schools (Lauermann & Konig, 2016). The good news is that teacher well-being is a malleable construct receptive to intervention (Fernandes et al., 2019).

This part of our chapter focuses on what can be done to reduce stress in teachers and promote wellness, giving them every chance to succeed with their students. Attention to teacher stress and wellness has expanded in recent years and it would be impossible to summarize the extant literature in this chapter (see McIntyre et al., 2017 for a comprehensive review). This portion of our chapter will focus on (1) first highlighting the role of coping with stress at a theoretical level, which will provide a context for our second purpose, (2) reviewing factors and interventions that have the potential to help teachers cope, generally and with respect to classroom management skills.

Coping Strategies for Addressing Classroom Management

Figure 11.1 depicted a process in which teachers who appraise classroom demands as exceeding their resources for coping are at risk for stress. To begin this section, we review the process of coping, which

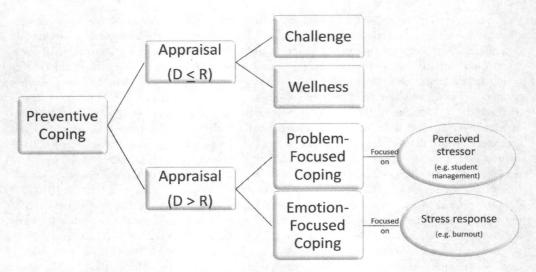

Figure 11.2 Preventive coping as antecedent to the appraisal process

refers to any effort to mitigate, less, or avoid whatever is causing stress. The various resources that teachers have for coping with job demands are hypothesized to be an important element of the stress process, both in the general population (Hobfoll et al., 1998) and in the teaching profession (Friedman, 2006). Additionally, supporting teachers with their ability to cope with demands and job stress also supports their overall well-being (Mattern & Bauer, 2014). So before reviewing specific factors that promote teacher well-being, a theoretical taxonomy of coping, drawn from transactional theory (Folkman et al., 1986), is provided in Figure 11.2, and each component of the figure is discussed in turn.

Preventive coping is depicted in Figure 11.2 as antecedent to the appraisal process. A movement towards positive psychology began several decades ago (Schwarzer & Taubert, 2002) which focuses more on cultivating wellness rather than simply reducing stress. Research by Fredrickson and Losada (2005) suggests a difference between "flourishing" and simply "coping" with stressful events—in other words, it is better to prevent stress than withstand it!

Scholars in this area have thus added preventive coping to the stress lexicon, which refers to "[employing] defensive and general strategies (saving resources for future needs)" (Gan et al., 2010, p. 644) to guard against future stress. Clunies-Ross et al. (2008) defined classroom management strategies into two categories: preventive and reactive. Preventive strategies are defined as strategies designed to prevent misbehavior from arising in the first place and generally give positive responses for appropriate behavior seen in students. Reactive strategies, on the other hand, are employed only after the teacher notices student misbehavior and usually require the teacher to respond in a negative, rather than a positive, way. The authors found that reactive strategies were associated with decreased on-task behavior from students and increased teacher stress, though proactive strategies failed to demonstrate a significant relationship with increased on-task behaviors and decreased stress (Clunies-Ross et al., 2008). Thus, preventive coping is shown as antecedent to the appraisal process, since possession of preventive resources reduces the likelihood that adequate resources are available to meet demands, resulting in "healthy" challenges that promote wellness.

Not all stress can be prevented, however, and is shown in Figure 11.2, once demands are appraised as exceeding resources, the coping that Clunies-Ross et al. (2008) describes as reactive ensues. Stress theories have a more charitable term for this type of coping: problem-focused and emotion-focused (Folkman & Lazarus, 1988a, 1988b). Figure 11.2 depicts both: emotion focused coping generally refers to efforts to tamp down the emotional reaction to stress, whereas problem-focused coping refers to efforts at changing the events that are causing stress. As an example, a teacher who is feeling stressed because of a student's behavior could attempt to use problem-focused coping by altering her or his classroom management practices attempting to stop the behavior, or emotion-focused coping such as taking a deep breath to attempt to calm their feelings of anxiety and frustration. Both problem-focused and emotion-focused coping strategies can be used together: a teacher might first need to calm themselves down (emotion-focused coping) before being able to employ classroom management techniques (problem-focused coping).

When it comes to emotion-focused coping, research suggests that there are certain socially and historically based norms for expressing emotions appropriately in the classroom. In general, during most interactions with students, teachers are expected to show positive emotions and suppress negative emotions (Aultman et al., 2009). Research by Sutton et al. (2004, 2009) examined emotion regulation and classroom management and found that emotion regulation is critical to teacher effectiveness. Their research indicated that teachers who believed in displaying their positive emotions to students also showed high levels of efficacy in classroom management. As the authors describe, *up-regulating* an emotion involves an attempt to increase the intensity or duration of an emotion. For example, a teacher may intentionally recall a student's recent reading growth to enhance a feeling of joy before retrieving her students from the lunchroom. *Down-regulating* an emotion is just the opposite, involving a person intentionally reducing the intensity or duration of a negative emotional experience (Sutton et al., 2009). Many teachers frequently down-regulate emotions (ex: frustration with student misbehavior) in order to successfully execute a lesson plan.

Early evidence from teachers suggests that self-regulation played an especially crucial role during the shift towards online instruction during the COVID-19 pandemic. In a series of interviews, teachers emphasized the importance of managing not only their own sense of self-efficacy while grappling with new modes of instruction, but also with balancing work-related demands with their own personal lives (Eblie Trudel et al., 2021). Additionally, teachers' manner of coping with additional stressors during the pandemic played a reciprocal role in their emotion regulation. MacIntyre and colleagues (2020) found that amongst an international sample of language teachers, teachers who reported the use of more avoidant coping strategies (i.e., disengagement or use of substances) were more likely to report feeling anger, anxiety, and sadness.

In the context of classroom management, problem-focused coping can be understood as the teacher directly addressing problematic student behaviors (see Figure 11.2). Lewis et al. (2011) found support for the notion that teachers are better off using problem-focused, rather than emotion-focused, coping in dealing with classroom management situations. They examined social problem solving, relaxation, and avoidant coping as strategies for coping with student misbehavior. Social problem-solving involved behaviors such as asking a mentor for help and finding a way to deal with the problem (problem-focused coping), while avoidant coping was defined as avoiding or worrying about the problem, and relaxation was defined as engaging in physical exercise and using humor (both emotion-focused strategies). Social problem solving was found to be the most effective strategy for dealing with student misbehavior (Lewis et al., 2011).

Resources that Promote Teacher Well-Being and Effective Classroom Management

Whether teachers engage in preventive or combative coping, they are more likely to cope successfully with a rich repertoire of resources. Researchers have found support for a number of stress management interventions that add to coping resources, through techniques such as meditation, relaxation, and mindfulness (Crain et al., 2016; Flook et al., 2013; Schussler et al., 2018; Sharp & Jennings, 2016). While detailing all of the literature on stress management for teachers could consume a book (c.f., Herman & Reinke, 2015), for the present purpose, we will describe teacher coping resources that are most relevant to classroom management. In judging relevance to classroom management, we examined factors that would be of use to teachers in the moment-to-moment reality of the classroom, in which the teacher is interacting with students, and in which stress-produced emotions can easily arise.

Social Support and Mentoring as a Protective Factor

Without adequate support from colleagues, new teachers may be more likely to appraise classroom management situations as more demanding and experience increased risk for stress (see Figures 11.1 and 11.2). Social support may be particularly salient for helping beginning teachers find their footing. Buchanan et al. (2013) found that a common theme among beginning teachers was the struggle to feel a sense of personal achievement during their first few years in the classroom. The beginning teachers in their longitudinal study noted a sense of helplessness in their work that was markedly different from that of veteran teachers. However, Buchanan and colleagues ultimately found overwhelming evidence that beginning teachers' job satisfaction increased over time via two critical factors: the opportunity for professional learning and the support of the work environment. In effect, the "supported stayers" in their study—those who had mentors and professional learning—were more likely to increase their effectiveness and sense of personal achievement than their non-mentored counterparts (Buchanan et al., 2013). Indeed, teachers who felt as though they had resources to match their demands likely experienced challenge and well-being (Figure 11.2), as opposed to burnout and stress. Social support as a resource for helping a new teacher manage their classroom demands may therefore decrease new teachers' risk for stress as it increases their confidence in their ability to execute efficacious classroom management.

Mentoring as a form of social support that promotes beginning teacher retention has also been explored. Teacher attrition is a known problem among beginning teachers (e.g. Chambers Mack et al., 2019), but prior research also suggests this issue extends beyond teachers' early career years (Bennett et al., 2013). While several areas have been studied as probable antecedents of teacher attrition, such as working in urban and high-needs schools (Simon & Johnson, 2015), insufficient opportunities for professional growth (Donaldson et al., 2008), and poor workplace conditions (Geiger & Pivovarova, 2018), mentoring may be preventive of teacher attrition. For example, effective mentoring practices have been noted as missing and inadequate in high-need schools (Kardos & Johnson, 2010; Wei et al., 2010), which may signal a trend of insufficient resources for teachers working in these environments. As depicted in Figure 11.2, teachers working in low-resource schools may lack the preventative coping that mentoring can provide and that is known to reduce risk for stress. For example, if a new teacher working in this type of setting found classroom management to be particularly demanding, having a mentor specifically assigned for their needs could mitigate the stress that such a demand can cause.

Mentoring has also been identified as a pertinent resource for more advanced teachers. Bressman and colleagues (2018) conducted a study of experienced teachers' professional needs and noted mentoring as a protective factor against burnout. Just as beginning teachers need resources to meet their job demands, veteran teachers benefit from the tailored support that mentoring can bring. Indeed, an experienced teacher who has mentoring as an available resource is likely able to enact stronger classroom management skills, create a more welcoming environment, and experience greater well-being (Figure 11.2). It follows that more experienced teachers can benefit from mentoring when navigating classroom management difficulties, too, as each new school year presents new students with new needs. In sum, social support, specifically mentoring, has a well-cited research base and is known for its potential to protect against teacher stress and turnover for teachers across their working lifespan.

Trauma-Informed Schools as a Resource for Teachers

Previously in this chapter, we noted that students with trauma histories may exhibit behaviors that are misinterpreted as acts of disobedience or defiance (Crosby, 2015). Schools have been identified as crucial settings for trauma-informed care. Teachers spend thousands of hours with students each year (OECD, 2017) and educators who recognize the signs of trauma can be in the role of first responder to mental health crises (Hydon et al., 2015). Baker and colleagues (2016) defined trauma-informed care as a means of interacting with individuals with trauma histories in ways that acknowledge the ongoing impact of trauma. Trauma-informed care is therefore a template for working with trauma-affected individuals that can be applied at an organizational (e.g., school) and individual (e.g. teacher) level (McInerny & McKlindon, 2014; Paccione-Dyszlewski, 2016).

However, successfully implementing this model requires equal emphasis on supporting the adults as much as the students (Chafouleas et al., 2016). Trauma-informed care resources are particularly necessary for teachers working with trauma-affected students (Wolpow et al., 2009). Yet, beginning and veteran teachers have historically experienced inadequate support and training for working with students who have experienced trauma and mental health issues (Koller et al., 2004). As a result, classroom management can become an exceptionally difficult hurdle for teachers who lack training and support when working with students with trauma histories.

Just as airlines recommend that adults put on their oxygen masks first in case of emergencies before helping children, teachers who work in schools in which trauma is present first require their own support and wellness in order to be able to later support others (Moreland-Capuia, 2019). It is crucial that teachers are able to promote wellness and healing in their own classroom, and Brunzell and colleagues argue that these actions stem from teachers who are taught to intentionally incorporate trauma-informed practices. This reality has borne out in a recent study by Salloum and colleagues (2019) who found more frequent use of trauma-informed self-care activities correlated with lower rates of teacher burnout. As we will detail later in this section, other experts have considered mind-body therapies, such as mindfulness, meditation, and yoga, as useful tools for individuals engaged in trauma-informed work (Justice et al., 2018; van der Kolk, 2014). In short, much of the foundation of trauma-informed care fits naturally into a classroom management system aimed at promoting the wellbeing of teachers and students alike.

Trauma-informed schools can provide a framework for both students and teachers to develop greater wellness and coping, thereby reducing the likelihood of classroom misconduct, which is a known stressor for teachers (West et al., 2014). Additionally, teacher support groups have been noted as a promising intervention for supporting teachers in their work with students (Hwang et al., 2017; McCarthy et al., 2016), which may foster a collective understanding of the effects of trauma that can occur within a school setting. Indeed, the greater the collective school knowledge of the ripple effects of trauma, the greater the likelihood for classroom management that centers students' diverse needs.

Mindfulness Based Stress Reduction as Resource for Teachers

Mindfulness is rooted in Buddhist philosophy and encourages intentional awareness of the present moment without judgement or filtering (Kabat-Zinn, 1994). Evidence suggests that mindfulness is linked to positive well-being, including cardiovascular health (Prazak et al., 2012) and lower anxiety (Prazak et al., 2012). Mindfulness-based interventions (MBIs) have also been developed (Fortney et al., 2013), with Kabat-Zinn's (1994) Mindfulness-Based Stress Reduction (MBSR) showing considerable promise in reducing psychological symptoms such as depression and anxiety (Burke, 2010; Hofmann et al., 2010). MBI interventions have also made their way into workplaces and have shown promising results in promoting employee job satisfaction (Hülsheger et al., 2013) and reducing stress and stress-associated symptoms (Flook et al., 2013; Fortney et al., 2013; Goodman & Schorling, 2012).

Roeser and colleagues (2012) suggested that the emotionally demanding and unpredictable nature of the teaching profession makes the concept of mindfulness especially effective for teachers. Mindfulness, as defined by Kabat-Zinn (1994), involves drawing attention and awareness to the present moment in a nonreactive and nonjudgmental manner that promotes emotion regulation, stress reduction, and healthy interpersonal interactions. Training programs that instruct teachers on mindfulness include instruction on how to regulate emotions and stress more effectively. A study that taught Mindfulness Based Stress Reduction (MBSR) strategies to a small group of emotionally distressed elementary school teachers yielded promising results (Gold et al., 2010). All teachers improved on scales of anxiety, depression, and stress, and for some participants the improvements were statistically significant.

Given its success in promoting occupational health, it is not surprising that MBI has also been used in schools with both students (Edwards et al., 2014) and teachers (Benn et al., 2012; Flook et al., 2013; Gold et al., 2010; Roeser et al., 2013). Roeser et al. (2012) noted that mindfulness could represent a "habit of mind" that includes, "tendencies to gather data through all of the senses, to be aware of and reflect on experience in a nonjudgmental manner, to be flexible when problem solving, to regulate emotion and be resilient after set-backs, and to attend to others with empathy and compassion" (p. 167). Such a skill set would allow teachers to interact with students, problem-solve when needed, regulate emotions, and use age-appropriate verbal and non-verbal behavior.

Supporting Roeser et al.'s (2012) contentions, randomized control studies suggest that MBI interventions have many positive outcomes necessary for effective classroom management, including great attention and working memory capacity, and effective teaching (Benn et al., 2012; Flook et al., 2013; Roeser et al., 2013). Qualitative studies also find that teachers report improved ability to manage conflict and anxiety (Napoli, 2004) and greater capacity to be aware of their emotional reactivity to students (Sharp & Jennings, 2016). MBIs are commonly offered in a group format, which can be important for teachers given the limited amount of time they have to interact with each other. For example, a study by Scholastic and the Bill and Melinda Gates Foundation (2012) suggested teachers spend only 3 percent of their day with each other.

One potential limitation of mindfulness programs for teachers is the length of time needed. Roeser et al. (2102) provide a sampling of mindfulness-based programs for teachers, including Jennings's Cultivating Awareness and Resilience in Education (CARE) program, which is a 4-day 36-hour program. Given the limited time that teachers have for professional development and the lack of relationship found between intervention hours and outcomes (Carmody & Baer, 2009), researchers such as Reiser et al. (2016) and Eyal et al. (2019) have proposed briefer (3–4 sessions, one hour) MBI groups with teachers.

Future Directions and Conclusions

Teacher stress has attained a prominence in the occupational health literature that was missing for many decades. In an era of limited educational budgets, accountability policies, growing emphasis on promoting educational equity, and high expectations for schools to play a role in the social and emotional lives of students, it is likely that even teachers with strong classroom management skills will experience high demand levels. Given inequities in US public schools that fall along racial/ethnic lines and the lack of diversity in the US teaching workforce, teachers will increasingly need training and resources that supplement traditional classroom management skills.

A number of supports, ranging from more traditional practices such as mentoring to more recent interventions such as mindfulness based stress reduction and trauma-informed schools, have been identified as effective in reducing teacher stress. However, beyond the literature on teacher self-efficacy, many interventions broadly address teacher stress as opposed to directly targeting teachers' need for classroom management support. Further, research into the factors contributing to teacher stress often do not include more systematic factors at the campus or community level.

Additionally, many extant interventions lack focus on specific pedagogical needs related to classroom management efficacy. It is therefore essential that researchers and all stakeholders in teacher welfare and effectiveness continue to research, promote, and support interventions for teachers experiencing stress and its consequences. Yet while there is hope for improving the overall occupational health of teachers so they can effectively manage their classrooms, public policy makers must make sustained investments in teachers' well-being and reimagine the educational environment to take advantage of such advances.

The COVID-19 pandemic in some ways has provided parents and caregivers with a sampling of classroom management demands, as many students learned from home and parents were essentially put in charge of managing their children's progress. Many understandably found these demands overwhelming, particularly when balanced with their own jobs and responsibilities. As society slowly adjusts to life following the pandemic, it will be important for campus leaders and administrators to attend to their teachers' occupational health for the sake of classroom management and their campus communities. In this way, the current paucity in interventions aimed at mitigating the stress resulting from classroom management demands may prove to become the next focal point for increasing teacher well-being.

References

Abdullah, A. S., & Ismail, S. N. (2019). A structural equation model describes factors contributing teachers' job stress in primary schools. *International Journal of Instruction, 12*(1), 1251–1262. https://doi.org/10.29333/iji.2019.12180a

Aldrup, K., Klusmann, U., Lüdtke, O., Göllner, R., & Trautwein, U. (2018). Student misbehavior and teacher well-being: Testing the mediating role of the teacher-student relationship. *Learning and Instruction, 58*(58), 126–136. https://doi.org/10.1016/j.learninstruc.2018.05.006

Aloe, A. M., Amo, L. C., & Shanahan, M. E. (2014). Classroom management self-efficacy and burnout: A multivariate meta-analysis. *Educational Psychology Review, 26*(1), 101–126. DOI: 10.1007/s10648-013-9244-0

Antoniou, A.-S., Polychroni, F., & Vlachakis, A.-N. (2006). Gender and age differences in occupational stress and professional burnout between primary and high-school teachers in Greece. *Journal of Managerial Psychology, 21*(7), 682. DOI: 10.1108/02683940610690213

Aultman, L. P., Williams-Johnson, M. R., & Schutz, P. A. (2009). Boundary dilemmas in teacher-student relationships: Struggling with "the line." *Teaching and Teacher Education, 25*, 636–646. https://doi.org/10.1016/j.tate.2008.10.002

Baker, C. N., Brown, S. M., Wilcox, P. D., Overstreet, S., & Arora, P. (2016). Development and psychometric evaluation of the attitudes related to trauma-informed care (ARTIC) scale. *School Mental Health, 8*(1), 61–76. https://doi.org/10.1007/s12310-015-9161-0

Bakker, A. B., & Demerouti, E. (2007). The job demands–resources model: State of the art. *Journal of Managerial Psychology, 22*(3), 309–328. https://doi.org/10.1108/02683940710733115

Barouch Gilbert, R., Adesope, O. O., & Schroeder, N. L. (2014). Efficacy beliefs, job satisfaction, stress and their influence on the occupational commitment of English-medium content teachers in the Dominican Republic. *Educational Psychology, 34*(7), 876–899. https://doi.org/10.1080/01443410.2013.814193

Benn, R., Akiva, T., Arel, S., & Roeser, R. W. (2012). Mindfulness training effects for parents and educators of children with special needs. *Developmental Psychology, 48*(5), 1476–1487. DOI: 10.1037/a0027537

Bennett, S.V., Brown Jr, J.J., Kirby-Smith, A., & Severson, B. (2013). Influences of the heart: Novice and experienced teachers remaining in the field. *Teacher Development, 17*(4), 562–576. DOI: 10.1080/13664530.2013.849613

Betoret, F. D. (2009). Self-efficacy, school resources, job stressors and burnout among Spanish primary and secondary school teachers: A structural equation approach. *Educational Psychology, 29*(1), 45–68. DOI: 10.1080/01443410802459234

Blaydes, M., Dillard, J. B., Gearhart, C., McCarthy, C. J., Mosley, K. C., & Playfair, E. (2021). [Teacher survey] [Unpublished raw data]. University of Texas at Austin.

Blömeke, S., & Klein, P. (2013). When is a school environment perceived as supportive by beginning mathematics teachers? Effects of leadership, trust, autonomy and appraisal on teaching quality. *International Journal of Science & Mathematics Education, 11*(4), 1029–1048. https://doi.org/10.1007/s10763-013-9424-x

Bottiani, J. H., Duran, C. A., Pas, E. T., & Bradshaw, C. P. (2019). Teacher stress and burnout in urban middle schools: Associations with job demands, resources, and effective classroom practices. *Journal of School Psychology, 77*, 36–51. https://doi.org/10.1016/j.jsp.2019.10.002

Boyle, G. J., Borg, M. G., Falzon, J. M., & Baglioni Jr, A. J. (1995). A structural model of the dimensions of teacher stress. *British Journal of Educational Psychology, 65*(1), 49–67. DOI: 10.1111/j.2044-8279.1995.tb01130.x

Buchanan, J., Prescott, A., Schuck, S., Aubusson, P., Burke, P., & Louviere, J. (2013). Teacher retention and attrition: Views of early career teachers. *Australian Journal of Teacher Education, 38*(3). http://dx.doi.org/10.14221/ajte.2013v38n3.9

Burke, C. A. (2010). Mindfulness-based approaches with children and adolescents: A preliminary review of current research in an emergent field. *Journal Of Child and Family Studies, 19*(2), 133–144. https://doi.org/10.1007/s10826-009-9282-x

Brackett, M. & Cipriano, C. (2020). Teachers are anxious and overwhelmed. They need SEL now more than ever. *Edsurge*. www.edsurge.com/news/2020-04-07-teachers-are-anxious-and-overwhelmed-they-need-sel-now-more-than-ever.

Bressman, S., Winter, J. S., & Efron, S. E. (2018). Next generation mentoring: Supporting teachers beyond induction. *Teaching and Teacher Education*, *73*, 162–170. https://doi.org/10.1016/j.tate.2018.04.003

Brouwers, A., & Tomic, W. (2000). A longitudinal study of teacher burnout and perceived self-efficacy in classroom management. *Teaching and Teacher Education*, *16*(2), 239–253. DOI: 10.1016/S0742-051X(99)00057-8

Brunetti, G. J. (2001). Why do they teach? A study of job satisfaction among long-term high school teachers. *Teacher Education Quarterly*, *28*(3), 49–74. www.jstor.org/stable/23478304

Brunzell, T., Waters, L., & Stokes, H. (2015). Teaching with strengths in trauma-affected students: A new approach to healing and growth in the classroom. *American Journal of Orthopsychiatry*, *85*(1), 3–9. https://doi.org/10.1037/ort0000048

Bullock, A., Coplan, R. J., & Bosacki, S. (2015). Exploring links between early childhood educators' psychological characteristics and classroom management self-efficacy beliefs. *Canadian Journal of Behavioural Science / Revue Canadienne Des Sciences Du Comportement*, *47*(2), 175–183. https://doi.org/10.1037/a0038547

Carmody, J., Baer, R. A., Lykins, E. L. B., & Olendzki, N. (2009). An empirical study of the mechanisms of mindfulness in a mindfulness-based stress reduction program. *Journal of Clinical Psychology*, *65*(6), 613–626. DOI: 10.1002/jclp.20579

Carver-Thomas, D. & Darling-Hammond, L. (2017). *Teacher turnover: Why it matters and what we can do about it.* Learning Policy Institute.

Centers for Disease Control and Prevention (2015). *Behavioral Risk Factor Surveillance System Survey ACE Data, 2009-2014.* U.S. Department of Health and Human Services, Centers for Disease Control and Prevention. www.cdc.gov/violenceprevention/aces/ace-brfss.html

Chafouleas, S. M., Johnson, A. H., Overstreet, S., & Santos, N. M. (2016). Toward a blueprint for trauma-informed service delivery in schools. *School Mental Health*, *8*(1), 144–162. https://doi.org/10.1007/s12310-015-9166-8

Chambers Mack, J., Johnson, A., Jones-Rincon, A., Tsatenawa, V., & Howard, K. (2019). Why do teachers leave? A comprehensive occupational health study evaluating intent-to-quit in public school teachers. *Journal of Applied Biobehavioral Research*, *24*(1). https://doi.org/10.1111/jabr.12160

Chang, M.-L. (2009). An appraisal perspective of teacher burnout: Examining the emotional work of teachers. *Educational Psychology Review*, *21*(3), 193–218. DOI: 10.1007/s10648-009-9106-y

Clunies-Ross, P., Little, E., & Kienhuis, M. (2008). Self-reported and actual use of proactive and reactive classroom management strategies and their relationship with teacher stress and student behaviour. *Educational Psychology*, *28*(6), 693–710. DOI: 10.1080/01443410802206700

Cobb-Clark, D. A., & Schurer, S. (2012). The stability of big-five personality traits. *Economics Letters*, *115*(1), 11–15. https://doi.org/10.1016/j.econlet.2011.11.015

Collie, R. J., Perry, N. E., & Martin, A. J. (2017). School context and educational system factors impacting educator stress. In T. M. McIntyre, S. E. McIntyre, & D. J. Francis (Eds.), *Educator stress: An occupational health perspective* (pp. 3–22). Springer. https://doi.org/10.1007/978-3-319-53053-6_1

Costa Jr., P. T. & McCrae, R. R. (2008). The revised NEO Personality Inventory (NEO-PI-R). In G. T. Boyle, G. Matthews, & D. H. Saklofske (Eds.), *The SAGE Handbook of Personality Theory and Assessment: Volume 2—Personality Measurement and Testing* (pp. 179–198). SAGE Publications Ltd. https://doi.org/10.4135/9781849200479

Costa Jr., P. T., & McCrae, R. R. (2009). The five-factor model and the NEO inventories. In J. N. Butcher (Ed.), *Oxford Handbook of Personality Assessment*. Oxford University Press. DOI: 10.1093/oxfordhb/9780195366877.013.0016

Covell, K., McNeil, J. K., & Howe, R. B. (2009). Reducing teacher burnout by increasing student engagement: A children's rights approach. *School Psychology International*, *30*(3), 282–290. https://doi.org/10.1177/0143034309106496

Crain, T. L., Schonert-Reichl, K. A., & Roeser, R. W. (2017). Cultivating teacher mindfulness: Effects of a randomized controlled trial on work, home, and sleep outcomes. *Journal of Occupational Health Psychology*, *22*(2), 138. DOI:10.1037/ocp0000043

Crawford, E. R., Lepine, J. A., & Rich, B. L. (2010). Linking job demands and resources to employee engagement and burnout: A theoretical extension and meta-analytic test. *Journal of Applied Psychology*, *95*(5), 834. DOI: 10.1037/a0019364

Crosby, S. D., Howell, P. B., & Thomas, S. (2020). Teaching through collective trauma in the era of COVID-19: Trauma-informed practices for middle level learners. *Middle Grades Review*, *6*(2). https://scholarworks.uvm.edu/mgreview/vol6/iss2/5

Deci, E. L., & Ryan, R. M. (2000). The "what" and "why" of goal pursuits: Human needs and the self-determination of behavior. *Psychological Inquiry*, *11*, 227–268. https://doi.org/10.1207/S15327965PLI1104_01

Dicke, T., Stebner, F., Linninger, C., Kunter, M., & Leutner, D. (2018). A longitudinal study of teachers' occupational well-being: Applying the job demands-resources model. *Journal of Occupational Health Psychology, 23*(2), 262–277. DOI: 10.1037/ocp0000070

Dillard, J. B., Mosley, K. C., Fitchett, P. G., Lambert, R. G., McCarthy, C. J. & Playfair, E. (2021, Apr 9-12) *A quasi-experimental examination of racial/ethnic teacher-student congruence and occupational stress* [Paper presented in Roundtable Session]. AERA Annual Meeting Virtual

Donaldson, M. L., Johnson, S. M., Kirkpatrick, C. L., Marinell, W. H., Steele, J. L., & Szczesiul, S. A. (2008). Angling for access, bartering for change: How second-stage teachers experience differentiated roles in schools. *Teachers College Record, 110*(5), 1088–1114.

Eblie Trudel, L., Sokal, L., & Babb, J. (2021). Teachers' voices: Pandemic lessons for the future of education. *Journal of Teaching and Learning, 15*(1), 4–19. https://doi.org/10.22329/jtl.v15i1.6486

Edwards, M., Adams, E. M., Waldo, M., Hadfield, O. D., & Biegel, G. M. (2014). Effects of a mindfulness group on Latino adolescent students: Examining levels of perceived stress, mindfulness, self-compassion, and psychological symptoms. *The Journal for Specialists in Group Work, 39*(2), 145–163. https://doi.org/10.1080/01933922.2014.891683

EdBuild (2019). 23 Billion (pp. 1–12). Retrieved from http://edbuild.org/content/23-billion.

EdWeek.org (2020). Map: Coronavirus and school closures in 2019–2020. www.edweek.org/leadership/map-coronavirus-and-school-closures-in-2019-2020/2020/03?override=web

Emmer, E. T., & Hickman, J. (1991). Teacher efficacy in classroom management and discipline. *Educational And Psychological Measurement, 51*(3), 755–765. DOI:10.1177/0013164491513027

Eyal, M., Bauer, T., Playfair, E., & McCarthy, C. J. (2019). Mind-body group for teacher stress: A trauma-Informed intervention program. *The Journal for Specialists in Group Work, 44*(3), 204–221. https://doi.org/10.1080/01933922.2019.1634779

Evers, W. J. G., Tomic, W., & Brouwers, A. (2004). Burnout among teachers: Students' and teachers' perceptions compared. *School Psychology International, 25*(2), 131–148. DOI: 10.1177/0143034304043670

Fernandes, L., Peixoto, F., Gouveia, M. J., Silva, J. C., & Wosnitza, M. (2019). Fostering teachers' resilience and well-being through professional learning: effects from a training programme. *The Australian Educational Researcher, 46*(4), 681–698. https://doi.org/10.1007/s13384-019-00344-0

Finkelhor, D., Turner, H. A., Shattuck, A., & Hamby, S. L. (2013). Violence, crime, and abuse exposure in a national sample of children and youth: An update. *JAMA Pediatrics, 167*(7), 614–621. DOI: 10.1001/jamapediatrics.2013.42

Fitchett, P. G., Dillard, J., McCarthy, C. J., Lambert, R. G., & Mosley, K. (2020). Examining the intersectionality among teacher race/ethnicity, school context, and risk for occupational stress. Education Policy Analysis Archives, *28*, 87. https://doi.org/10.14507/epaa.28.4999

Flook, L., Goldberg, S. B., Pinger, L., Bonus, K., & Davidson, R. J. (2013). Mindfulness for teachers: A pilot study to assess effects on stress, burnout, and teaching efficacy. *Mind, Brain, and Education, 7*(3), 182–195. DOI: 10.1111/mbe.12026

Folkman, S., & Lazarus, R. S. (1988a). Coping as a mediator of emotion. *Journal of Personality and Social Psychology, 54,* 466–475. https://doi.org/10.1037/0022-3514.54.3.466

Folkman, S., & Lazarus, R. S. (1988b). The relationship between coping and emotion: Implications for theory and research. *Social Science Medicine, 26*(3), 309–317. https://doi.org/10.1016/0277-9536(88)90395-4

Folkman, S., Lazarus, R. S., Dunkel-Schetter, C., DeLongis, A., & Gruen, R. J. (1986). Dynamics of a stressful encounter: Cognitive appraisal, coping, and encounter outcomes. *Journal of Personality and Social Psychology, 50*(5), 992–1003. DOI: 10.1037//0022-3514.50.5.992

Fortney, L., Luchterhand, C., Zakletskaia, L., Zgierska, A., & Rakel, D. (2013). Abbreviated mindfulness intervention for job satisfaction, quality of life, and compassion in primary care clinicians: a pilot study. *The Annals of Family Medicine, 11*(5), 412–420. DOI: 10.1370/afm.1511

Fredrickson, B. L., & Losada, M. F. (2005). Positive affect and the complex dynamics of human flourishing. *American Psychologist, 60,* 678–686. DOI: 10.1037/0003-066X.60.7.678

Freudenberger, H. J. (1974). Staff burn-out. *Journal of Social Issues, 30,* 159–165. https://doi.org/10.1111/j.1540-4560.1974.tb00706.x

Friedman, I. A. (1994). Conceptualizing and measuring teacher-perceived student behaviors: Disrespect, sociability, and attentiveness. *Educational and Psychological Measurement, 54*(4), 949–958. doi:10.1177/0013164494054004011

Friedman, I. A. (1995). Student behavior patterns contributing to teacher burnout. *Journal Of Educational Research, 88*(5), 281–289. https://doi.org/10.1080/00220671.1995.9941312

Friedman, I. A. (2006). Classroom management and teacher stress and burnout. In C. M. Evertson & C. S. Weinstein, C. S. (Eds.). *Handbook of classroom management: Research, practice, and contemporary issues* (pp. 925–944). Lawrence Erlbaum Associates.

Friedman, I. A., & Farber, B. A. (1992). Professional self-concept as a predictor of teacher burnout. *Journal of Educational Research, 86*(1), 28–35. DOI: 10.1080/00220671.1992.9941824

Friedman-Krauss, A. H., Raver, C. C., Morris, P. A., & Jones, S. M. (2014). The role of classroom-level child behavior problems in predicting preschool teacher stress and classroom emotional climate. *Early Education and Development, 25*(4), 530–552. DOI: 10.1080/10409289.2013.817030

Gan, Y., Hu, Y., & Zhang, Y. (2010). Proactive and preventive coping in adjustment to college. *The Psychological Record, 60*, 643–658. https://doi.org/10.1007/BF03395737

Geiger, T., & Pivovarova, M. (2018). The effects of working conditions on teacher retention. *Teachers and Teaching, 24*(6), 604–625. https://doi.org/10.1080/13540602.2018.1457524

Gold, E., Smith, A., Hopper, I., Herne, D., Tansey, G., & Hulland, C. (2010). Mindfulness-Based Stress Reduction (MBSR) for primary school teachers. *Journal Of Child And Family Studies, 19*(2), 184–189. DOI:10.1007/s10826-009-9344-0

Good, T. L., & Lavigne, A. L. (2017). *Looking in classrooms*. Routledge. DOI: 10.4324/9781315627519.

Goodman, M. J., & Schorling, J. B. (2012). A mindfulness course decreases burnout and improves well-being among healthcare providers. *The International Journal of Psychiatry in Medicine, 43*(2), 119–128. DOI: 10.2190/PM.43.2.b

Grant, A., Hann, T., Godwin, R., Shackelford, D., & Ames, T. (2020). A framework for graduated teacher autonomy: Linking teacher proficiency with autonomy. *The Educational Forum, 84*(2), 100–113. https://doi.org/10.1080/00131725.2020.1700324

Greenglass, E. R., & Burke, R. J. (2003). Teacher stress. In M. Dollard, H. R. Winefield, & A. H. Winefield (Eds.), *Occupational Stress in the Service Professions* (1st ed., pp. 227–250). CRC Press. https://doi.org/10.1201/9780203422809-11

Gross, J.J. (1998). The emerging field of emotion regulation: An integrative review. *Review of General Psychology, 2*, 271–299. DOI: 10.1037/1089-2680.2.3.271.

Gross, J. J. (2002). Emotion regulation: Affective, cognitive, and social consequences. *Psychophysiology, 39*(3), 281–291. DOI: 10.1017/S0048577201393198

Gross, J. J. (2008). Emotion regulation. In M. Lewis, J.M. Haviland-Jones, & L. Feldman Barret (Eds.) *Handbook of Emotions* (3rd ed.). Guilford Press.

Herman, K. C., & Reinke, W. (2015). *Stress management for teachers: A proactive guide*. Guilford Press.

Hobfoll, S. E., Schwarzer, R., & Chon, K. K. (1998). Disentangling the stress labyrinth: Interpreting the meaning of the stress as it is studied in the health context. *Anxiety, Stress, & Coping, 11*(3), 181–212. https://doi.org/10.1080/10615809808248311

Hofmann, S. G., Sawyer, A. T., Witt, A. A., & Oh, D. (2010). The effect of mindfulness-based therapy on anxiety and depression: A meta-analytic review. *Journal of Consulting and Clinical Psychology, 78*(2), 169–183. DOI: 10.1037/a0018555

Hong, J. Y. (2012). Why do some beginning teachers leave the school, and others stay? Understanding teacher resilience through psychological lenses. *Teachers and Teaching: Theory and Practice, 18*(4), 417–440. https://doi.org/10.1080/13540602.2012.696044

Hülsheger, U. R., Alberts, H. J., Feinholdt, A., & Lang, J. W. (2013). Benefits of mindfulness at work: the role of mindfulness in emotion regulation, emotional exhaustion, and job satisfaction. *Journal of Applied Psychology, 98*(2), 310–325. DOI: 10.1037/a0031313

Hwang, Y. S., Bartlett, B., Greben, M., & Hand, K. (2017). A systematic review of mindfulness interventions for in-service teachers: A tool to enhance teacher wellbeing and performance. *Teaching and Teacher Education, 64*, 26–42. https://doi.org/10.1016/j.tate.2017.01.015

Hydon, S., Wong, M., Langley, A. K., Stein, B. D., & Kataoka, S. H. (2015). Preventing secondary traumatic stress in educators. Child and adolescent psychiatric clinics of North America. *Child and Adolescent Psychiatric Clinics of North America, 24*(2), 319–333. http://dx.doi.org/10.1016/j.chc.2014.11.003

Ingersoll, R. M. (1996). Teachers' decision-making power and school conflict. *Sociology of Education, 69*, 159–176. https://doi.org/10.2307/2112804

Ingersoll, R. (2001). Teacher turnover and teacher shortages: An organizational analysis. *American Educational Research Journal, 38*(3), 499–534. https://doi.org/10.3102/00028312038003499

Ingersoll, R. M., & Smith, T. M. (2003). The wrong solution to the teacher shortage. *Educational Leadership, 60*(8), 30–33. Retrieved from https://repository.upenn.edu/gse_pubs/126

Justice, L., Brems, C., & Ehlers, K. (2018). Bridging body and mind: Considerations for trauma-informed yoga. *International Journal of Yoga Therapy, 28*(1), 39–50. DOI: 10.17761/2018-00017R2

Kabat-Zinn, J. (1994). *Wherever you go, there you are: Mindfulness meditation in everyday life*. Hyperion.

Kardos, S. M., & Johnson, S. M. (2010). New teachers' experiences of mentoring: The good, the bad, and the inequity. *Journal of Educational Change, 11*(1), 23–44. https://doi.org/10.1007/s10833-008-9096-4

Kauffman, D., Johnson, S. M., Kardos, S. M., Liu, E., & Peske, H. G. (2002). "Lost at sea": New teachers' experiences with curriculum and assessment. *Teachers College Record, 104*(2), 273–300. https://doi.org/10.1111/1467-9620.00163

Klassen, R. M. (2010). Teacher stress: The mediating role of collective efficacy beliefs. *The Journal of Educational Research, 103*(5), 342–350. https://doi.org/10.1080/00220670903383069

Klassen, R. M., & Chiu, M. M. (2010). Effects on teachers' self-efficacy and job satisfaction: Teacher gender, years of experience, and job stress. *Journal of Educational Psychology, 102*(3), 741–756. https://doi.org/10.1037/a0019237

Klassen, R. M., & Chiu, M. (2011). The occupation commitment and intention to quit of practicing and pre-service teachers: Influence of self-efficacy, job stress, and teaching context. *Contemporary Educational Psychology, 36*, 114–129. https://doi.org/10.1016/j.cedpsych.2011.01.002

Kokkinos, C. M. (2011). Job stressors, personality and burnout in primary school teachers. *British Journal of Educational Psychology, 77*(1), 229–243. https://doi.org/10.1348/000709905X90344

Kokkinos, C. M., Panayiotou, G., & Davazoglou, A. M. (2005). Correlates of teacher appraisals of student behaviors. *Psychology in the Schools, 42*(1), 79–89. DOI: 10.1002/pits.20031

Koller, J. R., Osterlind, S. J., Paris, K., & Weston, K. J. (2004). Differences between novice and expert teachers' undergraduate preparation and ratings of importance in the area of children's mental health. *International Journal of Mental Health Promotion, 6*(2), 40–45. DOI: 10.1080/14623730.2004.9721930

Kuzsman, F. J., & Schnall, H. (1987). Managing teachers' stress: Improving discipline. *The Canadian School Executive, 6*(3), 10.

Kyriacou, C. (2001). Teacher stress: Directions for future research. *Educational Review, 53*(1), 27–35. DOI: 10.1080/00131910120033628

Lambert, R. G., McCarthy, C. J., O' Donnell, M., & Wang, C. (2009). Measuring elementary teacher stress and coping in the classroom: Validity evidence for the classroom appraisal of resources and demands. *Psychology in the Schools, 46*, 973–988. https://doi.org/10.1002/pits.20438

Lauermann, F., & König, J. (2016). Teachers' professional competence and wellbeing: Understanding the links between general pedagogical knowledge, self-efficacy and burnout. *Learning and Instruction, 45*, 9–19. https://doi.org/10.1016/j.learninstruc.2016.06.006

Lazarus, R. S. (2000). Evolution of a model of stress, coping, and discrete emotions. In V. H. Rice (Ed) *Handbook of stress, coping, and health: Implications for nursing research, theory, and practice* (pp. 195–222). Sage Publications, Inc.

Lazarus, R. S., & Folkman, S. (1984). *Stress, appraisal, and coping.* Springer.

Lecavalier, L., Leone, S., & Wiltz, J. (2006). The impact of behaviour problems on caregiver stress in young people with autism spectrum disorders. *Journal of Intellectual Disability Research, 50*(3), 172–183. DOI: 10.1111/j.1365-2788.2005.00732.x

Lewis, R., Roache, J., & Romi, S. (2011). Coping styles as mediators of teachers' classroom management techniques. *Research In Education, 85*, 53–68. https://doi.org/10.7227/RIE.85.5

López, J. M. O., Castro, C., Santiago, M. J., & Villardefrancos, E. (2010). Exploring stress, burnout, and job dissatisfaction in secondary school teachers. *International Journal of Psychology and Psychological Therapy, 10*(1), 107–123.

López, J. M. O., Santiago, M. J., Godás, A., Castro, C., Villardefrancos, E., & Ponte, D. (2008). An integrative approach to burnout in secondary school teachers: Examining the role of student disruptive behaviour and disciplinary issues. *International Journal of Psychology & Psychological Therapy, 8*(2), 259–270.

Losen, D. J, Hodson, C. L, Keith II, M. A, Morrison, K., & Belway, S. (2015). Are we closing the school discipline gap? *UCLA: The Civil Rights Project / Proyecto Derechos Civiles.* Retrieved from https://escholarship.org/uc/item/2t36g571

Lowenstein, K. L. (2009). The work of multicultural teacher education: Reconceptualizing White teacher candidates as learners. *Review of Educational Research, 79*(1), 163–196. https://doi.org/10.3102/0034654308326161

MacIntyre, P. D., Gregersen, T., & Mercer, S. (2020). Language teachers' coping strategies during the Covid-19 conversion to online teaching: Correlations with stress, wellbeing and negative emotions. *System, 94*, 102352. https://doi.org/10.1016/j.system.2020.102352

Marzano, R. J., Marzano, J. S., & Pickering, D. (2003). *Classroom management that works: Research-based strategies for every teacher.* ASCD.

Maslach, C., Schaufeli, W. B., & Leiter, M. P. (2001). Job burnout. *Annual Review Of Psychology, 52*, 397–422. DOI:10.1146/annurev.psych.52.1.397

Mattern, J., & Bauer, J. (2014). Does teachers' cognitive self-regulation increase their occupational well-being? The structure and role of self-regulation in the teaching context. *Teaching and Teacher Education, 43*, 58–68. https://doi.org/10.1016/j.tate.2014.05.004

McCarthy, C. J., Dillard, J., Fitchett, P. G., Boyle, L., & Lambert, R. G. (2019). Associations between teacher–student racial/ethnic congruence and public school teachers' risk for stress. *Urban Education.* https://doi.org/10.1177/0042085919894049

McCarthy, C. J., Lambert, R. G., Mosley, K. C., Fitchett, P. G., & Dillard, J. B. (2021). Teacher appraisals of demand–resource imbalances in racially concentrated schools: An extension of transactional theory with Black, Hispanic, and White U.S. teachers. *International Journal of Stress Management, 28*(1), 24–31. https://doi.org/10.1037/str0000208

McCarthy, C. J., Lambert, R. G., O'Donnell, M., & Melendres, L. T. (2009). The relation of elementary teachers' experience, stress, and coping resources to burnout symptoms. *Elementary School Journal, 109*(3), 282–300. https://doi.org/10.1086/592308

McCarthy, C. J., Lambert, R. G., & Reiser, J. (2014). Vocational concerns of elementary teachers: Stress, job satisfaction, and occupational commitment. *Journal of Employment Counseling, 51*(2), 59–74. https://doi.org/10.1002/j.2161-1920.2014.00042.x.

McCarthy, C.J., Lambert, R.G., & Ullrich, A. (Eds.) (2012). *International perspectives on teacher stress.* Information Age Publishing, Inc.

McCormick, J., & Barnett, K. (2011). Teachers' Attributions for Stress and Their Relationships with Burnout. *International Journal of Educational Management, 25*(3), 278–293. https://doi.org/10.1108/09513541111120114

McCrae, R. R., & Costa, P.T., Jr. (2008). The five-factor theory of personality. In O. P. John, R. W. Robins, & L. A. Pervin (Eds.), *Handbook of Personality: Theory and Research* (p. 159–181). The Guilford Press.

McGrath, K. F., & Van Bergen, P. (2015). Who, when, why and to what end? Students at risk of negative student–teacher relationships and their outcomes. *Educational Research Review, 14,* 1–17. https://doi.org/10.1016/j.edurev.2014.12.001

McInerney, M., & McKlindon, A. (2014). Unlocking the door to learning: Trauma-informed classrooms & transformational schools. *Education Law Center,* 1–24. https://bit.ly/3PRr5DC

McIntyre, T., McIntyre, S., & Francis, D. (2017). *Educator stress: An occupational health perspective*: Springer.

Moreland-Capuia (2019). Training for change transforming systems to be trauma-informed, culturally responsive, and neuroscientifically. (1st ed.). Springer International Publishing. https://doi.org/10.1007/978-3-030-19208-2

Mosley, K. C., Dillard, J. B., McCarthy, C. J., Lambert, R. G., & Fitchett, P. G. (2021, April). *Associations between teacher-student racial/ethnic congruence and occupational stress among U.S. teachers.* Paper presented at the Annual Meeting of the American Educational Research Association, Virtual.

Moya–Albiol, L., Serrano, M. Á., & Salvador, A. (2010). Burnout as an important factor in the psychophysiological responses to a work day in teachers. *Stress and Health: Journal of the International Society for the Investigation of Stress, 26*(5), 382–393. DOI: 10.1002/smi.1309

Napoli, M. (2004). Mindfulness training for teachers: A pilot program. *Complementary health practice review, 9*(1), 31–42. DOI: 10.1177/1076167503253435

National Center for Education Statistics (2019a). Common Core of Data (CCD), "State Nonfiscal Survey of Public Elementary and Secondary Education," 1998-99 through 2017-18; and National Elementary and Secondary Enrollment by Race/Ethnicity Projection Model, 1972 through 2029. (This table was prepared December 2019.) Retrieved from https://nces.ed.gov/programs/digest/d19/tables/dt19_203.60.asp

National Center for Education Statistics. (2019b). Schools and Staffing Survey (SASS), "Public School Teacher Data File," "Charter School Teacher Data File," "Public School Data File," and "Charter School Data File," 1999–2000; and National Teacher and Principal Survey (NTPS), "Public School Teacher Data File," 2017–18. See Digest of Education Statistics 2019, table 209.22.

Newell, J. M., & MacNeil, G. A. (2010). Professional burnout, vicarious trauma, secondary traumatic stress, and compassion fatigue. *Best Practices in Mental Health, 6*(2), 57–68.

Ortet, G., Pinazo, D., Walker, D., Gallego, S., Mezquita, L., & Ibáñez, M. I. (2020). Personality and nonjudging make you happier: Contribution of the five-factor model, mindfulness facets and a mindfulness intervention to subjective well-being. *PLoS ONE, 15*(2). https://doi.org/10.1371/journal.pone.0228655

Paccione-Dyszlewski, M. R. (2016). Trauma-informed schools: A must. *The Brown University Child and Adolescent Behavior Letter, 32*(7), 8–8. https://doi.org/10.1002/cbl.30139

Parker, G. (2015). Teachers' autonomy. *Research in Education, 93*(1), 19–33. https://doi.org/10.7227/RIE.0008

Pearson, L. C., & Moomaw, W. (2005). The relationship between teacher autonomy and stress, work satisfaction, empowerment, and professionalism. *Educational Research Quarterly, 29*(1), 38–54.

Persson, P.B., & Zakrisson, A. (2016). Stress. *Acta Physiologica, 216,* 149–152. DOI: 10.1111/apha.12641

Pitt, A. (2010). On having one's chance: Autonomy as education's limit. *Educational Theory, 60*(1), 1–18. DOI: 10.1111/j.1741-5446.2009.00342.x

Prazak, M., Critelli, J., Martin, L., Miranda, V., Purdum, M., & Powers, C. (2012). Mindfulness and its role in physical and psychological health. *Applied Psychology: Health and Well-Being, 4*(1), 91–105. DOI: 10.1111/j.1758-0854.2011.01063.x

Reichl, C., Wach, F.-S., Spinath, F. M., Brünken, R., & Karbach, J. (2014). Burnout risk among first-year teacher students: The roles of personality and motivation. *Journal of Vocational Behavior*, *85*(1), 85–92. https://doi.org/10.1016/j.jvb.2014.05.002

Reiser, J. E., Murphy, S. L., & McCarthy, C. J. (2016). Stress prevention and mindfulness: A psychoeducational and support group for teachers. *The Journal for Specialists in Group Work*, *41*(2), 117–139. https://doi.org/10.1080/01933922.2016.1151470

Roeser, R. W., Schonert-Reichl, K. A., Jha, A., Cullen, M., Wallace, L., Wilensky, R., Oberle, E., Thomson, K., Taylor, C., & Harrison, J. (2013). Mindfulness training and reductions in teacher stress and burnout: Results from two randomized, waitlist-control field trials. *Journal of Educational Psychology*, *105*(3), 787. https://doi.org/10.1037/a0032093

Roeser, R. W., Skinner, E., Beers, J., & Jennings, P. A. (2012). Mindfulness training and teachers' professional development: An emerging area of research and practice. *Child Development Perspectives*, *6*(2), 167–173. DOI:10.1111/j.1750-8606.2012.00238.x

Schaufeli, W. B., & Bakker, A. B. (2004). Job demands, job resources, and their relationship with burnout and engagement: A multi-sample study. *Journal of Organizational Behavior*, *25*(3), 293–315. DOI: 10.1002/job.248

Schaufeli, W. B., & Enzmann, D. (1998). *The burnout component to study and practice*. Taylor & Francis.

Scholastic Inc. & Bill & Melinda Gates Foundation (2012). *Primary sources: America's teachers on the teaching profession*. Scholastic.

Schonfeld, I. S. (2001). Stress in 1st-year women teachers: The context of social support and coping. *Genetic, Social, and General Psychology Monographs*, *127*(2), 133–168.

Schussler, D. L., Greenberg, M., DeWeese, A., Rasheed, D., DeMauro, A., Jennings, P. A., & Brown, J. (2018). Stress and release: Case studies of teacher resilience following a mindfulness-based intervention. *American Journal of Education*, *125*(1), 1–28. https://doi.org/10.1086/699808

Schutz, P. A., Hong, J. Y., Cross, D. I., & Osbon, J. N. (2006). Reflections on investigating emotions among educational contexts. *Educational Psychology Review*, *18*, 343–360. https://doi.org/10.1007/s10648-006-9030-3

Schwarzer, R., & Hallum, S. (2008). Perceived teacher self-efficacy as a predictor of job stress and burnout. *Applied Psychology: An International Review*, *57*(Suppl 1), 152–171. DOI: 10.1111/j.1464-0597.2008.00359.x

Schwarzer, R., & Taubert, S. (2002). Tenacious goal pursuits and striving toward personal growth: Proactive coping. In E. Frydenberg (Ed.), *Beyond coping: Meeting goals, visions and challenges* (pp. 19–35). Oxford University Press.

Schwerdtfeger, A., Konermann, L., & Schönhofen, K. (2008). Self-efficacy as a health-protective resource in teachers? A biopsychological approach. *Health Psychology*, *27*(3), 358–368. DOI: 10.1037/0278-6133.27.3.358

Sharp, J. E., & Jennings, P. A. (2016). Strengthening teacher presence through mindfulness: What educators say about the cultivating awareness and resilience in education (CARE) program. *Mindfulness*, *7*(1), 209–218. https://doi.org/10.1007/s12671-015-0474-8

Shepard, W. B. (2018). Emerging issues that affect teachers' intrinsic motivation: A qualitative case study (Order No. 10784911). Available from ProQuest Dissertations & Theses Global. (2029884703). www.proquest.com/docview/2029884703/abstract/9409C1BD0D944D2BPQ/1

Siegrist, J. (1996). Adverse health effects of high-effort/low-reward conditions. *Journal of Occupational Health Psychology*, *1*(1), 27. DOI: 10.1037//1076-8998.1.1.27

Siegrist, J., Siegrist, K., & Weber, I. (1986). Sociological concepts in the etiology of chronic disease: The case of ischemic heart disease. *Social Science & Medicine*, *22*(2), 247–253. https://doi.org/10.1016/0277-9536(86)90073-0

Siemer, M., Mauss, I., & Gross, J. J. (2007). Same situation—different emotions: How appraisals shape our emotions. *Emotion*, *7*(3), 592. DOI: 10.1037/1528-3542.7.3.592

Simon, N., & Johnson, S. M. (2015). Teacher turnover in high-poverty schools: What we know and can do. *Teachers College Record*, *117*(3), 1–36.

Skaalvik, E. M., & Skaalvik, S. (2007). Dimensions of teacher self-efficacy and relations with strain factors, perceived collective teacher efficacy, and teacher burnout. *Journal of Educational Psychology*, *99*(3), 611–625. DOI: 10.1037/0022-0663.99.3.611

Skaalvik, E. M., & Skaalvik, S. (2014). Teacher self-efficacy and perceived autonomy: Relations with teacher engagement, job satisfaction, and emotional exhaustion. *Psychological Reports*, *114*(1), 68–77. https://doi.org/10.2466/14.02.PR0.114k14w0

Skaalvik, E. M., & Skaalvik, S. (2016). Teacher stress and teacher self-efficacy as predictors of engagement, emotional exhaustion, and motivation to leave the teaching profession. *Creative Education*, *7*(13), 1785–1799. DOI: 10.4236/ce.2016.713182

Sleeter, C. E. (2008). Preparing White teachers for diverse students. In M. Cochran-Smith, S. Feiman-Nemser, D. J. McIntyre, & K. E. Demers (Eds.), *Handbook of research on teacher education: Enduring questions in changing contexts*. (3rd ed.). Taylor & Francis Group.

Steinhardt, M. A., Smith Jaggars, S. E., Faulk, K. E., & Gloria, C. T. (2011). Chronic work stress and depressive symptoms: Assessing the mediating role of teacher burnout. *Stress and Health*, 27(5), 420–429. DOI: 10.1002/smi.1394

Sutton, R.E. (2004). Emotional regulation goals and strategies of teachers. *Social Psychology of Education*, 7, 379–398. https://doi.org/10.1007/s11218-004-4229-y

Sutton, R. E., Mudrey-Camino, R., & Knight, C. C. (2009). Teachers' emotion regulation and classroom management. *Theory Into Practice*, 48(2), 130–137. https://doi.org/10.1080/00405840902776418

Theorell, T., Karasek, R. A., & Eneroth, P. (1990). Job strain variations in relation to plasma testosterone fluctuations in working men-a longitudinal study. *Journal of Internal Medicine*, 227(1), 31–36. DOI: 10.1111/j.1365-2796.1990.tb00115.x

Tschannen-Moran, M., & Woolfolk-Hoy, A. (2001). Teacher efficacy: Capturing an elusive construct. *Teaching And Teacher Education*, 17(7), 783–805. DOI:10.1016/S0742-051X(01)00036-1

Tsouloupas, C. N., Carson, R. L., Matthews, R., Grawitch, M. J., & Barber, L. K. (2010). Exploring the association between teachers' perceived student misbehaviour and emotional exhaustion: The importance of teacher efficacy beliefs and emotion regulation. *Educational Psychology*, 30(2), 173–189. https://doi.org/10.1080/01443410903494460

Van der Kolk, B. (2014). *The body keeps the score: Mind, brain and body in the transformation of trauma*. Penguin UK.

van den Tooren, M., de Jonge, J., Vlerick, P., Daniels, K., & Van de Ven, B. (2011). Job resources and matching active coping styles as moderators of the longitudinal relation between job demands and job strain. *International Journal of Behavioral Medicine*, 18(4), 373–383. DOI: 10.1007/s12529-011-9148-7

von Känel, R., Bellingrath, S., & Kudielka, B. M. (2008). Association between burnout and circulating levels of pro- and anti-inflammatory cytokines in schoolteachers. *Journal of Psychosomatic Research*, 65(1), 51–59. DOI: 10.1016/j.jpsychores.2008.02.007

Wei, R. C., Darling-Hammond, L., & Adamson, F. (2010). Professional development in the United States: Trends and challenges. *National Staff Development Council*. https://edpolicy.stanford.edu/sites/default/files/publications/professional-development-united-states-trends-and-challenges.pdf

West, S. D., Day, A. G., Somers, C. L., & Baroni, B. A. (2014). Student perspectives on how trauma experiences manifest in the classroom: Engaging court-involved youth in the development of a trauma-informed teaching curriculum. *Children and Youth Services Review*, 38, 58–65. http://dx.doi.org/10.1016/j.childyouth.2014.01.013

Wolpow, R., Johnson, M. M., Hertel, R., & Kincaid, S. O. (2009). *The heart of learning and teaching: Compassion, resiliency, and academic success*. Office of Superintendent of Public Instruction (OSPI) Compassionate Schools.

Woods-Jaeger, B. A., Cho, B., Sexton, C. C., Slagel, L., & Goggin, K. (2018). Promoting resilience: Breaking the intergenerational cycle of adverse childhood experiences. *Health Education & Behavior*, 45(5), 772–780. DOI: 10.1177/1090198117752785

Zhai, F., Raver, C. C., & Li-Grining, C. (2011). Classroom-based interventions and teachers' perceived job stressors and confidence: Evidence from a randomized trial in Head Start settings. *Early Childhood Research Quarterly*, 26, 442–452. DOI: 10.1016/j.ecresq.2011.03.003

12

THE NEW JIM CROW IN SCHOOL[1]

Exclusionary Discipline and Structural Racism

Russell J. Skiba

INDIANA UNIVERSITY

Edward Fergus

TEMPLE UNIVERSITY

Anne Gregory

RUTGERS UNIVERSITY

Introduction

Since we last reviewed the literature on exclusionary discipline and disciplinary disparities for a chapter that appeared in the previous version of this Handbook (Skiba & Rausch, 2015), there has been a significant amount of new published research on the topic, with more sophisticated methodologies than had previously been available. But since that chapter was written, our society has also witnessed:

- The police killing of Michael Brown and resultant protests in Ferguson, Missouri, leading to the development of the national Black Lives Matter network.
- The Charlottesville "Unite the Right" rally and the death of Heather Heyer; President Donald Trump's response that there were "very fine people, on both sides."
- The murders of Eric Garner, Sandra Bland, Breonna Taylor, Ahmed Arbery, and 1,555 other Black men, women and children at the hands of police since 2016 .
- School closures across the nation, and over one million Americans, disproportionately Black and Brown, dying due to the COVID-19 pandemic.
- The murder of George Floyd by Derek Chauvin on May 24, 2020.
- At least 15 million people participating in more than 7,000 protests against police violence and in support of Black lives in the summer of 2020, often themselves met with police aggression and violence.
- The passing of Congressman and civil rights icon John Lewis.
- The election of the first Black/Asian woman as Vice President, and the election of the first Black senator from Georgia.
- An insurrection by white supremacists at the Capitol on January 6, 2021.

DOI: 10.4324/9781003275312-15

- Derek Chauvin convicted of the murder of George Floyd, one day after Daunte Wright was killed by police in Minneapolis.
- A dramatic increase in the rate of hate crimes across the nation, especially anti-Asian and anti-Semitic violence.
- Efforts underway or passed in 32 states to restrict education on racism, bias, the contributions of specific racial or ethnic groups to U.S. history, or information about race or racism that causes "discomfort" to students. (Education Week, 2022)

This turbulent period has also seen substantial growth in awareness of the pervasive and corrosive nature of racism, and an increased recognition of the historical forces that have left us with intractable racialized, often unconscious, belief systems, and ubiquitous structural racism. Coming on the heels of Michelle Alexander's groundbreaking work *The New Jim Crow* (Alexander, 2010), recent works, such as *Stamped from the Beginning* (Kendi, 2016), *The 1619 Project* (Hannah-Jones et al., 2021), and *Caste* (Wilkerson, 2020), have laid out in comprehensive detail our nation's history of slavery, oppression, genocide, and discrimination.

A host of new words and phrases have entered the lexicon during this period: "systemic racism," "structural racism," "Black Lives Matter," and a shift in usage of "white supremacy" to reference entire systems and historical patterns, rather than simply White nationalist hate groups. Despite variation in their usage in the popular press and scholarly literature, these emerging concepts signal a significant shift in our understanding of racism. They indicate a shift in focus from the personal—racism primarily as an issue of biased beliefs and discriminatory actions—to the structural/systemic—institutional policies and practices that reproduce inequity. At the same time, the phrase and movement "Black Lives Matter" draws attention away from racism as a concept ("Are we as a society still racist?") to the ongoing and very real consequences of racism to its victims ("Yes, clearly, we still are").

It is altogether fitting then to seek to understand the latest emerging scholarship on racialized discipline inequity in light of these paradigmatic shifts. Our purpose in this chapter is not only to review recent literature, but to place the most significant recent findings within the context of emerging understandings of the nature of racism and the mechanisms through which it is expressed. We begin with a focus on structural/systemic racism: What are the most common definitions of the construct? To what extent do racialized disparities in the use of exclusionary discipline act as an exemplar or component of structural racism? We then turn our attention to the central current expression of structural racism, *color-blind racism*: What is color-blind racism and how does it function? What are the consequences of attempting to remain color-blind in the face of continuing inequity? We go on to examine the most commonly used or recommended interventions for reducing exclusionary discipline and disciplinary disparities: To what extent are current disciplinary reform approaches reducing disproportionality in discipline (and why not)? Finally, we examine implications of the emerging paradigm of structural racism for policy and practice: In the face of the enduring and seemingly intransigent presence of structural racism, what do we do?

We begin with a focus on the emerging understanding of structural racism.

What is Structural Racism?

Emerging Awareness of Structural/Systemic Racism in Public Discourse

The events of the last six years, especially the national outrage after the death of George Floyd, appear to have created a dramatically increased awareness of the influence of systemic or structural, rather than merely individual, racism among both civil rights advocates (Yancey-Bragg, 2020), and in the public discourse (Worland, 2020). A Google search on the usage in the American media of the terms *systemic racism* or *structural racism* in the one-year period beginning May 24, 2020 (the day of George Floyd's death) to September 29, 2021 in News yielded about 154,000 results. A similar search for the *ten years* prior to that date (May 24, 2010–May 23, 2020) led to about one third the number of results, about 54,900.[2] Since Floyd's murder, the term has been applied in the popular press to address racial disparities in a wide variety of fields, including public health, immigration policy, COVID-19, banking, health care, education, criminal justice, professional sports, and scientific research (Bailey et al., 2021; Becker & Thompson, 2020; Editorial, 2021; Gross, 2021; Kamasaki, 2021; Sweet & Olson, 2020; Weller, 2020; Winthrop, 2020). The months following the murder of George Floyd saw a spate of announcements from professional organizations, businesses, and financial institutions recognizing the existence of structural or systemic racism and promising action to confront it, although the long-term commitment and follow-through in the wake of these pronouncements has clearly been variable (Demby et al., 2021).

The rapid growth of the terms structural or systemic racism in the popular press in no way guarantees that these terms will be defined in media entries. Indeed, it is not uncommon to see one or the other term used in a given news article without any attempt to define it. Definitions of terms and constructs are more likely to be found in the published literature.

Dimensions of the Terms Structural and Systemic Racism in Published Research

As with the popular press, citations for structural or systemic racism have grown tremendously in recent years. Prior to the publication of this chapter in the second edition of the Handbook (Skiba & Rausch, 2015), there were 948 citations for either structural or systemic racism in Google Scholar; since 2015, there have been 5,940. As in media reports, structural or systemic racism has been explored across a wide range of disciplines, including policing (Boyd, 2018), criminal justice (Rosino & Hughey, 2018), health (Yearby, 2018), education in general (Blaisdell, 2016), and the school-to-prison pipeline in particular (Schept et al., 2014) and inequities surrounding the COVID-19 pandemic (Emerson & Montoya, 2021).

There is not yet a single accepted definition of structural or systemic racism in the literature. A representative sampling of definitions appearing in published research may be found in Table 12.1. From a scan of Table 12.1, there appears to be no consistent difference in definitions of the two terms. Nor could we find any article that specifically distinguished between structural or systemic racism: The use of one or the other term appears to be arbitrary, based on the preference of the author.[3] Nevertheless, while there are clearly some differences among the definitions in Table 12.1, there are also a number of commonalities. From these commonalities, we propose the following definition:

> Structural racism is the interlocking constellation of institutional policies and practices and individual beliefs and behaviors, developed over at least 400 years that fabricated, and continues to fabricate, a racialized hierarchy that maintains the social and economic dominance of those with lighter skin color over those with darker skin color.
>
> Since recognition of the harms to others caused by structural racism may create ethical dissonance, one's participation in racialized structures—or even the existence of those structures—is denied or minimized through a process of *color-blind racism*, enabling individuals and institutions to remain unaware of their complicity in reproducing racialized practices. By minimizing individual and institutional contributions to racist practices and structures, the misfortunes of those assigned to lower ranks can be (and typically are) attributed to a personal or cultural flaw on their part.

In this section, we describe the components of the first half of the definition, then expand on the second half of the definition in the section on color-blindness.

Common beliefs and rules, shared across institutions. As opposed to the term *institutional racism*, which focuses on the effects of particular institutions, structural racism implies that

Table 12.1 Definitions of Structural or Systemic Racism in Published Literature Across Disciplines

Bonilla-Silva (1997)

"Racialized social systems: This term refers to societies in which economic, political, social, and ideological levels are partially structured by the placement of actors in racial categories or races.

In all racialized social systems, the placement of people in racial categories involves some form of hierarchy that produces definite social relations between the races. The race placed in the superior position tends to receive greater economic remuneration and access to better occupations and/or prospects in the labor market." (p. 470)

Saini & Vance (2020)

"Systemic racism is the residual effect of discriminatory legislation that reverberates through social, political, and financial systems. It includes the practice of discriminatory customs once rooted in law, and although these practices have changed over time, they continue to oppress people of color." (p. 53)

Churchwell et al. (2020)

"Structural racism refers to the normalization and legitimization of an array of dynamics–historical, cultural, institutional and interpersonal–that routinely advantage White people while producing cumulative and chronic adverse outcomes for people of color." (p. e455)

Feagin & Elias (2013)

"The concept of 'systemic racism' refers to the foundational, large-scale and inescapable hierarchical system of US racial oppression devised and maintained by whites and directed at people of color. Systemic racism is a material, social, and ideological reality that is well-embedded in major US institutions." (p. 936)

Gee & Hicken (2021)

"Structural racism is a system of interconnected institutions that operates with a set of racialized rules that maintain White supremacy. These connections and rules allow racism to reinvent itself into new forms and persist, despite civil rights interventions directed at specific institutions." (p. 293)

Wiecek & Hamilton (2014)

"Structural racism identifies the cause of such racial disparities in the processes, procedures, policies, historical conventions, assumptions, and beliefs regarding operational functioning that occur within, between, and among the social institutions that make up a society's infrastructure. It is the result of institutional arrangements that distribute resources unequally and inequitably." (p. 1106)

racist policies and practices are not limited solely to the influence of any single institution or field (e.g., medicine, criminal justice, education). Rather, the shared assumptions and beliefs maintaining a racialized hierarchy are deeply embedded across institutions and disciplines (Gee & Hicken, 2021), thereby decreasing the chance that the outcomes of structural racism will be noticed or examined. For example, frequent police stops for Black youth occur in concert with health disparities (Duarte et al., 2020). These connections and "racialized rules" shared across institutions "allow racism to reinvent itself into new forms and persist, despite civil rights interventions directed at specific institutions" (Gee & Hicken, 2021, p. 293).

Both individual and institutional. A debate has emerged in recent years over whether racism should be viewed primarily as an individual or an institutional level phenomenon. In reaction to a longstanding tradition of viewing racism, prejudice and bias as a problem of racist or prejudiced individuals (Bonilla-Silva, 1997; Powell, 2008), recent scholarship has emphasized the primacy of institutional or systemic racism and racist policy, that is, policies and practices that enforce a hierarchy of white dominance (Hammer, 2019; Kendi, 2019).

Yet organizations could not promulgate and enforce racist policies without their enactment by individual members. That enactment is premised upon the willing (if not always conscious) acceptance by group members of racialized biases and stereotypes. Longstanding stereotypes (e.g., the myth of the dangerous Black male, Carter et al., 2017) and biased perceptions serve as a perceptual filter, preventing individuals who accept those views from recognizing or directly confronting the blatantly differential treatment of a group of human beings—treatment that might otherwise be seen as a violation of personal or institutional ethics. The social sharing of those beliefs—whether it be attendance at a lynching, racist jokes at holiday gatherings with relatives, or accepting the belief that the overwhelmingly peaceful Black Lives Matter protests in the wake of George Floyd's murder were "violent"[4]—supports and perpetuates practices maintaining a racialized status quo.

Deeply rooted historically, adapting to current circumstances. Current stereotypic beliefs and harmful practices that create disparate negative outcomes for those made vulnerable by America's racialized hierarchy are not random or accidental. Rather they are rooted in a history of enslavement, colonialism, oppression, and discrimination going back at least 400 years. Current data during the pandemic indicates clear and troubling racialized discrepancies between Black and White patients both in the treatment and outcomes of COVID-19 (Emerson & Montoya, 2021). Yet discrimination in medical treatment has deep roots: the physician widely acknowledged as the father of modern gynecology made many of his most important discoveries by operating on enslaved Black women without anesthesia, many of them dying on the operating table (Washington, 2006).

The central thesis of *The New Jim Crow* (Alexander, 2010) is that the racialized effects of mass incarceration today recreate oppression and segregation similar in effect and scope to the earlier Jim Crow era. One component of that thesis is that the structures of racism endure over time by adapting and evolving to fit the particularities and circumstances of each period of history. Complete subjugation of all African Americans during the period of slavery was succeeded by the terror and legalized segregation of Jim Crow, which in turn has been superseded by a more "modern" form of structural racism as exemplified by the War on Drugs, zero tolerance, and mass incarceration. Scholars have argued that the current most common structural manifestation of racism is what has been termed *color-blind racism* (Bonilla-Silva, 2003).

Maintains a racialized hierarchy of human value based on skin color. Since systems of classifying human beings into ranked categories called "races" were first introduced by Linnaeus (1735) and Blumenbach (1776), the aim of scientific racism has been to amass evidence supporting the central presumption of white supremacy – that outward variations in skin color correlate with socially valued differences that demonstrate the supremacy of lighter over darker skin color. Over 200 years of vigorous exploration attempting to find biological or genetic markers that could distinguish between the "races" have failed to yield credible evidence of any physical or intellectual markers that could allow the ranking of individuals with differing skin colors as "better" or "worse."

While the acceptance that there are no biological differences favoring one group over another has been replaced in large measure by the idea that race is a social construct, that understanding does not in any way make the effects of a racial caste system any less real or devastating for those who have been placed on lower rungs of a skin-color based hierarchy. Indeed, the intransigence of structural racism, and the difficulty for those assigned to lower rungs of racialized status, to transcend its hierarchical boundaries has led some writers to refer to America's social structure as a *caste system* (Wilkerson, 2020), little different than the caste system of India or South African apartheid.

School Discipline as a Central Component of Structural Racism

Twenty years of research, and especially the most recent literature, on exclusionary discipline has demonstrated that longstanding and substantial disparities in rates of out-of-school suspension and expulsion for Black and Brown students represent a key component of structural racism; that is, the network of institutional policies, and individual beliefs and behaviors that have supported, and continue to support, a 400-year hierarchy of assigned worth based on skin color. In the following sections, we analyze the published literature on racialized disciplinary disparities—drawn primarily from peer-reviewed studies since the last edition of the Handbook—to examine the extent to which recent research findings from that field are consistent with and concretely actualize a definition of structural racism drawn from the conceptual literature.

Interlocking Constellation

The interlocking constellation of institutional policy and individual beliefs and actions that define structural racism is nowhere better expressed than in the process of interaction between schools and the criminal justice system known as the school-to-prison pipeline (STPP).

Reviews of research on short- and long-term outcomes of school exclusion have documented clear empirical relations between disciplinary exclusion and a host of negative short- and long-term outcomes (Skiba et al., 2016) that increase the probability of juvenile justice involvement. Exclusionary discipline has been found to be predictive of lower achievement (Hwang, 2018), poor attendance and dropout (Chu & Ready, 2018), lower chances of college attendance (Bacher-Hicks et al., 2019), increased chances of juvenile justice involvement (Cuellar & Markowitz, 2015; Novak & Krohn, 2020), and arrest and on probation up to 12 years later (Rosenbaum, 2020). Virtually *all* of these recent studies have included extensive controls, including poverty, previous behavior, and prior academic achievement, indicating that the exclusionary discipline is, *in and of itself*, a significant predictor of a host of short- and long-term negative consequences. In a meta-analysis examining the relation between exclusionary discipline and delinquent outcomes, Gerlinger et al. (2021) found exclusion to be a robust predictor of juvenile delinquency, leading them to conclude that "exclusionary discipline may inadvertently exacerbate rather than mollify delinquent behaviors" (p. 1493).

Both Institutional and Individual

There have been abundant discussions in recent years about whether racism should be viewed as primarily individual or primarily institutional. Research on disciplinary disparities has not, however, lacked for information on either school-wide disparities or on the individual stereotypes or bias expressed by staff within those institutions.

Institutional level. Racialized disparities in school discipline are ubiquitous. Significant racialized discipline disparities have been found in both urban and suburban locales (Annamma et al., 2014), highly resourced and economically disadvantaged schools and school districts (Skiba, Chung et al., 2014), at the elementary, middle, and secondary school levels (Losen et al., 2015), and in both public and charter schools (Losen et al., 2016). Indeed, a clear commonality across such studies is that the extent of over-representation of Black and Brown students in suspension covaries positively with the proportion in the enrollment of such students (Anderson & Ritter, 2017; Welch & Payne, 2010). Finally, school policies appear to play a significant role in disciplinary disparities, with higher disparities found in schools with principals and teachers who endorse zero tolerance disciplinary approaches (Huang & Cornell, 2021; Skiba, Chung et al., 2014).

Individual biases and stereotypes. Some widely shared biases and stereotypes—such as the myth of the dangerous Black male—have proven highly intransigent, and their persistence can reduce individual or institutional motivation to reform educational practices or policies that might well reduce disparities. The notion that higher rates of school suspension are due to poverty-induced differential behavior on the part of Black students has been consistently contradicted by data in both earlier (Skiba et al., 2002) and more recent investigations (Anderson & Ritter, 2017). Numerous multivariate studies have found that race remains a significant predictor of the probability of suspension even after controlling for indicators of poverty (e.g., Anderson & Ritter, 2017; Ksinan et al., 2019; Skiba et al., 2002; Wallace et al., 2008). Similarly, recent studies using rigorous methodology have continued to replicate earlier literature showing that disciplinary disparities cannot be explained by differential rates of infractions between Black and White students (Anderson & Ritter, 2017; Huang, 2020; Huang & Cornell, 2017).

Yet the persistent influence of the centuries-old stereotype of the dangerous Black male (Carter et al., 2017) continues to short-circuit policy discussion that could identify solutions. The Trump Administration Federal Commission on School Safety Report (2018), recommending recission of the

Obama Administration discipline guidance package (U.S. Department of Education, 2014), argued that disciplinary exclusions were likely not due to discrimination, but to a higher rate of prior problem behaviors on the part of students of color. Thus, despite abundant evidence to the contrary, the ancient underlying suspicion that disparate rates of punishment and exclusion are driven by higher rates of disruption among Black students—and thus differential punishment is somehow "earned"—makes it difficult to sustain the political will that would be necessary to truly reform school discipline for students of color.

Interaction of institutional and individual sources of racism. The notion that structural racism is supported and maintained by the *interaction* of racialized institutional policy and individual bias and stereotype begs the question: Is there empirical evidence of such interaction and the ways in which it might play out in real-life situations?

Recently, there have been some intriguing uses of the measures of implicit bias or historical racism to explore hypotheses about systemic distribution of exclusionary discipline and discipline disparities. In a study entitled "Teachers are People Too," Starck and colleagues (2020) found that the scores of teachers who had taken the Implicit Association Test could not be distinguished from the general population, leading (them) to two conclusions: Teachers are (a) no more biased than the population in general but (b) are also *no less biased*. In a study set in southern states, Ward et al. (2019) found that current rates of corporal punishment in schools are aligned with historical county rates of lynching between 1865 and 1950, that is, school districts that had the highest rates of lynching in the past have the highest rate of corporal punishment and the highest Black-White disparities in corporal punishment today.

Historical and Adaptive

Even after *Brown v. Board of Education*, integration proceeded glacially. As integration began to be enforced in earnest in the late 1960s and early 1970s, the increased use of school suspension and expulsion, particularly for Black students, became a frequently-used method through which school districts resisted desegregation (Black, 2016; Southern Regional Council and the Robert F. Kennedy Memorial, 1973). Exclusionary discipline that removed a disproportionate share of Black and Brown students from mainstream educational environments continued to evolve and grow once again in the 1990s with the rise of zero tolerance and its endorsement by all three branches of U.S. Government (Skiba et al., 2010).

Alexander (2010) makes the case that racialized disparities persist in part because the institutional structures that were originally designed to maintain a racial hierarchy persist long after the original racist rationale for those structures has faded; even though the racial discrimination of the 1990s War on Drugs has been recognized, and to a certain extent rejected, by policymakers on both sides of the aisle, institutional inertia continues to maintain exceedingly high and disproportionate rates of Black arrest and incarceration. In the same way, support for zero tolerance and the use of suspension and expulsion has dropped considerably since 2010 (Hirschfield, 2018). Disciplinary reforms have led to a 20% decrease in overall rates of suspension at the national level (Steinberg & Lacoe, 2017). Yet the size of the discipline gap has remained practically unchanged (U.S. Department of Education, 2020). One plausible explanation may be that, while evidence of the ineffectiveness of suspension and expulsion has diminished institutional and public support for its use in general, the institutional policies and individual belief systems reinforcing the discriminatory application of school discipline remain highly resistant to change (Skiba & White, in press).

Maintains a Racialized Hierarchy of Human Value Based on Skin Color

Despite an increasing awareness of the social constructedness of race, the structures of school discipline that have participated in the reproduction of disadvantage based on the shared illusion of "race" continue to create real and often catastrophic consequences for those on the lower rungs of the racialized hierarchy. Being convicted of a felony and incarcerated has lifelong consequences, ranging from restrictions on voting, to close—often electronic—supervision during parole, to a vastly decreased probability of getting a job that pays a living wage (Alexander, 2010). Out-of-school suspension predicts incarceration 12 years after the event and the relation between suspension and arrest is stronger for Black students (Rosenbaum, 2020). Research has estimated that students who are suspended from school are more likely to drop out of school, and that relation is stronger for Black students (Chu & Ready, 2018). School achievement predicts the likelihood of college attendance, and college attendance increases lifetime earnings: Out-of-school suspension predicts 20 percent of the opportunity gap in academic achievement (Morris & Perry, 2016) and significantly reduces the likelihood of college attendance (Bacher-Hicks et al., 2019). Given the number of serious negative consequences created for Black and Brown students due to a significantly higher rate of removal from educational opportunities, it is likely that the discipline gap is among the most potent contributing factors to a racialized hierarchy that predicts maintaining diminished economic and life opportunities for Black Americans.

School Policing and Other Manifestations of Structural Racism

While the focus of this analysis has been on school suspension, the same disparities, and their contribution to diminished life opportunities, appear to apply to every method of more severe and coercive form of discipline in American schools today. Both significant Black over-representation, and the negative consequences that flow from those disparities, have been demonstrated for corporal punishment (USDOE Office for Civil Rights, 2020), school security hardware (Kupchik & Ward, 2016), and school policing (Homer & Fisher, 2020).

Given the more extensive availability of research on school policing, further mention of that literature is instructive, however. While research on the effects of school policing prior was scant and inconsistent prior to 2010, there has been a dramatic increase in both the quantity and quality of published research in the past decade.

While space does not permit a thorough analysis cross walking the findings of the school policing literature and the conceptual components of structural analysis, there are clearly data points suggestive of that association.

- **Institutional and individual contributions**. Police in disadvantaged schools are more likely to engage primarily in law enforcement roles; those in more well-resourced schools more often engage in education and mentoring (Lynch et al., 2016). In predominantly White schools, school police see their role as protection from *external* threat; in predominantly Black enrollment schools, SROs see their role as protecting staff and students from *the students themselves* (Fisher et al., 2020).
- **Historical and adaptive**. *There have been racial disparities in perceptions and implementation of School Resource Officer programs from their beginnings in the late 1950s.* The first SRO program in Flint, Michigan was intended as a preventive intervention addressing juvenile delinquency; it was met with wide local and even national approval (Noble, 2017). But teachers and Black parents criticized and opposed the program, and Black students and their parents complained that the program targeted Black youth.
- **Maintains racialized hierarchy**. Like exclusionary discipline, school police presence is predictive of a broad range of negative outcomes. As school police presence increases, exclusionary discipline goes up more for Black and Latinx as compared to White students (Crosse et al., 2021). When school districts spend more on school police, minority students at the middle school level are disciplined more intensively for more minor incidents (Weisburst, 2019). When police are present in schools, the arrest rate goes up for all students, but more so for Black students than White or Latinx students (Fisher & Hennessy, 2016).

As noted, racism has taken on a different unique form during successive historic periods (Alexander, 2010): Physical bondage and torture during slavery, terror and physical segregation during Jim Crow, and differential surveillance and policing during the period of mass incarceration caused by the War on Drugs. Some scholars, most notably Eduardo Bonilla-Silva, have suggested that the form of racism most common in the current era might best be termed *color-blind racism*, the topic we explore in the following section.

Color Blindness

*Since recognition of the harms to others caused by structural racism may create ethical dissonance, one's participation in racialized structures—or even the existence of those structures—is denied or minimized through a process of **color-blind racism**, enabling individuals and institutions to deny their complicity in reproducing racialized practices. By minimizing individual and institutional contributions to racist practices and structures, the misfortunes of those assigned to lower ranks can be (and typically are) attributed to some element of flaw or failing on their part.*

On November 4, 2008, the *New York Times* declared in a byline, "Obama elected president as racial barrier falls" (*New York Times*, 2008). This proclamation of a post-racial period after Barack Obama's presidential victory marked an interesting inflection point in the legitimization of color blindness— that is, America does not see race, nor should it. The chief and most controversial provision of "anti-Critical Race Theory" bills introduced in 32 states (Education Week, 2022) bans any teaching about race and racism that may cause "discomfort, guilt, anguish, or any other form of psychological distress" for some (one would presume White) students.

The habits, ideology, and identity of color blindness have in some ways cemented new facets of racism. Specifically, when examining discipline practices and disparities, research highlights a thinking habit or an ideology that is being utilized to rationalize or legitimize these disparities. We argue color blindness ideology is serving as that thinking habit and it is imperative to understand how such an ideology operates in order to establish a terrain of remedies that address these disparities.

Features of Color Blindness

Eduardo Bonilla-Silva's (2003) groundbreaking research established color blindness as a new form of racial ideology that emerged after the civil rights era. Bonilla-Silva highlights two features of a color blindness ideology: (1) racism can be eliminated by omitting of race as a descriptor; and (2) education should highlight the individual characteristics and the meritocratic nature of society rather than acknowledging ongoing inequalities. This section describes the emergence of these complexities in the two major components of color blindness—i.e., removing race and legitimizing of inequalities.

The Strategy of Removing Race

One prominent feature of color-blind racism is ignoring race, in order to minimize one's awareness or recognition of racism or racist behaviors. Research has shown that the rationalization for "ignoring race" has shifted over time. Examining social surveys over the period between the 1960s to 2000s, Forman (2004) found that Whites in particular have decreased in their interest in responding to questions about racial attitudes. In a recent methodological study of social survey items on color blindness, Alexander (2018) finds that White participants have a higher prevalence of non-response to race-related items compared to their non-White peers.

Such patterns of "ignoring race," suggest that the purpose of removing race belies a desire among Whites to appear "unbiased." In four studies of cross-cultural social interactions, Apelfbaum, Sommers, and Norton (2008) find that Whites purposefully avoid talking about race in order to minimize potentially being viewed as biased. In fact, however the avoidance tactic is read by Black observers in the study as a sign of greater racial prejudice. The researchers concluded that "in situations where race is potentially relevant, Whites who think that avoiding race altogether will shield them from being perceived as biased should think again." (p. 930)

Color blindness also operates as a shared strategy when *race* is **not** a salient factor nor relevant in cross-cultural social interactions. The strategy of ignoring race gives Whites permission to deny or minimize the humanity of Black, Brown, and Indigenous populations. Faced with health crises such as the opioid epidemic, Curry and Curry (2018) argue that universalizing the dominant White narrative often ignores the realities of death and dying for Black, Brown, and Indigenous populations, but creates calls for policy reform when the victims are White.

A color-blind ideology in which Black, Brown and Indigenous populations are made invisible has a differential cost to those groups as opposed to the White population. In an experimental study, Holoien and Shelton (2011) reported that when Whites interacted with a racial/ethnic group member after being exposed to a color-blind ideology, the person of color experienced a cognitive depletion, while the White participant did not incur such a reduction. Similarly, Plaut et al. (2009) demonstrate that dominant group members, when primed to minimize group differences, heightened their group dominance and the minority group member's marginalization. Such findings highlight the differential cost of color blindness for Black and Brown individuals, in terms of cultural safety and cognitive growth.

Overall, the research on the removal of race as a strategy of the color-blindness ideology serves as an "impression management" for individuals, and, particularly for Whites, to minimize a gaze of being viewed as biased. The removal of race also creates a condition in which the humanity of lived experiences amongst racial/ethnic minority groups is ignored or removed, while the conditions and lived experiences of Whites carry significant humanity and is used to frame and rationalize public policy. Finally, the removal of race also comes at a cost for racial/ethnic minority populations; they experience cognitive depletion and culturally neutralizing environments.

Color Blindness as an Identity

Another dimension of color blindness is the way in which individuals, including teachers, embrace it as an identity. Stating "I am color blind" or "I don't see color" suggests not only ascription to an ideology, but also an attachment to an identity of sorts. Various studies demonstrate the presence of color-blindness ideology and its identity elements (e.g., Manning et al., 2015; Oh et al., 2010). Hartmann et al. (2017) explored color blindness "as a self-asserted identification, often proudly declared and less obviously tied to whiteness or other implicit ideologies and attachments" (p. 870). Their results include findings showing that: (1) across racial groups, most respondents ascribe to identifying or seeing themselves as color blind; (2) White and Latinx respondents identified more favorably to colorblind ideology than Black respondents; and (3) respondents who believe equal opportunity is well-established in American society are more likely to have a strong color-blind identification.

Color Blindness as a Strategy to Sustain Privilege: Examining Discipline Practices

By removing race and legitimizing inequities via individualism and meritocracy, Whites are able to utilize their identity-bound elements of individualism and meritocracy as centerpieces for moving through the social world, thus sustaining their placement on the highest rung of the racialized hierarchy. What are the ways in which school systems, and the educators within them, operate through a color-blind ideology to sustain this racial hierarchy?

Several studies of color-blindness ideology and discipline practices point to exploratory concepts of understanding this interaction. In a study of Alabama disciplinary practices, Baggett and Andrzjewski (2020) describe a pattern in which White educators' fears operated as a mechanism for activating color blindness. Specifically, a fear of losing entitlement to resources, a fear of Black bodies and framed as "dangerous," and a fear of being labeled as racist served to rationalize a color-blind ideology. Baggett and Andrzejewski (2020) thus suggest that discipline practices and policies be viewed as being a product of adult fear generated by color blindness.

What Is the Evidence on Interventions to Reduce Disciplinary Disparities?

School discipline reform has been dominated by three widely adopted practices for school discipline—Schoolwide Positive Behavioral Interventions and Supports (SWPBIS), Social Emotional Learning (SEL), and Restorative Practices (RP). Research suggests there can be positive discipline-related outcomes for all three initiatives, yet cumulative study has yet to demonstrate consistent gap-reducing effects. Other chapters in this volume contain complete descriptions of the three interventions; here we focus on the outcomes of those interventions for reducing disciplinary exclusions and disparities in those exclusions.

Schoolwide Positive Behavioral Interventions and Supports

Relative to other discipline reforms, the outcomes of SWPBIS have been the most extensively studied. In a meta-analysis, Noltemeyer et al. (2019) reported that, of 35 studies presenting findings related to exclusionary discipline, 91% reported significantly reduced rates of office disciplinary referrals (ODRs). Similarly, a recent review of high schools implementing SWPBIS found that all 16 included studies reported decreased ODRs (Estrapala et al., 2020). Gage et al. (2018) conducted a meta-analysis of experimental, group-design SWPBIS research focusing on disciplinary exclusion. Examining results from 90 elementary and high schools, they found a large treatment effect on suspensions: Schools implementing SWPBIS decreased suspensions by 16% relative to comparison schools.

Despite widespread utilization of SWPIBS, however, no randomized control trials have shown it reduces racial disparities in discipline. There is some evidence that Black and White discipline gaps can remain substantial in SWPBIS schools (McIntosh et al., 2018; Vincent & Tobin, 2011). In a national study of schools implementing SWPBIS, Skiba and colleagues (2011) found evidence that those schools were able to implement the program with fidelity, but racial/ethnic disparities in school suspension remained high.

Social Emotional Learning (SEL)

Research on SEL has not focused on exclusionary discipline but has examined a broader range of student outcomes (e.g., Durlak et al., 2011; Wigelsworth et al., 2016). The most recent meta-analysis, synthesizing findings from 82 SEL intervention studies (Taylor et al., 2017), reported positive outcomes lasting from 6 months to 18 years post-intervention. They found that SEL interventions were linked to student growth in SEL skills, social behavior, academic achievement, and college attendance, as well as lower rates of conduct problems, emotional distress, drug use, and arrest. Yet SEL studies have not specifically focused on how marginalized or minoritized groups who participate in SEL interventions fare relative to their peers. Indeed, program developers and scholars have only recently begun linking SEL and equity initiatives (Jagers et al., 2018).

Restorative Practices (RP)

Recent reviews have found growing evidence that restorative approaches to discipline can reduce the use of exclusionary discipline (Darling-Hammond et al., 2020; Gregory & Evans, 2020). For example, in a randomized control trial in Pittsburgh, Augustine and colleagues (2018) showed that the number of suspensions and days lost to suspension decreased more significantly in the program schools than in the control schools. Similarly, Gregory, Huang, and Ward-Seidel (2021a) found that one-year of RP implementation reduced discipline incidents in treatment schools relative to control schools.

Unfortunately, research on RP's promise for reducing racial disparities is not well-established with few studies showing evidence of having substantially narrowed Black/White gaps (for a review see Welsh & Little, 2018; Zakszeski & Rutherford, 2021). A noteworthy exception is the aforementioned Pittsburgh study. The evaluators found that relative to the comparison schools, program schools had steeper declines in the suspension rates of Black students and low-income students, primarily at the elementary levels. Yet, even with the steeper declines and narrowing of the disparities, the Black/White suspension gap remained substantial which has been the case in other districts as well (e.g., Gonzalez, 2015).

The Need for Race-conscious Programmatic Interventions

Cruz et al. (2021) examined the research on school discipline reform efforts and found little quality research that focused on disparity reduction. In addition, they conclude that discipline reforms have been largely "color-evasive" in their approach and they lament that lack of data "regarding the extent to which embedded structural and personal biases affect intervention effectiveness" (p. 417). Gregory et al. (2021b) concur, noting that, "school discipline reform, broadly speaking, is often implemented in a fragmented manner and often without sufficient attention to structural and cultural factors that undermine and contribute to the replication of inequity" (p. 207). Welsh and Little (2018) also critically examine the research on school discipline reforms and their promise for reducing disparities. They conclude that:

> Overall, there seems to be a mismatch between the theory of action of the alternative approaches and the causes of discipline disparities… The vast majority of the alternative approaches are most concerned with assisting students with assimilating to the school culture rather than crafting the school culture to fit the social, emotional, and cultural needs of students.
>
> *p. 773*

Given the lack of accumulative evidence that widespread school discipline initiatives are substantially reducing discipline disparities, educators and researchers are only recently developing and empirically testing race-conscious classroom and schoolwide initiatives. For example, with three urban elementary schools, Cook et al. (2018) augmented SW PBIS with teacher workshops and coaching with their GREET-STOP-PROMPT intervention targeting what they identified as root causes of racial disparities. They trained teachers to (a) proactively prevent problem behavior (GREET), (b) mitigate the impact of implicit bias on decision making (STOP), and (c) progressively respond to problem behaviors with interventions such as re-directing and teaching skills (PROMPT). Their single-case, experimental design study showed a reduction (but not elimination) of the odds Black males, relative to other students, were issued referrals. McIntosh and colleagues (2021) augmented SWPBIS in elementary schools with an equity-focused intervention. They trained and coached teachers in ReACT (Racial equity through Assessing data for vulnerable decision points, Culturally responsive behavior strategies, and Teaching about implicit bias and how to neutralize it). In their experimental trial, they found that the disparities in referrals issued to Black students relative to other students significantly reduced in treatment schools compared to control schools. In other words, they demonstrated their intervention successfully narrowed racial disparities in discipline referrals.

Conclusions and Recommendations

Racialized disproportionality has been referred to as a "wicked problem" (McCall & Skrtic, 2009). But it is not a problem in the way that term was used in previous generations ("the Negro problem" or "the American Indian problem") or even in its current color-blind incarnation ("the problem of the poor"). Together, the burgeoning body of literature on disciplinary disparities is drawing the field to the ineluctable conclusion that the locus of the problem of disparate discipline lies not within the individuals who are its victims, but rather in the interwoven institutional policies and individual beliefs that maintain a hierarchy of racialized disadvantage. To the extent that we fail to realize this understanding (as in "to bring into concrete existence"; Merriam-Webster, 2021), all of our interventions will fail, since our efforts and resources will continue to be brought to bear on the wrong question.

The real problem, the severely entrenched yet often unconscious patterns of institutional and personal behavior that reproduce a racialized hierarchy, is almost always avoided because it is complex, uncomfortable, and filled to the brim with the potential for interpersonal misunderstanding. Even well-meaning interventions that seek to address problems of racialized policies and behavior directly may fail because they underestimate how emotionally loaded and historically conditioned the issue is.

We would argue, in concert with much of the literature on problem solving, that massive yet urgent problems can be solved only through deep investigation into the nature and source of the problem. The process of root cause analysis has been used by NASA to address urgent, potentially life-and-death scenarios (NASA Technology Transfer Program, n.d.). The educational technology of functional behavioral assessment was originally developed to address the seemingly intransigent problem of self-injurious behavior (Carr, 1977; Iwata, 1994), but has come to be widely applied to develop interventions that are more precisely targeted at the underlying needs and functions of challenging behavior. The ongoing problem of dismantling structural racism is vastly more intricate, enduring, emotionally-laden and indeed more urgent than either of these problems. It deserves at least as much deep study of its root causes, and how those roots continue to be actualized every day in our societal and interpersonal interactions.

Dichotomous, "either/or" questions abound in the discussion of reforms targeting disciplinary inequity. Is disproportionality a greater problem in urban or suburban areas? Is it due more to between – school or within – school effects? Which makes a greater contribution: Biased individual beliefs, or systemic/structural racism? The answer in all cases is *both*, and both should be thoroughly explored. Research on disciplinary disproportionality has found evidence of differential treatment in both urban and suburban areas, present in both between-school and within-school effects, and expressed in both individual beliefs and institutional structures. Racial/ethnic inequity in America is ubiquitous. There is no school, no prison, no police station, no hospital in America in which there is not at least the potential for racial/ethnic inequity.

Biased individual beliefs and biased institutional policies are not independent. Both were forged in the crucible of White dominance, and mutually reinforce racialized disparities. Ultimately, what may be most fruitful in understanding and ultimately dismantling the levers of structural racism would be research that can shed light on the mutual influence of institutional policies and individual beliefs and actions. How do institutional policies supporting discrimination shape the beliefs and behaviors of individual actors within those institutions, and how do those individuals in turn speak and behave in ways that maintain institutional discrimination, or at least fail to challenge those policies and practices?

The paradigmatic popular and scholarly shift in how we think about racism, a shift that might well be marked by future generations as officially beginning at the moment of George Floyd's death, will also almost certainly include a fundamental shift in how issues of classroom management and school discipline are approached. Whether well-intentioned or not, zero tolerance, exclusionary discipline, corporal punishment, school hardening through electronic surveillance, and school policing all have their genesis in an attempt to *control* student behavior. As such, they are likely either to (a) have been developed as an explicit attempt to control the behavior of Black and Brown students, or (b) be subsumed by policies and beliefs shaping those strategies into practices that keep Black and Brown students trapped within the 400-year-old fabricated container of racialized hierarchy. The key question for school personnel, and especially for teacher trainers, is *what is the alternative?* How do we develop and implement approaches that nurture and support *all* students, especially those who have been made most vulnerable by structures that have institutionalized and reproduced white supremacy?

It is not yet fully clear what those alternative strategies and understandings will be—certainly there is insufficient quantitative study to apply the words *evidence-based* at the present time—but one highly promising approach is in the emerging literature on the teaching orientation known as "warm demander" teaching (Bondy & Ross, 2008; Bondy et al., 2012; Cosier, 2019; Hambacher et al., 2016). Mostly qualitative in nature at this point, research on the warm demander model points to teachers who demonstrate success in diverse classrooms (e.g., with *all* children) by holding high expectations, while simultaneously communicating that they believe all of their students can reach those expectations *and* that they will do whatever it takes to help them get there. Work on the effectiveness of *authoritative schools* (Gregory et al., 2010) suggests that the warm demanding model might be central to a new paradigm for schoolwide discipline as well.

Using the traditional descriptors *school discipline* or *classroom management* in no way implies endorsement of policies that seek to achieve order through control and coercion. The etymological origins of the word discipline come from the Latin *disciplina*, "learning or knowledge." There is no question that it is often important to teach children and youth how to interact successfully with others, just as it is frequently necessary, in a classroom of 30 children, to explicitly arrange the physical environment and manage the structure of the classroom so as to promote learning and minimize disruption. But there is also an emerging view (Basile, York, & Black, 2019; Bondy et al., 2007; Gregory & Fergus, 2017; Monroe, 2016) that it is possible to develop these strategies within a model that recognizes the need to instruct students in important social and behavioral skills, but does so through relationship-building and compassion, rather than coercion and control.

Recommendations and Future Directions

- **Practice: Institutional**. The lens of disciplinary reform must include:
  - Structural changes to behavioral support
  - An increased focus on the centrality of relationships both within the classroom, and with parents and the community
  - Local reform must include data-based self-analysis of sources of differential treatment at all levels (classroom, school, district, and state/federal policy)
- **Practice: Individuals**. Real reduction in discriminatory discipline will likely not be achieved without uncomfortable conversations:
  - Acknowledging the historical *and continuing* effects of White privilege/dominance/supremacy in school discipline
  - Consistently considering the possibility that individual educator bias, or institutional biased policy may play a key role in disciplinary disparity
  - Taking seriously data pointing to the need for police-free schools

- **Research**: Disciplinary reform without reduction/elimination of discipline disparities is not real reform:
  - **Disaggregation as a Universal Strategy**. Disciplinary interventions or strategies (e.g., SW, PBIS, RP, SEL) that can demonstrate reductions in overall exclusion, but have not shown a concomitant reduction in disciplinary disparities, should not be considered successful.
  - Assist teacher educators in identifying and evaluating alternative models of classroom management and school discipline that nurture and sustain *all* students, including Black and Brown students.
  - **All lives cannot matter until Black lives matter**: *If disciplinary reform does not eliminate racial disparities, it is not true disciplinary reform.*

- **Policy**: Policy focused on evidence-based practice with an attention to racial reconciliation, reparation, and humanity:
  - **Policy-makers**: Realize that freedom and civil rights are not partisan political issues
  - Base policy on evidence regarding disparity reduction, not fear and racist dog-whistles
  - **Researchers**: Increase the policy relevance of scholarly work by disseminating beyond purely academic venues. Take a stand in the face of political pressures, color-blind ideology, and racist policies.

Conclusion

In this chapter, we have attempted to trace the implementation of exclusionary discipline, the ideology of color blindness, and the failure of standard intervention approaches to explicitly recognize the structural nature of racism. These elements interact to prevent the field from recognizing the disproportionate application of exclusionary discipline for what it is—an integral part of the interlocking system of personal beliefs and institutional policies that act in concert with other social systems to maintain and reproduce a hierarchy of racialized disadvantage.

Overcoming the effects of 400-plus years of racial inequity will require a profound realization that race is not neutral in America. To overcome that 400-year head start, interventions attempting to combat disciplinary disparity will need to be grounded in exploration and a color-conscious approach, *deeply respectful of the history and heritage of all children*. As Kendi (2019) so aptly notes, anti-racism is not simply the absence of racism, but rather the willingness to engage in active efforts to dismantle the policies, practices, attitudes, and actions that build and maintain the structures of racism.

Notes

1 The derivative portion of this title was chosen purposefully. In formulating these analyses, we are indebted to Dr. Michelle Alexander for her cogent descriptions of processes and structures that create and maintain racialized disadvantage.
2 A search from May 24, 2001 to May 23, 2010 yielded 908 results, while a search prior to 2001 yielded no results.
3 For the remainder of the chapter, and in the title, we have chosen to use the term structural racism, for two reasons. First, there appears to be a longer scholarly tradition, with greater attention to definition, for the term structural racism. Second, we believe the term structural racism offers a greater degree of specificity than does the slightly more vague systemic racism (see also Kendi, 2019).
4 Of 7,750 Black Lives Matter protests in Summer 2020, 93 percent were entirely peaceful, with no recorded incidents of violence against persons or property (Mansoor, 2020).

References

Alexander, M. (2010). *The New Jim Crow: Mass incarceration in the era of colorblindness*. The New Press.

Alexander, E. (2018). Don't know or won't say? Exploring how colorblind norms shape item nonresponse in social surveys. *Sociology of Race and Ethnicity, 4,* 417–433.

Anderson, K. P., & Ritter, G. W. (2017). Disparate use of exclusionary discipline: Evidence on inequities in school discipline from a U.S. state. *Education Policy Analysis Archives, 25*(49). DOI:10.14507/epaa.25.2787

Annamma, S., Morrison, D., & Jackson, D. (2014). Disproportionality fills in the gaps: Connections between achievement, discipline and special education in the school-to-prison pipeline. *Berkeley Review of Education, 5*(1), 53–87.

Apfelbaum, E. P., Sommers, S. R., & Norton, M. I. (2008). Seeing race and seeming racist? Evaluating strategic colorblindness in social interaction. *Journal of Personality and Social Psychology, 95*(4), 918–932.

Augustine, C. H., Engberg, J., Grimm, G. E., Lee, E., Wang, E. L., Christianson, K., & Joseph, A. A. (2018). *Can restorative practices improve school climate and curb suspensions? An evaluation of the impact of restorative practices in a mid-sized urban school district*. RAND Corporation.

Bacher-Hicks, A., Billings, S. B., & Deming, D. J. (2019). *The school to prison pipeline: Long run impacts of school suspensions on adult crime* (No. w26257). National Bureau of Economic Research.

Baggett, H., & Andrzejewski, C. E. (2020) An exploration of white fear and school discipline in Alabama. *Whiteness and Education, 5*, 74–90.

Bailey, Z. D., Feldman, J. M., & Bassett, M. T. (2021). How structural racism works—racist policies as a root cause of US racial health inequities. *New England Journal of Medicine, 384*, 768–773

Basile, V., York, A., & Black, R. (2019). Who is the one being disrespectful? Understanding and deconstructing the criminalization of elementary school boys of color. *Urban Education,* 0042085919842627.

Becker, T., & Thompson, K. (2020, June 20). Criminal defense lawyers propose reforms to end systemic racism in the court system. *WBUR. www.wbur.org/news/2020/06/17/systemic-racism-criminal-defense-lawyers-reform*

Black, D. W. (2016). *Ending zero tolerance: The crisis of absolute school discipline.* University Press.

Blaisdell, B. (2016). Schools as racial spaces: Understanding and resisting structural racism. *International Journal of Qualitative Studies in Education, 29*(2), 248–272.

Blumenbach, J. F. (1776/1997). Degeneration of the species. In E. C. Eze (Ed.), *Race and the enlightenment: A reader* (pp. 79–90). Blackwell. (Original work published 1776.)

Bondy, E., & Ross, D. D. (2008). The teacher as warm demander. *Educational Leadership, 66*, 54–58.

Bondy, E., Ross, D. D., Gallingane, C., & Hambacher, E. (2007). Creating environments of success and resilience: Culturally responsive classroom management and more. *Urban Education, 42*(4), 326–348.

Bonilla-Silva, E. (1997). Rethinking racism: Towards a structural interpretation. *American Sociological Review, 62*, 465–80.

Bonilla-Silva, E. (2003). *Racism without racists.* Rowman & Littlefield.

Boyd, R. W. (2018). Police violence and the built harm of structural racism. *The Lancet, 392*, 258–259.

Carr, E. G. (1977). The motivation of self-injurious behavior: A review of some hypotheses. *Psychological Bulletin, 84*, 800–816

Carter, P. L., Skiba, R., Arredondo, M. I., & Pollock, M. (2017). You can't fix what you don't look at: Acknowledging race in addressing racial discipline disparities. *Urban Education, 52*(2), 207–235.

Chu, E. M., & Ready, D. D. (2018). Exclusion and urban public high schools: Short-and long term consequences of school suspensions. *American Journal of Education, 124*(4), 479–509.

Churchwell, K., Elkind, M. S., Benjamin, R. M., Carson, A. P., Chang, E. K., Lawrence, W., ... & American Heart Association (2020). Call to action: Structural racism as a fundamental driver of health disparities: A presidential advisory from the American Heart Association. *Circulation, 142*(24), e454–e468.

Cook, C. R., Duong, M. T., McIntosh, K., Fiat, A. E., Larson, M., Pullmann, M. D., & McGinnis, J. (2018). Addressing discipline disparities for Black male students: Linking malleable root causes to feasible and effective practices. *School Psychology Review, 47*(2), 135–152. http://doi.org/1010.17105/SPR-2017- 0026.V47-2

Cornell, D., Maeng, J., Huang, F., Shukla, K., & Konold, T. (2018). Racial/ethnic parity in disciplinary consequences using student threat assessment. *School Psychology Review, 47*, 183–195. http://doi.org/10.17105/SPR-2017-0030.V47-2

Cosier, K. (2019). On whiteness and becoming warm demanders. *Journal of Cultural Research in Art Education, 36*, 56–72.

Crosse, S., Gottfredson, D. C., Bauer, E. L., Tang, Z., Harmon, M. A., Hagen, C. A., & Greene, A. D. (2021). Are effects of school resource officers moderated by student race and ethnicity? *Crime & Delinquency,* 0011128721999346.

Cruz, R. A., Firestone, A. R., & Rodl, J. E. (2021). Disproportionality reduction in exclusionary school discipline: A best-evidence synthesis. *Review of Educational Research, 91*(3), 397–431. http://doi.org/10.3102/0034654321995255

Cuellar, A. E., & Markowitz, S. (2015). School suspension and the school-to-prison pipeline. *International Review of Law and Economics, 43*, 98–106.

Curry, T., & Curry, G. (2018). On the Perils of Race Neutrality and Anti-Blackness: Philosophy as an Irreconcilable Obstacle to (Black) Thought. *American Journal of Economics and Sociology, 77*, 657–687.

Darling-Hammond, S., Fronius, T. A., Sutherland, H., Guckenburg, S., Petrosino, A., & Hurley, N. (2020). Effectiveness of restorative justice in US K–12 Schools: A review of quantitative research. *Contemporary School Psychology, 24*, 295–308. https://doi.org/10.1007/s40688-020-00290-0

Demby, G. et al. (2021, June 9). The racial reckoning that wasn't. *NPR Code Switch.* www.npr.org/2021/06/08/1004467239/the-racial-reckoning-that-wasnt

Duarte, C. D. P., Salas-Hernández, L., & Griffin, J. S. (2020). Policy determinants of inequitable exposure to the criminal legal system and their health consequences among young people. *American Journal of Public Health, 110*, S43–S49.

Durlak, J. A., Weissberg, R. P., Dymnicki, A. B., Taylor, R. D., & Schellinger, K. B. (2011). The impact of enhancing students' social and emotional learning: A meta-analysis of school-based universal interventions. *Child Development, 82* (1), 405–432. https://doi.org/10.1111/j.1467-8624.2010.01564.x

Editorial (2021, May 26). Tackling systemic racism requires the system of science to change. *Nature. www.nature. com/articles/d41586-021-01312-4*

Education Week (2022). *Map: Where critical race theory is under attack.* Retrieved January 16, 2020 from www.edweek.org/policy-politics/map-where-critical-race-theory-is-under-attack/2021/06.

Emerson, M. A., & Montoya, T. (2021). Confronting legacies of structural racism and settler colonialism to understand COVID-19 Impacts on the Navajo Nation. *American Journal of Public Health, 111*(8), 1465–1469.

Estrapala, S., Rila, A., & Bruhn, A. L. (2021). A systematic review of Tier 1 PBIS implementation in high schools. *Journal of Positive Behavior Interventions, 23*, 288–302. https://doi.org/doi:10.1177/1098300720929684

Feagin, J., & Elias, S. (2013). Rethinking racial formation theory: A systemic racism critique. *Ethnic and Racial Studies, 36*(6), 931–960.

Fishbein, A,. & Bunce, H. (2001). Subprime Market Growth and Predatory Lending, in housing policy in the new millennium: conference proceedings 273 (U.S. Dep't of Hous. & Urban Dev. ed., 2001), available at www.huduser.org/Publications/pdf/brd/13Fishbein.pdf.

Fisher, B. W., & Hennessy, E. A. (2016). School resource officers and exclusionary discipline in US high schools: A systematic review and meta-analysis. *Adolescent Research Review, 1*, 217–233.

Fisher, B. W., Higgins, E. M., Kupchik, A., Viano, S., Curran, F. C., Overstreet, S., Plumlee, B., & Coffey, B. (2020). Protecting the flock or policing the sheep? Differences in school resource officers' perceptions of threats by school racial composition. *Social Problems, 1*(19). DOI: 10.1093/socpro/spaa062

Forman, T. A. (2004). Color-blind racism and racial indifference: The role of racial apathy in facilitating enduring inequalities. In Krysan, M., & Lewis, A. E. (Eds.), *The Changing Terrain of Race and Ethnicity* (pp. 43–66). Russell Sage.

Gage, N., Whitford, D. K., & Katsiyannis, A. (2018). A review of schoolwide positive behavior interventions and supports as a framework for reducing disciplinary exclusions. *The Journal of Special Education, 52*, 142–151.

Gee, G. C., & Hicken, M. T. (2021). Structural racism: The rules and relations of inequity. *Ethnicity & Disease, 31*(Suppl), 293–300.

Gerlinger, J., Viano, S., Gardella, J. H., Fisher, B. W., Curran, F.C., & Higgins, E. M. (2021). Exclusionary school discipline and delinquent outcomes: A meta analysis. *Journal of Youth and Adolescence, 50*, 1493–1509.

González, T. (2015). Socializing schools: Addressing racial disparities in discipline through restorative justice. In D. Losen (Ed.), *Closing the school discipline gap: Equitable remedies for excessive exclusion* (pp. 151–165). Teachers College Press.

Gregory, A., Cornell, D., Fan, X., Sheras, P. L, Shih, T., & Huang, F. (2010). Authoritative school discipline: High school practices associated with lower student bullying and victimization. *Journal of Educational Psychology, 102*, 483–496. DOI:10.1037/a0018562

Gregory, A., & Evans, K. R. (2020). *The starts and stumbles of Restorative Justice in Education: Where do we go from here?* National Education Policy Center. http://nepc.colorado.edu/publication/restorative-justice

Gregory, A., & Fergus, E. (2017). Social-emotional learning and equity in school discipline. *The Future of Children, 27*, 117–136. http://doi.org/

Gregory, A., Hafen, C. A., Ruzek, E. A., Mikami, A. Y, Allen, J. P., & Pianta, R. C. (2016). Closing the racial discipline gap in classrooms by changing teacher practice. *School Psychology Review, 45*, 171–191. https://doi.org/10.17105/SPR45-2.171-191.

Gregory, A., Huang, F., & Ward-Seidel, A. R. (2021a). *Evaluation of the Whole School Restorative Practices Project: One-Year Implementation and Impact on Discipline Incidents.* ERIC ED614590. https://eric.ed.gov/?id=ED614590

Gregory, A., Osher, D., Jagers, R. J., & Sprague. J. (2021b). Good intentions are not enough: Centering equity in school discipline reform. *School Psychology Review, 50*, 206–220, https://doi.org/10.1080/2372966X.2020.1861911

Gross, T. (2021, May 6). How systemic racism continues to determine health and wealth in Chicago. *National Public Radio.* www.npr.org/2021/05/06/994173342/how-systemic-racism-continues-to-determine-black-health-and-wealth-in-chicago

Hambacher, E., Acosta, M. M., Bondy, E., & Ross, D. D. (2016). Elementary preservice teachers as warm demanders in an African American school. *The Urban Review, 48*(2), 175–197.

Hammer, P. J. (2019). The Flint water crisis, the Karegnondi water authority and strategic–structural racism. *Critical Sociology, 45*(1), 103–119.

Hannah-Jones, N., Roper, C., Silverman, I., & Silverstein, J. (2021). *The 1619 Project: A new origin story.* One World.

Hartmann, D., Croll, P., Larson, R., Gerteis, J., & Manning, A. (2017). Colorblindness as identity: Key determinants, relations to ideology, and implications for attitudes about race and policy. *Sociological Perspectives, 60*, 866–888.

Hirschfield, P. (2018). Trends in school social control in the United States: Explaining patterns of decriminalization. In J. Deakin, E. Taylor, & A. Kupchik (Eds.), *The Palgrave International Handbook of School Discipline, Surveillance, and Social Control* (pp. 43–64). Palgrave MacMillan.

Holoien, D. S., & Shelton, J. N. (2012). You deplete me: The cognitive costs of colorblindness on ethnic minorities. *Journal of Experimental Social Psychology, 48*(2), 562–565.

Homer, E. M., & Fisher, B. W. (2020). Police in schools and student arrest rates across the United States: Examining differences by race, ethnicity, and gender. *Journal of School Violence, 19,* 192–204.

Huang, F. L. (2020). Prior problem behaviors do not account for the racial suspension gap. *Educational Researcher, 49*(7), 493–502.

Huang, F. L., & Cornell, D. G. (2017). Student attitudes and behaviors as explanations for the Black–White suspension gap. *Children and Youth Services Review, 73,* 298–308.

Huang, F. L., & Cornell, D. G. (2021). Teacher support for zero tolerance is associated with higher suspension rates and lower feelings of safety. *School Psychology Review, 50*(2–3), 388–405.

Hwang, N. (2018). Suspensions and achievement: Varying links by type, frequency, and subgroup. *Educational Researcher, 47*(6), 363–374.

Iwata, B. A., Dorsey, M. F., Slifer, K. J., Bauman, K. E., & Richman, G. S. (1994). Toward a functional analysis of self-injury. *Journal of Applied Behavior Analysis, 27,* 197–209.

Jagers, R. J., Rivas-Drake, D., & Williams, B. (2019). Transformative social and emotional learning (SEL): Toward SEL in service of educational equity and excellence. *Educational Psychologist, 54,* 162–184. https://doi.org/10.1080/00461520.2019.1623032

Kamasaki, C. (2021, Mar. 26). U.S. immigration policy: A classic, underappreciated example of structural racism. *Brookings. www.brookings.edu/blog/how-we-rise/2021/03/26/us-immigration-policy-a-classic-unappreciated-example-of-structural-racism/*

Kendi, I. X. (2016). *Stamped from the beginning: The definitive history of racist ideas in America.* Bold Type Books.

Kendi, I. X. (2019). *How to be an antiracist.* One World.

Ksinan, A. J., Vazsonyi, A. T., Jiskrova, G. K., & Peugh, J. L. (2019). National ethnic and racial disparities in disciplinary practices: A contextual analysis in American secondary schools. *Journal of School Psychology, 74,* 106–125.

Kupchik, A., & Ward, G. (2014). Race, poverty, and exclusionary school security: An empirical analysis of U.S. elementary, middle, and high schools. *Youth Violence and Juvenile Justice, 12,* 332–354.

Linnaeus, C. (1735/1970). *Systema naturae (A general system of nature: Through the three grand kingdoms of animals, vegetables, and minerals: Systematically divided into their several classes, orders, genera, species and varieties with their habitations, manners, economy, structure and peculiarities).* Lackington. (Original work published 1735)

Losen, D. J., Hodson, C., Keith, M. A., II, Morrison, K., & Belway, S. (2015). *Are we closing the school discipline gap?* University of California, The Civil Rights Project.

Losen, D. J., Keith, M. A., II, Hodson, C. L., & Martinez, T. E. (2016). *Charter schools, civil rights and school discipline: A comprehensive review.* University of California, The Civil Rights Project.

Lynch, C. G., Gainey, R. R., & Chappell, A. T. (2016). The effects of social and educational disadvantage on the roles and functions of school resource officers. *Policing: An International Journal of Police Strategies & Management, 39,* 521–535.

Manning, A., Hartmann, D., & Gerteis, J. (2015). Colorblindness in Black and White: An analysis of core tenets, configurations, and complexities. *Sociology of Race and Ethnicity, 1,* 532–546.

Mansoor, S. (2020, September 5). 93% of Black Lives Matter Protests Have Been Peaceful, New Report Finds. *Time.* https://time.com/5886348/report-peaceful-protests/

McCall, Z., & Skrtic, T. (2009). Intersectional needs politics: A policy frame for the wicked problem of disproportionality. *Multiple Voices for Ethnically Diverse Exceptional Learners, 11*(2), 3–23.

McIntosh, K., Gion, C., & Bastable, E. (2018). *Do schools implementing SWPBIS have decreased racial disproportionality in school discipline?* [PBIS evaluation brief]. OSEP TA Center on Positive Behavioral Interventions and Supports.

McIntosh, K., Girvan, E. J., Fairbanks Falcon, S., McDaniel, S. C., Smolkowski, K., Bastable, E., Santiago-Rosario, M. R., Izzard, S., Austin, S. C., Nese, R. N. T., & Baldy, T. S. (2021). Equity-focused PBIS approach reduces racial inequities in school discipline: A randomized controlled trial. *School Psychology, 36*(6), 433–444. https://doi.org/10.1037/spq0000466

Merriam–Webster Online (2021). Full definition of *realize.* www.merriam-webster.com/dictionary/realize.

Monroe, C. R. (2016). Race and color: Revisiting perspectives in Black education. *Theory Into Practice, 55*(1), 46–53.

Morris, E. W., & Perry, B. L. (2016). The punishment gap: School suspension and racial disparities in achievement. *Social Problems, 63,* 68–86.

Nagourney, A. (2008). "Obama Elected President as Racial Barrier Falls" in NYTimes, retrieved from: www.nytimes.com/2008/11/05/us/politics/05elect.html?pagewanted=print

NASA Technology Transfer Program (n.d.) *NASA root cause analysis tool (software).* https://software.nasa.gov/software/LEW-19737-1

Noble, A. K. (2017). *Policing the hallways: The origins of school-police partnerships in twentieth century american urban public schools.* [Unpublished doctoral dissertation]. University of Florida.

Noel, D. L. (Ed.) (1972). *The origins of American slavery and racism.* Merrill Publishing Company.

Noltemeyer, A., Palmer, K., James, A. G., & Wiechman, S. (2019). School-Wide Positive Behavioral Interventions and Supports (SWPBIS): A synthesis of existing research. *International Journal of School & Educational Psychology,* 7(4), 253–262. https://doi.org/10.1080/21683603.2018.1425169

Novak, A., & Krohn, M. (2020). Collateral consequences of school suspension: examining the "knifing off" hypothesis. *American Journal of Criminal Justice,* 1–20.

Oh, E., Chun-Chung, C., Neville, H. A., Anderson, C., & Landrum-Brown, J. (2010). Beliefs about affirmative action: A test of the groups self-interest and racism beliefs models. *Journal of Diversity in Higher Education,* 3(3), 163–76.

Plaut, V., Thomas, K., & Goren, M. (2009). Is multiculturalism or color blindness better for minorities? *Psychological Science,* 20(4), 444–446.

powell, j. a. (2008). Structural racism: Building upon the insights of john calmore. *North Carolina Law Review,* 86, 791–816.

Rosenbaum, J. (2020). Educational and criminal justice outcomes 12 years after school suspension. *Youth & Society,* 52(4), 515–547.

Rosino, M. L., & Hughey, M. W. (2018). The war on drugs, racial meanings, and structural racism: A holistic and reproductive approach. *American Journal of Economics and Sociology,* 77(3–4), 849–892.

Saini, V., & Vance, H. (2020). Systemic racism and cultural selection: A preliminary analysis of meta contingencies. *Behavior and Social Issues,* 29, 52–63.

Schept, J., Wall, T., & Brisman, A. (2014). Building, staffing, and insulating: An architecture of criminological complicity in the school-to-prison pipeline. *Social Justice,* 41, 96–115.

Skiba, R. J., Arredondo, M., & Williams (2016). In and of itself a risk factor: Exclusionary discipline and the School-to-Prison Pipeline. In K. J. Fasching-Varner, L. L. Martin, R. Mitchell, K. Bennett-Haron, & A. Daneshzadeh (Eds.) *Understanding, dismantling, and disrupting the Prison-to-School Pipeline* (pp. 109–126). Lexington Books

Skiba, R. J., Chung, C. G., Trachok, M., Baker, T. L., Sheya, A., & Hughes, R. L. (2014). Parsing disciplinary disproportionality: Contributions of infraction, student, and school characteristics to out-of-school suspension and expulsion. *American Educational Research Journal,* 51, 640–670. doi:10.3102/0002831214541670

Skiba, R., Eckes, S., & Brown, K. (2010). African American disproportionality in school discipline: The divide between best evidence and legal remedy. *New York Law School Law Review,* 54, 1071–1112.

Skiba, R. J., Horner, R. H. Chung, C. G., Rausch, M. K., May, S. L., & Tobin, T. (2011). Race is not neutral: A national investigation of African American and Latino disproportionality in school discipline. *School Psychology Review,* 40, 85–107.

Skiba, R. J., Michael, R. S., Nardo, A. C., & Peterson, R. L. (2002). The color of discipline: Sources of racial and gender disproportionality in school punishment. *Urban Review,* 34, 317–342. DOI:10.1023/A:1021320817372

Skiba, R. J., & Rausch, M. K. (2015). Reconsidering exclusionary discipline: The efficacy and equity of out-of-school suspension and expulsion. In E. Sabornie & E. Emmer (Eds.), *Handbook of Classroom Management (2nd. ed.).* Taylor and Francis Group.

Skiba, R., & White, A. L. (In press). Ever since Little Rock: The history of disciplinary disparities in America's schools. In N. A. Gage, L. J. Rapa, D. K. Whitford, & A. Katsiyannis (Eds.). *Disproportionality and Social Justice in Education.* Springer.

Southern Regional Council and the Robert F. Kennedy Memorial (1973). *The student pushout: Victim of continued resistance to desegregation.* Authors.

Starck, J. G., Riddle, T., Sinclair, S., & Warikoo, N. (2020). Teachers are people too: Examining the racial bias of teachers compared to other American adults. *Educational Researcher,* 49, 273–284.

Steinberg, M. P., & Lacoe, J. (2017). What do we know about school discipline reform? Assessing the alternatives to suspensions and expulsions. *Education Next,* 17(1), 44–53.

Stout, C. & LeMee, G. L. (2021, July 22). Efforts to restrict teaching about racism and bias have multiplied across the U.S. *Chalkbeat.* www.chalkbeat.org/22525983/map-critical-race-theory-legislation-teaching-racism

Sugai, G., & Horner, R. (2010). School-wide positive behavior support: Establishing a continuum of evidence-based practices. *Journal of Evidence-based Practices for Schools,* 11(1), 62–83.

Sweet, K., & Olson, J. (2020). J. P. Morgan puts $30B towards fixing banking's "systemic racism." *Associated Press.* https://apnews.com/article/race-and-ethnicity-small-business-charlotte-jamie-dimon-racial-injustice-3cf34a097380b3b0813a52994fbce648

Taylor, R. D., Oberle, E., Durlak, J. A., & Weissberg, R. P. (2017). Promoting positive youth development through school-based social and emotional learning interventions: A meta-analysis of follow-up effects. *Child Development,* 88(4), 1156–1171.

US Department of Education (2014). *Guiding principles: A resource guide for improving school climate and discipline.* Washington, DC. Retrieved from: www2.ed.gov/policy/gen/guid/school-discipline/guiding-principles.pdf

U.S. Department of Education, Office for Civil Rights (2020). *Civil Rights Data Collection, 2017–2018.* Retrieved from: www2.ed.gov/about/offices/list/ocr/docs/crdc-2017-18.html

Vincent, C. G., & Tobin T. J. (2011). The relationship between implementation of School-Wide Positive Behavior Support (SWPBS) and disciplinary exclusion of students from various ethnic backgrounds with and without disabilities. *Journal of Emotional and Behavioral Disorders, 19,* 217–232. DOI:10.1177/1063426610377329

Wallace, J. M., Jr., Goodkind, S., Wallace, C. M., & Bachman, J. G. (2008). Racial, ethnic, and gender differences in school discipline among U.S. high school students: 1991–2005. *The Negro Educational Review, 59*(1–2), 47–62.

Ward, G., Petersen, N., Kupchik, A., & Pratt, J. (2021). Historic lynching and corporal punishment in contemporary Southern schools. *Social Problems, 68,* 41–62. https://doi.org/10.1093/socpro/spz044

Washington, H. A. (2006). *Medical apartheid: The dark history of medical experimentation on Black Americans from colonial times to the present.* Anchor Books.

Weisburst, E. K. (2019). Patrolling public schools: The impact of funding for school police on student discipline and long-term education outcomes. *Journal of Policy Analysis and Management, 38*(2), 338–365.

Welch, K., & Payne, A. A. (2010). Racial threat and punitive school discipline. *Social Problems, 57*(1), 25–48. DOI:10.1525/sp.2010.57.1.25

Weller, C. (2020, June 18). Systemic Racism Makes Covid-19 Much More Deadly For African-Americans. *Forbes.* www.forbes.com/sites/christianweller/2020/06/18/systemic-racism-makes-covid-19-much-more-deadly-for-african-americans/?sh=149795617feb

Welsh, R. O., & Little, S. (2018). The School Discipline Dilemma: A Comprehensive Review of Disparities and Alternative Approaches. *Review of Educational Research, 88*(5), 752–794. https://doi.org/10.3102/0034654318791582

Wiecek, W. M., & Hamilton, J. L. (2013). Beyond the Civil Rights Act of 1964: Confronting structural racism in the workplace. *Louisiana Law Review, 74,* 1095–1160.

Wigelsworth, M., Lendrum, A., Oldfield, J., Scott, A., Ten Bokkel, I., Tate, K., & Emery, C. (2016). The impact of trial stage, developer involvement and international transferability on universal social and emotional learning programme outcomes: A meta-analysis. *Cambridge Journal of Education, 46,* 347–376.

Wilkerson, I. (2020). *Caste: The origins of our discontents.* Random House.

Winthrop, R. (2020, June 5). Learning to live together: How education can help fight systemic racism. *Brookings.* www.brookings.edu/blog/education-plus

Worland, J. (2020, June 11). America's Long Overdue Awakening to Systemic Racism. *Time Magazine.* https://time.com/5851855/systemic-racism-america/

Yancey-Bragg, N. (2020, June 15). What is systemic racism? Here's what it means and how you can help dismantle it. *USA Today.* www.usatoday.com/story/news/nation/2020/06/15/systemic-racism-what-does-mean/5343549002/

Yearby, R. (2018). Racial disparities in health status and access to healthcare: the continuation of inequality in the United States due to structural racism. *American Journal of Economics and Sociology, 77*(3–4), 1113–1152.

Zakszeski, B., & Rutherford, L. (2021). Mind the gap: A systematic review of research on restorative practices in schools. *School Psychology Review.* Published online: https://doi.org/10.1080/2372966X.2020.1852056

13

WHY EFFECTIVE CLASSROOM MANAGEMENT DEPENDS ON TEACHERS' ABILITIES TO ENGAGE FAMILIES

Joan Walker and Jennifer Pankowski

PACE UNIVERSITY

Every day, millions of US schoolchildren move between the social worlds of home and school. Shuttling between family and classroom is remarkably complex because it requires that children recognize, remember, and adapt to each setting's culture, language, and norms (Comer, 1996; Epstein, 2018). Children who have difficulty navigating between these two worlds, and regulating their behavior according to each one's expectations, can fall into two kinds of gaps: achievement and discipline (Gregory et al., 2010). For example, children and families whose language, culture, and related funds of knowledge do not align to the school curriculum are marginalized or excluded (Leonardo & Grubb, 2019). Similarly, children whose behavior does not conform to teacher expectations can be subject to increased disciplinary actions, which remove them from the classroom and further deny them opportunities to learn (Gilliam et al., 2016; Simson, 2020; Wun, 2016). In short, gaps between the two social worlds create and perpetuate inequity.

Teachers can narrow these gaps by functioning as a "living bridge" or developmental mesosystem that connects the social worlds of home and school (Bronfenbrenner, 1986; Walker & Hoover-Dempsey, 2006, 2014). Framed from this developmental and ecological perspective, this chapter asserts that effective classroom management depends on family engagement. Practically, student engagement and learning depends on effective classroom management; effective classroom management depends on teachers' knowledge of and relationships with students. Families are a critical resource for understanding students' talents, interests, needs, goals, and personality. Thus, teachers' abilities to engage families are the foundation of successful classroom management, and student and teacher success.

The two vignettes below illustrate the interdependence between family engagement and classroom management, their challenging social dynamics, and their importance for student and teacher success. Both vignettes introduce the hypothetical student, Javier Soto. The first lets us see Javier through the eyes of his teacher while the second shares his mother's perspective. We meet both teacher and mother as they each prepare for an upcoming parent-teacher conference. As you read, consider what is occurring in the classroom. How can the teacher describe this situation to the family? What can the teacher say and do to form a partnership that supports Javier? What are the potential consequences for Javier if a partnership is not achieved?

> You are a 5th grade teacher in your first year at Woodside Elementary. Among your class of 25 pupils, Javier Soto is a polite student who gets along well with his classmates. Aside from the occasional bout of silliness or inattention typical for a boy his age, his classroom social behavior is not an issue. Increasingly, however, he has refused to comply with your requests that he read aloud. Across the opening weeks of the school year, you have noted that while Javier is a strong performer in math, his reading skills are much weaker. His academic history indicates that he was below grade-level expectations in reading last year. Based on Javier's history and current performance, you decide to implement a reading intervention. For the next several weeks, you will try an intensive form of small group instruction with Javier and a few of his classmates who have a similar academic profile. Along the way, you will monitor his progress and then analyze the results. Your hope is that Javier will respond to this intervention and his reading skills will improve. If they do not, a potential next step is working with a reading specialist or referral for special education. To begin the reading intervention, you must inform Javier's family about his performance and your plans to help him. In educational jargon, you will conduct a pre-referral conference. The school is scheduling the first round of parent-teacher conferences for the year and Javier's mother, Carmen, has signed up for a 15-minute appointment next week. This is your chance to share your plans. You are nervous about this upcoming conversation because it's the first time you'll explain something like this to a family. While you learned about the legal and procedural aspects of Response-to-Intervention in your graduate program, you never actually had the chance to practice implementing them. You wish you had more resources than the one-page handout on parent-teacher conferences that your assistant principal distributed at that last faculty meeting.

Now, let's meet Javier's mother. The vignette offers a glimpse of what Javier's teacher *could* learn about him and his family in this upcoming conference.

> Carmen Soto is running late. She always seems to be running. She left work on time for her son's parent-teacher conference but traffic was bad and the bus was late. Carmen hurries toward Javier's school building and gets directions to his teacher's classroom. As she walks down the hall, Carmen takes a deep breath. A single mom who cooks at a hospital, Carmen is determined that Javier will have a better life than she has had. He is a bright boy who tinkers with mechanical objects and loves math. Math has always come easier for him than reading. Although Carmen reads whenever she can and has taken Javier to the library since he was a toddler, he just doesn't like to read. His reluctance frustrates her. She does not want Javier to experience the same shame and isolation that she felt as a student who struggled with learning in school. For her, learning English was challenging. But Javier seems comfortable with both Spanish and English. When Javier was younger, she asked his teachers how she could help with his reading, but they suggested something she had already tried or strategies that didn't fit with their daily routines. Carmen worries that Javier's teachers underestimate his abilities because he dislikes reading and can be shy. Low expectations will not get him to college. What is Javier's teacher like this year? Does she understand him? Carmen's attitude is, "Teachers have many children to care for. No one is going to look out for my son the way I will." A wary Carmen steps into the classroom.

These vignettes illustrate abiding tensions in teacher-family interactions. Teachers know that families matter yet they are often unsure of how to invite families as partners, especially when families differ from their own personal backgrounds and experiences (Amatea et al., 2012; D'Haem & Griswold, 2017; Kirmaci, 2019). For their part, families want teachers who know their children and who invite and value their knowledge about how their children learn and behave (Lightfoot, 2004; Zeitlin & Curcic, 2014). Yet, what they often experience is teachers who view communicating with parents as opportunities to address problems rather than opportunities to establish relationships that help them learn about the student and family (Guo, 2010; Martin et al., 2006).

Professional standards hold teachers accountable for the effective use of multiple social skills. For example, Interstate Teacher Assessment and Support Consortium standard 10 states, "the teacher understands that alignment of family, school and community … enhances student learning and discontinuity … interferes with learning" and "the teacher respects families' beliefs, norms and expectations" (CCSSO, 2011). Similarly, Standard 1 emphasizes the importance of knowing students as individuals (e.g., "The teacher creates … instruction that takes into account individual learners' strengths, interests, and needs and that enables each learner to advance …"). Similar professional responsibilities are part of in-service teacher standards (e.g., the Danielson framework for teaching; Danielson, 2007). Yet, teachers too are caught in a gap; a gap between their professional preparation and the socially situated and complex nature of their work with students and families. Unless we support teachers' capacity to meet the social demands of their work, students will continue to experience gaps between the social worlds of home and school.

Previous contributions to this Handbook linked the fields of classroom management and family engagement by drawing parallels between theories of parenting style and teachers' use of authority (Walker & Hoover-Dempsey, 2006) and by articulating families' and teachers' unique and interactive contributions to student outcomes (Walker & Hoover-Dempsey, 2014). Our purpose in this third edition is to focus on teachers with the aim of identifying the knowledge, skills, and dispositions they need to build positive and productive relationships with students and families. Certainly, building relationships in the context of education requires the participation of all parties—students, families, and teachers—because it is only when all are fully engaged and committed to sharing perspectives, knowledge, and information that each one's goals are achieved. However, we emphasize teachers' responsibilities in building relationships given that they hold a major share of knowledge and power essential to the effective education of students.

We structure our chapter in four sections. First, to understand better the gap between teachers' preparation and professional practice, we identify four barriers that impede teachers' ability to develop their professional social competencies. Second, to underscore the interconnection between family engagement and classroom management, we describe one of the most influential home-based forms of family engagement—academic socialization—and how it shapes student-teacher classroom interactions and student outcomes. In the third section, we turn to psychological research on social cognition, which is the foundation for social competence. Social cognition involves our perceptions of others and social situations, our ability to think about others' perspectives, mental states, emotions and experiences, and our ability to use that social information to make decisions and act. Social cognition is a fascinating characteristic of the human experience because it has both observable and implicit features. We can be fully aware of our social thoughts yet social thoughts below our conscious awareness can also determine our choices and behavior. This latter feature makes it challenging to teach and learn. We close this section by connecting social cognition to teachers' perceptions and actions as they navigate the professional challenges inherent to the social contexts of classroom management and family engagement.

Finally, we identify promising examples of efforts to develop teachers' social competencies for family engagement and in turn, successful classroom management. This section argues that advancing teachers' social competence requires two things: (1) an understanding of social cognition and interpersonal relationships and (2) well-structured and repeated opportunities to experience authentic, complex professional social situations. This section showcases innovations in teacher education including socially situated pedagogies ranging from technology-driven simulations and more traditional forms of experiential learning such as case studies and microteaching Throughout the chapter, we cite evidence from traditional research and teaching tools and highlight innovations in the measurement of teachers' social competence, including emerging trends in educational social neuroscience.

Our consideration of teachers' social competence across two social contexts, classroom management and family engagement, is important and timely. Since the last edition of the Handbook in 2014, the role of interpersonal skills in K–12 teaching, learning and professional success has received increased attention (Aldrup et al., 2020; National Academies of Sciences, Engineering, and Medicine, 2017). Simultaneously, psychological and educational research has developed tools that can elicit and assess specific aspects of teachers' social competence in real time (Davidesco et al., 2019; Dieker et al., 2014; Walker & Legg, 2018). New tools allow us to understand the social demands of teaching in new ways. They also allow us to prepare and support teachers by using situated pedagogies that demonstrate how, when and why to apply their professional content knowledge and pedagogical content knowledge. As we have argued elsewhere, continuing to prepare teachers in ways that marginalize the social context of teaching ignores decades of evidence about how people learn, spurns technological advances that offer ethical, durable and scalable models of professional education, and last but certainly not least, disregards the very real dilemmas faced by teachers, families and students (Walker, 2019).

Barriers to Developing Teachers' Social Competence

If we are going to support teachers' success at classroom management and family engagement, we need to acknowledge and address four barriers in their professional preparation (de Bruine et al., 2014; Walker, 2019). The first barrier to teachers' development of social competence is the educator preparation curriculum. Most educator preparation programs' curricula emphasize the development of novices' content knowledge and pedagogical content knowledge while offering relatively few sheltered avenues for experiencing the social demands of teaching and fewer still opportunities to practice using specific evidence-based strategies for effective classroom management and family engagement (Epstein & Sanders, 2006; Flanigan, 2007). Further, even when the social and relational context of teaching is addressed, these dynamics are often conveyed with traditional teaching methods such as lecture and reading. Given these features of the curriculum, it is no surprise that in-service teachers' report feeling unprepared for the social demands of the profession (Markow & Pieters, 2012; Stough et al., 2015). Closing this gap requires incorporating opportunities for prospective teachers to experience how and when the features of various social situations require adaptive use of their content knowledge and pedagogical content knowledge.

A second barrier to teachers' development of social competence is the quality of fieldwork experiences. Compared to other service professions such as counseling or medicine, prospective teachers receive few opportunities to enter the profession in well-structured, gradual ways (Grossman et al., 2009), which denies them opportunities to participate in establishing classroom management procedures and develop relationships with families. Moreover, fieldwork typically occurs late in candidates' preparation such as in the final year of study during student teaching, which hinders novices' abilities to apply the knowledge they have previously acquired in their pre-service training (Eyler, 2009). In psychological terms, this structure perpetuates the problem of inert knowledge, or knowing "what" but not "when" or "why" (Bereiter & Scardamalia, 1985). Finally, during fieldwork, prospective teachers learn from the role models, resources and situations in their immediate local context, which can result in the development of uneven knowledge, skills and impressions of families and students. To gain the most from fieldwork, prospective teachers need early, repeated, and well-structured opportunities to observe the dynamic and social nature of classroom management and family engagement.

A third barrier facing most pre- and in-service teachers is a growing mismatch between the demographics of the teaching profession and the students and families they serve. White middle-class females comprise most of the US teaching workforce (Goldring et al., 2013); yet our nation's student body includes an increasingly diverse array of children (Bitterman et al., 2013). Cultural mismatch can hinder effective teacher-family partnerships because teachers tend to have deeply held and often-implicit views about families' roles and abilities (Hoover-Dempsey et al., 2002). Similarly, cultural mismatch and linguistic differences can implicitly impact teachers' perceptions of students' abilities and behaviors, and in turn, their approaches to discipline and classroom management (Gilliam et al., 2016; Gregory et al., 2010; İnan-Kaya & Rubie-Davies, 2021). To mitigate the potentially negative impacts of this mismatch, teachers need opportunities to become *aware* of and concerned about implicit biases that can shape their perceptions and decision-making. Moreover, teachers need strategies that can help them replace personal assumptions with professional social skills, including the capacity to look at situations from multiple perspectives (Eberly et al., 2007; Plant & Devine, 2009).

A fourth barrier to developing teacher social competence is the inherent complexity of social interactions themselves. As illustrated in the opening vignettes, teachers' social interactions with students and families require significant social competence because they are often fraught with issues of power, equity, responsibility, and high-stakes decisions about students' educational trajectory. These issues can become even more complex when they intersect with issues of race, culture, and language (Li et al., 2021; Lightfoot, 2004). We address this complexity more fully in the section on social competence.

In sum, while teaching standards hold teachers accountable for practices that require significant social competence, teachers experience multiple barriers to developing their professional social skills. Without substantial professional supports, teachers are left to rely on their own personality and personal experiences, lessons learned from trial and error, and the social norms of their school for guidance on navigating classroom management and family engagement situations. Teachers, students, and families deserve better.

Aligning Home and School: Two Ways that Families Influence Classroom Management

This section returns to our central thesis that effective classroom management depends on family engagement by summarizing families' general contributions to student engagement and achievement, and how families and family-teacher interaction make a positive difference to student-teacher classroom interactions.

Family engagement in children's education matters because families uniquely contribute to student achievement across grade levels and ethnic groups (Christenson, 2004; Jeynes, 2012). For example, a meta-synthesis by Wilder (2014) found that the relationship between parental involvement and academic achievement was positive, regardless of a definition of parental involvement or measure of achievement. Importantly for classroom management, family–school engagement also predicts positive student behavior (e.g., prosocial skills) and decreases in challenging behaviors across the elementary and middle school years (Smith et al., 2019).

To understand families' contributions more fully, investigators have examined how, why, and when specific elements of families' home-based activities and family–school relationships support students' school success across the preschool through secondary years (Bryk & Schneider, 2002; Fan & Williams, 2010; Hoover-Dempsey & Sandler, 1995, 1997; Pomerantz et al., 2007; Sheridan et al., 2019). Underscoring the importance of bridging home and school, this work shows how student learning and engagement are enhanced when teachers and parents work together. Unfortunately, this line of work also shows how poor home-school alignment hinders student and teacher success (Christenson & Reschley, 2010; Henderson et al., 2007; Hughes & Kwok, 2007; Hughes et al., 2012). For example, Mantzicopoulos (2005) found that when kindergarten teachers reported poor relationships with families, their students were also more likely to report high levels of conflict with their teacher.

There is still much to learn about how productive teacher-family relationships are developed and how they function to align home and school in support of student and teacher success. The remainder of this section describes one of the most influential forms of family engagement—academic socialization—and how it can shape student-teacher classroom interactions and student outcomes.

Family Processes that Align Home and School: Academic Socialization

While many school and teacher efforts to invite families focus on family support of academic work (e.g., homework completion), some of the most powerful ways that families make a difference are not overtly related to academics (Hill, 2001; Hoover-Dempsey et al., 2005; Jeynes, 2010). Comparing various forms of parental involvement, Hill and Tyson's (2009) meta-analysis found that parental involvement in homework was unrelated to achievement whereas families' academic socialization efforts (Hill, 2001)—which include behaviors such as conveying the value of education, reinforcing student effort, modeling learning and communicating with teachers—had the strongest positive association with achievement. Similarly, a large-scale synthesis of 448 independent studies involving nearly 500,000 families found that family involvement was related more strongly to children's social and emotional adjustment than their academic adjustment (Barger et al., 2019). Thus, the impact of family engagement can be construed as indirectly relevant to achievement because it operates through students' "inner resources" (Grolnick et al., 1991).

There is growing evidence that the relationship between family engagement and student achievement is strongest when family engagement is defined as academic socialization (Boonk et al., 2018). Moreover, academic socialization is seen as a notable factor in closing the achievement gap observed along race and ethnicity (Cross et al., 2019; Hill & Torres, 2010; Jeynes, 2016). Demonstrating how well-designed family engagement interventions can deliberately use academic socialization to make a difference in students' academic trajectory, Harackiewicz and colleagues (2012) conducted an experimental field study that leverages academic socialization. They found that asking parent to convey the importance of mathematics and science courses led high school–aged children to take, on average, nearly one semester more of science and mathematics in the last two years of high school, compared with the control group. Academic socialization may be powerful because it represents the home's efforts to connect with the social world of school. It represents families' efforts to align their aspirations for the child's success with the school's expectations and it sends children the message that the school is a primary means whereby the child's educational success can be secured.

In sum, while teachers typically expect and value families' engagement in academic learning activities (e.g., reading at home and supervising homework), it is families' social support and engagement, or academic socialization, that makes the biggest contributions to children's educational success. This literature matters because of its potential to close the achievement gap: the forms of family engagement that matter most to student engagement and learning are those that every family possesses—aspirations for their children's education and success.

How Academic Socialization Shapes Classroom Interactions

In general, higher levels of family-teacher interaction predict more closeness in the teacher–child relationship whereas lower levels predict more teacher–child conflict (Dearing et al., 2005; Wyrick & Rudasill, 2009). Teacher-parent trust and communication appears particularly important in reducing two classroom management concerns, challenging child behaviors (Ogg et al., 2021) and on-task behavior (Fefer et al., 2020). Academic socialization appears to impact classroom processes by influencing the perceptions, motivation, and behaviors of both students and teachers.

How does this influence happen? Psychologically, if families have trusting, reciprocal relationships with teachers, they may convey this tone of partnership to students, which in turn, fosters students' trust, openness to learning and willingness to participate in classroom activities. Students' perceptions of their relationship with teachers plays a significant role in their engagement and learning. Children's perceptions of close relationships with teachers are important because they provide a developmental context in which children feel emotional security and can acquire self-regulation and social information-processing skills that promote successful social interactions (Buyse et al., 2011; Cornelius-White, 2007; O'Connor et al., 2012; Roorda et al., 2011, 2017; Walker, 2008). By contrast, if families have limited or negative interactions with teachers, children may not have access to this developmental context and resource.

Family–teacher interactions also influence teacher–child relationship quality through their effects on *teachers*. For example, positive parent-teacher relationships may encourage more positive teacher attention and interactions that are personalized to students' talents and interests. In one of the few studies to look at teachers' perceptions of the parent–teacher interactions as they relate to teachers' perceptions of student–teacher relational conflict, Thijs and Eilbracht (2012) found that teachers' perceptions of families could explain previously unaccounted for ethnic differences in student–teacher conflict. Similarly, teacher perceptions of parental involvement have been related more strongly to student achievement than parents' reports of their own behavior, suggesting that teacher perceptions of parents may be stereotyped and that such stereotypes affect academic results (Bakker et al., 2007). This work and related lines of research examining how differences in families' and teachers' social capital and demographics relate to teachers' management of classroom behavior (Gilliam et al., 2016; Marcucci, 2020) have potential to understand and narrow achievement and discipline gaps.

Finally, one of the most intriguing new avenues for understanding teacher-student relationship quality and its role in student learning and engagement is social educational neuroscience. Using portable imaging devices in classroom settings, this emerging line of research can advance fundamental research on education by providing biological evidence of what teacher-student interactions look like "under the hood." For example, neural caps worn by teachers and students during classroom interactions can measure the degree of joint attention or brain-to-brain synchrony, which can in turn be associated with learning outcomes (Bevilacqua et al., 2019; Pan et al., 2020). A central challenge in this emergent interdisciplinary field is weaving neural information about affiliative bonding between teachers and students with traditional measures such as observation and self-report.

In sum, this section demonstrated how family engagement can increase alignment between home and school. It introduced the construct of academic socialization and pointed to evidence of how this form or framing of family engagement can influence both student engagement and learning and teachers' classroom management practices. However, to reap the benefits of academic socialization, teacher must have significant social competence. This is the focus of the next section.

Defining Teacher Social Competence

Defining teacher social competence is important because if we want to improve teachers' readiness for the social demands of their work, then we must have a clear understanding of the outcomes we want to produce. As noted earlier, professional teaching standards offer general descriptions of critical professional social skills (e.g., "the teacher respects families' beliefs, norms and expectations;" "The teacher creates … instruction that takes into account individual learners' strengths, interests, and needs … that enables each learner to advance….," CCSSO, 2011). Educational and psychological research offer more tangible and nuanced definitions. For example, Zins and colleagues (2004) define teachers' social-emotional competence in terms of five emotional, cognitive, and behavioral competencies: self-awareness, social awareness, responsible decision-making, self-management, and relationship management (Zins et al., 2004). Taken as a whole, these five competencies represent (1) internally focused processes related to self-awareness and self-regulation, (2) externally focused skills such as awareness of social situations and others' mental states and emotions, and (3) integrative processes that translate self-focused and externally-focused information into real-time problem-solving decisions as social situations unfold.

Importantly, teacher social competence is associated not only with student success but also with teacher well-being. When teachers experience mastery over social and emotional challenges, they find teaching more enjoyable, and they feel more efficacious (Goddard et al., 2004). While teachers frequently experience intense social and emotional demands, they rarely receive support to address social and emotional issues in the classroom or other professional contexts (Sutton & Wheatley, 2003). Fortunately, efforts to address this gap are increasing. Particularly since the introduction of the Prosocial Classroom model, which highlights the importance of teacher's social-emotional competency and well-being (Jennings & Greenberg, 2009).

Understanding teacher social competence requires consideration of the quality of the social contexts in which their interpersonal relationships with students and families unfold. Communication between teachers and families is often 1:1, intermittent and reactive to sometimes challenging situations that involve student behavior, issues of power, equity, and high-stakes decisions about students' educational opportunities (Lightfoot, 2004). By contrast, teachers' relationships with students involve daily interactions in a group context involving conditions of complexity, immediacy, and simultaneity (Doyle, 1986). In a classroom, teachers are processing auditory and visual information from multiple sources at the same time, and they are expected to respond to this information quickly and appropriately. These features of the social context matter because they are precisely the conditions under which automatic social cognitive processes such as implicit bias are most likely to be activated and guide decision-making (Gawronski & Payne, 2011; Greenwald et al., 1998).

Cognitive science offers important guideposts for understanding both the social situations that teachers navigate and the nature of teachers' responses to these situations. For example, when we encounter other people, we form impressions of them based on our judgments of their behavior along two universal dimensions: warmth and competence (Fiske et al., 2007). Judgments of others' warmth are based on our perceptions of their intentions, including friendliness, helpfulness, sincerity, and trustworthiness. By contrast, judgments of their competence stem from our perceptions of their ability, including intelligence, skill, creativity, and efficacy. In general, judgments of warmth carry more weight than judgments of competence. That is, when we are deciding how to respond to someone, we consider questions of warmth such as, "does this person intend to harm or help me?" before we consider questions of competence such as, "Does this person have the ability to enact their helpful (or harmful) intentions?" Judgments of warmth and competence are important because of their behavioral consequences. Positive perceptions of warmth predict positive active behaviors such as helping whereas negative perceptions of warmth predict negative behaviors such as harm. Combinations of perceived warmth-competence dimensions can evoke a range of responses including pity (high warmth, low competence), contempt (low warmth, low competence) and admiration (high on both dimensions).

Another feature of social cognition is our innate tendency to quickly categorize others as "us versus them" (Mahajan & Wynn, 2012). These in-group and out-group judgments immediately and implicitly shape our behavior. For example, individuals tend to favor in-group members and disfavor out-group members (Balliet et al., 2014). In-group and out-group judgments also shape our responses to others' emotional expressions. If we perceive someone as an out-group member, we tend to be less aware of their emotional expressions (Richeson et al., 2007), which may also prompt discriminatory behavior via stereotyping and prejudice. Increasingly, neuroscience indicates that in-group and out-group judgments are part of our neural "hard wiring" and operate beneath our conscious control. For example, functional magnetic resonance imaging (fMRI) research found that social cognition about in-group and out-group members relates to distinctly different regions of the brain (Merritt et al., 2021).

Teachers and those who support their professional education need to be aware of these social cognition processes for two reasons: (1) it can help them to avoid forming potentially harmful biases based on brief and/or stressful interactions with students and families, and (2) it can help them to select behaviors that help students and families form favorable impressions of *them*, which can foster trust as the foundation for bridging home and school. Knowing more about these basic psychological processes can inform the specific kinds of social competencies that teachers need to acquire to form positive interpersonal relationships that support student success.

Teacher Social Competence in the Context of Classroom Management

Consistent with our tendency to appraise others on the dimensions of warmth and competence, the classroom management literature has long shown that effective managers balance two interrelated dimensions—warmth and demand (Kleinfeld, 1975; Ware, 2006). These two dimensions also align to developmental and psychological research that articulates warmth and demand as defining qualities of parenting style (Baumrind, 1991). In general, this research has noted that an authoritative style, marked by high levels of both warmth and demand, provides an optimal context for the development of student social and cognitive development (Walker, 2008; Wentzel, 2002). By contrast, authoritarian (high demand, low warmth) and permissive styles (low demand, moderate warmth) are associated with less adaptive patterns of development (Baumrind, 1991). The demand dimension involves behaviors that provide students with structure such as setting expectations, giving clear directions, and generally establishing order. Given its power to create time for learning, it makes sense that demand is positively associated with student learning and engagement (Emmer & Stough, 2001; Evertson & Weinstein, 2006). From the perspective of self-determination theory, teachers who provide structure help students understand what is required and offer guidance on how to achieve an expected outcome; these teacher characteristics, in turn, support learning because they foster students' sense of competence (Jang et al., 2010). Structure is often confused with control or the lack of student choice; however, in effectively managed classrooms, teacher structure and support for student autonomy are positively correlated. Both variables promote student engagement but in different ways (Jang et al., 2010; Walker, 2008).

As noted earlier, an important facet of teacher social competence is the capacity for self-regulation (Jennings & Greenberg, 2009; Sutton & Wheatley, 2003). Consistent with this idea, a meta-analysis of more than 100 studies of classroom management by Marzano, Marzano, and Pickering (2003) found that teachers' "mental set" had the largest effect on reductions in disruptive behavior. The construct of mental set, which is akin to metacognition and mindfulness, is central to effective classroom management because it involves "a heightened sense of situational awareness and a conscious control over one's thoughts and behavior relative to that situation" (Marzano et al., 2003, p. 65). By contrast, the absence of this situational and self-awareness implies a "mindlessness" or "automatic pilot" state where teachers operate with little conscious awareness. Mental set also includes emotional objectivity, which is valuable to teacher well-being. That is, rather than taking behaviors personally, effective classroom managers tend to address disciplinary issues in a straightforward and objective way. The quality of teachers' communication with students is a larger determining factor of positive classroom management than any particular management strategies teachers used (Zee & Koomen, 2016)

Finally, as Jennings and Greenberg (2009) defined it, "Socially and emotionally competent teachers ... develop supportive relationships with their students, design lessons that build on student strengths, establish, and implement behavioral guidelines that promote intrinsic motivation, ... encourage cooperation ... and act as a role model for respectful and appropriate communication." This relates back to the notion that skillful classroom managers are individuals who can integrate self-related processes with awareness of others/social situation in real time as social situations unfold. Efforts to help teachers to develop this complex set of competencies would do well to draw from psychological science's tradition of novice-expert comparisons and related evidence of what we have long known about how expert and novice managers view the classroom. Essentially, experts are more socially competent—they can recognize productive and unproductive patterns of student behavior and focus on prevention rather than reaction (Sabers et al., 1991; Stahnke & Blömeke, 2021). New tools offer new ways of understanding social competence. For example, neuroscience is able to demonstrate how expert and novice teachers differ in their ability to biologically attune to students' perspective during collaborative activities (Sun et al.,2020). Combining these new kinds of data with traditional methods such as self-reports on situational judgment tests (Aldrup et al., 2020) or hypothetical cases can illuminate the processes of self- and social awareness and inform the design of supports for teachers' professional education.

Teacher Social Competence in the Context of Family Engagement

As noted previously, family engagement often involves 1:1 interaction between adults who share a common interest in the education of a given child. Over the past decade, researchers have identified the hallmarks of effective and less effective teacher practices for family engagement in one social context, the parent-teacher conference. This is an important focal area for research given continued evidence that pre-service teachers often enter and exit their preparation programs with stereotypical views of people living in poverty, which are perceived by families and in turn, lead to "emotionally fraught" encounters (Hannon & O'Donnell, 2021).

For example, researchers have drawn from professional counseling standards. Gerich and Schmitz (2016) used four professional counseling criteria to assess pre-service teachers' family engagement competence: (1) *communication* (structuring the conversation), (2) *coping* (dealing with difficult situations), (3) *diagnostic* (defining the problem) and (4) *problem-solving* (searching for possible causes, taking cooperative actions). Mastery of these competencies was assessed with a Situational Judgment Test (SJT) or a set of short scenarios, commonly used in personnel training and selection to measure knowledge (e.g., what is the best way to respond to this situation?) and behavioral tendencies (e.g., which of the following actions would you be most likely to take?). Completing the SJT involved reading 13 parent-teacher conference scenarios and ranking a set of four possible responses from best to worst. Results indicated that these competencies were reliably measurable through observation and changed over time in relation to pre-service teachers' experiences with simulated parent-teacher conferences.

Drawing from the cognitive psychology literature of research on expertise, Walker and Dotger (2012) defined effective parent-teacher conference communication by asking a panel of experts in family engagement to identify the essential elements of a successful parent-teacher conference and by asking experts to explain how they would approach a range of conference scenarios. Content analysis revealed seven aspects of effective conference communication including a sequence of four strategies for initiating, developing and concluding any conference. The first aspect involves *opening* the conference by thanking parents for their time and clearly stating the conversation's goals for the student. The next two aspects focus on developing a dialogue by *sharing* and *gathering information*. Fourth, after exchanging information, the conversation closes with the establishment of a collaborative *action plan* that spells out the individual and shared responsibilities of the teacher, parent and student. Across this four-part sequence of socially competent behaviors, experts emphasized the importance of three underlying attitudes or dispositions: *empathy* or looking at the situation from the student and family perspective; *maintaining positive expectations* or focusing on the student's strengths, well-being and academic progress; and *managing flow*, which includes collaboration and ensuring that the conversation involves give-and-take.

Fundamental research that yields frameworks like these seven aspects are important because they articulate the dynamics of teacher-parent communication and the social competencies required for successful communication. Consistent with social cognition research which identified the universal dimensions of social cognition—warmth and competence (e.g., Fiske et al., 2007), subsequent survey research revealed that the seven aspects loaded on a two-factor structure of warmth and structure (DeConinck et al., 2020). Practically, such frameworks offer teachers a roadmap for developing specific social competencies as they navigate the unfamiliar terrain of family engagement.

Taken as a whole, the definitions and constructs involved in the research outlined immediately above are consistent with a recent meta-analysis of teacher training programs designed to enhance teachers' social competence for family engagement. This analysis showed that the training programs could influence teachers' family engagement knowledge, practices and attitudes and that three social competencies—communication strategies, collaborative planning, and problem solving—were consistently emphasized across the various training efforts (Smith & Sheridan, 2019).

Over the past decade, researchers have identified that productive parent-teacher conferences involve the key social competencies of two-way communication, perspective-taking, and shared action in the service of student success. Unfortunately, families report that these teacher competencies are often absent from their interactions with teachers. The gap between families' desire for teachers who know their child and listen to their concerns and the quality of their actual conference experiences with teachers is particularly true for families whose children have special needs (Spann et al., 2003; Zeitlin & Curcic, 2014). This dynamic is unfortunate because without family engagement, teachers' instructional and behavior management efforts may not realize their full potential. For example, Positive Behavior Intervention Supports (PBIS) and strategies for implementation encourage teacher mastery of strategies such as systematic data collection and analysis in the classroom; however, the PBIS framework also underscores the need for collaboration with multiple stakeholders including students' families to support behavioral expectations (Bethune, 2017). With increasing attention to a more inclusive educational environment, teachers and families need continued resources for the collaborative use of positive behavioral supports such as Positive Behavior Intervention Supports (PBIS), Functional Behavior Assessments (FBA), Behavior Intervention Plans (BIP) and the role of Response-to-Intervention in all classroom environments.

Promising Efforts to Support Teachers' Social Competence Family Engagement

Developing teachers' social competence in the service of their well-being and their effectiveness at both classroom management and family engagement requires opportunities to develop awareness and regulation of their own social, emotional, and relational capacities (Rodriguez et al., 2020). This section describes a sample of approaches that provide these opportunities. While some approaches involve new simulation technology and other digital tools, others are well within the reach of educator preparation programs without resources for the adoption of new technologies. Programs should select tools with awareness of their rewards and challenges. For instance, the long tradition of case-based instruction can provide benefits without technology (Merseth, 1991); however, technology can increase the reach of case-based pedagogy because well-designed cases offer opportunities to learn through vicarious reinforcement and structured observation (Walker & Marksbury, 2015). Digital multimedia environments are durable and can be scaled yet they require significant content development (Dede, 2006). Similarly, the emergent pedagogy of standardized simulations uses little technology but offer highly personalized learning experiences, which are resource intensive (Dotger et al., 2011).

Whether they involve technology or not, efforts to develop teachers' social competence should allow pre-service teachers early, repeated, and authentic opportunities to experience the social and emotional demands of the profession. These experiences should allow them to uncover implicit beliefs, and vicariously experience the consequences of their real-time decisions and behaviors without harm to themselves or others (Walker, 2019; Walker & Legg, 2018). A powerful three-part guiding structure for any experiential learning opportunity is: (1) eliciting prior knowledge, skills, and dispositions, (2) opportunities to observe or enact problem-solving strategies, and (3) revision and goal setting. Psychologically, this sequence is consistent with situated perspectives on learning, which argue that embedding professional knowledge in authentic social contexts facilitates understanding and task performance (Dewey, 2007; Ericsson, 2006).

Examples of technology-driven innovations in teacher education include tools such as mixed reality simulations (Dieker et al., 2014), multimedia online case studies (CAEP Family Engagement Mini-Course, 2021; Walker & Dotger, 2012;) and online coaching (Lang et al., 2020) as complements to traditional learning and professional development experiences. We illustrate how standardized, digital simulations can foster pre-service teachers' readiness for classroom management by describing how we designed a set of simulations that supported our students' understanding and use of the twin dimensions of warmth and competence (Pankowski & Walker, 2016).

Our series of classroom management simulation tasks immersed learners in two perennial classroom management challenges: motivating students to learn and dealing with non-compliance. To understand how simulation experiences fit the developmental needs of teachers on different preparation paths, we piloted them with graduate students enrolled in our institution's traditional and alternative certification programs. We found that initially, both groups defined classroom management primarily as teacher control of student behavior; however, their later definitions reflected an understanding that effective classroom management required a balance of warmth and control. Consistent with the idea that experiential learning fosters self-awareness, participants in the alternative certification group—who were serving as teachers of record while earning their degree—made significantly more references to the idea that classroom management involved teacher self-regulation. Finally, we learned how our students tended to approach different kinds of classroom management challenges. Both groups selected strategies aligned with the dimension of control or demand for addressing the non-compliance simulation; by contrast, they tended to choose tactics aligned with warmth to address the resistance to learning simulation.

Certainly, as new tools for teaching social competence and for understanding its physiological, psychological, and behavioral features emerge, teacher educators and professional development providers face challenges in incorporating these new methods appropriately and productively (Walker & Legg, 2018). Fruitful avenues of exploration include assessing pre-service teachers' perceptions of their simulation experiences as they relate to their learning and their field experiences (Kasperski & Crispel, 2021). Other emerging work seeks to develop machine learning and natural language processing tools that allow researchers and teacher educators to quickly make meaning from large data sets involving multiple forms of digital data (Sebastian & Datta, 2021).

Recalling the barrier or limited time for addressing social competence in traditional pre-service curricula, another promising line of work is integrating social competence training into existing traditional models of microteaching and rehearsal, which traditionally focus solely on teachers' content knowledge and pedagogical content knowledge (Howell et al., in press).

From a policy standpoint, roadmaps for progress exist but require commitment to implementation. In one of the most comprehensive summaries available to date, Weiss and colleagues offered five promising, high-leverage areas that can serve as "building blocks" for the next generation of family engagement strategies that have direct implications for classroom management. These five areas include reducing chronic absenteeism, data sharing about student and school climate indicators, the academic and social development of youth in and out of school, digital media, and the critical transition periods in children's learning pathways (Weiss et al., 2018). An example of concerted state-wide effort can be found in Kentucky's integrated, systemic, and sustainable Model of Transformational Family Engagement (Perry & Geller, 2021). Consistent with this chapter's focus on equity and social cognition, the model aims to fundamentally changes relationships between families and schools by interrupting deeply held beliefs about low-income, Black, Latinx, Indigenous, or immigrant families, each of which are rooted in systems of racism, classism, sexism, xenophobia, and their intersections.

Conclusion

This chapter asserts that effective classroom management depends on family engagement. To underscore the interdependent nature of classroom management and family engagement, we examined the knowledge, skills and dispositions that underlie teachers' abilities to build positive and productive relationships with both students and their families. Central to building interpersonal relationships in the service of student success is the construct of teachers' social competence. Drawing from social psychology, neuroscience and developmental and educational research, we defined teacher social competence in general, and how it manifests itself in the specific contexts of classroom management and family engagement. We also summarized challenges that pre- and in-service teachers face in developing their social competence and identified specific examples of contemporary efforts to its development. Our goal in writing this chapter was to underscore teachers' professional responsibility of functioning as a living bridge between children's social worlds of family and school. Until there is alignment between the content of teacher professional standards and teachers' opportunities to learn the social competencies needed for classroom management and family engagement, gaps in achievement and discipline will continue. This is why effective classroom management depends on teachers' family engagement skills.

References

Aldrup, K., Carstensen, B., Köller, M. M., & Klusmann, U. (2020). Measuring teachers' social-emotional competence: Development and validation of a situational judgment test. *Frontiers in Psychology, 11*, 892.

Amatea, E. S., Cholewa, B., & Mixon, K. A. (2012). Influencing pre-service teachers' attitudes about working with low-income and/or ethnic minority families. *Urban Education, 47*(4), 801–834.

Balliet, D., Wu, J., De Dreu C. K. W. (2014). In-group favoritism in cooperation: A meta-analysis. *Psychological Bulletin, 140*(6), 1556–1581.

Bakker, J., Denessen, E., & Brus-Laeven, M. (2007). Socio-economic background, parental involvement, and teacher perceptions of these in relation to pupil achievement. *Educational Studies, 33*(2), 177–192.

Barger, M. M., Kim, E. M., Kuncel, N. R., & Pomerantz, E. M. (2019). The relation between parents' involvement in children's schooling and children's adjustment: A meta-analysis. *Psychological Bulletin, 145*(9), 855.

Baumrind, D. (1991). The influence of parenting style on adolescent competence and substance use. *The Journal of Early Adolescence, 11*(1), 56–95.

Bereiter, C., & Scardamalia, M. (1985). Cognitive coping strategies and the problem of inert knowledge. *Thinking and Learning Skills, 2*, 65–80.

Bethune, K. S. (2017). Effects of coaching on teachers' implementation of tier 1 school-wide positive behavioral interventions and support strategies. *Journal of Positive Behavior Interventions, 19*(3), 131–142.

Bevilacqua, D., Davidesco, I., Wan, L., Chaloner, K., Rowland, J., Ding, M. ... Dikker, S. (2019). Brain-to-brain synchrony and learning outcomes vary by student–teacher dynamics: Evidence from a real-world classroom electroencephalography study. *Journal of Cognitive Neuroscience, 31*(3), 401–411.

Boonk, L., Gijselaers, H. J., Ritzen, H., & Brand-Gruwel, S. (2018). A review of the relationship between parental involvement indicators and academic achievement. *Educational Research Review, 24*, 10–30.

Bronfenbrenner, U. (1986). Ecology of the family as a context for human development: Research perspectives. *Developmental Psychology, 220*(6), 723–742.

Bryk, A. S., & Schneider, B. L. (2002). *Trust in schools: A core resource for improvement.* Russell Sage Foundation.

Buyse, E., Verschueren, K., & Doumen, S. (2011). Preschoolers' attachment to mother and risk for adjustment problems in kindergarten: Can teachers make a difference? *Social Development, 20*(1), 33–50.

CAEP Family Engagement Mini-Course (2021, August 2). Retrieved from www.caepnet.org/AboutFamilyEngagement

Council of Chief State School Officers (2011, April). *Interstate Teacher Assessment and Support Consortium (In TASC) Model Core Teaching Standards: A Resource for State Dialogue.* Author.

Christenson, S. L. (2004). The family-school partnership: An opportunity to promote the learning competence of all students. *School Psychology Review, 33*, 83–104

Christenson, S. L., & Reschly, A. L. (Eds.). (2010). *Handbook of family–school partnerships.* Routledge/Taylor & Francis.

Comer, J. P. (Ed.). (1996). *Rallying the whole village: The Comer process for reforming education.* Teachers College Press.

Cornelius-White, J. (2007). Learner-centered teacher-student relationships are effective: A meta-analysis. *Review of Educational Research, 77*(1), 113–143.

Cross, F. L., Marchand, A. D., Medina, M., Villafuerte, A., & Rivas-Drake, D. (2019). Academic socialization, parental educational expectations, and academic self-efficacy among Latino adolescents. *Psychology in the Schools, 56*(4), 483–496.

D'Haem, J., & Griswold, P. (2017). Teacher educators' and student teachers' beliefs about preparation for working with families including those from diverse socioeconomic and cultural backgrounds. *Education and Urban Society, 49*(1), 81–109.

Danielson, C. (2007). *Enhancing professional practice: A framework for teaching.* Association for Supervision and Curriculum Development.

Davidesco, I., Wan, L., Chaloner, K., Rowland, J., Ding, M., Poeppel, D., & Dikker, S. (2019). Brain-to-brain synchrony and learning outcomes vary by student–teacher dynamics: Evidence from a real-world classroom electroencephalography study. *Journal of Cognitive Neuroscience, 31*(3), 401–411.

Dearing, E., Kreider, H., Simpkins, S., & Weiss, H. B. (2006). Family involvement in school and low-income children's literacy: Longitudinal associations between and within families. *Journal of Educational Psychology, 98*(4), 653–664.

de Bruïne, E. J., Willemse, T. M., D'Haem, J., Griswold, P., Vloeberghs, L., & Van Eynde, S. (2014). Preparing teacher candidates for family–school partnerships. *European Journal of Teacher Education, 37*(4), 409–425.

De Coninck, K., Walker, J., Dotger, B., & Vanderlinde, R. (2020). Measuring student teachers' self-efficacy beliefs about family-teacher communication: Scale construction and validation. *Studies in Educational Evaluation, 64*, 100820.

Dede, C. (2006). *Online professional development for teachers: Emerging models and methods.* Harvard Education Press.

Dewey, J. (2007). *Experience and education.* Simon and Schuster.

Dieker, L. A., Rodriguez, J. A., Lignugaris/Kraft, B., Hynes, M. C., & Hughes, C. E. (2014). The potential of simulated environments in teacher education: Current and future possibilities. *Teacher Education and Special Education, 37*(1), 21–33.

Dotger, B. H., Harris, S., Maher, M., & Hansel, A. (2011). Exploring the emotional geographies of parent–teacher candidate interactions: An emerging signature pedagogy. *The Teacher Educator, 46*(3), 208–230.

Doyle, W. (1986). Classroom organization and management. In M. C. Wittrock (Ed.), *Handbook of Research on Teaching* (3rd ed., pp. 392–425). Macmillan.

Eberly, J. L., Rand, M. K., & O'Connor, T. (2007). Analyzing teachers' dispositions towards diversity: Using Adult Development Theory. *Multicultural Education, 14*(4), 31–36.

Elias, M. J., Zins, J. E., Weissberg, R. P., Frey, K. S., Greenberg, M. T., Haynes, N. M., ... Shriver, T. P. (1997). *Promoting social and emotional learning: Guidelines for educators.* ASCD.

Emmer, E. T., & Stough, L. M. (2001). Classroom management: A critical part of educational psychology, with implications for teacher education. *Educational Psychologist, 36*(2), 103–112.

Epstein, J. L. (2018). *School, family, and community partnerships: Preparing educators and improving schools.* Routledge.

Epstein, J. L., & Sanders, M. G. (2006). Connecting home, school, and community. In *Handbook of the Sociology of Education* (pp. 285–306). Springer US.

Ericsson, K. A. (2006). The influence of experience and deliberate practice on the development of superior expert performance. In K. A. Ericsson, N. Charness, P. J. Feltovich, & R. R. Hoffman (Eds.). *Cambridge Handbook of Expertise and Expert Performance* (pp. 683–703). Cambridge University Press.

Evertson, C. M, & Weinstein, C. S. (2006). *Handbook of classroom management: Research, practice, and contemporary issues.* Erlbaum.

Eyler, J. (2009). The power of experiential education. *Liberal Education, 95*(4), 24–31.

Fan, W., & Williams, C. M. (2010). The effects of parental involvement on students' academic self-efficacy, engagement and intrinsic motivation. *Educational Psychology, 30*(1), 53–74.

Fefer, S. A., Hieneman, M., Virga, C., Thoma, A., & Donnelly, M. (2020). Evaluating the effect of positive parent contact on elementary students' on-task behavior. *Journal of Positive Behavior Interventions, 22*(4), 234–245.

Fiske, S. T., Cuddy, A. J., & Glick, P. (2007). Universal dimensions of social cognition: Warmth and competence. *Trends in Cognitive Sciences, 11*(2), 77–83.

Flanigan, K. (2007). A concept of word in text: A pivotal event in early reading acquisition. *Journal of Literacy Research, 39*(1), 37–70.

Gawronski, B., & Payne, B. K. (Eds.). (2011). *Handbook of implicit social cognition: Measurement, theory, and applications.* Guilford Press.

Gerich, M., & Schmitz, B. (2016). Using simulated parent-teacher talks to assess and improve prospective teachers' counseling competence. *Journal of Education and Learning, 5*(2), 285–301.

Gilliam, W. S., Maupin, A. N., Reyes, C. R., Accavitti, M., & Shic, F. (2016). Do early educators' implicit biases regarding sex and race relate to behavior expectations and recommendations of preschool expulsions and suspensions. *Yale University Child Study Center, 9*(28), 1–16.

Goddard, R. D., Hoy, W. K., & Hoy, A. W. (2004). Collective efficacy beliefs: Theoretical developments, empirical evidence, and future directions. *Educational Researcher, 33*(3), 3–13.

Green, C. L., Walker, J. M. T., Hoover-Dempsey, K. V., & Sandler, H. M. (2007). Parents' motivations for involvement in children's education: An empirical test of a theoretical model of parental involvement. *Journal of Educational Psychology, 99*, 532–544.

Greenwald, A. G., McGhee, D. E., & Schwartz, J. L. K. (1998). Measuring individual differences in implicit cognition: The Implicit Association Test. *Journal of Personality and Social Psychology, 74*, 1464–1480

Gregory, A., Skiba, R. J., & Noguera, P. A. (2010). The achievement gap and the discipline gap: Two sides of the same coin? *Educational Researcher, 39*(1), 59–68.

Grolnick, W. S., Ryan, R. M., & Deci, E. L. (1991). Inner resources for school achievement: Motivational mediators of children's perceptions of their parents. *Journal of Educational Psychology, 83*(4), 508.

Grossman, P., Compton, C., Igra, D., Ronfeldt, M., Shahan, E., & Williamson, P. (2009). Teaching practice: A cross-professional perspective. *The Teachers College Record, 111*(9), 2055–2100.

Guo, Y. (2010). Meetings without dialogue: A study of ESL Parent-Teacher interactions at secondary school parents' nights. *School Community Journal, 20*, 121–141.

Hannon, L., & O'Donnell, G. M. (2021). Teachers, parents, and family-school partnerships: emotions, experiences, and advocacy. *Journal of Education for Teaching*, 1–15.

Harackiewicz, J. M., Rozek, C. S., Hulleman, C. S., & Hyde, J. S. (2012). Helping parents to motivate adolescents in mathematics and science: An experimental test of a utility-value intervention. *Psychological Science, 23*(8), 899–906.

Henderson, A. T., Mapp, K. L., Johnson, V. R., & Davies, D. (2007). *Beyond the bake sale: The essential guide to family—school partnerships*. The New Press.

Hill, N. E. (2001). Parenting and academic socialization as they relate to school readiness: The roles of ethnicity and family income. *Journal of Educational Psychology, 93*(4), 686.

Hill, N. E., & Torres, K. (2010). Negotiating the American dream: The paradox of aspirations and achievement among Latino students and engagement between their families and schools. *Journal of Social Issues, 66*(1), 95–112.

Hill, N. E., & Tyson, D. F. (2009). Parental involvement in middle school: a meta-analytic assessment of the strategies that promote achievement. *Developmental Psychology, 45*(3), 740.

Hoover-Dempsey, K. V., & Sandler, H. M. (1995). Parental involvement in children's education: Why does it make a difference? *Teachers College Record, 95*, 310–342.

Hoover-Dempsey, K. V., & Sandler, H. M. (1997). Why do parents become involved in their children's education? *Review of Educational Research, 67*(1), 3–42.

Hoover-Dempsey, K. V., Walker, J. M. T., Jones, K. P., & Reed, R. P. (2002). Teachers Involving Parents (TIP): An in-service teacher education program for enhancing parental involvement. *Teaching and Teacher Education, 18*, 843–867.

Hoover-Dempsey, K. V., Walker, J. M. T., Sandler, H. M., Whetsel, D., Green, C. L., Wilkins, A. S., & Closson, K. (2005). Why do parents become involved? Research findings and implications. *The Elementary School Journal, 106*(2), 105–130.

Howell, H., Francis, D. C., Bharaj, P. K., & Shekell, C. (in press). *Pre-service teacher learning to facilitate argumentation via simulation: exploring the role of understanding and emotion.*

Hughes, J., & Kwok, O. M. (2007). Influence of student–teacher and parent–teacher relationships on lower achieving readers' engagement and achievement in the primary grades. *Journal of Educational Psychology, 99*(1), 39–51.

Hughes, J. N., Wu, J. Y., Kwok, O. M., Villarreal, V., & Johnson, A. Y. (2012). Indirect effects of child reports of teacher–student relationship on achievement. *Journal of Educational Psychology, 104*(2), 350.

İnan-Kaya, G., & Rubie-Davies, C. M. (2021). Teacher classroom interactions and behaviours: Indications of bias. *Learning and Instruction*, 101516.

Jang, H., Reeve, J., & Deci, E. L. (2010). Engaging students in learning activities: It is not autonomy support or structure but autonomy support and structure. *Journal of Educational Psychology, 102*(3), 588.

Jennings, P. A., & Greenberg, M. T. (2009). The prosocial classroom: Teacher social and emotional competence in relation to student and classroom outcomes. *Review of Educational Research, 79*(1), 491–525.

Jeynes, W. H. (2007). Urban secondary school student academic achievement. *Urban Education, 42*(1), 82–110.

Jeynes, W. (2010). The salience of the subtle aspects of parental involvement and encouraging that involvement: Implications for school-based programs. *Teachers College Record, 112*(3), 747–774.

Jeynes, W. (2012). A meta-analysis of the efficacy of different types of parental involvement programs for urban students. *Urban Education, 47*(4), 706–742.

Jeynes, W. H. (2016). A meta-analysis: The relationship between parental involvement and African American school outcomes. *Journal of Black Studies, 47*(3), 195–216.

Kasperski, R., & Crispel, O. (2021). Preservice teachers' perspectives on the contribution of simulation-based learning to the development of communication skills. *Journal of Education for Teaching*, 1–14. https://doi.org/10.1080/02607476.2021.2002121

Kirmaci, M. (2019). Reporting Educators' Experiences Regarding Family-School Interactions with Implications for Best Practices. *School Community Journal, 29*(2), 129–156.

Kleinfeld, J. (1975). Effective teachers of Eskimo and Indian students. *The School Review*, *83*(2), 301–344.

Makoul, G. (2003). Communication skills education in medical school and beyond. *JAMA*, *289*(1), 93–93.

Lang, S. N., Jeon, L., Sproat, E. B., Brothers, B. E., & Buettner, C. K. (2020). Social emotional learning for teachers (SELF-T): A short-term, online intervention to increase early childhood educators' resilience. *Early Education and Development*, *31*(7), 1112–1132.

Leonardo, Z., & Grubb, W. N. (2018). *Education and racism: A primer on issues and dilemmas*. Routledge.

Li, L. W., Ochoa, W., McWayne, C. M., Priebe Rocha, L., & Hyun, S. (2021). "Talk to me": Parent–teacher background similarity, communication quality, and barriers to school-based engagement among ethnoculturally diverse Head Start families. *Cultural Diversity and Ethnic Minority Psychology*. https://doi.org/10.1037/cdp0000497

Lightfoot, S. L. (2004). *The essential conversation: What parents and teachers can learn from each other*. Ballantine Books.

Mahajan N., & Wynn, K. (2012). Origins of "us" versus "them": prelinguistic infants prefer similar others. *Cognition*, *124*(2), 227–33.

Mantzicopoulos, P. (2005). Conflictual relationships between kindergarten children and their teachers: Associations with child and classroom context variables. *Journal of School Psychology*, *43*(5), 425–442.

Martin, A. J., & Collie, R. J. (2019). Teacher–student relationships and students' engagement in high school: Does the number of negative and positive relationships with teachers matter? *Journal of Educational Psychology*, *111*(5), 861.

Martin, J. E., Van Dycke, J. L., Greene, B. A., Gardner, J. E., Christensen, W. R., Woods, L. L., & Lovett, D. L. (2006). Direct observation of teacher-directed IEP meetings: Establishing the need for student IEP meeting instruction. *Exceptional Children*, *72*(2), 187–200.

Marcucci, O. (2020). Parental involvement and the Black–White discipline gap: The role of parental social and cultural capital in American schools. *Education and Urban Society*, *52*(1), 143–168.

Marzano, R. J., Marzano, J. S., & Pickering, D. (2003). *Classroom management that works: Research-based strategies for every teacher*. ASCD.

Merritt, C., MacCormack, J., Stein, A. G., Lindquist, K., & Muscatell, K. (2021). The neural underpinnings of intergroup social cognition: an fMRI meta-analysis. https://doi.org/10.31234/osf.io/9rcj7

Merseth, K. K. (1991). *The Case for Cases in Teacher Education*. AACTE Publications.

National Academies of Sciences, Engineering, and Medicine (2017). *Supporting students' college success: The role of assessment of intrapersonal and interpersonal competencies*. National Academies Press.

O'Connor, E. E., Collins, B. A., & Supplee, L. (2012). Behavior problems in late childhood: The roles of early maternal attachment and teacher–child relationship trajectories. *Attachment & Human Development*, *14*(3), 265–288.

Ogg, J., Clark, K., Strissel, D., & Rogers, M. (2021). Parents' and teachers' ratings of family engagement: Congruence and prediction of outcomes. *School Psychology*, *36*(3), 142.

Pan, Y., Dikker, S., Goldstein, P., Zhu, Y., Yang, C., & Hu, Y. (2020). Instructor-learner brain coupling discriminates between instructional approaches and predicts learning. *NeuroImage*, *211*, 116657.

Pankowski, J., & Walker, J. T. (2016). Using simulation to support novice teachers' classroom management skills: Comparing traditional and alternative certification groups. Journal of the National Association for Alternative Certification, *11*(1), 3–20.

Perry, D. M., & Geller, J. (2021). Toward an Integrated, Systemic, and Sustainable Model of Transformational Family Engagement: The Case of the Kentucky Statewide Family Engagement Center. *Social Sciences*, *10*(10), 402.

Plant, E. A., & Devine, P. G. (2009). The active control of prejudice: Unpacking the intentions guiding control efforts. *Journal of Personality and Social Psychology*, *96*(3), 640–52.

Pomerantz, E. M., Moorman, E. A., & Litwack, S. D. (2007). The how, whom, and why of parents' involvement in children's academic lives: More is not always better. *Review of Educational Research*, *77*(3), 373–410.

Richeson J., Dovidio J. F., Shelton J. N., & Hebl M. (2007). Implications of in-group-out-group membership for interpersonal perceptions: faces and emotion. In U. Hess & P. Philippot, (Eds.), *Group Dynamics and Emotional Expression* (pp. 7–32). Cambridge University Press.

Rodriguez, V., Lynneth Solis, S., Mascio, B., Kiely Gouley, K., Jennings, P. A., & Brotman, L. M. (2020). With awareness comes competency: The five awarenesses of teaching as a framework for understanding teacher social-emotional competency and well-being. *Early Education and Development*, *31*(7), 940–972.

Roorda, D. L., Koomen, H. M., Spilt, J. L., & Oort, F. J. (2011). The influence of affective teacher–student relationships on students' school engagement and achievement: A meta-analytic approach. *Review of Educational Research*, *81*(4), 493–529.

Roorda, D. L., Jak, S., Zee, M., Oort, F. J., & Koomen, H. M. (2017). Affective teacher–student relationships and students' engagement and achievement: A meta-analytic update and test of the mediating role of engagement. *School Psychology Review*, *46*(3), 239–261.

Sabers, D. S., Cushing, K. S., & Berliner, D. C. (1991). Differences among teachers in a task characterized by simultaneity, multidimensional, and immediacy. *American Educational Research Journal, 28*(1), 63–88.

Saxe, R. (2006). Uniquely human social cognition. *Current opinion in neurobiology, 16*(2), 235–239.

Sheridan, S. M., Smith, T. E., Moorman Kim, E., Beretvas, S. N., & Park, S. (2019). A meta-analysis of family-school interventions and children's social-emotional functioning: Moderators and components of efficacy. *Review of Educational Research, 89*(2), 296–332.

Sebastian, R. & Datta, D. (2021). Scaling Teacher Candidates' Family Engagement Training Through Simulations and Artificial Intelligence. In E. de Vries, Y. Hod, & J. Ahn (Eds.), Proceedings of the 15th International Conference of the Learning Sciences—ICLS 2021. (pp. 903–904). Bochum, Germany: International Society of the Learning Sciences.

Simson, D. (2013). Exclusion, punishment, racism, and our schools: A critical race theory perspective on school discipline. *UCLA Law Review, 61*, 506.

Smith, T. E., & Sheridan, S. M. (2019). The effects of teacher training on teachers' family-engagement practices, attitudes, and knowledge: A meta-analysis. *Journal of Educational and Psychological Consultation, 29*(2), 128–157.

Smith, T. E., Reinke, W. M., Herman, K. C., & Huang, F. (2019). Understanding family–school engagement across and within elementary- and middle-school contexts. *School Psychology, 34*(4), 363–375.

Spann, S. J., Kohler, F. W., & Soenksen, D. (2003). Examining parents' involvement in and perceptions of special education services: An interview with families in a parent support group. *Focus on Autism and Other Developmental Disabilities, 18*(4), 228–237.

Stahnke, R., & Blömeke, S. (2021). Novice and expert teachers' situation-specific skills regarding classroom management: What do they perceive, interpret and suggest? *Teaching and Teacher Education, 98*, 103243.

Stough, L. M., Montague, M. L., Landmark, L. J., & Williams-Diehm, K. (2015). Persistent Classroom Management Training Needs of Experienced Teachers. *Journal of the Scholarship of Teaching and Learning, 15*(5), 36–48.

Sun, B., Xiao, W., Feng, X., Shao, Y., Zhang, W., & Li, W. (2020). Behavioral and brain synchronization differences between expert and novice teachers when collaborating with students. *Brain and Cognition, 139*, 105513.

Sutton, R. E., & Wheatley, K. F. (2003). Teachers' emotions and teaching: A review of the literature and directions for future research. *Educational Psychology Review, 15*(4), 327–358.

Tan, C. Y., Lyu, M., & Peng, B. (2020). Academic benefits from parental involvement are stratified by parental socioeconomic status: A meta-analysis. *Parenting, 20*(4), 241–287.

Thijs, J., & Eilbracht, L. (2012). Teachers' perceptions of parent–teacher alliance and student–teacher relational conflict: Examining the role of ethnic differences and "disruptive" behavior. *Psychology in the Schools, 49*(8), 794–808.

Walker, J. M. T. (2008). Looking at teacher practices through the lens of parenting style: Three case studies at entry to middle school. *Journal of Experimental Education, 76*, 218–240.

Walker, J. M. T. (2009). Authoritative classroom management: How control and nurturance work together. *Theory into Practice, 48*(2), 122–129.

Walker, J. M., & Dotger, B. H. (2012). Because wisdom can't be told: using comparison of simulated parent–teacher conferences to assess teacher candidates' readiness for family-school partnership. *Journal of Teacher Education, 63*(1), 62–75.

Walker, J. M. (2019). Recognizing Family Engagement as a Core Practice: Using Situated Pedagogies to Advance Candidates' Readiness to Invite Families. *The Wiley Handbook of Family, School, and Community Relationships in Education*, 623–646.

Walker, J. M. T., & Hoover-Dempsey, K. V. (2006). Why research on parental involvement is important to classroom management. In C. Evertson & C. Weinstein (Eds.), *The Handbook of Classroom Management* (pp. 665–684). Erlbaum.

Walker, J. M., & Hoover-Dempsey, K. V. (2014). Parental Engagement and Classroom Management: Unlocking the Potential of Family–School Interactions and Relationships. In *The Handbook of Classroom Management* (pp. 469–488). Routledge.

Walker, J. M., & Legg, A. M. (2018). Parent-teacher conference communication: A guide to integrating family engagement through simulated conversations about student academic progress. *Journal of Education for Teaching, 44*(3), 366–380.

Walker, J. M. T., & Marksbury, N. (2015). Can a case-based, online learning environment prompt positive change in pre-service teachers' knowledge and dispositions for parent-teacher communication?. Paper presented as part of the symposium, *Performance-based strategies to train and assess teacher-parent conversation competencies.* Annual Meeting of the American Educational Research Association, Chicago, IL.

Ware, F. (2006). Warm demander pedagogy: Culturally responsive teaching that supports a culture of achievement for African American students. *Urban Education, 41*(4), 427–456.

Weiss, H. B., Lopez, M. E., & Caspe, M. (2018). Joining Together to Create a Bold Vision for Next Generation Family Engagement: Engaging Families to Transform Education. *Global Family Research Project.*

Wentzel, K. R. (2002). Are effective teachers like good parents? Teaching styles and student adjustment in early adolescence. *Child Development, 73*(1), 287–301.

Wilder, S. (2013). Effects of parental involvement on academic achievement: A meta-synthesis. *Educational Review* (377–397), 1–21.

Wun, C. (2016). Unaccounted foundations: Black girls, anti-Black racism, and punishment in schools. Critical Sociology, *42*(4–5), 737–750.

Wyrick, A. J., & Rudasill, K. M. (2009). Parent involvement as a predictor of teacher–child relationship quality in third grade. *Early Education and Development, 20*(5), 845–864.

Zee, M., & Koomen, H. M. (2016). Teacher self-efficacy and its effects on classroom processes, student academic adjustment, and teacher well-being: A synthesis of 40 years of research. *Review of Educational Research, 86*(4), 981–1015.

Zeitlin, V. M., & Curcic, S. (2014). Parental voices on individualized education programs: 'Oh, IEP meeting tomorrow? Rum tonight!' *Disability & Society, 29*(3), 373–387.

Zheng, L., Liu, W., Long, Y., Zhai, Y., Zhao, H., Bai, X., Zhou, S., Li, K., Zhang, H., Liu, L., & Lu, C. (2020). Affiliative bonding between teachers and students through interpersonal synchronisation in brain activity. *Social Cognitive and Affective Neuroscience, 15*(1), 97–109

Zins, J. E., Weissberg, R. P., Wang, M. C., & Walberg, H. J. (2004). The scientific base linking social and emotional learning to school success. *Boys in Schools Bulletin, 7*(2), 34–43.

14

TEACHER TRAINING AND CLASSROOM MANAGEMENT

Marcia L. Montague and Andrew Kwok

TEXAS A&M UNIVERSITY

Introduction

Training and supporting teachers in classroom management is vital towards making this pedagogical skill come to fruition. As a practical skillset that has a solid base of empirical work to support why and how it should be enacted, it is pertinent for teachers to learn and develop these skills towards implementation (Brophy, 1988; Doyle, 1985; Emmer & Stough, 2001; Myers et al., 2017). Unfortunately, there have been consistent shortcomings, either in teacher preparation or throughout professional development, that have prevented integration and mastery of this skill (Simonsen et al., 2014). This knowledge-practice gap must be reduced for classroom management to have the impact it is stated to have (e.g., Korpershoek et al., 2016). In fact, continued research identifies how despite the importance of classroom management, it has yet to be fully embraced as a central training structure.

This chapter builds upon the previous editions' handbook chapters about classroom management support by examining current research in contemporary contexts. We identify whether there remains a need for classroom management training and then separately investigate different but related structures: pre-service teacher preparation and in-service professional development. We highlight prominent literature in these areas and offer new directions for this research. We conclude with several special considerations concerning classroom management training, specifically about the impetus for training in culturally responsive classroom management, inclusive classroom management, and Universal Design for Learning.

The Need for Classroom Management Training

Much research has found that teacher implementation of evidence-based classroom management strategies, such as providing clear expectations, behavior-specific praise, and numerous opportunities for response, results in positive outcomes for students (Office of Special Education Programs, 2015). In a meta-analysis of 54 classroom management interventions from 2003 to 2013, Korpershoek et al. (2016) found that many of these interventions positively affect student social-emotional and academic outcomes. Further, Gage et al. (2017) used latent class analysis and modeling of predictive relationships and found that teachers who implemented high rates of classroom management practices resulted in increased rates of student engagement during instruction.

Although this positive relationship exists, teachers often still struggle to successfully manage their classrooms (Gage & MacSuga-Gage, 2017). Over several decades, teachers have consistently reported that classroom management is a key concern (Dicke et al., 2014; Kee, 2011; Meister & Melnick, 2003; Veenman, 1984). Research has further documented disruptive student behavior as a primary reason for teacher attrition from a school campus or the teaching profession altogether (Ingersoll & May, 2012; Ramos & Hughes, 2020). Conversely, quality classroom management has been shown to decrease disruptive behavior as expected (Oliver et al., 2011; Sinclair et al., 2021).

Updated training in classroom management for both pre-service and in-service teachers is essential for their success in contemporary classrooms. When teacher skills are improved in classroom management, positive outcomes for students should follow. As education aims to support successful student outcomes, the need to provide high-quality teacher training in classroom management is indisputable. Training must be provided in management strategies that are responsive and based on current best practices and theory (Ficarra & Quinn, 2014). Two recent examples indicate how research in classroom management training has moved beyond standalone workshops of a particular strategy and now more often seeks to evaluate the impact of providing ongoing teacher training. Baker et al. (2016) provided a one-day professional development training to novice teachers, followed by 8 weeks of online support via discussion boards. Through this forum, teachers could support one another with suggestions for addressing classroom management challenges. In another approach to online educator training in classroom management, Pankowski and Walker (2016) provided pre-service and alternative certification teachers with the opportunity to practice their classroom management skills in a virtual simulation. Study participants were recorded during the simulations and provided the opportunity to review the video to engage in self-analysis and self-evaluation as reflective practice. These studies provide some evidence of how researchers are adapting traditional pre-service and in-service classroom management training to meet the needs of contemporary teachers.

Thus, we focus first on pre-service teacher preparation. We start here as the initial training experience for many who want to enter the profession. We explore how teacher preparation has changed within the past decade as well as outline potential avenues towards systematically and practically improving programs.

Pre-service Teacher Preparation

Pre-service preparation is a formative start for all teachers to learn about the profession. They are trained in various pedagogical and professional skills, but unfortunately, there is vast variation in the quality of classroom management preparation. Below, we outline issues specific to classroom management training, identify dedicated areas of current research, and highlight a framework to guide teacher preparation.

Issues within Classroom Management Preparation

Teachers often share how they feel unprepared prior to full-time teaching because of insufficient preparation (Atici, 2007; Kwok & Svjada-Hardy, 2021). Beginning teachers, in particular, continue to express concern with or hold limited beliefs in classroom management, both from pre-service teacher (PST) perspectives (Akdag & Haser, 2016) as well as in-service teachers reflecting on their preparation (Headden, 2014; Kwok & Hardy, 2019). PSTs are overwhelmingly focused on behavioral issues rather than more beneficial aspects such as relationships and student culture (Kwok, 2017, 2020; Kwok et al., 2020). This limited focus restricts their attention towards more effective strategies that they could otherwise implement. Moreover, much of these beliefs could stem from misinformed advice they hear about classroom management prior to preparation (Kwok, 2018). This includes taking guidance from family members or making assumptions about their time within the classroom, both which generally lead to a more behavioral conception of classroom management.

This understanding is ultimately concerning because of continually expanding teacher-related outcomes that are associated with classroom management. Beginning teachers tend to have lower management self-efficacy and a limited skill set that leads to emotional exhaustion, burnout, and reduced well-being (Aldrup et al., 2018; Dicke et al., 2015; Reinke et al., 2013). Therefore, these deficiencies point to teacher preparation as a logical avenue towards systematically improving the training of effective classroom management. Teacher education is often PSTs' first opportunity to learn about classroom management, and as a result, these programs should proactively seek to empirically develop future teachers.

Notably, classroom management courses are inconsistently offered in teacher education programs, leaving gaps in PSTs' understanding of effective classroom management based on the program they attend. Despite the apparent demand and need for quality training in classroom management, teacher preparation programs often fail to adequately address this needed skill set (Mitchell et al., 2017; Stevenson et al., 2020). For example, in a review of 31 teacher preparation programs in New York City, Hammerness (2011) found that only 45% offered any explicit classroom management training within their syllabi. Compounding this, many teachers do not complete a traditional teacher preparation program and do not receive equivalent training in classroom management knowledge and skill. Across the U.S., teachers trained via alternative certification programs leave the profession more often than their traditionally prepared counterparts (Carver-Thomas & Darling-Hammond, 2017).

Furthermore, previous handbook chapters (Jones, 2006; Stough, 2006; Stough & Montague, 2015), U.S. studies (Hammerness, 2011; Oliver & Reschly, 2010), and international studies (Ben-Peretz et al., 2011; O'Neil & Stephenson, 2012) consistently identify teacher preparation as deficient in the amount of coursework, time allotment, and requirements related to classroom management. For instance, the National Council of Teacher Quality conducted two audits of a sampling of U.S. university syllabi. In 2014, they analyzed 122 teacher education programs and found that nearly all programs mentioned classroom management, though the total time devoted to this skill roughly averaged to 40% of one course (Greenberg et al., 2014). Some of this content may have been integrated into other courses, but regardless, many programs largely fail to give classroom management much, if any, substantive attention. In 2020, the overall number of programs continued to struggle to instruct on this skill, but promisingly, 26% of universities have since integrated empirical classroom management practices into their curriculum (Pomerance & Walsh, 2020). This finding indicates that teacher preparation can evolve towards PST classroom management development.

Such absence of empirically focused management training could be attributed to U.S. states having few requirements addressing this skill set. Several studies have examined the prevalence of classroom management within state standards. While nearly every U.S. state has a policy referencing classroom management, only a few require alignment between classroom management and research-based information (Freeman et al., 2014; Gilmour et al., 2019; Greenberg et al., 2014; Pomerance & Walsh, 2020; Stough, 2006). Without this connection, there is little direction from policy towards incentivizing growth. Even in comparing alternative certification programs and traditional teacher education programs, there is a considerable variation in classroom management content. For instance, Flower et al. (2017) identified that most programs consistently teach about universal skills (i.e., classroom structures), but few teach specific skills of dealing with individual students, how to increase appropriate student behavior, or how to conduct behavioral assessments. This finding suggests the superficial nature of PSTs' preparation for classroom management and highlights the lack of policy supporting effective management training. This deficiency is also illustrated internationally. Woodcock and Reupert (2017) identified that PSTs across Australia, Canada, and the United Kingdom (UK) had significant differences in their use, confidence, and success of classroom management strategies. Specifically, UK PSTs had significantly more strategies to promote positive student behavior than the PSTs in the other countries, indicating potential teacher preparation differences. However, these differences could not necessarily be accounted for by program, which emphasizes how and what individual programs teach is innately important.

Recent Developments in Classroom Management Preparation

There is hope for programmatic change, as evidence indicates positive effects of classroom management preparation when available (Greenberg et al., 2014). For instance, Kwok (2020) surveyed PSTs as they matriculated through their program and found that they became less focused on behavior in their understanding of classroom management throughout teacher education. In another preparation program, Kwok et al. (2020) similarly identified that PSTs wrote more robust responses about how classroom management could adapt towards student diversity and focused more on the implementation of actions at the completion of the program compared to the start of the program. This reiterates previous evidence about the effect of teacher education on classroom management development (e.g., Jones & Vesilind, 1995) and continues to stress that programs need to be intentional with their training. This could include providing PSTs with opportunities to reflect on previous and implemented actions, teaching alternative strategies, providing a space to enact strategies, and fostering a collaborative learning environment (Girardet, 2018). Recently, studies have homed in on two areas of research to inform preparation programs.

First, contemporary evidence identifies or reiterates evidence-based classroom management techniques that should be taught in teacher preparation. For instance, praise is not consistently taught throughout programs (Pomerance & Walsh, 2020), even though it has been increasingly identified as an important skill (Floress et al., 2021; Gage et al., 2020; Markelz et al., 2017). Floress et al. (2017) reviewed the empirical research about teacher training of praise and stressed that most studies had positive results. Another important skill is teaching how to build relationships in the classroom (e.g., Wubbels et al., 2016), such as through positive greetings at the door (Cook et al., 2018). Most definitively, Kincade et al. (2020) conducted a meta-analysis on empirical teacher-student relationship studies and identified 44 practices that PSTs can learn to apply. The authors created a framework around categories of direct/indirect and proactive/teaching/consequent types of actions to guide researchers towards a consistent theory of action as well as practitioners in thinking about the multiple modes of implementation. This robust study should be foundational for training PSTs about the specific nuances required to facilitate all types of classroom interactions. A third skill is noticing or professional vision. Weber et al. (2018) identified the value of receiving expert feedback (compared to reflection or feedback from peers) in improving the ability to notice what is happening in the classroom through video-based self-reflection. Other studies relatedly compared PSTs' ability to notice against experienced teachers (Prilop et al., 2021; van Driel et al., 2021; Wolff et al., 2021) to develop this proactive strategy that recognizes potential misbehaviors and responds accordingly.

Second, an increasing area of study about classroom management preparation is the value of virtual simulations. Technological advances include software to allow PSTs to reflect or even interact with digital classrooms to develop skills (McGarr, 2020). Larson, Hirsch et al. (2020) measured PST confidence using a mixed-reality simulator to supplement guided practice opportunities. The authors found that this could be a potentially positive learning mode if adjustments were made to reduce stress and performance anxiety. More promisingly, Cohen et al. (2020), who conducted a pseudo-experimental study utilizing coaching within a simulated environment, best exemplified this. According to expert raters, practice sessions throughout teacher education led to a significant and considerable improvement in skills and faster pedagogical development in both skills and perceptions of addressing student behavior. Programs could consider integrating this type of technological tool to provide PSTs with practice implementing classroom management in a controlled environment.

Classroom Management Framework for Teacher Educators

To provide a more practical guide for classroom management preparation, Kwok (2021) proposed an overarching framework to aid programs. The Classroom Management Practice Relationships

Partnership (CM PReP) framework is derived from Jones (1989, 1996, 2006) and much of the afore-mentioned evidence in this field. Instead of focusing on individual teacher preparation strategies listed above, the author proposes five learning objectives for holistic curricular redesign of classroom management in teacher education:

1. **Culture:** Understanding how students' personal and cultural needs dictate how a classroom is managed
2. **Methods:** Implementing effective instructional methods to develop pre-service teachers in classroom management
3. **Practice:** Identifying practical strategies for pre-service teachers to create a safe, supportive classroom environment
4. **Relationships:** Creating positive teacher-student, student-student, and teacher-parent relationships
5. **Partnership:** Learning about and practicing how to respond to student misbehavior while in an authentic classroom environment

The Classroom Management Practice Relationships Partnership (CM PReP) explicitly guides teacher educators towards either implementing programmatic change from scratch or editing pre-existing courses. Each learning objective provides directions for the content of instruction, the type of instruction, or the context to enhance instruction with aims to develop effective managers for contemporary classrooms. While there is recognition that change within teacher education can be challenging, any minimal effort in this direction will undoubtedly be positive. And this framework is not intended to be a panacea, but rather a guide towards a semblance of guided and meaningful change. For PSTs to be sufficiently prepared in this vital skill, teacher education needs to prioritize such changes comparable to how many alternative certification programs have chosen to do so, though with varied success (Pomerance & Greenberg, 2020).

With such guidance, there remain areas for growth in researching classroom management training. Several studies identified an absence of a classroom management observation instrument, directly impacting how this skill is ultimately implemented (Gilmour et al., 2019; Pomerance & Walsh, 2020). This deficiency could be mitigated by the Classroom Management Observation Tool (CMOT; Simonsen, Freeman, Kooken, et al., 2020), which, through initial validation, provides a simple and efficient instrument evaluating vital components of classroom management. CMOT could pioneer more observation-based outcomes and a consistent framework towards understanding PST actions and corresponding development.

Another area for growth would be to explore innovative methods for classroom management training alongside objective measures of PST growth. Such methods could include additional technological enhancements (Cohen et al., 2020) or providing intentional clinical teaching support (e.g., Weber et al., 2018). While not necessarily innovative, another is also a necessity to examine classroom management textbooks or recent adoptions of textbooks that utilize empirical evidence (Evertson et al., 2021; Milner et al., 2018). Anecdotally, many programs still rely on outdated or theoretical textbooks, and so identifying the prevalence or change within a program after adopting a textbook could prompt policy improvements. However, this could only occur after documenting how previously barren programs integrate, troubleshoot, and improve much-needed classroom management curriculum. Program case studies could illuminate how programs navigate administrative and higher education structures, the trajectory of college student learning, and the integration of authentic practices.

Finally, objective growth measures are needed to identify whether programs (either integrating foundational curricula or innovative methods) indeed are producing more effective teachers, or more simply, whether an increase in available preparation learning yields positive PST development. Throughout the majority of studies about classroom management, particularly within preservice teacher learning, there were few notable outcomes that would be broadly accepted. While the field of teacher education largely struggles with iterating outcomes, classroom management is no different. But there could be some proactive opportunities to integrate how (a change in) classroom management curriculum is associated with proxies of (pre-service) teacher effectiveness, beliefs, or possibly even labor market outcomes. Classroom management research needs more precision in relating this pedagogical skill with meaningful outcomes to better inform necessary policy implications and programmatic change.

In-Service Teacher Professional Development

Professional development for in-service teachers supports ongoing professional growth, knowledge and skill development and refinement, and attitude or belief changes (Darling-Hammond et al., 2017; Desimone, 2009). Most educators have a continued need for classroom management training, in particular. Below, we describe the need for such training, review key components of quality professional development, and highlight several specific evidence-based professional development training practices.

Need for Ongoing Training

Beyond teacher preparation for certification, research has shown that teachers continue to need sustained professional development in classroom management (Stough et al., 2015). Student behavior remains a common concern for in-service teachers (Clunies-Ross et al., 2008). Additionally, we know that in-service teachers continue to learn and develop throughout their careers; that is, when teachers are practicing their craft, they can and do continue to hone their management skills. Teachers have reported that in-service (as opposed to pre-service) experiences are the primary source of their learning of evidence-based practices in classroom management (Ficarra & Quinn, 2014). Moreover, throughout their careers, professional development is the primary means by which teachers continue to improve their skills (Wilkinson et al., 2020).

Teachers' ongoing professional development needs often surface due to their beliefs about management. For example, narratives that teachers use (i.e., attachment, attribution, or efficacy) during classroom management situations may position the teacher as arrogant or submissive, powerful or weak (Romi et al., 2016). That is, teachers who adopt an attachment lens may interpret student misbehavior as rejection; teachers who adopt an attribution perspective may externalize blame and see students as troublemakers; and teachers who employ an efficacy narrative may see teacher aggression as an efficient reaction to student misbehavior. Professional development training that closely addresses the teachers' needs based on their beliefs about management is warranted. For example, professional development that focuses on relationship building may benefit teachers who have adopted an attachment narrative, whereas a focus on skill development would most closely meet the needs of teachers with an efficacy narrative, and a focus on beliefs about students would most closely meet the needs of teachers with an attribution belief system (Romi et al., 2016).

In a study of 97 teachers, Clunies-Ross et al. (2008) found that teachers' self-reports of practice mirror their actual practice of management strategies. Even more, the authors found that reactive management strategies are related to teacher stress and disruptive student behavior. Teachers often see classroom disturbances and disciplinary problems as major job stressors (Aldrup et al., 2018; Evans et al., 2019; Harmsen et al., 2018). Given this, teachers benefit from the opportunity to critically evaluate and discuss their beliefs about teaching, identity, and professional development as part of an ongoing learning process (Antoniou & Kyriakides, 2013). Providing teachers with professional development related to effective classroom management practices, based on current research, may reduce teacher stress and support positive student learning outcomes (Bentley-Edwards et al., 2020; Bottiani et al., 2019; Clunies-Ross et al., 2008; Harmsen et al., 2018; Ouellette et al., 2018).

The decision-making and actions that teachers enact stem from their beliefs about classroom management. Successful professional development training can encourage reflection and aid teachers in developing and implementing action plans, which will then improve their teaching skills alongside their classroom management (Antoniou & Kyriakides, 2013; Wilkinson et al., 2020). For instance, in a study of the Dynamic Integrated Approach (DIA) to professional development, Antoniou and Kyriakides (2013) found that through critical reflection, development of action plans, and coaching, teacher management (in this case, management of time) supported improved teaching skill and student outcomes were positively affected. Similarly, Nagro et al. (2019) describe how teachers can implement plans that incorporate research-based proactive classroom management strategies that support student engagement. The authors, for example, describe how teachers can intentionally plan whole-group response systems through the integration of movement, student choice, and visual supports. Ultimately, professional development, which stems from effective educational research and supports teacher development of action plans, can positively impact teachers' effectiveness and student outcomes (Gore, 2021).

Key Components of Professional Development

School leaders find it necessary to provide efficient professional development programs within schools to support educators in effective classroom management (Hirsch et al., 2019; Simonsen, Freeman, Myers, et al., 2020). However, providing professional development in a traditional sit-and-get, train-and-hope, or one-and-done framework is insufficient. That is, training offered in only one or two isolated events, where the trainer and school administrators hope the educators will implement the skills learned, does not support long-term development (Simonsen et al., 2014). Instead, more sustaining and comprehensive support is needed to promote quality change implementation (State et al., 2019). Effective professional development seeks to equip educators with classroom management skills, generalize them to their own classroom, and implement them consistently with fluency and fidelity (Mitchell et al., 2017). This is a tall order for school districts and campuses, especially given the myriad of demands regularly placed on school administrators and teachers. This makes quality, effective professional development training a challenging yet essential task.

Teachers need ongoing training in classroom management practices to implement evidence-based strategies with fidelity (Sanetti et al., 2018). Offering professional development in the school setting in a small group where teachers have opportunities to practice skills learned is a recommended practice (Kretlow et al., 2010), as is providing training that acknowledges culture and supports the enactment of culturally responsive classroom management (Larson, 2016). Additionally, the use of multimedia strategies, such as podcasts with video modeling, has been shown to support teachers' use of classroom management practices (Kennedy et al., 2017). Darling-Hammond et al. (2017) described recommendations that include offering professional development that is content-focused and includes active learning which employs adult learning theory. Content-focused professional development intentionally centers on learning within the context of the teachers' classroom, while active learning provides interaction with approaches that teachers can then apply in their own classroom context.

Further, Darling-Hammond et al. (2017) described that effective professional development supports collaboration through job-embedded contexts, "uses models and modeling of effective practices, provides coaching and expert support, offers opportunities for feedback and reflection, and is of sustained duration" (p. 14). By supporting collaboration, teachers can share their ideas and work and learn together. Models embedded into professional development give teachers the opportunity to see examples of best practice. Providing coaching and expert support allows evidence-based practices to be shared and then focused on a teacher's specific needs. Building in time for teachers to reflect and process the professional development knowledge and skills gained, they can ask for feedback, gain input, and consider changes to their practice. And finally, allowing adequate learning time (a sustained duration) is essential for processing information and considering how to implement strategies into practice.

Sustained Duration. When considering classroom management professional development, providing sufficient time to support the development of management knowledge and skills is paramount (Darling-Hammond et al., 2017). For instance, Simonsen, Freeman, Myers et al. (2020) found that teacher PD, which included direct training, coaching, performance feedback, and preliminary support, improved teacher use of positive classroom management approaches; however, maintenance of these skills did not result. That is, when teacher professional development moved on to focusing on a new skill, teacher increases in providing positive praise did not remain at the increased level (Simonsen, Freeman, Myers et al., 2020). This lack of skill maintenance highlights Darling-Hammond et al.'s (2017) recommendation for PD offered across a sustained timeframe. Even more, it is vital to ensure that investments to support teachers in the development and maintenance of classroom management skills should be additionally linked to the distal outcome of positive change in student behavior (Owens et al., 2020).

Evidence-Based Approaches

Selection and implementation of classroom management practices are often the responsibility of the individual classroom teacher (Cooper & Scott, 2017). When teachers struggle to manage students' challenging behaviors, they are often encouraged to seek assistance from a counselor or special educator (MacSuga-Gage et al., 2018). In response to this need for support, several training approaches exist that show a positive impact in equipping in-service teachers to be effective classroom managers. These job-embedded approaches to teacher training seek to improve teacher instructional quality (Kraft & Blazar, 2017; Wilkinson et al., 2020). The strategic delivery of supports based on a multi-tiered framework (e.g., Response to Intervention, Positive Behavior Interventions and Supports) has been suggested by a number of researchers within the last several years (Grasley-Boy et al., 2019; Samudre et al., 2021; Sanetti & Collier-Meek, 2015; Simonsen et al., 2014; State et al., 2019). Following are evidence-based approaches to teacher training that are often useful when supporting teachers who need additional assistance at the higher tiers, that is, those who need support either due to their own limited classroom management skill set or whose students present significant behavioral challenges.

Coaching. One-on-one coaching provides an evidence-based approach to support teachers in becoming effective classroom managers (Kraft & Blazar, 2017). Coaches are often those with advanced training or certification in areas such as applied behavior analysis, school psychology, or counseling (Samudre et al., 2021). However, educator peers have also served as coaches (Wilkinson et al., 2020). Through coaching, a coach observes a teacher in action and is then able to provide targeted feedback aimed at improving practice (Blazar & Kraft, 2015; Kraft & Blazar, 2017). This targeted feedback can include strengths noted during the observation, areas of needed improvement, and strategies useful for improving the implementation of the classroom management practice (Hirsch et al., 2019). Fallon et al. (2019) found that coaching through feasible implementation support, inclusive of direct training and as-needed booster training, positively influenced teacher demonstration and sustainable use of skills in a high-needs classroom setting. Alongside targeted professional development, coaching provides educators with the opportunity to adapt practices and receive input and feedback (Mitchell et al., 2017).

Coaching further aids the teacher in maintaining the practice with fidelity (Mitchell et al., 2017) by providing individual support following training (Kretlow & Bartholomew, 2010). Coaching supports teachers as they change and improve their classroom management skills as well as their implementation of classroom management prevention programs (Becker & Bradshaw, 2013). Additionally, coaching provides an alternative approach to traditional short-term professional development models (Kraft & Blazar, 2017; Kraft et al., 2018) and has been recommended for supporting teachers' inclusive classroom management practices, such as providing opportunities to respond (OTRs) and specific praise statements (McKenna et al., 2015).

Consultation. Research supports the use of problem-solving consultation along with teacher observation followed by performance feedback to improve teacher use of classroom management strategies (Owens et al., 2018; Sanetti et al., 2017). Within a multi-tiered framework, consultation can be provided as a Tier 3 training approach and is suggested for teachers with significant or chronic classroom management challenges (Grasley-Boy et al., 2019; Simonsen et al., 2014). In fact, Owens et al. (2020) suggest that when teachers struggle with classroom management challenges, current best practice involves the teacher engaging in problem-solving consultation with a school psychologist, along with observation and performance feedback to facilitate the use of classroom management strategies (Solomon et al., 2012).

Recent research supports these suggestions. For instance, Coles et al. (2015) sought to identify if delivering a multi-component consultation package could result in teachers' classroom management knowledge, skills, and beliefs. They found that consultation can impact all three factors, and some teachers need consultation to address all three factors for adequate classroom management improvements to result. In another study using a structured consultation approach, researchers again found that consultation can improve a teacher's classroom management. Additionally, Bradshaw et al. (2018) found that consultation support via the Double Check coaching model could increase teachers' proactive behavior management and responsiveness to student needs, as well as improvements in student cooperation and disruptive behavior. Kleinert et al. (2017), in extending previous work (Reinke et al., 2008), employed a structured consultation model (the Classroom Check-UP) paired with goal setting and in-vivo coaching to improve classroom management practices of three urban elementary school teachers. Taken together, it is evident that research has demonstrated the potential for consultation to aid teachers who need individualized support to improve their classroom management skills (Bradshaw et al., 2018; Coles et al., 2015; Kleinert et al., 2017; Reinke et al., 2008). To maintain skills teachers have developed, additional support may be warranted.

Self-Monitoring for Skill Maintenance. Teacher self-monitoring of skill implementation following professional development has been found to increase the use of specific skills in classroom management (Simonsen et al., 2013) and is a recommended practice to support fidelity of implementation (Samudre et al., 2021). In a study of four elementary teachers, Oliver et al. (2015) found that using a self-monitoring checklist supports the maintenance of evidence-based classroom management practice fidelity. Through this approach, a self-monitoring form serves as a prompt and reminder for teachers to use at each step as they enact evidence-based practices (Myers et al., 2017). Following a professional development training with performance feedback and then use of a self-monitoring checklist holds merit as a cost-effective and pragmatic approach to support teacher maintenance of effective classroom management skills (Oliver et al., 2015). Similarly, employing a single-case research design, researchers found that emailed delivery of prompts and performance feedback resulted in improved teacher implementation fidelity of classroom management interventions (Collier-Meek et al., 2017; Fallon et al., 2018). Self-monitoring checklists and emailed delivery of prompts offer two ways that researchers strive to improve the cost-effectiveness of consulting and coaching models of teacher training.

Special Issues in Classroom Management Training

Training for Inclusive Classrooms

Given contemporary US classroom diversity, ensuring that teachers are prepared to effectively educate students with disabilities through inclusive classroom management practices is essential. Educators teaching in inclusive settings must know and use evidence-based practices to provide students with disabilities, including those with behavioral challenges or emotional disturbance, the support and instruction needed to make meaningful educational progress (McKenna et al., 2019). Educators have frequently expressed their concerns about their perceived inability to meet individual student needs. In a 2012 survey of approximately 1,000 teachers, over 70% of educators reported that addressing the unique needs of diverse learners is one of the biggest challenges they face (MetLife Inc., 2013). Furthermore, in a study of 70 teachers, Westling (2010) found that teachers reported feeling unprepared to teach and manage behaviors of students with behavioral challenges.

However, in-service and pre-service preparation were predictive of both the confidence teachers had and the number of strategies they used to address challenging student behaviors. Similarly, Martinussen et al. (2010) found that general educators with moderate to in-depth training in attention-deficit hyperactivity disorder (ADHD) more often report using recommended management approaches. That is, knowledge of strategies is correlated with the reported use of strategies (Moore et al., 2017). Clearly, professional development in not only classroom management knowledge and skill is essential, but training in inclusive management approaches and support for students with disabilities is of critical importance (Flower et al., 2017). Likewise, holding high expectations for all learners and maintaining a positive environment provides for greater student—and ultimately, teacher success (Jones et al., 2013). In a study on several best practice classroom management strategies, Collier-Meek et al. (2018) found that class-wide academic engagement increases when teachers provide behavior-specific praise instead of error corrections.

Universal Design for Learning. The Universal Design for Learning (UDL) guidelines offer a framework meant to support student access and participation in learning (CAST, 2018). UDL guidelines include the provision of multiple means of engagement, representation, and action and expression (CAST, 2018). Universal Design can be seen as an approach that proactively accommodates diverse learners, whether through access to the physical space or to learning and instruction (McGuire et al., 2006). Providing teachers with training in UDL strengthens their ability to meet a broader range of student needs and support the student learning process (Capp, 2017).

Further, training in UDL supports teachers' ability to design lessons that are accessible for all students, including students with disabilities (Spooner et al., 2007). In a content analysis of the UDL framework, researchers found that even more than accessibility, UDL offers the opportunity for teachers to avoid student impulsive behavior and guide students to engage in risk-benefit processing (García-Campos et al., 2020). UDL also allows teachers to explore possibilities of individual autonomy and choice and organize classroom environments and resources (García-Campos et al., 2020), all of which directly relate to effective classroom management practices. Researchers have posited that UDL provides a helpful approach for educators seeking to address learner needs proactively and effectively manage their classrooms (Johnson-Harris & Mundschenk, 2014; Montague, 2009). More research, specifically on the interconnectedness of classroom management and Universal Design for Learning, as well as the impact of teacher training in these areas, is warranted.

Training in Culturally Responsive Classroom Management

Throughout this chapter, there has been an underlying perspective of honing classroom management to meet the needs of individual students. These adjustments highlight the relational nature of this skill so that all students feel welcomed. Thus, even if teachers know of behavioral structures but do not consider adapting those structures to their specific students during that year, it is arguable whether they are implementing effective classroom management.

Therefore, central to training effective classroom managers is guiding them towards an understanding that classrooms are defined by those particular students during that specific time (Evertson & Weinstein, 2006). For instance, establishing a classroom procedure may only be beneficial depending on the grade level and that group of students. Is the procedure meant to improve class time or to reduce misbehavior? Is it something that students would value, and is it worth enacting every day, even when half the class is not there because of a field trip? How have students previously responded to this procedure, and what is their energy like today? Effective classroom managers consider these questions among a multitude of other factors to determine what and how management techniques should be enacted. Each 8th-grade mathematics classroom varies as a result of students' demographics, previous experiences, personality traits, and interactions between one another. Even the same class on different days—whether because of the weather, an absent student, or a conflict between individuals outside of school—can dramatically change the dynamic. Management, therefore, is dependent on the classroom it is utilized in at that moment.

Equality-Based Approach. Training teachers to focus on these types of classroom differences requires a shift in perspectives. Teachers tend to conceive classroom management as a set of strategies to control students (Kwok, 2017). Thus, they assert their own conception of management and require students to assimilate to their vision of what a learner should be. That is, teachers often manage with the intention for all students to abide by teacher-created structures regardless of students' background, previous experiences, and interpersonal dynamics. They hold a mindset that prioritizes managing all students in the same way: All students deserve equal structures (Kwok et al., 2020). This colorblind or equality-based approach introduces classroom systems based on what best fits the teachers' style. This can be beneficial by reducing the cognitive load of novices and allowing them to prioritize aspects familiar to them (Kwok et al., 2020). These teachers may also believe that individual differences are unimportant because they want to treat everyone the same. While this paradigm appears noble in prioritizing equality, it negates the individual differences that make each classroom special and unique. A colorblind approach restricts the values that students bring, their specific needs, and their individuality when they are instead treated like one and the same. This approach also negates the historical and systemic structures within which students, families, and school communities must operate.

A colorblind approach can be exacerbated amidst a pronounced cultural gap defined by the diversifying student demographic juxtaposed against the stagnant White teaching workforce (Center for American Progress, 2017; Lowenstein, 2009). When schools are derived from a predominantly White American understanding of what defines misbehavior, such an educational context inherently handicaps students of color. Teachers, then, are relying on outdated approaches that can conflict with diverse students who hold different conceptions of what constitutes as engagement and misbehavior (Bottiani et al., 2018; Carter et al., 2017; Gregory et al., 2010, 2016; Larson, Pas et al., 2020). Teachers enter classrooms assuming their students know how to behave when, in fact, they are relying on their own perceptions of appropriate behavior. When students think they are acting innocently (e.g., yelling out the correct answer), but the teacher recognizes those actions as misbehavior, disputes are inevitable. Students may not only be confused about why they received a consequence (e.g., because they are accustomed to call and response tactics, or open discussions in other familiar settings), but they may then be frustrated by disagreement, promoting further issues. Consequently, throughout many classrooms in the U.S., students of color are likely to receive more frequent and harsher consequences (Santiago-Rosario et al., 2021; Skiba et al., 2011). These students miss instructional time—which is exacerbated amidst difficulties in catching up (Bell & Puckett, 2020)—and widens the achievement gap (Gregory et al., 2010). This is particularly salient in urban contexts (Milner, 2020) and figures to be prominent within beginning teachers' classrooms.

Equitable Perspective. Culturally relevant classroom management (CRCM) can be an alternative paradigm that embraces student differences. CRCM is the acknowledgment and utilization of race, culture, and context towards responsive management practices. These skills reframe teachers' attention towards utilizing individual differences to enhance classroom management strategies. That is, it shifts their attention from establishing authority regardless of the students towards building an environment-specific for that classroom of individuals. CRCM facilitates a learning environment based on intentional relationships based on prior experiences to construct appropriate, nuanced classroom structures (Cartledge et al., 2015).

Recent evidence solidifies that CRCM is associated with student achievement (Bell & Puckett, 2020; Larson et al., 2018), changes in teacher actions (Caldera et al., 2019), and an increase in both personalized interactions and positive student perspectives (Aronson, 2020; Larson et al., 2018). Furthermore, having teachers who view the cultural differences and experiences of their students as an additive part of the classroom can promote similar change within the school environment for both staff and students (Farinde-Wu et al., 2017). Dee and Penner (2017), in particular, focused on culturally relevant teaching within an ethnic studies course and its causal effects on positive student behavior and achievement. The authors used a regression discontinuity design from San Francisco Unified School District data to identify that the more ethic studies curriculum high school students took, there was an associated increase in the students' attendance, grade point average, and credits earned, on average. Larson et al. (2018) similarly took a large-scale quantitative approach but instead focused on using both culturally responsive teaching and proactive behavior management practices. Results from their structural equation models indicate these instructional practices were associated with observed positive student behaviors. Such studies promisingly provide some much-needed quantitative evidence about the scalability of culturally responsive curriculum and peripherally, CRCM.

Thus, a shift in paradigms is necessary to replace equal practices with equitable ones. Teachers need to reflexively consider their positionality amidst the classroom and the types of (potentially inequitable) experiences that their students matriculate through. An equitable mindset acknowledges students' differences and adjusts for their individual needs. Some students may need more praise as a form of motivation, whereas others may need proximity to encourage engagement. Equitable teachers factor what is required for each and every one of their students to be appropriately managed. It is a shift from *classroom* management to *student* management in the classroom. When all students are treated as unique individuals, and each class as a dynamic environment, equity is placed at the forefront. Classroom management that prioritizes the needs of the student regardless of race, ethnicity, disability, sexual orientation, gender, or background creates a space where individuals feel valued and a part of their own learning.

Training Culturally Responsive Classroom Managers. Unfortunately, there is little to no formal training in CRCM throughout teacher preparation (Siwatu et al., 2017), despite knowing it can require substantial effort to deconstruct equality or deficit-based beliefs (Kwok et al., 2020; Whitaker & Valtierra, 2018). Correspondingly, there is also a paucity of research about CRCM, though there have increasingly been case studies in this area. There is some peripheral evidence pointing to beginning teachers being capable of implementing CRCM or related actions in the classroom (Kwok, 2018; Milner & Tenore, 2010). But in-depth investigations are limited with just a handful of exceptions. For instance, Luet and Shealey (2018) studied the correlation between the management practices of urban teachers and their teacher preparation program. The authors found that programs that applied an asset-based frame to classroom management had graduates who advocated for their students and worked to change the deficit perception of colleagues.

Calls to mitigate disciplinary disproportionately (Gregory et al., 2010) have led to a gradual increase in CRCM-targeted programs. Though overwhelming, few induction or professional development programs contain content about or related to CRCM (Milner, 2015). While some studies focused exclusively on the behavioral components and did not integrate issues around race and culture (Carter et al., 2017), others have exhibited success. For instance, the Double Check program (Hershfeldt et al., 2009) supported culturally responsive practices through professional development and coaching. Evidence indicates that teachers undergoing this program are more proactive with behavior management, report less disruptive behavior, and have higher student cooperation (Bradshaw et al., 2018). While initially designed for a special education setting, it seemingly has had positive effects towards reducing racially-based disciplinary decisions, as echoed within similar studies (Knight-Manuel et al., 2019). Another prominent example is Kwok and Svajda-Hardy (2021), who examined one district's integration of classroom management coaching program from various administrative perspectives. They found that there was a persistent need to support beginning teachers in culturally understanding and managing that specific district's students. The study outlines the design, challenges, and strengths of their program and has implications for how other districts could consider supporting CRCM for beginning teachers.

These few successes indicate that developing CRCM is in the realm of possibility. Future research naturally should focus on exemplar programs exhibiting CRCM preparation and support for others to replicate or further develop. Moreover, there needs to be additional systematic documentation about the presence (or absence) of CRCM throughout programs and districts, as well as how intentional embedding makes tangible changes towards teacher and student growth.

These calls for future research coincide with how classroom management training similarly needs to be updated; CRCM should simultaneously be included alongside. With teacher preparation deficient in these areas, it will require a drastic overhaul. More importantly, knowing of such deficiencies and not doing anything is arguably unethical by perpetuating insufficient preparation. The route towards training effective classroom managers is evident, and now is a call to action for teacher educators to implement necessary changes. As stated within the CM PReP framework, even an incremental change is a step in a positive direction. The status quo for teacher training is unacceptable, and programs need to actively and intentionally make changes. Otherwise, they are altogether complicit in not providing the best they can towards educating all students.

Integrating Current Research into Past Findings

Promisingly, there has been substantial growth in research and overall knowledge base concerning classroom management training. Previous iterations of handbook chapters (Jones, 2006; Stough, 2006; Stough & Montague, 2015) focused more on the need for training and the existence of various support structures, occasionally drawing from non-peer-reviewed sources. However, in this instance, we more definitively identify the development and specifics of training within teacher preparation and professional development from some of the most rigorous peer-reviewed journals. This speaks to the proliferation and rigor of research in this area necessary to make monumental changes.

While some programs (pre-service and in-service alike) still lack recognizing the need to prioritize classroom management, others have made tremendous improvements and pushed the research agenda forward. We long for future research that focuses on the variation between programs as opposed to a dichotomy of programs that prioritize classroom management or not. Yet, we understand that change can take time and continue to press forward. We raise several areas towards the growth of classroom management training research.

First, there needs to be an established understanding and connection between classroom management and policy. Stough (2006) identified the lack of standards that address classroom management and corresponding competencies, with several recent studies reiterating this persistent finding. Thus, research needs to find ways of shifting policy towards mandating classroom management training for all pre-service and in-service teachers. Without standards, corresponding structures of teacher preparation and district support will be hesitant to shift away from the status quo. Policy-relevant research based on large-scale quantitative studies or experimental studies that isolate the impact of classroom management skills on student achievement could help to establish the argument needed for policymakers to spur action. Additionally, there could be a need for a common language across state standards that emphasize classroom management skills, as opposed to items related to behavior, discipline, or consequences. Disparate language or language focused on student misbehavior could limit the opportunities needed for teachers to comprehensively learn about classroom management.

Second, future research should examine learning about classroom management in remote settings. Given the prevalence of the COVID-19 pandemic and the abrupt change to solely virtual surroundings, educators were left with little resources. A previous Handbook chapter addressed the intersection between classroom management and technology (Mason Bolick & Bartels, 2014); however, the focus was exclusively on integrating technology into classrooms instead of specific learning or management techniques around technology. There have since been a handful of resources available that provided guidance for how teachers could manage classrooms (Center of Positive Behavioral Interventions and Supports, 2020; Goldman et al., 2021). Strategies include keeping the same school-wide behavioral expectations, using online activities, considering online-specific behavior, and teaching directly. However, these strategies have yet to be examined empirically within context. We anticipate forthcoming studies (e.g., Lathifah et al., 2021) addressing this glaring research gap, particularly as remote learning remains an option for the foreseeable future for some states and countries. Thus, researchers may want to expeditiously explore this area to alleviate challenges teachers face amidst uncertainty and the difficulties of virtual learning environments.

Third, continued research should explore the training, integration, and impact of CRCM. While separately discussed in the previous edition (Cartledge et al., 2014), the current evidence has allowed the burgeoning bridge between CRCM and training. A handful of studies have begun to identify concrete applications of (or components of) CRCM and the effects on teacher and student outcomes. Studies will need to determine the prevalence of pre-service and in-service programs that integrate this skill set and how it could be integrated within pre-existing structures towards teacher development. More research will be needed to build on this beginning foundation, particularly as policy efforts in some states seek to reduce the integration of culturally responsive actions within the classroom.

Conclusion

Across this chapter, our synthesis of recent research for both pre-service and in-service educators highlights the ongoing need for and the impact of quality training in classroom management. Current research builds upon decades worth of foundational work in classroom management research. Yet, there remains more work to be done to clearly understand the most effective, efficient, and fiscally responsible ways to provide classroom management training to pre-service and in-service teachers that yields direct positive outcomes for students. For example, more research is warranted in professional development for classroom management in high school settings (Freeman et al., 2018). Student developmental characteristics, differences in teacher training at that level, and school enrollment may affect the model for quality, effective classroom management training at that level. In addition, as was discussed above, other areas for future work in classroom management training remain (i.e., culturally responsive classroom management, inclusive classroom management, classroom management in remote learning environments, classroom management's relationship with universal design for learning, and the connection of classroom management with policy). We reiterate that solid progress in the research on classroom management teacher training has been made since the last edition of this handbook, but we look forward to continued strides in this area. One standing fact remains clear: teachers need effective training in classroom management appropriate for their teaching context. The role of researchers is to determine the most effective, cost-efficient models to provide such training.

Acknowledgments

We want to acknowledge Laura Stough and Megan Svajda-Hardy for their feedback on this chapter.

References

Akdağ, Z., & Haser, Ç. (2016). Beginning early childhood education teachers' classroom management concerns. *Teachers and Teaching: Theory and Practice*, 22(6), 700–715. https://doi.org/10.1080/13540602.2016.1158959

Aldrup, K., Klusmann, U., Lüdtke, O., Göllner, R., & Trautwein, U. (2018). Student misbehavior and teacher well-being: Testing the mediating role of the teacher-student relationship. *Learning and Instruction*, 58, 126–136. https://doi.org/10.1016/j.learninstruc.2018.05.006

Antoniou, P., & Kyriakides, L. (2013). A dynamic integrated approach to teacher professional development: Impact and sustainability of the effects on improving teacher behavior and student outcomes. *Teaching and Teacher Education*, *29*, 1–12. http://dx.doi.org/10.1016/j.tate.2012.08.001

Aronson, B. (2020). From teacher education to practicing teacher: What does culturally relevant praxis look like? *Urban Education*, *55*(8–9), 1115–1141. http://dx.doi.org/10.1177/0042085916672288

Atici, M. (2007). A small-scale study on student teachers' perceptions of classroom management and methods for dealing with misbehaviour. *Emotional and Behavioural Difficulties*, *12*(1), 15–27. https://doi.org/10.1080/13632750601135881

Baker, C., Gentry, J., & Larmer, W. (2016, Summer). A model for online support in classroom management: Perceptions of beginning teachers. *Administrative Issues Journal: Connecting Education, Practice, and Research*, *6*(1), 22–37. https://doi.org/10.5929/2016.6.1.3

Becker, K. D., Bradshaw, C. P., Domitrovich, C., & Ialongo, N. S. (2013). Coaching teachers to improve implementation of the good behavior game. *Administration and Policy in Mental Health and Mental Health Services Research*, *40*, 482–493. https://doi.org/10.1007/s10488-013-0482-8

Bell, C., & Puckett, T. (2020). I want to learn but they won't let me: Exploring the impact of school discipline on academic achievement. *Urban Education*, 1–30. https://doi.org/10.1177/0042085920968629

Ben-Peretz, M., Eilam, B., & Landler-Pardo, G. (2011). Teacher education for classroom management in Israel: Structures and orientations. *Teaching Education*, *22*(2), 133–150. http://dx.doi.org/10.1080/10476210.2011.567842

Bentley-Edwards, K. L., Stevenson, H. C., Thomas, D. E., Adams-Bass, V. N., & Coleman-King, C. (2020). Teaching scared: pre-service teacher appraisals of racial stress, socialization and classroom management self-efficacy. *Social Psychology of Education*, *23*(5), 1233–1257. https://doi.org/10.1007/s11218-020-09578-8

Blazar, D., & Kraft, M. A. (2015). Exploring mechanisms of effective teacher coaching: A tale of two cohorts from a randomized experiment. *Educational Evaluation and Policy Analysis*, *37*(4), 542–566. https://doi.org/10.3102/0162373715579487

Bottiani, J. H., Duran, C. A. K., Pas, E. T., & Bradshaw, C. P. (2019). Teacher stress and burnout in urban middle schools: Associations with job demands, resources, and effective classroom practices. *Journal of School Psychology*, *77*(September), 36–51. https://doi.org/10.1016/j.jsp.2019.10.002

Bradshaw, C. P., Pas, E. T., Bottiani, J. H., Debnam, K. J., Reinke, W. M., Herman, K. C., & Rosenberg, M. S. (2018). Promoting cultural responsivity and student engagement through double check coaching of classroom teachers: An efficacy study. *School Psychology Review*, *47*(2), 118–134. https://doi.org/10.17105/SPR-2017-0119.V47-2

Brophy, J. (1988). Educating teachers about managing classrooms and students. *Teaching and Teacher Education*, *4*(1), 1–18. https://doi.org/10.1016/0742-051x(88)90020-0

Caldera, A., Whitaker, M. C., & Conrad Popova, A. D. (2019). Classroom management in urban schools: proposing a course framework. *Teaching Education*. https://doi.org/10.1080/10476210.2018.1561663

Capp, M. J. (2017). The effectiveness of universal design for learning: a meta-analysis of literature between 2013 and 2016. *International Journal of Inclusive Education*, *21*(8), 791–807. https://doi.org/10.1080/13603116.2017.1325074

Carter, P. L., Skiba, R., Arredondo, M. I., & Pollock, M. (2017). You can't fix what you don't look at. *Urban Education*, *52*, 207–235. https://doi.org/10.1177/0042085916660350

Cartledge, G., Lo, Y., Vincent, C. G., & Robinson-Ervin, P. (2015). Culturally responsive classroom management. In E. Emmer & E. Sabornie (Eds.), *Handbook of classroom management* (pp. 411–430). Routledge.

Carver-Thomas, D., & Darling-Hammond, L. (2017). *Teacher turnover: Why it matters and what we can do about it.* Learning Policy Institute.

CAST (2018). Universal Design for Learning Guidelines version 2.2. Retrieved from http://udlguidelines.cast.org

Center for American Progress (2017). *Revisiting the persistent teacher diversity problem* [Data Set]. https://cdn.americanprogress.org/content/uploads/2017/09/18063438/TeacherDiversity-UPDATEDtablesSources.pdf?_ga=2.54309672.1212281783.1615395204-668828882.1615395204

Center on Positive Behavioral Interventions and Supports (March, 2020). Creating a PBIS Behavior Teaching Matrix for Remote Instruction. University of Oregon. www.pbis.org.

Clunies-Ross, P., Little, E., & Kienhuis, M. (2008). Self-reported and actual use of proactive and reactive classroom management strategies and their relationship with teacher stress and student behaviour. *Educational Psychology*, *28*, 693–710. http://dx.doi.org/10.1080/01443410802206700

Cohen, J., Wong, V., Krishnamachari, A., & Berlin, R. (2020). Teacher coaching in a simulated environment. *Educational Evaluation and Policy Analysis*, *42*(2), 208–231. http://dx.doi.org/10.3102/0162373720906217

Coles, E. K., Owens, J. S., Serrano, V. J., Slavec, J., & Evans, S. W. (2015). From consultation to student outcomes: The role of teacher knowledge, skills, and beliefs in increasing integrity in classroom management strategies. *School Mental Health*, *7*(1), 34–48. https://doi.org/10.1007/s12310-015-9143-2

Collier-Meek, M. A., Fallon, L. M., & DeFouw, E. R. (2017). Toward feasible implementation support: E-mailed prompts to promote teachers' treatment integrity. *School Psychology Review*, *46*(4), 379–394. https://doi.org/10.17105/SPR-2017-0028.V46-4

Collier-Meek, M. A., Johnson, A. H., Sanetti, L. H., & Minami, T. (2019). Identifying critical components of classroom management implementation. *School Psychology Review*, *48*(4), 348–361. https://doi.org/10.17105/spr-2018-0026.v48-4

Cook, C., Fiat, A., Larson, M., Daikos, C., Slemrod, T., Holland, E., Thayer, A., & Renshaw, T. (2018). Positive greetings at the door: Evaluation of a low-cost, high-yield proactive classroom management strategy. *Journal of Positive Behavior Interventions*, *20*(3), 149–159. http://dx.doi.org/10.1177/1098300717753831

Cooper, J. T., & Scott, T. M. (2017). The keys to managing instruction and behavior: considering high probability practices. *Teacher Education and Special Education: The Journal of the Teacher Education Division of the Council for Exceptional Children*, *40*(2), 102–113. https://doi.org/10.1177/0888406417700825

Darling-Hammond, L., Hyler, M. E., & Gardner, M. (2017). *Effective teacher professional development*. Learning Policy Institute.

Dee, T., & Penner, E. (2017). The causal effects of cultural relevance: Evidence from an ethnic studies curriculum. *American Educational Research Journal*, *54*(1), 127–166. https://doi.org/10.3102/0002831216677002

Desimone, L. M. (2009). Improving impact studies of teachers' professional development: Toward better conceptualizations and measures. *Educational Researcher*, *38*(3), 181–199. https://doi.org/10.3102/0013189x08331140

Dicke, T., Elling, J., Schmeck, A., & Leutner, D. (2015). Reducing reality shock: The effects of classroom management skills training on beginning teachers. *Teaching and Teacher Education*, *48*, 1–12. https://doi.org/10.1016/j.tate.2015.01.013.

Dicke, T., Parker, P. D., Marsh, H. W., Kunter, M., Schmeck, A., & Leutner, D. (2014). Self-efficacy in classroom management, classroom disturbances, and emotional exhaustion: A moderated mediation analysis of teacher candidates. *Journal of Educational Psychology*, *106*(2), 569–583. https://doi.org/10.1037/a0035504

Doyle, W. (1985). Recent research on classroom management. *Journal of Teacher Education*, *36*(3), 31–35. https://doi.org/10.1177/002248718503600307

Emmer, E. T., & Stough, L. M. (2001). Classroom management: A critical part of educational psychology, with implications for teacher education. *Educational Psychologist*, *36*(2), 103–112. https://doi.org/10.1207/s15326985ep3602_5

Evans, D., Butterworth, R., & Law, G. U. (2019). Understanding associations between perceptions of student behaviour, conflict representations in the teacher-student relationship and teachers' emotional experiences. *Teaching and Teacher Education*, *82*, 55–68. https://doi.org/10.1016/j.tate.2019.03.008

Evertson, C. M., Emmer, E. T., & Poole, I. (2021). *Classroom management for elementary teachers* (11th ed). Pearson.

Evertson, C. M., & Weinstein, C. S. (2006). Classroom management as a field of inquiry. In C. M. Evertson & Weinsteinstein (Eds.), *Handbook of classroom management: Research, practice, and contemporary issues* (pp. 3–15). Lawrence Erlbaum Associates.

Fallon, L. M., Collier-Meek, M. A., & Kurtz, K. D. (2019). Feasible coaching supports to promote teachers' classroom management in high-need settings: An experimental single case design study. *School Psychology Review*, *48*(1), 3–17. https://doi.org/10.17105/SPR-2017-0135.V48-1

Fallon, L. M., Collier-Meek, M. A., Kurtz, K. D., & DeFouw, E. R. (2018). Emailed implementation supports to promote treatment integrity: Comparing the effectiveness and acceptability of prompts and performance feedback. *Journal of School Psychology*, *68*, 113–128. https://doi.org/10.1016/j.jsp.2018.03.001

Farinde-Wu, A., Glover, C., & Williams, N. (2017). It's not hard work; It's heart work: Strategies of effective, award-winning culturally responsive teachers. *Urban Education*, *49*(2), 279–299. http://dx.doi.org/10.1007/s11256-017-0401-5

Ficarra, L., Quinn, K., (2014). Teachers' facility with evidence-based classroom management practices: An investigation of teachers' preparation programmes and in-service conditions. *Journal of Teacher Education for Sustainability*, *16*(2), 71–87. http://dx.doi.org/10.2478/jtes-2014-0012

Floress, M. T. & Beaudoin, M. M., & Bernas, R. S. (2021). Exploring secondary teachers' actual and perceived praise and reprimand use. *Journal of Positive Behavior Interventions*, *24*(1), 46–57. http://dx.doi.org/10.1177/10983007211000381

Floress, M. T., Jenkins, L. N., Reinke, W. M., & McKown, L. (2018). General education teachers' natural rates of praise: A preliminary investigation. *Behavioral Disorders*, *43*, 411–422. http://dx.doi.org/10.1177/0198742917709472

Flower, A., McKenna, J., & Haring, C. (2017). Behavior and classroom management: Are teacher preparation programs really preparing our teachers? *Preventing School Failure: Alternative Education for Children and Youth*, *61*(2), 163–169. https://doi.org/10.1080/1045988X.2016.1231109

Freeman, J., Kowitt, J., Simonsen, B., Wei, Y., Dooley, K., Gordon, L., & Maddock, E. (2018). A high school replication of targeted professional development for classroom management. *Remedial and Special Education*, *39*(3), 144–157. http://dx.doi.org/10.1177/0741932517719547

Freeman, J., Simonsen, B., Briere, D. E., & MacSuga-Gage, A. S. (2014). Preservice teacher training in classroom management: A review of state accreditation policy and teacher preparation program. *Teacher Education and Special Education*, *37*, 106–120.

Gage, N. A., Grasley-Boy, N., Lombardo, M., & Anderson, L. (2020). The effect of school-wide positive behavior interventions and supports on disciplinary exclusions: A conceptual replication. *Behavioral Disorders*, *46*(1), 42–53. http://dx.doi.org/10.1177/0198742919896305

Gage, N. A., Grasley-Boy, N., & MacSuga-Gage, A. (2018). Professional development to increase teacher behavior-specific praise: A single-case design replication. *Psychology in the Schools*, *55*(3), 264–277. http://dx.doi.org/10.1002/pits.22106

Gage, N. A., & MacSuga-Gage, A. S. (2017). Salient classroom management skills: Finding the most effective skills to increase student engagement and decrease disruptions. *Report on Emotional & Behavioral Disorders in Youth*, *17*(1), 13–18.

Gage, N. A, Scott, T., Hirn, R., & MacSuga-Gage, A. S. (2018). The relationship between teachers' implementation of classroom management practices and student behavior in elementary school. *Behavioral Disorders*, *43*(2), 302–315. http://dx.doi.org/10.1177/0198742917714809

García-Campos, M.-D., Canabal, C., & Alba-Pastor, C. (2020). Executive functions in universal design for learning: Moving towards inclusive education. *International Journal of Inclusive Education*, *24*(6), 660–674. https://doi.org/10.1080/13603116.2018.1474955

Gilmour, A., Majeika, C., Sheaffer, A., & Wehby, J. (2018). The coverage of classroom management in teacher evaluation rubrics. *Teacher Education and Special Education*, *42*(2), 161–174. http://dx.doi.org/10.1177/08884 06418781918

Girardet, C. (2018). Context and implications document for: Why do some teachers change and others don't? A review of students about factors influencing in-service and pre-service teachers' change in classroom management. *Review of Education*, *6*(1), 3–36. http://dx.doi.org/10.1002/rev3.3105

Goldman, S. E., Finn, J. B., & Leslie, M. J. (2021). Classroom management and remote teaching: Tools for defining and teaching expectations. *TEACHING Exceptional Children*, 00400599211025555. https://doi.org/10.1177/00400599211025555

Gore, J. (2021). The quest for better teaching. *Oxford Review of Education*, *47*(1), 45–60. https://doi.org/10.1080/03054985.2020.1842182

Grasley-Boy, N., Gage, N. A., & MacSuga-Gage, A. S. (2019). Multitiered support for classroom management professional development. *Beyond Behavior*, *28*(1), 5–12. https://doi.org/10.1177/1074295618798028

Greenberg, J., Putman, H., & Walsh, K. (2014). Training our future teachers: Classroom management. National Council of Teacher Quality.

Gregory, A., Hafen, C. A., Ruzek, E., Mikami, A. Y., Allen, J. P., & Pianta, R. C. (2016). Closing the racial discipline gap in classrooms by changing teacher practice. *School Psychology Review*, *45*(2), 171–191. https://doi.org/10.17105/SPR45-2.171-191

Gregory, A., Skiba, R. J., & Noguera, P. A. (2010). The achievement gap and the discipline gap: Two sides of the same coin? *Educational Researcher*, *39*(1), 59–68. http://dx.doi.org/10.3102/0013189X09357621

Hammerness, K. (2011) Classroom management in the United States: A view from New York City. *Teaching Education*, *22*(2), 151–167. http://dx.doi.org/10.1080/10476210.2011.567844

Harmsen, R., Helms-Lorenz, M., Maulana, R., & van Veen, K. (2018). The relationship between beginning teachers' stress causes, stress responses, teaching behaviour and attrition. *Teachers and Teaching: Theory and Practice*, *24*(6), 626–643. https://doi.org/10.1080/13540602.2018.1465404

Headden, S. (2014). Beginners in the classroom: What challenging demographics of teaching mean for schools, students, and society. Carnegie Foundation for the Advancement of Teaching. www.carnegiefoundation.org/wp-content/uploads/2014/09/beginners_in_classroom.pdf

Hershfeldt, P. A., Sechrest, R., Pell, K. L., Rosenberg, M. S., Bradshaw, C. P., & Leaf, P. J. (2009). Double-Check: A framework of cultural responsiveness applied to classroom behavior. *TEACHING Exceptional Children Plus*, *6*(2) Article 5.

Hirsch, S. E., Lloyd, J. W., & Kennedy, M. J. (2019). Professional development in practice. *The Elementary School Journal*, *120*(1), 61–87. https://doi.org/10.1086/704492

Ingersoll, R. M., & May, H. (2012). The magnitude, destinations, and determinants of mathematics and science teacher turnover. *Educational Evaluation and Policy Analysis*, *34*(4), 435–464. https://doi.org/10.3102/01623 73712454326

Johnson-Harris, K. M., & Mundschenk, N. A. (2014). Working effectively with students with BD in a general education classroom: The case for universal design for learning. *The Clearing House: A Journal of Educational Strategies, Issues and Ideas, 87*(4), 168–174. https://doi.org/10.1080/00098655.2014.897927

Jones, K. A., Jones, J. L., & Vermette, P. T. (2013, Summer). Exploring the complexity of classroom management: 8 components of managing a highly productive, safe, and respectful urban environment. *American Secondary Education, 41*(3), 21–33.

Jones, M. G., & Vesilind, E. (1995). Preservice teachers' cognitive frameworks for class management. *Teaching and Teacher Education, 11*(4), 313–330. https://doi.org/10.1016/0742-051X(94)00036-6

Jones, V. (1989). Classroom management: Clarifying theory and improving practice. *Education, 109*(3), 330–339.

Jones, V. (1996). Classroom management. In J. Sikula (Ed.), *Handbook of research on teacher education* (2nd edition, pp. 503–521). Macmillan.

Jones, V. (2006). How do teachers learn to be effective classroom managers? In C. M. Evertson & C. S. Weinstein (Eds.), *Handbook of classroom management: Research, practice, and contemporary issues* (pp. 887–907). Lawrence Erlbaum Associates. https://doi.org/10.4324/9780203874783.ch33

Kee, A. N. (2011). Feelings of preparedness among alternatively certified teachers: What is the role of program features? *Journal of Teacher Education, 63*(1), 23–38. http://dx.doi.org/10.1177/0022487111421933

Kennedy, M. J., Hirsch, S. E., Rodgers, W. J., Bruce, A., & Lloyd, J. W. (2017). Supporting high school teachers' implementation of evidence-based classroom management practices. *Teaching and Teacher Education 63*, 47–57. https://doi.org/10.1016/j.tate.2016.12.009

Kincade, L., Cook, C., & Goerdt, A. (2020). Meta-analysis and common practice elements of universal approaches to improving student-teacher relationships. *Review of Educational Research, 90*(5), 710–748. http://dx.doi.org/10.3102/0034654320946836

Kleinert, W. L., Silva, M. R., Codding, R. S., Feinberg, A. B, & St. James, P. S. (2017). Enhancing classroom management using the classroom check-up model with in-vivocoaching and goal setting components. *School Psychology Forum: Research in Practice, 11*(1), 5–19.

Knight-Manuel, M., Marciano, J., Wilson, M., Jackson, I., Vernikoff, L., Gavin Zuckerman, G., Watson, V. (2019). "It's all possible": Urban educators' perspectives on creating a culturally relevant, schoolwide, college-going culture for black and latino male students. *Urban Education, 54*(1), 35–64.

Korpershoek, H., Harms, T., De Boer, H., Van Kuijk, M., & Doolaard, S. (2016). A meta-analysis of the effects of classroom management strategies and classroom management programs on students' academic, behavioral, emotional, and motivational outcomes. *Review of Educational Research, 86*(3), 643–680. http://dx.doi.org/10.3102/0034654315626799

Kraft, M.A., & Blazar, D. (2017). Individualized coaching to improve teacher practice acrossgrades and subjects: New experimental evidence. *Educational Policy, 31*, 1033–1068. https://doi.org/10.1177/0895904816631099

Kraft, M. A., Blazar, D., & Hogan, D. (2018). The effect of teacher coaching on instruction and achievement: A meta-analysis of the causal evidence. *Review of Educational Research, 88*(4), 547–588. https://doi.org/10.3102/0034654318759268

Kretlow, A. G., & Bartholomew, C. C. (2010). Using coaching to improve the fidelity of evidence-based practices: A review of studies. *Teacher Education and Special Education: The Journal of the Teacher Education Division of the Council for Exceptional Children, 33*, 279–299. http://dx.doi.org/10.1177/0888406410371643

Kwok, A. (2017). Relationships between instructional quality and classroom management for beginning urban teachers. *Educational Researcher, 46*(7), 355–365. http://dx.doi.org/10.3102/0013189X17726727

Kwok, A. (2018). Promoting "quality" feedback: First-year teachers' self-reports on their development as classroom managers. *Journal of Classroom Interaction, 53*(1), 22–36.

Kwok, A., & Hardy, M. (2019) From why to how: Building relational capacity in beginning teachers. *Journal of the Effective Schools Project, 26*, 16–23.

Kwok, A. (2020). Pre-service teachers' classroom management beliefs and associated teacher characteristics. *Educational Studies, 47*(5), 609–626. http://dx.doi.org/10.1080/03055698.2020.1717932

Kwok, A. (2021). Managing classroom management preparation in teacher education. *Teachers and Teaching, 27*(1–4), 206–222. http://dx.doi.org/10.1080/13540602.2021.1933933

Kwok, A., McIntush, K., & Svajda-Hardy, M. (2020). Equitable or equal classroom management? Teacher candidates' contrasting beliefs about the impact of student demographics. *Learning Environments Research, 24*, 409–422. http://dx.doi.org/10.1007/s10984-020-09334-x

Kwok, A., & Svajda-Hardy, M. (2021). Classroom management coaching for first-year urban teachers: Purpose, design, and implementation. *Urban Education.* 1–32. https://doi.org/10.1177/00420859211058418

Larson, K. E. (2016). Classroom management training for teachers in urban environmentsserving predominately African American students: A review of the literature. *The Urban Review, 48*, 51–72. https://doi.org/10.1007/s11256-015-0345-6

Larson, K. E., Hirsch, S. E., McGraw, J. P., & Bradshaw, C. P. (2020). Preparing preservice teachers to manage behavior problems in the classroom: The feasibility and acceptability of using a mixed-reality simulator. *Journal of Special Education Technology, 35*(2), 63–75. https://doi.org/10.1177/0162643419836415

Larson, K., Pas, E., Bradshaw, C., Rosenberg, M., & Day-Vines, N. (2018). Examining how proactive management and culturally responsive teaching relate to student behavior: Implications for measurement and practice. *School Psychology Review, 47*(2), 153–166. https://doi.org/10.17105/SPR-2017-0070.V47-2

Larson, K. E., Pas, E. T., Bottiani, J. H., Kush, J. M., & Bradshaw, C. P. (2020). A multidimensional and multilevel examination of student engagement and secondary school teachers' use of classroom management practices. *Journal of Positive Behavior Interventions, 23*(3), 149–162. https://doi.org/10.1177/1098300720929352

Lathifah, Z. K., Helmanto, F., & Maryani, N. (2020). The practice of effective classroom management in COVID-19 time. *International Journal of Advanced Science and Technology, 29*(7), 3263–3271.

Lowenstein, K. L. (2009). The work of multicultural teacher education: Reconceptualizing white teacher candidates as learners. *Review of Educational Research, 79*(1), 163–196. https://doi.org/10.3102/0034654308326161

Luet, K., & Shealey, M. (2018). A matter of perspectives: Studying the persistence of fourth-hear urban teachers from two preparation programs. *Urban Education*, 1–30. http://dx.doi.org/10.1177/0042085918802630

MacSuga-Gage, A. S., Ennis, R. P., Hirsch, S. E., & Evanovich, L. (2018). Understanding and trumping behavioral concerns in the classroom. *Preventing School Failure: Alternative Education for Children and Youth, 62*(4), 239–249. https://doi.org/10.1080/1045988x.2018.1456398

Markelz, A., Riden, B., & Scheeler, M. C. (2017) Generalization training in special education teacher preparation: Does it exist? *Teacher Education and Special Education, 40*(3), 179–193. http://dx.doi.org/10.1177/0888406417703752

Martinussen, R., Tannock, R., & Chaban, P. (2011). Teachers' reported use of instructional and behavior management practices for students with behavior problems: Relationship to roleand level of training in ADHD. *Child & Youth Care Forum, 40*(3), 193–210. https://doi.org/10.1007/s10566-010-9130-6

Mason Bolick, C., & Bartels, J. Classroom management and technology. In E. Emmer & E. Sabornie (Eds.), *Handbook of classroom management: Research, practice, and contemporary issues* (pp. 446–458). Lawrence Erlbaum.

McGarr, O. (2021). The use of virtual simulations in teacher education to develop pre-service teachers' behaviour and classroom management skills: Implications for reflective practice. *Journal of Education for Teaching, 47*(2), 274–286. http://dx.doi.org/10.1080/02607476.2020.1733398

McGuire, J. M., Scott, S. S., & Shaw, S. F. (2006). Universal design and its applications in educational environments. *Remedial and Special Education, 27*(3), 166–175. https://doi.org/10.1177/07419325060270030501

McKenna, J. W., Muething, C., Flower, A., Bryant, D. P., & Bryant, B. (2015). Use and relationships among effective practices in co-taught inclusive high school classrooms. *International Journal of Inclusive Education, 19*(1), 53–70. https://doi.org/10.1080/13603116.2014.906665

McKenna, J. W., Solis, M., Brigham, F., & Adamson, R. (2019). The responsible inclusion of students receiving special education services for emotional disturbance: Unraveling the practice to research gap. *Behavior Modification, 43*(4), 587–611. https://doi.org/10.1177/0145445518762398

Meister, D. G., & Melnick, S. A. (2003). National new teacher study: Beginning teachers' concerns. *Action in Teacher Education, 24*(4), 87–94. https://doi.org/10.1080/01626620.2003.10463283

MetLife Inc. (2013). The MetLife Survey of the American teacher: Challenges of school leadership. Retrieved from: www.metlife.com/content/dam/microsites/about/corporate-profile/MetLife-Teacher-Survey-2012.pdf

Milner, H. R. (2015). Research on classroom management in urban schools. In E. Emmer & E. Sabornie (Eds.), *Handbook of classroom management* (pp. 167–185). Routledge.

Milner, H. R. (2020). Culturally responsive classroom management. *Oxford Research Encyclopedia of Education*, 1–20.

Milner, H. R., Cunningham, H. B., Delale-O'Connor, L., & Kestenberg, E. G. (2018). *"These Kids Are Out of Control": Why We Must Reimagine "Classroom Management" for Equity.* Corwin Press.

Milner, H. R., & Tenore, F. B. (2010). Classroom management in diverse classrooms. *Urban Education, 45*(5), 560–603. https://doi.org/10.1177/0042085910377290

Mitchell, B. S., Hirn, R. G., & Lewis, T. J. (2017). Enhancing effective classroom management in schools: Structures for changing teacher behavior. *Teacher Education and Special Education: The Journal of the Teacher Education Division of the Council for Exceptional Children, 40*(2), 140–153. https://doi.org/10.1177/0888406417700961

Montague, M. L. (2009). Expert secondary inclusive classroom management. Doctoral dissertation College Station, Texas A&M University. Available electronically at https://repository.tamu.edu/handle/1969.1/EDT-TAMU-2009-12-7343

Moore, T. C., Wehby, J. H., Oliver, R. M., Chow, J. C., Gordon, J. R., & Mahany, L. A. (2017). Teachers' reported knowledge and implementation of research-based classroom and behavior management strategies. *Remedial and Special Education, 38*(4), 222–232. https://doi.org/10.1177/0741932516683631

Myers, D., Freeman, J., Simonsen, B., & Sugai, G. (2017). Classroom management withexceptional learners. *TEACHING Exceptional Children, 49*(4), 223–230. https://doi.org/10.1177/0040059916685064

Myers, D., Sugai, G., Simonsen, B., & Freeman, J. (2017). Assessing teachers' behavior support skills. *Teacher Education and Special Education: The Journal of the Teacher EducationDivision of the Council for Exceptional Children, 40*(2), 128–139. https://doi.org/10.1177/0888406417700964

Nagro, S. A., Fraser, D. W., & Hooks, S. D. (2019). Lesson planning with engagement in mind: Proactive classroom management strategies for curriculum instruction. *Intervention in School and Clinic, 54*(3), 131–140. https://doi.org/10.1177/1053451218767905

Office of Special Education Programs (2015). Supporting and responding to behavior: Evidence-based classroom strategies for teachers. Retrieved from www.pbis.org/resource/supporting-and-responding-to-behavior-evidence-based-classroom-strategies-for-teachers

Oliver, R. M., & Reschly, D. J. (2010). Special education teacher preparation in classroommanagement: Implications for students with emotional and behavioral disorders. *Behavioral Disorders, 35*(3), 188–199. www.jstor.org/stable/43153818

Oliver, R. M., Wehby, J. H., & Nelson, J. R. (2015). Helping teachers maintain classroom management practices using a self-monitoring checklist. *Teaching and Teacher Education, 51*, 113–120.

Oliver, R. M., Wehby, J., & Reschly, D. J. (2011). Teacher classroom management practices: Effects on disruptive or aggressive student behavior. *Campbell Systematic Reviews, 7*(1), 1–55. https://doi.org/10.4073/csr.2011.4

O'Neill, S., & Stephenson, J. (2012). Classroom behaviour management content in Australian undergraduate primary teaching programmes. *Teaching Education, 23*(3), 287–308. http://dx.doi.org/10.1080/10476210.2012.699034

Ouellette, R. R., Frazier, S. L., Shernoff, E. S., Cappella, E., Mehta, T. G., Maríñez-Lora, A., Cua, G., & Atkins, M. S. (2018). Teacher job stress and satisfaction in urban schools: Disentangling individual-, classroom-, and organizational-level influences. *Behavior Therapy, 49*(4), 494–508. https://doi.org/10.1016/j.beth.2017.11.011

Owens, J. S., Evans, S. W., Coles, E. K., Holdaway, A. S., Himawan, L. K., Mixon, C. S., & Egan, T. E. (2020). Consultation for classroom management and targeted interventions: Examining benchmarks for teacher practices that produce desired change in student behavior. *Journal of Emotional and Behavioral Disorders, 28*(1), 52–64. https://doi.org/10.1177/1063426618795440

Pankowski, J., & Walker, J. T. (2016, Spring). Using simulation to support novice teachers' classroom management skills: Comparing traditional and alternative certification groups. *Journal of the National Association for Alternative Certification, 11*(1), 3–20

Pomerance, L., & Walsh, K. (2020). *2020 teacher prep review: Clinical practice and classroom management.* National Council on Teacher Quality. Retrieved from: www.nctq.org/publications/2020-Teacher-Prep-Review:-Clinical-Practice-and-Classroom-Management

Prilop, C. N., Weber, K. E., & Kleinknecht, M. (2021). The role of expert feedback in the development of pre-service teachers' professional vision of classroom management in an online blended learning environment. *Teaching and Teacher Education, 99*, 103276. http://dx.doi.org/10.1016/j.tate.2020.103276

Ramos, G. & Hughes, T. (2020, Spr). eJEP: eJournal of Education Policy, 21(1). https://doi.org/10.37803/ejepS2002

Reinke, W. M., Herman, K. C., Stormont, M., Newcomer, L., & David, K. (2013). Illustrating the multiple facets and levels of fidelity of implementation to a teacher classroom management intervention. *Administration and Policy in Mental Health and Mental Health Services Research, 40*, 494–506. http://dx.doi.org/10.1007/s10488-013-0496-2

Reinke, W. M., Lewis-Palmer, T., & Merrell, K. (2008). The classroom check-up: A classwide teacher consultation model for increasing praise and decreasing disruptive behavior. *School Psychology Review, 37*(3), 315–332. https://doi.org/10.1080/02796015.2008.12087879

Romi, S., Salkovsky, M., Lewis, R. (Rom). (2016). Reasons for aggressive classroom management and directions for change through teachers' professional development programmes. *Journal of Education for Teaching, 42*, 173–187. https://doi.org/10.1080/02607476.2016.1144633

Samudre, M. D., Burt, J. L., & Lejeune, L. M. (2021). An adaptation of multitiered systems of professional development to support teacher implementation of tier 2 behavioral supports. *Beyond Behavior*, 107429562110266. https://doi.org/10.1177/10742956211026672

Sanetti, L. M. H., & Collier-Meek, M. A. (2015). Data-driven delivery of implementation supports in a multitiered framework: A pilot study. *Psychology in the Schools, 52*(8), 815–828. https://doi.org/10.1002/pits.21861

Sanetti, L. M. H., Williamson, K. M., Long, A. C. J., & Kratochwill, T. R. (2018). Increasing in-service teacher implementation of classroom management practices throughconsultation, implementation planning, and participant modeling. *Journal of Positive Behavior Interventions, 20*(1), 43–59.

Santiago-Rosario, M. R., Whitcomb, S. A., Pearlman, J., & McIntosh, K. (2021). Associations between teacher expectations and racial disproportionality in discipline referrals. *Journal of School Psychology, 85*, 80–93. https://doi.org/10.1016/j.jsp.2021.02.004

Simonsen, B., Freeman, J., Kooken, J., Dooley, K., Gambino, A. J., Wilkinson, S., VanLone, J., Walters, S., Byun, S. G., Xu, X., Lupo, K., & Kern, L. (2020). Initial validation of the Classroom Management Observation Tool (CMOT). *School Psychology, 35*(3), 179–192. https://doi.org/10.1037/spq0000357

Simonsen, B., Freeman, J., Myers, D., Dooley, K., Maddock, E., Kern, L., & Byun, S. (2020). The effects of targeted professional development on teachers' use of empirically supported classroom management practices. *Journal of Positive Behavior Interventions, 22*(1), 3–14. https://doi.org/10.1177/1098300719859615

Simonsen, B., MacSuga, A. S., Fallon, L. M., & Sugai, G. (2013). Teacher self-monitoring to increase specific praise rates. *Journal of Positive Behavior Interventions, 15*, 3–13. https://doi.org/10.1177/1098300712440453

Simonsen, B., MacSuga-Gage, A. S., Briere, D. E., Freeman, J., Myers, D., Scott, T. M., & Sugai, G. (2014). Multitiered support framework for teachers' classroom-management practices. *Journal of Positive Behavior Interventions, 16*(3), 179–190. https://doi.org/10.1177/1098300713484062

Sinclair, J., Herman, K. C., Reinke, W. M., Dong, N., Stormont, M., (2021). Effects of a universal classroom management intervention on middle school students with or at risk of behavior problems. *Remedial and Special Education, 42*(1), 18–30. https://doi.org/10.1177/0741932520926610

Siwatu, K., Putman, S., Starker-Glass, T., & Lewis, C. (2017) The culturally responsive classroom management self-efficacy scale: Development and initial validation. *Urban Education, 52*(7), 862–888. http://dx.doi.org/10.1177/0042085915602534

Skiba, R. J, Horner, R. H, Chung, C. G, Rausch., M.K., May, S.L., & Tobin, T. (2011). Race is not neutral: A national investigation of African American and Latino disproportionality in school discipline. *School Psychology Review, 40*(1), 85–107. http://dx.doi.org/10.1080/02796015.2011.12087730

Solomon, B. G., Klein, S. A., & Politylo, B. C. (2012). The effect of performance feedback on teachers' treatment integrity: A meta-analysis of the single-case literature. *School Psychology Review, 41*, 160–175. http://dx.doi.org/10.1080/02796015.2012.12087518

Spooner, F., Baker, J. N., Harris, A. A., Ahlgrim-Delzell, L., & Browder, D. M. (2007). Effects of training in universal design for learning on lesson plan development. *Remedial and Special Education, 28*(2), 108–116. http://dx.doi.org/10.1177/07419325070280020101

State, T. M., Simonsen, B., Hirn, R. G., & Wills, H. (2019). Bridging the research-to-practice gap through effective professional development for teachers working with students with emotional and behavioral disorders. *Behavioral Disorders, 44*(2), 107–116. https://doi.org/10.1177/0198742918816447

Stevenson, N. A., VanLone, J., & Barber, B. R. (2020). A commentary on the misalignment of teacher education and the need for classroom behavior management skills. *Education and Treatment of Children, 43*(4), 393–404. https://doi.org/10.1007/s43494-020-00031-1

Stough, L. (2006). The place of classroom management and standards in teacher education. In C. Evertson & C. Weinstein (Eds.), *Handbook of classroom management research, practice, and contemporary issues* (pp. 909–923). Lawrence Erlbaum Associates.

Stough, L. M., & Montague, M. L. (2015). How teachers learn to be classroom managers. In E. Emmer & E. Sabornie (Eds.), *Handbook of classroom management: Research, practice, and contemporary issues* (pp. 446–458). Lawrence Erlbaum.

Stough, L. M., Montague, M. L., Landmark, L. J., & Williams-Diehm, K. (2015). Persistent classroom management training needs of experienced teachers. *Journal of the Scholarship of Teaching and Learning, 15*(5), 36–48. https://doi.org/10.14434/josotl.v15i5.13784

van Driel, S., Crasborn, F., Wolff, C. E., Brand-Gruwel, S., & Jarodzka, H. (2021). Exploring preservice, beginning and experienced teachers' noticing of classroom management situations from an actor's perspective. *Teaching and Teacher Education, 106*, 103435. https://doi.org/10.1016/j.tate.2021.103435

Veenman, S. (1984). Perceived problems of beginning teachers. *Review of Educational Research, 54*, 143–178. https://doi.org/10.3102/00346543054002143

Weber, K. E., Gold, B., Prilop, C. N., & Kleinknecht, M. (2018). Promoting pre-service teachers' professional vision of classroom management during practical school training: Effects of a structured online- and video-based self-reflection and feedback intervention. *Teaching and Teacher Education, 76*, 39–49. http://dx.doi.org/10.1016/j.tate.2018.08.008

Westling, D. L. (2010). Teachers and Challenging Behavior. *Remedial and Special Education, 31*(1), 48–63. https://doi.org/10.1177/0741932508327466

Whitaker, M. C., & Valtierra, K. M. (2018). Enhancing preservice teachers' motivation to teach diverse learners. *Teaching and Teacher Education, 73*, 171–182. https://doi.org/10.1016/j.tate.2018.04.004

Wilkinson, S., Freeman, J., Simonsen, B., Sears, S., Byun, S. G., Xu, X., & Luh, H. J. (2020). Professional development for classroom management: A review of the literature. *Educational Research and Evaluation, 26*(3–4), 182–212. https://doi.org/10.1080/13803611.2021.1934034

Wolff, C., Jarodzka, H., & Boshuizen, H. (2021). Classroom management scripts: A theoretical model contrasting expert and novice teachers' knowledge and awareness of classroom events. *Educational Psychology Review, 33*(1), 131–148. http://dx.doi.org/10.1007/s10648-020-09542-0

Woodcock, S., & Reupert, A. (2017). A tale from three countries: The classroom management practices of pre-service teachers from Australia, Canada and the United Kingdom. *Teacher Development*, *21*(5), 655–667. http://dx.doi.org/10.1080/13664530.2017.1308431

Wubbels, T., Brekelmans, M., den Brok, P., Wijsman, L., Mainhard, T., & van Tartwijk, J. (2015). Teacher-student relationships and classroom management. In E. Emmer & E. Sabornie (Eds.), *Handbook of classroom management: Research, practice, and contemporary issues* (pp. 363–386). Routledge.

15

SCHOOL ADMINISTRATION AND CLASSROOM MANAGEMENT

Lance D. Fusarelli

NORTH CAROLINA STATE UNIVERSITY

Lacey Seaton

VIRGINIA COMMONWEALTH UNIVERSITY

Claudia Saavedra Smith

NORTH CAROLINA STATE UNIVERSITY

Introduction

For much of the early history of public schooling in America, school administrators played little active role in classroom management or instructional leadership. School administrators, be they superintendents or principals, were largely responsible for the efficient organization and management of the school system. Matters pertaining to the classroom, including pedagogy and classroom management, were the province of teachers. Although Ellwood Cubberley created one of the first evaluation forms to evaluate teachers in the 1920s (Cubberley, 1923; Marzano et al., 2011), the loosely coupled nature of schooling afforded teachers a great deal of autonomy in how they ran their classrooms, what they taught, and how they taught it (Lortie, 1975).

This situation held true throughout much of the twentieth century, where the principal's role in instructional supervision and classroom management largely consisted of principals checking off extensive checklists including whether the teacher had a lesson plan, whether they covered the material they were supposed to in the curriculum, and classroom organization and management, with little attention paid to student learning (Lewis & Fusarelli, 2010), a practice Zepeda (2006) derisively called "pseudo-supervision" (p. 68). Although models of principal supervision became more prominent, much of it was pro forma. Systematic evaluation of teacher performance was the exception rather than the rule (Weick, 1976). The principal's role in classroom management largely consisted of telling teachers to maintain order and discipline. If students were not running out of control, and if parents were not complaining to the principal about the teacher, then the principal largely left teachers alone (Fusarelli & Fusarelli, 2019).

DOI: 10.4324/9781003275312-18

Classroom Management and Instructional Supervision

The late 1980s and 1990s saw states try to improve teaching and learning through more tightened command and control structures under the label of systemic reform (Cibulka & Derlin, 1995), which represented an effort to more tightly couple a loosely coupled educational system (Fusarelli, 2002; Weick, 1976). The dawn of a new century brought about No Child Left Behind in 2001 under President Bush and Race to the Top in 2009 under President Obama—reforms which directly impacted classrooms through increased use of standardized testing, assessment, and quantifiable measures of productivity. The competition for Race to the Top funding, with the Obama administration's emphasis on reforming teacher evaluation, led 36 states and the District of Columbia to change their teacher evaluation systems (Laine & Behrstock-Sherratt, 2012).

These reforms affected teachers as well as their students (Lavigne, 2014; Lewis & Fusarelli, 2010) and included comprehensive instructional design and curriculum frameworks, high-stakes testing, performance-based accountability, and disaggregation of student data including public reporting of student performance by subgroup (Cohen & Spillane, 1992; Fusarelli & Fusarelli, 2015; Robbins & Alvy, 2004; Wong, 2004). School performance data, including value-added models, are now regularly incorporated into teacher and administrator evaluations, despite the limitations of such measures, including measurement concerns (variation in teacher ratings from class to class and year to year), student characteristics, and class assignment (Darling-Hammond, 2012, 2013). The reforms had a profound impact on schooling and fundamentally changed the nature of instructional supervision toward a focus on results (Zepeda, 2013). The emphasis on student test scores quickly became the focus of both teacher and school leader evaluation systems which led them to become more tightly linked to state accountability systems (Lewis & Fusarelli, 2010; McGuinn, 2012).

Effective classroom management skills are generally recognized as an essential component of effective instructional leadership, yet pose a significant challenge, particularly for beginning teachers (Wolff et al., 2015). Effective instruction of students is dependent on effective management of the classroom. In a study of teacher effectiveness and student achievement, Stronge, Ward, and Grant (2011) found that top-quartile teachers scored significantly higher on two dimensions related to classroom management: (1) establishing routines, efficiently and effectively using time, and monitoring student behavior; and (2) ensuring availability of resources for students, making effective use of space, and the classroom layout. Top-quartile teachers had better classroom management skills, experienced fewer classroom disruptions, and developed better relationships with their students than their less effective peers. These findings are consistent with previous research demonstrating the connection between effective classroom management and student achievement (Fidler, 2002).

The pressure on principals to be instructional leaders highlights a tension inherent in the hiring process between principals' concerns about high-quality instructional leadership and effective classroom management. Studies of principals' preferences in hiring suggest that principals give more weight to teachers' dispositional characteristics such as a caring demeanor, classroom management skills, and willingness to go the extra mile than they do to teachers' content knowledge or effectiveness as measured by student performance (Engel, 2012). In a mixed method study of principals' hiring preferences in Chicago, over half of principals failed to mention teaching skills as an essential hiring criterion. Classroom management skills were identified as easy to assess during interviews through questions or responses to scenarios (Engel, 2012). Engel also identified principals in low-performing schools as placing more emphasis on classroom management skills than principals in high-performing schools; classroom management skills were cited nearly three times more often by principals in low-performing schools. These differences have important implications for equity and paint a disturbing picture of teachers as disciplinarians or managers rather than instructional leaders in schools with higher concentrations of students of color and those living in poverty. In the next section, we explore how principals can support effective classroom management so that teachers can focus more on instructional leadership in the classroom.

Principal Support for Effective Classroom Management

Since many novice teachers struggle with classroom management, principals and assistant principals play a key role in providing support to beginning teachers, particularly when the consequences of failure are high not only for students but for the teachers and leaders themselves (Sebastian et al., 2019). "In the past decade, school discipline policies and practices have garnered increasing attention because of well-documented racial, gender, and income disparities in disciplinary outcomes" (Welsh & Little, 2018, p. 752). Therefore, educational leaders need to be knowledgeable regarding equitable classroom management practices to support teachers because effective classroom management strategies have a positive impact on student learning outcomes (Gage et al., 2018; Korpershoek et al., 2016). In addition to equitable practices, consistent implementation of expectations throughout the schools increases appropriate social behaviors as students and teachers both have a clear understanding of the intended norms and behaviors (Franklin & Harrington, 2019; Gage et al., 2018; Kehoe et al., 2018; Wong, 2007; Wong et al., 2012). School leaders can support beginning teachers through effective teacher induction systems.

Teacher Induction Systems

The challenges presented for novice teachers in learning effective classroom management strategies, and the accompanying well-documented stress experienced by beginning teachers, make creation of effective teacher induction systems crucial (Reitman & Karge, 2019). Research has shown that within the first three years of teaching 20–25 percent of novice teachers abandon the profession (Clark, 2012). When expanding the timeframe to the first five years, the figure nearly doubles to 39 percent (Clark, 2012). The growing teacher turnover rates are alarming especially in low-income schools when compared to higher-income schools (Clark, 2012). "The experiences of novice teachers are considered to be the most difficult time in a teacher's career (Gavish & Friedman, 2010) and have been described in the research literature as 'sink or swim' (Lawson, 1992; Lortie, 1975), 'baptism of fire,' or 'trial of fire' experiences (Hall, 1982; Pataniczek & Isaacson, 1981)" (Clark, 2012, p. 197). One of the main causes of teacher churn stems from insufficient training pertaining to classroom management strategies (Sebastian et al., 2019). Lack of effective classroom management skills is frequently cited by principals as a hindrance to successful teaching (Range et al., 2012; Torff & Sessions, 2005). In addition to teacher ineffectiveness, erroneous classroom management skills can lead to exclusionary discipline practices which can lead to both short-term and long-term effects, such as impacting students' cognitive and noncognitive outcomes, school climate, labor market outcomes, and more (Welsh & Little, 2018). Therefore, it is imperative that districts and school leaders provide the means, support, and opportunities for new teachers to grow into their role as classroom teachers.

A key component in retaining novice teachers is to provide the necessary support through high-quality teacher induction programs. "Induction is the term used to describe all the processes through which a new teacher is introduced to the policies and culture of the school district, including the individual school, the staff, curriculum, and the community" (Bland et al., 2014, p. 4). The orientation process must begin as soon as the new teacher is hired to provide ample time for acclimating and learning about the student population and community context in which they will be serving. Induction training provides the opportunity for school and district leaders to create cohesion on how to respond to tensions as they arise in a culturally appropriate manner despite what biases new hires may bring.

Another way principals can provide support for new teachers is by assigning the right mentor, specifically one that works to overcome deficit thinking, implicit bias, and is skilled at implementing restorative practices. "Mentoring is perceived as an effective method for supporting novice teachers as it aims at fostering a relationship of ongoing support and facilitating collaboration and the development of knowledge and skills that translate into improved teaching strategies" (Gholam, 2018,

p. 2). Mentors have been found to improve retention among beginning teachers; one study found a 15 percent increase in the likelihood that a beginning teacher paired with an experienced mentor would remain in the field by the fifth year (Gray et al., 2015). The mentor must be someone who is nurturing, provides constructive feedback in a non-evaluative way, and is skilled in the areas of classroom management, differentiated instruction, and parent involvement—areas which principals identify as particularly challenging for beginning teachers (Shepherd & Devers, 2017). Ensuring both parties have uninterrupted time to observe each other, reflect, and converse will help provide the novice teacher with the reassurance, confidence, and knowledge needed to succeed.

Being assigned to a grade-level professional learning community (PLC) that is a mutual fit can also help bring out the best qualities in a novice teacher and provide some of the emotional support needed to perform the multitude of tasks required on any given day. Clark (2012) states, "most beginning teachers are left alone to succeed or fail" (p. 198). School leaders must prioritize team building and collaboration in order to create a sense of unity where teachers learn and support each other as they strive to achieve common goals. "Most importantly, this must be a community willing to accept and value perspectives offered by new teachers" (Bland et al., 2014, p. 5). PLCs also offer the perfect opportunity for teachers to model lessons prior to implementation in order to receive constructive feedback as it relates to student engagement and cultural relevance; hopefully, resulting in decreased student disruption and disengagement. Ensuring time is properly allocated to not only establish but to strengthen these support systems throughout the year is critical in creating collaborative PLCs. Although not always an easy task, the benefits reaped from these high-functioning grade-level teams can be immense.

All teachers are on a continuum of growth. One hopes that teachers progress on this continuum with the support of a variety of learning opportunities, such as professional development (PD), conferences, and strategic coaching. School leaders must be intentional in investing in PD opportunities for all teachers, but especially novice teachers. Feiman-Nemser states, "new teachers have two jobs—they have to teach, and they have to learn to teach" (Feiman-Nemser, 2001, as cited in Clark, 2012, p. 198). Even though providing novice teachers with the necessary support and resources can be costly upfront, teacher attrition rates are high and teacher turnover is estimated to cost more than $7 billion annually (Reitman & Karge, 2019). "The message for administrators is that to ensure teachers remain in the field, we need to put time and effort into planned professional learning, based on solid research and individualized support, for teachers during the first five years of their careers" (Reitman & Karge, 2019, p. 17). Teachers not only need professional learning opportunities, but they also need time to put these strategies into practice, receive feedback, and reflect on the pedagogy learned and applied. With our nation's population quickly diversifying, policies continuously changing, and best practices constantly being refined, it is imperative that teachers receive PD that is reflective of our current times and student population. Investing in teachers will help foster and grow the skills required to be successful in the classroom.

Principals, second only to classroom teachers, are the most influential school-level personnel impacting student learning (Costa et al., 2019). School administrators have the authority, responsibility, and birds-eye view needed to establish the processes to streamline the work and run the ship, per se (Clark, 2012). These include, but are not limited to, school rules, parental involvement and communication, grade level planning, and much more. "New teachers need guidance and clear expectations, but they must also find freedom and empowerment to determine how they meet these expectations" (Bland et. al., 2014, p. 5). As a result, school administrators must create a nurturing environment where novice teachers feel unafraid to embark on the challenge and whirlwind adventure that is the teaching profession. Teaching is a multifaceted career where a single being is required to possess multiple hats such as teacher, nurse, counselor, and more. Reutzel and Clark state that:

> Classroom teachers are ordinary people who do extraordinary things. They are passionate and committed individuals who truly want to make a difference in the lives of their students.

Many novice teachers enter the field of teaching with wide-eyed optimism, only to have their idealism dashed.

2011 as cited in Clark, 2012, p. 199

Ensuring that proper support is in place for new teachers should be a top priority for all school administrators in order for teachers to flourish and students to thrive. Principals' knowledge of effective classroom management strategies is key in providing such support.

Classroom Strategies

Student learning and academic achievement cannot occur in classrooms that are mismanaged and continually disrupted by behavioral misconduct (Korpershoek et al., 2016). In order for educational leaders to create schoolwide expectations regarding classroom management and provide guidance to teachers who struggle with maintaining a calm and orderly classroom, one must be aware of the strategies that researchers and practitioners suggest are most effective to employ. This section will highlight practical strategies that can be implemented in classrooms with an emphasis on preventative measures to maintain a structured environment (Korpershoek et al., 2016; Sebastian et al., 2019).

Educational leaders' awareness of effective practices for classroom management will ensure that they are supporting and training teachers on the best ways to prevent and address behavioral concerns that distract from the instructional aspect of teaching. School communities need to emphasize the importance of preventative measures pertaining to classroom management in order to be proactive instead of reactive (Anderson et al., 2019; Korpershoek et al., 2016; Sebastian et al., 2019). "Considerations such as seating layout, classroom displays, group allocations, coupled with a clear understanding of rules, routines, procedures and consequences all fall under the umbrella of prevention" (Franklin & Harrington, 2019, p. 7). Such strategies should have a direct connection to the cultural norms of the community in which the school is situated, including permitting call and response opportunities, representation throughout the curriculum, and allowing students to have a voice regarding how their behavior should be redirected.

Extant research urges teachers and school leaders alike to establish classroom procedures from the very beginning of the school year (Wong, 2007; Wong et al., 2012). Such processes require great detail to all aspects of the classroom environment. Students need to be trained from day one in how they will respond to various prompts and stimuli in their new classroom (Franklin & Harrington, 2019) and be given a chance to practice each expected routine (Wong, 2007). For example, students should have a clear understanding of how the teacher will seek their attention, where and when to submit assignments, how to move into group activities, and what to do when they walk into the classroom each morning, just to name a few (Wong, 2007; Wong et al., 2012). Payne (2008) emphasizes the importance of directly teaching students how rules and expectations may change depending on the various environments within the school such as the classroom, cafeteria, or gym, and depending on whom one is speaking to, such as another student, different teachers, or school administrators. When routines and procedures within the classroom are clear and consistent for students from the beginning of the school year, students feel comfortable about what to expect each day which decreases opportunity for behavioral outbursts due to uncertainty (Carter et al., 2017; Wong, 2007; Wong et al., 2012).

Building relationships is a simple yet critical strategy in creating a more harmonious environment and decreasing disruptions (Izard, 2016; Payne, 2008). Bass states, "Genuine relational or interpersonal caring for students is the precursor to winning student trust, providing a forum for student voice, and enhancing student efficacy and interest in school" (2012, p. 73). Being intentional about knowing each child's home life, interests, and aspirations, then connecting that information in the classroom, leads to increased student engagement in school (Morris, 2016). One simple way to build relationships with students is to greet them by their preferred name and with a smile (Hansuvadha

& Slater, 2012; Payne, 2008). Educational leaders should model what this looks like for teachers and encourage all staff to start each day with a joyful greeting for each child within their classroom. Students are more likely to actively engage in a lesson when they know the teacher cares about them (Parrett & Budge, 2012). Through relationships, teachers are able to learn about students who might be struggling with basic health or nutritional needs and address such issues prior to causing a disruption due to challenges like hunger or lack of sleep (Jensen, 2009, 2013). Moreover, as relationships develop, teachers can become more aware of the triggers that might be present within a classroom for any given student and work towards resolving issues before they arise.

When students are provided with proactive praise, they are likely to repeat the desired behavior in order to gain additional positive reinforcement (Franklin & Harrington, 2019; Sebastian et al., 2019). Students benefit from increased opportunities to interact with a lesson through answering questions or presenting to the class (Gage et al., 2018), curriculum that is relevant to their life experiences (Franklin & Harrington, 2019), and incorporating elements of student choice (Franklin & Harrington, 2019; Izard, 2016). Providing students with choices regarding which activities they will complete in addition to how they will complete the tasks help them experience a sense of control (Izard, 2016). This is especially important for students who feel everything else is spiraling out of their control and causing high stress. Students need structured time to interact with peers that allow for demonstration of the desired learning outcomes (Franklin & Harrington, 2019), yet such activities need to be well planned to avoid off-task behaviors including procedures for transitioning between tasks (Wong et al., 2012). Intentional opportunities for movement help prevent restlessness, but again students need to receive direct instruction regarding permissible behaviors during such times (Franklin & Harrington, 2019). Sometimes assumptions are made that children come to school with sound knowledge regarding social interactions, when in fact educators ought to explicitly teach emotional regulation strategies and prosocial skills (Sebastian et al., 2019).

Even in the most well-organized and structured classrooms, behavioral infractions are still likely to occur throughout the course of an academic year. As such, principals need to help prepare all school staff on how to respond to various levels of misconduct. Teachers and leaders need to be aware of the ways that their responses to minor incidents have the potential to de-escalate or heighten any given situation.

> Teacher judgment regarding the severity of misbehavior and whether or not misbehavior can be handled at the classroom level is influenced by (a) student behavior patterns, (b) the immediate context of the behavior, (c) teacher tolerance level and skills in behavior management, and (d) the resources available to the teacher for managing disruptive behavior.
>
> *Welsh & Little, 2018, p. 764*

All educators need to be cognizant of their reactions to perceived noncompliant behavior to avoid escalation or entering into a power struggle with a student. For minor disruptions a teacher's use of proximity, nonverbal communication, and eye contact (Franklin & Harrington, 2019) can help redirect the student without utilizing unnecessary exclusionary consequences, such as zero tolerance policies which exacerbate inequities. Zero tolerance policies, which were first brought into schools in 1989, required all offenses be punished uniformly despite the gravity of the behavior (Bass, 2012). These policies have been shown to be especially harmful to disadvantaged populations (Bass, 2012).

Some research has identified gender differences in how male and female principals respond to disruptive behaviors in schools. In interviews with 16 primary school principals in Israel, Oplatka and Atias (2007) found that female principals focused on listening, caring, human proximity, and emotions to diminish such behavior, while male principals focused on obedience, hierarchy, and sanctions, which the authors conclude "coincides, to a certain degree, with models of masculine and feminine leadership styles" (p. 10), a finding consistent with other studies of gender and school leadership (Regan & Brooks, 1995; Shakeshaft, 1989). When consequences are warranted they ought to be short, to the point, and consistently implemented in response to a particular behavior (Franklin & Harrington, 2019). Educators should refrain from withholding recess as a form of punishment (Love, 2019); children need physical activity and social interaction that is experienced during recreational play time (Izard, 2016). Teachers and leaders should avoid positively reinforcing the negative behavior by giving it too much attention (Franklin & Harrington, 2019). When students utilize attention-seeking behaviors, teachers need to be all the more vigilant to give such students their attention for positive behaviors as opposed to primarily responding to a disturbance. Following disciplinary actions, educational leaders should take time to engage in a reflective process with each teacher around the antecedents of the disruption and how their contributions could lead to alternative outcomes in the future (Carter et al., 2017).

Teachers should be provided with a chance to practice classroom management strategies within the safe environment of professional learning communities (PLCs). Additionally, educators benefit from the opportunity to observe peer educators' implementation of management skills in order to hone their own craft (Cansoy & Parlar, 2018; Sebastian et al., 2019). Professional development regarding classroom management must be coupled with ongoing support provided by the leadership team to garner positive outcomes such as increased academic achievement and decreased behavioral misconduct (Sebastian et al., 2019). Raising and maintaining high expectations for each student to ensure academic achievement through engaging and relevant instruction helps decrease behavioral disruptions (Skiba & Losen, 2016) and increase academic achievement (Medina et al., 2014). All too often teachers set too low of a bar for students, especially in high poverty schools (Jensen, 2009; Parrett & Budge 2012), which can lead to distraction and disengagement.

School leaders are responsible for establishing a school climate that promotes an environment suited for academic acceleration (Alhosani et al., 2017). The involvement of parents can contribute to a positive school climate and an increased commitment to educational outcomes when students, parents, teachers, and leaders work together for student success (Alhosani et al., 2017; Leithwood et al., 2020). Likewise, teachers appreciate being included in the decision-making process (Alhosani et al., 2017; Cansoy & Parlar, 2018). More specifically, as educators increase their sense of control, they also increase their sense of efficacy (Cansoy & Parlar, 2018). When teachers experience an increased involvement in the decision-making process throughout a school, Alhosani and colleagues (2017) purport that these educators have an increased commitment to implementing expectations pertaining to climate and classroom management.

Data Analysis and Student Engagement

Educators who experience success in the realm of classroom management must have an astute awareness of the linkage to student academic achievement (Sun et al., 2016). One potential trigger for behavioral misconduct within the classroom is a lack of student understanding regarding that academic content (DeMatthews et al., 2017; Franklin & Harrington, 2019). A principal who is focused on instructional leadership must train educators to recognize this association and how to address such challenges through strategic instructional design (Franklin & Harrington, 2019). When data analysis is used effectively, teachers are able to understand the individualized academic and social needs of students which can alleviate stress and reduce behavioral outbursts (Sun et al., 2016). Furthermore, strategic analysis of discipline data can help shine light on disparities occurring within particular classrooms or pertaining to any particular population subgroups (Carter et al., 2017; Skiba & Losen, 2016). Such an in-depth understanding of classroom management challenges as they pertain to disciplinary actions can guide initiatives that are targeted to specific needs within a given school (Skiba & Losen, 2016).

Data analysis should ensure that educators are hyper aware of the specific learning needs of each student within their classroom in order to effectively individualize the learning experience (Franklin & Harrington, 2019). Educational leaders have an obligation to grant teachers access to pertinent student information in a timely manner to ensure that students have access to appropriate support and interventions without delay (Sun et al., 2016). Such analyses require access to data from a variety of sources and training around how to interpret convergence of these points to understand each child as whole, as opposed to analyzing the various sources in isolation. In conjunction with data analysis across sources, teachers should be encouraged to collaborate with specialty teachers, special education teachers, English language instructors, gifted educators and psychologists to maximize resources and student success through data analysis and classroom management support.

Educational leaders ought to encourage creativity during lesson planning and implementation as a way to optimize the likelihood of student engagement (Franklin & Harrington, 2019). When students become disengaged, teachers should commit time to self-reflection regarding the interest level of the instructional design and the antecedents that led to inattentiveness (Franklin & Harrington, 2019). Educators need to be aware of their projected level of interest regarding any given lesson, meaning if the teacher finds the topic to be boring and describes the content in a droll manner, then students are likely to become disengaged (Franklin & Harrington, 2019).

Principals and assistant principals need to encourage teachers to develop strong personalized relationships with each student in their classroom (Franklin & Harrington, 2019; Ramsay-Jordon, 2020; Sebastian et al., 2019). When students feel valued and cared for personally by their teachers, they are more engaged in the learning process (Bass, 2012). Franklin and Harrington indicate that, "When teachers initiate discussion and allow room for students to use their voice, they are afforded valuable insight into how students think and what they already know" (2019, p. 4). Furthermore, when teachers know their students on an individual level, they are able to make the curriculum more relevant to their students' background and interests. Likewise, a lack of understanding of students' cultural experiences outside of the school environment prevents educators from being able to connect the academic content with the lived experiences of students (Ramsay-Jordan, 2020). Student involvement in data analysis gives ownership of goal setting and attainment to the learner, which often leads to greater effort and possibility of attainment (Franklin & Harrington, 2019).

Data audits are a great way to analyze disparities occurring in an educational environment (Skrla et al., 2009; Theoharis et al., 2020). However, this data analysis must be completed carefully so as to not reinforce deficit beliefs focusing on achievement gaps of certain subgroups (Roegman et al., 2018). Skrla and colleagues (2009) specifically encourage auditing programmatic, teacher quality, and achievement equity at the school level by disaggregating the data in comparison to the total school population. Confidential student information should only be shared with the necessary individuals, as a way of maintaining dignity and respect for any given student. When considering data audits at the school level, leaders need to be cognizant of tracking of students by gender, race, disabilities, linguistic abilities, or socio-economic status, and the potential influences of tracking on classroom management as it relates to disengagement (Ramsay-Jordon, 2020). One particularly interesting data point that principals should consider is the diversity of staff employed because of the impact that having teachers who are representative of the student population has on student attainment (Egalite et al., 2015). Principals ought to establish an ongoing professional development agenda that focuses on training teachers to analyze data and apply what they have learned within the classroom (Sun et al., 2016). Attending such professional development opportunities and mastering the content demonstrates a commitment by the leadership team which can be motivating for teachers to implement the newly acquired strategies (Sun et al., 2016). Throughout this chapter, we have highlighted some of the inequities that can result from poor classroom management. We turn now to the principal's role in redressing these inequities.

The Principal's Role in Redressing Inequities Caused by Poor Classroom Management

Due to the racial inequities produced by ineffective classroom management (poor student performance, disproportional referrals and suspensions, higher dropout rates, etc.) (Carter et al., 2017;

DeMatthews et al., 2017; Skiba & Losen, 2016) and the principal's role in addressing these inequities, we offer research-based recommendations for how school leaders can help teachers become more effective in their classrooms. School leaders are in the unique position of indirectly influencing the educational experience of students through the enforcement of expectations including those pertaining to classroom management (Leithwood et al., 2020). The principal is charged with ensuring that a consistent framework for classroom management is established and implemented throughout a school (Gage et al., 2018; Kervick et al., 2020). Such consistency is especially important due to the swift spread of undesired responses to misbehavior and the impacts such negativity has on the culture and climate of the school (Smith et al., 2015).

Understanding Bias

Educators and leaders alike need to remain astutely aware of the many ways their personal biases impact the behavior and decision-making process within schools (Carter et al., 2017; DeMatthews et al., 2017; Fergus, 2017; Franklin & Harrington, 2019; Skiba & Losen, 2016). Understanding bias is especially important for White educators who make up the majority of the teaching profession, yet whose racial and cultural identity and expectations are in contrast to the students they teach (Ramsay-Jordan, 2020). Personal biases of educators lead to assumptions about students' home life, academic capability, aspirations, and interests (Ramsay-Jordan, 2020). Educational leaders should consider themselves responsible for ensuring that every teacher spends time reflecting on their biases and working towards preventing such perspectives from negatively influencing their classroom management. The three primary biases that Fergus (2017) indicates that educators need to be especially aware of and address are color blindness, deficit thinking, and poverty disciplining. Furthermore, intentionality regarding the cultural makeup of a particular school context should be embedded in curriculum decisions and throughout all aspects of the school.

According to Gay (2013), "Within the context of U.S. history, society, and education, race is one of the most powerful, pervasive, and problematic manifestations of human difference" (p. 61). As educators, we must acknowledge race and the pivotal role it plays in our students' lives, in our classrooms, and in our teaching. Teachers need to be aware that one's beliefs and attitudes influence the way instruction is delivered; oftentimes what they teach is a reflection of themselves and the subject matter (Gay, 2013).

Racial biases can often manifest themselves in classroom management practices (Carter et al., 2017). In two experimental studies pertaining to stereotyping, researchers Okonofua and Eberhardt (2015) found that Black students were significantly more likely to invoke a teacher's desire to refer them to the office after their second minor infraction than their White counterparts. Likewise, Black students were more likely than their White peers to be considered to be troubled or labeled as students who should receive increased disciplinary attention in their future (Okonofua & Eberhardt, 2015). Data shows that Black students are 3.8 times more likely than their White classmates to be suspended in a K-12 setting (Delale-O'Connor et al., 2017). "Research has demonstrated that teachers tend to refer students of color to the office more for subjective infractions (being disrespectful) but White students are referred to the office for more objective ones (being tardy to class; Milner, 2015, Skiba, 2000; Skiba & Williams, 2014)" (Delale-O'Connor et al., 2017, p. 179).

Teachers must be prepared to respond to and address incidents of conscious and unconscious bias. Gay (2013) states, "racism is so deeply ingrained in U.S. institutions, culture, and life that it is normalized, and often difficult to recognize, especially by dominant and privileged European Americans" (p. 60). Malouff (2008) suggests external influences such as if the student is kind, hardworking, has done well in other classes, as well as their ethnic status or gender could consciously or unconsciously affect the grade a college or university professor assigns. While Malouff's experience specifically refers to higher education, the same bias awareness in grading could be of concern in the K-12 setting (2008). One way school leaders can assist teachers in counteracting these measures of bias is by participating in community immersion experiences where teachers further develop their sociopolitical consciousness (Delale-O'Connor et al., 2017). Delale-O'Connor and colleagues (2017) believe, "Community immersion may assist teachers in better interpreting students' behaviors because, as Milner (2015) noted, teachers' 'views of student behavior can be racially and culturally shaped' resulting in unnecessary conflicts" (p. 183). By engaging in activities outside of the school building, such as participating in local community-service projects, attending community meetings, or visiting students at their afterschool programs, teachers can develop a better understanding of the context surrounding a student's life outside of the school setting (Delale-O'Connor et al., 2017).

While bias commonly presents itself in matters of race, it may also present itself in matters of gender. "Children develop their own ideas about gender at an early age, as evidenced by the clothes they wear, their dramatic play, their playground talk, and their classroom work" (Frawley, 2005, p. 221). Educators must be aware of their own biases and how they may, intentionally or not, sway a child's belief in their own capabilities (Frawley, 2005). Educators must also be cognizant of the gender stereotypes they may be perpetuating daily through the "hidden curriculum—the subtle lessons that children encounter every day through teachers' behaviors, feedback, classroom segregation, and instructional materials" (Frawley, 2005, p. 221). Educators must strive to create an environment that is equitable and free of sex-role stereotypes in order to maximize student performance (Frawley, 2005; Morris, 2016).

In order to recognize one's own biases, school leaders must provide teachers with learning opportunities where one can reflect on their practices, converse with others, and push their thinking. "Teaching requires an obligation to question deeply rooted sexist attitudes and a willingness to use a variety of teaching strategies to help children understand that sexism and stereotypes have harmful personal and social effects and consequences" (Frawley, 2005, p. 226). Teaching also requires an ongoing commitment to analyzing one's own teaching, cultural competencies, and instructional materials to ensure gender and racial biases are not being (consciously or unconsciously) cemented into the minds of our youth.

Cultural Competencies

Hansuvadha and Slater (2012) define cultural competence as "the knowledge, behaviors, and dispositions necessary to effectively interact with other cultural groups" (p. 174). The importance of cultural competence in education has been emphasized in the literature for the last few decades; unfortunately, the implementation of such practices has not been generalized throughout all schools (Ramsay-Jordan, 2020). Skiba and Losen (2016) assert that "by integrating students' racial/ethnic, gender, and sexual identities into curricula, resources, and school events, effective schools find that students feel safer, report lower rates of victimization and discrimination, and have higher achievement" (p. 8). Yet, all too often teachers graduate from preparation programs without truly learning about cultures outside of their own (Love, 2019), and as such the responsibility to ensure that teachers know how to actualize such concepts lies in the hands of educational leaders.

"The five basics of culturally responsive teaching as laid out by Gay (2000) are the following: (1) cultural competence, (2) culturally relevant curriculum, (3) supportive learning community, (4) cultural congruity, and (5) effective instruction" (DeCapua & Marshall, 2015, p. 359). In order for educators and leaders to demonstrate cultural competence, one must develop an understanding of their students' customs and traditions that go beyond the surface. DeCapua and Marshall (2015) compare culture to an iceberg: "heroes and holidays" are viewed as the narrow peak, visible to outsiders; however, the bulk of the weight is hidden below the surface, just like the nuance of one's culture.

Teachers must be intentional about infusing meaningful content and elements of their students' culture into the curriculum (DeCapua & Marshall, 2015; Gay, 2013). By connecting the student's home life to the curriculum, teachers are recognizing the value brought by students instead of ignoring their heritage (DeCapua & Marshall, 2015; Gay, 2013). Consequently, by using resources with which students can identify, teachers can enrich the curriculum (DeCapua & Marshall, 2015). Other methods can also improve learning accessibility; teachers, for example, can implement cultural scaffolding to present content and language students are familiar with and the funds of knowledge students bring are purposefully permeated into the school day (DeCapua & Marshall, 2015). By drawing on a student's funds of knowledge, one is utilizing content and life experiences gathered in their home life and incorporating it into their learning environment (DeCapua & Marshall, 2015).

Another piece of culturally responsive teaching is providing educators and students the knowledge and tools to where they feel empowered to view strategies and teaching resources with a critical lens while addressing any information that may be lacking (Gay, 2013). Often times, resources provided and available to teachers provide a skewed view of people from diverse cultural backgrounds (Gay, 2013). Teachers should be constantly reviewing the curriculum to ensure accurate information is being taught in order to counteract the falsehoods perpetuated in schools and in society (Gay, 2013). "Beyond those individual characteristics of academic achievement and cultural competence, students must develop a broader sociopolitical consciousness that allows them to critique the cultural norms, values, mores, and institutions that produce and maintain social inequities" (Ladson-Billings, 1995, p. 162).

In order for students to be active learners, teachers must create a safe and positive learning community where students feel comfortable being their authentic self (DeCapua & Marshall, 2015; Gay, 2013; Ladson-Billings, 1995). If teachers are unaware of cultural differences, then certain student behaviors can be misinterpreted as defiant or disrespectful (DeCapua & Marshall, 2015; Ladson-Billings, 1995). Teacher-student relationships are key to the academic success and well-being of students. Teachers must also make every effort to pronounce their students' names correctly; if mispronounced, students may believe their teacher lacks care for them, their family, or their culture (Hansuvadha & Slater, 2012).

School administrators must serve as advocates for their students and staff. Administrators serving our schools are predominantly white and classrooms are becoming increasingly diverse; therefore, it is up to the school leaders to "monitor and model attitudes and practices that promote cultural diversity" (Hansuvadha & Slater, 2012, p. 175). Districts can support school administrators in becoming more culturally competent by providing them with a mentor who understands the "hidden curriculum" and providing carefully planned cross-cultural experiences where leaders gain a deeper understanding of an unfamiliar culture without reinforcing stereotypes (Hansuvadha & Slater, 2012).

Restorative Practices

Principals, particularly assistant principals, often spend a disproportionate amount of time dealing with discipline issues, some if not most of which would not have become issues had teachers utilized more effective classroom management techniques. Exclusionary discipline disproportionately impacts students from groups that have been historically marginalized, such as students of color or students who have been identified with a disability (Carter et al., 2017; Fergus, 2017; Kervick et al., 2020; Ramsay-Jordan, 2020; Skiba & Losen, 2016; Smith et al., 2015; Welsh & Little, 2018). Suspension has been found to be linked to greater risk of negative student outcomes, for example, incarceration, drop out, additional suspensions, or lower academic achievement (Anderson et al., 2019; DeMatthews et al., 2017; Ramsay-Jordan, 2020; Skiba & Losen, 2016). In an effort to combat such disparities, restorative practices (RP) are being emphasized to establish environments that value keeping students in the classroom (Englehart, 2014; Skiba & Losen, 2016). Kervick and colleagues (2020) state that "schoolwide RP practices draw from the community-based restorative justice model in criminal justice, utilizing prevention and intervention strategies to build community, strengthen relationships among students and adults, and reduce punitive discipline" (p. 156). They go on to say, "whole school restorative practices promote positive and healthy school climates focused on relationship building and repairing harm when behavioral infractions occur (Kidde, 2017)" (Kervick et al., 2020, p. 156).

Students who attend schools that implement restorative practice report an increased awareness of their behavior and are adept at producing more positive outcomes through mastering socially appropriate responses (Kehoe et al., 2018). Benefits of restorative practice implementation in education include reduction in behavioral outbursts, bullying, depression, and anxiety, while increasing students' time in school, academic achievement, social skills, and a more positive culture and climate for both students and staff (Kehoe et al., 2018; Skiba & Losen, 2016). Restorative practices provide students with the space to reflect on their negative behaviors and learn ways to respond to such triggers or incidences differently in the future (Englehart, 2014; Kehoe et al., 2018; Smith et al., 2015). Alternative ways to solve conflicts that do not end in suspension or expulsion are emphasized using restorative practices (Skiba & Losen, 2016). Restorative circles are one of the more prominent elements from restorative practices that schools employ (Kehoe et al., 2018; Kervick et al., 2020). The use of circles in schools gives teachers and students the opportunity to discuss behavioral expectations, direct teach what socially acceptable behaviors look like in schools, practice ways to resolve conflicts as they arise, and to be cognizant of escalating tension to learn ways to de-escalate an incident before disruption occurs (Kehoe et al., 2018; Smith et al., 2015). McCluskey and colleagues (2008) suggest the use of restorative conferencing as a way to repair damaged relationships following any form of conflict.

Principals and assistant principals must model for the school community what such practices should look like in action when addressing disciplinary referrals. If school leaders revert back to the historic practice of suspension, restorative practices will not persist (Kervick et al., 2020; McCluskey et al., 2008). Non-instructional personnel should also be included in training pertaining to the implementation of the restorative practice model in order to ensure that such a mindset permeates the total school (Ramsay-Jorden, 2020; Skiba & Losen, 2016); especially school resource officers because their presence in schools has been linked to increased criminalization of student behaviors (Carter et al., 2017). As school leaders embark upon implementing restorative practices, consideration of the various elements and frameworks in regards to existent research should be in conjunction with the context and needs of their specific school (Kervick et al., 2020). Principals will likely face some resistance when pursuing implementation of restorative practices (DeMatthews et al., 2017; McCluskey et al., 2008), yet the ultimate positive outcomes for the school community make it worth persisting (Kehoe et al., 2018). Principals ought to be cognizant that successful implementation of restorative practices in schools requires at least three to five years to begin to see positive outcomes at the whole school level (Blood & Thorsborne, 2005 as cited in Kehoe et al., 2018). Throughout this chapter, we have highlighted various ways in which principals can support effective classroom management. We turn now to the limitations principals face in providing such support.

Limitations of Principals' Supervision of Teachers' Classroom Management Performance

Although principals may want to be more involved in helping teachers with classroom management and instruction, several barriers exist, both structural and cultural, which limit such efforts. One such structural barrier is lack of time. The time demands on principals and assistant principals to fully engage with the more elaborate teacher evaluation systems currently practiced have expanded dramatically (Kersten & Israel, 2005; Range, et al., 2012; Weisberg et al., 2009). Observing teachers multiple times throughout the year can be a full-time job itself and can affect the quality and depth of feedback (Kraft & Gilmour, 2016). Principals have little time to be dealing with unruly classrooms. Thus, it comes as no surprise that many principals place a priority on classroom management skills in the hiring process.

School culture and norms are also limiting factors in supervision of classroom management and teacher evaluation. Principals may be reluctant to provide critical feedback and negative evaluation ratings, which require extensive documentation (Donaldson, 2009). Further, principal-teacher interactions operate within a micropolitical context shaped by "contracts, state and district personnel policies, and precedents set by local experiences with teacher dismissals" (Cooper et al., 2005, p. 112). Since principals in some states such as North Carolina are evaluated in part by teacher satisfaction as measured in the Teachers Working Conditions Survey, there is a degree of self-interest in maintaining good relationships between principals and teachers (Sartain et al., 2011). Some principals simply prefer to avoid conflict altogether, particularly if the behavior is unlikely to change (Danielson & McGreal, 2000). As a result, many principals prefer less confrontational methods to remove teachers, such as counseling them out of the school or profession or relying on voluntary retirement (Range, et al., 2012).

School context also matters. Hard to staff schools, often in high poverty urban or rural areas, have a difficult time attracting and retaining teachers, regardless of ability or performance (Fusarelli & Fusarelli, 2019; Sutcher et al., 2019). Faced with limited options, principals are more likely to tolerate uneven instruction or problematic classroom management practices. Unfortunately, this situation creates inequities in instructional delivery and student performance and further exacerbates differences in the experiences of students in high poverty versus high wealth schools.

Conclusion

Regardless of the strategy being implemented, recurring professional development for educators in a variety of formats is paramount to the success of any initiative in education including classroom management (Kervick et al., 2020; Sebastian et al., 2019; Skiba & Losen, 2016; Sun et al., 2016). Furthermore, the school leader's ability to model any given strategy consistently for the community including teachers, students, and parents enhances the likelihood of increased success pertaining to classroom management (Kerick et al., 2020; Sun et al., 2016). Principals should strive to influence policy changes that would reduce the use of exclusionary discipline procedures for minor infractions (Skiba & Losen, 2016) and emphasize alternative measures that address the behavioral concern but keep students in the classroom learning (Anderson et al., 2019). Educational leaders carry the weight of their school on their shoulders, and it is our hope that by providing them with the aforementioned strategies they will feel empowered to create a lasting effect that transcends their school walls and positively impacts society at large.

References

Alhosani, A. A., Singh, S. K., & Al Nahyan, M. T. (2017). Role of school leadership and climate in student achievement: The mediating role of parental involvement. *International Journal of Educational Management*, *31*(6), 843–851. http://dx.doi.org.prox.lib.ncsu.edu/10.1108/IJEM-05-2016-0113

Anderson, K. P., Ritter, G. W., & Zamarro, G. (2019). Understanding a vicious cycle: The relationship between student discipline and student academic outcomes. *Educational Researcher*, *48*(5), 251–262. http://dx.doi.org.prox.lib.ncsu.edu/10.3102/0013189X19848720

Bass, L. (2012). When care trumps justice: The operationalization of black feminist caring in educational leadership. *International Journal of Qualitative Studies in Education (QSE)*, *25*(1), 73–87. http://dx.doi.org.prox.lib.ncsu.edu/10.1080/09518398.2011.647721

Bland, P., Church, E., & Luo, M. (2014). Strategies for attracting and retaining teachers. *Administrative Issues Journal: Connecting Education, Practice, and Research*, *4*(1), 545–555. https://doi-org.proxy.library.vcu.edu/10.5929/2014.4.1.2

Cansoy, R., & Parlar, H. (2018). Examining the relationship between school principals' instructional leadership behaviors, teacher self-efficacy, and collective teacher efficacy. *International Journal of Educational Management*, *32*(4), 550–567. http://dx.doi.org/10.1108/IJEM-04-2017-0089

Carter, P. L., Skiba, R., Arredondo, M. I., & Pollock, M. (2017). You can't fix what you don't look at: Acknowledging race in addressing racial discipline disparities. *Urban education*, *52*(2), 207–235. http://dx.doi.org.prox.lib.ncsu.edu/10.1177/0042085916660350

Cibulka, J. G., & Derlin, R. L. (1995). State educational performance reporting policies in the U.S.: Accountability's many faces. *International Journal of Educational Research*, *23*(6), 479–492. https://doi.org/10.1016/0883-0355(96)89554-1

Clark, S. K. (2012). The plight of the novice teacher. *Clearing House: A Journal of Educational Strategies, Issues and Ideas*, *85*(5), 197–200. www-tandfonline-com.prox.lib.ncsu.edu/doi/abs/10.1080/00098655.2012.689783

Cohen, D. K., & Spillane, J. P. (1992). Chapter 1: Policy and practice: The relations between governance and instruction. *Review of Research in Education*, *18*(1), 3–49. https://doi-org.proxy.library.vcu.edu/10.2307/1167296

Cooper, B. S., Ehrensal, P. A., & Bromme, M. (2005). School-level politics and professional development: Traps in evaluating the quality of practicing teachers. *Educational Policy*, *19*(1), 112–125. http://dx.doi.org.prox.lib.ncsu.edu/10.1177/0895904804272231

Costa, E., Almeida, M., Pinho, A. S., & Pipa, J. (2019). School leaders' insights regarding beginning teachers' induction in Belgium, Finland and Portugal. *Eurasian Journal of Educational Research*, *19*(81), 57–77. https://doi-org.proxy.library.vcu.edu/10.14689/ejer.2019.81.4

Cubberley, E. P. (1923). *The principal and his school: The organization, administration, and supervision of instruction in an elementary school*. The Riverside Press.

Danielson, C., & McGreal, T. L. (2000). *Teacher evaluation to enhance professional practice*. Association for Supervision and Curriculum Development.

Darling-Hammond, L. (2012). *Creating a comprehensive system for evaluating and supporting effective teaching*. Stanford Center for Opportunity Policy in Education. https://edpolicy.stanford.edu/publications/pubs/591

Darling-Hammond, L. (2013). *Getting teacher evaluation right: What really matters for effectiveness and improvement*. Teachers College Press. http://store.tcpress.com/0807754463.shtml

DeCapua, A., & Marshall, H. W. (2015). Reframing the conversation about students with limited or interrupted formal education: From achievement gap to cultural dissonance. *NASSP Bulletin*, *99*(4), 356–370. http://dx.doi.org.prox.lib.ncsu.edu/10.1177/0192636515620662

Delale-O'Connor, L. A., Alvarez, A. J., Murray, I. E., & Milner, H. R., IV (2017). Self-efficacy beliefs, classroom management, and the cradle-to-prison pipeline. *Theory Into Practice*, *56*(3), 178–186. http://dx.doi.org.prox.lib.ncsu.edu/10.1080/00405841.2017.1336038

DeMatthews, D. E., Carey, R. L., Olivarez, A., & Moussavi Saeedi, K. (2017). Guilty as charged? Principals' perspectives on disciplinary practices and the racial discipline gap. *Educational Administration Quarterly*, *53*(4), 519–555. http://dx.doi.org.prox.lib.ncsu.edu/10.1177/0013161X17714844

Donaldson, M. L. (2009). *So long, Lake Wobegon? Using teacher evaluation to raise teacher quality*. Center for American Progress. www.americanprogress.org/issues/education/reports/2009/06/25/6243/so-long-lake-wobegon/

Egalite, A. J., Kisida, B., & Winters, M. A. (2015). Representation in the classroom: The effect of own-race teachers on student achievement. *Economics of Education Review*, *45*, 44–52. https://doi.org/10.1016/j.econedurev.2015.01.007

Engel, M. (2012). Problematic preferences? A mixed method examination of principals' preferences for teacher characteristics in Chicago. *Educational Administration Quarterly*, *49*(1), 52–91. http://dx.doi.org.prox.lib.ncsu.edu/10.1177/0013161X12451025

Englehart, J. M. (2014). Attending to the affective dimensions of bullying: Necessary approaches for the school leader. *Planning & Changing*, *45*(1), 19–30. http://education.illinoisstate.edu/planning/articles/vol45.php

Fergus, E. (2017). The integration project among white teachers and racial/ethnic minority youth: Understanding bias in school practice. *Theory into Practice*, *56*(3), 169–177. http://dx.doi.org.prox.lib.ncsu.edu/10.1080/00405841.2017.1336036

Fidler, P. (2002). *The relationship between teacher instructional techniques and characteristics and student achievement in reduced size classes*. Los Angeles Unified School District, CA. Program Evaluation and Research Branch. ERIC Document ED 473 460.

Franklin, H., & Harrington, I. (2019). A review into effective classroom management and strategies for student engagement: Teacher and student roles in today's classrooms. *Journal of Education and Training Studies*, *7*(12), 1–12. https://doi.org/10.11114/jets.v7i12.4491

Frawley, T. (2005). Gender bias in the classroom: Current controversies and implications for teachers. *Childhood Education*, *81*(4), 221–227. https://doi.org/10.1080/00094056.2005.10522277

Fusarelli, L. D. (2002). Tightly coupled policy in loosely coupled systems: Institutional capacity and organizational change. *Journal of Educational Administration*, *40*(6), 561–575. https://doi.org/10.1108/09578230210446045

Fusarelli, L. D., & Fusarelli, B. C. (2015). Federal education policy from Reagan to Obama: Convergence, divergence, and "control." In B. S. Cooper, J. G. Cibulka, & L. D. Fusarelli (Eds.), *Handbook of education politics and policy* (2nd ed., pp. 189–210). Routledge.

Fusarelli, L. D., & Fusarelli, B. C. (2019). Instructional supervision in an era of high-stakes accountability. In S. J. Zepeda and J. A. Ponticell (Eds.), *The Wiley Handbook of Educational Supervision* (pp. 131–156). Wiley Blackwell.

Gage, N. A., Scott, T., Hirn, R., & MacSuga-Gage, A. S. (2018). The relationship between teachers' implementation of classroom management practices and student behavior in elementary school. *Behavioral Disorders*, *43*(2), 302–315. http://journals.sagepub.com.prox.lib.ncsu.edu/doi/full/10.1177/0198742917714809

Gavish, B., & Friedman, I A. (2010). Novice teachers' experience of teaching: A dynamic aspect of burnout. *Social Psychology of Education*, *13*(2), 141–167. https://10.1007/s11218-009-9108-0

Gay, G. (2013). Teaching to and through cultural diversity. *Curriculum Inquiry*, *43*(1), 48–70. https://doi.org/10.1111/curi.12002

Gholam, A. (2018). A mentoring experience: From the perspective of a novice teacher. *International Journal of Progressive Education*, *14*(2), 1–12. https://doi.org/10.29329/ijpe.2018.139.1

Gray, L., Taie, S., & O'Rear, I. (2015). *Public school teacher attrition and mobility in the first five years: Results from the first through fifth waves of the 2007-08 beginning teacher longitudinal study.* U.S. Department of Education, National Center for Education Statistics.

Hall, G. E. (1982). Induction: The missing link. *Journal of Teacher Education*, *33*(3), 53–55. https://doi.org/10.1177%2F002248718203300311

Hansuvadha, N., & Slater, C. L. (2012). Culturally competent school leaders: The individual and the system. *The Educational Forum*, *76*(2), 174–189. http://dx.doi.org.prox.lib.ncsu.edu/10.1080/00131725.2011.653094

Izard, E. (2016). *Teaching children from poverty and trauma.* National Education Association. https://files.eric.ed.gov/fulltext/ED594465.pdf

Jensen, E. (2009). *Teaching with poverty in mind: What being poor does to kids' brains and what schools can do about it.* ASCD.

Jensen, E. (2013). *Engaging students with poverty in mind: Practical strategies for raising achievement.* ASCD.

Kehoe, M., Bourke-Taylor, H., & Broderick, D. (2018). Developing student social skills using restorative practices: A new framework called HEART. *Social Psychology of Education*, *21*(1), 189–207. http://dx.doi.org.prox.lib.ncsu.edu/10.1007/s11218-017-9402-1

Kersten, T. A., & Israel, M. S. (2005). Teacher evaluation: Principal's insights and suggestions for improvement. *Planning and Changing*, *36*(1&2), 47–67. http://education.illinoisstate.edu/planning/

Kervick, C. T., Garnett, B., Moore, M., Ballysingh, T. A., & Smith, L. C. (2020). Introducing restorative practices in a diverse elementary school to build community and reduce exclusionary discipline: Year one processes, facilitators, and next steps. *The School Community Journal*, *30*(2), 155–183. http://proxy.library.vcu.edu/login?url=https://search.ebscohost.com/login.aspx?direct=true&AuthType=ip,url,cookie,uid&db=ehh&AN=147493819&site=ehost-live&scope=site

Korpershoek, H., Harms, T., de Boer, H., van Kuijk, M., & Doolaard, S. (2016). A meta-analysis of the effects of classroom management strategies and classroom management programs on students' academic, behavioral, emotional, and motivational outcomes. *Review of Educational Research*, *86*(3), 643–680. http://dx.doi.org.prox.lib.ncsu.edu/10.3102/0034654315626799

Kraft, M. A., & Gilmour, A. F. (2016). Can principals promote teacher development as evaluators? A case study of principals' views and experiences. *Educational Administration Quarterly*, *52*(5), 711–753. https://doi.org/10.1177/0013161X16653445

Ladson-Billings, G. (1995). But that's just good teaching: The case for culturally relevant pedagogy. *Theory Into Practice*, *34*(3), 159–165. https://doi.org/10.3102/00028312032003465

Laine, S., & Behrstock-Sherratt, E. (2012). Strengthening teacher evaluation in the age of accountability. Retrieved August 22, 2016 from www.advanc-ed.org/source/strengthening-teacher-evaluation-age-accountability

Lavigne, A. L. (2014). Exploring the intended and unintended consequences of high-stakes teacher evaluation on schools, teachers, and students. *Teachers College Record*, *116*, 1–29. www.tcrecord-org.proxy.library.vcu.edu/library/content.asp?contentid=17294

Lawson, H. A. (1992). Beyond the new conception of teacher induction. *Journal of Teacher Education*, *43*(3), 163–172. https://doi.org/10.1177%2F0022487192043003002

Leithwood, K., Harris, A., & Hopkins, D. (2020). Seven strong claims about successful school leadership revisited. *School Leadership & Management*, *40*(1), 5–22. http://dx.doi.org.prox.lib.ncsu.edu/10.1080/13632434.2019.1596077

Lewis, W. D., & Fusarelli, L. D. (2010). Leading schools in an era of change: Toward a "new" culture of accountability? In S. D. Horsford (Ed.), *New perspectives in educational leadership: Exploring social, political, and community contexts and meaning* (pp. 111–125). Peter Lang.

Lortie, D. C. (1975). *Schoolteacher: A sociological study.* University of Chicago Press.

Love, B. L. (2019). *We want to do more than survive: Abolitionist teaching and the pursuit of educational freedom.* Beacon Press.

Malouff, J. (2008). Bias in grading. *College Teaching*, *56*(3), 191–192. https://doi.org/10.3200/CTCH.56.3.191-192

Marzano, R. J., Frontier, T., & Livingston, D. (2011). *Effective supervision: Supporting the art and science of teaching.* ASCD.

McCluskey, G., Lloyd, G., Kane, J., Riddell, S., Stead, J., & Weedon, E. (2008). Can restorative practices in schools make a difference? *Educational Review*, *60*(4), 405–417. www.informaworld.com.prox.lib.ncsu.edu/open url?genre=article&id=doi:10.1080/00131910802393456

McGuinn, P. (2012). Stimulating reform: Race to the top, competitive grants and the Obama education agenda. *Educational Policy*, *26*(1), 136–159. http://dx.doi.org.prox.lib.ncsu.edu/10.1177/0895904811425911

Medina, V., Martinez, G., Murakami, E. T., Rodriguez, M., & Hernandez, F. (2014). Principals' perceptions from within: Leadership in high-need schools in the USA. *Management in Education*, *28*(3), 91–96. http://dx.doi.org.prox.lib.ncsu.edu/10.1177/0892020614537664

Milner, H. R. (2015). *Rac(e)ing to class: Confronting poverty and race in schools and classrooms*. Harvard Educational Press.

Morris, M. (2016). *Pushout: The criminalization of Black girls in schools*. The New Press.

Okonofua, J. A., & Eberhardt, J. L. (2015). Two strikes: Race and the disciplining of young students. *Psychological Science*, *26*(5), 617–624. https://doi.org/10.1177/0956797615570365

Oplatka, I., & Atias, M. (2007). Gendered views of managing discipline in school and classroom. *Gender & Education*, *19*(1), 41–59. www.informaworld.com.prox.lib.ncsu.edu/openurl?genre=article&id=doi:10.1080/09540250601087751

Parrett, W. H., & Budge, K. M. (2012). *Turning high-poverty schools into high-performing schools*. ASCD.

Pataniczek, D., & Isaacson, N. S. (1981). The relationship of socialization and the concerns of beginning secondary teachers. *Journal of Teacher Education*, *32*(3), 14–17. https://doi.org/10.1177%2F002248718103200303

Payne, R. (2008). Nine powerful practices. *Educational Leadership*, *65*(7), 48–52. www.ascd.org/portal/site/ascd/menuitem.a4dbd0f2c4f9b94cdeb3ffdb62108a0c/

Ramsay-Jordan, N. (2020). Understanding the impact of differences: Using tenets of critical race pedagogy to examine white pre-service teachers' perceptions of their black students' race & culture. *Multicultural Education*, *27*(2), 2–17. www.caddogap.com/periodicals.shtml

Range, B. G., Duncan, H. E., Scherz, S. D., & Haines, C. A. (2012). School leaders' perceptions about incompetent teachers: Implications for supervision and evaluation. *NASSP Bulletin*, *96*(4), 302–322. http://dx.doi.org.prox.lib.ncsu.edu/10.1177/0192636512459554

Regan, H. B., & Brooks, G. H. (1995). *Out of women's experience: Creating relational leadership*. Corwin Press.

Reitman, G. C., & Karge, B. D. (2019). Investing in teacher support leads to teacher retention: Six supports administrators should consider for new teachers. *Multicultural Education*, *27*(1), 7–18. https://vcu.primo.exlibrisgroup.com/permalink/01VCU_INST/6i0npe/cdi_proquest_journals_2366666286

Robbins, P., & Alvy, H. (2004). *The new principal's fieldbook: Strategies for success*. Association for Supervision and Curriculum Development.

Roegman, R., Samarapungavan, A., Maeda, Y., & Johns, G. (2018). Color-neutral disaggregation? Principals' practices around disaggregating data from three school districts. *Educational Administration Quarterly*, *54*(4), 559–588. http://dx.doi.org.prox.lib.ncsu.edu/10.1177/0013161X18769052

Sartain, L., Stoelinga, S. R., & Brown, E. R. (2011). *Rethinking teacher evaluation in Chicago: Lessons learned from classroom observations, principal-teacher conferences, and district implementation*. University of Chicago Consortium on Chicago School Research.

Sebastian, J., Herman, K. C., & Reinke, W. M. (2019). Do organizational conditions influence teacher implementation of effective classroom management practices: Findings from a randomized trial. *Journal of School Psychology*, *72*, 134–149. https://doi-org.prox.lib.ncsu.edu/10.1016/j.jsp.2018.12.008

Shakeshaft, C. (1989). *Women in educational administration*. Corwin Press.

Shepherd, D., & Devers, C. J. (2017). Principal perceptions of new teacher effectiveness. *Journal of Education*, *197*(2), 37–47. www.bu.edu/journalofeducation/current-issues/

Skiba, R. J. (2000, August). *Zero tolerance, zero evidence: An analysis of school disciplinary practice*. Indiana Education Policy Center, Policy Research Report #SRS2, ED 469 537. www.academia.edu/62771760/Zero_tolerance_zero_evidence_an_analysis_of_school_disciplinary_practice

Skiba, R. J., & Losen, D. J. (2016). From reaction to prevention: Turning the page on school discipline. *American Educator*, *39*(4), 4–11. http://proxy.library.vcu.edu/login?url=https://search.ebscohost.com/login.aspx?direct=true&AuthType=ip,url,cookie,uid&db=ehh&AN=112081042&site=ehost-live&scope=site

Skiba, R. J., & Williams, N. T. (2014). *Are Black kids worse? Myths and facts about racial differences in behavior*. The Equity Project at Indiana University. www.indiana.edu/~atlantic/wp-content/uploads/2014/03/African-American-Differential-Behavior_031214.pdf

Skrla, L., McKenzie, K. B., & Scheurich, J. J. (Eds.) (2009). *Using equity audits to create equitable and excellent schools*. Corwin Press.

Smith, D., Fisher, D., & Frey, N. (2015). *Better than carrots or sticks: Restorative practices for positive classroom management*. ASCD.

Stronge, J. H., Ward, T. J., & Grant, L. W. (2011). What makes good teachers good? A cross-case analysis of the connection between teacher effectiveness and student achievement. *Journal of Teacher Education, 62*(4), 339–355. http://dx.doi.org.prox.lib.ncsu.edu/10.1177/0022487111404241

Sun, J., Przybylski, R., & Johnson, B. J. (2016). A review of research on teachers' use of student data: From the perspective of school leadership. *Educational Assessment, Evaluation and Accountability, 28*(1), 5–33. http://dx.doi.org.prox.lib.ncsu.edu/10.1007/s11092-016-9238-9

Sutcher, L., Darling-Hammond, L., & Carver-Thomas, D. (2019). Understanding teacher shortages: An analysis of teacher supply and demand in the United States. *Education Policy Analysis Archives, 27*(35), 1–40. https://doi.org/10.14507/epaa.27.3696

Theoharis, G., Causton, J., Woodfield, C., & Scribner, S. (2020). Inclusive leadership and disability. In G. Theoharis and M. Scanlan (Eds.), *Leadership for increasingly diverse schools* (2nd edition, pp. 17–56). Routledge.

Torff, B., & Sessions, D. N. (2005). Principals' perceptions of the causes of teacher ineffectiveness. *Journal of Educational Psychology, 97*(4), 530–537. http://content.apa.org.prox.lib.ncsu.edu/journals/edu/97/4

Weick, K. E. (1976). Educational organizations as loosely coupled systems. *Administrative Science Quarterly, 21,* 1–19. https://doi.org/10.2307/2391875

Weisberg, D., Sexton, S., Mulhern, J., & Keeling, D. (2009). *The widget effect: Our national failure to acknowledge and act on differences in teacher effectiveness.* The New Teacher Project. www.carnegie.org/publications/widget-effect/

Welsh, R. O., & Little, S. (2018). The school discipline dilemma: A comprehensive review of disparities and alternative approaches. *Review of Educational Research, 88*(5), 752–794. http://dx.doi.org.prox.lib.ncsu.edu/10.3102/0034654318791582

Wolff, C. E., van den Bogert, N., Jarodzka, H., & Boshuizen, H. P. A. (2015). Keeping an eye on learning: Differences between expert and novice teachers' representations of classroom management events. *Journal of Teacher Education, 66*(1), 68–85. http://dx.doi.org.prox.lib.ncsu.edu/10.1177/0022487114549810

Wong, H. K. (2007). The well-managed classroom. *Excerpt from The First Days of School.* Retrieved May 9, 2021, from http://go.hrw.com/resources/go_sc/gen/HSTPR034.PDF

Wong, H., Wong, R., Rogers, K., & Brooks, A. (2012). Managing your classroom for success. *Science and Children, 49*(10), 60–64. www.nsta.org/publications/browse_journals.aspx?action=issue&id=10.2505/3/sc12_049_09

Wong, K. K. (2004). The politics of education. In V. Gray and R. L. Hanson (Eds.), *Politics in the American states* (8th ed., pp. 357–388). Congressional Quarterly.

Zepeda, S. J. (2006). High stakes supervision: We must do more. *International Journal of Leadership in Education, 9*(1), 61–73. www.informaworld.com.prox.lib.ncsu.edu/openurl?genre=article&id=doi:10.1080/136031 20500448154

Zepeda, S. J. (2013). *The principal as instructional leader.* Routledge.

16

THE CONTRIBUTION OF SCHOOL AND CLASSROOM DISCIPLINARY PRACTICES TO THE SCHOOL-TO-PRISON PIPELINE

David Osher

AMERICAN INSTITUTES FOR RESEARCH

Stephen Plank

ANNIE E. CASEY FOUNDATION

Candace Hester

AMERICAN INSTITUTES FOR RESEARCH

Scott Houghton

AMERICAN INSTITUTES FOR RESEARCH

Schools and school practices contribute in major ways to the disproportionate and high level of incarceration of historically marginalized groups, including Black, Latinx, and Native American people (Girvan et al., 2017; Mallett, 2017; Raphael & Stoll, 2013; Skiba et al., 2011).[1] Although factors including mass incarceration and racist policing practices also give rise to these disparities, school-generated or school-amplified pipelines are important (Barnes & Motz, 2018; Duffy, 2021; Osher et al., 2002). Schools' contributions begin in preschool, where Black, Latinx, and Native students are suspended, expelled, or labeled as behaviorally problematic at higher rates than are other students (Gilliam et al., 2016; Giordano et al., 2021; Wiley et al., 2013). Differential treatment of students, including disparities in use of exclusionary discipline practices, continue throughout schooling (Duffy, 2021; Petras et al., 2011).

The school-to-prison pipeline involves systematic patterns of school policies, processes, and practices contributing to youth and young adults becoming involved with the juvenile or adult correctional systems (Alexander et al., 2016; Rocque, 2018; Skiba et al., 2014; Wald & Losen, 2006). Contextual influences on the pipeline start before birth (National Research Council, 2015; Osher, Cantor, et al., 2020). Context includes historical, social, cultural, and institutional factors and interpersonal relationships (Bronfenbrenner, 1986; National Academies of Sciences, Engineering, and Medicine, 2019, Roeser et al., 2000; Spencer et al., 1997). Schools play an especially prominent

DOI: 10.4324/9781003275312-19

pipeline role because they are universal, emotionally high stakes, and provide access to learning opportunities and supports while also serving certifying, sorting, and gatekeeping functions (Osher et al., 2002, 2014; Skiba et al., 2014). While all aspects of school are important, the dynamic interactions between and among students and teachers in classrooms are particularly important (Farmer et al., 2020; Wubbels, 2017). These interactions shape and are shaped by school discipline policies, student–teacher relationships, teacher pedagogy, and classroom management (González et al., 2019; Osher, Cantor, et al., 2020; Spilt et al., 2011).

In this chapter we address racialized classroom interactions that are a key part of the pipeline. Doing this requires addressing the school and socio-cultural factors that drive racialized classroom interactions and amplify their effects. To do so we first address the connection between racism and the construction and operationalization of schools and other institutions. We examine the roots of the school-to-prison pipeline through a phenomenological ecological lens that addresses how historical and macroprocesses of institutionalized racism and privilege play out and are remade in the dynamic interactions and co-actions between and among adults and youth in classrooms, nested within schools and communities. We synthesize empirical findings on school climate and conditions for learning and classroom management. We suggest how educators can address the pipeline by focusing on factors that systematic reviews (e.g., Cruz et al., 2021; Valdebenito et al., 2019) indicate are critical:

- disciplinary and instructional practices and interpersonal dynamics between teachers (and other adults in schools) and students, and
- school-related factors that affect how teachers and students interact as well as whether and for how long students are suspended.

Factors Affecting Development and Outcomes

Development and learning are shaped by dynamic interactions and co-actions among environmental factors, relationships, and learning opportunities experienced by youth and young adults, both in and out of school, along with interdependent physical, psychological, cognitive, social, and emotional processes (Cantor & Osher, 2021a; Fischer & Bidell, 2007; Rose et al., 2013). Rather than compartmentalizing these developmental processes and analyzing them in isolation from one another, it is important to examine how tightly interrelated they are and how they jointly produce educational and developmental outcomes inclusive of social and emotional health, attachment to and engagement with schooling, academic achievement, educational attainment, and involvement with the juvenile justice system or other institutionalized settings (Lerner & Callina, 2013).

The phenomenological relational developmental systems perspective unpacks and connects these factors, with attention to sociocultural factors while providing a conceptual bridge linking the macro–historical, meso, and micro (Cantor & Osher, 2021a). This perspective connects bio-ecological and cultural processes to social structures of opportunity and constraint (e.g., relational support and opportunities to learn in classrooms) that play out and are understood within social and cultural contexts (Darling-Hammond et al., 2020; Lee et al., 2020; Losen & Martinez, 2020).

Children's development is embodied, contextualized, and socially and culturally situated (Bornstein, 2015; Bronfenbrenner & Morris, 2006; Cairns, 1979; Ford & Lerner, 1992; Overton, 2015). These dynamics and effects include sociocultural processes, social and emotional states, appraisal, and other school and classroom factors associated with the development of students individually as well as their experiences as members of sociologically ascribed groups (Barbarin et al., 2020; Cantor & Osher, 2021b; Gaylord-Harden et al., 2018; Spencer, 1995, 2008). The experiences students and teachers have with classroom management and exclusionary discipline, and how they understand and react to these experiences, shape student behavioral and learning trajectories. For some youth and young adults, interactions with school systems set them on a path that is more likely to lead to adjudication within the justice system and confinement than it is to lead toward college or engaged citizenship. For others, schooling often privileges students' backgrounds as it amplifies existing assets, builds new assets, and provides an affirming environment that can support a successful transition to emancipated adulthood and attaining some piece of the American dream (Cantor & Osher, 2021a, b).

For every context or relationship that can benefit a young person's learning and development, there also exist possible contexts or qualities of relationship that can derail or harm trajectories (Cantor et al., 2021; Cantor & Osher, 2021a). These negative and damaging conditions undergird the school-to-prison pipeline, as schools provide unique and repetitive experiences that can be either challenging or positive depending on the degree of alignment between a student's personal characteristics and preferences and school practices. The fit between school and student influences the dynamic interactions between and among students and teachers and affects student attitudes and beliefs about themselves, age-peers, and adults.

How adults and students interact affects student development. It is important to understand a student's school experience within general developmental processes. Development is a cascade of changes over time that emerges through school transactions between an individual and their social and physical contexts (e.g., Lavigne et al., 2016). The fit between a child and the environment that the child experiences is consequential (e.g., Byrd & Chavous, 2011). Contexts come together through relationships, and these relationships are affected by both positive and negative ecological factors (e.g., stress, attunement, and support). Children develop as individuals and as members of groups, in cultures and contexts, producing unique individual developmental pathways that reflect their own adaptation and meaning making across the lifespan (Overton, 2015). Children thrive when they have healthy, engaging, supportive opportunities to learn and grow; children stagnate, develop maladaptive dispositions, or even wither when opportunities are unhealthy, aversive, and unsupported. Even when conditions are difficult, supportive adults can buffer the effects of challenging conditions and support healthy development and learning (Osher, Cantor, et al., 2020; Spencer, 2008).

Development is individual, but socially contextualized. People's life journeys are socially contextualized but individually unique (Cantor et al., 2019; Lewin, 2013). Individuals influence each other and help each other make meaning; they contribute to and are influenced by the individualized pathways of others as well as how others experience environments and make sense of their individual and collective experience. There is a "web of group experience" (Simmel, 1955) that is dynamic and affected by the individualized experiences of each group member (Cantor & Osher, 2021b).

Schools as Creators, Amplifiers, and Buffers of Risk

Schools are socially constructed environments that provide messages through language and social-cultural traditions, and spontaneous or unplanned interactions (Carey, 2019; Gray et al., 2018, 2020). Decoding these messages requires constant processing and interpretation. This decoding and meaning making does not occur only in schools, but rather is "ever present" (Spencer, 2008, p. 696). Meaning making should be unpacked if we are to understand how school-related factors affect teacher behavior and student trajectories (Gehelbach & Robinson, 2016; Lodato et al., 2021; Osher, Cantor, et al., 2020; Spencer, 2008).

Schools provide powerful contexts through which stress can be created, amplified, or buffered, neural integration and connectivity supported, and individual development nurtured or undermined. Culture, cultural responsiveness, and cultural competence are critical components of context and are profoundly important in shaping the experiences through which children grow. Micro- and macro-contexts create risks as well as assets. Assets serve as protective factors and can prevent the actualization or impacts of risk. These assets reduce a child's net vulnerability (Spencer, 2008), foster resilience, and support well-being. Contexts such as schools can either support or hinder healthy development (Fischer & Bidell, 2007; Spencer et al., 2015).

Children's development is responsive to relationships, experience, and meaning making throughout their lives, and this plasticity offers opportunities to buffer and overcome the effects of risk factors throughout development. Adversity affects development, mental and physical health, and learning. Resilience and thriving in the face of adversity are possible and are a product of children's internal assets and supports from individuals and institutions within the social environment (Causadias & Umaña-Taylor, 2018; DaViera et al., 2020; Harris & Kruger, 2021).

Adults' ability to buffer stress plays a central role in healthy child development. Therefore, building and supporting teacher capacity to provide for students is central to enabling student success. Teachers may also experience adversity and stress that affect how teachers respond to students' behavior and support students (Jennings et al., 2019; Osher, Cantor, et al., 2020).

Schooling Processes and the School-to-Prison Pipeline

Schools and other social institutions reflect and operationalize institutionalized racism and privilege, which are often baked into staff training, recruitment, and supervisory processes, and reflected in teachers' responses to students (Delpit, 2006; Osher, Coggshall, et al., 2012). Racialized narratives, constructs, research, policies, and protocols shape the design and implementation of schools, attitudes, and expectations regarding learning. Further, social constructions of race and racism shape perceptions of appropriate behavior in school and society, school discipline, and social control (Cantor & Osher, 2021a; Hirschfield, 2008; Rosenbaum, 2020). These cumulative privilege-sustaining and victim-blaming processes that rationalize and legitimate social outcomes play out in the excessive use of punitive and exclusionary discipline, disciplinary disparities, and related disparities in both academic attainment and incarceration (Anderson et al., 2019; Curran, 2016; Gregory et al., 2010; LiCalsi et al., 2021; Mowen & Brent, 2016; Osher, Coggshall, et al., 2012).

Institutionalized racism and privilege in US society and institutions run deep and have always affected schools. Racism and settler colonialism are fundamentally tied to the founding and development of the nation (Kendi, 2016; Lefevre, 2015; Painter, 2010; Takaki, 2018). The creation and evolution of US education and policing embedded explicit and de facto policies based on race, culture, and class (Carter, 2012; Hinton & Cook, 2021; Kendi, 2016; Massey & Denton, 1993; Rothman, 2017; Wilkerson, 2020). The ties between race, schooling, and criminal justice are arguably among the most pernicious aspects of the American story (Alexander, 2011; Davis & Friedman, 2021; Van Cleve & Mayes, 2015). White militias and police patrolled slaves before slavery ended (Kendi, 2016; Reichel, 1988) while schooling for Black Americans (and other minoritized groups) was forbidden, segregated, or limited, and decontextualizing (Spring, 2016; Takaki, 2018). De facto and explicit race-based policies were replicated and reinforced even after the 13th and 14th Amendments. This historical through-line can be seen in overt and subtle instances that include:

- racialized recruitment and promotion patterns
- disparate regulation and criminalization of social behaviors
- disproportionate surveillance, segregation, and discipline
- harsher policing of communities of color
- "subtractive schooling"
- implicit biases' effects on police and educator perceptions, judgments, and behaviors (Alexander, 2011; Glaser, 2015; Kendi, 2016; Rios, 2011; Valenzuela, 2010).

The historical and macro contexts that contribute to the pipeline involve the social construction of race and institutionalized racism but are also more broadly about opportunity, access, resources, and privilege. Societal and educational structures in the United States privilege some and not others

(Bowles & Gintis, 1976; Rothstein, 2017). Schools and school systems were designed for sorting and selecting, based on racist and classist beliefs and assumptions that are victim blaming (Cantor & Osher, 2021b). The issue here is more than White fragility. Bouie's framing is apt:

> Our society was built on the racial segmentation of personhood. Some people were full humans, guaranteed non-enslavement, secured from expropriation and given the protection of the law, and some people—Blacks, Natives and other non-Whites—were not. That unequal distribution of personhood was an economic reality as well. It shaped your access to employment and capital; determined whether you would be doomed to the margins of labor or given access to its elevated ranks; marked who might share in the bounty of capitalist production and who would most likely be cast out as disposable (Bouie, 2020).

Community, Neighborhood, and School Factors

Children's life chances are defined largely by zip code (Bronfenbrenner & Crouter, 1983; Chetty et al., 2018; Manduca & Sampson, 2019). Neighborhood or geographic location within a larger county, metropolitan area, or city often dictates which schools children can and will attend; funding levels and resources within those schools; quality of housing, water supply, and available food; access to high-quality health care; and the depth of formal community resources that exist to support families (Sampson, 2016a, 2016b). Adults and children in low-income communities with large Black, Latinx, and Native populations have experienced centuries of injustice due to systemic and institutional racist housing practices and education, health care, and economic policies; police control and brutality; segregation; minoritization; and marginalization.

These injustices cause high levels of adversity and persistent stress, which can compromise community well-being (Duncan et al., 2015; Galea et al., 2020; Murry et al., 2015). Although individuals and community organizations often display great resilience, the challenges created by food deserts, environmental toxins, persistent racism and classism, community stigma and segregation, and inequitable tax revenue are consequential biologically and sociologically (Adamson & Darling-Hammond, 2012; Belfield et al., 2011; Bifulco, 2005; Osher, Cantor, et al., 2020; Rothstein, 2015; Spencer, 2001). These factors significantly and persistently affect disparities in school resources, processes, and outcomes (Blake et al., 2016; Osher, Fisher, et al., 2015; Schanfield et al., 2019). There are, however, malleable school-based factors that can mitigate or avert the negative impact of these factors (Chang et al., 2019; Gregory et al., 2017).

The geographical institutionalization of racism as well as neighborhood effects constrain life chances (Cantor & Osher, 2021b; DeLuca et al., 2016; Hoxby & Avery, 2012; Leventhal & Brooks-Gunn, 2003). Funding, organization, policy, practice, and community resources affect opportunity pathways and attainment (Danieli et al., 2019; Osher & Chasin, 2015; Osher, Pittman et al., 2020). Each malleable factor affects school discipline practices and educational outcomes and can be altered by equity-oriented policy decisions (Osher, Fisher, et al., 2015).

School funding facilitates or undermines equitable access to high-quality schooling (Lee et al., 2021). Econometric studies of the effects of funding reform on students' educational attainment indicate meaningful and longstanding benefits of providing adequate funding for schools, particularly for students in low-income school districts (Jackson et al., 2016; Lafortune et al., 2018). Nevertheless, place-based schooling has been fundamental to segregating schools before and following *Brown v. Board of Education* (Johnson, 2019; Rothstein, 2017). And despite recent improvements in funding inequities, starting in the 1970s and 1980s and continuing through the 2000s (Fiske & Ladd, 2014; Lafortune et al., 2018), the aftermath of *San Antonio Independent School District v. Rodriguez* (411 U.S. 1973) established the sustained conditions for school funding inequity by allowing the continued connection between school resources and property tax values.

The public school system as designed focused on bureaucratic order, disciplined behavior, and social control (e.g., Tropea, 1987; Tyack & Cuban, 1995). Educational decisions have often been shaped by frameworks and belief systems that include culturally uninformed or racist views of child development, which are then reinforced by generalized victim-blaming thinking. Educators and policymakers often apply assumptions that are inconsistent with what we now know about how children learn and develop (Bailey et al., 2019; Jones & Kahn, 2017). As a result, educators often design, adopt, or accept unquestioningly policies and procedures that reinforce rather than undermine racial, gender, and income disparities (Cantor & Osher, 2021b; Fergus, 2019; Haeny et al., 2021). The issues here are systemic but addressable, although not easily (Fullan, 2020; Tyack & Cuban, 1995).

Community-related factors affect conditions and characteristics of schools and classrooms. Such factors include (a) reliance on local property taxes in many states, which limits resource availability as well as equitable distribution of resources; (b) clustering of schools according to neighborhood designations, which are often coupled with insufficient resources and organizational capacity to educate and support students who have experienced adversities related to poverty; (c) a disconnect between the student body and their families on the one hand and teachers and administrators on the other hand, particularly when educators do not come from minoritized communities and may view these communities and their people as a set of deficits; and (d) militarization of many schools and their lack of green space (Kupchik & Ward, 2014; Oakes et al., 2017; Osher & Boyd-Brown (in press); Sass et al., 2012). Community-level racial bias has been empirically related to office disciplinary referrals and out-of-school suspensions (Girvan et al., 2020).

The Role of Schools

Schools function as ecological risk and protective factors, which are experienced differentially by individual students and by different groups of students (Espelage, 2014; Gottfredson & Gottfredson, 2001; Gottfredson et al., 2005; Osher et al., 2014; Osher, Van Acker, et al., 2004). While the traditional criminological risk paradigm did not address most aspects of the school ecology and focused on student outcomes rather than school inputs or school–student co-actions, more recent work in criminology addresses the impact of school-related factors, including school climate and approaches to discipline and policing (e.g., Bacher-Hicks et al., 2019; Devlin & Gottfredson, 2018; Murray & Farrington, 2010; Skiba et al., 2016).

Schools can be stressful places that function as a risk factor as youth adapt their behaviors to relatively inflexible bureaucratic structures and adult-driven demands within a high-stakes environment that can be identity threatening and culturally undermining (e.g., Eccles & Midgely, 1989; Gray et al., 2018, 2020; Osher et al., 2014). Schools can expose students to physical and emotional violence, identity threat and micro-aggressions, boredom, alienation, academic frustration, negative relationships with adults and peers, teasing, bullying, academic humiliation and failure, harsh punishment, chaotic transitions, and adult insensitivity and sarcasm. When schools operate in these ways they create and amplify social, emotional, and academic risk (Balfanz et al., 2015; Osher, Van Acker, et al., 2004). Punitive and exclusionary discipline embody this by labeling and treating some students as problematic and creating a recursive cycle that involves troubling behavior, punishment, and misbehavior in response to the punishment (LiCalsi et al., 2021; Matsueda, 2014; Okonofua et al., 2016; Osher, Van Acker, et al., 2004; Valdebenito et al., 2019).

Research specifies the kinds of strategies and practices that support positive relationships and learning opportunities and in doing so promote children's healthy development and transferable learning (e.g., National Academies of Sciences, Engineering, and Medicine, 2019.) This research also documents structures and cultures in schools that are exclusionary, punitive, stigmatizing, and likely to result in discouragement and disengagement. The opposite of a young person thriving often takes the form of messages from adults and institutions that the young person does not have potential or is not worthy of acceptance, which contributes to a shutting down of receptivity to trust-based attachments and normal learning, disengagement from school, and a path toward society's institutionalized settings for those labelled bad, delinquent, or dangerous (Bryan, 2020; Ferguson, 2020; Gregory & Ripski, 2008; Gregory & Weinstein, 2008; Osher, 2015).

Schools that have poor school climates, weak conditions for learning, and limited opportunity structures (Astor et al., 2020) create or amplify problem behavior and social, emotional, and academic ill-being and the use of exclusionary discipline (Osher, Poirier, et al., 2015; Osher, Cantor, et al., 2020; Martinez et al., 2016; Pyne, 2019). Schools need not function in this way; schools can be safe havens where community is built and supported while providing caring, healing, grounding, voice, a sense of community, engaging and supportive opportunities to learn and understand, and opportunity structures and systems that engender positive learning pathways (Cairns & Cairns, 1994; McKinney de Royston et al., 2021; Nasir et al., 2020; Oakes et al., 2017; Osher et al., 2014). Many studies document schools and teachers that promote thriving and well-being (Ancess et al., 2019; Burns et al., 2019; Podolsky et al., 2019; Ross et al., 2016). These schools often have leadership that builds school and teacher readiness to address the needs of the whole child and to do so in a manner that is culturally competent and responsive, is family and student driven, and supports teacher and student well-being (Osher et al., 2018, 2001).

School Leadership, Policy, and Practice

Principal leadership, as well as that of other building-level administrators, affects the adoption and implementation of all policies and practices, and can have significant effects on student outcomes, including suspension outcomes (Skiba, Chung, et al., 2014; Taylor et al., 2017; Williams et al., 2020). Leadership creates organizational conditions associated with student suspensions being frequent or infrequent (Sorensen et al., 2020). Principals and superintendents determine or sign off on suspension dosage, with higher dosage contributing to additional behavioral offenses and suspensions, poorer attendance and grades, and more dropout (Jarvis & Okonofua, 2020; LiCalsi et al., 2021). Principals' attitudes contribute to high variability in school suspension rates within schools even with similar contexts by being "tough" or by focusing on restorative and inclusive practices (e.g., Jarvis & Okonofu, 2020; Mukuria, 2002). Principals can collaborate with teachers and prioritize the training and support essential for culturally responsive, restorative, and engaging teaching and provide students with the support necessary for their behavioral and academic success (DeMatthews, 2016). Principals can distribute leadership while ensuring the high-quality implementation of interventions and while creating and supporting a problem-solving approach to continuous improvement (Osher et al., 2004).

Equity-focused principals create the conditions for an inclusive culture that can stimulate a nourishing environment for student development (Barbour et al., 2018; Irby et al., 2020; Sebring et al., 2006). Principals' explicit attention to culture, social context, and equity can play a significant role in enabling student success. To provide a palpably inclusive and supportive culture for diverse students requires that leaders ensure that all members of the school community participate in active and continuous reexamination of policies, practices, and effects on all students. This includes engaging and collaborating with students and community groups and addressing the marginalization of the voices of culturally and linguistically diverse families (e.g., Marcucci, 2020; Mayo & Osher, 2018; Osher & Hanley, 2001). These examinations must extend to disparities, examination of which students or groups are not being well-served, and what can be done. Failure to develop such inclusive and supportive culture will perpetuate and reproduce inequity and injustice (DeMatthews, 2016; Gregory, Osher, et al., 2021).

"Hardening" and Exclusionary Discipline

School safety concerns inappropriately drive or justify exclusionary discipline. While safety is an appropriate concern, an overwhelming body of evidence indicates that promotion and prevention are the best approaches, rather than "getting tough" or "hardening schools" (Flannery et al., 2019; Nickerson et al., 2016; Noguera, 1995; Osher, Dwyer, et al., 2012). Unfortunately, "hard," criminal justice–like enforcement strategies, including zero-tolerance, punitive, and subjective adult-centered codes of conduct, and the misuse or overuse of police in schools, are still found in US schools, and they directly influence the school-to-prison pipeline (Curran, 2016; Gottfredson et al., 2005; Skiba, Arredondo, & Williams, 2014; Sorensen et al., 2022).

Punitive, exclusionary, segregating, and hardening policies are ineffective or harmful, exacerbate disparities, and undermine equitable access to opportunities to engage and learn, including developmentally valuable learning from mistakes (National Academies of Sciences, Engineering, and Medicine, 2019; Sharkey & Fenning, 2012). Hardening policies and practices often undermine emotional and identity safety. They also use resources that could be better used for promotion and prevention and can constrain the policies that allow staff to respond flexibly to students' needs (e.g., Casella, 2003). Although they may seem to make sense and may sometimes be well intentioned, from an intervention perspective they are iatrogenic (Valdebenito et al., 2019; Welsh et al., 2020).

Exclusionary discipline is unequal and especially so for subjective offenses such as defiance, for which there is no concrete referent (Girvan et al., 2017). Black, Latinx, and Native students are more likely to receive harsh penalties, including suspension and expulsion (Carter et al., 2017; Hoffman, 2014; Liu et al., 2021; Losen & Martinez, 2013; Shi & Zhu, 2021; Skiba et al., 2000; Wallace et al., 2008), even after accounting for behavior, socioeconomic status, and achievement (Bradshaw et al., 2010; Fabelo et al., 2011; Finn & Servoss, 2015; Skiba et al., 2018). Discipline disparities are linked to racial biases and cultural clashes (Fabelo et al., 2011; Golann, 2015; Gregory & Mosely, 2004; Gregory & Thompson, 2010; Nichols et al., 2006; Okonofua & Eberhardt, 2015; Skiba, Chung, et al., 2014; Staats, 2014).

Discipline disparities are exacerbated by suspension for minor offenses as well as by inappropriate, disproportionate, and segregating special education services (Artiles et al., 2010; Bornstein, 2017; Osher, Cartledge, et al. 2004; Skiba, Artiles, et al., 2016). For example, Black students are suspended for minor infractions at higher rates than White students who commit similar infractions, which has negative impacts on future grades and perceptions of school climate (Del Toro & Wang, 2021). This inequity produces stark racial disparities in lost instruction time associated with out-of-school suspensions, including 82 more days of lost instructional time per 100 students enrolled for Black students relative to White students (Losen & Martinez, 2020). Black students are also disproportionately identified as needing services under one particularly stigmatizing special education category, emotional disturbance; once identified, they receive more segregating environments, fewer mental health services, and greater levels of behavioral control than are experienced by similarly identified White peers. The over-identification and disparate services, which reflect the impact of cultural bias and a lack of cultural competence, contribute to a particularly high rate of suspension, dropout, and justice contact for these students (Artiles et al., 2010; Nelson et al., 2002; Osher, Cartledge, et al., 2004; Osher et al., 2002).

Addressing Exclusionary Discipline

Root causes of discipline disparities can be identified and addressed (Meyers & VanGronigen, 2021; Osher, Fisher, et al., 2015). Addressing root causes and sustaining change requires systemic and comprehensive strategies and approaches. Strategies should avoid the all-too-common pitfall of focusing on fixing student behavior and assimilating students into school culture rather than adjusting structures and practices to support students' social and emotional needs (Cook et al., 2018; Cruz et al., 2021; Voulgarides et al., 2017; Welsh & Little, 2018). Systematic reviews and expert syntheses indicate the importance of addressing the classroom, which is the origin of many disparities (Anyon et al., 2018). Together, these reviews indicate the particular importance of building and leveraging:

- authentic and positive student–teacher relationships
- academic challenge for all students
- teacher and staff cultural competence and responsiveness
- teacher capacity to teach diverse students and create supportive classrooms
- restorative approaches and practices, social and emotional learning (SEL), skill development, and positive behavioral support to address discipline challenges
- trauma sensitivity and trauma-informed mental health support
- inclusive school and classroom climates
- actively engaged student and family voice
- data-based planning, problem-solving, and continuous improvement
- multi-tiered approaches (e.g., Gregory et al., 2017, 2021; Valdebenito et al., 2019).

These research reviews support focusing on promotion and prevention strategies, which were also recommended by the multi-stakeholder consensus report organized by the Council of State Governments (Cohen et al., 2014). Given the demands on teacher and staff time, these strategies and approaches need to be implemented in a coherent and aligned manner (e.g., Gregory, Osher, et al., 2021; Osher et al., 2010, Osher & Berg, 2017; Osher, Guarino, et al., 2020).

Schoolwide Support for Classroom Practices that Reduce the Pipeline

Schools can build and support educator and school readiness, which involves motivation, individual and organizational and capacity to implement these strategies (Osher, 2018). Schools foster positive student behavior and school safety through promotional/preventative approaches that support social competence and intervene in a caring, supportive, and culturally competent and trauma–sensitive manner (e.g., Osher et al., 2002; Osher et al., 2008, 2016; Quinn et al., 1998). Schools that are well equipped to implement restorative practices around student behavior, as well as promote social, emotional, and cognitive development, have school–wide foundations that capacitate all staff and students to be caring; culturally proficient leadership and staff; culturally competent programming, curricula, and pedagogy; staff collaboration; and a student-centered school community (Dwyer & Osher, 2000; Lindsey et al., 1999; Nickerson et al., 2016; Osher et al., 2002, 2008). Research identifies school-level approaches, including SEL, positive behavioral approaches, restorative practices, and tiered mental health supports, which help create such an environment (Gregory, Osher, et al. 2021; Osher et al, 2010.) These are described in Darling-Hammond et al. (2020, 2021) and the examples in Osher et al. (2019) and Osher, Moroney, and Williamson (2018).

Restorative and inclusionary approaches work best when there are strong conditions for learning (Osher & Kendziora, 2010) and equitable opportunities to learn, and when student and adult emotional and behavioral challenges are addressed. Creating such a school requires a multi-tiered approach that is trauma-sensitive, culturally responsive, and underpinned by universal programming or interventions adapted to the contexts of individual schools. This foundation should employ universal design principles (Rose, 2000) and use targeted universalism (Powell, 2008) for planning, monitoring, and assessment, all of which should include active and inclusive stakeholder engagement. The schoolwide foundation should be conceptually and emotionally coherent and provide a common language and approach for social, emotional, and academic learning that can be employed across intervention tiers. It also makes it easier to identify and serve students and staff needing additional support, while reducing the costs of removing students from common learning and relationship-building activities (Osher et al., 2004). The foundation makes it easier for restorative approaches and more selective interventions to work (Osher et al., 2002).

The schoolwide foundation employs universal approaches to support teacher and staff cultural competence, school climate, and conditions for learning where students experience connectedness and support; physical, emotional, and identity safety; academic challenge and engagement; peer and adult social, emotional, and cultural competence. This foundation supports the development and use of these competencies and the use of culturally responsive and restorative approaches to behavior. The foundation provides the base for early and intensive intervention, as well as the ability to address discipline problems and warning signs in positive and supportive rather than punitive and exclusionary ways. For students with more intensive needs, these schools offer individualized supports such as special education services, mental health services, and strengths-based wraparound supports (Campbell-Whatley & Comer, 2000; Darling-Hammond et al., 2020; Osher et al., 2002, 2018).

The foundation is considered tier one in Multi-Tiered Systems of Support (MTSS) and by similar multi-tiered approaches that employ collaborative, iterative, and data-based decision-making to provide high-quality supports tied to identified level of student needs (Flannery et al., 2019; Jackson et al., 2018; Nese et al., 2019; Osher et al., 2008). These multi-tiered supports can undergird equitable restorative approaches, but only when implemented in a manner that is strengths based, culturally competent and responsive, family- and student-driven (Mayo & Osher, 2018; Osher & Osher, 2002) and in a manner that prevents stigma and self-fulfilling prophecies (Jackson et al., 2018; Salinger & Osher, 2018; Welsh & Little, 2018).

Restorative Practices

Even in supportive environments, some students may still commit disciplinary infractions. Schools can treat infractions as opportunities for learning, development, and inclusion (Darling-Hammond et al., 2020; Rimm-Kaufman et al., 2014). Restorative approaches emphasize reflection, communication, community building, relational-based discipline, and making amends instead of relying on punishment and exclusion (Darling-Hammond et al., 2020; Fronius et al., 2016; Gregory, Clawson, et al., 2016). When a strong schoolwide foundation is in place, it is easier for restorative practices to be effective if an emphasis has been placed on:

- effective implementation of practices and tiered approaches to restorative practices
- support for student and faculty skills as they participate
- well-being and ensuring physical, social, and emotional safety preventively
- centering equity (Gregory, Ward-Seidel, et al., 2021; Morrison & Riestenberg, 2019; Nese et al., in press).

Restorative practices are currently unequally available. Whether restorative approaches are employed, and for which students, has been influenced by student and school socioeconomic status (Gregory, Clawson, et al., 2021; Payne & Welch, 2013; Welsh & Little, 2018). This inequity reflects the same factors that lead to harsh discipline in schools serving minoritized students, as well as the effects of implicit bias and aversive racism, which contribute to pernicious, although unacknowledged, sorting processes (e.g., which students are viewed as appropriate candidates for restorative practices). The collection and analysis of quantitative data regarding who receives restorative interventions is necessary to help identify these continued contributors to disproportionality. And prior scholarship has warned of the limits of restorative practices if schools don't target social and racial justice (Cruz et al., 2021; Gregory et al., 2019), and suggests the need to proactively address sociohistorical conditions and institutions (Gregory, Osher, et al., 2021). Some restorative programs attempt to accomplish this by increasing educator and student awareness about the nature and manifestations of inequality. This includes increasing understanding of educators' own implicit bias and discussions about racism and oppression during restorative justice circles (Gregory, Osher, et al., 2021).

Classroom Policy, Practice, and Interpersonal Relationships

A student's experience within classrooms and with teachers and classroom peers is profoundly formative. While learning takes place in all environments (e.g., Spier et al., 2018), the continuous interactions between and among students and teachers in the classrooms are particularly important because they are regular, high dosage, emotionally salient, and high stakes emotionally and in terms of life chances (Cantor & Osher, 2021b; Osher et al., 2017). Classroom interactions create advantages or disadvantages and exacerbate or buffer the effects of adversity, including adversity encountered in other parts of a young person's life. Teachers are particularly important as they structure learning, allocate cultural resources, act as gatekeepers regarding current and future learning opportunities, and affect peer relationships (Farmer et al., 2011; Osher et al., 2016, 2017).

Environment, Relationships, and Classroom Management

Classrooms are the context for most disciplinary referrals (Anyon et al., 2018; Gregory, Clawson, et al., 2016; Osher et al., 2003; Osher, Coggshall, et al., 2012; Scott & Gage, 2020). The school-to-prison pipeline includes negative teacher–student and peer interactions as well as poor classroom conditions for teaching, learning, and engagement. These inequity-producing emotional and relational processes drive, reflect, and co-act with school and community factors—all of which contribute to school disengagement, dropout, arrest, and incarceration (MacSuga–Gage & Simonsen, 2015; Osher, Pittman, et al., 2020; Schanfield et al., 2019; Scott & Gage, 2020). A punitive classroom environment constrains students' opportunities to manage their individual and collective behavior and develop a sense of self-responsibility (Darling-Hammond et al., 2020; Lewis, 2001; Mayer, 1995; Osher et al. 2010). Punishment breaks vectors of classroom learning and increases student stress levels, which inhibits capacity to learn (Darling-Hammond et al., 2020; Osher et al. 2010; Pennington et al., 2016).

Supportive Classroom Conditions

Student emotions and relationships with teachers and students as well as conditions for learning and opportunities to learn and engage affect behavior, learning, and thriving (Arnold & Gagnon, 2020; Cantor & Osher, 2021a; Immordino-Yang et al., 2019; Immordino-Yang & Gotlieb, 2020; Lerner, 2020; Nasir, 2020; National Academies of Sciences, Engineering, and Medicine, 2019). Supportive classrooms engender physical, emotional, and identity safety; the experience of connectedness; culturally responsive academic, social, and emotional learning opportunities that are challenging, engaging, and experienced as being personally relevant; an inclusive and culturally responsive classroom environment that is trauma-sensitive and addresses problems proactively and restoratively; and attention to the social-emotional well-being and competence of students and teachers (Darling-Hammond et al., 2020; Osher & Kendziora, 2010).

Students learn best when teachers scaffold learning, attending to each student's dynamic zone of proximal development (ZPG) (De Valenzuela, 2006; Shabani et al., 2010; Vygotsky, 1978), as well as that of the class. ZPG involves both cognitive/skill-related elements and emotional ones such as mood and emotion, both of which change during the day and week as well as over time. Teachers' capacity to understand and respond to individual student and classroom ZPG is affected both by (1) teacher planning, bandwidth, and emotional state, and (2) the social emotional conditions for learning and teaching, including student and teacher ability to communicate with each other about what students need to facilitate learning and engagement. Teacher social and emotional competence, which includes their being culturally self-aware and competent (Osher, Coggshall, et al., 2012; Yoder et al., 2018), helps teachers attune to the strengths and needs of culturally and linguistically diverse students.

Teachers' ability to develop strong relationships with students of color depends upon teachers' cultural responsiveness and humility as well as their social-emotional competencies (Wacker & Olson, 2019). Teachers disrupt the pipeline to prison and promote thriving both by what they avoid doing (react aggressively, punish, demean, humiliate, micro-aggress, and exclude) and what they do to create supportive, inclusive learning communities filled with caring and micro-affirmations (Huber et al., 2021; Milner et al., 2018) that engulf students individually and collectively in active learning that develops agency and supports groundedness.

Supportive teachers engage students in creating civil classrooms and employ developmental, authoritative, positive, and restorative approaches to discipline. Classroom management is approached as "something done *with* students and not *to* them" (Darling-Hammond et al., 2020). Supportive teachers emphasize student participation, agency, and leadership; promote respectful relationships between students and teachers and among students; and support student responsibility rather than compliance (Darling-Hammond et al., 2020; Hamedani et al., 2015; LePage et al., 2005; Noguera et al., 2017).

Supportive teachers and classrooms foster learning and development by creating identity-safe environments filled with safety and micro-affirmations (Steele & Cohn-Vargas, 2013). These teachers have the capacity to attune to students and collaborate with students and their families. These collaborations help teachers support students in a manner that is responsive to their social, emotional, and cognitive zones of proximal development. Supportive teachers foster deeper learning by focusing on academic challenge (that includes but is not limited to high standards) and promoting student cultural competence and critical and metacognitive thinking. These teachers scaffold learning and focus on the cognitive, emotional, and social components of academic engagement (Fredricks et al., 2004; Hernandez, 2015; Mehta & Fine, 2019; Nasir et al., 2021; Osher, 2015; Osher, Pittman, et al., 2020; Velez et al., 2020).

Supportive and transformative classroom environments promote robust equity (Osher, Pittman, et al., 2020) when they are safe, respectful, and inclusive, and when they affirm and support all students (Darling-Hammond et al., 2020). Teachers promote robust equity through culturally responsive pedagogy that addresses dominant social hierarchies and distributions of power and privilege (Gorski, 2008; Lee, 2007). Scholarship on transformative, culturally responsive education indicates the importance of drawing upon student funds of knowledge, including their cultural knowledge; engaging students in critical reflection about their own lives and societies (Hernandez, 2015); and facilitating students' cultural competence and their ability to reveal and challenge oppressive systems through the critique of discourses of power, both individually and collectively (Aronson & Laughter, 2016; Osher, Pittman, et al., 2020). These environments prioritize student voices while viewing students' perspectives and experiences as assets (Darling-Hammond et al., 2020). Culturally responsive instruction promotes cultural well-being; supports positive racial identity; cultivates academic motivation, interest, and confidence; and creates a safe environment for academic and social-emotional learning (Hammond, 2014, 2020; Jagers et al., 2019).

Strong, trusting relationships can foster learning and development while buffering the impact of adverse childhood experiences and even trauma (SoLD Alliance, 2021). The quality of student–teacher relationships affects classroom behavior, motivation, engagement, learning, and achievement (Allen et al., 2007; Cornelius-White, 2007; Osher, Cantor, et al., 2020; Roorda et al., 2011). Strong, culturally responsive teacher–student relationships diminish stereotype threat (Steele, 2010), buffer victimization effects (Norwalk et al., 2016), and support engagement of disengaged learners (Romero, 2018; Roorda et al., 2011; Osher, Pittman, et al., 2020). Developmental relationships characterized by enduring emotional attachment, reciprocity, and power balance (Li & Julian, 2012; Osher, Cantor, et al., 2020) foster student confidence, engagement, and ability to self-regulate (Institute of Medicine & National Research Council, 2015; Merritt et al., 2012; Pekel et al., 2018; Scales et al., 2020; Tsai & Cheney, 2012). Developmental relationships are supported by teacher sensitivity, warmth, high expectations, and support for student and staff capacity to care (Bergin & Bergin, 2009; Quinn et al. 1998).

Poor Conditions for Learning and Engagement

Negative student emotions and relationships with teachers and classmates as well as poor conditions for learning undermine behavior, engagement, and learning. Students of color are more likely than others to receive messages that cause belonging uncertainty (Gray et al., 2018). They experience unequal interpersonal classroom interactions including unwarranted low educational expectations, micro-aggressions, implicit bias, stereotype threat, and colorblind legitimating rationales (Bryan, 2017; Compton-Lilly, 2020; Kohli & Solórzano, 2012; Jagers et al., 2019; Turetsky et al., 2021). These experiences drive social identity threat, which engenders stress, anxiety, depression, and challenging behavior that results from students' attempts to protect their identity or dignity (Darling-Hammond et al., 2020; Major & Schmader, 2018; Sennet & Cobb, 1993).

Cultural misunderstanding contributes to deficit orientations, low expectations, as well as problematic student behavior resulting from the misunderstanding (Cartledge et al., 2000; Noguera, 1995; Townsend, 2000). Teachers may incorrectly perceive students' behavior and academic ability (Allen & Boykin, 1992; Boykin et al., 2005; Tyler et al., 2006) and treat Black and Latinx students less positively and with lower expectations (Gregory et al., 2010; Irvine, 2003; Kaplan et al., 2002; Tenenbaum & Ruck, 2007). When teachers insufficiently understand student cultural context, personal assets and challenges, and developmental needs, they may apply developmentally inappropriate behavioral expectations, misinterpret student behavior, and escalate behavioral incidents (Bergin & Bergin, 2009; Gerber & Semmel, 1984; Osher, Coggshall, et al., 2012; Osher, Van Acker, et al., 2004). For example, teachers may react to minor misconduct or troubling behavior as official (formalized and recorded) infractions despite evidence demonstrating that such responses contribute to criminalization and more defiant behavior (Amemiya et al., 2020; Hirschfield, 2008). These negative encounters can be exacerbated by racial stress and unconscious counter-aggressive responses when adults feel threatened, are angered, humiliated, or disrespected (Carter et al., 2020; Dârjan, 2013; Osher, Van Acker et al., 2004).

Reactive teacher responses drive a negative cascade of transactions that include limiting opportunities to learn, student disengagement, dropping out, exclusionary discipline, and incarceration (Conduct Problems Prevention Research Group, 2015; Del Toro & Wang, 2021; Kellam et al., 2008; Okonofua et al., 2016). These outcomes coact and contribute to justice system involvement. For example, disengagement contributes to poor attendance, suspensions, and dropout (Kendziora et al., 2014; Osher, Pittman, et al., 2020; Schanfield et al., 2019), and suspension contributes to behavior problems, school absence, experience of rejection, academic disengagement, grade retention, negative peer socialization, dropout, delinquency, and arrest (LiCalsi et al., 2021; Mallett, 2015; Osher et al., 2014, 2020; Osher, Pittman, et al., 2020; Osher et al., 2002).

Improving Academic Engagement

Classrooms and teachers can promote academic engagement, which contributes to learning and prosocial behavior. This can be done by creating a safe and supportive environment; developing close and affirming teacher–student relationships; and supporting caring and connecting peer relationships (Darling-Hammond et al., 2020; Osher et al., 2010). Culturally responsive instruction increases student motivation, interest in and ability to engage content, and academic confidence, which promote student engagement (Aronson & Laughter, 2016). Instruction that builds on children's prior knowledge and experiences helps scaffold and broaden student engagement and learning (Darling-Hammond et al., 2020; Nasir et al., 2020).

Meaningful challenge promotes academic engagement and on-task behavior when it is accompanied by motivating opportunities and sufficient support to address barriers to learning. Teachers should sustain a growth mindset tied to high expectation, communicate their expectations to students *while* providing meaningful support to help students realize those expectations. For example, offering actionable feedback emphasizing teacher's high standards *and* belief that students could meet those standards supports task persistence and quality (Romero, 2018; Yeager et al., 2014). Alternatively, interventions to address deficits for students perceived "at risk," can, if not carefully implemented, undermine motivation and learning (Salinger & Osher, 2018).

Creating such classrooms and supporting equitable learning hinges upon supporting teachers' capacity to care, have growth mindsets, and teach in a manner that is engaging, culturally responsive, trauma-sensitive, and personalized (Cantor et al., 2019; Quinn et al., 1998; Santiago-Rosario, 2021). It also hinges on schools providing the necessary supports to students, including access to culturally responsive and strengths-based community and school-based emotional, mental health, behavioral, social, and academic support (Cramer et al., 2014; Woodruff et al., 1999).

Supporting Teacher Capacity

Teacher well-being and support for changing practice is important. In the absence of ongoing professional development and support for teachers, teachers may teach in a culturally unresponsive manner and respond to student misbehavior punitively rather than supportively (Coggshall & Ott, 2010; Okonofua & Eberhardt, 2015; Osher, Coggshall, et al., 2012; Public Agenda, 2004). Teachers experience high levels of stress, which affect their well-being and burnout (Jennings et al., 2019) and student achievement and behavior (Corbin et al., 2019; Schonert-Reichl, 2017; Sutton & Wheatley, 2003). Stress affects discipline (Osher et al., 2008), and awareness of bias (Yu, 2016). Teacher stress can be caused by challenges related to inequitable funding and school leadership, policies, and practices (Jennings et al., 2019). These challenges include:

- school job leadership and an approach to collaboration
- teacher job press (e.g., test-based accountability)
- lack of teacher autonomy
- teacher capacity to manage stress (Greenberg et al., 2016).

Supporting teachers' well-being and capacity requires individual and organizational strategies. These include teacher empowerment and a process of continuous improvement focused on identifying and improving teaching conditions (e.g., Hirsch & Emerick, 2007; Jennings et al., 2019; Yoder et al., 2018). Building teachers' social-emotional capacity can help teachers manage stress and relationships with students (Domitrovich et al., 2009; Hagelskamp et al., 2013).

Mindfulness-based professional development can promote teacher well-being and teacher–student relationships (Harris et al., 2016; Jennings et al., 2013; Jennings et al., 2017; Roeser et al., 2013). Interventions designed to promote teacher stress management, social-emotional competencies, and well-being have improved educators' mindfulness, relationships, positive affect, classroom management, and distress tolerance (Harris et al., 2016; Jennings et al., 2017; Jennings et al., 2019; Roeser et al., 2013). Burnout, motivation, and stress are contagious (Burgess et al., 2018). Teacher burnout affects student motivation and achievement; reducing teacher stress appears to reduce student stress (Madigan & Kim, 2021; Oberle et al., 2020; Oberle & Schonert-Reichl, 2016). Addressing teacher morale and stress are insufficient when teachers are also influenced by racial bias and stereotype priming (Eberhardt, 2020; FitzGerald et al., 2019). Poor racial synchronicity between White teachers and Black students contributes to negative academic and behavioral outcomes (Coopersmith, 2009; Egalite & Kisida, 2018). Improving synchronicity involves building teacher social, emotional, and cultural competencies with attention to equity (Gregory & Fergus, 2017).

Equity-oriented capacity building improves teacher-student relationship quality and reduces disparities in exclusionary discipline (Destin, 2020; Okonofua et al., 2020) and achievement gaps under the right conditions (Gehlbach et al., 2016; Gregory et al., 2019; Turetsky et al., 2021). For example, a 70-minute social–psychological intervention focused on teachers' understanding of student perspectives and sustaining positive relationships when students misbehave reduced disciplinary disparities by 45% (Okonofua et al., 2016, 2021), and an intervention targeting teacher–student interactions that focused on positive climate, teacher sensitivity, and instructional supports reduced discipline referrals and disparities when readiness conditions were in place (Dymnicki et al., 2017; Gregory et al., 2019; Gregory, Hafen et al., 2016).

Capacity building should be done with and not to teachers who need to actively embrace changes while being supported in the very hard work of changing beliefs and practices (e.g., Atallah et al., 2019). There are effective approaches to supporting change such as the concerns-based adoption model (CBAM) which can be leveraged in support of this work (Butler et al., 2019; Caverly & Osher, 2021).

Positive Behavioral Approaches

Positive behavioral approaches can help teachers understand and manage troubling behaviors that contribute to suspensions (Kellam et al., 2008; Osher et al., 2004; Quinn et al. 1998). Positive Behavioral Interventions and Supports (PBIS) is a prevalent positive behavioral approach that can reduce disciplinary referrals that drive disparities (Osher et al., 2010). When PBIS intentionally targets racial equity, it can reduce discipline disparities (McIntosh et al., 2021). PBIS systemically uses positive behavioral approaches and avoidance of negative reactive approaches to behavioral problems. PBIS's core elements are clearly defining, teaching, and rewarding positive behaviors and providing clearly defined consequences for negative behavior (Bradshaw et al., 2009; Horner et al., 2009; Horner et al., 2015; Sprague et al., 1999).

PBIS' core elements do not address students' intrinsic motivation or engagement in learning (Petrasek et al., 2021) or mitigate discipline disparities (Cruz et al., 2021). Relational, culturally responsive approaches to PBIS try to remedy this by focusing on practitioner sociocultural identity awareness, student voice, supportive environment, data disaggregation, and culturally responsive behavioral expectations (Gregory, Osher, et al., 2021; Leverson et al., 2019; McIntosh et al., 2014; Rose et al., 2020). This remedy will be most effective when it helps to establish trust between teachers and students *and* assists teachers in changing behaviors that contribute to disparities (Gion et al., 2022; McIntosh et al., 2018; Vincent et al., 2015).

Social and Emotional Learning

Social and Emotional Learning (SEL) approaches can address problematic encounters that drive the school-to-prison pipeline, in particular when SEL provides students and teachers with tools to manage their behavior and skills, become more self-aware, and collaborate with others in bicultural and multicultural contexts. SEL programs can contribute to reduced problem behavior, enhanced social competence, and improved academic performance (Durlak et al., 2011; Sklad et al., 2012; Taylor et al., 2017; Wigelsworth et al., 2016). SEL programs are more effective when they are administered by teachers who have had opportunities to develop their own SEL skills, are integrated into other instruction (Darling-Hammond et al., 2020), attend to classroom and conditions for learnings, and involve culturally competent and culturally affirming practices (Berg et al., 2017a; Jagers et al., 2019; Osher et al., 2016; Osher & Berg, 2017).

Although SEL programs were first created to foster social competence (Osher et al., 2016) schools and districts sometimes use SEL programs—problematically—with a focus on managing or fixing students (e.g., Jagers et al., 2018; Welsh & Little, 2018), rather than supporting student agency and fostering the cultural assets of economically disadvantaged students of color (Ginwright, 2018; Jagers,

2016; Jagers et al., 2019; Kirshner, 2015; Rivas-Drake et al., 2019). SEL programs can lack conceptions of cultural orientation and identity, and most SEL frameworks do not address privilege (Berg et al., 2017b; Jagers et al., 2019; Rivas-Drake & Umaña-Taylor, 2019). Gregory and Fergus (2017) found that districts employing traditional SEL programs to address racial disparities in suspensions reduce the number of overall suspensions but not racial disparities, highlighting the critical need for SEL programming that explicitly addresses cultural difference and equity, including teacher education programs, and racial biases (Baird & Kracen, 2006; Nosek et al., 2007).

Transformative SEL approaches target equitable expressions of SEL competencies, such as agency, identity, and belonging (Jagers et al., 2019). Transformative SEL emphasizes educator and student awareness of culture and racism and focuses on culturally informed SEL practice (Gregory & Fergus, 2017; Gregory, Osher, et al., 2021; Osher et al., 2018). Transformative SEL prioritizes factors that have the potential to cultivate deeper belonging, which promotes student motivation, self-efficacy, well-being, and school engagement and success, and in so doing, can help disrupt the pipeline. Key ingredients are student-directed learning, power-sharing between students and faculty, student agency, and creating an identity-safe learning environment (Duchesneau, 2020; Jagers et al., 2019; Osher, Pittman, et al., 2020). Transformative SEL can be aligned with universal trauma-sensitive approaches that also focus on individual and collective agency and healing (Osher, Guarino, et al., 2020). Equitable SEL approaches can also be integrated into MTSS if MTSS avoids labeling and is equity focused, strengths based, individualized, and culturally affirming (Jackson et al., 2018; Weist et al., 2019).

Equitable approaches to SEL (Simmons et al., 2018) can be integrated into restorative classroom practices, for example, via the co-creation of classroom norms and class meetings (Rimm-Kaufman et al., 2014), which have the potential to successfully address exclusionary discipline (Colombi et al., 2018; Gregory et al., 2021; Osher et al., 2020). An educative, restorative, trauma-sensitive approach offers students and teachers problem-solving and restorative solutions; it interacts with students in a nonthreatening way while aiming for a safe, empowering environment (Darling-Hammond et al., 2020; Jones et al., 2018; Turnaround for Children, 2016).

Conclusion

Schools function as risk or protective factors, and are experienced differently by different students, both individually and collectively. Schools create or feed a pipeline to prison or alternatively enable pathways to thriving. Schools are dynamic environments that co-act both with students and the broader social–historical environment in which schools and school staff are nested. While all school processes and aspects of the school structure, culture, and climate play a pivotal and addressable role in creating negative pipelines, classroom management and how students are supported and treated are particularly important, as are school discipline policies and conditions for learning and teaching. The solution requires supporting not fixing students and staff, while attending to the impacts of institutionalized racism on all members of the school community.

The negative processes that create and fuel the pipeline from the classroom to prison are systemic. They can be eliminated. Doing so requires transformative approaches that address the impacts of institutionalized prejudice and privilege and building and supporting the ability of teachers to attune to and support every student in their uniqueness and as members of groups (Cruz et al., 2021; Gregory, Osher, et al., 2021; Milner et al., 2018; Welsh & Little, 2018).

Note

1 The views expressed in this chapter are those of the authors alone and do not reflect the views of the American Institutes for Research or the Annie E. Casey Foundation.

References

Adamson, F., & Darling-Hammond, L. (2012). Funding disparities and the inequitable distribution of teachers: Evaluating sources and solutions. *Education Policy Analysis Archives, 20*, 37.

Alexander, M. (2011). The new Jim Crow. *Ohio State Journal of Criminal Law, 9*, 7.

Alexander, S. N., Arredondo, M. I., Bernstein-Danis, T., Castek, J., Chandler, J., Clark, C., ... Washington, A. (2016). *Understanding, dismantling, and disrupting the prison-to-school pipeline.* Lexington Books.

Allen, B. A., & Boykin, A. W. (1992). African-American children and the educational process: Alleviating cultural discontinuity through prescriptive pedagogy. *School Psychology Review, 21*(4), 586–596.

Allen, M., Witt, P. L., Wheeless, L. R., Allen, M., Witt, P. L., & Wheeless, L. R. (2007). The role of teacher immediacy as a motivational factor in student learning: Using meta-analysis to test a causal model. *Communication Education, 55*(1), 21–31.

Amemiya, J., Mortenson, E., & Wang, M. T. (2020). Minor infractions are not minor: School infractions for minor misconduct may increase adolescents' defiant behavior and contribute to racial disparities in school discipline. *American Psychologist, 75*(1), 23.

Ancess, J., Rogers, B., Duncan Grand, D., & Darling-Hammond, L. (2019). Teaching the way students learn best: Lessons from Bronxdale High School. *Learning Policy Institute.*

Anderson, K. P., Ritter, G. W., & Zamarro, G. (2019). Understanding a vicious cycle: The relationship between student discipline and student academic outcomes. *Educational Researcher, 48*(5), 251–262.

Anyon, Y., Lechuga, C., Ortega, D., Downing, B., Greer, E., & Simmons, J. (2018). An exploration of the relationships between student racial background and the school sub-contexts of office discipline referrals: A critical race theory analysis. *Race Ethnicity and Education, 21*(3), 390–406.

Arnold, M. E., & Gagnon, R. J. (2020). Positive youth development theory in practice: An update on the 4-H Thriving Model. *Journal of Youth Development, 15*(6), 1–23.

Aronson, B., & Laughter, J. (2016). The theory and practice of culturally relevant education: A synthesis of research across content areas. *Review of Educational Research, 86*(1), 163–206.

Artiles, A. J., Kozleski, E. B., Trent, S. C., Osher, D., & Ortiz, A. (2010). Justifying and explaining disproportionality, 1968–2008: A critique of underlying views of culture. *Exceptional Children, 76*(3), 279–299.

Astor, R. A., Noguera, P., Fergus, E., Gadsden, V., & Benbenishty, R. (2020). A call for the conceptual integration of opportunity structures within school safety research. *School Psychology Review*, 1–19.

Atallah, D. G., Koslouski, J. B., Perkins, K. N., Marsico, C., & Porche, M. V. (2019). *An Evaluation of Trauma and Learning Policy Initiative's (TLPI) Inquiry-Based Process: Year Three.* Boston University, Wheelock College of Education and Human Development.

Bacher-Hicks, A., Billings, S. B., & Deming, D. J. (2019). *The school to prison pipeline: Long-run impacts of school suspensions on adult crime* (No. w26257). National Bureau of Economic Research.

Bailey, R., Meland, E. A., Brion-Meisels, G., & Jones, S. M. (2019). Getting developmental science back into schools: Can what we know about self-regulation help change how we think about "no excuses"? *Frontiers in Psychology, 10*, 1885.

Baird, K., & Kracen, A. C. (2006). Vicarious traumatization and secondary traumatic stress: A research synthesis. *Counselling Psychology Quarterly, 19*(2), 181–188.

Balfanz, R., Byrnes, V., & Fox, J. H. (2015). Sent home and put off track. In Losen, D.J. (Ed.), *Closing the school discipline gap: Equitable remedies for excessive exclusion* (pp. 17–30). New York: Teachers College Press.

Barbarin, O. A., Tolan, P. H., Gaylord-Harden, N., & Murry, V. (2020). Promoting social justice for African-American boys and young men through research and intervention: A challenge for developmental science. *Applied Developmental Science, 24*(3), 196–207.

Barbour, C., Dwyer, K., & Osher, D. (2018). Leading, coordinating, and managing for equity with excellence. In D. Osher, D. Moroney, & S. Williamson (Eds.), *Creating safe, equitable, engaging schools: a comprehensive, evidence-based approach to supporting students* (pp. 25–34). Harvard Education Press.

Barnes, J. C., & Motz, R. T. (2018). Reducing racial inequalities in adulthood arrest by reducing inequalities in school discipline: Evidence from the school-to-prison pipeline. *Developmental Psychology, 54*(12), 2328.

Belfield, C., Hollands, F., & Levin, H. (2011). *Providing comprehensive educational opportunity to low-income students. What are the social and economic returns?* The Campaign for Educational Equity. Teachers College. www.centerforeducationalequity.org/publications/expanding-opportunity-comprehensive-strategies-for-improving-education/18664_Final4belfield.pdf

Berg, J., Osher, D., Moroney, D., & Yoder, N. (2017a). *The intersection of school climate and social and emotional development.* American Institutes for Research.

Berg, J., Osher, D., Same, M. R. N. E., Benson, D., & Jacobs, N. (2017b). *Identifying, defining, and measuring social and emotional competencies* (Final report prepared for the Robert Wood Johnson Foundation). American Institutes for Research.

Bergin, C., & Bergin, D. (2009). Attachment in the classroom. *Educational Psychology Review, 21*(2), 141–170.

Bifulco, R. (2005). District-level Black–White funding disparities in the United States, 1987–2002. *Journal of Education Finance, 31*(2), 172–194.

Blake, J. J., Gregory, A., James, M., & Hasan, G. W. (2016, September). Early warning signs: Identifying opportunities to disrupt racial inequities in school discipline through data-based decision making. In *School Psychology Forum* (Vol. 10, No. 3).

Bornstein, J. (2017). Entanglements of discipline, behavioral intervention, race, and disability. *Journal of Cases in Educational Leadership, 20*(2), 131–144.

Bornstein, M. H. (2015). Children's parents. In R. M. Lerner (Editor-in-Chief) & M. H. Bornstein & T. Leventhal (Vol. Eds.), *Handbook of child psychology and developmental science: Vol. 4. Ecological settings and processes in developmental systems* (7th ed., pp. 55–132). Wiley.

Bouie, J. (2020, June 26). Beyond "white fragility." *The New York Times.* Retrieved from www.nytimes.com/2020/06/26/opinion/black-lives-matter-injustice.html

Bowles, S., & Gintis, H. (1976). *Schooling in capitalist America: Educational reform and the contradictions of economic life.* Basic Books.

Boykin, A. W., Tyler, K. M., & Miller, O. (2005). In search of cultural themes and their expressions in the dynamics of classroom life. *Urban Education, 40*(5), 521–549.

Bradshaw, C. P., Koth, C. W., Thornton, L. A., Leaf, P. J. (2009). Altering school climate through School-Wide Positive Behavioral Interventions and Supports: Findings from a group-randomized effectiveness trial. *Prevention Science, 10*(2), 100–115. https://doi.org/10.1007/s11121-008-0114-9

Bradshaw, C. P., Mitchell, M. M., O'Brennan, L. M., & Leaf, P. J. (2010). Multilevel exploration of factors contributing to the overrepresentation of Black students in office disciplinary referrals. *Journal of Educational Psychology, 102*(2), 508.

Bronfenbrenner, U. (1986). Ecology of the family as a context for human development: Research perspectives. *Developmental Psychology, 22*(6), 723–742.

Bronfenbrenner, U., & Crouter, A. C. (1983). Evolution of environmental models in developmental research. *Handbook of child psychology: formerly Carmichael's manual of child psychology / Paul H. Mussen, editor.*

Bronfenbrenner, U., & Morris, P. A. (2006). The bioecological model of human development. In W. Damon & R. M. Lerner (Eds.), *Handbook of child psychology: Vol. 1. Theoretical models of human development* (6th ed., pp. 793–828). Wiley.

Bryan, N. (2017). White teachers' role in sustaining the school-to-prison pipeline: Recommendations for teacher education. *The Urban Review, 49*(2), 326–345.

Bryan, N. (2020). Shaking the bad boys: Troubling the criminalization of black boys' childhood play, hegemonic white masculinity and femininity, and the school playground-to-prison pipeline. *Race Ethnicity and Education, 23*(5), 673–692.

Burgess, L. G., Riddell, P. M., Fancourt, A., & Murayama, K. (2018). The influence of social contagion within education: A motivational perspective. *Mind, Brain, and Education, 12*(4), 164–174.

Burns, D., Darling-Hammond, L., & Scott, C. (2019). *Closing the opportunity gap: How positive outlier districts in California are pursuing equitable access to deeper learning.* Positive Outliers Series. Learning Policy Institute.

Butler, A. R., Johnson, J., & Hall, G. E. (2019). Getting to outcomes: planning, continuous improvement, and evaluation, in D. Osher, M. J. Mayer, R. J. Jagers, K. Kendziora, & L. Wood (Eds.), *Keeping students safe and helping them thrive: A collaborative handbook on school safety, mental health, and wellness*, volume II, 413–432.

Byrd, C. M., & Chavous, T. (2011). Racial identity, school racial climate, and school intrinsic motivation among African American youth: The importance of person–context congruence. Journal of Research on Adolescence, 21(4), 849–860.

Cairns, R. B. (Ed.). (1979). *The analysis of social interactions: Methods, issues, and illustrations.* Lawrence Erlbaum.

Cairns, R. B., & Cairns, B. D. (1994). *Lifelines and risks: Pathways of youth in our time.* Cambridge University Press.

Campbell-Whatley, G. D., & Comer, J. (2000). Self-concept and African-American student achievement: Related issues of ethics, power and privilege. *Teacher Education and Special Education, 23*(1), 19–31.

Cantor, P., Lerner, R. M., Pittman, K. J., Chase, P. A., & Gomperts, N. (2021). *Whole-child development, learning, and thriving: A dynamic systems approach.* Cambridge University Press.

Cantor, P., & Osher, D. (Eds.). (2021a). *The science of learning and development: Enhancing the lives of all young people.* Routledge.

Cantor, P., & Osher, D. (2021b). The future of the science of learning and development: Whole-child development, learning, and thriving in an era of collective adversity, disruptive change, and increasing inequality. In *The science of learning and development* (pp. 233–254). Routledge.

Cantor, P., Osher, D., Berg, J., Steyer, L., & Rose, T. (2019). Malleability, plasticity, and individuality: How children learn and develop in context. *Applied Developmental Science, 23*(4), 307–337.

Carey, R. L. (2019). Imagining the comprehensive mattering of Black boys and young men in society and schools: Toward a new approach. *Harvard Educational Review, 89*(3), 370–396.

Carter, P. L. (2012). *Stubborn roots: Race, culture, and inequality in U.S. and South African schools.* Oxford University Press.

Carter, P. L., Skiba, R., Arredondo, M. I., & Pollock, M. (2017). You can't fix what you don't look at: Acknowledging race in addressing racial discipline disparities. *Urban Education, 52*(2), 207–235.

Carter, R. T., Roberson, K., & Johnson, V. E. (2020). Race-based stress in White adults: Exploring the role of White racial identity status attitudes and type of racial events. *Journal of Multicultural Counseling and Development, 48*(2), 95–107.

Cartledge, G., Kea, C. D., & Ida, D. J. (2000). Anticipating differences—Celebrating strengths: Providing culturally competent services for students with serious emotional disturbance. *Teaching Exceptional Children, 32*(3), 30–37.

Casella, R. (2003). Zero tolerance policy in schools: Rationale, consequences, and alternatives. *Teachers College Record, 105*(5), 872–892.

Causadias, J. M., & Umaña-Taylor, A. J. (2018). Reframing marginalization and youth development: Introduction to the special issue. *American Psychologist, 73*(6), 707.

Caverly, S., & Osher, D. (2021, January 25). Why a system level approach is needed to counter racism within the education system. American Institutes for Research. www.air.org/resource/field/why-system-level-approach-needed-counter-racism-within-education-system

Chang, H. N., Osher, D., Schanfield, M., Sundius, J., & Bauer, L. (2019). Using chronic absence data to improve conditions for learning. *Attendance Works & American Institutes for Research.*

Chetty, R., Friedman, J. N., Hendren, N., Jones, M. R., & Porter, S. R. (2018). *The opportunity atlas: Mapping the childhood roots of social mobility* (No. w25147). National Bureau of Economic Research.

Coggshall, J. G., & Ott, A. (with Lasagna, M.). (2010). *Retaining teacher talent: Convergence and contradictions in teachers' perceptions of policy reform ideas.* Learning Point Associates & Public Agenda.

Cohen, R., Morgan, M., Plotkin, N., & Salomon, N. (2014). *The school discipline consensus report.* Council of State Governments.

Colombi, G., Mayo, R. V., Tanyu, M., Osher, D., & Mart, A. (2018). Building and restoring school communities. In D. Osher, D. Moroney, & S. Williamson (Eds.), *Creating safe, equitable, engaging schools: A comprehensive, evidence-based approach to supporting students* (pp. 147–162). Harvard Education Press.

Compton-Lilly, C. (2020). Microaggressions and macroaggressions across time: The longitudinal construction of inequality in schools. *Urban Education, 55*(8–9), 1315–1349.

Conduct Problems Prevention Research Group. (2015). Impact of early intervention on psychopathology, crime, and well-being at age 25. *The American Journal of Psychiatry, 172*(1), 59–70. https://doi.org/10.1176/appi.ajp.2014.13060786

Cook, C. R., Duong, M. T., McIntosh, K., Fiat, A. E., Larson, M., Pullmann, M. D., & McGinnis, J. (2018). Addressing discipline disparities for Black male students: Linking malleable root causes to feasible and effective practices. *School Psychology Review, 47*(2), 135–152.

Coopersmith, J. (2009). *Characteristics of public, private, and Bureau of Indian Education elementary and secondary school teachers in the United States: Results from the 2007–08 Schools and Staffing Survey. First Look.* NCES 2009-324. National Center for Education Statistics.

Corbin, C. M., Alamos, P., Lowenstein, A. E., Downer, J. T., & Brown, J. L. (2019). The role of teacher-student relationships in predicting teachers' personal accomplishment and emotional exhaustion. *Journal of School Psychology, 77*, 1–12.

Cornelius-White, J. (2007). Learner-centered teacher-student relationships are effective: A meta-analysis. *Review of Educational Research, 77*(1), 113–143.

Cramer, E. D., Gonzalez, L., & Pellegrini-Lafont, C. (2014). From classmates to inmates: An integrated approach to break the school-to-prison pipeline. *Equity & Excellence in Education, 47*(4), 461–475.

Cruz, R. A., Firestone, A. R., & Rodl, J. E. (2021). Disproportionality reduction in exclusionary school discipline: A best-evidence synthesis. *Review of Educational Research, 91*(3), 397–431.

Curran, F. C. (2016). Estimating the effect of state zero tolerance laws on exclusionary discipline, racial discipline gaps, and student behavior. *Educational Evaluation and Policy Analysis, 38*(4), 647–668.

Danieli, O., Devi, T., & Fryer Jr, R. G. (2019). *Getting beneath the veil of intergenerational mobility: Evidence from three cities.* The Pinchas Sapir Center for Development, Tel Aviv University.

Dârjan, L. P. I. (2013). Oppositional interactions: Aggression and counter aggression in conflict cycle. *SPECTO 2013*, 239.

Darling-Hammond, L., Cantor, P., Hernández, L. E., Theokas, C., Schachner, A., Tijerina, E., & Plasencia, S. (2021). *Design principles for schools: Putting the science of learning and development into action.* Learning Policy Institute & Turnaround for Children.

Darling-Hammond, L., Flook, L., Cook-Harvey, C., Barron, B., & Osher, D. (2020). Implications for educational practice of the science of learning and development. *Applied Developmental Science, 24*(2), 97–140.

DaViera, A. L., Roy, A. L., Uriostegui, M., & Fiesta, D. (2020). Safe spaces embedded in dangerous contexts: How Chicago youth navigate daily life and demonstrate resilience in high-crime neighborhoods. *American Journal of Community Psychology, 66*(1–2), 65–80.

Davis, M. H., & Friedman, A. B. (2021). Not Staying in Their Place: An Historic Analysis of Mechanisms of Controlling Movement of Black Men in America through the Lenses of Social Identity and Gender. *Journal of Black Studies*, 00219347211021091.

De Valenzuela, J. (2006). Sociocultural views of learning. *The SAGE Handbook of Special Education.* SAGE Publications.

Del Toro, J., & Wang, M. T. (2021). The roles of suspensions for minor infractions And school climate in predicting academic performance among adolescents. *American Psychologist, 77*(2), 173–185.

Delpit, L. (2006). *Other people's children: Cultural conflict in the classroom.* The New Press.

DeLuca, S., Clampet-Lundquist, S., & Edin, K. (2016). *Coming of age in the other America.* Russell Sage Foundation.

DeMatthews, D. (2016). Effective leadership is not enough: Critical approaches to closing the racial discipline gap. *The Clearing House: A Journal of Educational Strategies, Issues and Ideas, 89*(1), 7–13.

Destin, M. (2020) Identity research that engages contextual forces to reduce socioeconomic disparities in education. *Current Directions in Psychological Science. 29,* 161–166.

Devlin, D. N., & Gottfredson, D. C. (2018). Policing and the school-to-prison pipeline. In *The Palgrave International Handbook of School Discipline, Surveillance, and Social Control* (pp. 291–308). Palgrave Macmillan.

Domitrovich, C. E., Gest, S. D., Gill, S., Bierman, K. L., Welsh, J., & Jones, D. (2009). Fostering high quality teaching in Head Start classrooms: Experimental evaluation of an integrated curriculum. *American Education Research Journal, 46,* 567–597. https://doi.org/10.3102%2F0002831208328089

Duchesneau, N. (2020). *Social, emotional, and academic development through an equity lens.* Education Trust.

Duffy, H. J. (2021). *Cycles of punishment: Understanding the mechanisms and relationship between school suspensions and juvenile justice and how it varies by student identity* (Doctoral dissertation, Rice University).

Duncan, G. J., Magnuson, K., & Votruba-Drzal, E. (2015). Children and socioeconomic status. In M. H. Bornstein, T. Leventhal, & R. M. Lerner (Eds.), *Handbook of child psychology and developmental science* (7th Edition) (pp. 534–566). Wiley.

Durlak, J. A., Weissberg, R. P., Dymnicki, A. B., Taylor, R. D., & Schellinger, K. B. (2011). The impact of enhancing students' social and emotional learning: A meta-analysis of school-based universal interventions. *Child Development, 82*(1), 405–432.

Dwyer, K. P., & Osher, D. (2000). *Safeguarding our children: An action guide: Implementing early warning timely response.* US Department of Education.

Dymnicki, A., Wandersman, A., Osher, D., & Pakstis, A. (2017). Bringing interventions to scale: Implications and challenges for the field of community psychology. In Bond, M., Keyes, C. B., Serano-Garcia, I., & Shinn, M. (Eds)., *APA handbook of school psychology* (Volume II, pp. 297–310). American Psychological Association.

Eberhardt, J. L. (2020). *Biased: Uncovering the hidden prejudice that shapes what we see, think, and do.* Penguin Books.

Eccles, J. S., & Midgley, C. (1989). Stage-environment fit: Developmentally appropriate classrooms for young adolescents. In C. Ames & R. Ames (Eds.), *Research on motivation in education: Goals and cognitions* (Vol. 3, pp. 139–186). Academic.

Egalite, A. J., & Kisida, B. (2018). The effects of teacher match on students' academic perceptions and attitudes. *Educational Evaluation and Policy Analysis, 40*(1), 59–81.

Espelage, D. L. (2014) Ecological theory: Preventing youth bullying, aggression, and victimization. *Theory Into Practice, 53*(4), 257–264. https://doi.org/10.1080/00405841.2014.947216

Fabelo, T., Thompson, M. D., Plotkin, M., Carmichael, D., Marchbanks, M. P., III, & Booth, E. A. (2011). *Breaking schools' rules: A statewide study of how school discipline relates to students' success and juvenile justice involvement.* Council of State Governments Justice Center Publications.

Farmer, T. W., Gatzke-Kopp, L., & Latendresse, S. J. (2020). The development, prevention, and treatment of emotional and behavioral disorders: An interdisciplinary developmental systems perspective. In T. W. Farmer, M. A. Conroy, E. M. Z. Farmer, & K. S. Sutherland (Eds.), *Handbook of research on emotional and behavioral disorders* (pp. 3–22). Routledge.

Farmer, T. W., Lines, M. M., & Hamm, J. V. (2011). Revealing the invisible hand: The role of teachers in children's peer experiences. *Journal of Applied Developmental Psychology, 32*(5), 247–256.

Fergus, E. (2019). Confronting our beliefs about poverty and discipline. *Phi Delta Kappan, 100*(5), 31–34.

Ferguson, A. A. (2020). *Bad boys: Public schools in the making of Black masculinity.* University of Michigan Press.

Finn, J. D., & Servoss, T. J. (2015). Security measures and discipline in American high schools. *Closing the school discipline gap: Equitable remedies for excessive exclusion,* 44–58.

Fischer, K. W., & Bidell, T. R. (2007). Dynamic development of action and thought. *Handbook of Child Psychology, 1.*

Fiske, E. B., & Ladd, H. F. (2014). Education equity in an international context. In *Handbook of research in education finance and policy* (pp. 313–330). Routledge.

FitzGerald, C., Martin, A., Berner, D., & Hurst, S. (2019). Interventions designed to reduce implicit prejudices and implicit stereotypes in real world contexts: A systematic review. *BMC Psychology, 7*(1), 1–12.

Flannery, D. J., Bear, G., Benbenishty, R., Astor, R. A., Bradshaw, C. P., Sugai, G.,… Cornell, D. G. (2019). The scientific evidence supporting an eight point public health oriented action plan to prevent gun violence. In Osher, D., Mayer, M. J., Jagers, R. J., Kendziora, K., & Wood, L. (Eds.), *Keeping students safe and helping them thrive: A collaborative handbook on school safety, mental health, and wellness* (Vol. 2, pp. 227–255). Praeger/ABC-CLIO.

Ford, D. H., & Lerner, R. M. (1992). *Developmental Systems Theory: An integrative approach.* Sage Publications.

Fredricks, J. A., Blumenfeld, P. C., & Paris, A. H. (2004). School engagement: Potential of the concept, state of the evidence. *Review of Educational Research, 74*(1), 59–109.

Fronius, T., Persson, H., Guckenburg, S., Hurley, N., & Petrosino, A. (2016). *Restorative Justice in U.S. Schools: A Research Review.* WestEd.

Fullan, M. (2020). System change in education. *American Journal of Education, 126*(4), 653–663.

Galea, S., Merchant, R. M., & Lurie, N. (2020). The mental health consequences of COVID-19 and physical distancing: The need for prevention and early intervention. *JAMA Internal Medicine, 180*(6), 817–818.

Gaylord-Harden, N. K., Barbarin, O., Tolan, P. H., & Murry, V. M. (2018). Understanding development of African American boys and young men: Moving from risks to positive youth development. *American Psychologist, 73*(6), 753.

Gehlbach, H., Brinkworth, M. E., King, A. M., Hsu, L. M., McIntyre, J., & Rogers, T. (2016). Creating birds of similar feathers: Leveraging similarity to improve teacher–student relationships and academic achievement. *Journal of Educational Psychology, 108*(3), 342–352. https://doi.org/10.1037/edu0000042

Gehlbach, H., & Robinson, C. D. (2016). Commentary: The foundational role of teacher-student relationships. *Handbook of social influences in school contexts: Social-emotional, motivation, and cognitive outcomes,* 230–238.

Gerber, M. M., & Semmel, M. I. (1984). Teacher as imperfect test: Reconceptualizing the referral process. *Educational Psychologist, 19,* 137–148.

Gilliam, W. S., Maupin, A. N., Reyes, C. R., Accavitti, M., & Shic, F. (2016). Do early educators' implicit biases regarding sex and race relate to behavior expectations and recommendations of preschool expulsions and suspensions. *Yale University Child Study Center, 9*(28), 1–16.

Ginwright, S. (2018). *The future of healing: Shifting from trauma informed care to healing centered engagement.* Occasional Paper. https://ginwright.medium.com/the-future-of-healing-shifting-from-trauma-informed-care-to-healing-centered-engagement-634f557ce69c

Gion, C., McIntosh, K., & Falcon, S. (2022). Effects of a multifaceted classroom intervention on racial disproportionality. *School Psychology Review, 51*(1), 67–83.

Giordano, K., Interra, V. L., Stillo, G. C., Mims, A. T., & Block-Lerner, J. (2021). Associations between child and administrator race and suspension and expulsion rates in community childcare programs. *Early Childhood Education Journal, 49*(1), 125–133.

Girvan, E. J., Gion, C., McIntosh, K., & Smolkowski, K. (2017). The relative contribution of subjective office referrals to racial disproportionality in school discipline. *School Psychology Quarterly, 32*(3), 392.

Girvan, E. J., McIntosh, K., & Santiago-Rosario, M. R. (2020). Community-level implicit and explicit racial biases predict racial disparities in school discipline. *School Psychology Review.* https://doi.org/10.1080/2372966X.2020.1852852

Glaser, J. (2015). *Suspect Race: Causes and consequences of racial profiling.* Oxford University Press.

Golann, J. W. (2015). The paradox of success at a no-excuses school. *Sociology of Education, 88,* 103–119. https://doi.org/10.1177%2F0038040714567866

González, T., Etow, A., & De La Vega, C. (2019). Health equity, school discipline reform, and restorative justice. *The Journal of Law, Medicine & Ethics, 47*(2_suppl), 47–50.

Gorski, P. C. (2008). Good intentions are not enough: A decolonizing intercultural education. *Intercultural Education, 19*(6), 515–525.

Gottfredson, G. D., & Gottfredson, D. C. (2001). What schools do to prevent problem behavior and promote safe environments. *Journal of Educational and Psychological Consultation, 12*(4), 313–344.

Gottfredson, G. D., Gottfredson, D. C., Payne, A. A., & Gottfredson, N. C. (2005). School climate predictors of school disorder: Results from a national study of delinquency prevention in schools. *Journal of Research in Crime and Delinquency, 42*(4), 412–444.

Gray, D. L., Hope, E. C., & Byrd, C. M. (2020). Why Black adolescents are vulnerable at school and how schools can provide opportunities to belong to fix it. *Policy Insights from the Behavioral and Brain Sciences, 7*(1), 3–9.

Gray, D. L., Hope, E. C., & Matthews, J. S. (2018). Black and belonging at school: A case for interpersonal, instructional, and institutional opportunity structures. *Educational Psychologist, 53*(2), 97–113.

Greenberg, M. T., Brown, J. L., & Abenavoli, R. M. (2016). *Teacher stress and health effects on teachers, students, and schools.* Edna Bennett Pierce Prevention Research Center, Pennsylvania State University.

Gregory, A., Clawson, K., Davis, A., & Gerewitz, J. (2016). The promise of restorative practices to transform teacher–student relationships and achieve equity in school discipline. *Journal of Educational and Psychological Consultation, 26*(4), 325–353.

Gregory, A., & Fergus, E. (2017). Social and emotional learning and equity in school discipline. *The Future of Children, 27*(1), 117–136.

Gregory, A., Hafen, C. A., Ruzek, E., Mikami, A. Y., Allen, J. P., & Pianta, R. C. (2016). Closing the racial discipline gap in classrooms by changing teacher practice. *School Psychology Review, 45*(2), 171–191.

Gregory, A., & Mosely, P. M. (2004). The discipline gap: Teachers' views on the overrepresentation of African American students in the discipline system. *Equity & Excellence in Education, 37,* 18–30. https://doi.org/10.1080/10665680490429280

Gregory, A., Osher, D., Bear, G. G., Jagers, R. J., & Sprague, J. R. (2021). Good intentions are not enough: Centering equity in school discipline reform. *School Psychology Review, 50*(2–3), 206–220.

Gregory, A., & Ripski, M. B. (2008). Adolescent trust in teachers: Implications for behavior in the high school classroom. *School Psychology Review, 37*(3), 337–353.

Gregory, A., Ruzek, E. A., DeCoster, J., Mikami, A. Y., & Allen, J. P. (2019). Focused Classroom Coaching and Widespread Racial Equity in School Discipline. *AERA open, 5*(4), 1–15. https://doi.org/10.1177/2332858419897274

Gregory, A., Skiba, R. J., & Mediratta, K. (2017). Eliminating disparities in school discipline: A framework for intervention. *Review of Research in Education, 41*(1), 253–278.

Gregory, A., Skiba, R. J., & Noguera, P. A. (2010). The achievement gap and the discipline gap: Two sides of the same coin?. *Educational Researcher, 39*(1), 59–68.

Gregory, A., & Thompson, A. R. (2010). African American high school students and variability in behavior across classrooms. *Journal of Community Psychology, 38,* 386–402. https://doi.org/10.1002/jcop.20370

Gregory, A., Ward-Seidel, A. R., & Carter, K. V. (2021). Twelve indicators of restorative practices implementation: A framework for educational leaders. *Journal of Educational and Psychological Consultation, 31*(2), 147–179.

Gregory, A., & Weinstein, R. S. (2008). The discipline gap and African Americans: Defiance or cooperation in the high school classroom. *Journal of School Psychology, 46,* 455–475. https://doi.org/10.1016/j.jsp.2007.09.001

Haeny, A. M., Holmes, S. C., & Williams, M. T. (2021). The need for shared nomenclature on racism and related terminology in psychology. *Perspectives on Psychological Science: A Journal of the Association for Psychological Science, 16*(5), 886–892. https://doi.org/10.1177/17456916211000760

Hagelskamp, C., Brackett, M. A., Rivers, S. E., & Salovey, P. (2013). Improving classroom quality with the RULER approach to social and emotional learning: Proximal and distal outcomes. *American Journal of Community Psychology, 51,* 530–543. https://doi.org/10.1007/s10464-013-9570-x

Hamedani, M. G., Zheng, X., Darling-Hammond, L., Andree, A., & Quinn, B. (2015). *Social emotional learning in high school: How three urban high schools engage, educate, and empower youth.* Stanford Center for Opportunity Policy in Education.

Hammond, Z. (2014). *Culturally responsive teaching and the brain: Promoting authentic engagement and rigor among culturally and linguistically diverse students.* Corwin Press.

Hammond, Z. (2020). The power of protocols for equity. *Educational Leadership, 77*(7), 45–50.

Harris, A. R., Jennings, P. A., Katz, D. A., Abenavoli, R. M., & Greenberg, M. T. (2016). Promoting stress management and wellbeing in educators: Feasibility and efficacy of a school-based yoga and mindfulness intervention. *Mindfulness, 7*(1), 143–154.

Harris, J., & Kruger, A. C. (2021). Exploring the influence of racial–ethnic and gender identity on the prosocial behaviors of African American adolescent males. *Youth & Society, 53*(3), 512–535.

Hernandez, P. (2015). *The pedagogy of real talk: Engaging, teaching, and connecting with students at-promise: First edition.* Corwin Press.

Hinton, E., & Cook, D. (2021). The mass criminalization of Black Americans: A historical overview. *Annual Review of Criminology, 4,* 261–286.

Hirsch, E., & Emerick, S. (2007). *Teacher working conditions are student learning conditions: A report on the 2006 North Carolina Teacher Working Conditions Survey.* Center for Teaching Quality.

Hirschfield, P. J. (2008). Preparing for prison? The criminalization of school discipline in the USA. *Theoretical Criminology, 12*(1), 79–101.

Hoffman, S. (2014). Zero benefit: Estimating the effect of zero tolerance discipline polices on racial disparities in school discipline. *Educational Policy, 28*(1), 69–95.

Horner, R. H., Sugai, G., & Lewis, T. (2015). Is school-wide positive behavior support an evidence-based practice. *Positive Behavioral Interventions and Supports.*

Horner, R. H., Sugai, G., Smolkowski, K., Eber, L., Nakasato, J., Todd, A. W., Esperanza, J. (2009). A randomized, wait-list controlled effectiveness trial assessing school-wide positive behavior support in elementary schools. *Journal of Positive Behavior Interventions, 11*(3), 133–144. https://doi.org/10.1177/1098300709332067

Hoxby, C. M., & Avery, C. (2012). *The missing "one-offs": The hidden supply of high-achieving, low income students* (No. w18586). National Bureau of Economic Research.

Huber, L. P., Gonzalez, T., Robles, G., & Solórzano, D. G. (2021). Racial microaffirmations as a response to racial microaggressions: Exploring risk and protective factors. *New Ideas in Psychology, 63*, 100880.

Immordino-Yang, M. H., Darling-Hammond, L., & Krone, C. R. (2019). Nurturing nature: How brain development is inherently social and emotional, and what this means for education. *Educational Psychologist, 54*(3), 185–204.

Immordino-Yang, M. H., & Gotlieb, R. J. (2020). Understanding emotional thought can transform educators' understanding of how students learn. In *Educational Neuroscience* (pp. 244–269). Routledge.

Institute of Medicine & National Research Council (2015). *Investing in the health and well-being of young adults.* The National Academies Press.

Irby, D. J., Meyers, C. V., & Salisbury, J. D. (2020). Improving schools by strategically connecting equity leadership and organizational improvement perspectives: Introduction to special issue. *Journal of Education for Students Placed at Risk (JESPAR), 25*(2), 101–106.

Irvine, J. J. (2003). *Educating teachers for diversity: Seeing with a cultural eye.* Teachers College Press.

Jackson, S., Berg, J., Williamson, S. K., & Osher, D. (2018). Multi-tiered systems of support. In Osher, D., Moroney, D., & Williamson, S. (Eds.), *Creating safe, equitable, engaging schools: A comprehensive, evidence-based approach to supporting students* (pp. 177–186). Harvard Education Press.

Jackson, C. K., Johnson, R. C., & Persico, C. (2016). The effects of school spending on educational and economic outcomes: Evidence from school finance reforms. *The Quarterly Journal of Economics, 131*(1), 157–218.

Jagers, R. J. (2016). Framing social and emotional learning among African-American youth: Toward an integrity-based approach. *Human Development, 59*(1), 1–3. https://doi.org/10.1159/000447005

Jagers, R. J., Rivas-Drake, D., & Borowski, T. (2018). *Equity & social and emotional learning: A cultural analysis.* CASEL Assessment Work Group Brief series.

Jagers, R. J., Rivas-Drake, D., & Williams, B. (2019). Transformative social and emotional learning (SEL): Toward SEL in service of educational equity and excellence. *Educational Psychologist, 54*(3), 162–184.

Jarvis, S. N., & Okonofua, J. A. (2020). School deferred: When bias affects school leaders. *Social Psychological and Personality Science, 11*(4), 492–498.

Jennings, P. A., Brown, J. L., Frank, J. L., Doyle, S., Oh, Y., Davis, R.,…Greenberg, M. T. (2017). Impacts of the CARE for Teachers program on teachers' social and emotional competence and classroom interactions. *Journal of Educational Psychology.* Advance online publication. http://dx.doi.org/10.1037/edu0000187

Jennings, P. A., Frank, J. L., Snowberg, K. E., Coccia, M. A., & Greenberg, M. T. (2013). Improving classroom learning environments by Cultivating Awareness and Resilience in Education (CARE): Results of a randomized controlled trial. *School Psychology Quarterly, 28*(4), 374.

Jennings, P. A., & Greenberg, M. T. (2009). The prosocial classroom: Teacher social and emotional competence in relation to student and classroom outcomes. *Review of Educational Research, 79*, 491–525. https://doi.org/10.3102%2F0034654308325693

Jennings, P., Minnici, A. & Yoder, N. (2019). Creating the working conditions to enhance teacher social and emotional well-being. In D. Osher, M. J. Mayer, R. J. Jagers, K. Kendziora, & L. Wood (Eds.), *Keeping students safe and helping them thrive: A collaborative handbook on school safety, mental health, and wellness*, volume I, 210–239. Praeger/ABC-CLIO.

Johnson, R. C. (2019). *Children of the Dream: Why School Integration Works.* Hachette.

Jones, S. M., & Kahn, J. (2017). The evidence base for how we learn: Supporting students' social, emotional, and academic development. Consensus statements of evidence from the Council of Distinguished Scientists. *Aspen Institute.*

Jones, W., Berg, O., & Osher, D. (2018). *TLPI Trauma-Sensitive Schools Descriptive Evaluation.* American Institutes for Research.

Kaplan, A., Gheen, M., & Midgley, C. (2002). Classroom goal structure and student disruptive behaviour. *The British Journal of Educational Psychology, 72*(Pt 2), 191–211.

Kellam, S. G., Brown, C. H., Poduska, J. M., Ialongo, N. S., Wang, W., Toyinbo, Petras,…Wilcox, H. C. (2008). Effects of a universal classroom behavior management program in first and second grades on young adult behavioral, psychiatric, and social outcomes. *Drug and Alcohol Dependence, 95*(Suppl. 1), S5–S28. https://doi.org/10.1016/j.drugalcdep.2008.01.004

Kendi, I. X. (2016). *Stamped from the BEginning: The definitive history of racist ideas in America.* Hachette.

Kendziora, K., Osher, D., & Carey, M. (2014). *Say yes to education student monitoring system: Updated literature review.* American Institutes for Research.

Kirshner, B. (2015). *Youth activism in an era of education inequality.* New York University Press.

Kohli, R., & Solórzano, D. G. (2012). Teachers, please learn our names! Racial microaggressions and the K-12 classroom. *Race Ethnicity and Education, 15*(4), 441–462.

Kupchik, A., & Ward, G. (2014). Race, poverty, and exclusionary school security: An empirical analysis of US elementary, middle, and high schools. *Youth Violence and Juvenile Justice, 12*(4), 332–354.

Lafortune, J., Rothstein, J., & Schanzenbach, D. W. (2018). School finance reform and the distribution of student achievement. *American Economic Journal: Applied Economics, 10*(2), 1–26.

Lavigne, J. V., Gouze, K. R., Hopkins, J., & Bryant, F. B. (2016). A multidomain cascade model of early childhood risk factors associated with oppositional defiant disorder symptoms in a community sample of 6-year-olds. *Development and Psychopathology, 28*(4pt2), 1547–1562.

Lee, A., Gage, N. A., McLeskey, J., & Huggins-Manley, A. C. (2021). The impacts of school-wide positive behavior interventions and supports on school discipline outcomes for diverse students. *The Elementary School Journal, 121*(3), 410–429.

Lee, C. D. (2007). *Culture, literacy, and learning: Taking bloom in the midst of the whirlwind.* Teachers College Press.

Lee, C. D., Meltzoff, A. N., & Kuhl, P. K. (2020). The braid of human learning and development: Neuro-physiological processes and participation in cultural practices. In *Handbook of the Cultural Foundations of Learning* (pp. 24–43). Routledge.

Lefevre, T. A. (2015). *Settler Colonialism* (pp. 9780199766567–0125). Oxford University Press.

LePage, P., Darling-Hammond, L., & Akar, H. (2005). Classroom management. In L. Darling-Hammond & J. Bransford, (Eds.), *Preparing teachers for a changing world: What teachers should learn and be able to do* (pp. 327–357). Wiley.

Lerner, R. M. (2020). A roadmap for youth thriving: A commentary on the Arnold and Gagnon Vision for Positive Youth Development. *Journal of Youth Development, 15*(6), 147–161.

Lerner, R. M., & Callina, K. S. (2013). Relational developmental systems theories and the ecological validity of experimental designs. *Human Development, 56*(6), 372–380.

Leventhal, T., & Brooks-Gunn, J. (2003). Moving to opportunity: An experimental study of neighborhood effects on mental health. *American Journal of Public Health, 93*(9), 1576–1582.

Leverson, M., Smith, K., McIntosh, K., Rose, J., & Pinkelman, S. (2019). *PBIS cultural responsiveness field guide: Resources for trainers and coaches.* OSEP Technical Assistance Center on Positive Behavioral Interventions and Supports. www.pbis.org/resource/pbis-cultural-responsiveness-field-guide-resources-for-trainers-and-coaches

Lewin, K. (2013). *Principles of Topological Psychology.* Read Books.

Lewis, R. (2001). Classroom discipline and student responsibility: The students' view. *Teaching and Teacher Education, 17*(3), 307–319.

Li, J., & Julian, M. M. (2012). Developmental relationships as the active ingredient: A unifying working hypothesis of "what works" across intervention settings. *The American Journal of Orthopsychiatry, 82*(2), 157–166. https://doi.org/10.1111/j.1939-0025.2012.01151.x

LiCalsi, C., Osher, D., & Bailey, P. (2021). *An empirical examination of the effects of suspension and suspension severity on behavioral and academic outcomes.* American Institutes for Research.

Lindsey, R. B., Robins, K. N., & Terrell, R. D. (1999). *Cultural proficiency: A manual for school leaders.* Corwin Press.

Liu, J., Hayes, M., & Gershenson, S. (2021). *From Referrals to Suspensions: New Evidence on Racial Disparities in Exclusionary Discipline.* IZA Discussion Papers, No. 14619, Institute of Labor Economics (IZA), Bonn.

Lodato, B. N., Harris, K., & Spencer, M. B. (2021). Human development perspectives on public urban education. In H. R. Milner & K. Lomotez (Eds.), *Handbook of Urban Education* (pp. 84–96). Routledge.

Losen, D. J., & Martinez, P. (2020). *Lost opportunities: How disparate school discipline continues to drive differences in the opportunity to learn.* Learning Policy Institute.

Losen, D. J., & Martinez, T. E. (2013). *Out of school and off track: The overuse of suspensions in American middle and high schools.* University of California.

MacSuga-Gage, A. S., & Simonsen, B. (2015). Examining the effects of teacher-directed opportunities to respond on student outcomes: A systematic review of the literature. *Education and Treatment of Children, 38*(2), 211–239.

Madigan, D. J., & Kim, L. E. (2021). Does teacher burnout affect students? A systematic review of its association with academic achievement and student-reported outcomes. *International Journal of Educational Research, 105*, 101714.

Major, B., & Schmader, T. (2018). Stigma, social identity threat, and health. In *The Oxford handbook of stigma, discrimination, and health.* Oxford University Press.

Mallett, C. A. (2015). The school-to-prison pipeline: A critical review of the punitive paradigm shift. *Child and Adolescent Social Work Journal, 33*(1), 15–24. https://doi.org/10.1007/s10560-015-0397-1

Mallett, C. A. (2017). The school-to-prison pipeline: Disproportionate impact on vulnerable children and adolescents. *Education and Urban Society*, *49*(6), 563–592.

Manduca, R., & Sampson, R. J. (2019). Punishing and toxic neighborhood environments independently predict the intergenerational social mobility of black and white children. *Proceedings of the National Academy of Sciences*, *116*(16), 7772–7777.

Marcucci, O. (2020). Parental involvement and the Black–White discipline gap: The role of parental social and cultural capital in American schools. *Education and Urban Society*, *52*(1), 143–168.

Martinez, A., McMahon, S. D., & Treger, S. (2016). Individual-and school-level predictors of student office disciplinary referrals. *Journal of Emotional and Behavioral Disorders*, *24*(1), 30–41.

Massey, D., & Denton, N. A. (1993). *American Apartheid: Segregation and the making of the underclass*. Harvard University Press.

Matsueda, R. L. (2014). The natural history of labeling theory. In D. P. Farrington & J. Murray (Eds.), *Labelling theory. empirical tests. Advances in criminological theory*. volume 18 (pp. 11–44). Transaction Publishers.

Mayer, G. R. (1995). Preventing antisocial behavior in the schools. *Journal of Applied Behavior Analysis*, *28*(4), 467–478.

Mayo, R. V., & Osher, D. (2018). Engaging students in creating sage, equitable, and excellent schools. In Osher, D., Moroney, D., & Williamson, S. (Eds.), *Creating safe, equitable, engaging schools: A comprehensive, evidence-based approach to supporting students* (pp. 87–94). Harvard Education Press.

McIntosh, K., Moniz, C., Craft, C. B., Golby, R., & Steinwand-Deschambeault, T. (2014). Implementing school-wide positive behavioral interventions and supports to better meet the needs of indigenous students. *Canadian Journal of School Psychology*, *29*(3), 236–257.

McIntosh, K., Gion, C., Bastable, E. (2018). *Do schools implementing SWPBIS have decreased racial and ethnic disproportionality in school discipline?* Technical Assistance Center on Positive Behavioral Interventions and Supports (ERIC Document Reproduction Service No. ED591154). https://eric.ed.gov/?id=ED591154

McIntosh, K., Girvan, E. J., McDaniel, S. C., Santiago-Rosario, M. R., St. Joseph, S., Fairbanks Falcon, S., ... & Bastable, E. (2021). Effects of an equity-focused PBIS approach to school improvement on exclusionary discipline and school climate. *Preventing School Failure: Alternative Education for Children and Youth*, *65*(4), 354–361.

McKinney de Royston, M., Madkins, T. C., Givens, J. R., & Nasir, N. I. S. (2021). "I'm a teacher, I'm gonna always protect you": Understanding Black educators' protection of Black children. *American Educational Research Journal*, *58*(1), 68–106.

Mehta, J., & Fine, S. (2019). *In Search of Deeper Learning*. Harvard University Press.

Merritt, E. G., Wanless, S. B., Rimm-Kaufman, S. E., Cameron, C., & Peugh, J. L. (2012). The contribution of teachers' emotional support to children's social behaviors and self-regulatory skills in first grade. *School Psychology Review*, *41*(2), 141–159.

Meyers, C. V., & VanGronigen, B. A. (2021). Planning for what? An analysis of root cause quality and content in school improvement plans. *Journal of Educational Administration*, *59*(4), 437–453.

Milner IV, H. R., Cunningham, H. B., Delale-O'Connor, L., & Kestenberg, E. G. (2018). *"These kids are out of control": Why we must reimagine" classroom management" for equity*. Corwin Press.

Morrison, B., & Riestenberg, N. (2019). Reflections on twenty years of restorative justice in schools. In *Keeping students safe and helping them thrive: A collaborative handbook on school safety, mental health, and wellness*, 295–327.

Mowen, T., & Brent, J. (2016). School discipline as a turning point: The cumulative effect of suspension on arrest. *Journal of Research in Crime and Delinquency*, *53*(5), 628–653.

Mukuria, G. (2002). Disciplinary challenges: How do principals address this dilemma? *Urban Education*, *37*(3), 432–452.

Murray, J., & Farrington, D. P. (2010). Risk factors for conduct disorder and delinquency: key findings from longitudinal studies. *The Canadian Journal of Psychiatry*, *55*(10), 633–642.

Murry, V. M., Hill, N. E., Witherspoon, D., Berkel, C., & Bartz, D. (2015). *Children in diverse social contexts*. In R. M. Lerner (Ed. In chief) & M. H. Bornstein & T. Leventhal (Eds.), Ecological settings and processes in developmental systems. Volume 4 of the *Handbook of child psychology and developmental science* (pp. 416–454). Hoboken.

Nasir, N. I. S. (2020). Teaching for equity: Where developmental needs meet racialized structures. *Applied Developmental Science*, *24*(2), 146–150.

Nasir, N. I. S., Lee, C. D., Pea, R., & McKinney de Royston, M. (2021). Rethinking learning: What the interdisciplinary science tells us. *Educational Researcher*, *50*(8), 557–565.

Nasir, N. S., de Royston, M. M., Barron, B., Bell, P., Pea, R., Stevens, R., & Goldman, S. (2020). Learning pathways. *Handbook of the Cultural Foundations of Learning*, 201–218.

National Academies of Sciences, Engineering, and Medicine. (2019). *The promise of adolescence: Realizing opportunity for all youth*. National Academies Press. https://doi.org/10.17226/25388

National Research Council. (2015). *Transforming the workforce for children birth through age 8: A unifying foundation*. National Academies Press.

Nelson, C. M., Jordan, D., & Rodrigues-Walling, M. (2002). Expand positive learning opportunities and results. *Journal of Child and Family Studies, 11*(1), 13–22.

Nese, R. N., Nese, J. F., McIntosh, K., Mercer, S. H., & Kittelman, A. (2019). Predicting latency of reaching adequate implementation of Tier I schoolwide positive behavioral interventions and supports. *Journal of Positive Behavior Interventions, 21*(2), 106–116.

Nese, R. N. T., McDaniel, S., Hirsch, S., Green, A., Sprague, J., & McIntosh, K. (2019). Major systems for facilitating safety and pro-social behavior: Positive school wide behavior. In Osher, D., Mayer, M. J., Jagers, R. J., Kendziora, K., & Wood, L. (Eds.), *Keeping students safe and helping them thrive: A collaborative handbook on school safety, mental health, and wellness* (Vol. 2, pp. 256–276). Praeger.

Nichols, J. D., Ludwin, W. G., & Iadicola, P. (2006). A darker shade of gray: A yearend analysis of discipline and suspension data. *Equity & Excellence in Education, 32*(1), 43–55. https://doi.org/10.1080/106656899 0320105

Nickerson, A. B., Mayer, M. J., Cornell, D. G., Jimerson, S. R., Osher, D., & Espelage, D. L. (2016). Violence prevention in schools and communities: Multicultural and contextual considerations. In M. Casas, L. Suzuki, C. Alexander, & M. Jackson (Eds.), *Handbook of multicultural counseling* (4th ed., pp. 323–331). Sage.

Noguera, P. (1995). Preventing and producing violence: A critical analysis of responses to school violence. *Harvard Educational Review, 65*(2), 189–213.

Noguera, P., Darling-Hammond, L., & Friedlaender, D. (2017). Equal opportunity for deeper learning. In R. Heller, R. Wolfe, & A. Steinberg (Eds.), *Rethinking Readiness: Deeper Learning for College, Work, and Life* (pp. 81–104). Harvard Education Press.

Norwalk, K., Hamm, J., Farmer, T., & Barnes, K. (2016). Improving the school context of early adolescence through teacher attunement to victimization. *Journal of Early Adolescence, 36*(7), 989–1009. https://doi.org/10.1177%2F0272431615590230

Nosek, B. A., Greenwald, A. G., & Banaji, M. R. (2007). The Implicit Association Test at age 7: A methodological and conceptual review. In J. A. Bargh (Ed.), *Social psychology and the unconscious: The automaticity of higher mental processes* (pp. 265–292). Psychology Press.

Oakes, J., Maier, A., & Daniel, J. (2017). *Community schools: An evidence-based strategy for equitable school improvement.* National Education Policy Center.

Oberle, E., Gist, A., Cooray, M. S., & Pinto, J. B. (2020). Do students notice stress in teachers? Associations between classroom teacher burnout and students' perceptions of teacher social–emotional competence. *Psychology in the Schools, 57*(11), 1741–1756.

Oberle, E., & Schonert-Reichl, K. A. (2016). Stress contagion in the classroom? The link between classroom teacher burnout and morning cortisol in elementary school students. *Social Science & Medicine, 159*, 30–37.

Okonofua, J. A., Perez, A. D., & Darling-Hammond, S. (2020). When policy and psychology meet: Mitigating the consequences of bias in schools. *Science advances, 6*(42), eaba9479.

Okonofua, J. A., & Eberhardt, J. L. (2015). Two strikes: Race and the disciplining of young students. *Psychological Science, 26*(5), 617–624.

Okonofua, J. A., Goyer, J. P., Lindsay, C. A., Haugabrook, J., & Walton, G. M. (2022). A scalable empathic-mindset intervention reduces group disparities in school suspensions. *Science Advances, 8*, eabj0691.

Okonofua, J. A., Walton, G. M., & Eberhardt, J. L. (2016). A vicious cycle: A social–psychological account of extreme racial disparities in school discipline. *Perspectives on Psychological Science, 11*(3), 381–398.

Osher, D. (2015). The pedagogy of real talk and the promotion of student well-being and success. In P. Hernandez, *The pedagogy of real talk: Engaging, teaching, and connecting with students* at risk. Corwin.

Osher, D. (2018). Building readiness and capacity. In Osher, D., Moroney, D., & Williamson, S. (Eds.), *Creating safe, equitable, engaging schools: A comprehensive, evidence-based approach to supporting students* (pp. 235–252). Harvard Education Press.

Osher, D., Bear, G. G., Sprague, J. R., & Doyle, W. (2010). How can we improve school discipline? *Educational Researcher, 39*(1), 48–58.

Osher, D., & Berg, J. (2017). *School climate and social and emotional learning: The integration of two approaches.* Edna Bennet Pierce Prevention Research Center, Pennsylvania State University.

Osher, D., & Boyd-Brown, M. (Manuscript submitted for publication). *The relationship between thriving, equity, and human learning.*

Osher, D., Cantor, P., Berg, J., Steyer, L., & Rose, T. (2020). Drivers of human development: How relationships and context shape learning and development. *Applied Developmental Science, 24*(1), 6–36.

Osher, D., Cantor, P., Berg, J., Steyer, L., Rose, T., & Nolan, E. (2017). *Science of learning and development: A synthesis.* American Institutes for Research.

Osher, D., Cartledge, G., Oswald, D., Sutherland, K. S., Artiles, A. J., & Coutinho, M. (2004). Cultural and linguistic competency and disproportionate representation. In Rutherford Jr., R.B., Quinn, M.M., & Mathur, S.R. (Eds) *Handbook of research in emotional and behavioral disorders* (pp. 54–77). New York: Guilford.

Osher, D., & Chasin, E. (2015). Bringing together schools and the community: The case of Say Yes to Education. In *Comprehensive community initiatives for positive youth development* (pp. 82–113). Routledge.

Osher, D., Coggshall, J., Colombi, G., Woodruff, D., Francois, S., & Osher, T. (2012). Building school and teacher capacity to eliminate the school-to-prison pipeline. *Teacher Education and Special Education*, *35*(4), 284–295.

Osher, D., Dwyer, K. P., Jimerson, S. R., & Brown, J. A. (2012). Developing safe, supportive, and effective schools: Facilitating student success to reduce school violence. In S. R. Jimerson, A. B. Nickerson, M. J. Mayer, & M. J. Furlong (Eds.), *Handbook of School Violence and School Safety: International Research and Practice* (2nd ed., pp. 27–44). Routledge.

Osher, D., Fisher, D., Amos, L., Katz, J., Dwyer, K., Duffey, T., & Colombi, G. D. (2015). *Addressing the root causes of disparities in school discipline: An educator's action planning guide*. National Center on Safe Supportive Learning Environments.

Osher, D., Guarino, K., Jones, W., & Schanfield, M. (2020). *Trauma-sensitive schools and social and emotional learning: An integration*. Edna Bennet Pierce Prevention Research Center, Pennsylvania State University.

Osher, D., & Hanley, T. V. (2001). Implementing the SED national agenda: Promising programs and policies for children and youth with emotional and behavioral problems. *Education and Treatment of Children*, 374–403.

Osher, D., & Kendziora, K. (2010). Building conditions for learning and healthy adolescent development: Strategic approaches. In B. Doll, W. Pfohl, & J. Yoon (Eds.), *Handbook of Youth Prevention Science* (pp. 121–140). Routledge.

Osher, D., Kendziora, K., Spier, E., & Garibaldi, M. L. (2014). School influences on child and youth development. In Z. Sloboda & H. Petras (Eds.), *Advances in Prevention Science Vol. 1: Defining Prevention Science* (pp. 151–170). Springer.

Osher, D., Kidron, Y., DeCandia, C. J., Kendziora, K., & Weissberg, R. P. (2016). Interventions to promote safe and supportive school climate. In K. R. Wentzel & G. B. Ramani (Eds.), *Handbook of social influences in school contexts* (pp. 384–404). Routledge.

Osher, D., Mayer, M. J., Jagers, R. J., Kendziora, K., & Wood, L. (2019). *Keeping students safe and helping them thrive: A collaborative handbook on school safety, mental health, and wellness (2 vols.)*. Praeger/ABC-CLIO.

Osher, D., Moroney, D., & Williamson, S. (2018). *Creating safe, equitable, engaging schools: A comprehensive, evidence-based approach to supporting students*. Harvard Education Press.

Osher, D., Morrison, G., & Bailey, W. (2003). Exploring the relationship between student mobility and dropout among students with emotional and behavioral disorders. *Journal of Negro Education*, *72*(1), 79–96.

Osher, T. W., & Osher, D. M. (2002). The paradigm shift to true collaboration with families. *Journal of Child and Family Studies*, *11*(1), 47–60.

Osher, D., Pittman, K., Young, J., Smith, H., Moroney, D., & Irby, M. (2020). *Thriving, robust equity, and transformative learning & development*. American Institutes for Research and Forum for Youth Investment.

Osher, D., Poirier, J. M., Jarjoura, G. R., Haigt, M. S., & Mitchell, D. (2015). *Follow-up assessment of conditions for learning in the Cleveland Metropolitan School District*. American Institutes for Research.

Osher, D., Sandler, S., & Nelson, C. (2001). The best approach to safety is to fix schools and support children and staff. *New Directions in Youth Development*, *92*, 127–154.

Osher, D., Sprague, J., Weissberg, R. P., Axelrod, J., Keenan, S., Kendziora, K., & Zins, J. E. (2008). A comprehensive approach to promoting social, emotional, and academic growth in contemporary schools. In A. Thomas & J. Grimes (Eds.), *Best practices in school psychology V* (vol. 4, pp. 1263–1278). National Association of School Psychologists.

Osher, D., Van Acker, R., Morrison, G. M., Gable, R., Dwyer, K., & Quinn, M. (2004). Warning signs of problems in schools: Ecological perspectives and effective practices for combating school aggression and violence. *Journal of School Violence*, *3*(2–3), 13–37.

Osher, D., Woodruff, D., & Sims, A. E. (2002). Schools make a difference: The overrepresentation of African American youth in special education and the juvenile justice system. *Racial Inequity in Special Education*, 93–116.

Overton, W. F. (2015). Processes, relations and relational–developmental-systems. In W. F. Overton & P. C. M. Molenaar (Eds.), *Handbook of child psychology and developmental science: Vol. 1. Theory and method* (7th ed., pp. 9–62). Wiley.

Painter, N. I. (2010). *The history of white people*. W. W. Norton & Company.

Payne, A. A., & Welch, K. (2013). The impact of schools and education on antisocial behavior over the lifecourse. *Handbook of life-course criminology*, 93–109.

Pekel, K., Roehlkepartain, E. C., Syvertsen, A. K., Scales, P. C., Sullivan, T. K., & Sethi, J. (2018). Finding the fluoride: Examining how and why developmental relationships are the active ingredient in interventions that work. *American Journal of Orthopsychiatry*, *88*(5), 493–502.

Petras, H., Kellam, S. G., Brown, C. H., Muthén, B. O., Ialongo, N. S., & Poduska, J. M. (2008). Developmental epidemiological courses leading to antisocial personality disorder and violent and criminal behavior: Effects by young adulthood of a universal preventive intervention in first-and second-grade classrooms. *Drug and Alcohol Dependence, 95,* S45–S59.

Petras, H., Masyn, K. E., Buckley, J. A., Ialongo, N. S., & Kellam, S. (2011). Who is most at risk for school removal? A multilevel discrete-time survival analysis of individual- and context-level influences. *Journal of Educational Psychology, 103*(1), 223.

Petrasek, M., James, A., Noltemeyer, A., Green, J., & Palmer, K. (2021). Enhancing motivation and engagement within a PBIS framework. *Improving schools,* 13654802211002299.

Pennington, C. R., Heim, D., Levy, A. R., & Larkin, D. T. (2016). Twenty years of stereotype threat research: A review of psychological mediators. *PLoS One, 11*(1), e0146487. https://doi.org/10.1371/journal.pone.0146487

Podolsky, A., Darling-Hammond, L., Doss, C., & Reardon, S. (2019). *California's positive outliers: Districts beating the odds.* Positive Outliers Series. Learning Policy Institute.

Powell, J. A. (2008). Post-racialism or targeted universalism. *Denver University Law Review, 86,* 785.

Public Agenda. (2004). *Teaching interrupted: Do discipline policies in today's schools foster the common good.*

Pyne, J. (2019). Suspended attitudes: Exclusion and emotional disengagement from school. *Sociology of Education, 92*(1), 59–82.

Quinn, M. M., Osher, D., Hoffman, C. C., & Hanley, T. V. (1998). *Safe, drug-free, and effective schools for all students: What Works!* Center for Effective Collaboration and Practice, American Institutes for Research.

Raphael, S., & Stoll, M. A. (2013). *Why are so many americans in prison?* Russell Sage Foundation.

Reichel, P. L. (1988). Southern slave patrols as a transitional police type. *American Journal of Police, 7,* 51.

Rimm-Kaufman, S. E., Larsen, R. A., Baroody, A. E., Curby, T. W., Ko, M., Thomas, J. B.,… DeCoster, J. (2014). Efficacy of the responsive classroom approach: Results from a 3-year, longitudinal randomized controlled trial. *American Educational Research Journal, 51*(3), 567–603. https://doi.org/10.3102%2F0002831214523821

Rios, V. M. (2011). *Punished: Policing the lives of Black and Latino boys.* NYU Press.

Rivas-Drake, D., Jagers, R., & Martinez, K. (2019). Race, ethnicity, and socioemotional health. In D. Osher, M. Mayer, K. Osher, R. Jagers, & K. Kendziora (Eds.), *Keeping students safe and helping them thrive: A collaborative handbook for education, mental health, safety, and justice professionals, families, and communities.* Praeger.

Rivas-Drake, D., & Umaña-Taylor, A. J. (2019). *Below the surface: Talking with teens about race, ethnicity, and identity.* Princeton University Press.

Roeser, R. W., Eccles, J. S., & Sameroff, A. J. (2000). School as a context of early adolescents' academic and social-emotional development: A summary of research findings. *The Elementary School Journal, 100*(5), 443–471.

Roeser, R. W., Schonert-Reichl, K. A., Jha, A., Cullen, M., Wallace, L., Wilensky, R., Oberle, E., Thomson, K., Taylor, C., & Harrison, J. (2013). Mindfulness training and reductions in teacher stress and burnout: Results from two randomized, waitlist-control field trials. *Journal of Educational Psychology, 105*(3), 787–804. https://doi.org/10.1037/a0032093

Romero, C. (2018). *What we know about belonging from scientific research.* Mindset Scholars Network, Center for Advanced Study in the Behavioral Sciences, Stanford University. https://studentexperiencenetwork.org/wp-content/uploads/2018/11/What-We-Know-About-Belonging.pdf

Roorda, D. L., Koomen, H. M., Spilt, J. L., & Oort, F. J. (2011). The influence of affective teacher–student relationships on students' school engagement and achievement: A meta-analytic approach. *Review of Educational Research, 81*(4), 493–529. https://doi.org/10.3102%2F0034654311421793

Rocque, M. (2018). The prison school: Educational inequality and school discipline in the age of mass incarceration. *Journal of Criminal Justice Education, 29*(3), 476–479.

Rose, D. (2000). Universal design for learning. *Journal of Special Education Technology, 15*(3), 45–49.

Rose, J., Leverson, M., & Smith, K. (2020). *Embedding culturally responsive practices in tier I.* Center on Positive Behavioral Interventions and Supports.

Rose, L. T., Rouhani, P., & Fischer, K. W. (2013). The science of the individual. *Mind, Brain, and Education, 7*(3), 152–158.

Rosenbaum, J. (2020). Educational and criminal justice outcomes 12 years after school suspension. *Youth & Society, 52*(4), 515–547.

Ross, K. M., Nasir, N. I. S., Givens, J. R., de Royston, M. M., Vakil, S., Madkins, T. C., & Philoxene, D. (2016). "I do this for all of the reasons America doesn't want me to": The organic pedagogies of Black male instructors. *Equity & Excellence in Education, 49*(1), 85–99.

Rothman, D. J. (2017). *The discovery of the asylum: Social order and disorder in the New Republic.* Routledge.

Rothstein, R. (2015). The racial achievement gap, segregated schools, and segregated neighborhoods: A constitutional insult. *Race and Social Problems, 7*(1), 21–30.

Rothstein, R. (2017). *The color of law: A forgotten history of how our government segregated America.* Liveright Publishing.

Salinger, T., & Osher, D. (2018). Academic interventions—Use with care. In Osher, D., Moroney, D., & Williamson, S. (2018). *Creating safe, equitable, engaging schools: A comprehensive, evidence-based approach to supporting students.* Harvard Education Press.

Sampson, R. J. (2016a). Individual and community economic mobility in the Great Recession era: The spatial foundations of persistent inequality. In *Economic mobility: Research and ideas on strengthening families, communities and the economy* (pp. 261–287). Federal Reserve Bank.

Sampson, R. J. (2016b). Neighborhood inequality and public policy: What can Milwaukee learn from Chicago and Boston? *Marquette Lawyer*, summer, 9–20.

Santiago-Rosario, M. R., Whitcomb, S. A., Pearlman, J., & McIntosh, K. (2021). Associations between teacher expectations and racial disproportionality in discipline referrals. *Journal of School Psychology*, *85*, 80–93.

Sass, T. R., Hannaway, J., Xu, Z., Figlio, D. N., & Feng, L. (2012). Value added of teachers in high-poverty schools and lower poverty schools. *Journal of Urban Economics*, *72*(2–3), 104–122.

Scales, P. C., Pekel, K., Sethi, J., Chamberlain, R., & Van Boekel, M. (2020). Academic year changes in student–teacher developmental relationships and their linkage to middle and high school students' motivation: A mixed methods study. *The Journal of Early Adolescence*, *40*(4), 499–536.

Schanfield, M., Chang, H., & Osher, D. (2019). How student and teacher social and emotional competencies contribute to student engagement. In J. Fredricks, A. Reschly, & S. Christenson, *Handbook of student engagement interventions: Working with disengaged youth* (pp. 183–198). Academic Press.

Schonert-Reichl, K. A. (2017). Social and emotional learning and teachers. *The Future of Children*, 137–155.

Science of Learning and Development (SoLD) Alliance (2021). *What we've learned*. www.soldalliance.org/what-weve-learned

Scott, T. M., & Gage, N. (2020). An examination of the association between teacher's instructional practices and school-wide disciplinary and academic outcomes. *Education and Treatment of Children*, *43*(3), 223–235.

Sebring, P. B., Allensworth, E., Bryk, A. S., Easton, J. Q., & Luppescu, S. (2006). *The essential supports for school improvement*. Research Report. Consortium on Chicago School Research.

Sennett, R., & Cobb, J. (1993). *The Hidden Injuries of Class*. WW Norton & Company.

Shabani, K., Khatib, M., & Ebadi, S. (2010). Vygotsky's zone of proximal development: Instructional implications and teachers' professional development. *English Language Teaching*, *3*(4), 237–248.

Sharkey, J. D., & Fenning, P. A. (2012). Rationale for designing school contexts in support of proactive discipline. *Journal of School Violence*, *11*(2), 95–104. https://doi.org/10.1080/15388220.2012.646641

Shi, Y., & Zhu, M. (2021). *Equal time for equal crime? Racial bias in school discipline*. IZA—Institute of Labor Economics.

Siegel, D. J. (2012). *The developing mind: How relationships and the brain interact to shape who we are* (2nd ed.). Guilford.

Simmel, G. (1955). *Conflict and the web of group-affiliations*. Free Press.

Simmons, D. N., Brackett, M. A., & Adler, N. (2018.) *Applying an equity lens to social, emotional, and academic development*. Edna Bennett Pierce Prevention Research Center, The Pennsylvania State University. www.rwjf.org/en/library/research/2018/06/applying-an-equity-lens-to-social-emotional-and-academic-development.html

Skiba, R. J., Arredondo, M. I., Gray, C., & Rausch, M. K. (2018). Discipline disparities: New and emerging research in the United States. In *The Palgrave international handbook of school discipline, surveillance, and social control* (pp. 235–252). Palgrave Macmillan.

Skiba, R. J., Arredondo, M. I., & Williams, N. T. (2014). More than a metaphor: The contribution of exclusionary discipline to a school-to-prison pipeline. *Equity & Excellence in Education*, *47*(4), 546–564.

Skiba, R. J., Arredondo, M. I., Williams, N. T. (2016). In and of itself a risk factor. Exclusionary discipline and the school-to-prison pipeline (Chapter 10). In K. J. Fasching-Varner et al. (Eds.), *Understanding, dismantling, and disrupting the prison-to-school pipeline*. Lexington Books.

Skiba, R. J., Artiles, A. J., Kozleski, E. B., Losen, D. J., & Harry, E. G. (2016). Risks and consequences of oversimplifying educational inequities: A response to Morgan et al. (2015). *Educational Researcher*, *45*(3), 221–225.

Skiba, R. J., Chung, C. G., Trachok, M., Baker, T. L., Sheya, A., & Hughes, R. L. (2014). Parsing disciplinary disproportionality: Contributions of infraction, student, and school characteristics to out-of-school suspension and expulsion. *American Educational Research Journal*, *51*, 640–670. https://doi.org/10.3102%2F0002831214541670

Skiba, R. J., Horner, R. H., Chung, C. G., Rausch, M. K., May, S. L., & Tobin, T. (2011). Race is not neutral: A national investigation of African American and Latino disproportionality in school discipline. *School Psychology Review*, *40*(1), 85–107.

Skiba, R. J., Michael, R. S., Nardo, A. C., & Peterson, R. (2000). *The color of discipline: Sources of racial and gender disproportionality in school punishment*. Policy Research Report.

Sklad, M., Diekstra, R., Ritter, M. D., Ben, J., & Gravesteijn, C. (2012). Effectiveness of school-based universal social, emotional, and behavioral programs: Do they enhance students' development in the area of skill, behavior, and adjustment?. *Psychology in the Schools*, *49*(9), 892–909.

Smeding, A., Darnon, C., Souchal, C., Toczek-Capelle, M. C., & Butera, F. (2013). Reducing the socio-economic status achievement gap at university by promoting mastery-oriented assessment. *PLoS One*, *8*(8), e71678.

Sorensen, L. C., Shen, Y., & Bushway, S. D. (2020). Making schools safer and/or escalating disciplinary response: A study of police officers in North Carolina schools. *Educational Evaluation and Policy Analysis*. https://doi.org/10.3102%2F01623737211006409

Sorensen, L. C., Bushway, S. D., & Gifford, E. J. (2022). Getting tough? The effects of discretionary principal discipline on student outcomes. *Education Finance and Policy*, 17(2), 255–284.

Spencer, M. B. (1995). Old issues and new theorizing about African American youth: A phenomenological variant of ecological systems theory. *Black youth: Perspectives on their status in the United States* (pp. 37–69). Westport, CA: Praeger.

Spencer, M. B. (2001). Resiliency and fragility factors associated with the contextual experiences of low-resource urban African–American male youth and families. In Booth, A., & Crouter, A. C. (Eds), *Does it take a village: Community effects on children, adolescents, and families*, (pp. 51–77). New Jersey: Lawrence Erlbaum.

Spencer, M. B. (2008). Phenomenology and ecological systems theory: Development of diverse groups. In W. Damon & R. M. Lerner (Eds.), *Child and adolescent development: An advanced course* (pp. 696–735). Wiley Publishers.

Spencer, M. B., Dupree, D., & Hartmann, T. (1997). A phenomenological variant of ecological systems theory (PVEST): A self-organization perspective in context. *Development and Psychopathology*, 9(4), 817–833.

Spencer, M. B., Swanson, D. P., & Harpalani, V. (2015). Conceptualizing the self: Contributions of normative human processes, diverse contexts and social opportunity. In M. Lamb, C. G. Coll, & R. Lerner (Eds.), *Handbook of child psychology and developmental science* (pp. 750–793). John Wiley.

Spier, E., González, R., & Osher, D. (2018). The role of the community in learning and development. In G. Hall (Ed.), *Handbook of teaching and learning* (pp. 79–106). Wiley Blackwell.

Spilt, J. L., Koomen, H. M., & Thijs, J. T. (2011). Teacher wellbeing: The importance of teacher–student relationships. *Educational Psychology Review*, 23(4), 457–477.

Sprague, J. R., Sugai, G., Horner, R., & Walker, H. M. (1999). Using office discipline referral data to evaluate school-wide discipline and violence prevention interventions. *OSSC Bulletin*, 42(2), n2.

Spring, J. (2016). *Deculturalization and the struggle for equality: A brief history of the education of dominated cultures in the United States*. Routledge.

Staats, C. (2014). *Implicit racial bias and school discipline disparities* (Special report). Kirwan Institute.

Steele, C. (2010). *Whistling Vivaldi: And other clues to how stereotypes affect us*. Norton.

Steele, D. M., & Cohn-Vargas, B. (2013). *Identity safe classrooms, grades K-5: Places to belong and learn*. Corwin Press.

Sutton, R. E., & Wheatley, K. F. (2003). Teachers' emotions and teaching: A review of the literature and directions for future research. *Educational Psychology Review*, 15(4), 327–358.

Takaki, R. T. (2018). *A different mirror* (pp. 213–224). Routledge.

Taylor, R. D., Oberle, E., Durlak, J. A., & Weissberg, R. P. (2017). Promoting positive youth development through school-based social and emotional learning interventions: A meta-analysis of follow-up effects. *Child Development*, 88(4), 1156–1171.

Tenenbaum, H. R., & Ruck, M. D. (2007). Are teachers' expectations different for racial minority than for European American students? A meta-analysis. *Journal of Educational Psychology*, 99(2), 253–273.

Townsend, B. (2000). The disproportionate discipline of African American learners: Reducing school suspensions and expulsion. *Exceptional Children*, 66(3), 381–392.

Tropea, J. L. (1987). Bureaucratic order and special children: Urban schools, 1890s–1940s. *History of Education Quarterly*, 27(1), 29–53.

Tsai, S. F., & Cheney, D. (2012). The impact of the adult–child relationship on school adjustment for children at risk of serious behavior problems. *Journal of Emotional and Behavioral Disorders*, 20(2), 105–114.

Turetsky, K. M., Sinclair, S., Starck, J. G., & Shelton, J. N. (2021). Beyond students: how teacher psychology shapes educational inequality. *Trends in Cognitive Sciences*, 25(8), 697–709.

Turnaround for Children. (2016). *Classroom and Behavior Management (CBM) unit overview*.

Tyack, D. B., & Cuban, L. (1995). *Tinkering toward utopia: A century of public school reform*. Harvard University Press.

Tyler, K. M., Boykin, A. W., & Walton, T. R. (2006). Cultural considerations in teachers' perceptions of student classroom behavior and achievement. *Teaching and Teacher Education*, 22(8), 998–1005.

Valdebenito, S., Eisner, M., Farrington, D. P., Ttofi, M. M., & Sutherland, A. (2019). What can we do to reduce disciplinary school exclusion? A systematic review and meta-analysis. *Journal of Experimental Criminology*, 15(3), 253–287.

Valenzuela, A. (2010). *Subtractive schooling: US-Mexican youth and the politics of caring*. Suny Press.

Van Cleve, N. G., & Mayes, L. (2015). Criminal justice through "colorblind" lenses: A call to examine the mutual constitution of race and criminal justice. *Law & Social Inquiry*, 40(2), 406–432.

Velez, G., Hahn, M., Recchia, H., & Wainryb, C. (2020). Rethinking responses to youth rebellion: Recent growth and development of restorative practices in schools. *Current Opinion in Psychology*, 35, 36–40.

Vincent, C. G., Sprague, J. R., Pavel, M., Tobin, T. J., & Gau, J. M. (2015). Effectiveness of schoolwide positive behavior interventions and supports in reducing racially inequitable disciplinary exclusion. In *Closing the school discipline gap: Equitable remedies for excessive exclusion*, 207, 1–34.

Voulgarides, C. K., Fergus, E., & Thorius, K. A. K. (2017) Pursuing equity: Disproportionality in special education and the reframing of technical solutions to address systemic inequities. *Review of Research in Education*, *41*(1), 61–87.

Vygotsky, L. S. (1978). *Mind in society: The development of higher psychological processes*. Harvard University Press.

Wacker, C., & Olson, L. (2019). Teacher mindsets: How educators' perspective shape student success. *Future Ed*, Georgetown University.

Wald, J., & Losen, D. J. (2006). Out of sight: The journey through the school-to-prison pipeline (Ch. 2). In S. Books (Ed.), *Invisible children in the society and its schools* (pp. 23–37). Routledge.

Wallace Jr, J. M., Goodkind, S., Wallace, C. M., & Bachman, J. G. (2008). Racial, ethnic, and gender differences in school discipline among US high school students: 1991–2005. *The Negro Educational Review*, *59*(1–2), 47.

Weist, M. D., Shapiro, C. J., Hartley, S. N., Bode, A. A., Miller, E., Huebner, S., Terry, J., Hills, K., & Osher, D. (2019). Assuring strengths- and evidence-based approaches in child, adolescent and school mental health. In Osher, D., Mayer, M. J., Jagers, R. J., Kendziora, K., & Wood, L. (Eds.), *Keeping students safe and helping them thrive: A collaborative handbook on school safety, mental health, and wellness*. Praeger/ABC-CLIO.

Welsh, R. O., & Little, S. (2018). The school discipline dilemma: A comprehensive review of disparities and alternative approaches. *Review of Educational Research*, *88*(5), 752–794.

Welsh, B. C., Yohros, A., & Zane, S. N. (2020). Understanding iatrogenic effects for evidence-based policy: A review of crime and violence prevention programs. *Aggression and Violent Behavior*, *55*, 101511.

Whitford, D. K., & Emerson, A. M. (2019). Empathy intervention to reduce implicit bias in pre-service teachers. *Psychological Reports*, *122*(2), 670–688.

Wigelsworth, M., Lendrum, A., Oldfield, J., Scott, A., Ten Bokkel, I., Tate, K., & Emery, C. (2016). The impact of trial stage, developer involvement and international transferability on universal social and emotional learning programme outcomes: A meta-analysis. *Cambridge Journal of Education*, *46*(3), 347–376.

Wiley, A. L., Brigham, F. J., Kauffman, J. M., & Bogan, J. E. (2013). Disproportionate poverty, conservatism, and the disproportionate identification of minority students with emotional and behavioral disorders. *Education and Treatment of Children*, *36*(4), 29–50.

Wilkerson, I. (2020). *Caste: The origins of our discontents*. Random House.

Williams III, J. A., Davis, A., Richardson, S. C., & Lewis, C. W. (2020). Can assistant principals' years of experience make a difference in school suspensions? A state-wide analysis of North Carolina assistant principals. *Journal of School Leadership*. https://doi.org/10.1177%2F1052684620969931

Woodruff, D. W., Osher, D., Hoffman, C. C., Gruner, A., King, M., Snow, S., & McIntire, J. C. (1999). *The role of education in a system of care: Effectively serving children with emotional or behavioral disorders*. Center for Effective Collaboration and Practice, American Institutes for Research.

Wubbels, T. (2017). A knowledge base for teachers on teacher-student relationships. In *Teacher education for the changing demographics of schooling* (pp. 67–81). Springer.

Yeager, D. S., Purdie-Vaughns, V., Garcia, J., Apfel, N., Brzustoski, P., Master, A., ... Cohen, G. L. (2014). Breaking the cycle of mistrust: Wise interventions to provide critical feedback across the racial divide. *Journal of Experimental Psychology: General*, *143*(2), 804.

Yoder, N., Holdheide, L., & Osher, D. (2018). Educators matter. In Osher, D., Moroney, D., & Williamson (Eds.), *Creating safe, equitable, engaging schools: A comprehensive, evidence-based approach to supporting students* (pp. 213–234). Harvard Education Press.

Yu, R. (2016). Stress potentiates decision biases: A stress induced deliberation-to-intuition (SIDI) model. *Neurobiology of Stress*, *3*, 83–95.

17

RETHINKING K-12 DISCIPLINARY POLICIES AND PRACTICES IN VIRTUAL SCHOOL SETTINGS

Initial School Responses to the COVID-19 Pandemic

Kevin P. Brady

UNIVERSITY OF ARKANSAS

Introduction

It is well established that public school students do not shed their constitutional rights at the schoolhouse door. But what about when the "schoolhouse door" is a computer screen, with students entering and exiting the learning environment from the comfort of their homes through an internet-enabled device? The rise of virtual learning, expediated by the COVID-19 pandemic, raises questions about when and how constitutional rights apply to public school students in the virtual setting.

Peggy Nicholson, 2021, p. 133

In March 2020, an extremely contagious virus, COVID-19, spread into an alarming and deadly international pandemic. An early request by the American Federation of Teachers (AFT) for additional federal guidance to school officials in dealing with the COVID-19 pandemic was largely unsuccessful (Jones, V. M., 2020). With little guidance from the federal government, state and especially local school officials were afforded significant discretion in determining how and whether K-12 schools would proceed with in-person schooling during the ongoing COVID-19 pandemic. On March 12, 2020, Ohio became the first state to officially mandate statewide public K-12 school closures. By the end of March 2020, approximately 50.8 million students were impacted as every state in the nation mandated public K-12 school closures (Jameson, Stegenga, Ryan, & Green, 2020). In a matter of days and with little or no specialized training, teachers nationwide were required to transform their physical brick-and-mortar classrooms to fully virtual learning environments. So, too, teachers nationwide are having to continually adjust and adapt their usual classroom management and disciplinary practices and strategies due to the COVID-19 pandemic.

As it specifically relates to school discipline, the abrupt shift to virtual instruction has dramatically blurred the existing lines between students' school and homes lives, which has forced teachers to make very difficult decisions about whether to intervene in situations involving their students witnessed over Zoom or some other comparable online platform. While instances of student misbehavior did not vanish during the shift to virtual learning, school officials have found themselves in unchartered territory when it comes to managing and attempting to apply disciplinary practices to fully virtual school environments (Jones, C., 2020). Often, teachers have not received specific guidance nor specialized professional development or training from school administrators on how to both effectively and equitably handle student disciplinary concerns taking place in virtual learning environments.

There is initial evidence that an increasing number of school districts are beginning to update their school discipline policies to substantially reduce harsh, punitive disciplinary expulsions and suspensions as well as police presence in schools, including school resource officers (Preston & Butrymowicz, 2021). For instance, in Florida, the Miami-Dade County Public School System recorded a total of 114 student arrests during the 2019 school year and in 2020 when the school district transitioned to become fully online, the number of student arrests was recorded at only 5 (Preston & Butrymowicz, 2021). Some argue that these significant reductions in student arrests are largely artificial and in large part due to public school districts not having in-person instruction.

Virtual instruction and the recent return in 2021 during the months of August and September of students and school staff to public schools with differing COVID-19 protocols in place has radically changed the school discipline landscape in many schools nationwide. For example, one Louisiana public school teacher commented, "For me it feels unethical to discipline students who are online for circumstances that are beyond their control, like noise in their home environment or if they are late" (Preston & Butrymowicz, 2021, p. 1). Another serious concern for returning students to schools after one full school year of virtual instruction and learning is initial concerns over the perceived lack of student mental health services (Preston & Butrymowicz, 2021). Dan Losen, Director of the Center for Civil Rights Remedies at UCLA's Civil Rights Project, predicts there will be a significant increase in student behavioral issues as well as punitive disciplinary practices, including long-term out-of-school suspensions and expulsions if appropriate student mental health services are not provided to returning students (Preston & Butrymowicz, 2021).

While this chapter will discuss the emerging legal issues unique to virtual teaching environments as it relates to the COVID-19 pandemic, including varying individual state mask mandates, the primary sources of law related to school discipline remain largely the same as they were prior to the COVID-19 pandemic. The following discussion will present a preliminary background as to how the existing law applies to K-12 student disciplinary concerns.

Sources of Law

The three sources of law that have direct relevance and applicability to school discipline in the USA include constitutional law, statutory law, and case law. These three legal sources exist on the federal and state levels.

Constitutional Law

The US Constitution is a major source of law in the US legal system. All 50 states have their own separate state constitutions, each of which plays a role similar to the federal constitution. Usually, state constitutions tend to be more detailed compared to the federal Constitution. For example, many state constitutions commonly address the day-to-day operations of state government, including public education (McCarthy, Eckes, & Decker, 2019). As a result, every state has its own unique collection of laws relating to school disciplinary practices in K-12 schools. In 1975, the Due Process Clause of the Fourteenth Amendment of the US Constitution was first applied to the area of school discipline at the K-12 level by the US Supreme Court in the case, *Goss v. Lopez*, where the Court ruled in 1975 that student suspensions of up to ten days require that the disciplined student be given both notice and a hearing under the Due Process Clause of the US Constitution's Fourteenth Amendment (Nicholson, 2021).

Statutory Law

The US Constitution affords Congress the legal authority to make laws. The laws that are passed or enacted by Congress are referred to as *statutes*. In Congress, the formal process begins with the introduction of a bill by either a senator or representative. A particular bill is assigned a designation as originating in either the House of Representatives (H.R.) or the Senate (S.). If a bill passes both the House of Representatives and the Senate but in different forms, a conference committee comprised of both representatives and senators is appointed to develop what is known as a "compromise bill." The compromise bill is then voted on again, and the final version of the bill is sent to the President, who either signs or vetoes the bill. State statutes or laws are created and enacted in a similar manner to federal statutes. Most statutes concerning matters of public education are state as opposed to federal laws.

Case Law

Case law refers to the published opinions of judges in court cases. Analogous to constitutional and statutory law, there is one federal court system and a court system in each of the 50 states. The opinions that arise from either federal or state court cases are used to interpret federal or state statutes. The US legal system relies heavily on these decisions because they establish legal precedents that other courts located across the country often follow or use as legal guidance. The importance of case law comes from the English tradition known as the "common law." Once a particular legal principle or precedent is established, it applies to legal cases with similar facts by subsequent courts.

Although the Constitution does not explicitly address public education and contains no federal provisions for it, the basic legal rights that the US Constitution guarantees to citizens do affect and influence education. Three federal constitutional amendments, in particular, the 1st, 4th, and 14th Amendments, have a collective influence on educational policies and practices, including classroom management practices and policies as it relates to student discipline.

The highest court in the United States, the US Supreme Court has repeatedly emphasized the legal authority of school officials and educators to control student conduct in public K-12 schools. An especially important Supreme Court case in student discipline is *Goss v. Lopez* (1975), in which the Supreme Court noted that the 14th Amendment of the US Constitution forbids states from depriving any student of life, liberty, or property without due process of law. More specifically, when a state provides a free public education to its citizens, it essentially is a legal right that a state or local educational agency may not deprive a citizen, including minor students without also providing due process protections to ensure the fairness and equity of the school disciplinary process. In the next section, the specific due process rights of students will be discussed and how the law directly influences schoolwide disciplinary polices and classroom management practices.

Student Due Process Protections in the School Disciplinary Process

The US Supreme Court in *Goss v. Lopez* (1975) ruled that students have constitutional protections in the form of due process rights when school officials use disciplinary procedures, such as student expulsions and suspensions. The due process protections afforded students, however, are limited by the state's interest in maintaining order and discipline in the schools. The courts, therefore, have had to strike the often-difficult balance between acknowledging student rights with the legitimate needs of protecting the overall safety of students and school staff.

The two general areas of due process rights afforded students are classified as (1) procedural due process and (2) substantive due process. In terms of student discipline, *procedural due process* refers to the fairness of methods and procedures used by the schools; *substantive due process* refers to the legal protection of student rights from violation by school officials and involves the reasonableness of the disciplinary processes (Valente & Valente, 2005). School authorities, however, are vested with broad and discretionary authority for establishing appropriate rules and procedures to maintain order and discipline in the school environment. Unless students can show through evidence that they were deprived of a liberty or property interest, there is no student right to due process. According to a federal district court in Tennessee, "teachers should be free to impose minor forms of classroom discipline, such as admonishing students, requiring special assignments, restricting activities, and denying certain privileges, without being subjected to structures of due process" (*Dickens v. Johnson Board of Education*, 1987, p. 157).

Procedural Due Process: The Right to Fair Procedures in the Disciplinary Process

The importance of education to a student's future certainly requires that disciplinary actions resulting in the student being deprived of an education (e.g., suspension, expulsion) be subjected to the standards of due process. The primary purpose of due process procedures is to ensure that disciplinary decisions, including punishments and sanctions are made in a fair and non-arbitrary manner. Due process procedures in school settings do not require the full range of legal protections a person would receive in a formal court trial (e.g., representation by legal counsel, cross-examination of witnesses, etc.). Due process procedures in school settings do, however, include the basic legal protections of notice and a hearing.

The US Supreme Court in *Goss v. Lopez* (1975) outlined the due process protections, which must be extended to all K–12 students. The *Goss* case involved nine high school students in Columbus, Ohio, who were suspended from school without any type of informal or formal hearing. The students filed a lawsuit claiming they had been denied due process of law under the US Constitution's Fourteenth Amendment. The Supreme Court agreed, ruling that the students had the right to at least minimal due process protections in cases of student suspension. The high court stated: "Having chosen to extend the right to an education ... [the state] may not withdraw the right on grounds of misconduct absent fundamentally fair procedures to determine whether the misconduct had occurred" (p. 574).

The Court noted that schools have broad legal authority to prescribe and enforce standards of behavior. However, in their decision, the Supreme Court held that students are entitled to public education as a property interest, which is protected by the Fourteenth Amendment. Because education is protected, it may not be taken away without adhering to the due process procedures required by the Constitution. The school's lawyers had argued that a 10-day suspension was only a minor and temporary interference with the student's education; the high court disagreed, stating that a 10-day suspension was a serious event in the life of the suspended child. When school officials impose 10-day suspensions, therefore, they must grant the suspended student the fundamental requisite of due process of law, the opportunity to be heard.

The opportunity to be heard, when applied to the school setting, involves the right to notice and hearing. The right to notice and hearing requires that students are presented with the charges against them and have an opportunity to state their case (Yudof, Kirp, & Levin, 1992). These legal protections will not shield students from properly imposed suspensions. The protections will, however, protect them from an unfair or mistaken suspension. The court in *Goss* recognized the necessity of order and discipline and the need for immediate and effective action, stating that suspension is a "necessary tool to maintain order [and] a valuable educational device" (p. 572). The prospect of imposing lengthy and cumbersome hearing requirements on every suspension case was a concern to the Court. However, the majority believed that school officials should not have the power to act unilaterally, free of notice and hearing requirements. The Court held that when students are suspended for a period of 10 days or less, therefore, the school must give them oral or written notice of the charges, an explanation of the reasons for the suspension, and an opportunity to present their side of the story.

The notice and hearing requirement does not mean that a formal notice to a student and a meeting must always precede suspension. It is permissible to have a reasonable delay between the time the notice is given and the student's hearing. For example, if the behavior poses a threat to other students or the academic process, a student can be immediately removed from school. The notice and hearing should then follow within 24 to 72 hours. A teacher or an administrator who is disciplining the student could also informally discuss the misconduct with the student immediately after the behavior occurred. This would give the student notice and an opportunity to explain his or her version of the facts before the teacher or administrator carried out the disciplinary sanction. In this case, the notice and hearing would precede the discipline.

It is important to remember that the basic due process protections outlined by the Supreme Court in *Goss* only apply to short suspensions of under 10 school days. According to the Court, longer suspensions, or expulsions, require more extensive and formal notices and hearings. Disciplinary procedures such as time-out, detention, response cost, and overcorrection do not require that due process procedures be extended to students. It is a reasonable assumption that when using in-school suspension the notice and hearing procedures should be followed. These school disciplinary procedures apply to all students, disabled and nondisabled alike.

Substantive Due Process: The Right to Reasonableness in the Disciplinary Process

The courts have tended to give great legal authority to teachers and school officials to write rules that govern student behavior in school. Additionally, courts have granted school officials the authority to develop and impose consequences on students who break their rules. There is a limit to this power, however. These rules and consequences must not violate students' constitutional principles discussed earlier (e.g., privacy, due process, expression). Generally, rules and consequences will not violate students' constitutional rights when they are reasonable. Reasonable rules and consequences have a carefully considered rationale and a school-related purpose. Schools may not prohibit or punish behavior that has no adverse effect on the school environment. Furthermore, schools cannot use disciplinary penalties or restraints that are unnecessary or excessive to achieve safety and order in school. In other words, reasonable rules and consequences are rational and fair and they are not excessive for a school environment.

Rules must be sufficiently clear and specific to allow students to distinguish permissible from prohibited behavior. School rules that are too vague or general may result in the violation of students' rights because students will not have a clear understanding of them. Appropriate school rules are specific and definitive. They provide students with information regarding behavioral expectations.

In the next section, a discussion of school disciplinary issues and legal concerns arising from the ongoing COVID-19 pandemic are discussed.

Specific School Disciplinary Issues Arising from the COVID-19 Pandemic

School disciplinary practices and strategies are noticeably different compared to when students are in a brick-and-mortar classroom. For example, instead of a student being sent to the school principal's office or being sent to an in-school suspension room within a school building, educators teaching in fully virtual school settings have had to resort to muting a student's audio on Zoom or turn off the student's video (Cohen, 2020; Klein, 2020). While some see the ongoing COVID-19 pandemic as a unique opportunity for school officials to rethink existing disciplinary practices, other school districts nationwide have simply extended their existing school disciplinary codes, policies, and classroom managerial practices to the virtual classroom setting with little or no modifications that factor in the uniqueness of the virtual setting where most students are logging in from their homes. For instance, some school districts retain long-standing student dress code policies, which now include not wearing pajamas during virtual instructional sessions.

Traditionally, the nation's courts have recognized the invaluable importance of schools maintaining a safe and orderly educational environment and have granted considerable discretion to teachers in exercising this control through the use of disciplinary policies and practices. Courts, however, have also recognized that students, while at school, have legal rights that must be respected. Such rights include the right to (a) reasonable expectations of student privacy, (b) due process procedures, and (c) student free speech and expression. Both school leaders and teachers are faced with the difficult task of balancing students' rights with the need to maintain safety and order in the school environment. Unquestionably, the COVID-19 pandemic has brought new and difficult considerations for school officials as well as students attempting to balance a safe and orderly educational environment with a reasonable level of student legal rights and protections. Since initial evidence suggests that the COVID-19 pandemic has significantly disrupted the lives of students, many school mental health and safety professionals are calling for more trauma-informed practices as well as much more lenient and considerably less punitive approaches to school discipline (Arundel, 2020).

During the ongoing COVID-19 pandemic, students are being disciplined for a growing number of infractions that did not exist prior to the pandemic, including students being disciplined for removing their masks in schools, talking inappropriately during a Zoom session, or failing to properly socially distance themselves from other students or school staff while on school property. Some state political officials argue that these disciplinary actions should receive harsh disciplinary punishment, even criminal sanctions. For example, the Governor of Utah, Gary Herbert, in 2020 enacted a state law making it possible for K-12 students and teachers to be charged with a criminal misdemeanor for not wearing a mask within a school building (Arundel, 2020).

A Student's Right to Privacy in Virtual School Settings: The Case of Ka'Mauri Harrison

One of the emerging legal issues related to school officials disciplining students in a virtual learning environment has been gauging a student's right to privacy in a virtual school setting where the student is receiving live, online instruction while the student is at home. Some recent cases involving disciplining a student in virtual school environments involve whether school officials can legally regulate what objects are allowed in a student's home, including weapons (Jones, V. M., 2020). Another issue involving student privacy in a virtual school environment is whether school officials can use images of students recorded during virtual instruction, such as a Zoom session without the student or parents' consent as evidence that a student violated a particular school or district-level code of disciplinary conduct.

In a 2020 Louisiana case receiving considerable national media attention, a nine-year-old African-American child was suspended when his teacher saw a BB gun in his bedroom during a Google Meets virtual instructional session (Crespo, 2020). On September 11, 2020, Ka'Mauri Harrison, a fourth grader at Woodmere Elementary School, located in the Jefferson Parish Public Schools System (JPPSS), Louisiana's largest public school district. The student, Ka'Mauri Harrison was attending his virtual social studies class while at home and getting prepared to take an English exam online on his computer. While taking his English exam, Ka'Mauri's younger brother entered the bedroom they shared and tripped over a BB gun. After picking up the BB gun, Ka'Mauri accidently placed the gun in the view of his computer's video camera, where it was seen by his teacher as well as his fellow classmates. Soon after witnessing what appeared to be real gun, Ka'Mauri's teacher disconnected him from his virtual class (Peiser, 2020). Ka'Mauri's parents were notified soon after that he was suspended from attending any further virtual school sessions for a total of six days. The student was also recommended for a long-term expulsion for being in the possession of an unauthorized weapon.

Ka'Mauri's parents disagreed with the suspension and a hearing was held, which was attended by his teacher, the school's principal, Ka'Mauri, his parents, as well as an attorney representing Ka-Mauri. A hearing officer upheld the student's six-day suspension for "displaying a facsimile weapon while receiving virtual instruction." The hearing officer also amended Ka'Mauri's punishment to include a social work assessment.

Ka'Mauri's parents sought a formal appeal to the school board's suspension on his record and the requirement that he be assessed by a social worker. Ka'Mauri's parents responded to the local school board's decision by filing an injunction and temporary restraining order (TRO) in the civil court of Jefferson Parish against the school board. As a result of this disciplinary incident, Ka'Mauri, his father, and their attorney testified before the Louisiana State Legislature in support of what was to be called, House Bill 83, which gives students the legal right to appeal their suspensions to the local school board prior to seeking judicial relief. More specifically, this bill requires public K–12 school districts in Louisiana to develop virtual school discipline policies. Additionally, House Bill 83 allows families to collect attorney's fees if a school official's use of discipline was found to be grossly negligent. House Bill 83, which is commonly referred to as the "Ka'Mauri Harrison Act" received bipartisan support in the Louisiana House of Representatives and Senate. The Ka'Mauri Harrison Act was signed into law by Louisiana Governor, John Bel Edwards on November 5, 2020. With the passage of the Ka'Mauri Harrison Act, the family again sought to appeal his suspension before the local school board. However, the school board ultimately upheld Ka'Mauri's suspension and upheld the hearing officer's decision to keep both the suspension and weapons charge on Ka'Mauri's school record.

Despite the fact that the JPPSS school system decided to uphold Ka'Mauri's suspension and the weapons charge, the passage of the Ka'Mauri Harrison Act did result in the creation of the JPPSS's *Virtual Discipline Policy and Code of Conduct*. Some of the prohibited student behaviors detailed in the school district's new virtual discipline policy and code of conduct include: harassing or discriminatory language used while in a virtual learning environment, displaying online images of pornography or images of nudity, handling or displaying weapons, including toy or facsimile weapons, sharing assignments or questions/answers online in violation of the district's academic honesty policy, interference with a virtual instructional audio or video, or violations of the district's acceptable use policy or technological device contract. In the aftermath of the passage of the Ka'Mauri Harrison Act, other school districts nationwide have begun developing new disciplinary rules and regulations based on the unique context and considerations found in virtual student learning environments.

The Increasing Adoption of Virtual Student Disciplinary Codes of Conduct

Fortunately, there are growing examples of public school districts recognizing the importance of having specific procedures outlined for student discipline early in the COVID-19 pandemic (Nicholson, 2021). For example, in 2020, Tennessee's Shelby County Schools, which includes the city of Memphis, created a virtual disciplinary code of conduct called *Virtual Student Conduct Expectations* which details Shelby County Schools disciplinary policies specifically tailored to virtual school environments and disciplinary situations. The school district's guidance established and defined new categories for discipline within virtual school settings, including virtual detention as well as virtual in-school suspension. An important legal factor in Shelby County's *Virtual Student Conduct Expectations* document is that the guidance requires that both the virtual in-school suspensions as well as supervised study environments be conductive for student learning and provide students with ongoing online instruction throughout the duration of the student's suspension or expulsion (Nicholson, 2021).

Since students still have the opportunity to learn during virtual in-school suspensions under Shelby County's virtual discipline policy, the stated policies and practices legally satisfy the student due process guidelines of notice and a hearing and thus do not violate a student's procedural due process rights under the US Constitution. Additional evidence suggests that keeping students connected to learning during virtual student disciplinary removals is also likely to help improve student outcomes (Morgan et al., 2014).

Shelby County Schools' current virtual discipline policies indicate student behaviors that could potentially result in disciplinary actions specifically in virtual school environments, including cyberbullying, wearing clothing that reveal underwear as seen in video cameras during virtual class sessions, repeated lateness to virtual classes, inappropriate use of electronic media, and the intentional

Table 17.1 Major Virtual Discipline Categories: Shelby County Public Schools (Tennessee)

Category A: (Serious)

Any student who commits a Category A offense must receive a mandatory 180 day suspension. Category A offenses include: possession of drugs, aggravated assault of staff and possession of a firearm on school property/event.

Category C: (Moderate–Serious)

#1. Threatening bodily harm to school personnel, including transmitting by an electronic device any communication containing a credible threat to cause bodily injury or death to a school employee and the transmission of such threat creates actual disruptive activity at the school that requires administrative intervention;

#2. Malicious destruction of or damage to school property, including electronic media, or the property of any person attending or assigned to the school;

#3. Stealing or misappropriation of school or personal property (regardless of intent to return);

Consequences of these behaviors cam result in:

- Parent–Principal Conference (Virtual/in-person/hybrid)
- Virtual Supervised Study/Detention
- Virtual In–School Suspension
- In–School Suspension
- Out-of–School Suspension
- Remand to Alternative School

Category D (Minor–Moderate):

#1. Threatening bodily harm to another student, including transmitting by an electronic device any communication containing a credible threat to cause bodily injury or death to a student and the transmission of such threat creates actual disruptive activity at the school that requires administrative intervention;

#2. Inappropriate use of electronic media, including but not limited to, all calls (land line, cellular or computer generated), instant messaging, text messaging, video/audio recording devices, IPods, MP3s or any type of electronic music or entertainment device, and cameras and camera phones;

#3. Bullying/cyberbullying, intimidation, and harassment;

#4. Inciting, advising or counseling of others to engage in any acts in Categories A or C using any means to send or receive spoken or written messages, including, but not limited to, notes, letters, texts, online or in-person group chats or conferencing, electronic messaging, audio messaging, video messaging, social media posts/streams, or other similar forms of communication;

Category E (Minor):

#1. Habitual and/or excessive tardiness;

#2. Class cutting;

#3. Intentional disturbance of class, cafeteria or school activities;

#4. Possession of and access to beepers, cellular phones or other electronic communication devices during school hours without permission of the principal or in violation to district/school policy;

#5. Dress code violation, including wearing, while on school grounds during the regular school day, clothing that exposes underwear or body parts in an indecent manner that disrupts the learning environment.

Consequences for these behaviors can result in:

- Parent–Principal Conference (Virtual/in-person/hybrid)
- Virtual Supervised Study/Detention
- Virtual In–School Suspension

Source: Shelby County Schools, Virtual Student Conduct Expectations (2020).

disturbance of a virtual class (Heim & Straus, 2020). In order to address specific virtual student conduct expectations, the Shelby County Schools have classified virtual discipline into various categories. As detailed in Table 17.1, prohibited student behaviors within virtual school environments include: Category A (requiring a mandatory 180-day student suspension); Category C (moderate-serious); Category D (minor-moderate); and Category E (minor).

As a direct result of the COVID-19 pandemic and the transition to remote, online learning, more school districts nationwide are expanding or adjusting their student disciplinary codes of conduct and practices to include the unique considerations of virtual learning environments. The Denver Public Schools, for example, have created a set of policies, *Student Discipline in a Virtual Classroom*, recognizing that safe, secure, and welcoming school environments must include virtual as well as face-to-face environments. More specifically, the Denver Public Schools acknowledge the added stress the COVID-19 pandemic has had on students and strongly encourage the use of restorative as well as trauma-informed practices when addressing student misbehavior(s) in virtual learning environments (Denver Public Schools, 2021, p. 1).

School Mask Requirements During COVID-19: Implications for School Discipline

As the 2021–22 school year begins at the time of writing, a volatile debate continues to polarize students, parents, and staff involving the issue of whether local school officials can or should require students to wear masks while attending schools. While the American Academy of Pediatrics and the Centers for Disease Control (CDC) have argued that masks are a proven way to mitigate the spread of COVID-19, mask mandates for both students and school staff continue to generate controversy nationwide. Some argue that the decision of whether or not to require masks should be left to individual students, school staff members, or students' parents (Decker, 2021). As Table 17.2 illustrates, individual states are divided over whether or not to require masks in public school environments. As of September 2021, five states, including Florida, Oklahoma, South Carolina, Tennessee, and Utah currently ban public school districts from implementing universal mask mandates. Presently, four states, Arizona, Arkansas, Iowa, and Texas have had their mask mandates temporarily blocked, suspended, or are not being enforced. A total of 16 states (California, Connecticut, Delaware, Hawaii, Illinois, Louisiana, Maryland, Massachusetts, Nevada, New Jersey, New Mexico, Oregon, Pennsylvania, Rhode Island, Virginia, and Washington) and the District of Columbia currently requires masks be worn in public schools.

Some individual school districts have actively defied their own state's mask mandate ban in public schools. For example, in Tennessee, a state where masks are not mandated in public schools, the Nashville Public Schools have decided to not follow current state law and adopted a discipline policy for students who refuse to comply with the district's mask requirement. More specifically, the Nashville Public Schools COVID-19 protocols, in part, state "refusing to wear a mask or maintain social distancing, leaving a designated area or intentionally exchanging "bodily fluids," such as coughing or sneezing, are considered violations of the school district's protocols. Students who violate the district's COVID-19 protocols could possibly face discipline proceedings, including a student-teacher conference for the first offense; a parent-teacher conference for the second offense; and a suspension or expulsion for multiple incidents.

Table 17.2 Mask Mandates in Public Schools: By State

School mask mandate type	State
Masks not mandated in public schools	Florida, Oklahoma, South Carolina, Tennessee, Utah
Mask mandates in have been blocked, suspended, or not being enforced	Arizona, Arkansas, Iowa, Texas
Mask mandates are required in public schools	California, Connecticut, Delaware, District of Columbia, Hawaii, Illinois, Louisiana, Maryland, Massachusetts, Nevada New Jersey, New Mexico, Oregon, Pennsylvania, Rhode Island, Virginia, Washington

Source: Education Week (2021).

The Call for More Equitable Approaches to Student Discipline During the Pandemic

Considering that peer-reviewed research has consistently shown a disparity in discipline by race for the same offenses, media reports demonstrating the overreaction of districts and schools to remote behavior by children suggests that students of color are readily being identified as troublemakers instead of children in need of mild discipline and/or restorative interventions.

Julian Vasquez Heilig, Dean, University of Kentucky College of Education

There are genuine and growing concerns that the COVID-19 pandemic has actually magnified existing disciplinary inequities among students in public K–12 education. As such, there have been increasing calls for more equitable disciplinary practices that avoid a punitive approach to suspending or expelling students (Heim & Strauss, 2020). More specifically, it is recommended that schools adopt more trauma-informed practices rather thàn punitive approaches to school discipline, especially in the wake of the COVID-19 pandemic and its suggested negative impacts on the mental health of students and school officials (Arundel, 2020). For instance, some school districts have implemented online materials that focus on students' social and emotional needs, including the use of restorative justice practices, which focus on repairing the harm a student has caused to others and teaching the student to learn from these experiences (Heim & Strauss, 2020). Kelly Valliancourt Strobach, Director of Policy and Advocacy for the National Association of School Psychologists, contends, "By focusing on prevention and intervention, educators can better support students who are struggling emotionally and behaviorally during the pandemic. It's not that the student is giving you a hard time, it's that the student is having a hard time. The goal…should be to identify kids who need support and get them that support." Based on the immeasurable emotional toll of the pandemic on students and educators alike, an increasing number of educators and school leaders are fundamentally rethinking school disciplinary practices and the direct impact of these practices on students, especially the nation's most vulnerable students, including students of color and those with disabilities.

Although there is no one model of schoolwide discipline used in schools, there are three basic professional practices that are often suggested to foster effective school disciplinary systems (Horner et al., 2000; Walker, Colvin, & Ramsey, 1995). First, schools with effective policies invest in preventing problem behavior by defining, teaching, and supporting student behavior. This means school personnel develop important expectations or rules concerning student behavior and clearly communicate these expectations to students. Moreover, school officials recognize students who adhere to these expectations, and respond effectively when students do not. Second, effective schoolwide discipline systems have rapid, effective support systems for identifying and addressing the needs of students who are at risk of developing problem behavior. According to Lewis and Sugai (1999), these procedures often involve increased adult monitoring and group behavior support. Third, schools using effective discipline systems have support for high-intensity problem behavior. Such systems focus on a small number of students who display high rates of disruptive behavior and include specialized individual behavior programs (e.g., FBAs and BIPs).

Adopting Clear School District Disciplinary Policies and Procedures, Including Virtual School Environments

District and school-level administrators should develop clearly written policies and procedures for teaching appropriate behavior and disciplining students when they violate school disciplinary rules. These policies and procedures must ensure that schools maintain safe and orderly environments while continuing to provide students with an appropriate public education. These policies should include rules of student conduct, and disciplinary sanctions when those rules are broken. Developing the policies with the participation of administrators, teachers, parents, and students will help to ensure that they are reasonable and related to a legitimate educational function. Teachers, administrators, staff, and parents should have access to, and understand, information in the school district's discipline policy. Methods to ensure parental access include mailing discipline policy brochures to district parents and having teachers explain the procedures in parent-teacher conferences. It is important that school disciplinary policies and procedures apply equally to all students and that they be administered in a fair and consistent manner.

(1) **Proactively Address Problem Student Behavior.** We must remember that the purpose of discipline is to teach. As educators our goal should not be solely the elimination of problem behavior. Rather it should be the elimination of problem behavior and the teaching of positive prosocial behaviors. Positive behavioral programming (e.g., conflict resolution training, anger control training) should be an important part of our school district practices.

(2) **Document Disciplinary Actions Involving Students.** When using disciplinary procedures with students with and without disabilities, teachers must keep thorough written records of all disciplinary actions taken. An examination of court cases and administrative rulings in disciplinary matters indicates that in many instances, decisions turned on the quality of the school's records (Yell, 2006). That is, when a school district is sued over a particular disciplinary incident, the court will examine the rules and consequences of the school to determine whether they are fair and reasonable. Often they will also examine the records that were kept, if any, on the particular behavior incident. Records on emergency disciplinary actions are also important. Such records should contain an adequate description of the incident, disciplinary action taken, and the signatures of witnesses present.

(3) **Evaluate the Effectiveness of Student Disciplinary Interventions.** Finally, it is crucial that school officials and teachers evaluate the effectiveness of the schoolwide policies and procedures and individual students' discipline plans. If schoolwide discipline plans, classroom rules and consequences, and individualized student programs are to be effective, school personnel should develop and implement a set of procedures for monitoring program effectiveness (Drasgow & Yell, 2002). The collection of meaningful data will allow school officials and teachers to determine the efficacy of the schoolwide policies and to maintain effective components of the program while eliminating the ineffective components.

There are several reasons for collecting data on an ongoing basis. To make decisions about whether a disciplinary intervention is reducing target behaviors in the school or for a student, teachers need data collected during the course of the intervention. If formative data not collected, school officials and teachers will not know with certainty if the procedures they use are actually achieving the desired results.

Teachers and administrators are accountable to supervisors, parents, and communities; data collection is useful for these purposes. From a legal standpoint it is imperative that school officials and teachers collect such data. Courts do not readily accept anecdotal information, and data-based decisions certainly would be viewed much more favorably (Drasgow & Yell, 2001).

Conclusion

The COVID-19 pandemic is continually causing educators nationwide to rethink school disciplinary policies and practices. Given the recent availability of vaccines for school-aged children ranging from 5 to 11 years old, many students have returned to in-person learning with an increased sense of protection against COVID-19. Nevertheless, many school districts nationally continue to provide virtual offerings for students who request them (Nicholson, 2021). There is also a sense of wariness that schools may once again have to abruptly return to fully virtual environments. School districts, administrators, and teachers have legal rights as well as responsibilities to ensure that their students attend safe and orderly school environments, whether they be in-person, hybrid, or fully virtual. Regardless of the delivery method of instruction, the common goal is that all students receive a meaningful and non-disruptive education. During these challenging times, it is strongly encouraged that today's school officials use this time to reconsider the role of managing discipline policies, practices, and its effects on students. In the current era of COVID-19, K-12 schools need to also acknowledge the unusually severe emotional impacts on students and school officials and implement trauma-informed practices. In order to effectively address the mental health of students, school officials must be mindful of this "new age" in school discipline and the adverse as well as possibly long-term consequences of punitive disciplinary practices during this challenging period of history.

As virtual school environments continue to remain a viable option during the ongoing COVID-19 pandemic, school officials need to consider the following three recommendations for considering the unique impact of virtual disciplinary policies and practices, including:

(1) Developing clear discipline policies and practices for virtual school environments.
(2) Proving comprehensive and updated training for teachers and school administrators in the best practices of virtual classroom management and discipline policies and practices.
(3) Updating monitoring and accountability systems for collecting and reporting student discipline data that accounts for student suspensions and expulsions because of disciplinary infractions in virtual school environments.

As schools continue to deal with the COVID-19 pandemic, schools must take proactive steps to develop disciplinary policies and practices that are unique to virtual school environments. School officials must acknowledge that disciplinary management does not cease when the student learning environment moves to a fully virtual platform. However, school officials must also consider the unique disciplinary considerations of virtual school setting and that student due process considerations must also be legally protected in these environments. While everyone affiliated with schools realize that we are venturing through muddled and unchartered territory, there are growing examples of public school districts that recognize the unique nature of the virtual school environment and are proposing new and innovative ways of managing discipline in the "new normal" of the nation's schools.

Appendix
Shelby County Schools
Virtual Student Conduct Expectations

STUDENT EXPECTATIONS

Students must maintain virtual settings and behaviors that are conducive for instruction and that minimize distractions.

Virtual Work Settings

1. Working stations must be free of foreign objects that are not being utilized for instruction.
2. The recording device being used for instruction must be positioned to allow teachers to observe both the working space and student, especially during testing.
3. Eating and drinking are not allowed during virtual courses. This is hazardous to electronic devices and can also be distracting during instruction.
4. When possible, students are encouraged to work in areas that are isolated from other individuals and pets. If circumstances exist that do not allow complete seclusion, the parent will need

to share this information separately with the instructor. Instructors will only require what the parent can reasonably provide.

5. Additional electronic devices should not be kept or used within the visible working area, unless they are being utilized for instruction/are teacher approved. This includes the use of speakers, phones, earphones and other devices that may provide distractions from teacher lead instruction.

6. Students will follow daily guidance from their teachers regarding best methods of communicating and participating during virtual schooling. Instructions regarding when and how to interact verbally and how to use audio and camera options will be dependent on the design of instruction and direction of the teacher.

Student Dress & Conduct

7. Students are to wear appropriate dress, that does not distract from the virtual learning process. Inappropriate attire including but not limited to the following are prohibited: clothing with profanity; derogatory terms; racial slurs; sexual content; and clothing that is transparent or overly revealing. School uniforms will not be required for Virtual Schooling.

8. Students should refrain from engaging in any of the behaviors identified in SCS Policy 6022 while engaged in virtual schooling. Traditional school rules and behavioral expectations still apply. Behavior that is disruptive to the virtual schooling setting will be addressed using progressive discipline measures.

9. Students are to remain positively engaged in instruction and participate.

TEACHER EXPECTATIONS

Every teacher will continue to hold student's accountable for misconduct during virtual courses, as authorized in TCA § 49-6-4102. Teachers must continue to implement reasonable classroom management interventions prior to referring students to administration.

Virtual Classroom Management & Restorative Practices

1. Teachers will regularly communicate behavior expectations to students. Expectations should be briefly stated at the beginning of each virtual course to remind students of protocol and appropriate use of their devices.

2. Teachers may utilize audio and video features on the technological platform to limit a student's interaction, if the student's behavior is disruptive to the virtual schooling process.

3. Teachers will remain cognizant of the social emotional needs of students, even while interacting within the virtual setting.

4. Teachers will continue to monitor, implement and revisit interventions and restorative (i.e., Bright Bytes etc.) practices as a deterrent to removing students completely from virtual class.

5. Teachers will maintain Virtual ISS folders that contain rigorous class assignments that meet local and state standards. Teachers will communicate deadlines for assignments to be returned and collect ISS assignments electronically from students.

Teacher Reporting & Communication

6. Teachers will routinely communicate student behaviors to parents and involve them in the development of behavior support plans and intervention strategies.

7. Teachers will report persistent misbehavior to administration, only after varied interventions and supports have been implemented and failed.

8. Teachers will report any instances of harassment, bullying, intimidation and any forms of harassment based on discrimination to administration within 24 hours.
9. Teachers will report possible criminal offenses, abuse, and neglect to DCS/law enforcement. Please see the following policy for more specifics SCS Policy 7005.
10. Teachers will NOT penalize students academically for misbehavior in the virtual setting; However, students who miss virtual schooling due to suspension, run the risk of missing assignments, which can lead to academic decline.
11. A restorative credit/grade process should be established for first time offenders that will allow students to participate in grade/credit recovery. Teachers/Administrators may create reasonable stipulations that coincide with make-up work opportunities (i.e., reflective essays, community service if applicable, SHAPE etc.).
12. Teachers will continue to abide by all 504 and IDEA stipulations when responding to virtual conduct, just as required within the traditional school environment.

ADMINISTRATIVE EXPECTATIONS (i.e. Principals, Assistant Principals and Vice-Principals)

Virtual Restorative Practices & Discipline Response

1. Administrators will work to ensure that teachers have thoroughly implemented restorative practices and interventions before referring students to administration. (unless the severity of the misconduct warrants immediate action per Policy Categories).
2. Administrators will investigate virtual misconduct that has escalated beyond the teacher's responsibility and provide virtual due process to students.
3. Administrators will review teacher referrals to determine the appropriate response/consequences/interventions to misbehavior and will also assist teachers in the development of virtual interventions.
4. Administrators will collaborate virtually with students, parents and teachers when developing behavior support plans
5. Administrators may collaborate with teachers to create reasonable stipulations that coincide with make-up work opportunities (i.e., reflective essays, community service if applicable, SHAPE etc.) and may develop restorative credit programs.
6. Administrators may assign students to Virtual Supervised Study/ISS for misbehavior.
7. Administrators will be responsible for entering any behavior that is deemed worthy of becoming a part of the student's disciplinary history into PowerSchool. Suspensions must be entered with 24 hours.
8. Administrators may conduct, schedule and manage Virtual ISS/supervised study when support staff are unavailable or identify and train appropriate others. Administrator Reporting & Communication
9. Principals will conduct virtual appeal conferences for parents who desire to appeal short-term exclusionary consequences, or other disciplinary consequences that do not warrant formal due process.
10. Administrators will report any instances of harassment, bullying, intimidation and any forms of harassment based on discrimination appropriately, document and investigate following policy guidelines.
11. Administrators will report possible criminal offenses, abuse, and neglect to DCS/law enforcement. Please see the following policy for more specifics SCS Policy 7005.
12. Administrators (only) will make SHAPE referrals, levy suspensions or remove students from the virtual schooling setting.

13. Administrators will Virtually participate in Formal Due Process Hearings and will be responsible for presenting evidence that justifies severe exclusionary consequences. As always, schools have flexibility when developing restorative practices. Creativity and resourcefulness can be used when developing virtual intervention strategies, when strategies coincide with SCS policy.

References

Arundel, A. (August 5, 2020). Avoid punitive approaches to school discipline during the pandemic, *District Administrator*. https://districtadministration.com/avoid-punitive-approach-to-school-discipline-during-the-pandemic/

Cohen, J. S. (July 14, 2020). A teenager didn't do her online homework. So a judge sent her to juvenile detention. *ProPublica*. www.propublica.org/article/a-teenager-didnt-do-her-online-schoolwork-so-a-judge-sent-her-to-juvenile-detention

Cole v. Greenfield-Central Community Schools, 657 F.Supp. 56 (S.D. Ind. 1986).

Crespo, G. (October 4, 2020). Parents sue Louisiana school district after 4th grader suspended for BB gun during virtual class at home, *CNN*. www.cnn.com/2020/10/04/us/student-suspended-gun-virtual-lawsuit-trnd/index.htmlCresCr

Decker, S. (August 20, 2021). Which states ban mask mandates in schools, and which require masks? *Education Week*. www.edweek.org/policy-politics/which-states-ban-mask-mandates-in-schools-and-which-require-masks/2021/08

Denver Public Schools (2021). *Student discipline in a virtual classroom*. http://thecommons.dpsk12.org/cms/lib/CO01900837/Centricity/Domain/52/SOP%20for%20Student%20Discipline%20in%20a%20Virtual%20Classroom.pdf

Dickens v. Johnson Board of Education, 661 F. Supp. 155 (ER.D.TN 1987).

Drasgow, E., & Yell, M. L. (2001). Functional behavioral assessment: Legal requirements and challenges. *School Psychology Review*, 30(2), 239–251. https://doi.org/10.1080/02796015.2001.12086112

Drasgow, E., & Yell, M. L. (2002). School-wide behavior support: Legal implications. *Child and Family Behavior Therapy*, 24(1), 129–145. https://doi.org/10.1300/J019v24n01_09

Goss v. Lopez, 419 U.S. 565 (1975). *Harrison v. Jefferson Parish School Board,* 2020 WL 7053298 (E.D. La. 2020) .

Heim, J., & Strauss, V. (September 15, 2020). School discipline enters new realm with online learning. *The Washington Post*. www.washingtonpost.com/education/school-discipline-enters-new-realm-with-online-learning/2020/09/14/e19a395e-f393-11ea-999c-67ff7bf6a9d2_s

Horner, R. H., Sugai, G., & Horner, H. F. (2000). A school-wide approach to student discipline. *The School Administrator*, 57(2), 20–23.

Jameson, J. M., Stegenga, S. M., Ryan, H., & Green, A. (2020). Free appropriate public education in the time of COVID-19. *Rural Special Education Quarterly*, 39(4), 181–192. https://doi.org/10.1177/8756870520959659

Jones, C. (November 17, 2020). How school discipline-and student behavior-- has changed during the pandemic, *EdSource*. https://edsource.org/2020/how-school-discipline-and-student-misbehavior-has-changed-during-the-pandemic/643758

Jones, V. M. (2020). COVID-19 and the "virtual" school-to-prison pipeline. *Children Legal Rights Journal*, 41(2), 105–126. www.childrenslegalrightsjournal.com/childrenslegalrightsjournal/volume_41_issue_2/MobilePagedReplica.action?pm=2&folio=105#pg22

Klein, R. (August 11, 2020). The new school suspension: Blocked from online classrooms. *Huffington Post*. www.huffpost.com/entry/school-discipline-remote-learning_n_5f329829c5b64cc99fde4d64?guccounter=1

Lewis, T. J., & Sugai, G. (1999). Effective behavior support: A systems approach to proactive school-wide management. *Focus on Exceptional Children*, 31(6), 1–24. https://doi.org/10.17161/foec.v31i6.6767

McCarthy, M. M., Eckes, S. E., & Decker, J. R (2019). *Legal rights of school leaders, teachers, and students (8th ed.)*. Pearson.

Morgan, E., Salomon, N., Plotkin, M., and Cohen, R. (2014). *The school discipline consensus report: Strategies from the field to keep students engaged in school and out of the juvenile justice system*. The Council of State Governments Justice Center. https://safesupportivelearning.ed.gov/sites/default/files/The_School_Discipline_Consensus_Report.pdf

Nicholson, P. (2021). When virtual discipline becomes virtual suspension: Protecting the due process rights of virtual learners. *Journal of Law and Education*, 50(2), 133–169.

Peiser, J. (September 8, 2020). A Black seventh-grader played with a toy gun during a virtual class. His school called the police. *The Washington Post*. www.washingtonpost.com/nation/2020/09/08/black-student-suspended-police-toy-gun/

Preston, C. & Butrymowicz, S. (February 2, 2021). How the pandemic has altered school discipline–perhaps forever. *Huffington Post*. www.huffpost.com/entry/pandemic-school-discipline_n_60300a72c5b6cc8bbf3b83a6

Sugai, G., Sprague, J. R., Horner, R. H., & Walker, H. M. (2000). Preventing school violence: The use of office discipline referrals to assess and monitor school-wide discipline interventions. *Journal of Emotional and Behavioral Disorders, 8*(2), 94–102. https://doi.org/10.1177/106342660000800205

Valente, W. D., & Valente, C. M. (2005). *Law in the schools* (6th ed.). Merrill/Prentice Hall.

Walker, H. M., Colvin, G., & Ramsey, E. (1995). *Antisocial behavior in school: Strategies and best practices*. Brooks/Cole.

Walker, H. M., & Epstein, M. H. (2001). *Making schools safer and violence free: Critical issues, solutions, and recommended practices*. Pro-Ed.

Yell, M. L. (2006). *The law and special education* (6th ed.). Merrill/Prentice Hall.

Yudof, M. G., Kirp, D. L., & Levin, B. (1992). *Education policy and the law* (3rd ed.). West.

18

USING MULTIMEDIA TO SUPPORT TEACHER CANDIDATES' KNOWLEDGE AND USE OF EVIDENCE-BASED CLASSROOM MANAGEMENT PRACTICES

Michael J. Kennedy, Rachel L. Kunemund, and Lindsay M. Carlisle

UNIVERSITY OF VIRGINIA

Introduction

A critical window for helping teachers gain the skills and competence needed to successfully learn and implement evidence-based classroom management practices is during preparation programs (Myers et al., 2017). Although nearly all preparation programs require at least one course in classroom or behavior management, the content and quality of those courses with respect to specific pedagogies used by instructors is highly variable (Stough & Montague, 2015). Candidate outcomes (and corresponding impact on K–12 student outcomes) in terms of verifiable implementation of evidence-based classroom management practices they learned during preparatory programs are also in short supply (Nelson et al., 2015; Reinke et al., 2013).

Within the broad field of education there is an opportunity to address initial preparation methods to develop teachers' use of evidence-based classroom management practices (Moore et al., 2017; Yoon et al., 2007). Without high-quality initial preparation and ongoing professional development (PD), we will continue to see poorly prepared teachers leaving the field after only a short period of time, often citing classroom management as a primary reason (Ingersoll & Merrill, 2010). However, a larger issue is the harm teachers can cause during the time they are employed stemming from poor or limited classroom management knowledge and skills—especially to students with disabilities.

Teachers with poor classroom management skills often rely on reactive disciplinary strategies (e.g., office discipline referrals), which result in student suspensions, frayed student relationships, and substantial loss of instructional time (Polirstok & Gottlieb, 2006). Students with disabilities usually begin the year behind their peers academically; therefore, teachers whose actions (or lack thereof) result in missed instructional time and students being removed from the classroom often result in these vulnerable students falling even further behind. Given these concerns, additional research is needed to develop more evidence-based pedagogy and instructional materials to help faculty members adequately prepare teacher candidates and in-service teachers with the knowledge and skills

DOI: 10.4324/9781003275312-21

Table 18.1 Instructional Design Principles of the Cognitive Theory of Multimedia Learning (Mayer, 2020)

Instructional Goal	Instructional Design Principles	Description of Instructional Design Principles
Reduce extraneous processing	Coherence principle (N = 18; ES = 0.86)	Exclude irrelevant or extraneous information.
	Signaling principle (N = 15; ES = 0.69)	Use cues to highlight the organization of content.
	Redundancy principle (N = 5; ES = 0.72)	Use graphics and narration rather than graphics, narration, *and* text when possible.
	Spatial contiguity principle (N = 9; ES = 0.82)	Place related words and images in close proximity to one another.
	Temporal contiguity principle (N = 8; ES = 1.31)	Present related words and images together.
Manage essential processing	Segmenting principle (N = 7; ES = 0.67)	Structure lessons to present small bits of information at a time.
	Pre-training principle (N = 10; ES = 0.78)	Review relevant background knowledge to support understanding of new concepts.
	Modality principle (N = 18; ES = 1.00)	Pair images with narration rather than printed text when possible.
Foster generative processing	Personalization principle (N = 13; ES = 1.00)	Use conversational rather than formal speech.
	Voice principle (N = 6; ES = 0.74)	Use human voice rather than computer-generated voice whenever possible.
	Embodiment principle (N = 16; ES = 0.58)	On-screen characters should embody human characteristics, if used to present content.
	Multimedia principle (N = 13; ES = 1.35)	Use of corresponding words *and* images supports learning more than words alone.
	Generative activity principle (N = 37; ES = 0.71)	Use generative learning activities (e.g., summarizing, mapping, drawing) to support knowledge retention.

Note: N = the number of tests conducted for each principle; ES = the median effect size found for each principle.

needed to implement and sustain high-quality classroom management (Nelson et al., 2015; Reinke et al., 2013).

Multimedia is an intriguing option to support the repertoire of faculty and other instructors supporting teacher candidates' development of evidence-based classroom management practices and dispositions (Hirsch et al., 2019). One reason why is its portability and flexibility. For example, instructors can assign modeling and instructional videos to help bolster assigned readings and lectures (Kennedy et al., 2011). Multimedia also enables candidates to watch their teaching, in simulated situations, or with children, and then reflect on the extent to which their practices were used with fidelity and quality (Nagro et al., 2017).

To compose this chapter, we reviewed empirical research from general and special education teacher preparation domains, with a focus on studies where multimedia was a key component in design and delivery of instruction regarding classroom management practices. Three key domains of practices emerged: (a) content acquisition podcasts, (b) use of simulations, and (c) video reflection. Other uses of multimedia exist, but domains used herein provided multiple studies that form robust evidence for review. Additional reviews related to novice (e.g., Hirsch et al., 2021) and in-service teachers (e.g., Cho et al., 2020) have recently been published. In the conclusion we discuss findings from similar reviews in the in-service space and contrast with the literature reviewed herein.

Content Acquisition Podcasts

Content acquisition podcasts (CAPs) are a form of enhanced podcasts (visuals in time with audio) that can be used to deliver instruction for any topic area, including classroom management (Kennedy et al., 2011). Typically 5 to 15 minutes in length, CAPs are short multimedia vignettes and can be viewed on any Internet-connected device. However, CAPs are set apart from generic use of podcasting technology in important ways. To illustrate, CAPs are planned, designed, and delivered to reflect Mayer's (2008) cognitive theory of multimedia learning (CTML) and associated instructional design principles. These principles are laid out in Table 18.1 with effect sizes for each principle as reported by Mayer (2008). These design principles are used to shape the looks and sounds of each CAP. For example, each CAP has a clear, but simple image that represents the content being taught at any given time. Images change quickly during the video to correspond to content being taught. In addition, there is sparing on-screen text, and lots of clear cues and signals throughout. Only essential information is presented.

The CTML holds that learners benefit from instruction that leverages images (including text) and narration designed to maximize active learning processes and minimize extraneous cognitive processing that distracts from learning (Mayer, 2008). Extraneous cognitive processing can occur when narration is too fast, includes too much new or unknown information, or is off topic relative to the main content being presented (DeLeeuw & Mayer, 2008). Because all instruction carries a level of intrinsic load for the learner, it is essential that multimedia instruction not add unnecessary cognitive processing demands (Sweller, 2020). We expand on this point below, and for a fuller description of how cognitive load impacts learners and the mitigating factor of multimedia, see Kennedy and Romig (2021), and Carlisle et al. (2021). A screenshot of a CAP is shown in Figure 18.1 and a sample CAP can be viewed at https://vimeo.com/344402025.

Use of CAPs in Teacher Education

When first introduced, CAPs provided university instructors and students a flexible option for delivering or learning key content about a specific topic (e.g., positive behavioral supports, Kennedy & Thomas, 2012) or specific evidence-based practice (e.g., functional behavioral assessments, Hirsch et al., 2020). Teacher candidates, as they learn about evidence-based classroom management practices, are subject to substantial cognitive overload. This is because of the volume of practices they need to master and develop an understanding of the appropriate time and place for their use. When teachers are cognitively overloaded, they are unlikely to use evidence-based practices (Feldon, 2007). Therefore, building teacher fluency with key knowledge and practices related to classroom management is essential, and CAPs are designed to support this goal. CAPs can be found on www.spedintro.com, or created new by instructors.

There are four published studies where CAPs were used specifically within teacher preparation coursework or field experiences to support knowledge and implementation of practices related to behavior management. Each illustrates the efficacy of this intervention to support knowledge of teacher candidates.

Kennedy and Thomas (2012) randomly assigned 164 teacher candidates from two universities to either watch a CAP on aspects of positive behavior interventions and supports (PBIS), or read a chapter containing the same content. Results revealed the teacher candidates who learned using CAPs scored significantly higher on a dependent measure of knowledge at post-test and maintenance several weeks later. Although this study did not evaluate learners' cognitive load directly, based on Mayer's CTML, positive results in favor of the CAP condition indicate learning processes were supported at a level higher than peers who only read the same content.

In the first of two conceptual replication studies, Hirsch et al. (2015) completed a quasi-experimental test of the impact of CAPs on teacher candidates' (n = 97) knowledge of functional

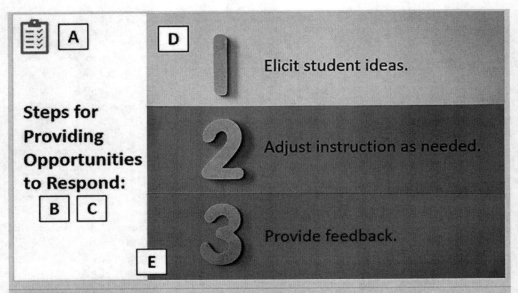

Figure 18.1 Example of a CAP Slide with Description of Formatting Components

A. Visual cue reminding viewers that this is the portion of the lesson describing the steps for a classroom management practice.

B. Large (36 point), plain font-type.

C. Font color is a clear contrast to the background color of the slide.

D. Large, clear image placed with corresponding text.

E. Image has a clear connection to the text, and the text matches language used in the speaker notes.

behavior analysis (FBA) content. Group 1 watched a CAP containing key information regarding FBA content. Group 2 listened to a live lecture by a professor of the same content. Results favored the CAP group, who demonstrated an increase in their knowledge of FBAs. In a follow up, Hirsch and colleagues (2020) conducted a quasi-experiment with 94 teacher candidates in an attempt to understand the roles of CAPs for supporting knowledge of FBA components. One group watched CAPs with embedded questions (to support engagement and memory), and the other watched a traditional CAP. Researchers did not observe a difference in performance on their dependent measure of candidate knowledge between the two groups. Both studies again lend credibility to the notion that this multimedia approach is effective for the task of boosting teachers' knowledge of important content.

In a final quasi-experimental study, Firestone and Rodl (2020) randomly assigned participants to one of three conditions to learn about PBIS-related content: CAP plus professor-facilitated discussion, CAP plus professor-facilitated application activity, and CAP alone. Results demonstrated teacher candidates in the two CAP plus formats scored higher on a measure of knowledge than the CAP only group. In each study, completed by different research teams across several years' time, CAPs demonstrated efficacy for supporting teacher candidate learning.

Where do we go from here? Researchers and teacher educators utilize CAPs in a wide variety of ways (Nagro, 2020). The aforementioned studies illustrate the positive impact of this intervention on teacher candidates' learning of content related to classroom management practices and topics. Currently, teacher educators can use CAPs with teacher candidates with the expectation that CAPs will help improve candidate classroom management knowledge. However, more research should be conducted to determine if CAPs can be used to help teacher candidates implement new evidence-based practices in real settings with students. Some research (see Hirsch et al., 2019; Kennedy et al., 2017) has used CAPs to address this question with in-service teachers and found positive effects. To illustrate, Kennedy et al. (2017) compared the use of CAPs as PD presentation to a traditional workshop-style PD. In both settings, the PD delivered instruction on the use of three EBPs for classroom management: opportunities to respond, behavior specific praise statements, and pre-correction statements. Across all three practices, teachers in the CAPs group implemented them with greater frequency than the teachers who received traditional (i.e. lecture and discussion-driven) PD.

Despite promising results in both pre-service and in-service settings, further work needs to be done to determine whether the impact of CAPs on candidate knowledge can transfer into skills in the classroom. Therefore, additional replications should be completed with the additional use of applied skill to determine the extent to which CAPs can support candidate implementation of key practices—particularly related to classroom management skill. In addition, more research teams not affiliated with Kennedy and team should conduct independent evaluations of this intervention.

Simulations in Teacher Preparation

When it comes to teacher preparation, simulations offer teacher candidates an opportunity to practice their classroom management skills in real time prior to entering an actual classroom with students. There are many benefits to using simulations aimed at improving classroom management in teacher preparation programs. For example, the ability to engage in low-stakes practice enables teacher candidates to fine tune instructional strategies and decision-making in novel situations like those they may face upon entering the classroom. Simulations provide a means for filling in the gap between learning and action. While simulation is a relatively new tool for teacher education, the idea of practice before actual, live teaching is not new. In the same way you may practice an interview or presentation in front of friends or colleagues, simulations offer teacher candidates an opportunity to practice classroom management in front of fictitious "students."

History of Simulations in Teacher Education

Simulations have been used by teacher educators for decades, although it has only been in recent years that we have seen simulations using advanced technology (e.g. hypermedia theater, computer-based; Arvola et al., 2018; Hughes et al., 2015) as the medium continues to mature. Cruikshank (1969) describes early efforts to use simulations a part of teacher preparation, specifically as a replacement for portions of student teaching. It appears that even in these earlier years in teacher education, there was a preference for this type of pre-teaching practice. Early versions of simulations involved recorded videos, paper-based problems to solve, and role playing. The logic behind these early simulations remains the same today; it provides teacher candidates an opportunity to practice and refine their technical skills without the pressures of a real-world classroom environment and the ability to stop, reflect, and try again.

As technology continued to advance into the 1990s and early twenty-first century, simulations began to take on a new format with simulated virtual classroom environments (Ferry et al., 2004). Ferry and colleagues highlight the benefits of simulations in providing teacher candidates an opportunity to practice instructional decision making, see the result of their decisions, and then revise. In their recent systematic literature review, Theelen et al. (2019) examined studies from 2004 to 2016. They found that teacher-candidate use of simulations during teacher preparation improved their classroom management and their sense of self-efficacy. In sum, the long history of simulations and their continued advancement from paper-based to virtual reality demonstrates a promising method for preparing teacher candidates and encouraging thoughtful decision-making.

Current Use of Simulations for Teacher Candidates

Simulations, such TeachLivE and Interactive Virtual Training for Teachers (IVT-T), have been shown to be effective in improving the classroom management skills of teachers already in classrooms (Dawson & Lignugaris/Kraft, 2017; Shernoff et al., 2021). Simulations may be useful when developing classroom management skills in teacher candidates as they often feel unprepared to manage a classroom and behavior, perhaps due to a lack of proficiency in applying classroom management strategies in real-time scenarios (Hudson et al., 2019). Because they provide students with increased opportunities to implement strategies and receive feedback, simulations may be the much-needed answer teacher educators have desired, particularly as school-based practice opportunities are increasingly difficult to arrange (Kaufman & Ireland, 2016). There are three aspects to consider when selecting a simulation for use in teacher preparation work: (a) ability to customize to an individual candidate's learning needs, (b) realistic scenarios or portrayals, and (c) embedded ongoing practice, feedback, and reflection opportunities (Dieker et al., 2014). When using simulations, the course instructor should personalize the experience (e.g., provide specific behavioral challenges) to best support a teacher candidate with their specific areas of need in skill development.

Often, simulations may target a specific scenario, context, or lesson, and these are known as situational simulations (Alessi & Trollip, 2001; Kaufman & Ireland, 2016). These are particularly useful when practicing different applications of classroom management strategies. Kaufman and Ireland identify three broad categories of situational simulations: scenario roleplay, standardized students, and computer-based clinical. In scenario-roleplay simulations, the teacher-candidate may act in a role (e.g., student, teacher, parent) and problem solve a specific dilemma. This type of simulation is particularly useful for not only broadening perspective-taking, but also sharpening candidates' ability to apply and adapt their classroom management skills to a variety of situations. Standardized student simulations are useful for practice and feedback of skills in situations or events that are common in educational settings. Here, a teacher-candidate may respond to a standardized student or parent situation while the teacher educator monitors progress using a fixed list of items. Finally, computer-based clinical simulations are what most educators think of when the term "simulation" is used. Computer-based simulations provide realistic classroom experiences using avatars, virtual reality, or other digital scenarios to engage a learner in an interactive experience. Student responses or behaviors are dependent on teacher candidate actions, reflecting a more realistic teacher-student interaction. The teacher candidate can repeatedly practice the same scenario and change their classroom management response and see how the student responds, enabling teacher candidates to refine their skills in a low-risk environment. While each type of simulation has its strengths, teacher educators should carefully consider their instructional goals as well as resources available before selecting a simulation.

Mursion, formerly *TeachLivE*, enables avatars, scenarios, and students to be customized by teacher educators based on the desired learning experience for the teacher candidate (Hudson et al,. 2019). Mursion provides users with an interactive experience in which the teacher and student avatar actions are based on teacher decisions and the simulation scenario being used. Mursion uses a live "interactor" who controls the avatars and responds to prompts from teachers based on predetermined scripts provided by the instructor.

Hudson and colleagues (2019) looked at teacher candidates' perceptions of Mursion. While positive perceptions decreased over the course of three simulation practice opportunities, it seems students in general education preparation viewed the simulations more favorably than those in the special education training. In a related study, Larson et al. (2020) noted that teacher candidates rated the potential usefulness of TeachLivE higher prior to using its simulations, and such scores dropped after the candidates participated in the simulation. Additionally, the introduction of simulations into the program contributed to increased levels of stress and anxiety prior to use and led the authors to suggest that teacher educators take this into consideration when adopting simulations into programs. It should be noted this finding is based on one team's relatively small-scale study and has not been reported widely by other teams; and should therefore be considered an area for future study.

As discussed in the previous section, self-reflection is a crucial component of teaching as it supports teacher candidates' ability to consider their own decision making in the classroom and evaluate those decisions in terms of student response and need (Nagro et al., 2017). The use of simulations in teacher preparation may be another way to improve teacher candidates' self-reflective ability. In an exploratory study, Arvola et al. (2018) investigated the use of scenario-based SIMPROV in teacher candidates' classroom management self-reflection. In a "choose-your-own adventure" style, teacher candidates interacted with voice-recorded scenarios focused on classroom management. In response to the recorded scenario, candidates worked in pairs to choose a pre-written teacher action. Each decision they made led to the next scenario. Candidates would engage in ongoing reflection of their classroom management decision and associated outcome throughout the simulation activity. Teacher candidates in this study also reported high levels of self-reflection and increases in their classroom management learning.

Where do we go from here? While recent research has certainly laid the groundwork for understanding how to utilize simulations to prepare future teachers, much more exploration is needed. Simulations offer students a step between didactically learning skills in a teacher preparation program and applying them in an actual classroom setting (Hudson et al., 2019). Early research on the ability of simulations to enhance pre-service teachers' reflective ability for classroom management decision-making is promising (see Arvola et al., 2018). However, more work needs to be done in this area to determine whether these self-reflective skills transfer to the classroom. As more technology becomes available, teacher educators and universities should carefully consider the quality and accuracy of commercially available simulations. In addition, the costs of programs like Mursion are a barrier for some to utilize this practice. As the technology continues to mature, and more options enter the marketplace, it can be anticipated that costs will come down, and become more available to a wider swath of potential users.

Video Reflection

Video reflection is an important technology-based method for supporting teacher candidates' knowledge and implementation of effective classroom management practices. Video reflection has also been referred to as video analysis, video-based evaluation, or microteaching, with differences relating to the type of reflective activity involved, including reflecting on others or self-reflecting on one's own teaching practice observed in a video-recorded lesson or lesson segment (Christ et al., 2017; Kleinknecht & Gröschner, 2016; Nagro et al., 2017; Prilop et al., 2021; Wiens et al., 2021). Regardless of name and activity type, however, all video reflection activities share the same general purpose of increasing teachers' ability to observe and identify the strengths and weaknesses of a lesson, in addition to using that information to improve their fidelity with implementing evidence-based practices across various instructional contexts (Gaudin & Chaliès, 2015; Kleinknecht & Gröschner, 2016).

Evidence suggests that video reflection methods result in more detailed and specific reflections when compared to reflecting on an expert teacher's instruction, or a teacher candidate's memory of their own instruction (Nagro et al., 2017). Using videos allows teacher candidates to view and review the exact teaching moves that occur across a variety of classroom situations and contexts, supporting development of their professional vision of classroom management (van Es & Sherin, 2002, 2010; Weber et al., 2018). However, it is not simply repeated opportunities to reflect on video-recorded instruction that supports teacher candidates' professional vision development (deBettencourt & Nagro, 2018). Rather, teacher candidates must understand what is occurring and which occurrences are significant in a given scenario—a concept referred to as *noticing* (van Es & Sherin, 2002, 2010). To develop noticing skills, teacher candidates critically evaluate evidence-based practice implementation by (a) identifying noteworthy situations in video-recordings of classroom instruction, and (b) connecting what they know about the situational context to their theoretical knowledge of underlying instructional principles (van Es & Sherin, 2002, 2010).

Researchers have studied the use of video reflection to improve teacher candidates' knowledge and implementation of evidence-based practices for several decades (see Nagro & Cornelius, 2013). However, recent empirical studies evaluated the use of different combinations of activities involving video reflection with the specific intent of providing teacher candidates with the knowledge and skills needed to effectively manage classrooms (Gold et al., 2021; Kleinknecht & Gröschner, 2016; Nagro et al., 2017; Prilop et al., 2021; Weber et al., 2018, 2021). These methods of video reflection fall into two broad categories—video reflection of others and self, and video reflection plus feedback—and are summarized below.

Video Reflection of Others and Self

In two recent studies, researchers evaluated video self-reflection, video reflection of others' instruction, or some combination of these methods (Gold et al., 2021; Wiens et al., 2021). Gold et al. (2021) conducted a mixed methods study investigating how different perspectives influence development of teacher candidates' professional vision and knowledge of classroom management. Teacher candidates participated in one of three treatment conditions, which involved analyzing: (a) videos of their own and others' teaching ($n = 52$); (b) videos of others' teaching only ($n = 36$); and (c) one's own teaching from memory, without video support ($n = 46$). Teacher candidates who analyzed videos of themselves and others' teaching demonstrated the greatest gains across three time points, followed by those recalling the lesson from memory, and candidates who analyzed others' teaching only. These results suggest that the multiple perspectives afforded by viewing one's own and others' teaching provided the greatest level of support for developing candidates' professional vision of classroom management. Further, while all treatment groups increased their knowledge of classroom management after the first two assessments, candidates who reflected based on memory demonstrated the greatest knowledge increase, followed by candidates who reflected on others' practice, and those who reflected on others plus themselves. Though unsurprising, as all three treatment groups received the same theoretical knowledge base via participation in classroom management coursework, the result suggests that self-reflecting on one's own teaching was most effective for maintaining knowledge of effective classroom management, even if only self-reflecting from memory (Gold et al., 2021).

Wiens et al. (2021) sought to determine if there was a relationship between noticing other teachers' effective classroom interactions and teacher candidates' ($n = 130$) own effective classroom interaction skills. They used the Classroom Assessment Scoring System (CLASS; Hamre et al., 2007) to analyze the quality of interactions (i.e., emotional support, classroom organization, and instructional support) and the Video Assessment of Interactions and Learning (VAIL; Jamil et al., 2015) to measure teacher candidates' skill in identifying effective interactions. The VAIL comprised three selected videos of expert teachers implementing a range of practices that support three classroom management domains—Emotional Support (e.g., relationships, affect, flexibility), Classroom Organization (e.g., clear expectations, student engagement), and Instructional Support (e.g., feedback, scaffolding, discourse). Using hierarchical regression analyses to examine the relationship between skill in identifying and skill in implementing effective classroom interactions, a significant relationship was found in Emotional Support and Instructional Support, revealing a link between teacher candidates' ability to notice effective classroom management enacted by others and implement such in their own classrooms (Wiens et al., 2021).

Video Reflection Plus Feedback

Several studies evaluated the effects of video reflection plus some type of feedback (e.g., peer or expert feedback) on teacher candidates' knowledge and implementation of classroom management practices (Nagro et al., 2017; Prilop et al., 2021; Weber et al., 2018). Nagro et al. (2017) used a quasi-experimental design to determine if expert guidance provided during video self-reflection activities improved teacher candidates' reflective abilities and instructional skills. Participants in both groups video-recorded their instruction during teaching internships on four occasions and wrote corresponding reflections for each video; however, the treatment group received directed guidance and feedback to supplement their video analyses. The authors evaluated teacher candidates' ability to reflect on their use of classroom management practices (e.g., communicating expectations and directions, questioning and prompting students) across four dimensions of reflection: (a) describing past teaching choices, (b) analyzing why teaching choices were made, (c) judging the success of those choices based on student outcomes, and (d) applying conclusions about necessary adjustments to future lesson plans. Results indicated that teacher candidates who participated in the guided video self-reflection condition demonstrated significant increases across time in their perceived professional ability, reflective ability, and instructional skills. Additionally, although all teacher candidates demonstrated increases in their perceived professional ability and instructional skills, reflective ability decreased among teacher candidates who did not receive expert guidance in the self-reflection process. Thus, expert guidance in the process of self-reflection may be a necessary component for fostering this skillset and maximizing the benefits of self-reflection on teacher practice for the long-term.

Weber et al. (2018), used a quasi-experimental pre-post-design to compare the effects of an online video-based self-reflection program incorporating peer feedback (V-Reflect), or expert feedback (V-Reflect+), to a traditional teaching internship supervision approach that did not use videos, on teacher candidates' ($n = 110$) professional vision of classroom management. After receiving instruction in evidence-based classroom management practices through coursework, teacher candidates practiced using learned strategies in professional placements, self-reflected with peer or expert feedback, and were assessed in their noticing of others' classroom management skills. No significant effects were found among teacher candidates who participated in the traditional supervision and feedback experience. However, large effects were found among candidates who participated in the V-Reflect+ group ($n = 25$), with significant gains noted across all areas assessed: professional vision of classroom management, establishing rules and routines, managing momentum, and monitoring. Additionally, though a large significant effect was found among teacher candidates in the V-Reflect group ($n = 16$) for the area of monitoring, no significant effects were identified in the other areas assessed (Weber et al., 2018). Based on these results, the combination of video reflection on others' teaching practice, video self-reflection on personal implementation, and expert feedback throughout both of these reflection activities may be a powerful tool for improving teacher candidates' classroom management expertise.

In Prilop et al. (2021), teacher candidates analyzed videos of other teachers' classroom management practice implementation (i.e., establishing rules and routines, monitoring, and managing momentum) and received expert feedback on their analyses with the intent of refining their professional vision of classroom management through improvements to their video analysis skills. After watching a video recording, candidates in the treatment group ($n = 25$) analyzed expert teachers' use of classroom management practices via a three-step process (i.e., describe observations, evaluate and explain, then describe future adjustments needed), received feedback from course instructors, and then extended their analyses based on feedback. Comparison group participants ($n = 29$) also watched and analyzed videos of other teachers implementing classroom management practices, but they did not receive expert feedback on their analyses. Teacher candidates who received expert feedback on their analyses demonstrated significant changes to their professional vision of classroom management and all facets comprised therein: monitoring, managing momentum, and establishing rules and routines. Comparison group participants, however, demonstrated no significant changes to their professional vision or the three measured components. Results reveal that expert feedback on teacher candidates' analyses of others' classroom management practice implementation supported improvements to noticing and, in turn, their own professional vision of classroom management.

Where Do We Go From Here?

Video reflection of expert teachers' and teacher candidates' own implementation of evidence-based classroom management practices is a powerful method for bridging the gap between theoretical knowledge and application in authentic contexts. Repeated exposure to video reflection opportunities, however, does not suffice for such change to occur (deBettencourt & Nagro, 2018). Connecting knowledge to practice requires that teacher candidates *learn to notice* significant classroom interactions across a variety of contexts and critically evaluate actions noticed to adjust future implementation accordingly (van Es & Sherin, 2002, 2010). The studies summarized in the preceding sections suggest that teacher candidates' knowledge and implementation of classroom management practices improves whether reflecting on videos of others (Wiens et al., 2021), or videos of themselves (Gold et al., 2021). Yet, more significant changes occurred when experts provided teacher candidates with guidance on how to reflect and offered feedback on ways to improve their reflections (Nagro et al., 2017; Prilop et al., 2021; Weber et al., 2018). In fact, as one study revealed (i.e., Nagro et al., 2017), candidates' reflective ability actually decreased when expert guidance was not provided.

To maximize benefits of video reflection though, it appears that teacher candidates' participation in a combination of activities (i.e., reflecting on others' teaching and self-reflecting on their own teaching thereafter) with provision of expert feedback throughout both experiences is necessary. Thus, teacher educators should consider a three-step process when using video reflection as a method for training teacher candidates in evidence-based classroom management: (a) support candidates' development of noticing skills through video reflections of others' classroom management practice implementation; (b) use video reflections of others as an opportunity to refine candidates' reflection skills by guiding them on how to reflect and ways to improve their reflections; and (c) continue providing guidance and feedback while candidates self-reflect on their own classroom management practice implementation to ensure reflective abilities are maintained. Additional research to support this multifaceted practice within teacher preparation should be completed and disseminated.

Conclusion and Future Directions

With many teacher candidates entering the profession feeling unprepared to manage the classroom and challenging behavior (Hudson et al., 2019), it is imperative that teacher preparation programs focus on developing these skills in their students. Given the rate of teacher burnout associated with addressing challenging classroom behaviors among new teachers (Aloe et al., 2014), it is crucial that teachers learn skills related to effective classroom management. Incorporating technology into teacher preparation programs is one promising method for helping to teach, refine, and master such skills. With increasing numbers of teacher candidates enrolling in virtual learning, technology offers students varied means of remotely accessing quality content that can improve their knowledge and skills. Additionally, technology provides teacher candidates realistic practice opportunities (e.g. through simulations) before being ready to enter a classroom. In sum, technology in teacher preparation provides teacher candidates and faculty with access to high-quality and effective instructional methods that can have a lasting impact on pedagogical practices for years to come.

The three educational technologies reviewed in this chapter (i.e., CAPs, simulations, reflections) offer clear benefits to candidates within preparation programs. However, teacher preparation programs should consider using these technologies together to provide a well-rounded program of learning, practice, and reflection. In this concluding section, we lay out a vision for how a teacher preparation program could consider combining these evidence-based practices into a coherent roadmap for preparing candidates for the challenges they are sure to face once assuming control of their own classroom.

Using the Research to Build a Stronger Foundation in Classroom Management Practices

In our vision of a multimedia-informed approach to developing candidates' classroom management skills across a teacher preparation program, CAPs play an early and repeated role. Given their demonstrated efficacy for building candidates' declarative knowledge, faculty and other instructors can count on this tool to help supplement readings, lectures, and other early interactions with evidence-based practices and related content for classroom management. Instructors of introductory courses in special education, classroom management, and general methods could find CAPs that suit their instructional objectives and assign them to supplement other learning activities. A library of CAPs (and other content) is available free on www.spedintro.com, and www.pbisvideos.com. Instructors can also create their own CAPs.

As noted, CAPs are capable of bolstering declarative knowledge, but there is less evidence to support their use for implementing new practices among teacher candidates. Therefore, we recommend pairing CAPs with the opportunity to implement practice within simulated teaching activities. The instructor can utilize whatever simulation mode is most readily available (e.g., Mursion, microteaching, role play), document candidate use of practice, and deliver feedback. The feedback can be accompanied by a recommendation to re-watch key CAPs, or segments of CAPs to be reminded of what the practice entails and see a model of its use. This type of on-demand professional development is likely to provide candidates with a flexible learning option and be an ongoing support that does not require time or energy from the instructor.

Finally, the instructor using CAPs and simulations should also have students use video recordings of teaching sessions to reflect on their practice. Again, the instructor can assign CAPs as an on-demand remedy to help support limited implementation of practice(s), and also call upon a round of simulated teaching to solve documented problem areas. For a teacher in training who may be facing a crisis situation in terms of poor implementation in a school during a practicum, returning to the safe space of simulated teaching, paired with on-demand PD resources such as CAPs may offer comfort, and the right combination of structured practice. Figure 18.2 provides a graphical look at this proposed model.

Contrast with Previous Reviews

As the availability of education technology increases and research on the effectiveness of these technologies continues to become available, teacher educators should carefully consider which technology would best promote classroom management skill development. Existing research points to increased knowledge gains and self-reflective ability following use of educational technology for the development of classroom management skills. However, future work should continue to examine the effectiveness of these technologies and whether they have lasting effects as teacher candidates move into the classroom. Other research teams have published systematic reviews beyond the scope of this chapter, but still hold relevance for our overall search for effective practices in the multimedia space for teacher candidates to learn classroom management practices.

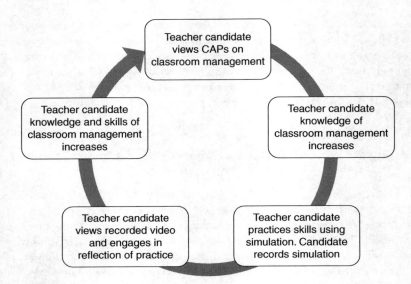

Figure 18.2 Technology Cycle: Learn, Practice, Reflect

For example, in a systematic review, Hirsch et al. (2021) identified seven studies that used an experimental design to support teachers' knowledge and use of classroom management practices. Of the seven, six used technology applications. These studies used CAPs (Hirsch et al., 2019), video reflection (Rathel et al., 2014), and hand-held counters for self-management (Briere et al., 2015). Faculty and instructors within teacher preparation programs using our above model (see Figure 18.1) could create CAPs on how to use handheld counters, and then have students practice within a simulated lesson. Reflection following the simulation could give the instructor and candidate strong feedback on their performance, and reinforce their use of high-quality practice.

Cho et al. (2020) found 22 qualitative and quantitative sources using technology to support teachers' knowledge and use of skills in the domain of classroom management. The largest number of studies (n = 7) used video in some capacity to deliver instruction to the teachers. Cho and team also documented several studies (n = 5) that used simulations. The authors concluded that multimedia has a key role in the preparation of teachers for understanding and implementing classroom management skills.

Summary and Next Steps

Multimedia is everywhere in our world—teacher preparation coursework and practicum experiences are no exception. The documented use of multimedia is relatively limited, at least using published empirical literature as a guide. We recommend that researchers bring fresh thinking to this line of inquiry, as far more high-quality research is needed. Simply using technology to deliver static content to teacher candidates is important, but much more is possible. As an example, many possible research questions regarding how teacher candidates can apply their learning, and then measure the corresponding impact on student performance, should be pursued.

Next steps for faculty members engaged in preparation of teachers to implement evidence-based classroom management practices include documenting use and effectiveness of the practices noted within this chapter, and others yet to be designed. Different combinations of multimedia practices being deployed to help teach properties and implementation of various evidence-based practices should be carefully studied. It is possible, perhaps likely, that some evidence-based practices (e.g., using handheld counters) may work well when taught using CAPs, but other practices (e.g., using behavior-specific feedback) are better deployed following CAPs plus simulation practice. There are infinite combinations of practices and multimedia delivery mechanisms, but this is a logical starting place for developing a more robust evidence base in this field.

References

Aloe, A. M., Shisler, S. M., Norris, B. D., Nickerson, A. B., & Rinker, T. W. (2014). A multivariate meta-analysis of student misbehavior and teacher burnout. *Educational Research Review, 12*, 30–44. https://doi.org/10.1016/j.edurev.2014.05.003

Alessi, S. M., & Trollip, S. R. (2001). *Multimedia for learning: Methods and development.* Allyn & Bacon.

Arvola, M., Samuelsson, M., Nordvall, M., & Ragnemalms, E. L. (2018). Simulated provocations: A hypermedia radio theatre for reflection on classroom management. *Simulation & Gaming, 49*(2), 98–114. https://doi.org/10.1177/1046878118765594

Briere, D. E., Simonsen, B., Sugai, G., & Myers, D. (2015). Increasing new teachers' specific praise using a within-school consultation intervention. Journal of Positive Behavior Interventions, *17*(1), 50–60. https://doi.org/10.1177/1098300713497098

Carlisle, L. M., VanUitert, V. J., McDonald, S. M., Kunemund, R., & Kennedy, M. J. (2021). Using multimedia to create explicit and culturally responsive content area vocabulary lessons. *TEACHING Exceptional Children,* 00400599211038322. https://doi.org/10.1177/00400599211038322

Cho, V., Masfield, K. C., & Claughton, J. (2020). The past and future technology in classroom management and school discipline: A systematic review. Teaching and Teacher Education, *90*, 1–11 https://doi.org/10.1016/j.tate.2020.103037

Christ, T., Arya, P., & Chiu, M. M. (2017). Video use in teacher education: An international survey of practices. *Teaching and Teacher Education, 63*, 22–35. https://dx.doi.org/10.1016/j.tate.2016.12.005

Cruickshank, D. R. (1969). The use of simulation in teacher education: A developing phenomenon. *Journal of Teacher Education, 20*(1), 23–26. https://doi/pdf/10.1177/002248716902000105

Dawson, M. R., & Lignugaris/Kraft, B. (2017). Meaningful practice: Generalizing foundation teaching skills from TLE TeachLivE™ to the classroom. *Teacher Education and Special Education, 40*(1), 26–50. https://doi.org/10.1177/0888406416664184

deBettencourt, L. U., & Nagro, S. A. (2018). Tracking special education teacher candidates' reflective practices over time to understand the role of theory in clinically-based teacher preparation. *Remedial and Special Education, 40*(5), 277–288. https://doi.org/10.1177/0741932518762573

DeLeeuw, K. E., & Mayer, R. E. (2008). A comparison of three measures of cognitive load: Evidence for separable measures of intrinsic, extraneous, and germane load. *Journal of Educational Psychology, 100*(1), 223–234. https://doi.org/10.1037/0022-0663.100.1.223

Dieker, L. A., Rodriguez, J. A., Lignugaris/Kraft, B., Hynes, M. C., & Hughes, C. E. (2014). The potential of simulated environments in teacher education: Current and future possibilities. Teacher Education and Special Education, *37*(1), 21–33. https://doi.org/10.1177%2F0888406413512683

Feldon, D. F. (2007). Cognitive load and classroom teaching: The double-edged sword of automaticity. *Educational Psychologist, 42*, 123–137. https://doi.org/10.1080/00461520701416173

Ferry, B., Kervin, L., Cambourne, B., Turbill, J., Puglisi, S., Jonassen, D., & Hedberg, J. (2004, March). Online classroom simulation: The next wave for pre-service teacher education. In *Beyond the comfort zone: Proceedings of the 21st ASCILITE Conference* (pp. 294–302). Australian Society for Computers in Learning in Tertiary Education.

Firestone, A., & Rodl, J. (2020). Integrating with purpose: Leveraging content acquisition podcasts to enhance preservice teachers' knowledge of positive behavior interventions and supports with three different instructional conditions. *Journal of Technology and Teacher Education, 28*(1), 5–32. www.learntechlib.org/p/210406/

Gaudin, C., & Chaliès, S. (2015). Video viewing in teacher education and professional development: A literature review. *Educational Research Review, 16*, 41–67. https://dx.doi.org/10.1016/j.edurev.2015.06.001

Gold, B., Pfirrmann, C., & Holodynski, M. (2021). Promoting professional vision of classroom management through different analytic perspectives in video-based learning environments. *Journal of Teacher Education, 72*(4), 431–447. https://doi.org/10.1177/0022487120963681

Hamre, B. K., Pianta, R. C., Mashburn, A. J., & Downer, J. T. (2007). *Building a science of classrooms: Application of the CLASS framework in over 4,000 U.S. early childhood and elementary classrooms.* www.fcd-us.org/assets/2016/04/BuildingAScienceOfClassroomsPiantaHamre.pdf

Hirsch, S. E., Randall, K., Bradshaw, C., & Lloyd, J. W. (2021). Professional learning and development in classroom management for novice teachers: A systematic review. *Education and Treatment of Children.* https://doi.org/10.1007/s43494-021-00042-6

Hirsch, S. E., Lloyd, J. W., & Kennedy, M. J. (2019). Professional development in practice: Improving novice teachers' use of universal classroom management. *The Elementary School Journal, 120*(1), 61–87. https://doi.org/10.1086/704492

Hirsch, S. E., Randall, K. N., Common, E. A., & Lane, K. L. (2020). Results of practice-based professional development for supporting special educators in learning how to design functional assessment–based interventions. *Teacher Education and Special Education, 43*(4), 281–295. https://doi.org/10.1177/0888406419876926

Hirsch, S. E., Kennedy, M. J., Haines, S. J., Thomas, C. N., & Alves, K. D. (2015). Improving preservice teachers' knowledge and application of functional behavioral assessments using multimedia. *Behavioral Disorders, 41*(1), 38–50. https://doi.org/10.17988/0198-7429-41.1.38

Hudson, M. E., Voytecki, K. S., Owens, T. L., & Zhang, G. (2019). Preservice teacher experiences implementing classroom management practices through mixed-reality simulations. *Rural Special Education Quarterly, 38*(2), 79–94. https://doi.org/10.1177/8756870519841421

Hughes, C. E., Nagendran, A., Dieker, L. A., Hynes, M. C., & Welch, G. F. (2015). Applications of avatar mediated interaction to teaching, training, job skills and wellness. In *Virtual Realities* (pp. 133–146). Springer. https://doi.org/10.1007/978-3-319-17043-5_8

Ingersoll, R., & Merrill, L. (2010). Who's teaching our children? *Educational Leadership, 67*(8), 14–20. www.ascd.org/el/articles/whos-teaching-our-children

Jamil, F. M., Sabol, T. J., Hamre, B. K., & Pianta, R. C. (2015). Assessing teachers' skills in detecting and identifying effective interactions in the classroom: Theory and measurement. *The Elementary School Journal, 115*(3), 407–432. https://doi.org/10.1086/680353

Kaufman, D., & Ireland, A. (2016). Enhancing teacher education with simulations. *TechTrends, 60*(3), 260–267. https://doi.org/10.1007/s11528-016-0049-0

Kennedy, M. J., Hart, J. E., & Kellems, R. O. (2011). Using enhanced podcasts to augment limited instructional time in teacher preparation. *Teacher Education and Special Education, 34*(2), 87–105. https://doi.org/10.1177/0888406410376203

Kennedy, M. J., Rodgers, W. J., Romig, J. E., Lloyd, J. W., & Brownell, M. T. (2017). The effect of a multimedia professional development package on middle school science teachers' instructional practices. Journal of Teacher Education, 68(2), 213–230. https://doi.org/10.1177%2F0022487116687554

Kennedy, M. J., & Romig, J. E. (2021). *Cognitive load theory: An applied reintroduction for special and general educators.* TEACHING Exceptional Children. https://doi.org/10.1177%2F00400599211048214

Kennedy, M. J., & Thomas, C. N. (2012). Effects of content acquisition podcasts to develop preservice teachers' knowledge of positive behavioral interventions and supports. Exceptionality, 20, 1–19. https://doi.org/10.1080/09362835.2011.611088

Kleinknecht, M., & Gröschner, A. (2016). Fostering preservice teachers' noticing with structured video feedback: Results of an online- and video-based intervention study. *Teaching and Teacher Education, 59*, 45–56. https://dx.doi.org/10.1016/j.tate.2016.05.020

Larson, K. E., Hirsch, S. E., McGraw, J. P., & Bradshaw, C. P. (2020). Preparing preservice teachers to manage behavior problems in the classroom: The feasibility and acceptability of using a mixed-reality simulator. *Journal of Special Education Technology, 35*(2), 63–75. https://doi.org/10.1177/0162643419836415

Mayer, R. E. (2008). Applying the science of learning: Evidence-based principles for the design of multimedia instruction. *American Psychologist, 63*, 760–769. https://doi.org/10.1037/0003-066X.59.1.14

Mayer, R. E. (2020). *Multimedia Learning* (3rd edition). Cambridge University. https://doi.org/10.1017/978131 6941355

Moore, T. C., Wehby, J. H., Oliver, R. M., Chow, J. C., Gordon, J. R., & Mahany, L. A. (2017) Teachers' reported knowledge and implementation of research-based classroom and behavior management strategies. *Remedial and Special Education, 38*, 222–232. https://doi.org/10.1177/0741932516683631

Myers, D., Freeman, J., Simonsen, B., & Sugai, G. (2017). Classroom management with exceptional learners. *Teaching Exceptional Children, 49*(4), 223–230. https://doi.org/10.1177/0040059916685064

Nagro, S. A. (2020). Reflecting on others before reflecting on self: Using video evidence to guide teacher candidates' reflective practices. Journal of Teacher Education, 71(4), 420–433. https://doi.org/10.1177/00224 87119872700

Nagro, S. A., & Cornelius, K. E. (2013). Evaluating the evidence base of video analysis: A special education teacher development tool. *Teacher Education and Special Education, 36*(4), 312–329. https://doi.org/10.1177/08884 06413501090

Nagro, S. A., DeBettencourt, L. U., Rosenberg, M. S., Carran, D. T., & Weiss, M. P. (2017). The effects of guided video analysis on teacher candidates' reflective ability and instructional skills. *Teacher Education and Special Education, 40*(1), 7–25. https://doi.org/10.1177/0888406416680469

Nelson, J. R., Oliver, R. M., Hebert, M. A., & Bohaty, J. (2015). Use of self-monitoring to maintain program fidelity of multi-tiered systems of support. *Remedial and Special Education, 36,* 14–19. https://doi.org/10.1177/0741932514544970

Prilop, C. N., Weber, K. E., & Kleinknecht, M. (2021). The role of expert feedback in the development of preservice teachers' professional vision of classroom management in an online blended learning environment. *Teaching and Teacher Education, 99.* https://dx.doi.org/10.1016/j.tate.2020.103276

Polirstok, S., & Gottlieb, J. (2006). The impact of positive behavior intervention training for teachers on referral rates for misbehavior, special education evaluation, and student reading achievement in the elementary grades. *International Journal of Behavioral and Consultation Therapy, 2,* 354–361. https://doi.org/10.1037/h0100789

Rathel, J. M., Drasgow, E., Brown, W. H., & Marshall, K. J. (2014). Increasing induction-level teachers' positive-to-negative communication ratio and use of behavior-specific praise through e-mailed performance feedback and its effect on students' task engagement. *Journal of Positive Behavior Interventions, 16*(4), 219–233. https://doi.org/10.1177/1098300713492856

Reinke, W. M., Herman, K. C., & Stormont, M. (2013). Classroom-level positive behavior supports in schools implementing SW-PBIS: Identifying areas for enhancement. *Journal of Positive Behavior Interventions, 15*(1), 39–50. https://doi.org/10.1177/1098300712459079

Shernoff, E. S., Frazier, S. L., Lisetti, C., Delmarre, A., Bibi, Z., & Gabbard, J. (2021). Supporting the Implementation of Evidence-Based Behavior Management Practices through Simulation: A Mixed Method Study. *Journal of Educational and Psychological Consultation,* 1–35. https://doi.org/10.1080/10474412.2021.1875840

Stough, L. M., & Montague, M. L. (2015). How teachers learn to be classroom managers. In E. T. Emmer & E. J. Sabornie (Eds.), *Handbook of classroom management: Research, practice, and contemporary issues* (2nd ed.). Routledge.

Sweller, J. (2020). Cognitive load theory and educational technology. *Educational Technology Research and Development, 68*(1), 1–16. https://doi.org/10.1007/s11423-019-09701-3

Theelen, H., Van den Beemt, A., & den Brok, P. (2019). Classroom simulations in teacher education to support preservice teachers' interpersonal competence: A systematic literature review. *Computers & Education, 129,* 14–26. https://doi.org/10.1016/j.compedu.2018.10.015

van Es, E. A., & Sherin, M. (2002). Learning to notice: Scaffolding new teachers' interpretations of classroom interactions. *Journal of Technology and Teacher Education, 10,* 571–596.

van Es, E. A., & Sherin, M. (2010). The influence of video clubs on teachers' thinking and practice. *Journal of Math Teacher Education, 13,* 155–176. https://doi.org/10.1007/s10857-009-9130-3

Weber, K. E., Gold, B., Prilop, C. N., & Kleinknecht, M. (2018). Promoting preservice teachers' professional vision of classroom management during practical school training: Effects of a structured online- and video-based self-reflection and feedback intervention. *Teaching and Teacher Education, 76,* 39–49. https://dx.doi.org/10.1016/j.tate..2018.08.008

Wiens, P. D., LoCasale-Crouch, J., Cash, A. H., & Escudero, F. R. (2021). Preservice teachers' skills to identify effective teaching interactions: Does it relate to their ability to implement them? *Journal of Teacher Education, 72*(2), 180–194. https://doi.org/10.1177/0022487120910692

Yoon, K. S., Duncan, T., Lee, S. W.-Y., Scarloss, B., & Shapley, K. (2007). *Reviewing the evidence on how teacher professional development affects student achievement* (Issues & Answers Report, REL 2007–No. 033). U.S. Department of Education, Institute of Education Sciences, National Center for Education Evaluation and Regional Assistance, Regional Educational Laboratory Southwest. Retrieved from http://ies.ed.gov/ncee/edlabs

19

INTERNATIONAL RESEARCH ON THE FOCI AND EFFECTIVENESS OF CLASSROOM MANAGEMENT PROGRAMS AND STRATEGIES

Hanke Korpershoek, Jolien M. Mouw, and Hester De Boer

UNIVERSITY OF GRONINGEN

Introduction

Effective classroom management is generally aimed at establishing a positive classroom environment encompassing effective teacher-student relationships (Wubbels et al., 1999) enabling effective teaching and learning. Effective classroom management is conditional for student learning. Evertson and Weinstein (2006) defined classroom management as "the actions teachers take to create an environment that supports and facilitates both academic and social-emotional learning" (pp. 4–5). Evertson and Weinstein distinguish five types of teacher actions: (a) develop caring, supportive relationships with and among students; (b) organize and implement instruction in ways that optimize students' access to learning; (c) encourage students' engagement in academic tasks; (d) promote the development of students' social skills and self-regulation; and (e) use appropriate interventions to assist students with behavior problems. Both preventive and reactive classroom management strategies are needed to optimize learning opportunities in the classroom, although preventive strategies are generally considered more effective than reactive strategies.

The meta-analysis "A meta-analysis of the effects of classroom management strategies and classroom management programs on students' academic, behavioral, emotional, and motivational outcomes" of Korpershoek et al. (2016) was based on Evertson and Weinstein's broad definition of classroom management, and summarized the effects of various classroom management interventions on student outcomes. The meta-analysis included 54 (non-)random controlled intervention studies published between 2003 and 2013. It confirmed the effectiveness of classroom management interventions on student outcomes in primary education. Across all interventions, the overall effect was $g = 0.22$ ($SE = 0.02$, $p < .01$), which is a small effect size. The overall effect was 0.17 after taking publication bias into account. There were no significant differences between various outcome categories (academic, behavioral, social-emotional, and motivational outcomes). Moderator analyses revealed that interventions focused on the social-emotional development of the students were somewhat

DOI: 10.4324/9781003275312-22

more effective than interventions without this component, in particular regarding social–emotional outcomes. All included programs (School-Wide Positive Behavior Support [SWPBS], Promoting Alternative Thinking Strategies, Good Behavior Game, Second Step, Zippy's Friends, and other programs) were equally effective, except for SWPBS, which was not found to have an effect on overall student outcomes (see Korpershoek et al., 2016, pp. 668–669).

Building on the earlier meta-analysis, this chapter presents an up-to-date overview of recent classroom management studies, incorporating studies evaluating the effectiveness of classroom management programs (CMP) and of multimodal social–emotional learning (SEL) programs in which (in our view) relevant classroom management elements were included. Since 2014, new CMPs may have been developed and tested. Moreover, an important question is whether the positive effects that were reported for most programs are replicated in more recent studies. Therefore, our first research question is: Do recent whole-classroom intervention studies on classroom management support previous reported significant overall effects on students' academic, behavioral, social–emotional, and/or motivational outcomes in primary education?

Furthermore, we aim to identify possible changes in foci of the interventions since the prior meta-analysis. In Korpershoek et al. (2016, p. 646), the interventions were coded for the presence or absence of four categories of classroom management strategies. These categories are not considered to be mutually exclusive, as most interventions fit into more than one category; however, such a classification helps to identify differential effects for different types of interventions, as one category or combination of categories might be more effective than others. The four categories are based on the five teacher actions for high–quality classroom management distinguished by Evertson and Weinstein (2006), but in line with the majority of the current interventions, a clearer distinction between teacher-focused and student-focused actions was made (see also Wubbels, 2011). For example, we distinguished between "developing caring, supportive relationships *with* students" and "developing caring, supportive relationships *among* students." The rationale behind this is that in the category 2 interventions (see below), usually a combination of teacher- and student-centered approaches are used to improve teacher–student relationships, whereas in the category 4 interventions (see below), the approaches are generally student-centered only (i.e. with no particular focus on improving teacher behavior). See also Wubbels' (2011) six approaches to classroom management, with a similar distinction between teacher-focused and student-focused approaches. The categories introduced by Korpershoek et al. (2016) are:

(1) Teachers' behavior-focused interventions. The focus of these interventions is on improving teachers' classroom management (e.g., keeping order, introducing rules and procedures, disciplinary interventions) and thus on changing teachers' behaviors, in line with Evertson and Weinstein's (2006) teacher actions "organize and implement instruction in ways that optimize students' access to learning" and "encourage students' engagement in academic tasks." Both preventive and reactive interventions are included in this category.

(2) Teacher–student relationship-focused interventions. The focus of these interventions is on improving the interaction between teachers and students and, thus on developing caring, supportive relationships, in line with teacher action "develop caring, supportive relationships *with* students." Only preventive interventions are included in this category.

(3) Students' behavior-focused interventions. The focus of these interventions is on improving student behavior, for example, via group contingencies or improving self-control among all students, in line with the teacher action "use appropriate interventions to assist students with behavior problems." Both preventive and reactive interventions are included in this category.

(4) Students' social–emotional development-focused interventions. The focus of these interventions is on improving students' social–emotional development, such as enhancing

empathic and prosocial skills, and improving peer relations, thus in line with the teacher actions "develop caring, supportive relationships *among* students" and "promote the development of students' social skills and self-regulation." Both preventive and reactive interventions are included in this category.

One of the surprising findings in the original meta-analysis was that, although many (practically all) included papers stressed the importance of establishing positive teacher-student relationships, only very few interventions actually included activities stimulating or improving these relationships directly. Wubbels (2011) also noted the relational approach as an effective classroom management practice. Furthermore, Korpershoek et al. (2016) observed a trend towards more student-centered approaches rather than teacher-centered approaches. Hence, our second research question is: What are the foci of the current intervention studies on classroom management? In line with the prior meta-analysis, intervention studies conducted in various countries are included in this chapter, as to identify similarities and dissimilarities in foci of the intervention studies across the globe. In some countries, for example, the interventions may concentrate on different classroom management strategies (e.g., more teachers' behavior-focused or more students' behavior-focused) than in other countries.

All in all, this chapter presents a scoping review that synthesizes the literature published from 2014 onwards, largely replicating the search strategy (search terms and inclusion criteria) of the Korpershoek et al. (2016) meta-analysis. This review provides new insights into the current state and development of international research on the effectiveness of classroom management strategies and programs.

Method

Literature searches were conducted in the online databases ERIC, Web of Science, and PsycINFO (from January 1, 2014 until June 1, 2021) using a broad range of search terms. Eligibility criteria were as follows. First, the focus of the study should be on teachers' classroom management strategies or relevant programs implemented by teachers in regular, primary-school classrooms. Second, the interventions needed to focus on (basically) all students in the classroom: in other words, interventions aimed at changing individuals' or small groups' behaviors were not eligible. Third, the outcome variable had to include measures of academic outcomes (e.g., achievement tests), behavioral outcomes (e.g., on-task/off-task behavior, disruptive behavior, self-control), social-emotional outcomes (social skills, social competence, emotion recognition, coping, and empathy), motivational outcomes (e.g., engagement, motivation, sense of belonging), or other relevant student outcomes (e.g., time-on-task, self-efficacy, peer acceptance). Fourth, the studies had to be (quasi-)experimental designs with control groups (no treatment or treatment as usual), which we operationalized as (a) participants were randomly assigned to treatment and control or comparison conditions, (b) or were matched into treatment and control conditions and the matching variables included a pretest for the outcome variable, or pretest differences were statistically controlled for using analyses of covariance, (c) if subjects were not randomly assigned or matched, the study needed to have a pre-post-test design providing sufficient statistical information to derive an effect size or to estimate group equivalence from statistical significance tests.

We concentrated on interventions in which at least one of the categories of classroom management strategies (Korpershoek et al., 2016) was present (i.e., teachers' behavior-focused, students' behavior-focused, teacher-student relationship-focused, students' social-emotional development-focused). There is one exception, that is that interventions that *only* focused on students' social-emotional development, were only considered when also one or more of the other foci (e.g., students' behavior-focused) were present. These SEL programs are thus included not because they are CMPs, but because they included elements that we considered relevant classroom management strategies to improve student outcomes. Several recent meta-analyses consistently report on positive effects of SEL programs on students' social-emotional outcomes (e.g., Taylor et al., 2017), although these approaches are not without critique. For a discussion on the assumption that social and emotional attributes are malleable by means of educational interventions and relevant analyses, see Scheerens et al. (2020).

School-wide anti-bullying interventions and programs that aimed to improve students' social skills were excluded, as these are generally not seen as CMPs. Moreover, social skills training is usually concentrated on enhancing mental resilience rather than general social-emotional development such as showing prosocial behavior and empathy in class. If training social skills was part of an overarching program that did meet our inclusion criteria, the studies were not excluded. School-wide programs with a primary focus on improving academic skills such as reading or mathematics were also excluded, although these programs sometimes include classroom management training and as part of their universal approach (e.g., see Veldman et al., 2020, studying the effects of Success for All on Dutch students' prosocial behavior).

In total, 1481 papers (ERIC 267, PsychINFO 477, Web of Science 737) were found. After deleting duplicates and initial screening of the titles and abstracts to eliminate off-topic papers, 71 papers were selected for further inspection by two researchers. A third researcher was consulted when necessary. Twenty papers met all inclusion criteria. The main reasons for excluding the other papers were: they (a) did not report on a relevant intervention or were not conducted in regular primary education (criterion 1) but, for example, special education or preschool; (b) did not meet the research design criteria (criterion 4), for example, because they used ABA designs, multiple baseline designs, or designs without control group, had no equal groups for comparison, because they reported on a single case (one teacher), or because it were ethnographic studies; (c) focused on teachers' or school leaders' outcomes (thus not on students) or focused on individual students with specific behavioral characteristics (criterion 2); (d) did not include student data or reported student outcomes that we thought irrelevant for this review (e.g., bullying, suicide prevention, executive functioning; criterion 3); (e) reported on the same intervention study as already included papers, without additional relevant student data for this review, or (f) the full paper was not available. Last, the reference lists of the selected studies and websites of the selected programs were consulted to find additional studies that met the inclusion criteria, which resulted in three additional studies, bringing the total to 23 included papers.

We start the results with an overview table of the studies that met all inclusion criteria. Subsequently, for each program, a program description is provided and a classification following the four classroom management strategies specified by Korpershoek et al. (2016). Each program was assessed and classified by at least two researchers following the program descriptions, and discussed until mutual agreement was reached. In some cases, additional information was identified via program websites and other publications, that is, when the included studies lacked sufficient details on the content of the program itself. The classification followed from the program content, not from the goals of the program, as the presented goals in some cases were much broader than the actual actions and activities included in the program. For example, the importance of improving teacher-student relationships is highlighted in most studies, but not all of them actually included intervention components that explicitly addressed this aspect.

Each intervention study that implemented the program is summarized, reporting the research design, samples, research methods, and main findings. In these summaries, the main findings at student level are reported, leaving out data regarding effectiveness at the teacher level. This decision follows from the perspective that improved classroom management should be beneficial for students and thus should result in improved student outcomes (e.g., improved classroom behavior, social-emotional development, motivation, or academic outcomes). For conciseness and our search for CMPs that benefit (basically) all students in the classroom, we only report findings for the overall student sample. For more information about the differential effects for specific student groups (e.g., regarding gender, ethnic background, socioeconomic status, or students with behavioral problems) we refer to the primary studies. For consistency, intervention effects are reported when statistically significant at $p < .05$ (i.e., some studies reported on marginally significant effects at $p < .1$). When effect sizes are reported in the primary studies, they are reported here as well. The summaries are followed by a concluding remark about the effectiveness of the program, based on the presented studies.

Results

Overview of the Included Papers

The 23 included papers (see Table 19.1) together report on 18 intervention studies on nine different CMPs or programs that include classroom management strategies in their SEL intervention. The studies by Aasheim et al. (2018, 2019, 2020), are counted as one intervention study, because the reported results are based on the same sample. The only difference between these studies is the outcome variables reported. The same applies to the studies by Low et al. (2015, 2019) and Cook et al. (2018), and to the studies of Cappella et al. (2015) and McCormick et al. (2015). The study of Ialongo et al. (2019) counts as two intervention studies, as the paper includes two experimental conditions (with the same control group). None of the included intervention studies focused on SWPBS (reported on in the previous meta-analysis), although some studies mentioned that PBS interventions had previously been implemented at the participating schools. Bradshaw et al. (2015) did conduct a randomized controlled trial on the effects of SWPBS on student outcomes, but used a person-oriented approach (LPA) to analyze the data. We also did not find any new experimental studies on Zippy's Friends, the Color Wheel System, or the Consistency Management & Cooperative Discipline program, that is, at least not reported in studies that met our inclusion criteria. Although most studies

Table 19.1 Overview of Included Papers

Program	Intervention studies	Country	Grade level
Incredible Years Teacher Classroom Management	Aasheim et al. (2018), Aasheim et al. (2019), and Aasheim et al. (2020)	Norway	Grades 1–3
	Hickey et al. (2017)	Ireland	Kindergarten
	Ford et al. (2019)	UK	Kindergarten–grade 3
	Reinke et al. (2018)	USA	Kindergarten–grade 3
	Murray et al. (2018)	USA	Kindergarten–grade 2
Teacher–Child Interaction Training	Fernandez et al. (2015)	USA	Kindergarten–grade 1
Adler–Dreikurs Classroom Management Techniques	Soheili et al. (2015)	Iran	Grades 1–5
Irie Classroom Toolbox	Baker-Henningham et al. (2019)	Jamaica	Grade 1
Promoting Alternative Thinking Strategies	Humphrey et al. (2016)	UK	Grades 2–4
	Berry et al. (2016)	UK	Kindergarten
	Schonfeld et al. (2015)	USA	Grades 3–6
	Fishbein et al. (2016)	USA	Kindergarten
PAX Good Behavior Game	Weis et al. (2015)	USA	Grades 1–3
	Ialongo et al. (2019)	USA	Kindergarten–grade 5
Second Step + Proactive Classroom Management training	Low et al. (2015), Cook et al. (2018), and Low et al. (2019)	USA	Kindergarten–grade 2
Insights	Cappella et al. (2015) and McCormick et al. (2015)	USA	Kindergarten–grade 1
Class–Wide Function–Related Intervention Teams	Kamps et al. (2015)	USA	Kindergarten–grade 5
	Wills et al. (2018)	USA	Kindergarten–grade 6

were conducted in the USA, we found a variety of studies conducted in Europe (Norway, Ireland, UK) and two studies in other regions (Jamaica, Iran).

Incredible Years Teacher Classroom Management

Program Description

The Incredible Years Teacher Classroom Management (IY-TCM) program is a universal CMP that covers a comprehensive series of interventions designed to promote teachers' use of effective classroom management practices and to prevent and reduce disruptive and aggressive behavior and conduct problems in young children (Webster-Stratton, 1994, 2012). The interventions include teacher training components as well as child and parent training components. Teachers receive various workshops, covering topics such as building positive relationships with students and parents (e.g., how to build trust, fostering students' sense of responsibility for the classroom and their peers, sharing positive feelings), proactive classroom management strategies (e.g., encouragement and praise), effective use of incentives to motivate students, applying effective disciplinary strategies (e.g., ignoring and redirecting, and inappropriate behavior followed through with consequences), and social and emotional coaching of students (e.g., emotion regulation, social skills, and problem solving). The design of the program is based on the premise that establishing positive relationships with students and parents has to precede other teaching strategies and that teachers' attention should be directed more frequently to positive rather than negative student behavior (Webster-Stratton, 2012). In-service coaching by trained facilitators, assisting the teachers in translating the learned skills to their own classroom context, is generally included (Webster-Stratton et al., 2011). For more information see www.incredibleyears.com.

Classification

We classified the IY-TCM program in all four categories, that is, "teachers' behavior focused," "teacher–student relationship focused," "students' behavior focused," and "students' social–emotional development focused," as this is the most comprehensive program explicitly focusing on both teachers and students, and offering a broad range of classroom management strategies.

Effect Studies

The studies of Aasheim et al. (2018, 2019, 2020) evaluated the effects of the IY-TCM program in Norway in a large-scale quasi-experimental pre–post design. The intervention study was conducted in grades 1 to 3 and included 302 teachers from 44 schools. The overall student sample included 1,396 students (random samples of 7 students per classroom). Participating students were on average 7.3 years old and 5.5% were non-Norwegian.

Aasheim et al. (2018) used the Student–Teacher Relationship Scale, short form (Pianta, 1996), with subscales closeness and conflict to measure teachers' perceptions of their relationship with individual students. Significant main positive effects were found for student–teacher relationships, on the subscale closeness ($p = .03$; $d_w = 0.22$) as well as on the subscale conflict ($p = .02$; $d_w = 0.15$).

Aasheim et al. (2019) reported on the intensity subscale of the Sutter-Eyberg Student Behavior Inventory (SESBI; Eyberg & Pincus, 1999) evaluating the frequency of various problem behaviors, the Teacher Report Form (Achenbach & Rescorla, 2001) evaluating students' behavioral difficulties (subscales: aggression, attention problems, academic performance), and the Social Skills Rating System (Gresham & Elliott, 1990) with subscales cooperation, assertion, and self-control of students. A significant positive effect was found on the intensity of problem behaviors ($p < .01$; $d_w = 0.08$), thus a decreased intensity of problem behaviors after receiving the intervention. Furthermore, a positive, small effect in reducing attention problems ($p < .01$; $d_w = 0.08$) was found, but not for the level of aggressive behavior or academic performance. The intervention had a significant positive effect on cooperation ($p < .01$; $d_w = 0.17$) and self-control ($p < .05$; $d_w = 0.20$), but not on assertion.

Aasheim et al. (2020) reported on the Problem Behavior in the Classroom and Problem Behavior in the School Environment scales based on Grey and Sime (1989) and Ogden (1998). No significant effects were found.

Hickey et al. (2017) studied the effects of the IY-TCM program in Ireland, applying a randomized controlled trial (RCT). Eleven schools participated in the study, of which the majority served students from low SES-backgrounds. The participating classrooms ($N = 22$ teachers) were junior and senior infant classes (comparable to Kindergarten), randomly assigned to the experimental or control condition. From each participating class, approximately 12 students were selected for data collection on student outcomes (balancing students with low, medium, and high levels of behavioral problems; rated by the teachers using the Strengths and Difficulties Questionnaire; SDQ, Goodman, 1997), resulting in an overall sample of 227 students (average age: 5.3 years old). The SDQ subscales emotional symptoms, conduct problems, hyperactivity, peer problems, and prosocial behavior, were measured at pre- and post-test. Moreover, the Teacher-Pupil Observational Tool (Martin et al., 2010) was used. Composite variables were created for negative behaviors, positive behaviors, compliance, and non-compliance. The findings revealed no significant main effects of the IY-TCM intervention in favor of the experimental condition.

Ford et al. (2019) evaluated the effectiveness of IY-TCM in the UK with a RCT (randomization at school level). Eighty schools participated in the study, focusing on (pre-)Kindergarten to third-grade classrooms (i.e. Reception to year 4 in the UK). The student sample consisted of 2,075 who were 4-9 years old. Data were collected after 9, 18, and 30 months, using the SDQ (Goodman, 2001) and the Pupil Behaviour Questionnaire (PBQ; Allwood et al., 2018), for which teachers rated classroom-based disruptive behaviors. Significant positive effects on all time points were found for the SDQ subscale overactivity ($p = .02$). The positive effects at the SDQ peer relations and prosocial subscales were significant after 9 months ($p = .02$), but not anymore after 18 or 30 months. The results also showed a positive effect on reducing disruptive behavior ($p = .04$) at each time point.

Reinke et al. (2018) evaluated the effects of IY-TCM in the USA using a group RCT. The sample consisted of K-3 children in an urban area. An important remark is that all schools (in the experimental and control condition) were implementing Positive Behavioral Interventions and Supports (Sugai et al., 2002). Nine schools with 105 teachers participated in the study. Participating students ($N = 1,817$) were on average 7 years old. Sixty-one percent received free or reduced lunches (FRL), 76% were African-American, 22% White, and 2% had other backgrounds. The Teacher Observation of Classroom Adaptation-Checklist (TOCA-C; Koth et al., 2009) was used to evaluate students' social behavior (subscales: disruptive behaviors, concentration problems, emotional dysregulation, and prosocial behavior), and the Revised Social Competence Scale-Teacher version (Gifford-Smith, 2000) was used to measure teacher perceptions of students' social competence and academic competence. Academic achievement (reading and math) was measured using the Woodcock Johnson III Normative Update Tests of Achievement (Woodcock et al., 2007). Main positive significant effects were found for prosocial behavior ($p = .04$; $d = 0.13$), social competence ($p = .03$; $d = 0.13$), and emotional dysregulation ($p < .001$; $d = 0.14$), but not for disruptive problems, concentration problems, academic competence or academic achievement. In Chuang et al. (2020), that also report on this intervention study, student observations were conducted to assess students' physically or verbally aggressive behavior towards objects, peers, or the teacher to act as moderator in subsequent analyses. By adding this moderator, the main effect of the intervention on other student outcomes was not significant anymore.

Murray et al. (2018) evaluated the IY-TCM program in the USA. A pretest- posttest control group design was used to study the effects of the IY-TCM program on students' social competence and their level of inattention. Randomization was conducted at the grade level within each school. Ninety-one teachers from 11 rural and semi-rural schools participated in the study. The sample of 1,192 students consisted of Kindergarten (mean age 5.2 years), grade 1 (M_{age} = 6.2 years), and grade 2 (mean age 7.1 years) students. Forty-nine percent of them received FRL. Ethnic backgrounds were: 55% non-Hispanic White, 21% Hispanic, 20% African-American, and 4-5% other. The Social Competence Scale (Conduct Problems Prevention Research Group, 1995) was used to measure students' emotion regulation (e.g., thinks before acting), prosocial behavior (e.g., resolves peer problems), and academic competence (e.g., solving math problems, turning in homework). Furthermore, the DSM-IV Inattentive Scale from the Conners' Teacher Rating Scale (Conners, 2001) was used to assess students' cognitive self-regulation. Multilevel analyses revealed no significant effects of the intervention on these student outcomes.

In conclusion, positive effects of the IY-TCM program have been reported in three of the presented studies, for example, on teacher-student relationships, student behavior, or social skills. Two studies did not report significant effects on student outcomes.

Teacher-Child Interaction Training

Program Description

The Teacher-Child Interaction Training (TCIT) was adapted from Parent-Child Interaction Therapy (developed by Eyberg et al., 1995). TCIT is designed to improve teachers' skills to create a more constructive classroom environment (which will improve student behavior) and to provide teachers with behavior management skills that promote positive teacher-student relationships. Via individual training, teachers learn how to shape student behavior with attention and through modeling (Fernandez et al., 2015). The training includes two phases. Each phase starts with a teaching session outside the classroom and continues with in-service coaching sessions. The first phase, Child-Directed Interaction (CDI), focuses on teaching skills that strengthen teacher-student relationships and promote prosocial behavior of students. Praising positive behavior (i.e., labeled praise) and establishing positive teacher-student relationships (e.g., showing enjoyment in positive interactions with students) are seen as important ways to improve on-task behavior and reduce disruptive behavior. These skills are practiced extensively until teachers achieve CDI mastery. The second phase, Teacher-Directed Interaction (TDI), focuses on teaching skills to reduce problem behaviors (e.g., using "If-then" statements for students to earn privileges or as a warning of negative consequences of disruptive behavior). Skills are again practiced until teachers achieve mastery of the TDI skills (for details, see Fernandez et al., 2015). For more information about the program, see www.tcit.org.

Classification

We classified the TCIT program as "teachers' behavior focused" and "teacher-student relationship focused."

Effect Study

Fernandez et al. (2015) examined the effects of the TCIT in a small-scale RCT (randomization at the classroom level). The study was conducted in the USA, using a sample of K-1 teachers (N = 11) and students (total N = 70) from three urban public schools. The majority of the students received FRL. The authors distilled demographic information from publicly available data and reported that the majority of students identified as Hispanic/Latino (60%), other students identified as Black (20%), White (10%), or Asian (7%). Pre- and post-tests were conducted to evaluate the effects of TCIT on the frequency of disruptive behavior in the classroom and whether the frequency of the behavior was problematic according to the teachers, using the SESBI (Eyberg & Pincus, 1999). The results revealed no significant effects of the intervention on the intensity of disruptive behavior, but TCIT did have a significant positive effect on teachers' perception of how bothersome students' behaviors were ($p = .01$; $d = 0.62$). The authors suggest that this could be explained by the direct effect of the TCIT training on teacher distress, which was significantly decreased from pre- to post-test.

Based on this one study, the TCIT program has not demonstrated significant positive effects on student behavior, though teachers perceived students' disruptive behaviors as less bothersome.

Adler-Dreikurs Classroom Management Techniques

Program Description

The Adler-Dreikurs approach is a teacher-directed approach which trains teachers to apply democratic principles and techniques to their classroom (Dreikurs et al., 1999). Dreikurs et al. (2004) argue that teacher-student relationships can be improved by applying principles of democratic relationships and mutual respect. Soheili et al. (2015) developed a teacher training based on these principles. Using logical consequences for (mis)behavior is one of the strategies for establishing democratic relationships. Choice of consequence, and their purpose and rationale are discussed with the students, following the democratic principles (Dreikurs & Grey, 1968). The training helps teachers to establish and promote democratic relationships in the classroom, in which mutual respect and a sense of community are felt by both teachers and students. The approach (for a detailed description, see Soheili et al., 2015, pp. 458–461) addresses different leadership styles (promoting the democratic style) and focuses on recognizing and determining students' goals and needs. Natural and logical consequences of misbehavior are identified, in order to correct students in a respectful and reasonable way. These consequences need to be discussed with the students in order to avoid students experiencing it as a punishment. In the training sessions, attention goes to positive parental involvement as well. The training consists of lectures, presentations, group discussions, and hand-outs (Soheili et al., 2015) and the following reading materials: *Discipline without Tears* (Dreikurs et al., 2004) and *Maintaining Sanity in the Classroom* (Dreikurs et al., 1999). Moreover, the teachers received in-service guidance to practice and apply the Adler-Dreikurs methods and principles.

Classification

We classified the intervention as "teachers' behavior focused" and "teacher-student relationship focused."

Effect Studies

Soheili et al. (2015) studied the effects of the Adler-Dreikurs classroom management techniques in Iran, applying a RCT with randomization at the class level. Thirty teachers from four primary schools participated in the study. In total, 745 first- to fifth-grade students were included (average age: 9.3 years). The My Classroom Scale (Burnett, 2002) evaluated students' perceptions of the classroom environment. We only report on the subscale evaluating students' perception of the student-teacher relationship: the subscale evaluating students' perception of the classroom environment was deemed less relevant for this summary. Students' academic performance on reading, spelling, writing, mathematics, science, and art were retrieved from the school administration. The results revealed a significant positive effect on student-teacher relationships ($p < .01$; $\eta^2 = .69$) and on students' academic performance ($p < .008$ for all school subjects; $\eta^2 = .63$).

Based on this study, the Adler-Dreikurs training demonstrated promising positive effects on student-teacher relationships, as well as on students' academic outcomes.

Irie Classroom Toolbox

Program Description

Baker-Henningham (2018) developed the Irie Classroom Toolbox, a school-based teacher training program. "Irie" is a Jamaican word that describes feeling at peace and in harmony with oneself and with the world in general (Baker-Henningham, 2018, pp. 180-181). The program focuses on the use of positive and proactive teaching strategies to promote positive behavior and prevent negative behavior among students. The key concepts are: (a) teaching rules and routines, (b) using praise in the classroom and paying attention to positive behavior, (c) being proactive to prevent child behavior problems, (d) promoting children's social-emotional competence, (e) interactive storybook reading, and (f) promoting children's active participation in teaching and learning activities (p. 8). The toolbox includes different materials for teachers, such as a tools book with guidelines, a problem-solving stories book, an activities book with songs, games, activities, and lesson plans, and picture cards to support children remembering the classroom rules, developing friendship skills, and understanding emotions. For a detailed description see Baker-Henningham et al. (2019). Teachers receive training before implementing the program and also receive (in-service) support and some classroom assignments during the implementation (including text message prompts to remind and encourage them to use the strategies). For more information see www.irietoolbox.com.

Classification

We classified the Irie Classroom Toolbox as "teachers' behavior focused," "students' behavior focused," and "students' social-emotional development focused."

Effect Study

Baker-Henningham et al. (2019), of which the first author is the developer of the Irie Classroom Toolbox, studied the effects of the program in Jamaica. In the study, only the training on promoting positive behavior was implemented and tested. The study included 14 primary schools, randomly assigned to experimental and control conditions. Twenty-eight first-grade teachers participated in the study. The student sample included 220 students (a random sample of four students per classroom participated in the data collection), they were on average 7 years old. In a post-test only design, observations of child aggression and prosocial behavior were conducted, as well as teacher-reported behavioral difficulties and prosocial skills of participating students (SDQ; Goodman & Scott, 1999), after teachers had finished the program. The study also included math and language achievement tests (Woodcock et al., 1994, 2001, 2004), and students' self-regulation skills (Smith-Donald et al., 2007) were rated by independent observers. No significant effects were reported in the study.

Based on this study, the Irie Classroom Toolbox has not demonstrated significant positive effects on students' behavior and social-emotional functioning.

Promoting Alternative Thinking Strategies

Program Description

Promoting Alternative Thinking Strategies (PATHS; Greenberg & Kusché, 1993; Kusche & Greenberg, 1994) is one of the most widely implemented interventions in schools to prevent behavioral and social-emotional problems. The aim of the curriculum is to promote social-emotional competence among students by developmental integration of affect, emotion language, behavior, and cognitive understanding (Greenberg & Kusché, 1993). Achieving self-control and social problem solving (i.e. increasing prosocial behavior) may ultimately prevent the development of violent and aggressive behavior in children. PATHS is based on the Affective-Behavioral-Cognitive-Dynamic (ABCD) model of development (Greenberg & Kusché, 1993). Early emotional development is identified as a precursor to other ways of thinking. In many of the activities, students learn how to verbally identify and label feelings and emotions, in order to be able to manage their own feelings and emotions (Riggs et al., 2006). The curriculum utilizes a "spiral" model, including an extensive package of lessons and homework activities teaching students social and emotional skills throughout the school year, and can be implemented as a school-wide intervention. The developers emphasize the necessity of endorsing the social-emotional skills also outside the classroom and not only during the PATHS lessons. There are materials available for teachers (e.g., an implementation guidance manual) as well as for parents to support students' social-emotional development. Lesson activities include (among others) storytelling, direct instruction, discussions, video presentations, and role-playing. Teachers receive initial and (often in-service) follow-up training. For more information see www.pathstraining.com.

Classification

We classified PATHS as "students' behavior focused" and "students' social-emotional development focused."

Effect Studies

Humphrey et al. (2016) conducted a RCT (randomization at school level) in the UK, focusing on year 3 to 5, corresponding with grades 2 to 4 in the US system. Forty-five schools participated in the study, with a sample of 4,516 students. Students' age ranged from 7–9 years at the start of the intervention. The child-rated Social Skills Improvement System (SSIS) scale (Gresham & Elliot, 2008) was used, with subscales on communication, cooperation, assertion, responsibility, empathy, engagement, and self-control. Second, the SDQ (Goodman, 1997) was used. Third, the Social and Emotional Competence Change Index, developed by the Evidence-based Prevention and Intervention Supports center (2014), was rated by the teachers, which is part of the PATHS program evaluation tool. The results revealed no statistically significant positive effects of the intervention on the student outcomes measured by the SSIS or SDQ. There were two significant effects favoring the control group regarding peer problems ($p = .03$; $d = 0.07$) and emotional symptoms ($p = .01$; $d = 0.10$). Teachers' perception of students' social-emotional competence did increase by means of the intervention ($p = .01$; $d = 0.47$).

Berry et al. (2016) also conducted a RCT (randomization at school level) in the UK, applying pre-K PATHS, as this version was more appropriate for the youngest students that participated in the study. Fifty-six schools participated in the study. The participating children ($N = 5,074$) were Reception and Year One students (comparable to Kindergarten) who were followed for two school years (average age: 5 years at the start of the intervention). About half of the students received FRL. Data collection included the SDQ (Goodman, 1997) and the PATHS Teacher Rating Scale (PTRS) to measure children's behavior and social and emotional development (subscales: emotion regulation, prosocial behavior, social competence, aggressive behavior, internalizing/withdrawn, relational aggression, peer relations, inattention–hyperactivity, impulsivity–hyperactivity, learning behaviors, and academic performance). The effects of the intervention after 12 months were not significant for the SDQ scales. For 6 out of 11 subscales of the PTRS, significant positive effects were found after 12 months, namely on social competence, aggressive behavior, inattention–hyperactivity, impulsivity–hyperactivity, peer relations, and learning behaviors (all $p < .05$). The follow-up results after 24 months revealed that the effects on SDQ were still not significant, and the effects on the PTRS subscales were not significant anymore.

Schonfeld et al. (2015) conducted a study in the USA on the effects of PATHS on students' academic performance, with random assignment of 24 schools to treatment and control conditions. The intervention started in the third grade (students' average age: 8.9 years) and students were followed until they were in the sixth grade. The student sample ($N = 705$) included 48% African–Americans, 41% Hispanic/Latino-Americans, 9% Caucasians, and 13% other backgrounds. Sixty-eight percent received FRL. Students' academic performance in the fourth, fifth, and sixth grade was examined with the State Mastery Test (Hendrawan & Wibowo, 2013), measuring students' ability to use problem-solving skills for academic tasks in math, reading, and writing. The students in the experimental condition had higher scores on reading and writing in the fifth and sixth grade (not in the fourth grade) compared to the students in the control condition. For math, students in the experimental condition outperformed the control condition students in the fourth grade, but not in the fifth or sixth grade.

Fishbein et al. (2016) conducted a RCT on the effects of PATHS in Kindergarten classrooms in the USA, using pre-K PATHS. Four schools were randomly assigned to treatment or control conditions, all schools serving a high-poverty urban student population ($N = 327$). The majority of the students were African-American. The Teacher Observation of Child Adaptation-Revised (TOCA-R; Werthamer-larsson et al., 1991) was used, measuring overt aggression and internalizing behavior. Moreover, various teacher-rated measures were used. The Social Competence Scale (Conduct Problems Prevention Research Group, 1995) measuring prosocial behavior and emotion regulation, the ADHD Rating Scale (DuPaul, 1991) measuring attention problems and impulsivity, the Student-Teacher Relationship Scale (Pianta, 2001) measuring closeness and conflict, the Peer Relations Questionnaire (Ladd & Profilet, 1996) measuring the quality of peer relations and the Academic Competence Evaluation Scales (DiPerna & Elliot, 1999) measuring academic skills. Finally, students conducted the FACES task (Ekman & Friesen, 1975) at the posttest, measuring students' ability to accurately identify emotional expressions. The results revealed positive effects on social competence (on both subscales; $p < .001$), closeness (in student-teacher relationships; $p < .001$), peer relations ($p < .001$) and academic skills $p < .05$) and positive effects on reducing student aggression ($p < .001$), internalizing behavior ($p < .001$), inattention ($p < .01$), impulsivity ($p < .01$), and conflict (in student-teacher relationships; $p < .05$). No significant differences between the groups were found on emotional recognition.

The four studies discussed here presented mixed findings regarding the effectiveness of PATHS on student outcomes. In the two UK papers, the effects of students' behavior and social-emotional outcomes were short-term and/or not significant, although in one study, teachers' perceptions of change in students' social-emotional competence did change by means of the intervention. In the two USA papers, some positive effects on students' academic outcomes, behavior, and social-emotional outcomes were found.

PAX Good Behavior Game

Program Description

The Good Behavior Game (GBG) is a classroom-based universal program targeting the prevention of and early intervention in aggressive and disruptive behavior. Barrish et al. (1969) developed the original GBG game, and defined it as "a classroom behavior management technique, based on reinforcers natural to the classroom, other than teacher attention" (p. 119). GBG is administered by teachers during regular classroom activities. Interdependent group contingencies are used to improve students' behavior in class. Appropriate student behavior and classroom rules during an activity are explicitly defined and explained to (and sometimes together with) the students. Demonstrating appropriate student behavior is then systematically rewarded, though not individually but as a team effort, thus by the teams' collective success. Peer pressure (group self-regulation) may help students to avoid engaging in disruptive or inappropriate behavior. The teams compete for small prizes and privileges. In the studies of Weis et al. (2015) and Ialongo et al. (2019), the PAX-GBG version of GBG was implemented (Embry et al., 2003; Biglan et al., 2012; Embry & Biglan, 2008). PAX stands for Peace, Productivity, Health, and Happiness, emphasizing that student teams work cooperatively to comply with classroom rules and show appropriate behavior. PAX-GBG contains some additional components compared to the original GBG, for example, activities for teachers and students to establish the classroom rules together and the use of transition cues and hand signals to speed-up lesson transitions. Moreover, teachers are stimulated to write praise notes to acknowledge appropriate student behavior. Parental involvement is steered towards generalization of self-regulation skills at home (Embry, 2010, 2013). For more information see www.paxis.org/pax-good-behavior-game.

Classification

We classified the PAX GBG program as "teachers' behavior focused" and "students' behavior focused."

Effect Studies

Weis et al. (2015) evaluated the effects of PAX-GBG in the USA in a RCT during one school year in first- to third-grade classrooms. Six schools participated in the study, with a random selection of 27 classrooms to implement the intervention. Additionally, 22 classrooms were matched for comparison. The participating student sample ($N = 949$) had a high percentage of White (82%) students, as well as 7% African-American, 2% Latino, and 1% Asian-American students. Students' reading and mathematics achievement was measured with the Measures of Academic Progress tests (Northwest Evaluation Association, 2013). The results revealed a small and positive effect on students' reading skills ($p < .001$; $\eta^2 = .03$), but not on their mathematics skills.

Ialongo et al. (2019) studied the effects of PAX-GBG only condition and a PATHS-to-PAX condition (an integrated approach) compared to a control condition in the USA, applying a RCT. The 27 schools were randomly assigned to one of the three conditions. In the PATHS-to-PAX condition, the PATHS curriculum on developing social and emotional skills, such as self-control, emotion regulation and social problem solving was implemented in addition to the PAX-GBG activities. In total, 5,611 K-5 students and 331 teachers participated in the study. Most students were African-American (89.6%) and the majority received FRL (86.5%). Classroom observations of student behavior were conducted (Conduct Problems Prevention Research Group, 1999; Tapp et al., 1995) by independent observers, focusing on on-task, disruptive, and verbally and physically aggressive behaviors. The readiness to learn subscale (i.e., attention-concentration problems) and authority acceptance subscale (i.e., oppositional defiant/conduct problems behavior) from the TOCA-R (Werthamer-Larsson et al., 1991) were administered. The Social Health Profile Social Competence Scale (Conduct Problems Prevention Research Group, 1999), including the student social competence and emotion regulation subscales, were rated by the teachers. Comparing the PAX-GBG only condition with the control group revealed no significant effects on any of the student outcomes. The integrated PATHS-to-PAX condition did reveal a significant effect as compared to the control condition on reducing students' problem behavior, as measured by the behavior observations ($p < .05$; $d = 0.08$), but not for the social competence scales.

All in all, the PAX-GBG program was found to improve students' reading (but not math) skills. No significant effects were found for student behavior or social-emotional development in these recent studies. The integrated PATHS-to-PAX program showed promising results on improving student behavior, though not for social-emotional outcomes.

Second Step

Program Description

Second Step (Committee for Children, 2016) is a social-emotional program that aims to strengthen students' social-emotional skills and prosocial behavior via a comprehensive SEL-curriculum.

Students receive direct instruction in social-emotional skills and practice those skills in various activities. By learning and practicing these skills and behaviors, the program may help to prevent maladaptive behavior and conduct problems in students' school careers and adult lives. The studies reported on here used the K-5 program (Second Step Elementary), which is a scripted program including lesson plans organized around the following units: (a) skills for learning; (b) empathy; (c) emotion management; and (d) problem solving. The lessons are implemented by the teachers as part of the normal classroom activities. There are individual and small group activities in which students learned and practiced social-emotional skills. Positive behavior is supported as well, for example, by positive reinforcement and modeling by the teacher. Teachers are encouraged to reinforce skills throughout the day. This applies to parents as well, as they receive weekly handouts with information on what students learned that week. For more information see www.seconds tep.org.

Classification

We classified the Second Step program as "students' behavior focused" and "students' social-emotional development focused." The Second Step + Proactive Classroom Management (PCM) training (see the effect studies below) also includes elements of a "teachers' behavior focused" intervention.

Effect Studies

The studies of Low et al. (2015, 2019) and Cook et al. (2018) reported on the same intervention study conducted in the USA, evaluating the effects of Second Step (fourth edition) in combination with a PCM training, which was an additional teacher training, providing an overview of classroom management strategies such as attention signals and behavioral praise. The RCT was conducted in K-2 classrooms, with randomization at the school level. Sixty-one schools participated in the study, including 310 participating teachers. Participating students ($N = 7,213$) were, on average, 6.2 years old. The majority of the students received FRL (varying from 50% to 78% across subsamples in different regions). Ethnic backgrounds were diverse.

Low et al. (2015) reported on the effects after one year intervention, using the teacher-rated Devereux Student Strengths Assessment-Second Step edition (DESSA; developed by the Devereux Center for Resilient Children), measuring skills for learning, empathy, emotional management, and problem solving, and on the SDQ scales (Goodman, 1997). Student observations were conducted using the academic time engaged (on-task behavior) scale of the Behavioral Observation of Students in Schools (BOSS; Shapiro & Kratochwill, 2000). Low et al. (2015) applied the Benjamini-Hochberg procedure to control for false discoveries, and reported a significant positive effect of the intervention on reducing students' SDQ hyperactivity (adjusted $p = .015$).

Cook et al. (2018) reported on student achievement in oral reading fluency and math computational skills (curriculum-based measurement tests) after one year intervention. There were no significant main effects of the intervention on these academic outcomes.

Low et al. (2019) conducted a follow-up study after two years of intervention, using all of the above-mentioned measurements. After applying the Benjamini-Hochberg procedure to control for false discoveries, they found significant positive effects on SDQ emotional symptoms (adjusted $p = .0004, g = -0.07$), DESSA skills for learning (adjusted $p = .0138, g = 0.10$), and DESSA emotion management (adjusted $p = .0138, g = 0.13$), but not for the other included variables (e.g., academic outcomes).

Based on this intervention study, it can be concluded that the Second Step Elementary + PCM training intervention demonstrated promising effects on students' behavior and social-emotional development. The combined programs did not demonstrate significant positive effects on students' academic outcomes.

Insights

Program Description

Insights is a SEL intervention that aims to enhance the development of young children in low-income schools (McClowry et al., 2005). Insights is based on temperament theory and research, focusing on improving students' social-emotional skills and behaviors by matching the environment and the child's temperament. As stated by Cappella et al. (2015), it is expected that "improving goodness of fit between teaching practices and children's temperaments would enable teachers to provide more emotional support and create a more organized classroom for students" (p. 221). The Insights curriculum includes classroom activities as well as parent-child activities. The teacher and parent programs consist of three parts: (a) the 3Rs of child management (recognize, reframe, and respond); (b) gaining compliance (behavioral management strategies that match a child's temperament); and (c) giving control (supporting students when they encounter challenges, scaffolding a child through demanding situations, expanding their skills; McClowry et al., 2010). The classroom curriculum runs parallel, with 45-minute sessions per week. Students are introduced to four puppets that represent common temperaments, view videotaped vignettes demonstrating each puppet's reactions to challenging situations, and interact with the puppets and their peers to practice ways to approach and resolve daily dilemmas (McClowry et al., 2005). For more information see www.insightsintervention.com.

Classification

We classified Insights as "teachers' behavior focused," "teacher-student relationship focused," and "students' social-emotional development focused."

Effect Studies

Cappella et al. (2015) and McCormick et al. (2015) evaluated the effects of Insights in a RCT in the USA (see also O'Connor et al., 2014). The study included 22 schools, 120 teachers, and 435 students. Randomization took place at the school level. It was a longitudinal study, following Kindergarten children into the first grade. At the start of the intervention, students were on average 5.4 years old. The control condition was an attention-control condition, receiving a ten-week supplementary reading program after school. The majority of the students were eligible for FRL (87%).

In Cappella et al. (2015) classwide behavioral engagement and classwide off-task behavior were measured with the BOSS instrument (Shapiro, 2004). The results showed no significant main effects on classwide behavioral engagement or off-task behaviors.

McCormick et al. (2015) reported on measures of students' reading and math achievement, using the Woodcock-Johnson III Tests of Achievement-Form B (Woodcock et al., 2001). Moreover, child behavior problems were rated by the teachers using the SESBI (Eyberg & Pincus, 1999). There were no significant main effects of Insights on these student outcomes.

Based on these intervention studies, we conclude that the Insights program did not demonstrate significant positive effects on student outcomes.

Class-Wide Function-Related Intervention Teams

Program Description

The Class-Wide Function-Related Intervention Teams (CW-FIT) program is a group contingency CMP (Wills et al., 2009) aiming to improve students' on-task behavior as well as to increase teachers' recognition of appropriate behavior. Key components include teaching specific behavioral skills (e.g., following directions), increasing teacher attention to appropriate behavior and reducing teacher (and peer) attention to inappropriate behavior, and differentially reinforcing behavioral skills via points, goal setting, and interdependent group contingencies (Kamps et al., 2015). Students are taught appropriate behaviors in class, which are then reinforced by using a game format. These activities were scheduled 3–4 times per week. Student teams of 2 to 5 students can earn tokens when all team members engage in appropriate behaviors within short time frames of 2–3 minutes. The team with the best score at the end of the class period receives a group reward or privilege.

Classification

We classified CW-FIT as "teachers' behavior focused" and "students' behavior focused."

Effect Studies

Kamps et al. (2015) studied the effects of CW-FIT in a RCT in the USA. The study took four years, focusing on K–5 classrooms at 17 schools (also including several special education classrooms), serving urban and culturally diverse communities. A total of 159 teachers participated in the study. The majority of the students received FRL (79%). Considering the reported average class size, we estimated that over 3,000 students participated in the study. Classroom observations were conducted in late fall and early spring in each school year, to assess group on-task behavior. The results revealed a significant positive effect of the CW-FIT intervention on students' behavior ($p < .0001$).

Wills et al. (2018) replicated the study of Kamps et al. (2015) in a sample of 21 schools in the USA (again including several special education classrooms). In total, 157 K–6-teachers participated in the study. Ninety-six percent of the students received FRL. We estimated based on reported average class size that about 1,800 students were included in the study. Based on the classroom observations, it can be concluded that the CW-FIT intervention had a significant positive effect on students' behavior in the classroom ($p < .0001$; $d = 1.54$).

Based on these two studies, the CW-FIT program demonstrated promising positive effects on student behavior in the classroom.

Conclusions

Table 19.2 summarizes the foci of the interventions (from the authors' perspective). All the interventions had different foci, from which we draw the tentative conclusion that effective classroom management interventions should target both teachers and students. A focus on changing

Table 19.2 Focus of the Interventions (from the Authors' Perspective)

	Teacher behavior	Teacher-student relationship	Student behavior	Student social-emotional development
IY-TCM	X	X	X	X
TCIT	X	X		
Adler-Dreikurs Classroom Management Techniques	X	X		
Irie Classroom Toolbox	X		X	X
PATHS			X	X
PAX–GBG	X		X	
Second Step + PCM	X		X	X
Insights	X	X		X
CW-FIT	X		X	

teacher behavior, thus improving teachers' classroom management strategies and skills, is basically part of every program (note that we did not see this explicitly in the PATHS program). About two third of the interventions (also) focused on changing student's behavior and/or improving their social-emotional development. In four programs, there were specific activities included that aimed to improve teacher-student relationships (though basically all program developers acknowledged the importance of positive teacher-student relationships in their program descriptions), which we consider as a positive development in this field. The observed trend in Korpershoek et al. (2016) toward more student-centered approaches rather than teacher-centered approaches in CMPs continued over the last decade (see also Freiberg et al., 2020).

The intervention studies presented in this chapter confirm and expand previous findings (Korpershoek et al., 2016) that whole-classroom interventions on classroom management (or SEL interventions with classroom management elements) can significantly improve student behavior, social-emotional functioning, and academic performance, as well as improve teacher-student relationships. Positive main effects on relevant student outcomes were (generally) found for IY-TCM, PATHS, CW-FIT, the Adler-Dreikurs training, Second Step Elementary + PCM training, and the PAX-to-PATHS curriculum. No positive main effects were found for TCIT, Irie, PAX-GBG, and Insights, though we need to point out that this conclusion is based on only one (TCIT, Irie, Insights) or two (PAX-GBG) intervention studies. Several new CMPs were found since 2014, strengthening the knowledge base on effective classroom management strategies. Note that most programs included in this chapter were not only targeting teachers and students, but also parents in guiding their children in their social-emotional development or behavior in line with the programs' approach. Intervention effects are thus not exclusively caused by improved classroom practices. Nevertheless, the overall findings are promising.

We included 11 intervention studies from the USA and seven from other countries (Norway, UK, Ireland, Jamaica, Iran), as to identify similarities and dissimilarities in foci of the intervention studies across the globe. Although the number of studies outside the USA and Europe was very small, a tentative conclusion could be that the focus of interventions on improving students' behavior and/or students' social-emotional development in the classroom is more prominent in North American and European studies.

With ever-changing educational practices and contexts, replication studies are necessary to further improve implementation quality and to confirm effects in other student samples. Collecting empirical evidence among student samples from various educational, cultural, and societal contexts across the globe will contribute to a more comprehensive knowledge base on the effectiveness of the interventions, as transferability to other contexts is not necessarily always successful (Wigelsworth et al., 2016). Another recommendation for future studies is to include motivational outcomes in classroom management studies, as these were largely lacking in the included studies. Student motivation (e.g., Howard et al., 2021) and having a sense of school belonging (e.g., Korpershoek et al., 2020) are adaptive, and are associated with a broad range of favorable student outcomes.

Although we did not focus on intervention effects on teachers' classroom management skills, we would like to express that teacher training in effective classroom management strategies is essential, as it takes time for teachers to develop their knowledge and practice their skills. New technologies offer a broad variety of learning opportunities for teachers to reflect on their classroom practices. Mouw et al. (2021), for example, developed a Virtual-Reality Kindergarten environment for pre-service teachers to practice their classroom management skills as part of their teacher training program.

A limitation is that relevant research reports were not included, as we limited our search to peer-reviewed publications. Furthermore, the effects of the programs were, in many cases, also investigated using non-experimental or other research designs (multiple baseline designs, quasi-experimental designs, etc.). We concentrated on RCTs and pretest–posttest control group designs, as these are the only research designs that can provide strong empirical support for the effectiveness of an intervention on student outcomes. We realize that this stringent inclusion criterion does not do justice to the broad range of relevant papers. We refer readers to the program websites, recent review studies, and research databases for more complete overviews of conducted works, including papers addressing teacher outcomes, effective implementation strategies, and differential effects on specific student groups (e.g., students with behavioral problems) and in specific educational settings (e.g., special education schools). Despite these limitations, we hope that the international focus of this chapter provides some new perspectives and insights on recently developed as well as long-established interventions on classroom management.

We conclude this chapter by presenting some practical implications for teachers, teacher educators, and education administrators (e.g., school leaders, school boards). First of all, this scoping review may help education administrators and their school teams to compare the effectiveness of the different types of programs and make an evidence-informed decision on which program presumably would best fit the local context and the objectives the school is striving to reach. The rapidly growing trend towards evidence-informed practice in education (Nelson & Campbell, 2017) is an impulse for researchers to provide educational administrators and teachers with straightforward review studies and handbooks that summarize the vast amount of scientific literature available, as this could be helpful for deciding on the implementation of specific programs.

Based on the studies included in the current review, we recommend administrators and teachers who aim to improve both student behavior and social–emotional functioning to consider implementing a comprehensive, multimodal program such as IY-TCM or the combined PAX-to-PATHS curriculum. These integrative approaches focusing on improving teachers' general skills, applying preventative and reactive classroom management strategies, and a prescribed student curriculum (e.g., on prosocial behavior) seem most beneficial. Our review revealed that comprehensive programs can significantly improve a variety of student outcomes as well as improve the quality of teacher–student relationships. Although the number of randomized controlled trials and whole-classroom implementations were limited, the findings of the included studies suggest that all students may benefit from such programs, and not only those with maladaptive behavior and conduct problems.

Irrespective of the potential of specific programs for improving student behavior, it is important to take into account teachers' perspectives on classroom management when selecting a CMP, because teacher perceptions determine their willingness and ability to adapt their classroom management approach. Martin et al. (2016) identified five perspectives on precursors to teacher actions; for example, teachers may hold a more relational perspective of classroom management, or view classroom management from a developmental, culturally responsive perspective. To what extent these perspectives are represented in the CMPs that we included lies outside the scope of this chapter, but we recommend schools take teachers' perspectives into account when selecting a CMP, and not just teachers' classroom management skills or student behavior.

Moreover, given the effectiveness of programs explicitly including components focusing on improving teacher–student relationships, it is recommended that teacher educators integrate this more explicitly in their curriculum, and assist pre-service and beginning teachers in developing skills to improve their relationship with their students. Good practices to build positive teacher–student relationships, for example, include trust-building activities and the establishment of a shared responsibility for the classroom atmosphere and learning environment (see also Wubbels, 2011). Finally, we recommend teacher educators incorporate the empirical knowledge base on effective strategies and different CMPs in primary school teacher-training programs, as negative experiences with classroom management and resulting teacher stress and low levels of self-efficacy are important reasons why many beginning teachers leave the teaching profession within 5 to 10 years (Aloe et al., 2014; Dicke et al., 2014).

References

Aasheim, M., Drugli, M.-B., Reedtz, C., Helge Handegård, B., & Martinussen, M. (2018). Change in teacher-student relationships and parent involvement after implementation of the Incredible Years Teacher Classroom Management programme in a regular Norwegian school setting. *British Educational Research Journal*, 44(6), 1064–1083. https://doi.org/10.1002/berj.3479

Aasheim, M., Fossum. S., Reedtz, C., Helge Handegård, B., & Martinussen, M. (2020). Examining the Incredible Years Teacher Classroom Management Program in a regular Norwegian school setting: Teacher-reported behavior management practice, problem behavior in classroom and school environment, teacher self- and collective efficacy, and classroom climate. *SAGE Open, 10*(2). Article 215824402092742. https://doi.org/10.1177/2158244020927422

Aasheim, M., Reedtz, C., Helge Handegård, B., Martinussen, M., & Mørch, W.-T. (2019). Evaluation of the Incredible Years Teacher Classroom Management Program in a regular Norwegian school setting. *Scandinavian Journal of Educational Research, 63*(6), 899–912. https://doi.org/10.1080/00313831.2018.1466357

Achenbach, T. M., & Rescorla, L. A. (2001). *Manual for the ASEBA School-Age Forms & Profiles.* University of Vermont, Research Center for Children, Youth, & Families.

Allwood, M., Allen, K., Price, A., Hayes, R., Edwards, V., Ball, S., Ukoumunne, O.C., & Ford, T. (2018) The reliability and validity of the pupil behaviour questionnaire: a child classroom behaviour assessment tool. *Emotional and Behavioural Difficulties, 23*(4), 361–371. https://doi.org/10.1080/13632752.2018.1478945

Aloe, A. M., Amo, L. C., & Shanahan, M. E. (2014). Classroom management self-efficacy and burnout: A multivariate meta-analysis. *Educational Psychological Review, 26,* 101–126. https://doi.orgl/10.1007/s10648-013-9244-0

Baker-Henningham, H. (2018). The Irie Classroom Toolbox: Developing a violence prevention, preschool teacher training program using evidence, theory, and practice. *Annals of the New York Academy of Sciences, 1419*(1), 179–200. https://doi.org/10.1111/nyas.13713

Baker-Henningham, H., Scott, Y., Bowers, M., Francis, T. (2019). Evaluation of a violence-prevention programme with Jamaican primary school teachers: A cluster randomised trial. *International Journal of Environmental Research and Public Health, 16*(15). Article 2797. https://doi.org/10.3390/ijerph16152797

Barrish, H. H., Saunders, M., & Wolf, M. M. (1969). Good behavior game: Effects of individual contingencies for group consequences on disruptive behavior in a classroom. *Journal of Applied Behavior Analysis, 2,* 119–124. http://doi.org/10.1901/jaba.1969.2-119

Berry, V., Axford, N., Blower, S., Taylor, R. S., Edwards, R. T., Tobin, K., Jones, C., & Bywater, T. (2016). The effectiveness and micro-costing analysis of a universal, school-based, social-emotional learning programme in the UK: A cluster-randomised controlled trial. School Mental Health, 8(2), 238–256. https://doi.org/10.1007/s12310-015-9160-1

Biglan, A., Flay, B. R., Embry, D. D., & Sandler, I. N. (2012). The critical role of nurturing environments for promoting human well-being. *American Psychologist, 67,* 257–271. https://doi.org/10.1037/a0026796

Bradshaw, C. P., Waasdorp, T., & Leaf, P. (2015). Examining the variation in the impact of school-wide positive behavior interventions and supports: Finding from a randomized controlled effectiveness trial. *Journal of Educational Psychology, 2,* 546–557. https://doi.org/10.1037/a0037630

Burnett, P. C. (2002). Teacher praise and feedback and students' perceptions of the classroom environment. *Educational Psychology, 22*(1), 5–16. https://doi.org/10.1080/01443410120101215

Cappella, E., O'Connor, E. E., McCormick, M. P., Turbeville, R., Collins, A. J., McClowry, S. G. (2015). Classwide efficacy of INSIGHTS: Observed teacher practices and student behaviors in kindergarten and first grade. *The Elementary School Journal, 116*(2), 217–241. https://doi.org/10.1086/683983

Chuang, C.-C., Reinke, W. M., & Herman, K. C. (2020). Effects of a universal classroom management teacher training program on elementary children with aggressive behaviors. *School Psychology, 35*(2), 128–136. https://doi.org/10.1037/spq0000351

Committee for Children (2016). *Second Step social-emotional programming.* Committee for Children.

Conduct Problems Prevention Research Group (1995). *Fast track project.* https://fasttrackproject.org/techrept/s/sct/

Conduct Problems Prevention Research Group (1999). Initial impact of the Fast Track prevention trial for conduct problems: II. Classroom effects. *Journal of Consulting and Clinical Psychology, 67,* 648–657. https://doi.org/10.1037/0022-006X.67.5.648

Conners, C. K. (2001). *Conners' rating scales revised.* Multi-Health Systems.

Cook, C. R., Low, S., Buntain-Ricklefs, J., Whitaker, K., Pullmann, M. D., & Lally, J. (2018). Evaluation of second step on early elementary students' academic outcomes: A randomized controlled trial. *School Psychology Quarterly, 33*(4), 561–572. https://doi.org/10.1037/spq0000233

Dicke, T., Parker, P. D., Marsh, H. W., Kunter, M., Schmeck, A., & Leutner, D. (2014). Self-efficacy in classroom management, classroom disturbances, and emotional exhaustion: A moderated 3 mediation analysis of teacher candidates. *Journal of Educational Psychology, 106*(2), 569–583. https://doi.org/10.1037/a0035504

DiPerna, J. C., & Ellliott, S. N. (1999). Development and validation of the Academic Competence Evaluation Scales. *Journal of Psychoeducational Assessment, 17*(3), 207–225. https://doi.org/10.1177/073428299901700302

Dreikurs, R., Cassel, P., & Ferguson, E. (2004). *Discipline without tears: How to reduce conflict and establish cooperation in the classroom.* John Wiley & Sons.

Dreikurs, R., & Grey, L. (1968). *The new approach to discipline: Logical consequences.* Hawthorne.

Dreikurs, R., Grunwald, B. B., & Pepper, F. C. (1999). *Maintaining sanity in the classroom: classroom management techniques* (2nd ed.). Taylor and Francis.

DuPaul, G. (1991). Parent and teacher ratings of ADHD symptoms: Psychometric properties in a community-based sample. *Journal of Clinical Child Psychology, 20,* 245–253. https://doi.org/10.1207/s15374424jccp2003_3

Ekman, P., & Friesen, W. V. (1975). *Pictures of facial affect.* Consulting Psychologists Press.

Embry, D. D. (2010). *PAX manual for behavioral supports for users of the PAX Good Behavior Game.* Johns Hopkins Center for Prevention and Early Intervention.

Embry, D. D. (2013). *PAX Plus Good Behavior Game kit.* PAXIS Institute.

Embry, D. D., & Biglan, A. (2008). Evidence-based kernels: Fundamental units of behavioral influence. *Clinical Child and Family Psychology Review, 11,* 75–113. https://doi.org/10.1007/s10567-008-0036-x

Embry, D. D., Staatemeier, G., Richardson, C., Lauger, K., & Mitich, J. (2003). *The PAX good behavior game* (1st ed.). Hazelden.

EPIS Center (2014). Promoting alternative thinking strategies. www.episcenter.psu.edu/ebp/paths

Evertson, C. M., & Weinstein, C. S. (Eds.). (2006). *Handbook of classroom management: Research, practice, and contemporary issues.* Lawrence Erlbaum.

Eyberg, S. M., Boggs, S. R., & Algina, J. (1995). Parent-child interaction therapy: A psychosocial model for the treatment of young children with conduct problem behavior and their families. *Psychopharmacology Bulletin, 31,* 83–91.

Eyberg, S. M. & Pincus, D. (1999) *Eyberg Child Behavior Inventory (ECBI) and Sutter–Eyberg Student Behavior Inventory-Revised (SESBI-R).* Psychological Assessment Resources.

Fernandez, M. A., Adelstein, J. A., Miller, S. P., Areizaga, M. J., Gold, D. C., Sanchez, A. L., Rothschild, S. A., Hirsch, E., & Gudiño, O. G. (2015). Teacher-Child Interaction Training: A pilot study with random assignment. *Behavior Therapy, 46*(4), 463–477. https://doi.org/10.1016/j.beth.2015.02.002

Fishbein, D. H., Domitrovich, C., Williams, J., Gitukui, S., Guthrie, C., Shapiro, D., & Greenberg, M. (2016). Short-term intervention effects of the PATHS curriculum in young low-income children: Capitalizing on plasticity. *The Journal of Primary Prevention, 37*(6), 493–511. https://doi.org/10.1007/s10935-016-0452-5

Ford, T., Hayes, R., Byford, S., Edwards, V., Fletcher, M., Logan, S., Norwich, B., Pritchard, W., Allen, K., Allwood, M., Ganguli, P., Grimes, K., Hansford, L., Longdon, B., Norman, S., Price, A., & Ukoumunne, O. C. (2018). The effectiveness and cost-effectiveness of the Incredible Years® Teacher Classroom Management programme in primary school children: results of the STARS cluster randomised controlled trial. *Psychological Medicine, 49*(5), 828–842. https://doi.org/10.1017/S0033291718001484

Freiberg, H. J., Oviatt, D., & Naveira, E. (2020). Classroom management meta-review continuation of research-based programs for preventing and solving discipline problems. *Journal of Education for Students Placed at Risk, 25*(4), 319–337. https://doi.org/10.1080/10824669.2020.1757454

Gifford-Smith, M. (2000). *Teacher social competence scale, fast track project technical report.* Duke University.

Goodman, R. (1997). The Strengths and Difficulties Questionnaire: A research note. *Journal of Child Psychology and Psychiatry, 38*(5), 581–586. https://doi.org/10.1111/j.1469-7610.1997.tb01545.x

Goodman, R. (2001). Psychometric properties of the strengths and difficulties questionnaire. *Journal of the American Academy of Child & Adolescent Psychiatry, 40,* 1337–1345. https://doi.org/10.1097/00004583-200111000-00015

Goodman, R. & Scott, S. (1999). Comparing the Strengths and Difficulties Questionnaire and the Child Behaviour Checklist: Is small beautiful? *Journal of Abnormal Child Psychology, 27,* 17–24. https://doi.org/10.1023/a:1022658222914

Greenberg, M. T., & Kusche, C. A. (1993). *Promoting social and emotional development in deaf children: The PATHS project.* University of Washington Press.

Gresham, F. M., & Elliott, S. N. (1990). *Social skills rating system manual.* American Guidance Service.

Gresham, F. M., & Elliott, S. N. (2008). *Social skills improvement system: Rating scales manual.* Pearson.

Grey, J., & Sime, N. (1989). *Discipline in schools. Report of the committee of enquiry chaired by Lord Elton.* www.educationengland.org.uk/documents/elton/elton1989.html

Hendrawan, I., & Wibowo, A. (2013). *The Connecticut Mastery Test: Technical Report.* Connecticut State Board of Education.

Hickey, G., McGilloway, S., Hyland, L., Leckey, Y., Kelly, P., Bywater, T., Comiskey, C., Lodge, A., Donnelly, M., & O'Neill, D. (2017). Exploring the effects of a universal classroom management training programme on teacher and child behaviour: A group randomised controlled trial and cost analysis. *Journal of Early Childhood Research, 15*(2), 174–194. https://doi.org/10.1177/1476718x15579747

Howard, J. L., Bureau, J., Guay, F., Chong, J. X. Y., & Ryan, R. M. (2021). Student motivation and associated outcomes: A meta-analysis from self-determination theory. *Perspectives on Psychological Science,* 174569162096678. https://doi.org/10.1177/1745691620966789

Humphrey, N., Barlow, A., Wigelsworth, M., Lendrum, A., Pert, K., Joyce, C., Stephens, E., Wo, L., Squires, G., Woods, K., Calam, R., & Turner, A. (2016). A cluster randomized controlled trial of the Promoting Alternative Thinking Strategies (PATHS) curriculum. *Journal of School Psychology*, *58*, 73–89. https://doi.org/10.1016/j.jsp.2016.07.002

Ialongo, N. S., Domitrovich, C., Embry, D., Greenberg, M., Lawson, A., Becker, K. D., & Bradshaw, C. (2019). A randomized controlled trial of the combination of two school-based universal preventive interventions. *Developmental Psychology*, *55*(6), 1313–1325. https://doi.org/10.1037/dev0000715

Kamps, D., Wills, H., Dawson-Bannister, H., Heitzman-Powell, L., Kottwitz, E., Hansen, B., & Fleming, K. (2015). Class-Wide Function-Related Intervention Teams "CW-FIT" efficacy trial outcomes. *Journal of Positive Behavior Interventions*, *17*(3), 134–145. https://doi.org/10.1177/1098300714565244

Korpershoek, H., Canrinus, E. T., Fokkens-Bruinsma, M., & De Boer, H. (2020). The relationships between school belonging and students' motivational, social–emotional, behavioural, and academic outcomes in secondary education: A meta-analytic review. *Research Papers in Education*, *6*, 641–680. https://doi.org/10.1080/02671522.2019.1615116

Korpershoek, H., Harms, G.J., De Boer, H., Van Kuijk, M.F., & Doolaard, S. (2016). A meta-analysis of the effects of classroom management strategies and classroom management programs on students' academic, behavioural, emotional, and motivational outcomes. *Review of Educational Research*, *86*, 643–680. https://doi.org/10.3102/0034654315626799

Koth, C.W., Bradshaw, C.P., & Leaf, P.J. (2009). Teacher observation of classroom adaptation–checklist: Development and factor structure. *Measurement and Evaluation in Counseling and Development*, *42*(1), 15–30. https://doi.org/10.1177/0748175609333560

Kusche, C., & Greenberg, M.T. (1994). *The PATHS curriculum*. Developmental Research and Programs.

Ladd, G.W., & Profilet, S. M. (1996). The Child Behavior Scale: A teacher-report measure of young children's aggressive, withdrawn, and prosocial behaviors. *Developmental Psychology*, *32*(6), 1008–1024. https://doi.org/10.1037/0012-1649.32.6.1008

Low, S., Cook, C. R., Smolkowski, K., & Buntain-Ricklefs, J. (2015). Promoting social–emotional competence: An evaluation of the elementary version of Second Step®. *Journal of School Psychology*, *53*(6), 463–477. https://doi.org/10.1016/j.jsp.2015.09.002

Low, S., Smolkowski, K., Cook, C., & Desfosses, D. (2019). Two-year impact of a universal social–emotional learning curriculum: Group differences from developmentally sensitive trends over time. *Developmental Psychology*, *55*(2), 415–433. https://doi.org/10.1037/dev0000621

Martin, P.A., Daley, D., Hutchings, J., Jones, K., Eames, C., & Withaker, C. J. (2010) The Teacher–Pupil Observation Tool (T-POT): Development and testing of a new classroom observation measure. *School Psychology International*, *31*(3), 229–249. https://doi.org/10.1177/0143034310362040

Martin, N. K., Schafer, N. J., McClowry, S., Emmer, E. T., Brekelmans, M., Mainhard, T., & Wubbels, T. (2016). Expanding the definition of classroom management: Recurring themes and new conceptualizations. *Journal of Classroom Interaction*, *51*(1), 31–41. www.jstor.org/stable/26174348

McClowry, S. G., Snow, D. L., & Tamis-LeMonda, C. S. (2005). An evaluation of the effects of INSIGHTS on the behavior of inner city primary school children. *Journal of Primary Prevention*, *26*(6), 567–584. https://doi.org/10.1007/s10935-005-0015-7

McClowry, S. G., Snow, D. L., Tamis-LeMonda, C. S., & Rodriguez, E.T. (2010). Testing the efficacy of INSIGHTS on student disruptive behavior, classroom management, and student competence in inner city primary grades. *School Mental Health*, *2*, 3–35. https://doi.org/10.1007/s12310-009-9023-8

McCormick, M. P., Cappella, I., O'Connor, E. E., & McClowry, S. G. (2015). Social-emotional learning and academic achievement. *AERA Open*, *1*(3). Article 233285841560395. https://doi.org/10.1177/2332858415603959

Mouw, J. M., Fokkens-Bruinsma, M., & Snippe, A. (2021). *Assessing complex skills in a virtual reality context: Capturing the development of pre-service teachers' classroom management strategies* [Manuscript submitted for publication]. GION Education/Research, University of Groningen.

Murray, D. W., Rabiner, D. L., Kuhn, L., Pan, Y., & Forooz Sabet, R. (2018). Investigating teacher and student effects of the Incredible Years Classroom Management Program in early elementary school. *Journal of School Psychology*, *67*, 119–133. https://doi.org/10.1016/j.jsp.2017.10.004

Nelson, J., & Campbell, C. (2017). Evidence-informed practice in education: meanings and applications. *Educational Research*, *59*, 127–135. https://doi.org/10.1080/00131881.2017.1314115

Northwest Evaluation Association (2013). *Measures of academic progress manual*. Northwest Evaluation Association.

O'Connor, E. E., Cappella, E., McCormick, M. P & McClowry, S. G. (2014). An examination of the efficacy of INSIGHTS in enhancing the academic and behavioral development of children in early grades. *Journal of Educational Psychology*, *106*(4), 1156–1169. https://doi.org/10.1037/a0036615

Ogden, T. (1998). *Elevatferd og læringsmiljø: Læreres erfaringer med og syn på elevatferd og læringsmiljø i grunnskolen.* [Student behavior and learning environment: Teachers' experiences and view of student behavior and learning environment in elementary school]. www.regjeringen.no/no/doku-menter/elevatferd-og-laringsmiljo/id105365/

Pianta, R. C. (1996). *Manual and scoring guide for the student–teacher relationship scale.* University of Virginia.

Pianta, R. C. (2001). *Student–teacher relationship scale.* Psychological Assessment Resources.

Reinke, W. M., Herman, K. C., & Dong, N. (2018). The Incredible Years Teacher Classroom Management Program: Outcomes from a group randomized trial. *Prevention Science, 19*(8), 1043–1054. https://doi.org/10.1007/s11121-018-0932-3

Riggs, N. R., Greenberg, M. T., Kusché, C. A., & Pentz, M. A. (2006). The mediational role of neurocognition in the behavioral outcomes of a socialemotional prevention program in elementary school students: Effects of the PATHS Curriculum. *Prevention Science, 7,* 91–102. https://doi.org/10.1007/s11121-005-0022-1.

Scheerens, J., van der Werf, G., & De Boer, H. (2020). Soft skills in education: Putting the evidence in perspective. Springer.

Schonfeld, D. J., Adams, R. E., Fredstrom, B. K., Weissberg, R. P., Gilman, R., Voyce, C., Tomlin, R., & Speese-Linehan, D. (2015). Cluster-randomized trial demonstrating impact on academic achievement of elementary social-emotional learning. *School Psychology Quarterly, 30*(3), 406–420. https://doi.org/10.1037/spq0000099

Shapiro, E. S. (2004). *Academic skills problems: Direct assessment and intervention* (3rd ed.). Guilford.

Shapiro, E. S., & Kratochwill, T. R. (Eds.). (2000). *Behavioral assessment in schools: Theory, research, and clinical foundations.* Guilford Press.

Smith-Donald, R., Raver, C. C., Hayes, T., & Richardson, B. (2007). Preliminary construct and concurrent validity of the Preschool Self-regulation Assessment (PSRA) for field-based research. *Early Childhood Research Quarterly, 22,* 173–187. https://doi.org/10.1016/j.ecresq.2007.01.002

Soheili, F., Alizadeh, H., Murphy, J. M., Salimi Bajestani, H., & Dreikurs Ferguson, E. (2015). Teachers as leaders: The impact of Adler-Dreikurs classroom management techniques on students' perceptions of the classroom environment and on academic achievement. *The Journal of Individual Psychology, 71*(4), 440–461. https://doi.org/10.1353/jip.2015.0037

Sugai, G., Horner, R., & Gresham, F. (2002). Behaviorally effective school environments. In M. Shinn, H. Walker, & G. Stoner (Eds.), *Interventions for academic and behavior problems II: Prevention and remedial approaches* (pp. 315–350). NASP.

Tapp, J., Wehby, J., & Ellis, D. (1995). A multiple option observation system for experimental studies: MOOSES. *Behavior Research Methods, Instruments & Computers, 27,* 25–31. https://doi.org/10.3758/BF03203616

Taylor, R. D., Oberle, E., Durlak, J. A., & Weissberg, R. P. (2017). Promoting positive youth development through school-based social and emotional learning interventions: A meta-analysis of follow-up effects. *Child Development, 88,* 1156–1171. https://doi.org/10.1111/cdev.12864

Veldman, M. A., Hingstman, M., Doolaard, S., Snijders, T. A. B., & Bosker, R. J. (2020). Promoting students' social behavior in primary education through Success for All lessons. *Studies in Educational Evaluation, 67.* Article 100934. https://doi.org/10.1016/j.stueduc.2020.100934

Webster-Stratton, C. (1994). *The Incredible Years Teacher Training series.* Incredible Years, Inc.

Webster-Stratton, C. (2012). *Incredible teachers: Nurturing children's social, emotional, and academic competence.* Incredible Years, Inc.

Webster-Stratton, C., Reinke, W. M., Herman, K. C., & Newcomer, L. L. (2011). The Incredible Years Teacher Classroom Management Training: The methods and principles that support fidelity of training delivery. *School Psychology Review, 40*(4), 509–529. https://doi.org/10.1080/02796015.2011.12087527

Weis, R., Osborne, K. J., & Dean, E. L. (2015). Effectiveness of a universal, interdependent group contingency program on children's academic achievement: A countywide evaluation. *Journal of Applied School Psychology, 31*(3), 199–218. https://doi.org/10.1080/15377903.2015.1025322

Werthamer-Larsson, L., Kellam, S., & Wheeler, L. (1991). Effect of first-grade classroom environment on shy behavior, aggressive behavior, and concentration problems. *American Journal of Community Psychology, 19*(4), 585–602. https://doi.org/10.1007/bf00937993

Wigelsworth, M., Lendrum, A., Oldfield, J., Scott, A., Ten Bokkel, I., Tate, K., & Emery, C. (2016). The impact of trial stage, developer involvement and international transferability on universal social and emotional learning programme outcomes: a meta-analysis. *Cambridge Journal of Education, 46*(3), 347–376. https://doi.org/10.1080/0305764x.2016.1195791

Wills, H., Kamps, D., Caldarella, P., Wehby, J., & Swinburne Romine, R. (2018). Class-wide Function-Related Intervention Teams (CW-FIT): Student and teacher outcomes from a multisite randomized replication trial. *The Elementary School Journal, 119*(1), 29–51. https://doi.org/10.1086/698818

Wills, H. P., Kamps, D., Hansen, B., Conklin, C., Bellinger, S., Neaderhiser, J., & Nsubuga, B. (2009). The Classwide Function-Based Intervention Team Program. *Preventing School Failure: Alternative Education for Children and Youth, 54*(3), 164–171. https://doi.org/10.1080/10459880903496230

Woodcock, R. W., Mather, N., & Schrank, F. (2004). *Woodcock-Johnson III Diagnostic Reading Battery*. Riverside Publishing.

Woodcock, R. W., McGrew, K. S., & Mather, N. (2001). *Woodcock-Johnson III Tests of Achievement*. Riverside Publishing.

Woodcock, R. W., McGrew, K. S., & Mather, N. (2007). *Woodcock-Johnson III Test of Achievement*. Riverside Publishing.

Woodcock, R. W., McGrew, K. S., & Werder, J. (1994). *Woodcock-McGrew-Werder Mini-Battery of Achievement*. Riverside Publishing.

Wubbels, T. (2011). An international perspective on classroom management: What should prospective teachers learn? *Teaching Education, 22*, 113–131. https://doi.org/10.1080/10476210.2011.567838

Wubbels, T., Brekelmans, M., Tartwijk, J. van, & Admiraal, W. (1999). Interpersonal relationships between teachers and students in the classroom. In H. C. Waxman & H. J. Walberg (Eds.), *New directions for teaching practice and research* (pp. 151–170). McCutchan.

PART IV

Social Perspectives of Classroom Management

20

TRANSFORMATIVE SOCIAL-EMOTIONAL LEARNING AND CLASSROOM MANAGEMENT

Dorothy L. Espelage, Luz E. Robinson, and Alberto Valido

UNIVERSITY OF NORTH CAROLINA AT CHAPEL HILL

Introduction

Social-emotional learning (SEL) programs have been regarded as an effective intervention for schools and classrooms, showing positive changes in both social and academic outcomes (Corcoran et al., 2018; Durlak et al., 2011; Schonert-Reichl, 2019; Taylor et al., 2017). However, SEL programs have been criticized for not explicitly addressing the relational and cultural dynamics of power and oppression endured by marginalized and historically under-resourced students (Hoffman, 2009). Further, most SEL programs have been developed with a Eurocentric lens and do not fully reflect how culture impacts the recognition and processing of emotions. Hoffman observed:

> Debates over the basis for and effectiveness of.... SEL aside, the diffusion of SEL programs across schools in the United States raises other important questions that have been largely ignored in the literature. These issues concern implicit ideologies of selfhood and their links to cultural norms for emotional expression, as well as questions of power and the structuring of educational opportunity in the United States.
>
> *p. 357*

Social-emotional learning programming is becoming increasingly common in the U.S. However, as a response to the blatant social and educational inequities during the COVID-19 pandemic and the national outcry for racial justice, the Collaborative for Academic, Social, and Emotional Learning (CASEL) refined their conceptualization of SEL to Transformative SEL (TSEL), a form of SEL that centers diversity, equity, and inclusion (Jagers et al., 2019, 2021). Transformative SEL is aimed at redistributing power to promote social justice through increased engagement in school and civic life. It emphasizes the development of identity, agency, belonging, curiosity, and collaborative problem-solving within individuals and within communities (Jagers et al., 2019).

Transformative social-emotional learning is rooted in the notion of justice-oriented citizenship, and issues of culture, identity, agency, belonging, and wellbeing as relevant expressions of the CASEL 5 core competencies: self-awareness, self-management, social awareness, relationship

DOI: 10.4324/9781003275312-24

skills, and responsible decision making (Jagers et al., 2019). Identity is multifaceted and is reflected across all five SEL competencies. Agency is a critical component of self-management and relationship skills. Belonging and engagement require social awareness and responsible decision making. To achieve educational equity in the U.S., every student should have what they need when they need it, regardless of ability, race, gender, ethnicity, language, family background, or family income (The Aspen Education & Society Program and the Council of Chief State School Officers, 2017). As classrooms in the U.S. continue to become more diverse, it is imperative for teachers, administrators, and other school staff (e.g., paraprofessionals, school security) to understand and approach cultural differences through a trauma-informed, strengths-based lens while centering educational equity.

This chapter will serve as a foundational resource in increasing the understanding and capacity of teachers, administrators, and school-community partners to support marginalized students in today's classrooms through TSEL. The outline for the chapter includes: (a) introduction and overview of the TSEL literature, (b) discussion of TSEL implemented systematically across a Multi-Tiered System of Support (MTSS) framework, (c) integrating data from multiple stakeholders to inform TSEL work in classrooms and schools, (d) SEL as a critical component to successful classroom management, (e) strategies in TSEL for classroom management and restorative justice, and (f) next steps.

Introduction and Overview of the Transformative SEL Literature

Social-emotional learning is the process by which children and adults practice interrelated skills such as self-awareness, self-management and regulation, social awareness, building relationships, and responsible decision making (Weissberg et al., 1989). Social-emotional learning skills are multifaceted and critical for well-being, learning, and academic success (Jones et al., 2017). Social-emotional learning can be taught formally at school (i.e., SEL curriculum) or informally in a variety of contexts throughout development (i.e., socialization). While formal SEL programming is marketed to schools to teach strategies across the five SEL skills, some scholars have criticized its lack of explicit consideration for equity and diversity (Hoffman, 2009; Shriver & Weissberg, 2020; Simmons, 2019). Of note, the efficacy of SEL programs yield modest effect sizes (Durlak et al., 2011; Taylor et al., 2017), especially in randomized clinical trials (Corcoran et al., 2018). These modest effect sizes could be attributed partly to the high levels of diversity among students in U.S. schools and the lack of diversity among implementers, including teachers and school practitioners (e.g., school psychologists, social workers). Initiatives to diversify the teaching profession as well as school practitioners are critical to serving diverse students and the need for SEL programming that centers equity and social justice is long overdue (Camangian & Cariaga, 2021; Hoffman, 2009). During the COVID-19 pandemic and the ongoing national outcry for institutional accountability regarding discriminatory practices against students of color and their communities demands that education center equity, diversity, and inclusion in all its practices, including SEL (Kennedy, 2019). Thus, in 2020 the CASEL modified their definition of SEL to include elements of transformative or equity-focused SEL and called for systemic approaches to SEL implementation (Jagers et al., 2021).

Transformative social-emotional learning is defined as "a process whereby students and teachers build strong, respectful relationships founded on an appreciation of similarities and differences; learn to critically examine root causes of inequity; and develop collaborative solutions to community and social problems" (Jagers et al., 2018, p. 2). Further, TSEL emphasizes the need for direct connections between individual cultural assets and social and emotional development (Jagers et al., 2019). The updated definition incorporates specific language for the role of SEL-centered school-family-community partnerships in promoting equity in education and promotes student agency while recognizing that environment and history shape students' academic, social, and emotional growth.

Social-emotional learning competencies are developed and expressed in various ways depending on biological (e.g., developmental stages) and social (e.g., race, class, gender, country, etc.) characteristics. This framework affirms that social and emotional competencies differ by culture, and intentionally shapes SEL programming through a culturally responsive, equity-focused lens. Therefore, it is critical to utilize a form of SEL that transforms individuals and institutions in ways that support optimal human development and functioning for all children and adults regardless of their abilities, circumstances, or backgrounds (e.g., Jagers, 2016; Jagers et al., 2018).

Transformative SEL Implemented Systematically across a Multi-Tiered System of Support (MTSS) Framework

Transformative social-emotional learning is optimized when implemented with fidelity which requires a systemic approach to combat the systemic issues that have been designed to oppress and marginalize students and families, either intentionally or unintentionally (Elias, 2019; Jagers et al., 2019). An MTSS framework is a systemic, continuous-improvement approach in which data-driven problem solving is practiced across all levels of the educational system to support student academics and wellbeing. Specifically, MTSS serves as a prevention-based framework of team-driven data-based decision making for improving the outcomes of every student through family, school, and community partnerships and a layered continuum of evidence-based practices applied at the individual, classroom, school, district, and state level (Eagle et al., 2015; McCart & Choi, 2020). The MTSS framework utilizes high-quality evidence-based instruction, intervention, and assessment practices to ensure educational equity where every student receives the appropriate level of support to be successful in school and beyond. A MTSS framework helps schools and districts organize their resources through alignment of academic standards and behavioral expectations, implemented with fidelity and sustained over time, to enable every child to successfully reach their fullest potential at school (Freeman et al., 2015).

The general MTSS framework structure includes five different elements (Harris, 2020) that can be implemented to meet the needs of marginalized students in a school (see Table 20.1). These five elements can be leveraged to include TSEL at the school and classroom level.

The CASEL has worked closely with US state education agencies (SEAs) to develop policies and practices to facilitate the implementation of TSEL in classrooms, schools, and districts (Yoder et al., 2020). These state collaborations yielded a Theory of Action (TOA) aligned with four focus areas. These focus areas are presented below with a description as to how each is relevant for educators at the classroom and school level.

Area 1: Build Foundational Support and Plan for SEL

Implementing TSEL requires effort and support of an interdisciplinary team of teachers, students, parents, and school staff across all schools in a district. At the district level, there must be a shared commitment to SEL, academics, and equity by creating a shared vision of TSEL as a lever for academic success, meaningful relationships, and workforce development (Yoder et al., 2020). The CASEL recommends building a diverse TSEL team to work collaboratively within the school to build a shared understanding and community surrounding TSEL. When students have social and emotional skill deficits, they may be more likely to engage in disruptive behavior in the classroom (Malti & Song, 2018). Educators and other school staff (e.g., administrators, school security) have a significant level of discretion in the disciplinary process; therefore, it is fundamental that they be included in a TSEL team at their schools to shape the disciplinary measures that are appropriate for the students they serve.

Table 20.1 MTSS Elements

1) A holistic approach to assessment, instruction, and interventions	Using Whole Child measures that have been validated with marginalized populations to analyze academic, behavioral and social–emotional skill development (Darling-Hammond & Cook-Harvey, 2018), a Comprehensive Assessment System to include a variety of assessment tools which allow for prevention and early intervention among marginalized students, and tiered instruction and supports for all students (Tier 1, 2, and 3) to create a system-level approach that aligns student services with student individual need.
2) Cultivating a positive classroom and school climate and culture	Incorporating culturally and linguistically appropriate practices to support marginalized students and their families, focusing on their emotional, physical and mental wellness through a trauma-informed and strengths-based lens, and implementing effective bullying prevention strategies to students both in school and online (Bradshaw et al., 2021).
3) Collaborative stakeholder engagement	Utilizing school-based teams that include a variety of stakeholders engaged in systematic data collection and analysis of trends to implement a system-level strategic action plan that facilitates progress monitoring and responsive intervention implementation. A collaborative and dedicated review of resource allocation should include data-driven decision making around programming, staff, and other resources, along with capacity building and clear communication of expectations to ensure schoolwide buy-in and implementation fidelity.
4) Intentionally integrated infrastructure	Collaborating with various stakeholders to provide professional learning opportunities to facilitate educators in their role supporting students learning and well-being, well-aligned policies, communication and data process procedures that streamline assessment and intervention practices. In addition, intervention and program evaluations are intentionally integrated to ensure practices are effective and sustainable in a specific classroom or school.
5) Student, family, and community partnerships	Including collaborative processes and shared responsibility to extend student support beyond the classroom and school into the family and community. Transparency of progress and goal setting should include parents and communities in data collection and analysis. Student identity, voice, and choice is actively involved to support students as the main stakeholder in their learning, well-being and academic success.

Source: Harris, 2020.

Area 2: Strengthen Adult SEL Competencies and Capacities

The success of implementation and adoption of TSEL hinges on the quality of training, amount of ongoing support, and level of understanding of TSEL by all adults in a school (Yoder et al., 2020). Social-emotional learning in schools is a formal and informal process embedded within relationships between and among students, teachers, and staff. As such, every adult working with the students would benefit from ongoing professional development on TSEL to gain awareness of the benefits of SEL and its important role in education as a lever for equity. At the school level, the transformative SEL team can survey staff to identify what topics staff need support with and distribute schoolwide professional development (PD) on TSEL to all staff. It is critical also for individuals in the educator and school practitioner pipeline (e.g., pre-service teachers and social workers) to be exposed to TSEL throughout their coursework, internships, practicum, and student teaching. Educators and practitioners need to have explicit and consistent instruction on how to build and maintain respectful relationships with colleagues and students. These relationships must embrace individual and cultural similarities and differences through reflexive activities that examine root causes of inequities and collaborate on solutions to address social justice issues (Jagers et al., 2021).

Area 3: Promote SEL for Students

Transformative social-emotional learning can be integrated into the curriculum and schools' educational practices to permeate and abolish systemic inequities. It can be incorporated through both formal and informal interactions with students and will be more successful if it is woven into their overall educational experiences (Ferreira et al., 2020). Support and funding from state and federal agencies for evidence-based SEL programs have grown significantly in the last decade and SEL programming development and implementation are increasing through school-community partnerships (Benavides et al., 2020). These partnerships include youth and family services, afterschool and summer programs, youth leadership initiatives, and community sports and arts programs.

Two common issues with SEL programming are (a) fragmented implementation, and (b) over-focusing on the individuals within classrooms (Jones & Bouffard, 2012). Transformative SEL is most effective and sustainable when it is integrated into academics, promoted in all social interactions, reinforced by daily routines and school structures, and explicitly incorporated into school policies. The primary outcome of TSEL integration is a positive classroom and school climate and comprehensive programming that is delivered sequentially across grade levels and across school settings to intentionally support historically marginalized students.

Area 4: Reflect on Data for Continuous Improvement

Finally, schools need to develop policies, tools, and resources to support successful implementation by collecting and reflecting on data for continual improvement. Transformative SEL programming requires sustained efforts that are adapted as school climates, classrooms, and students need evolve. Creating metrics can help ensure that educators and staff alike do not drift from the established practices and support the goal of continuous improvement through progress monitoring. This includes regular booster training for all staff on how to best relate to students with a variety of identities and needs.

The implementation of TSEL, with a particular emphasis on cultural competence and equity, is essential to the successful academic, social, and emotional development of students. By aligning with these four focus areas, schools can effectively involve a multifaceted team in assessing and addressing needs for TSEL implementation. By educating and including the often-underrepresented staff population (e.g., paraprofessionals, school security, administrators), families and community organizations, schools will have a more balanced perspective about the population of students they serve and can work toward creating meaningful relationships that emphasize inclusion and positive identity formation in every aspect of the educational context. Adults who work with children and adolescents need to have the capacity to analyze historical underpinnings of inequity in education and develop competencies and practices to counteract social -isms (e.g., racism, ableism, sexism, heterosexism, classism) and discrimination in classrooms and communities.

Integrating Data from Multiple Stakeholders to Inform TSEL

Through a TSEL framework, students, families, and communities work together to foster positive change that advances equity and diversity. Research-practice partnerships (RPP) between researchers and local stakeholders such as school administrators, districts, and families can inform the implementation of TSEL in classrooms and schools (Jagers et al., 2021; Oberle et al., 2016; Williams & Jagers, 2020). Collaborative partnerships can be established at every level of a TSEL program from the foundation to include planning, implementation, and continuous improvement phases (Jagers et al., 2021). For programming to be successful in schools and classrooms, it is important to establish clear lines of communication between all stakeholders during the planning stage that continue as the program evolves into the implementation and improvement stages. However, these efforts must go beyond clear communication and must encourage active participation and sharing of responsibilities among diverse stakeholders. Implementation research suggests a framework for active RPP collaboration that includes: (a) a focus on local needs and problems instead of research-centered "best practices"; (b) an active role of practitioners and stakeholders in the program to track continuous improvement; (c) a cyclical process for setting goals, assessing progress, and adjusting action; and (d) encouraging systemic change beyond the classrooms in schools and communities (Jagers et al., 2021; Yurkofsky et al., 2020). Transformative social-emotional learning can draw on these principles to bring together diverse opinions and expertise from a range of stakeholders and practitioners.

Transformative social-emotional learning emphasizes family-school-community partnerships through collective action and systemic change (Jagers et al., 2021). Another purpose of TSEL is to extend the development of social, emotional, and cultural competencies to adults in the social ecosystems of students and their families (Jagers et al., 2021). This work recognizes that SEL does not occur only in schools, and that families and communities are critical in the development and support of TSEL skills reinforced in the classroom. The involvement of families in the SEL development process can enable educators and families to jointly create welcoming learning environments that honor families' funds of knowledge and support their participation as role models and advocates (Jagers et al., 2021). Families and educators can also form authentic partnerships by engaging in discussions and collaborative projects that acknowledge the importance of the home in the development of SEL while recognizing the cultural values of families within their communities and schools.

Participatory action research and student-led project-based learning at the classroom level are also part of the culturally responsive education framework behind TSEL (Jagers et al., 2019, 2021; Larmer et al., 2015). By engaging in service-related activities, collaborative problem-solving, and project-based learning, students can integrate TSEL skills to solve real-world problems that impact them and their communities (Elias et al., 2006). Student agency is further enhanced by these activities, which enable communication and collaboration among culturally diverse students to reach common goals (Jagers et al., 2021). Youth participatory action research is also an important tool to create a sense of cohesion and collaboration between youth and adult facilitators that promote the goals of TSEL (Jagers et al., 2021). The goals of participatory action research include involving youth in the research process and empowering them to use their lived experiences and knowledge to solve issues and problems directly relevant to them. Transformative social-emotional learning as an equity-centered SEL program is a new approach to SEL. Thus, there are no randomized control trials (RCTs) on TSEL programs yet.

The Connection Between TSEL and Classroom Management

This chapter is a follow-up of the contribution on social-emotional learning and classroom management by Schwab and Elias (2015) in the second edition of the *Handbook of Classroom Management*. We are in agreement with Schwab and Elias' "more holistic and student-centered goal for classroom management: to create a classroom environment that fosters students' learning of academic, social, and emotional skills and the ability to put them to positive use in the world around them" (p. 95). While numerous definitions of classroom management have been articulated over the last 50 years, many conceptualizations of classroom management point to the importance of developing and fostering social-emotional competencies in students over the sole focus on controlling student behavior (Schwab & Elias, 2015). For example, Wubbels and colleagues (2015) defined essential features of classroom management as "all teacher and associated cognitions and attitudes involving in creating the social-emotional aspect of the learning environment" (p. 363). These authors argue that SEL is seen not as an add-on to classroom management, but is at the core of effective classroom management. That is, SEL-focused classroom management builds healthy interactions between students and teachers, fosters positive relationships, routines, and processes that are established so everyone feels cared for, respected, and valued. These processes are put into place on the first day of school and reinforced on a daily basis. SEL-focused classroom management involves teaching students how to listen, to respect everyone, to identify and regulate a wide range of emotions, including strong emotions like anger or feeling upset, and to learn effective forms of communication, problem-solving, and decision-making (Schwab & Elias, 2015). When these skills are integrated into the academic content that is required, students have frequent opportunities to practice these skills and learn to see events and situations from more than one perspective, and start to integrate these skills into their own lives and the decisions that they make both academically and socially (Schwab & Elias, 2015).

Schwab and Elias (2015) described four areas of action that demonstrate the integration among SEL, classroom management, and academic learning. First, SEL skills need to be taught explicitly, with opportunity to practice each skill, get feedback, refine the skill, and attempt to generalize the skill to new situations. Second, SEL will be successful as a classroom management tool if skill instruction unfolds with classrooms where caring, supportive relationships exist between teachers and students, and also among students. Third, SEL and classroom management enables the teacher to set and establish firm, fair, and equitable boundaries, and is exactly where TSEL can inform efforts to address inequities in the classroom. Finally, teachers need to assume responsibility with the students as partners in creating caring relationships among all members of the classroom. This could be as simple as creating classroom norms centered around respectful, inclusive behaviors and attitudes.

It is also important that teachers strive to develop their own SEL competencies while demonstrating these skills to their students. Teachers with high SEL competencies have a higher degree of self-awareness, are better able to recognize their own emotional strengths and weaknesses, and how their emotions impact students around them (Jennings & Greenberg, 2009). When teachers are aware of and can regulate their own emotional reactions they are better able to cope with professional demands, have lower levels of burnout, and stress which is conducive to more effective classroom management practices (Brackett et al., 2010).

Teachers with high SEL skills are also culturally sensitive, aware of power imbalances in the classroom and how language and cultural barriers may affect student interactions. As part of culturally sensitive pedagogy, instructors address how their own cultural values and biases influence how they engage with students (Weinstein et al., 2014). Another aspect is learning about students' cultural backgrounds and offering a curriculum that is relevant to their lives and experiences (Skiba et al., 2016). Teachers who remain abreast of the larger societal context and how it uniquely impacts students from minoritized backgrounds are also better equipped to recognize discriminatory incidents and take appropriate action (Skiba et al., 2016).

It is crucial that teachers are provided with professional development that provides explicit training about how to develop their own SEL competencies and how to integrate them into their instructional practices (Murano et al., 2019). However, teachers often report not receiving sufficient training in SEL competencies or SEL informed classroom management strategies (Schonert-Reichl et al., 2015). Providing early and ongoing TSEL professional development for teachers, especially within a culturally sensitive classroom management approach, can be an effective strategy to foster a positive classroom climate and teacher–student relationships.

Strategies in TSEL for Classroom Management and Restorative Justice

Historically, schools in the U.S. have reinforced inequitable social structures by supporting ableist, middle-class American culture and offering culturally relevant education for White middle-income children and youth (Jagers et al., 2019). Students who diverge from this normative standard, such as those from diverse cultural and linguistic backgrounds as well as those with disabilities often experience unreasonably low expectations, microaggressions, discrimination, and implicit biases from peers and adults (Allen et al., 2013; Skiba et al., 2011). These experiences at school reproduce and exacerbate existing educational, social, and economic inequities that threaten the physical and psychological safety of all students. In addition to the aforementioned inequitable social structures that exist within schools, there has also been an overreliance on traditionally punitive disciplinary measures that disproportionately impact students of color and students with disabilities (Gregory et al., 2018). Transformative social-emotional learning and restorative justice can be used for classroom management.

Restorative justice (RJ) in classrooms is a process that is based on creating and repairing relationships, rather than enforcing rules and punishments. Restorative practices are designed to teach empathy and understanding, as well as to respond to conflict by empowering those who cause harm to make things right, and in the process, support the healing of those who were harmed (Gregory et al., 2016; Song et al., 2020). On the other hand, traditional punitive discipline reacts to conflict by excluding students and using rewards to gain compliance to school rules. Traditional punitive discipline does not prepare youth with the SEL skills needed to be successful in school and beyond. Conflict and disruptive behaviors approached through restorative practices can be opportunities for TSEL. To implement RJ in the classroom requires a careful examination and deconstruction of the power dynamics between teachers, administrators, school staff, and students (Morrison & Vaandering, 2012). This cultural shift allows for the democratization of power and the recognition of the agency and dignity of students through the use of narratives that separate the individuals from the problem being addressed (Cohen, 2018). To prevent inflicting harm, students are required to have self-awareness, self-control, and an awareness of how they affect others. This is difficult for young people because their brains are not fully developed and even more difficult among those who have experienced Adverse Childhood Experiences (ACEs). To enable self-control is to promote empathy and compassion which are generated in a supportive and caring environment. Caring classroom and school climates can provide students, especially those from marginalized identities, the opportunity to heal from discrimination, generational trauma, and develop their social and emotional skills (Cohen, 2018).

Some strategies for RJ in the classroom include circles, conversations, mediations, and conferences (Anfara et al., 2013). Circles are collective sessions that allow for students to be heard, learn to listen and understand others. Teachers can introduce check-in circles at the beginning or end of the school day to give students a chance to get in touch with their feelings and, if difficulties are occurring in their lives, to speak their troubles into existence. If the student sees the circle from a mindfulness perspective, a safe non-judgmental space (Anfara et al., 2013), they can feel safe to speak their mind. Given that many children do not have these safe spaces at home, schools can provide them a place to process challenges while also learning they are not alone and that their peers and teachers also experience hardship. It is possible that at first, some students may feel reluctant to speak up, but with time and practice, students can begin to trust and feel empathy toward themselves, their peers, and their teacher. For some students, circles may be the first time they have dealt with conflict or stress in this way, and potentially the first time they have felt supported in their efforts to cope. Circles help students strengthen their social and emotional skills while talking through stressors and negative experiences (Cohen, 2018).

Conversations are private discussions held between a student and a teacher or administrator to uncover personal problems that may not feel appropriate to share in public spaces like circles (Erb & Erb, 2018). Conversations allow for deeper and often more personal reflections while promoting trust and mutual respect. Educators and other school staff can help validate student feelings and help them understand that they are not the problem, rather the problem is the problem. Asking students about their lives outside of school and having a conversation around their problems and coping strategies can reinforce that the student has the ability, or can at least work on their ability, to cope with their problems in healthy ways. In this restorative practice, the teacher can assist the student with positive emotional development, interpersonal skills, and distress tolerance. During conversations, teachers, administrators, and supportive school staff need to be aware of how trauma, cultural values, and different ways of expressing emotions impact students' learning styles and behaviors (Cohen, 2018).

Mediations are smaller circles that take place when others are harmed (Johnson & Johnson, 2012; Payne & Welch, 2015). The students involved and a mediator who is a trained teacher, student or administrator participate objectively to facilitate a discussion on what preceded the incident, the incident and how all the students involved have been affected (e.g., physically, socially and/or emotionally) (Payne & Welch, 2015). By guiding the discussion with empathy and understanding, as opposed to shame and blame, the message to all students involved should be that what happened was the problem rather than internalizing that they are the problem as well as ensuring that every student feels like the mediator cares about their wellbeing. This type of interaction works best when it has previously been reinforced by earlier circle or conversation practices and within a school climate that encourages a growth mindset and restorative justice. As in all restorative practices, trust and understanding can be established by always focusing on the "problem" not the person. By focusing on the problem in this way, it is easier for students to take responsibility for the harm caused without making demoralizing self-judgments about perpetration and/or victimization. Mediators can lead the students involved into an exercise that delineates the students' strengths and abilities to resolve past, present and future problems in a non-aggressive manner. This strategy can empower students to take responsibility, not out of fear of punishment, but out of the realization that they can manage their thoughts, feelings and behaviors. In short, a common understanding is achieved by first naming the problem, deconstructing the problem (the context), and formulating appropriate outcomes for conflict resolution (Cohen, 2018).

Conferences are in response to more severe harm or repetitive patterns of harm or if the student has been suspended or incarcerated and returning to school (Morrison et al., 2005). Conferences are spaces where family members and other supportive people can facilitate a discussion with both the party(s) harmed and the party(s) causing the harm. This responsive and collaborative practice, like all restorative practices, focuses on the relational situation where all individuals are respected and listened to. Because the focus is not on blame, nor is the result motivated by fear of punishment, those causing harm can be empowered to become part of the solution and be accountable for their behavior. Conferences provide the opportunity for all parties to heal from an incident. As in conversations and mediations, relying on externalizing practices, deconstruction, and searching for appropriate outcomes, those who caused or experienced harm can begin to see negative behaviors and experiences as just that, behaviors and experiences that exist separate from themselves. Once the behavior and experience are separated, they are less likely to internalize it and can see themselves and others as individuals with the agency to make better choices (Cohen, 2018).

The shift from punitive to restorative practices in schools and districts is increasing at varying speeds and modalities across the country, but a few states (e.g., California, Colorado, Illinois, Minnesota, and Pennsylvania) have been implementing restorative practice for several years and have developed large-scale programs to determine efficacy. Darling-Hammond et al. (2020) conducted a recent review of research published since 1999 on the effectiveness of RJ in K-12, US schools. Their review included studies which utilized quantitative methods (e.g., regression analyses, nonparametric models, t-tests, and analyses of variance) to measure the effectiveness of RJ on student and school-level outcomes including student misbehavior, exclusionary discipline, bullying, racial discipline disparities, student attendance, school climate, and academics. The bulk of extant RJ studies are correlational in nature and thus causal inferences cannot be drawn. However, nearly all the empirical studies reviewed from the past two decades reported a decrease in exclusionary discipline and youth violence after implementing a RJ program. Augustine et al. (2018) indicated a statistically significant reduction (16%) in days lost to suspension after RJ implementation. Goldys (2016) reported a 55% decrease in office referrals after implementing an RJ program at an elementary school.

There is a dearth of research that has directly examined the effect of RJ on bullying, but extant literature is mixed (Darling-Hammond et al., 2020). Acosta et al. (2019) conducted an RCT with seven middle schools in Maine and found no statistically significant difference on bullying outcomes between the RJ program and control group. However, students with more exposure to RJ did experience statistically significantly less physical and cyber bullying. The research on the effect of RJ at reducing racial discipline disparities is also mixed but is largely supported as effective. Augustine et al. (2018) found that RJ implementation led to reduction in the racial discipline gap between Black and White students in an RCT with 22 intervention and 22 control schools. Gregory et al. (2018) analyzed Denver public school data and found that suspension rates decreased for all racial categories and that the discipline gap between Black and White students lowered from 9% to 5% after implementing RJ throughout the district. However, another study in a large urban school district (Anyon et al., 2016), found that although discipline rates decreased overall, the racial discipline gap did not.

Across studies, the effectiveness of RJ on school attendance is supported (Darling-Hammond et al., 2020). Baker (2009) reported that students who experienced at least three RJ interventions during the school year had a 50% decrease in absenteeism and a 64% decrease in tardiness during the first year of implementation. Similarly, Jain et al. (2014) found that Oakland (CA) middle schools that implemented RJ reported a 24% decrease in absenteeism and schools not implementing RJ reported a 62.3% increase in absenteeism during the same period. Although the evidence is limited, there are studies that suggest that RJ improves school climate and safety. Augustine et al. (2018) found that RJ practices were associated with a statistically significant increase in teachers' perception of school climate. However, while Acosta et al. (2019) did not find a statistically significant improvement in school climate after RJ implementation, they did find that students who experienced more RJ practices reported statistically significantly higher levels of school connectedness, positive peer relations, and peer attachment.

The effectiveness of RJ on academics is also mixed but largely in favor of RJ practices. Jain et al. (2014) found that Oakland (CA) schools implementing RJ had (a) reading levels increase by 128% over three years compared to schools without RJ which increased only by 11% over the same time frame; (b) four-year graduation rates increased by 60% in RJ schools while it only increased by 7% in non-RJ schools; and (c) high school dropout rates decreased by 56% in RJ high schools compared to 17% in non-RJ high schools. Armour (2014) examined middle schools and found that 6th graders exposed to RJ for a year improved standardized reading scores by 11% and math scores by 13%. The academic improvements in the study were most significant among marginalized students: Black students (8% increase), Hispanic students (13% increase) economically disadvantaged students (13% increase), and among students in special education who increased significantly in both reading (42%) and math (50%) scores. However, Augustine et al. (2018) found that RJ did *not* have a positive impact on reading and math scores and, instead, was associated with reductions in elementary and middle school math outcomes and particularly worse academic outcomes for Black elementary and middle school students. Given the variability in implementation of RJ in schools, and the variability of US school contexts and the limitations of the reported research designs, RJ still provides a promising strategy for schools and districts.

When K-12 classroom disruption occurs, teachers have the power to utilize restorative practices as effective prevention and intervention strategies to not only restore justice but to also allow students to strengthen their social and emotional skills. Transformative social–emotional learning focuses on equity by addressing issues of culture, identity, agency, belonging, and engagement. Cultivating a positive classroom environment and school climate assists students in viewing their problems as things they can change and solve rather than viewing problems and conflict as part of who they are. Every student has the ability to make prosocial and positive choices, but it is the responsibility of the adults who support them to foster these spaces that enable them to do so.

Next Steps

In the past few years, there has been increased attention in the field of SEL to implement TSEL in K–12 settings to promote academic and social development and to create safe classrooms for all students, teachers, and paraprofessionals. However, most of the empirical literature in support of SEL in K-12 settings has not focused on evaluating the value-added of a transformative approach or lens. So, first and foremost, concerted efforts must be made to deliberately develop and evaluate integration or adaptation of transformative approaches to SEL. As TSEL is simply a lens by which curricula and other approaches are delivered, it would be important for scholars and clinicians to document how best to adopt this lens and support the fidelity of programming.

In addition, evaluations of TSEL must begin having conversations about how to augment current SEL measures and assessments to capture the transformative aspects of programs and approaches. It would also be important to identify barriers to implementation and scaling-up of efficacious approaches (Elias, 2019). More than ever, it is important to also attend to the social-emotional competencies of adults in K-12 settings that spend time with students. It is imperative that this training is informed by researchers and practitioners and offered in colleges and universities. Pre-service teacher training programs need to infuse discussions of TSEL in their educator preparation programs and continue post-graduation in the induction and retention phases through ongoing professional development and communities of practice on TSEL (Schonert-Reichl, 2019). The work does not stop with pre-service teachers and should also include administrators, school counselors, social workers, and psychologists (Bowers et al., 2017).

References

Acosta, J., Chinman, M., Ebener, P., Malone, P. S., Phillips, A., & Wilks, A. (2019). Evaluation of a whole-school change intervention: findings from a two-year cluster-randomized trial of the restorative practices intervention. *Journal of Youth and Adolescence, 48*, 876–890. https://doi.org/10.1007/s10964-019-01013-2.

Allen, A., Scott, L. M., & Lewis, C. W. (2013). Racial microaggressions and African American and Hispanic Students in urban schools: A call for culturally affirming education. *Interdisciplinary Journal of Teaching and Learning, 3*(2), 117–129.

Anfara Jr, V. A., Evans, K. R., & Lester, J. N. (2013). Restorative justice in education: What we know so far. *Middle School Journal, 44*(5), 57–63.

Anyon, Y., Gregory, A., Stone, S., Farrar, J., Jenson, J. M., McQueen, J., Downing, B., Greer, E., & Simmons, J. (2016). Restorative interventions and school discipline sanctions in a large urban school district. *American Educational Research Journal, 53*(6), 1663–1697. https://doi.org/10.3102/0002831216675719.

Armour, M. (2014). *Ed White Middle School restorative discipline evaluation: implementation and impact, 2012/2013 sixth & seventh grade.* The Institute for Restorative Justice and Restorative Dialogue. Retrieved from http://sites.utexas.edu/irjrd/ files/2016/01/Year-2-Final-EW-Report.pdf

The Aspen Education & Society Program and the Council of Chief State School Officers (2017). *Leading for equity: Opportunities for state education chiefs.* Washington, D.C.

Augustine, C. H., Engberg, J., Grimm, G. E., Lee, E., Wang, E. L., Christianson, K., & Joseph, A. A. (2018). *Can restorative practices improve school climate and curb suspensions? An evaluation of the impact of restorative practices in a mid-sized urban school district.* RAND Corporation. www.rand.org/pubs/research_reports/RR2840.html

Baker, M. (2009). *DPS Restorative Justice Project: year three.* Denver Public Schools.

Benavides, V., Meghjee, S., Johnson, T., Joshi, A., Ortiz, C., & Rivera, V. (2020). Social and emotional learning in afterschool settings: Equity evaluations, recommendations, and critiques. *Afterschool Matters, 33*, 1–8.

Bowers, H., Lemberger-Truelove, M. E., & Brigman, G. (2017). A social-emotional leadership framework for school counselors. *Professional School Counseling, 21*(1b), 1–10.

Brackett, M. A., Palomera, R., Mojsa-Kaja, J., Reyes, M. R., & Salovey, P. (2010). Emotion-regulation ability, burnout, and job satisfaction among British secondary-school teachers. *Psychology in the Schools, 47*(4), 406–417.

Bradshaw, C. P., Cohen, J., Espelage, D. L., & Nation, M. (2021). Addressing school safety through comprehensive school climate approaches. *School Psychology Review, 50*(2–3), 221–236.

Camangian, P., & Cariaga, S. (2021). Social and emotional learning is hegemonic miseducation: Students deserve humanization instead. *Race Ethnicity and Education*, 1–21. https://doi.org/10.1080/13613324.2020.1798374

Cohen, R. (2018). The transformative nature of restorative narrative justice in schools. *Journal for Leadership, Equity, and Research, 4*(1), 1–11. Retrieved from https://journals-sfu-ca.libproxy.lib.unc.edu/cvj/index.php/cvj/article/view/37

Corcoran, R. P., Cheung, A. C., Kim, E., & Xie, C. (2018). Effective universal school-based social and emotional learning programs for improving academic achievement: A systematic review and meta-analysis of 50 years of research. *Educational Research Review, 25*, 56–72.

Darling-Hammond, L., & Cook-Harvey, C. M. (2018). *Educating the whole child: Improving school climate to support student success.* Learning Policy Institute. Retrieved from https://learningpolicyinstitute.org/product/educating-whole-child

Darling-Hammond, S., Fronius, T. A., Sutherland, H., Guckenburg, S., Petrosino, A., & Hurley, N. (2020). Effectiveness of restorative justice in US K–12 schools: A review of quantitative research. *Contemporary School Psychology, 24*, 295–308.

Durlak, J. A., Weissberg, R. P., Dymnicki, A. B., Taylor, R. D., & Schellinger, K. B. (2011). The impact of enhancing students' social and emotional learning: A meta-analysis of school-based universal interventions. *Child Development, 82*(1), 405–432.

Eagle, J. W., Dowd-Eagle, S. E., Snyder, A., & Holtzman, E. G. (2015). Implementing a multi-tiered system of support (MTSS): Collaboration between school psychologists and administrators to promote systems-level change. *Journal of Educational and Psychological Consultation, 25*(2–3), 160–177.

Elias, M. J. (2019). What if the doors of every schoolhouse opened to social-emotional learning tomorrow: Reflections on how to feasibly scale up high-quality SEL. *Educational Psychologist, 54*(3), 233–245.

Elias, M. J., O'Brien, M. U., & Weissberg, R. P. (2006). Transformative leadership for social-emotional learning. *Principal Leadership, 7*(4), 10–13.

Erb, C. S., & Erb, P. (2018). Making amends: A restorative justice approach to classroom behavior. *Teacher Educators' Journal, 11*, 91–104.

Ferreira, M., Martinsone, B., & Talić, S. (2020). Promoting sustainable Social-emotional Learning at school through relationship-centered learning environment, teaching methods and formative assessment. *Journal of Teacher Education for Sustainability, 22*(1), 21–36.

Freeman, R., Miller, D., & Newcomer, L. (2015). Integration of academic and behavioral MTSS at the district level using implementation science. *Learning Disabilities: A Contemporary Journal, 13*(1), 59–72.

Goldys, P. (2016). Restorative practices: from candy and punishment to celebration and problem-solving circles. *Journal of Character Education, 12*(1), 75–80.

Gregory, A., Clawson, K., Davis, A., & Gerewitz, J. (2016). The promise of restorative practices to transform teacher-student relationships and achieve equity in school discipline. *Journal of Educational and Psychological Consultation, 26*(4), 325–353.

Gregory, A., Huang, F. L., Anyon, Y., Greer, E., & Downing, B. (2018). An examination of restorative interventions and racial equity in out-of-school suspensions. *School Psychology Review, 47*(2), 167–182.

Harris, J. (2020, January 16). What is MTSS? How to Explain MTSS to Almost Anyone. Illuminate Education. www.illuminateed.com/blog/2020/01/what-is-mtss-education/

Hoffman, D. M. (2009). Reflecting on social-emotional learning: A critical perspective on trends in the United States. *Review of Educational Research, 79*(2), 533–556.

Jagers, R. J. (2016). Framing social and emotional learning among African-American youth. *Human Development, 59*(1), 1–3.

Jagers, R. J., Rivas-Drake, D., & Borowski, T. (2018). Equity and social and emotional learning: A cultural analysis. CASEL.

Jagers, R. J., Rivas-Drake, D., & Williams, B. (2019). Transformative social and emotional learning (SEL): Toward SEL in service of educational equity and excellence. *Educational Psychologist, 54*(3), 162–184.

Jagers, R. J., Skoog-Hoffman, A., Barthelus, B., & Schlund, J. (2021). Transformative social and emotional learning in pursuit of educational equity and excellence. *American Educator, 6*(2021), 7.

Jain, S., Bassey, H., Brown, M., & Kalra, P. (2014). *Restorative justice in Oakland schools: implementation and impacts.* Oakland Unified School District. Retrieved from www.ousd.org/cms/lib/CA01001176/Centricity/Domain/134/OUSD-RJ%20Report% 20revised%20Final.pdf

Jennings, P. A., & Greenberg, M. T. (2009). The prosocial classroom: Teacher social and emotional competence in relation to student and classroom outcomes. *Review of Educational Research, 79*(1), 491–525.

Johnson, D. W., & Johnson, R. T. (2012). Restorative justice in the classroom: Necessary roles of cooperative context, constructive conflict, and civic values. *Negotiation and Conflict Management Research, 5*(1), 4–28.

Jones, S. M., & Bouffard, S. M. (2012). Social and Emotional Learning in schools from programs to strategies. *Social Policy Report, 26*(4), 1–33.

Jones, S., Brush, K., Bailey, R., Brion-Meisels, G., McIntyre, J., Kahn, J., ... & Stickle, L. (2017). Navigating SEL from the inside out. *Looking Inside and Across, 25*, 1–328.

Kennedy, K. (2019). Centering equity and caring in leadership for social-emotional learning: Toward a conceptual framework for diverse learners. *Journal of School Leadership, 29*(6), 473–492.

Larmer, J., Mergendoller, J. R., & Boss, S. (2015). Gold standard PBL: Essential project design elements. *Buck Institute for Education*, 1–4.

Malti, T., & Song, J-H. (2018). Social-emotional development and aggression. In *Handbook of Child and Adolescent Aggression* (pp. 127–144). Guilford Press.

McCart, A. B., & Choi, J. H. (2020). State-wide social and emotional learning embedded within equity-based MTSS: Impact on student academic outcomes. Research Brief. *SWIFT Education Center*.

Morrison, B., Blood, P., & Thorsborne, M. (2005). Practicing restorative justice in school communities: Addressing the challenge of culture change. *Public Organization Review, 5*(4), 335–357.

Morrison, B. E., & Vaandering, D. (2012). Restorative justice: Pedagogy, praxis, and discipline. *Journal of School Violence, 11*(2), 138–155.

Murano, D., Way, J. D., Martin, J. E., Walton, K. E., Anguiano-Carrasco, C., & Burrus, J. (2019). The need for high-quality pre-service and inservice teacher training in social and emotional learning. *Journal of Research in Innovative Teaching & Learning, 12*(2), 111–113.

Oberle, E., Domitrovich, C. E., Meyers, D. C., & Weissberg, R. P. (2016). Establishing systemic social and emotional learning approaches in schools: A framework for schoolwide implementation. *Cambridge Journal of Education, 46*(3), 277–297.

Payne, A. A., & Welch, K. (2015). Restorative justice in schools: The influence of race on restorative discipline. *Youth & Society, 47*(4), 539–564.

Schonert-Reichl, K. A. (2019). Advancements in the landscape of social and emotional learning and emerging topics on the horizon. *Educational Psychologist, 54*(3), 222–232.

Schonert-Reichl, K. A., Hanson-Peterson, J. L., & Hymel, S. (2015). SEL and preservice teacher education. In Durlak, J. A., Domitrovich, C.E., Weissberg, R.P., & Gullotta, T.P. (Eds.), *Handbook of social and emotional learning: Research and practice*, 406–421. Guildford.

Shriver, T. P., & Weissberg, R. P. (2020). *A response to constructive criticism of social and emotional learning.* Retrieved from https://kappanonline.org/response-constructive-criticism-social-emotional-learning-sel-shriver-weissberg/

Schwab, Y., & Elias, M. J. (2015). From compliance to responsibility: Social-emotional learning and classroom management. In E. T. Emmer & E. J. Sarbonie (Eds.), *Handbook of classroom management* (pp. 94–115). Routledge.

Simmons, D. (2019). Why we can't afford whitewashed social-emotional learning. *ASCD Education Update, 61*(4), 2–3. Retrieved from www.ascd.org/publications/newsletters/education_update/apr19/vol61/num04/Why _We_Can't_Afford_Whitewashed_Social-Emotional_Learning.aspx

Skiba, R. J., Horner, R. H., Chung, C. G., Rausch, M. K., May, S. L., & Tobin, T. (2011). Race is not neutral: A national investigation of African American and Latino disproportionality in school discipline. *School Psychology Review, 40*(1), 85–107.

Skiba, R., Ormiston, H., Martinez, S., & Cummings, J. (2016). Teaching the social curriculum: Classroom management as behavioral instruction. *Theory Into Practice, 55*(2), 120–128.

Song, S.Y., Eddy, J. M., Thompson, H. M., Adams, B., & Beskow, J. (2020). Restorative consultation in schools: A systematic review and call for restorative justice science to promote anti-Racism and social justice. *Journal of Educational and Psychological Consultation, 30*(4), 462–476.

Taylor, R. D., Oberle, E., Durlak, J. A., & Weissberg, R. P. (2017). Promoting positive youth development through school-based social and emotional learning interventions: A meta-analysis of follow-up effects. *Child Development, 88*(4), 1156–1171.

Weinstein, C. S., Tomlinson-Clarke, S., & Curran, M. (2004). Toward a conception of culturally responsive classroom management. *Journal of Teacher Education, 55*(1), 25–38.

Weissberg, R. P., Caplan, M. Z., & Sivo, P. J. (1989). A new conceptual framework for establishing school-based social competence promotion programs. In L. A. Bond & B. E. Compas (Eds.), *Primary prevention and promotion in the schools* (pp. 255–296). Sage Publications, Inc.

Williams, B. V., & Jagers, R. J. (2020). Transformative social and emotional learning: Work notes on an action research agenda. *Urban Education.* https://doi.org/10.1177/0042085920933340

Wubbels, T., Brekelmans, M., Brok, P. den, Wijsman, L., Mainhard, T., & Tartwijk, J. van. (2015). Teacher–student relationships and classroom management. In E. T. Emmer & E. J. Sarbonie (Eds.), *Handbook of classroom management* (pp. 363–386). Routledge.

Yoder, N. Dusenbury, L., Martinez-Black, T., & Weissberg, R. P. (2020). *State education agency theory of action.* Collaborative for Academic, Social, and Emotional Learning, Chicago, IL.

Yurkofsky, M. M., Peterson, A. J., Mehta, J. D., Horwitz-Willis, R., & Frumin, K. M. (2020). Research on continuous improvement: Exploring the complexities of managing educational change. *Review of Research in Education, 44*(1), 403–433.

21

CLASSROOM MANAGEMENT AT DIFFERENT TIMESCALES

An Interpersonal Perspective

Theo Wubbels

UTRECHT UNIVERSITY

Tim Mainhard

LEIDEN UNIVERSITY

Perry den Brok

WAGENINGEN UNIVERSITY AND RESEARCH

Luce Claessens

UTRECHT UNIVERSITY

Jan van Tartwijk

UTRECHT UNIVERSITY

Introduction

In the chapter "An Interpersonal Perspective on Classroom Management in Secondary Classrooms in the Netherlands," in the first edition of the Handbook of Classroom Management, (Wubbels, Brekelmans et al., 2006), we and our colleagues described an interpersonal approach to classroom management and summarized research findings.[1] The interpersonal approach analyses teaching, and more specifically classroom management, in terms of the relationships and interactions between teachers and their students.

In the present chapter, we review and summarize the considerable amount of research that has been carried out on classroom management from an interpersonal perspective since 2006 and show how interpersonal dynamics between teachers and students can be understood and described at different timescales: at the level of moment-to-moment interactions, at the level of relationships developing over weeks and months and at the level of a teacher's professional life. We start this chapter with an introduction of the basic concepts and mechanisms of interpersonal theory and its application to teaching and classroom management. We also describe how using concepts derived

DOI: 10.4324/9781003275312-25

from social dynamic systems theory can help understand how teacher and student behaviors feed into classroom interactions and are associated with teacher-student relationships (TSRs), and with a teacher's interpersonal style, which develops over the teacher's professional life.

We are aware that there is a lot of research based on perspectives like the interpersonal perspective that have results adjacent to the studies we summarize in this chapter. Because of space limitations we confine this chapter to research from an interpersonal perspective.

Concepts and Mechanisms

Interpersonal Theory

Interpersonal theory describes the perceptions of behavior of persons in the vicinity of others (Horowitz & Strack, 2011). A basic premise of this theory is that all interpersonal behavior can be described along two orthogonal dimensions, together forming the basis of a circular structure (e.g., Gurtman, 2009; Leary, 1957; Sadler et al., 2011). Depending on the context (e.g., psychiatry, family, education) the dimensions are designated differently with "agency" and "communion" as meta-level labels (Fournier et al., 2011; Gurtman, 2009). Agency refers to someone who is individuated, dominant, and strives for power and control, whereas communion means someone is social, and strives for union, friendliness, and affiliation (Gurtman, 2009). Each behavior communicates inter-personal messages with a specific blend of agency and communion. Thus, all behaviors people might show during interactions can be ordered along the circumference of the circular structure, referred to as the interpersonal circle (IPC, see Figure 21.1). When teachers, for example, are perceived as behaving "compliant," their behavior conveys relatively little agency and moderately high commu-nion. Compliant behavior has some similar qualities to behavior that is perceived as understanding (positive communion) and uncertain behaviors (low agency) and therefore these behaviors are close to each other on the IPC. Further, behaviors that are perceived as very agentic and communicating moderately low communion, can be qualified as "imposing" and have an opposite position at a max-imum distance from each other on the IPC.

Figure 21.1 (left) shows how we currently refer to the dimensions and eight positions along the circumference of the IPC, when we use it to describe teacher behavior from an interpersonal per-spective. Wubbels et al. (2012) explained how and why changes in the labels occurred over time. The words on the IPC are prototypical and should be understood as placeholders of similar behaviors. For example, the label "directing" for behavior is very similar to concepts such as "structuring" or "leading" that therefore also could have been used as labels. A similar IPC can be used for describing student behavior from an interpersonal perspective (Figure 21.1, right). Some student labels differ from the teacher IPC labels because some of these teacher labels are not terms that are commonly used to describe student behaviors, for example, for high agency and moderately low teacher behavior we use "imposing" whereas for students we use "critical." However, the underlying circular structure is universal for describing the interpersonal meaning of behavior.

Social Dynamic Systems: Behavior, Interaction, and Relationships

In their bio-ecological theory, Bronfenbrenner and Morris (1998) describe how interaction (the moment-to-moment timescale) is the primary engine of development, and therefore the basis for macro-social outcomes on a longer timescale. When applying this to the context of the classroom, this means that teacher-student interactions, which can be conceptualized as exchanges of inter-personal messages through behavior, are underlying characteristics of the classroom social climate and TSRs, teacher job satisfaction, and student emotional wellbeing. Any human development can be viewed as being hierarchically nested in time, and interactions can be regarded as the building blocks of relationships (Granic & Hollenstein, 2003). In this dynamic process, interactions not only

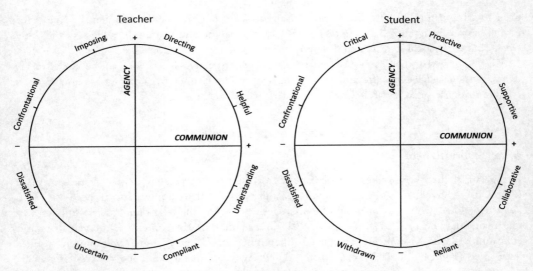

Figure 21.1 The Interpersonal Circle (IPC) for the Teacher (left) and for the Student (right)
Source: Pennings et al., 2018

form, renegotiate and change relationships, but relationships also constrain real-time processes such as interactions (Hollenstein & Lewis, 2006; Mainhard et al., 2012). In classrooms, the typical teacher and student roles as well as the nature of specific TSRs, make certain interactions and interpersonal behaviors more likely than others. For example, in a "cold" TSR, interactions are likely to be more hostile than friendly and at the same time such hostile interactions perpetuate a cold relationship. Relationships become manifest in recurring patterns of classroom interactions.

Figure 21.2 visualizes how the different aspects of TSRs can be understood as being nested in each other. At the core of social classroom processes lie behaviors which convey interpersonal messages. Interpersonal messages can be communicated with words, but also nonverbally, e.g., through facial expressions, body posture, gestures, distance to others, gaze, voice volume and intonations (van Tartwijk, 1993; van Tartwijk et al., 2010). These verbal and nonverbal behaviors happen from moment to moment and together form a stream of actions of teacher or student. These behaviors are embedded in teacher-student interaction, which can be regarded as an integrated moment-to-moment stream of actions and reactions. Interactions, in turn, are situated in the context of (dyadic) TSRs which represent the *generalized* perceptions a teacher may have of the interactions with a specific student (or classroom group: teacher-class relationship) or a student may have of the interactions with a specific teacher. Together, all the relationships in a classroom can be understood as the building blocks of the classroom social climate. More technically, the classroom social climate can be viewed as the average or shared student perception across several lessons and students. Relationships, on the other hand, also include the idiosyncratic way a student views the teacher, for example as being more friendly or less imposing than most other students view the teacher (Mainhard et al., 2018). Finally, the way teachers tend to teach all their classes represents the teacher interpersonal style. A teacher's interpersonal style can, for instance, be assessed by averaging student perceptions of the teacher's agency and communion over several lessons and for several groups of students. A teacher's interpersonal style can be considered as a rather stable trait, which does develop slowly over a teacher's professional life. Lower levels in the scheme (e.g., behavior) are more dynamic than higher levels (e.g., the classroom climate or teacher style). In dynamic systems thinking, adjacent levels or timescales are independent as explained above, for the reciprocal dependency of teacher-student interactions and TSRs.

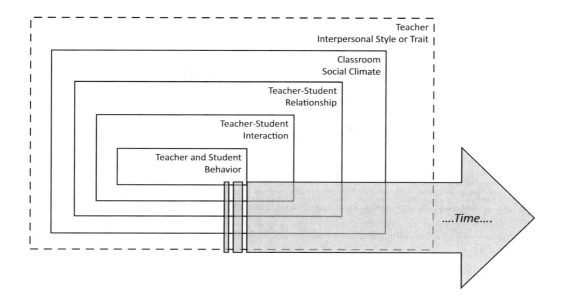

Note. Adjacent levels are interdependent and lower levels change and develop faster than higher levels.

Figure 21.2   Levels and Components of Teacher–Student Variables

In the remainder of this chapter, we highlight classroom management from an interpersonal perspective in terms of three timescales. First, we focus on teacher–student interactions, then on relationships and the classroom social climate, and finally on changes in interactions and relationships and during teachers' professional lives.

Teacher-Student Interactions

Measurement and Representation

To map teacher–student interactions in terms of the IPC for the teacher and for the student (Figure 21.1), Mainhard et al. (2012), following earlier work by van Tartwijk et al. (1998), rated teacher and student agency and communion on a five-point scale and the combination of these scores defined the position in the circle. van Tartwijk et al. (1998) scored behavior per eight-second fragments, while Mainhard et al. (2012) rated every change that occurred in either student or teacher agency or communion. There are two methodological innovations that made the study and visualization of classroom interactions from an interpersonal perspective more accessible, and which sparked new lines of study.

Most importantly, Sadler et al. (2009) innovated the observation of interpersonal interaction. Rather than summarizing entire lessons or larger periods of time (e.g., Pianta et al., 2008), they developed an observational method for coding videotaped interpersonal behaviors in terms of agency and communion continuously from moment-to-moment (Continuous Assessment of Interpersonal Dynamics, CAID). While observing a person, the researcher moves a joystick device over the interpersonal circle and agency and communion values are automatically stored twice per second, resulting in a stream of changing agency and communion values. The coding for classroom observations is done separately for the teacher and the class. This method made it possible to quantify interactions and study the nature of interactions directly. Questions that can be studied, for instance, are: how variable is teacher behavior; how are teacher and student behaviors aligned interpersonally; and how are interactions and relationships interrelated?

It should be emphasized that what trained observers register when using CAID to code classroom interaction is not the same as what students perceive and what teachers report about themselves (Donker et al., 2021). While teacher agency is relatively similar from these three perspectives, observers, students, and teachers agree to a lesser degree on the level of teacher communion. Specifically, what observers register in terms of communion while watching a classroom video differ from teachers' self-perceived communion.

A second innovation was the introduction of the State Space Grid (SSG) by Hollenstein and colleagues (Hollenstein, 2013; Lamey et al., 2004). SSGs allow a researcher to visualize and summarize data from continuous behavior observation of two parties in an interaction. A certain behavior exhibited during interaction is called a state and the set of all possible behaviors is referred to as the state space. Originally developed to capture child–parent interactions, SSGs have also been used to describe classroom interaction (Mainhard et al., 2012; Pennings & Mainhard, 2016; Turner & Christensen, 2020; Pennings & Hollenstein, 2020). With SSGs it is possible, for example, to make the differences in interactional patterns of two classrooms tangible. Figure 21.3 depicts communion during the interaction between teacher and class in two different classrooms. Communion is scaled to run from 1 to 5 for both the class and the teacher (Mainhard et al., 2012). Each dot in the grid represents a specific combination of teacher and class communion; the larger the dot, the longer the interaction resided in this specific state. The lines represent the sequence of the interactions over time. While the interaction in the left panel is rather stable and concentrates on states that represent intermediate high teacher and student communion (states 3,3 and 4,3), the interaction in the other classroom is clearly more variable and dispersed over the entire state space grid. In this classroom, states involving low teacher communion occur more frequently. While the climate in the classroom depicted in the left panel could be described as mellow and friendly with only few and short instances where the teacher corrects student behavior, the climate in the other classroom is at times clearly positive as well; nonetheless, also negative interactions occur frequently, which contribute to an overall more chaotic atmosphere.

In sum, CAID and SSGs make it possible to study not only the interpersonal content of interactions (i.e., the levels of agency and communion) but also the variability and predictability of classroom interaction (Mainhard et al., 2012).

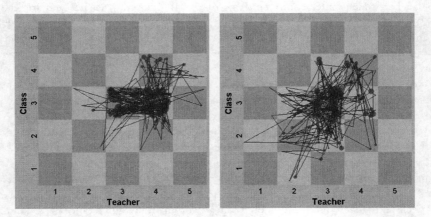

Figure 21.3 Example of two State Space Grids for Teacher and Student Communion in Different Classrooms
Source: Mainhard et al., 2012

The General Classroom Climate and the Nature of Classroom Interaction

In line with general expectations of teachers in their professional role, teachers usually refrain from hostility and subordinate behavior in class (Pennings et al., 2018). The level of agency and communion teachers exhibit in class during interaction corresponds to how their students perceive them on a more general level (i.e., the TSR as assessed with the QTI), with moderate correlations for both agency and communion (e.g., Donker et al., 2021; Pennings & Hollenstein, 2020).

In addition, there is a clear tendency of teachers with less preferred classroom climates (i.e., relatively low levels of agency and communion in the TSR, see Wubbels, Brekelmans et al., 2006) to also show more variable interpersonal behavior (Mainhard et al., 2012; Pennings & Hollenstein, 2020). In class, when teachers move often between different levels of agency and communion, this seems to indicate more chaotic teacher behavior and a more chaotic classroom social climate with more frequent and more pronounced negative interaction sequences (i.e., low teacher communion; Mainhard et al., 2012).

Adaptation of Teacher and Student Behavior

Next to studying how agency and communion of teachers and students during interaction relate to the classroom climate and the nature of TSRs, the way teachers and students adapt their interpersonal behavior to each other can be studied. We present two examples: interpersonal complementarity and answering the question: who is following who?

Teacher-Student Adaptation and Interpersonal Complementarity

A core concept of interpersonal theory is complementarity (Carson, 1969; Horowitz & Strack, 2011). This principle states that if someone shows high levels of communion, the most likely reaction of interaction partners is reciprocated high levels of communion. That is, it is very hard to be hostile with someone who is genuinely friendly. On the other hand, the more agentic (i.e., dominant) one interaction partner is, the more likely it is that the other will respond in a submissive way (and vice versa).

A general assumption of interpersonal theory is that more complementary interactions will result in more positive relationships (Kiesler, 1996; Sadler et al., 2009). Indeed, also in classrooms this seems to be the case (Pennings et al., 2018; Roorda et al., 2011). Figure 21.4 depicts two time series that summarize the first ten minutes of a lesson of teacher and student agency (upper panel) and communion (lower panel). These time series represent highly complementary interactions. The communion time series of teacher and class are highly positively correlated and follow each other closely over time. The agency time series are highly negatively correlated: Whenever a teacher or students take on an agentic position, the other is more subordinate.

Pennings et al. (2018) showed that most non-complementary interaction occurs in classrooms with less preferred climates. There is however also evidence for an important exception: teachers who according to their students have relatively more agency and communion, are more likely to remain agentic and friendly in the face of negative or dissatisfied student behavior (i.e., a non-complementary reaction). Of the 35 teachers included in their study, about two thirds refrained from hostile behavior in the face of hostile student behavior and did not react subordinately when confronted with dominant student behavior. This means that these teachers were able to break unfavorable patterns of complementary interactions. It is noteworthy that such a reaction (staying high on communion and agency) also implies less variable teacher behavior. Students, on the other hand, seem to accommodate more readily with a teacher's agency when the teacher is also more friendly (Pennings et al., 2018; Thijs et al., 2011). That is, students are more likely to show subordinate behaviors as a response

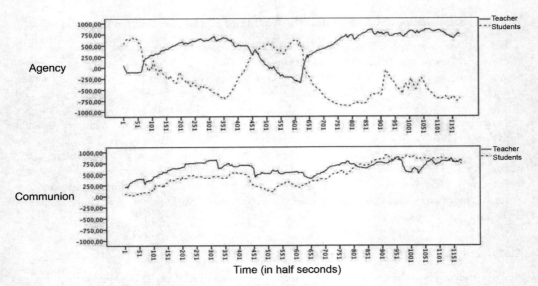

Figure 21.4 Teacher and Student Behaviors in Complementary Relationships
Source: Pennings et al., 2018

to teacher agency when they perceive the TSR as generally positive and warm (i.e., as high on communion; see also Roorda et al., 2013).

Regarding classroom management, an unfriendly or impatient reaction towards a student with low motivation or who is dissatisfied, would be complementary and at the same time, it would be unproductive. In the case of such a complementary reaction, student and teacher can be expected to get caught in negative interaction cycles, because unfriendly behavior invites more unfriendly behavior. However, an agentic and positive teacher reply that is genuinely friendly and offers behavioral alternatives to the student may invite the student to become more cooperative as well.

Teacher-Student Adaptation: Who Is Following Who?

An interesting question is whether teachers or students are in the lead during classroom interaction. Do teachers high on agency cause low student agency, or do students low on agency invite the teacher to be high on agency? Similarly, do teachers become angry because of a bid of student misbehavior or the other way around? In a study by Pennings et al. (2018) classrooms had a varied pattern regarding who was leading the interactions during the lesson start. In classrooms with more preferred interpersonal classroom climates, teachers were more often leading on agency (overall, 17% of the studied classrooms teachers were leading in agency). In the kindergarten setting, Roorda et al. (2011) found that children were more inclined to respond in friendly ways to teacher's communion than teachers were inclined to do so as a response to student communion. For agency, this pattern was reversed. However, in more positive TSRs, children were inclined to behave more subordinately when the teachers increased their agency.

Context and Teacher-Student Interaction

In the 2006 edition of the Handbook of Classroom Management, Doyle (2006) described an ecological perspective to classroom management. In this perspective, the context of the classroom is considered a habitat or "behavioral setting" with specific features and "programs of action" that structure interactions. Other contexts in education, for instance teachers meeting students in the informal settings of the school corridors or during field trips, can also be regarded as behavioral settings with their own programs of actions.

Within the classroom behavioral setting, more specific settings can be distinguished that each have their own programs of action. Examples of such settings are common classroom activities such as lecturing, recitation, seatwork, and the lesson start and transitions between lesson phases. According to Doyle (2006), order in the classroom means that students are following the program of action of that particular classroom activity. This implies that the interpersonal meaning of specific teacher or student (nonverbal) behavior may differ depending on the classroom activity in which it is situated. van Tartwijk et al. (1998) studied associations between teacher agency in the TSRs with the level of agency communicated through teacher behavior during whole class teaching and group work. Only teacher agency in behavior during whole class teaching turned out to be predictive for students' perceptions of teacher agency in the TSR. Van Tartwijk et al. (2010) also compared the association between the relative frequency of teacher nonverbal behavior during various classroom activities with students' perceptions of their relationship with their teacher. They found that this association was quite different within various classroom activities. They, for instance, established a strong correlation between student perceptions of teacher communion in the TSR and their teachers' frequency of smiling or laughing during informal situations (e.g., when students are entering the classroom). However, no correlation was found during whole class teaching of non-verbal behaviors and communion perceptions.

Research investigating the interpersonal significance of teacher-student interactions outside the classroom is scarce. A noteworthy exception is research by Claessens et al. (2017). They interviewed 28 teachers about the quality of their relationships with specific students. It turned out that teachers define the quality of these relationship mostly by the level of communion in the TSR. In teachers' perceptions, positive and problematic relationships also differed with the context where interactions take place and the topic of the interaction. Contrary to interactions in problematic TSRs, interactions in positive relationships were mostly situated outside the classroom context and conversations during these encounters covered a wide range of topics.

All these studies point at the importance of considering the context when studying the interpersonal significance of (non-)verbal behavior and of the character of teacher-student interactions.

Outcomes and Teacher and Student Interaction

Student Behavior

How teachers and students interact is related to students' engagement with their classwork. In a study with 179 kindergartners, Roorda et al. (2017) coded teacher and student behavior in small group interaction. They found that teacher agency was associated with child engagement and task performance, while the teacher's communion was largely unrelated to the children's behavior, possibly due to ceiling effects in teacher communion. Interestingly, the more subordinate teachers behaved while children took on a more agentic role (i.e., the stronger complementarity was in these situations), the better children performed. This latter finding may be due to an overlap between the agency and engagement constructs, which both imply active involvement and may result in better performance. In another article on the same sample, Roorda et al. (2013) studied how teachers behaved differently with children showing relatively more internalizing or externalizing behaviors than their peers. As expected, teachers were more friendly and agentic with children showing internalizing behavior. While children with externalizing behavior problems showed no less communion or friendliness towards their teachers, they nonetheless were treated in less friendly ways by their teachers. Apparently, it is more difficult for teachers to show communion towards children with externalizing than with internalizing problems.

Teacher Emotional Responses

Classroom interaction and negative TSRs can be the cause of considerable teacher stress and negative emotions (Skaalvik & Skaalvik, 2015). While for most teachers lecturing in front of the class goes together with extra alertness, teachers differ largely in what kind of interpersonal interaction and student behavior they experience as stressful (Junker et al., 2021).

To understand how classroom interaction and teachers' emotions and wellbeing are intertwined, Donker and colleagues (Donker, Erisman et al., 2020; Donker, van Gog et al., 2020; Donker et al., 2018) not only used questionnaires on teacher emotions, but also assessed heart rate to pinpoint moments during the lesson that teachers experienced as important and potentially stressful. Heart rate is increasingly used as indicator of psychological phenomena such as emotions and psychological arousal (Cacioppo et al., 2017; Ebner-Priemer & Kubiak, 2007; Mauss & Robinson, 2009). An increased heart rate is not so much an indicator of positive or negative emotions, but signals personal importance, urgency, or task engagement. Figure 21.5 illustrates the heart rate every 5 seconds in combination with a teacher's interpersonal behavior during one entire lesson. The more agency the teacher showed in class, the higher this teacher's heart rate tended to be (r.=.68), and the more communion this teacher showed, the more relaxed this teacher was (i.e., a lower heart rate; r.= -.65) (Donker, Van Gog et al., 2020).

Importantly, the association between teachers' heart rate and their interpersonal behavior is linked to how teachers feel about their teaching. The higher a teacher's heart rate is during moments of friendly and communal behavior, the more teachers are inclined to report stress and disappointment about their lesson. On the other hand, a positive association between teacher agency and teacher heart rate was linked to more positive teacher emotions and satisfaction (Donker, Erisman et al., 2020).

From a classroom management perspective, this result may indicate that teachers compare their own behavior to what they think is desired classroom behavior (Barber et al., 2011; Chang & Davis, 2009; Hagenauer & Volet, 2014). Showing friendly behavior while being stressed may trigger what is referred to as emotional labor (Keller et al., 2014), because teachers feel compelled to act friendly while actually not feeling friendly. Regarding agency, apparently being able to take the lead in class despite a certain level of stress or arousal may reflect a mastery experience and as

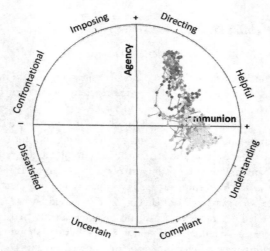

Figure 21.5 Dots Representing Heart Rate Values with Corresponding Interpersonal Behavior During an Entire Lesson. The Darker the Dot, the Higher the Heart rate at that Moment.

Source: Donker, Van Gog et al., 2020

a result, teachers may feel good about having been able to meet a challenge. Generally, teachers with, according to students, more agency in class also report lower levels of emotional exhaustion (Donker, Van Gog et al., 2020). Divoll and Ribeiro (2021) provide strategies to help teachers overcome emotional stress.

Culture and Classroom Interaction

What we discussed so far mostly stems from research in western classrooms, but there are indications that similar teacher behaviors may convey different interpersonal meanings in different cultures. A few studies directly compared interpersonal processes in Western and East Asian classrooms (McIntyre et al., 2017, 2020; Sun et al., 2018). For example, in Chinese classrooms, "the acceptance of the legitimacy of hierarchy and the valuing of perseverance and thrift" (Franke et al., 1991, p. 167) may be more pronounced and students may expect and at the same time accept more agentic teacher behavior (Wei et al., 2009, 2015). Indeed, in Chinese classrooms teachers frequently showed agentic behavior and there were only very few or no instances of low agency, which do occur frequently in western classrooms. At the same time, teacher behavior was also perceived as being relatively communal or friendly which resembled teacher behavior in the western context. Overall, Chinese teachers showed more stable and predictable behavior than western teachers, mostly due to the lack of subordinate behaviors (Sun et al., 2018).

McIntyre et al. (2020) used eye-tracking glasses during real-life classes to investigate the association between teacher gaze and TSRs. Generally, teachers had more agency according to students when they maintained eye contact with students while asking questions. Eye contact during lecturing, on the other hand, was associated with teacher communion. Interestingly, and against what could be expected (see for example Hofstede, 1986; Miellet et al., 2013), McIntyre et al. (2020) did not find any differences between UK and Hong Kong teachers in the effect of their gaze: making eye contact had a similar effect in all classrooms.

Thus, concerning classroom management, what works in western settings at least to some degree may be transferable to other cultural settings.

Interaction in Multicultural Classrooms

Research was also carried out into what interaction strategies are effective when teaching in multicultural classrooms. It seems that the multicultural classroom puts heavier demands on teachers' interpersonal competence than a less diverse classroom (Wubbels, den Brok et al., 2006). This research was carried out in the Netherlands among teachers who were considered experts in classroom management by their principals and their students (van Tartwijk et al., 2009). Although these teachers were aware of the importance of providing clear rules and correcting student behavior whenever necessary, they also felt the need to reduce potential negative influences of correcting undesirable student behavior on the classroom social climate. To do this, they used strategies such as using small rather than intense corrections, use humor to make corrections less grave, and use rational rather than power arguments. They also invested in getting to know students better and in building positive personal relationships with students.

Most of these Dutch expert teachers seemed reluctant to refer to the cultural and ethnic background of their students and they presented themselves as "color blind" (cf. Milner, 2006). Van Tartwijk et al. (2009) attributed this to the dominant discourse in Dutch society at that time, in which it was regarded inappropriate to take students' cultural or ethnic background into consideration when discussing student misbehavior, because this might reinforce prejudice. This is quite different from the dominant discourse in the USA where teachers are urged to be aware of and respond to their students' ethnic and cultural characteristics (Brown, 2003).

Teacher-Student Relationships and the Classroom Social Climate

In this section, we first describe how students' and teachers' perceptions of the TSR can be assessed with the Questionnaire on Teacher Interaction. Subsequently, we review research on associations of the TSRs with other student, teacher and class variables. Then we describe research on how TSRs can change from lesson to lesson.

Measurement

Teachers' and students' perceptions of the TSR can be measured with the Questionnaire on Teacher Interaction (QTI) (see Wubbels & Levy, 1991). Over the years the QTI has been translated into many different languages and has been used in several countries and cultural contexts (see for some of the most recent adaptations: China, Sun et al., 2018; Greece, Charalampous & Kokkinos, 2013, Kyriakides, 2006; Indonesia, Maulana et al., 2012; Iran, Safa & Doosti, 2017; Italy, Passini et al., 2015; Malaysia, Jailani & Abdullah, 2019; Pakistan, Bahoo et al., 2020; Saudi Arabia, AlDhafiri, 2015; Slovakia, Brestovanský, 2020; Spain, García Bacete et al., 2014; Thailand, Santiboon & Ekakul, 2017; Turkey, Telli et al., 2007). In addition to the original version developed for secondary education, there are versions for primary (e.g., Charalampous & Kokkinos, 2013; Zijlstra et al., 2013) and higher education (e.g., Laudadío & Mazzitelli, 2018; Mainhard et al., 2009) and for the measurement of the relationship during specific situations (e.g., Mainhard et al., 2014).

The items of the QTI are divided into eight scales corresponding with eight octants of the IPC depicted in Figure 21.6. Based on these scale scores, agency and communion dimension scores can be calculated (Wubbels & Brekelmans, 2005). The questionnaire can be used to assess students' perceptions of their relationship with their teacher (i.e., the degree of agency and communion a teacher usually conveys in class) and to measure teachers' self-perceptions and teacher ideals.

Studies on the reliability and validity of the QTI (e.g., den Brok, Fisher et al., 2006; den Brok, Brekelmans et al., 2006; Fulmer & Lang, 2015; Passini et al., 2015; Sivan et al., 2017) usually show

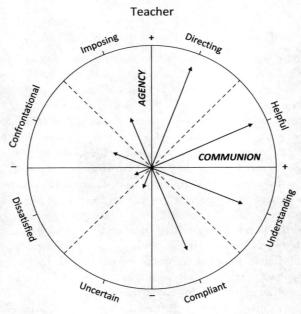

Figure 21.6   QTI Scores in the IPC's Octants
Source: after Brekelmans, 1989

acceptable to good reliability of the scales and dimensions at the student level and good to excellent reliabilities at the class level. Regarding the circular structure of the model for the QTI, in most cases adjacent scales have the highest positive correlations, whereas diametrically opposite scales the highest negative ones (Charalampous et al., 2016). Testing of the assumption that the scales are ordered in a circumplex structure usually shows a fit of a circular model, but the scales are not ordered equi-distantly on a circle (Wubbels et al., 2012). Especially with younger students, there is a tendency for more differentiation in the student perceptions on the communion than the agency dimension (Zijlstra et al., 2013). Furthermore, the structure differs slightly across countries (e.g., den Brok, Fisher et al., 2006) and these between-country differences might reflect different meanings or connotations attached to the words describing TSRs (see Hui & Triandis, 1985).

Teacher and Student Outcomes and Teacher-Student Relationships

Since the first edition of the Handbook of Classroom Management appeared in 2006 (Everston & Weinstein, 2006), a wealth of studies has been published on associations between student or teacher perceptions of the TSR, gathered with the QTI, and other student, class, or teacher variables. Because of the scarcity of longitudinal and experimental studies that would allow for more causal inferences, we present what we call correlates of TSRs. Further, many studies have investigated the associations in terms of the eight QTI scales or octant scores. Because of the theoretically assumed and empirically confirmed collinearity between the scales (Wubbels, Brekelmans et al., 2006) it is preferable to use the statistically independent measures of agency and communion, and therefore we only included studies referring to these two dimensions or using just one or two sub-scales. Many studies did not report effect sizes, but sometimes we were able to estimate these from the results.

Student Variables

STUDENT BACKGROUND CHARACTERISTICS

Student gender is related to students' perceptions of their teacher's agency and communion; girls generally perceive more teacher agency and communion than boys, although effect sizes are small (Charalampous & Kokkinos, 2014; de Jong et al., 2014; den Brok et al., 2009; den Brok, Taconis, & Fisher, 2010; Fisher et al., 2006). One study (den Brok, Taconis, & Fisher, 2010) reported that younger students experienced less teacher communion than older students, while other studies (den Brok et al., 2009) found that older students saw less agency. Indicating cultural differences, den Brok and Levy (2005) showed in a meta-analysis that students in the USA and Australia, with a background from non-western countries, reported more teacher agency than students originating from the majority, western culture. According to Fisher et al. (2006), Australian students who do not speak English at home perceived lower agency and communion in the TSR. On the other hand, the same study reported that when students' mothers were from Southeast Asia, they perceived higher agency in their teachers. In a study in the Netherlands, den Brok et al. (2009) found that Moroccan students perceived their teachers higher on agency than students from other countries. Students with a Surinamese background perceived their teachers relatively higher on communion.

In Greece, Charampolous and Kokkinos (2014) investigated associations between student person-ality and their perceptions of the TSR and math achievement. Student extraversion was positively, and neuroticism negatively related to student perceived teacher communion. The association of extraver-sion with the TSR positively mediated the relationship between student extraversion and their math achievement. In China, Wang et al. (2020) found that student emotional intelligence was negatively related to teacher communion. Finally, students' parental attachment perceptions (Charalampous et al., 2016) were associated with the perception of the relationship with their teacher. The more students felt trust in and communication with their parents and the lower their alienation from their parents, the more they perceived communion in the relationship with their teachers.

STUDENT ACHIEVEMENT

In the 2006 presentation of work regarding the QTI, we concluded that higher student cognitive and affective outcomes were associated with students' perceptions of high teacher agency and communion (Wubbels, Brekelmans et al., 2006). Since then, also in other studies in several countries, generally positive associations have been reported between students' perceptions of teacher agency and communion and student achievement, with slightly stronger associations for the communion dimension (Ethiopia: Gedamu & Shure, 2015; Greece: Charalampous & Kokkinos, 2014, 2018; Kyriakides, 2006; Italy: Molinari et al., 2013; Malaysia: Jailani & Abdullah, 2019). In the United Kingdom (Creech & Hallam, 2011) and in Spain (García Bacete & Rosel Remírez, 2021) only associations were found with communion. In the latter study, the relationship was partly mediated by achievement motivation. In all, it seems that the 2006 conclusions that higher student cognitive and affective outcomes are associated with students' perceptions of high teacher agency and communion still holds today. However, it should be noted that the effect sizes are generally small. An exception is a study by Slof et al. (2016) that reported no association between student achievement and teacher interpersonal relationships in computer-supported collaborative learning environments. The different character of such an environment might well explain the different result.

Differential effects of TSRs on student achievement and attitudes have been reported for students with different ethnic backgrounds in the Netherlands. Overall, the positive effects of both teacher agency and communion on student outcomes was larger for students with parents born in non-western countries than for students whose parents were born in the Netherlands (den Brok, van Tartwijk et al., 2010). Thus, it can be concluded that the TSR is more important for students with a non-Dutch background than for students with a Dutch background, and it appeared also more for second-generation than for first-generation immigrant students. For these students, the TSR may function as a protective factor (Roorda et al., 2017) that, for example, is needed because of lower parent support at home for these students.

STUDENT ATTITUDES AND EMOTIONS

It was consistently found across countries that student motivation and emotions (e.g., attitude toward the teacher, lesson or subject matter, enjoyment, attitude toward inquiry in project work, peer relations, school attachment, and school adjustment) were positively related to the students' perceptions of teacher agency and communion, again, with usually stronger associations for communion than for agency (Australia: Fisher et al., 2006; China: Wei et al., 2009; Greece: Kyriakides, 2006; Indonesia: Maulana et al., 2011, 2012, 2014; Italy: Molinari et al., 2013; Netherlands: Hendrickxs et al., 2016; Hopman et al., 2018, van Uden et al., 2014; Turkey: Telli et al., 2010, with an exception for career interest; UK: Creech & Hallam, 2011; USA: Tyler et al., 2016).

More specifically, Wijsman et al. (2014) reported for a Dutch sample, that although at the individual level the relationship between teacher agency and communion and student-controlled motivation could vary between classes, generally there was a positive relationship of controlled motivation with agency and a negative association with communion, which was positively related to autonomous motivation. In another longitudinal study in the Netherlands, Opdenakker et al. (2012) found indications for a relationship between TSRs and student autonomous motivation, but not controlled motivation. So, these two studies report mixed results. Research in Turkey (Telli, 2016) showed a differential effect across subjects taught by the teacher. Whereas agency was positively related to student motivation in sciences and literature and languages, it was unrelated for arts and sports. Communion, however, was positively related to motivation in all four subject areas.

Some studies investigated the association between TSRs and student achievement goals, i.e., approach and avoidance goals that both can be oriented toward mastery or performance (Elliot, 1999). Shukla et al. (2020), in a large study in India with two measurement occasions, showed that student self-efficacy and mastery goal orientation were influenced negatively by low teacher communion, specifically the degree of perceived teacher confrontation and dissatisfaction, with about 25% of the variance in goals explained. Other scales of the QTI were not included. In a study by Mainhard (2015), a considerable amount of variance in student achievement goals was related to the students' perceived teacher communion and agency, with a positive relationship of agency and a negative relationship of communion with approach goals. This relationship was found for students' individual perceptions of teacher agency and communion, and for the difference with a student's perception with the class mean of the students' perception. Personally liking a generally tough teacher added the most to mastery approach goals. In general, perceiving more agency combined with communion in teachers was positively associated with approach goals. Regarding avoidance goals, next to generally being perceived as high on agency and a bit low on communion was related to stronger mastery avoidance. Mainhard (2015) concluded that:

> It is not simply perceiving support that connects to a student's goals; whether the teacher substantiates support with relatively high levels of agency is also important. In general, low agency adds to avoidance goals, and high agency adds to approach goals whereas communion is positively associated with approach goals and negatively associated with avoidance goals.
>
> *p. 570*

Regarding student emotions, we finally highlight two studies on student enjoyment and anxiety. In a Dutch study, Mainhard et al. (2018) reported that perceived teacher agency and communion were positively related to student enjoyment and negatively to student anxiety with a stronger association for communion. The amounts of explained variance were 45% for enjoyment and 20% for anxiety. These results were corroborated in a Chinese sample by Sun et al. (2020). Additionally, student boredom was negatively related to teacher communion. An interaction effect between agency and communion on enjoyment and anxiety indicated that the two interpersonal dimensions strengthened each other's effect.

STUDENT BEHAVIOR

Studies on student behavior and the TSR from an interpersonal perspective are relatively scarce. Student bullying and victimization were associated negatively only with teacher communion and peer trust and peer communication were positively related to teacher communion. Effect sizes were rather small. Van Aalst et al. (2021) investigated teacher communion and corroborated the finding of a negative association with bullying and victimization. Regarding student problem behavior, negative associations between boys' externalizing problem behavior and teacher communion were found in special education (Hopman et al., 2019). Agency and communion were negatively related to students' behavioral, emotional and social problems (Poulou, 2014) and positively to prosocial behavior (Hendrickx et al., 2016). Glock and Pit-ten Cate (2021) investigated student teachers' intended behaviors toward fictious students presented to them. These students differed in being placed in special education or not, and having internalizing or externalizing problem behaviors. The student teachers wanted to show more intense behavior in all octants of the IPC for students placed in special education and with externalizing problematic behavior. This is a surprising outcome because usually when on certain scales teachers behave or want to behave more, they want to show less behavior on octants placed opposite in the model (i.e., if one intends to be more imposing, this usually entails also being less compliant).

Class Variables

Class-level variables have been studied far less than individual student characteristics. Studies including class level variables generally take into account the nested character of data (students in classes in schools) by performing multilevel analyses. The higher the class achievement level, the more students see teacher communion (García Bacete & Rosel Remírez, 2021). The lower the ratio between boys and girls, the more students perceive agency and communion (Fisher et al., 2006). Regarding class size, the bigger a class, the less teacher agency is perceived by students (Fisher et al., 2006) and for the ratio of student ethnicity, the more non-native speakers in a class, the more teacher agency tends to be reported (Fisher et al., 2006). Similarly, in the Netherlands den Brok et al. (2009) found that teachers in multi-ethnic classes were perceived as being higher on agency and communion compared to teachers in more homogeneous classes.

Teaching and Teacher Variables

Associations between students' perceptions of the curricular orientation in the lessons and teacher agency and communion were studied by Overman et al. (2014). Students in "knowledge development chemistry-based" chemistry classrooms perceived their teachers as having less agency than students in traditional chemistry classrooms. Students in "chemistry technology and society-based" classrooms perceived their teachers as being lower on communion than students in traditional classrooms.

Regarding the subject taught, Telli (2016) found no relationship with students' perceptions of agency and communion. den Brok, Taconis, and Fisher (2010), however, reported students' perceptions of agency and communion to be slightly lower for science teachers, in line with Fisher et al. (2006) who found lower communion scores for science teachers as compared to other teachers. Moreover, for teachers' self-perceptions, few differences across subjects were found (Fisher et al., 2006).

For teacher educators in Iran, Khodamorado et al. (2020) reported strong negative associations of student teacher personality (neuroticism and conscientiousness) with student perceptions of communion and positive associations of communion with agreeableness. These associations were weaker for teacher self-perceptions of agency and communion. However, De Jong et al. (2014) reported no relationship of teacher personality (extraversion and agreeableness) and student perceptions of teacher agency and communion. Regarding teachers' moral beliefs, paternalist beliefs were shown to be positively related to teachers' self-perception of their agency while liberal beliefs were negatively related with students' perceptions of teachers' communion (Pantić & Wubbels, 2012). Thus, all in all results on teachers' beliefs and personality are mixed.

Also, for teacher self-efficacy, results on associations with the TSR are mixed. Van Uden et al. (2013) found positive associations between teacher self-perceived agency and communion and their self-efficacy, but Hopman et al. (2018) found no such associations with students' perceptions. Veldman et al. (2017) reported that teacher self-efficacy was related positively to the degree of realization of their ideals for agency and communion (the difference between their self-perception and ideal of the TSR). Teacher self-perceived teaching competence (van Uden et al., 2013) and the students' perceived teacher's use of complex instructional strategies (van der Lans et al., 2020) were positively related to the levels of agency and communion in the TSR.

Associations between TSRs and teacher job satisfaction consistently point to good relationships concurring with high job satisfaction (Spilt et al., 2011). Admiraal et al. (2019) showed a positive relationship of teacher job satisfaction with the quality of the TSR and Hopman et al. (2018) reported communion to be negatively related to later emotional exhaustion. Veldman et al. (2016) found that the smaller the distance between teachers' ideals and their self-perception of the TSR, the higher their job satisfaction, i.e., the more they felt they realized their ideal the higher their job satisfaction was. Korthagen and Evelein (2016) reported on the association between teacher-perceived needs fulfillment (need for competence, relatedness, and autonomy) and the TSR. Overall, they found a positive association between agency and communion and the degree of needs fulfillment. An exception was that fulfillment of autonomy was negatively related to the degree of agency.

Regarding teacher disciplinary actions, student-perceived teacher punishment and recognition of students were both positively related to teacher agency, and the latter also to communion (de Jong et al., 2014). Aggression was negatively related to both agency and communion and punishment was negatively associated with communion.

Reflections on Teacher-Student Relationships Studies

There is a wealth of evidence for associations between student, class, and teacher characteristics with the TSR. The outcomes of studies generally support each other, but there are a few areas where results are mixed, for example about teacher personality. The associations of student perceptions with student and class variables alert researchers not to interpret student perceptions too easily as the general view of a class. Although most effect sizes are small, class perceptions may be influenced by student characteristics.

Most of the studies on associations of TSRs with other variables are correlational in origin and therefore do not allow for causal inferences. For some variables (e.g., gender or ethnicity), causality might be plausible, but it cannot be ruled out that a third variable explains the association. For example, student enjoyment of a lesson might be higher for girls than boys and thus explain that female students see higher teacher communion than boys in the TSR. Also, this association between enjoyment and teacher communion can be interpreted in two different ways: positive student enjoyment of lessons could provide high teacher communion or a high communal TSR might lead to high student enjoyment.

Reflecting on the methods used in QTI studies, we can conclude that considerable progress has been made in the way data are analyzed. Whereas to take the nested character of data in consideration, before 2006 data often were analyzed separately at the individual and the class or teacher level, now multilevel analyses are quite common to cater for the nested structure of data and simultaneously analyze effects on student and class or teacher level. The amount of variance is usually much larger on the student than the class level and at the teacher and school level much smaller than the class level. For example, Fisher et al. (2006) reported about 2/3 of the variance to be at the student and 1/3 at the class level with a very small amount at the school level.

Despite this progress, several points need to be considered for strengthening the results. First, because of the collinearity of the QTI scales it is essential to include dimension scores in the analyses. Second, to investigate causality in the associations between TSR and other variables, longitudinal studies are asked for. Finally, there is a need for the use of valid achievement outcome measures instead of the often-used teacher grades or student-perceived outcomes.

Changes in Teacher-Student Relationships over Time

Overall, the nature of the classroom social climate and TSRs are rather stable over time (Wubbels, Brekelmans et al., 2006). At the same time, not all lessons are the same, and not all students perceive the teacher similarly in every lesson. In the area of classroom management, thinking in terms of changes from lesson to lesson was first highlighted when Evertson and Veldman (1981) reported on the changes in the quality of classroom management over the course of a school year. They saw an increase in misbehavior among students and a decrease in the time students spent on their tasks but also noted that "although life in classrooms deteriorated towards the end of the year, these changes were not dramatic" (p. 162). Patrick, Ryan, and colleagues (Patrick et al., 2003; Ryan & Patrick, 2001) focused more specifically on interpersonal aspects of teaching. Their general conclusion was that student perceptions of teacher support remain rather stable over time: teachers who showed more support and care at the start of a school year had also a more positive classroom climate later on.

Two separate studies looked specifically at the development of teacher agency and communion from lesson to lesson in new secondary schools (Mainhard, Brekelmans, den Brok & Wubbels, 2011; Opdenakker et al., 2012). By using multilevel growth modelling, these studies were able to provide a more intimate picture of change.

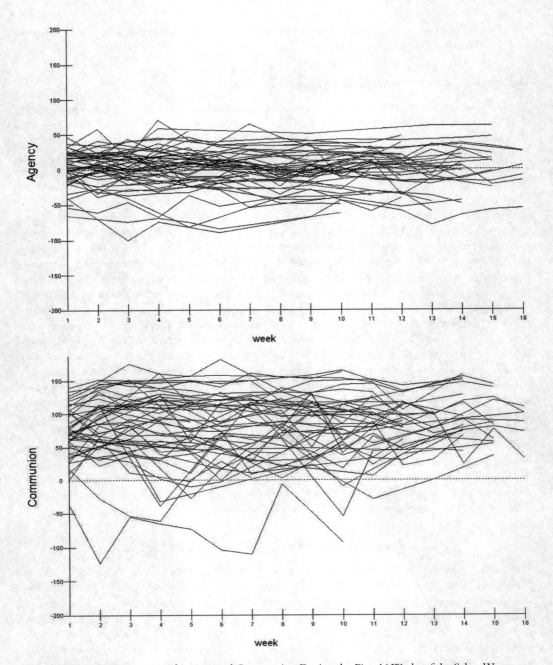

Figure 21.7 Raw Trajectories of Agency and Communion During the First 16 Weeks of the School Year
Source: Adapted from Mainhard, Brekelmans, den Brok & Wubbels, 2011

Mainhard, Brekelmans, den Brok and Wubbels (2011) also found the general theme of stability of the classroom social climate. They assessed teacher agency and communion in 48 classrooms on a weekly basis for 16 weeks starting from the first lesson at the start of the school year. Overall, the nature of the classroom climate during the first lesson was like that in all other lessons with correlations around .80. Nonetheless, when looking at what happened in these classrooms from week to week, it is clear that much is going on. Figure 21.7 depicts the raw trajectories.

What is clearly visible, is that, according to students, teachers differed more in terms of communion (lower panel) than in terms of agency (upper panel). Also, it is visible that within a classroom rather pronounced differences from lesson to lesson could occur; again, this was more pronounced for communion. Thus, the general finding of stability at the level of the sample is clearly not an adequate description of what happened within each of the classrooms. Indeed, about one third of the variability in agency and communion was due to weekly changes. On the other hand, this change was not systematic, and the classroom climate quality had no clear tendency to increase or decrease over time. Interestingly, for teachers with classroom climates characterized by relatively lower agency and communion at the end of the first lesson, it was more likely that agency and communion would further decline.

Diverting somewhat more from the general findings of stability, Opdenakker and colleagues (2012) found that agency and communion of 20 middle school teachers decreased steadily over the course of the school year. The decrease was more pronounced for communion than for agency, and for such teachers a bad start predicted a stronger subsequent decline in agency and communion.

An interesting question is if what happens during class affects changes in the quality of the TSR and the classroom social climate. Mainhard and colleagues (Mainhard, Brekelmans & Wubbels, 2011) used teacher coercion (yelling, using punishment or sarcasm) and interpersonal support to understand possible links between teacher behavior and the general classroom climate. Both teacher coercion and support in a lesson were clearly related to student-perceived teacher communion in that same lesson, and in the lesson one week later. Interestingly, coercion did not help to increase teacher agency, while increasing agency may be the primary reason for teachers to engage in coercion. In fact, two consecutive lessons with teacher coercion were associated with decreased teacher agency according to students. This result is in line with work of Lewis et al. (2005) and Miller et al. (2000) which suggests that teacher coercion does not help to confine student misbehavior but may in fact even further increase this.

Overall, these findings have implications for teachers and their classroom management. A continuous negative classroom climate, characterized by both low teacher agency and communion, is likely to hamper a positive development of students in class. First of all, it is not likely that TSRs and the classroom climate as such will improve during the course of a school year, despite (sometimes pronounced) differences between single lessons of teachers. Being more stern and even coercive will almost certainly further deteriorate teacher communion, while it is unlikely to help establishing teacher agency and authority. Investing in positive relationships from day one on and in a clear structure for students (agency) is key. For student-teaching placement in teacher education it might be important to consider that a continuous negative classroom climate may hamper student-teachers' development of classroom management competencies. Therefore, if things get too tough for a student teacher in the TSR, it may be advisable to change student-teaching classes. Indeed, especially for early career teachers, the classroom climate quality may differ largely between classrooms (Mainhard et al., 2018), and thus changing to a different class, ideally in combination with strong behavioral support, could be beneficial.

It is sometimes concluded that, based on the findings of relative stability of the classroom social climate, the first impression a teacher makes in class is crucial for the subsequent quality of the classroom social climate (c.f., Everston & Emmer, 1982; Hargreaves, 1972; Patrick et al., 2003). This conclusion is however somewhat questionable, because it is not clear whether a causal relation exists between the nature of interpersonal teacher behavior during the first and subsequent lessons. The first lesson is just (or already) a fairly good indicator of what the classroom climate usually looks like in a specific classroom. This has also been confirmed in studies with experimental designs using what is called 'thin slices' (i.e., very short video clips) of teacher behavior to predict more general teaching quality (Begrich et al., 2021; Mainhard et al., 2014).

Teacher Interpersonal Style during the Professional Life

In the section on concepts and mechanisms used to study teacher-student communication, we referred to teacher interpersonal style as the way teachers tend to teach their different classes. Interpersonal style is a stable trait which develops slowly over a teacher's professional life. In this section, we focus on this development.

There is a long tradition of research into how teachers develop throughout their professional lives (for an overview see, for example, van Tartwijk et al., 2017). Much of this research was inspired by the work of Fuller and her colleagues (Fuller, 1969; Fuller & Bown, 1975), who identified several stages in the concerns teachers have about their development and functioning during their professional lives. As a first stage, Fuller and Bown (1975) distinguish the period before prospective teachers start teaching. In this stage, their primary concern is their own progress as students. Once they have started teaching the second phase, their concerns are mainly about their survival as a teacher. They focus on class control and being liked by students, and on the quality of their teaching techniques. This is the stage in which classroom management, and more specifically the interpersonal dynamics with their students are what they worry about most. Subsequently, a mastery phase can be distinguished in which they focus on being able to perform well as a teacher. In the final phase of the Fuller model, teachers focus on student learning and development. Several authors have built on Fuller's work, such as Fessler and Christensen (1992) and, more recently, Day and Gu (2010) and van de Grift and colleagues (see Van der Lans et al., 2017).

A pitfall when conceptualizing the development of teachers' expertise in terms of stages, is that it suggests that after teachers have mastered a routine that is central in a specific developmental stage, they can move to the next stage and no more attention needs to be paid to the routines that are mastered in the earlier stages. Day (2008) found that most teachers maintain their effectiveness throughout their professional lives, but do not necessarily become more effective over time. He warns that teachers in later years are even at greater risk of becoming less effective. Research into the development of expertise and expert performance using a cognitive psychological perspective, shows that expertise may continue to develop with experience, provided that targeted efforts are made to develop performance (Ericsson, 2018). The targeted efforts that are made to improve performance are referred to as "deliberate practice" and during this practice, prospective experts develop perceptual and behavioral routines which help to perform tasks without having to spend limited working memory capacity. Experience is necessary for automatizing these routines but without deliberate practice, performance tends to stabilize after a relatively short period and may even decline later: the pattern that Day (2008) warned about.

In earlier research into the development of teachers' interpersonal styles throughout their professional lives, Brekelmans and her colleagues used both cross-sectional and longitudinal Dutch secondary school teachers QTI data (Brekelmans et al., 1992; Brekelmans et al., 2005). They established that, during the first three years of teaching, mean students' perceptions of teacher agency significantly increased every successive year. After these three years, mean differences between years got smaller but still increased until about six years of experience and then stabilized for most teachers. Their analyses showed, however, that there was significant individual variation around the mean. Compared with students' perceptions of agency, the students' perceptions of their teachers' interpersonal styles in terms of communion showed far less variation during teachers' professional lives. On average, perceptions of communion slightly increased during the first ten years of teaching and became slightly lower afterwards. Differences were large between teachers, but the variation across years for specific teachers were small.

More recently, Veldman and her colleagues combined interview data from veteran teachers about their job satisfaction and their interpersonal relationship with their students throughout their professional lives, with data gathered with the QTI (Veldman et al., 2013, 2016). For some of these teachers, these authors retrieved QTI data which were gathered at several points earlier in their career. Teachers' job satisfaction appeared positively related to the self-reported quality of the TSR, although these self-perceptions did not always coincide with student perceptions. Some of the teachers involved in the 2016 study with relatively low job satisfaction, reported that the emotional distance between them and the students had increased over the years. To avoid low job satisfaction, some of them reduced the number of tasks that were directly related to teaching students.

These research findings did show that early in their teaching career, teachers need to develop routines in classroom management that are related to students' perceptions of teacher agency in the TSR. This is in line with studies on stages in the development of teacher expertise, pointing at the importance of the development of routines early in the career (e.g., Fuller & Bown, 1975; Van der Lans, et al., 2017). Research using the QTI and interviews did not show that agency-related routines (e.g., providing students with structure) declined later in the career. Rather the increasing emotional distance to their students, i.e., the communion aspect of the relationship, can be problematic for veteran teachers.

Conclusion and Future Research

The research reported in this chapter shows that the interpersonal approach to study classroom management is fruitful in providing insights for theory and practice. The Interpersonal Circle, measurement tools for interactions and their representation in State Space Grids and mapping TSRs with the QTI were developed for research purposes but can be used also for feedback to teachers. The notions of adaptation and complementarity provide teachers and student teachers with important anchors for understanding how they communicate with students and how this communication can be improved if needed. Especially being able to avoid negative forms of complementarity in the interactions from moment-to-moment is an important competence for teachers to build a positive social climate in class.

There is a wealth of evidence suggesting that teachers should be seen by students as relatively high on agency and communion in their TSR. For these teachers, high levels of agency and communion are seen during teaching, with relatively low variability of these behaviors and few negative incidents. For all teachers, separate lessons may differ to some degree, but overall relationships are relatively stable from lesson to lesson.

In the early years of the professional career of teachers, the level of agency is likely to increase every year until, on average, the sixth year. Differences between teachers, however, are large. For some veteran teachers, the level of communion in the relationship decreases toward the end of the career, which has a major impact on their job satisfaction. How student teachers can be assisted in developing routines related to agency has not been studied. Techniques such as video-simulation (Theelen et al., 2020) and in-ear coaching (Coninx et al., 2013) might be useful techniques for deliberate practice of these routines, but additional research is needed on this topic.

Future research could also further explore the significance for classroom communication processes of teachers' and the students' cultural background, specifically in multicultural and urban classrooms. For teachers, building productive working relationships with their students in such classrooms seems to be challenging. More knowledge on what culturally sensitive teaching strategies work in these classrooms and why they work, can help teacher education programs better prepare prospective teachers for these contexts.

All changes in the classroom climate and relationships between students and teachers are initiated during interaction and, ultimately, it is a teacher's behavior that, as part of the interaction, affects students' social-emotional well-being and learning. Therefore, future research on classroom management from an interpersonal perspective could delve deeper into the moment-to-moment characteristics of favorable interpersonal teacher behavior. For example, research could investigate the circumstances that allow a teacher to avoid negative interaction cycles with students and how teachers could be trained to resist to reply to negative student behavior with an equally negative attitude. Learning to re-appraise student behavior and being able to take students' perspectives may be at the core of this. Further, research is needed that investigates the bio-physiological basis and correlates of classroom interaction and social processes. There is a growing body of research that has examined cortisol levels of teachers (Catherine et al., 2012; Qi et al., 2017; Wettstein et al., 2020), and students (Hatfield et al., 2013; Hatfield & Williford, 2017; Oberle & Schonert-Reichl, 2016), to gauge longer-term stress experiences and how these are connected to TSRs. To understand stress as it occurs during teaching and interaction with students, especially heart rate and skin conductance, are interesting because these measures are highly susceptible to short-term situational changes (Donker et al., 2020). A new and exciting line of research has taken neurological measures to the classroom (e.g., Raufelder et al., 2016). How teachers and students adapt to each other cannot only be traced via their interpersonal behavior, but also via the level of brain-to-brain synchrony (Belivacqua et al., 2019). Understanding how interpersonal teacher behavior affects neurological processes that underly positive student emotions and engagement could inform theory and practice of teaching and classroom management in new and exciting ways.

Note

1 We are grateful to an anonymous reviewer for very helpful comments on an earlier version of this chapter.

References

Admiraal, W., Veldman, I., Mainhard, T., & Tartwijk, J. van. (2019). A typology of veteran teachers' job satisfaction: Their relationships with their students and the nature of their work. *Social Psychology of Education, 22*(2), 337–355.

AlDhafiri, N. R. (2015). The role of interpersonal EFL teacher behaviour in enhancing saudi students' learning. *International Journal of English Language Teaching, 2*(1), 47–55.

Bahoo, R., Nasim, I, Shaheen, R, Latif Javed, M. (2020). A confirmatory factor analysis of interpersonal teacher behaviour scale: Validation of the Urdu translation of secondary school students' perspectives. *Review of Economics and Development Studies, 6*(3), 715–725.

Barber, L. K., Grawitch, M. J., Carson, R. L., & Tsouloupas, C. N. (2011). Costs and benefits of supportive versus disciplinary emotion regulation strategies in teachers. *Stress and Health, 27*(3), 173–187.

Begrich, L., Kuger, S., Klieme, E., & Kunter, M. (2021). At a first glance – How reliable and valid is the thin slices technique to assess instructional quality? *Learning and Instruction, 74*, 101466.

Bevilacqua, D., Davidesco, I., Wan, L., Chaloner, K., Rowland, J., Ding, M., ... & Dikker, S. (2019). Brain-to-brain synchrony and learning outcomes vary by student–teacher dynamics: Evidence from a real-world classroom electroencephalography study. *Journal of cognitive neuroscience, 31*(3), 401–411.

Brekelmans, M. (1989). *Interpersonal teacher behavior in the* classroom [in Dutch]. W.C.C.

Brekelmans, M., Holvast, A., & Tartwijk, J. van. (1992). Changes in teacher communication styles during the professional career. *Journal of Classroom Interaction, 27*(1), 13–22.

Brekelmans, M., Wubbels, T., & Tartwijk, J. van. (2005). Teacher-student relationships across the teaching career. *International Journal of Educational Research, 32*(1–2), 55–71.

Brestovanský, M. (2020). Relations between the teacher-student relationship and school achievement: The attachment and motivation perspectives. *Československá Psychologie, 64*(4), 668–689.

Bronfenbrenner, U., & Morris, P. A. (1998). The ecology of developmental processes. In W. Damon (Series Ed.) & R. M. Lerner (Vol. Ed.), *Handbook of child psychology, Vol. 1. Theoretical models of human development (5th ed.)* (pp. 993–1028). Wiley.

Brown, D. F. (2003). Urban teachers' use of culturally responsive management strategies. *Theory into Practice, 42*(4), 277–282.

Brok, P. den, Brekelmans, M., & Wubbels, T. (2006). Multilevel issues in studies using students' perceptions of learning environments: The case of the Questionnaire on Teacher Interaction. *Learning Environments Research, 9*(3), 199–213.

Brok, P. den, Fisher, D., Brekelmans, M., Wubbels, T., & Rickards, T. (2006). Secondary teachers' interpersonal behaviour in Singapore, Brunei and Australia: a cross-national comparison. *Asia-Pacific Journal of Education, 26*(1), 79–95.

Brok, P. den, & Levy, J. (2005). Teacher-student relationships in multicultural classes: Reviewing the past, preparing the future. *International Journal of Educational Research, 43*(1–2), 72–88.

Brok, P. den, Taconis, R., & Fisher, D. (2010). How well Do Science Teacher Do. Differences in teacher-student interpersonal behavior between Science Teachers and teachers of other (school) subjects. *The Open Education Journal, 3*(1), 44–53.

Brok, P. den, Tartwijk, J. van, Wubbels, Th., & Veldman, I. (2010). The differential effect of the teacher–student interpersonal relationship on student outcomes for students with different ethnic backgrounds. *British Journal of Educational Psychology, 80*(2), 199–221.

Brok, P. den, Wubbels, T., Veldman, I., & Tartwijk, J. van. (2009). Perceived teacher-student interpersonal relationships in Dutch multi-ethnic classes. *Educational Research and Evaluation*, *15*(2), 119–135.

Cacioppo, J. T., Tassinary, L. G., & Berntson, G. G. (2017). Strong inference in psychophysiological science. In J. T. Cacioppo, L. G. Tassinary, & G. G. Berntson (Eds.), *Handbook of psychophysiology* (4th ed., pp. 3–15). Cambridge University Press.

Carson, R. C. (1969). *Interaction concepts of personality*. Aldine.

Catherine, N. L., Schonert-Reichl, K. A., Hertzman, C., & Oberlander, T. F. (2012). Afternoon cortisol in elementary school classrooms: Associations with peer and teacher support and child behavior. *School Mental Health*, *4*(3), 181–192.

Chang, M. L., & Davis, H. A. (2009). Understanding the role of teacher appraisals in shaping the dynamics of their relationships with students: Deconstructing teachers' judgments of disruptive behavior/students. In P. A. Schutz & M. Zembylas (Eds.), *Advances in teacher emotion research: The impact on teachers' lives* (pp. 95–127). Springer.

Charalampous, K., & Kokkinos, C. M. (2013). The Model of Interpersonal Teacher Behaviour: A qualitative cross-cultural validation within the Greek elementary education context. *British Educational Research Journal*, *39*(1), 182–205.

Charalampous, K., & Kokkinos, C. M. (2014). Students' Big Three Personality Traits, Perceptions of Teacher Interpersonal Behavior, and Mathematics Achievement: An Application of the Model of Reciprocal Causation, *Communication Education*, *63*(3), 235–258.

Charalampous, K. & Kokkinos, C.M. (2018). The structure of pre-adolescents' perceptions of their teacher's interpersonal behaviours and their relation to pre-adolescents' learning outcomes, *Educational Studies*, *44*(2), 167–189.

Charalampous, K., Kokkinos, C. M., Apota, E., Iliadou, A., Iosifidou, M., Moysidou, S., & Vriza, E. (2016). Pre-adolescents' representations of multiple attachment relationships: the role of perceived teacher interpersonal behaviour. *Learning Environments Research*, *19*(1), 63–86.

Claessens, L.C., Tartwijk, J. van, van der Want, A.C., Pennings, H.J., Verloop, N., Brok, P.J. den. & Wubbels, T. (2017). Positive teacher–student relationships go beyond the classroom, problematic ones stay inside. *Journal of Educational Research*, *110*(5), 478–493.

Coninx, N., Kreijns, K., & Jochems, W. (2013). The use of keywords for delivering immediate performance feedback on teacher competence development. *European Journal of Teacher Education*, *36*(2), 164–182.

Creech, A., & Hallam, S. (2011). Learning a musical instrument: The influence of interpersonal interaction on outcomes for school-aged pupils. *Psychology of Music*, *39*(1), 102–122.

Day, C. (2008). Committed for life? Variations in teachers' work, lives and effectiveness. *Journal of Educational Change*, *9*(3), 243–260.

Day, C., & Gu, Q. (2010). *The new lives of teachers*. Routledge.

Divoll, K. A., & Ribeiro, A. R. (2021). Strategies to overcome middle school teachers' classroom management stress. In C. B. Gaines, & K. M. Hutson (Eds.), *Promoting positive learning experiences in middle school education* (pp. 217–235). IGI.

Donker, M. H., Erisman, M. C., Van Gog, T., & Mainhard, T. (2020). Teachers' emotional exhaustion: associations with their typical use of and implicit attitudes toward emotion regulation strategies. *Frontiers in Psychology*, *11*, 867.

Donker, M. H., Van Gog, T., Goetz, T., Roos, A.-L., & Mainhard, T. (2020). Associations between teachers' interpersonal behavior, physiological arousal, and lesson-focused emotions. *Contemporary Educational Psychology*, *63*, 101906.

Donker, M. H., Van Gog, T., & Mainhard, M.T. (2018). A quantitative exploration of two teachers with contrasting emotions: Intra-individual process analyses of physiology and interpersonal behavior. *Frontline Learning Research*, *6*(3), 162–184.

Donker, M. H., van Vemde, L., Hessen, D. J., Van Gog, T., & Mainhard, T. (2021). Observational, student, and teacher perspectives on interpersonal teacher behavior: Shared and unique associations with teacher and student emotions. *Learning and Instruction*, *73*, 101414.

Doyle, W. (2006). Ecological approaches to classroom management. In C. M. Evertson & C. S. Weinstein (Eds.), *Handbook of classroom management: Research, practice, and contemporary issues* (pp. 97–126). Lawrence Erlbaum Associates.

Ebner-Priemer, U. W., & Kubiak, T. (2007). Psychological and psychophysiological ambulatory monitoring: A review of hardware and software solutions. *European Journal of Psychological Assessment*, *23*(4), 214–226.

Elliot, A. J. (1999). Approach and avoidance motivation and achievement goals. *Educational Psychologist*, *34*(3), 169–189.

Ericsson, K. A. (2018). The differential influence of experience, practice and deliberate practise on the development of superior individual performance of experts. In K. A. Ericsson, R. R. Hoffman, A. Kozbelt, & A. M.

Williams (Eds.), *The Cambridge handbook of expertise and expert performance* (2nd ed., pp. 745–769). Cambridge University Press.

Evertson, C. M., & Emmer, E. T. (1982). Effective management at the beginning of the school year in junior high schools. *Journal of Educational Psychology, 74*(4), 485–498.

Evertson, C.M. & Veldman, D.J. (1981). Changes over time in process measures of classroom behavior. *Journal of Educational Psychology, 73*(2), 156–163.

Evertson, C.M. & Weinstein, C.S. (Eds.), *Handbook of classroom management: Research, practice, and contemporary issues.* Lawrence Erlbaum Associates.

Fessler, R., & Christensen, J. (1992). *The teacher career cycle: Understanding and guiding the professional development of teachers.* Allyn & Bacon.

Fisher, D., Brok, P. den, & Rickards, T. (2006). Factors influencing students' perceptions of thier teachers' interpersonal behaviour: A multilevel analysis. In D. Fisher & M. Swe Khine (Eds.), *Contemporary approaches to research on learning environments* (pp. 51–74). World Scientific.

Fournier, M.A., Moskowitz, D.S., & Zuroff, D.C. (2011). Origins and applications of the interpersonal circumplex. In L.M. Horowitz, & S. Strack (Eds.), *Handbook of interpersonal psychology* (pp. 37–56). Wiley.

Franke, H. F., Hofstede, G., & Bond, M. H. (1991). Cultural roots of economic performance: A research note. *Strategic Management Journal, 12*(S1), 165–173.

Fuller, F. F. (1969). Concerns of teachers: A developmental conceptualization. *American Educational Research Journal, 6*(2), 207–226.

Fuller, F. F., & Bown, O. H. (1975). Becoming a teacher. In K. Ryan (Ed.), *Teacher education* (pp. 25–52). University of Chicago Press.

Fulmer, G. W., Lang Q. C., (2015). Testing the multidimensionality in teacher interpersonal behavior: Validating the questionnaire on Teacher Interaction using the Rasch measurement model. *Journal of Applied Measurement 16*(4), 416–431.

García Bacete, F. J., Ferrá, P., Monjas, M. I., & Maranda, G. (2014). Teacher student relationships in first and second grade classrooms: Adaptation of the Questionnaire on Teacher Interaction Early Primary. *Revista de Psicodidactica, 19*(1), 211–231.

García Bacete, F. J., & Rosel Remírez, J. F. (2021). Validación en español del Questionnaire on Teacher Interaction en los cursos superiores de educación primaria (QTI-P) y cómo esta interacción influye en el rendimiento académico. *Anales de Psicología / Annals of Psychology, 37*(1), 101–113.

Gedamu, A. D. Shure, M. (2015). The Association between EFL Teachers' Interpersonal Behavior and Students' Achievement in English Language: Selected Secondary Schools in Focus. *Science, Technology and Arts Research Journal, 4*(3), 222–229.

Glock, S., & Pit-ten Cate, I. M. (2021, online ahead of print) What's in a diagnosis: The effect of externalizing and internalizing students' behaviour on pre-service teachers' classroom management and interaction strategies. *British Journal of Educational Psychology,* e12412.

Granic, I., & Hollenstein, T. (2003). Dynamic systems methods for models of developmental psychopathology. *Development and Psychopathology, 15*(3), 641–669.

Gurtman, M. B. (2009). Exploring personality with the interpersonal circumplex. *Social Psychology Compass, 3*(1), 601–619.

Hagenauer, G., & Volet, S. E. (2014). Teacher–student relationship at university: An important yet under-researched field. *Oxford Review of Education, 40*(3), 370–388.

Hargreaves, D. H. (1972). *Interpersonal relations and education.* Routledge & Kegan Paul.

Hatfield, B. E., Hestenes, L. L., Kintner-Duffy, V. L., & O'Brien, M. (2013). Classroom Emotional Support predicts differences in preschool children's cortisol and alpha-amylase levels. *Early Childhood Research Quarterly, 28*(2), 347–356.

Hatfield, B. E., & Williford, A. P. (2017). Cortisol patterns for young children displaying disruptive behavior: Links to a teacher-child, relationship-focused intervention. *Prevention Science, 18*(1), 40–49.

Hendrickx, M. M. H. G., Mainhard, T., Boor-Klip, H. J., Cillessen, A. H. M., & Brekelmans, M. (2016). Social dynamics in the classroom: Teacher support and conflict and the peer ecology. *Teaching and Teacher Education, 53*, 30–40.

Hofstede, G. (1986). Cultural differences in teaching and learning. *International journal of intercultural relations, 10*(3), 301–320.

Hollenstein, T. (2013). *State Space Grids.* Springer.

Hollenstein, T., & Lewis, M. D. (2006). A state space analysis of emotion and flexibility in parent–child interactions. *Emotion, 6*(4), 663–669.

Hopman, J. A. B., Tick, N. T., Van der Ende, J., Wubbels, T., Verhulst, F. C., Maras, A., Breeman, L. D., & Van Lier, P. A. C. (2018). Special education teachers' relationships with students and self-efficacy moderate associations between classroom–level disruptive behaviors and emotional exhaustion. *Teaching and Teacher Education*, *75*, 21–30.

Hopman, J. A. B., Tick, N. T., Van der Ende, J., Wubbels, T., Verhulst, F. C., Maras, A., Breeman, L. D., & Van Lier, P. A. C. (2019). Developmental links between externalizing behavior and student–teacher interactions in male adolescents with psychiatric disabilities. *School Psychology Review*, *48*(1), 68–80.

Horowitz, M. L., & Strack, S. (2011). *Handbook of interpersonal psychology*. Wiley.

Hui, C. H., & Triandis, H. C. (1985). Measurement in cross–cultural psychology: A review and comparison of strategies. *Journal of Cross-Cultural Psychology*, *16*(2), 131–152.

Jailani, A. I. & Abdullah, N. (2019). Students' perception of their English lecturer's interpersonal behaviour and achievement In English as a subject. *Pertanika Journal Social Sceinces & Humanities*, *27*(T2), 83–102.

Junker, R., Donker, M. H., & Mainhard, T. (2021). Potential classroom stressors of teachers: An audiovisual and physiological approach. *Learning and Instruction*, *75*, 101495.

Jong, R. de, Mainhard, T., Van Tartwijk, J., Veldman, I., Verloop, N., & Wubbels, T. (2014). How pre–service teachers' personality traits, self–effi cacy, and discipline strategies contribute to the teacher–student relationship. *British Journal of Educational Psychology*, *84* (2), 294–10.

Keller, M. M., Chang, M.-L., Becker, E. S., Goetz, T., & Frenzel, A. C. (2014). Teachers' emotional experiences and exhaustion as predictors of emotional labor in the classroom: An experience sampling study. *Frontiers in Psychology*, *5*(1442), 1–10.

Khodamoradi, A., Talebi, S. H., & Maghsoudi, M. (2020). The relationship between teacher personality and teacher interpersonal behavior: The case of Iranian teacher educators. *Applied Research on English Language*, *9*(3), 325–348.

Kiesler, D. J. (1996). *Contemporary interpersonal theory and research: Personality, psychopathology, and psychotherapy*. John Wiley & Sons.

Korthagen, F. A. J., & Evelein, F. G. (2016). Relations between student teachers' basic needs fulfillment and their teaching behavior. *Teaching and Teacher Education*, *60*, 234–244.

Kyriakides, L. (2006). Measuring the learning environment of the classroom and its effect on cognitive and affective outcomes of schooling. In: D. Fisher, and M. Swe Khin (Eds.), *Contemporary approaches to research on learning environments: Worldviews* (pp. 369–408). World Scientific.

Lamey, A., Hollenstein, T., Lewis, M. D., & Granic, I. (2004). *GridWare* [Computer software].

Laudadío, J. & Mazzitelli, C. (2018). Adaptation and validation of the Questionnaire on Teacher Interaction in higher education. *Interdisciplinaria*, *35*(1), 153–170.

Leary, T. (1957). *An interpersonal diagnosis of personality*. Ronald Press.

Lewis, R., Romi, S., Qui, X., & Katz, Y. J. (2005). Teachers' classroom discipline and student misbehavior in Australia, China and Israel. *Teaching and Teacher Education*, *21*(6), 729–741.

Mainhard, T. (2015). Liking a tough teacher: interpersonal characteristics of teaching and students' achievement goals. *School Psychology International*, *36*(6), 559–574.

Mainhard, M. T., Brekelmans, M., Brok, P. den, & Wubbels, T. (2011). The development of the classroom social climate during the first months of the school year. *Contemporary Educational Psychology*, *36*(3), 190–200.

Mainhard, T., Brekelmans, M., & Wubbels, T. (2011). Coercive and supportive teacher behaviour: Within- and across-lessons associations with the classroom social climate. *Learning and Instruction*, *21*(3), 345–354.

Mainhard, T., Oudman, S., Hornstra, L., Bosker, R. J., & Goetz, T. (2018). Student emotions in class: The relative importance of teachers and their interpersonal relations with students. *Learning and Instruction*, *53*, 109–119.

Mainhard, M. T., Pennings, H. J. M., Wubbels, T., & Brekelmans, M. (2012). Mapping control and affiliation in teacher–student interaction with state space grids. *Teaching and Teacher Education*, *28*, 1027–1037.

Mainhard, T., Van der Rijst, R. M., Tartwijk, J. van, & Wubbels, T. (2009). A model for the supervisor-doctoral student relationship. *Higher Education*, *58*(3), 359–373.

Mainhard, T., Wubbels, T., & Brekelmans, M. (2014). The role of the degree of acquaintance with teachers on students' interpersonal perceptions of their teacher. *Social Psychology of Education*, *17*(1), 127–140.

Maulana, R., Opdenakker, M., Brok, P. den, (2012). Teacher–student interpersonal relationships in Indonesian lower secondary education: Teacher and student perceptions. *Learning Environments Research*, *15*(2), 251–271.

Maulana, R., Opdenakker, M., Brok, P. den, Bosker, R. (2011) Teacher–student interpersonal relationships in Indonesia: profiles and importance to student motivation, *Asia Pacific Journal of Education*, *31*(1), 33–49.

Maulana, R., Opdenakker, M., & Bosker, R. (2014). Teacher–student interpersonal relationships do change and affect academic motivation: A multilevel growth curve modelling. *British Journal of Educational Psychology*, *84*(3), 459–482.

Mauss, I. B., & Robinson, M. D. (2009). Measures of emotion: A review. *Cognition & Emotion*, *23*(2), 209–237.

McIntyre, N. A., Mainhard, M. T., & Klassen, R. M. (2017). Are you looking to teach? Cultural, temporal and dynamic insights into expert teacher gaze. *Learning and Instruction*, *49*, 41–53.

McIntyre, N.A., Mulder, K.T., & Mainhard, M.T. (2020). Looking to relate: Teacher gaze and culture in student-rated teacher interpersonal behaviour. *Social Psychology of Education, 23*(2), 411–431.

Miellet, S., Vizioli, L., He, L., Zhou, X., & Caldara, R. (2013). Mapping face recognition information use across cultures. *Frontiers in Psychology, 4*, 34.

Miller, A., Ferguson, E., & Byrne, I. (2000). Pupils' causal attributions for difficult classroom behaviour. *British Journal of Educational Psychology, 70*(1), 85–96.

Milner, H. R. (2006). Classroom management in urban schools. In C. M. Evertson, & C. S. Weinstein (Eds.), *Handbook of classroom management: Research, practice, and contemporary issues* (pp. 491–522). Lawrence Erlbaum Associates.

Molinari, L., Speltini, G., & Passini, S. (2013). Do perceptions of being treated fairly increase students' outcomes? Teacher–student interactions and classroom justice in Italian adolescents. *Educational Research and Evaluation, 19*(1), 58–76.

Oberle, E., & Schonert-Reichl, K. A. (2016). Stress contagion in the classroom? The link between classroom teacher burnout and morning cortisol in elementary school students. *Social Science & Medicine, 159*, 30–37.

Opdenakker, M., Maulana, R., & Brok, P. den. (2012). Teacher–student interpersonal relationships and academic motivation within one school year: developmental changes and linkage. *School effectiveness and school improvement, 23*(1), 95–119.

Overman, M., Vermunt, J.D., Meijer, P.C., Bulte, A.M.W., & Brekelmans, M. (2014) Students' perceptions of teaching in context-based and traditional chemistry classrooms: Comparing content, learning activities, and interpersonal perspectives. *International Journal of Science Education, 36*(11), 1871–1901.

Pantic, N., & Wubbels, T. (2012). The role of teachers in inculcating moral values: operationalisation of concepts. *Journal of Beliefs and Values, 33*(1), 55–69.

Passini, S., Molinari, L. & Speltini, G. (2015). A validation of the Questionnaire on Teacher Interaction in Italian secondary school students: The effect of positive relations on motivation and academic achievement. *Social Psychology of Education, 18*(3), 547–559.

Patrick, H., Turner, J. C., Meyer, D. K., & Midgley, C. (2003). How teachers establish psychological environments during the first days of school: Associations with avoidance in mathematics. *Teachers College Record, 105*(8), 1521–1558.

Pennings, H. J. M., Brekelmans, M., Sadler, P., Claessens, L. C. A., van der Want, A. C., & Tartwijk, J. van, (2018). Interpersonal adaptation in teacher-student interaction. *Learning and Instruction, 55*, 41–57.

Pennings, H. J. M., & Hollenstein, T. (2020). Teacher-student interactions and teacher interpersonal styles: A State Space Grid analysis. *The Journal of Experimental Education, 88*(3), 382–406.

Pennings, H. J. M., & Mainhard, T. (2016). Analyzing teacher–student interactions with State Space Grids. In M. Koopmans & D. Stamovlasis (Eds.), *Complex Dynamical Systems in Education: Concepts, Methods and Applications* (pp. 233–271). Springer International Publishing.

Pianta, R.C., La Paro, K.M. & Hamre, B.K. (2008). *Classroom Assessment Scoring System [CLASS]: Manual, pre-K*. Brookes Publishing.

Poulou, M. (2014). The effects on students' emotional and behavioural difficulties of teacher–student interactions, students' social skills and classroom context. *British Educational Research Journal, 40*(6), 986–1004.

Qi, X., Ji, S., Zhang, J., Lu, W., Sluiter, J. K., & Deng, H. (2017). Correlation of emotional labor and cortisol concentration in hair among female kindergarten teachers. *International Archives of Occupational and Environmental Health, 90*(1), 117–122.

Raufelder, D., Hoferichter, F., Romund, L., Golde, S., Lorenz, R. C., & Beck, A. (2016). Adolescents' socio-motivational relationships with teachers, amygdala response to teacher's negative facial expressions, and test anxiety. *Journal of Research on Adolescence, 26*(4), 706–722.

Roorda, D. L., Jak, S., Zee, M., Oort, F. J., & Koomen, H. M.Y. (2017). Affective Teacher–Student Relationships and Students' Engagement and Achievement: A Meta-Analytic Update and Test of the Mediating Role of Engagement. *School Psychology Review, 46*(3), 239–261.

Roorda, D. L., Koomen, H. M.Y., Spilt, J. L., & Oort, F. J. (2011). The influence of affective teacher–student relationships on students' school engagement and achievement. *Review of Educational Research, 81*(4), 493–529.

Roorda, D. L., Koomen, H. M.Y., Thijs, J. T., & Oort, F. J. (2013). Changing interactions between teachers and socially inhibited kindergarten children: An interpersonal approach. *Journal of Applied Developmental Psychology, 34*(4), 173–184.

Ryan, A. M., & Patrick, H. (2001). The classroom social environment and changes in adolescents' motivation and engagement during middle school. *American Educational Research Journal, 38*(2), 437–460.

Sadler, P., Ethier, N., Gunn, G.R., Duong, D. & Woody, E. (2009). Are we on the same wavelength? Interpersonal complementarity as shared cyclical patterns during interactions. *Journal of Personality and Social Psychology, 97*(6), 1005–1020.

Sadler, P., Ethier, N., & Woody, E. (2011). Interpersonal complementarity. In L. M. Horowitz, & S. Strack (Eds.), *Handbook of interpersonal psychology* (pp. 123–142). Wiley.

Safa, M.A, & Doosti, M. (2017). A culturally-adaptive Iranian version of the Questionnaire on Teacher Interaction to investigate English teachers' interpersonal behaviour. *Learning Environments Research, 20*(2), 199–219.

Santiboon, T. & Ekakul, P. (2017). Appropriating characteristics of the 21st century teachers to transform the Thailand 4.0 policies. *European Journal of Education Studies, 3*(5), 648–672.

Shukla, K. D., Kuril, S., & Chand, V. S. (2020). Does negative teacher behavior influence student self-efficacy and mastery goal orientation? *Learning and Motivation, 71*, 101653.

Sivan, A., Cohen, A., Chan, D. W. K., & Kwan, Y. W. (2017). The circumplex model of the Questionnaire on Teacher Interaction among Hong Kong students: A multidimensional scaling solution. *Learning Environments Research, 20*(2), 189–198.

Skaalvik, E. M., & Skaalvik, S. (2015). Job satisfaction, stress and coping strategies in the teaching profession – What do teachers say? *International Education Studies, 8*(3), 181–192.

Slof, B., Nijdam, D., & Janssen, J. (2016). Do interpersonal skills and interpersonal perceptions predict student learning in CSCL-environments? *Computers & Education, 97*, 49–60.

Spilt, J. M., Koomen, M. Y., & Thijs, J. T. (2011). Teacher wellbeing: The importance of teacher–student relationships. *Educational Psychology Review, 23*(4), 457–477.

Sun, X., Hendrickx, M. M., Goetz, T., Wubbels, T., & Mainhard, T. (2020). Classroom social environment as student emotions' antecedent: Mediating role of achievement goals. *The Journal of Experimental Education*, 1–12. Published online: February 25, 2020.

Sun, X., Mainhard, T., & Wubbels, T. (2018). Development and evaluation of a Chinese version of the Questionnaire on Teacher Interaction (QTI). *Learning Environments Research, 21*(1), 1–17.

Tartwijk, J. van. (1993). The interpersonal significance of nonverbal behaviour in the classroom [in Dutch]. WCC.

Tartwijk, J. van., Brekelmans, M., Wubbels, T., Fisher. D.L., & Fraser, B.J. (1998). Students perceptions of teacher interpersonal style: The front of the classroom as the teacher's stage. *Teaching and Teacher Education, 14*(6), 607–617.

Tartwijk, J. van, Brok, P. den, Veldman, I., & Wubbels, T. (2009). Teachers' practical knowledge about classroom management in multicultural classrooms. *Teaching and Teacher Education, 25*(3), 453–460.

Tartwijk, J. van, Wubbels, T., Mainhard, T., & Brekelmans, M. (2010). *Teacher nonverbal behaviour and students' perceptions of teacher interpersonal styles.* (Paper presentation), 2010 Annual Meeting of the American Educational Research Association, Denver CO.

Tartwijk, J. van, Wubbels, T., & Zwart, R. C. (2017). Developing teachers' competences with the focus on adaptive expertise in teaching. In D. J. Clandinin & J. Husu (Eds.), *The SAGE Handbook of Research on Teacher Education* (pp. 820–835). Sage.

Telli, S. (2016). Students' perceptions of teachers' interpersonal behaviour across four different school subjects: Control is good but affiliation is better. *Teachers and Teaching, 22*(6), 729–744.

Telli, S., Brok, P. den, & Cakiroglu, J. (2007). Students' perceptions of science teachers' interpersonal behaviour in secondary schools: Development of a Turkish version of the Questionnaire on Teacher Interaction. *Learning Environments Research, 10*(2), 115–129.

Telli, S., Brok, P. den, & Cakiroglu, J. (2010) The importance of teacher–student interpersonal relationships for Turkish students' attitudes towards science. *Research in Science & Technological Education, 28*(3), 261–276.

Theelen, H., Van den Beemt, A., & Brok, P. den. (2020). Developing preservice teachers' interpersonal knowledge with 360-degree videos in teacher education. *Teaching and Teacher Education, 89*, 102992.

Thijs, J., Koomen, H., Roorda, D., & ten Hagen, J. T. (2011). Explaining teacher–student interactions in early childhood: An interpersonal theoretical approach. *Journal of Applied Developmental Psychology, 32*(1), 34–43.

Turner, J. C., & Christensen, A. L. (2020). Using state space grids to analyze teacher–student interaction over time. *Educational Psychologist, 55*(4), 256–266.

Tyler, K.M., Stevens-Morgan, R., & Brown-Wright, L. (2016) Home-School Dissonance and Student-Teacher Interaction as Predictors of School Attachment among Urban Middle Level Students. *RMLE Online, 39*(7), 1–22.

van Aalst, D. A. E., Huitsing, G., Mainhard, T., Cillessen, A. H. N., & Veenstra, R. (2021). Testing how teachers' self-efficacy and student-teacher relationships moderate the association between bullying, victimization, and student self-esteem. *European Journal of Developmental Psychology, 18*(6), 928–947.

van der Lans, R. M., Cremers, J., Klugkist, I., & Zwart, R. (2020). Teachers' interpersonal relationships and instructional expertise: How are they related? *Studies in Educational Evaluation, 66*, 100902.

van der Lans, R. M., Van de Grift, W. J. C. M., & Van Veen, K. (2017). Individual differences in teacher development: An exploration of the applicability of a stage model to assess individual teachers. *Learning and Individual Differences, 58*, 46–55.

van Uden, J. M., Ritzen, H., & Pieters, J. M. (2013). I think I can engage my students. Teachers' perceptions of student engagement and their beliefs about being a teacher. *Teaching and Teacher Education, 32*, 43–54.

van Uden, J. M., Ritzen, H., & Pieters, J. M. (2014). Engaging students: The role of teacher beliefs and interpersonal teacher behavior in fostering student engagement in vocational education. *Teaching and Teacher Education*, *37*, 21–32.

Veldman, I., Admiraal, W., Mainhard, T., Wubbels, T., & Tartwijk, J. van. (2017). Measuring teachers' interpersonal self-efficacy: Relationship with realized interpersonal aspirations, classroom management efficacy and age. *Social Psychology of Education*, *20*(2), 411–426.

Veldman, I., Admiraal, W., Tartwijk, J. van, Mainhard, T., & Wubbels, T. (2016). Veteran teachers' job satisfaction as a function of personal demands and resources in the relationships with their students. *Teachers and Teaching: Theory and Practice*, *22*(8), 913–926.

Veldman, I., Tartwijk, J. van, Brekelmans, M., & Wubbels, T. (2013). Job satisfaction and teacher–student relationships across the teaching career: Four case studies. *Teaching and Teacher Education*, *32*, 55–65.

Wang, X., Wang, L., Zhang, J., & Wang, J. (2020). A multilevel analysis on the evaluation and promotion of emotional intelligence among Chinese school adolescents. *Youth & Society*, 0044118X20982316.

Wei, M. Brok, P. den, Zhou, Y (2009). Teacher interpersonal behaviour and student achievement in English as a Foreign Language classrooms in China. *Learning Environments Research*, *12*(3), 157–174.

Wei, M., Zhou, Y., Barber, C., & Brok, P. den. (2015). Chinese students' perceptions of teacher–student interpersonal behavior and implications. *System*, *55*, 134–144.

Wettstein, A., Kühne, F., Tschacher, W., & La Marca, R. (2020). Ambulatory assessment of psychological and physiological stress on workdays and free days among teachers. A preliminary study. *Frontiers in neuroscience*, *14*, 112.

Wijsman, L., Mainhard, T., & Brekelmans, M. (2014). Stimulating autonomous motivation in the classroom: The role of interpersonal teacher agency and communion. In D. Zandvliet, P. den Brok, T. Mainhard, & J. van Tartwijk (Eds.), *Interpersonal relations in education: From theory to practice* (pp. 231–249). Sense Publishers.

Wubbels, Th., & Brekelmans, M. (2005). Two decades of research on teacher–student relationships in class. *International Journal of Educational Research*, *43*(1–2), 2005.

Wubbels, Th., Brekelmans, M., Brok, P. den, Levy, J., Mainhard, T., & Tartwijk, J. van. (2012). Let's make things better: developments in research on interpersonal relationships in education. In Th. Wubbels et al. (Eds.), *Interpersonal Relationships in Education: An Overview of Contemporary Research* (pp. 225–250). Sense Publishers.

Wubbels, Th., Brekelmans, M., Brok, P. den, & Van Tartwijk, J. (2006). An interpersonal perspective on classroom management in secondary classrooms in the Netherlands. In C. M. Evertston & C. S. Weinstein (Eds.), *Handbook of classroom management: Research, practice, and contemporary issues* (pp. 1161–1191). Lawrence Erlbaum Associates.

Wubbels, T., Brok, P. den, Veldman, I., & Tartwijk, J. van. (2006). Teacher interpersonal competence for Dutch secondary multicultural classrooms. *Teachers and Teaching: Theory and Practice*, *12*(4), 207–433.

Wubbels, T. & Levy, J. (1991). A comparison of interpersonal behavior of Dutch and American teachers. *International Journal of Intercultural Relations*, *15*(1), 1–18.

Zijlstra, H., Wubbels, T., Brekelmans, M., & Koomen H.M.Y. (2013) Teacher Interpersonal Behavior and Associations with Mathematics Achievement in Dutch Early Grade Classrooms. *The Elementary School Journal*, *113*(4), 517–540.

22

TEACHER AGGRESSION AND CLASSROOM MANAGEMENT

Kent Divoll

UNIVERSITY OF HOUSTON-CLEAR LAKE

Introduction

Being an educator is a complex job wherein teachers and principals frequently quit the profession because of the stress (Carver-Thomas & Darling-Hammond, 2017, 2019; Divoll & Ribeiro, 2021, in press-a; Klassen & Chiu, 2011; Sutcher et al., 2016).[1] One of the common stressors of being a teacher is issues with student motivation and discipline (Albright et al., 2017; Brill & McCartney, 2008; Chang, 2009; Divoll & Ribeiro, 2021; Kraft et al., 2016; Kukla-Acevedo, 2009; McCarthy et al., 2015; Ribeiro & Divoll, 2020). For a comprehensive review of teacher stress, see Chapter 11 of this handbook. Given the stress of teaching, it is not surprising how easy it is to find examples of a teacher's aggressive behavior on social media platforms today.

According to Riley et al. (2012), the use of aggressive classroom management techniques seems to be increasing. Teacher aggression is viewed as "any form of overt communication intended to psychologically injure a student who is motivated to avoid such treatment, including verbal or non-verbal attacks on the self-concept of a student" (Montuoro & Lewis, 2018, p. 439). Teacher aggression is not an issue that is exclusive to one country but is studied worldwide (Bekiari, 2016, 2017; Bekiari & Petanidas, 2016; Bekiari & Tsaggopoulou, 2016; Bekiari & Tsiana, 2016; Choi, 2021; Deliligka et al., 2017; Geiger, 2017; Gershoff et al., 2019; Kaltenbach et al., 2018; Kambuga et al., 2018; Lewis et al., 2008; Mainhard et al., 2011; Mazer & Stow, 2016; Montuoro, 2016, 2017; Montuoro & Lewis, 2015, 2018; Montuoro & Mainhard, 2017; Piekarska, 2000; Romi et al., 2011, 2016; Seyrek & Ersanh, 2020). Despite the application of teacher aggression in so many countries, literature on the subject clearly suggests that teacher aggression negatively impacts students in a number of ways. For example, the following can be impacted by teacher aggression: a student's (a) behavior (Choi, 2021; Lewis, 2001, 2006; Lewis & Riley, 2009; Lewis et al., 2005, 2008; Riley, 2009; Romi et al., 2009; Sava, 2002; Wubbels et al., 2006); (b) achievement (Aysan et al., 2001; Kearney et al., 1991; Sava, 2002; Stipek & Miles, 2008); (c) distraction from work (Lewis & Riley, 2009; Lewis et al., 2008; Montuoro & Lewis, 2018); (d) attitude toward school (Lewis, 2001; Lewis et al., 2005, 2008; Romi et al., 2009, 2011); (e) hatred of subject matter (Henderson et al., 2000;); (f) focus on school work (Clunies-Ross et al., 2008; Lewis, 2001; Romi et al., 2011); (g) poor relationships with the teacher/loss of respect (Cothran et al., 2003; Lewis, 2006; Lucas-Molina et al., 2015; Romi et al., 2011); (h) personal responsibility (Lewis, 2001); (i) self-esteem (Neto & Mullet, 2004; Parrott et al., 1988; Szabados, 1990); and (j) peer victimization (Lucas-Molina et al., 2015). Moreover, teacher aggression does not only impact the students receiving the aggression, but also the bystander of that aggression (Clunies-Ross et al., 2008; Cothran et al., 2003; Lewis, 2001; Mainhard et al., 2011; Montuoro & Lewis, 2018; Romi et al., 2011). Additionally, teacher aggression runs counter to much of the teacher-student relationships and classroom management literature (Caskey & Anfara, 2014; Divoll, 2010; Eccles & Roeser, 2011; Ellerbrock, 2016; Emmer & Evertson, 2017; Emmer & Gerwels, 2006; Hamre & Pianta, 2006; Kesner, 2000; Pianta, 2006; Watson & Ecken, 2003; Woolfolk Hoy & Weinstein, 2006; Wong & Wong, 2018).

According to the aforementioned literature base, there is no excuse for and no place for teacher aggression in schools. Despite this, discussing teacher aggression and conducting future research on teacher aggression is needed because: (a) students are still experiencing teacher aggression (Bekiari, 2016, 2017; Bekiari & Tsiana, 2016; Deliligka et al., 2017; Geiger, 2017; Kambuga et al., 2018; Montuoro & Lewis, 2018); (b) there are teachers who view aggressive classroom management strategies as necessary (Deliligka et al., 2017, Kambuga et al., 2018; Suryaningrat et al., 2020); (c) it is a worldwide issue; and (d) there is societal acceptance of teacher aggression (Choi, 2021; Gershoff et al., 2019; Kambuga et al., 2018; Suryaningrat et al., 2020). Essentially, until teacher aggression is eradicated from the classroom, understanding more about teacher aggression, its effects, and ways to prevent it are needed. Therefore, this chapter will summarize and synthesize recent research on teacher aggression. The chapter also will include recent definitions of teacher aggression and a breakdown of the recent research by theme. The teacher aggression themes include verbal aggression, philosophy and traits of teacher aggression, a group of three studies that do not fit into the other categories (i.e., professional development, bystanders, and acceptable behaviors), and teacher corporal punishment.

Defining Teacher Aggression

Previous investigations into teacher aggression focused on: teacher aggression, teacher misbehavior (Lewis & Riley, 2009), teacher hostility, teacher cohesion (Lewis 2001), and legal teacher aggression (Riley et al., 2010). In recent research, the term *teacher aggression* seems to be the most prevalently used. Montuoro and Lewis (2018) define teacher aggression as "any form of overt communication intended to psychologically injure a student who is motivated to avoid such treatment, including verbal or nonverbal attacks on the self-concept of a student" (p. 439). This definition also seems to be an umbrella term for other characterizations of teacher aggression (i.e., verbal abuse and verbal aggression). Additionally, recent research provided examples of teacher aggression:

> Such behaviours include the use of derogatory language, publicly or privately embarrassing or insulting students, and verbal harassment of students. Such aggressive behaviours harm students physically, psychologically or educationally and may even include such negative behaviours as hair pulling, slapping, insulting or throwing chalk.
>
> *Romi et al., 2016, p. 174*

Out of the 14 recent studies on teacher aggression (see Table 22.1), six used the same definition or one that is similar. This is not surprising, given that four of the six were conducted in Australia with either Roman Lewis or Paul Montuoro as one of the authors (see Montuoro 2017; Montuoro & Lewis, 2018; Montuoro & Mainhard, 2017; Romi et al., 2016). The fifth and sixth studies are from Turkey and Indonesia with different authors (i.e., Seyrek & Ersanh, 2020; Suryaningrat et al., 2020).

Eight of the studies focused on one aspect of teacher aggression, i.e., verbal aggression. These studies referred to teacher aggression as verbal aggressiveness (see Bekiari, 2016, 2017; Bekiari & Petanidis, 2016; Bekiari & Tsaggopoulou, 2016; Bekiari & Tsiana, 2016; Deliligka et al., 2017; Mazer & Stowe, 2016) or verbal abuse (see Geiger, 2017). The studies that used the term verbal aggressiveness were from Greece and the United States, whereas the term verbal abuse was used in the study from Israel. In these studies, the common definition of verbal aggression is to "attack a person's self-concept of the

Table 22.1 Teacher Aggression Studies

Author(s)	Year	Title	Location	Participants	Methodology
Bekiari	2016	Insights into instructors' verbal aggressiveness and students' Machiavellianism through leadership style and motivational climate	Greece	Students	Quantitative
Bekiari	2017	Verbally aggressive instructors and Machiavellian students: Is the socio-communicative style an over-bridging?	Greece	Students	Quantitative
Bekiari & Petanidis	2016	Exploring teachers' verbal aggressiveness through interpersonal attraction and students' intrinsic motivation	Greece	Students	Quantitative
Bekiari & Tsaggopoulou	2016	Verbal aggressiveness and affective learning in physical education	Greece	Students	Quantitative
Bekiari & Tsiana	2016	Exploring instructors' verbal aggressiveness and students' personal orientations and reasons of discipline in physical education class	Greece	Students	Quantitative
Deliligka, Bekiari, & Syrmpas	2017	Verbal aggressiveness and argumentativeness in physical education: Perceptions of teachers and students in qualitative and quantitative exploration	Greece	Students and Teachers	Mixed Methods
Geiger	2017	Sixth graders in Israel recount their experience of verbal abuse by teachers in the classroom	Israel	Students	Qualitative
Mazer & Stowe	2016	Can teacher immediacy reduce the impact of verbal aggressiveness? Examining effects on student outcomes and perceptions of teacher credibility	United States	College Students	Quantitative
Montuoro	2017	Failure to replicate ego depletion in the mechanism underlying teacher aggression: A conditional process analysis	Australia	Teachers	Quantitative
Montuoro & Lewis	2018	Personal responsibility and behavioral disengagement in innocent bystanders during classroom management events: The moderating effect of teacher aggressive tendencies	Australia	Students	Quantitative
Montuoro & Mainhard	2017	An investigation of the mechanism underlying teacher aggression: Testing 13 theory and the general aggression model	Australia	Teachers	Quantitative
Romi, Salkovsky, & Lewis	2016	Reasons for aggressive classroom management and directions for change through teachers' professional development programmes	Australia	Teachers	Quantitative
Seyrek & Ersanh	2020	Examining the relationship between the teachers' emotional reactivity and aggression levels	Turkey	Teachers	Quantitative
Suryabingrat, Mangunsong, & Riantoputra	2020	Teachers' aggressive behaviors: what is considered acceptable and why?	Indonesia	Teachers and Parents	Quantitative

other in order to cause psychological pain" (Bekiari & Tsiana, 2016, p. 159). This attack can be based on a person's "character, competence, physical appearance" (Bekiari & Tsiana, 2016, p. 159), "deficient scholastic abilities, work habits, and achievements" (Geiger, 2017, p. 97), and/or capability (Deliligka et al., 2017). Verbal aggression can come in the form of "disregard, derision, threats, obscenity, curses, loud voices, teasing gestures" (Deliligka et al., 2017, p. 1695), ridicule (Bekiari & Tsiana, 2016), and/or "putdowns, name-calling, yelling, and scapegoating" (Geiger, 2017, p. 97).

Teacher Verbal Aggression

Although eight of the studies looked at teacher aggression in terms of verbal aggression, each of the studies had focused on different aspects. In the first, Geiger (2017) interviewed 60 sixth-graders in Israel about their experiences with verbal abuse by teachers. According to Geiger, research on verbal aggression is an understudied area in Western countries, it is often integrated into teacher-student relationship research, and little research has been conducted on this topic with elementary school students in Israel. As explained by Geiger: "The importance of this study cannot be overemphasized since it aims at providing important information about a disturbing and often neglected form of abuse—verbal/emotional maltreatment in an under-studied population of elementary school children" (p. 97). In addition, interviewing students about teacher verbal aggression is not common in the recent literature.

Geiger's (2017) results add to the literature on teacher aggression and specifically teacher verbal aggression. The students explained the typical times and forms that teachers used verbal aggression. Reasons for incurring the wrath of the teacher's verbal abuse often occurred when students lost attention, did not complete their class or homework, and/or when they did not earn good grades. The common teacher verbal abuse methods reported by the students included yelling at students, embarrassing the students in front of their peers, scapegoating, using putdowns, and calling the students names—all of which are not commonly advocated for in teacher-student relationships literature or research on classroom management (Caskey & Anfara, 2014; Divoll, 2010; Eccles & Roeser, 2011; Ellerbrock, 2016; Emmer & Evertson, 2017; Emmer & Gerwels, 2006; Hamre & Pianta, 2006; Kesner, 2000; Pianta, 2006; Watson & Ecken, 2003; Wong & Wong, 2018; Woolfolk Hoy & Weinstein, 2006). The students saw the aforementioned behaviors as cruel and a form of public humiliation.

Although the students believed that the aggressive behaviors displayed by the teachers were humiliating and insensitive, the students rarely "fought back." Rather, the students covertly protested the teacher's actions and were afraid to report the teacher to their parents or the principal because they worried that nothing would be done and their attempt would result in teacher reprisals. Since these students are in sixth grade, they might have had teachers in the past that were verbally abusive and nothing was done when they complained. It would be interesting to repeat this study in other countries to determine if this is unique to Israel or if this finding is common among students in other countries. However, Choi (2021) explained that in Korean culture, a teacher's authority is strong; thus, such a finding might not be unique.

Geiger (2017) provided two interesting perspectives about teacher aggression. First, she explained that hearing from the students provides a powerful understanding of their reactions to teacher verbal abuse. Second, Geiger viewed teacher aggression in terms of students' rights:

> This study reinforces the guidelines included in the United Nations Convention of the Rights of the Child (1989), that views children's rights to express their views as a necessary condition to achieve its primary goal—the best interests of children.
>
> *p. 102*

Looking at teacher aggression in terms of students' rights, rather than as inappropriate practices of teaching, is unique. Additionally, studies addressing teacher aggression are typically published with the hopes of making a change in practices or policy. However, Geiger published the article and became an advocate when she reported the findings to the Israeli Children Protection Agency.

Given that teacher aggression studies highlight unprofessional and harmful behaviors by teachers toward a population that needs to be protected by adults, more researchers who focus on teacher aggression should take a similar approach. This should be especially true when considering that Geiger (2017) viewed such behavior as a form of abuse. In addition to her advocacy, Geiger also suggested two ways to reduce verbal aggression: (a) "include emotional/verbal abuse prevention programs in teacher education programs with courses on emotional learning, emphatic listening, and interpersonal communication skills"; and (b) use various ways to screen out potentially abusive teachers in the hiring process (p. 103). The second recommendation is unique and a potential unexplored area of research. If schools complete background checks on teachers before they are hired in the hope of protecting students, why not develop and/or use some existing measures to eliminate potentially aggressive teachers? Additionally, studies like this one that provide the students' voice explain: (a) why they do not report a teacher's aggressive behaviors and (b) the impact that the behavior has on students. Such studies will hopefully result in more of a focus on recognizing and removing aggressive teachers. Thus, more studies providing the students' voices are needed.

In the second study, Mazer and Stowe (2016) used quantitative methods with 242 undergraduate college students to investigate whether specific classroom management strategies (i.e., immediacy) reduced the impact of teacher verbal aggression. This study investigated a new line of research in teacher aggression literature, i.e., does a teacher's use of immediacy reduce the negative impact of teacher verbal aggression. Having college students read a narrative about a teacher while completing a survey that focused on motivation, affective learning, and classroom climate is unique. Thus, repeating this study using students at the primary and secondary levels with the narratives, as well as using real teachers rather than a narrative about a fictitious teacher, would be beneficial. Mazer and Stowe explained that teacher "immediacy typically is described as a set of nonverbal behaviors including the use of direct eye contact, facial expressions, vocal variety, and movement" (p. 22). Research suggests that teachers who use immediacy perceive the classroom to be more positive (Mazer, 2012, 2013a, 2013b; Mottet et al., 2006; Titsworth et al., 2010; Titsworth et al., 2013). Mazer and Stowe suggested the following about immediacy: (a) "Conclusions stemming from decades of immediacy research generally suggest that teachers should increase their immediacy behaviors for optimum communication success in the classroom" (p. 22) and (b) "In essence, immediate teachers create an environment where student motivation, engagement, and learning can flourish" (p. 22–23). In contrast, verbal aggression is related to: (a) issues with the classroom climate (Kearney et al., 1991; Myers & Rocca, 2001); (b) the teacher being viewed as being credible (Myers, 2001); (c) reduced student motivation (Myers, 2002; Myers & Rocca, 2001); (d) reduced student satisfaction (Myers, 2002; Myers & Knox, 2000); and (e) decreased learning (Kearney et al., 1991; Myers, 2002). Thus, the authors posited that "teacher verbal aggressiveness has overwhelming negative effects on students and their perceptions of teachers' credibility" (p. 23).

The results of this study suggested similar findings to other studies in that the students reported "significantly less motivation and affective learning, the classroom climate as significantly less positive, and the teacher as significantly less credible" (p. 31). However, the results also suggested something new, i.e., that "teachers' use of immediacy potentially can offset the negative effects of verbal aggressiveness on students" (p. 31). More specifically, the students suggested that motivation, affective learning, classroom climate, and teacher credibility all increased when teachers used more versus less immediacy. The highest levels of motivation and affective learning occurred when teachers used the greatest amount of immediacy without any verbal aggression. However, when immediacy was combined with verbal aggression, students reported higher levels of motivation and affective learning than when verbal aggression was used without immediacy. Not surprising, teachers who were perceived to use immediacy frequently without verbal aggression were given the highest ratings of classroom climate.

However, the use of immediacy with teacher aggression did reduce the negative impact of the use of verbal aggression as it did with motivation and affective learning. Mazer and Stowe (2016) explained a possible rationale for the different results with motivation, affective learning, and classroom climate: "Put simply, teacher immediacy behaviors do little to subdue the negative effects of verbal aggression with respect to effects on students' perceptions of the classroom climate" (pp. 31–32). Mazer and Stowe also suggested, similar to the findings of Geiger (2017), that verbal aggression might result in student short-term compliance, with the negative outcomes outweighing the short-term benefits. Mazer and Stowe's final takeaway from this study was that although immediacy does have an impact on the use of lower levels of verbal aggression, it is not an excuse to use verbal aggression because immediacy does not mitigate high levels of teacher aggression.

In the third study on teacher verbal aggression, Deliligka et al. (2017) used a mixed methods approach (interviewing 15 physical education teachers and surveying 894 students) to investigate the relationship between verbal aggression and argumentativeness in physical education teachers. The authors of this study suggested that the purpose of the qualitative investigation was to determine the teachers' perceptions of their verbal aggressiveness and argumentativeness, whereas the goal of the quantitative portion of the study was to determine if there were differences in the students' views of the teachers' verbal aggression and argumentativeness in terms of gender, school, and level. The authors proposed that argumentativeness is "defined as a person's tendency to support its beliefs on debatable disputes and at the same time trying to prove false the opinions of the interlocutor" (p. 1695). The results of the qualitative analysis revealed that argumentativeness and verbal aggression simultaneously exist in a physical education teacher's behavior. Teachers who understand how to argue can do so without verbally attacking the student, but those who do not know how to argue tend to resort to verbal aggression (Bekiari, 2017; Infante & Rancer, 1993; Infante & Rancer, 1996; Syrmpas & Bekiari, 2015).

Deliligka et al. (2017) suggested that teachers who avoid arguments include: "withdrawing from expressing arguments with students, insisting on their point of view thinking that it's the right thing to do and imposing their opinion through punishments, threats or yelling" (p. 1706). The authors explained that "the higher verbally aggressive teachers are, the more verbally aggressive messages are using [sic] and in these messages are included attacks on students' character, competence attacks, irony, cursing, swearing, threats, ridicule, teasing and nonverbal emblems" (p. 1707). Sadly, this finding is not unique in the literature (Infante et al., 1990, 1992; Infante & Rancer, 1993). The authors also suggested that female teachers use verbal aggressiveness at a higher rate than men and that men use argumentativeness more than women. When the student survey data were compared to the teacher self-perception data, most of the profiles were in alignment. Junior high school teachers were perceived to have higher verbal aggression and high school teachers as more argumentative rather than aggressive. Future research in this area could include exploring the same concept with teachers from different subjects to determine if there is a difference between perceptions of these teachers to physical education teachers.

In the fourth study on teacher verbal aggression, Bekiari and Tsiana (2016) used quantitative methodology to investigate students' views of physical education teachers' verbal aggression and the reasons for discipline compared to their personal orientations (i.e., task and ego). The authors justified the need for this study by suggesting that:

> students' personal orientations and discipline reasons during physical education lessons has not yet being linked with verbal aggressiveness of physical education instructors as perceived by students.
>
> p. 161

Thus, although this type of research has been conducted in other areas, it is unique in the field of physical education. The results of the study suggested that:

perceived instructors' verbal aggressiveness was positively related to students' ego orientation, external reasons, introjected reasons, no reasons, and self-responsibility reasons for discipline, but was negatively related to students' task orientation, intrinsic reasons and caring reasons for discipline. Moreover, perceived instructors' verbal aggressiveness could significantly predict the variables of students' personal orientations and external reasons, intrinsic reasons and self-responsibility reasons for discipline.

p. 163

Finally, Bekiari and Tsiana suggested that future research examining their study be repeated with larger sample sizes to verify the results. Moreover, additional research investigating the suggested typology in physical education and other fields would add to the literature.

The remaining four studies also had Bekiari as the lead author, but all of these studies seem to focus on aspects of verbal aggression in a physical education setting in Greece that are all related to each other; in addition, the studies all follow a similar pattern. Thus, rather than taking a deep dive into each study, as has been the case in this chapter, the studies will be discussed collectively. Each of these studies is quantitative, used questionnaires with students ranging from 9–17 years old (i.e., 9–12, 10–12, 12–14, or 14–17), and focused on verbal aggression combined with at least one additional aspect (i.e., Machiavellianism, socio-communication style, interpersonal attraction, internal motivation, motivational climate, leadership style, and/or affective learning).

Two of these studies, Bekiari (2016, 2017), focused on the concept of Machiavellianism. Machiavellianism is defined as a person that is "characterized by the ability to influence other people and control them, and self-interest is the key motive of his behavior" (p. 94). Bekiari (2016) investigated the relationship between teacher verbal aggression, leadership style, climate, and student Machiavellianism. Bekiari suggested that a teacher's level of verbal aggression was directly related to their leadership style and classroom climate. A teacher who uses a high level of verbal aggression is more likely to have a classroom that values "interpersonal competition, public valuation, and normative review" (Bekiari, 2016, p. 93) and an autocratic leadership teaching style.

Bekiari (2017) investigated the teachers' communication style and verbal aggressiveness compared to the teachers' and students' level of Machiavellianism. The author found that a teacher's verbal aggressiveness was positively associated with the teacher being viewed as someone who has: desire for control, distrust of others, desire for status, and unethical behavior if he/she believes that it will help him/her succeed (all of which are Machiavellian behaviors). Furthermore, teachers who were perceived this way also had students who were more likely to exhibit these behaviors. Both Bekiari (2016) and Bekiari (2017) found that male students were more likely than female students to view their teachers as being verbally aggressive, assertive, and autocratic. This finding is not surprising given that previous research has found that educators are more likely to use verbal aggression toward male students than female students (Bekiari, 2014; Bekiari & Petanidis, 2016; Hasanagas & Bekiari, 2016). Moreover, in both studies, a teacher's use of verbal aggression also seemed to result in having more students with Machiavellian tendencies than teachers who implemented verbal aggressive behaviors at a lower level, thus, creating a cycle wherein the teacher and students are negatively influencing each other's behaviors (Bekiari & Petanidis, 2016; Choi, 2021; Lewis, 2001; Lewis et al., 2005; Nesdale & Pickering, 2006).

In the final two studies, Bekiari and Tsaggopoulou (2016) focused on teacher verbal aggression compared to student affective learning, while Bekiari and Petanidis (2016) addressed verbal aggression compared to interpersonal attraction and intrinsic motivation. Bekiari and Tsaggopoulou explained that the affective domain:

includes the ability of a person to listen, respond to others, demonstrate appropriate behaviors and attitudes, maintain balances and show interest, as well as to be consistent on a daily basis, and at the same time willing to reconsider his opinions and changes the behavior suitably whenever new situations occur…Therefore, affective learning concerns the sentimental area of learning which reflects upon the students' beliefs, values, interests and behaviors.

p. 407

The results of this study suggested that a teacher's verbal aggression has an influence on student affective learning (i.e., affect toward course content, recommended course behavior, and instructor). A teacher who is perceived as being verbally aggressive results in students having a lower affect for the course content, recommended course behavior, and instructor.

In the final study in this group, Bekiari and Petanidis (2016) explained that interpersonal attraction is (a) "considered to be a person's tendency or disposition to evaluate favorably or negatively others or their personality traits" (p. 73) and (b) composed of physical (i.e., how the student perceives how the teacher looks), social, and task attraction. The results show that a teacher's verbal aggression negatively impacts social attraction, task attraction, physical attraction, "enjoyment/importance," "effort/interest," and competence, while also increasing "pressure/tension." Finally, Bekiari and Petanidis suggested that urban schools have higher levels of stress and pressure during physical education courses than students in suburban and rural areas and that students in suburban and rural areas have higher levels of effort and interest than that of their peers who live in urban areas.

The eight studies that focused on verbal aggression investigated different aspects of teacher aggression. Collectively, these eight studies suggest that teachers who: (a) use immediacy have the potential to mitigate some of the negative impacts that teacher aggression has on students and (b) exhibit verbal aggression have an autocratic teaching style, are not good at arguing, and exhibit Machiavellian behaviors. This collection of studies also posits that students who experience teacher aggression: (a) have a lower affect for the course content, recommended course behavior, and the instructor, (b) do not always report teacher aggressive behaviors because they fear repercussions by the teacher and worry that they will not be believed, and (c) experience more "pressure/tension" and less enjoyment.

Philosophies of Teacher Aggression

Three of the recent studies about teacher aggression investigated the philosophies/traits of teacher aggression. In the first study, Montuoro and Mainhard (2017) surveyed 249 teachers to investigate the causes of teacher aggression (i.e., I^3 theory and the General Aggression Model [GAM]). The authors explained why this study was needed: "the psychological mechanism underlying teacher aggression remains unknown, and knowledge of this mechanism may be critical to reducing the incidence of this dysfunctional behaviour" (p. 498). The authors suggested that I^3 theory:

was used to test whether the mechanism underlying teacher aggression follows a moderating pathway, whereby an instigating trigger (high misbehaviour provocation), an impelling force (low caregiving responsiveness), and a disinhibiting force (low trait self-control) spontaneously align, leading to teacher aggression.

p. 498

In I^3 theory, there is an interaction between three events that result in aggression: investigating triggers, compelling forces, and inhibiting forces (Finkel, 2014; Montuoro, 2016). The authors explained that GAM:

was used to test whether the mechanism follows a mediating pathway, whereby a preliminary antecedent variable (low caregiving responsiveness) increases the likelihood that a teacher will experience higher misbehaviour provocation and lower trait self-control, in turn leading to aggression. It is hoped that ultimately the identification of the mechanism will improve the effectiveness of teacher education programmes and reduce the incidence of teacher aggression.

p. 498

GAM theory suggests that aggression is influenced by characteristics of an individual (Anderson & Bushman, 2002; Anderson & Carnagey, 2004; Anderson & Huesmann, 2003; Montuoro, 2016).

In their investigation of I³ and GAM, Montuoro and Mainhard (2017) explored three predictors of teacher aggression, i.e., the attachment and caregiving behaviors systems, misbehavior provocation, and trait self-control. The results of the study provided evidence that aggressive behavior is partly a result of the aforementioned three predictors of aggression. This means that teacher aggression can be conceptualized as Anderson and Bushman (2002) suggested, i.e., the person in the situation. Thus, a person who has low caregiving responsiveness, which results from their past experiences with caregivers (Divoll, 2010; Howes & Spieker, 2018; Slater Ainsworth & Bowlby, 1991; Watson & Ecken, 2003), when mediated with higher misbehavior provocation (student behavior issue) and lower trait self-control (lack of ability of self-control), results in aggressive behaviors. The authors explained the interaction of the three aforementioned factors and how they impact teacher aggression:

> From the perspective of the GAM, this suggests that the mechanism underlying teacher aggression is based on, and proceeds from, lower caregiving responsiveness as a preliminary antecedent variable, which negatively influences the affective, cognitive, and arousal states through which the individual perceives and interprets student misbehaviour as a situational factor. This also suggests that the tendency to experience these internal states, in turn, negatively influences the appraisal and decision process by constraining trait self-control, leading to immediate appraisals and impulsive actions, instead of effortful reappraisals and thoughtful actions.

p. 510

The authors also suggested a new aspect for teacher aggression literature, i.e., that a countertransference occurs, which is typically used in psychotherapy (see Fauth, 2006; Gelso & Hayes, 2007), wherein the teacher subconsciously allows attitudes about previous relationships to influence their reactions to and relationships with students. The authors posited a need for a new perspective on teacher education programs if GAM is a predictor of teacher aggression, in that these programs would need to: "foster the self-development of the whole person, and to recognize that every teacher has a unique personal history that leads to unconscious biases, personal issues, and unresolved conflicts" (p. 512). Finally, Montuoro and Mainhard also suggested three recommendations for future study: (a) investigating the experiences of teachers who respond aggressively to students, (b) repeating the same study using qualitative methods of multiple instances, and (c) an additional investigation using observations and/or a psychological measure.

In the second study, Seyrek and Ersanh (2020) used quantitative methods with 266 teachers to investigate how teachers' emotional reactivity relates to aggression levels. The authors explained that:

> Emotional reactivity involves individual's emotions for a series of stimuli, intensity of these emotions, and the time passed until the individual goes back to the stimulation level which was before they encountered the series of stimuli that caused them to feel the emotion in question.

p. 461

Teachers interact with many situations during a school day, which may result in an emotional reaction; having an emotional reaction to a situation could result in a harsh reaction to a classroom management situation (Divoll & Ribeiro, 2021, in press-a,). The results of the study are similar to that of Geiger (2017) in that there was a difference in emotional reactivity in terms of gender. Females had a higher mean score of emotional reactivity than males. Other studies found similar results between men and women (Hasta & Güler, 2013; Yurdakul & Üner, 2015). Additionally, male levels of aggression were higher than that of females. However, the levels of emotional activity and aggression did not differ by years of teaching. Seyrek and Ersanh explained why these results matter:

> Facing obstacles and experiencing conflict is by nature of being a human. In such cases, teachers' ability to recognize and manage their own feelings in a healthy manner is an important skill for an environment which facilitates the achievement of the desirable and expected goals of education, and it can be a preventive factor for violence in schools.
>
> *p. 466*

Two areas of additional study are recommended by the authors: (a) using a larger sample size to repeat the study and (b) a repeated study that investigates the emotional reaction and aggression of non-teachers as a comparison. Finally, they suggested that if teachers learn to recognize and manage their own feelings, then it could reduce teacher aggression. As Seyrek and Ersanh suggested, this type of emotional awareness training could be done by psychological counselors.

In the final study, Montuoro (2017) used quantitative analysis with 110 teachers to determine the impact that ego depletion has on teacher aggression. More specifically, the author suggested, "The present study investigated whether ego depletion influences the mechanism underlying teacher aggression, and specifically whether depleted teachers are more likely than nondepleted teachers to respond aggressively to students who misbehave" (p. 1). Investigating ego depletion is a new line of research in teacher aggression. Ego depletion, simply put, is the concept that "self-control depends on a limited energy resource" (p. 2). Montuoro suggested that the depletion effect did not influence teacher aggression and that the results support Montuoro and Mainhard's (2017) finding that "lower caregiving responsiveness indirectly led to higher teacher aggression through higher misbehaviour provocation, controlling for the covariates" (p. 12). Montuoro concluded: "This null finding may simply be evidence that ego bolstering occurs 'naturally' in the teaching profession, or that teachers are less likely to experience motivated switching because they place high value on their role" (p. 14). Additionally, the results of this study support the idea that GAM influences teacher aggression. Although this study resulted in a null finding, eliminating aspects that influence teacher aggression is just as important as determining them.

These three studies analyzed teacher aggression from three different perspectives (i.e., characteristics of the teacher, emotional reactivity, and ego deletion). Collectively, these studies provide an explanation for the cause of teacher aggression. Simply put, teachers with lower caregiver responsiveness tend to have an emotional reaction to student behaviors and react impulsively.

Teacher Aggression: Professional Development, Bystanders, and Acceptable Behaviors

The next three studies were very different investigations of teacher aggression than the previous 11. In the first study, Montuoro and Lewis (2018) conducted a quantitative analysis with 528 students about the impact that teacher aggression had on innocent bystanders (i.e., a student who sees or hears the teacher's aggression, but is not a direct recipient of the aggression). Previous research suggested that innocent bystanders, even though they know the teacher's aggression is not directed at them, still experience negative impacts (Clunies-Ross et al., 2008; Cothran et al., 2003; Lewis, 2001; Mainhard et al., 2011; Romi et al., 2011). Although research on innocent bystanders is not new, this study approaches this topic from a new perspective, i.e., the perceptions of teacher aggression by innocent bystanders and how it is shaped by the student's sense of personal responsibility and behavioral disengagement. Previous literature on classroom management has investigated the influence of both personal responsibility (Lewis et al., 2013; Romi et al., 2009) and behavioral engagement (Dotterer & Lowe, 2011; Hughes et al., 2008; Openakker & Minnaert, 2011; Reyes et al., 2012; Wang & Holcombe, 2010). The authors provided the following definitions for behavioral engagement and personal responsibility: (a) "behavioral engagement refers to students' efforts to follow classroom norms and participate and engage in classroom activities, including attending to the teacher, concentrating on and persisting with educational tasks, and making contributions to classroom discussion" (p. 440) and (b) personal responsibility, which is "a sense of agency that allows them to overcome peripheral distractions" (p. 440). The results of this study suggested that innocent bystanders with a high level of personal responsibility who witness teacher aggression ended up with lower levels of behavior disengagement. Additionally, the authors explained that:

> The present finding is the first evidence that increasing levels of teacher aggression have a progressively detrimental effect on students. In fact, the present finding indicates that relatively high levels of teacher aggression can even destabilize autonomous and self-directed innocent bystanders who have the highest levels of personal responsibility.
>
> *p. 444*

Oddly enough, a teacher's "aggressive tendencies moderated the inverse relationship between personal responsibility and behavioral disengagement until teacher aggressive tendencies was particularly high" (p. 444). The authors suggested two possible reasons for this: (a) the student could be fearful of the teacher and (b) students in this type of classroom could be so disengaged that the acts of aggression no longer influence behavior disengagement.

In the second study, Romi et al. (2016) conducted a quantitative analysis with 192 teachers to determine if teachers' reasons for aggression could be used to target classroom management related to professional development. The teachers were categorized into three approaches, i.e., attachment, attribution, and efficacy, in the hopes of clarifying teacher reasoning for aggression. For a comprehensive understanding of these three theories, please see Lewis and Riley (2009). In attachment theory, "insecurely attached teachers are more likely to behave inappropriately, as their emotional resources to deal with relationship difficulties are not well developed and they may interpret students' misbehaviour as rejection" (p. 175); thus, the teacher may react harshly to behaviors. In attribution theory, a teacher "focuses on students' characteristics as causal factors for both positive and negative classroom behaviour and outcomes" (p. 175). Teachers who adopt efficacy theory focus on identifying techniques to help them manage the classroom, and they tend to be more likely to be aggressive toward students (Riley et al., 2010). The results indicated that teachers who accepted the attribute narrative were less likely to believe that they would benefit from professional development about student misbehavior, yet teachers with an efficacy narrative felt that they would benefit from such information. Teachers with an attachment narrative did not have a specific preference. The authors posited that professional development might need to be tailored to teachers based on their aggression narrative. However, all teachers, regardless of their narrative, believed that they would benefit from professional development on teacher-student relationship and skill development in classroom management. Finally, the authors advocated that a follow-up study be conducted with qualitative methods to broaden the picture.

In the third study, Suryaningrat et al. (2020) conducted a quantitative analysis with 203 teachers and 293 parents at the secondary level in Indonesia to determine their view of which aggressive behaviors were acceptable for use by teachers. Suryaningrat et al. found that both parents and teachers were more accepting of verbal aggressive behaviors than physical aggressive behaviors and that parents were more accepting of verbal behaviors than teachers. The results also showed that parents and teachers who have had high exposure to aggressive behaviors and/or had a bachelor's degree rather than a master's degree were more likely to be accepting of physical and verbal aggression by teachers. Given these results, it is not surprising that students are reluctant to report aggressive teacher behaviors (Geiger, 2017). The authors also suggested that there were cultural differences in the views of teacher (i.e., the Javanese culture was more accepting of aggressive behaviors). Finally, the authors recommended that future research explore the differences between teacher proactive and reactive aggressive behaviors, as well as a further examination of the teachers and parent's education level versus view of acceptable teacher aggression. Although these three studies are grouped together because they did not relate to the previous themes, they do provide some interesting results. Collectively, these three investigations of teacher aggression suggest that: (a) innocent bystanders with a high level of personal responsibility experience behavior disengagement, (b) targeted classroom management professional development might be the key to reducing teacher aggression, and (c) teacher and parents both believe that some forms of teacher aggressions are acceptable.

Teacher Corporal Punishment as Aggression

I am proposing an additional aspect that needs to be discussed with teacher aggression, i.e., teacher corporal punishment. This would be specific to corporal punishment used by teachers in the class-room, but not corporal punishment in general. Currently, teacher aggression literature does not seem to include a teacher's use of corporal punishment and is an independent line of research. This could be a result of the specialization of those researching each topic, the favorable view of corporal punishment by advocates of its implementation (Gershoff, 2017; Kambuga et al., 2018), or the cultural acceptance of corporal punishment (Choi, 2021). In schools where teacher corporal punishment is sanctioned, such as in one third of the world's countries including Australia, Tanzania, South Korea, and the United States (Choi, 2021; Gershoff, 2017; Gershoff et al., 2019; Kambuga et al., 2018), it is not viewed as teacher aggression, but rather a form of discipline or a method to improve student performance (Gershoff, 2017; Kambuga et al., 2018).

Given the aforementioned definitions of teacher aggression: (a) "any form of overt communica-tion intended to psychologically injure a student who is motivated to avoid such treatment, including verbal or nonverbal attacks on the self-concept of a student" (Montuoro & Lewis, 2018, p. 439) and the list of behaviors (b) "derogatory language, publicly or privately embarrassing or insulting students, and verbal harassment of students. Such aggressive behaviours harm students physically, psychologically or educationally and may even include such negative behaviours as hair pulling, slapping, insulting or throwing chalk" (Romi et al., 2016, p. 174), corporal punishment by teachers is a match for teacher aggression. Additionally, with all of the evidence that suggests corporal pun-ishment has negative consequences for students (Choi, 2021; Gershoff et al., 2019; Kaltenbach et al., 2018; Kambuga et al., 2018), one would have a difficult time arguing that corporal punishment by teachers is not a form of overt communication intended to psychologically harm. Straus (1994) defined corporal punishment as "the use of physical force with the intention of causing a child to experience pain but not injury for the purposes of correction or control of the child's behavior" (p. 4). Moreover, Choi (2021) expands this definition and advocated that the definition of corporal pun-ishment should include direct (physical) and indirect forms. Putting all of these definitions together, the line between teacher aggression and teacher use of corporal punishment seems to intersect. Since corporal punishment by teachers can be seen as a form of teacher aggression, many of the same afore-mentioned consequences of teacher aggression would apply. For example, as Divoll (2010) suggested, for teacher-student relationships to be effective, teachers need to be explicit about the fact that they want to create positive teacher-student relationships and show that they care. However, doing so would be very difficult in a setting wherein the teacher is also physically aggressive, in this example using corporal punishment, toward the students. Moreover, teachers who use aggressive tactics are seen as less credible (Mazer & Stowe, 2016); thus, students who are in classrooms wherein the teacher

Table 22.2 Corporal Punishment Studies

Author(s)	Year	Title	Location	Participants	Methodology
Choi	2021	*Cycle of violence in schools: Longitudinal reciprocal relationship between student's aggression and teacher's use of corporal punishment*	Korea	Student	Quantitative
Gershoff, Sattler, & Holden	2019	*School corporal punishment and its associations with achievement and adjustment*	United States	Adults	Quantitative
Kaltenbach, Hermenau, Nkuba, Goessmann, & Hecker	2018	*Improving interaction competencies with children—a pilot feasibility study to reduce school corporal punishment*	Tanzania	Teachers	Quantitative
Kambuga, Manyengo, & Mbalamula	2018	*Corporal punishment as a strategic reprimand used by teachers to curb students' misbehaviours in secondary schools: Tanzanian case*	Tanzania	Teachers and Students	Quantitative

uses corporal punishment will most likely not "trust" (Watson & Ecken, 2003) their teacher's interest in creating positive teacher-student relationships.

Since including corporal punishment with teacher aggression is unique, the four studies (see Table 22.2) that meet the criteria for inclusion (i.e., studies with a focus on corporal punishment used by teachers in the classroom) are discussed in a separate section rather than with the teacher aggression studies. In the first study, Choi (2021) conducted a quantitative analysis of 4,051 Korean secondary students, investigating the relationship between student aggression and teachers' use of corporal punishment. Choi's investigation of corporal punishment focused on the potential cycle of aggression caused by corporal punishment and student aggressive behaviors. Previous research suggested that teachers use aggressive techniques when a student acts aggressively toward the teacher (Lewis, 2001; Lewis et al., 2005; Nesdale & Pickering, 2006).

Moreover, this study was also unique because it used an autoregressive cross-lagged model, which, according to the author, has not been used in empirical studies. Choi (2021) explained that there has been little research that examines the relationship between a teacher's use of corporal punishment and student aggression. The results suggested that students who engage in aggressive behavior "provoke" a teacher's use of corporal punishment and that a teacher's use of corporal punishment results in student aggression, which Choi posits creates a cycle of violence. Thus, rather than correct behaviors, teachers are actually creating more problems for themselves if they use corporal punishment in the classroom. The author also suggested that future research should "find the moderating variables that could buffer the paths from student's aggressions to teacher's use of corporal punishments" (p. 1180).

In the second study, Kambuga et al. (2018) used quantitative methods with 50 teachers and 99 students to compare teacher and student views of corporal punishment in Tanzania. Kambuga et al. suggested that in Tanzania:

> corporal punishment is the punishment that is supposed to be administered by teachers in schools as it aims to cause deliberate pain or discomfort in response to undesired behaviour shown by students. It is administered by striking the pupil either across the buttocks or on the palms.
>
> *p. 184*

The results suggested that other than the frequency (80% of students have had corporal punishment used on them at least three times in the past year) and behaviors that elicited a corporal punishment response (both minor and major issues), teachers and students had very different views of corporal punishment. Teachers concluded that there was not an alternative to corporal punishment, while students suggested that a more nurturing approach be used. Interestingly enough, this is another example of when students have a better understanding of what teachers should do than the teachers themselves (Montuoro & Lewis, 2015; Woolfolk Hoy & Weinstein, 2006).

In the third study, Kaltenbach et al. (2018) used quantitative methods to study a new professional development model to curb teacher use of corporal punishment in Tanzania. Thus, the previous study essentially set up the need for teachers to learn about alternatives to corporal punishment, and this study tested the impact of such a professional development program. The authors suggested that there are not many professional development programs that specifically address teachers' use of corporal punishment and even fewer that have been researched. Kaltenbach et al. explained that the professional development program, ICC-T, "is a comprehensive training workshop for teachers aiming at preventing corporal punishment and at improving the teacher–student relationship in school settings" (p. 47). The participants were surveyed before, immediately after the training, and three months later. The professional development program resulted in improved student behaviors, improvements in teacher–student relationships, and a high rate of participant implementation of the core ideas.

In the fourth study, Gershoff et al. (2019) used quantitative methods to study 876 adults in the United States between the ages of 18 and 23 in the 19 states where corporal punishment is legal, to better understand the types and frequencies of corporal punishment and the association between corporal punishment and achievement and adjustment. The authors suggested that little is known about how corporal punishment is implemented in the country and that this is the first investigation in the country of outcomes linked with experiences of school corporal punishment. The findings of this study are as follows: (a) an administrator implemented the corporal punishment 41% of the time, (b) a teacher administered the corporal punishment 39% of the time, (c) 16% experienced corporal punishment, (d) 79% reported an object being used, (e) 82% suggested the experience was very or extremely painful, (f) 25 % experienced bruising after the punishment, and (g) having experienced corporal punishment was linked with lower high school GPA, higher current depressive symptoms, and greater likelihood of spanking their own children. Finally, Gershoff et al. suggested that "this study has demonstrated that corporal punishment in schools is linked with substantial risk for physical, psychological, and academic harm as well as with the perpetuation of violence in future generations" (p. 7) and advocated for the use of alternative strategies rather than corporal punishment.

Collectively, these four studies suggest: (a) teachers are administrating corporal punishment in the classroom because they deem it necessary, (b) students believe that teachers should be using alternatives to corporal punishment, and (c) comprehensive workshops that provide alternatives to corporal punishment have the potential to curb teacher behaviors.

Conclusion

As an education professor who teaches classroom management, teachers displaying aggression as part of their strategies, either intentionally or as a result of stress and/or attachment issues that result in a momentary reaction, runs contrary to everything that I believe and what research on classroom management and teacher–student relationships suggests (Caskey & Anfara, 2014; Divoll, 2010; Eccles & Roeser, 2011; Ellerbrock, 2016; Emmer & Evertson, 2017; Emmer & Gerwels, 2006; Hamre & Pianta, 2006; Kesner, 2000; Pianta, 2006; Watson & Ecken, 2003; Wong & Wong, 2018; Woolfolk Hoy & Weinstein, 2006; Wubbels et al., 2015). Thus, knowing that students are still suffering from issues with teacher aggression, despite all of the previous research on negative consequences for students, is unnerving.

Recent literature on teacher aggression added some new concepts to the literature. Montuoro (2016) and Montuoro and Mainhard (2017) suggested that GAM better explains teacher aggression than the I³ theory. If GAM is the mechanism behind teacher aggression, then aggression is about the person in the situation and how they are influenced by their characteristics (Anderson & Bushman, 2002; Anderson & Carnagey, 2004; Anderson & Huesmann, 2003; Montuoro, 2016), e.g., prior attachments (Divoll, 2010; Howes & Spieker, 2018; Slater Ainsworth & Bowlby, 1991; Watson & Ecken, 2003). The recent studies provided a number of recommendations for professional development programs to address teacher aggression. These include professional development that: (a) is targeted toward the teacher's narrative (i.e., attribution, attachment, or efficacy) (Romi et al., 2006), (b) instructs teachers how to argue (Deliligka et al., 2017), (c) promotes the use of immediacy (Mazer & Stowe, 2016), and (d) is specific to teacher aggression (Kaltenbach et al., 2018). Additionally, Montuoro (2016) suggested that teachers' professional development needs to include an introspective into the self to better understand their classroom management tendencies. One possible way to have a teacher better understand his/her aggressive tendencies and make changes in his/her practices would be to write an adapted best-loved self story (see Divoll & Ribeiro, in press-b). Such a practice might help teachers reflect on their attachments and experiences to understand the "why" behind their reactions in the classroom.

Furthermore, teachers who use aggressive classroom management techniques are creating a cycle that results in additional student misbehavior (Bekiari 2016, 2017; Bekiari & Petanidis, 2016; Choi, 2021; Lewis, 2001; Lewis et al., 2005; Nesdale & Pickering, 2006). Thus, teachers who use aggression in the classroom might receive initial student compliance, but they are creating negative long-term consequences for themselves, i.e., additional behavior problems. The problems caused by teacher aggression not only impact students who are the receiver of the aggression, but also impacts innocent bystanders (Montuoro & Lewis, 2018). Although this is not a new concept, Montuoro and Lewis's (2018) finding that students with higher levels of personal responsibility negate some of the effects of teacher aggression is novel.

Reviewing recent literature on teacher aggression yielded future directions for research. Much of the recent literature on teacher aggression comes from Greece and focuses on physical education. One issue with the transferability of teacher aggression research in physical education settings to non-physical education classrooms is that the activities and classroom management can be very different. More research is needed that focuses on teacher aggression in other classroom settings such as special education, English language learning settings, and other subject areas. Additionally, more research is needed about the influence that teacher aggression has on different demographic groups (e.g., socio-economic status, ethnic groups). As research suggests, students of color experience higher suspension rates (Gregory et al., 2011; Mendez et al., 2002); thus, the assumption is that students of color would also experience teacher aggression more frequently.

The lack of studies on preservice teachers and their understanding of teacher aggression, their attachment history, and levels of aggression is another area that does not appear much in recent research. Although Montouro (2017) and Montouro and Mainhard (2017) investigated the mechanisms underlying teacher aggression, recent research does not focus on when teachers become aggressive. Jaleel and Verghis (2017) suggested that preservice teachers have above-average aggression levels. A longitudinal study tracking teacher aggression levels from their time as a preservice teacher into their teaching careers would add to the literature. Additional studies that investigate the assumption that teachers with lower caregiver responsiveness tend to have an emotional reaction to student behaviors and react impulsively (Montouro & Mainhard, 2017; Seyrek & Ersanh, 2020) is also needed. If future research confirms this assumption, then targeting interventions to stop teacher aggression might be possible. Furthermore, more research is also needed to determine if current professional development models (e.g., Kaltenbach et al., 2018) or new models based on a teacher's style (Romi et al., 2016), which includes training teachers to implement immediacy strategies (Mazer & Stowe, 2016) and how to argue (Deliligka et al., 2017), can reduce teacher aggression. Since teacher aggression might be a result of a teachers' previous attachments (Montuoro & Mainhard, 2017) and thus embedded into a teacher's identity, changing his/her aggressive behaviors might be difficult in traditional professional development models. Thus, additional investigations into professional development targeted at reducing teacher aggression is also needed.

The repetition of most of the studies in this chapter in multiple countries is needed to better understand teacher aggression. One issue with teacher aggression is that views of what is appropriate can be cultural and different based on the country and/or regional within a country (Choi, 2021; Gershoff et al., 2019; Suryaningrat et al., 2020). For example, determining if students in other countries also do not report teacher aggression because they worry about teacher reprisals and assume that their complaints will be ignored (Geiger, 2017) is important. Thus, repeating these studies in other countries would be beneficial. With so few recent studies on teacher aggression in the United States, this is another area that needs to be explored. Additionally, the lack of inclusion of teacher corporal punishment literature into the teacher aggression literature, as I proposed, also warrants further investigation.

Recent research on teacher aggression provided perspectives on teacher aggression from the view of teachers, students, and parents. However, perspectives from administrators and preservice teachers are not prevalent in the recent research on teacher aggression and could add to the literature base. Specifically, learning more about how administrators: (a) view teacher aggression, (b) deal with aggressive teachers, (c) handle complaints by students, and (d) what efforts they take to avoid hiring aggressive teachers are areas for future research. More qualitative investigations of teacher aggression are needed to provide a richer understanding of teacher, preservice teachers, students, parents, and administrators views of and experiences with teacher aggression.

In conclusion, the recent and previous research is clear, i.e., teacher aggression does not belong in classrooms today. In addition to developing and implementing professional development to provide teachers with alternatives to aggressive classroom management practices (Kaltenbach et al., 2018), researchers, school administrators, and policymakers need to find ways to prevent aggressive teachers from entering the profession and remove teachers who practice aggression. However, if students believe that their reports about teacher aggression will be diminished or ignored, this might be complicated to achieve (Geiger, 2017).

Note

1 The charge of this chapter was to review research since the previous Handbook on Classroom Management (Emmer & Sabornie, 2015); thus, when the term *previous* is used, it refers to literature before 2015 and *recent* refers to literature since 2015. Also, much of the research included in this chapter occurred outside of the United States, and thus British English is frequently used in quotes and in names of the instruments used in some of the studies.

References

Ainsworth, M. D., & Bowlby, J. (1991). An ethological approach to personality development. *American Psychologist*, *46*(4), 333–341. https://doi.org/10.1037/0003-066X.46.4.333

Albright, J. L., Safer, L. A., Sims, P. A., Tagaris, A., Glasgow, D., Sekulich, K. M., & Zaharis, M. C. (2017). What factors impact why novice middle school teachers in a large midwestern urban school district leave after their initial year of teaching. *The International Journal of Educational Leadership Preparation*, *12*(1), 53–68.

Anderson, C. A., & Bushman, B. J. (2002). Human aggression. *Annual Review of Psychology*, *53*(1), 27–51. https://doi.org/10.1146/annurev.psych.53.100901.135231

Anderson, C. A., & Carnagey, N. L. (2004). Violent evil and the general aggression model. In A. Miller (Ed.), *The social psychology of good and evil* (pp.168–192). The Guilford Press.

Anderson, C. A., & Huesmann, L. R. (2003). Human aggression: A social–cognitive view. In M. A. Hogg & J. Cooper (Eds.), *The sage handbook of social psychology* (pp. 296–323). Sage.

Aysan, F., Bàban, A., Savage, G., & Van De Vijver, F. (2001). Causes of student failure: A cross-cultural comparative study of Turkish, South-African and Romania students. *Cogniţie Creier Comportament, 5*(2), 125–136.

Bekiari, A. (2014). Verbal aggressiveness and leadership style of sports instructors and their relationship with athletes' intrinsic motivation. *Creative Education, 5*(2), 114–121. https://doi.org/10.4236/ce.2014.52018

Bekiari, A. (2016). Insights into instructors' verbal aggressiveness and students' machiavellianism through leadership style and motivational climate. *European Scientific Journal, 12*(25), 90–110. https://doi.org/10.19044/esj.2016.v12n25p90

Bekiari, A. (2017). Verbally aggressive instructors and Machiavellian students: Is the socio-communicative style an over-bridging? *Psychology, 8*(10), 1437–1454. https://doi.org/10.4236/psych.2017.810095

Bekiari, A., & Petanidis, D. (2016). Exploring teachers' verbal aggressiveness through interpersonal attraction and students' intrinsic motivation. *Open Journal of Social Sciences, 4*(12), 72–85. http://dx.doi.org/10.4236/jss.2016.412007

Bekiari, A., & Tsaggopoulou, T. (2016). Verbal aggressiveness and affective learning in physical education. *Advances in Physical Education, 6*(4), 406–418. http://dx.doi.org/10.4236/ape.2016.64041

Bekiari, A., & Tsiana, I. (2016). Exploring instructors' verbal aggressiveness and students' personal orientations and reasons of discipline in physical education class. *Advances in Physical Education, 6*(3), 158–168. http://dx.doi.org/10.4236/ape.2016.63018

Brill, S., & McCartney, A. (2008). Stopping the revolving door: Increasing teacher retention. *Politics & Policy, 36*(5), 750–774. https://doi.org/10.1111/j.1747-1346.2008.00133.x

Carver-Thomas, D., & Darling-Hammond, L. (2017). *Teacher turnover: Why it matters and what we can do about it.* Learning Policy Institute. https://files.eric.ed.gov/fulltext/ED606805.pdf

Carver-Thomas, D., & Darling-Hammond, L. (2019). The trouble with teacher turnover: How teacher attrition affects students and schools. *Education Policy Analysis Archives, 27*(36), 1–22. http://dx.doi.org/10.14507/epaa.27.3699

Caskey, M., & Anfara, V. A. (2014). *Developmental characteristics of young adolescents.* Association for Middle Level Education. www.amle.org/developmental-characteristics-of-young-adolescents/

Chang, M. L. (2009). An appraisal perspective of teacher burnout: Examining the emotional work of teachers. *Educational Psychology Review, 21*(3), 193–218. https://doi.org/10.1007/s10648-009-9106-y

Choi, B. (2021). Cycle of violence in schools: Longitudinal reciprocal relationship between student's aggression and teacher's use of corporal punishment. *Journal of Interpersonal Violence, 36*(3–4), 1168–1188. https://journals.sagepub.com/doi/pdf/10.1177/0886260517741627

Clunies-Ross, P., Little, E., & Kienhuis, M. (2008). Self-reported and actual use of proactive and reactive classroom management strategies and their relationship with teacher stress and student behavior. *Educational Psychology, 28*(6), 693–710. https://doi.org/10.1080/01443410802206700

Cothran, D. J., Kulinna, P. H., & Garrahy, D. A. (2003). "This is kind of giving a secret away…": Students' perspectives on effective class management. *Teaching and Teacher Education, 19*(4), 435–444.

Deliligka, S., Bekiari, A., & Syrmpas, I. (2017). Verbal aggressiveness and argumentativeness in physical education: Perceptions of teachers and students in qualitative and quantitative exploration. *Psychology, 8*, 1693–1717. https://doi.org/10.4236/psych.2017.811112

Divoll, K. A. (2010). *Creating classroom relationships that allow students to feel known* [Doctoral dissertation, University of Massachusetts-Amherst]. https://scholarworks.umass.edu/cgi/viewcontent.cgi?article=1273&context=open_access_dissertations

Divoll K. A., & Ribeiro, A. R. (in press-a). Applying brain research and positive psychology to promote the well-being of principals. In B. Carpenter, J. Mahfouz, & K. Robinson (Eds.), *Supporting leaders for school improvement.* Information Age Publishing.

Divoll K. A., & Ribeiro, A. R. (in press-b). Exploring your past to strengthen your best-loved self. In C. Craig, D. McDonald, & G. Curtis (Eds.), *Best-loved self: Learning and leading in teaching and teacher education.* Palgrave Macmillan.

Divoll, K. A., & Ribeiro, A. R. (2021). Strategies to overcome middle school teachers' classroom management stress. In C. Gaines & K. Hutson (Eds.), *Promoting positive learning experiences in middle school education* (pp. 217–235). IGI Global.

Dotterer, A. M., & Lowe, K. (2011). Classroom context, school engagement, and academic achievement in early adolescence. *Journal of Youth and Adolescence, 40*(12), 1649–1660. https://link.springer.com/content/pdf/10.1007/s10964-011-9647-5.pdf

Eccles, J. S., & Roeser, R. W. (2011). Schools as developmental contexts during adolescence. *Journal of Research on Adolescence, 21*(1), 225–241. https://doi.org/10.1111/j.1532-7795.2010.00725.x

Ellerbrock, C. R. (2016). Relationships. In S. B. Mertens, M. M. Caskey, & N. Flowers (Eds.), *The encyclopedia of middle grades education* (pp. 311–314). Information Age Publishing.

Emmer, E. T., & Evertson, C. M. (2017). *Classroom management for middle and high school teacher* (10th ed.). Pearson.

Emmer, E. T., & Gerwels, M. C. (2006). Classroom management in middle and high school classrooms. In C. M. Evertson & C. S. Weinstein (Eds.), *Handbook of classroom management: Research, practice, and contemporary issues* (pp. 407–437). Lawrence Erlbaum Associates.

Emmer, E. T., & Sabornie, E. J. (2015). Teacher–student relationships and classroom management. *The handbook of classroom management* (2nd ed). Routledge.

Fauth, J. (2006). Toward more (and better) countertransference research. Psychotherapy: Theory, Research, & Practice, *43*(1), 16–31. https://doi.org/10.1037/0033-3204.43.1.16

Finkel, E. J. (2014). The I3 model: Metatheory, theory, and evidence. In J. M. Olson & M. P. Zanna (Eds.), *Advances in experimental social psychology* (Vol. 49, pp. 1–104). Academic Press. https://doi.org/10.1016/B978-0-12-800052-6.00001-9

Geiger, B. (2017). Sixth graders in Israel recount their experience of verbal abuse by teachers in the classroom. *Child Abuse & Neglect, 63*, 95–105. https://doi.org/10.1016/j.chiabu.2016.11.019

Gelso, C. J., & Hayes, J. A. (2007). Countertransference and the therapist's inner experience: Perils and possibilities. Erlbaum.

Gershoff, E. (2017). School corporal punishment in global perspective: Prevalence, outcomes, and efforts at intervention. *Psychology, Health & Medicine, 22*(sup1), 224–239. https://doi.org/10.1080/13548506.2016.1271955

Gershoff, E., Sattler, K. M., & Holden, G. W. (2019). School corporal punishment and its associations with achievement and adjustment. *Journal of Applied Developmental Psychology, 63*, 1–8. https://doi.org/10.1016/j.appdev.2019.05.004

Gregory, A., Cornell, D., & Fan, X. (2011). The relationship of school structure and support to suspension rates for Black and White high school students. *American Educational Research Journal, 48*(4), 904–934. https://doi.org/10.3102/0002831211398531

Hamre, B. K., & Pianta, R. C. (2006). Student–Teacher Relationships. In G. G. Bear & K. M. Minke (Eds.), *Children's needs III: Development, prevention, and intervention* (pp. 59–71). National Association of School Psychologists.

Hasanagas, N., & Bekiari, A. (2015). Depicting determinants and effects of intimacy and verbal aggressiveness target through social network analysis. *Sociology Mind, 5*(3), 162–175. https://doi.org/10.4236/sm.2015.53015

Hasta, D., & Güler, M. E. (2013). Aggression: An investigation in terms of interpersonal styles and empathy. *Ankara University Journal of Institute of Social Sciences, 4*(1), 64–104.

Henderson, D., Fisher, D., & Fraser, B. (2000). Interpersonal behaviour, laboratory learning environments, and student outcomes in senior biology. *Journal of Research in Science Teaching, 37*(1), 26–43. https://doi.org/10.1002/(SICI)1098-2736(200001)37:1<26::AID-TEA3>3.0.CO;2-I

Howes, C., & Spieker, S. (2018). Attachment relationships in the context of multiple caregivers. In J. Cassidy & P.R. Shaver (Eds.), *Handbook of attachment: Theory, research, and clinical application* (3rd ed., pp. 314–329). Guilford Publications.

Hughes, J. N., Luo, W., Kwok, O. M., & Loyd, L. K. (2008). Teacher–student support, Effortful engagement, and achievement: A 3-year longitudinal study. *Journal of Educational Psychology, 100*(1), 1–14. https://doi.org/10.1037/0022-0663.100.1.1

Infante, D. A., Hartley, K. C., Martin, M. M., Higgins, M. A., Bruning, S. D., & Hur, G. (1992). Initiating and reciprocating verbal aggression: Effects on credibility and credited valid arguments. *Communication Studies, 43*(3), 182–190. https://doi.org/10.1080/10510979209368370

Infante, D. A, & Rancer, A. S. (1982). A conceptualization and measure of argumentativeness. *Journal of Personality Assessment, 46*(1), 72–80. https://doi.org/10.1207/s15327752jpa4601_13

Infante, D. A., & Rancer, A. S. (1993). Relations between argumentative motivation, and advocacy and refutation on controversial issues. *Communication Quarterly, 41*(4), 415–426. https://doi.org/10.1080/01463373909369902

Infante, D. A., & Rancer, A. S. (1996). Argumentativeness and verbal aggressiveness: A review of recent theory and research. *Annals of the International Communication Association, 19*(1), 319–352. https://doi.org/10.1080/23808985.1996.11678934

Infante, D. A., Sabourin, T. C., Rudd, J. E., & Shannon, E. A. (1990). Verbal aggression in violent and nonviolent marital disputes. *Communication Quarterly, 38*(4), 361–371. https://doi.org/10.1080/01463379009369773

Jaleel, S., & Verghis, A. M. (2017). Comparison between emotional intelligence and aggression among student teachers at secondary level. *Universal Journal of Educational Research, 5*(1), 137–140.

Kaltenbach, E., Hermenau, K., Nkuba, M., Goessmann, K., & Hecker, T. (2018). Improving interaction competencies with children—a pilot feasibility study to reduce school corporal punishment. *Journal of Aggression, Maltreatment & Trauma, 27*(1), 35–53. https://doi.org/10.1080/10926771.2017.1357060

Kambuga, Y. M., Manyengo, P. R., & Mbalamula, Y. S. (2018). Corporal punishment as a strategic reprimand used by teachers to curb students' misbehaviours in secondary schools: Tanzanian case. *International Journal of Education and Research, 6*(4), 183–194.

Kearney, P., Plax, T. G., Hays, E. R., & Ivey, M. J. (1991). College teacher misbehaviors: What students don't like about what teachers say and do. *Communication quarterly*, *39*(4), 309–324. https://doi.org/10.1080/014633 79109369808

Kesner, J. E. (2000). Teacher characteristics and the quality of child–teacher relationships. *Journal of school psychology*, *38*(2), 133–149. https://doi.org/10.1016/S0022-4405(99)00043-6

Klassen, R. M., & Chiu, M. M. (2011). The occupational commitment and intention to quit of practicing and pre-service teachers: Influence of self-efficacy, job stress, and teaching context. *Contemporary Educational Psychology*, *36*(2), 114–129. https://doi.org/10.1016/j.cedpsych.2011.01.002

Kraft, M. A., Marinell, W. H., & Shen-Wei Yee, D. (2016). School organizational contexts, teacher turnover, and student achievement: Evidence from panel data. *American Educational Research Journal*, *53*(5), 1411–1449. https://doi.org/10.3102/0002831216667478

Kukla-Acevedo, S. (2009). Leavers, movers, and stayers: The role of workplace conditions in teacher mobility decisions. *The Journal of Educational Research*, *102*(6), 443–452. https://doi.org/10.3200/JOER.102.6.443-452

Lewis, R. (2001). Classroom discipline and student responsibility: The students' view. *Teaching and Teacher Education*, *17*(3), 307–319. https://doi.org/10.1016/S0742-051X(00)00059-7

Lewis, R. (2006). Classroom discipline in Australia. In C. Evertson & C. S. Weinstein (Eds.), *International handbook of classroom management: Research, practice and contemporary issues* (pp. 1193–1214). Lawrence Erlbaum.

Lewis, R., Montuoro, P., & McCann, P. (2013). Self-predicted classroom behavior without external controls: Imagining a "Lord of the Flies" scenario. *Australian Journal of Education*, *57*, 270–291. https://doi.org/10.1177/0004944113496175

Lewis, R., & Riley, P. (2009). Teacher misbehavior. In I. J. Saha & A. G. Dworkin (Eds.), *The international handbook of research on teachers and teaching* (pp. 417–431). Springer.

Lewis, R., Romi, S., Katz, Y. J., & Qui, X. (2008). Students' reaction to classroom discipline in Australia, Israel, and China. *Teaching and Teacher Education: An International Journal of Research and Studies*, *24*(3), 715–724. https://doi.org/10.1016/j.tate.2007.05.003

Lewis, R., Romi, S., Qui, X., & Katz, Y. J. (2005). Teachers' classroom discipline and student misbehavior in Australia, China and Israel. *Teaching and Teacher Education*, *21*(6), 729–741. https://doi.org/10.1016/j.tate.2005.05.008

Lucas-Molina, B., Williamson, A. A., Pulido, R., & Pérez-Albéniz, A. (2015). Effects of teacher–student relationships on peer harassment: A multilevel study. *Psychology in the Schools*, *52*(3), 298–315. https://doi.org/10.1002/pits.21822

Mainhard, M. T., Brekelmans, M., & Wubbels, T. (2011). Coercive and supportive teacher behaviour: Within-and across-lesson associations with the classroom social climate. *Learning and Instruction*, *21*(3), 345–354. https://doi.org/10.1016/j.learninstruc.2010.03.003

Mazer, J. P. (2012). Development and validation of the student interest and engagement scales. *Communication Methods and Measures*, *6*(2), 99–125. https://doi.org/10.1080/19312458.2012.679244

Mazer, J. P. (2013a). Associations among teacher communication behaviors, student interest, and engagement: A validity test. *Communication Education*, *62*(1), 86–96. https://doi.org/10.1080/03634523.2012.731513

Mazer, J. P. (2013b). Student emotional and cognitive interest as mediators of teacher communication behaviors and student engagement: An examination of direct and interaction effects. *Communication Education*, *62*(3), 253–277. https://doi.org/10.1080/03634523.2013.777752

Mazer, J. P., & Stowe, S. A. (2016). Can teacher immediacy reduce the impact of verbal aggressiveness? Examining effects on student outcomes and perceptions of teacher credibility. *Western Journal of Communication*, *80*(1), 21–37. https://doi.org/10.1080/10570314.2014.943421

McCarthy, C. J., Lineback, S., & Reiser, J. (2015). Teacher stress, emotion, and classroom management. In E. T. Emmer & E. J. Sabornie (Eds.), *Handbook of classroom management* (2nd ed., pp. 301–321). Taylor & Francis.

Mendez, L. M. R., Knoff, H. M., & Ferron, J. M. (2002). School demographic variables and out-of-school suspension rates: A quantitative and qualitative analysis of a large, ethnically diverse school district. *Psychology in the Schools*, *39*(3), 259–277. https://doi.org/10.1002/pits.10020

Montuoro, P. (2016). *The causal process of teacher aggression: A mixed methods analysis*. [Unpublished doctoral dissertation]. La Trobe University. http://arrow.latrobe.edu.au:8080/vital/access/manager/Repository/latrobe:41952

Montuoro, P. (2017). Failure to replicate ego depletion in the mechanism underlying teacher aggression: A conditional process analysis. *Journal of Articles in Support of the Null Hypothesis*, *14*(1). 1–18. www.jasnh.com/pdf/Vol14-No1-article1.pdf

Montuoro, P. & Lewis, R. (2015). Student perceptions of misbehavior and classroom management. In E. T. Emmer & E. J. Sabornie (Eds.), *Handbook of classroom management* (2nd ed., pp. 344–362). Taylor & Francis.

Montuoro, P., & Lewis, R. (2018). Personal responsibility and behavioral disengagement in innocent bystanders during classroom management events: The moderating effect of teacher aggressive tendencies. *The Journal of Educational Research*, *111*(4), 439–445. https://doi.org/10.1080/00220671.2017.1291486

Montuoro, P., & Mainhard, T. (2017). An investigation of the mechanism underlying teacher aggression: Testing I3 theory and the general aggression model. *British Journal of Educational Psychology*, *87*(4), 497–517. https://doi.org/10.1111/bjep.12161

Mottet, T. P., Frymier, A. B., & Beebe, S. A. (2006). Theorizing about instructional communication. In T. P. Mottet, V. P. Richmond, & J. C. McCroskey (Eds.), *Handbook of instructional communication* (pp. 255–282). Pearson.

Myers, S. A. (2001). Perceived instructor credibility and verbal aggressiveness in the college classroom. *Communication Research Reports*, *18*(4), 354–364. https://doi.org/10.1080/08824090109384816

Myers, S. A. (2002). Perceived aggressive instructor communication and student state motivation, learning, and satisfaction. *Communication Reports*, *15*(2), 113–121. https://doi.org/10.1080/08934210209367758

Myers, S. A., & Knox, R. L. (2000). Perceived instructor argumentativeness and verbal aggressiveness and student outcomes. *Communication Research Reports*, *17*(3), 299–309. https://doi.org/10.1080/08824090009388777

Myers, S. A., & Rocca, K. A. (2001). Perceived instructor argumentativeness and verbal aggressiveness in the college classroom: Effects on student perceptions of climate, apprehension, and state motivation. *Western Journal of Communication*, *65*(2), 113–137. https://doi.org/10.1080/10570310109374696

Nesdale, D., & Pickering, K. (2006). Teachers' reactions to children's aggression. *Social Development*, *15*(1), 109–127. https://doi.org/10.1111/j.1467-9507.2006.00332.x

Neto, F., & Mullet, E. (2004). Personality, self-esteem, and self-construal as correlates of forgivingness. *European Journal of Personality*, *18*(1), 15–30. https://doi.org/10.1002/per.500

Openakker, M. C., & Minnaert, A. (2011). Relationship between learning environment characteristics and academic engagement. *Psychological Reports*, *109*(1), 259–284. https://doi.org/10.2466/09.10.11.PR0.109.4.259-284

Parrott, W. G., Sabini, J., & Silver, M. (1988). The roles of self-esteem and social interaction in embarrassment. *Personality and Social Psychology Bulletin*, *14*(1), 191–202. https://doi.org/10.1177/0146167288141019

Pianta, R. C. (2006). Classroom management and relationships between children and teachers: Implications for research and practice. In C. M. Evertson, & C. S. Weinstein (Eds.), *Handbook of classroom management: Research, practice, and contemporary issues* (pp. 685–710). Lawrence Erlbaum Associates.

Piekarska, A. (2000). School stress, teachers' abusive behaviors, and children's coping strategies. *Child Abuse & Neglect*, *24*(11), 1443–1449. https://doi.org/10.1016/S0145-2134(00)00201-5

Ribeiro, A. & Divoll, K. (2020). Keeping your sanity: 6 strategies to promote well-being. *New Teacher Advocate*, Winter, 14–15.

Riley, P. (2009). An adult attachment perspective on the student-teacher relationship and classroom management difficulties. *Teaching and Teacher Education*, *25*(5), 626–635. https://doi.org/10.1016/j.tate.2008.11.018

Riley, P., Lewis, R., & Brew, C. (2010). Why did you do that? Teachers explain the use of legal aggression in the classroom. *Teaching and Teacher Education*, *26*(4), 957–964. https://doi.org/10.1016/j.tate.2009.10.037

Riley, P., Watt, H. M., Richardson, P. W., & De Alwis, N. (2012). Relations among beginning teachers' self-reported aggression, unconscious motives, personality, role stress, self-efficacy and burnout. In T. Wubbels, P. den Brok, J. van Tartwijk, J. Levy (Eds.) *Interpersonal relationships in education* (pp. 149–166). Brill Sense.

Romi, S., Lewis, R., & Katz, Y. J. (2009). Student responsibility and classroom discipline in Australia, China, and Israel. *Compare*, *39*(4), 439–453. https://doi.org/10.1080/03057920802315916

Romi, S., Lewis, R., Roache, J., & Riley, P. (2011). The impact of teachers' aggressive management techniques on students' attitudes to schoolwork. *Journal of Educational Research*, *104*(4), 231–240. https://doi.org/10.1080/00220671003719004

Romi, S., Salkovsky, M., & Lewis, R. (2016). Reasons for aggressive classroom management and directions for change through teachers' professional development programmes. *Journal of Education for Teaching*, *42*(2), 173–187. https://doi.org/10.1080/02607476.2016.1144633

Sava, F. A. (2002). Causes and effects of teacher conflict-inducing attitudes toward pupils: A path analysis model. *Teaching and Teacher Education*, *18*(8), 1007–1021. https://doi.org/10.1016/S0742-051X(02)00056-2

Seyrek, Ö. D., & Ersanh, E. (2020). Examining the relationship between the teachers' emotional reactivity and aggression levels. *International Journal of Progressive Education*, *16*(5), 459–471. https://pdfs.semanticscholar.org/b521/bd1a1c2c4b90333235cb97f66d7fe7690977.pdf

Stipek, D., & Miles, S. (2008). Effects of aggression on achievement: Does conflict with the teacher make it worse? *Child Development*, *79*(6), 1721–1735. https://doi.org/10.1111/j.1467-8624.2008.01221.x

Straus, M. A. (1994). *Beating the devil out of them: Corporal punishment in American families*. Lexington Books.

Suryaningrat, R. D., Mangunsong, F. M., & Riantoputra, C. D. (2020). Teachers' aggressive behaviors: what is considered acceptable and why? *Heliyon*, *6*(10), 1–9. https://doi.org/10.1016/j.heliyon.2020.e05082

Sutcher, L., Darling-Hammond, L., & Carver-Thomas, D. (2016). *A coming crisis in teaching? Teacher supply, demand, and shortages in the US*. Learning Policy Institute. https://learningpolicyinstitute.org/sites/default/files/productfiles/A_Coming_Crisis_in_Teaching_REPORT.pdf

Syrmpas, I., & Bekiari, A. (2015). The relationship between perceived physical education teacher's verbal aggressiveness and argumentativeness with students' interpersonal attraction. *Inquiries in Sport & Physical Education, 13*(2), 21–32.

Szabados, B. (1990). Embarrassment and self-esteem. *Journal of Philosophical Research, 15,* 341–349. https://doi.org/10.5840/jpr_1990_3

Titsworth, B. S., McKenna, T., Mazer, J. P., & Quinlan, M. M. (2013). The bright side of emotion in the classroom: How teachers influence students' enjoyment, hope, and pride. *Communication Education, 62*(2), 191–209. https://doi.org/10.1080/03634523.2013.763997

Titsworth, B. S., Quinlan, M. M., & Mazer, J. P. (2010). Emotion in teaching and learning: Development and validation of the Classroom Emotions Scale. *Communication Education, 59*(4), 431–452. https://doi.org/10.1080/03634521003746156

United Nations Convention on the Rights of the Child (1989). *Entry into force September 2nd, 1990, in accordance with article 49.* United Nations Human Rights. www.ohchr.org/EN/ProfessionalInterest/Pages/CRC.aspx

Wang, M. T., & Holcombe, R. (2010). Adolescents' perceptions of school environment, engagement, and academic achievement in middle school. *American Educational Research Journal, 47*(3), 633–662. https://doi.org/10.3102/0002831209361209

Watson, M., & Ecken, L. (2003). *Learning to trust: Transforming difficult elementary classrooms through developmental discipline.* Jossey-Bass.

Wong, H. K., & Wong, R. T. (2018). *The classroom management book* (2nd ed.). Harry K. Wong Publishing, Inc.

Woolfolk Hoy, A. & Weinstein, C. S. (2006). Student and teacher perceptions on classroom management. In C. M. Evertson, & C. S. Weinstein (Eds.), *Handbook of classroom management: Research, practice, and contemporary issues* (pp. 181–219). Lawrence Erlbaum Associates.

Wubbels, T., Brekelmans, M., den Brok, P., & van Tartwijk, J. (2006). An interpersonal perspective on classroom management in secondary classrooms in the Netherlands. In C. M. Evertson & C. S. Weinstein (Eds.), *Handbook of classroom management: Research, practice, and contemporary issues* (pp. 1161–1191). Lawrence Erlbaum Associates.

Yurdakul, A., & Üner, S. (2015). Sağlık yüksekokulu öğrencilerinin duygusal tepkisellik durumlarının değerlendirilmesi [Evaluation of emotional reactivity status of health school students]. *TAF Preventive Medicine Bulletin, 14*(4), 300–307.

23

AN EQUITY-DRIVEN BEHAVIOR MANAGEMENT APPROACH TO CLOSE THE DISCIPLINE GAP

Anna Long and Kelly Clark

LOUISIANA STATE UNIVERSITY

Introduction

It only takes one or two kids who are very hyperactive or very undisciplined to almost ruin it for everybody. You know, and it really has a big impact on even good kids … when they see other kids come to school and they get exposed to those different personalities and different ways of doing things and they pick it up a lot of times.

Tillery et al., 2010, p. 92

A negative behavior … requires a negative response. Be it a loss of a privilege or the loss of a treat or … play time or something else … I think they have to learn that it is accompanied by a consequence … it's something that I feel like they need to learn at a very young age.

Tillery et al., 2010, p. 98

As the opening quotations illustrate, student disruptive behavior is common, and teachers often have a negative emotional and behavioral reaction to it. When problem behavior is experienced as chronic and unmanageable by the adults in their environment, it is associated with multiple outcomes that teachers find aversive, including loss of precious instructional time, heightened stress, and diminished job satisfaction and confidence in their ability to control the outcomes of their classrooms (Cook et al., 2015; Long, Renshaw et al., 2018; Okonofua et al., 2016). It is well established that opportunities to learn are related to academic success (Greenwood et al., 2002). Therefore, behavioral disruptions not only result in problematic social interactions, upsetting the classroom climate, but also reduced academic achievement. In an age of accountability, teachers feel heightened pressure to ensure their classrooms achieve the expected academic outcomes. Thus, anything that threatens a loss of instructional time and students' learning opportunities can be particularly stress-inducing. In fact, in a national study (Johnson et al., 2010), student problem behavior was a major contributing factor to discontent among teachers, with teacher stressors significantly contributing to the rising crisis of teacher shortages (Sutcher et al., 2016). Teachers with little preparation for the classroom tend to leave at rates two to three times higher than those appropriately prepared for the job (Sutcher et al., 2016). Despite this, recent research reveals that teachers continue to receive inadequate pre-service

DOI: 10.4324/9781003275312-27

training and insufficient support on the job to effectively manage student behavior (Flower et al., 2017; Mitchell & Bradshaw, 2013).

To manage student classroom behavior, teachers employ a variety of strategies; yet one type of strategy continues to reign supreme: the use of punishment (Reinke et al., 2013; Skiba & Losen, 2016). Punishment procedures often try to capitalize on social control and are reactive (i.e., aversive consequence is applied *after* a challenging behavior occurs), rather than proactive (i.e., desirable antecedent is provided to reinforce adaptive behavior, thereby preventing occurrence of challenging behavior). A particularly concerning form of punitive behavior management is exclusionary discipline, or the removal of a student from the learning environment because of a behavioral infraction. Examples of exclusionary discipline include sending a student to the hallway or office disciplinary referrals (e.g., "go to the principal's office"), as well as suspensions and even expulsion.

An overreliance on punishment procedures, particularly exclusionary discipline, undermines the teacher-student relationship and contributes to student disengagement (Cook et al., 2018). Furthermore, research consistently shows that the use of punitive and exclusionary practices disproportionately impacts students of color and those from lower socioeconomic backgrounds or with disabilities (Welsh & Little, 2018). For instance, there are significantly higher rates of and disproportionalities in the application of corporal punishment and alternate sanctions to exclusionary discipline for Black students. Ironically, punitive disciplinary strategies not only lack empirical evidence of effectiveness at reducing challenging student behaviors, but these strategies are associated with poorer academic, social, and behavioral functioning for students (e.g., Hirschfield, 2008; Hirschfield & Celinska, 2011; Lewis et al., 2005; Skiba & Rausch, 2006). In this chapter, we discuss the challenges that teachers are often faced with, followed by an examination of the reasons why punitive discipline practices continue to pervade our schools and the subsequent racial discipline gap they produce. We conclude by outlining potential pathways forward that are supportive of students and teachers and attend to the dynamic interchange between them.

The Challenges of Teaching

The need to attend to the behavioral health of youth as foundational to ensuring their school success has been brought to the forefront by the COVID-19 pandemic. Research suggests that roughly one in five youth have diagnosable mental health disorders (Kessler et al., 2005; Merikangas et al., 2010), and more than one-third have experienced childhood adversity or trauma (Kessler et al., 2010). Notably, these estimates were established prior to the COVID-19 pandemic. Since the onset of the pandemic, children, families, and schools have experienced unprecedented collective trauma, social isolation, economic stress, and life disruption. Furthermore, rates of adverse childhood experiences have significantly increased (Song et al., 2020). Adverse childhood experiences include, but are not limited to, abuse (e.g., physical, emotional, sexual), neglect, loss of a loved one, parental incarceration, chronic environmental stressors (e.g., domestic or community violence), and familial situations (e.g., divorce, mental illness, or substance abuse). When children are exposed to traumatic experiences, the effects can permeate throughout their lives, inhibiting their learning, disrupting their core self-regulatory functioning, and impacting their interpersonal relations with others (Devi et al., 2019; Ford et al., 2012). Given the significant life stressors across the pandemic, it is likely that the prevalence and severity of behavioral health challenges in youth have only expanded. Therefore, teachers are likely to observe more internalizing (e.g., fear, depression, somatic complaints) and externalizing (e.g., anger, aggression, defiance, conduct issues, substance use) problems in their classrooms.

Studies of the actual incidence and prevalence for specific problem behaviors experienced by teachers in the classroom are infrequent, especially compared to epidemiological studies of the prevalence of childhood mental health disorders and trauma. However, one study conducted of a nationally representative sample of youth in classrooms across the U.S. revealed roughly 8% of children often worried, and 8% of teens often displayed silly behavior, while substantial percentages of children and adolescents were distractable or engaged in excessive movement (Harrison et al., 2012). Unsurprisingly, disruptive, hyperactive, or acting out behaviors were found to be the most common problems, of greatest concern to teachers, and most frequent reasons for office discipline referrals. Taken together, it is clear that all teachers face a spectrum of challenging student behavior, from mild and slightly interruptive behaviors to severely disruptive and even dangerous behaviors.

Discouraging for teachers, a bidirectional influence between problem behavior and academic underperformance can develop. More specifically, as problem behavior interrupts students' learning, their skill development is compromised; in turn, this lack of academic proficiency is associated with higher levels of off-task and disruptive behaviors, as students are frustrated by academic demands that exceed their abilities (Claessens & Dowsett, 2014). Thus, a recursive cycle can develop, leading to the repeated loss of learning opportunities, as behavior impacts academic skill development, and lack of skill development impacts behavior. Notably, beyond the direct adverse effects on students' learning who are engaged in these problem behaviors, their behavior also disrupts the education of their peers and has a detrimental impact on teachers. For instance, students have reported their peers' disruptive behaviors make it difficult to concentrate and interrupt their learning and instructional time (Bru, 2009). For teachers, problem behaviors in the classroom are associated with elevated stress, increased emotional exhaustion and depersonalization, and lower perceived self-efficacy, all of which contribute to leaving the field (Sanetti et al., 2020). Among teachers leaving the profession in their first five years of experience, as many as 50% report occupational stress as a prime reason for leaving (Algozzine et al., 2011). Devastatingly, teacher turnover rates are significantly higher in schools serving primarily students of color and those from low-income backgrounds (Simon & Johnson, 2015). Equally concerning are the documented higher attrition rates of teachers of color who disproportionately serve in high-poverty and high-minority schools (Sutcher et al., 2016).

As noted earlier, teachers today are held accountable for student academic outcomes. Frequently, the data collected by schools related to standardized testing or performance goals are used as part of teachers' evaluations (Von der Embse et al., 2016). Unfortunately, stress is generated from accountability measures, which only heightens for teachers if a student (or students) regularly disrupts the learning environment. One of the strongest predictors of teachers' effectiveness is their ability to manage their classroom (Kane et al., 2013). Therefore, disruptive behaviors are a threat to teachers' ability to maintain control and maximize their students' learning—learning for which they will be judged and held accountable. Hence, in the service of protecting instructional time, teachers must respond to student disruptive behavior and maintain classroom control. In point of fact, students receiving office discipline referrals and other punitive actions overwhelmingly receive them due to their disruptive classroom behaviors (Harrison et al., 2012). Although disciplinary procedures, such as exclusionary practices or zero-tolerance policies, have been widely criticized and proven ineffectual, they continue to be used at concerningly high rates (Cook et al., 2018). One major reason for this is that educators often deem them necessary to ensure learning and promote safety (Welsh & Little, 2018). Also, educators are under the mistaken impression that by setting an example, other students, in addition to those punished, will be discouraged from breaking rules or misbehaving in the future (Gregory et al., 2010). Moreover, teachers may react with punitive discipline procedures, especially if they lack the training and support to use alternate proactive strategies (Flower et al., 2017; Reinke et al., 2013).

The Discipline Gap: An Urgent Problem

The use of swift and severe punishments for student misbehavior gained prominence following the 1980s War on Drugs, a spike in school violence in the 1990s, and as a result of several high-profile school shooting cases in the U.S. (Skiba & Peterson, 1999; Welsh & Little, 2018). Since then, the use of exclusionary discipline remains all too prevalent in today's schools. Exclusionary discipline refers to any school penalization that removes or excludes a student from the learning environment (e.g., office discipline referrals, suspensions, expulsions). Recent work suggests that about one-third of students are expected to receive at least one out-of-school suspension at some point in their education (Welsh & Little, 2018). When narrowed to adolescent years, about one-third of students receive at least one out-of-school suspension between 7th and 12th grades, and more than half of students (54%) receive at least one in-school suspension during this time (Fabelo et al., 2011).

Decades of research have documented racial disparities in exclusionary discipline among African American, Latinx, and Indigenous students compared to White students (Wegman & Smith, 2019); however, the disproportionality is most severe among youth identifying as Black or African American (Achilles et al., 2007; Bradshaw et al., 2010; Hirschfield, 2018). Evidence of the discipline gap was clearly shown by Fabelo and colleagues' study (2011), as African American males and females were disproportionately more likely than Hispanic and White males and females to receive an exclusionary disciplinary measure—altogether, African American students were 31% more likely to receive exclusionary discipline than Hispanic and White peers. Systemic inequities in exclusionary discipline are likely rooted in school staff's differential responses for the same behavioral infractions depending on student's race; for example, White youth are more likely to receive a non-exclusionary form of discipline (e.g., written warning), whereas African American youth are significantly more likely to receive exclusionary forms of discipline (e.g., suspension) for the same behavioral infraction (Wegman & Smith, 2019). Beyond the racial/ethnic disparities that consistently place Black and African American youth at greater risk for punitive and exclusionary disciplinary action, disproportionalities also have been well-evidenced among boys compared to girls, as well as among youth with disabilities compared to those without (e.g., Achilles et al., 2017). This means that Black and African American boys, and especially those with disabilities, are at greatest risk for being the recipients of punitive strategies and exclusionary discipline.

Beyond the use of exclusionary methods like suspension and expulsion, school personnel are legally allowed to use physical means to inflict pain (i.e., corporal punishment) as a disciplinary method in 19 states in the U.S.—a decision permitted on a state-by-state basis by the U.S. Supreme Court when it ruled in favor of the constitutionality of school-based corporal punishments in 1977 (*Ingraham v. Wright*; Gershoff & Font, 2016). Moreover, there is widespread racial disproportionality in the use of such discipline, as Black children are between 2 and 5 times more likely than White children to receive corporal punishment at school (Gershoff & Font, 2016).

Educators have been placed under a proverbial microscope, as researchers and policymakers alike work to understand the multifaceted causes of systemic education inequity (Welsh & Little, 2018). But despite the longstanding attention to this educational rights issue, punitive discipline and its disproportionate allocation continues to be present (Cook et al., 2018), with some research suggesting exclusionary procedures such as suspensions have doubled in frequency since the 1970s (Losen, 2013). As previously described, exclusionary discipline lacks empirical evidence for reducing challenging student behaviors; paradoxically, exclusionary discipline is actually associated with *increases* in the frequency and severity of students' challenging behaviors (Lewis et al., 2005), as well as involvement in the juvenile justice system (Fabelo et al., 2011) and criminal justice system (Pettit & Western, 2004). A recent meta-analysis demonstrated that exclusionary discipline exacerbated, rather than reduced, challenging behaviors among youth receiving it (Gerlinger et al., 2021). Not only is exclusionary discipline an ineffective deterrent of misbehavior (Fisher & Hennessy, 2016), but it is also associated with poorer academic performance and engagement, as well as an increased risk for school dropout (Hirschfield, 2008; Perry & Morris, 2014; Skiba & Rausch, 2006). This is likely because exclusionary discipline removes students from the learning environment, thereby decreasing their access to instruction, and diminishes their educational engagement. The scientific evidence is clear that exclusionary discipline strategies do not improve students' functioning, and instead worsen their behavioral health and educational performance.

The use of exclusionary discipline is associated with poorer school climate not only as perceived by students who are the recipients of such practices, but also among students who observe it (Mitchell & Bradshaw, 2013). This is in contrast to common beliefs among teachers that they are *setting an example* through punitive disciplinary procedures. Other unintended school-wide consequences of puni-tive exclusionary discipline methods include decreased overall academic achievement and increased anxiety for all students, not just those who are the recipients of exclusionary punishment (Perry & Morris, 2014). Further demonstrating detrimental school-wide effects, the use of exclusionary discip-line is inversely linked to all students' connectedness with teachers and other staff (Anyon et al., 2016).

Recent research also suggests a bidirectional link between the use of exclusionary discipline and teachers' stress and emotional exhaustion; teachers reporting high stress are likely to have reduced tol-erance for students' behavioral infractions (Eddy et al., 2020; Kokkinos et al., 2005) and may be more reliant on exclusionary methods such as office disciplinary referrals and suspensions for individual students (Eddy et al., 2020) and expulsions at the school level (Zinnser et al., 2019). Because such exclusionary practices are shown to actually worsen students' behavior, this likely leads to a recursive intensification of teachers' stress levels.

Contributors to Racial Disparities and Pathways Forward

Why do US public schools continue to perpetuate well-known racial disparities in student discipline, despite widespread criticism and scrutiny? As with all longstanding school problems, explanations are complex and multi-faceted, especially when the dynamic interchange between students and their teachers and schools is considered, and contributing factors are placed in the broader social and his-torical context. Thus, an equity-driven approach to behavior management will sharpen educators' focus on identifying disparities associated with race and ethnicity in schools and ensure they are involved in deliberate, strategic activities that analyze and target contributing factors within and out-side the school walls (Gay, 2018; Jagers et al., 2018).

Many school characteristics associated with racial disparities in discipline are connected to historical structural oppression and its vestiges. For instance, school demographics such as higher percentages of students eligible for free or reduced lunch (Christle et al., 2005), lower school academic achievement (Christle et al., 2005), more urbanicity (Noltemeyer & Mcloughlin, 2010), and a greater number of racial minorities in the student body (especially a higher percentage of Black students; Welsh & Little, 2018) have all been shown to explain rates of and disparities in punitive discipline practices. Sadly, the concentration of low-income and racial minority students into select schools is connected to societal practices that racially segregate and create unequally treated communities. According to the US Department of Education, roughly 60% of Black and Hispanic students attend schools, with greater than 75% of students identifying as racial or ethnic minorities (McFarland et al., 2017). This heightened segregation of students by race and ethnicity violates the accomplishments of Brown v. Board of Education (1954) and harkens back to redlining housing practices (Nardone et al., 2020) that produce a de facto segregation of students that persists nearly 70 years after the momentous *Brown v. Board* decision.

The aftereffects of housing redlining continue to undermine neighborhood schools today, as they erode the tax base for education and often provide opportunities for families with more financial means to flee to higher-quality educational contexts, taking their resources and social capital with them. Furthermore, low-income families, often families of color, are constrained to underperforming schools through attendance zone boundaries within school districts and through school district line drawing itself (Burke & Schwalbach, 2021). These practices further educational inequity and create a new type of redlining—educational redlining—perpetuating school segregation by race and socio-economic status (Kummings & Tienken, 2021). For instance, compared with other schools, racially isolated or segregated minority schools are under-resourced, offer fewer advanced and high-quality educational opportunities, less enrichment activities, serve a sizable proportion of students living in poverty, and a less qualified and stable teaching workforce (Burke & Schwalbach, 2021; Simon & Johnson, 2015; U.S. Government Accountability Office, 2016). Also, these schools are housed in communities that experience systemic inequities in transportation, employment, healthcare, and environmental injustices, in addition to housing inequality that produces transience in school attendance and instability in exposure to academic curricula (Carter, 2007). The combination of a concentration of higher educational needs coupled with limited resources, school functionality, and teaching competency readily results in excessive and ineffective discipline practices.

Because structural factors tied to historical oppression are not readily malleable to change, educational advocates and researchers have identified points of intervention that may be more readily remediated (Cook et al., 2018). Several school-, student-, and teacher-related factors have consistently been associated with discipline disparities. However, educators have touted the benefits of targeting contributors most proximal to students, including their lived experiences and teachers' practices and classroom interactions, as what happens in the classroom often results in the biggest improvements in student outcomes (Darling-Hammond, 2003). Thus, doing everything possible to develop, support, and retain good teachers is paramount. Still, it is also critical to interrogate the school discipline policies and philosophies within which teachers must function if equity efforts towards resolving racial discipline disparities is to be optimized (Sevon et al., 2021).

Research indicates that school discipline policies and philosophies are intricately associated with racial discipline disparities and that these disparities are found across grade levels, and even as early as preschool (Skiba, 2015). For instance, a review of zero-tolerance school discipline policies found that mandating predetermined and harsh consequences for student transgressions was not only ineffective and harmful, but consistently targeted youth of color, particularly Black males (APA Zero Tolerance Taskforce, 2008). Furthermore, this disproportionate impact could not be explained by differences in socioeconomic status or racial differences in misbehavior rates. Though the popularity of zero-tolerance policies has waned, the reliance on exclusionary practices with the intent of deterring or reducing problem behaviors remains. Furthermore, the range in the severity and type of behaviors that exclusionary discipline is applied to has expanded, including delivery for relatively minor and subjective behavioral infractions (Skiba et al., 2014). In relation, differences in the philosophies of principals also influence the use of exclusionary discipline. For example, principals that strictly adhere to harsh disciplinary policies or focus on eliminating distractions in their schools have higher rates of exclusionary discipline and more significant problems with disproportionality (Welsh & Little, 2018). In contrast, Mukuria (2002) found that lower rates of exclusionary discipline were associated with principals promoting the use of effective strategies and the development of positive student–teacher and school–family relationships. Furthermore, school policies that promote positive behavioral approaches are perceived by students as fairer and support the formation and maintenance of positive student–teacher relationships, in addition to helping remediate the use of exclusionary discipline (Gage et al., 2018; Mitchell & Bradshaw, 2013). For instance, in a study examining the effects of implementing PBIS in 35 middle schools, the use of proactive in place of reactive behavior management procedures led to a decrease in the rates of exclusionary discipline for Latino and American Indian/Alaska Native students, but not for African American students (as cited in Skiba & Losen, 2016).

In summary, research to date reveals that interrogation of school discipline policies and philosophies and aligning them with proactive and positive behavior support methods is one way to improve the disproportionate use of punitive disciplinary practices. Yet, targeted in isolation remains an insufficient approach. Therefore, below proximal targets for eliminating discipline disparities are reviewed, including supporting students' social-emotional and positive behavioral development (Center on PBIS, 2022; Durlak et al., 2011; Taylor et al., 2017), providing effective teacher classroom management training and support (Cook et al., 2015; Long et al., 2019), and reducing the chance of counterproductive interactions between teachers and minoritized students (Cook et al., 2018; Darling-Hammond et al., 2020; Okonofua et al., 2016). While attending to these more proximal contributors alone may not solve longstanding and deep-seated inequities found in broader society, they can and do go a long way in transforming the experiences and disciplinary outcomes of racial and ethnic minority students.

Student Social-Emotional Competencies and Behavior

Statement of the Problem. Many factors result in punitive and exclusionary practices, including disruptive behaviors students display. For several students of color living in poverty, a constellation of structural inequities can influence the development of vital social-emotional competencies and place them at risk for heightened rates of problem behavior (McGrath & Elgar, 2015; Okonofua et al., 2016). For instance, many of these students must deal with chronic stressors and are at greater risk for trauma exposure, discriminatory events, and inequitable access to necessary resources (Aspen Institute, 2018). Indeed, countless students bring their traumatic experiences and chronic stressors to school with them and sometimes even have these experiences in schools themselves. For instance, students of color disproportionately face housing instability, food insecurity, exposure to toxins, and inadequate access to healthcare, along with other stressors correlated with low socioeconomic status (Levy et al., 2016).

Plus, within schools, students of color may encounter low expectations, unsafe environments, and mistreatment (Aspen Institute, 2018). There is a well-established link between stressful life events and displays of child problem behavior (e.g., Little & Maunder, 2021). Yet, contrary to a common misconception, student behaviors associated with these experiences do not fully account for the discipline disparities regularly found (Cook et al., 2018; Huang & Cornell, 2017; Welsh & Little, 2018).

Several emotional concerns, acting out and executive functioning challenges, posttraumatic stress symptoms, and interpersonal problems can result from traumatic stress (Levy et al., 2016; Price et al., 2013). Using longitudinal data of a diverse sample of children and adolescents, Price et al. (2013) found a number of factors relevant to the relationship between childhood traumatic experiences and the psychological symptoms and impairment expressed, including, but not limited to, socioeconomic status. Furthermore, this study revealed that interpersonal traumas were associated with externalizing problems (i.e., defiance and conduct problems) in particular. Students of color living in economically disadvantaged communities are at elevated risk of exposure to interpersonal traumas not only stemming from community and domestic violence but also from race-based stressors (Levy et al., 2016), including microaggressions (i.e., commonplace slights, insults, putdowns, invalidations, and offensive behaviors; Sue, 2019) and mega-threats (adverse, large-scale, race-related events, such as police brutality against Black Americans; Leigh & Melwani, 2019). Research evidence shows that racism-related trauma can and does cause significant psychological harm that detrimentally impacts children's functioning and academic performance (Carter & Sant-Barket, 2015; Levy et al., 2016; Sue, 2019). Therefore, scholars point to the importance of building students' social-emotional and behavioral skills and setting up a school environment and contingencies for maintaining them (Cook et al., 2015; Taylor et al., 2017). By doing so, children at risk can develop the tools they need to be resilient and academically persist in the face of challenges.

Pathway Forward. An equity-driven approach to supporting students' behavior is two-pronged. It strengthens desired student behaviors by developing internal competencies and delivering appropriate external support. This approach to managing behavior emphasizes understanding and opportunities for growth over punishment, and integrating social-emotional learning (SEL) lessons with positive behavioral supports (PBS) to great effect. In fact, Cook et al. (2015) demonstrated empirically that the combination of universal SEL and PBS programming produced superior results to the business-as-usual, SEL alone or PBS alone conditions. Specifically, students in the combined condition displayed better overall mental health and a more significant reduction in externalizing behaviors when compared to the other study conditions.

SEL intervention. Social-emotional competencies comprise specific skills students need to function successfully in social contexts and positively develop (Aspen Institute, 2018). Five social-emotional competencies are now widely recognized in education and disseminated by the Collaborative for Academic, Social, and Emotional Learning (CASEL; https://casel.org): (1) *self-awareness*, or the ability to understand oneself and contributors to one's behavior, including emotions, thoughts, and values; (2) *self-management*, or the ability to regulate one's feelings, thoughts, and behaviors adaptively; (3) *social awareness*, or the ability to take perspectives and show empathy; (4) *relationship skills*, including the ability to get along with others and have healthy relationships; and (5) *responsible decision-making*, including the ability to make constructive choices and problem-solve. Much research has demonstrated the benefits of directly teaching social-emotional competencies, for instance, in a large-scale meta-analysis involving over 270,000 K-12 students (Durlak et al., 2011), students who participated in SEL programs demonstrated significantly improved pro-social skills, attitudes, behavior regulation, and academic performance in comparison to controls. Also, engagement in SEL programming has helped buffer against the development of mental health problems and risky behaviors as examined in a follow-up meta-analysis involving over 97,000 students (Taylor et al., 2017). Notably, the significant durability of these positive effects has also been established, with student improvements persisting post-intervention for up to as many as 195 weeks (Taylor et al., 2017).

However, equitable SEL is not simply about delivering lessons but also ensuring students' backgrounds, social identities, and cultures are affirmed (Aspen Institute, 2018). This means that the SEL programming and its delivery must be culturally responsive. That is, it must use the "cultural knowledge, prior experiences, frames of reference, and performance styles of ethnically diverse students to make learning encounters more relevant to and effective for them" (Gay, 2018, p. 36). Furthermore, SEL lessons should help students recognize, critique, and feel empowered to address mistreatment and inequities within and beyond their schools (Ladson-Billings, 2021). Finally, content of the SEL lessons should think about how to best address unique needs of minoritized students brought on by heightened exposure to stress and trauma and race-based stressors. For instance, some scholars have found that mindfulness can be an effective tool for decreasing racism-related stress (e.g., Hwang & Chan, 2019; Zapolski et al., 2019). Mindfulness is commonly defined as paying attention to the present moment without reactivity or judgement (Kabat-Zinn, 2003).

Positive behavioral intervention. While SEL lessons build the internal tools' children need to take on life challenges and thrive, PBS ensure students encounter teacher practices grounded in well-established behavioral principles that create positive and structured learning environments (Gage et al., 2020; Sugai & Horner, 2002). PBS, also commonly referred to as Positive Behavioral Interventions and Supports (PBIS), are rooted in applied behavior analysis, and focus on explicitly teaching, modeling, prompting, and reinforcing desired behaviors (Sugai & Horner, 2009). This behavioral approach emphasizes identifying and eliminating triggers for problem behavior and creating environmental contingencies that encourage appropriate behavior over punishing inappropriate behavior (Center on PBIS, 2022; Long, Sanetti et al., 2018). When problem behavior does occur, the goal is to respond in the least intrusive and reinforcing manner as possible to diminish the likelihood of the behavior reoccurring and safeguard the relationship between the teacher and student (Long, Sanetti et al., 2018). PBS are particularly effective in reducing externalizing problems in a manner that is not reactive or punitive (Gage et al., 2020). For instance, in a meta-analytic review of classroom behavior management strategies tested in majority racial and ethnic minority classrooms, positive behavioral interventions demonstrated large effects on reducing students' disruptive behaviors (Long et al., 2019).

Another benefit of implementing PBS to manage student behavior is evidence suggesting it reduces disproportionately in the allocation of exclusionary discipline by student race (McIntosh et al., 2018; Vincent et al., 2015). Furthermore, the implementation of PBS helps to counter a negative history of teacher-student interactions by shifting the focus from catching and punishing problem behaviors to acknowledging and reinforcing desirable ones (Jolivette et al., 2014). Despite these benefits, eliminating racial discipline disparities requires intentional exploration of its potential root causes, in particular the disaggregation of discipline data by student subgroup (Welsh & Little, 2018). For example, disaggregation of discipline data can improve educators' ability to recognize patterns and tailor behavioral supports (Boneshefski & Runge, 2014; McIntosh et al., 2018). For instance, equity audits at the classroom or school levels can expose which teachers struggle the most with discipline and what students are most often receiving behavioral infractions (Blake et al., 2016). Scott et al. (2012) found that revamping office discipline referrals to include information regarding the time, location, grade level, and student ethnicity by incident permitted the exposure of racial disparities and contextual factors predicting problem behaviors. This information could then be used to make data-driven adjustments to PBS, ensuring a consistent decrease in behavioral problems and dismantling of causes to discipline disparities. In addition to data disaggregation, a critical evaluation is necessary of educator cultural norms informing the development of behavioral expectations and interpretations of student behavior.

Teacher Behavior Management Training and Support

Statement of the Problem. Inadequate teacher training and support is another hypothesized contributor to the discipline gap in schools (Cook et al., 2018). Many teachers are insufficiently prepared to handle problem behaviors in their classrooms (Flower et al., 2017; Freeman et al., 2014). This lack of behavior management preparation and competency is even more pronounced for teachers working in high-poverty schools. For instance, teachers with weaker credentials disproportionately serve low-income and minority students, and first-year teachers are nearly twice as likely to be assigned to high-poverty schools than low-poverty schools (Almy et al., 2010). Given this, teacher professional development and support are critical to ensuring their success, particularly in classrooms where students have higher academic and behavioral needs. When teachers have inadequate preparation and training to deal with student behavior, research shows they rely on punishment strategies (Cook et al., 2018). For example, Arcia (2007) analyzed suspension data within a large urban district to understand variations between schools in the percentage of Black students suspended. This study revealed that educators' average years of experience were related to suspensions, such that the use of suspensions declined as years of experience increased. When educators are provided with appropriate training to use positive behavioral interventions, a reduction in racial disparities in exclusionary discipline can follow. In point of fact, an investigation of a two-year classroom management coaching program found that teachers in the treatment group showed no differences in discipline referrals between Black and non-Black students by the conclusion of the study. In contrast, teachers in the control group did (Gregory, Hafen et al., 2016).

Pathway Forward. Clearly, the provision of practical and adequate classroom management training and support shows promise for improving the equity of teacher behavior towards discipline. However, two domains critical to ensuring the effective and equitable delivery of PBS are often left unattended in the provision of teacher behavior management training. First, research consistently shows that training alone does not result in the successful and sustained implementation of teaching practices (Long et al., 2016). Teachers often require ongoing implementation support to integrate new behavioral strategies into their classrooms effectively. Second, the cultural backgrounds of teachers and students is not usually considered. This lack of deliberate attention to culture can result in the application of color-blind or race-neutral behavioral strategies that ignore the basis upon which disparities in discipline exist in the first place (Skiba, 2015).

Supporting Implementation. Teachers who simply read aloud lessons from an empirically supported SEL curriculum or do not implement a behavioral strategy in keeping with the underlying behavioral principles should not expect to see desired changes in student behavior (Upright et al., 2020). A systematic review of research on training in schools has shown that standard professional development is inadequate for changing teachers' behavior in the classroom (Joyce & Showers, 2002). Therefore, effectively supporting teachers' implementation of SEL or PBS practices starts with adequate training. Adequate training involves the use of direct training procedures which are interactive and go beyond didactic instruction to include modeling and rehearsal or practice with feedback (Fallon, Kurtz et al., 2018). Although direct training procedures are more time and labor intensive, the benefits to teachers' implementation promotion far outweigh these costs.

Following training, the provision of time-limited, but ideally, ongoing implementation supports is required (Long et al., 2016). Two time-limited implementation supports have shown promise in creating higher levels of teacher fidelity to intervention content and procedures: implementation planning and commitment emphasis (as cited in Upright et al., 2020). These methods are carried out with teachers immediately following intervention training and share features that require teachers to reflect on the importance of implementing practices as designed and think through what they need to implement successfully (Upright et al., 2020). When engaging in implementation planning, for example, teachers are asked to work through the logistical details of carrying out intervention procedures (i.e., action planning) and anticipate possible implementation barriers and strategies for resolving them (i.e., coping planning; Sanetti et al., 2015). Lastly, ongoing implementation supports typically involve teacher coaching or performance feedback across multiple weeks. For performance feedback, a coach or consultant will help teachers monitor and assess the integrity of their intervention implementation and identify needs for adjustment and support to ensure accurate delivery (Noell & Gansle, 2014).

Attending to Culture. Cultural mismatches between educators and students may also contribute to discipline disparities when left unresolved (Cook et al., 2018). For example, using ethnographic fieldwork, Golann (2015) attributed associations between culture, class, and discipline to the adherence and promotion of middle-class Eurocentric values within schools. He purported that the mismatch between students' home cultures and their schools resulted in a clash between what teachers and students viewed as acceptable and normative behaviors. However, by taking deliberate steps to understand students' cultures and the association to behavior, educators can more accurately interpret their students' behavior and incorporate their voice and cultural norms in the development of behavioral expectations and responses (Fallon et al., 2012; Fallon, Cathcart et al., 2018; Sugai et al., 2012). In support of this culturally informed approach, preliminary evidence has shown a significant association between observed culturally responsive teaching and proactive behavior management with positive student behaviors in classrooms (Larson et al., 2018).

Implicit Racial Bias and Negative Teacher-Student Interactions

Statement of the Problem. Although students' race and socioeconomic background are both associated with their likelihood of receiving punitive discipline, research indicates that race is dominant over other student characteristics in explaining disparities (Welsh & Little, 2018). In fact, students' race is one of the most significant factors in understanding discipline disparities (Chin et al., 2020) and remains predictive of receipt of exclusionary discipline even after controlling for socioeconomic status (Huang & Cornell, 2017). Furthermore, racial differences in discipline cannot be explained by differential types of student behaviors (e.g., fighting, threatening others, and substance possession), involvement in high-risk behaviors (e.g., carrying a weapon, consuming alcohol, or using marijuana), or aggressive or hostile attitudes by race (Huang & Cornell, 2017). Given these findings, research has examined the role of teachers' racial implicit biases, finding that higher levels of implicit (and explicit) racial bias are associated with greater discipline inequalities, particularly when comparing White and Black students (Chin et al., 2020; Welsh & Little, 2018).

Implicit racial bias is the social cognitive process of associating stereotypes and attitudes with racial groups without conscious awareness (Greenwald & Krieger, 2006). Implicit biases can become automatically activated in one's mind and result in prejudicial behaviors or judgments that elude one's knowledge and awareness (Greenwald & Krieger, 2006). Thus, these unconscious biases place teachers at risk of making unjust decisions or engaging in racially unfair practices, actions aligned with stereotypes even when teachers' intentions, values, and beliefs may be at odds with them (Cook et al., 2018). Gullo and Beachum (2020) nicely summarized that implicit racial bias is associated with many undesirable teacher behaviors including, "lower student expectations (van den Bergh, Denessen, Hornstra, Voeten, & Holland, 2010), increased incidences of office referrals (Blake et al., 2016), more frequent monitoring for problem behaviors (Gilliam et al., 2016), biased tracking decisions (Tetlock & Mitchell, 2009), and other forms of differential treatment" (p. 4). Furthermore, they found that school administrators' implicit racial bias explained differences in the severity of discipline assigned for subjective behaviors and that administrators often held pro-White implicit biases (Gullo & Beachum, 2020). Concerningly, Gregory and Mosely (2004) discovered that most teachers believed negative social forces working against minoritized students were the primary contributor to racial discipline disparities, with few appreciating the significant contributions of teacher and school discriminatory practices. Therefore, despite many educators' good intentions, implicit racial bias still plays a key role in the inequitable racial discipline patterns observed.

Educators can be ill-prepared and biased, and students of color at times can display disruptive behaviors that require teachers' management. Therefore, a singular focus on teacher professional development or student supports is inadequate for resolving discipline disparities (Cook et al., 2015, 2018). Instead, a focus on the reciprocal dynamic between teachers and students is necessary, especially since negative interactions based on bias and stereotyping can self-perpetuate and undermine the teacher-student relationship (Okonofua et al., 2016). For instance, a considerable challenge for students with stigmatized (or commonly stereotyped) identities concerns being prepared for and responding to prejudice and discrimination in school (Aspen Institute, 2018). A related challenge for teachers is to consistently operate in ways that reflect egalitarian values and are fair and equitable, despite unconscious biases (Chin et al., 2020; Okonofua et al., 2016).

According to Garcia and Crocker (2006), interactions between stigmatized and non-stigmatized parties can be perilous. Racially stigmatized students are often caught between two unacceptable alternatives—react and confront or internalize and overlook perceived mistreatment. Confronting a teacher about a misinterpretation or mistreatment of one's behavior may result in the fulfillment of stereotypes and a greater likelihood of receiving punitive discipline, as confrontation can create teacher discomfort and spark conflict. Yet, standing up for themselves also helps students maintain their self-worth, value, and agency. In contrast, a student attempting to ignore or absorb unfair treatment creates challenges of its own. Withdrawing and stifling oneself may help keep the peace, but this can be at the cost of one's self-esteem, take an emotional and psychological toll, and lead to heightened vigilance to protect oneself from prejudice or discrimination in the future (Garcia & Crocker, 2006; Pitoňák, 2017). Over time, student feelings of rejection and devaluation may influence their classroom behavior and lead to counter control behaviors (e.g., a racially stigmatized student actively opposing or resisting a teacher's attempts to regulate their behavior; Delprato, 2002). Furthermore, the anticipation of being the target of negative stereotypes creates a social threat that undermines student performance, as documented in the stereotype threat literature (Spencer et al., 2016). For example, meta-analyses have found that the effect size of stereotype threat for African American and Latinx students on intellectual tests is significant and ranges from d = 0.46 to d = 0.52 (Spencer et al., 2016).

Non-stigmatized parties, such as teachers, can approach interactions with students with apprehension or a need to regain control (Okonofua et al., 2016). Thus, they may operate based on two social pressures: (1) the desire to avoid acting on implicit biases or running the risk of being perceived as prejudicial, and (2) the need to eliminate behavior disrupting the learning environment swiftly. Both social motivations can result in counterproductive teaching behaviors. First, worrying about acting upon implicit biases can lead to discomfort in interactions with minority students and the suppression of thoughts and inhibition of normal behavioral expressions (Crocker & Gracia, 2006). Research suggests that the monitoring and suppression of stereotypic thoughts in the hopes of preventing them from influencing judgments and behavior can backfire, such that stereotype inhibition leads to a rebound effect in which the unwanted stereotype subsequently reappears with greater intensity (Macrae et al., 1994). Second, teachers are under heightened pressure to achieve target academic outcomes in their classrooms and are held accountable for missing benchmarks. Thus, when a student disrupts class learning, teachers may react aggressively in an attempt to regain control quickly (Okonofua et al., 2016). Over time, the activation and enactment of stereotypes by both teachers and students can undermine the objectivity and constructiveness of school/teacher–student relationships, leading to misinterpretations and a breakdown in trust (Okonofua et al., 2016).

Pathway Forward. In identifying implicit racial bias and counterproductive teacher–student interactions as key contributors to disciplinary inequities, the above analysis exposes two pathways forward. The first is implementing strategies to reduce the chance that teachers will process and respond to the misbehaviors of students of color in stereotypic or pejorative ways. The second is improving teacher–student communications and relationships.

Implicit Racial Bias Reduction. A significant body of research has investigated mechanisms for reducing implicit racial bias with mixed success (Burns et al., 2017; Lai et al., 2014; Pettigrew & Tropp, 2006). For example, Lai et al. (2014) held a research contest to compare interventions for reducing implicit racial prejudice experimentally. A total of 17 investigated interventions were submitted, with eight of the 17 found effective—the most successful interventions associated Black individuals with positivity or invoked high self-involvement. For example, repeated exposure to exemplars or counterstereotypes can reduce implicit bias, as can interventions that facilitate bias awareness and increase one's negative self-directed affect, resulting in the motivation to self-regulate stereotype application (Burns et al., 2017; Lai et al., 2014). However, questions about the durability of these improvements linger (Lai et al., 2016). In contrast, a meta-analytic test of intergroup contact theory found that intergroup contact consistently reduces intergroup prejudice (Pettigrew & Tropp, 2006).

Intergroup contact theory speculates that interracial experiences or contacts under the right conditions can result in mutual understanding and regard and reduce prejudice (Pettigrew & Tropp, 2006). Allport (1954) formulated the optimal intergroup conditions to include equal status between social groups in a situation, shared goals, intergroup cooperation, and authority or institutional support and reinforcement. These conditions have stood the test of time and research. The meta-analytic results decisively show that intergroup contact typically reduces prejudice and that the effects often generalize beyond participants in the immediate contact situation and can reduce bias in various intergroup situations and contexts (Pettigrew & Tropp, 2006). Furthermore, although Allport's conditions are not essential for intergroup contact to achieve positive outcomes, markedly higher mean effects of these interventions are observed when these conditions are met.

Targeting Relationships with Restorative Practices. Existing evidence shows that using discipline as an opportunity to promote students' growth and further positive teacher–student relationships, a practice known as restorative justice, is advantageous (Welsh & Little, 2018). For example, teachers implementing restorative practices have better relationships with their minoritized students and issue them fewer office discipline referrals (Gregory, Clawson et al., 2016). Similarly, Jain et al. (2014) showed that these practices result in improvements in the way students relate to and resolve conflicts with their teachers and peers, in addition to helping close inequitable gaps in student discipline. Finally, a recent review of empirical studies on restorative practices found that in most cases these practices lead to a reduction in discipline disparities (Darling-Hammond et al., 2020).

Restorative practices can take on various shapes and forms; however, it is helpful to identify core features consistently associated with positive effects. As revealed in Darling-Hammond and colleagues' review (2020), these features include practices to help students gain prosocial skills for adaptively managing conflicts, educator practices to guide and resolve disputes, and educator and school practices to promote connectedness and inclusivity. In essence, restorative practices facilitate teachers operating as warm demanders (or empathetic discipliners; Okonofua et al., 2016) who have trusting relationships with their students and open, constructive communication. Restorative interventions set aside time (e.g., restorative circles or meetings) to deepen relationships and repair harm, engage in empathy and introspection, and learn strategies for resolving conflicts (Tyler, 2006).

Conclusion

Research clearly demonstrates that discipline disparities are best understood to be multiply influenced. Factors contributing to the perpetuation of these disparities include, but are not limited to, school discipline policies and philosophies, teacher preparation and implicit racial bias, and student characteristics such as the heightened risk for problem behaviors, poverty, and race/ethnicity. Although the responsibility for the discipline gap may be placed at the hands of systemic inequities internal and external to the educational setting, a two-sided approach is needed to successfully eliminate the discipline gap. This approach targets both teachers and students in attempt to interrupt counterproductive dynamics between them. Such an approach attends to a neglected point of intervention: the interchange between unintentionally biased schools and educators and students' genuine apprehensions about and reactions to being the target of bias. Through culturally responsive SEL and PBS, educators may shift from an overreliance on ineffective, inequitable punitive disciplinary practices and toward evidence-based proactive strategies which have clear positive effects on students' overall functioning.

References

Achilles, G. M., McLaughlin, M. J., & Croninger, R. G. (2007). Sociocultural correlates of disciplinary exclusion among students with emotional, behavioral, and learning disabilities in the SEELS national dataset. *Journal of Emotional and Behavioral Disorders*, *15*, 33–45.

Algozzine, B., Wang, C., & Violette, A. S. (2011). Reexamining the relationship between academic achievement and social behavior. *Journal of Positive Behavior Interventions*, *13*(1), 3–16. https://doi.org/10.1177/109830070 9359084

Allport, G. W. (1954). *The nature of prejudice*. Addison Wesley.

Almy, S., Theokas, C., & Education Trust. (2010). Not Prepared for Class: High-Poverty Schools Continue to Have Fewer In-Field Teachers. *In Education Trust*. Education Trust.

American Psychological Association Zero Tolerance Task Force (2008). Are zero tolerance policies effective in the schools? An evidentiary review and recommendations. *American Psychologist*, *63*(9), 852–862. https://doi. org/10.1037/0003-066X.63.9.852

Anyon, Y., Zhang, D., & Hazel, C. (2016). Race, exclusionary discipline, and connectedness to adults in secondary schools. *American Journal of Community Psychology*, *57*(3–4), 342–352. https://doi.org/10.1002/ajcp.12061

Arcia, E. (2007). Variability in schools' suspension rates of Black students. *The Journal of Negro Education*, *76*(4), 597–608. https://doi.org/68.108.234.118

Aspen Institute (2018). Pursuing social and emotional development through a racial equity lens: A call to action. www.aspeninstitute.org/wp-content/uploads/2018/05/Aspen-Institute_Framing-Doc_Call-to-Action.pdf

Blake, J. J., Gregory, A., James, M., & Hasan, G. W. (2016). Early warning signs: Identifying opportunities to disrupt racial inequities in school discipline through data-based decision making. *School Psychology Forum: Research In Practice*, *10*(3), 289–306.

Boneshefski, M. J., & Runge, T. J. (2014). Addressing disproportionate discipline practices within a school-wide positive behavioral interventions and supports framework: A practical guide for calculating and using disproportionality rates. *Journal of Positive Behavior Interventions*, *16*(3), 149–158.

Bradshaw, C. P., Mitchell, M. M., & Leaf, P. J. (2010). Examining the effects of schoolwide positive behavioral interventions and supports on student outcomes: Results from a randomized controlled effectiveness trial in elementary schools. *Journal of Positive Behavior Interventions*, *12*(3), 133–148. https://doi.org/10.1177/10983 00709334798

Brown v. Board of Education, 347 U.S. 483 (1954).

Bru, E. (2009). Academic outcomes in school classes with markedly disruptive pupils. *Social Psychology of Education*, *12*(4), 461–479. https://doi.org/10.1007/s11218-009-9095-1

Burke, L. M., & Schwalbach, J. (2021). *Housing redlining and its lingering effects on education opportunity*. The Heritage Foundation. Backgrounder No. 3594. The Foundation.

Burns, M. D., Monteith, M. J., & Parker, L. R. (2017). Training away bias: The differential effects of counterstereotype training and self-regulation on stereotype activation and application. *Journal of Experimental Social Psychology*, *73*, 97–110. https://doi.org/10.1016/j.jesp.2017.06.003

Carter, R. T. (2007). Racism and psychological and emotional injury: Recognizing and assessing race-based traumatic stress. *The Counseling Psychologist*, *35*(1), 13–105.

Carter, R. T., & Sant-Barket, S. M. (2015). Assessment of the impact of racial discrimination and racism: How to use the Race-Based Traumatic Stress Symptom Scale in practice. *Traumatology*, *21*(1), 32–39. https://doi.org/10.1037/trm0000018

Center on PBIS (2022). Supporting and responding to student's social, emotional, and behavioral needs: Evidence-based practices for educators (Version 2). Center on PBIS, University of Oregon. www.pbis.org.

Chin, M. J., Quinn, D. M., Dhaliwal, T. K., & Lovison, V. S. (2020). *Bias in the Air: A Nationwide Exploration of Teachers' Implicit Racial Attitudes, Aggregate Bias, and Student Outcomes*. (Ed Working Paper: 20–205). Retrieved from Annenberg Institute at Brown University: https://doi.org/10.26300/n3fe-vm37

Christle, C. A., Jolivette, K., & Nelson, C. M. (2005). Breaking the school to prison pipeline: Identifying school risk and protective factors for youth delinquency. *Exceptionality*, *13*(2), 69–88. https://doi.org/10.1207/s15327035ex1302_2

Claessens, A., & Dowsett, C. (2014). Growth and change in attention problems, disruptive behavior, and achievement from kindergarten to fifth grade. *Psychological Science*, *25*(12), 2241–2251. https://doi.org/10.1177/0956797614554265

Cook, C. R., Duong, M. T., McIntosh, K., Fiat, A. E., Larson, M., Pullmann, M. D., & McGinnis, J. (2018). Addressing discipline disparities for Black male students: Linking malleable root causes to feasible and effective practices. *School Psychology Review*, *47*(2), 135–152. https://doi.org/10.17105/SPR-2017-0026.V47-2

Cook, C. R., Frye, M., Slemrod, T., Lyon, A. R., Renshaw, T. L., & Zhang, Y. (2015). An integrated approach to universal prevention: Independent and combined effects of PBIS and SEL on youths' mental health. *School Psychology Quarterly*, *30*(2), 166–183. https://doi.org/10.1037/spq0000102

Crocker, J., & Garcia, J. A. (2006). Stigma and the social basis of the self: A synthesis. In S. Levin & C. van Laar (Eds.), *Stigma and group inequality: Social psychological perspectives* (pp. 287–308). Lawrence Erlbaum Associates Publishers.

Delprato, D. J. (2002). Countercontrol in behavior analysis. *The Behavior Analyst*, *25*(2), 191–200.

Devi, F., Shahwan, S., Teh, W. L., Samasivam, R., Zhang, Y. J., Lau, Y. W., Ong, S. H., Fung, D., Gupta, B., Chong, S. A., & Subramaniam, M. (2019). The prevalence of childhood trauma in psychiatric outpatients. *Annals of General Psychiatry*, *18*, 15. https://doi.org/10.1186/s12991-019-0239-1

Darling-Hammond, L. (2003). Keeping Good Teachers: Why It Matters, What Leaders Can Do. *Educational Leadership*, *60*(8), 6–13.

Darling-Hammond, S., Fronius, T. A., Sutherland, H., Guckenberg, S., Petrosino, A., & Hurley, N. (2020). Effectiveness of restorative justice in U.S. K-12 schools: A review of quantitative research. *Contemporary School Psychology*, *24*, 295–308. doi:10.1007/s40688-020-00290-0

Durlak, J. A., Weissberg, R. P., Dymnicki, A. B., Taylor, R. D., & Schellinger, K. B. (2011). The impact of enhancing students' social and emotional learning: A meta-analysis of school-based universal interventions. *Child Development*, *82*(1), 405–432.

Eddy, L. H., Bingham, D. D., Crossley, K. L., Shahid, N. F., Ellingham-Khan, M., OttesleV, A., ... & Hill, L. J. (2020). The validity and reliability of observational assessment tools available to measure fundamental movement skills in school-age children: A systematic review. *PloS one*, *15*(8), e0237919. https://doi.org/10.1371/journal.pone.0237919

Fabelo, T., Thompson, M. D., Plotkin, M., Carmichael, D., Marchbanks, M. P., & Booth, E. A. (2011). Breaking schools' rules: A statewide study of how school discipline relates to students' success and juvenile justice involvement. Council of State Governments Justice Center.

Fallon, L. M., Cathcart, S. C., DeFouw, E. R., O'Keeffe, B. V., & Sugai, G. (2018). Promoting teachers' implementation of culturally and contextually relevant class-wide behavior plans. *Psychology in the Schools*, *55*(3), 278–294. https://doi.org/10.1002/pits.22107

Fallon, L. M., Kurtz, K. D., & Mueller, M. R. (2018). Direct training to improve educators' treatment integrity: A systematic review of single-case design studies. *School Psychology Quarterly*, *33*(2), 169–181. doi:10.1037/spq0000210

Fallon, L. M., O'Keeffe, B. V., & Sugai, G. (2012). Consideration of culture and context in school-wide positive behavior support: A review of current literature. *Journal of Positive Behavior Interventions*, *14*(4), 209–219. https://doi.org/10.1177/1098300712442242

Fisher, B. W., & Hennessy, E. A. (2016). School resource officers and exclusionary discipline in US high schools: A systematic review and meta-analysis. *Adolescent Research Review*, *1*(3), 217–233. https://doi.org/10.1007/s40894-015-0006-8

Flower, A., McKenna, J. W., & Haring, C. D. (2017). Behavior and classroom management: Are teacher preparation programs really preparing our teachers? *Preventing School Failure: Alternative Education for Children and Youth*, *61*(2), 163–169.

Ford, J. D., Chapman, J., Connor, D. F., & Cruise, K. R. (2012). Complex trauma and aggression in secure juvenile justice settings. *Criminal Justice and Behavior*, *39*(6), 694–724.

Freeman, J., Simonsen, B., Briere, D. E., & MacSuga-Gage, A. S. (2014). Pre-service teacher training in classroom management: A review of state accreditation policy and teacher preparation programs. *Teacher Education and Special Education*, *37*(2), 106–120.

Gage, N. A., Grasley-Boy, N., Lombardo, M., & Anderson, L. (2020). The effect of school-wide positive behavior interventions and supports on disciplinary exclusions: A conceptual replication. *Behavioral Disorders*, *46*(1), 42–53.

Gage, N. A., Whitford, D. K., & Katsiyannis, A. (2018). A review of schoolwide positive behavior interventions and supports as a framework for reducing disciplinary exclusions. *Journal of Special Education*, *52*(3), 142–151.

Gay, G. (2018). *Culturally Responsive Teaching: Theory, Research, and Practice* (3rd ed.). Teachers College Press.

Gerlinger, J., Viano, S., Gardella, J. H., Fisher, B. W., Curran, F. C., & Higgins, E. M. (2021). Exclusionary school discipline and delinquent outcomes: A meta-analysis. *Journal of Youth and Adolescence*, *50*, 1493–1509.

Gershoff, E. T., & Font, S. A. (2016). Corporal punishment in U.S. public schools: Prevalence, disparities in use, and status in state and federal policy. *Social Policy Report*, *30*, 1–37.

Gilliam, W. S., Maupin, A. N., Reyes, C. R., Accavitti, M., & Shic, F. (2016). Do early educators' implicit biases regarding sex and race relate to behavior expectations and recommendations of preschool expulsions and suspensions? (Research Study Brief). Yale University Child Study Center. Retrieved from https://medicine. yale.edu/childstudy/zigler/publications/Preschool%20Implicit%20Bias%20Policy%20Brief_final_9_26_276 766_5379_v1.pdf

Golann, J. W. (2015). The paradox of success at a no-excuses school. Sociology of Education, *88*(2), 103–119.

Greenwald, A. G., & Krieger, L. H. (2006). Implicit bias: Sci. foundations. CA Law Rev, *94*, 945–967.

Greenwald, A. G., Nosek, B. A., & Sriram, N. (2005). Consequential validity of the Implicit Association Test. Retrieved from: https://osf.io/preprints/psyarxiv/tnfgr/download

Greenwood, C. R., Horton, B. T., & Utley, C. A. (2002). Academic engagement: Current perspectives on research and practice. *School Psychology Review*, *31*(3), 328–349.

Gregory, A., Clawson, K., Davis, A., & Gerewitz, J. (2016). The promise of restorative practices to transform teacher–student relationships and achieve equity in school discipline. *Journal of Educational and Psychological Consultation*, *26*(4), 325–353. https://doi.org/10.17105/SPR45-2.171-191

Gregory, A., Hafen, C. A., Ruzek, E., Mikami, A. Y., Allen, J. P., & Pianta, R. C. (2016). Closing the racial discipline gap in classrooms by changing teacher practice. *School Psychology Review*, *45*(2), 171–191. https://doi.org/ 10.17105/SPR45-2.171-191

Gregory, A., & Mosely, P. M. (2004). The discipline gap: Teachers' views on the over-representation of African American students in the discipline system. Equity & Excellence in Education, *37*(1), 18–30.

Gregory, A., Skiba, R. J., & Noguera, P. A. (2010). The achievement gap and the discipline gap: Two sides of the same coin?. *Educational Researcher*, *39*(1), 59–68. https://doi.org/10.3102/0013189X09357621

Gullo, G. L., & Beachum, F. D. (2020). Does implicit bias matter at the administrative level? A study of principal implicit bias and the racial discipline severity gap. *Teachers College Record*, *122*(3), 1–28.

Harrison, J. R., Vannest, K., Davis, J., & Reynolds, C. (2012). Common problem behaviors of children and adolescents in general education classrooms in the United States. *Journal of Emotional and Behavioral Disorders*, *20*(1), 55–64. doi:10.1177/1063426611421157

Hirschfield, P. J. (2008). Preparing for prison? The criminalization of school discipline in the USA. *Theoretical Criminology*, *12*(1), 79–101. https://doi.org/10.1177/1362480607085795

Hirschfield, P. J., & Celinska, K. (2011). Beyond fear: Sociological perspectives on the criminalization of school discipline. *Sociology Compass*, *5*(1), 1–12. https://doi.org/10.1111/j.1751-9020.2010.00342.x

Huang, F. L., & Cornell, D. G. (2017). Student attitudes and behaviors as explanations for the Black–White suspension gap. *Children and Youth Services Review*, *73*, 298–308. https://doi.org/10.1016/j.childyouth.2017.01.002

Hwang, W.-C., & Chan, C. P. (2019). Compassionate meditation to heal from race-related stress: A pilot study with Asian Americans. *American Journal of Orthopsychiatry*, *89*(4), 482–492. https://doi.org/10.1037/ort0000372

Jagers, R. J., Rivas-Drake, D., and Borowski, T. (2018). Equity and social-emotional learning: A cultural analysis. CASEL Assessment Work Group Brief Series. doi:10.1037/t67831-000. https://measuringsel.casel.org/wp-content/uploads/2018/11/Frameworks-Equity.pdf

Jain, S., Bassey, H., Brown, M. A., & Pretty, K. (2014). *Restorative justice in Oakland schools: Implementation and impact.* Oakland Unified School District.

Johnson, J., Yarrow, A., Rochkind, J., & Ott, A. (2010). Teaching for a living: How teachers see the profession today. *Education Digest: Essential Readings Condensed for Quick Review, 75(5)*, 4–8.

Jolivette, K., Patterson, D. P., Swoszowski, N. C., McDaniel, S. C., Kennedy, C., & Ennis, R. P. (2014). School-wide positive behavioral interventions and supports in a residential school for students with emotional and behavioral disorders: First years of implementation and maintenance follow-up focus groups. *Residential Treatment for Children & Youth, 31*, 63–79. https://doi.org/10.1080/0886571X.2014.878584

Joyce, B. R., & Showers, B. (2002). *Student achievement through staff development* (3rd ed.). Association for Supervision and Curriculum Development.

Kabat-Zinn, J. (2003). Mindfulness-based interventions in context: Past, present, and future. *Clinical Psychology: Science and Practice, 10*, 144–156. https://doi.org/10.1093/clipsy.bpg016

Kane, T. J., McCaffrey, D. F., Miller, T., & Staiger, D. O. (2013). Have we identified effective teachers? Validating measures of effective teaching using random assignment. Research Paper. MET Project. *Bill & Melinda Gates Foundation.*

Kessler, R. C., Chiu, W. T., Demler, O., & Walters, E. E. (2005). Prevalence, severity, and comorbidity of 12-month DSM-IV disorders in the National Comorbidity Survey Replication. *Archives of General Psychiatry, 62*, 617–627. https://doi.org/10.1001/archpsyc.62.6.617

Kessler, R. C., McLaughlin, K. A., Green, J. G., Gruber, M. J., Sampson, N. A., Zaslavsky, A. M., . . . Williams, D. R. (2010). Childhood adversities and adult psychopathology in the WHO World Mental Health Surveys. *British Journal of Psychiatry, 197*, 378–385.

Kokkinos, C. M., Panayiotou, G., & Davazoglou, A. M. (2005). Correlates of teacher appraisals of student behaviors. *Psychology in the Schools, 42*(1), 79–89. https://doi.org/10.1002/pits.20031

Kummings, J. K., & Tienken, C. H. (2021). Redlining education. *Kappa Delta Pi Record, 57*(3), 100–103. https://doi.org/10.1080/00228958.2021.1935176

Ladson-Billings, G. (2021). *Culturally relevant pedagogy: Asking a different question.* Teachers College Press.

Lai, C. K., Marini, M., Lehr, S. A., Cerruti, C., Shin, J.-E. L., Joy-Gaba, J. A., Ho, A. K., Teachman, B. A., Wojcik, S. P., Koleva, S. P., Frazier, R. S., Heiphetz, L., Chen, E. E., Turner, R. N., Haidt, J., Kesebir, S., Hawkins, C. B., Schaefer, H. S., Rubichi, S., . . . Nosek, B. A. (2014). Reducing implicit racial preferences: I. A comparative investigation of 17 interventions. *Journal of Experimental Psychology: General, 143*(4), 1765–1785. https://doi.org/10.1037/a0036260

Lai, C. K., Skinner, A. L., Cooley, E., Murrar, S., Brauer, M., Devos, T., Calanchini, J., Xiao, Y. J., Pedram, C., Marshburn, C. K., Simon, S., Blanchar, J. C., Joy-Gaba, J. A., Conway, J., Redford, L., Klein, R. A., Roussos, G., Schellhaas, F. M. H., Burns, M., . . . Nosek, B. A. (2016). Reducing implicit racial preferences: II. Intervention effectiveness across time. *Journal of Experimental Psychology: General, 145*(8), 1001–1016. https://doi.org/10.1037/xge0000179

Larson, K. E., Pas, E. T., Bradshaw, C. P., Rosenberg, M. S., & Day-Vines, N. L. (2018). Examining how proactive management and culturally responsive teaching relate to student behavior: Implications for measurement and practice. *School Psychology Review, 47*(2), 153–166.

Leigh, A., & Melwani, S. (2019). #BlackEmployeesMatter: Mega-threats, identity fusion, and enacting positive deviance in organizations. *The Academy of Management Review, 44*(3), 564–591. https://doi.org/10.5465/amr.2017.0127

Levy, D. J., Heissel, J. A., Richeson, J. A., & Adam, E. K. (2016). Psychological and biological responses to race-based social stress as pathways to disparities in educational outcomes. *American Psychologist, 71*(6), 455–473. http://dx.doi.org/10.1037/a0040322

Lewis, R., Romi, S., Qui, X., & Katz, Y. J. (2005). Teachers' classroom discipline and student misbehavior in Australia, China and Israel. *Teaching and Teacher Education, 21*(6), 729–741.

Little, S., & Maunder, R. E. (2021). Why we should train teachers on the impact of childhood trauma on classroom behaviour. *Educational & Child Psychology, 38*(1), 54–61.

Long, A. C., Miller, F. G., & Upright, J. J. (2019). Classroom management for ethnic-racial minority students: A meta-analysis of single-case design studies. School Psychology, 34(1), 1.

Long, A. C., Renshaw, T. L., & Camarota, D. (2018). Classroom management in an urban, alternative school: A comparison of mindfulness and behavioral approaches. *Contemporary School Psychology, 22*(3), 233–248. https://doi.org/10.1007/S40688-018-0177-Y

Long, A. C. J., Sanetti, L. M. H., Collier-Meek, M. A., Gallucci, J., Altschaefl, M., & Kratochwill, T. R. (2016). An exploratory investigation of teachers' intervention planning and perceived implementation barriers. *Journal of School Psychology, 55*, 1–26. https://doi.org/10.1016/j.jsp.2015.12.002

Long, A. C. J., Sanetti, L. M. H., Lark, C. R., & Connolly, J. J. G. (2018). Examining behavioral consultation plus computer-based implementation planning on teachers' intervention implementation in an alternative school. *Remedial and Special Education, 39*(2), 106–117.

Losen, D. J. (2013). Discipline policies, successful schools, racial justice, and the law. *Family Court Review, 51*, 388–400.

McFarland, J., Hussar, B., De Brey, C., Snyder, T., Wang, X., Wilkinson-Flicker, S., ... Hinz, S. (2017). *The Condition of Education 2017*. NCES 2017-144. *National Center for Education Statistics*.

Macrae, C. N., Bodenhausen, G. V., Milne, A. B., & Jetten, J. (1994). Out of mind but back in sight: Stereotypes on the rebound. *Journal of Personality and Social Psychology, 67*(5), 808–817.

McGrath, P. J., & Elgar, F. J. (2015). Effects of socio-economic status on behavior problems. In J. D. Wright (Ed.), *International Encyclopedia of the Social & Behavioral Sciences* (2nd ed., pp. 477–480). https://doi.org/10.1016/B978-0-08-097086-8.23052-3

McIntosh, K., Gion, C., & Bastable, E. (2018). Do schools implementing SWPBIS have decreased racial and ethnic disproportionality in school discipline? In *Technical Assistance Center on Positive Behavioral Interventions and Supports*, 1–6.

Merikangas, K. R., He, J. P., Burstein, M., Swanson, S. A., Avenevoli, S., Cui, L., & Swendsen, J. (2010). Lifetime prevalence of mental disorders in US adolescents: Results from the National Comorbidity Survey Replication-Adolescent Supplement (NCS-A). *Journal of the American Academy of Child & Adolescent Psychiatry, 49*, 980–989. https://doi.org/10.1016/j.jaac.2010.05.017

Mitchell, M. M., & Bradshaw, C. P. (2013). Examining classroom influences on student perceptions of school climate: The role of classroom management and exclusionary discipline strategies. *Journal of School Psychology, 51*(5), 599–610. https://doi.org/10.1016/j.jsp.2013.05.005

Mukuria, G. (2002). Disciplinary challenges: How do principals address this dilemma? *Urban Education, 37*, 432–452. https://doi.org/10.1177/00485902037003007

Nardone, A., Chiang, J., & Corburn, J. (2020). Historic redlining and urban health today in U.S. cities. *Environmental Justice, 13*(4), 109–119. https://doi.org/10.1089/env.2020.0011

Noell, G. H., & Gansle, K. A. (2014). The use of performance feedback to improve intervention implementation in schools. In L. M. H. Sanetti & T. R. Kratochwill (Eds.), *Treatment integrity: A foundation for evidence-based practice in applied psychology* (pp. 161–183). American Psychological Association.

Noltemeyer, A., & Mcloughlin, C. S. (2010). Patterns of exclusionary discipline by school typology, ethnicity, and their interaction. *Penn GSE Perspectives on Urban Education, 7*(1), 27–40.

Okonofua, J. A., Walton, G. M., & Eberhardt, J. L. (2016). A vicious cycle: A social-psychological account of extreme racial disparities in school discipline. *Perspectives on Psychological Science, 11*(3), 381–398. https://doi.org/10.1177/1745691616635592

Perry, B. L., & Morris, E. W. (2014). Suspending progress: Collateral consequences of exclusionary punishment in public schools. *American Sociological Review, 79*, 1067–1087. https://doi.org/10.1177/0003122414556308

Pettigrew, T. F., & Tropp, L. R. (2006). A meta-analytic test of intergroup contact theory. *Journal of Personality and Social Psychology, 90*(5), 751–783. https://doi.org/10.1037/0022-3514.90.5.751

Pettit, B., & Western, B. (2004). Mass imprisonment and the life course: Race and class inequality in US incarceration. *American Sociological Review, 69*(2), 151–169.

Pitoňák, M. (2017). Mental health in non-heterosexuals: Minority stress theory and related explanation frameworks review. *Mental Health and Prevention, 5*, 63–73. https://doi.org/10.1016/j.mhp.2016.10.002

Price, M., Higa-McMillan, C., Kim, S., & Frueh, B. C. (2013). Trauma experience in children and adolescents: An assessment of the effects of trauma type and role of interpersonal proximity. *Journal of Anxiety Disorders, 27*(7), 652–660. https://doi.org/10.1016/j.janxdis.2013.07.009

Reinke, W. M., Herman, K. C., & Stormont, M. (2013). Classroom-level positive behavior supports in schools implementing SW-PBIS: Identifying areas for enhancement. *Journal of Positive Behavior Interventions, 15*(1), 39–50.

Sanetti, L. M. H., Charbonneau, S., Knight, A., Cochrane, W. S., Kulcyk, M. C., & Kraus, K. E. (2020). Treatment fidelity reporting in intervention outcome studies in the school psychology literature from 2009 to 2016. *Psychology in the Schools, 57*(6), 901–922.

Sanetti, L. M. H., Collier-Meek, M. A., Long, A. C. J., Byron, J., & Kratochwill, T. R. (2015). Increasing teacher treatment integrity of behavior support plans through consultation and Implementation Planning. *Journal of School Psychology, 53*(3), 209–229. https://doi.org/10.1016/j.jsp.2015.03.002

Scott, T. M., Hirn, R. G., & Barber, H. (2012). Affecting disproportional outcomes by ethnicity and grade level: Using discipline data to guide practice in high school. *Preventing School Failure, 56*(2), 110–120.

Sevon, M. A., Levi-Nielsen, S., & Tobin, R. M. (2021). Addressing racism and implicit bias--Part 1: A response to the framework for effective discipline. *Communique, 49*(5), 10–12.

Simon, N. S., & Johnson, S. M. (2015). Teacher turnover in high-poverty schools: What we know and can do. *Teachers College Record, 117*(3), 1–36.

Skiba, R. J. (2015). Interventions to address racial/ethnic disparities in school discipline: Can systems reform to be race neutral? In R. Bangs, & L. E. Davis (Eds.), *Race and social problems: Restructuring inequality* (pp. 107–124). Springer Science + Business Media.

Skiba, R. J., Arredondo, M. I., & Williams, N. T. (2014). More than a metaphor: The contribution of exclusionary discipline to a school-to-prison pipeline. *Equity & Excellence in Education, 47*(4), 546–564.

Skiba, R. J., & Losen, D. J. (2016). From reaction to prevention: Turning the page on school discipline. *American Educator, 39*, 4–44.

Skiba, R., & Peterson, R. (1999). The dark side of zero tolerance: Can punishment lead to safe schools? *The Phi Delta Kappan, 80*(5), 372–382.

Skiba, R. J., & Rausch, M. K. (2006). Zero tolerance, suspension, and expulsion: Questions of equity and effectiveness. In C. M. Evertson & C. S. Weinstein (Eds.), *Handbook of classroom management: Research, practice, and contemporary issues* (pp. 1063–1089). Lawrence Erlbaum Associates Publishers.

Song, S. Y., Wang, C., Espelage, D. L., Fenning, P., & Jimerson, S. R. (2020). COVID-19 and school psychology: Adaptations and new directions for the Field. *School Psychology Review, 49*(4), 431–437. https://doi.org/10.1080/2372966X.2020.1852852

Spencer, S. J., Logel, C., & Davies, P. G. (2016). Stereotype threat. *Annual Review of Psychology, 67*, 415–437.

Sue, D. W. (2019). Microaggressions and student activism: Harmless impact and victimhood controversies. In G. C. Torino et al. (Eds.), *Microaggression theory: Influence and implications.* Wiley.

Sugai, G., & Horner, R. (2002). The evolution of discipline practices: School-wide positive behavior supports. *Child & Family Behavior Therapy, 24*(1–2), 23–50.

Sugai, G., & Horner, R. H. (2009). Responsiveness-to-intervention and schoolwide positive behavior supports: Integration of multi-tiered system approaches. *Exceptionality, 17*, 223–227. http://dx.doi.org/10.1080/09362830903235375

Sugai, G., O'Keeffe, B. V., & Fallon, L. M. (2012). A contextual consideration of culture and school-wide positive behavior support. *Journal of Positive Behavior Interventions, 14*(4), 197–208. https://doi.org/10.1177/1098300711426334

Sutcher, L., Darling-Hammond, L., & Carver-Thomas, D. (2016). *A coming crisis in teaching? Teacher supply, demand, and shortages in the U.S.* Learning Policy Institute. https://learningpolicyinstitute.org/product/coming-crisis-teaching

Taylor, R. D., Oberle, E., Durlak, J. A., & Weissberg, R. P. (2017). Promoting positive youth development through school-based social and emotional learning interventions: A meta-analysis of follow-up effects. *Child Development, 88*(4), 1156–1171.

Tetlock, P. E., & Mitchell, G. (2009). Implicit bias and accountability systems: What must organizations do to prevent discrimination? *Research in Organizational Behavior, 29*, 3–38.

Tillery, A. D., Varjas, K., Meyers, J., & Collins, A. S. (2010). General education teachers' perceptions of behavior management and intervention strategies. *Journal of Positive Behavior Interventions, 12*(2), 86–102. https://doi.org/10.1177/1098300708330879

Tyler, T. (2006). Restorative justice and procedural justice: Dealing with rule breaking. *Journal of Social Issues, 62*(2), 307–326.

United States Government Accountability Office (2016). Better use of information could help agencies identify disparities and address racial discrimination (GAO-16-345). Author.

Upright, J. J., Long, A. C. J., & La Salle, T. P. (2020). Treatment integrity in school-based interventions: Assessing and supporting teacher intervention implementation. In C. Maykel & M. A. Bray (Eds.), *Promoting mind-body health in schools: Interventions for mental health professionals* (pp. 27–43). American Psychological Association. https://doi.org/10.1037/0000157-003

Van den Bergh, L., Denessen, E., Hornstra, L., Voeten, M., & Holland, R. W. (2010). The implicit prejudiced attitudes of teachers: Relations to teacher expectations and the ethnic achievement gap. *American Educational Research Journal, 47*(2), 497–527.

Vincent, C. G., Sprague, J. R., CHiXapkaid (Pavel, M.), Tobin, T. J., & Gau, J. (2015). The effectiveness of school-wide positive behavior interventions and supports in reducing racially inequitable disciplinary exclusion. In D. J. Losen (Ed.), *Closing the school discipline gap: Equitable remedies for excessive exclusion* (pp. 207–221). Teachers College Press.

Von der Embse, N., Sandilos, L. E., Pendergast, L., & Mankin, A. (2016). Teacher stress, teaching-efficacy, and job satisfaction in response to test-based educational accountability policies. *Learning and Individual Differences, 50*, 308–317. https://doi.org/10.1016/j.lindif.2016.08.001

Wegmann, K. M., & Smith, B. (2019). Examining racial/ethnic disparities in school discipline in the context of student-reported behavior infractions. *Children and Youth Services Review, 103*, 18–27. https://doi.org/10.1016/j.childyouth.2019.05.027

Welsh, R. O., & Little, S. (2018). The school discipline dilemma: A comprehensive review of disparities and alternative approaches. *Review of Educational Research, 88*(5), 752–794. https://doi.org/10.3102/0034654318791582

White, J. M., Li, S., Ashby, C. E., Ferri, B., Wang, Q., Bern, P., & Cosier, M. (2019). Same as it ever was: The nexus of race, ability, and place in one urban school district. *Educational Studies: Journal of the American Educational Studies Association*, *55*(4), 453–472. https://doi.org/10.1080/00131946.2019.1630130

Zapolski, T.C.B., Faidley, M.T. & Beutlich, M.R. (2019). The experience of racism on behavioral health outcomes: The moderating impact of mindfulness. *Mindfulness*, 10, 168–178. https://doi.org/10.1007/s12 671-018-0963-7

Zinsser, K. M., Zulauf, C. A., Das, V. N., & Silver, H. C. (2019). Utilizing social-emotional learning supports to address teacher stress and preschool expulsion. *Journal of Applied Developmental Psychology*, *61*, 33–42. https://doi.org/10.1016/j.appdev.2017.11.006

PART V

The Classroom Management and Student Type Interaction

24

CRITICAL RACE THEORY INSIGHTS ON ISSUES OF CLASSROOM MANAGEMENT

Patricia L. Marshall and Brittani N. Clark

NC STATE UNIVERSITY

Introduction

Contemporary PK–12 student demographics are distinguished by a level of diversity that spans a wider range of social axes than any previous period in US history.[1] Yet the axis of *race* consistently heightens angst over both work and interpersonal relationships in the nation's schools. Arguably, nowhere is this more prominent than in conjunction with activities that come under the realm of classroom management. Race complicates. And when it comes to the management of classrooms, complications associated with race have resulted in a plethora of unfair advantages, inequities, and missed opportunities that diminish the overall experience of school for untold numbers of children and youth. Race can be isolated as a singularly complicating factor in classroom management, but this in no way means that race operates in isolation. Rather, race typically intersects with other social identity axes creating intricacies that take on a normalized character in the everyday activities and commonplace interactions in schools. In turn, through its intersections with other axes, race can present chicken–egg illusions that sow doubt in the minds of some about the depth of its influences and reverberations. A challenge for scholars is to interrogate these intersections, and illuminate how they function in schools. In this chapter, we explore whether and how concepts from Critical Race Theory have been deployed to do just that as we analyze how race has been situated, troubled, and theorized in contemporary classroom management discourses.

Critical Race Theory: A Brief Overview

The first part of this chapter has three sections. First, we expose contours of a recent campaign directed, ostensibly, at protecting citizens from the purportedly corrupting influences of critical race theory. We explain how through legal decrees issued by officials at the highest levels of US government, this campaign has become a full-fledged social issue that has amassed supporters throughout the USA and beyond. Next, we explore the question *what is critical race theory?* and discuss some of its basic concepts and tenets. Finally, we present an overview of critical race theory in the field of education.

DOI: 10.4324/9781003275312-29

An Imminent Threat to US Democracy?

The mid-1970s marked the emergence of a project in legal scholarship focused on provoking "dialogical engagement with liberal race discourse and Critical Legal Studies"[2] (Crenshaw, 2002, p. 1343). In part, its purpose was to expose the complex anatomy of racialist underpinnings in the structures, interpretations, and applications of US jurisprudence. This project would become *Critical Race Theory*, although in a retrospective review of its development one of its founding scholars noted that "the name Critical Race Theory, …, was basically made up, fused together to mark a possibility" (Crenshaw, 2002, p. 1361). From its inception Critical Race Theory (CRT) was a highly contested project and, in its earliest days, leading advocates received harsh criticism from other legal scholars (Farber & Sherry, 1993; Kennedy, 1989) and from those in other academic disciplines who questioned some of its tenets (Gates, 1994). Critique of CRT took a detour into the abyss of partisan politics, however, when on September 4, 2020 a memorandum was issued by the Director of the United States Office of Management and Budget (OMB). The memorandum called for "all agencies … to begin to identify all contracts or other agency spending related to any training on 'critical race theory'," Under threat of defunding, the OMB memorandum decreed that in agency activities all references to critical race theory, direct or implied, were to be discontinued. Some two weeks later, the OMB memorandum was reinforced by Presidential Executive Order 13950, *Combating Race and Sex Stereotyping.*

That the OMB memorandum and Executive Order 13950 offered critique of CRT was not the problem; rather, it was the deliberate *distortions of CRT* that were concerning. To be clear, no mention of CRT is found in Executive Order 13950, yet on September 20, 2020 (just two days prior to the Order's release), President Trump made multiple direct references to the offending framework in a speech delivered at the White House Conference on American History. Among his comments was the following:

> Students in our universities are inundated with critical race theory. This is a Marxist doctrine holding that America is a wicked and racist nation, that even young children are complicit in oppression, and that our entire society must be radically transformed. Critical race theory is being forced into our children's schools, it's being imposed into workplace trainings, and it's being deployed to rip apart friends, neighbors, and families.
>
> *White House Event, 2020*

Trump's remarks exposed a direct connection between the OMB memorandum and the issuance of Executive Order 13950. Attacking "a possibility" that until then had been limited to academic discourses positioned CRT as an easy foil for a conservative political agenda. It was an agenda that, through its silence on the real issue of growing white nationalism, did more to stoke racial tensions in the USA than to de-escalate them. Nowhere in Executive Order 13950 is there mention of entrenched patterns of systemic racial terrorism and discrimination throughout US history. Nor is there a hint at how reverberations of those realities manifest in present-day US society. In the lives of contemporary African Americans, for example, unemployment levels that are consistently double that of the white population; extrajudicial killings of unarmed citizens by law enforcement officers; separate and unequal schooling; and most recently disproportionate risks for infection and death from the Covid-19 pandemic all offer compelling counterstories. Executive Order 13950 ignores these realities of US life and instead decontextualizes and distorts CRT tenets in service to ginning up fear and hysteria over a supposed threat to peace and racial harmony. Thus, the campaign against CRT can be seen as an effort to shut down discourse around features of US society that perpetuate what one scholar calls "the lie."[3] This is to say the language in the OMB Memorandum and Executive Order 13950 entrenches "the 'value gap' … that in America white lives have always mattered more than the lives of others, … [and that *the lie* is a] … broad and powerful architecture of false assumptions by which the value gap is maintained" (Glaude, 2020, p. 7). A question begged is *why a campaign against*

Critical Race Theory? The answer is traceable, in part, to backlash directed at The 1619 Project, a long-form journalism project that appeared in the August 18, 2019 issue of the *New York Times*.

Publication of The 1619 Project was timed to coincide with the landing (roughly 400 years prior) of the first 20 Africans off the shore of what is now the US state of Virginia. Developed and organized by award-winning journalist and McArthur Fellow Nikole Hannah-Jones, The 1619 Project is a collection of essays that detail the expansiveness of the system of Black enslavement and its connection to prominent sectors of US society including economics; law; medicine; housing; education; and entertainment. According to the authors of the essays, the strength of the foundation of these various sectors is traceable to exploitation of Black labor during the 250-year period of enslavement along with the 150-year post-Emancipation period that was bookended by roughly a decade of Reconstruction, and a nearly 90-year span of US-style racial apartheid better known as the era of Jim Crow. The latter formed the legally-sanctioned architecture that defined the second-class citizenship status, complete with discrimination, subjugation, and racial terrorism, reserved for the descendants of the enslaved.

Response to The 1619 Project was swift and varied. Although some renowned historians disputed the veracity of some of its details, others allowed that by and large its essays presented an accurate accounting of the role and influence of Black enslavement in the development of US society. Less than a year after publication of The 1619 Project, the White House Conference on American History where President Trump indicted CRT was held. In response, the American Historical Association Council issued a statement (co-signed by over 40 prominent professional associations including Phi Beta Kappa Society, Modern Language Association, and Southern Historical Association) that was decidedly not in alignment with the thrust of the Conference in general, and Trump's remarks in particular.[4]

Approximately 18 months after publication of The 1619 Project, and four months after issuance of the OMB Memorandum and the White House Conference on American History, President Joseph R. Biden issued Executive Order 13985, "Advancing Racial Equity and Support for Underserved Communities Through the Federal Government." Signed on his first day in office, Section 10 reads, "Executive Order 13950 of September 22, 2020 [issued by former President Donald Trump], … is hereby revoked" (Executive Order 13985). Issuance of the latter Executive Order might have constituted a full-circle moment in the anti-CRT campaign, yet as decisive as it may have been meant to be, Executive Order 13985 in no way marked the end of the politically tinged indictments of CRT. Just one month later, an article in the *New York Times* prompted comments from over 2,000 readers and illustrated how CRT had clearly emerged as the newest political wedge issue not just in the USA, but in the politics of other western democracies.[5] *Inside Higher Education* reported "[l]awmakers in 16 states have introduced or passed legislation … seeking to limit the teaching of critical race theory within public institutions" (Flaherty, 2021). In an interview in May 2021 on *Black News Tonight*, gubernatorial candidate for the state of Georgia, Vernon Jones, expressed pointed opposition to Critical Race Theory. When ask by his interviewer, Temple University associate professor and political commentator Marc Lamont Hill, to clarify exactly *what is critical race theory* the would-be governor responded:

> Well actually, I think it's different depending on who's teaching it and how they're teaching it … But there are those who are using their own ideology and their own party affiliation to go to the extreme. … but it's left up to you to understand [what is critical race theory] I can't make you understand. Fact of it is, the Critical Race Theory even on its basis should not be taught in our schools—period.

The convolutedness of this response mirrors that of many others who have joined the campaign against Critical Race Theory. In the next sections we offer a response to the question, and clarify CRT's central concepts and tenets.

So, What Is *Critical Race Theory*, and Is that Even the Question to Be Asking?

A number of pithy albeit opaque two–word responses to the question *what is critical race theory* can be found throughout the professional literature. Among them are *analytic tool* (Chapman, 2013; Ladson–Billings & Tate, 1995); *analytic framework* (Marshall, et al., 2016; Solórzano, 2013); *intellectual movement* (Brown & Jackson, 2013); *methodological frame* (Cook, 2013); *productive space* (Subedi, 2013); *theoretical framework* (Laughter & Han, 2019; Muñoz, 2009); and *theorizing counterspace* (Cabrera, 2018). Strictly speaking, each answers the question *what is CRT*, yet even a cursory review of academic scholarship reveals a more pressing question, which is, *how can CRT be used to dismantle systems of oppression*? In other words, most scholars concern themselves with the *justice ends* toward which CRT can be directed. In light of this we offer that while it's important to know what CRT is, many scholars are equally (if not more) concerned with *what can CRT be deployed to do?*

Central Concepts and Themes of CRT

Deployment of CRT by scholars across disciplines and institutions consistently has been structured around and guided by a collection of foundational concepts and themes drawn from diverse areas of study. Delgado & Stefancic (2017) note "critical race theory builds on insights of two previous movements, critical legal studies and radical feminism…. It also draws from certain European philosophers and theorists … as well as the American radical tradition exemplified by such figures as Sojourner Truth, Frederick Douglass, W.E.B. DuBois, César Chávez, Martin Luther King, Jr., and the Black Power and Chicano movements of the sixties and early seventies" (p. 5). Citing the foremost early foci of CRT, Crenshaw (2002) noted, "[c]ritiques of neutrality, objectivity, colorblindness, meritocracy, and formal equality constituted the most common themes that linked our work" (p. 1363).[6] CRT scholars (like CLS advocates before them) argue against the notion that US jurisprudence is free from personal bias and subjectivity. Further CRT scholars hold that notions of meritocracy and formal equality have been used historically to justify and entrench white racial advantage through the assumption that jurisprudence and the law itself is neutral and colorblind.

Two of the more well-known concepts associated with CRT are *structural determinism* and *whiteness as property*. The former essentially refers to the imperviousness of institutional protocols to change in ways that will contradict the interests they were designed originally to serve and protect. In part, the absence of change can be attributed to the fact that prior to CRT certain concepts used to introduce or advance change simply did not exist as part of legal nomenclature and therefore the phenomenon itself (e.g., multiple marginalizations) could not be acknowledged as a factor that mitigated against "colorblind justice" in the extant legal canon. As such, litigants who put forth claims for redress in regard to actions or outcomes that the law was never designed to consider were perpetually frustrated and their injuries further entrenched by the inertia inherent in structurally deterministic foundations of the law itself (Delgado & Stefancic, 2001). The concept of *whiteness as property* was detailed by legal scholar Cheryl Harris (1993) through an extensive description of similarities between the legally protected rights designated to persons with land ownership and those who hold white racial classification. Among the similar *property* rights are disposition, use and enjoyment, reputation and status, and right to exclude (pp. 1731–1736).

CRT's Basic Tenets

Various writers have detailed basic tenets of CRT with each noting that not all who deploy CRT in their work necessarily embrace or draw upon these tenets equally or similarly. In this overview we include four tenets that appear to run across most descriptions of CRT reviewed for this chapter.

These are: (1) *Racism is normal and commonplace*; (2) *Interest convergence*; (3) *Social construction of race*; and (4) *Counterstorying and the centrality of experiential knowledge*.

The tenet that is probably most directly and most consistently associated with CRT is the notion that *racism is a normal* (rather than aberrant and intermittent) feature of US society. Because of its normalcy often racism is undetectable to those whose interests it serves while at the same time it is highly visible to those whom it affects adversely. Related to this first tenet is the idea that irrespective of individual white people's status relative to each other, all white people benefit, albeit in different ways, from racism and thereby as a collective population they have little incentive to end it. Another tenet that is also commonly associated with CRT is *interest convergence*. This idea is attributed to the late legal scholar Derrick A. Bell, and it holds that progress around civil rights and equality for Blacks has been and will be realized only to the extent that said progress simultaneously advances the interests of the dominant white population (Bell, 1995).

Social construction of race as a central tenet of CRT is consistent with ideas drawn from anthropology and sociology. It holds that *race* as an explanation for fundamental human group differences has no basis in scientific fact. *Race* is neither immutable nor biologically rooted; rather, it is the core of an irresolute classification scheme that is vulnerable to and determined by socio-political exigencies as linked to dominant group interests. The race designation and related status of any collective population can be (and many have been) shifted to serve economic or political interests while maintaining status quo group hierarchies. *Anti-essentialism*, a related idea to this third tenet, is the notion that there is no prototypical minority experience around race and racism. Instead, the different "non-white" ethnoracial minority groups have unique histories and contemporary circumstances marked by conflict and tension with the white dominant population and, to some degree, with each other as individual groups are afforded skin-color privilege. Finally, the tenet of the *centrality of experiential knowledge* and the concept of *counterstorying* holds that those who are adversely affected by racism have an important perspective that needs to be forefronted and that is counter to (and at turns opposite to) the understandings, interactions, and engagements with race as understood, experienced and normalized by the dominant white population. *Counterstorying* in CRT is a discursive tool often used to detail, illuminate, and elevate the experiences (give voice to) those whose worldviews and realities have been excluded (through conscious intent or happenstance) or otherwise interpreted and filtered through a dominant culture screen (the core of the structural determinism) that does not serve the interests of minorities. Other themes that run across descriptions of CRT include *intersectionality*. This concept holds that existing power structure is sustained by interlocking systems of oppression (e.g., racism, classism, sexism, and so on) that produce multiple realms of marginalization for those who do not hold dominant status within, across, and at the spaces where these various social axes overlap. Advocates of CRT call for its deployment in scholarship that draws on these various tenets yet also fuses them with social activism in service to fashioning a defense against (and ultimately the elimination of) oppressive power structures. (Crenshaw, 2002, 2011; Delgado & Stefancic, 2001, 2017).

Since its introduction, interest in CRT has spawned several compelling off-shoot "intellectual sibling" frameworks including LatCrit (Oliva et al., 2013); TribalCrit (Brayboy, 2013); and DisCrit (Migliarini & Annamma, 2019) which have been introduced and used in analyses of academic scholarship, and the framing of research questions and methodology across a wide range of fields. For example, Migliarini & Annamma (2019) in describing DisCrit (Disability Critical Race theory) noted that "perceptions about race often influence how one's ability (in thinking, learning and behavior) is imagined, surveilled, and evaluated" (p. 6). They explain direct alignments between tenets of DisCrit and those long championed by CRT scholars. Among these are, DisCrit "rejects the understanding of both race and disability as primarily biological facts and recognizes the social construction of both as society's response to 'differences' from the norm" (p. 9). Likewise, DisCrit acknowledges that "historically and legally whiteness and ability have been used to deny rights to those that have been constructed as raced and disabled." Finally, DisCrit "recognizes whiteness and ability as 'property', conferring rights to those that claim those statuses and disadvantaging those who are unable to access them" (p. 10). Today CRT and its various sibling off-shoot frameworks are being deployed across a wide range of disciplines and professional fields including law, medicine, social work, and architecture. Education is one field where discourses around CRT took off quickly and spread rapidly.

Making Space for Analysis of Race in a Nice Field Like Education

Introduction of CRT to the field of education can be traced to three works (in order of publication): Ladson-Billings and Tate (1995); Tate (1997); and Ladson-Billings (1998). As a collective, these works prompted many education scholars to re-direct their focus away from liberal diversity discourses and toward engagements with entrenched systemic racism in classrooms, schools, and other realms of the education enterprise. To be sure, the pathway for the earliest advocates of CRT in education had been prepared through decades of foot-traffic by ethnic studies and multicultural education scholars including James A. Banks; Barbara Sizemore; H. Prentice Baptiste; Carl Grant; Geneva Gay; Sonia Nieto; and Christine Sleeter to name a few. The difference with CRT in education, however, was that it marked a turn toward an unflinching analysis of "how race is deliberately exploited and/or subversively implicated in the perpetuation and entrenchment of systems of oppression" (Marshall, et al., 2016, p. 68) across various contexts in education. Ladson-Billings (1998) described CRT as a "powerful explanatory tool" through which scholars can illuminate longstanding inequities in schools around such areas as "curriculum, instruction, assessment, school funding, and desegregation" (p. 18).

A complete discussion of the uses of CRT specific to education scholarship is beyond the scope of this chapter; however, in the over 25 years since publication of Ladson-Billings and Tate (1995), works addressing CRT in education have included an edited handbook (Lynn & Dixson, 2013) and at least two retrospective reviews (Dixson & Rousseau Anderson, 2018; Ledesma & Calderon, 2015). Likewise, CRT has been taken up in edited volumes addressing social studies education (Ladson-Billings, 2002); mathematics education (Davis & Jett, 2019); and education research methods (DeCuir-Gunby, et al., 2018; Leonardo, 2013 as cited in Gray, 2018; Parker, et al., 1999) demonstrating that it is now well-infused into how education phenomena are conceptualized and studied. Furthermore, not unlike legal scholars before them, education scholars too have offered critique of CRT.

For example, in the provocatively titled article, "Where is the racial theory in critical race theory? A constructive criticism of the Crits," Cabrera (2018) proposed that CRT is missing "an explicit theory of racism" (p. 213) and as a result, some conceptual tensions within the framework go largely unacknowledged (and thereby unaddressed) by education scholars. Drawing principally on student affairs scholarship, he details how "Crits frequently refer to systemic racism/White supremacy as the cause of race-based educational inequality, but offer little in terms of the nature of this oppressive social force within their central tenets." (p. 214). According to Cabrera, a tension in CRT is that analysis stops short of providing a theoretical explanation for how racism is perpetuated in institutions despite the significant and arguably substantive changes in US society and institutions since passage of 1950s and 1960s Civil Rights legislation. For Cabrera, there is "an internal logical tension within CRT that arises when the paradigm is applied to an extreme example" (p. 215). Moreover, he proposes "there has been a strong reliance on Bell's thesis [permanence of racism] at the expense of exploring how the nature of White supremacy has evolved over the past 50 years" (pp. 219–220). To address this tension, Cabrera offers "hegemonic Whiteness as a theoretical perspective on the contemporary nature of systemic racism." He takes full aim at the centrality of experiential knowledge along with anti-essentialism around minority experience and perspective to illustrate how whiteness in many respects (and particularly in its reproduction) represents an ideology that can be taken up and perpetuated by both white and non-white actors alike. Concluding, Cabrera advises that it is "increasingly important that Crits be explicit about what they mean by race/racism, and hegemonic Whiteness helps clarify this issue" (p. 227).

We believe Cabrera's discussion of a theory of racism enhances the explanatory power of CRT as a framework in education discourses and, in light of the growing attacks on CRT, additional scholarship in this vein likely will be forthcoming. In the next sections we turn to whether and how CRT has been deployed in classroom management discourse.

Classroom Management through the Lens of Critical Race Theory

There is a high degree of consistency among definitions of classroom management and descriptions of its broad purposes. Even so, missing are references to how race figures in this ineluctable facet of the work of teachers in schools. In the main, the absence of explicit mention of race is understandable since definitions, essentially, are intended to delineate component parts of a phenomenon. However, the absence may also suggest that to fully grasp the nature of how race operates in classroom management requires attending to *implied* associations or linkages between and among definitions, enactments, and results.

Getting a Handle on What Is (Implied by) Classroom Management

One of the most frequently cited definitions of classroom management, formulated by Evertson and Weinstein (2006), identifies five interrelated tasks including: (1) "develop relationships ...(2) organize and implement instruction... (3) use group management ... (4) promote social skills and self-regulation; and ... (5) use appropriate interventions [for] ... behavior problems. Clearly classroom management is a multifaceted endeavor" (pp. 4–5). More recently, Martin, et al. (2016) called for the incorporation of cultural responsiveness along with teachers' cognitive and emotional states as related to classroom decision making. Postholm (as cited in Postholm et al., 2017) notes that classroom management "refers to the set of strategies used by the teacher to increase students' cooperation and engagement and to decrease students' disruptive behaviors, thus keeping an appropriate learning environment" (pp. 470–471). The issue of *behavior* is alluded to, or mentioned directly, in each definition despite the claim that classroom management "is far more complex than... [the] control of students' behavior" (Evertson & Weinstein, 2006, p. 5).

Many teachers, and the general public-at-large, perceive classroom management as synonymous with behavior management or discipline protocols in schools (Casey et al., 2013). Indeed, the term *classroom management* often is used interchangeably with *behavior management* (Egeberg et al., 2016; Landrum & Kauffman, 2006; Postholm, 2013) and this can probably be attributed to the fact that behaviorists were the first to conduct research explicitly focused on the various tasks that are now accepted as part and parcel of classroom management. Hence, drawing on these various definitions, we offer that behavior management, used interchangeably with classroom management, represents the efforts deployed by teachers to maintain order, quell disruptive behavior, and increase student engagement. Put differently, in any given classroom the teacher is obligated to establish and maintain order in service to promoting student engagement and learning. Yet in contemporary schools where the ethnoracial, cultural, and experiential backgrounds of teachers and their students are often highly dissimilar, behavior management for maintaining order is disturbingly weighted by the socio-historical baggage associated with race in the larger society. Specifically, throughout history *maintaining order* has been used as an excuse to justify all manner of physically and psychologically assaultive acts directed at sustaining and entrenching the subordinate status of ethnoracial minorities in general, and the collective Black population in particular (Alexander, 2012; Kendi, 2016; Wilkerson, 2020).

In the book *Effective Classroom Management: The Essentials*, Tracy Garrett (2014) outlines five components of classroom management: physical design of the classroom; rules and routines; relationships; engaging and motivating instruction; and discipline. The definitions and components Garrett details serve as backdrop for our interpretation of classroom management for this chapter.

Most notable among the components are *rules, routines, and discipline*. According to Garrett (2014) rules are meant to structure features of behavior around such issues as "classroom safety, respect, and making appropriate effort" (p. 30). Routines are similar to rules in that they offer insight on how teachers perceive classrooms *should* operate (e.g., answering a question, permission to use the restroom, or how to secure class materials). A primary purpose of routines is to provide explicit *steps of order* for engaging with and within the classroom space. Thus, routines can be interpreted as a device to coerce students to comport themselves in ways that are consistent with a set of standards that may (or may not) take into account their individual identities. Rules, routines, and discipline work in tandem to create and reinforce a certain normality around how students "should be" in classrooms. Moreover, they are implemented, and intended to be adhered to, through rigorous practice. Garrett (2014) indicates that for teachers to be considered effective, they must "invest a considerable amount of time having students practice routines" (p. 36). Using rules, routines, and discipline to maintain order (or, maintaining order through rules, routines, and discipline) has been at the core of how classroom management has been conceptualized historically (See for example: Bear, 2014; Brophy, 2006; Doyle, 1986; 2006; Emmer & Sabornie, 2014; Schwab & Elias, 2015).

At this juncture we reiterate that our exploration in this chapter is one of how CRT presents in classroom management discourses. We do not presume that the aforementioned components necessarily imply race, and certainly not in any *inherently* problematic way. At the same time, however, recent scholarship demonstrates linkages between the enactment of school behavior management protocols and race. Youngsters most likely to suffer the severest consequences of discipline and behavior management protocols in schools (ostensibly due to violations of rules and routines), and those who eventually interface with the juvenile justice system (Bryan, 2017; DeMatthews, 2016; Gray, 2016; Okilwa & Robert, 2017; Whitford et al., 2016), are disproportionately from ethnoracial minority backgrounds. The concept of "school-to-prison-pipeline" references how some discipline and behavior management protocols in schools (i.e., zero tolerance practices) seem to offer preparation for entry into carceral institutions (e.g., alternative school sites; juvenile detention centers; juvenile prisons) for many Black and Brown youngsters who, disproportionately, are sanctioned for infractions of classroom/behavior management rules and protocols (Berlowitz et al., 2017; Hines-Datiri & Carter Andrews, 2017; Skiba, 2014). In short these linkages unveil a troubling association between classroom (behavior) management and race. Casey et al. (2013), in seeking to understand the origins of the focus on "managing" students' behavior in schools, trace that history to the social structure found on plantations and white overseers' emphases on controlling and maintaining compliance among enslaved peoples. This connection provides thought-provoking insights into how race, albeit implicitly, enters into the what and how of classroom management.

A Coded Race Discourse Around Classroom Management?

Rather than address it outright, writers allude to race as an intervening and complicating factor in the conceptualization and enactment of classroom management (Cartledge et al., 2014; Deckman 2017; Delale-O'Connor et al., 2017; Migliarini & Annamma, 2019; Milner, 2006, 2014). For example, multicultural education theorist Geneva Gay (2006), in a chapter titled "Connections Between Classroom Management and Culturally Responsive Teaching," reports that although classroom management encompasses far more than discipline and behavior management, much interaction in classrooms around these two components have connections to differences in the ethnoracial/cultural backgrounds of teachers and students. According to Gay, "problems" arise with classroom management when teachers' ill-conceived and poorly executed pedagogical moves fail to take into account the backgrounds of students in relation to other classroom management components such as grouping, curriculum selection, interpersonal interaction patterns, and so on. Gay makes implicit reference to race but stops short of mentioning CRT as she details the connections between cultural responsiveness and classroom management.

Direct mentions of race in definitions of classroom management are absent, yet a certain implicit *race discourse* does surround the concept. Twine and Warren (2000) defined race discourse as "the way people talk about race, their racial vocabularies, racial narratives, and their definitions of racism" (p. 20). The notion of implicit race is helpful here in that we identify in descriptions of classroom management a certain *non-race* race referencing that is most discernable when the concept is situated in (and filtered through) the broader socio-political and historical contexts of schools. Flanked by the normality of racism in US mainstream culture, use of such terms as *behavior management, maintaining order, safety, and zero tolerance,* offer clear evidence that although not mentioned explicitly, *race* has held a central if obscured place in classroom management discourse.

In Search of Explicit Deployment of CRT in Classroom Management Scholarship

Our project was to understand and detail whether and how CRT has been deployed as analytic framework, methodological tool, or theorizing space in classroom management (CM) discourse as accessible through published writing. To this end we searched the professional literature targeting the most recent CM scholarship represented by empirical studies and conceptual papers published over a roughly seven-year period from 2014 (the last edition of this Handbook) to 2021. The search occurred in two rounds, the second of which generated the collection of works used in this chapter. Platforms used were Education Database and EBSCO*host* (e.g., ERIC; Teachers Reference Center; Social Work Abstracts; APA PsycArticles; and PsycInfo).

First round search terms ("critical race theory" OR "CRT") AND ("classroom management") yielded 90 results. Examination of them revealed "CRT" is commonly used in reference to *culturally relevant teaching* therefore we abandoned that acronym. For the second round we used the terms ("critical race theory") AND ("classroom management" OR "behavior management" OR "classroom discipline" OR "student discipline"). While the term *classroom management* was used in the initial search, *behavior management, classroom discipline,* and *student discipline* were added to include the multiple ways classroom management is conceptualized and discussed in the literature. These steps yielded 107 sources each of which was studied to determine whether both concepts (e.g., classroom management and critical race theory) were addressed. After multiple rounds of evaluation for appropriateness and fit, the selection used in this chapter (each designated by an asterisk in the References) all met the primary criterion of being inquiries where scholars deployed CRT in service to critical study, analysis, critique, or evaluation of some aspect of CM.

CM through the Lens of CRT

One-quarter of the articles represented "conceptual pieces" whereas 75 percent were empirical research studies. Research involving data collection from students ranged from a study focused on two kindergarteners, to studies that targeted all students (K-12) holding a particular status during the span of an academic year in large urban school districts. The overwhelming majority of studies were characterized by the researchers as qualitative (e.g., ethnographies; critical ethnography; interpretivist qualitative; case study; qualitative ethnographic case study) and a plethora of data collection protocols were employed including one-on-one interviews; focus groups; extensive classroom observations; and even shadowing members of school leadership teams. Across the qualitative studies, half involved data collected from K-12 students exclusively; 25% drew data from school staff including principals, teachers, social workers; 8.3% focused on School Resource Officers and students; 8.3% on students and their parents; and 8.3% from students, staff, and parents. One study was characterized as a sequential mixed methods design and it included district-level data drawn from all students enrolled in the largest urban school district within a western state. In that study quantitative statistical analyses (e.g., multinomial logistic regression modeling) were used on a portion of the data, whereas qualitative methods (e.g., critical discourse analysis) was used to interpret definitions of the office referral categories under which students had incurred discipline infractions.

School levels varied among the studies as well. Those highlighted were elementary; middle school; secondary/high school; elementary and middle; K–12, and middle/secondary. Physical locations were scattered across all five regions of the US as defined by the National Geographic Society with the highest percentage situated in the West (33.3%); followed by the Midwest (16.6%); Southeast (16.6%); Northeast (16.6%), and Southwest (8.3%). There was only one study in the collection where the researchers did not disclose its geographic location.

Defining CM through the Lens of CRT

Notwithstanding the various definitions of classroom management (Evertson & Weinstein, 2006; Martin, et al., 2016), in all but one source the concept was distilled down to activities undertaken by school personnel in service to managing student behavior and comportment. In a word, CM was conceptualized as *discipline*. This typically was captured in the notion of *maintaining safety* in classrooms and the school broadly. To this end, behavior management and discipline were shown not to rest with teachers exclusively nor even primarily. Rather most commonly discipline comes under the purview of non-classroom personnel including Principals; Assistant Principals; School Counselors; Social Workers; and School Resource Officers. The latter are typically fire-arm outfitted personnel charged to provide "school-based policing."

To gain additional insight on how CM as behavior management/discipline is operationalized, we surveyed the entire collection of articles for terminology used along with the accompanying "thick descriptions." This yielded 34 different terms. Some were exclusive to the context of a single study or article (e.g., carceral logics; code of conduct; traumatization; targeting; withholding of academic and behavioral supports); whereas various others were used across multiple articles (e.g., disparities; disproportionality; office referrals; out-of-school suspension; school-to-prison pipeline; removal from school; surveillance). Thus, while CM was uniformly characterized as *discipline*,[7] when we mined all the articles in search of deeper insights we found layering within that broad conceptualization.

As synthesized across the articles, *discipline* represents the consequences (penalties) students receive for being charged with, and found guilty of, violating written and/or tacit rules, codes, and protocols established and used by adults in schools to govern student behavior and comportment. Scholars detail what can best be described as deeply troubling patterns undergirding both the conceptualization and enforcement of student discipline protocols in many of the nation's pre-collegiate school districts. For example, various qualitative studies involving extensive interviews with and observations of school personnel revealed widespread embrace and defense of *colorblind or race-neutral ideology* in the language and ostensibly the intent of school discipline protocols. Researchers often exposed clear evidence of the influence of race in the interpretation and enforcement of those same protocols (DeMatthews et al., 2017; Gray, 2016; Howard, 2020; Kennedy et al., 2019; Wiley, 2021). Most striking were instances when researchers pointed out distinctly racial patterns of inequity in discipline, yet explanations for such findings were recast by school personnel as nonracial. In some cases, researchers detailed how school personnel were at a loss to explain how and why particular consequences had been perceived to be consistent with the ostensible broad reason (e.g., school safety) for imposing the discipline in the first place (Anyon et al., 2018; DeMatthews et al, 2017).

An especially prominent focus in much of the literature was the widespread phenomenon of racial disproportionality among students selected for discipline sanctions. Typically, researchers identified disproportionality when the percentage of a particular group of students sanctioned for behavioral protocol violations far exceeds the percentage of that same group within the school's overall student population. All of the sources used in this review referenced the disproportionality of ethnic and racial minority students in school discipline incidents as a major problem. For the most part, scholars present convincing arguments and evidence that disproportionality in school discipline is influenced by, if not patterned after, socio-cultural pathologies (e.g., racism, classism, and patriarchy) that have long plagued the larger US society. Through deployment of CRT concepts and tenets, scholars detail how unfair and biased enforcement of discipline protocols in the nation's schools both targets and traumatizes untold numbers of students at the intersections of various identity markers including race/ethnicity, economic class, gender, and disability status.

Several discussions highlight that school personnel routinely *interpret* classroom and school discipline rules and protocols (and they impose consequences on violators of said protocols), sans providing fair opportunities for students or students' parents to offer alternative interpretations of the ostensible violation. Researchers detail how the foreclosure of opportunities to present counterstories invariably leaves particular students vulnerable to a range of disciplinary consequences. Among the more extreme are consignment to segregated spaces within the school that are designated for problem students (Wiley, 2021); suspension and expulsion from school property including alternative school placements (Annamma et al., 2019; Anyon et al., 2018; Kennedy et al., 2019); and in the most severe cases transfer to juvenile justice/carceral institutions (Annamma, 2016, 2019, 2020; Gray, 2016).

Deploying CRT in CM Discourse

Across the collection of empirical articles, just over half used CRT as a framework or lens through which research findings were interpreted. For example, Martinez et al. (2016) used CRT as "methodological/interpretive grounding" for a quantitative study in which they tested three hypotheses to illuminate individual and school predictors (using Positive Behavior Intervention Support sites only) of office disciplinary referrals for African American versus Latinx students. Anyon et al. (2018) drew on CRT concepts, most prominently *structural or systemic racism* and *colorblind ideology*, in an extensive exploration of the relationship between student race and the sub-contexts in which students are disciplined within a large urban school district. On the other hand, Annamma et al. (2019) drew on CRT and FemCrit theory to situate their research both historically and socially in an exploration of mechanisms in schools that move Black girls through a "Pipeline" where they end up in carceral institutions.

About one quarter of researchers used CRT as a *theoretical framework* with particular focus on CRT tenets such as the interdependent nature of racism and whiteness as property (Annamma, 2016) and whiteness as property and constructions of race (Gray, 2016). Likewise, three studies (Annamma, 2016; Gray, 2016; Kennedy et al., 2019) all quantitative, drew on CRT (or its offshoots including DisCrit and FemCrit) as *method* or *methodological grounding* (Martinez et al., 2016). In the former cases where CRT was directly drawn on as method the idea of *counterstories* or *counternarratives* served as prominent components in the data collection protocol. Indeed, counter-story/counternarrative was mentioned in 40 percent of the articles reviewed. Even when not specifically employed as a data collection method, the concept was mentioned as an idea central to gaining full and critical understanding of the complex nature of the *failure of classroom management* as manifested in disproportionality in disciplinary matters in schools.

Prominent CRT Tenets and Concepts in CM Discourse

We conducted multiple readings of all the articles to determine the diversity of CRT concepts scholars employed. This involved isolating those concepts used or alluded to in study findings or in conclusions to conceptual discussions. Twenty-four CRT concepts were identified across the entire collection. To be sure there was some overlap and even instances where terms were used slightly differently from how they have been interpreted by foundational CRT scholars (e.g., Crenshaw, 1989, 1991, 2002, 2011; Delgado & Stefancic, 2001, 2017). Still and all, among the more frequently cited CRT concepts drawn upon were *whiteness as property* and *intersectionality*.

One prominent feature of whiteness as property is the right to use and enjoy (Harris, 1993; Ladson-Billings, 1998) and in the context of schools this can be translated as the right not to be disturbed in nor ejected from the learning environment. In CM discourse, this particular concept has been used to explain and critique the subjectivity in discipline protocols when directed at students who *do not* possess whiteness. The severity of consequences they face result in students of color being disproportionately stigmatized by discipline incidents when compared to their white peers. Consequently, students of color are highly vulnerable to negative interpretations and judgements of their behavior and personhood in ways that foreclose (rather than confer) access to opportunities (the right to use and enjoyment) of the benefits of schooling. Foreclosed access to opportunity for such students manifests further in them not being given the benefit of the doubt by their teachers and other school personnel in discipline matters.

Researchers report how subjective interpretations of the behavior of Black and Latino students gets judged by and contrasted with notions of white goodness and white innocence (Annamma, 2016; Annamma et al., 2020; Gray, 2016) while at the same time such judgement is cloaked in the veneer of colorblindness (Gray, 2016). The physical presence of students of color (Annamma, 2016) and their actions are interpreted through longstanding valuation of white classification that is deeply entrenched in the US racial caste culture (Wilkerson, 2020). Not uncommonly, the property value of whiteness then allows misbehavior among white students to be characterized as youthful horseplay or adolescent cheekiness, while similar behaviors among students of color are interpreted through a lens of adultification overlayed by longstanding race-based stereotypes including Black males as insubordinate and disruptive (Martinez et al., 2016); Latino youth as criminally gang-oriented (Gray, 2016); Black females as disobedient and defiant (Annamma et al., 2019); and Black parenting as deficient (DeMatthews et al., 2017). This devaluation makes Black students more vulnerable to being *perceived* as running afoul of and existing in opposition to the accepted (and expected) behavior protocols in schools (Annamma, 2016; Annamma et al., 2019; Annamma et al., 2020; Fergus, 2021; Gray, 2016; Kennedy, 2019).

Freidus' (2020) ethnography of two kindergartners, one a white female the other a Black male, explores how "discursive frames" around discipline including disposition, medicalization, and family/ community work in ways that advantage and create a kind of privilege free-pass for whiteness. Here its property value worked to excuse misbehavior of the white child casting her explicit rule violations as being beyond her control. By contrast, the same "beyond the child's control" explanation was not granted for the Black child. Freidus concluded that the differential framing of misbehaviors coming from a White versus a Black child creates a double-standard where teachers and staff relax rules for the former that are rigidly enforced for the latter.

We hasten to note that in at least one qualitative study, the problem of racial disproportionality was attributed to *whiteness as property* and *white privilege* sans convincing illustration. The study used data collected from Black students who had received out-of-school suspensions and the parents of those students. Its purpose was to explore and analyze "how ... Black students and their parents perceive school discipline" (Bell, 2020, p. 3). Among the conclusions offered was "structural barriers and pervasive marginalization described by parents of Black students further demonstrates the privilege to exclude others as indicated in the Whiteness as property tenet of critical race theory." (p. 6) Unfortunately, the results do not offer concrete illustration of how the exclusion manifests in a way that discriminately favors (or privileges) white students.

The CRT concept of *intersectionality* was deployed in interpretations of findings from studies of associations and links between and among ethnicity/race, sex/gender, disability, and economic status of students identified as violators of classroom management/school discipline protocols. Nearly all writers who explored and critiqued the intersections of various identity axes in school discipline also identified pervasive subjectivity both in how school personnel interpret what constitutes behavior code violations, and in how they dole out related sanctions or punishments. Researchers explain that irrespective of the ethnoracial demographics of a schools' population, classroom management failure (as manifested in office discipline referrals) is characterized by practices and protocols that are wildly subjective and disproportionately punitive when directed at students from ethnoracial minority backgrounds. This pattern holds especially for African American students, although within the collection of literature we reviewed for this chapter studies were conflicting regarding the intersections of race and gender for African American girls (Annamma et al., 2019; Martinez et al., 2016).

A particularly disturbing finding in the literature is that many school discipline protocols appear to be aligned with and informed by *carceral logics* wherein the language, purpose, theoretical underpinnings, and outcomes (focused on punishment) are informed by protocols commonly associated with and found among prisons and other carceral institutions (Annamma, 2016; Annamma et al., 2019, 2020; Wiley, 2021). Across multiple studies where Annamma et al. (2019, 2020) found disproportionality among Black girls in exclusionary disciplinary outcomes, students' stories about their schooling journeys and experiences were revealing. According to the researchers, using a CRT framework allowed them to gain insight into deep inequities inherent in racially disproportionate discipline because it illuminated students' "historical and social location and that of others with whom they interact in their world" (Annamma et al., 2019, p. 216).

Unreality Around the Reality of Race

Cartmill (1998) explained that many cultural and physical anthropologists dismiss race as a biological fact and reject its use as a definitive marker and substantive explanation for fundamental human differences. At the same time, many people who *are raced* (in that they hold minority status) experience negative psycho-social and material challenges that show them race is a highly consequential reality in their lives. In the collection of articles reviewed for this chapter, scholars described how discipline protocols and practices often playout in ways where race takes on an illusory if not *delusory* quality resulting in divergent and at times contradictory interpretations of its very existence and impact. Our final observation, then, surrounds interrelationships between and among several CRT concepts namely *colorblindness* and the *construction of race/essentialization of race* and how scholars revealed a certain unreality of the reality of race (Marshall, 2002) about CM vis-à-vis discipline in schools.

Various scholars detailed that despite widely-known facts of racial disproportionality in discipline outcomes in schools broadly, and even in the light of confirming statistics in their own school sites or district, some school personnel claimed not to know of racial disparities. Likewise, claims of colorblindness gave rise to outright denial of the impact of race on discipline outcomes. Through counternarrative qualitative interviews and focus groups with African American girls Annamma et al. (2020) unveiled what the girls perceived as unwillingness of school personnel to engage in any dialogue or action to address racism and inequity in how behavior protocol violations are addressed in schools. Likewise, girls describe problems with teachers withholding academic supports or teachers being inequitable in their offerings of behavioral supports. Anyon et al. (2018), through quantitative analysis of school data detail how discipline reform recommendations are implemented in a way that does not attend to the issues of race including disproportionality of students color and the subjective nature of the offenses for which they are disciplined. Whereas DeMatthews et al. (2017) identified colorblindness in qualitative interviews of principals who rejected race explanations for racial disproportionality in discipline outcomes. In the face of pronounced racial disparities around discipline in their schools, principals emphasized their focus on "fair" and "uniform" implementation of codes of conduct.

Researchers describe how even though school personnel deny seeing color, having personal racial bias, or being otherwise aware of racist mechanisms at play in discipline protocols, they employ descriptions of students that reflect a definite construction of race. Moreover, the construction is essentialized in that it represents narrow conceptualizations of group characteristics. Broad, essentialized notions of race vis-à-vis behavioral expectations for African American, Latino, and White students are apparent in the way discipline consequences are differentiated. For example, analysis and critique by Annamma et al. (2019) of subjective discipline violations makes clear that Black students (girls) are perceived as threatening, disrespectful, or defiant. Other writers identify associations of racial whiteness with goodness and appropriate behavior worthy of emulation by other (non-white) students (Wiley, 2021), whereas Black and Latinos boys are criminalized (DeMatthews et al., 2017) with the latter being associated with street gangs (Gray, 2016). In the one study where CM is conceptualized as classroom placements, teachers' perceptions of students' behaviors and "legitimate" status to be classified as racially Black or white routinely reflected essentialized race stereotypes (Wiley, 2021).

Conclusion: Critical Race Analysis of Classroom Management in an Age of Racial Retrenchment

Racism has been recognized, studied, critiqued, and appropriately indicted for the prominent and troubling position it holds in operations deemed central to schooling. Specifically, when it comes to discipline and behavior management protocols and practices, CRT analyses reveal that the presence and impact of racism is ubiquitous and insidious, yet curiously for some it seems to be hidden in plain sight. Ideas in schools about what constitutes correct student behavior and comportment (versus *which students'* behavior and comportment are at odds with those ideas) are often grounded in and supported by some of the most deeply entrenched and pernicious group stereotypes that, while historical, remain prevalent in contemporary US society. The personal beliefs and professional training offered to school personnel at all levels, but particularly those charged with enacting sanctions for students deemed to be in violation of behavior policies, expose support for (rather than critique of) a status quo that perpetuates inequities. Most critical, through use of CRT as methodological grounding, with a focus on capturing counterstories and counternarratives, we now know that the students who become entangled in discipline webs have an important perspective to share. It is one that reveals how, despite gross power differentials that invariably render them exceptionally vulnerable to the severest punishments, these students often exercise a kind of agency. They resist negative characterizations that accompany out-of-school suspension and interfaces with carceral institutions, and they maintain a sense of hope and purpose through self-affirmation.

The literature reveals that race is insinuated in CM in contrasting ways. For some students, it is the traumatizing weapon at the core of discipline encounters that are subjective, inequitable, and unfair; while for others, race serves as a dependable protection, a cushion as it were, from the severest consequences of school discipline rules and regulations. At the outset of this chapter, we noted that race rarely operates in isolation; instead, it often is implicated subversively at the intersections of multiple social identity axes. Our exploration of the literature fully supported this claim. In empirical studies of discipline protocols, whether multivariate analysis of district-level data drawn from thousands of students, or ethnographic case studies of individual classrooms focused on just a few, the CRT lens exposes unequivocal intersections between race, gender, and economic class. It reveals that the comportment of Black male students, more commonly than any other segment of student populations, are identified and sanctioned for violations of school discipline and behavior guidelines and rules. Critically, however, a series of studies deploying CRT via its sibling off-shoots DisCrit and BlackFemCrit, demonstrate that Black female students with disabilities are sanctioned for discipline and behavior violations at particularly high rates and nearly exclusively for subjective "offenses" most of which align with some of the basest stereotypes of Black women (Collins, 2009; Donovan, 2011) including belligerence, defiance, and threat. Scholars reveal a reverse outcome at the intersections of race and gender in schools when it comes to white girls. Commonly they are the least likely of all students to receive out-of-school suspensions or discipline for infractions across all categories.

CRT as analytic and methodological framing has been especially central in demonstrating the ubiquity of problematic discourses around classroom management and discipline in schools. Various scholars have interrogated the "logics" (Annamma, 2016; Wiley, 2021) and "hegemonic norms associated with bureaucracy and managerialism" (DeMatthews et al., 2017, p. 526) at the core of common discipline and behavior protocols in schools. The notion of "carceral logics" denotes an organizational culture, including nomenclature, written guidelines, interpersonal talking points, actions, and justifications, that establish and support a deterministic prison-aligned structure around discipline and behavior management. Gray (2016) described how language itself is imbued with "coded narratives of racial difference and violence ... [which allow school folk to claim personal innocence because race narratives have] already been established in the popular imagination through the media, music and literature" (p. 70). Various scholars detailed how sanctions imposed on particular students are routinely and demonstratively inequitable yet school personal rationalize and defend such inequity in the name of "maintaining safety" and "protecting the rights of students to learn." A chilling set of racist realities has been exposed through CRT analysis of the logics that undergird CM as behavior management. Among them is the perception that students from certain backgrounds pose a threat to school safety. These same students are perceived as compromising the right of other students *from different backgrounds* to learn to such an extent that students in the former group are subjected to close surveillance that invariably warrants their being physically removed from classroom and school spaces.

Another point we made in the opening is that through its intersections with other social axes, the insidious nature of race can present as a chicken-egg illusion that sows doubt in the minds of some about the depth of its influence. Scholars effectively demonstrate this reality through qualitative studies involving one-on-one and focus group interviews with school personnel who, even in the face of school district data to the contrary, insist that something *other than race* (typically economic class and poor parenting) explains gross *racial* disproportionality where students of color are those most commonly (and most severely) sanctioned for behavior code violations.

Questions we face now include, what directions should CRT analysis vis-à-vis CM discourses take in the future? We would hope that future treatment of CRT in CM discourse will take up the praxis and social action obligations of the framework, while extending analyses beyond the prism of behavior management as an element of CM. Indeed, we were struck by the difficulties we encountered in identifying literature that brought CRT analysis to such features of CM as grouping for instruction; curriculum selection; or teacher promotion of socio-emotional learning. Such studies, we believe, will be best structured as qualitative inquiries involving extensive ethnographic observation along with considerable opportunities to capture teachers' but especially students' perspectives in order to gain the most useful and the fullest insights on how and where race enters in the various elements of classroom management.

Finally, in a now germinal article published in 1998, Gloria Ladson-Billings described challenges education scholars interested in critical race theory would likely face in their quest to effect change and substantive movement toward true equity and justice for all children and youth in the nation's schools. Opining on the future of CRT in education, she wrote:

> I doubt if it will go very far into the mainstream. Rather, CRT in education is likely to ... continue to generate scholarly papers and debate, and never penetrate the classrooms and daily experiences of students of color. But, students of color, their families, and communities cannot afford the luxury of CRT scholars' ruminations ... where the ideas are laudable but the practice leaves much to be desired.
>
> *p. 22*

It seems fair to say her prediction has largely proven accurate even though much has occurred in the intervening years that might have portended a different, more hopeful and progressive, story vis-à-vis race in education. Yet in those same years the nation experienced some of its most socio-politically regressive events around race since before the introduction of CRT. This includes near-epidemic police brutality against unarmed African American citizens; racially motivated violence against Asian Americans and Muslim Americans; open protests by neo-Nazis and white nationalists with the imprimatur of elected politicians and media leaders; a health pandemic that has been especially ravaging in communities of color; and the storming of the nation's capital building by a violent mob in protest of the results of the 2020 Presidential election.

As we see it, a certain irony surrounds the present status of CRT in education. The framework has most certainly entered the "mainstream," but in a way intended to undermine and distort its every tenet. The current campaign against CRT derives from partisan-politics, and it appears bent on opposing social advancement and racial reconciliation in this nation (Harris, 2021). Ladson-Billings (1998) was prophetic in her prediction that "it will never penetrate into the classrooms and daily experiences of students of color." We add, nor, most assuredly, in those of white students. In the light of these realities, and to the extent that the fever pitch of the anti-CRT campaign is sustained, it may turn out to be an understatement to say that writers who insist on deploying CRT as a framework in connection with education scholarship can expect to be met with a barrage of resistance. Ladson-Billings predicted that too when she noted, "[w]e may be pilloried ...,[and] vilified for these stands. Ultimately, ... we may have to ... hear our ideas distorted and misrepresented" (p. 22). We urge those who would bring a critical lens to classroom management discourse to continue to fight the good fight. Resist being silent if for no other reason than because the children—*all of the children*—are watching. In the words of James Baldwin, "we can't tell the children there's no hope."

Notes

1 Included among the axes are racial; ethnic; social; cultural; economic; linguistic; sexual orientation; gender identity; gender expression; and legal status. This is not to suggest that many of these axes are *new* to school environments; rather we contend that in contemporary schools these (and other) axes of diversity have attained a salience that is palpable, insistent, acknowledged, and (to some degree) affirmed in ways that heretofore was not the case in US schools.
2 Critical Legal Studies emerged in the 1970s and challenged foundational principles of jurisprudence including the notion of value neutrality as suggested in the adage "justice is blind."
3 Glaude's use of "the lie" is distinguished from "the big lie." The latter phrase came in vogue in 2021 in reference to former President Trump's claim that it was he who won the 2020 US presidential election, contrary to all polls, ballot recounts, and State Election Commissioner certifications. As of the writing of this chapter the former President, along with high- and low-ranking members of the Republican party, maintain the 2020 Presidential Election was "stolen" by the Democratic party candidate and certified winner, Joseph R. Biden.
4 [We address] this "conference" and the president's ill-informed observations about American history and history education reluctantly and with dismay. The event was clearly a campaign stunt, ..., to draw distinctions between the two political parties on education policy, tie one party to civil disorder, and enable the president to explicitly attack his opponent. ...... [T]his political theater stokes culture wars that are meant to distract Americans from other, more pressing current issues. The AHA only reluctantly gives air to such distraction; we are not interested in inflating a brouhaha that is a mere sideshow to the many perils facing our nation at this moment. (American Historical Society, 2020).
5 "... [T]he conservative government in Britain [has] declared some uses of critical race theory in education illegal"; whereas stateside "... a number of House and Senate offices, ... are working on their own anti-critical race theory bills,... ." (Goldberg, 2021, p. 3). "In the UK, critical race theory is a relatively marginal intellectual current, and a term most people are unlikely to have encountered until now. Yet the Conservative government, no doubt glancing across the Atlantic, has decided to co-opt this bogeyman into the culture it enthusiastically pursues on several fronts, whether it's against 'lefty lawyers' who represent migrants in court, or against the 'north London metropolitan liberal elite'" (Trilling, 2020).
6 For comprehensive treatment of CRT see Crenshaw, K. W. (2002). The first decade: Critical reflections, or "a foot in the closing door'. *UCLA Law Review*, 49, 1341–1372; and Crenshaw, K.W. (2011). Twenty years of critical race theory: Looking back to move forward. *Connecticut Law Review*, *43*(5), 1253–1352. Combined, these two retrospective reviews chronicle the origins, growth, and expansion of CRT from its emergence as a focus in legal scholarship to its contemporary interdisciplinary and cross-institutional dynamics.
7 The one article that did not focus on discipline highlighted student classroom assignment patterns (Wiley, 2021).

References

Alexander, M. (2012). *The new Jim Crow: Mass incarceration in the age of colorblindness.* The New Press.

American Historical Society (2020). *AHA issues statement on recent 'White House Conference on American History'.* Retrieved on May 11, 2020 www.historians.org/news-and-advocacy/aha-advocacy/aha-statement-on-the-recent-white-house-conference-on-american-history-(september-2020

Annamma, S. (2016). Disrupting the carceral state through education journey mapping. *International Journal of Qualitative Studies in Education, 29*(9), 1210–1230. DOI:10.1080/09518398.2016.1214297 (★)

Annamma, S.A., Anyon, Y., Joseph, N.M., Farrar, J., Greer, E., Downing, B., & Simmons, J. (2019). Black girls and school discipline: The complexities of being overrepresented and understudied. *Urban Education, 54*(2), 211–242. DOI:10.1177/0042085916656610 (★)

Annamma, S., Handy, T., Miller, A. L., & Jackson, E. (2020). Animating discipline disparities through debilitating practices: Girls of color and inequitable classroom interactions. *Teachers College Record, 122*(5), 1–17. (★)

Anyon, Y., Lechuga, C., Ortega, D., Downing, B., Greer, E., & Simmons, J. (2018). An exploration of the relationships between student racial background and the school sub- contexts of office discipline referrals: A critical race theory analysis. *Race, Ethnicity & Education, 21*(3), 390–406. DOI: 10.1080/13613324.2017.1328594 (★)

Bear, G. G. (2014). Preventative and classroom-based strategies. In E. T. Emmer & E. J. Sabornie (Eds.), *Handbook of classroom management* (pp. 15–39). Routledge.

Bell, C. (2020). Maybe if they let us tell the story I wouldn't have gotten suspended: Understanding black students' and parents' perceptions of school discipline. *Children and Youth Services Review, 110*, 1–11. (★)

Bell, D. A., Jr. (1995). Brown v. board of education and the interest convergence dilemma. In K. Crenshaw, N. Gotanda, G. Peller, & K. Thomas (Eds.), *Critical race theory: The key writings that formed the movement* (pp. 20–29). The New Press.

Berlowitz, M. J., Frye, R., Jette, K. M. (2017). Bullying and zero-tolerance policies: The school to prison pipeline. *Multicultural Learning and Teaching, 12*(1), 7–25.

Brayboy, B. M J. (2013). Tribal critical race theory: An origin story and future directions. In M. Lynn & A. D. Dixon (Eds.), *Handbook of critical race theory in education* (pp. 88–100). Routledge/Taylor & Francis Group.

Brophy, J. (2006). History of research on classroom management. In C. M. Evertson & C. S. Weinstein (Eds.), *Handbook of classroom management. Research, practice, and contemporary Issues* (pp. 17–43). Lawrence Erlbaum Associates.

Brown, K, & Jackson, D. D. (2013). The history and conceptual elements of critical race theory. In M. Lynn & A. D. Dixon (Eds.), *Handbook of critical race theory in education* (pp. 9–22). Routledge/Taylor & Francis Group.

Bryan, N. (2017). White teachers' role in sustaining the school-to-prison pipeline: Recommendations for teacher education. *The Urban Review, 49*(2), 326–345. http://dx.doi.org.prox.lib.ncsu.edu/10.1007/s11 256-017-0403-3

Cabrera, N. L. (2018). Where is the racial theory in critical race theory? A constructive criticism for the crits. *The Review of Higher Education, 42*(1), 209–233.

Cartledge, G., Lo, Y.-y., Vincent, C. G., & Robinson-Ervin, P. (2014). Culturally responsive classroom management. In E. T. Emmer & E. J. Sabornie (Eds.), *Handbook of classroom management* (411–430). Routledge.

Cartmill, M. (1998). The status of the race concept in physical anthropology. *American Anthropologist, 100*(3), 651–660.

Casey, Z. A., Lozenski, B. D., & McManimon, S. K. (2013). From neoliberal policy to neoliberal pedagogy: Racializing and historicizing classroom management. *Journal of Pedagogy, 4*(1), 36-n/a. http://dx.doi.org.prox.lib.ncsu.edu/10.2478/jped-2013-0003

Chapman, T. (2013). Origins of and connections to social justice in critical race theory education. In M. Lynn & A. D. Dixon (Eds.), *Handbook of critical race theory in education* (pp. 101–112). Routledge/Taylor & Francis Group.

Collins, P. H. (2009). *Black feminist thought: Knowledge, consciousness, and the politics of empowerment.* Routledge.

Cook, D. A. (2013). Blurring the boundaries: The mechanics of creating composite characters. In M. Lynn & A. D. Dixon (Eds.), *Handbook of critical race theory in education* (pp. 181–194). Routledge/Taylor & Francis Group.

Crenshaw, K. W. (1989). Demarginalizing the intersection of race and sex; A Black feminist critique of antidiscrimination doctrine, feminist theory and antiracist politics. *University of Chicago Legal Forum,* 139–167.

Crenshaw, K. W. (1991). Mapping the margins: Intersectionality, identity politics, and violence against women of color. *Stanford Law Review, 43*(6), 1241–1299.

Crenshaw, K. W. (2002). The first decade: Critical reflections, or "a foot in the closing door." *UCLA Law Review, 49*, 1341–1372.

Crenshaw, K. W. (2011). Twenty years of critical race theory: Looking back to move forward. *Connecticut Law Review, 43*(5), 1253–1352.

Davis, J., & Jett, C. C. (Eds.). (2019). *Critical race theory in mathematics education.* Routledge.

Deckman, S. L. (2017). Managing race and race-ing management: Teachers' stories of race and classroom conflict. *Teachers College Record, 119*(12), 1–40.

DeCuir-Gunby, J. T., Chapman, T. K., & Schutz, P. A. (Eds.) (2018). *Understanding critical race research methods and methodologies: Lessons from the field*. Routledge.

Delale-O'Connor, L. A., Alvarez, A. J., Murray, I. E., & Milner, R., IV. (2017). Self-efficacy beliefs, classroom management and the cradle-to-prison pipeline. *Theory Into Practice, 56*(3), 178–186.

Delgado, R., & Stefancic, J. (2001). *Critical race theory: An introduction*. New York University Press.

Delgado, R., & Stefancic, J. (2017). *Critical race theory: An introduction*. (3rd ed.) New York University Press.

DeMatthews, D. (2016). Effective leadership is not enough: Critical approaches to closing the racial discipline gap. *The Clearing House, 89*(1), 7–13. (★)

DeMatthews, D. E., Carey, R. L., Olivarez, A., & Moussavi Saeedi, K. (2017). Guilty as charged? Principals' perspectives on disciplinary practices and racial discipline gap. *Educational Administration Quarterly, 53*(4), 519–555. (★)

Dixson, A. D., & Rousseau Anderson, C. (2018). Where are we? Critical race theory in education 20 years later. *Peabody Journal of Education, 93*(1), 121–131.

Donovan, R. A. (2011). Tough or tender: (Dis)similarities in white college students' perceptions of black and white women. *Psychology of Women Quarterly, 35*(3), 458–468.

Doyle, W. (1986). Classroom organization and management in M.C. Wittrock (Ed.), *Handbook of research on teaching* (pp.392–431). Macmillan.

Doyle, W. (2006). Ecological approaches to classroom management. In C. M. Evertson & C.S. Weinstein (Eds.), *Handbook of classroom management: Research, practice, and contemporary issues* (pp. 97–126). Lawrence Erlbaum Associates, Publishers.

Dutil, S. (2020). Dismantling the school-to-prison pipeline: A trauma-informed, critical race perspective on school discipline. *Children & Schools, 42*(3), 171–178. (★)

Egeberg, H.M., McConney A., & Price, A. (2016). Classroom management and national professional standards for teachers: A review of the literature on theory and practice. *Australian Journal of Teacher Education, 41*(7), pp.1–18.

Emmer, E.T., & Sabornie, E. J. (Eds.) (2014). *Handbook of classroom management* (2nd. ed.). Routledge.

Evertson, C. M. & Weinstein, C. S. (2006). Classroom management as a field of inquiry. In C. M. Evertson & C. S. Weinstein (Eds.), *Handbook of classroom management: Research, practice, and contemporary issues* (pp. 3–15). Lawrence Erlbaum Associates, Publishers.

Executive Order No. 13950, 85 Fed Reg, 188 (September 22, 2020). p. 60683. *Combating race and sex stereotyping.*

Executive Order No. 13985, 86 Fed Reg, 14 (January 25, 2021) p. 7009. *Advancing racial equity and support for underserved communities through the federal government.*

Farber, D. A., & Sherry, S. (1993). Telling stories out of school: An essay on legal narratives. *Stanford Law Review, 45*, 807–855.

Flaherty, C. (2021). Legislating against critical race theory. *Inside Higher Ed.* www.insidehighered.com/news/2021/06/09/legislating-against-critical-race-   theory-curricular-implications-somestates?utm_source-Inside+Higher_Ed&utm_   campaign=ab420cc161-DNU_2021_COPY_03&utm_medium=email&utm_term=0 _1fcbc04421-ab420cc161-234552857&mc_cid=ab420cc161&mc_eid=312a0eee5

Fergus, E. (2021). The beliefs about race and culture operating in our discipline strategies. A Commentary. *Preventing School Failure, 65*(3).

Freidus, A. (2020). 'Problem children' and 'children with problems': Discipline and innocence n a gentrifying elementary school. *Harvard Educational Review, 90*(4), 550–572, 691. (★)

Garrett, T. (2014). *Effective classroom management: The essentials*. Teachers College Press.

Gates, H. L., Jr. (1994). War of words: Critical race theory and the first amendment. In H. L. Gates, Jr. et al. (Eds.), *Speaking of race, speaking of sex: Hate speech, civil rights, and civil liberties* (pp. 17–57). New York University Press.

Gay, G. (2006). Connections between classroom management and culturally responsive teaching. In C. M. Evertson & C. S. Weinstein (Eds.), *Handbook of classroom management: Research, practice, and contemporary issues* (pp. 343–370). Lawrence Erlbaum Association, Publishers.

Glaude, E. S., Jr. (2020). *Begin again: James Baldwin's America and its urgent lessons for our own*. Crown.

Goldberg, M. (February 28, 2021) The campaign to cancel wokeness: How the right is trying to censor critical race theory. *New York Times*, Section SR, p. 3.

Gray, M.S. (2016). Saving the lost boys: Narratives of discipline disproportionality. *Educational Leadership and Administration, 27*, 53–80. (★)

Gray, M. S. (2018). *Discretion, discourse, decision-making and disproportionality: A critical ethnography of student discipline* (Order No. 10182826) [Doctoral dissertation, University of California Davis]. ProQuest Dissertations and Theses Global.

Harris, A. (2021). The GOP's 'Critical Race Theory' obsession: How conservative politicians and pundits became fixated on an academic approach. *The Atlantic.* www.theatlantic.com/politics/archive/2021/05/gops-critical-race-theory-fixation-explained/618828/

Harris, C. I. (1993). Whiteness as property. *Harvard Law Review, 106*(8), 1707–1791.

Hines-Datiri, D., & Carter Andrews, D. J. (2017). The effects of zero tolerance policies on Black girls: Using critical race feminism and figured worlds to examine school discipline. *Urban Education, 55*(10), 1419–1440. https://doi.org/10.1177/0042085917690204

Howard, J. (2020). The way it was done: Considering race in classroom placement. *Teacher Education Quarterly, 47*(1), 27–47. (★)

Kendi, I.X. (2016). *Stamped from the beginning: The definitive history of racist ideas in America.* National Books Publishing.

Kennedy, B. L., Acosta, M. M., & Soutullo, O. (2019). Counternarratives of students' experiences returning to comprehensive schools from an involuntary disciplinary alternative school. *Race, Ethnicity, & Education, 22*(1), 130–149. (★)

Kennedy, R. L. (1989). Racial critiques of legal academy. *Harvard Law Review, 102*(8), 1745–1819.

Ladson-Billings, G. (1998). Just what is critical race theory and what's it doing in a *nice* field like education? *Qualitative Studies in Education, 11*(1), 7–24.

Ladson-Billings, G. (Ed.). (2002). *Critical race theory perspectives on social studies: The profession, policies, and curriculum.* Information Age Publishing.

Ladson-Billings, G., & Tate, W. F., IV. (1995). Toward a critical race theory of education. *Teachers College Record, 97*(1), 47–68.

Landrum, T. J., & Kauffman, J. M. (2006). Behavioral approaches to classroom management in C. M. Evertson & C. S. Weinstein (Eds.). *Handbook of classroom management: Research, practice, and contemporary issues* (pp. 47–72). Lawrence Erlbaum Associates, Publishers.

Laughter, J., & Han, K.T. (2019). Critical race theory in teacher education: Coalitions for the future. In K.T. Han & J. Laughter (Eds.), *Critical race theory in teacher education: Information classroom culture and practice* (pp. 1–10). Teachers College Press.

Ledesma, M. C., & Calderon, D. (2015). Critical race theory in education: A review of past literature and a look to the future. *Qualitative Inquiry, 21*(3), 206–222.

Leonardo, Z. (2013). *Race frameworks: A multidimensional theory of racism and education.* NY Teachers College Press.

Lopes, J., Silva, E., Oliveira, C., Sass, D., & Martin, N. (2017) Teacher's classroom management behavior and students' classroom misbehavior: A study with 5th through 9th- grade students. *Electronic Journal of Research in Educational Psychology, 15*(3), 467–490.

Lynn, M. & Dixson, A. D. (Eds.). (2013). *Handbook of critical race theory in education.* Routledge.

Marshall, P. L. (2002). *Cultural diversity in our schools.* Wadsworth/Thomson Publishers.

Marshall, P. L., Manfra, M. M., & Simmons, C. G. (2016). No more playing in the dark: Twenty-first century citizenship, critical race theory, and the future of the social studies methods course. In A. R. Crowe & A. Cuenca (Eds.), *Rethinking social studies teacher education in the twenty-first century* (pp. 61–79). Springer International Publishing AG.

Martin, N. K., Schafer, N. J., McClowry, S., Emmer, E. T., et al. (2016). Expanding the definition of classroom management: Recurring themes and new conceptualizations. *The Journal of Classroom Interaction, 51*(1), 31–41.

Martinez, A., McMahon, S.D., & Treger, S. (2016). Individual-and-school level predictors of student office disciplinary referrals. *Journal of Emotional and Behavior Disorders, 24*(1), 30–41. (★)

Migliarini V., & Annamma S.A. (2019). Classroom and behavior management: (Re)conceptualization through disability critical race theory. In R. Papa (Ed.) *Handbook on promoting social justice in education.* Springer. https://doi.org/10.1007/978-3-319-74078-2_95-1

Milner, H. R. (2006). Classroom management in urban classrooms. In C. M. Evertson & C. S. Weinstein (Eds.), *Handbook of classroom management: Research, practice, and contemporary issues* (pp. 491–522). Lawrence Erlbaum Association, Publishers.

Milner, H. R., IV. (2014). Research on classroom management in urban schools. In E. T. Emmer & E. J. Sabornie (Eds.), *Handbook of classroom management* (pp. 167–185). Routledge.

Muñoz, F. M. (2009). Critical race theory and landscapes of higher education. *The Vermont Connection:* vol. 30, Article 6. https://scholarworks.uvm.edu/tvc/vol30/iss1/6.

Okilwa, N. S. & Robert, C. (2017). School discipline disparity: Converging efforts for better student outcomes. *Urban Review, 49,* 239–262.

Oliva, N., Pérez, J. C. & Parker, L. (2013). Educational policy contradictions: A LatCrit perspective on undocumented Latino students. In M. Lynn & A. D. Dixon (Eds.), *Handbook of critical race theory in education* (pp. 140–152). Routledge/Taylor & Francis Group.

Parker, L. Deyhle, D., & Villenas, S. (Eds.) (1999). *Race is—race isn't: Critical race theory and qualitative studies in education.* Westview Press.

Postholm, M. B. (2013). Classroom management: What does research tell us? *European Educational Research Journal, 12*(3), 389–402.

Schwab, Y. & Elias, M. J. (2015) Reconsidering exclusionary discipline: The efficacy and equity of out-of-school suspension and expulsion in E. T. Emmer & E. J. Sabornie (Eds.), *Handbook of classroom management* (pp. 116–138). Routledge.

Skiba, R. J. (2014). The failure of zero tolerance. *Reclaiming Children and Youth, 22*(4), 27–33.

Solózano, D. G. (2013). Critical race theory's intellectual roots: My email epistolary with Derrick Bell. In M. Lynn & A. D. Dixon (Eds.), *Handbook of critical race theory in education* (pp. 48–68). Routledge/Taylor & Francis Group.

Subedi, B. (2013). The racialization of South Asian Americans in a post-9/11 era. In M. Lynn & A. D. Dixon (Eds.), *Handbook of critical race theory in education* (pp. 167–180). Routledge/Taylor & Francis Group.

Tate, W. F., IV. (1997). Critical race theory and education: History, theory, and implications. In M. W. Apple (Ed.), *Review of research in education* (pp. 195–247). American Educational Research Association.

Trilling, D. (October 23, 2020). Why is the UK government suddenly targeting "critical race theory"? *The Guardian*, www.theguardian.com/commentisfree/2020/oct/23/uk-critical-race-theory-trump-conservatives-structural-inequality

Twine, F. W., & Warren, J. W. (Eds.). (2000). *Racing research, researching race: Methodological dilemmas in critical race studies.* New York University Press.

White House Event. (September 18, 2020). www.whitehouse.gov/briefings-statements/remarks-president-trump-white-house-conference-american-history/. [Retrieved on April 28, 2021 from www.c-span.org/video/?475934-1/president- trump-announces-1776-commission-restore-patriotic-education-nations-schools]

Whitford, D. K., Katsiyannis, A., & Counts, J. (2016). Discriminatory discipline: Trends and issues. *National Association of Secondary School Principals. NASSP Bulletin, 100*(2), 117–135. http://dx.doi.org.prox.lib.ncsu.edu/10.1177/0192636516677340

Wiley, K. E. (2021). A tale of two logics: School discipline and racial disparities in a 'mostly white' middle school. *American Journal of Education, 127*(2), 163–192. (★)

Wilkerson, I. (2020). *Caste: The origins of our discontents.* Random House Publishers.

25

CLASSROOM MANAGEMENT INSTRUCTION IN TEACHER EDUCATION

A Culturally Responsive Approach

Bettie Ray Butler

THE UNIVERSITY OF NORTH CAROLINA AT CHARLOTTE

Deondra Gladney

THE UNIVERSITY OF NORTH CAROLINA AT CHARLOTTE

Ya-yu Lo

THE UNIVERSITY OF NORTH CAROLINA AT CHARLOTTE

Altheria Caldera

HOWARD UNIVERSITY

Introduction

Classroom management instruction in teacher education has traditionally taken a race–neutral stance. Despite the growing diversity in United States (US) schools, the content presented in university classroom management courses remains White and heavily Eurocentric. Because student behavior is culturally influenced, teacher educators who neglect to integrate explicit knowledge about cultural diversity within their curriculum, in turn, do little to prepare preservice teachers (PSTs) to effectively teach and successfully engage students from different cultures.

Although almost all teacher education programs provide some form of instruction on classroom management, PSTs continue to express a general lack of confidence in their classroom management skills (Siwatu et al., 2017). The National Council on Teacher Quality reported that approximately 40 percent of new teachers, many of whom were presumably recent teacher education graduates, felt unprepared by their program to handle classroom management and discipline concerns (Greenberg et al., 2014). This is especially true in schools with high levels of cultural diversity (Milner, 2006; Siwatu, 2011). While this is not a new finding (Merrett & Wheldall, 1993), the issue of teacher unpreparedness has resurfaced in recent years in response to the current and projected demographic shifts in K–12 student enrollment.

DOI: 10.4324/9781003275312-30

477

Today's schools are rapidly becoming more racially, ethnically, and linguistically diverse; and yet, the teaching force remains overwhelmingly White, middle class, and monolingual (US Department of Education, 2016). Given the evolving demography of the K-12 student population, teacher educators—who are also mostly White—are now challenged to rethink and reimagine how they teach classroom management (Howard & Milner, 2021; Milner et al., 2019). Although some teacher education programs have certainly given attention to the sociocultural context of K-12 schools and its anticipated impact on the future teaching profession, research has shown that other programs approach diversity very differently. In many instances, the discussion of diversity is narrowly focused (King & Butler, 2015), limited to a single course (Caldera et al., 2020), and/or introduced primarily by teacher educators of color (Young, 2020). The study of diversity in teacher education must be intentional, deliberate, and integrated throughout the general curriculum; currently this is not being done consistently. This is why scholars (Cochran-Smith, 2001; Milner, 2010) have argued that what is being taught in teacher education "needs to be drastically and radically reformed in order to meet the needs of culturally diverse learners" (Howard & Milner, 2021, p. 204). Unless this happens, matters of culture will remain at the margins of teaching and learning broadly, and classroom management instruction specifically. Without significant reform, PSTs will continue to graduate without the necessary competencies to understand and mitigate potential cultural conflicts in diverse classrooms, and by default, adopt colorblind practices known to produce and perpetuate disparities in education (Ladson-Billings, 2009; Weinstein et al., 2004). Gay (1993) fervently asserted that, "no one should be allowed to graduate from a teacher [education] program or be licensed to teach without being well grounded in how the dynamic of cultural conditioning operates in teaching and learning" (p. 292).

This chapter emphasizes the importance of centering culturally responsive practices—an approach that recognizes and builds upon the "cultural knowledge, prior experiences, frames of reference, and performance styles of [racially], ethnically, [and linguistically] diverse students to make learning encounters more relevant to and effective for them" (Gay, 2018, p. 36)—in classroom management instruction. Beyond mere rules and procedures, when we refer to *classroom management* from here on out we mean "teachers' ability to develop and [co]construct innovative, emancipatory classroom spaces that cultivate students' opportunities to learn and develop" (Milner, 2014 as cited in Delale-O'Connor et al., 2017). Considering this definition, it is unlikely that PSTs will develop the necessary competencies to implement effective, equitable, and culturally responsive classroom management on their own, which is why this knowledge should be communicated in a deliberate and methodical manner prior to entering into the classroom. The onus falls chiefly on teacher educators to design classroom management courses though a cultural lens. However, not much has been written in this regard. There is growing recognition that teacher educators need guidance on what knowledge needs to be integrated within these courses to ensure that they are attending to their PSTs' cultural development. Herein lies the premise of this chapter.

To begin, we highlight data concerning the widening racial and linguistic gap between K-12 students and teachers and the resulting implications (i.e., test score gaps, disparities in special and gifted education, and disproportionality in school discipline) of this incongruence. Next, we review the literature on culturally responsive practices in education giving specific attention to instruction and classroom management. We conclude with a brief overview outlining several broad culturally responsive classroom management (CRCM) practices that every teacher educator should integrate within their curriculum to help better prepare PSTs to approach classroom management in a culturally responsive way.

The Changing Demographic Profile of US Schools

Racial Incongruence

The cultural landscape of US schools is changing. For the first time in history, White students are no longer the majority. What's more, their enrollment is projected to continue to decrease in years to come. The National Center for Education Statistics (NCES) reported that between 2000 (61%) and 2018 (47%) the percent of White students in public elementary and secondary schools declined by 14 points, making them the new numerical "minority" in US schools (Hussar et al., 2020; Irwin et al., 2021). By 2029, White students are projected to make up just 44 percent of total student body (Hussar et al., 2020). This precipitous decline in White enrollment means that students of color will collectively comprise the largest student group in K–12 schools. Latinx students are expected to nearly double in size between 2000 and 2029, increasing from 16 percent to 28 percent. When considered all together, the combined Latinx (28%), Black (15%), Asian (7%), Indigenous (1%), and multiracial (6%) student population is projected to become 57 percent of the total public elementary and secondary school enrollment within the next decade (Hussar et al., 2020).

Notwithstanding the above demographic shifts in student enrollment, the teaching workforce has remained homogeneous (Putman et al., 2016). In 2000, approximately 15 percent of teachers identified as non-White (Hussar et al., 2020). Nearly two decades later, this percentage increased marginally, rising to 21 percent. In 2018, Latinx teachers comprised 9 percent, and Black teachers made up 7 percent, of the total teaching profession. By comparison, there were far fewer Asian (2%), Indigenous (1%), and multiracial (2%) teachers. Although schools with more racial/ethnic diversity in their student population generally employed more teachers of color (i.e., the percentage of non-White teachers was highest in schools with 90% or more students of color), the fact that the proportion of racial/ethnic diversity make-up in the teacher workforce is significantly less than the racial/ethnic diversity in student enrollment is a clear indication of a student-teacher racial gap (Irwin et al., 2021). This means that K–12 students are, and will likely continue to be, taught by a predominantly White teacher workforce. To be more precise, the White teacher population is more than three times that of non-White teachers (Hussar et al., 2020). In 2000, 84 percent of the teaching profession was White. While there was a slight decline in the percent of White teachers (79%) in 2018, their numbers are projected to remain steady as they continue to occupy the majority of the teaching positions in public elementary and secondary schools.

Linguistic Incongruence

Just as in the case of race, the data also reflect a linguistic mismatch between students and teachers. English language learners (ELLs)—students whose native language is not English, but who are actively learning the English language—represent the fastest-growing, most diverse student group in the USA. In 1993, there were 2.1 million ELLs enrolled in public schools and in 2018 nearly 5 million students—80 percent of whom were Latinx—identified as ELLs (NCES, 2004). This represents an alarming growth of 138 percent within just 15 years. Demographers estimate that by 2025 nearly 1 in every 4 students will identify as an ELL, accounting for 25 percent of the total student enrollment (National Education Association [NEA], 2020). Given these projections, there is a grave concern that there are not enough qualified teachers to meet the unique needs of this student subgroup.

Currently, the majority of public school teachers are monolingual English speakers. Only 13 percent reported having fluency in multiple languages (Barros et al., 2020). Moreover, less than 2 percent of all teachers are English as a Second Language (ESL)/bilingual education (BLE) instructors (de Brey et al., 2021). This means that there is a severe shortage of teachers who are certified to teach ELLs.

The growing racial and linguistic diversity among K–12 students has outpaced that of teachers. This cultural incongruence has illuminated opportunity gaps—the inequitable distribution of resources (inputs)—which have produced widespread racial and ethnic disparities in education (Carter & Welner, 2013; Milner, 2020). Students of color broadly, Black and Latinx students specifically, have consistently scored lower on standardized tests, repeatedly received more referrals for special education and fewer referrals for gifted education, and are more frequently subjected to harsher school punishment in comparison to White students.

Racial and Ethnic Disparities in Education

Standardized Tests

Data from the National Assessment of Education Progress (NAEP) showed that during the 1970s up though the mid-1980s, Black and Latinx students made substantial academic gains in reading and in math, while White students' achievement levels remained relatively flat (Lee, 2002). In the 1990s, however, this trend shifted as test score gaps between Black–White and Latinx–White students eventually stabilized and then started to slowly widen. Since 1992, Black and Latinx students' test scores have steadily dropped. Their 4th, 8th, and 12th grade reading scores have consistently fallen below those of White students (NAEP, 2021). Data from 2019 showed that Black students scored, on average, 26–31 points below White students, whereas Latinx students scored 20–21 points below White students. Similar trends existed for math scores. In 2019, Black and Latinx students also scored 18 points or more below White students on math assessments.

Test score gaps are also common between ELL and non-ELL students. In 2003, across all grade levels (i.e., 4th, 8th, and 12th grades), non-ELLs outperformed ELLs on both math and reading assessments (NAEP, 2021). In reading, ELLs scored between 36–41 points below non-ELLs. In math, the test score gaps widened by as much as 15 points with ELLs scoring, on average, 22–37 points below non-ELLs. While test scores remained relatively stable for ELLs in 2019 in comparison to 2003, the gaps between ELLs and non-ELLs grew. In 2019, the reading test score gap between ELLs and non-ELLs was roughly 33–52 points; meaning, the gap between these two groups grew by 6 points (120%) from 2003 to 2019. In the same year, the math test score gap between ELLs and non-ELLs was 24–42 points; indicating that the gap, though more narrow than reading, still grew by 3 points (20%) from 2003 to 2019.

The interpretation of test score gaps, however, should be done with extreme caution. Recognizing differences in testing performance between groups is not as important as understanding the reasons why these gaps exist in the first place. Performance on standardized tests alone tells us very little about what students actually know and even less about what they can do. Scholars contend that test scores are poor measurements of intelligence, but clear indicators of the limited access to equitable learning opportunities (Carter & Welner, 2013). Systemic barriers—such as implicit bias, racism, discrimination, academic grouping, and cultural incongruence—work against students of color and prevent them from reaching their full academic potential. Low test scores, Gay (2018) argues, are really just "symptoms of, not causes of" larger institutional problems (p. 17).

Gifted and Special Education

The underrepresentation of racially, ethnically, and linguistically diverse (RELD) students for gifted and talented education and their overrepresentation for special education services are both symptoms of institutional dysfunction. These issues were first raised more than 50 years ago, when scholars drew attention to the disproportionate representation of Black students in gifted (Baldwin, 1977) and special education programs (Dunn, 1968). Since then, research has attempted to better understand the causes of racial disparities in selection and identification, often pointing to systemic inequity as a possible culprit (Artiles & Trent, 1994; Ford, 1998). Student placement in gifted and special education is thought to be highly variable and subjective. The reliance on teacher referrals (Andrews et al., 1997; Ford, 1998) and the centering of Whiteness (Cavendish et al., 2020) operate in tandem to privilege some students while marginalizing others. To dismantle systems that undergird disproportionality in gifted and special education, critical attention must be given to the racially biased practices that have historically upheld and normalized Whiteness (Wright et al., 2022).

Measures to deny Black students high-quality classroom instruction intensified after the US Supreme Court's landmark decision in *Brown v. Board of Education* (1954). The *Brown* decision ruled that separating students on the basis of their race was a violation of the Fourteenth Amendment and thus considered unconstitutional. Still, after this ruling, schools—and by extension, teachers—continued to engage in racially biased practices, such as homogenous grouping/ability tracking (Oakes, 1985) and intelligence testing (Baldwin, 1977). Black and other marginalized students (i.e., Latinx, Indigenous, ELLs, and students experiencing poverty) were labeled based on perceived competencies and deficits (Anderson & Oakes, 2014). Such perceptions have resulted in their persistent placement in special education and unequal access to advanced learning opportunities.

It is largely believed that teachers who hold deficit-oriented beliefs about RELD students tend to over-refer them for special education services and under-refer them for gifted programs (Fish, 2019; Scott & Ford, 2011). In this instance, racial, cultural, and/or language differences are viewed as obstacles, rather than assets, to learning; yet the real obstacle is oftentimes teachers' lack of competency in supporting RELD students. It is well known that the interplay of low expectations, biases, and subjectivity influences which students teachers identify as gifted and talented and which ones they identify as having a learning disability. Because these labels to some extent are socially constructed (Sleeter, 1986), teachers have considerable discretion in removing students whom they consider difficult to teach from general classroom instruction. Teachers also have autonomy in preventing students, whose giftedness may not fit into their own perceptions of intelligence, from accessing honors and advanced level courses. Teachers must understand that high scores on IQ tests are not the only sign of giftedness, and undesirable behaviors are not always an indication of a special need. These traditional indicators of intelligence and disability are inherently flawed and demonstrate a misunderstanding or lack of awareness of diverse learning styles and culturally influenced behaviors. Without a deeper understanding of culture, access to advanced learning opportunities are considerably diminished for students who have, for far too long, been left on the margins.

School Discipline

School discipline in many ways works alongside the aforementioned selection and identification processes to (re)produce and maintain educational inequities (Skiba, 2002). Disparities in school discipline, much like the overidentification for special education and the underrepresentation in gifted education, is a symptom of a broken educational system. For quite some time now research has provided evidence of a racial and gender discipline gap. The first national investigation to identify a racial discipline gap was conducted by the Children's Defense Fund (CDF) in 1975. Several important findings emerged from the CDF (1975) report including: (1) Black students, in comparison to White students, are more frequently and severely punished often for relatively minor, non-violent offenses; (2) the Black–White gap in out-of-school suspensions are, in part, a result of the pervasive intolerance by teachers for students whose culture is different than their own; and (3) suspensions are counterproductive to student success and, in most cases, largely unnecessary. These findings are as relevant today as they were in the 1970s—suggesting that little has changed. A substantial body of research now exists that still suggests Black students disproportionately experience more punitive and aversive discipline when compared to other students (Skiba et al., 2011; Wallace et al., 2008). In fact, if disaggregating the data by gender, the conditions seem to have worsened since the CDF report.

In analyzing disciplinary patterns, Lewis and colleagues (2010) found that Black male students were twice as likely as White male students to receive a disciplinary sanction. Similar disciplinary patterns exist for Black female students. Blake and her team of researchers (2011) found that Black female students, in comparison to White female students, were twice as likely to receive an out-of-school suspension, but four times more likely to receive an in-school suspension. In both studies, Black male (Lewis et al., 2010) and female (Blake et al., 2011) students were sanctioned oftentimes for subjectively defined infractions, such as disobedience and defiance—implying that teacher discretion (and perhaps, racial and gender bias) play a critical role in determining who gets suspended and why. Moreover, the loss of instructional time is known to have negative short- and long-term effects (Losen, 2015). It is evident that the resulting consequences of school discipline for Black students, male and female alike, are severe. And judging by the persistence in which the racial/gender discipline gap has been maintained—these disparities appear far from resolved.

Throughout the years, racial and gender disparities in school discipline have drawn widespread interest and concern over the differential treatment of Black students in exclusionary discipline. This is true across all grade levels including even the most vulnerable of youth—preschool and primary (K-2) aged students (Butler et al., 2012).

According to national data from the Office for Civil Rights (OCR), Black preschool students were almost 4 times more likely to receive at least one or more out-of-school suspensions than White preschool students (OCR, 2016). Although Black students only represented 19 percent of preschool enrollment, they accounted for over 47 percent of out-of-school suspensions. Comparatively, White students represented over 41 percent of preschool enrollment, yet they only accounted for 28 percent of out-of-school suspensions. These disciplinary trends are not unique by any means. In fact, similar disparities in suspensions are also evident as Black students become older and enroll in public elementary (3–5) and secondary schools.

Based on OCR data, Black K-12 students were almost 4 times more likely than White K-12 students to receive one or more out-of-school suspensions (OCR, 2016). Young and colleagues (2018) found this to be a fairly stable disciplinary pattern in elementary and secondary schools. In their meta-analysis of research on school discipline disproportionality between Black and White students, they synthesized a total of 29 published research studies. The following criteria were used to select studies for inclusion: (1) the study had to juxtapose discipline practices between that of Black and White students exclusively; (2) the study had to directly assess students' discipline; (3) the study had to include disaggregated data for specific student discipline outcomes (e.g., expulsions and suspension); and (4) the study had to present sufficient quantitative information to calculate odds ratio effect sizes (Young et al., 2018). The results of their analysis substantiated both empirical and practical claims that Black students were more likely to receive school discipline sanctions relative to White students, and that this gap started early and was sustained across multiple grade levels.

In a similar vein, Skiba and colleagues (2011) led a national investigation of 436 elementary (K-6) and 69 middle schools to provide a comprehensive look at disproportionality in school discipline across racial and ethnic categories, as well as school levels. The authors found that Black students were twice as likely to receive an office discipline referral (ODR) at the elementary level and almost four times more likely to be referred to the office at the middle school level. In addition to this finding, their data also suggested that even when exhibiting similar behaviors Black students were more likely than White students to be suspended or expelled irrespective of grade level. This was typical for subjective and vaguely defined infractions. They concluded that differential selection by teachers significantly contributed to increased ODRs for Black students which led to their overrepresentation in school discipline.

Beyond the disciplinary trends found between Black and White students, scholars have found that other racial groups have been subject to overrepresentation in exclusionary discipline. A number of studies have showed that students from Latinx and Indigenous cultures receive suspensions at a rate higher than expected based on the proportion of their student enrollment (Brown & Di Tillio, 2013; Wallace et al., 2008). Extending this work, Whitford and colleagues (2019) investigated the rates of disciplinary exclusion specifically for Indigenous students with and without disabilities. Using school discipline data from OCR they found that Indigenous students were substantially overrepresented in suspensions and expulsions relative to White students. The researchers also discovered that Indigenous students with and without disabilities had the greatest risk of receiving an expulsion (Whitford et al., 2019). Another study (i.e., Nguyen et al., 2019) explored discipline patterns for Asian and Pacific Islander (AAPI) students. After close examination Nguyen and her team found that when discipline data were disaggregated, and Asian and Pacific Islander students were analyzed separately, Pacific

Islanders were nearly twice as likely as White students to receive a school sanction—a finding that would have been masked had the two groups remained coupled together. As a result of their findings, the authors challenged researchers to "rearticulate" (Omi & Winant, 2015 as cited in Nguyen et al., 2019, p. 1991) racial subgroups when exploring discipline trends. They suggested that through the process of rearticulation scholars are able to better understand the unique and sometimes varied ways that different groups of students experience school discipline.

Due to the exclusionary and often discriminatory nature of school discipline, it is not surprising that RELD students who have been suspended and/or expelled also drop out of school at higher rates and experience frequent and disproportionate contact with the juvenile and criminal justice system. Theory holds that implicit bias, coupled with racial incongruence, causes teachers to perceive some students' behaviors more negatively than others even when the behaviors are otherwise similar. Those students labeled as troublemakers get pushed out of the classroom through exclusionary discipline. The loss in instructional time causes them to fall significantly behind in their coursework, increasing their risk of dropout. Without a high school diploma the path to upward mobility is stalled and many find themselves experiencing poverty. As residents in an under-resourced community they become targets of hyper-surveillance by law enforcement. If arrested, notwithstanding the charge, they are likely to receive more punitive sentences. This narrative, though somewhat oversimplified here, is the very crux of what some call the "school-to-prison pipeline" (Wald & Losen, 2003).

Skiba et al. (2014) among others (Nicolson-Crotty et al., 2009; Wald & Losen, 2003) have traced the link between school and prison. Skiba and his co-authors conducted a systematic literature review to examine the evidence surrounding the assumption that exclusionary discipline is correlated with increased student involvement in the juvenile justice system. They highlighted research that indicated that out-of-school suspensions and expulsions resulted in a number of negative developmental outcomes including dropout and juvenile justice involvement. The authors suggested that exclusionary practices may be a key predictive factor for future contact with law enforcement and involvement with the justice system.

The parallels between education and criminal justice institutions are undeniable and noteworthy (Nicholson-Crott et al., 2009). Research has made clear the blurred boundary between schools and prisons. Any effort to dismantle the school-to-prison pipeline must begin as early as preschool. Children as young as two years old are being suspended and expelled from their childcare program because of perceived behavioral challenges, hence the term "*cradle*-to-prison" pipeline (Giordano et al., 2020). Regardless of when the pipeline begins, it almost always originates with teachers—those primarily responsible for issuing discipline referrals. Beyond setting behavioral expectations, teachers have a responsibility to ensure that all students receive an equitable and just education.

Teachers stand on the frontlines in educating students from all cultural backgrounds, which is why it is important that they are armed with the right knowledge and skills to effectively engage diverse learners. The best means to do so, according to a host of scholars (Ladson-Billings, 2021a; Milner, 2020; Sleeter, 2012), is to honor students' lived experiences by bridging home culture (i.e., out-of-school living; Gay, 2013) with school culture (i.e., in-school-learning; Gay, 2013) to provide meaningful opportunities to learn that support student growth and success. The fight against racial and ethnic disparities in testing, special and gifted education, and school discipline begins in the classroom and rests largely on teachers' willingness to commit to doing the work of becoming more culturally responsive.

Culturally Responsive Practices: Instruction and Classroom Management

To achieve an emancipatory learning environment that provides *all* students—no matter their race, ethnicity, language, ability, or economic status—with equitable opportunities to learn and develop, it is imperative that instruction and classroom management be complementary to, not independent of, each other. Good teaching does not occur in isolation (Ladson-Billings, 1995b) and successful classroom management does not happen by chance (Weinstein et al., 2004). Although highly effective instruction mitigates classroom conflict, it does not eliminate it altogether (Emmer & Stough, 2001). Effective teachers possess well-balanced competencies in both pedagogy and management. Effective teachers also acknowledge that good teaching and successful classroom management does not exist apart from understanding the different learning styles and culturally influenced behaviors of RELD students.

Instruction

Culturally responsive instruction emerged in the field of education as a way of thinking about how to leverage a student's unique cultural background to improve their educational experiences (Gay, 2018; Ladson-Billings, 1995a). Since its inception, the concept of culturally responsive instruction has been widely accepted by education scholars and practitioners around the world and used to inform research and practice. Though conceptually straightforward, educators have struggled to understand what culturally responsive instruction looks like in practice. This explains why in recent years there has been extended discussion about its application. Paris and Alim (2017), for example, advance understanding around culturally *sustaining* pedagogies, placing emphasis on practices that go beyond "relevance" and "responsiveness" (presumably, understood as adjectives) to maintenance and social critique (verbs). They suggest that "it is possible to be relevant [responsive] to something without ensuring its continuing and critical presence in … practice, and its presence in … classrooms and communities" (Paris & Alim, 2017, p. 5). With attention to sustaining the cultural ways of being of students of color, Paris and Alim position cultural pluralism (literacy and language) and the centrality of youth culture (voice) as vital to the social transformation of schooling. The authors make clear that culture is not static, but fluid and constantly evolving—spanning across time, location, race, and ethnicity. With this acknowledgement, Paris and Alim call on educators—and those alike—to "reimagine schools as sites where diverse, heterogeneous practices are not only valued but sustained" (p. 3). Similar to Paris and Alim, Hammond also extends the conversation on culturally responsive instruction. Her rationale for doing so was based largely on her own observations of teachers having difficulty translating culturally responsive principles into teaching practices. Having a desire to bridge theory with practice, Hammond describes the relationship between culture, learning, and neurological science to show how brain-based learning, when coupled with rigorous culturally responsive instruction, can aid in closing the "achievement [opportunity]" gap for underperforming students of color and help them become self-directed, independent learners (p. 3). Hammond lays out a very practical framework (Ready for Rigor) with specific tools and strategies for putting culturally responsive instruction into actionable steps that provide guidance to teachers on what students need to more actively engage and take ownership of their learning process. While these extended discussions have certainly been meaningful contributions to the discourse on culturally responsive instruction, without an understanding of the earlier frameworks on which Paris and Alim (2017) and Hammond (2015) have based their claims there can be no real comprehension of why culture is vital to teaching and learning.

To fully understand culturally responsive instruction, it is necessary to become familiar with the major conceptual frameworks that have been germane to research and practice concerned with improving the academic performance of diverse learners. Gloria Ladson-Billings and Geneva Gay both pioneered research and popularized language around culturally responsive instruction. To date, their conceptualizations of culturally relevant pedagogy (Ladson-Billings, 1995a, 1995b) and culturally responsive teaching (Gay, 2015, 2018) are two of the most prominent and well-established frameworks on culturally responsive instructional practices.

Gloria Ladson-Billings' Culturally Relevant Pedagogical Framework

In *Dreamkeepers*, one of the most seminal and influential texts of our time, Ladson-Billings (2009) set out to demonstrate that there were teachers that could effectively teach Black students and help them to achieve high levels of academic success while also maintaining a positive self-concept. At the time of her study, she stated that "most of the scholarly literature positions [Black] students as problems and seeks to determine what is wrong—with their education, their families, their culture, and their minds" (p. vii). To break up this monotony and fill a much-needed void in the research, Ladson-Billings (2009) provided an ethnographic account of teachers who were revered by parents and administration as effective teachers of Black students. A total of eight teachers were identified for her study. Five were Black and three were White and all were women. Some had experience teaching in suburban schools, others in urban settings. Despite these differences, Ladson-Billings (2009) found that each of the eight teachers shared common teaching characteristics. All of their pedagogical practices had a strong focus on student learning, developing cultural competence, and cultivating students' sociopolitical awareness. These three teaching methods laid the groundwork to provide a useful heuristic for both teachers and teacher educators who desire to "[empower] students intellectually, socially, emotionally, and politically by using cultural referents to impart knowledge, skills, and attitudes" (Ladson-Billings, 2009, p. 20). This train of thought developed the framework for what we now know as *culturally relevant pedagogy*.

Ladson-Billings' (1995b) culturally relevant pedagogical framework rests upon three propositions: (1) students must experience academic success; (2) students must develop and/or maintain cultural competence; and (3) students must develop a critical consciousness that disrupts the status quo. To break this down further, culturally relevant pedagogy promotes high expectations. Teachers who possess this attribute will view all students as capable of learning and demand, reinforce, and produce academic excellence in each of them (Ladson-Billings, 1995b). A culturally relevant pedagogy will also "utilize students' culture as a vehicle for learning" (Ladson-Billings, 1995b, p. 161). Teachers who possess this attribute find ways to connect a student's home culture and school culture in their teaching practices to make learning engaging. A culturally relevant pedagogy helps students to "critique the cultural norms, values…and institutions that produce and maintain social inequities" (Ladson-Billings, p. 162). Teachers who possess this attribute will teach students how to critically think so that they can become producers of knowledge, not just consumers. Altogether, a culturally relevant pedagogical framework helps teachers to understand their positionality in relation to their students and their students' families. It also shows teachers how to build a community of learners through meaningful social interactions within the classroom. Lastly, a culturally relevant pedagogical framework encourages teachers to go beyond the traditional curriculum to see knowledge as fluid and open to critique so that they can help students to promote positive change within their schools, communities, families, and individual lives (Ladson-Billings, 2009).

Over 20 years have passed since Ladson-Billings began constructing the three tenets, named above, that would become the basis by which culturally relevant pedagogy is understood today (Ladson-Billings, 1990, 1995a). The concept, though it has grown increasingly popular in recent years, has not always been applied as originally designed. Notably, some educators have "dull[ed] its critical edge or omitt[ed] it altogether" (Ladson-Billings, 2014, p. 77). Seemingly dissatisfied with this discontinuity, Ladson-Billings found it necessary to r(e)volutionize, remix, and reintroduce culturally relevant pedagogy to a new generation of teachers and teacher educators (Ladson-Billing, 2014, 2017, 2021a). In doing so, she now draws attention to youth culture in a way that she had not done in her earlier work; recognizing, more explicitly, the vitality of youth voice in engaging in critical conversations that offer new pedagogical insight. Ladson-Billings (2014) does not imply that her original conceptualization was deficient, rather due to the fluidity of culture and changing systems it was necessary to take her previously developed idea and synthesize it to create new understandings. Engaging with scholars like Django Paris and Samy Alim, Ladson-Billings (2021a) views contemporary cultural frameworks, like culturally sustaining pedagogy, as both timely and relevant. These progressive frames help to push the boundaries of culturally relevant pedagogy beyond static notions of culture to facilitate growth in the field and improve praxis.

Geneva Gay's Culturally Responsive Teaching Framework

Gay's (2018) highly acclaimed text, *Culturally Responsive Teaching*, has through the years become another staple in schools and colleges of education globally. Using research findings, theoretical claims, practical experiences, and personal stories of teachers who work with RELD students, Gay (2018) identifies six specific components of her culturally responsive teaching framework: (1) social and academic empowerment; (2) multidimensional learning; (3) learning that validates every student's cultural experiences; (4) learning that engages the whole child; (5) learning that is transformative of social inequities; and (6) learning that grounds itself in emancipatory practice. Each of these essential principles were developed with teachers and teacher educators in mind.

The first principle, *social and academic empowerment*, refers to the idea that teachers are expected to have the highest expectations for their students' success as a form of empowerment for each student to achieve their goals in adulthood. The second principle, *multidimensional learning*, relates to the need for teachers to use a number of different perspectives, views, and experiences within their content and instruction to engage students. The third principle, *validating cultural experiences*, calls on teachers to employ students' own culture and communities to help them locate themselves within what is being taught. The fourth principle, *engaging the whole child*, speaks to the need for teachers to engage the whole child in the learning process, rather than merely providing academic instruction. This includes attending to social and emotional needs as well as incorporating the needs of students' communities within their learning. The fifth principle, *transformative learning*, refers to the idea that teachers are capable of helping their students by advocating for changes within the education system through leveraging students' unique abilities to direct instructional practices, assessment, and changes to curriculum. Finally, the sixth principle, *emancipatory learning*, emphasizes the need for teachers to provide instruction that can help students engage in social justice for themselves and empower them to combat oppressive ideologies and norms embedded within the educational system.

Gay (2013, 2018) recently revisited her culturally responsive teaching framework. In doing so, she explained how it is necessary for every teacher to identify their implicit biases and deficit mindsets to contextualize instruction more broadly to capture larger social justice aims in education. Gay also somewhat unapologetically admitted that while her earlier writings were more curriculum specific, given that this focus was consistent with the most pressing educational needs at the time, she has always had a firm grasp of the benefits of culturally responsive teaching in other areas of educational practice, such as classroom management. However, it was Carol Weinstein who would lead the efforts to formally conceptualize a framework for culturally responsive classroom management (Weinstein et al., 2004).

Classroom Management

Although the studies discussed in the previous section emphasize the importance of culturally responsive instruction for improving the academic performance of students from different racial and ethnic backgrounds, researchers have identified a further need to address culturally responsive instruction in the context of classroom management (Bondy et al., 2007). Because classroom management is about fostering equitable, just, and inclusive classrooms (Milner et al., 2019), the phrase "management" in some regard is an apparent misnomer. Classroom management is more about collaboration and relationship building and less about control and/or coercion.

For years there was no frame of reference or model available to guide classroom management in diverse learning spaces. Weinstein and her co-authors (2004) explain this further:

[T]he literature on multicultural education has tended to ignore issues of classroom management. Numerous educators have called for culturally responsive or culturally sensitive pedagogy, but they have primarily focused on curriculum content and teaching strategies. Although there has been some discussion of how culturally responsive teachers foster connectedness, community, and collaboration and how students and teachers perceive disciplinary conflict, other issues of classroom management (e.g., organizing the physical environment, defining and teaching expectations for behavior, preventing minor confrontations, and communicating with families) have not been thoroughly explored.

p. 26

To extend discussions of culturally responsive teaching to include classroom management, Weinstein and colleagues (2003) introduced CRCM as a framework to situate classroom management through a cultural lens.

Weinstein and Colleagues' CRCM Framework

In their original article, *Culturally Responsive Classroom Management: Awareness into Action*, Weinstein and co-authors (2003) built upon Ladson-Billings' and Gay's culturally responsive instructional frameworks to identify practical approaches and strategies for implementing CRCM. Even while the authors themselves refer to CRCM as a "set of strategies or practices," the underlying premise of the framework is that CRCM is as much as, if not more so, a "frame of mind" positioned within justice-oriented teaching practices (Weinstein et al., 2003, p. 275). Using knowledge gained from their professional and personal backgrounds, the authors construct five essential principles around CRCM: (1) recognition of one's (teachers') own ethnocentrism and biases; (2) knowledge of students' cultural backgrounds; (3) awareness of the broader social, economic, and political context; (4) ability and willingness to use culturally appropriate management strategies; and (5) commitment to building caring classrooms (Weinstein et al., 2004).

First, the *recognition of one's own ethnocentrism and biases* is a deeply reflective process that challenges teachers' to consider their beliefs, values, and assumptions about a student's behavior. The authors argue that when teachers bring their "implicit, unexamined cultural biases to a conscious level, [they] are less likely to misinterpret the behaviors of…culturally diverse students and treat them inequitably" (Weinstein et al., 2004, p. 29). Next, the *knowledge of student's cultural background* is a participatory process that encourages teachers to get to know their students and their families. Engaging in cross-cultural communication is necessary to appreciate and respect others' culture. The authors maintain that this level of dialogue "can sensitize [teachers] to the possibility that cultural values and norms underlie behavior that, on the surface, looks like a lack of interest in school" (Weinstein et al., 2004, p. 30). Third, the *awareness of the broader social, economic, and political context* is a holistic process wherein teachers see schools as a microcosm of society. The authors point out that education "reflects and often perpetuates discriminatory practices of the larger society" (Weinstein et al., 2004, p. 31). Thus, teachers need to understand how school policies, as well as their individual pedagogical practices might work to create and reinforce systemic racism. Fourth, the *ability and willingness to use culturally appropriate management strategies* is an evaluative process that forces teachers to assess a situation and determine the most appropriate response. The authors warn that teachers must learn how to "question traditional assumptions of 'what works' in classroom management and be alert to possible mismatches between conventional management strategies and students' cultural backgrounds" (Weinstein et al., 2004, p. 32). Therefore, teachers must carefully observe their verbal (and nonverbal) dispositions to ensure that their practices are both inclusive and equitable. Last, the *commitment to building caring classroom communities* is a relational process that teachers should establish early in the school year. There is an old adage that says *students don't care what you know, until they know that you care.* The same is true here as the authors remind us that when students are, "[f]aced with directives from the teacher, they resist or cooperate, ignore or acquiesce—and the key factor determining which option they choose is often their perception of the teacher's caring" (Weinstein et al., 2004, p. 33).

Implications of Culturally Responsive Instruction and Classroom Management

Academic and Behavioral Effects

The cultural frameworks offered by Ladson-Billings (1995a) and Gay (2018) have enticed a number of researchers to study the relationship between cultural responsiveness and student outcomes. Despite the abundance of scholarship in favor of using culturally responsive practices, only a handful of studies have established a causal relationship between culture-specific interventions and academic and behavioral outcomes. Some scholars have suggested that more robust research is needed in this area (Morrison et al., 2008; Pas et al., 2016).Yet, of the limited number of studies that do exist, the use of culturally responsive approaches have been found to be generally favorable for students, particularly RELD students and Black students with disabilities.

Among the extant scholarship, researchers have found positive effects on academic (Cartledge et al., 2015; Dee & Penner, 2017) and social/behavioral outcomes (Lo et al., 2011) for students of color when using culturally responsive approaches to instruction (e.g., integration of multicultural literature, student input, cooperative learning groups, peer modeling, and knowledge application). Studies have reported significant improvement in student reading scores for RELD students (Bui & Fagan, 2013), as well as increased ability to follow adult directions among Black students with emotional and behavioral disorders (Robinson-Erwin et al., 2016). Furthermore, when instruction is supplemented with coaching around culturally responsive social skill development, researchers have noted a decline in disruptive behaviors (Bradshaw et al., 2018) and rule violations (Gladney et al., 2021).

In addition to instruction, a few researchers have investigated the effects of culturally responsive approaches to classroom management. For example, Pas and colleagues (2016) conducted a study that looked at teachers' willingness to implement CRCM in their classes. They argued that improving teachers use of CRCM strategies could operate as a preventative method that reduces disparities in school discipline for RELD students with disabilities. The findings from their study were mixed. When offering professional development that combined traditional classroom management strategies with culturally responsive strategies (e.g., relevant curriculum, authentic relationships, reflection, effective communication, and cultural sensitivity), Pas and her team found that teachers were more inclined to set goals around general expectations for positive behavior than around cultural proficiency—an indication that teachers may be less comfortable addressing culture, which implies that more support should be provided to teachers during their preservice education training.

In light of these findings, it is critical that teachers receive the necessary preparation to integrate culturally responsive practices before they enter the classroom. Because this knowledge is largely transmitted through teacher education programs, teacher educators have a responsibility to design curricula, specifically classroom management instruction, to foreground issues of race, culture, equity, and social justice (Alvarez, 2019). In the final section of this chapter, we outline several broad CRCM practices that teacher educators should integrate within their curriculum to aid PSTs in understanding classroom management in a culturally responsive way.

Teacher Education and Traditional Classroom Management

At the conclusion of their article, Weinstein and her co-authors (2004) issued a call to disrupt traditional ideas about classroom management instruction, asking teacher educators to consider:

> How [they] can sensitize (mostly White, middle-class) [PSTs] to their own biases, assumptions, and stereotypes so that they undergo genuine personal transformation…[provide] knowledge about cultural differences in worldviews, communication patterns, and customs without perpetuating stereotypes and essentializing cultural differences…[and]

opportunities for [PSTs] to gain awareness of the broader social, economic, and political context in which they, their students, and educational institutions exists.

p. 36

The motivation behind this chapter, thus, is to help teacher educators respond to this call by moving away from traditional classroom management instruction to a more culturally responsive approach.

Contemporary scholars in teacher education propose culturally responsive approaches to classroom management because culture:

> Plays a role in disciplinary judgments; in some cases, "inappropriate behaviors" may reflect a cultural mismatch between the norms of the school and the norms of a student's home culture. Teachers can better understand the relationship between culture and discipline by working on a related critical practice: self-awareness and cultural competency.
>
> *Teaching Tolerance, 2021*

To be clear, teachers can only be effective classroom "managers" (loosely used) if they are knowledgeable of students' cultural backgrounds. They should make every attempt to "go out of their way to understand the culture … of the community that makes up the school" (Sieberer-Nagler, 2016, p. 170). Ladson-Billings (2017) even contends that learning culture "takes deliberate study" (p. 143). She further points out that "no teacher education course can ever cover every potential cultural conflict. Thus … teachers [must] take the initiative to learn about the communities where they work" (Ladson-Billings, 2017, p. 144). Teacher education classroom management instruction should be shaped—as much as possible—around opportunities to critically engage culturally responsive approaches to classroom management. It is through approaching classroom management in this way that teachers can create humanizing school cultures and begin to disrupt racial and ethnic disparities in education.

Culturally Responsive Classroom Management Instruction

Weinstein and colleagues (2004) urged teachers and teacher educators to question what they believe works when teaching RELD students and to be willing to supplement their existing strategies with promising CRCM practices that challenge deficit thinking, promote greater equity, and embrace principles of social justice. Caldera and her co-authors (2019), inspired by the work led by Carol Weinstein and colleagues (2004) and the larger body of scholarship on culturally responsive approaches (Gay, 2018; Ladson-Billings, 2021a), put forth several ideas for developing different units of study they believed to be essential in aiding teacher educators to prepare PSTs to teach in urban schools. Guided by these proposed units, the next section provides a discussion on four classroom management practices—restorative discipline, culturally responsive positive behavior interventions and supports (CRPBIS), mindfulness, and anti-racism—that teacher educators should integrate fully within their general curriculum to reflect a more critical and culturally responsive approach to classroom management instruction. Each of the practices discussed, though distinct, are closely interrelated; and when used together their combined effects generally yield more favorable outcomes for students at the greatest risk of experiencing inequitable treatment in school.

Proposing the Integration of Promising CRCM Practices into the Curriculum

Restorative Discipline

Restorative discipline is a promising approach that reflects the tenets of CRCM. Unlike zero tolerance practices that seek to control students with the threat of removal, restorative discipline encourages interconnectedness to guide responses to conflict (Evans & Vaandering, 2016). Restorative discipline, adapted from early biblical and indigenous customs and principles of restorative justice (Zehr, 1990), seeks to (Amstutz & Mullet, 2015):

- Recognize the purposes of misbehavior;
- Address the needs of those harmed;
- Work to put right the harm;
- Aim to improve the future;
- Seek healing;
- Use collaborative processes; and
- Make *changes to the system* when it contributes to the harm.

Each of these goals are intended to emphasize social engagement over social control, placing relationships over rules, and people over policies (Evans & Vaandering, 2016). More than just an alternative to zero tolerance, restorative discipline aims to strengthen social and emotional competencies, reduce gender and racial disparities in discipline, and increase access to equitable and supportive environments for all students, but especially those from marginalized groups (Gregory & Evans, 2020).

Restorative discipline has both a proactive and a reactive component which has made the use of this approach relatively successful in schools (Darling-Hammond et al., 2020). Although there are a variety of approaches that fall under restorative discipline, the most widely used in schools are Circles. Circle processes allow members of the school community to "come together as equals to have honest exchanges about difficult issues and painful experiences in an atmosphere of respect and concern for everyone" (Pranis, 2005, p. 6). Wachtel (2016) suggests that while Circles have been traditionally used for conflict resolution, healing, and support (reactive), they can also be used to guide decision-making, exchange information and develop relationships (proactive).

Despite the potential of restorative discipline to positively transform the schooling experiences of marginalized students, its implementation has been challenging for educators. Winn (2018) has argued that PSTs should be trained in restorative discipline and circle process facilitation while in their teacher education program. Yet, this is rarely accomplished; which explains why restorative discipline is sometimes mis-implemented. When restorative discipline is not implemented as intended, or designed, its transformative power is lost (Butler, 2021, in press). Some common misapplications of restorative discipline include: (1) misalignment of restorative values; (2) narrow focus on one restorative practice; (3) disconnection to racial justice; (4) minimal ongoing support; and (5) no long-term investment (Gregory & Evans, 2020). Teacher educators desiring to integrate restorative discipline within their curriculum should take heed to these cautions; remembering that restorative discipline is a mindset, not a program; a compass, not a map; it is proactive, not simply reactionary; and that it is for everyone, not just students (Butler, 2021; Zehr, 2015).

Culturally Responsive Positive Behavior Interventions and Supports

Another promising practice that is undergirded by CRCM principles is culturally responsive positive behavior interventions and supports (CRPBIS). CRPBIS is a relatively new approach to Positive Behavior Intervention Supports (PBIS)—a multi-tier, schoolwide system approach that "aims to reduce problem behaviors and improve school climate" by establishing a team to oversee behavioral issues and to make data driven decisions (Bal et al., 2021, p. 278). CRPBIS was developed in response to growing interest in the intersection of culture and PBIS implementations. Scholars have noted that while PBIS has been used in schools widely, students from diverse backgrounds still have high discipline rates leading some to conclude that its culture-neutral approach makes it less effective for

RELD students (Cramer & Bennett, 2015). This critique forced scholars to think critically about how PBIS could be implemented in more culturally responsive ways that produce greater equity in student outcomes, and giving specific attention to disparities in school discipline.

Bal (2018) presents CRPBIS as a paradigm shift in the service delivery of PBIS. He states that CRPBIS moves away from surface level analysis of disparities to focusing on the very processes that perpetuate them. Ultimately, the shift that Bal proposes calls on researchers and educators to "comprehensively understand and address complex and adaptive enduring equity issues that are reproduced in/though schooling" (Bal, 2018, p. 154). To fully dismantle systemic inequities, Bal makes clear that schools must build capacity around inclusive, data-based decision-making that centers the voices of students and their families and affirms their cultural values. This form of coalition building, however, is not intuitive. Teachers need training to facilitate participatory engagement between students, families, school-based teams, and the larger community.

As students in schools become more heterogenous, teacher educators play an important role in training PSTs to engage and produce knowledge with people whose culture may be different from their own. By integrating this training within the curriculum, PSTs are able to work towards prioritizing students and families' needs, closing opportunity gaps, and advocating for socially just systemic change.

Mindfulness

Mindfulness, like restorative discipline and CRPBIS, can be used to further equity work in schools (Duane et al., 2021). Its focus on reflexivity, self-awareness, and fostering a safe environment aligns closely with CRCM principles. Kabat-Zinn (2015) defines mindfulness as, "moment-to-moment, non-judgmental awareness, cultivated by paying attention in a specific way, that is, in the present moment, and as non-reactively, as non-judgmentally, and as openheartedly as possible" (p. 1481). Over the years, more and more individuals have recognized the benefits of mindfulness and have integrated it within their practices within and outside of schools.

Mindfulness can be a valuable approach for everyone, including those who have been exposed to trauma and adverse life events. For Black people specifically, mindfulness has reduced depressive symptoms and suicidal ideation associated with race-related stressors (Watson-Singleton, 2019). In school-settings mindfulness can help all students, particularly urban youth and youth experiencing poverty, with sustained attention, socioemotional development, executive functioning, and self-regulation (Armstrong, 2019; Mendelson et al., 2010). Mindfulness, in many ways, teaches the brain how to relax so it can grow and think.

Notwithstanding these benefits, mindfulness—if not used correctly—can be detrimental and even harmful. Oftentimes mindfulness practices are deeply entrenched in White experiences and social references. Therefore, when mindfulness is implemented in schools without the appropriate sociopolitical and racial context it can be weaponized and used "unintentionally and inadvertently…to manipulate, coerce, or commit acts of emotional, psychological, and curricular violence" (Duane et al., 2021, p.5). Duane and colleagues (2021) offer examples of this weaponization, describing times when teachers: tell a student in crisis to close their eyes and "just" breathe, downplaying their emotional needs; mandate that students use mindfulness while subjecting them to oppressive practices and policies that disempower them (e.g., eating lunch silently or walking in a straight line); or punish students who make use of mindfulness strategies when it is inconvenient for the teacher. The mere adoption of mindfulness strategies bears no actual weight unless there is a deliberate focus on culture. For mindfulness to be effective in schools, with students of color especially, its implementation must be done with the intention to disrupt the racial injustice in education.

Given the newness of mindfulness in schools, PSTs should be trained in advance prior to attempting to use this practice in the classroom. Teacher educators should thoughtfully integrate a mindfulness curriculum that is rooted in both trauma-informed practices and culturally responsive approaches (Duane et al., 2021), as a part of their classroom management instruction. This type of early exposure can protect students from well-meaning teachers who do more harm than good when facilitating mindfulness as a behavioral strategy but fail to consider the cultural implications associated with its use.

Anti-Racism

Teachers will at times state affirmatively that they are not racist, but whether they are anti-racist is debatable. Anti-racism as a practice is based on what one does, not what one professes. Anti-racist educators work to dismantle structures, policies, institutions, and systems that create and sustain racial inequities among students of color (Kendi, 2019). This stance, like the aforementioned practices, embodies the tenets of CRCM. Weinstein and colleagues (2004) have highlighted the importance of teachers understanding how "the educational enterprise reflects and often perpetuates discriminatory practices of the larger society" (p. 31). With regard to classroom management, the Weinstein et al. push teachers to reexamine the ways that their current practices and policies reinforce oppressive and marginalizing behaviors. Yet, constantly reflecting and reexamining teaching practices, alone, does not make one anti-racist; rather protecting, advocating, and leveraging resources, power, and influence to the benefit of marginalized students is what determines whether an educator engages in anti-racism.

It is problematic when teachers believe that being race-neutral, or colorblind, is not oppressive. These teachers tend to conflate equity and equality, believing that "treating all students the same" is good practice. Some consider neutrality a safe place wherein to position their classroom management. Yet, Kendi (2019) states that "there is no in-between safe space of 'not racist'" (p. 9). To borrow from Freire (1970), teaching [classroom management] is, in and of itself, a political act; and is never neutral.

Teachers who practice anti-racism in education understand the impact of race on opportunity, confront racism without reservation or risk of ostracism, and challenge structural systems that perpetuate racism (Blakeney, 2005). Becoming anti-racist does not happen overnight. Anti-racism is a daily practice that must be cultivated early and continuously. To prepare PSTs of all races to engage in anti-racism, teacher educators must first become aware of their own social position and critically reflect on it; understanding that their "socialization and intersecting identities (including internalized racial superiority and internalized racial inferiority)" impact how and what they teach (Kishimoto, 2018, p. 543).

Recent conversations about anti-racism in teacher education, and education in general, have sparked national debate (Ray & Gibbons, 2021). Several political officials, mostly conservative, have attempted to undo decades of racial progress made possible by critical race scholars who have established the need to call out and counter racism in schools. Yet, the opposition to critical race theory does not void its significance; it makes the discussion of anti-racism that much more salient and necessary. Teacher education programs should not shy away from training PSTs to practice anti-racism, rather they should make a conscious decision to integrate principles of anti-racism throughout its all of its courses—classroom management included. Teacher educators should be prepared to name racism as the main contributor to educational disparities. Naming race and racism are essential to dismantling factors that are deeply embedded in teaching practices (Welton et al., 2018). Discussions that center race and/or people of color should not be tokenized but fully integrated within the curriculum (Kishimoto, 2018). Kishimoto (2018) contends that teacher educators adopt an anti-racist position in their pedagogy, must not only teach it to PSTs but they should model it in their department, research, and interactions with their colleagues—an often omitted, but core component, of anti-racism.

Conclusion

In sum, though additional research is needed to strengthen the argument for cultural responsiveness in classroom management, existing studies, many of which are included in this chapter, offer evidence in support of this approach. Consequently, teacher educators must be able to re-envision the way they prepare PSTs to be effective classroom managers who relate to RELD students in humanizing ways. Given the growing diversity in schools, it is no longer justifiable to accept classroom management as it is. Teacher educators and teachers must reimagine classroom management as it could be. Greene (1995) offers this poignant reflection:

> To tap into imagination is to become able to break with what is supposedly fixed and finished, objectively and independently real. It is to see beyond what the imaginer has called normal or "common-sensible" and to carve out new orders in experience. Doing so, a person may become freed to glimpse what might be, to form notions of what should be and what is not yet. And the same person may, at the same time, remain in touch with what presumably is.
>
> *p. 19*

If classroom management is expected to change, so should classroom management instruction. Such change then necessitates that teacher educators' approach to classroom management instruction shift away from race- and culture-neutrality. To move the field forward it is, in no uncertain terms, absolutely imperative to give greater attention to race, racism, and social justice in teacher education. Teacher educators have a responsibility to shepherd PSTs beyond their margins of comfort to explore what classroom management for equity could be in the lives of students (Milner et al., 2019). PSTs who learn classroom management practices beyond traditional approaches (e.g., structuring their daily schedule, organizing physical space, compliance, punishment/rewards) are better equipped to disrupt longstanding disparities in education (i.e., testing, special and gifted education, and school discipline). A deliberate and intentional focus on restorative discipline, CRPBIS, mindfulness, and anti-racism within classroom management instruction is certain to aid in the advancement of research and the improvement of practice. To move from what is, to what could be, requires what Ladson-Billings (2021b) refers to as a "hard re-set" in our thinking, in our practices, and in our policies. And the only way to do this is by approaching classroom management instruction in a more culturally responsive way.

References

Alvarez, A. (2019). Teacher educator responsibilities for preparing teachers to center race. In P. M. Jenlink (Ed.)., *Teacher preparation at the intersection of race and poverty in today's schools* (pp. 95–98). Rowman & Littlefield.

Amstutz, L., & Mullet, J. (2015). *The little book of restorative discipline for schools: Teaching responsibility; creating caring climates.* Good Books.

Anderson, L., & Oakes, J. (2014). The truth about tracking. In P. Gorski & K. Zenkov (Eds.), *The big lies of school reform: Finding better solutions for the future of public education* (pp. 109–128). Routledge.

Andrews, T., Wisniewski, J., & Mulick, J. (1997). Variables influencing teachers' decisions to refer children for school psychological assessment services. *Psychology in Schools, 34*(3), 239–244. https://doi.org/10.1002/(SICI)1520-6807(199707)34:3<239::AID-PITS6>3.0.CO;2-J

Armstrong, T. (2019). *Mindfulness in the classroom: Strategies for promoting concentration, compassion, and calm.* ASCD.

Artiles, A., & Trent, S. (1994). Overrepresentation of minority students in special education: A continuing debate. *The Journal of Special Education, 27*(4), 410–437. https://doi.org/10.1177/002246699402700404

Bal, A. (2018). Culturally responsive positive behavioral interventions and supports: A process-oriented framework for systemic transformation. *Review of Education, Pedagogy, and Cultural Studies, 40*(2), 144–174. https://doi.org/10.1080/10714413.2017.1417579

Bal, A., Afacan, K., Clardy, T., & Cakir, H. (2021). Inclusive future making: Building a culturally responsive behavioral support system at an urban middle school with local stakeholders. *Cognition and Instruction, 39*(3), 275–305. https://doi.org/10.1080/ 07370008.2021.1891070

Baldwin, A.Y. (1977). Tests can underpredict: A case study. *The Phi Delta Kappan, 58*(8), 620–621. www.jstor.org/stable/20298721

Barros, S., Domke, L. Symons, C., & Ponzio, C. (2020). Challenging monolingual ways of looking an multilingualism: Insights for curriculum development in teacher preparation. *Journal of Language, Identity, & Education, 20*(4), 239–254. https://doi.org/10.1080/15348458.2020.1753196

Blake, J., Butler, B. R., Lewis, C., & Darensbourg, A. (2011). Unmasking the inequitable discipline experiences of urban Black girls: Implications for urban educational stakeholders. *The Urban Review, 43,* 90–106. https://doi.org/10.1007/s11256-009-0148-8

Blakeney, A. (2005). Antiracist pedagogy: Definition, theory, and professional development. *Journal of Curriculum and Pedagogy, 2*(1), 119–132. https://doi.org/10.1080/15505170.2005.10411532

Bondy, E., Ross, D. D., Gallingane, C., & Hambacher, E. (2007). Creating environments of success and resilience: Culturally responsive classroom management and more. *Urban education, 42*(4), 326–348. https://doi.org/10.1177%2F0042085907303406

Bradshaw, C. P., Pas, E. T., Bottiani, J. H., Debnam, K. J., Reinke, W. M., Herman, K. C., & Rosenberg, M. S. (2018). Promoting cultural responsivity and student engagement through Double Check coaching of classroom teachers: An efficacy study. *School Psychology Review, 47*(2), 118–134. https://doi.org/10.17105/SPR-2017-0119.V47-2

Brown, C. A., & Di Tillio, C. (2013). Discipline disproportionality among Hispanic and American Indian students: Expanding the discourse in U.S. research. *Journal of Education and Learning, 2*(4), 47–59. https://doi.org/10.5539/jel.v2n4p47

Bui, Y. N., & Fagan, Y. M. (2013). The effects of an integrated reading comprehension strategy: A culturally responsive teaching approach for fifth-grade students' reading comprehension. *Preventing School Failure: Alternative Education for Children and Youth, 57*(2), 59–69. https://doi.org/10.1080/1045988X.2012.664581

Butler, B. R. (2021). Bridging the divide between data and solutions: A closer look at a restorative justice framework for school discipline. In T. Heafner, L. Handler, & T. Rock (Eds.), *The divide within: Intersections of realties, facts, theories, and practices* (pp. 251–264). Information Age Publishing.

Butler, B. R. (in press). Restorative philosophy in education. In H. R. Milner & J. Bennett (Eds.), *Encyclopedia for social justice in education: Teaching and teacher education.* Bloomsbury.

Butler, B. R., Lewis, C. W., III Moore, J. L., & Scott, M. (2012). Assessing the odds: Disproportional discipline practices and implications for educational stakeholders. *The Journal of Negro Education, 81*(1), 11–24. https://doi.org/10.7709/jnegroeducation. 81.1.0011

Caldera, A., Whitaker, M. C., & Conrad Popova, D. A. D. (2020). Classroom management in urban schools: Proposing a course framework. *Teaching Education, 31*(3), 343–361. https://doi.org/10.1080/10476210.2018.1561663

Carter, P., & Welner, K. (Eds.). (2013). *Closing the opportunity gap: What American must do to give every child an even chance.* Oxford University Press.

Cartledge, G., Bennett, J. G., Gallant, D. J., Ramnath, R., & Keesey, S. (2015). Effects of culturally relevant materials on the reading performance of second-grade African Americans with reading/special education risk. *Multiple Voices for Ethnically Diverse Exceptional Learners, 15*(1), 22–43. https://doi.org/10.5555/2158-396X.15.1.22

Cavendish, W., Connor, D., Gonzalez, T., Jean-Pierre, P., & Card, K. (2020). Troubling the problem of racial overrepresentation in special education: A commentary and call to rethink research. *Educational Review, 72*(5), 567–582. https://doi.org/10.1080/00131911.2018.1550055

Children's Defense Fund (1975). *School suspensions: Are they helping children?* Washington Research Project.

Cochran-Smith, M. (2001). Learning to teach against the (new) grain. *Journal of Teacher Education, 52*(1), 3–4. https://doi.org/10.1177/0022487101052001001

Cramer, E., & Bennett, K. (2015). Implementing culturally responsive positive behavior interventions and supports in middle school classrooms. *Middle School Journal, 46,* 18–24. https://doi.org/10.1080/00940771.2015.11461911

Darling-Hammond, S., Fronius, T., Sutherland, H., Guckenburg, S., Petrosino, A., & Hurley, N. (2020). Effectiveness of restorative justice in US K-12 schools: A review of quantitative research. *Contemporary School Psychology, 24,* 295–308. https://doi.org/10.1007/s40688-020-00290-0

De Brey, C., Snyder, T. D., Zhang, A., & Dillow, S. A. (2021). *Digest of Education Statistics, 2019* (NCES 2021-009). National Center for Education Statistics, Institute of Education Sciences, U.S. Department of Education. https://nces.ed.gov/ pubs2021/2021009.pdf

Dee, T. S., & Penner, E. K. (2017). The causal effects of cultural relevance: Evidence from an ethnic studies curriculum. *American Educational Research Journal, 54*(1), 127–166. https://doi.org/10.3102/0002831216677002

Delale-O'Connor, L., Alvarez, A., Murray, I., & Milner IV, H. (2017). Self-efficacy beliefs, classroom management, and the cradle-to-prison pipeline. *Theory to Practice, 56*(3), 178–186. https://doi.org/10.1080/00405841.2017.1336038

Duane, A., Casimir, A., Mims, L, Kaler-Jones, C., & Simmons, D. (2021). Beyond deep breathing: A new vision for equitable, culturally responsive, and trauma-informed mindfulness practice. *Middle School Journal, 52*(3), 4–14. https://doi.org/10.1080/00940771.2021.1893593

Dunn, L. (1968). Special education for the mildly retarded—is much of it justifiable? *Exceptional Children, 35*(1), 5–22. https://doi.org/10.1177/001440296803500101

Emmer, E. T., & Stough, L. M. (2001). Classroom management: A critical part of educational psychology, with implications for teacher education. *Educational Psychologist, 36*(2), 103–112. https://doi.org/10.1207/S15326985EP3602_5

Evans, K., & Vaandering, D. (2016). *The little book of restorative justice in education: Fostering responsibility, healing, and hope in schools.* Good Books.

Fish, R. (2019). Standing out and sorting in: Exploring the role of racial composition in racial disparities in special education. *American Educational Research Journal, 56*(6), 2573–2608. https://doi.org/10.3102/0002831219847966

Ford, D. (1998). The underrepresentation of minority students in gifted education: Problems and promises in recruitment and retention. *The Journal of Special Education, 32*(1), 4–14. https://doi.org/10.1177/002246699803200102

Freire, P. (1970). *Pedagogy of the oppressed* (2nd ed.). Penguin Press.

Gay, G. (1993). Building cultural bridges: A bold proposal for teacher education. *Education and Urban Society, 25*(3), 285–299. https://doi.org/10.1177/0013124593025003006

Gay, G. (2013). Teaching to and through cultural diversity. *Curriculum Inquiry, 43*(1), 48–70. https://doi.org/10.1111/curi.12002

Gay, G. (2015). The what, why, and how of culturally responsive teaching: International mandates, challenges, and opportunities. *Multicultural Education Review, 7*(3), 123–139. https://doi.org/10.1080/2005615X.2015.1072079

Gay, G. (2018). *Culturally responsive teaching: Theory, research, and practice* (3rd ed.). Teachers College Press.

Giordano, K., Vega, V., & Gubi, A. (2020). Expelled from childcare: Suspension and expulsion practices in one state's community childcare centers. *Early Childhood Education Journal, 50*, 135–144. https://doi.org/10.1007/s10643-020-01134-5

Gladney, D., Lo, Y., Kourea, L., & Johnson, H. N. (2021). Using multilevel coaching to improve general education teachers' implementation fidelity of culturally responsive social skill instruction. *Preventing School Failure: Alternative Education for Children and Youth, 65*(2), 175–184. https://doi.org/10.1080/1045988X.2020.1864715

Greenberg, J., Putman, H., & Walsh, K. (2014). *Training our teachers: Classroom management.* National Council on Teacher Quality. www.nctq.org/dmsView.do?id=152076

Greene, M. (1995). *Releasing the imagination: Essays on education, the arts, and social change.* Jossey-Bass.

Gregory, A., & Evans, K. (2020). *The starts and stumbles of restorative justice in education: Where do we go from here?* National Education Policy Center. http://nepc.colorado.edu/ publication/restorative-justice

Hammond, Z. (2015). *Culturally responsive teaching and the brain: Promoting authentic engagement and rigor among culturally and linguistically diverse students.* Corwin.

Howard, T., & Milner IV, H. R. (2021). Teacher preparation for urban schools. In H. R. Milner & K. Lomotey (Eds.), *Handbook of urban education* (pp. 195–211). Routledge.

Hussar, B., Zhang, J., Hein, S., Wang, K., Roberts, A., Cui, J., Smith, M., Bullock Mann, F., Barmer, A., & Dilig, R. (2020). *The condition of education 2020* (NCES 2020-144). National Center for Education Statistics, Institute of Education Sciences, U.S. Department of Education. https://nces.ed.gov/pubs2020/2020144.pdf

Irwin, V., Zhang, J., Wang, X., Hein, S., Wang, K., Roberts, A., York, C., Barmer, A., Bullock Mann, F., Dilig, R., & Parker, S. (2021). *Report on the Condition of Education 2021* (NCES 2021-144). National Center for Education Statistics, Institute of Education Sciences, U.S. Department of Education. https://nces.ed.gov/pubs2021/2021144.pdf

Kabat-Zinn, J. (2015). Mindfulness. *Mindfulness, 6*, 1481–1483. https://doi.org/10.1007/s12671-015-0456-x

Kendi, I. (2019). *How to be an antiracist.* One World.

King, E., & Butler, B. R. (2015). Who cares about diversity? A preliminary investigation of diversity exposure in teacher preparation programs. *Multicultural Perspectives, 17*(1), 46–52. https://doi.org/10.1080/15210960.2015.994436

Kishimoto, K. (2018). Anti-racist pedagogy: From faculty's self-reflection to organizing within and beyond the classroom. *Race, Ethnicity, and Education, 21*(4), 540–554. https://doi.org/10.1080/13613324.2016.1248824

Ladson-Billings, G. (1990). Like lightening in a bottle: Attempting to capture the pedagogical excellence of successful teachers of Black students. *International Journal of Qualitative Studies in Education, 3*(4), 335–344. https://doi.org/10.1080/0951839900030403

Ladson-Billings, G. (1995b). But that's just good teaching! The case for culturally relevant pedagogy. *Theory into Practice, 34*(3), 159–165. https://doi.org/10.1080/00405849509543675

Ladson-Billings, G. (1995a). Toward a theory of culturally relevant pedagogy. *American Educational Research Journal, 32*(3), 465–491. https://doi.org/10.3102/00028312032003465

Ladson-Billings, G. (2009). *Dreamkeepers: Successful teachers of African American children* (2nd.). Jossey-Bass.

Ladson-Billings, G. (2014). Culturally relevant pedagogy 2.0: aka the Remix. *Harvard Educational Review, 84*(1), 74–84. https://doi.org/10.17763/haer.84.1.p2rj131485484751

Ladson-Billings, G. (2017). The (r)evolution will not be standardized: Teacher education, hip hop pedagogy, and culturally relevant pedagogy 2.0. In D. Paris & S. Alim (Eds.), *Culturally sustaining pedagogies: Teaching and learning for justice in a changing world* (pp. 141–156). Teachers College Press.

Ladson-Billings, G. (2021a). *Culturally relevant pedagogy: Asking a different question.* Teachers College Press.

Ladson-Billings, G. (2021b). I'm here for the hard re-set: Post pandemic pedagogy to preserve our culture. *Equity & Excellence in Education, (54)*1, 68–78. https://doi.org/10.1080/10665684.2020.1863883

Lee, J. (2002). Racial and ethnic achievement gap trends: Reversing the progress toward equity? *Educational Researcher, 31*(1), 3–12. https://doi.org/10.3102/0013189X031001003

Lewis, C., Butler, B. R., Bonner, F., & Joubert, M. (2010). African American male discipline patterns and school district responses resulting impact on academic achievement: Implications for urban educators and policy makers. *Journal of African American Males in Education, 1*(1), 7–25. https://jaamejournal.scholasticahq.com/article/18394.pdf

Lo, Y., Mustian, A. L., Brophy, A., & White, R. B. (2011). Peer-mediated social skill instruction for African American males with or at risk for mild disabilities. *Exceptionality, 19*(3), 191–209. https://doi.org/10.1080/09362835.2011.579851

Losen, D. J. (Ed.). (2015). *Closing the school discipline gap.* Teachers College Press.

Marchbanks III, M. P., Blake, J. J., Booth, E. A., Carmichael, D., Seibert, A. L., & Fabelo, T. (2015). The economic effects of exclusionary discipline on grade retention and high school dropout. In Losen, D. J. (Ed.), *Closing the school discipline gap: Equitable remedies for excessive exclusion* (pp. 59–74). Teachers College Press.

Mendelson, T. Greenberg, M. Dariotis, J., Gould, L. Rhoades, B., & Leaf, P. (2010). Feasibility and preliminary outcomes of a school-based mindfulness intervention for urban youth. *Journal of Abnormal Child Psychology, 38*, 985–994. https://doi.org/10.1007/s10802-010-9418-x

Merrett, F., & Wheldall, K. (1993). How do teachers learn to manage classroom behavior? A study of teachers' opinions about their initial training with special reference to classroom behavior management. *Educational Studies, 19*(3), 91–107. https://doi.org/10.1080/0305569930190106

Milner IV, H. R. (2006). Classroom management in urban schools. In C. Evertson & C. Weinstein, *Handbook of classroom management: Research, practice, and contemporary issues* (pp. 491–522). Routledge.

Milner IV, H. R. (2010). What does teacher education have to do with teaching? Implication for diverse students. *Journal of Teacher Education, 61*(1–2), 118–131. https://doi.org/10.1177/0022487109347670

Milner IV, H. R. (2020). *Start where you are but don't stay there: Understanding diversity, opportunity gaps, and teaching in today's classrooms* (2nd ed.). Harvard Education Press.

Milner IV, H. R., Cunningham, H. B., Delale-O'Connor, L., & Gold Kestenberg, E. (2019). *"These kids are out of control": Why we must reimagine "classroom management" for equity.* Corwin Press.

Morrison, K. A., Robbins, H. H., & Rose, D. G. (2008). Operationalizing culturally relevant pedagogy: A synthesis of classroom-based research. *Equity & Excellence in Education, 41*(4), 433–452. https://doi.org/10.1080/10665680802400006

National Assessment of Educational Progress (2021). *Achievement Gaps Dashboard* (2003–2019). The Nations Report Card. www.nationsreportcard.gov/dashboards/ achievement_gaps.aspx

National Center for Education Statistics (2004). *English language learner students in U.S. public schools: 1994 and 2000* (NCES 2004-035). National Center for Education Statistics, Institute of Education Sciences, U.S. Department of Education. https://nces.ed.gov/pubs2004/2004035.pdf

National Education Association (2020). *English language learners.* NEA. www.nea.org/resource-library/english-language-learners

Nicholson-Crotty, S., Birchmeier, Z., & Valentine, D. (2009). Exploring the impact of school discipline on racial disproportion in the juvenile justice system. *Social Science Quarterly, 90*(4), 1003–108. https://doi.org/10.1111/j.1540-6237.2009.00674.x

Nguyen, B. M. D., Noguera, P., Adkins, N., & Teranishi, R. T. (2019). Ethnic discipline gap: Unseen dimensions of racial disproportionality in school discipline. *American Educational Research Journal, 56*(5), 1973–2003. https://doi.org/10.3102/0002831219833919

Oakes, J. (1985). *Keeping track: How schools structure inequality.* Yale University Press.

Office for Civil Rights (2016). *2013-2014 civil rights data collection: A first look.* U.S. Department of Education. www2.ed.gov/about/offices/list/ocr/docs/2013-14-first-look.pdf

Omi, M., & Winant, H. (2015). *Racial formation in the United States.* Routledge.

Paris, D., & Alim, S. (2017). *Culturally sustaining pedagogies: Teaching and learning for justice in a changing world.* Teachers College Press.

Pas, E. T., Larson, K. E., Reinke, W. M., Herman, K. C., & Bradshaw, C. P. (2016). Implementation and acceptability of an adapted classroom check-up coaching model to promote culturally responsive classroom management. *Education and Treatment of Children, 39*(4), 467–491. https://doi.org/10.1353/etc.2016.0021

Pranis, K. (2005). *The little book of circle processes: A new/old approach to peacemaking.* Good Books.

Putman, H., Hansen, M., Walsh, K., & Quintero, D. (2016). *High hopes and harsh realities: The real challenges to building a diverse workforce.* The Brown Center on Education Policy and Brookings. www.nctq.org/publicati ons/High-Hopes-and-Harsh-Realities:-The-real-challenges-to-building-a-diverse-workforce

Ray, R., & Gibbons, A. (2021, November 21). *Why are states banning critical race theory?* Brookings. www.brooki ngs.edu/blog/fixgov/2021/07/02/why-are-states-banning-critical-race-theory/

Robinson-Ervin, P., Cartledge, G., Musti-Rao, S., Gibson Jr, L., & Keyes, S. E. (2016). Social skills instruction for urban learners with emotional and behavioral disorders: A culturally responsive and computer-based intervention. *Behavioral Disorders, 41*(4), 209–225. https://doi.org/10.17988/bedi-41-04-209-225.1

Scott, M. T., & Ford, D. (2011). Preparing teacher education candidates to work with students with disabilities and gifts and talents. In A. Ball & C. Tyson (Eds.), *Studying diversity in teacher education* (pp. 201–218). American Educational Research Association.

Sieberer-Nagler, K. (2016). Effective classroom-management and positive teaching. *English Language Teaching, 9*(1), 163–172. http://doi.org/10.5539/elt.v9n1p163

Siwatu, K. O., Putman, S. M., Starker-Glass, T. V., & Lewis, C. W. (2017). The culturally responsive classroom management self-efficacy scale: Development and initial validation. *Urban Education, 52*(7), 862–888. https://doi. org/10.1177% 2F0042085915602534

Siwatu, K. O. (2011). Preservice teachers' sense of preparedness and self-efficacy to teach in America's urban and suburban schools: Does context matter? *Teaching and Teacher Education, 27*(2), 357–365. https://doi.org/ 10.1016/j.tate.2010.09.004

Skiba, R. J. (2002). Special education and school discipline: A precarious balance. *Behavioral Disorders, 27*(2), 81–97. https://doi.org/10.1177/019874290202700209

Skiba, R. J., Arredondo, M. I., & Williams, N. T. (2014). More than a metaphor: The contribution of exclusionary discipline to a school-to-prison pipeline. *Equity & Excellence in Education, 47*(4), 546–564. https://doi.org/ 10.1080/10665684.2014.958965

Skiba, R. J., Horner, R. H., Chung, C.-G., Rausch, M. K., May, S. L., & Tobin, T. (2011). Race is not neutral: A national investigation of African American and Latino disproportionality in school discipline. *School Psychology Review, 40*(1), 85–107. https://doi.org/10.1080/02796015.2011.12087730

Sleeter, C. E. (1986). Learning disabilities: The social construction of special education category. *Exceptional Children, 53*(1), 46–54. https://doi.org/10.1177/001440298605300105

Sleeter, C. E. (2012). Confronting the marginalization of culturally responsive pedagogy. *Urban Education, 47*(3), 562–584. https://doi.org/10.1177/0042085911431472

Teaching Tolerance (2021). *Critical practices for anti-bias education.* Learning for Justice. www.learningforjustice.org/ magazine/publications/critical-practices-for-antibias-education/classroom-culture

United States Department of Education, Office of Planning, Evaluation and Policy Development, Policy and Program Studies Service (2016). *The state of racial diversity in the educator workforce.* US Department of Education. www2.ed.gov/rschstat/eval/highered/racial-diversity/state-racial-diversity-workforce.pdf

United States Department of Education, Institute of Education Sciences, National Center for Education Statistics, National Assessment of Educational Progress (n.d.). *The National's Report Card: Achievement gap results, 1990–2019 Mathematics and 1992–2019 Reading.* The Nations Report Card. www.nationsreportcard.gov/dashboa rds/ achievement _gaps.aspx

Vincent, C. G., Sprague, J., & Tobin, T. (2012). Exclusionary discipline practices across students' racial/ethnic backgrounds and disability status: Findings from the pacific northwest. *Education and Treatment of Children, 35*(4), 585–601. https://doi.org/10.1353/etc.2012.0025

Wachtel, T. (2016). *Defining restorative.* International Institute for Restorative Practices. www.nassauboces.org/ cms/lib/NY01928409/Centricity/Domain/1699/Defining%20Restorative.pdf

Wald, J., & Losen, D. J. (2003). Defining and redirecting a school-to-prison pipeline. In J. Wald & D. J. Losen (Eds.). *New directions for youth development* (No. 99; Deconstructing the school-to-prison pipeline) (pp. 9–15). Jossey-Bass.

Wallace, J. M., Goodkind, S., Wallace, C. M., & Bachman, J. G. (2008). Racial, ethnic, gender difference in school discipline among U.S. high school students: 1991-2005. *The Negro Educational Review, 59*(1–2), 47–62. https:// pubmed.ncbi.nlm.nih.gov/19430541/

Watson-Singleton, N. Black, A., & Spivey, B. (2019). Recommendations for culturally-responsive mindfulness-based intervention for African Americans. *Complementary Therapies in Clinical Practice*, *34*, 132–138. https://doi.org/10.1016/j.ctcp.2018.11.013

Weinstein, C., Curran, M., & Tomlinson-Clarke, S. (2003). Culturally responsive classroom management: Awareness into action. *Theory Into Practice*, *42*(4), 269–276. https://doi.org/10.1207/s15430421tip4204_2

Weinstein, C., Tomlinson-Clarke, S., & Curran, M. (2004). Toward a conception of culturally responsive classroom management. *Journal of Teacher Education*, *55*(1), 25–38. https://doi.org/10.1177/0022487103259812

Welton, A. D., Owen, D. R., & Zamani-Gallaher, E. M. (2018). Anti-racist change: A conceptual framework for educational institutions to take systemic actions. *Teachers College Record*, *120*, 1–22. www.tcrecord.org/content.asp?contentid=22371

Whitford, D. K., Gage, N. A., Katsiyannis, A., Counts, J., Rapa, L. J., & McWhorter, A. (2019). The exclusionary discipline of American Indian and Alaska Native (AI/AN) students with and without disabilities: A Civil Rights Data Collection (CRDC) national analysis. *Journal of Child and Family Studies*, *28*(12), 3327–3337. https://doi.org/10.1007/s10826-019-01511-8

Winn, M. (2018). *Justice on both sides: Transforming education through restorative justice*. Harvard Education Press.

Wright, B., Ford, D., & Moore, J. L. (2022). Hidden in plain sight: Increasing equitable representation of underrepresented students in gifted and talented education. In J. Nyberg & J. Manzone (Eds.), *Creating equitable services for the gifted: Protocols for identification, implementation, and evaluation* (pp. 11–19). IGI Global.

Young, J. L. (2020). Evaluating multicultural education courses: Promise and possibilities for portfolio assessment. *Multicultural Perspectives*, *22*(1), 20–27. https://doi.org/10.1080/15210960.2020.1728274

Young, J. L., Young, J. R., & Butler, B. R. (2018). A student saved is not a dollar earned: A meta-analysis of school disparities in discipline practice toward Black children. *Taboo: The Journal of Culture & Education*, *17*(4), 95–112. http://doi.org/10.31390/taboo.17.4.06

Zehr, H. (1990). *Changing lenses: A new focus for crime and justice*. Herald Press.

Zehr, H. (2015). *The little book of restorative justice*. Good Books.

26

CLASSROOM MANAGEMENT TO SUPPORT STUDENTS WITH DISABILITIES

Empowering General and Special Educators

Kathleen Lynn Lane

UNIVERSITY OF KANSAS

Holly M. Menzies

CALIFORNIA STATE UNIVERSITY, LOS ANGELES

Lucia Smith-Menzies

CALIFORNIA STATE UNIVERSITY, SAN BERNARDINO

Katie Scarlett Lane

UNIVERSITY OF CONNECTICUT

Introduction

Students with disabilities receive instruction in a variety of instructional settings. For example, students receiving special education services as defined in the Individuals with Disabilities Education Improvement Act (IDEA, 2004) may be afforded learning opportunities via (a) inclusive programming in general education settings with typically developing peers, (b) supports provided on a pull-out basis in which students receive assistance in more private settings outside of the general education classroom, as well as (c) more restrictive settings such as self-contained classrooms where students spend most or all of their instructional day with other students receiving special education services. To facilitate instructional programming for students receiving special education in all contexts, classroom management goes beyond procedures for organizing the learning environment (e.g., room arrangement, traffic patterns, and posted expectations) and requires careful consideration of students' behavior patterns and use of instructional strategies, as well as the overall school- or class-wide system approach.

While most students come to school well-prepared to meet academic, behavioral, and social expectations throughout the school day, there are many school-age youth who struggle (Walker et al., 2004). Even before the pandemic, as many as 20 percent of students demonstrated externalizing

DOI: 10.4324/9781003275312-31

(e.g., aggressive and noncompliant) and/or internalizing challenges (e.g., extremely shy, anxious, and withdrawn; Forness et al., 2012). While externalizing behaviors are more likely to be recognized by teachers given the overt nature of these behaviors, internalizing behavior patterns are no less serious in their impact on students' school experiences (Walker et al., 2014; Weist et al., 2017). Moreover, students' instructional experiences are inextricably connected to teachers' ability to manage behavior because several qualifying disorders under IDEA feature behavioral characteristics (e.g., hyperactivity, inattention, limited self-regulation skills, and social skills deficits) that may negatively impact academic performance (e.g., Perfect et al., 2016). In fact, these collective challenges—behavioral excesses and deficits, limited social skills, and academic underachievement—create difficulties that lead general education teachers to refer students to be evaluated for additional supports and services (Walker et al., 2004).

In addition to effective practices for managing classrooms, which are applicable for students with special needs as well as their typically developing peers, the field of special education has developed methods of behavioral change such as functional assessment-based interventions (e.g., FABI; Umbreit et al., 2007). Such interventions are theoretically grounded in applied behavior analysis (ABA), creating a technology of positive behavior supports which, when implemented as designed, result in dramatically improved outcomes for students academically, behaviorally, and socially (Horner & Sugai, 2015). Many of these methods can be used across instructional settings, from inclusive to more restrictive placements, and incorporated into every educator's classroom management practices.

We begin the chapter with a discussion of the disability characteristics that can pose challenges for educators, particularly for those whose teacher preparation programs did not equip them with a full set of classroom management skills to prevent and respond to challenging behaviors (Lane, Menzies et al., 2015). We detail negative outcomes associated with reactive and/or punitive discipline and provide a brief historical overview of the shift from reactive to proactive approaches to meeting students' multiple needs. We discuss positive behavior interventions and supports (PBIS) and its evolution from applied behavior analysis, including the subsequent focus on examining the context within which behavior occurs, along with the personal characteristics a student brings to the situation. We address the importance of using an integrated, tiered system approach to supporting students that includes a universal plan for classroom management (Lane, Buckman, et al., 2020) and review several research-based practical, low-intensity strategies all teachers can use as part of daily instruction and interactions to extend and enhance their classroom management skills. We include a brief discussion of more intensive interventions that can be used to effect behavioral change when primary (Tier 1) prevention efforts are insufficient (see Chapter 7 by Simonsen). We conclude by considering structural approaches (including cultural responsiveness) that can support teachers in creating optimal learning environments for all students—including those with high-incidence disabilities (e.g., specific learning disabilities, emotional disturbances).

Challenging Behavioral Characteristics: The Impact of Behavioral Support

Disability is a complicated mix of biological, genetic, environmental, familial, and school factors that manifest differently for each individual. Several disabilities under IDEA (e.g., intellectual disability, autism, emotional disturbance, and learning disability) may include characteristics such as impulsivity, hyperactivity, lack of ability to self-regulate, aggression, and limited social skills. These characteristic behavior patterns can make a student's school experience challenging as they often lead to conflict with teachers and peers; yet recognizing behavior is affected by factors such as biological predispositions and genetics is key (Kauffman, 2020). Otherwise, teachers may believe a student is willfully choosing to exhibit problem behavior when the reality is they may have more difficulty than typical students with recognizing, monitoring, and controlling undesirable behavior. It is not to say students with disabilities cannot be held responsible for their behavior, but it is crucial to understand how a behavior functions for a particular student, and to provide explicit instruction and reinforcement for changing or managing the target behavior, as well as providing support for acquiring and demonstrating prosocial behaviors with fluency. Well thought-out classroom management strategies and practices (e.g., routines and procedures), along with targeted strategies for promoting and supporting prosocial behavior, can help students overcome these potential areas of deficit. We briefly describe specific behavioral characteristic of students with disabilities and discuss challenges associated with these patterns if left unchecked and unsupported.

Challenging Behavioral Patterns

Some students come to school well prepared with behavioral skills sets that facilitate instruction. For example, being able to listen to and follow instructions, resolve conflicts with peers and adults, and make assistance needs known facilitate the smooth flow of instruction (Gresham & Elliott, 2008). In contrast, behaviors such as impulsivity, hyperactivity, limited self-regulation skills, aggression, and limited social skills impede instruction (Walker et al., 2004).

Impulsivity is acting without first thinking about the consequences of the act. As the brain matures, individuals develop a greater capacity to think before taking action, but students with disabilities may experience delays in this area. Impulsivity manifests in a variety of ways in the classroom and can negatively affect a student's social competence, academic work, and sometimes even their safety (Walker et al., 2004). For example, a student may respond with an inappropriate verbal comment to a classmate or the teacher, be more prone to hit or use a physical response, and may even leave the classroom without permission. These are all actions that occur because the student has limited ability to consider the appropriateness or implications of their actions in the moment, and they are actions that lead to problems in school.

Similarly, hyperactivity (excessive physical movement where the individual is restless, moves about, fidgets, or talks more than is typical) impedes instruction and learning. Students with hyperactivity find it difficult to contain their movement so settings like a classroom can be challenging if it does not allow sufficient opportunity to move physically or interact with others. Hyperactivity can be bothersome to classmates and the teacher as students with hyperactivity tend to interrupt others, have trouble working quietly, and find it hard to wait their turn or to refrain from talking. It is not surprising they may be perceived as rule violators. Yet, their intent often is not willful, but a manifestation of their inability to control the hyperactivity.

Limited self-regulation skills (the brain's ability to monitor one's behavioral and emotional processes) also negatively impact the instructional environment. In ideal conditions, as students grow and learn, they increase their ability to self-regulate and become more proficient at monitoring their behavior and manifesting an appropriate response. Self-regulation is particularly important in academic work because planning, monitoring, and reflecting on a learning task improves one's competence in completing it successfully. It is equally important for self-managing behavior (managing aggressive thoughts) and developing social competencies.

Aggressive behavior in school is especially problematic as sustained levels of aggression are likely to lead to removal from the classroom (see Chapter 10 by Skiba regarding exclusionary discipline) and negatively affect relations with peers and teachers. Aggression can be overt, such as acting out physically by hitting, fighting, or throwing a tantrum, and yelling or being verbally abusive, and it can be covert, when children or young adults engage in secretive antisocial behaviors such as lying, destroying property, or stealing. Generally speaking, noncompliance and disobedience characterize aggression, as well as behaviors that alienate others such as teasing, non-cooperation, bullying, and being physically rough. Yet systematically and proactively addressing behavioral issues by building social skills, rather than relying on reactive discipline, can ameliorate or prevent the negative outcomes so strongly correlated with antisocial behavior.

In terms of social skills, it is long established that learning disabilities, emotional disturbances, and intellectual disabilities are comorbid with social skills deficits which lead to judgements of negative social competence (Gresham & Elliott, 2008). Establishing social competence in school encompasses skills related to interacting with peers and adults as well as to academic tasks. Skills associated with social competence in learning include listening and self-regulation, while those needed for inter-personal relations include cooperating, sharing, and communicating effectively. Social competence is associated with academic success, positive peer relationships, and positive school adjustment (Legkauskas & Magelinskaitė-Legkauskienė, 2019).

When students present with these often co-occurring behavioral characteristics, they struggle to engage constructively with task demands as well as interactions with peers and adults. These clashes between teacher expectations and student performance can create tension for teachers who feel ill-prepared with the knowledge, skills, and confidence needed to prevent and respond to learning and behavior challenges (Menzies et al., 2020). In studies of professional learning needs, teachers have reported the need for strategies, practices, and programs to prevent and respond to challenging behavior (e.g., de-escalation skills; Lane, Carter, et al., 2015). Recently, Common et al. (2021) conducted a professional learning survey of a geographically diverse sample of educators. The top three needs identified by educators were de-escalation techniques, small-group social skill instruction, and strategies for supporting students with internalizing needs. Moreover, administrators and teachers alike desired practical strategies for increasing engagement and minimizing disruption such as behavior specific praise, precorrection, active supervision, instructional choices, and increased opportunities to respond (Lane, Carter et al., 2015). These strategies are the building blocks of (a) effective classroom management plans for general and special educators as well as (b) de-escalation plans to interrupt the acting out cycle, providing teachers with specific skills to know when and how to prevent and respond to challenging behavior (Colvin & Scott, 2004; Walker et al., 2004). Fluent use of these low-intensity strategies is important as the consequences of poor classroom management can be devastating for students and educators.

Consequences of Poor Behavior Management

Thoughtful and consistent classroom management practices are powerful in supporting students who have trouble in the areas discussed above as they are all related to successful achievement in academic and social domains. In addition to providing the necessary foundation for an atmosphere conducive to learning, good classroom management is critical for alleviating several negative outcomes for students. Classrooms characterized by harsh and exclusionary discipline as a means of managing student behavior can cause or exacerbate troubling conditions such as social disruption, learned helplessness, and an increase in aggression (Walker et al., 2004). Harsh and exclusionary discipline practices also contribute to a poor classroom climate and potentially to the school-to-prison pipeline (Okonofua & Eberhardt, 2015). Next, we briefly discuss each.

One unintended consequence of punishment is social disruption (Pierce & Cheney, 2017). While a teacher may use punishment with the intent of extinguishing an unacceptable behavior, it can become associated with both the setting (e.g., classroom or school) as well as the person administering the punishment or consequence (e.g., teacher or principal). This may lead to escape-motivated behavior in which a student to tries to avoid the associated person (e.g., teacher) and place (e.g., school). For example, some students increase their disruptive behavior so they will be suspended and others may present with somatic complaints so they can stay home or go to the school nurse's office. Other students are frequently tardy or truant, and some simply stop attending school at all. Social disruption is compounded over time, so a student whose misbehavior is problematic will encounter more negative teacher attention thereby increasing the chances of social disruption for that individual (referred to as a negative reinforcement cycle) and may set the stage for learned helplessness

Learned helplessness occurs when a student will not attempt tasks or will do so at a level inconsistent with what they are capable of achieving (Sutherland et. al., 2004) because they are worried about a teacher's reaction to their attempts. Compounding the problem, teachers may not provide immediate and specific reinforcement when students do respond correctly either for fear of inadvertently triggering a negative interaction or because they do not believe in praising students for expected behavior (Lane, Menzies, et al., 2015). Missing the opportunity to provide behavior-specific praise when desired behaviors occur can create an environment where a student does not recognize the relationship between their own actions and subsequent events (Sutherland et. al., 2004); they assume everything they do will be viewed negatively. Eventually, a student may develop a severe lack of motivation or persistence due to repeated past failures (Licht & Kistner, 1986).

In addition, harsh and inconsistent school discipline can actually increase aggression. Students learn how to behave by emulating the example of the adults around them (Landrum & Kauffman, 2006), and angry verbal and physical responses can become a normal mode of interaction between a student and teacher. Aggressive student behavior may initially stem from academic problems, in which students act out to escape too difficult or too easy tasks (Umbreit et al., 2004). In other instances, students who experience frequent negative feedback from teachers may develop a negative self-conception about their academic ability. These contentious relationships can develop as early as kindergarten and have been associated with academic and behavior problems that continue to middle school and beyond (Hamre & Pianta, 2001). Stressors such as economic hardship can also result in physically aggressive behavior as a coping mechanism, especially for primary-age students who are still learning emotional regulation skills (Brooks-Gunn & Duncan, 1997; Wildeman, 2010). If schools and teachers react with a negative model of interaction through angry reprimands, shaming, or excluding students, they may not have an opportunity to learn or practice appropriate responses.

These effects contribute to negative school climates—in sharp contrast to positive, productive classroom environments that facilitate teaching and learning. Even cooperative students develop negative perceptions about school when exclusionary practices such as sending students out of the classroom and suspension are used frequently. Strikingly, students have been found to attribute peers' inappropriate behavior *to* the use of punitive strategies by their teachers (Mitchell & Bradshaw, 2013). Poor school climate becomes a self-perpetuating cycle characterized by decreased student engagement and increased truancy, dropout, delinquency, and bullying (Bradshaw et al., 2008; Bradshaw et al., 2009).

As discussed in Chapter 21 by Rousch in this handbook, we note the importance of the role of the school in influencing students' experiences with the justice system. The school-to-prison pipeline, which refers to the connection between the education and justice systems, is created by punitive and exclusionary discipline practices in schools which disproportionally affects students of color and those with disabilities (National Council on Disability, 2015; Rivera-Calderon, 2019). This pipeline can be literal and immediate such as when students are arrested on school grounds. In other cases, a student's experience with suspension has been shown to decrease their engagement in school and increase their risk of dropping-out, and predicts involvement with the justice system during their school years and later in life. An analysis of several studies on the effects of exclusionary practices found a direct and significant association between exclusionary discipline practiced in schools and student contact with the justice system (Fabelo et al., 2011; Monahan et al., 2014; Novak, 2018). Laub and Sampson (1993) characterize exclusionary discipline as a negative turning point in an individual's life, which denies them prosocial opportunities. These unfortunate outcomes have been estimated to cost the United States $11 billion in fiscal impacts and $35.7 billion in social impacts (Rumberger & Losen, 2016) as well as untold costs to the students and their families (Walker et al., 2014). Exclusionary discipline alienates students, provoking negative emotions and feelings of being misunderstood or not wanted. Students who feel alienated from their teacher and school are denied the opportunity to participate academically and socially in ways that could be gratifying and productive. Recent work examining the effectiveness of culturally responsive schoolwide programs emphasizes the importance of addressing policies and beliefs that contribute to the school-to-prison pipeline (Fetterman et al., 2020).

In summary, many students with and at risk for disabilities demonstrate behavioral characteristics that pose challenges for themselves as learners and impede the instructional experiences of others. This is exacerbated when teachers may not have fully developed classroom management skill sets or when the school system is not structured to prevent and respond to learning and behavioral challenges. Throughout much of the 1970s and 1980s, teacher preparation programs focused on a consequence-based approached to challenging behaviors, such programs did not emphasize a proactive or instructional approach to behavior management, other than basic classroom management (Lane, Buckman, et al., 2020). During this same era, school systems relied on a wait-to-fail approach in which students typically received assistance only after the discrepancy between current and desired levels of performance were substantial enough to call for special education supports (Lane & Walker, 2015). Fortunately, the field of special education has moved away from these less-than-optimal approaches, with a focus on integrated systems that empower teachers—general and special educators—with clearly articulated approaches for preventing *and* responding to challenges using a cascade of progressively more intensive supports according to individual students' needs, including students receiving special education services (Lane, Buckman, et al., 2020).

In the next section we discuss the historical shift away from reactive to instructive approaches for supporting desired behaviors. We begin by introducing the concept of positive behavior interventions and support (PBIS) and explain its origins and subsequent use in schools (Walker et al., 1996). We follow with recommendations for using classroom management and positive behavior support strategies effective for all students—including those with disabilities—to help them acquire and use prosocial behaviors essential to school success.

Historical Context: A Shift from Reactive to Proactive Approaches

Positive behavior interventions and supports (PBIS) is a well-established approach to working with individuals to expand the use of prosocial behaviors to improve their quality of life by ameliorating challenging or inappropriate behavior in the school, home, and work settings (Horner & Sugai, 2015). The use of PBIS is now widespread in schools and focuses on examining the classroom and school environments in addition to working individually with students to effect behavior change. Importantly, PBIS emphasizes the need for proactive instruction to promote prosocial behavior compared to a reactive approach to managing challenging behavior. It does this, partly, through classroom management procedures as well as through targeted strategies and specific interventions (Simonsen et al., 2019).

Carr and Dunlap and colleagues published several articles (Carr, 1997; Carr et al., 2002; Dunlap et al., 2008) explaining the genesis of PBIS from three areas: (a) applied behavior analysis, (b) the inclusion movement, and (c) a person-centered emphasis when programming for services. These disparate areas have informed an approach that honors an individual's specific needs in settings relevant to their life. This is especially important in school because a fundamental goal when working with students with disabilities is to educate them in the least restrictive environment using methods that have high social validity for all stakeholders including students, parents, and teachers (Wolf, 1978).

PBIS relies on several techniques from ABA which operates on the premise that behavior can be changed by analyzing the setting event (that which sets the stage for a given behavior to occur), the behavior (how one reacts), and the type of reinforcement that follows (what occurs as a result of one's reaction—consequence; accessing or avoiding attention, tangibles or activities, as well as sensory experiences; Umbreit et al., 2007). In ABA terms, this is called functional assessment (Carr, 1977). In other words, it is a close examination of the *function* of the behavior: what does the student gain or avoid as a result of their behavior? By determining this information, a new, prosocial behavior can be taught and practiced so that an individual replaces socially problematic behavior with behavior that is functional for them (meets their needs) as well as acceptable to those around them so that they solicit naturally occurring reinforcers.

ABA heralded a dramatic change in thinking about behavior. It gave clinicians a method for determining the function (or why) of a behavior as well as effective strategies for teaching clients how to replace maladaptive behaviors with prosocial behaviors. In essence, it set the stage for moving toward an instructional approach to behavior: setting expectations, teaching and practicing expectations explicitly, and acknowledging (reinforcing) students when they demonstrated established expectations (Horner & Sugai, 2015). This was a novel departure from using reactive, punitive measures to change behavior that involved waiting for a challenging behavior to occur and then responding. Instead, the field shifted to an instructional, proactive approach to "teaching" behavior and arranging the context to set the stage for more desirable, socially valid behaviors to occur.

PBIS uses many of these techniques but also emphasizes the importance of ecological and social validity (Dunlap et al., 2008). Behavior change methods must be acceptable and feasible, for the parents and teachers implementing them and students they are meant to assist. If procedures, strategies, or interventions are too difficult (e.g., complex, time consuming) to use in the school setting, then it is highly unlikely they will be used at all. As with ABA, a PBIS approach analyzes problematic behaviors for their function and designs interventions based on a student's specific needs. While some interventions may need to be intensive (e.g., Tier 3 supports), many can be embedded into everyday instruction in the classroom, and others can be part of routine practice. (Specific practices and interventions are discussed in the next sections.)

Another PBIS premise is that the intervention to change behavior happens when the challenging behavior is *not* occurring. Students must have an opportunity to understand the replacement behavior, practice it, and develop fluency before they can be expected to demonstrate it consistently. Additionally, to self-regulate behavior, students must be taught to recognize their emotions, note their physical response, reflect on their thoughts and feelings, and respond acceptably (as determined by classroom norms and teacher expectations). In the moment when challenging behaviors occur, de-escalation strategies are used to help students calm themselves and engage productively (Colvin & Scott, 2004), but once a student has some proficiency with using newly acquired prosocial behaviors, a teacher can use prompts and cues in situations she knows will prove challenging to the student. A PBIS approach also evaluates practices and interventions for their effectiveness to be sure they are providing the level of support the student requires.

The Shift to Comprehensive Approaches to Preventing Challenging Behaviors: Integrated Instruction Within and Beyond Integrated Tiered Systems

Twenty-five years ago, Walker and colleagues (1996) issued a clarion call in a seminal article in the *Journal of Emotional and Behavioral Disorders* about the complex problem of youth violence and anti-social behavior. They stressed the urgent need for schools to address the issue by moving away from reactive, punitive, and exclusionary school policies for addressing problem behavior. They also recommended what is now widely known as a tiered approach to prevention and treatment which was adapted from the mental health field: primary (Tier 1) prevention for all to prevent harm, secondary (Tier 2) prevention for some to reverse harm, and tertiary (Tier 3) prevention for a few to reduce harm. This paved the path for Response to Intervention (RTI) and PBIS models of prevention. It began an historic change for educators. Rather than each teacher devising their own discipline plan or being solely responsible for identifying students who might need intervention or treatment, and perhaps being the only one to figure out what that additional assistance might be, schools and districts moved to design custom, but comprehensive and graduated support to all students who need it. This system approach is now well-known for use with PBIS (Horner & Sugai, 2015) and teaching reading (e.g., Response to Intervention) as well as for integrated systems such as Comprehensive,

Integrated, Three-tiered (Ci3T) that combine academics, behavior, and social emotional well-being learning domains (Lane, Menzies, et al., 2020).

Ci3T is a tiered system comprised of three levels of prevention (Tiers 1, 2, and 3), each consisting of validated strategies, practices, and programs tailored to the specific school or district content and needs of its students. For example, at the universal level, in addition to clearly articulated roles and responsibilities in the academic domain, there is a schoolwide PBIS behavioral with clearly stated expectations, a system for reinforcing desired behavior, and consistently applied consequences along with a social skills curriculum in the social-emotional well-being domain. Expectations are explicitly taught and modeled by faculty and staff at each school. They provide consistency and continuity throughout the grades and across school settings. Students know what the expectations are no matter which classroom or school area they are in ranging from the school bus to the lunchroom. A social skills curriculum ensures all students have the opportunity to become competent in the social and emotional well-being skills which are indispensable for social success in and beyond the school setting. Teachers develop integrated lessons plans, featuring academic, behavioral, and social domain objectives that create opportunities for students to develop their social and behavioral competencies within daily instructional tasks (e.g., using self-regulation skills during small group instruction and independent activities; Lane, Oakes, et al., 2018).

For students who require more support, the secondary level increases in intensity by offering either more time, individualized instruction, or a special curriculum to address their needs. Examples might include Check/In Check/Out (e.g., Hawken et al., 2007) and repeated reading interventions to improved oral reading fluency. The tertiary level is for students with the most intensive intervention needs (e.g., functional assessment-based interventions; Umbreit et al., 2007), which might necessitate specialized personnel or coordination with outside agencies. In systems implementing Ci3T, these validated Tier 2 and 3 strategies, practices, and programs are made transparent in intervention grids (descriptions to follow; see Table 26.1). In this way, if Tier 1 effort are insufficient for meeting students' needs, there is clarity on what other interventions are available.

Then, instead of "guessing" who might need more, there are two other components integral to tiered systems to identify students who need additional assistance: systematic screening and data-informed decision making. Screening all students to detect behavioral issues ensures support is offered to any student in need of it, often before the behavior escalates in intensity or frequency. In the past, relying solely on teacher recommendation meant some students would not be identified as each teacher's knowledge and expertise is different, and in this situation, students with internalizing behaviors are often overlooked given the covert nature of their behavior (e.g., anxious, withdrawn) relative to externalizing behaviors (McIntosh et al., 2010). Using schoolwide data to connect students to supports ensures all students are considered for additional supports three times a year (fall, winter, and spring) by analyzing screening data alongside other data collected as part of regular school practices (e.g., attendance, office discipline referrals). This is important: if our goal is to reduce gaps in student performance, we must reduce gaps in access to supports (Lane, Oakes, & Menzies, 2021). Screening is also an opportunity to determine whether a *teacher* may benefit from the more intentional use of low-intensity strategies as part of daily instruction. For example, if more than 20 percent of students in a class screen in to moderate- or high-risk categories for internalizing and/or externalizing behaviors, a teacher might increase the use of behavior specific praise, offer students instructional choices, use precorrection to facilitate transitions, and practice active supervision.

Data are used for a variety of purposes including identification of students in need of support, effectiveness of interventions, and potential areas of faculty learning. In addition to universal screening data (for both behavior and academics), other data sources such as a nurse and counselor visits, office discipline referrals, and attendance are collected and analyzed. With multiple data sources, students with both internalizing and externalizing behaviors can be accurately identified and connected to appropriate supports at the earliest sign of concern. These same data are used as outcome data when

Table 26.1 Secondary (Tier 2) Intervention Grid: For Elementary Students

Support	Description	School-wide Data: Entry Criteria	Data to Monitor Progress	Exit Criteria
Check/in Check/out	Participating students check in and out with a mentor each day on targeted goals. During check-in, students receive a daily progress report that they take to each class for feedback on their progress meeting the school-wide Ci3T model expectations.	**Behavior:** ☐ SRSS-E7 score: Moderate (4–8) ☐ SRSS-I5 score: Moderate (2–3) or ☐ SRSS-E7 score: High (9–21) ☐ SRSS-I5 score: High (4–15) or ☐ 2 or more office discipline referrals (ODR) in a 5-week period Or ☐ 2 or more tardies or absences per quarter AND/OR **Academic:** ☐ Progress report: 1 or more course failures ☐ Progress report: Targeted for Growth for academic learning behaviors	**Student measures:** Daily progress reports **Treatment integrity:** Coach completes checklist of all BEP steps and whether they were completed each day (percentage of completion computed) **Social Validity:** Teacher: IRP-15 Student: CIRP	SRSS-E7 score: Low (0–3) SRSS-I5 score: Low (0–1) With 8 weeks of data, student has made their CICO goal 90% of the time and there have not been any office discipline referrals. The teacher is then contacted for their opinion about if exiting is appropriate or if CICO should continue.

Note: From www.ci3t.org. Reprinted with permission. [Alt] A sample Secondayr (Tier 2) Intervention Grid Illustrating how to use screening data along with other data collected as part of regular school practices to connect students to validated interventions such as Check/in Check/out collected on a regular basis and compared to baseline to see whether a school has made progress in reducing risk status.

Collecting treatment integrity data is recommended so schools can determine whether their plan is being implemented as designed (Buckman et al., 2021). If there is no improvement in reducing overall risk status, integrity data will indicate whether the practices and interventions are actually in place. This is a necessary step before changing current policies or adopting new practices. Treatment integrity data along with social validity data (stakeholders' views regarding goals, procedures, and outcomes) can also be used to inform professional learning for faculty, staff, and administrators. Later in the chapter, we discuss using a variety of data to inform professional learning.

In a Ci3T model, these collective data sources (treatment integrity, social validity, and student-level data) are used to guide students' instructional experiences as well as to support teachers' data-informed, professional learning needs. A tiered system of support is intended to be tailored to each school's context as it is not a specific curriculum, but a collection of practices administered with intentionality and consistency. We suggest the Ci3T model which features academic, behavioral, and social and emotional well-being learning domains, is an effective, efficient model for addressing all the essential components of a student's educational experience in a manner that also supports teachers' well-being as evidenced by lower rates of teacher burnout and increased sense of self-efficacy (e.g., Lane, Oakes, Royer, et al., 2020). For a detailed description of a Comprehensive, Integrated, Three-Tiered Model of Prevention see Lane, Menzies et al. (2020).

While not every school or district may be implementing an integrated tiered system of support featuring data-informed instruction for students and professional learning for adults, we contend it is possible to empower teachers with teacher-delivered, low-intensity supports to facilitate engagement and minimize disruption. In the next section, we detail five such strategies and connect readers with free-access, on-demand resources to support implementation efforts (see www.ci3t.org/pl). Again, we emphasize these are important building blocks of strong classroom management and de-escalation plans.

Low-Intensity, Teacher-Delivered Strategies to Increase Engagement and Decrease Disruption

By systematically focusing on prevention, teachers can create a classroom environment that is highly engaging and reinforcing for all students and avoid reactive interactions that disrupt instruction. Below we review five research-based, low-intensity, teacher-delivered strategies designed to increase engagement and minimize disruptive behavior. Behavior-specific praise, precorrection, active supervision, increasing opportunities to respond, and instructional choice are appropriate for all learners and grade levels, with sufficient evidence suggesting that if implemented as designed, these strategies will likely yield the desired outcomes.

Teachers can implement these strategies classwide to support students, including students with disabilities, in a range of instructional settings (e.g., inclusive classroom, self-contained classrooms) with school-age youth—including those with emotional disturbances (see systematic reviews by Allen et al., 2020; Common et al., 2020; Ennis et al., 2018, 2020; Royer et al., 2017). Multiple treatment outcomes conducted using single case and group design methodology have demonstrated these proactive strategies leave less opportunity for disruptive behavior because they increase student engagement, allowing teachers to focus on instruction rather than reactive reprimands. Not only are these strategies easy to learn—requiring little teacher training time—they are easy to maintain and can have immediate, lasting results (Haydon & Kroeger, 2016). See Lane, Menzies and colleagues (2015) for step-by-step instructions for using each of these strategies as part of in-person instruction as well as www.ci3t.org/pl for free-access, on-demand professional learning resources. Most recently, these strategies have been adapted for use as part of teacher-led remote instruction and for families supporting instruction and engagement in the COVID-19 era (see www.ci3t.org/covid). Next, we provide brief descriptions of each strategy.

Behavior-Specific Praise

Behavior-specific praise (BSP) acknowledges appropriate behavior. It is a feedback statement delivered contingent upon a given behavior occurring, specifically identifying the desired behavior. For example, a teacher might say, "I appreciate you using a quiet voice during small group time, Ana." Though a minor change, the use of specific statements rather than general statements such as "Good job!" helps orient students to what is desirable and provides feedback when students make appropriate choices. This way, students are cognizant of why they are receiving praise and understand what behavior they should continue to engage in (Lane, Menzies, et al., 2015). Being specific helps increase the probability of the behavior occurring by building student mastery and fluency of skills (Royer et al., 2017). It is a strategy that can be used across school contexts and grade levels (Ennis et al., 2020). Teachers should maximize its effectiveness by giving behavior-specific praise as soon as they see the desired behavior. Furthermore, the praise should be delivered frequently, and with eye contact and enthusiasm to communicate sincerity (Marchant & Anderson, 2012). BSP is a good way to ensure a 4:1 frequency of positive feedback to negative or corrective feedback (Myers et al., 2011).

Precorrection

Precorrection is a technique to prevent problem behaviors that can be used in all school settings. This strategy is effective for decreasing disruption, particularly during transitions, by reminding students of expectations and of the desired behavior (Ennis et al., 2018). The strategy targets the antecedent by identifying environments or situations that may trigger a problem. A brief reminder can cue students to what is expected before a problem occurs. For example, a teacher might remind students they need to use quiet voices before entering the library or that they should walk, not run in the hallway. Precorrection may also involve modifying the environment by changing the classroom arrangement, altering teacher behavior, or incorporating visual cues (Lane et al, 2015). Rather than relying on reactive responses to inappropriate behavior, a precorrection avoids tense or stressful interactions with students thus contributing to a more positive learning environment. It is a proactive way to illustrate what a teacher expects to see and orient students to what they should do rather than delivering a reprimand after they fail to meet expectations (Ennis et al., 2018).

Active Supervision

Active supervision employs the use of scanning, escorting, and interacting to support appropriate student behavior both in the classroom and in unstructured areas of the school such as the playground and hallways (Colvin et al., 1997). The goal of active supervision is to prevent problem behavior through consistent monitoring of student activity (Kounin, 1977). Intentional and systematic supervision is a powerful tool for ensuring student safety by decreasing disruption and increasing engagement (Allen et al., 2020). Active supervision is most effectively used when there are already basic routines and procedures in place. This way students are aware of the expectations and the teacher can provide precorrection or quickly prompt depending on the setting or activity. Teachers use their physical presence, or proximity, to prompt students to expectations. Proximity or other nonverbal gestures can be an effective reminder for students to engage in appropriate behavior. The teacher continuously moves around, scans the area, and monitors student interactions. In doing this, the teacher is looking for potentially problematic situations or inappropriate behavior that can be averted with quick intervention. This strategy focuses on circumventing the antecedent events that can escalate or trigger problems. It actively helps students identify and remember appropriate behavior and expectations, with demonstrated positive outcomes for school-age youth. Moreover, teachers can use active supervision to provide reinforcement and motivate students to be engaged.

Increasing Opportunities to Respond

Research on opportunities-to-respond shows that an appropriate instructional pace leads to a decrease in off-task behaviors (Common et al., 2020). Instruction that is engaging and provides immediate feedback supports both positive behavior and academic achievement (Sutherland et al., 2008). Opportunities to respond is an instructional strategy that optimizes student engagement by providing multiple points of participation that are quick and targeted (Messenger et al., 2017). It is best used with content that students already have familiarity with. The teacher identifies the target content and develops several questions, cues, and/or prompts that allow students to practice the material. The teacher poses the questions or cues to which students respond in a rapid sequence. Students can respond individually or together (choral responding) using a range of response techniques (i.e., thumbs up or down, individual whiteboards, response cards, oral response, or other digital response tool). The teacher scans the responses and provides succinct feedback. Pressure to provide the correct answer is reduced because the teacher is quickly providing corrective feedback without pinpointing individual responses. OTR is a versatile strategy that can be employed across instructional settings and grade levels.

Instructional Choice

Providing students with choices when completing their academic tasks decreases inappropriate behavior and has been shown to increase academic engagement for both students with disabilities and their typical peers (Royer et al., 2017). Choices can be offered across activities as well as within activities (Jolivette et al., 2002). With across-choice, students are offered several different ways of completing an assignment. For example, they can choose whether they want to type a written response or create a slideshow with images. When providing choice within activities, students might choose the order in which they will complete their assigned tasks. Other types of choices include allowing students to choose which materials to use for an assignment such as a marker or a pen. Or they can be given choice of where they complete a task, for example, sitting on the carpet or at the small group desk. These choices may not seem consequential, but giving students even minimal opportunities to make their own choices during the school day can reduce behavior issues and provide an opportunity to engage in self-determined behaviors (Lane et al., 2018).

Comprehensive, Integrated Use of Low-Intensity Supports

As mentioned previously, teachers can incorporate these and other low-intensity strategies into daily instruction as part of regular school practices, as part of Tier 1 instruction and classroom management (Simonsen et al., 2019). In addition, these strategies can be used as Tier 2 targeted supports collecting additional data to obtain students' views about the goals, procedures, and intended outcomes (e.g., social validity data; Wolf, 1978); ensure the procedures are implemented as planned (treatment integrity); as well as frequent, repeated assessment to monitor student progress.

Yet, even with a suite of proactive and culturally responsive low-intensity supports built into the fabric of daily instruction and social interactions, teachers will still need access to additional evidence-based strategies, practices, and programs at Tier 2 as well as the most intensive interventions at Tier 3, many of which feature these same low-intensity supports. For example, behavior-specific praise is a key component of many Tier 2 and Tier 3 supports.

As part of a Ci3T model of prevention, teachers have access to Secondary (Tier 2) and Tertiary (Tier 3) Intervention Grids delineating available supports (Lane et al., 2014; Oakes et al., 2014). These grids include: the name of the support, a brief description, entry criteria specifying which schoolwide data (e.g., academic and behavior screenings, office discipline referrals, nurse visit, attendance) to review to determine if this support might be useful for student data to monitor progress (e.g., social validity, treatment integrity, and progress monitoring), as well as exit criteria to determine when to conclude or fade this extra support (e.g., successfully met outcomes, or another more intensive intervention if warranted; see Table 26.1 for an illustration). For example, this list may include a Check/In Check/Out intervention at Tier 2 as well as functional assessment-based intervention (FABI) to support students who needed more than Tier 1 (and perhaps even more than Tier 2) had to offer.

These intervention grids feature not only behavioral supports, but also well-researched interventions to meet students' academic and social emotional well-being needs, often in an integrated fashion. For example, a student with higher-than-average internalizing issues according to a systematic screening tool (e.g., Student Risk Screening Scale—Internalizing subscale score in the moderate risk range; Lane et al., 2019) may require a Tier 2 support. The teacher may reach out to the parents to explore the possibility of putting in place a self-monitoring intervention coupled with instruction on how to recognize anxious feelings and learn relaxation strategies to support students within internalizing issues be more comfortably engaged academically and socially (see Lane, Buckman, et al., 2020). Similarly, another student with Tier 3 needs in reading comprehension may receive reading instruction four days a week for 45 minutes using a validated reading intervention coupled with a self-monitoring intervention to support engagement. These are but two illustrations of how to address students' multiple needs in an integrated fashion. In optimal conditions, district- and school-leaders implementing Ci3T or other integrated tiered systems would have access to a range of strategies, practices, and programs at Tier 2 and Tier 3. Each would be delineated in Secondary (Tier 2) Intervention Grids and Tertiary (Tier 3) Intervention Grids to support communication and transparencies between teachers, families, administrators, and students themselves. In addition, teachers and others would have access to a range of high-quality professional learning offerings (e.g., on-demand webinars, coaching, instructional videos) to assist educators with implementation (see Common et al., 2021).

Culturally Responsive Practices in Integrated Tiered Systems

A fundamental premise of positive behavior support—the center stone of Ci3T—is a strong contextual fit between the individual and the supportive practices (Dunlap et al. 2008). In addition to empowering teachers with low-intensity supports and using structures such as intervention grids to make transparent validated Tier 2 and Tier 3 supports, this requires school communities have an awareness and understanding of the various backgrounds and cultures of students and their families. Cultural responsiveness also ensures schools establish equitable practices that safeguard students from punitive discipline practices that contribute to the school-to-prison pipeline and other deleterious outcomes (Walker et al., 2004). This includes developing reactive plans with respectful procedures for responding to challenging behaviors. In Ci3T models this often includes the following sequence: show empathy to the student who is struggling, keep instruction moving forward, restate expectations, acknowledge students meeting expectations, and reinforce the student who was struggling as soon as they re-engaged in desired behaviors. While the literature on culturally responsive practices is longstanding (Gay, 2010; Ladsen-Billings, 2009; Nieto, 2000), the Center on PBIS has released a field guide on how to implement Tier 1 practices that address cultural responsiveness (Leverson et al., 2021), an area that had not previously been comprehensively addressed in tiered systems. The guide specifies five core components to guide cultural responsiveness: identity, voice, supportive environment, situational appropriateness, and data for equity. Next, we briefly explain each of these components.

Identity

One's identity is not only comprised of elements such as race or ethnicity, but also gender, language, religion and other salient markers that shape our beliefs and worldview. In addition to understanding students' identities, practitioners must also be conscious of their own identity and how their own cultural values are manifested in the classroom. Only when there is an awareness of the complex interplay of identity between students and school personnel will educators be able to determine whether their practice is responsive.

Voice

As a valued part of the school community, students and their families must be offered substantive opportunities to contribute their ideas, opinions, and partake in leadership roles. This facilitates authentic engagement and promotes an inclusive partnership whose effects will be felt schoolwide. Efforts should be made to encourage participation if stakeholders do not engage on their own. School personnel must have an awareness of various community members' values and concerns to be able to engage with the community in a meaningful way. In schools implementing Ci3T, both a student and their family member serves on the Ci3T Leadership Team, participating in the manualized building process as well as facilitating implementation in the years ahead.

Supportive Environment

A supportive school environment includes the establishment of a schoolwide approach to addresses student needs rather than requiring each teacher to work independently. The school community is guided by a common mission with an emphasis on helping students acquire the knowledge and skills they need to be successful. School staff make a deliberate effort to communicate to students that they are valued and that students' success is everyone's success. In Ci3T models, the Ci3T Implementation Manuals have clearly defined roles and responsibilities of all key stakeholders—students, faculty and staff, families, and administrators—to facilitate transparency.

Situational Appropriateness

This is the awareness that families may have views that differ from those of school staff as to how various situations should be handled, and those views are respected even if staff are not in agreement with them. While school expectations are taught and students are supported in learning and demonstrating those expectations, staff do not make judgements about differences between home and school expectations. A salient aspect of situational appropriateness is that students are taught to recognize and meet school expectations while in school, even if the expectations are different from what is valued at home. At the same time, students are not made to feel uncomfortable about the differences between the home and school cultures. Differences can arise in several areas including social interaction norms, behavioral issues, and linguistic and communication styles. Situational appropriateness requires school staff be respectful of families' perspectives while helping students learn how to successfully navigate the school environment.

Data for Equity

The school community uses both fidelity of implementation data and student outcome data to ensure all students receive the attention and support they need. As illustrated above, school teams use implementation data to examine whether Tier 1 efforts are in place as intended and can be helpful in designing professional learning opportunities for faculty and staff. In schools implementing Ci3T models, data are analyzed for the school as a whole, for grade levels, and individual levels. In addition, these data are disaggregated to determine whether there are discrepancies among groups so action planning can be done at a systems level. In addition, outcome data are used to design individual and classroom interventions as needed. Reviewing behavioral, social-emotional, and academic outcomes helps schools address students' needs in these important domains.

Considerations

In this chapter, we provided a brief discussion of the history of classroom management practices in special education settings which relied heavily on responding to challenging behavior rather than preventing such challenges from occurring initially. Students with disabilities have behavioral characteristics such as impulsivity, hyperactivity, limited self-regulation skills, aggression, and social skill deficits that often pose substantial challenges to even the most well-prepared teacher. As such, the shift from consequence-based, reactive approaches to managing behavior towards proactive, system approaches was an innovative approach in the field of education. These coordinated frameworks offer collaborative structures to facilitate communication between general educators, special educators, families, and administrators.

In recent years, integrated tiered systems such as Ci3T have garnered attention. In fact, the Institute of Education Sciences (IES) invested 20 million dollars into integrated systems inquiry to determine how best to design, implement, and evaluate integrated systems at the elementary level to meet students' academic, behavioral, and social emotional well-being. Such models hold particular promise for supporting students receiving special education services (IDEA, 2004), as these models empower all educators to incorporate effective, efficient, research-based strategies into daily instruction. Many of our district partners design district-wide professional learning plans to provide a range of opportunities (e.g., presentations, web-based learning experiences, practice guides, and informational graphics) for all educators to learn strategies such as: behavior specific praise, precorrection, active supervision, increased opportunities to respond, and instructional choices (Lane et al, 2015). These strategies have been tested in a range of contexts from inclusive classrooms to self-contained classroom and schools. In addition, educators and families will also need access to additional, practical, and effective strategies to assist students needing more than Tier 1 has to offer—even when low-intensity supports are in place as planned as part of classroom management practices. With the support of high-quality professional learning, including coaching, general and special education teachers can be empowered to prevent and respond to challenging behaviors with confidence.

Ultimately, the successful implementation of these strategies can facilitate inclusive programming, which may be one of the greatest benefits of establishing proactive practices within integrated tiered systems of support such as Ci3T. Such systems move away from the refer-test-place model, and are focused on data-informed decision making to determine how best to meet students' multiple needs—efficiently and effectively. In addition, such systems also hold the benefit of providing educators with the information they are looking for with the use of data-informed professional learning efforts.

References

Allen, G. E., Common, E. A., Germer, K. A., Lane, K. L., Buckman, M. M., Oakes, W. P., & Menzies, H. M. (2020). A systematic review of the evidence base for active supervision in PK–12 settings. *Behavioral Disorders*, *45*(3), 167–182. https://doi.org/10.1177/0198742919837646 online first 2019

Bradshaw, C. P., O' Brennan, L. M., & McNeely, C. A. (2008). Core competencies and the prevention of school failure and early school leaving. *New Directions for Child and Adolescent Development*, *2008* (122), 19–32. https://doi.org/10.1002/cd.226

Bradshaw, C. P., Sawyer, A. L., & O' Brennan, L. M. (2009). A social disorganization perspective on bullying-related attitudes and behaviors: The influence of school context. *American Journal of Community Psychology*, *43*(3), 204–220. https://doi.org/10.1007/s10464-009-9240-1

Brooks-Gunn, J., & Duncan, G. J. (1997). The effects of poverty on children. *The Future of Children*, *7*(2), 55–71. https://doi.org/10.2307/1602387

Buckman, M. M., Lane, K. L., Common, E. A., Royer, D. J., Oakes, W. P., Allen, G. E., Lane, K. S., & Brunsting, N. (2021). Treatment integrity of primary (tier 1) prevention efforts in tiered systems: Mapping the literature. *Education and Treatment of Children*.

Carr, E. G. (1997). The evolution of applied behavior analysis into positive behavior support. *Journal of the Association for Persons with Severe Handicaps*, *22*(4), 208–209.

Carr, E. G., Dunlap, G., Horner, R. H., Koegel, R. L., Turnbull, A. P., Sailor, W., Anderson, J. L., Albin, R. W., Koegel, L. K., & Fox, L. (2002). Positive Behavior Support: Evolution of an applied science. *Journal of Positive Behavior Interventions, 4*(1), 4. https://doi-org.mimas.calstatela.edu/10.1177/109830070200400102

Colvin, G., & Scott, T. M. (2004). *Managing the cycle of acting out behavior in the classroom.* Behavior Associates.

Colvin, G., Sugai, G., Good, R. H., & Lee, Y. (1997). Using active supervision and precorrection to improve transition behaviors in an elementary school. *School Psychology Quarterly, 12,* 344–363. https://doi.org/10.1037/h0088967

Common, E. A., Buckman, M. M., Lane, K. L., Oakes, W. P., Royer, D. J., Chafouleas, S., Briesch, A., & Sherod, R. (2021). Project ENHANCE: Assessing professional learning needs for implementing Comprehensive, Integrated, Three-tiered (Ci3T) Prevention modules. *Education and Treatment of Children, 44,* 125–144.

Common, E. A., Lane, K. L., Cantwell, E. D., Brunsting, N., Oakes, W. P., Germer, K. A. & Bross, L. A., (2020). Teacher-delivered strategies to increase students' opportunities to respond: A systematic methodological review. *Behavioral Disorders, 45*(2), 67–84. https://doi.org/10.1177/0198742919828310 online first 2019

Dunlap, G., Carr, E. G., Horner, R. H., Zarcone, J. R., & Schwartz, I. (2008). Positive Behavior Support and Applied Behavior Analysis: A familial alliance. *Behavior Modification, 32*(5), 682–698. https://doi.org/10.1177/0145445508317132

Ennis, R. P., Lane, K. L., Menzies, H. M., & Owens, P. P. (2018). Precorrection: An effective, efficient, low-intensity strategy to support student success. *Beyond Behavior, 27*(3), 146–152. https://doi.org/10.1177/1074295618799360

Ennis, R. P., Lane, K. L., Oakes, W. P., & Flemming, S. C. (2020). Empowering teachers with low-intensity strategies to support instruction: Implementing across-activity choices in 3rd grade reading. *Journal of Positive Behavioral Interventions, 22*(2), 78–92. https://doi.org/10.1177/1098300719870438

Ennis, R. P., Royer, D. J., Lane, K. L., & Dunlap, K. D. (2020). Behavior-specific praise in K–12 settings: Mapping the 50-year knowledge base. *Behavioral Disorders, 45*(3), 131–147. https://doi.org/10.1177/0198742919843075

Fabelo, T., Thompson, M. D., Plotkin, M., Carmichael, D., Marchbanks, M. P., & Booth, E. A. (2011). *Breaking schools' rules: A statewide study of how school discipline relates to students' success and juvenile justice system involvement.* CGS Justice Center. https://csgjusticecenter.org/publications/breaking-schools-rules/

Fetterman, H., Ritter, C., Morrison, J. Q., & Newman, D. S. (2020). Implementation fidelity of culturally responsive school-wide positive behavior interventions and supports in a Spanish-language magnet school: A case study emphasizing context. *Journal of Applied School Psychology, 36*(1), 89–106. https://doi.org/10.1080/15377903.2019.1665607

Forness, S. R., Freeman, S. F. N., Paparella, T., Kauffman, J. M., & Walker, H. M. (2012). Special education implications of point and cumulative prevalence for children with emotional or behavioral disorders. *Journal of Emotional and Behavioral Disorders, 20,* 4–18. https://doi.org/10.1177/1063426611401624

Gay, G. (2010). *Culturally responsive teacher: Theory, research, and practice* (2nd ed.). Teachers College Press.

Gresham, F. M., & Elliott, S. N. (2008). *Social Skills Improvement System (SSiS) Rating Scales.* PsychCorp Pearson Education.

Hamre, B. K., & Pianta, R. C. (2001). Early teacher–child relationships and the trajectory of children's school outcomes through eighth grade. *Child Development, 72*(2), 625–638. doi:10.1111/1467-8624.00301

Hawken, L. S., MacLeod, K. S., & Rawlings, L. (2007). Effects of the Behavior Education Program (BEP) on office discipline referrals of elementary school students. *Journal of Positive Behavior Interventions, 9,* 94–101.

Haydon, T., & Kroeger, S. D. (2016). Active supervision, precorrection, and explicit timing: A high school case study on classroom behavior. *Preventing School Failure, 60*(1), 70–78.

Horner, R. H., & Sugai, G. (2015). School-wide PBIS: An example of applied behavior analysis implemented at a scale of social importance. *Behavior Analysis Practice, 8*(1), 80–85. https://doi.org/10.1007/s40617-015-0045-4

Individuals with Disabilities Education Improvement Act of 2004, Pub. L. No. 20 U.S.C. 1400 et seq. (2004).

Jolivette, K., Strichter, J. P., & McCormick, K. M. (2002). Making choices – improving behavior – engaging in learning. *Teaching Exceptional Children, 34,* 24–30.

Kauffman, J. M. (2005). *Characteristics of children's behavior disorders* (7th ed.). Merrill.

Kauffman, J. M. (2020). *On educational inclusion: Meanings, history, issues, and international perspectives.* Routledge Taylor & Francis.

Kounin, J. (1977). *Discipline and group management in classrooms.* Holt, Rinehart, & Winston.

Ladsen-Billings, G. (2009). Toward a theory of culturally relevant pedagogy. *American Educational Research Journal, 32*(3), 465–491.

Landrum, T. J., & Kauffman, J. M. (2006). Behavioural approaches to classroom management. In C.M. Everton & C.S. Weinstein (Eds.), *Handbook of classroom management: Research, practice, and contemporary issues.* Erlbaum.

Lane, K. L., Buckman, M. M., Oakes, W. P., & Menzies, H. M. (2020). Tiered systems and inclusion: Potential benefits, clarifications, and considerations. In J. M. Kauffman (Ed.). *On educational inclusion: Meanings, history, issues, and international perspectives* (pp. 85–106). Routledge Taylor & Francis.

Lane, K. L., Carter, E., Jenkins, A., Magill, L., & Germer, K. (2015). Supporting comprehensive, integrated, three-tiered models of prevention in schools: Administrators perspectives. *Journal of Positive Behavior Interventions*, 17(4), 209–222. https://doi.org/10.1177/1098300715578916

Lane, K. L., Menzies, H. M., Ennis, R. P., & Oakes, W. P. (2015). *Supporting behavior for school success: A step-by-step guide to key strategies*. Guilford Press.

Lane, K. L., Menzies, H. M., Ennis, R. P., Oakes, W. P., Royer, D. J., & Lane, K. S. (2018). Instructional choice: An effective, efficient, low-intensity strategy to support student success. *Beyond Behavior*, 27, 160–167. https://doi.org/10.1177/1074295616786965

Lane, K. L., Menzies, H. M., Oakes, W. P., & Kalberg, J. R. (2020). *Developing a schoolwide framework to prevent and manage learn and behavior problems (2nd Edition)*. Guilford Press.

Lane, K. L., Oakes, W. P., Buckman, M. M., & Lane, K. S. (2018). *Supporting school success: Engaging lessons to meet students' multiple needs*. Council for Children with Behavior Disorders (CCBD) Newsletter.

Lane, K. L., Oakes, W. P., Cantwell, E. D., Royer, D. J., Leko, M., Schatschneider, C., & Menzies, H. M. (2019). Predictive validity of Student Risk Screening Scale for Internalizing and Externalizing scores in secondary schools. *Journal of Emotional and Behavioral Disorders*, 27(2), 86–100. https://doi:10.1177/1063426617744746

Lane, K. L., Oakes, W. P., Ennis, R. P., & Hirsch, S. E. (2014). Identifying students for secondary and tertiary prevention efforts: How do we determine which students have Tier 2 and Tier 3 needs? *Preventing School Failure*, 58(3), 171–182. https://doi.org/10.1080/1045988X.2014.895573

Lane, K. L., Oakes, W. P., & Menzies, H. M. (2021). Considerations for systematic screening PK-12: Universal screening for internalizing and externalizing behaviors in the COVID-19 era. *Preventing School Failure: Alternative Education for Children and Youth*, 65(3), 275–281. https://doi.org/10.1080/1045988X.2021.1908216

Lane, K. L., Oakes, W. P., Menzies, H. M., Buckman, M. M., & Royer, D. J. (2020). Systematic screening for behavior: Considerations and commitment to continued inquiry. Practice Brief available on www.ci3t.org/screening.

Lane, K. L., Oakes, W. P., Royer, D. J., Menzies, H. M., Brunsting, N., Buckman, M. M., Common, E. A., Lane, N. A., Schatschneider, C., & Lane, K. S. (2020). Secondary teachers' self-efficacy during initial implementation of comprehensive, integrated, three-tiered models of prevention. *Journal of Positive Behavior Interventions*. 1–13 https://doi.org/10.1177/1098300720946628

Lane, K. L., & Walker, H. M. (2015). The connection between assessment and intervention: How does screening lead to better interventions? In B. Bateman, M. Tankersley, & J. Lloyd (Eds.), *Enduring issues in special education: Personal perspectives* (pp. 283–301). Routledge.

Laub, J. H., & Sampson, R. J. (1993). Turning points in the life course: Why change matters to the study of crime. *Criminology*, 31(3), 301–325. https://doi.org/10.1111/j.17459125.1993.tb01132.x

Legkauskas, V., & Magelinskaitė-Legkauskienė, Š. (2019). Importance of social competence at the start of elementary school for adjustment indicators a year later. *Issues in Educational Research*, 29(4), 1262–1276.

Leverson, M., Smith, K., McIntosh, K., Rose, J., & Pinkelman, S. (March, 2021). *PBIS cultural responsiveness field guide: Resources for trainers and coaches*. Center on PBIS, www.pbis.org.

Licht, B. G., & Kistner, J. A. (1986). Motivational problems of learning disabled children: Individual differences and their implications for treatment. In Torgesen, J. K., Wong, B. Y. L. (Eds.), *Psychological and educational perspectives on learning disabilities* (pp. 225–255). Academic Press.

Marchant, M., & Anderson, D. H. (2012). Improving social and academic outcomes for all learners through the use of teacher praise. *Beyond Behavior*, 21, 22–28. https://doi.org/10.1177/107429561202100305

McIntosh, K., Filter, K. J., Bennett, J. L., Ryan, C., & Sugai, G. (2010). Principles of sustainable prevention: Designing scale-up of school-wide positive behavior support to promote durable systems. *Psychology in the Schools*, 47(1), 5–21. https://doi.org/10.1002/pits.20448

Menzies, H. M., Oakes, W. P., Lane, K. L., Royer, D. J., Cantwell, E. D., & Buckman, M. M. (2020). Elementary teachers' perceptions of comprehensive, integrated, three-tiered models: A need to clarify PBIS. *Remedial and Special Education*, 1–13. https://doi.org/10.1177/0741932519896860

Messenger, M., Common, E. A., Lane, K. L., Oakes, W. P., Menzies, H. M., Cantwell, E. D., & Ennis, R. P. (2017). Increasing opportunities to respond for students with internalizing behaviors: The utility of choral and mixed responding. *Behavioral Disorders*, 42(4), 170–184. https://doi.org/10.1177/0198742917712968

Mitchell, M. M., & Bradshaw, C. P. (2013). Examining classroom influences on student perceptions of school climate: the role of classroom management and exclusionary discipline strategies. *Journal of School Psychology*, 51(5), 599–610. https://doi.org/10.1016/j.jsp.2013.05.005

Monahan, K.C., VanDerhei, S., Bechtold, J., & Cauffman, E. (2014). From the school yard to the squad car: School discipline, truancy, and arrest. *Journal of Youth and Adolescence*, 43(7), 1110–1122. https://doi.org/10.1007/s10964-014-0103-1

Myers, D. M., Simonsen, B., & Sugai, G. (2011). Increasing teachers' use of praise with a response-to-intervention approach. *Education & Treatment of Children*, 34(1), 35–59.

National Council on Disability (2015). *Breaking the school-to-prison pipeline for students with disabilities*. www.ncd. gov/publications/2015/06182015

Nieto, S. (2000). Affirming diversity. The sociopolitical context of multicultural education (3rd ed.). Addison Wesley Longman.

Novak, A. (2018). The association between experiences of exclusionary discipline and justice system contact: A systematic review. *Aggression and Violent Behavior, 40*, 73–82. https://doi.org/10.1016/j.avb.2018.04.002

Oakes, W. P., Cantwell, E. D., Lane, K. L., Royer, D. J., & Common, E. A. (2020). Examining educator's views of classroom management and instructional strategies: School-site capacity for supporting students' behavioral needs. *Preventing School Failure, 64*(1), 1–11. https://doi.org/10.1080/1045988X.2018.1523125

Oakes, W. P., Lane, K. L., & Germer, K. (2014). Developing the capacity to implement Tier 2 and Tier 3 supports: How do we support our faculty and staff in preparing for sustainability? *Preventing School Failure, 58*(3), 183–190. https://doi.org/10.1080/1045988X.2014.895575

Okonofua, J. A., & Eberhardt, J. L. (2015). Two strikes: Race and the disciplining of young students. *Psychological Science, 26*(5), 617–624. doi:10.1177/0956797615570365

Perfect, M. M., Turley, M. R., Carlson, J. S., Yohanna, J., & Saint Gilles, M. P. (2016). School-related outcomes of traumatic event exposure and traumatic stress symptoms in students: A systematic review of research from 1990 to 2015. School Mental Health, 8(1), 7–43. https://doi.org/10.1007/s12310-016-9175-2

Pierce, W. D., & Cheney, C. D. (2017). *Behavior analysis and learning: A biobehavioral approach (6th ed.)*. Routledge.

Rivera-Calderón, N. (2019). Arrested at the Schoolhouse Gate: Criminal School Disturbance Laws and Children's Rights in Schools. *National Lawyers Guild Review, 75*(3), 1–41.

Royer, D. J., Lane, K. L., Cantwell, E. D., & Messenger, M. (2017). A systematic review of the evidence base for instructional choice in k–12 settings. *Behavioral Disorders, 42*(3), 89–107. https://doi.org/10.1177/019874291 6688655

Rumberger, R. W., & Losen, D. J. (2016). The high cost of harsh discipline and its disparate impact. UCLA: The Civil Rights Project / Proyecto Derechos Civiles. Retrieved from https://escholarship.org/uc/item/ 85m2m6sj

Simonsen, B., Freeman, J., Swain-Bradway, J., George, H. P., Putnam, R., Lane, K. L., Sprague, J., & Hershfeldt, P. (2019). Using data to support teachers' implementation of Positive Classroom Behavior Support (PCBS) practices. *Education and Treatment of Children, 42*(2), 265–290. https://doi.org/10.1353/etc.2019.0013

Sutherland, K. S., Lewis-Palmer, T., Stichter, J., & Morgan, P. L. (2008). Examining the influence of teacher behavior and classroom context on the behavioral and academic outcomes for students with emotional or behavioral disorders. *The Journal of Special Education, 41*(4), 223–233. https://doi.org/10.1177/002246690 7310372

Sutherland, K. S., Singh, N. N., Conroy, M., & Stichter, J. P. (2004). Learned helplessness and students with emotional or behavioral disorders: Deprivation in the classroom. *Behavioral Disorders, 29*(2), 169–181. https://doi. org/10.1177/019874290402900208

Umbreit, J., Ferro, J., Liaupsin, C., & Lane, K. (2007). *Functional behavioral assessment and function-based intervention: An effective, practical approach*. Prentice-Hall.

Umbreit, J., Lane, K. L., & Dejud, C. (2004). Improving classroom behavior by modifying task difficulty: The effects of increasing the difficulty of too-easy tasks. *Journal of Positive Behavior Interventions, 6*, 13–20.

Walker, H. M., Forness, S. R., & Lane, K. L. (2014). Design and management of scientific research in applied school settings. In B. Cook, M. Tankersley, and T. Landrum (Eds.), Advances in learning and behavioral disabilities (vol. 27, pp. 141–169). Emerald.

Walker, H. M., Horner, R. H., Sugai, G., Bullis, M., Spragues, J. R., Bricker, D., & Kaufman, M. J. (1996). Integrated approaches to preventing antisocial behavior patterns among school-age children and youth. *Journal of Emotional and Behavioral Disorders, 4*(4), 194–209.

Walker, H. M., Ramsey, E., & Gresham, F. M. (2004). *Antisocial behavior in school: Evidence-based practices* (2nd ed.). Wadsworth Publishing Company.

Weist, M. D., Garbacz, S. A., Lane, K. L., & Kincaid, D. (Eds.). (2017). *Aligning and integrating family engagement in Positive Behavioral Interventions and Supports (PBIS): Concepts and strategies for families and schools in key contexts*. Center for Positive Behavioral Interventions and Supports Office of Special Education, Programs, U.S. Department of Education. University of Oregon Press.

Wildeman, C. (2010). Paternal incarceration and children's physically aggressive behaviors: Evidence from the fragile families and child wellbeing study. *Social Forces, 89*(1), 285–309. https://doi.org/10.1353/sof.2010.0055

Wolf, M. M. (1978). Social validity: The case for subjective measurement or how applied behavior analysis is finding its heart. *Journal of Applied Behavior Analysis, 11*(2), 203–214.

27

STUDENTS WITH AUTISM AND CLASSROOM MANAGEMENT

Edward J. Sabornie

NC STATE UNIVERSITY

Glennda K. McKeithan

UNIVERSITY OF KANSAS

Jamie N. Pearson

NC STATE UNIVERSITY

Introduction

One may question the need for a separate chapter on classroom management related to students with autism spectrum disorder (ASD); however, over the past decade, the number of students with ASD has doubled in US public schools (Maenner et al., 2021), and the increased prevalence of ASD has heightened the need for more educational and therapeutic interventions for such individuals (Steinbrenner et al., 2020). Autism is a lifelong neurodevelopmental disability characterized by support needs related to social-emotional cognition and communication, sensory processing, restricted patterns of interest, and activities daily living (Scheuermann et al., 2019). Autism occurs approximately once in every 44 (about 2%) of children (Maenner et al., 2021). In fact, evidence suggests the prevalence of school aged children in the United States with ASD may be higher (Travers & Krezmien, 2018). The discrepancy may be due to cultural, ethnic, and gender differences and the fact that many students with ASD who have the ability to meet academic expectations go undiagnosed. Although research findings demonstrate the benefits of early ASD diagnoses and early intervention, many children with ASD are not diagnosed until school age (Hammond et al., 2013; Siddiqua et al., 2021). A delay in diagnoses is particularly prevalent among Black and Latinx children, and those from low-income families (Pearson, 2015; Travers & Krezmien). The timing of ASD diagnoses has important implications for teachers and related service providers because the age of diagnosis, age during onset of treatment, and the intensity of treatment predict outcomes for students with ASD (Yingling et al., 2018). Schools have an obligation to engage in practices to help facilitate timely diagnosis, and to promote more positive, long-term outcomes for students with ASD—many of which can be fostered through the implementation of effective classroom management strategies. The rapid increase in ASD diagnoses in recent years has also required schools to develop and implement appropriate, evidence-based practices (EBPs), including classroom management strategies, for such students in all types of classroom settings (Steinbrenner et al., 2020). Given its neurodevelopmental nature (i.e., as a

DOI: 10.4324/9781003275312-32

"spectrum disorder"), there are many support needs and related disorders among students with ASD. Students with ASD often experience varying levels of social communication challenges. In some cases, students with ASD have a variety of social-affective problem behaviors and exhibit disruptive behavior that can adversely impact the classroom environment (e.g., noncompliance, aggression, echolalia, tantrums, elopement, sarcasm; McKeithan & Sabornie, 2020). Given the issues mentioned above related to school-aged students with ASD, this chapter will discuss the classroom management strategies and EBPs that effectively support the needs of such students. Classroom-based research will be reviewed to highlight what has been shown to be successful in managing students with ASD in classrooms at all levels and internationally.

Educational Service Delivery for Students with ASD

In recent years, there has been an emphasis on inclusive models of education that focus on placing students with disabilities in general education to the greatest extent possible (Meindl et al., 2020). As a result, students with ASD are increasingly being served in general education classrooms (McKeithan & Sabornie, 2020). Findings suggest that nearly 40% of students with ASD in US public schools spend 80% or more of their time in general education classrooms (Snyder et al., 2018). Research has shown that when students with ASD (across the spectrum) are placed in inclusive classroom settings, they often demonstrate higher levels of social interaction and academic skill development (Morningstar et al., 2017).

Support Needs among Students with ASD

Educational support needs vary greatly among students with ASD. Many students with ASD experience multiple areas of needed support related to social skills, behavior, and communication that make it difficult for teachers to develop and maintain high-quality interactions that influence both the quantity and quality of learning opportunities for their learners (Bouck & Park, 2018; Leifler et al., 2020).

Behavior

Evidence shows that general education teachers may struggle to address the social-behavioral needs of students with ASD (Byrne, 2020; McKeithan & Sabornie, 2020). In addition, many students on the spectrum (80%) often present with co-occurring conditions commonly associated with emotional and behavioral disorders (EBD), including generalized anxiety disorder, attention deficit hyperactivity disorder, bipolar disorder, conduct disorder, depression, and oppositional defiant disorder (Sesso et al., 2020). Findings indicate that the prevalence of EBD among students with ASD is higher than those rates for the general pediatric population (Rosen et al. 2018; Sesso et al.). There is a dearth of guidance around how school personnel can implement effective classroom management procedures along with a continuum of evidence-based supports for students with ASD and co-occurring emotional and behavioral support needs. As a result, students with ASD and co-occurring EBD may struggle to access the least restrictive setting (Steinbrenner et al., 2020).

Classroom Management for Students with ASD

Research indicates that some teachers (i.e., particularly those in general education) have low to intermediate levels of knowledge about ASD and the best EBPs to meet the needs of students (Steinbrenner et al., 2020). Teachers report that they are unprepared to handle behavior problems in the classroom, that student misbehavior interferes with teaching, and that they are not accepting of students who exhibit challenging behavior (Gilmour et al., 2019). In many cases, general education

teacher preparation programs provide little to no preparation in classroom and behavior management, which likely contributes to daily challenges teachers face regarding these domains (Sabornie
& Pennington, 2015).

For students with and without disabilities, classrooms characterized by frequent disruptive behaviors
and poor classroom management can lead to negative learning outcomes among students (Gilmour
et al., 2019). Moreover, research has shown that some teachers hold less-than-positive feelings toward
students engaged in frequent classroom misbehavior (Scherzinger & Wettstein, 2019). Low teaching
performance reviews are typical among teachers who struggle with classroom management (Gilmour
et al.). Establishing successful classroom management is critical for school-aged students with ASD,
but effective classroom management depends on factors such as established behavioral expectations
that enhance the classroom environment and lead to desired behaviors (Aspiranti et al., 2019).

Given the challenges that educators face regarding classroom management for students with ASD,
it is critical to identify evidence-based strategies to support student needs, to enhance the positive
culture of the classroom environment, and to improve the likelihood of positive student outcomes
(Steinbrenner et al., 2020). Although some research indicates that teachers are often unprepared to
manage classroom behavior, there also exists a large body of empirical investigations that have identified effective classroom management interventions (Cooper & Scott, 2017; Mitchell et al., 2017). In
the next section we review research on classroom management interventions and other related issues
that can strengthen educational outcomes for students with ASD.

Research on Classroom Management and Students with ASD

There is a history in the available research literature on classroom management—regardless of the focus on
student type (e.g., students with disabilities)—that the term "classroom management" is frequently used
synonymously with "behavior management" (see Brophy, 2006; Divoll & Ribeiro, 2021; Postholm, 2013).
Among many other aspects of pedagogy and activity in schools, classroom management includes issues
beyond simple teacher-student interactions and physical organization of instructional environments. The
definition of classroom management by Divoll and Ribeiro "includes but is not limited to dealing with
student behavior, classroom community, classroom relationships, teaching strategies, attention strategies,
and interactive lessons" (p. 235). This is particularly true in the study of those with ASD for much of the
focus on improving classroom management conditions for such students involves interventions related
to their overt behavior in classrooms. Another caveat of classroom and behavior management research
involving students with ASD is that most studies used single case design (SCD) research protocols and
applied behavior analysis (ABA) interventions (e.g., positive reinforcement) to change student behavior.
Applied behavior analysis research has a long history of association with ASD. Therefore, most studies
reviewed below involve SCD and the application of some type of ABA to improve students' behavior
and, in so doing, enhance the classroom environment through successful management.

The research reviewed below is related to classroom and behavior management of students with
ASD and the following additional factors: (a) social aspects of behavior, (b) behavior compliance, and
(c) self-management of behavior. In an attempt to be as current as possible, all the studies reviewed
below have been published since the 2nd edition of the *Handbook of Classroom Management* (Emmer
& Sabornie, 2015) was initially in production (i.e., 2013).

Social Behavior Research and Classroom Management

Gengoux (2015) used a brief "priming" intervention in an attempt to improve the social interactions
of students with ASD among their peers without disabilities in an inclusive summer day camp.
Behavioral observation and intervention settings included classrooms as well as school athletic fields
where art, music, games, and sports activities occurred under teacher supervision. Four students (3
males, one female; aged 6–8) with ASD, with delayed social skills based on a standardized assessment

of adaptive behavior, were the participants of interest among a larger sample of peers without disabilities at the day camp.

The priming intervention consisted of instructing a participant with ASD how to play a certain game (i.e., "Bumparena," "Carriboo," or the card game "Chomp"), at home, the day before they were to engage a peer without disabilities to play the same game at camp. The priming instruction (i.e., how to play the game) lasted from 10 to 30 minutes for each participant and was provided by the primary investigator. After the priming instruction occurred, the author reminded the student with ASD to play the game tomorrow and invite a fellow day camper to join him or her while playing the game. The behavioral data collected included the rate of social initiations made by the participant with ASD toward a peer without disabilities, and statements toward a peer without disability which showed expertise in playing a game. A multiple baseline across participants SCD was used in the research.

Results showed that during baseline, the four students with ASD demonstrated less than one conversation initiation per minute with peers. Following the baseline phase, however, the target participants increased their conversation initiation to at least the average normative rate (i.e., when compared with students without disabilities) while using the priming intervention. In other words, the priming intervention was successful in increasing conversation initiations among students with ASD matching those of their peers without disabilities. Daily classroom and behavior management of students with ASD may not lend itself easily to frequent priming of conversations with peers, but assisting such students in social integration and student-to-student relationships in classrooms is a worthy goal of schooling.

Sadler (2019) used video self-modeling (VSM) and functional behavior assessment (FBA) as interventions to decrease aggression and increase a replacement behavior (i.e., acts of self-management) of two boys (aged 7 and 12) with ASD (and intellectual disability) in a non-inclusive (i.e., self-contained) public school. A multiple baseline across stimulus conditions with participant replication was used to determine whether VSM together with FBA can modify the aggressive classroom behaviors of two students with ASD. Aggressive behavior was defined as acts of physical contact (e.g., biting, hitting), and the replacement behavior variable was identified as when the participant with ASD requested a "break" from the ongoing activity, or used deep breathing with a ball to squeeze as a calming, substitute behavior. Partial interval recording (i.e., 10 sec. in length) was used for data collection. A VSM recording of their appropriate classroom behavior was shown to each participant at the beginning of each school day during the SCD intervention phase; the video showed the student displaying an appropriate replacement behavior instead of aggression.

Results showed participants with ASD decreased the frequency of aggressive behaviors during the intervention phase when the VSM intervention was in place at the beginning of each school day. The results for the use of a replacement behavior to decrease classroom aggression, however, were mixed in that one participant did not use his replacement behavior at a high rate to prevent aggressive tendencies. In essence, the VSM treatment assisted in decreasing aggression in both participants, but it did not increase the use of a replacement behavior (i.e., to decrease aggression in the classroom) in one participant. Student aggressive behavior is a challenge in any classroom, and effective classroom management needs to address this type of danger so all are safe. Perhaps using VSM to reduce aggression among those with ASD should be further examined to determine its effectiveness on a larger scale. Using the VSM intervention with a large number of students, though, may be too cumbersome for teachers serving many students with ASD in classrooms.

Diorio et al. (2019), in another VSM study, used the intervention to determine whether it could increase behavioral compliance with classroom-based requests among students with ASD (see below for more on compliance behavior instruction in classrooms). Three boys with ASD (two in kindergarten and one in grade four), with a tendency for noncompliance to teacher requests in classrooms, were the participants. The VSM independent variable included four or five action scenes, each lasting approximately 30s in length, where the participant with ASD was shown responding appropriately to a specific request from the paraprofessional in the classroom. Each participant with ASD watched his personal VSM immediately prior to an instructional period when, historically, noncompliant behavior was likely to be demonstrated. The dependent variable was the percent of behavioral compliance to classroom-based requests measured via event recording. The participant observation sessions lasted 45 minutes, and a multiple baseline across participants SCD was used.

Results indicated that the VSM was successful in increasing compliance behavior across the three participants with ASD. Effect size estimates using TauU, and percentages of nonoverlapping data across experimental phases with the three participants, however, indicated only modest positive effects of the VSM intervention. It is noteworthy that both the teachers and classroom paraprofessionals viewed the VSM intervention as socially valid despite questionable strength of behavior change. Perhaps the students with ASD were not motivated to respond as desired, or the actual VSMs lacked stimulation for the students to enjoy watching session after session. Whatever the reason, and in combination with the results of Sadler (2019) above, it appears VSM interventions need additional examination to determine whether it is a true evidence-based practice for frequent use in classrooms.

McCurdy and Cole (2014) used a peer social support system in an attempt to decrease the off-task and disruptive behavior of three boys with high-functioning ASD (aged 7–11) in general education classrooms. A few of the off-task behaviors that were included in the dependent variable group included playing with objects on the child's desk, random talking unrelated to the lesson, looking out the classroom windows, reading materials not associated with the current classroom focus, and other off-task behaviors. The off-task behavior recording sessions were conducted in general education classrooms for 20 minutes each day, five days per week.

Each student with ASD was assigned a trained peer support person of similar age in the intervention classroom. The peer sat near the target participant with ASD during instruction and gently prompted the target student when he was off-task and not paying attention to the teacher's instruction. The prompt was a simple redirection of the student with ASD by gently tapping on the instructional material on the student's desk. When the participant with ASD complied with the peer support prompt during a lesson, he received verbal praise and a "thumbs-up" gesture from the peer. Frequency of off-task behavior was the dependent variable in the multiple baseline across participants' SCD research.

Results showed that the peer social support intervention dramatically reduced the off-task behavior of the three target students with ASD to levels similar to students without disabilities in the classroom. The peer social support persons reported that they enjoyed working with their classmates with ASD, the pair became friends, and they played together subsequent to the investigation. The classroom teachers, target students with ASD, and the peer social supporters all found the intervention project to be positive and acceptable for changing a student's behavior. With such positive social results for the target students, the peer support intervention appears to be worthy of improving the classroom management routine of any teacher in general education serving students with high-functioning ASD.

In a group research, classroom management-oriented project with students with ASD, Irvin et al. (2015) examined the connection between adult talk in preschool classrooms and "socially competent behavior" among students with ASD in attendance. A total of 73 children were identified as having ASD; 37 scored in the mild range, 12 were functioning in the moderate to severe range, and 24 were classified in the mild-moderate to severe range. The students attended a total of 33 classrooms. One classroom type followed the *Learning Experiences: Alternative Program for Preschoolers and Parents* (LEAP; Strain & Hoyson, 2000) protocols, and the other type of classroom was named "business as usual" wherein it was "typically used for children with ASD in public schools" (Irvin et al., 2015, p. 133). The preschool participants with ASD had an average age of 48 months.

Each preschool student with ASD was videotaped for approximately 30 minutes in "center time" where he or she interacted with adults or other participants with ASD. Teachers were instructed to perform their normal activities in the classrooms. The video recordings of each student were then subdivided into 10-second intervals for subsequent partial interval behavioral calculations. Results of the assessment of behavioral recordings showed that students with ASD engaged in far more "socially competent" behavior with adults versus their peers. However, very little appropriate social behavior of students with ASD followed conversations with teachers and adults in the classroom. One very interesting finding was that when teachers engaged in "behavior management talk" with students with ASD early in the school year, it was subsequently associated with reduced social awareness by the end of the school year. By comparison, students with ASD who received supporting play talk from adults at the beginning of the school year were observed to demonstrate better social communication and motivation months later. It appears that the content and style of the way teachers communicate with preschoolers with ASD over time influences how later classroom and behavioral management evolves.

In another small *n*, group design study in Australia, Vivanti et al. (2019) examined whether preschoolers with ASD differed in behavioral outcomes over time when receiving a specific early intervention program in different settings—inclusion classrooms versus ASD-specific school placements. Forty-four preschoolers (*M* age = 24–26 months) participated in the study, and 22 students with ASD were randomly assigned to either early intervention inclusive classrooms or specialized settings specifically for students with ASD. Both experimental groups received the *Group-Early Start Denver Model* (G-ESDM) intervention, which is an adaptation of the *Early Start Denver Model* (Rogers & Dawson, 2010). The G-ESDM intervention is a specific set of teaching procedures and curricula to address the developmental needs of students with ASD. Skills taught in the program include various social skills, and verbal and non-verbal communication, among others. The participants with ASD attended both types of the early intervention research sites over a 15-week period, five hours per day, three days per week over 10–11 months.

Regarding child behavioral outcomes over time and across instructional settings, the results showed that the two groups of students with ASD in both settings improved in social interaction, imitation, and vocalizations, but a specific experimental effect was not shown for type of learning placement. In other words, students with ASD can improve their social functioning regardless of the type of instructional setting if a robust, evidence-based intervention is used in the classroom. Improved social functioning in school among students with ASD can then lead to smoother classroom management.

A qualitative research design (i.e., interpretive case study) was used by Myburgh et al. (2020) to understand the social skill instruction of students with ASD (in early elementary grades, Pre-K to grade 3) in South Africa. The researchers specifically examined the methodology of three teachers (two in rural areas, one in an urban school setting) as they taught social skills to students with high functioning ASD. Structured interviews (i.e., open-ended, one-on-one interviews) of the teachers as well as classroom observations were used in data collection. The researchers were explicitly interested in the teachers' perspectives concerning the following social domain variables of their students with ASD: sharing, independence, behavioral etiquette, and self-esteem. Three interviews with the teachers (with subsequent member checks) as well as three classroom observations formed the data collection procedures.

Myburgh et al. (2020) provided four distinct, narrative vignettes of how social skills instruction related to sharing, independence, behavioral etiquette, and self-esteem was implemented by the three teacher participants. Results indicated that, to ensure success and skill acquisition of the students with ASD, each teacher was actively involved in scaffolding the level of social skill instruction to address each of the four domains with their students. The teachers provided flexible learning environments to enhance the students' social skill acquisition, as well as consistently including the pupils with ASD in all learning activities. When students with ASD share materials with peers appropriately and demonstrate proper etiquette among peers and adults in classrooms, as shown by Myburgh et al., classroom and behavioral management is made easier for any teacher.

Social Stories™ and Students with ASD

Perhaps the most frequently used single intervention to improve classroom and behavior management, and social interactions of students with ASD, are Social Stories. To demonstrate the popularity of social stories as an intervention, we conducted an online library literature search using "Social Stories for children with autism" as the single descriptor. This one search term yielded 766 related journal articles, chapters, reports, dissertations, and books (since the 1990s) covering the topic.

Social Stories are "short, personalized stories designed to teach children with autism how to manage their behavior during social situations" (Litras et al., 2010, p. 1). Students with ASD using Social Stories in instruction receive (a) cues to display certain social behaviors (e.g., saying thank you after someone helps a student), (b) descriptions of where a newly learned social behavior is to be displayed, (c) instructions on how the situation will occur where the social behavior is required for appropriate responding, and (d) the ways in which others will respond subsequent to performance of a learned social behavior (see Bakar & Zubair, 2018). The actual "stories" can be written in a descriptive manner (e.g., "My name is Jamal. I go to Main Street Elementary School."), as an affirmative statement (e.g., "I really like this candy."), and in a directive manner (e.g., "When I don't know how to get somewhere, I can ask for directions first."), among other choices (Bakar & Zubair). Additionally, among just a few focus areas, Social Stories can be written related to (a) getting in line at school properly; (b) making eye contact with a speaker; (c) starting a conversation with a peer at the appropriate time in school; (d) chatting with peers about playground games, cafeteria food, and computer games; and (e) reinforcing a classmate for performing desirable classroom behavior. To ensure that the student with ASD understands the information found in a Social Story, frequent rehearsal is required under teacher supervision, and the stories include illustrations (as in a comic strip), photos, pictures maps, computer animations, and anything needed to ensure student understanding and the subsequent display of appropriate behavior or reduction in disruptive behavior.

As an example of Social Stories research, Thompson and Johnston (2017) explored whether a traditional social story presentation on paper was more effective than one provided on a computer screen (i.e., via an iPad) to reduce the frequency of "undesired" classroom behavior of four, early childhood students (boys) with ASD (N.B.: The exact undesirable behaviors were not described in the narrative.). Each participant consistently demonstrated at least two undesirable behaviors that challenged the teachers and interrupted instructional activities and the schedule in early childhood, special education classrooms. Each participant with ASD received two Social Stories written for him to address two selected, undesirable classroom behaviors; the stories were read to each participant by an "interventionist." An "adapted alternating treatment" SCD was used to test whether the four students with ASD acquired the new, Social Stories-learned appropriate behaviors better through the traditional paper-based pedagogy versus the iPad-based instruction. The students with ASD received equal amounts or instructional time using both Social Stories presentation methodologies.

Results across all four participants showed that both types of Social Stories instructional methods were equally effective in decreasing the measured undesired behaviors. Inappropriate student behavior among students with ASD can lead to numerous classroom management problems for teachers, and it appears that Social Stories—delivered through either traditional means or via technology in classrooms—can lead to a more appropriate and consistent behavioral atmosphere.

Hanrahan et al. (2020) used a small *n* (i.e., 14 males, 1 female, aged 4–10), quasi-experimental, randomized control trial (RCT) between students with ASD to examine the efficacy of "digitally mediated" (i.e., use of an iPad) Social Stories on various maladaptive and appropriate classroom behaviors (e.g., study time, frequency of behaviors, intensity of behavior, understanding of behavior, behavior related anxiety). When the Hanrahan study was published it represented the only RCT ever conducted (albeit on a very small scale) to examine the appropriate and inappropriate behavior of students with ASD in a classroom environment using Social Stories. The study was conducted over six weeks in England; all participants with ASD attended a special school. Nine students were randomly assigned to receive an intervention which included a unique social story delivered on an iPad meant to increase appropriate social behavior and reduce inappropriate conduct in school. Example titles of the Social Stories created include, "Sharing my Toys," "I Can Stay Focused and on Task," "When I Don't Get My Way," and "Personal Space," among others (the Appendix provided by Hanrahan et al.

includes all Social Stories created). The control group was exposed to a poem of equal length (i.e., in comparison to the Social Stories) that they read on an iPad while the treatment group received the stories. Four weeks of intervention were followed by a follow-up participant assessment six weeks after the intervention period.

Results showed that the computer-delivered Social Stories group exceeded the behavior displayed by the control group over ten weeks in terms of exhibiting global appropriate behavior and understanding of behavior. At the same time, the experimental group also displayed less inappropriate behavior and less intensity of inappropriate behavior over the same period. Lastly, the intervention group showed less behavior-related anxiety over time. Given the impressive results in the Hanrahan et al. (2020) study, educators should not hesitate to deliver comprehensive, well-designed, computer-driven Social Stories to students with ASD. Classroom and behavioral management of students with ASD are likely to improve if Social Stories are implemented with fidelity.

The positive results of Social Stories research related to classroom and behavior management of students with ASD reviewed herein arrive with a stipulation. That is, Leaf et al. (2015) called into question the results of the majority of 41 SCD studies using Social Stories to increase appropriate and decrease inappropriate behaviors of students with ASD. Leaf et al. found that over 92% of SCD studies examining Social Stories lacked a sufficient demonstration of the overall efficacy of the interventions due to "poor implementation of the various research designs" (p. 134). Leaf et al. also found that just over one-half of the 41 SCD studies reviewed could not clearly show that a social story intervention was solely responsible for changing the behavior of students with ASD. A total of 41% of studies in the Leaf et al. sample were capable of partial demonstration of an experimental effect of Social Stories, and only 7% of studies showed a "convincing demonstration" of the efficacy of Social Stories for students with ASD. In other words, Leaf et al. concluded that SCD research (i.e., prior to 2015) is insufficient in terms of providing empirical evidence in support of Social Stories. Perhaps the SCD research on Social Stories with students with ASD post-2015 has been conducted with stronger research designs and better control of confounding variables. It appears that the Social Stories intervention paradigm used to decrease disruptive behaviors and increase appropriate overt behavior does have merit, but a comprehensive reappraisal of such research with students with ASD since 2015 is highly recommended.

Self-Monitoring and Self-Management Research and Classroom Management

Another area of research related to classroom and behavioral management of students with ASD concerns assisting them in being aware of their own overt behavior. When students are aware of their actions and they are actively engaged in counting or measuring such activities, and they receive positive reinforcement when their actions are appropriate, it can lead to higher levels of appropriate behavior and lower levels of inappropriate behavior in classrooms. That is the intent of the cognitive behavior management program known as self-monitoring of behavior, and selected studies dealing with this type of intervention, along with self-management of behavior, are reviewed below.

Clemons et al. (2016) used self-monitoring of behavior with a high school male student with ASD (aged 17) to improve classroom engagement and academic outcomes using the *I-Connect* program on an electronic tablet. The I-Connect program includes a timer that is set to remind a student about appropriate behavior at selected times set by the researcher or teacher. In the Clemons et al. study, for example, the participant with ASD was prompted by the I-Connect program every one-minute interval by flashing on the screen, "Are you on task?" The on-task target behavior of the participant in the classroom included sitting at one's desk and completing teacher-assigned academic work. The observation sessions lasted 30 minutes, and a 15-second momentary time sampling behavioral recording system was implemented in an ABAB withdrawal SCD. Two other adolescents with disabilities (without ASD) were also included as participants in the study.

Results showed that the self-monitoring with technology intervention was successful in maintaining the on-task behavior of the participant with ASD. Student satisfaction while using the I-Connect program was positive and showed that he also improved work completion and accuracy of performance, and his class grades. Moreover, at 2- and 4-week maintenance probes after the formal reversal design experiment was removed, the on-task behavior of the participant was found to be at 93% and 100% of the desired target behavior level. It appears that the use of self-monitoring of classroom behavior with the I-Connect program is worth implementing in classrooms serving adolescents with ASD.

In another self-monitoring of behavior study comparable to Clemons et al. (2016), Rosenbloom et al. (2019) also used the I-Connect program with four adolescent males with ASD who demonstrated verbal and physical-motor disruptive behavior in classrooms. Rosenbloom et al. used an ABAB withdrawal design with a maintenance phase, and demonstrated a functional relation between the introduction of the I-Connect intervention with task completion and on-task behavior of the four participants. One of the four participants also decreased his disruptive classroom behaviors, and all participants and teachers expressed satisfaction with the students' change in classroom behavior. Once again, empirical evidence shows that a simple, yet effective intervention such as self-monitoring of behavior with the I-Connect program holds promise in serving older students with ASD with classroom-based, inappropriate behavior.

Osborne et al. (2019) used a multi-treatment (a.k.a. multi-component or changing conditions) SCD to measure the efficacy of a "Stay, Play, Talk" (SPT) treatment (with self-monitored contingencies and variations) on the socially oriented behaviors of two preschool children (one 4-year-old girl, and one 5-year-old boy) with ASD. The self-monitored group contingency involved teaching the students with ASD to be in close physical proximity of a peer (i.e., Stay), engage with a peer and participate in a similar activity (i.e., Play), and verbally comment or ask a question about what the peer was doing, or say the peer's name in conversation (i.e., Talk). A self-monitoring group contingency was taught to the students with ASD in that they decided, individually, whether the play groups behaved in such a way that all participants earned a predetermined award (i.e., they engaged in Stay, Play, and Talk at criterion levels) after a brief period in the classroom. Another experimental comparison condition involved recorded reminders to the participants to Stay, Play, and Talk and a cue to remember the group contingency that was to be determined at the end of the period. Observation sessions lasted five minutes in duration across all phases of the multi-treatment SCD study which included baseline, a Stay, Play, Talk measurement phase, a Stay, Play, Talk with self-monitored group contingency phase, and a Stay, Play, Talk, with recorded reminders. Various other combinations of the multi-component interventions were also implemented.

Results showed that in terms of Play behavior, the Stay, Play, and Talk intervention(s) did not show a functional relationship with the participants' with ASD behavior. Regarding the Stay behavior measured, the recorded reminders to the two students with ASD stabilized their level of "staying with" their play peer. The presence of the recorded reminders also demonstrated a functional relationship with the boy with ASD in terms of his Talk with classmates. Given the multi-treatment interference possible with three different SCD treatment phases, and changing three different target behaviors as the goal, perhaps it is not surprising that the change in the dependent variable in the study was minimal. The interventions, collectively, improved the stability of the target behaviors across the two participants with ASD, but additional research is necessary to determine if the group of selected treatments, in the manner used in the study, is worthwhile. The self-monitoring group contingency implemented in the Osborne et al. (2019) study, in particular, needs further experimentation and development among students with ASD.

Carr et al. (2014) conducted a meta-analysis of 23 SCD studies that examined self-management (which included self-monitoring of various classroom behaviors) interventions among students with ASD. The researchers concentrated on only studies that attempted to increase appropriate or positive behavior in students with ASD. It should be noted that there are several meta-analysis and individual study effect size calculation methods (e.g., nonparametric methods, standardized mean difference measurement, regression model methods) present in the existing literature. Likewise, there are many opinions on the best way in which to perform a SCD research meta-analysis. Given the choice, Carr et al. used the percentage of non-overlapping data in their individual study effect size calculations. Study dependent variables included self-monitoring, self-recording and reinforcement, academic skills, social skills, and others. In addition, studies were separated into concentrating on either high- or low-functioning students with ASD.

Results of the Carr et al. (2014) meta-analysis show that self-management procedures of various types can be considered "effective treatment" for increasing numerous desired behaviors among students of all ages with ASD. Remarkably, five studies included in the meta-analysis also reported a collateral *decrease* in inappropriate classroom behavior (which was not a goal of the self-management research) among the study participants. The self-management interventions were most effective with adolescents, followed by other ages of school-aged pupils. More robust self-management effect sizes were shown with the students with ASD who were higher functioning (vs. lower functioning students). Interventions such as self-recording, self-reinforcement, prompting, and peer involvement all showed high effect sizes when chosen as part of the intervention package for students with ASD. In essence, the Carr et al. findings show that if a teacher wants to improve the classroom behavior of students with ASD and, at the same time, allow the student to control his or her own behavior, look no further than self-management techniques. Students with ASD managing their own behavior can lead directly to effective classroom management of such learners.

Imasaka et al. (2020) used self-management of behavior to increase classroom behavioral compliance (see next section for more on compliance behavior instruction in classrooms) and on-task behavior of two students (i.e., 8-yr.-old boys) with ASD and attention-deficit hyperactivity disorder (ADHD) in general education, second-grade settings, in Australia. The researchers used event recording to count the students' compliance behavior in a multiple baseline across three, 40-minute instructional settings design. A 10s momentary time sampling recording system was also implemented to simultaneously tabulate on-task classroom behavior of the two participants with ASD. The students were provided sheets to self-record their displayed compliance behavior in the classrooms. The participants with ASD were told to place a smiley face on a prepared recording sheet for each time they complied with their teachers' request in the classroom. The compliance response to teacher instructions and the students' on-task behavior (e.g., staying in one's seat, among other overt behaviors) were the dependent variables.

Imasaka et al. (2020) showed that both participants with ASD increased in behavioral compliance and on-task attention as a result of the self-management intervention, and the level of behavioral improvement of both students was maintained after the intervention was faded. Likewise, regarding the external validity of the experimental behavioral change post intervention, both participants' levels of on-task behavior in class also compared favorably to those of their peers (i.e., who did not receive the intervention) over time. If self-management procedures are implemented vigilantly over time, it appears that the inappropriate behaviors of young students with ASD can be reduced, and classroom management for elementary level teachers can advance.

Xu et al. (2017) used a changing criterion SCD to investigate whether a self-monitoring of overt behavior intervention could increase academic engagement and decrease disruptive classroom behavior of a student with ASD (i.e., a 9-year-old boy) in China. The participant's engagement and disruptive behaviors were measured in a public elementary school; he was taught the behavioral self-recording methodology at a university-affiliated autism research center. The target behaviors that the young boy was to display during the classroom observation periods included (a) "I did not play with things; (b) I sat on the chair nicely; (c) I looked at the teacher, blackboard, or PPT; and (d) I did what the teacher said" (p. 109). A one-minute, whole interval behavior recording system was taught to the participant with ASD and, when accurate in recording and increasing the level of his academic engagement in a session, the participant received desired reinforcement that was pre-selected. Both the experimenter and the partici-pant engaged in the same classroom behavior recording system; the experimenter signaled the partici-pant at the end of each one-minute observation to record whether he displayed the engaged academic behavior and did not engage in any disruptive behavior during the previous one-minute observation period.

Results showed that the self-monitoring of engaged academic behavior and inappropriate dis-ruptive conduct was instrumental in improving the participant's behavior over five phases of the SCD study, and during a maintenance period. The participant with ASD improved from a baseline average of below 20% academic engaged behavior to well over 70% in the closing phases of the study. Regarding social validity assessment of the entire project, the participant's teacher, mother, and grand-father were also satisfied with the self-management of troublesome behavior results displayed by the participant with ASD. Improvement in a child's behavior over time is simple enough evidence to be pleasing to significant others in the child's life, and self-management of behavior can deliver such progress. It is therefore suggested for use with students with ASD as an aide in effective classroom management.

For those interested, Schulze (2016) provides researchers and educators additional information on implementation of self-management classroom strategies for students with ASD.

Classroom Management and Behavioral Compliance of Students with ASD

Classroom behavior compliance issues among students of all ages with ASD has had a long history in educational research. Because of the tendency of students with ASD to display undesirable behaviors in classrooms, teachers and researchers have used many successful treatments to reduce such inappro-priate behavior. Below we review studies that used a variety of interventions to improve the behav-ioral compliance of students with ASD.

Vargo and Brown (2020) evaluated variations of the *Good Behavior Game* (GBG) to decrease the classroom problem behaviors of six (male) high school students. The students selected for the SCD research were educated in a "structured learning classroom," and had a history of inappropriate behaviors that prevented their inclusion in general education classrooms. The disruptive behaviors that were common among the participants included refusal to follow directions, out-of-seat behavior, making noises, noncompliance, and arguing with adults. A multi-element (with a reversal condition) research design was used with the GBG game in the classroom. Briefly, the GBG operated in such a manner that team points were earned for every occurrence of a disruptive behavior in the class-room. The team with the lowest number of points at the end of an observation period earned the special reinforcement from the teacher. After examining the baseline levels of disruptive behaviors demonstrated, the teacher set a behavioral goal for the two GBG teams in the classroom (with 3 students on each team) at 50% of the total of inappropriate behaviors demonstrated during a 40-minute math period. A 30-second partial interval recording system was used to count the students' inappropriate behavior occurrences. The GBG variations used to determine the specific type of intervention included (a) traditional GBG; (b) a *ClassDoJo* version where the interactive computer tool, ClassDoJo, was used to tabulate inappropriate behavior points; and (c) a *ClassBadges* GBG, where team points were displayed on another electronic screen similar to that used with ClassDoJo.

Vargo and Brown (2020) showed that during the initial baseline, inappropriate behavior occurred, on average, during 55% of the recording intervals. When the interventions were applied, the disruptive classroom behavior decreased to 7% (i.e., of all observed intervals) during trad-itional GBG and during the ClassBadges phases, and just 4% during the ClassDoJo intervention. Four of the six participants favored the singular use of ClassDoJo, and two students preferred the traditional GBG alone to reduce their inappropriate behavior in the classroom. The GBG plus the addition of ClassDoJo technology, therefore, appears to be a viable intervention package to decrease the inappropriate behaviors (including noncompliance) of students with ASD in classrooms. Fewer disruptive behaviors displayed in the classroom leads directly to better classroom management.

An oft-used classroom management intervention related to rules and expectations, the Color Wheel System (CWS), was applied to students with ASD in Aspiranti et al. (2019). When used in classrooms, the CWS provides structure so that students know what is expected behaviorally throughout instructional periods, and reminds students how to act in the classroom environment throughout the entire school day. In Aspiranti et al., the researchers implemented the CWS in three separate classrooms (i.e., in two, K-2 settings, and one in a grade 3–5 setting; in a special school for students with ASD) with sets of rules (i.e., red, yellow, green) that were dependent on the activity occurring in classrooms. The classroom rules specific to the red condition included "eyes on teacher," "in seat," and "no talking;" yellow rules comprised "inside voices," "hands and feet to self," and "follow directions;" and the green rules involved "use inside/quiet voices" and other behaviors duplicated in the other color conditions. The intent of the CWS was to encourage students to behave in certain appropriate ways dependent upon the activity occurring in the classroom, and to allow for smooth transitions from one activity to the next throughout the school day.

Aspiranti et al. (2019) used a 20-second partial interval behavior recording procedure in a multiple baseline across classrooms SCD. Observation and recording sessions lasted 20 minutes. Disruptive behaviors (i.e., inappropriate vocalizations in two classrooms, and out-of-seat behavior in one setting) were recorded and graphed to determine whether the CWS had a functional relationship with reducing the two, specific disruptive behaviors related to compliance. Results showed that the two types of inappropriate behavior consistently decreased under the CWS intervention. Moreover, the reduced disruptive behavior across the three selected classrooms lasted into a maintenance phase. Overall effect sizes were medium to large across the three classrooms. The CWS system provides for flexibility in student compliance classroom management and, when implemented with fidelity, is recommended as an evidence-based practice with students with ASD. Of particular benefit is its ease of implementation across many different types of classrooms.

Additional Concerns Related to Classroom Management of Students with ASD

It should be noted that other issues arise when considering classroom management and related topics of students with ASD. Schwartz (2019), for example, concluded that while many teachers understand the importance of the social-emotional competence of their students, few know the ways in which it can be taught in classrooms—even teachers not serving students with ASD. Many teachers have difficulty addressing the psychological and behavioral distress of students regardless of whether a student has ASD, and such students strain the pedagogical skill of teachers (Schwartz, 2019). This omission in the skills of teachers of all types falls on teacher training institutions of higher education. In fact, the teacher training programs found in many colleges and universities do not require students to develop classroom management skills as part of degree requirements (Stevenson et al., 2020). Unfortunately, this important issue remains: the social, behavioral, and emotional competence of students with ASD must be constantly addressed in school and, by training pre-service and in-service teachers in how to deal with such issues, classroom behavior management will benefit.

The social validity of the research reviewed herein also needs to be addressed to completely understand its contribution to the knowledge base and body of interventions known to be efficacious for classroom management of students with ASD. Social validity as a construct pertaining to research has been described in many ways—for decades—using various terms such as social significance, educational relevance, and cultural validity, among others (see Carter & Wheeler, 2019). Another way to examine the social validity of intervention research, such as that reviewed above, is to ask the question: If you had to repeat a student-behavior change study, and include all the steps and separate factors in the research design, (e.g., selecting the specific intervention, gaining permission from all concerned, repeatedly measuring the target behavior, instructing fellow investigators, etc.) is it worth doing again? Behavior change research is difficult and time consuming, just as preserving the newly learned classroom-based behavior of a student with ASD can be challenging. Maintaining the learned behavior of a student with ASD over time is also a form of social validity and must not be ignored in judging the contribution of any study (Kennedy, 2002).

To provide just one example of what is meant by social validity in the research reviewed above, and its difficulty, consider the experimental steps that were necessary in the Xu et al. (2017) study. To change the behavior in the desired direction of the 9-year-old participant with ASD, Xu et al. stated that it was necessary to conduct 29, 15-minute, self-monitoring training sessions for the participant *before the actual behavioral recording in the study occurred.* That equals 7 hours and 15 minutes, and such a research component could be viewed as a *very* arduous element of the study. Reflecting on such an important issue, perhaps the social validity of the entire study needs to be reconsidered in addition to the success of the intervention. Other studies with even greater complexity surely exist pertaining to classroom and behavior management of students with ASD, and an informed interpreter of research needs to consider all the factors of a study before claiming its efficacy, merit for replication, and robustness of social validity. Moreover, it is also wise to grasp that complexity of research methodology is not validation of scholarly contribution. The concept of social validity, therefore, is important to keep in mind whenever reviewing classroom management research no matter who the target participant, sample, or population (i.e., students with ASD) may be.

An additional issue related to classroom management of students with ASD needs to be considered. While most studies reviewed above used ABA techniques to affect change in students' behavior and therefore improve classroom management (which we wholeheartedly approve), a constructivist perspective of classroom management also exists (see Postholm, 2013). Constructivism is not behaviorism. In a constructivist view of education, students are involved in shaping their own learning and teachers fill secondary roles not as direct instructors but as facilitators and scaffolders of student learning in classrooms. A constructivist philosophy may be successful with typical students without disabilities, but for many students with ASD, who have difficulties in cognitive functioning, social interactions, and communication (among other issues), it may be difficult to adopt such a mindset when instructing such students. Embracing constructivism in classroom management for students with ASD, therefore, may be too challenging even for the most effective general or special education teacher.

Conclusions

This chapter reviewed research related to behaviorally oriented interventions that attempted to support the needs of students with ASD in classrooms. The treatments found in the research cited above should be used to enhance effective classroom management needed to maximize the potential for student success in school. Although most of the research reviewed above is directed toward younger learners with ASD and their intensive support needs, the studies highlight important tools that can be used to address the various needs of such students. Improperly serving students with ASD in school can cause classroom management problems and negatively impact other student outcomes (Bouck & Park, 2018).

Establishing successful classroom management is critical for teachers of students with ASD, but effective classroom management also depends on factors such as established behavioral expectations that enhance the classroom environment and lead to desired behaviors (Aspiranti et al., 2019; Myburgh et al., 2020; Sabornie & Pennington, 2015). Direct instruction and repetition of social-behavioral expectations is needed for learners with ASD across settings. Students with ASD cannot be expected to incidentally learn and follow classroom rules that are not regularly reviewed and reinforced, and the unwritten social code that exists in schools may be difficult for them to master (Byrne, 2020). The research reviewed above also reinforces the need for continuous professional development in classroom management and other associated issues (e.g., applied behavior analysis) pertaining to students with ASD. In doing so, educational outcomes should improve for students with ASD related to social aspects of behavior, behavior compliance, and self-management of behavior (Irvin et al., 2015; Myburgh et al., 2020; Steinbrenner et al., 2020).

Assisting students with ASD to understand and identify the verbal and nonverbal clues others may demonstrate when they are offended, misunderstand, and experience frustration must also be an essential component of instruction for proper classroom behavior management (Aspiranti et al., 2019; Myburgh et al., 2020; Vargo & Brown, 2020). Teachers concerned with classroom management of students with ASD must teach and integrate social skills instruction into their practice on a regular basis (Dean & Chang, 2021; Steinbrenner et al., 2020). Other skills to be taught to students with ASD that can assist teachers in effective classroom management include behavioral modeling (Diorio et al., 2019; Irvin et al., 2015; Sadler, 2019), social narratives (Aspiranti et al., 2019; Myburgh et al., 2020), self-management techniques (Vargo & Brown, 2020), and contingent reinforcement to help students recognize when they are stressed and how to effectively manage their emotions (Xu et al., 2017). The regular use of "teacher talk" to emphasize and explain thinking, reasoning, and problem solving can be used to teach learners the "thinking process" (metacognition) needed to monitor and correct problems in their understanding. Teaching learners to use and manage their own supports can assist them in regulating their emotions and reducing undesired behaviors in the classroom (Irvin et al., 2015; Steinbrenner et al., 2020).

The social, behavioral, and emotional competence of students with ASD must be constantly addressed in educational settings so teachers can provide effective instruction (Stevenson et al., 2020). In other words, without constant attention directed toward the plethora of students' educational needs—of all types—effective classroom management related to students with ASD will be difficult to demonstrate.

References

Aspiranti, K. B., Bebech, A., Ruffo, B., & Skinner, C. H. (2019). Classroom management in self-contained classrooms for children with autism: Extending research on the color wheel system. *Behavior Analysis in Practice*, *12*(1), 143–153. https://doi.org/ 10.1007/s40617-018-0264-6

Bakar, R. A., & Zubair, H. D. (2018). Social stories: A creative way in minimizing disruptive behaviours among autisitc learners. In R. A. Bakar & H. A. Zubair (Eds.), *Creativity in Teaching and learning: A blueprint for success* (pp. 9–14). University Teknologi, Malaysia.

Bouck, E. C., & Park, J. (2018). Exploring post-school outcomes across time out of school for students with autism spectrum disorder. *Education and Training in Autism and Developmental Disabilities*, *53*(3), 253–263. https://doi.org/10.2307/26563466

Brophy, J. (2006). History of research on classroom management. In C. M. Evertson & C. S. Weinstein (Eds.), *Handbook of classroom management. Research, practice, and contemporary issues* (pp. 17–43). Lawrence Erlbaum Associates.

Byrne, J. P. (2020). Perceiving the social unknown: How the hidden curriculum affects the learning of autistic students in higher education. *Innovations in Education and Teaching International*, 1–8. https://doi.org/10.1080/14703297.2020.1850320

Carr, M. E., Moore, D. W., & Anderson, A. (2014). Self-management interventions on students with autism: A meta-analysis of single-subject research. *Exceptional Children*, *81*(1), 28–44. https://doi.org/10.1177/001440 2914532235

Carter, S. L., & Wheeler, J. J. (2019). *The social validity manual: Subjective evaluation of interventions* (2nd ed.). Academic Press.

Clemons, L. L., Mason, B. A., Garrison-Kane, L., & Wills, H. P. (2016). Self-monitoring for high school students with disabilities: A cross-categorical investigation of *I-Connect*. *Journal of Positive Behavior Interventions*, *18*(3), 145–155. https://psycnet.apa.org/ doi/10.1177/1098300715596134

Cooper, J. T., & Scott, T. M. (2017). The keys to managing instruction and behavior: Considering high prob-ability practices. *Teacher Education and Special Education*, *40*(2), 102–113. https://doi.org/10.1177%2F08884 06417700825

Dean, M., & Chang, Y. C. (2021). A systematic review of school-based social skills interventions and observed social outcomes for students with autism spectrum disorder in inclusive settings. *Autism*, *25*(7), 1828–1843. https://doi.org/10.1177/13623613211012886

Diorio, R., Bray, M., Sanetti, L., & Kehle, T. (2019). Using video self-modeling to increase compliance to classroom requests in students with autism spectrum disorder. *International Journal of School & Educational Psychology*, 7(1), 145–157. https://doi.org/10.1080/21683603.2018.1443857

Divoll, K. A., & Ribeiro, A. R. (2021). Strategies to overcome middle school teachers' classroom management stress. In C. B. Gaines, & K. M. Hutson, (Eds.), *Promoting positive learning experiences in middle school education* (pp. 217–235). IGI Global. http://doi:10.4018/978-1-7998-7057-9.ch012

Emmer, E. T., & Sabornie, E. J. (Eds.) (2015). *Handbook of classroom management* (2nd. ed.). Routledge.

Gengoux, G. W. (2015). Priming for social activities: Effects on interaction between children with Autism and typically developing peers. *Journal of Positive Behavior Interventions*, 17(3), 181–192. https://doi.org/10.1177%2F1098300714561862

Gilmour, A. F., Majeika, C. E., Sheaffer, A. W., & Wehby, J. H. (2019). The coverage of classroom management in teacher evaluation rubrics. *Teacher Education and Special Education*, 42(2), 161–174. https://doi.org/10.1177%2F0888406418781918

Hammond, R. K., Campbell, J. M., & Ruble, L. A. (2013). Considering identification and service provision for students with autism spectrum disorders within the context of response to intervention. *Exceptionality*, 21(1), 34–50. https://doi.org/10.1080/09362835. 2013.750119

Hanrahan, R., Smith, E., Johnson, H., Constantin, A., & Brosnan, M. (2020). A pilot randomized control trial of digitally-mediated social stories for children on the autism spectrum. *Journal of Autism and Developmental Disorders*, 50, 4243–4257. https://doi.org/10.1007/s10803-020-04490-8

Imasaka, T., Leen, P. L., Anderson, A., Wong, C. W. R., Moore, D. W., Furlonger, B. N., & Bussaca, M. (2020). Improving compliance in primary school students with autism spectrum disorder. *Journal of Behavioral Education*, 29(4), 763–786. https://doi. org/10.1007/s10864-019-09346-5

Irvin, D. W., Boyd, B. A., & Odom, S. L. (2015). Adult talk in the inclusive classroom and the socially competent behavior of preschoolers with autism spectrum disorder. *Focus on Autism and Other Developmental Disabilities*, 30(3), 131–142. https://doi.org/10.1177%2F1088357614547890

Kennedy, C. H. (2002). The maintenance of behavior change as an indicator of social validity. *Behavior Modification*, 26(5), 594–604. https://doi.org/10.1177/014544502236652

Leaf, J. B., Oppenheim-Leaf, M. L., Leaf, R. B., Taubman, M., McEachin, J., Parker, T., Waks, A. B., & Moutjoy, T. (2015). What is the proof? A methodological review of studies that have utilized social stories. *Education and Training in Autism and Developmental Disabilities*, 50(2), 127–141. www.jstor.org/stable/24827530

Leifler, E., Carpelan, G., Zakrevska, A., Bölte, S., & Jonsson, U. (2020). Does the learning environment 'make the grade'? A systematic review of accommodations for children on the autism spectrum in mainstream school. *Scandinavian Journal of Occupational Therapy*, 1–16. https://doi.org/10.1080/11038128.2020.1832145

Litras, S., Moore, D. W., & Anderson, A. (2010). Using video self-modelled social stories to teach social skills to a young child with autism. *Autism Research and Treatment*, 2010, 1–9. https://dx.doi.org/10.1155%2F2010%2F834979

Maenner, M., Shaw, K., Bakian, A., Bilder, D. A., Durkin, M. S., Esler, A., Furnier, S. M., Hallas, L., Hall-Lande, J., Hudson, A., Hughes, M. M., Patrick, M., Pierce, K., Poynter, J. N., Salinas, A., Shenouda, J., Vehorn, A., Warren, Z., Costantino, J. N., …Cogswell, M. E. (2021). Prevalence and characteristics of Autism Spectrum Disorder among children aged 8 years. Autism and Developmental Disabilities Monitoring Network, 11 Sites, United States, 2018. *MMWR Surveill Summ 2021*; 70(No. SS-11), 1–16. http://dx.doi.org/10.15585/mmwr.ss7011a1

McCurdy, E. E., & Cole, C. L. (2014). Use of a peer support intervention for promoting academic engagement of students with autism in general education settings. *Journal of Autism and Developmental Disorders*, 44, 883–893. https://doi.org/10.1007/s10803-013-1941-5

McKeithan, G. K., & Sabornie, E. J. (2020). Social–behavioral interventions for secondary-level students with high-functioning autism in public school settings: A meta-analysis. *Focus on Autism and Other Developmental Disabilities*, 35(3), 165–175. https://doi.org/10.1177/1088357619890312

Meindl, J. N., Delgado, D., & Casey, L. B. (2020). Increasing engagement in students with autism in inclusion classrooms. *Children and Youth Services Review*, 111, 104854. https://doi.org/10.1016/j.childyouth.2020.104854

Mitchell, B. S., Hirn, R. G., & Lewis, T. J. (2017). Enhancing effective classroom management in schools: Structures for changing teacher behavior. *Teacher Education and Special Education*, 40(2), 140–153. https://doi.org/10.1177/0888406417700961

Morningstar, M. E., Kurth, J. A., & Johnson, P. E. (2017). Examining national trends in educational placements for students with significant disabilities. *Remedial and Special Education*, 38(1), 3–12. https://doi.org/10.1177/0741932516678327

Myburgh, L., Condy, J., & Barnard, E. (2020). Pedagogical approaches to develop social skills of learners with autism spectrum disorder: Perceptions of three foundation phase teachers. *Perspective in Education*, 38(2), 241–254. https://doi.org/10.18820/ 2519593X/pie.v38.i2.16

Osborne, K., Ledford, J. R., Martin, J., & Thorne, K. (2019). Component analysis of stay, play, talk interventions with and without self-monitored group contingencies and recorded reminders. *Topics in Early Childhood Special Education, 39*(1), 5–18. https://doi.org/10. 1177%2F0271121418815236

Pearson, J. N. (2015). Disparities in diagnoses and access to services for African American Children with Autism Spectrum Disorder. *DADD Online Journal, 2*, 52–65.

Postholm, M. B. (2013). Classroom management: What does research tell us? *European Educational Research Journal, 12*(3), 389–402. http://dx.doi.org/10.2304/ eerj.3013.12.3.389

Rogers, S. J., & Dawson, G. (2010). *Early Start Denver Model for young children with autism: Promoting language, learning, and engagement.* Guilford.

Rosen, T. E., Mazefsky, C. A., Vasa, R. A., & Lerner, M. D. (2018). Co-occurring psychiatric conditions in autism spectrum disorder. *International Review of Psychiatry, 30*(1), 40–61. https://doi.org/10.1080/09540 261.2018.1450229

Rosenbloom, R., Wills, H. P., Mason, R., Huffman, J. M., & Mason, B. A. (2019). The effects of a technology-based self-monitoring intervention on on-task, disruptive, and task-completion behaviors for adolescents with autism. *Journal of Autism and Developmental Disorders, 49*(12), 5047–5062. https://doi.org/10.1007/s10 803-019-04209-4

Sabornie, E. J., & Pennington, M. L. (2015). Classroom and behavior management research in special education environments. In E. T. Emmer & E. J. Sabornie (Eds.), *Handbook of classroom management* (2nd ed.; pp. 186–204). Routledge.

Sadler, K. M. (2019). Video self-modeling and functional behavior assessment to modify aggressive behaviors in students with autism spectrum disorder and intellectual disabilities. *Education and Training in Autism and Developmental Disabilities, 54*(4), 406–419. www.daddcec.com/uploads/2/5/2/0/2520220/ etadd_december_54_4_2019.pdf

Scheuermann, B., Webber, J., & Lang, R. (2019). *Autism: Teaching makes a difference.* Cengage Learning.

Scherzinger, M., & Wettstein, A. (2019). Classroom disruptions, the teacher–student relationship and classroom management from the perspective of teachers, students and external observers: A multimethod approach. *Learning Environments Research, 22*(1), 101–116. https://doi.org/10.1007/s10984-018-9269-x

Schulze, M. A. (2016). Self-management strategies to support students with ASD. *Teaching Exceptional Children, 48*(5), 225–231. https://doi.org/10.1177%2F0040059916640759

Schwartz, S. (2019). Teachers support social–emotional learning, but say students in distress strain their skills. *Education Week, 38*(37), 1, 12–13. www.edweek.org/leadership/ teachers-support-social-emotional-learning-but-say-students-in-distress-strain-their-skills/2019/07

Sesso, G., Cristofani, C., Berloffa, S., Cristofani, P., Fantozzi, P., Inguaggiato, E., Narzisi, A., Pfanner, C., Ricci, F., Tacchi, A., Valente, E., Viglione, V., Milone, A., & Masi, G. (2020). Autism spectrum disorder and disruptive behavior disorders comorbidities delineate clinical phenotypes in attention-deficit hyperactivity disorder: Novel insights from the assessment of psychopathological and neuropsychological profiles. *Journal of Clinical Medicine, 9*(12), 3839. https://doi.org/10.3390/jcm9123839.

Siddiqua, A., Janus, M., Mesterman, R., Duku, E., Georgiades, K., Saxena, F., ... & Saunders, N. (2021). Primary care provider and child characteristics associated with age of diagnosis of autism spectrum disorder: A population-based cohort study. *Journal of Autism and Developmental Disorders*, 1–15. https://doi.org/10.1007/ s10803-021-05165-8

Snyder, T. D., de Brey, C., and Dillow, S. A. (2018). *Digest of Education Statistics 2016* (NCES 2017-094). National Center for Education Statistics, Institute of Education Sciences, U.S. Department of Education. Washington, DC.

Steinbrenner, J. R., Hume, K., Odom, S. L., Morin, K. L., Nowell, S. W., Tomaszewski, B., Szendrey, S., McIntyre, N. S., Yucesoy-Ozkan, S., & Savage, M. N. (2020). *Evidence-based practices for children, youth, and young adults with autism.* The University of North Carolina at Chapel Hill, Frank Porter Graham Child Development Institute, National Clearinghouse on Autism Evidence and Practice Review Team.

Stevenson, N. A., VanLone, J., & Barber, B. R. (2020). A commentary on the misalignment of teacher education and the need for classroom behavior management skills. *Education and Treatment of Children, 43*(4), 393–404. https://doi.org/10.1007/s43494-020-00031-1

Strain, P. S., & Hoyson, M. (2000). The need for longitudinal, intensive social skills intervention: LEAP follow-up outcomes for children with autism. *Topics in Early Childhood Special Education, 20*, 116–122. https://doi.org/ 10.1177% 2F027112140002000207

Thompson, R., & Johnston, S. S. (2017). Examination of social story format on frequency of undesired behaviors. *Journal of the American Academy of Special Education Professionals*, Spr-Sum, 83–107.

Travers, J., & Krezmien, M. (2018). Racial disparities in autism identification in the United States during 2014. *Exceptional Children, 84*(4), pp. 403–419. https://doi.org/10.1177/0014402918771337

Vargo, K., & Brown, C. (2020). An evaluation of and preference for variations of the Good Behavior Game with students. *Behavioral Interventions, 35*(4), 560–570. https://doi.org/10.1002/bin.1740

Vivanti, G., Dissanayake, C., Duncan, E., Feary, J., Capes, K., Upson, S., Bent, C. A., Rogers, S. J., & Hudry, K. (2019). Outcomes of children receiving Group-Early Start Denver Model in an inclusive versus autism-specific setting: A pilot randomized controlled trial. *Autism, 23*(5), 1165–1175. https://doi.org/10.1177/1362361318801341

Xu, S., Wang, J., Lee, G. T., & Luke, N. (2017). Using self-monitoring with guided goal setting to increase academic engagement for a student with autism in an inclusive classroom in China. *The Journal of Special Education, 51*(2), 106–114. https://doi.org/10.1177/0022466916679980

Yingling, M. E., Hock, R. M., & Bell, B. A. (2018). Time-lag between diagnosis of autism spectrum disorder and onset of publicly-funded early intensive behavioral intervention: do race–ethnicity and neighborhood matter?. *Journal of Autism and Developmental Disorders, 48*(2), 561–571. https://doi.org/10.1007/s10803-017-3354-3

28

CLASSROOM MANAGEMENT IN EARLY CHILDHOOD EDUCATION

Marissa A. Bivona and Amanda P. Williford

UNIVERSITY OF VIRGINIA

Introduction

In settings that serve young children, classroom management (CM) is rooted in everyday routines and connections that serve as points of reference for the group. As children separate from caregivers, wash their hands, listen to stories, work together in centers, share meals, greet classmates, and rest and play, they deepen their understanding of how their needs connect to those of a larger community. Educators play an essential role in this process, as they work to understand and meet young children's physical and emotional needs, and create opportunities for children to care for themselves and others.

Classroom management is often defined as the strategies and systems used by educators to promote on-task behavior, and prevent and manage disruptive behaviors, with the goal of maximizing time children spend engaged in learning (Henley, 2007; Skiba et al., 2016; van Driel et al., 2021). However, this definition does not map entirely onto early childhood education (ECE) settings where learning is not separate from being cared for and occurs during all parts of the day (e.g., during meals and transitions). Additionally, young children are learning how to be with others in a group, while navigating the classroom environment (Blair & Raver, 2016; Jung, 2020; Rosanbalm & Murray, 2018). Educators use CM practices to meet children's needs and support their cognitive and social-emotional development. Practices that help children to feel physically and emotionally safe, cared for, heard, unconditionally accepted, and connected to themselves, their teachers, and their peers, are part of effective CM.

In this chapter, we examine CM from a child–centered perspective which shifts from the goal of maintaining order to providing opportunities for each child to fully develop and find their role within the classroom community. Approaching CM from a child–centered perspective means that teachers trust young children to consider and act on deep questions, including how their actions impact others, how to respond to injustice, and what it means to have agency (Adair & Sachdeva, 2021; Neuman et al., 2000; Shalaby, 2020). Shalaby (2020) captures this conceptualization when she asserted that CM is a response to the questions: "'How will we be in a genuine community together?', 'How will we keep everyone safe, happy and well?', 'What will we do when harm or conflict happens in our community?', and 'How will we take extra care of the most vulnerable among us?'" (p.43).

DOI: 10.4324/9781003275312-33

In this chapter we: (a) review CM in ECE, exploring how children's behaviors are perceived and regulated, and the ways that methods not grounded in an understanding of context have been harmful; (b) describe current tensions in conceptualizing and enacting CM practices in ECE; (c) offer frameworks to guide understanding of CM; (d) outline key strategies aligned with these frameworks; and (e) acknowledge constraints unique to ECE as well as resources that can facilitate a shift toward CM from a child- and community-centered orientation.

CM in an ECE Context

The birth to five period lays the foundation for children's cognitive and social-emotional development (Denham et al., 2003; Diamond, 2012). The relationships teachers form with children, and the priorities and norms they set within the classroom, serve as the primary context outside of the home for young children to make sense of the world around them and how they fit into it (Hamre & Pianta, 2001; Housman, 2017; McNally & Slutsky, 2018; Williford et al., 2013, 2017). Access to affirming experiences and care in well-managed classrooms provides space for young children to continue developing their sense of self and role within the community (Diamond & Lee, 2011; Shonkoff & Philips, 2000; Zelazo & Carlson, 2012). In ECE, this learning is woven throughout the everyday routines, and interpersonal exchanges that occur as children care for themselves and their peers (The National Association for the Education of Young Children, 2005; Neuman et al., 2000; Shalaby, 2020). Explicit scaffolding of children's capacities such as conflict resolution, communication, empathy, and assertiveness support children's skills to relate to others and therefore is part of CM. The emphasis on the link between children's physical and mental well-being and their engagement with learning has expanded beyond ECE through social-emotional curricula (Prothero, 2021; Regenstein, 2019).

Approaching CM from a child-centered and relational perspective that is integrated into curriculum and classroom routines is beneficial not just in ECE, but for children of all ages. This framework rests on the assumptions that children are entitled to affirming care and learning experiences, engage in behaviors that are not inherently positive or negative, and are capable of fulfilling their potential when provided with strengths-based, culturally relevant expectations and support.

Reframing Challenging Behavior

Challenging behavior is defined as the behaviors and patterns of behavior that interfere with students' learning and relationships with others (Hemmeter et al., 2008; The National Institute for Care and Health Excellence, 2015). Discussions of CM often center around preventing or stopping behaviors adults perceive as challenging or disruptive. However, this definition is adult-centered and does not consider that children's behaviors are a response to their environment and convey important information about what they need to be successful within their environment (Jiron et al., 2013; Kaiser & Rasminsky, 2021). Behaviors can elicit assistance, support, attention, or sensory stimulation, and may help a child to avoid something they find distressing or too difficult (The National Institute for Care and Health Excellence, 2015). Young children are sensitive to external stimuli, and still developing the skills to consistently communicate their needs and regulate their emotions (The National Institute for Care and Health Excellence, 2015; Whitters, 2020). When goals of CM shift from decreasing challenging behavior to understanding function to meet children's needs, behavior is reframed as communication (Center on the Social and Emotional Foundations for Early Learning, n.d.; Jiron et. al., 2013). Observing behavior in context allows teachers to gather information about what is working or not working for a child or the group in the current environment (Shalaby, 2017).

Notably, some behaviors cause physical harm or threaten the safety and well-being of others in the community (e.g., biting, hitting, kicking), and children should be told these behaviors are not permitted and why. However, whether many other behaviors are deemed challenging depends on when and where they occur, and the adult's attributions for them. These include non-compliance and emotion dysregulation, which are frequently cited as behavioral concerns in ECE settings (Buyuktaskapu-Soydan et al., 2018; The National Institute for Care and Health Excellence, 2015).

Adult interpretations of and responses to children's behaviors are influenced by a variety of factors, including cultural norms and values. Adults decide if a child's behavior is acceptable and determine the consequences. Adults' personal experiences and biases shape their attributions and the ways they respond to children which has implications for their development and well-being (Allen et al., 2021; Essien, 2019). If an adult deems a behavior disruptive and attributes it to something internal to the child and unlikely to change (as opposed to attributing the behavior to the environment), this may cause tension or conflict, leading to restriction of freedom and fewer opportunities for the child to engage with others (Jung, 2020; Miller et al., 2017). Lack of access to these experiences means that the child misses opportunities for learning and connection that would support their social and emotional development. Unfortunately, exclusion from social and learning experiences or loss of access to materials is often used a consequence for engaging in behavior teachers perceive as disruptive (Acavitti & Williford, 2020; Emerson & Einfeld, 2011).

In practice, CM too often includes punitive responses to behaviors such as verbal reprimands, excluding children from social or learning opportunities, threatening punishment, and removing or restricting privileges. Such practices often exacerbate behaviors or create coercive cycles characterized by negative interactions with peers and adults in the environment (James et al., 2019a; Meek & Gilliam, 2016; Pierce et al., 2021). Even if these practices increase compliance or decrease the occurrence of behaviors that adults deem to be challenging, they do not support children's well-being, do not help children learn the skills they need to be successful, and are often delivered in ways that exacerbate inequities (Neitzel, 2018; Williford et al., 2021; Wymer et al., 2020). When a child is excluded, shamed, or labelled as a troublemaker, it has negative implications for their engagement in the classroom and their reputation with peers and adults (MacLure et al., 2012). Time out is a practice that falls into this category. There is evidence that brief (e.g., one to three minutes) and calmly delivered time outs provide children a break to calm down, increase compliance, and decrease behaviors that adults see as aggressive (Kazdin, 2013, 2017). However, time outs are typically not a logical consequence, do not repair harm done, and are often not used as intended. While having the choice to leave the group and calm down in a designated area (e.g., a calm down or cozy corner) can support children's ability to regulate, these areas have a tendency to be misused, with teachers sending children to them as a consequence, and thus implementing time out with a different name (Wymer et al., 2020). Conversely, CM practices that provide children with choices and opportunities to see and repair the consequences of their actions, while remaining connected to the community, meet the needs of the group and individual children (Carter & Doyle, 2006; Hemmeter et al., 2006).

Developmentally Appropriate Practice and Curriculum as CM

It is difficult to differentiate between CM curriculum and high-quality care in ECE. An enriching, developmentally appropriate curriculum and environment support CM by engaging children while giving them ownership over their experiences (Burchinal et al., 2014; Carter & Doyle, 2006; Skiba et al., 2016). Understanding expectations, demonstrating empathy, resolving conflicts, and sharing ideas support children to be part of a group and engage in learning. These capacities are also learning objectives for young children who require intentional scaffolding and explicit instruction for proper development (Blair & Raver, 2016; Rosanbalm & Murray, 2018).

An educator's approach to curriculum and teaching shape their expectations and support for children's learning, autonomy, and engagement, which sets the stage for CM (Reeve & Jang, 2006; Vitiello et al., 2012). If children are required to engage in activities that are a mismatch for their developmental stage, they will respond by engaging in behaviors that adults perceive as challenging

(The National Institute for Care and Health Excellence, 2015). Conversely, if children have the freedom to play, explore the world around them, and have a say over what happens in the classroom, they are more likely to sustain their engagement (Gagné, 2003). Agency over activities and classroom experiences allows children to practice modulating their actions and working toward goals (Savina, 2021). Providing opportunities for children to be agents of their learning conveys trust while affirming children's strengths and abilities (Benard & Slade, 2009; Bondy et al., 2007).

The process through which CM is established should be developmentally appropriate and intentional. Similar to curriculum or supporting children's learning in other areas, educators gather information and engage in reflection on practices in order to individualize for each child's needs (Escamilla & Meier, 2018).

Systemic Inequities and Biases: Barriers to Equitable CM

Structural inequities and individual biases related to race, ethnicity, income, disability status, linguistic background, and gender simultaneously shape how families, children, and behavior are perceived, and restrict access to high-quality ECE experiences that support equitable CM (The National Association for the Education of Young Children, 2016; Shewark et al., 2018). Biases impact how adults interpret and respond to behavior, including to what they attribute behavior and the type and severity of discipline they use with children (Acavitti & Williford, 2020; Dobbs & Arnold, 2009; Gilliam et al., 2016). Caregivers provide information explicitly and implicitly to young children about the world around them, including cultural norms and expectations (Belsky & Cassidy, 1994). Established norms for behavior, and practice, most often reflect the beliefs and values of the dominant culture. Notably, much of the research on child development and professional knowledge in the ECE field is based on the experiences of English-speaking, white, middle-class children and their families (The National Association for the Education of Young Children, 2019; Jipson, 1991). When these perspectives are presented as objective truths, privilege is given to the values and experiences of certain children and their families (Fleer, 2003; Kincheloe et al., 2017; Soto & Swadener, 2002).

Structural inequities restrict access to ECE programs and shape classroom processes to impact children's experiences differentially depending on ethnic, racial, linguistic, and gender identities in devastating ways (Barnett et al., 2013; Johnson-Staub, 2017; Ready & Wright, 2011). Children in the same classroom have different experiences related to autonomy over their learning and freedom of movement (Early et al., 2010; Skiba et al., 2016; Tonyan & Howes, 2003). Classroom compositions consisting of a greater proportion of children coming from lower-income households and African American or Latino children were associated with children having less free play time, less choice, more teacher-assigned activities, and adult-centered teaching approaches (Early et al., 2010).

In addition, preschool teachers' goals have been found to focus on individual needs for children from middle socio-economic status backgrounds, and on preparation for kindergarten math and literacy for children from lower socio-economic status backgrounds (Lee & Ginsberg, 2007). Teachers used more didactic and adult-directed teaching strategies with children who were not white, and child-directed scaffolding with white children (Early et al., 2010). White children over three in childcare tended to have more interactions with adults, and more time for free play, while African American children spent less time playing and less time in educational, learning, and goal-directed activities (Tonyan & Howes, 2003; Winsler & Carlton, 2003). Gender biases have also been observed to shape children's experiences in childcare, with boys engaging in more non-educational activities, and girls engaging in more language arts and creative play (Tonyan & Howes, 2003). These inequities in access to culturally responsive and developmentally appropriate care are unjust, do not meet children's needs, and detrimentally impact children from minoritized groups. It is increasingly likely that children will engage in behaviors that adults see as challenging in these settings because expectations are unfair and inappropriate (Lerkkanen et al., 2016).

Ineffective and inequitable CM practices also lead to exclusion through expulsion or suspension (Zinsser et al., 2014). Suspension and expulsions occur at alarming rates that are more frequent in early childhood settings than in older grades (Gilliam & Shahar, 2006; Stegelin, 2018). In a survey of 345 center directors, 82.9% of directors reported at least one suspension request, and 64% reported at least one expulsion request in response to challenging behavior in the previous 12 months (Clayback & Hemmeter, 2021). In addition, many children are suspended and expelled informally when a family is asked to leave a program (with the explanation that a program is not "a good fit" for the child), repeatedly pick their child up early, or told that their child's needs cannot be met within a program (Neitzel, 2018). This is, in effect, the same as expulsion and occurs in settings that do not allow formal suspensions or expulsions. Suspension and expulsion are harmful to children's development and result in negative long-term outcomes. These include lack of engagement, increased conflict, and escalation of behavioral challenges in school settings (Gilliam, 2005). Suspension and expulsion disproportionately impact children from minoritized groups, including Black boys, English-language learners, and children with disabilities; thus, these children are more likely to be excluded from early learning opportunities (Clayback & Hemmeter, 2021; Gillliam & Shahar, 2006; The National Association for the Education of Young Children, 2019).

A major issue in the field of ECE is how to enact CM in ways that limit how individual and systemic biases adversely impact children's access to and experiences in early care, while giving each child opportunities to bring strengths and perspectives to learn alongside others (The National Association for the Education of Young Children, 2019). Eliminating individual bias is not possible. However, moving toward a child-centered framework of CM where teachers reflect on systemic and personal biases and how they attribute child behavior provides a starting point to meet every child's needs, create an environment that is conducive to equitable CM, and choose more effective responses to behavior.

Frameworks for Understanding and Enacting Equitable CM in ECE Settings

Critical Awareness of Context and Commitment to Promoting Equity in CM

Awareness of the ways in which systemic inequities impact the daily lives of individuals is a key precursor to engaging in equitable CM practices (Iruka et al., 2020). Classroom management in ECE is often framed as community building. The goal of community building is for all children to feel a sense of safety, belonging, and ownership. This requires educators to explore and be aware of historical oppression and present-day inequities, and how these forces shape the realities of children in their care (Shalaby, 2020). Reflection on individual identity, personal biases, and the ways they shape interactions within the classroom should inform CM (Friedman & Mwenelupembe, 2020; hooks, 2003; Iruka et al., 2020). Recognizing that all people bring beliefs and practices influenced by identity and experience promotes meaningful changes in perspective and practice (Gonzalez-Mena & Shareef, 2005). When paired with ongoing action and reflection cycles, awareness of individual prejudices and motivation to change can decrease bias in decision-making (Wymer et al., 2020).

Culturally responsive CM practices include drawing on child and family strengths, and the ways in which culture shapes experience and identity. By recognizing nuance, and being curious about what informs children and families' identities and perspectives, care providers can better understand and learn from children and families (Derman-Sparks, 1989; Iruka et al., 2020).

Engaging in critical awareness and reflection on individual and structural biases as part of CM and curriculum serves several functions: (a) it disrupts individual biases that shape the ways educators perceive and respond to children and families, (b) it makes educators aware of the values and skills they prioritize and center in their classroom, and (c) it gives educators a framework to support young children as they explore questions related to justice, identity, and belonging (Freire, 1970; hooks, 2003; Ladson-Billings, 1994, 1995).

Although some adults may feel discomfort addressing issues of diversity and equity with children, or believe they are not developmentally ready to understand these concepts, young children recognize similarities and differences and strive for fairness and compassion (Adair & Sachdeva, 2021; Payne, 2018). Without intervention or explicit guidance, children become aware of and internalize biased messages communicated about gender, race, class, and ethnicity (Dunham et al., 2013; Shutts, 2015). For example, infants recognize others from their own race and begin to show own race preference between 6–13 months (Katz & Kofkin, 1997; Xiao et al., 2018). Five-year-olds randomly assigned to two groups were able to discern subtle nonverbal cues of teacher approval, and demonstrated group preference based on their observations (Brey & Pauker, 2019). Young children are capable of and uniquely positioned to engage in social justice work, including questioning inequities and working toward fairness and the collective good (Adair & Sachdeva, 2021; Payne et al., 2020; Shalaby, 2020).

All children benefit from a curriculum that explicitly acknowledges similarities and differences, addresses gender, race, and cultural biases, and works toward justice. Racial ethnic socialization, cultural socialization, and acknowledgement of systemic biases are tied to positive outcomes for children from minoritized groups (Hughes et al., 2006; Umaña-Taylor & Hill, 2020). Children of all races and ethnicities were more likely to recognize discrimination and intervene after being given messages about the value of diversity (Apfelbaum et al., 2010). Children's awareness of and attunement to adults' and systemic biases make it important to address these issues as part of CM. Developing authentic relationships, creating space to engage in culturally responsive practices, and addressing behaviors from a place of care requires educators to be dedicated to identifying and disrupting inequities so as not to replicate them in their interactions.

Community

Applying a critical lens to building inclusive ECE classroom communities requires connection, listening, and accountability (Bettez, 2011). Care, including meeting the physical and emotional needs of each child and the group, is a priority. Goals and values aligned with child-centered CM include promoting empathy, self-awareness, perspective-taking, social and group problem solving, curiosity, and exploration (Wahman & Steed, 2016; Wisneski & Goldstein, 2004). Each community member plays a role that impacts others. Building genuine community requires the establishment of shared values while viewing differences as an asset or strength. Effective teachers and classroom managers show students that they are valued for being themselves and caring for others as part of the community (Martin et al., 2012; National Association for the Education of Young Children, 2009; Wahman & Steed, 2016).

Relationships as a Foundation for Community Building

During the first few years of life, children depend on adults in their environment to meet their physical and emotional needs. Within close relationships, caregivers provide comfort in the moment, support children's regulation, and help them see the world as safe and predictable (Feldman, 2007). Co-regulation supports infants and young children to regulate physiological reactions to stress (Feldman et al., 2011). Later, relationships with a supportive adult scaffold children as they learn to regulate their emotions, manage behaviors, and use coping strategies to work through distress (Erdmann & Hertel, 2019; Gillespie, 2015). Caregiver attunement (i.e., attention to children's emotional states and responsiveness to their needs) is associated with long-term social and emotional outcomes, including empathy (Feldman & Eidelman, 2007). Research shows that children in emotionally supportive daycare classrooms experience less stress over the course of the day than those in settings with less responsive caregiving (Hatfield et al., 2013; Hatfield & Williford, 2017). These supportive interactions, grounded in warm and connected relationships, form the foundation of CM in ECE.

When children's needs are met through consistent responsive interactions, they develop self-efficacy and autonomy (Downer et al., 2010; Hamre et al., 2014; McNally & Slutsky, 2018). These interactions require caregivers to notice subtle cues and respond in sensitive and supportive ways, form authentic connections, and be aware of each child's interests, preferences, and abilities (Hamre & Pianta, 2001). Teacher–child relationship quality is consistently linked to social and emotional outcomes, which in turn support children's participation in the classroom community and their ability to have empathy and to care for others (Burchinal et al., 2014; Rucinski et al., 2018). Close relationships between teachers and the children they perceive as having behavioral challenges, support children's social development and act as a protective factor; despite the fact that such relationships may be more difficult to develop and sustain (Myers & Pianta, 2008; Nurmi, 2012).

It is common to conceptualize relationships as being contained between dyads and influenced by individual characteristics of each dyad member. The reality within classrooms is that relationships form an interconnected web, and interactions create ripple effects felt by the community. A strained relationship between a teacher and child has an impact on the whole class by requiring additional time and energy, increasing teacher stress, and sending messages about expectations and belonging to all children. Teachers cultivate community by setting the tone for peer relationships and group dynamics in the classroom (Howes et al., 2011). Teacher–child closeness, and teachers' behavior management practices, were associated with children's perceptions of their relationships with peers, and with perceptions of stronger peer relationships and support from peers (Hughes & Chen, 2011).

Although research in different contexts points to the importance of relationships in fostering children's sense of belonging and engagement with learning, research has also explored the ways in which cultural values shape these relationships (Graves & Howes, 2011; Gregoriadis et al., 2019; Ikegami & Rivalland, 2016). Identities and experiences of educators and children matter in how relationships are formed and sustained. Research shows that teacher and child race match is associated with teacher ratings of relationship quality (Murray & Murray, 2004; Howes & Shivers, 2006; Saft & Pianta, 2001), as well as teacher ratings of children's social and emotional competence and behavior (Graves & Howes, 2011). Relationships can protect against educator bias. When teachers and students had a close relationship, teachers rated aggression in Black and Hispanic students as lower (Meehan et al., 2003). Teachers may vary the strategies they use in their interactions with children depending on how they perceive that child and their identity. For example, Langeloo and colleagues (2019) found that educators individualized the strategies they used during interactions to support multilingual children, including speaking in the child's home language, and using nonverbal communication. However, the authors also found that children whose native language was not English were exposed to unequal interactions and learning opportunities.

Collaboration between school and home is both an extension of teacher–child relationships and an integral part of CM in ECE settings (Fantuzzo et al., 2000; Ma et al., 2016). A child's caregivers and close relations are the main system in which they develop (Allen & Steed, 2016; Price & Steed, 2016). Respecting families, including asking about and prioritizing their values, communicates that their perspective and input are welcome in the classroom (Cardona et al., 2012; Sheridan & Krawochowill, 2007). Being flexible and responsive to families' needs and choices, including hearing about their expectations and how they understand their child's behavior, is part of CM. Conversations with families about children's strengths, communicating on a daily basis, and sharing positive information shows families that the educator genuinely knows and cares about their child (Fantuzzo et al., 2000). Teacher's positive perceptions of a child's caregivers was associated with a lower rated risk for expulsion, especially for Black boys who had not been previously expelled (Zulauf-McCurdy & Zinsser, 2021). Close relationships between teachers and families promote empathy and understanding.

Classroom community extends to children's families, and CM should reflect their vision for their child's care and education.

In sum, the relationships established between caregivers and young children serve multiple functions in the context of CM. First, by consistently responding to and meeting children's needs, adults help children self-regulate. Genuine relationships in which an adult knows about and conveys acceptance of all aspects of a child's identity, fosters connection and belonging to the classroom community. The ways in which educators frame and scaffold social interactions between children shape how they relate to one another and the group. Relationships with families grounded in mutual respect establish a working alliance necessary to understand and meet each child's needs. Such mutual respect aides in establishing effective CM.

Key Strategies and Applications of Classroom Management

An Inclusive and Culturally Sensitive Environment

Young children learn through directly observing and experiencing ideas and concepts. When children feel safe and their needs are met, they are eager to explore the world around them. Thus, classroom organization and the environment play a central role in CM in ECE (Berti et al., 2019; Doctoroff, 2001). The classroom environment can convey acceptance by being accessible to children of different abilities, and by meaningfully reflecting the multiple identities of children and their families (Biermeier, 2015; Drew & Rankin, 2004; Mukhanji et al., 2016). Documenting and displaying children's work communicates the value of children's' learning processes and encourages conversations and reflection with caregivers (Katz & Chard, 1996; Schroeder-Yu, 2008).

Classroom organization should be guided by and facilitate daily routines (Petrakos & Howe, 1996). Furniture and materials can be intentionally arranged to align with priorities and expectations. For example, classroom set up can afford opportunities for children to practice particular skills and ways of relating to others, while limiting opportunities for engaging in unsafe behaviors (Berti et al., 2019; Schroeder-Yu, 2008). Actions and activities are directed by making boundaries and expectations clear, and safety to explore independently fosters children's autonomy in developmentally appropriate ways (Greenman, 1988). By presenting a variety of attractive, organized, accessible, hands-on materials, children are given freedom to experiment and direct their learning (Barrable, 2020; Beaty-O'Ferrall et al., 2010; Isbell & Raines, 2012; Mukhanji et al., 2016). Maintaining organization and labelling spaces for materials supports children's planning as they find, use, and return items (Epstein, 2007). Increased amounts of time spent in free choice is positively associated with children's abilities to regulate their actions (Goble & Pianta, 2017). Educators promote children's regulation by keeping the classroom organized and clean; they limit stimulation by keeping lighting, temperature, and sound at appropriate levels (Wohlfarth, 1986). Because young children are still developing the ability to self-regulate, attention to sensory aspects of the environment such as light, clutter, and colors are necessary for creating an environment conducive to positive CM (Greenman, 1988; Wohlfarth, 1986).

Creating a variety of large and small spaces to facilitate independent, parallel, and cooperative play allows children to select a space that meets their needs in the moment. This provides opportunities for children to negotiate for space and materials, communicate their needs, share ideas, cooperate, and work to resolve conflicts (The National Association for the Education of Young Children, 2009).

Young children are developing their identity and sense of self in relation to the world around them. Classroom management practices in ECE support children as they explore classroom environs. A classroom environment that is safe and stimulating supports engagement, and offers opportunities for children to assert and express ideas and needs. When young children see the ways they shape their environment, they are better able to weigh and understand the consequences of their actions, which is an essential part of CM (Solomon & Henderson, 2016; Wohlwend, 2015).

Routines and Structure to Facilitate Classroom Management

Child-centered routines give children a sense of control and predictability (Brouwers & Tomic, 2000; Hemmeter et al., 2006). Knowing that their needs will be met allows children to fully engage in the classroom community and learning activities. Educators can be mindful when creating a schedule and intentionally sequencing activities. Setting aside long periods of time for children to become immersed in free play, and limiting transitions, can prevent difficulties that may arise (The National Association for the Education of Young Children, 2009). Seeing everyday routines and activities as opportunities for learning encourages educators to slow down the pace, and not rush children through the care routines that are important to them.

Routines are everyday occurrences (e.g., mealtime, rest time, toileting, handwashing) that offer opportunities for connection and community building. Keeping consistent routines supports children in knowing what behavior is expected at different times. Such consistency, however, needs to be balanced with flexibility and adaptation to suit children's needs in the moment (Tonyan, 2015). Making sure that children understand the schedule by posting a visual guide, referencing the schedule, and asking children what comes next are all strategies that support children's understanding of daily routines that scaffold CM.

Care routines that are co-constructed by teachers, children, and families with children's needs in mind foster connection. They provide opportunities for children to care for themselves and others while developing social-emotional skills (Howell & Reinhard, 2015). Creating shared meaning during a routine strengthens emotional bonds and children's sense of belonging to the community (Spagnola & Fiese, 2007). For example, routines for greeting children and families when they arrive to the classroom, and hearing from families regarding how they prefer to separate and say goodbye to their child, can support children to manage emotions and make the transition into the classroom during a sensitive time (Hemmeter et al., 2006; National Association for the Education of Young Children, 2013). Routines have salient meaning for children when educators take children's identity and culture into account when creating them. Inviting families into the classroom to share their own traditions, including holiday celebrations, special events, stories, music, and recipes, offers opportunities for sharing knowledge and culture (Derman-Sparks, 1989).

Transitions between activities are also an important part of the classroom routine to consider from a child's perspective. Transitions can be an especially difficult time for young children. Expectations may be less clear, and demands may increase (e.g., following multi-step directions; Vitiello et al., 2012). Children are vulnerable to becoming dysregulated due to physical needs such as sleepiness or hunger, or emotional reactions, such as disappointment at needing to leave an activity (Feldman, 2007). Preparing for transitions, including giving a warning ahead of time or setting a timer, gives children the opportunity to get ready. Making expectations simple and clear and incorporating games or activities to decrease wait time helps children move smoothly to the next activity (Center on the Social and Emotional Foundations for Early Learning, n.d; The National Association for the Education of Young Children, 2009).

Creating Clear and Reasonable Expectations

Adults' ideas about young children, how they learn, and their capabilities are shaped by cultural context. It is easy for a teacher to make assumptions about children's understanding and awareness of expectations and social norms (Benard & Slade, 2009; Bondy et al., 2007; Henderson, 2012). Noncompliance, frequently reported as a "challenging behavior" in EC settings, can be a result of a variety of issues, including misunderstood, unclear, or unrealistic expectations (Yilmaz et al., 2021).

Collectively establishing expectations is a potential solution. Creating and discussing reasoning for expectations as a group weaves together empathy and collective problem solving. By engaging in this process, children understand the purpose of expectations and how they serve the community (Gable et al., 2009; Kane, 2016). Expectations should be developmentally appropriate and explained clearly. The reason for establishing and agreeing upon expectations is linked to keeping everyone safe and respecting the environment (Shalaby, 2017, 2020). The goal of establishing rules jointly in the context of CM is to provide opportunities for children to share and reflect on their responsibility to others, and how each individual's behavior impacts others within the community (Alter & Haydon, 2017). Creating rules together offers an opportunity to establish and affirm values that are reflective of the multiple identities within the group, and support for autonomy has been shown to foster internalization of rules (Laurin & Joussemet, 2017).

Expectations should be consistently revisited so that children can remember and reflect on them. Educators can do this by clarifying expectations and using reminders (e.g., having rules posted clearly, using cues and visuals, providing reminders before a change in expectations; Downer et al., 2010; Hamre et al., 2014). Class meeting time can be used by educators to scaffold developmentally appropriate discussions about violations of community agreements and to brainstorm potential solutions (Martin et al., 2016; Shalaby, 2017).

Understanding Strengths, Needs, and Behavior in Context

Part of the educator's role within CM is to know and understand the children in their care and how to support them. Setting aside time for open-ended observation of one-on-one time with each child strengthens relationships and helps providers learn about the children in their care (Hojnoski et al., 2020; Voorhees et al., 2013). Notably, dyadic interventions in which teachers spend time with children show positive outcomes related to teacher-child relationships and teacher perceptions of children's behavior (Cook et al., 2018; Davidson et al., 2021; Williford et al., 2017).

Observation helps educators better understand behavior in context. Specific observation tools can be used to better understand behaviors, but this information should always be paired with knowledge of the particular child and the environment. Functional Behavior Assessments (FBAs) should also be used to document the context surrounding a child's patterns of behavior. Use of FBAs assists adults (i.e., teachers and family members) to better understand if something that happened before or after a specific behavior under scrutiny made it more likely for the behavior to occur (Head Start, Early Childhood Learning, & Knowledge Center, n.d.; Gettinger & Stoiber, 2006; Kaiser & Rasminsky, 2003).

The goal of FBAs should be to determine how adults respond to behavior and how the environment plays a role in the occurrence of target behaviors. Educators can use FBA information in planning to adjust and assess the effectiveness of changes to (a) the environment, (b) classroom routines, and (c) teaching practices that have been shown to reduce the behaviors teachers perceived as challenging (Lambert et al., 2012; Voorhees et al., 2013). Documenting behaviors and surrounding ecologies in this way helps to understand behavior as communicating a need, and works to find an alternate way to meet that need to support a child's well-being (Arthur-Kelly et al., 2017a; Hirschland, 2015). Recording and reflecting on context via the FBA process should also capture a child's strengths. Using the FBA as a lens, teachers can understand under what circumstances the child is able to demonstrate their skills, cope with distress, and fully engage in classroom routines. When completed intentionally, and paired with reflection, documenting behaviors through FBAs helps educators decrease bias in their reporting and perceptions of behaviors. Capturing data in this way may assist in the realization that a behavior is not as extreme or occurring as frequently as initially perceived. Strong relationships with families are also essential in this process. Open communication regarding families' expectations and strategies for managing behavior at home, as well as current stresses or changes affecting a child, may impact how they interact within the classroom environment.

Universal screenings and formative assessments of children's development across domains are also ways of gathering information to identify and meet children's needs. When administered and interpreted appropriately, screening measures can identify children who might benefit from additional support or interventions (Nores & Fernandez, 2018). However, measures must be intentionally selected to ensure that they are age-appropriate, measure relevant constructs, and apply to the population of children with whom they are being used (Denham et al., 2016; The National Association for the Education of Young Children, 2019).

Collecting data on trends within a classroom, program, or district can inform training and professional development (PD), and provide information on whether resources and support are being equitably distributed (Yun et al., 2021). Data can inform supports for individual children and changes in teacher practice and the environment, but care must be shown with language and framing of results (Meloy & Schachter, 2019; Yun et al., 2021). Universal screening measures are intended to provide information about a child's demonstration of a skill or knowledge in a particular context at a particular time, and in relation to other children their age. Results do not present a full picture of a child's functioning or capacities. Ideally, assessments reveal both areas where children need additional support to further develop their abilities, and also strengths unique to a child that might be leveraged to support their learning (Yun et al., 2021). Assessment results support child-centered CM when they are used with other sources of information. Educators can use this information to plan learning activities, and individualize support.

Responding to Behavior: Genuine Feedback and Community Problem Solving

Adult and peer reactions are powerful drivers of behavior (Duncan et al., 2000). Young children are attuned to the responses of others in their environment and learn from social feedback (Hester et al., 2009). It is by trial and error, or making mistakes and seeing how others react, that young children determine boundaries and the impact of their actions on others. Engaging with others provides opportunities for children to receive and respond to social feedback (Howe & Mercer, 2007; La Paro et al., 2012; Stirrup et al., 2017). Children learn from one another. Adults can draw on the richness of children's strengths by being attuned to the group and interactions, pointing out when children demonstrate empathy, resolve a conflict or navigate a difficult social situation, and by scaffolding or mediating interactions that are too complex or challenging for children to navigate independently.

Classroom management that is child-centered and strength-based promotes caregivers to deliver positive social feedback in the context of warm and responsive relationships (Sigler & Aamidor, 2005). When children have secure relationships with caregivers, they feel accepted and will be more likely to respond positively to praise and constructive feedback. Research shows that intentional and specific praise reinforces behaviors, increasing the likelihood that they will occur again (Kazdin, 2013, 2017). However, use of praise, behaviors typically praised, and the type of praise used (e.g., individual versus group) may differ based on culture (Clegg et al., 2021). Within child and community-centered CM, praise can be used intentionally to emphasize shared values and draw attention to actions that are aligned with those values, such as caring for others in the community. Actions of individual children or the group can be acknowledged through educators' use of praise that specifically describes the behavior. The impact of actions on others and the community should be emphasized above compliance, for example, pointing out how a child's action impacted a peer.

Adults often unintentionally focus on and respond to the behaviors they perceive as negative. This may reinforce those behaviors by focusing on them rather than on constructive behaviors, thus increasing the likelihood they will occur again (Okonofu & Eberhadt, 2015; Gilliam, 2005). Pausing before responding to a behavior when safety is not an issue can act as a safeguard against harsh, instinctive, or rushed responding. In doing so, educators give children time to problem solve and give themselves time to assess whether the behavior is interfering with the child's learning or their relationships with others.

An educator's response to one child's behavior has implications for the whole community, for it sends a message about how violations of expectations or harm to another are addressed (Pautz, 2009; Shalaby, 2017). When a child's behavior puts physical or emotional well-being of others at risk, it is essential to bring this to the child's attention and set a limit. This supports the safety and well-being of the child who was hurt and establishes expectations for how to treat others in the community. Subsequently, the child who displayed the behavior can be given an opportunity to repair the harm done (Lawrence & Hinds, 2016). Social problem solving can also be used to help children talk about the situation, label related emotions, and brainstorm solutions. Educators can provide scaffolding to determine solutions in the form of a solutions kit (National Center for Pyramid Model Innovations, n.d). Such problem solving involves perspective taking, and develops the strategies children need to demonstrate with future issues (Costello & Wachtel, 2009; James et al., 2019a; 2019b).

After clearly identifying the behaviors that are harmful to children's safety, or interfere with a child's ability to engage fully in learning or relationships with others, it is helpful for educators to plan how to respond. Context should be taken into account to understand the underlying need that the child is conveying through his or her behavior. When determining a response to behavior in the moment, consider the following:

- What feelings is this child's behavior causing for me and why?
- What factors are influencing how I am perceiving this behavior?
- What are my reasons for wanting the child to stop this behavior?
- Are these reasons aligned with my CM objectives and our community values?
- What way of responding (or not responding) would be aligned with the outcome I want, or the message I want to convey?
- How can my practice meet both the needs of this particular child and the group in this moment?

Engaging in self-evaluation and reflection on practice is a crucial part of CM (Arthur et al., 2017b; Escamilla & Meier, 2018; Ryan & Grieshaber, 2004). Although interactions are bi-directional, the teacher has the power to stop negative cycles. Educators can use information about the child and their strengths and challenges to tailor future interactions to support the child's well-being, success, and inclusion in the classroom community.

Challenges and Supports for EC Educators

Early childhood educators demonstrate resilience in the face of limited resources, high demands, and inadequate compensation (Whitebook et al., 2018). These issues of educator equity are directly linked to the same systemic injustices that shape children's experiences in EC settings (The National Association for the Education of Young Children, 2019). Educators working in early childhood settings report that lack of benefits such as paid planning time, and professional requirements, detract from their interactions with children and use of effective CM practices (Jeon et al., 2018a, 2018b; Johnson, 2021; Whitebook et al., 2018). Educators' reports of challenging behaviors are linked to low professional investment, and work-related stress (Clayback & Williford, 2021; Friedman-Krauss et al., 2014; Jeon et al., 2018b; Roberts et al., 2016). In- and pre-service ECE teachers consistently report needing more training to support children with regard to their behavior in the classroom (Hemmeter et al., 2006; Soydan, 2017). Requirements for provider training and experience vary, and degree and credential educational training programs may not comprehensively address CM practices (Jeon et al., 2018a; Roberts et al., 2016). It is also unclear how much training educators receive regarding culturally-responsive CM practices, including acknowledging and disrupting bias in the classroom (Derman-Sparks, 1989; Derman-Sparks et al., 2015; Kissinger, 2017).

Training and support, whether in the form of effective applied professional development, consultation, coaching, colleague mentoring, or formal preparation and credentialling programs, should focus on supporting educators to develop CM practices that are relevant to the communities in which they are working (Joyce & Showers, 2002). Educators require support and resources to engage in these practices. This includes systems and policies that prioritize teacher mental health and well-being, including adequate compensation, class size, and appropriate work hours (Whitebook et al., 2018). Moreover, the above well-being parameters decrease educator stress, which is linked to impairment and bias in decision making (Yu, 2016). Support from leadership, and a collegial workplace culture are associated with educator agency and efficacy, which are both linked to supportive CM practices (Ransford et al., 2009; Schachter et al., 2021; Whitaker et al., 2015).

We briefly describe two scalable educator support systems that can serve to enhance educators' CM in group-based EC settings: The Pyramid Model for Promoting Young Children's Social Emotional Competence (Pyramid Model), and the Early Childhood Mental Health Consultation (ECMHC) paradigm. The Pyramid Model is a multi-tiered system of support that uses a continuum of evidence-based practices matched to student needs to improve outcomes for all students. This framework is specifically designed for ECE and care settings for use by teachers, home visitors, coaches, behavior specialists, mental health consultants, and program leaders to support young children's social and emotional development (Fox et al., 2003; Hemmeter et al., 2006). The Pyramid Model starts with universal strategies to support all children in the classroom and moves toward more targeted interventions for children who require additional support (Fox & Hemmeter, 2009). Previous research consistently finds that children in classrooms that implement the Pyramid Model display better social skills and fewer challenging behaviors compared to children in classrooms that do not use the model (Hemmeter et al., 2016, 2021).

Increasingly, ECMHC is being used at scale in states to support children who are reported to display challenging behaviors, support children's mental health and well-being, and prevent suspensions and expulsions from group-based early care and education settings. In ECMHC, a mental health professional (i.e., "consultant") is paired with the adults (i.e., caregivers, teachers, and families) who work with infants and young children in the settings where they grow and learn (Cohen & Kaufmann, 2005; Duran et al., 2009). By working with children and adults in a natural setting, consultants interpret behavior in context and draw on resources in the child's environment. The consultant's role is to establish an equal partnership that values the family's perspective.

The use of ECMH consultation improves children's social, emotional, behavioral, and mental health outcomes by building the capacity of the adults who interact with children and their families. Consultants use a strengths-based approach to problem-solve mental health or behavioral concerns with the adults who care for children, and guide them to interpret and respond to children's challenging behaviors using an EC developmental perspective. In this way, ECMH consultation seeks to build on the ongoing, daily interactions between children and their caregivers to support children's optimal development (Duran et al., 2009). Consultants' work is responsive to the specific context, culture, and needs of the child and their setting. Early childhood mental health consultation is associated with decreases in teacher reports of challenging behavior and increases in positive social and emotional outcomes for young children, including increases in social skills, communication, and self-control (Hepburn et al., 2013; Perry et al., 2010). Families also report improvements in parent-child relationships (Hepburn et al., 2013). In addition, ECMH consultation is associated with improvements in the quality of teacher's relationships with students, teacher-child interactions, and improvements in teaching practices related to social-emotional learning, classroom climate, and classroom quality (Brennan et al., 2008; Hepburn et al., 2013). Finally, ECMH is associated with decreases in educator stress and turnover, and has been studied as a potential way to decrease the use of exclusionary discipline (Albritton et al., 2019; Brennan et al., 2008).

Both the Pyramid Model and ECMHC are intended to be implemented in ways that promote equity in how adults respond to children's behaviors, thus promoting effective CM that serves all children. The Pyramid Model practices include awareness and understanding of cultural factors that shape children's behavior and development. Consultants use a reflection tool in their work with educators to identify and address areas of concern related to equity, including countering implicit bias and engaging in culturally responsive practices (The National Center for Pyramid Model Innovations, n.d). Pyramid Model coaches and ECMHC consultants develop trusting partnerships with educators that allow for adults to examine their beliefs, attitudes, and biases about a child which, in turn, may lead to behavior change for both the educator and the child (Duran et al., 2009; The National Center for Pyramid Model Innovations, n.d).

Conclusion

Effective CM practices include caring for and interacting with children, individualizing learning for each child, and responding to challenging behaviors with patience and creativity. These practices require knowledge of child development, mindfulness in the moment, and time for planning and reflection. Educators engaging in equitable CM practices problem solve and balance complex and competing demands while caring for children's physical and emotional needs throughout the day (Faulkner et al., 2016; Johnson, 2021).

This chapter reviewed aspects of CM unique to ECE settings, the role of care in CM, and the ways in which young children learn through everyday routines and hands-on experiences. The importance of addressing issues of equity and decreasing bias through culturally responsive and social justice-oriented CM was emphasized, as were the roles of autonomy, care, and relationships in cultivating genuine community. We conclude that child-oriented CM makes the shift from behavioral compliance to understanding behaviors in context and responding in ways that meet children's needs.

References

Accavitti, M. R., & Williford, A, P. (2020). Teacher perceptions of externalizing behavior subtypes in preschool: considering racial factors, *Early Child Development and Care*, 1–15. https://doi.org/10.1080/03004430.2020.1825405

Adair, J. K., & Sachdeva, S. (2021). Agency and power in young children's lives: Five ways to advocate for social justice as an early childhood educator, *Advancing Equity in Early Childhood Education*, 76(2), 40–48. www.proquest.com/openview/581cc06c905380f5cff9729fc367e0b0/1?pq-origsite=gscholar&cbl=27755

Albritton, K., Mathews, R. E., & Anhalt, K. (2019). Systematic review of early childhood mental health consultation: Implications for improving preschool discipline disproportionality. *Journal of Educational and Psychological Consultation*, 29(4), 444–472. https://doi.org/10.1080/10474412.2018.1541413

Allen, R., Shapland, D. L., Neitzel, J., & Iruka, I. U. (2021). Creating anti-racist early childhood spaces. *YC: Young Children*, 76(2), 49–54. www.naeyc.org/resources/pubs/yc/summer2021/viewpoint-anti-racist-spaces

Allen, R., & Steed, E. A. (2016). Culturally responsive pyramid model practices: Program–wide positive behavior support for young children. *Topics in Early Childhood Special Education*, 36(3), 165–175. https://doi.org/10.1177/0271121416651164

Alter, P., & Haydon, T. (2017). Characteristics of effective classroom rules: A review of the literature. *Teacher Education and Special Education*, 40(2), 114–127. https://doi.org/10.1177/0888406417700962

Apfelbaum, E. P., Pauker, K., Sommers, S. R., & Ambady, N. (2010). In blind pursuit of racial equality? *Psychological Science*, 21(11), 1587–1592. https://doi.org/10.1177/0956797610384741

Arthur, L., Beecher, B., Death, E., Dockett, S., & Farmer, S. (2017b). *Programming and planning in Early Childhood settings*. Cengage Learning Australia.

Arthur-Kelly, M., Farrell, G., De Bortoli, T., Lyons, G., Hinchey, F., Ho, F. C., Opartkiattikul, W., Baker, F., & Fairfax, W. (2017a). The reported effects of a systematic professional learning program on the knowledge, skills, and concerns of Australian early childhood educators who support young children displaying or at risk of challenging behaviours. *International Journal of Disability, Development and Education*, 64(2), 131–149. https://doi.org/10.1080/1034912X.2016.1181258

Barnett, S., Carolan, M., & Johns, D. (2013). *Equity and excellence: African-American children's access to quality preschool*. National Institute for Early Education Research, Center on enhancing early learning outcomes. http://ceelo.org/wp-content/uploads/2013/11/CEELO-NIEERequityExcellence-2013.pdf

Barrable, A. (2020). Shaping space and practice to support autonomy: Lessons from natural settings in Scotland. *Learning Environments Research*, 23(3), 291–305. https://doi.org/10.1007/s10984-019-09305-x

Beaty-O'Ferrall, M. E., Green, A., & Hanna, F. (2010). Classroom management strategies for difficult students: Promoting change through relationships. *Middle School Journal*, *41*(4), 4–11. https://files.eric.ed.gov/fulltext/EJ887746.pdf

Belsky, J., & Cassidy, J. (1994). Attachment and close relationships: An individual-difference perspective. *Psychological Inquiry*, *5*(1), 27–30. www.jstor.org/stable/1449077

Benard, B., & Slade, S. (2009). Listening to Students: Moving from resilience research to youth development practice and school connectedness. In M. J. Furlong, & E. S. Huebner (Eds.), *Handbook of positive psychology in schools* (pp. 353–371). Routledge. https://doi.org/10.4324/9780203884089

Berti, S., Cigala, A., & Sharmahd, N. (2019). Early Childhood Education and Care Physical Environment and Child Development: State of the art and Reflections on Future Orientations and Methodologies. *Educational Psychology Review*, *31*(4), 991–1021. 10.1007/s10648-019-09486-0

Bettez, S. C. (2011). Critical community building: Beyond belonging. *Educational Foundations*, *25*(3–4), 3–19. https://doi.org/10.1177/1086482220906151

Biermeier, M.A. (2015). Inspired by Reggio Emilia: Emergent curriculum in relationship-driven learning environments. *YC: Young Children*, *70*(5), 72–79. www.naeyc.org/resources/pubs/yc/nov2015/emergent-curriculum

Blair, C., & Raver, C. C. (2016). Poverty, Stress, and brain development: New directions for prevention and intervention. *Academic Pediatrics*, *16*(3), 30–36. https://doi.org/10.1016/j.acap.2016.01.010

Bondy, E., Ross, D. D., Gallingane, C., & Hambacher, E. (2007). Creating environments of success and resilience: Culturally responsive classroom management and more. *Urban Education*, *42*(4), 326–348. https://doi.org/10.1177/0042085907303406

Brennan, E. M., Bradley, J. R., Allen, M. D., & Perry, D. F. (2008). The evidence base for mental health consultation in early childhood settings: Research synthesis addressing staff and program outcomes. *Early Education and Development*, *19*(6), 982–1022. https://doi.org/10.1080/10409280801975834

Brey, E., & Pauker, K. (2019). Teachers' nonverbal behaviors influence children's stereotypic beliefs. *Journal of Experimental Child Psychology*, *188*, 104671. https://doi.org/10.1016/j.jecp.2019.104671

Brouwers A., & Tomic, W. (2000). A longitudinal study of teacher burnout and perceived self-efficacy in classroom management. *Teaching and Teacher Education*, *16*(2), 239–253. https://doi.org/10.1016/S0742-051X(99)00057-8

Burchinal, M., Vernon-Feagans, L., Vitiello, V., & Greenberg, M. (2014). Thresholds in the association between child care quality and child outcomes in rural preschool children. *Early Childhood Research Quarterly*, *29*(1), 41–51. https://doi.org/10.1016/j.ecresq.2013.09.004

Buyuktaskapu Soydan, S., Alakoc, P., Ozturk Samur, A., & Angin, D. E. (2018). Pre-school teachers' classroom management competency and the factors affecting their understanding of discipline. *Eurasian Journal of Educational Research 73*, 149–171. 10.14689/ejer.2018.73.9

Cardona, B., Jain, S., & Canfield-Davis, K. (2012). Home-School relationships: A qualitative study with diverse families. *Qualitative Report*, *17*(35), 1–20. https://doi.org/10.46743/2160-3715/2012.1738

Carter, K., & Doyle, W. (2006). Classroom management in early childhood and elementary classrooms. In C. M. Evertson & C. S. Weinstein (Eds.), *Handbook of classroom management: Research, practice, and contemporary issues* (pp. 373–406). Erlbaum.

Center on the Social and Emotional Foundations for Early Learning (CSEFEL) (n.d.). Understanding your child's behavior: Reading your child's cues from birth to age 2. http://csefel.vanderbilt.edu/documents/reading_cues.pdf

Clayback, K. A., & Hemmeter, M. L. (2021). Exclusionary discipline practices in early childhood settings: A survey of child care directors. *Early Childhood Research Quarterly*, *55*(2), 129–136. https://doi.org/10.1016/j.ecresq.2020.11.002

Clayback, K. A. & Williford, A. P. (2021) Teacher and classroom predictors of preschool teacher stress. *Early Education and Development*, https://doi.org/10.1080/10409289.2021.1972902

Clegg, J. M., Wen, N. J., DeBaylo, P. H., Alcott, A., Keltner, E. C., & Legare, C. H. (2021). Teaching through collaboration: Flexibility and diversity in caregiver–child Interaction across cultures. *Child Development*, *92*(1), 56–75. https://srcd.onlinelibrary.wiley.com/doi/epdf/10.1111/cdev.13443

Cohen, E., & Kaufmann, R.K. (2005). Early childhood mental health consultation (Department of Health and Human Services Publication Number CMHS-SVP0151). Center for Mental Health Services, Substance Abuse and Mental Health Services Administration.

Cook, C. R., Coco, S., Zhang, Y., Fiat, A. E., Duong, M. T., Renshaw, T. L., Long, A. C., & Frank, S. (2018). Cultivating positive teacher–student relationships: Preliminary evaluation of the establish–maintain–restore (EMR) method. *School Psychology Review*, *47*(3), 226–243. https://doi.org/10.17105/SPR-2017-0025.V47-3

Copple, C., Jerlean, D., & Tomlinson, H. B. (2007). Revisiting the NAEYC Position Statement on developmentally appropriate practice. *YC:Young Children*, *61*(5), 63–63. www.jstor.org/stable/42729997

Costello, B., J., & T. Wachtel. (2009). *The restorative practices handbook for teachers, disciplinarians, and administrators.* International Institute for Restorative Practices.

Davidson, B. C., Davis, E., Cadenas, H., Barnett, M., Sanchez, B. E. L., Gonzalez, J. C., & Jent, J. (2021). Universal teacher–child interaction training in early special education: A pilot cluster-randomized control trial. *Behavior Therapy, 52*(2), 379–393. https://doi.org/10.1016/j.beth.2020.04.014

Denham, S. A., Blair, K. A., DeMulder, E., Levitas, J., Sawyer, K., Auerbach-Major, S., & Queenan, P. (2003). Preschool emotional competence: Pathway to social competence? *Child Development, 74*(1), 238–256. www.jstor.org/stable/3696354

Denham, S. A., Ferrier, D. E., Howarth, G. Z., Herndon, K. J., & Bassett, H. H. (2016). Key considerations in assessing young children's emotional competence. *Cambridge Journal of Education, 46*(3), 299–317. http://dx.doi.org/10.1080/0305764X.2016.1146659

Derman-Sparks, L. (1989). *Anti-bias curriculum: Tools for empowering young children.* National Association for the Education of Young Children.

Derman-Sparks, L., LeeKeenan, D., & Nimmo, J. (2015). *Leading ANTI-BIAS Early Childhood programs: A guide for change.* Teachers College Press.

Diamond, A. (2012). Activities and programs that improve children's executive functions. *Current Directions in Psychological Science, 21*(5), 335–341. https://doi.org/10.1177/0963721412453722

Diamond, A., & Lee, K. (2011). Interventions shown to aid executive function development in children 4-12 years old. *Science, 333*(6045), 959–964. https://doi.org/10.1126/science.1204529

Dobbs, J., & Arnold, D. H. (2009). Relationship between preschool teachers' reports of children's behavior and their behavior toward those children. School Psychology Quarterly, 24(2), 95–105. https://doi.org/10.1037/a0016157

Doctoroff, S. (2001). Adapting the physical environment to meet the needs of all young children for play. *Early Childhood Education Journal, 29*(2), 105–110. https://doi.org/10.1023/A:1012524929004

Downer, J., Sabol, T. J., & Hamre, B. (2010). Teacher–child interactions in the class- room: Toward a theory of within- and cross-domain links to children's developmental outcomes. *Early Education and Development, 21*(5), 699–723. https://doi.org/10.1080/10409289.2010.497453

Drew, W. F., & Rankin, B. (2004). Promoting creativity for life using open-ended materials. *Young Children, 59*(4), 38–45. www.jstor.org/stable/i40102758

Duncan, T. K., Kemple, K. M., & Smith, T. M. (2000). Reinforcement in developmentally appropriate early childhood classrooms. *Childhood Education, 76*(4), 194–203. https://doi.org/10.1080/00094056.2000.10521162

Dunham, Y., Chen, E. E., & Banaji, M. R. (2013). Two signatures of implicit intergroup attitudes: Developmental invariance and early enculturation. *Psychological Science, 24*(6), 860–868. https://doi.org/10.1177/0956797612463081

Duran, F., Hepburn, K., Irvine, M., Kaufmann, R., Anthony, B., Horen, N., & Perry, D. F. (2009). *What works? A study of effective early childhood mental health consultation programs.* Georgetown University Center for Child and Human Development. https://gucchd.georgetown.edu/products/FINAL%20formatted%20executive%20summary.pdf

Early, D., Iruka, I., Ritchie, S., Barbarin, O., Winn, D. M., Crawford, G., Frome, P., Clifford, R., Burchinal, M., Howes, C., Bryant, D., & Pianta, R. (2010). How do pre-kindergarteners spend their time? Gender, ethnicity, and income as predictors of experiences in pre-kindergarten classrooms. *Early Childhood Research Quarterly, 25*(2), 177–193. https://doi.org/10.1016/j.ecresq.2009.10.003

Emerson, E., & Einfeld, S. L. (2011). *Challenging behaviour, Third Edition.* Cambridge University Press. https://doi.org/10.1017/CBO9780511861178

Epstein, A. S. (2007). *The intentional teacher: Choosing the best strategies for young children's learning.* National Association for the Education of Young Children.

Erdmann, K. A., & Hertel, S. (2019). Self-regulation and co-regulation in early childhood–development, assessment and supporting factors. *Metacognition and Learning, 14*(3), 229–238. https://doi.org/10.1007/s11409-019-09211-w

Escamilla, I. M., & Meier, D. (2018). The promise of teacher inquiry and reflection: Early childhood teachers as change agents. *Studying Teacher Education: Journal of Self-Study of Teacher Education Practices, 14*(1), 3–21. https://doi.org/10.1080/17425964.2017.1408463

Essien, I. (2019). Pathologizing culture in early childhood education: Illuminating microaggressions from the narratives of the parents of black children. *Western Journal of Black Studies, 43*(1–2), 9–21. http://proxy.library.cpp.edu/login?url=www-proquest- com.proxy.library.cpp.edu/scholarly-journals/pathologizing-culture-early- childhood-education/docview/2362907107/se-2?accountid=10357

Fantuzzo, J., Tighe, E., & Childs, S. (2000). Family Involvement Questionnaire: A multivariate assessment of family participation in early childhood education. *Journal of Educational Psychology, 92*(2), 367–376. https://doi.org/10.1037/0022-0663.92.2.367

Faulkner, M., Gerstenblatt, P., Lee, A., Vallejo, V., & Travis, D. (2016). Childcare providers: Work stress and personal well-being. *Journal of Early Childhood Research*, *14*(3), 280–293. https://doi.org/10.1177/14767 18X14552871

Feldman, R. (2007). Parent–infant synchrony and the construction of shared timing; physiological precursors, developmental outcomes, and risk conditions. *Journal of Child Psychology and Psychiatry*, *48*(3-4), 329–354. https://doi.org/10.1111/j.1469-7610.2006.01701.x

Feldman, R., & Eidelman, A. I. (2007). Maternal postpartum behavior and the emergence of infant–mother and infant–father synchrony in preterm and full-term infants: The role of neonatal vagal tone. *Developmental Psychobiology*, *49*(3), 290–302. https://doi.org/10.1002/dev.20220

Feldman, R., Magori-Cohen, R., Galili, G., Singer, M., & Louzoun, Y. (2011). Mother and infant coordinate heart rhythms through episodes of interaction synchrony. *Infant Behavior and Development*, *34*(4), 569–577. https://doi.org/10.1016/j.infbeh.2011.06.008

Fleer, M. (2003). Early childhood education as an evolving 'community of practice' or as lived 'social reproduction': Researching the 'taken-for-granted'. *Contemporary Issues in Early Childhood*, *4*(1), 64–79. https://doi.org/10.2304/ciec.2003.4.1.7

Fox, L., Dunlap, G., Hemmeter, M. L., Joseph, G. E., & Strain, P. S. (2003). The Teaching Pyramid: A model for supporting social competence and preventing challenging behavior in young children. *YC: Young Children*, *58*(4), 48–52. https://challengingbehavior.cbcs.usf.edu/docs/TeachingPyramid_yc_article_7_2003.pdf

Fox, L., & Hemmeter, M. L. (2009). A program-wide model for supporting social emotional development and addressing challenging behavior in early childhood settings. In W. Sailor, G. Dunlap, G. Sugai, & R. Horner (Eds.), *Handbook of positive behavior support* (pp. 177–202). Springer.

Freire, P. (1970). *Pedagogy of the oppressed*. Bloomsbury Publishing.

Friedman, S. & Mwenelupembe, A. (2020). *Each & every child: Using an equity lens when teaching preschool*. National Association for the Education of Young Children.

Friedman-Krauss, A. H., Raver, C. C., Morris, P. A., & Jones, S. M. (2014). The role of classroom-level child behavior problems in predicting preschool teacher stress and classroom emotional climate. *Early Education and Development*, *25*(4), 530–552. https://doi.org/10.1080/10409289.2013.817030

Gable, R. A., Hester, P. H., Rock, M. L., & Hughes, K. G. (2009). Back to basics: Rules, praise ignoring, and reprimands revisited. *Intervention in School and Clinic*, *44*(4), 195–205. https://doi.org/10.1177/105345120 8328831

Gagné, M. (2003). The role of autonomy support and autonomy orientation in prosocial behavior engagement. *Motivation and Emotion*, *27*(3), 199–223. https://doi.org/10.1023/A:1025007614869

Gettinger, M., & Stoiber, K. C. (2006). Functional assessment, collaboration, and evidence-based treatment: Analysis of a team approach for addressing challenging behaviors in young children. *Journal of School Psychology*, *44*(3), 231–252. https://doi.org/10.1016/j.jsp.2006.03.001

Gillespie, L. (2015). The role of co-regulation in building self-regulation skills. *YC: Young Children*, 94–96. www.naeyc.org/system/files/RR-0715.pdf

Gilliam, W.S. (2005). *Pre-kindergarteners left behind: Expulsion rates in state prekindergarten systems*. Yale University Child Study Center. www.ziglercenter.yale.edu/publications/ National%20Prek%20Study_expulsion_tcm350-34774_tcm350-284-32.pdf.

Gilliam, W. S., Maupin, A. N., Reyes, C. R., Accavitti, M., & Shic, F. (2016). Do early educators' implicit biases regarding sex and race relate to behavior expectations and recommendations of preschool expulsions and suspensions. *Yale University Child Study Center*, *9*(28), 1–16. https://medicine.yale.edu/childstudy/zigler/publications/Preschool%20Implicit%20Bias%20Policy%20Brief_final_9_26_276766_5379_v1.pdf

Gilliam, W. S., & Shahar, G. (2006). Prekindergarten expulsion and suspension: Rates and predictors in one state. *Infants and Young Children* *19*(3), 228–245. https://medicine.yale.edu/childstudy/zigler/publications/Gilliam%20and%20Shahar%20%202006%20Preschool%20and%20Child%20Care%20Expulsion%20and%20Suspension%20Rates%20and%20Predictors%20in%20One%20State_251491_5379_v3.pdf

Goble, P., & Pianta, R. C. (2017). Teacher–Child interactions in free choice and teacher-directed activity Settings: Prediction to school readiness. *Early Education & Development*, *28*(8), 1035–1051. https://doi.org/10.1080/10409289.2017.1322449

Gonzalez-Mena, J., & Shareef, I. (2005). Discussing diverse perspectives on guidance. *YC: Young Children*, *60*(6), 34–38. www.jstor.org/stable/42729312

Graves Jr, S. L., & Howes, C. (2011). Ethnic differences in social-emotional development in preschool: The impact of teacher child relationships and classroom quality. *School Psychology Quarterly*, *26*(3), 202–214. https://doi.org/10.1037/a0024117

Greenman, J. (1988). *Caring spaces, learning places: Children's environments that work*. Exchange Press.

Gregoriadis, A., Grammatikopoulos, V., Tsigilis, N., & Zachopoulou, E. (2019). Assessing teacher–child relationships: A cultural context perspective. In O. N. Saracho (Ed.), *Handbook of research on the education of young children* (4th ed., pp. 322–332). Routledge.

Hamre, B., Hatfield, B., Pianta, R., & Jamil, F. (2014). Evidence for general and domain-specific elements of teacher–child interactions: Associations with preschool children's development. *Child Development, 85*(3), 1257–1274. https://doi.org/10.1111/cdev.12184

Hamre, B. K., & Pianta, R. C. (2001). Early teacher–child relationships and the trajectory of children's school outcomes through eighth grade. *Child Development, 72*(2), 625–638. https://doi.org/10.1111/1467-8624.00301

Hatfield, B. E., Hestenes, L. L., Kintner-Duffy, V. L., & O'Brien, M. (2013). Classroom emotional support predicts differences in preschool children's cortisol and alpha- amylase levels. *Early Childhood Research Quarterly, 28*(2), 347–356. https://doi.org/10.1016/j.ecresq.2012.08.001

Hatfield, B. E., & Williford, A. P. (2017). Cortisol patterns for young children displaying disruptive behavior: Links to a teacher–child, relationship-focused intervention. *Prevention Science, 18*(1), 40–49. https://doi.org/10.1007/s11121-016-0693-9

Head Start, Early Childhood Learning, & Knowledge Center (ECLKC) (n.d.). Child Screening & Assessment. US Department of Health & Human Services, Administration for Children and Families. https:// eclkc.ohs.acf.hhs.gov/child-screening-assessment/article/ screening-assessment-evaluation-observation

Hemmeter, M. L., Fox, L., Snyder, P., Algina, J., Hardy, J., Bishop, C., & Veguilla, M. (2021). Corollary child outcomes of the Pyramid Model professional development efficacy trial. *Early Childhood Research Quarterly, 54*, 204–218. https://doi.org/10.1016/j.ecresq.2020.08.004

Hemmeter, M. L., Ostrosky, M., & Fox, L. (2006). Social and emotional foundations for early learning: A conceptual model for intervention. *School Psychology Review, 35*(4), 583–601. https://doi.org/10.1080/02796015.2006.12087963

Hemmeter, M. L., Santos, R. M., & Ostrosky, M. M. (2008). Preparing early childhood educators to address young children's social-emotional development and challenging behavior: survey of higher education programs in nine states. *Journal of Early Intervention, 30*(4), 321–340. https://doi.org/10.1177/1053815108320900

Hemmeter, M. L., Snyder, P. A., Fox, L., & Algina, J. (2016). Evaluating the implementation of the Pyramid Model for promoting social-emotional competence in early childhood classrooms. *Topics in Early Childhood Special Education, 36*(3), 133–146. https://doi.org/10.1177/0271121416653386

Henderson, N. (2012). Resilience in schools and curriculum design. In M. Ungar (Ed.), *The social ecology of resilience: A handbook of theory and practice* (pp. 297–306). Springer Science and Business Media. https://doi.org/10.1007/978-1-4614-0586-3_23

Henley, M. (2007). *Classroom management: A proactive approach*. Pearson.

Hepburn, K. S., Perry, D. F., Shivers, E. M., & Gilliam, W. S. (2013). Early childhood mental health consultation as an evidenced-based practice: Where does it stand? *Zero to Three, 33*(5), 10–18.

Hester, P. P., Hendrickson, J. M., & Gable, R. A. (2009). Forty years later--The value of praise, ignoring, and rules for preschoolers at risk for behavior disorders. *Education and Treatment of Children, 32*(4), 513–535. www.jstor.org/stable/42900038

Hirschland, D. (2015). *When young children need help: Understanding and addressing emotional, behavioral, and developmental challenges*. Redleaf Press.

Hojnoski, R. L., Missall, K. N., & Wood, B. K. (2020). Measuring engagement in early education: Preliminary evidence for the behavioral observation of students in schools–early education. *Assessment for Effective Intervention, 45*(4), 243–254. https://doi.org/10.1177/1534508418820125

hooks, B. (2003). *Teaching community: A pedagogy of hope*. Routledge.

Housman, D. (2017). The importance of emotional competence and self-regulation from birth: case for the evidence-based emotional cognitive social early learning approach. *International Journal of Child Care and Education Policy. 11*(13). https://doi.org/10.1186/s40723-017-0038-6

Howe, C., & Mercer, N. (2007). *Children's social development, peer interaction and classroom learning*. (Primary Review Research Survey), University of Cambridge Faculty of Education.

Howell, J. & Reinhard, K. (2015). *Rituals and traditions: Fostering a sense of community in preschool*. National Association for the Education of Young Children.

Howes, C., & Shivers, E. M. (2006). New child–caregiver attachment relationships: Entering childcare when the caregiver is and is not an ethnic match. *Social Development, 15*(4), 574–590. https://doi.org/10.1111/j.1467-9507.2006.00358.x

Howes, C., Wishard, A., Fuligni, A., Zucker, E., Lee, L., Obregon, N., & Spivak, A. (2011). Classroom dimensions predict early peer interaction when children are diverse in ethnicity, race, and home language. *Early Childhood Research Quarterly, 26*(4), 399–408. https://doi.org/10.1016/j.ecresq.2011.02.004

Hughes, J. N., & Chen, Q. (2011). Reciprocal effects of student–teacher and student–peer relatedness: Effects on academic self-efficacy. *Journal of Applied Developmental Psychology*, *32*(5), 278–287. https://doi.org/10.1016/j.appdev.2010.03.005

Hughes, D., Rodriguez, J., Smith, E. P., Johnson, D. J., Stevenson, H. C., & Spicer, P. (2006). Parents' ethnic-racial socialization practices: a review of research and directions for Future study. *Developmental Psychology*, *42*(5), 747–770. https://doi.org/10.1037/0012-1649.42.5.747

Ikegami, K., & Rivalland, C. (2016). Exploring the quality of teacher–child interactions: The Soka discourse in practice. *European Early Childhood Education Research Journal*, *24*(4), 521–535. https://doi.org/10.1080/1350293X.2016.1189719

Iruka, I., Escayg, K., Durden, T., & Curenton, S. (2020). *Don't look away: Embracing anti-bias classrooms.* Gryphon House.

Isbell, R., & Raines, S. C. (2012). *Creativity and the arts with young children.* Cengage.

James, A. G., Noltemeyer, A., Ritchie, R., Palmer, K., & University, M. (2019b). Longitudinal disciplinary and achievement outcomes associated with school-wide PBIS implementation level. *Psychology In the Schools*, *56*(9), 1512–1521. https://doi.org/10.1002/pits.22282

James, V., Williams, S., Earl, K., Lewis, K., Garrett, C., & McKnight, K. (2019a). *Guiding practices in early childhood discipline.* NC Department of Public Instruction.

Jeon, L., Buettner, C. K., & Grant, A. A. (2018a). Early childhood teachers' psychological well-being: Exploring potential predictors of depression, stress, and emotional exhaustion. *Early Education and Development*, *29*(1), 53–69. https://doi.org/10.1080/10409289.2017.1341806

Jeon, L., Buettner, C. K., Grant, A. A., & Lang, S. N. (2018b). Early childhood teachers' stress and children's social, emotional, and behavioral functioning. *Journal of Applied Developmental Psychology*, *61*, 21–32. https://doi.org/10.1016/j.appdev.2018.02.002

Jipson, J. (1991) Developmentally appropriate practice: Culture, curriculum, connections, *Early Education and Development*, *2*(2), 120–136. 10.1207/s15566935eed0202_4

Jiron, A., Brogle, B., & Giacomini, J. (2013). *How to understand the meaning of your child's challenging behavior.* Technical Assistance Center on Social Emotional Intervention (TACSEI) for Young Children. http://challengingbehavior.fmhi.usf.edu/do/resources/documents/bkpk_understand_meaning.pdf

Johnson, D. (2021) To whom little is given, much is expected: ECE teacher stressors and supports as determinants of classroom quality. *Early Childhood Research Quarterly*, *54*(1), 13–30. https://doi.org/10.1016/j.ecresq.2020.07.002

Johnson-Staub, C. (2017). Equity starts early: Addressing racial inequities in child care and early education policy. *Center for Law and Social Policy, Inc. (CLASP).* www.clasp.org/sites/default/files/publications/2017/12/2017_EquityStartsEarly_0.pdf

Joyce, B. R., & Showers, B. (2002). Student Achievement Through Staff Development. In B. R. Joyce & B. Showers (Eds.), *Designing training and peer coaching: Our needs for learning.* National College for School Leadership.

Jung, L.A. (2020). There's More to Emotional Self-Regulation than meets the eye. *Educational Leadership*, *78*(3), 46–51. www.ascd.org/el/articles/theres-more-to-emotional-self-regulation-than-meets-the-eye

Kaiser, B., & Rasminsky, J. S. (2003). Opening the culture door. *YC: Young Children*, *58*(4), 53–56.

Kaiser, B., & Rasminsky, J. S. (2021). *Addressing challenging behavior in young children: The leader's role.* NAEYC.

Kane, K. (August 16, 2016). Back to school: Why creating classroom community is so important. National Association for the Education of Young Children. www.naeyc.org/resources/blog/why-creating-classroom-community-so-important

Katz, L. G., & Chard, S. C. (1996). *The contribution of documentation to the quality of early childhood education.* ERIC Clearinghouse on Elementary an Early Childhood Education, University of Illinois. https://nla.gov.au/nla.cat-vn4119868

Katz, P. A., & Kofkin, J. A. (1997). Race, gender, and young children. In S. S. Luthar, J. A. Burack, D. Cicchetti, & J. R. Weisz (Eds.), *Developmental psychopathology: Perspectives on adjustment, risk, and disorder* (pp. 51–74). Cambridge University Press.

Kazdin, A.E. (2013). *Behavior modification in applied settings* (7th ed.). Waveland Press.

Kazdin, A.E. (2017). Parent management training and skills. In J.R. Weisz & A.E. Kazdin (Eds.). *Evidence-based psychotherapies for children and adolescents* (3rd ed., pp. 142–158). Guilford Press.

Kissinger, K. (2017). *Anti-bias education in the early childhood classroom: Hand in hand, Step by Step.* Routledge.

Kincheloe, J. L., McLaren, P., Steinberg, S. R., & Monzó, L. (2017). Critical pedagogy and qualitative research: Advancing the bricolage. In N. K. Denzin & Y. S. Lincoln (Eds.), *The SAGE Handbook of Qualitative Research* (5th ed.; pp. 235–260). Sage.

La Paro, K. M., Maynard, C., Thomason, A., & Scott-Little, C. (2012). Developing teachers' classroom interactions: A description of a video review process for early childhood education students. *Journal of Early Childhood Teacher Education*, *33*(3), 224–238. http://doi.10.1080/10901027.2012.705809

Ladson-Billings, G. (1994). *The dreamkeepers*. Jossey-Bass Publishing.

Ladson-Billings, G. (1995). Towards a theory of culturally relevant pedagogy, *American Educational Research Journal, 32*(3). https://doi.org/10.3102/00028312032003465

Lambert, J. M., Bloom, S. E., & Irvin, J. (2012). Trial-based functional analysis and functional communication training in an early childhood setting. *Journal of Applied Behavior Analysis, 45*(3), 579–584. https://doi.org/10.1901/jaba.2012.45-579

Langeloo, A., Mascareño Lara, M., Deunk, M. I., Klitzing, N. F., & Strijbos, J. W. (2019). A systematic review of teacher–child interactions with multilingual young children. *Review of Educational Research, 89*(4), 536–568. https://doi.org/10.3102/0034654319855619

Laurin, J.C., & Joussemet, M. (2017). Parental autonomy-supportive practices and toddlers' rule internalization: A prospective observational study. *Motivation and Emotion, 41*(5), 562–575. https://doi.org/10.1007/s11031-017-9627-5

Lawrence, E., & Hinds, T. (2016). From punish and discipline to repair and restore. *Principal, 96*(2), 20–23. www.naesp.org/sites/default/files/LawrenceHinds_ND16.pdf

Lee, J. S., & Ginsburg, H. P. (2007). what is appropriate mathematics education for four-year olds?: pre-kindergarten teachers' beliefs. *Journal of Early Childhood Research, 5*(1), 2–31. https://doi.org/10.1177/1476718X07072149

Lerkkanen, M. K., Kiuru, N., Pakarinen, E., Poikkeus, A. M., Rasku-Puttonen, H., Siekkinen, M., & Nurmi, J. E. (2016). Child-centered versus teacher-directed teaching practices: Associations with the development of academic skills in the first grade at school. *Early Childhood Research Quarterly, 36*(3), 145–156. https://doi.org/10.1016/j.ecresq.2015.12.023

Lubeck, Sally. (1998). Is developmentally appropriate practice for everyone? *Childhood Education, 74*(5), 283–292. https://doi.org/10.1080/00094056.1998.10521952

Lutton, A., & The National Association for the Education of Young Children (2012). *Advancing the early childhood profession: NAEYC standards and guidelines for professional development*. National Association for the Education of Young Children.

Ma, X., Shen, J., Krenn, H. Y., Hu, S., & Yuan, J. (2016). A meta-analysis of the relationship between learning outcomes and parental involvement during early childhood education and early elementary education. *Educational Psychology Review, 28*(4), 771–801. https://doi.org/10.1007/s10648-015-9351-1

MacLure, M., Jones, L., Holmes, R., & MacRae, C. (2012). Becoming a problem: Behaviour and reputation in the early years classroom, *British Educational Research Journal, 38*(3), 447–471. https://doi.org/10.1080/01411926.2011.552709

Martin, N.K., Sass, D.A., & Schmitt, T.A., (2012). Teacher efficacy in student engagement, instructional management, student stressors, and burnout: A theoretical model using in-class variables to predict teachers' intent-to-leave. *Teaching and Teacher Education, 28*(4), 546–559. http://dx.doi.org/10.1016/j.tate.2011.12.003

Martin, N., Schafer, N., McClowry, S., Emmer, E., Brekelmans, M., Mainhard, T., & Wubbels, T. (2016). Expanding the definition of classroom management: Recurring themes and new conceptualizations. *The Journal of Classroom Interaction, 51*(1), 31–41. www.jstor.org/stable/26174348

McFarland, L., Saunders, R. & Allen, S. (2009). Reflective practice and self-evaluation in learning positive guidance: Experiences of early childhood practicum students. *Early Childhood Education Journal, 36*(6), 505–511. https://doi.org/10.1007/s10643-009-0315-2.

McNally, S., & Slutsky, R. (2018). Teacher–child relationships make all the difference: Constructing quality interactions in early childhood settings. *Early Child Development and Care, 188*(5), 508–523. https://doi.org/10.1080/03004430.2017.1417854

Meehan, B. T., Hughes, J. N., & Cavell, T. A. (2003). Teacher–student relationships as compensatory resources for aggressive children. *Child Development, 74*(4), 1145–1157. www.jstor.org/stable/3696214

Meek, S. E., & Gilliam, W. S. (2016). Expulsion and suspension as matters of social justice and health equity. Discussion Paper, National Academy of Medicine, Washington, DC. https://nam.edu/wp-content/up-loads/2016/10/Expulsion-and-Suspension-in-Early- Education-as-Matters-of-Social-Justice-and-Health- Equity.pdf.

Meloy, B., & Schachner, A. (2019). *Early Childhood Essentials: A Framework for Aligning Child Skills and Educator Competencies*. (fact sheet). Learning Policy Institute.

Miller, S., Smith-Bonahue, T., & Kemple, K. (2017). Preschool teachers' responses to challenging behavior: The role of organizational climate in referrals and expulsions. *International Research In Early Childhood Education, 8*(1), 38–57. https://files.eric.ed.gov/fulltext/EJ1173675.pdf

Mukhanji, J. M., Ndiku, J. M., & Obaki, S. (2016). Effect of increased student enrollment on teaching and learning resources in Maseno University, Kenya. *Journal of Learning for Development. 8*(1), 192–203. https://files.eric.ed.gov/fulltext/EJ1294986.pdf

Murray, C., & Murray, K. M. (2004). Child level correlates of teacher–student relationships: An examination of demographic characteristics, academic orientations, and behavioral orientations. *Psychology in the Schools, 41*(7), 751–762. https://doi.org/10.1002/pits.20015

Myers, S. S., & Pianta, R. C. (2008). Developmental commentary: Individual and contextual influences on student–teacher relationships and children's early problem behaviors. *Journal of Clinical Child & Adolescent Psychology, 37*(3), 600–608. https://doi.org/10.1080/15374410802148160

The National Association for the Education of Young Children (NAEYC) (2005). *Early childhood program standards and accreditation criteria: the mark of quality in early childhood education*. National Association for the Education of Young Children.

The National Association for the Education of Young Children (NAEYC) (2009). *Position statement: Developmentally appropriate practice in early childhood programs serving children from birth through age 8*. National Association for the Education of Young Children.

The National Association for the Education of Young Children (NAEYC) (2013). Copple, C., Bredekamp, S., Koralek, D., & Charner, K. (Eds.). *Position statement: Developmentally appropriate practice in early childhood programs serving children from birth through age 8*. National Association for the Education of Young Children.

The National Association for the Education of Young Children (NAEYC) (2019). *Position statement: Advancing Equity in Early Childhood Education*. National Association for the Education of Young Children.

National Center for Pyramid Model Innovations (NCPMI) (n.d.). Statement on equity and inclusion: Implementation with equity, implicit bias, disproportionate discipline. https://challengingbehavior.cbcs.usf.edu/Implementation/Equity/index.html

National Institute for Care and Health Excellence (NICHE), United Kingdom, Collaborating Centre for Mental Health (UK) (2015). Challenging behaviour and learning disabilities: prevention and interventions for people with learning disabilities whose behaviour challenges. www.ncbi.nlm.nih.gov/books/NBK355392/

Neitzel, J. (2018) Research to practice: understanding the role of implicit bias in early childhood disciplinary practices, *Journal of Early Childhood Teacher Education, 39*(3), 232–242, 10.1080/10901027.2018.1463322

Nelson, C. A., Zeanah, C. H., & Fox, N. A. (2019). How early experience shapes human development: The case of psychosocial deprivation. Neural Plasticity, *1*(67), 62–85. https://doi.org/10.1155/2019/1676285

Neuman, S., Copple, C., & Bredekamp, S. (2000). *Learning to read and write: Developmentally appropriate practices for young children*. National Association for the Education of Young Children.

Nores, M., & Fernandez, C. (2018). Building capacity in health and education systems to deliver interventions that strengthen early child development. *Annals of the New York Academy of Sciences, 1419*(1), 57–73. https://doi.org/10.1111/nyas.13682

Nurmi, J. E. (2012). Students' characteristics and teacher–child relationships in instruction: A meta-analysis. *Educational Research Review, 7*(3), 177–197. http://dx.doi.org/10.1016/j.edurev.2012.03.001

Obaki, S. O. (2017). Impact of classroom environment on children's social behavior. *International Journal of Education and Practice, 5*(1), 1–7. http://doi. 10.18488/journal.61/2017.5.1/61.1.1.7

Okonofua, J. A., & Eberhardt, J. L. (2015). Two strikes: Race and the disciplining of young students. *Psychological Science, 26*(5), 617–624. https://doi.org/10.1177/0956797615570365

Pautz, M.I. (2009). *Empowering the next generation: Restorative practices in a preschool*. Restorative Practices Eforum. www.iirp.edu/iirpWebsites/web/uploads/article_pdfs/93908_rp_preschool.pdf.

Payne, K. A. (2018) Young children's everyday civics. *The Social Studies, 109*(2), 57–63, 10.1080/00377996.2018.1446897

Payne, K. A., Adair, J. K., Colegrove, K. S. S., Lee, S., Falkner, A., McManus, M., & Sachdeva, S. (2020). Reconceptualizing civic education for young children: Recognizing embodied civic action. *Education, Citizenship and Social Justice, 15*(1), 35–46, https://doi.org/10.1177/1746197919858359

Perry, D. F., Allen, M. D., Brennan, E. M., & Bradley, J. R. (2010). The evidence base for mental health consultation in early childhood settings: A research synthesis addressing children's behavioral outcomes. *Early Education and Development, 21*(6), 795–824. https://doi.org/10.1080/10409280903475444

Petrakos, H., & Howe, N. (1996). The influence of the physical design of the dramatic play center on children's play. *Early Childhood Research Quarterly, 11*(1), 63–77. https://doi.org/10.1016/S0885-2006(96)90029-0

Pierce, H., Jones, M. S., & Gibbs, B. G. (2021). Early adverse childhood experiences and exclusionary discipline in high school. *Social Science Research, 101*(102621), https://doi.org/10.1016/j.ssresearch.2021.102621

Prothero, A. (2021). Older students need social-emotional learning, too. Are they getting it? *Education Week, 41*(9), 3–6. www.edweek.org/leadership/middle-and-high-school-students-need-social-emotional-learning-too-are-they-getting-it/2021/10

Price, C. L., & Steed, E. A. (2016). Culturally responsive strategies to support young children with challenging behavior. *YC: Young Children, 71*(5), 36–43. www.naeyc.org/resources/pubs/yc/nov2016/culturally-responsive-strategies

Ransford, C. R., Greenberg, M. T., Domitrovich, C. E., Small, M., & Jacobson, L. (2009). The role of teachers' psychological experiences and perceptions of curriculum supports on the implementation of a social and emotional learning curriculum. *School Psychology Review, 38*(4), 510–532. https://link.gale.com/apps/doc/A215844828/AONE?u=anon~d81eaed2&sid=googleScholar&xid=498a9626

Ready, D. D., & Wright, D. L. (2011). Accuracy and inaccuracy in teachers' perceptions of young children's cognitive abilities: The role of child background and classroom context. *American Educational Research Journal, 48*(2), 335–360. https://doi.org/10.3102/0002831210374874

Reeve, J., & Jang, H. (2006). What teachers say and do to support students' autonomy during a learning activity. *Journal of Educational Psychology, 98*(1), 209–218. https://doi.org/10.1037/0022-0663.98.1.209

Regenstein, E. (2019). *How early childhood education uses social and emotional learning.* The American Enterprise Institute. https://files.eric.ed.gov/fulltext/ED602773.pdf

Ritchie, S., & Howes, C. (2003). Program practices, caregiver stability, and child–caregiver relationships. *Journal of Applied Developmental Psychology, 24*(5), 497–516. https://doi.org/10.1016/S0193-3973(03)00028-5

Roberts, A., LoCasale-Crouch, J., Hamre, B., & DeCoster, J. (2016). Exploring teachers' depressive symptoms, interaction quality, and children's social-emotional development in Head Start. *Early Education and Development, 27*(5), 642–654. https://doi.org/10.1080/10409289.2016.1127088

Rosanbalm, K. D., & Murray, D. W. (2018). Promoting self-regulation in the first five years: A practice brief (OPRE Brief #2017–79). Office of Planning, Research and Evaluation, Administration for Children and Families, U.S. Department of Health and Human Services. https://files.eric.ed.gov/fulltext/ED583624.pdf

Rucinski, C. L., Brown, J. L., & Downer, J. T. (2018). Teacher–child relationships, classroom climate, and children's social-emotional and academic development. *Journal of Educational Psychology, 110*(7), 992–1004. https://doi.org/10.1037/edu0000240

Ryan, S., & Grieshaber, S. (2004). It's more than child development: Critical theories, research, and teaching young children. *YC: Young Children, 59*(6), 44–52. www.journal.naeyc.org/search/item-detail.asp?page=1&docID=2991&sesID=1170733121813

Saft, E. W., & Pianta, R. C. (2001). Teachers' perceptions of their relationships with students: Effects of child age, gender, and ethnicity of teachers and children. *School Psychology Quarterly, 16*(2), 125–141. https://doi.org/10.1521/scpq.16.2.125.18698

Savina, E. (2021). Self-regulation in preschool and early elementary classrooms: Why it is important and how to promote it. *Early Childhood Education Journal, 49*(3), 493–501. https://doi.org/10.1007/s10643-020-01094-w

Schachter, R. E., Jiang, Q., Piasta, S. B., & Flynn, E. E. (2021). We're more than a daycare: Reported roles and settings for early childhood professionals and implications for professionalizing the field. *Early Childhood Education Journal, 20*(34), 1–14. https://doi.org/10.1007/s10643-021-01252-8

Schroeder-Yu, G. (2008). Documentation: Ideas and applications from the Reggio Emilia approach. *Teaching Artist Journal, 6*(2), 126–134. https://doi.org/10.1080/15411790801910735

Shalaby, C. (2017). *Troublemakers: Lessons in Freedom from Young Children at School.* The New Press.

Shalaby, C. (2020). Classroom management as a curriculum of care. *Educational Leadership, 78*(3), 40–45. www.ascd.org/publications/educational-leadership/nov20/vol78/num03/Classroom-Management-as-a-Curriculum-of-Care.aspx

Sheridan, S. M., & Kratochwill, T. R. (2007). Family–school partnerships in prevention and intervention. In *Conjoint Behavioral Consultation: Promoting Family–School Connections and Interventions* (pp. 1–19). Springer. https://doi.org/10.1007/978-0-387-71248-2_1

Shewark, E. A., Zinsser, K. M., & Denham, S. A.. (2018). Teachers' perspectives on the consequences of managing classroom climate. *Child and Youth Care Forum, 47*(6), 787–802. http://dx.doi.org/10.1007/s10566-018-9461-2

Shonkoff, J. P., & Phillips, D. A. (Eds.). (2000). *From Neurons to Neighborhoods: The Science of Early Childhood Development.* National Academy Press. http://doi.10.17226/9824

Shutts, K. (2015). Young children's preferences: Gender, race, and social status. *Child Development Perspectives, 9*(4), 262–266. https://doi.org/10.1111/cdep.12154

Sigler, E. A., & Aamidor, S. (2005). From positive reinforcement to positive behaviors: An everyday guide for the practitioner. *Early Childhood Education Journal, 32*(4), 249–253. http://dx.doi.org/10.1007/s10643-004-0753-9

Skiba, R. J., Ormiston, H., Martinez, S. & Cummings, J. (2016). Teaching the social curriculum: Classroom management as behavioral instruction. *Theory Into Practice, 55*(2), 120–128, http://doi.10.1080/00405841.2016.1148990

Smith, B., & Fox, L. (2003). *Systems of service delivery: A synthesis of evidence relevant to young children at risk of or who have challenging behavior.* Center for Evidence-Based Practice: Young Children with Challenging Behavior,

University of South Florida. https://ohiofamilyrights.com/Reports/Special-Reports-Page-4/Systems-of-Service-Delivery-A-Synthesis-of-Evidence-Relevant-to-Young.pdf

Solomon, J., & Henderson, B. (2016). Gender identity and expression in the early childhood classroom. *YC: Young Children, 71*(3), 61. www.naeyc.org/resources/pubs/yc/jul2016/gender-identity

Soto, L. D., & Swadener, B. B. (2002). Toward liberatory early childhood theory, research and praxis: Decolonizing a field. *Contemporary Issues in Early Childhood, 3*(1), 38–66. https://doi.org/10.2304/ciec.2002.3.1.8

Soydan, S. B. (2017). Some variables predicting the school readiness of preschool children. *Ankara University Journal of Faculty of Educational Sciences (JFES), 50*(1), 189–208. https://dergipark.org.tr/en/download/article-file/508577

Spagnola, M., & Fiese, B. H. (2007). Family routines and rituals: A context for development in the lives of young children. *Infants & Young Children, 20*(4), 284–299. https://doi.org/10.1097/01.IYC.0000290352.32170.5a

Stegelin, D. A. (2018). Preschool suspension and expulsion: Defining the issues. Institute for Child Success. www.instituteforchildsuccess.org/wpcontent/uploads/2018/12/ICS-2018-PreschoolSuspensionBrief-WEB.pdf

Stirrup, J., Evans, J., & Davies, B. (2017). Learning one's place and position through play: Social class and educational opportunity in early years education. *International Journal of Early Years Education, 25*(4), 343–360. https://doi.org/10.1080/09669760.2017.1329712

Tonyan, H. A. (2015). Everyday routines: A window into the cultural organization of family child care. *Journal of Early Childhood Research, 13*(3), 311–327. https://doi.org/10.1177/1476718X14523748

Tonyan, H. A., & Howes, C. (2003). Exploring patterns in time children spend in a variety of child care activities: Associations with environmental quality, ethnicity, and gender *Early Childhood Research Quarterly, 18*(1), 121–142. https://doi.org/10.1016/S0885-2006(03)00006-1

Umaña-Taylor, A. J., & Hill, N. E. (2020). Ethnic–racial socialization in the family: A decade's advance on precursors and outcomes. *Journal of Marriage and Family, 82*(1), 244–271. https://doi.org/10.1111/jomf.12622

US Department of Health and Human Services, Substance Abuse and Health Services Administration, by the Center of Excellence for Infant and Early Childhood Mental Health Consultation (2017). Center of Excellence Equity Statement. www.samhsa.gov/sites/default/files/programs_campaigns/IECMHC/center-excellence-equity-framing-statement.pdf

Van Driel, S. & Crasborn, F., Wolff, C. & Brand-Gruwel, S., & Jarodzka, H. (2021). Exploring preservice, beginning and experienced teachers' noticing of classroom management situations from an actor's perspective. *Teaching and Teacher Education, 106*, 103435. https://doi.org/10.1016/j.tate.2021.103435

Vitiello, V. E., Moas, O., Henderson, H. A., Greenfield, D. B., & Munis, P. M. (2012). Goodness of fit between children and classrooms: Effects of child temperament and preschool classroom quality on achievement trajectories. *Early Education and Development, 23*(3), 302–322. http://dx.doi.org/10.1080/10409289.2011.526415

Voorhees, M. D., Walker, V. L., Snell, M. E., & Smith, C. G. (2013). A demonstration of individualized Positive Behavior Support Interventions by Head Start staff to address children's challenging behavior. *Research and Practice for Persons with Severe Disabilities, 38*(3), 173–185. https://doi.org/10.1177/154079691303800304

Whitters, H. G. (2020). *Adverse childhood experiences, attachment, and the early years Learning environment: Research and inclusive practice.* Routledge.

Wahman, C. & Steed, E. (2016). Culturally responsive strategies to support young children with challenging behavior. *YC: Young Children, 71*(5), 36–43. www.naeyc.org/resources/pubs/yc/nov2016/culturally-responsive-strategies

Whitaker, R. C., Dearth-Wesley, T., & Gooze, R. A. (2015). Workplace stress and the quality of teacher–children relationships in Head Start. *Early Childhood Research Quarterly, 30*(1), 57–69. https://doi.org/10.1016/j.ecresq.2014.08.008

Whitebook, M., McLean, C., Austin, L. J., & Edwards, B. (2018). *Early Childhood Workforce Index 2018.* Center for the Study of Child Care Employment, University of California at Berkeley. https://cscce.berkeley.edu/wp-content/uploads/2018/06/2018-Index-Executive-Summary.pdf

Williford, A. P., Alamos, P., Whittaker, J. E., & Accavitti, M. R. (2021). Who's left out of learning? Racial disparities in teacher's' reports of exclusionary discipline strategies beyond suspensions and expulsions. EdWorkingPaper 21–472. https://doi.org/10.26300/pep2-w676

Williford, A. P., LoCasale-Crouch, J., Whittaker, J. V., DeCoster, J., Hartz, K. A., Carter, L. M. Wolcott, C. S., & Hatfield, B. E. (2017). Changing teacher–child dyadic interactions to improve preschool children's externalizing behaviors. *Child Development, 88*(5), 1544–1553. https://doi.org/10.1111/cdev.12703

Williford, A. P., Maier, M. F., Downer, J. T., Pianta, R. C., & Howes, C. (2013). Understanding how children's engagement and teachers' interactions combine to predict school readiness. *Journal of Applied Developmental Psychology, 34*, 299–309. doi:10.1016/j.appdev.2013.05.002.

Winsler, A., & Carlton, M. P. (2003). Observations of children's task activities and social interactions in relation to teacher perceptions in a child-centered preschool: Are we leaving too much to chance? *Early Education and Development, 14*(2), 155–178. https://doi.org/10.1207/s15566935eed1402_2

Wisneski, D. B., & Goldstein, L. S. (2004). Questioning community in early childhood education. *Early Child Development and Care*, *174*(6), 515–526. https://doi.org/10.1080/0300443042000187031

Wohlfarth, H. (1986). Colour and light effects on students' achievement, behavior and physiology. Alberta Department of Education, Edmonton. https://files.eric.ed.gov/fulltext/ED272312.pdf

Wohlwend, K. E. (2015). *Playing their way into literacies: Reading, writing, and belonging in the early childhood classroom.* Teachers College Press.

Wymer, S. C., Williford, A. P., & Lhospital, A. S. (2020). Exclusionary discipline practices in early childhood. *YC:Young Children*, *75*(3), 36–44. www.naeyc.org/resources/pubs/yc/jul2020/exclusionary-discipline-practices-early-childhood?r=1&Site=NAEYC

Xiao, N. G., Quinn, P. C., Liu, S., Ge, L., Pascalis, O., & Lee, K. (2018). Older but not younger infants associate own-race faces with happy music and other-race faces with sad music. *Developmental Science*, *21*(2). https://doi.org/10.1111/desc.12537

Yılmaz, A., Şahin, F., Buldu, M., Ülker Erdem, A., Ezmeci, F., Somer Ölmez, B., Aydos, E. H., Buldu, E., Unal, B. H., Aras, S., Baldu, M., & Akgül, E. (2021). An examination of Turkish early childhood teachers' challenges in implementing pedagogical documentation. Early Childhood Education Journal, *49*(6), 1047–1059. https://doi.org/10.1007/s10643-020-01113-w

Yu, R. (2016). Stress potentiates decision biases: A stress induced deliberation-to-intuition (SIDI) model. *Neurobiology of Stress*, *3*, 83–95. https://doi.org/10.1016/j.ynstr.2015.12.006

Yun, C., Melnick, H., & Wechsler, M. (2021). *High-quality early childhood assessment: Learning from states' use of kindergarten entry assessments.* Learning Policy Institute.

Zelazo, P. D., & Carlson, S. M. (2012). Hot and cool executive function in childhood and adolescence: Development and plasticity. *Child Development Perspectives*, *6*(4), 354–360. https://doi.org/10.1111/j.1750-8606.2012.00246.x

Zeng, S., Pereira, B., Larson, A., Corr, C. P., O'Grady, C., & Stone-MacDonald, A. (2021). Preschool suspension and expulsion for young children with disabilities. *Exceptional Children*, *87*(2), 199–216. https://doi.org/10.1177/0014402920949832

Zinsser, K. M., Shewark, E. A., Denham, S. A., & Curby, T. W. (2014). A mixed-method examination of preschool teacher beliefs about social-emotional learning and relations to observed emotional support. *Infant & Child Development*, *23*(5), 471–493. https://doi.org/10.1002/icd.1843

Zinsser, K. M., Zulauf, C. A., Nair Das, V., & Silver, H. C. (2017). Utilizing social-emotional learning supports to address teacher stress and preschool expulsion. Journal of Applied *Developmental Psychology*, *61*, 33–42. https://doi.org/10.1016/j.appdev.2017.11.006

Zulauf-McCurdy, C. A., & Zinsser, K. M. (2021). How teachers' perceptions of the parent-teacher relationship affect children's risk for early childhood expulsion. *Psychology in the Schools*, *56*(6), 69–88. https://onlinelibrary.wiley.com/doi/epdf/10.1002/pits.22440

INDEX

Note: Figures are indicated by *italics* and tables by **bold type**. Endnotes are indicated by the page number followed by "n" and the note number e.g., 159n22 refers to note 22 on page 159. The acronyms "CM", "CRCM", and "SEB" are used for "classroom management", "culturally relevant classroom management", and "Social, Emotional, and Behavior" respectively.

1619 Project, The 212, 459

AAPI (Asian and Pacific Islander) students 482–483
ABA (applied behavior analysis) **122**, 256, 353, 443, 500, 504–505, 519, 529–530
ABCD (Affective-Behavioral-Cognitive-Dynamic) model of development 360
ability and willingness to use culturally appropriate management strategies, CRCM essential principle of 487
absenteeism 61–62, 64, 242, 384
abuse, verbal 416, **417**, 418, 419
academic achievement 20, 35, 36, 40, 46, 56, 61, 63, 88–89, 95, 139, 155, 167, 169, 171–172, 216, 218, 221, 235, 275, 277, 281, 282, 289, 356, 436, 440, 510
academic attainment 161–163, 278, 289, 291, 292
academic competence 81, 84, 356, 357, 361
academic engaged time (AET) 78, 81, 84
academic engagement 56, 75, 84, **108**, 141, 172, 258, 510, 526–527; and positive behavioral interventions 88–89, 94–95, 96; and school-to-prison pipeline 299, 300–303
academic instruction 3, 16, *104*, **119**, 486n
academic motivation 20, 21, 299
academic outcomes 95, 130, 152, 177, 179, 249, 375, 384, 512, 524; and CM programs and strategies 352, 353, 358, 361, 363; and discipline gap 436, 438, 447; and restorative practices 57, 63–64
academic performance 87, **118**, 129, 134, 172, 302, 439, 442, 443, 484, 486, 500; and CM programs and strategies 355–356, 358, 360–361, 366; and First Step 78, 79, 84; prevention strategies for 41, 46, 48; and restorative practices 64, 66, 69

academic skills **109**, **112**, **121**, 353, 361, 526
academic socialization 233, 236–237
academic success 154, 281, 294, 376, 377, **378**, 436, 485, 502
acceptable behaviors 282, 416, 424–426
accountability: for discriminatory practices 376; for misbehavior 54; of school staff 90, 154, 202, 272, 330, 436, 438, 539; for social harm 69
ACEs (Adverse Childhood Experiences) 299, 382, 437
achievement: academic *see* academic achievement; student *see* student achievement
Achievement First (AF) 152, 155–156
action planning 89, 90, 93, **108**, 134, 240, 255, **378**, 445, 512
active engagement 6, 22–23, **23**, **119**
active supervision **112**, **118**, 129, 136–137; and disabilities 502, 506, 508, 509, 513; and positive behavioral interventions 88, 89, 91, 94
ADHD *see* Attention Deficit Hyperactive Disorder (ADHD)
Adler-Dreikurs CM Techniques **354**, 358
administrative support 79, 83, 178
adolescence 39, 167, 169
adult learning element, of school climate improvement process 178
Adverse Childhood Experiences (ACEs) 299, 382, 437
adversity 291, 292, 298, 437
AET (academic engaged time) 78, 81, 84
AF (Achievement First) 152, 155–156
Affective-Behavioral-Cognitive-Dynamic (ABCD) model of development 360
affective learning **417**, 419–420, 421–422

affective outcomes 400

African-Americans 78, 324, 356, 357, 361, 362; *see also* Black students; Black teachers

AFT (American Federation of Teachers) 319

agency: educator 546; student 302–303, 376–377, 380, *390*, 391, 393, 394; teacher *see* teacher agency

aggression: micro- 35, 381–382, 442; social 62; student 168, 170, 171, 172, 173, 174, 175, 176, 177, 178; teacher 10–11, 254, 415–430, **417**, **427**

agreeableness 194, 402

Albuquerque Public Schools (APS) 78, 80

American Federation of Teachers (AFT) 319

antecedent strategies 31–36, 103, 116

anti-bullying 171, 176, 178, 353

"anti-Critical Race Theory" bills 219, 472n5

anti-racism 162, 489, 492

antisocial behavior 175, 194, 501

anxiety 8, 68, **112**, 116, 171, 172, 252, 282, 300, 341, 401, 440, 523, 524; disorders of 81–82, 84, 518; and prevention strategies 32, 38, 39, 43; and teacher stress 189–190, 199, 201, 202

applied behavior analysis (ABA) **122**, 256, 353, 443, 500, 504–505, 519, 529–530

appraisals, of demands and resources 190–191, 193, 194

APS (Albuquerque Public Schools) 78, 80

argumentativeness **417**, 420

ASD (Autism Spectrum Disorder) 81, 170, 517–530

Asian and Pacific Islander (AAPI) students 482–483

aspirations 236, 275, 279

assets, of children 290, 291, 299, 300, 481, 539; cultural 170, 302–303, 376

at-risk students 74, 75, 81, 161–162, 178

attachment: emotional 299; parental 399; peer 60, 62, 384; school 400

attachment history 429

attachment narrative 254, 423, 425, 428, 429

attainment: academic 161–163, 278, 289, 291, 292; educational 161–163, 278, 289, 291, 292; student 163, 278

attendance, school *see* school attendance

Attention Deficit Hyperactive Disorder (ADHD) 80–81, 83, 84, 258, 361, 526; *see also* hyperactivity

Australia 251, 399, 400, 416, **417**, 426, 522, 526

autism 11, 81, 84, 143, 170, 500, 517–530

autistic boys 520–521, 523, 526

autonomy: student 155, 239; teacher 195–196, 197, 301

autoregressive cross-lagged model 427

avatars 340

avoidance behaviors 168

awareness of broader social, economic, and political context, CRCM essential principle of 487, 489

barriers: to equitable CM 537–538; to developing teachers' social competence 234–235

Behavior and Academic Support and Enhancement (BASE) intervention 78

Behavior Intervention Plans (BIPs) 241, 328

behavior management (BM): and autism 519, 520, 522–523, 524, 528, 529, 530; and critical race theory 463, 464, 465, 466, 470, 471; equity-driven 436–448; poor 502–504; proactive 257, 260; reactive 93, 96

behavior patterns 74, 75, 276, 499, 500, 501–502

behavior protocols 468, 469, 471

behavior rules, anchored to larger expectations *18*

behavior support plan (BSP) 103, 331, 332, 509

behavioral analysis: applied (ABA) **122**, 256, 353, 443, 500, 504–505, 519, 529–530; functional (FBA) 103, 241, 328, 337–338, 520, 543

behavioral assessment 5, 103, 116, 223, 251, 337

behavioral challenges 79–80, 131, 256, 258, 296, 340, 483, 504, 538, 540

behavioral change 79, 84, 143, 500, 504, 505, 521, 526, 528–529, 547

behavioral characteristics 74, 353, 500–501, 502, 504, 513

behavioral compliance, of students with autism 519, 520, 521, 526, 527–528

behavioral data 89, 520

behavioral development 172–173, 179, 441

behavioral difficulties 355, 359

behavioral disengagement **417**, 425

behavioral disorders 81, 83, 140, 488, 518

behavioral distress 528

behavioral expectations 6, 7, 33, 37, **132**, 139, 141, 159, 241, 262, 282, 300, 302, 323, 331, 377, 444, 445, 470, 483, 519, 529

behavioral infractions 93, 276, 281, 437, 439, 440, 441, 444

behavioral interventions 6, 80; *see also* Positive Behavioral Interventions and Supports (PBIS)

behavioral misconduct 275, 277

behavioral observations 77, 78, 519–520

behavioral outbursts 275, 277, 282

behavioral outcomes 39, 80, 95, 171, 301, 352, 488, 522

behavioral patterns, challenging 501–502

behavioral practices 134, 154, 159

behavioral problems 4, 6, 59, 302, 353–354, 356, 367, 444; *see also* disruptive behavior problems

behavioral regulation 46, 47, 136

behavioral strategies 62, 137, 444, 492

behavioral support 9, 87, 131, 224, 296, 405, 444, 466, 469; and disabilities 500–501, 511, 518; *see also* Positive Behavioral Interventions and Supports (PBIS)

behaviorism 137, 463, 529

behavior-specific praise 92, 249, 258, 503, 508, 509, 510

beliefs: about class 292; deficit-based 260, 278, 481; of families 233, 237; and identity 511, 538, 547; liberal 402; moral 402; paternalist 402; about race 212, 213–214, **214**, 215, 216, 223, 225, 192; student 290, 422; teacher 136, 241, 242, 250, 254, 255, 257, 279, 402, 440, 446, 470, 487

best practices 10, 154, 189, 250, 255, 257, 258, 274, 330, 380 biases: cultural 295, 487, 539; educator 224, 540; implicit *see* implicit bias; implicit racial 445–448; personal 20, 222, 279, 460, 538; racial 11, 293, 301, 445–448, 469–470; systemic 538, 539; and victimization 169

BIPs (Behavior Intervention Plans) 241, 328

Black boys, disciplining of 538, 540

Black female students with disabilities, disciplining of 470

Black Lives Matter 211, 212, 215, 225n4

Black students 35, 170–171, 301, 384, 468, 470; discipline gap 437, 440, 444, 445; exclusionary discipline for 56, 124, 130, 216, 217, 218, 222, 279, 295, 437; New Jim Crow 216, 217, 218, 222; restorative practices 56, 60, 63, 64, 67, 69; teacher education 480–481, 482, 484–485, 488

BM *see* behavior management (BM)

boys 61, 78, 399, 401, 402, 403, 439, 470, 537; with autism 520–521, 523, 526; Black 538, 540

brain breaks 43–44, 44–45, 45–47, *46*, 48

brain-to-brain synchrony 237, 408

breathing 37, 40, 41, 43–45, *44*, *45*, *46*, 47, **120**, 520

Brown v. Board of Education 217, 292, 440, 480–481

BSP (behavior support plan) 103, 331, 332, 509

building relationships 21, 34–36, 139, 171, 233, 254, 275–276, 376

bullying 9, 143, 282, 293, **326**, 332, 353, 383–384, 401, 501, 503; emerging issues in research prevention of 9, 60, 167–179, **378**; restorative practices for 57, 59–60, 64, 66, 69

burnout *see* teacher burnout

bystanders 174, 175, 416, **417**, 424–426, 429

CAID (Continuous Assessment of Interpersonal Dynamics) 391–392

CAPs (content acquisition podcasts) 10, 143, 336, 337–339, *338*

carceral logics 466, 469, 471

caregiver attunement 539

caregiver concerns 65–66

caregiver responsiveness 424, 429

caregivers 66, 203, 423, 534, 537, 539, 540–541, 544, 546

caring 25, 26, 63, 136, 174, 381, 382, 421, 487; and CM programs and strategies 350, 351, 352; in early childhood education 539, 544, 547; and school administration 272, 275, 276; and school-to-prison pipeline 294, 296, 299, 300

Carter, Samuel Casey 154–155

CASEL *see* Collaborative for Academic, Social, and Emotional Learning (CASEL)

case law 320, 321

caste system 215

CBAM (concerns-based adoption model) 302

CCU (Classroom Check-Up) **132**, 137–138, 143, 257

CDC (Centers for Disease Control) 168, 193, 327

CDF (Children's Defense Fund) 481

Center on Reinventing Public Education (CRPE) 154, 157, 158

Center on the Social and Emotional Foundations for Early Learning (CSEFEL) 535, 542

Centers for Disease Control (CDC) 168, 193, 327

certification programs 242, 251, 253

challenging behaviors 9, 21, 22, 27, 33, 35, 129, 235, 256, 439; and disabilities 500, 504, 505–508, **507**, 511, 513; and early childhood education 545, 546, 547; patterns of 501–502; and social, emotional and behavior (SEB) growth **118**, **119**, **120**; character strengths 36

Charter Management Organizations (CMOs) 152, 153, 154, 155, 157, 158–159, 160, 161–162, 163

charter networks 59, 62, 64, 153, 155

charter school heterogeneity 154

charter schools 9, 59, 152–163, 216

"Check-In/Check-Out" (CICO) 6, 87, 506, **507**, 511; and social, emotional and behavior (SEB) growth 110, **111**, **112**, **113**, **114**, **115**, **117**, **118**, **120**

child behavior problems 359, 364

child development 160, 291, 293, 537, 547; *see also* children's development

childcare 483, 537

children's assets 290, 291, 299, 300, 481, 539; cultural 170, 302–303, 376

Children's Defense Fund (CDF) 481

children's development 193–194, 289, 291, 538, 543–544; *see also* child development

children's learning 242, 536, 537

Ci3T (Comprehensive, Integrated, Three-tiered) 11, 506, **507**, 508, 510, 511, 512, 513

CICO *see* "Check-In/Check-Out" (CICO)

circles 136, 282, 297, 382, 383, 448, 490; and prevention strategies 36–37, 43–44, 48; and restorative practices 56, 66, 67, 68, 69

civil rights 212, **214**, 214, 219, 225, 461, 462

CLASS (Classroom Assessment Scoring System) 342

CLASS (Contingencies for Learning Academic and Social Skills) Program 77

classroom activities **113**, 237, 361, 363, 364, 395, 425

Classroom Assessment Scoring System (CLASS) 342

Classroom Check-Up (CCU) **132**, 137–138, 143, 257

classroom climate 9, 35, 47, 96, 197, 381, 419–420, 421, 436, 502, 546; and CM at different timescales 390, 393, 403, 404–405, 407

classroom community 19, 35, **105**, **111**, 519, 534, 540, 541, 542, 545

classroom conflicts 48, 65, 67, 484

classroom demands *190*, 190, 191, 194, 197, 200

classroom discipline 322, 465; *see also* discipline

classroom environment 253, 275, 380, 384, 508, 534, 541, 543; and autism 518, 519, 523, 528, 529; and CM programs and strategies 518, 519, 523, 528, 529; inclusive 20, 298; positive 10, 350; punitive 298; and social, emotional and behavior (SEB) growth **105**, **108**, **111**

classroom expectations 17, 18, 33, 48, 94

classroom instruction 8, **27**, 342, 480–481

classroom interaction 252, 289, 300, 342, 344, 441; and CM at different timescales 389, 390, 391; and family engagement 233, 235, 236, 237

classroom management curriculum 253, 254

classroom management framework, for teacher educators 252–254

classroom management instruction 91, 477–493

classroom management interventions 4, 249, 257, 331, 350, 365, 519, 528

classroom management knowledge 251, 257, 258, 335, 339

classroom management observation tool (CMOT) 91, 253

Classroom Management Practice Relationships Partnership (CM PReP) framework 253, 261

classroom management preparation 250–252; *see also* Classroom Management Practice Relationships Partnership (CM PReP) framework

classroom management professional development 143–144, **144**, 256, 426

classroom management programs (CMPs) 144, 350–367, **354**, **365**

classroom management self-efficacy 194, 195, 197

classroom management skills 6, 143, 366, 367, 477, 500, 528; and multimedia 335, 339, 340, 343, 345; and school administration 272, 273, 282; and teacher stress 191, 197, 200, 202; and teacher training 250, 255, 256, 257, 261

classroom management strategies 36, 198, 273, 275, 277, 340, 350–367, **354**, **365**; and delivery across contexts 128, 129–130, 136, 137, 139, 142, 143, 144; and positive behavioral interventions 87, 91, 92, 93; and teacher training 249, 251, 255, 257, 258, 259

classroom management stress 191, 192–194

classroom management support 39, 202, 249, 278, 351

classroom management teacher training 262

classroom management training 96, 136, 141, 142, 143, 144, 353, **354**, 441, 444; need for 249–250; special issues in 257–261; in teacher training 251, 253, 254, 262

classroom managers 4, 5, 6, 17, 40, 195, 239, 493, 539; and teacher training 256, 258–259, 260, 261

classroom norms 303, 381, 425, 505; and social, emotional and behavior (SEB) growth *104*, **106**, **107**, **112**, **113**, **118**, **119**, **120**

classroom observations 92, 163, 362, 365, 391, 465, 522

classroom organization 271, 342, 541

classroom practices 94, 95, 123, 124, 296–303, 366

classroom processes 236, 390, 537

classroom routines 6, 41, 47, 131, 535, 542, 543; and social, emotional and behavior (SEB) growth **106**, **107**, **111**, **117**, **121**, 124

classroom rules 3, 4, 7, 33, 34, 75, 176, 329, 359, 361, 362, 463, 528, 529

classroom social climate: and CM at different timescales 389, 390, 391, 393, 397, 398–403, *398*,

404, 405; effective instruction in 16, 17–18, *18*, **19**, 21, 25, 27

classroom space structuring 31–32

classroom strategies 131, 275–277, 527

classroom structures 88, 174, 251

classroom systems 90, 139, 259

classroom-level predictors, and bullying/peer victimization 174

Class-Wide Function-Related Intervention Teams (CW-FIT) 94–95, **354**, 364–365, **365**

Class-wide Positive Behavioral Intervention and Supports (CWPBIS) 9, 87, 88–95, *90*, 96

clear and reasonable expectations 542–543

closeness 35, 236, 355, 361, 540

CM PReP (Classroom Management Practice Relationships Partnership) framework 253, 261

CMOs (Charter Management Organizations), 152, 154–55, 157–58, 160, 163–66

CMOT (classroom management observation tool) 91, 253

CMPs (classroom management programs) 144, 350–367, **354**, **365**

coaching, in effective classroom management 5, 6

coded race discourse, around classroom management 464–465

coercion 224, 405, 486

cognition 41, 46, 48, 168, 517; social 233, 238–239, 240, 242

cognitive theory of multimedia learning (CTML) **336**, 337

Collaborative for Academic, Social, and Emotional Learning (CASEL) 176–177, 375, 376, 377, 443

college attendance 216, 218, 221

colorblind ideology 160, 219, 220–221, 225, 466, 467

colorblind racism 10, 212, 213, 215, 219

colorblindness 160, 219, 220–221, 225, 279, 460, 468, 469

Color Wheel System (CWS) 354–355, 528

commitment to building caring classroom communities, CRCM essential principle of 487

communication skills 173, 174, 175, 177, 179, 419

communion 389, *390*, 390, 391, 392, *392*, 393–394, *394*, 395, 396, 397, *398*, 399–401, 402–403, *404*, 404–405, 406, 407

community building 36, 37, 56, 67, 68, 69, 297, 538, 539–541, 542

community partnerships 178, 377, **378**, 379, 380

community problem solving 544–545

competence: academic 81, 84, 356, 357, 361; cultural 280, 281, 290, 295, 296–297, 299, 379, 485; social-emotional 237, 298, 359, 360, 361, 528, 530, 540, 546

complementarity, interpersonal 393–394, *394*, 395, 407

compliance 36, 57, 60, 64, 299, 356, 364, 382, 420, 429, 464, 493, 536, 544; behavioral 519, 520, 521, 526, 527–528, 530, 547; non- 158, 242, 535–536

comprehensive assessment 103, 116, **117**, **118**, **119**, **122**, **378**

Comprehensive, Integrated, Three-tiered (Ci3T) 11, 506, **507**, 508, 510, 511, 512, 513

comprehensive student support plan, for SEB 116, 123

Comprehensive Support Plan Development **117**, **118**, **120**, **122**

computers 41, 134, 138, 319, 324, **326**, 340, 400, 523–524, 527

concerns-based adoption model (CBAM) 302

conflict 83, 382, 384, 424, 446, 461, 487, 500; classroom 48, 65, 67, 484; cultural 137, 195, 478, 489; in early childhood education 534, 536, 538, 544; and family engagement 235, 236, 237; interpersonal 176, 194; resolution of 16, 36, 63, 329, 383, 490, 535; and restorative practices 36, 48, 54, 55, 62, 65, 68, 282

constitutional law 320

content acquisition podcasts (CAPs) 10, 143, 336, 337–339, *338*

content knowledge 234, 242, 272

contextualized information 17–18, *18*

Contingencies for Learning Academic and Social Skills (CLASS) Program 77

Continuous Assessment of Interpersonal Dynamics (CAID) 391–392

continuous improvement 294, 296, 301, 377, 379, 380

continuous professional development (CPD) 56, 67, 529–530

conversations, role in restorative justice of 382, 383, 385

coping: emotion-focused 199; preventive *198*, 198; problem-focused 198–199; resources for 199–202

corporal punishment *see* teacher corporal punishment

correction 25–26, 88, **108**, **120**, 426; pre- 136, 339, 502, 506, 508, 509, 513

counseling criteria, of Gerich and Schmitz 240

counterstorying, in Critical Race Theory 461

"Counting Blessings" 38

COVID-19 pandemic 8, 10, 68, 128, 138, 156, 261, 375, 376, 437, 458, 508; and discipline in virtual settings 319–333, **326**, **327**; and New Jim Crow 211, 213, 215; and teacher stress 189, 192–193, 199, 203

CPD (continuous professional development) 56, 67, 529–530

CRCM (culturally relevant classroom management) 259–261, 262

CRCM (Culturally Responsive Classroom Management) 478, 487, 488, 489–492

criminal justice system 54, 213, 214, 216, 281, 291, 295, 300, 439, 483; *see also* juvenile justice system

Critical Race Theory (CRT) 11, 160, 219, 457–473, 492

CRPBIS (culturally responsive positive behavior interventions and supports) 489, 490–491, 493

CRPE (Center on Reinventing Public Education) 154, 157, 158

CRT (Critical Race Theory) 11, 160, 219, 457–473, 492

CSEFEL (Center on the Social and Emotional Foundations for Early Learning) 535, 542

CTML (cognitive theory of multimedia learning) **336**, 337

cultural backgrounds 136, 281, 381, 444, 464, 483, 487, 489

cultural biases 295, 487, 539

cultural competence 280, 281, 290, 295, 296–297, 299, 379, 485

cultural conflict 137, 195, 478, 489

cultural contexts 142, 289, 300, 398, 542

cultural differences 160, 260, 281, 303, 376, 399, 426, 488–489

cultural diversity 137, 281, 477

cultural norms 275, 281, 375, 444, 445, 485, 536, 537

cultural values 40, 171, 380, 381, 382, 487, 491, 512, 536, 537, 540

culturally relevant classroom management (CRCM) 259–261, 262

culturally relevant pedagogical framework, of Ladson-Billings 484–485

Culturally Responsive Classroom Management (CRCM) 478, 487, 488, 489–492

Culturally Responsive Classroom Management Framework, of Weinstein and colleagues 487

Culturally Responsive Classroom Management Instruction 489

culturally responsive instruction 299, 300, 484, 486, 488

culturally responsive positive behavior interventions and supports (CRPBIS) 489, 490–491, 493

culturally responsive teaching framework, 450, 464, 486, 495

culturally sensitive meditation 39–41

culturally-responsive practices framework 137–138

culture change 65, 69

current classroom management 8

curriculum 20, **107**, **112**, 359–360, 538–539; CM 253, 254; CRCM practice integration into 489–492; developmentally appropriate 536–537; educator preparation 234; hybrid 31; and school administration 271, 272, 273, 275, 276, 278, 279, 280–281; social and emotional learning **144**, 177; in teacher education 477, 478, 485, 486, 487, 488; in teacher training 251, 253, 254, 260

CW-FIT (Class-Wide Function–Related Intervention Teams) 94–95, **354**, 364–365, **365**

CWPBIS (Class-wide Positive Behavioral Intervention and Supports) 9, 87, 88–95, *90*, 96

CWS (Color Wheel System) 354–355, 528

cyberbullying 68, 168, 169, 325–326, **326**

daily progress report (DPR) 110, **111**, **112**, **113**, **114**, **118**, **120**, **507**

data disaggregation 272, 302, 444

data for equity 511, 512

data-based decision making (DBDM) 9, 87, 88, 89, 93, 138, 297, 377, 491

DBRs (direct behavior ratings) 89, **121**

DCPD (Double Check Professional Development) 137, 138
defiant behavior 158, 194, 300
deficit-based beliefs 260, 278, 481
delinquency 216, 218, 300, 503
Denver Public Schools 327
Departments of Education 6–7, 65, 168, 176
depression 8, 38, 39, 82, 116, 168, 169, 171, 172, 194, 201, 202, 282, 300, 437, 518
development: Affective-Behavioral-Cognitive-Dynamic model of development 360; behavioral 172–173, 179, 441; child *see* child development; children's *see* children's development; CM professional 143–144, **144**, 256, 426; Comprehensive Support Plan **117**, **118**, **120**, **122**; Double Check Professional (DCPD) 137, 138; emotional *see* emotional development; human *see* human development; in-service teacher professional 254–257; Multitiered Support for Professional (MTS-PD) 141–143; professional *see* professional development (PD); skill *see* skill development; social 242, 384–385, 540; student 290, 294; targeted professional (TPD) 143, 256; teacher 255, 262; teacher professional 89, 128, **132**, 254–257, 444, 446; zone of proximal (ZPD) 298
developmental outcomes 82, 289, 483
developmental stages 377, 406, 536–537
developmentally appropriate curriculum 536–537
developmentally appropriate practice 536–537
DIA (Dynamic Integrated Approach) 255
direct behavior ratings (DBRs) 89, **121**
disabilities 335–336, 381–382; autism 518, 519–520, 521, 524, 529; and bullying 169–170, 173, 177, 178; CM to support 499–513, **507**; and delivery across contexts 129, 130, 131, 140; exclusionary discipline 56, 60, 61, 328, 439, 470, 538; inclusive environments for 257–258; and social, emotional and behavior (SEB) growth 102, **108**, 116, 124
Disability Critical Race theory (DisCrit) 461–462, 467, 470
disadvantaged schools 216, 218
disaggregation: and disciplinary reform 224; of student data 272, 302, 444
disciplinary disparities *see* discipline disparities
disciplinary disproportionality 10, 60, 93, 138, 212, 223, 441, 467, 478; ethnic 466–467, 482; racial 222–223, 288, 297, 439, 466–467, 468, 469, 471, 480, 482
disciplinary policies 11, 136, 153, 161, 273, 289, 303, 448; K-12 319–333, **326**, **327**, 441
disciplinary practices 220–221, 273, 288, 292, 482; and disabilities 502, 503, 511; and discipline gap 437, 440, 441, 448; in no-excuses charter schools 152–153, 155, 156, 157, 160, 161, 162, 163; and school-to-prison pipeline 288–303; in virtual settings 319, 320, 323, 328, 330
disciplinary procedures 321, 323, 329, 438, 440
disciplinary process 321–323, 377

disciplinary reform 212, 216, 217, 220, 221, 222, 224, 469
disciplinary strategies 9, 10, 335, 355, 437, 439
discipline: classroom 322, 465; exclusionary *see* exclusionary discipline; no-excuses 153, 157, 158–162, 163; punitive 65, 281, 382, 437, 438, 439, 440, 445, 446, 500, 503, 511; restorative 137, 297, 328, 447–448, 489–490, 491, 493; school *see* school discipline; student *see* student discipline; virtual 325–327, **326**; zero tolerance *see* zero tolerance discipline
discipline data 138, 277, 330, 444, 482–483
discipline disparities 11, 291, 295, 302, 383, 384, 490; and discipline gap 440, 441, 442, 444, 445, 446, 447, 448; and New Jim Crow 211, 212, 215, 216, 217, 222, 224; and restorative practices 56, 57, 60–61, 64, 65, 66, 68, 69
discipline gap 61, 217, 218, 384, 436–448, 481, 482
discipline policies *see* disciplinary policies
discipline practices *see* disciplinary practices
discipline rates 58, 60, 61, 66, 384, 490–491
discipline strategies 9, 10, 335, 355, 437, 439
discrimination 169, 179, 280, 332, 379, 381–382, 446, 480; ethnic 170, 539; institutional 223; racial 170, 212, 215, 217, 458, 459, 539
DisCrit (Disability Critical Race theory) 461–462, 467, 470
disengagement, student *see* student disengagement
disparities: disciplinary *see* discipline disparities; ethnic 221, 439, 479, 480–483, 489; racial *see* racial disparities; racial discipline 383, 384, 441, 444, 446
disproportionality, disciplinary *see* disciplinary disproportionality
disruptive behavior problems, and First Step program 74–84
distractions 40, 41, **105**, **111**, **117**, 330, 331, 425, 441
distress 48, 168, 190, 201–202, 219, 221, 301, 358, 382, 528, 535, 539, 543
District Systems Fidelity Inventory (DSFI) 90, 95
diversity 375, 376, 379, 472n1, 493, 539: cultural 137, 281, 477; linguistic 479; racial/ethnic 479; student *see* student diversity 130, **132**, 135, 138, 169, 176, 177, 179, 252, 257, 457; teacher 156, 202, 278, 479; and teacher education 478
Double Check CARES framework **132**, 137
Double Check Professional Development (DCPD) 137, 138
DPR (daily progress report) 110, **111**, **112**, **113**, **114**, **118**, **120**, **507**
dropout 61, 63, 116, 216, 278–279, 384, 439, 483, 503; and school-to-prison pipeline 294, 295, 298, 300
DSFI (District Systems Fidelity Inventory) 90, 95
Dynamic Integrated Approach (DIA) 255
dynamic interactions, between students and teachers 10, 289, 290

early childhood education (ECE) 11, 534–547
Early Childhood Inventory (ECI) 81–82

Early Childhood Mental Health Consultation (ECMHC) 546–547
early intervention, for young students with behavior problems 74–84
Early Start Denver Model 522
EBD (emotional and behavioral disorders) 140, 488, 518
EBPs *see* evidence-based practices (EBPs)
ECE (early childhood education) 11, 534–547
ECI (Early Childhood Inventory) 81–82
ECMHC (Early Childhood Mental Health Consultation) 546–547
educational attainment 161–163, 278, 289, 291, 292
educational equity 202, 376, 377
educational inequality 462
educational outcomes 277, 292, 519, 530
educational performance 439
educational policy 472n4
educational redlining 440–441
educator agency 546
educator bias 224, 540
educator preparation curriculum 234
educator preparation programs *see* preparation programs
effective classroom management: principal support for 273–278; and teacher well-being 197–202, *198*
effective instruction 15–27, *18*, **19**, **23**, **27**
effective instructional feedback 23–24
effective professional development 142, 255
effective teachers 17, 253, 426, 484, 485, 539
effectiveness, of CM programs and strategies 350–367, **354**, **365**
elementary schools **27**, 63, 82, 174, 324, 383, 526
elementary teachers 92, 138, 159, 202, 257
ELLs (English language learners) 479, 480, 481
emancipatory learning 483–484, 486
emotion regulation 177, 199, 201, 355, 357, 360, 361, 362
emotional and behavioral disorders (EBD) 140, 488, 518
emotional attachment 299
emotional disturbances 258, 295, 500, 502, 508
emotional dysregulation 356
emotional exhaustion 189, 192, 195, 251, 397, 402, 438, 440
emotional expression 238, 361, 375; written 38–39, 48
emotional reactivity 202, **417**, 423–424
emotional support 274, 342, 364
emotion-focused coping 199
empathy 37, 60, 202, 240, 382, 383, 443, 448, 511; and bullying 175, 176, 177, 178; and CM programs and strategies 352, 353, 360, 363; and early childhood education 535, 536, 539, 540, 542–543, 544
engagement: academic *see* academic engagement; active 6, 22–23, **23**, **119**; of families 231–243; school 171, 235, 303; student *see* student engagement
engaging multiple stakeholders element, of school climate improvement process 178

engaging the whole child, component of Gay's culturally responsive teaching framework 486
English language learners (ELLs) 479, 480, 481
environment: classroom *see* classroom environment; inclusive and culturally sensitive 541; remote learning 131–133, **132**; rural 133, 134, 135, **144**, 283, 422, 522; supportive 136, 297, 490; urban 135–136, 137; virtual school 10, 320, 324, 325–326, 328–329, 330
equality-based approach, to CM 259
equitable classroom management 136, 259–260, 273, 537–541, 547
equity-driven behavior management 436–448
ethnic discrimination 170, 539
ethnic disparities 221, 439, 479, 480–483, 489
ethnic groups 169, 170, 171, 173, 212, 235, 429
ethnocentrism 16, 136, 487
evaluation, teacher *see* teacher evaluation
evidence-based classroom management practices 91, 92, 93, 96, 129, 130, 335–347, **336**, *338*, *346*
evidence-based practices (EBPs) **119**, 124, 128, 135, 377, 517, 518, 546; involving multimedia 337, 339, 341, 342, 345, 346–347; in positive behavioral interventions 88, 92, 94, 96; in teacher training 254, 255, 257–258
example selection 18–20, **19**
example sequencing 18–20, **19**
exclusionary discipline 273, 281, 283, 383, 482, 483, 546; addressing of 295–296; and charter schools 152, 153; and disabilities 56, 60, 61, 328, 439, 470, 538; and discipline gap 437, 438, 439–440, 441, 442, 443, 444, 445; and "hardening" 294–295; and Positive Behavioral Interventions and Supports (PBIS) 87, 96; and restorative practices 56, 57–58, 59, 60, 65, 67, 68–69; and school-to-prison pipeline 288, 289–290, 291, 293, 300, 301–302, 303; and structural racism 10, 211–225, **214**; and student misbehavior 57
Executive Orders: 13950, of United States Office of Management and Budget 458–459; 13985, of President Joseph R. Biden 459
expert feedback 252, 343–344
explicit instruction 9, 16–17, 37, 91, 92, 94, *104*, **107**, **119**, 501, 536
expulsions 124, 153, 163, 439, 440, 482, 483, 538, 546; in virtual settings 320, 321, 323, 330
externalizing behaviors 395, 442, 500, 506–507
extraversion 194, 399, 402

FABI (functional assessment-based intervention) 500, 506, 511
family characteristics, and bullying/peer victimization 173–174
family engagement 110, 231–243
Family Group Conferencing 58, 62–63
family voice **118**, 296
family-school-community partnerships 380
family-teacher interaction 235, 236, 237

FBA (functional behavior assessment) 103, 241, 328, 337–338, 520, 543

feedback: effective instructional 23–24; expert 252, 343–344; negative 25, 26–27, **27**, 88, 503; performance 6, 91, 92, 94, 96, 124, 143, 256, 257, 445; positive 24, 25, 26–27, **27**, *104*, **107**, 136–137, 509

First Step Next (FSN) 9, 75, 76–77, 77–78, 79–84

First Step Program 74–84

Floyd, George 156, 162, 211, 212–213, 215, 223

Four Cs 157–158, 159

free or reduced lunches (FRL) 356, 357, 360, 361, 362, 363, 364, 365

FSN (First Step Next) 9, 75, 76–77, 77–78, 79–84

functional assessment-based intervention (FABI) 500, 506, 511

functional behavior assessment (FBA) 103, 241, 328, 337–338, 520, 543

funding, of schools 66, 89, 90, 130, 134, 135, 195, 272, 292, 301, 379, 462

GAM (General Aggression Model) **417**, 422–423, 424, 429

Gay, Geneva 279, 280, 281, 440, 443, 464, 511; and teacher education 478, 480, 483, 484, 486, 488, 489

GBG (Good Behavior Game) 351, **354**, 361–362, 527

gender discipline gap 481, 482

General Aggression Model (GAM) **417**, 422–423, 424, 429

general and special educators, empowering of 499–513, **507**

general classroom climate 393, 405; *see also* classroom climate

G-ESDM (Group-Early Start Denver Model) 522

gifted and special education 478, 480, 483, 493

girls 60, 62, 78, 399, 402, 403, 439, 467, 469, 470, 537

Good Behavior Game (GBG) 351, **354**, 361–362, 527

Goss v. Lopez (1975) 320, 321, 322

gratitude writing 38

Greece 398, 399, 400, 416, **417**, 421, 429

GREET-STOP-PROMPT intervention 222

Group-Early Start Denver Model (G-ESDM) 522

group work 31, 32, **105**, 395

guided imagery 37–38, 48

harassment 168, **326**, 332, 416, 426

"hardening," of schools 223, 294–295

Harrison, Ka'Mauri 324–325

healing 36, 201, 294, 303, 382, 490

health: mental *see* mental health; mind-body 36–37, 39, 48

Hierarchy of Needs, of Maslow 31, 32

high schools: bullying in 171, 174, 175; restorative practices in 58, 59, 61, 62, 63, 64

higher education 4, 5, 7, 253, 279–280, 398, 528

high-performing schools 272

high-poverty 135, 137, 361, 438, 444

Hispanic students 63, 80–81, 384, 440, 540

Holland *see* Netherlands

homework 17, **105**, **113**, 138–139, 236, 357, 360, 418

human development 34, 377, 389–390

human value, based on skin color 215, 217–218

hybrid curriculum 31

hyperactivity 41, 48, 81, 356, 360, 363, 500, 501, 513; *see also* Attention Deficit Hyperactive Disorder (ADHD)

ICERs (incremental cost-effectiveness ratios) 83

I³ theory **417**, 422–423

ID (intellectual disabilities) 170, 500, 502, 520

IDEA (Individuals with Disabilities Education Improvement Act) 332, 499, 500, 513

identity-based victimization 169–171

IES (Institute for Education Sciences) 74, 78, 513

IIRP (International Institute of Restorative Practices) 57, 59, 66

implementation fidelity 37, 64, 79–80, 88, 90, *90*, 92, 95, 96, 114, **257**, **378**

implementation support **115**, **122**, 256, 344, 444, 445

Implicit Association Test 217

implicit biases 35, **108**, **114**, 124, 217, 222, 238, 273, 297, 300, 301, 447, 480, 483

implicit racial bias 445–448

impulsivity 178, 360, 361, 500, 501, 513

inclusive and culturally sensitive environment 541

inclusive classrooms 20, 141, 257–258, 298, 486, 513, 522

inclusive practices 39, 294, 556

Incredible Years Teacher Classroom Management (IY-TCM) 355–357, **365**, 366, 367

incremental cost-effectiveness ratios (ICERs) 83

independence **106**, **118**, 156, 159, 522

Indigenous populations 36, 220, 242

Indigenous students 288, 295, 439, 441, 479, 481, 482–483; *see also* Native students

individualized behavior plan **119**, **120**

individualized comprehensive support plans **117**, **118**, **120**, **121**, **122**, 123

individualized SEB support 110–123, **111–115**, **117–122**

Individuals with Disabilities Education Improvement Act (IDEA) 332, 499, 500, 513

inequalities 195, 219, 297, 441, 445, 462; structural 159–160

inequities: structural 135, 379, 439, 441, 442, 448, 491, 537–538; systemic 379, 439, 441, 448, 491, 537–538

innocent bystanders **417**, 424–425, 426, 429

in-service teachers 9, 91, 143, 234–235, 243, 336, 339, 528; professional development of 254–257; training of 250, 254, 256, 261, 262

Insights program **354**, 364, **365**, 366

Institute for Education Sciences (IES) 74, 78, 144, 513

Institute of Positive Education 46, 47

institutional discrimination 223

institutional policies 212, 213, 215, 217, 223, 225

institutional racism 213

instruction: academic 3, 16, *104*, **119**, 486; classroom 8, **27**, 342, 480–481; culturally responsive 299, 300, 484, 486, 488, 489; effective 15–27, *18*, **19**, **23**, **27**; explicit 9, 16–17, 37, 91, 92, 94, *104*, **107**, **119**, 501, 536; social skills 37, 110, **111**, **112**, **113**, **114**, **115**, 522, 530

instructional choice 502, 506, 508, 510, 513

instructional leadership 271, 272

instructional materials **105**, **106**, 280, 335, 521

instructional practices 15, 16, 27, **132**, 260, 289, 381, 484, 486

instructional strategies 22, 339, 402, 499, 510

instructional supervision 271, 272

instructional time 96, 154, 176, 178, 259, 295, 335–336, 436, 438, 482, 483, 523

integrated tiered systems 505–508, **507**, 511–512, 513

intellectual disabilities (ID) 170, 500, 502, 520

intelligence 238, 399, 480, 481

interests, of students 134, 139, 231, 233, 237, 275, 278, 279, 422

intergroup contact theory 447

interlocking constellation, of institutional policy and individual beliefs and actions that define structural racism 213, 216

International Institute of Restorative Practices (IIRP) 57, 59, 66

interpersonal attraction **417**, 421–422

interpersonal behavior 389, 390, 391, 393, 396, 408

Interpersonal Circle (IPC) 389, *390*, 391–392, 407

interpersonal complementarity 393–394, *394*, 395, 407

interpersonal conflict 176, 194

interpersonal interactions 10, 201, 223, 391, 396, 464

interpersonal relationships 178, 233, 238, 239, 243, 288, 298–303, 400, 457

interpersonal style 389, 390, *391*, 405

interpersonal teacher behavior 405, 407, 408

interpersonal theory 388, 389, 393

intersectionality 461, 468–469

intervention effectiveness 83, 222

intervention effects 78, 80, 177, 354, 366

intervention grids 506, **507**, 510, 511

intervention implementation 167, **378**, 445

intervention programs 82, 167, 175–176, 445, 522

intervention strategies 130, 281, 331, 333, 384

interventions: behavioral 6, 74–84; CM 4, 249, 257, 331, 350, 365, 519, 528; functional assessment-based (FABI) 500, 506, 511; GREET-STOP-PROMPT 222; mindfulness-based (MBIs) 201, 202; preventive 218, 351; race-conscious programmatic 222; restorative 297, 328, 447–448

intrinsic motivation 161, 196, 239, 302, **417**, 421–422

iPads 523–524

IPC (Interpersonal Circle) 389, *390*, 391–392, 407

Irie Classroom Toolbox **354**, 359, **365**

Israel 276, 416, **417**, 418

IY-TCM (Incredible Years Teacher Classroom Management) 355–357, **365**, 366, 367

Jefferson Parish Public Schools System (JPPSS) 324–325

job stress 198, 254

JPPSS (Jefferson Parish Public Schools System) 324–325

justice system 54, 213, 214, 216, 281, 291, 295, 300, 439, 483; *see also* juvenile justice system

juvenile delinquency 216, 218, 300, 503

juvenile justice system 36, 55, 289, 290, 439, 464, 483, 503

K-12 disciplinary policies and practices 319–333, **326**, **327**

K-12 schools, restorative justice in 55

Ka'Mauri Harrison Act 325

KIPP (Knowledge is Power Program) 152, 155–156, 157, 161, 162

knowledge: CM 251, 257, 258, 335, 339; content 234, 242, 272; teacher 136

Knowledge is Power Program (KIPP) 152, 155–57, 161, 165

knowledge of student's cultural background, CRCM essential principle of 487

knowledge-to-practice gap 249

Ladson-Billings, Gloria 471–472, 484–485, 487, 488, 489, 493

Latinx students 218, 300, 446, 467, 479, 480

law, sources of 320–321

LD (learning disabilities) 170, 500, 502

leadership 36, 59, 62, 66, 178, 196, 276, 277, 546; instructional 271, 272; and school-to-prison pipeline 294, 296, 299, 301

leadership style 358, **417**, 421

leadership teams 110, 144, 277, 278, 465, 512; and positive behavioral interventions 87, 89–90, *90*, 93, 96

LEAP (Learning Experiences: Alternative Program for Preschoolers and Parents) 521

learning: adult 178, 255; affective **417**, 419–420, 421–422; children's 242, 536, 537; emancipatory 483–484, 486; multidimensional 486; multimedia **336**, 337, 338; online *see* online learning; professional *see* professional learning; remote 131–133, *132*; social 74–75; social and emotional *see* social and emotional (SEL); Transformational Social Emotional (TSEL) 10, 375–385, **378**; transformative 486; Universal Design for (UDL) 10, 249, 258, 262

learning disabilities (LD) 170, 500, 502

Learning Experiences: Alternative Program for Preschoolers and Parents (LEAP) 521

legal rights 321, 324, 329–330

lesbian, gay, bisexual, transgender, queer or questioning (LGBTQ+) community 169, 171

lesson planning 22, 93, **107**, 199, 271, 278, 343, 359, 363

LGBTQ+ (lesbian, gay, bisexual, transgender, queer or questioning) community 169, 171

linguistic diversity, among K–12 students 479
linguistic incongruence 479
"living bridge," connecting home and school 231, 243
loving kindness meditation 41
low-intensity strategies 500, 502, 506, 510
low-intensity supports 508, 510–511, 513
low-intensity, teacher-delivered strategies 508–511
lynching 215, 217

Machiavellianism 421
mask mandates 320, 324, 327, **327**
mass incarceration 215, 219, 288
math 17, 24, 36, 63, 64, 232, 384, 399, 480, 527, 537;
    and CM programs and strategies 356, 361, 363, 364
MBIs (mindfulness-based interventions) 201, 202
MBSR (Mindfulness Based Stress Reduction)
    201–202
measurement practices element, of school climate
    improvement process 178
meditation 41, 47, 48, 199, 201; culturally sensitive
    39–41; loving kindness 41; mindfulness 37, 41
memory 338, 341, 342; working 39, 46, 202, 406
mental health 8, 32, 38, **132**, 193, 201, 301, 546; and
    bullying 169, 171, 172, 174, 179; disorders of 437,
    438, 442, 443; services for 133, 295, 297, 320; and
    social, emotional and behavior (SEB) growth **105**,
    116, **122**, 123; supports for 134–135, 296; training
    for **144**; in virtual settings 324, 328, 330
mentoring 66, 124, 137, 200, 202, 218, 273–274,
    545–546
microaggressions 35, 381–382, 442
middle schools, restorative practices in 59, 60, 61, 62,
    63, 64
mind-body health 36–37, 39, 48
mindfulness-based interventions (MBIs) 201, 202
Mindfulness Based Stress Reduction (MBSR)
    201–202
mindfulness meditation 37, 41
mindfulness practice 491; *see also* Relaxation and
    Guided Imagery (RGI)
minoritized groups 102, 221, 291, 537, 538, 539
minority students 93, 195, 218, 440, 442, 444, 446,
    466–467
monitoring: progress 116, **121**, 123; self- *see*
    self-monitoring
motivation: academic 20, 21, 299; intrinsic 161, 196,
    239, 302, **417**, 421–422; student 34, 300, 301, 303,
    366, 400, 415, 419
motivational outcomes 3, 350, 351, 352, 366
movement breaks 45–47, *46*
MTS-PD (Multitiered Support for Professional
    Development) 141–143
MTSS (Multi-Tiered System of Supports) 102–125,
    104, **105–109**, **111–115**, **117–122**
multicultural classrooms, interaction in 397
multicultural education 462, 464, 486–487
multidimensional learning 486
multimedia 241, 242, 255, 335–347, **336**, *338*,
    346

multimedia learning (CTML), cognitive theory of
    336
Multitiered Support for Professional Development
    (MTS-PD) 141–143
Multi-Tiered System of Supports (MTSS) 102–125,
    104, **105–109**, **111–115**, **117–122**
murder, of George Floyd 156, 162, 211, 212–213,
    215, 223
Mursion 340–341, 345
mutual respect 21, 358, 382, 541

NACSA (National Association of Charter School
    Authorizers) 155
NAEP (National Assessment of Education Progress)
    480
NAEYC *see* National Association for the Education
    of Young Children (NAEYC)
NASEM *see* National Academies of Sciences,
    Engineering, and Medicine (NASEM)
National Academies of Sciences, Engineering, and
    Medicine (NASEM) 167, 168, 173, 175, 176, 234,
    288, 293, 295, 298
National Assessment of Education Progress (NAEP)
    480
National Association for the Education of Young
    Children (NAEYC) 535, 537, 538, 539, 541, 542,
    545
National Association of Charter School Authorizers
    (NACSA) 155
National Center for Pyramid Model Innovations
    (NCPMI) 545, 547
National Center on Educational Statistics (NCES) 4,
    133, 169, 195, 479
National Institute for Health and Care Excellence
    (NICE) 535, 536, 537
National Research Council 288, 299
National School Climate Council 178
Native students 288, 295, 439, 441, 479, 481,
    482–483; *see also* Indigenous students
NCES (National Center on Educational Statistics) 4,
    133, 169, 195, 479
NCPMI (National Center for Pyramid Model
    Innovations) 545, 547
needs fulfillment 402
negative behaviors 141, 238, 277, 282, 302, 356, 359,
    383, 436
negative emotions 38, 192, 199, 396, 436, 503
negative feedback 25, 26–27, **27**, 88, 503
negative interactions 237, 392, 393, 394, 407, 446,
    503, 536
negative teacher-student interactions 445–448
Netherlands 397, 399, 400, 402
neuroscience 234, 237, 240, 243
neuroticism 194, 399, 402
New Jim Crow 211–225
NICE (National Institute for Health and Care
    Excellence) 535, 536, 537
no-excuses charter schools 9, 59, 152–163, 216
no-excuses discipline 153, 157, 158–162, 163

non-compliance 158, 242, 535–536
nonverbal behaviors 390, 395, 419
norms: classroom *104*, **106**, **107**, **112**, **113**, **118**, **119**, **120**, 303, 381, 425, 505; cultural 275, 281, 375, 444, 445, 485, 536, 537; and family engagement 231, 233, 237; school *104*, **106**, **119**, 282; social 173, 235, 542; and social, emotional and behavior (SEB) growth *104*, **106**, **107**, **111**, **112**, **113**, **118**, **119**, **120**; and teacher education 486, 487, 489
Norway 176, **354**, 355, 366
novice teachers 15, 152, 159, 160, 161, 240, 250, 273–274, 274–275
nurturing 21, 62, 69, 274, 428

OBPP (Olweus Bullying Prevention Program) 176
occupational stress 195, 438
ODRs *see* office disciplinary referrals (ODRs)
offenders 54, 55, 332
offenses 55, 59, 276, 294, 295, **326**, 327, 328, 332, 469, 470, 481
office disciplinary referrals (ODRs) 59, 141, 177, 221, 293, 335, 467, 469, 482; and disabilities 506, **507**, 510–511; and discipline gap 437, 438, 439, 440, 444, 447; and positive behavioral interventions 87, 88–89, 93
Olweus Bullying Prevention Program (OBPP) 176
OMB (United States Office of Management and Budget) 458–459
online learning 9, 11, 68, 144, 192–193, 327; challenges faced in 138–140; support for 142, 143, 250; *see also* remote learning environments, schooling in
on-task behavior **106**, 141, 198, 236, 300, 357, 363, 364, 365, 525, 526, 534
opportunities to respond (OTR) 7, 22–23, **23**, **106**, **108**, 124, 131, **132**, 140, 257, 339; and disabilities 502, 508, 510, 513; and positive behavioral interventions 88, 89, 91, 94
Oregon Research Institute (ORI) 76, 77
Oregon Social Learning Center (OSLC) 76, 77
ORI (Oregon Research Institute) 76, 77
OSLC (Oregon Social Learning Center) 76, 77
OTR *see* opportunities to respond (OTR)
outcomes: academic *see* academic outcomes; affective 400; behavioral 39, 80, 95, 171, 301, 352, 488, 522; developmental 82, 289, 483; educational 277, 292, 519, 530; motivational 3, 350, 351, 352, 366; social 36, 291, 389; social–emotional 162–163, 351, 352, 353, 361, 362
out-of-school suspensions 56, 293, 295, 320, 468, 470, 481, 482, 483

pandemic *see* COVID-19 pandemic
parental attachment 399
parental involvement 178, 235, 236, 237, 274, 358, 362
parenting 75, 135, 173–174, 274, 468, 471
parenting style 233, 239
parent-teacher conferences 232, 240, 241, 329

participatory action research 380
paternalism 154, 158, 402
PATHS (Promoting Alternative Thinking Strategies) 351, **354**, 359–361
PATHS Teacher Rating Scale (PTRS) 360
PAX Good Behavior Game (PAX–GBG) **354**, 361–362, **365**, 366
PBIS *see* Positive Behavioral Interventions and Supports (PBIS)
PBS *see* positive behavioral supports (PBS)
PCM (Proactive Classroom Management) 7, 93, 255, **354**, 355, 363, **365**, 366
PCP (Person-Centered Planning) **118**, 125n3
PD *see* professional development (PD)
pedagogy 141, 163, 195, 241, 271, 274, 335, 381, 519, 523; and school-to-prison pipeline 289, 296, 299; and teacher education 484, 485, 487, 492
peer attachment 60, 62, 384
peer characteristics, and bullying/peer victimization 174–175
peer relationships 60, **118**, 298, 300, 502, 540
Peer Restorative Justice (Peer RJ) 58
peer victimization 167–169, 169, 169–170, 171–173, 178, 415
performance feedback 6, 91, 92, 94, 96, 124, 143, 256, 257, 445
personal bias 20, 222, 279, 460, 538
personal responsibility 175, 415, **417**, 425, 426, 429
personality: student 7, 231, 259, 399; student teacher 402; teacher 191, 194, 235, 402, 403; traits of 36, 422
Person-Centered Planning (PCP) **118**, 125n3
physical activity 46, 277
physical education 46, **417**, 420–421, 422, 429
Pierson, Rita 34, 35
planning: action 89, 90, 93, **108**, 134, 240, 255, **378**, 445, 512; lesson 22, 93, **107**, 199, 271, 278, 343, 359, 363; Person-Centered (PCP) **118**, 125n3
PLCs (professional learning communities) 56, 142, 178, 274, 277
policing, of schools 68, 69, 218–219, 223, 224, 291, 293, 295, 320, 466
policy: disciplinary *see* disciplinary policies; educational 472n4; institutional 212, 213, 215, 217, 222, 223, 225; school 9, 60, 62, 196, 216, 288, 294, **326**, 379, 441, 487, 505; school discipline 11, 153, 273, 289, 303, 320, 325, 441, 448
poor behavior management 502–504
poor classroom management 197, 278–281, 335, 502, 519
positive behavioral approaches 296, 302, 441
positive behavioral interventions 65, 87–96, *90*, 103; *see also* Positive Behavioral Interventions and Supports (PBIS)
Positive Behavioral Interventions and Supports (PBIS) 34, 87–96, *90*; framework for 33, 34, 88, 131, 134, 135, 177–178, 241; implementation of 87, 96, 134
positive behavior support 103, 131, 441, 504, 511

positive behavioral supports (PBS) 241, 296, 337, 442; *see also* functional behavior assessment (FBA); Positive Behavioral Interventions and Supports (PBIS)

positive classroom environment 10, 350

positive feedback 24, 25, 26–27, **27**, *104*, **107**, 136–137, 509

positive psychology 35–36, 189–190, 198

positive relationships 21–22, 35–36, 65, 67, 178, 293, 302, 355, 380–381, 393, 395, 405

positive teacher-student relationships 135, 352, 357, 366, 367, 426, 427, 447

poverty 61, **132**, 133, 152, 216, 240, 293, 441, 442, 448; high- 135, 137, 361, 438, 444; and school administration 272, 277, 279, 283; and teacher education 481, 483, 491

practice: behavioral 134, 154, 159; best 10, 154, 189, 250, 255, 257, 258, 274, 330, 380; classroom 94, 95, 123, 124, 296–303, 366; culturally-responsive 137–138; developmentally appropriate 536–537; disciplinary *see* disciplinary practices; evidence-based *see* evidence-based practices (EBPs); evidence-based CM 91, 92, 93, 96, 129, 130, 335–347, **336**, *338*, *346*; inclusive 39, 294, 556; instructional 15, 16, 27, **132**, 260, 289, 381, 484, 486; proactive 102, 124, 513; restorative *see* restorative (RP); school 60, 66, 67, 288, 290, 294, 447, 506, **507**, 510; school-based restorative 54–56; teacher 93, 141, 240, 443; teaching 15, 364, 444, 484, 485, 487, 492, 543, 546

praise: behavior-specific 92, 249, 258, 503, 508, 509, 510; teacher 25, 75, 76; verbal 25, **106**, **107**, 521

precorrection 136, 339, 502, 506, 508, 509, 513

prejudice 133, 214, 220, 238, 303, 397, 446, 447, 538

preparation programs 27, 251, 252, 280, 385, 500, 504, 519; and family engagement 234, 240, 241; multimedia in 335, 339, 344–345, 346

preschool 169, 170, 235, 288, 353, 441, 482, 483, 521–522, 525, 537; *see also* First Step Next

pre-service teacher preparation 249, 250–254

pre-service teachers (PSTs) 5, 143, 195, 240, 241, 242, 253, 341, 366, 378, 385

prevention strategies 9, 31–48, *42*, *43*, *44*, *45*, *46*, 198, 296, **378**

preventive coping *198*, 198

preventive interventions 218, 351

preventive strategies *see* prevention strategies

primary education 350–351, 353

privacy, right to 323, 324–325

privilege (advantage) 10, 220–221, 224, 461, 468, 480, 537; and school-to-prison pipeline 289, 290, 291–292, 299, 303

privileges (benefits) 25, 26, 157, 322, 357, 361, 365, 436, 536

proactive behavior management 257, 260

Proactive Circle 37

Proactive Classroom Management (PCM) 7, 93, 255, **354**, 355, 363, **365**, 366

proactive practices 102, 124, 513

problem behaviors: and CM programs and strategies 355–356, 357, 362; and disabilities 500, 505, 509; and discipline gap 436, 437–438, 441, 442, 443–444, 446, 448; and First Step 74, 78, 80, 81, 82, 83

problem-focused coping 198–199

problem-solving: for bullying 176, 177, 178; in CM programs and strategies 355, 359–360, 362, 363; and delivery across contexts 134, 139, 141; in early childhood education 539, 542–543, 544–545; family engagement for 238, 240, 241; and school-to-prison pipeline 294, 296, 303; and transformative social-emotional learning 377, 380, 381

procedural due process, in student disciplinary process 321, 322–323

professional development (PD): CM 143–144, **144**, 256, 426; continuous (CPD) 56, 67, 529–530; Double Check (DCPD) 137, 138; effective 142, 255; in-service teacher 254–257; Multitiered Support for (MTS-PD) 141–143; programs for 255, 260, **417**, 428, 429; targeted (TPD) 143, 256; teacher 89, 128, **132**, 254–257, 444, 446; training for 142, 250, 254–55, 257

professional learning 5, 12, 200, 274, **378**, 502, 508, 511, 512, 513; communities of (PLCs) 56, 142, 178, 274, 277

program/practice gap 66–67, 69

programs: certification 242, 251, 253; CM 144, 350–367, **354**, **365**; Contingencies for Learning Academic and Social Skills (CLASS) 77; First Step 74–84; Insights **354**, 364, **365**, 366; intervention 82, 167, 175–176, 445, 522; Knowledge is Power (KIPP) 152, 155–57, 161, 165; Olweus Bullying Prevention (OBPP) 176; preparation *see* preparation programs; teacher education 137, 251, 303, 407, 419, 423, 477, 478, 488, 492; teacher preparation *see* preparation programs; teacher training 4, 241, 359, 366, 367, 385, 528

progress monitoring 116, **121**, 123

Promoting Alternative Thinking Strategies (PATHS) 351, **354**, 359–361

prosocial behaviors 38, 62, 67, 141, 175, 177, 300, 329, 401, 501, 504–505; and CM programs and strategies 353, 356, 357, 359–360, 361, 362–363, 367

Prosocial Classroom model 238

prosocial education element, of school climate improvement process 178

prosocial skills **121**, 235, 276, 352, 359, 443, 447

protests 156, 211, 215, 225n4, 472

PSTs (pre-service teachers) 5, 143, 195, 240, 241, 242, 253, 341, 366, 378, 385

PTRS (PATHS Teacher Rating Scale) 360

public education 39, 153, 154, 320, 321, 322, 328

punishment *see* teacher corporal punishment

punitive classroom environment 298

punitive discipline 65, 281, 382, 500, 503, 511; and discipline gap 437, 438, 439, 440, 445, 446

Pyramid Model 546–547

QTI (Questionnaire on Teacher Interaction) 393, 398–399, *398*, 400, 401, 403, 406, 407
qualitative research, 30, 69, 552
Questionnaire on Teacher Interaction (QTI) 393, 398–399, *398*, 400, 401, 403, 406, 407

race-conscious programmatic interventions 222
race-neutral ideology 160, 466, 467
racial bias 11, 293, 301, 445–448, 469–470
racial discipline disparities 383, 384, 441, 444, 446
racial discipline gap 61, 384, 437, 481
racial discrimination 170, 212, 215, 217, 458, 459, 539
racial disparities 221, 439, 479, 480–483, 489
racial disproportionality 439, 466, 468, 469, 471
racial incongruence 478–479, 483
racial retrenchment 470–472
racial minority students 195, 440, 466
racial/ethnic diversity 479
racialization 10, 156, 162, 289, 291; and New Jim Crow 212, 213, 215, 219
racialized disproportionality 222–223, 223–224, 225
racialized hierarchy, of human value 215, 217–218, 218–219, 220
racially, ethnically, and linguistically diverse (RELD) students 480, 481, 483, 484, 486, 488, 489, 491, 493
randomized controlled trials (RCTs) 78, 81, 82, 93, 383–384, 523; and CM programs and strategies 354, 356, 357–358, 360, 361, 362, 363, 364, 365; and restorative practices 57, 60–61, 62, 64, 66, 67
reactive behavior management 93, 96, 441
reading 46, 63, 64, 78, 79, 232, 384, 480, 488, 506, 511; and CM programs and strategies 353, 356, 358, 361, 362, 363, 363
Real Talk 4 Girls 62
recognition of one's own ethnocentrism and biases, CRCM essential principle of 487
redlining, in education 440–441
reflective ability 341, 343, 344, 345
reform 153, 177–178, 272, 292, 478; disciplinary 212, 216, 217, 220, 221, 222, 224, 469
relationships: building of 21, 34–36, 139, 171, 233, 254, 275–276, 376; interpersonal 178, 233, 238, 239, 243, 288, 298–303, 400, 457; peer 60, **118**, 298, 300, 502, 540; supportive 139, 174, 239, 350, 351, 352, 381; teacher-child 236, 237, 540, 543; teacher-student *see* teacher-student relationships (TSRs)
relaxation 41, 43, 47, 199, 511
relaxation and guided imagery (RGI) 37–38, 48
RELD students *see* racially, ethnically, and linguistically diverse (RELD) students
remote learning environments, schooling in 131–133, **132**; *see also* online learning
replacement behavior 34, 505, 520
research-practice partnerships (RPP) 379, 380
Response to Intervention (RTI) 232, 241, 256, 505–506
restorative discipline 137, 297, 328, 447–448, 489–490, 491, 493

restorative interventions 297, 328, 447–448
restorative justice (RJ): in no-excuses charter schools 157, 162, 163; as root of restorative practices 54–56; TSEL strategies for 381–385
restorative practice research 64–65
restorative practices (RP) 9, 36, 48, 54–69, 221–222, 296, 297, 447–448; and delivery across contexts 136, 141, 142, **144**; and school administration 273, 281–282; and transformative social-emotional learning 382, 383, 384; virtual 331, 332–333
rewards 34, 36, 75, 157, 158, 190, 365, 382, 493
RGI (relaxation and guided imagery) 37–38, 48
right to privacy, in virtual school settings 324
rights: civil 212, 214, 219, 225, 461, 462; legal 321, 324, 329–330; student [incl seven rights]
RJ *see* Restorative Justice (RJ)
role models 171, 234, 239, 380
RP *see* restorative practices (RP)
RPP (research-practice partnerships) 379, 380
RTI (Response to Intervention) 232, 241, 256, 505–506
rules: classroom *see* classroom rules; school 161, 274, 323, 331, 382
rural environments 133, 134, 135, **144**, 283, 422, 522
rural schools 133–134, 134–135, 138, 144, 357
rural Tier 1 support 134

San Antonio Independent School District v. Rodriguez 292
SCD (single case design) 519, 520, 521, 523, 524, 525–526, 527, 528
school adjustment 167, 400, 502
school administration 271–283
school attendance 35, **108**, 193, 260, 294, 300, 383, 384, 440, 441, 506; and New Jim Crow 215, 216, 218, 221; and restorative practices 215, 216, 218, 221
school bullying 167–179
school characteristics, and bullying/peer victimization 174
school climate: and no-excuses charter schools 159, 161, 162; and restorative practices 55–56, 57, 59, 61, 62–63, 64, 68, 69; and school-to-prison pipeline 289, 293, 295, 296–297; and transformational social-emotional learning **378**, 379, 383, 384
school closures 193, 211, 319
school connectedness 60, 62–63, 384
school counselors 75, 135, 385, 466
school culture 155, 159, 222, 282–283, 295, 483, 485, 489, 512
school discipline: policies 11, 153, 273, 289, 303, 320, 325, 441, 448; protocols 466, 468, 469; reform 221, 222
school engagement 171, 235, 303
school funding 66, 89, 90, 130, 134, 135, 195, 272, 292, 301, 379, 462
school leadership 62, 110, 144, 196, 276, 294, 301, 465
school norms *104*, **106**, **119**, 282

school performance 75, 80, 167, 172, 272

school policing 68, 69, 218–219, 223, 224, 291, 293, 295, 320, 466

school policy 9, 60, 62, 196, 216, 288, 294, **326**, 379, 441, 487, 505

school practices 60, 66, 67, 288, 290, 294, 447, 506, **507**, 510

school reform *see* reform

school resource officers (SROs) 68–69, 218

school rules 161, 274, 323, 331, 382

school safety 62, 294–295, 296, 466, 471

school security 218, 376, 377, 379

school success 75, 76, 77, 235, 437, 504

school suspensions 56, 293, 295, 320, 468, 470, 481, 482, 483

school systems 33, 220, 290, 292, 504; to support Tier 2 110; to support Tier 3 123

school teachers: gender of 5; language skills of 479

school violence 172, 175–176, 177–178, 438–439

school-based restorative practices 54–56

school-to-prison pipeline (STPP) 36, 55, 216, 288–303, 464, 466, 483; and students with disabilities 502, 503, 504, 511

School-Wide Positive Behavioral Intervention and Supports (SWPBIS) 87, 88, 89, 93, 95, 96, 221, 222

SDQ (Strengths and Difficulties Questionnaire) 356, 359, 360, 363

seated yoga sequences 41–42, *42*, *43*

SEB (Social, Emotional, and Behavior) growth 102–125, *104*, **105–109**, **111–115**, **117–122**

secondary schools 59, 479, 482

Second Step 351, **354**, 362–363, **365**, 366

segregation 215, 219, 280, 291, 292, 295, 440–441, 467

SEL *see* Social and Emotional Learning (SEL)

self-awareness 176–177, 237–238, 239, 242, 376, 381, 382, 443, 489, 491, 539

self-control 351, 352, 355–356, 359–360, 362, 382, 422, 423, 424

self-management 110, **115**, **122**, 135, 176–177, 237–238, 346, 376, 443; and autism 519, 520, 530; and positive behavioral interventions 87, 91–92, 93–94; research in 524–527

self-monitoring **122**, 142, 143–144, 257, 511, 529; and positive behavioral interventions 89, 92, 93–94, 94–95, 96; research in 524–527

self-reflection 20, 21, 252, 278, 341, 342, 343

self-regulation 31, 41, 48, 194, 199, 463; and CM programs and strategies 350, 352, 357, 359, 361, 362; and disabilities 500, 501, 502, 513; and family engagement 237–238, 239, 242

SES *see* socioeconomic status (SES)

seven rights of our students 35

shaming 54–55, 158, 160, 161–162, 503

Shelby County Public Schools 325–326, 326, 330–333

simulations: for teacher candidates 340–341; in teacher education 339–340; in teacher preparation 339

single case design (SCD) 519, 520, 521, 523, 524, 525–526, 527, 528

situational appropriateness 511, 512

Situational Judgment Test (SJT) 240

1619 Project, The 212, 459

SJT (Situational Judgment Test) 240

skill development 46, 169, 176, 178–179, 254, 296, 340, 345, **378**, 425, 438, 488, 518

skin color 213, 215, 217–218, 461

social aggression 62

social and academic empowerment 486

social and emotional competence 298, 360, 540

social and emotional learning (SEL) 65, **144**, 176, 177, 178, 296, 298, 302–303; *see also* Collaborative for Academic, Social, and Emotional Learning (CASEL)

social and emotional skills 10, 63, 67, 169, 176, 360, 362, 380, 382, 384

social and emotional well-being 298, 407, 506, 508, 511, 513

social awareness 176, 237, 240, 376, 443

social behavior research 519–524

social behaviors 18, 221, 232, 273, 291, 356, 523

social climate 389, 390, *391*, 391, 393, 397; and teacher-student relationships 398–405, *398*, *404*, 407

social cognition 233, 238–239, 240, 242

social communication 518, 522

social competence, of teachers 234–235, 237–242

social control 291, 293, 437, 490

social demands 233, 234, 237

social development 242, 384–385, 540

social dynamic systems 10, 389

Social, Emotional, and Behavior (SEB) growth 102–125, *104*, **105–109**, **111–115**, **117–122**

social justice 9–10, 375, 376, 378, 486, 488, 489, 493, 539

social learning 74–75

social norms 173, 235, 542

social outcomes 36, 291, 389

social problems 376, 401

social skills deficits 500, 502

social skills instruction 37, 110, **111**, **112**, **113**, **114**, **115**, 522, 530

Social Skills Rating System (SSRS) 78, 81, 355

Social Stories™ 522–524

social structures 174, 289, 381–382

social support 56, 161, 172, 174–175, 200, 236, 521

social validity, 94, 96, 99–101, 123, 528–29, 531; and disabilities 505, 507–8, 510, 516

social work 75, **111**, 116, 123, 324, 325, 376, 378, 385, 462, 465, 466

social worlds 220, 231, 233, 236, 243

social-ecology perspective, on bullying and peer victimization 172

social-emotional competence 237, 298, 359, 360, 361, 528, 530, 540, 546

social-emotional development 351, 352, 353, 355, 359, 360, 362, 363, 364, **365**, 366, 535 social–emotional learning 10, 129, 135, 136, **144**, 176–177, 224, 299, 350, 351, 442, 546; transformative 375–385, **378**

social–emotional outcomes 162–163, 351, 352, 353, 361, 362

social–emotional well-being 298, 407, 506, 508, 511, 513

socioeconomic status (SES) 35, 95, 169, 178, 195, 295, 297, 429; and CM programs and strategies 353–354, 356; and discipline gap 440–441, 442, 445

space structuring, of the classroom 31–32

special and general educators, empowering of 499–513, **507**

special and gifted education 478, 480, 483, 493

special education: multimedia use in 336, 340, 345; restorative practices for 61, 63, 65, 68, 69; services for 170, 295, 297, 480, 481, 499, 504, 513

SROs (school resource officers) 68–69, 218

SSGs (State Space Grids) 392, *392*, 407

SSRS (Social Skills Rating System) 78, 81, 355

standardized tests 171, 479, 480

State Space Grids (SSGs) 392, *392*, 407

statutory law 320, 321

stereotypes 170–171, 237, 280, 281, 468, 470, 488–489; and discipline gap 445–446, 446–447; and New Jim Crow 214–215, 216–217; and school-to-prison pipeline 299, 300, 301

stigma **119**, 133, 142, 169, 171, 292, 293, 295, 297, 446, 468

STPP *see* school-to-prison pipeline (STPP)

Strengths and Difficulties Questionnaire (SDQ) 356, 359, 360, 363

stress: management of 141, 199, 301; student 298, 301; teacher 8, 189–203, *190*, *198*, 254, 301, 367, 396, 415, 540

stress process, and teacher appraisals 190–191, 196, 198

stressors: student 39, 382, 437, 442, 443, 491, 503; teacher 197, 199, 254, 415, 436

structural inequalities 159–160

structural inequities 135, 379, 439, 441, 442, 448, 491, 537–538

structural racism 10, 211–225, 214

student achievement 48, 155, 159, 235, 236, 237, 260, 261, 272, 301, 363, 400–401

student agency 302–303, 376–377, 380, *390*, 391, 393, 394

student aggression 168, 170, 171, 172, 173, 174, 175, 176, 177, 178

student attainment 163, 278

student autonomy 155, 239

student beliefs 290, 422

student culture 10, 128, 137, 154, 250

student development 290, 294

student discipline 154, 161, 189, 440, 447, 465, 466, 482; in virtual settings 321–322, 325, 327, 328, 330

student disengagement 199, 274, 277, 278, **417**, 425, 426, 437; and school-to-prison pipeline 293–294, 298, 300

student diversity 130, **132**, 135, 138, 169, 176, 177, 179, 252, 257, 457

student due process protections, in school disciplinary process 321–322

student emotions 137, 298, 300, 401, 408

student engagement: and data analysis 277–278; and disabilities 503, 508, 510; Double Check 137–138; and family engagement 231, 235, 236, 237, 239; and school administration 274, 275–276; strategies for increasing 140

student enrollment 477, 479, 482

student interests 134, 139, 231, 233, 237, 275, 278, 279, 422

student misbehavior: and CM at different timescales 394, 397, 405; and exclusionary discipline 57–59; and teacher stress 192, 193, 194, 198, 199; and teacher training 253, 254, 261; in virtual settings 319–320, 327

student motivation 34, 300, 301, 303, 366, 400, 415, 419

student personality 7, 231, 259, 399

student rights 321–322

student safety 68, 69, 159, 509

student social–emotional competencies 442–444

student stress 298, 301

student stressors 39, 382, 437, 442, 443, 491, 503

student success 3, 161, 277, 278, 291, 294, 481, 529; and effective instruction 15, 21–22, 25, 27; and family engagement 238, 239, 241, 243

student suspensions 294, 320, 322, 326, 330, 335

student teachers 4, 401, 402, 405, 407

student voice 136, 162, 275, 299, 302

student well-being 40, 294

substantive due process, in student disciplinary process 321–322, 323

suicidal ideation 116, 168, 169, 171, 491

suicide 133, 353

supportive environments 136, 297, 490

supportive relationships 139, 174, 239, 350, 351, 352, 381

suspensions: out-of-school 56, 293, 295, 320, 468, 470, 481, 482, 483; student 294, 320, 322, 326, 330, 335

sustainability, of First Step Next program usage 82–83

sustained duration, of CM professional development 255, 256

SWPBIS *see* Schoolwide Positive Behavioral Interventions and Supports (SWPBIS)

systematic screening 78, 506, 511

systemic bias 538, 539

systemic inequities 379, 439, 441, 448, 491, 537–538

systemic racism 212–215, 225n3, 462, 467, 487

tailored improvement goals element, of school climate improvement process 178

targeted professional development (TPD) 143, 256

targeted SEB support 103–110, **105–109**

TCIT (Teacher-Child Interaction Training) **354**, 357–358, **365**, 366

TDI (Teacher-Directed Interaction) 357

teacher agency *390*, 391, 392, 393–394, 395, 396, *398*, 399, 400, 401, 402, 403, 404, 405, 406–407

teacher aggression 10–11, 254, 415–430, **417**, **427**; studies of **417**, 419, 427

teacher appraisals, of demands and resources 190–191, 193, 194

teacher attrition 4, 135–136, 200, 250, 274

teacher autonomy 195–196, 197, 301

teacher behavior management *see* behavior management (BM)

teacher beliefs 136, 241, 242, 250, 254, 255, 257, 279, 402, 440, 446, 470, 487

teacher burnout 27, 129, 141, 251, 301, 344, 381, 508; *see also* teacher stress

teacher candidates 4, 335–347, **336**, *338*, *346*

teacher capacity 291, 296, 301–302

teacher communion *see* communion

teacher coping *see* coping, teacher

teacher corporal punishment 11, 130, 217, 218, 223, 416, 430, 437, 439; as aggression 426–428, **427**

teacher development 255, 262

teacher diversity 156, 202, 278, 479

teacher education 477–493; programs of 137, 251, 303, 407, 419, 423, 477, 478, 488, 492

teacher effectiveness 199, 254, 272

teacher efficacy 196–197

teacher evaluation 91, 272, 282–283

teacher expectations 75, 231, 331–332, 502, 505

teacher induction systems 273–275

teacher interpersonal styles 405–407

teacher knowledge 136

teacher personality 191, 194, 235, 402, 403

teacher practices 93, 141, 240, 443

teacher praise 25, 75, 76

teacher preparation: pre-service 249, 250–254; programs for *see* preparation programs; simulations in 339–344, 345, 346

teacher professional development 89, 128, **132**, 444, 446; in-service 254–257

teacher quality 196, 251, 278, 477

teacher ratings 78, 81, 84, 177, 272, 540

teacher self-efficacy 196–197, 402

teacher shortages 436–437

teacher social competence 234–235, 237–242

teacher stress 8, 189–203, *190*, *198*, 254, 301, 367, 396, 415, 540; *see also* teacher burnout

teacher stressors 197, 199, 254, 415, 436

teacher success 231–233, 235, 236, 258

teacher support 88, 94–95, 133, 160, 171, 201, 403

teacher training 4, 5, 7, 8, 10, 94, 136, 241, 385, 444, 508, 528; and CM 249–262; programs for 4, 241, 355, 358, 359, 363, 366, 367, 385, 528

teacher turnover 156, 273, 274, 438

teacher verbal aggression 418–422, 426

teacher well-being 189–190, 195, 197–202, *198*, 203, 238, 239, 301

Teacher-Child Interaction Training (TCIT) **354**, 357–358, **365**, 366

teacher–child relationship 236, 237, 540, 543

Teacher-Directed Interaction (TDI) 357

teacher-student adaptation 393–394, *394*

teacher-student interaction 237, 302, 340, 443–444, 519; and CM at different timescales 389, 390, 391–397, *392*, *394*, *396*; and implicit racial bias 445–448

teacher-student relationships (TSRs): changes over time in 403–405, *404*; and classroom social climate 398–399, *398*; and CM programs and strategies 350, 351, 352, 353, 357, 358, 366, 367; and school-to-prison pipeline 299, 300, 301; studies of 403; and teacher aggression 418, 426–427, 428; and teacher and student outcomes 399–403

teacher-student variables *391*

teaching practices 15, 364, 444, 484, 485, 487, 492, 543, 546

TeachLivE see *Mursion*

technology cycle *346*

theory: cognitive **336**, 337; Critical Race (CRT) 11, 160, 219, 457–473, 492; Disability Critical Race (DisCrit) 461–462, 467, 470; I³ **417**, 422–423; intergroup contact 447; interpersonal 388, 389, 393; transactional 190, 191, 198

Theory of Action (TOA) 222, 252, 377

Tier I training supports 142

Tier II training supports 142

Tier III training supports 142–143

TOA (Theory of Action) 222, 252, 377

TPD (targeted professional development) 143, 256

traditional classroom management 136–137, 202, 488–489

training: CM *see* classroom management training; CM teacher 262; mental health **144**; teacher *see* teacher training; Teacher-Child Interaction (TCIT) **354**, 357–358, **365**, 366

transactional theory 190, 191, 198

transformative learning, CRCM essential principle of 486

Transformative Social Emotional Learning (TSEL) 10, 375–385, **378**

transparent, democratically informed leadership element, of school climate improvement process 178

trauma histories, students with 192, 193–194, 200–201

trauma sensitive spaces 32–33

trauma-informed schools 200–201, 202

TSEL (Transformative Social Emotional Learning) 10, 375–385, **378**

TSRs *see* teacher-student relationships TSRs)

UDL (Universal Design for Learning) 10, 249, 258, 262

Uncommon Schools 152, 156, 162

Universal Design for Learning (UDL) 10, 249, 258, 262

universal SEB support, in Tier 1 103

urban environments 135–136, 137

urban schools 4, 9, 135, 136, 137, 144, 152, 159, 422, 489
US Constitution 320, 321, 325
US Department of Education 124, 129, 138, 168, 217, 440, 478
US Office of Management and Budget (OMB) 458–459
US Supreme Court 320, 321, 322, 439

VAIL (Video Assessment of Interactions and Learning) 342
validating cultural experiences, CRCM essential principle of 486
values, cultural 40, 171, 380, 381, 382, 487, 491, 512, 536, 537, 540
verbal abuse 416, **417**, 418, 419
verbal aggression 416–418, **417**; teacher 418–422, 426
verbal harassment 416, 426
verbal praise 25, **106**, **107**, 521
victimization: bias-based 169; bullying 60, 171; identity-based 169–171; peer 167–169, 169–170, 171–173, 178, 415
victims 55, 59, 168, 169, 173–174, 175, 212, 220, 223
Video Assessment of Interactions and Learning (VAIL) 342
video reflection 336, 341–344, 346
video self-modeling (VSM) 520–521
virtual discipline 325–327, **326**
virtual school environment 10, 320, 324, 325–326, 328–329, 330
virtual school settings 319–333, **326**, **327**
Virtual Student Conduct Expectations (Shelby County Schools) 325, **326**, 326, 330–333
virtual student disciplinary codes of conduct 325–327, **326**
VSM (video self-modeling) 520–521

warmth 32, 238, 239, 240, 242, 299
well-being: emotional 46, 545; psychological 43, 46; social–emotional 298, 407, 506, 508, 511, 513; student 40, 294; teacher 189–190, 195, 197–202, *198*, 203, 238, 239, 301
wellness 110, 141, 197, 198, 201, **378**
What Works Clearinghouse (WWC) 74, 80, 84
White House Conference on American History 458, 459
White privilege 224, 468
Whiteness 220, 462, 468, 470, 480; as property 460, 461–462, 467, 468
White schools 129, 195, 218
White students 61, 69, 129–130, 170, 279, 295, 384, 439; and critical race theory 468, 470, 472; and culturally responsive teacher education 478–479, 480, 481, 482–483; and New Jim Crow 216, 218, 219
White supremacy 212, **214**, 215, 223, 462
White teachers 129–130, 195, 301, 479
Whole School Restorative Justice (WSRJ) 58
working memory 39, 46, 202, 406
workplace conditions 200
Written Emotional Expression 38–39, 48
WSRJ (Whole School Restorative Justice) 58
WWC (What Works Clearinghouse) 74, 80, 84

yoga 41–45, *42*, *43*, *44*, *45*, 48, 201
youth violence 176, 383, 505

zero tolerance discipline 36, 136, 154, 276, 295, 438, 441, 464, 465; and New Jim Crow 215, 216, 217, 223
zone of proximal development (ZPD) 298